DOMESTIC VIOLENCE AND THE LAW:
THEORY AND PRACTICE

SECOND EDITION

by

ELIZABETH M. SCHNEIDER
Rose L. Hoffer Professor of Law
Brooklyn Law School

CHERYL HANNA
Professor of Law
Vermont Law School

JUDITH G. GREENBERG
Associate Dean and Professor of Law
New England School of Law

CLARE DALTON
George J. and Kathleen Waters Matthews
Distinguished University Professor of Law
Northeastern University School of Law

FOUNDATION PRESS
75TH ANNIVERSARY

THOMSON

WEST

© 2001 FOUNDATION PRESS
© 2008 By FOUNDATION PRESS
   395 Hudson Street
   New York, NY 10014
   Phone Toll Free 1–877–888–1330
   Fax (212) 367–6799
   foundation–press.com
Printed in the United States of America

ISBN 978–1–59941–028–9

TEXT IS PRINTED ON 10% POST CONSUMER RECYCLED PAPER

To Tom, Anna and Matthew

- from E.M.S.

To Paul, Samira, Elias, Mom and Carrie

- from C.H.

To my family: Ken, Laura, Dustin, Amy, Arthur and Lisa

- from J.G.G.

To my sons Adam and Sam, and their father, Bob

- from C.D.

And also to the many activists and scholars who have labored to create this field, and to the women and men whose experiences are recorded here, and whose courage and resilience are reflected on every page.

- from all of us.

*

PREFACE

This book has been a product of many generative collaborations and wonderful connections over many years. The seed for this book was first planted in 1991, when Liz Schneider taught one of the country's very first courses on Battered Women and the Law at Harvard Law School. The materials for this and subsequent courses were expanded little by little and ultimately formed the core of the book. Clare Dalton, a professor at Northeastern University Law School and later Director of Northeastern's Domestic Violence Institute integrated domestic violence materials into an experimental first-year curriculum at Northeastern Law School and drew on the materials that Liz had prepared. The two then decided that this was a book whose time had come. The first edition of this casebook, co-authored by Liz Schneider and Clare Dalton, was published in 2001 as BATTERED WOMEN AND THE LAW. In preparing the first edition, Liz and Clare developed the book from courses that they were each teaching on domestic violence and on their experiences as lawyers in the field. The book was a careful mix of theory and practice that has been useful in teaching courses and programs on domestic violence to law students, lawyers, judges and activists in this country and across the globe.

This second edition adds Cheryl Hanna and Judi Greenberg as new co-authors and changes the book's title to DOMESTIC VIOLENCE AND THE LAW: THEORY AND PRACTICE. Cheryl Hanna was a student in that first class on Battered Women and the Law that Liz taught at Harvard Law School. After serving as a domestic violence prosecutor, she is now a law professor at Vermont Law School. Judi Greenberg, a professor at New England School of Law, has taught seminars on domestic violence for more than 15 years, originally from the materials Liz first developed in the early 1990s. The new collaboration among us has resulted in significant changes in this second edition of the book. We are delighted to celebrate the many dimensions of our personal and intellectual connections over many years that are reflected in these pages.

There have been many people who have helped us complete this edition and we are grateful to each one of them.

Liz Schneider thanks her many students in Battered Women and the Law over the years at Brooklyn, Harvard and Columbia Law Schools who have generated ideas that are reflected in this new edition of the book and many colleagues in the field who have given helpful feedback. Stephanie Farrior, Stacy Caplow and Dan Smulian made important contributions to the chapters on Immigration, Asylum and International Human Rights and Deb Widiss provided helpful materials for the chapter on Employer Liability. Lauren Edgerton, Emily Roberts, Kristin Delaney, Grace Albinson, Nahal Batmanghelidj, and Anita Nabha were great research assistants. Charles Krause was, as always, an enormous help and support on every phase of this project. Minna Kotkin, Stacy Caplow, Susan Herman and Nan Hunter were especially supportive colleagues. The Dean's Summer Research Stipend Program generously supported work on this book.

Cheryl Hanna thanks her wonderful research assistants Sarah Flint, Kathryn Kent, Jamelea Westerhold, Johanna Evans Thibault, Julie Van Erden, Gretchen Staft, Jessica Dexter, and Gina Pasquantonio for all of their hard work and enthusiastic optimism. She is also grateful to the many students in the Domestic Violence and the Law course at Vermont Law School who contributed ideas and comments as we developed this edition. In particular, she is grateful to Kimberly Perdue, whose work on domestic violence and reproductive rights is included in this book and Wynona Ward, a former student and founder of Have Justice Will Travel, who continues to provide ideas and inspiration. Naomi Flint Neff, Ginny Burnham, and Wendy Smith provided crucial support for the book's completion. The VLS library staff, particularly Glenn Marvel, was invaluable to this project. She also thanks Dean Jeff Shields and Vice-Dean Stephanie Willbanks for their generous support and encouragement. Finally, she thanks the Vermont Law School community, which continues to be a source of inspiration and hope.

Judi Greenberg thanks her great research assistants, Jessica Price, Talia Simonds, and Jeffrey Zahler. She also thanks Barry Stearns and Brian Flaherty, her ever-helpful librarians. In addition, Pat Gresham has provided all kinds of staff support and Jean Guttman who helped with proof-reading.

Clare Dalton offers special thanks to her many colleagues at Northeastern's Domestic Violence Institute, especially its current director Lois Kanter, Pualani Enos, Karin Raye and Kathy Garren, and the dedicated students who have worked with them. That work, in Dorchester Court, in the Boston Medical Center's Emergency Department, in the community and in the classroom, has expanded the services available to those who experience abuse in their intimate relationships and our understanding of how to respond to and partner with them in changing their lives.

ACKNOWLEDGEMENTS

We gratefully acknowledge the authors and publishers who graciously granted us permission to reprint their works.

al-Hibri, Azizah Y., *An Islamic Perspective on Domestic Violence*, 27 Fordham International Law Journal 195 (2003). Reprinted by permission.

Ammons, Linda L., *Why Do You Do the Things You Do? Clemency for Incarcerated Battered Women: A Decade's Review*, 11 American University Journal Gender, Social Policy and Law 533 (2003). Reprinted by permission.

Anderson, Michelle J., *Marital Immunity, Intimate Relationships, and Improper Inferences: A New Law on Sexual Offenses by Intimates*, 54 Hastings Law Journal 1465 (2003). Reprinted by permission.

Aulivola, Michele, *Outing Domestic Violence: Affording Appropriate Protections to Gay and Lesbian Victims*, 42 Family Court Review 162 (2004). Reprinted by permission.

Balos, Beverly, *Domestic Violence Matters: The Case for Appointed Counsel in Protective Order Proceedings,* 15 Temple Political and Civil Rights Law Review 557 (2006). Reprinted by permission.

Bancroft, Lundy, WHY DOES HE DO THAT? Copyright © 2002 by Lundy Bancroft. Used by permission of G.P. Putnam & Sons, a division of Penguin Group (USA) Inc.

Boka, Wendy, *Domestic Violence in Farming Communities: Overcoming The Unique Problems Posed By A Rural Setting*, 9 Drake Journal of Agricultural Law 389 (2004). Reprinted by permission.

Boland, Beth I.Z., *Battered Women Who Act Under Duress*, 28 New England Law Review 603 (1994). Reprinted by permission.

Bowermaster, Janet M., *Relocation Custody Disputes Involving Domestic Violence*, 46 University of Kansas Law Review 433 (1998). Reprinted by permission of Kansas Law Review and Janet M. Bowermaster.

Boxer-Macomber, Laurie, *Revisiting the Impact of California's Mandatory Custody Mediation Program on Victims of Domestic Violence through a Feminist Positionality Lens*, 15 St. Thomas Law Review 883 (2003). Reprinted by permission.

Brandl, Bonnie, & Tess Meuer, *Domestic Abuse Later in Life*, 8 Elder Law Journal 297 (2000). Reprinted by permission.

Braver, Sanford L., Peter Salem, Jessica Pearson, and Stephanie R. DeLuse, *The Content of Divorce Education Programs: Results of a Survey,* 34 Family & Conciliation Courts Review 41 (1996). Reprinted by permission.

Brown, Margaret F., *Domestic Violence Advocates' Exposure to Liability for Engaging in the Unauthorized Practice of Law*, 34 Columbia Journal of Law & Social Problems 279 (2001). Reprinted by permission.

Browne, Angela, from WHEN BATTERED WOMEN KILL (1987) McMillan Free Press, a division of Simon & Shuster (1987). Reprinted by permission.

Buel, Sarah M., *Effective Assistance of Counsel for Battered Women Defendants: A Normative Construct*. Copyright 2003 The President and Fellows of Harvard Law School, and the Journal of Law and Gender, formerly the Harvard Women's Law Journal. Reprinted by permission.

Buel, Sarah M., *Fifty Obstacles to Leaving, a.k.a., Why Abuse Victims Stay*, 28 Colorado Lawyer 19 (1999). Reprinted by permission.

Burke, Alafair S., *Rational Actors, Self-Defense, & Duress: Making Sense Not Syndromes Out of the Battered Woman*, 81 North Carolina Law Review 211 (2002). Reprinted by permission.

Clymer, Steven D., *Unequal Justice: The Federalization of Criminal Law*, 70 Southern California Law Review 643 (1997). Reprinted by permission.

Coker, Donna, *Enhancing Autonomy for Battered Women: Lessons Learned From Navajo Peacemaking*, 47 UCLA Law Review 1 (1999). Reprinted by permission.

Copelon, Rhonda, *International Human Rights Dimensions of Intimate Violence: Another Strand in the Dialectic of Feminist Law Making*, 11 American University Journal of Gender, Social Policy and Law 865 (2003). Reprinted by permission.

Crenshaw, Kimberle, *Mapping the Margins: Intersectionality, Identity Politics, and Violence Against Women of Color*, 43 Stanford Law Review 1241 (1993). Reprinted by permission.

Dalton, Clare, *When Paradigms Collide: Protecting Battered Parents and Their Children in the Family Court System*, 37 Family & Conciliation Courts Review 273 (1999). Reprinted by permission.

Decasas, Michelle, *Protecting Hispanic Women: The Inadequacy of Domestic Violence Policy*, 24 Chicano-Latino L. Rev. 61 (2003). Reprinted by permission.

Dinnerstein, Julie, *Working with Immigrant Victims of Domestic Violence* LAWYER'S MANUAL ON DOMESTIC VIOLENCE REPRESENTING THE VICTIM (eds. Jill Laurie Goodman and Dorchen A. Leidholdt) (2005 4th ed.). Reprinted by permission.

Domestic Abuse Intervention Project, Power and Control and Equality Wheels. Reprinted with permission of the Domestic Abuse Intervention Project, 202 E. Superior Street, Duluth, MN 55802.

Duthu, Kathleen Finley, *Why Doesn't Anyone Talk About Gay and Lesbian Domestic Violence,* 18 Thomas Jefferson Law Review 23 (1996). Reprinted by permission.

Easterling, Michelle W., *For Better or Worse: The Federalization of Domestic Violence,* 98 West Virginia Law Review 933 (1996). Reprinted by permission.

Ellman, Ira Mark, and Stephen D. Sugarman, *Spousal Emotional Abuse as a Tort?* 55 Maryland Law Review 1268 (1996). Reprinted by permission.

Faizi, Nooria, *Domestic Violence in the Muslim Community*, 10 Texas Journal of Women and the Law 209 (2001). Reprinted by permission.

Findlater, Janet, and Susan Kelly, *Child Protective Services and Domestic Violence,* 9 The Future of Children 84 (1999) Copyright by the David and Lucille Packard Foundation. Reprinted with the permission of the David and Lucile Packard Foundation.

Fine, Michelle, Rosemarie A. Roberts, and Lois Weis, *Puerto Rican Battered Women Redefining Gender, Sexuality, Culture, Violence, and Resistance*, in Sokoloff, Natalie J. ed. Domestic Violence at the Margins: Readings on Race, Class, Gender, and Culture. Copy right © 2005 by Natalie J. Sokoloff. Reprinted by permission of Rutgers University Press.

Finn, Peter; Colson, Sarah, Civil Protection Orders: Legislation, Current Court Practice, and Enforcement. National Institute of Justice, March 1990. Reprinted by permission.

Fischer, Karla; Vidmar, Neil; Ellis, Rene, *The Culture of Battering and the Role of Mediation in Domestic Violence Cases.* Originally appearing in Vol. 46, No. 5 of the Southern Methodist University Law Review. Reprinted with permission from the SMU Law Review and the Southern Methodist University School of Law.

Flamme, Alexandra Blake, *Hernandez v. Ashcroft: A Construction of "Extreme Cruelty" Under the Violence Against Woman Act and Its Potential Impact on Immigration and Domestic Violence Law*, 40 New England Law Review 571 (2006). Reprinted by permission.

Franklin, Marnie J., *The Closet Becomes Darker for the Abused: A Perspective on Lesbian Partner Abuse*, 9 Cardozo Women's Law Journal 299 (2003). Reprinted by permission.

Fuhrmann, Geri S.W., Joseph McGill, Mary E. O'Connell, *Parent Education's Second Generation*, 37 Family & Conciliation Courts Review 24 (1999). Reprinted by permission.

Gionis, Thomas & Anthony Zito, *A Call for the Adoption of Federal Rule of Evidence 702 for the Admissibility of Mental-Health Professional Expert Testimony in Illinois Child-Custody Cases*, 27 Southern Illinois University Law Journal 1 (2002). Reprinted by permission.

Goelman, Deborah M., *Shelter from the Storm: Using Jurisdictional Statutes to Protect Victims of Domestic Violence after the Violence Against Women Act of 2000*, 13 Columbia Journal of Gender and Law (2004). Reprinted by permission.

Goldfarb, Sally F., *Violence Against Women and the Persistence of Privacy*, 61 Ohio State Law Journal 1 (2000). Reprinted by permission.

Goldfarb, Sally, *The Supreme Court, the Violence Against Women Act, and the Use and Abuse of Federalism*, 71 Fordham Law Review 57 (2002). Reprinted by permission.

Goldscheid, Julie, "The Civil Rights Remedy of the 1994 Violence Against Women Act" by Julie Goldscheid, published in Family Law Quarterly, Volume 39, No. 1, Spring 2005. Copyright © 2005 by the American Bar Association. Reprinted with permission.

Gondolf, Edward with Ellen Fisher, BATTERED WOMEN AS SURVIVORS: AN ALTERNATIVE TO TREATING LEARNED HELPLESSNESS (1988), Lexington Books, an Imprint of MacMillian, Inc. Reprinted by permission.

Gorelick, Jamie, and Harry Litman, *Prosecutorial Discretion and the Federalization Debate*, 46 Hastings Law Journal 967 (1995). Reprinted by permission.

Greenberg, Judith G., *Domestic Violence and the Danger of Joint Custody Presumptions*, 25 Northern Illinois University Law Review 403 (2005). Reprinted by permission.

Grillo, Trina, *The Mediation Alternative: Process Dangers for Women*, 100 Yale Law Journal 1545 (1991). Reprinted by permission of The Yale Law Journal Company and William S. Hein Company from The Yale Law Journal, Vol. 100.

Guthartz-Cohen, Capt. Stacey A., Judge Advocate, US Army, *Domestic Violence and the Jewish Community*, 11 Michigan Journal of Gender and Law 27 (2004). Reprinted by permission.

Gwinn, Casey, and Sgt. Anne O'Dell, *Stopping the Violence: The Role of the Police Officer and the Prosecutor*, 20 Western State Law Review 297 (1993). Reprinted by permission.

Hanna, Cheryl, *No Right to Choose: Mandated Victim Participation in Domestic Violence Prosecutions,* 109 Harvard Law Review 1849 (1996). Reprinted by permission.

Hanna, Cheryl, *Sex Before Violence: Girls, Dating Violence, and (Perceived) Sexual Autonomy*, 33 Fordham Urban Law Journal 437 (2006). Reprinted by permission.

Hanna, Cheryl, *The Paradox of Hope: The Crime and Punishment of Domestic Violence,* 39 William & Mary Law Review 1505 (1998). Reprinted by permission.

Hart, Barbara, *State Codes on Domestic Violence: Analysis, Commentary and Recommendations*, 1992 Juvenile and Family Court Journal 3 (1992). Reprinted by permission of the National Council of Juvenile and Family Court Judges.

Hastings, Cynthia Grover, *Letting Down Their Guard*, 24 Boston College Third World Law Journal 283 (2004). Reprinted by permission.

Herman, Judith Lewis, Trauma and Recovery. Copyright © 1992 by Basic Books, a division of HarperCollins Publishers. Reprinted by permission.

Island, David and Patrick Letellier, The Neighbors Call the Police, Men Who Beat the Men Who Love Them (1991). Harworth Press, Inc. Reprinted by permission.

Jablow, Pamela M., *Victims of Abuse and Discrimination: Protecting Battered Homosexuals Under Domestic Violence Legislation*, 28 Hofstra Law Review 1095 (2000). Reprinted by permission.

Jones, Ann, NEXT TIME SHE'LL BE DEAD: BATTERING AND HOW TO STOP IT (2000) Beacon Press. Reprinted by permission.

Kelly, Linda, *Disabusing the Definition of Domestic Abuse: How Women Batter Men and the Role of the Feminist State,* 30 Florida State University Law Review 791 (2003). Reprinted by permission.

Kelly, Linda, *Stories From the Front: Seeking Refuge for Battered Immigrants in the Violence Against Women Act*, 92 Northwestern University Law Review 665 (1998). Reprinted by special permission of Northwestern University School of Law, Northwestern University Law Review.

King, Carol J., *Burdening Access to Justice: The Cost of Divorce Mediation on the Cheap*, 73 St. John's Law Review 375 (1999). Reprinted by permission.

Koh, Harold Hongju, *Why America Should Ratify the Women's Rights Treaty*, 34 Case Western Reserve Journal of International Law 263 (2002). Reprinted by permission.

Kurz, Demie, FOR RICHER FOR POORER: MOTHERS CONFRONT DIVORCE (1995) Routledge Press. Reprinted by permission.

Lehrman, Fredrica, DOMESTIC VIOLENCE PRACTICE AND PROCEDURE, Thomson West (1996) (2005 Supplement). Reprinted by permission.

Lemon, Nancy K. D., *Statutes Creating Rebuttable Presumptions Against Custody to Batterers: How Effective Are They?* 28 William Mitchell Law Review 601 (2001). Reprinted by permission.

Lightman, Lisa and Francine Byrne, *Addressing the Co-Occurrence of Domestic Violence & Substance Abuse: Lessons from Problem-Solving Courts*, 6 Journal of the Center for Families, Children & the Courts 53 (2005). Reprinted by permission.

Lininger, Tom, *Prosecuting Batterers After Crawford*, 91 Virginia Law Review 747 (2005). Reprinted by permission.

Lundy, Sandra, *Abuse That Dare Not Speak Its Name: Assisting Victims of Lesbian and Gay Domestic Violence in Massachusetts*, 28 New England Law Review 273 (1993). Reprinted by permission.

Lutz, Victoria L. and Cara E. Gady, *Necessary Measures and Logistics to Maximize the Safety of Victims of Domestic Violence Attending Parent Education Programs*, 42 Family Court Review 363 (2004). Reprinted by permission.

Mahoney, Martha R., *Legal Images of Battered Women: Redefining the Issue of Separation*, 90 Michigan Law Review 1 (1991). Reprinted by permission.

Maldonado, Solangel, *Beyond Economic Fatherhood: Encouraging Divorced Fathers to Parent*, 153 University of Pennsylvania Law Review 921 (2005). Reprinted by permission.

Marcus, Isabel, *Reframing "Domestic Violence": Terrorism in the Home;* in THE PUBLIC NATURE OF PRIVATE VIOLENCE (M. A. Fineman and R. Mykitiuk, eds. 1994), Routledge Press. Reprinted by permission.

Margulies, Peter, *Battered Bargaining: Domestic Violence and Plea Negotiations in the Criminal Justice System*, 11 Southern California Review of Law and Women's Studies 153 (2001). Reprinted by permission.

McConnell, Joyce, *Beyond Metaphor: Battered Women, Involuntary Servitude and the Thirteenth Amendment,* 4 Yale Journal of Law and Feminism 207 (1992). Reprinted by permission.

Meier, Joan S., *Domestic Violence, Child Custody, and Child Protection: Understanding Judicial Resistance and Imagining the Solutions*, 11 American University Journal of Gender, Social Policy and the Law 657 (2003). Reprinted by permission.

Meier, Joan, *Notes From the Underground: Integrating Psychological and Legal Perspectives on Domestic Violence in Theory and Practice*, 121 Hofstra Law Review 1295 (1993). Reprinted by permission.

Melissa, Rachel L., *Oregon's Response to the Impact of Domestic Violence on Children*, 82 Oregon Law Review 1125 (2003). Reprinted by permission.

Merry, Sally Engle, *Constructing A Global Law--Violence Against Women and the Human Rights System*, 28 Law and Social Inquiry 941 (2003). Reprinted by permission.

Miccio, G. Kristian, *A House Divided: Mandatory Arrest, Domestic Violence, and the Conservativization of the Battered Women's Movement*, 42 Houston Law Review 237 (2005). Reprinted by permission.

Mills, Linda, *Killing Her Softly: Intimate Abuse and the Violence of State Intervention*, 113 Harvard Law Review 550 (1999). Reprinted by permission.

Moore, Shelby A.D., *Understanding the Connection between Domestic Violence, Crime, and Poverty: How Welfare Reform May Keep Battered Women from Leaving Abusive Relationships*, 12 Texas Journal of Women and the Law 451 (2003). Reprinted by permission.

Mordini, Nichole Miras, *Mandatory State Interventions for Domestic Abuse Cases: An Examination of the Effects on Victim Autonomy & Safety*, 52 Drake Law Review 295 (2004). Reprinted by permission.

Moriarty, Jane Campbell, *While Dangers Gather: The Bush Preemption Doctrine, Battered Women, Imminence, and Anticipatory Self-Defense*, 30 New York University Review of Law and Social Change 1 (2005). Reprinted by permission.

Murphy, Jane C., *Lawyering for Social Change: The Power of the Narrative in Domestic Violence Law Reform*, 21 Hofstra Law Review 1243 (1993). Reprinted by permission.

Musalo, Karen, *Protecting Victims of Gendered Persecution: Fear of Floodgates or Call to (Principled) Action?* 14 Virginia Journal of Social Policy & Law 119 (2007). Reprinted by permission.

Nash, Jennifer C., *From Lavender to Purple: Privacy, Black Women, and Feminist Legal Theory*, 11 Cardozo Women's Law Journal 303 (2005). Reprinted by permission.

Newsome, Holli B., *Mail Dominance: A Critical Look at the International Marriage Broker Regulation Act and It's Sufficiency in Curtailing*

Mail-Order Bride Domestic Abuse, 29 Campbell Law Review 291 (2007). Reprinted by permission.

Nutter, Karen, *Domestic Violence in The Lives of Women With Disabilities: No (Accessible) Shelter From The Storm*, 13 Southern California Review of Law and Women's Studies 329 (2004). Reprinted by permission.

Orloff, Leslye E., Mary Ann Dutton, Giselle Aguilar Hass, & Nawal Ammar, *Battered Immigrant Women and the Police Response*, 13 UCLA Women's Law Journal 43 (2003). Reprinted by permission.

Perdue, Kimberly D., *The Impact of Violence on Reproductive Decision-Making* (2006)(unpublished paper). Reprinted by permission.

Picard, Ken, *In Harm's Way: Elder Abuse – Outing the Other Domestic Violence, Seven Days*, Burlington, Vermont, June 9, 2004. Reprinted by permission.

Rabin, Bonnie, *Violence Against Mothers Equals Violence Against Children; Understanding the Connections*, 58 Albany Law Review (1995). Reprinted by permission.

Raeder, Myrna S., *The Better Way: The Role of Batterers' Profiles and Expert "Social Science Framework" Background in Cases Implicating Domestic Violence*, 68 University of Colorado Law Review (1997). Reprinted with permission of the University of Colorado Law Review.

Ramsey, Carolyn B., *Intimate Homicide: Gender and Crime Control, 1880 – 1920*, 77 University of Colorado Law Review 101 (2006). Reprinted with permission of the University of Colorado Law Review.

Richie, Beth, COMPELLED TO CRIME: THE GENDER ENTRAPMENT OF BATTERED BLACK WOMEN (1996) Routledge Press. Reprinted by permission.

Roberts, Dorothy E., *Mothers Who Fail to Protect Their Children*, from MOTHER TROUBLES (Julia E. Hanisberg and Sara Ruddick, eds. 1999) Beacon Press. Reprinted by permission.

Robson, Ruthann, *Lavender Bruises: Intra-Lesbian Violence, Law and Lesbian Legal Theory*, 20 Golden Gate University Law Review 567 (1990). Reprinted by permission.

Rodriguez, Cynthia, *Cynthia's Story*, 3 Whittier Journal of Child and Family Advocacy 123 (2003). Reprinted by permission.

Sack, Emily J., *Domestic Violence Across State Lines: The Full Faith and Credit Clause, Congressional Power, and Interstate Enforcement of Protective Orders*, 98 Northwestern University Law Review 827 (2004). Reprinted by special permission of Northwestern University School of Law, Northwestern University Law Review.

Sack, Emily J., *Battered Women and the State: The Struggle for the Future of Domestic Violence Policy*, 2004 Wisconsin Law Review 1657. Copyright 2004 by The Board of Regents of the University of Wisconsin System; Reprinted by permission of the Wisconsin Law Review.

Schachter, Oscar, United Nations Law, 88 America Journal of International Law 1 (1994). Reproduced with permission from the © American Society of International Law.

Shalleck, Ann, *Theory and Experience in Constructing the Relationship Between Lawyer and Client: Representing Women Who Have Been Abused*, 64 Tennessee Law Review 1019 (1997). Reprinted by permission.

Schechter, Susan, WOMEN AND MALE VIOLENCE: THE VISIONS AND STRUGGLES OF THE BATTERED WOMEN'S MOVEMENT, Boston, MA © 1982, Reprinted with permission from South End Press.

Schmidt, Janell D. and Lawrence W. Sherman, *Does Arrest Deter Domestic Violence?* in DO ARRESTS AND RESTRAINING ORDERS WORK? (E.S. Buzawa & C.G. Buzawa, eds. 1996). Sage Publications, Inc. Reprinted by permission.

Schneider, Elizabeth M., BATTERED WOMEN AND FEMINIST LAWMAKING (2000) Yale University Press. Reprinted by permission.

Schneider, Elizabeth M., *Transnational Law as a Domestic Resource: Thoughts on the Case of Women's Rights*, 38 New England Law Review 689 (2004). Reprinted by permission.

Sharp, Paula, from the book CROWS OVER A WHEATFIELD, by Paula Sharp. Copyright © 1996 Paula Sharp. Reprinted by permission of Hyperion. All rights reserved.

Sherman, Lawrence W., *Domestic Violence and Restorative Justice: Answering Key Questions*, 8 Virginia Journal of Law and Social Policy 263 (2000). Reprinted by permission.

Siegel, Reva B., *"The Rule of Love": Wife Beating As Prerogative and Privacy,* 105 Yale Law Journal 2117 (1996). Reprinted by permission.

Sinden, Amy, *"Why Won't Mom Cooperate?": A Critique of Informality in Child Welfare Proceedings*, 11 Yale Journal of Law and Feminism 339 (1999). Reprinted by permission.

Smith, Judith A., *Battered Non-Wives and Unequal Protection-Order Coverage: A Call for Reform*, 23 Yale Law and Policy Review 93 (2005). Reprinted by permission.

Spears, Linda, *Building Bridges Between Domestic Violence Organizations and Child Protective Services, Violence Against Women Online Resources* (2000), available at http://www.vaw.umn.edu/documents/dvcps/dvcps.html#id76318. Reprinted by permission.

Srikantiah, Jayashri, *Perfect Victims and Real Survivors: The Iconic Victim in Domestic Human Trafficking Law,* 87 Boston University Law Review 157 (2007). Reprinted by permission.

Thomas, Dorothy Q. and Michele E. Beasley, *Domestic Violence As a Human Rights Issue*, 58 Albany Law Review 1119 (1995). Reprinted by permission.

Tuerkheimer, Deborah, *Recognizing and Remedying the Harm of Battering: A Call to Criminalize Domestic Violence*, 94 Journal of Criminal Law and Criminology 959 (2004). Reprinted by permission.

Tuerkheimer, Deborah, *Reconceptualizing Violence Against Pregnant Women*, 81 Indiana Law Journal 667 (2006). Reprinted by permission.

Walker, Lenore, TERRIFYING LOVE: WHY BATTERED WOMEN KILL AND HOW SOCIETY RESPONDS. Copyright © 1990 by Lenore E. Auerbach Walker. HarperCollins Publishers, Inc. Reprinted by permission.

Walker, Lenore, *The Battered Women Syndrome is a Psychological Consequence of Abuse*, CURRENT CONTROVERSIES ON FAMILY VIOLENCE (R.J. Gelles & D.R. Loseke, EDS., Sage Publications 1993). Reprinted by permission.

Walker-Wilson, Molly J., *An Evolutionary Perspective on Male Domestic Violence: Practical and Policy Implications*, 32 American Journal of Criminal Law 291 (2005). Reprinted by permission.

Wang, Karin, *Battered Asian American Women: Community Responses from the Battered Women's Movement and the Asian American Community*, 3 Asian Law Journal 151 (1996). Reprinted by permission.

West, Robin, *Toward an Abolitionist Interpretation of the Fourteenth Amendment*, 94 West Virginia Law Review 111 (1991). Reprinted by permission.

Wriggins, Jennifer, *Domestic Violence Torts*, 75 Southern California Law Review 121 (2001). Reprinted by permission.

Zorza, Joan, *The Criminal Law of Misdemeanor Violence*, 1970-1990, 83 Journal of Criminal Law & Criminology 46 (1992). Reprinted by permission.

*

SUMMARY OF CONTENTS

PREFACE v
ACKNOWLEDGEMENTS vii
TABLE OF CASES xxxix

CHAPTER ONE. Domestic Violence in Historical and Social Context 4

A. Experiences with Domestic Violence 5
B. The Pervasiveness of Domestic Violence 8
C. Domestic Violence: A Historical Perspective 13
D. History of the Current Domestic Violence Movement 18
E. Current Controversies 23
F. The U.S. Supreme Court and Domestic Violence 28

CHAPTER TWO. The Dynamics of Abusive Relationships 38

A. Women's Experiences of Abusive Relationships 41
B. Men's Experiences as Abusers 72

CHAPTER THREE. Dimensions of the Battering Experience 85

A. Battering in Same–Sex Relationships 86
B. Race, Culture, Immigration, Religion and the Experience of Abuse ... 97
C. Teens, Elders, and Individuals with Disabilities as Victims of Domestic Violence 127
D. Battered Women and Poverty 140

CHAPTER FOUR. Domestic Violence, Reproductive Rights and Sexual Autonomy 154

A. Sexual Consent and Marital Rape 155
B. Access to Birth Control and Disease Prevention 164
C. Reproductive Rights 171
D. Battering During Pregnancy 178

CHAPTER FIVE. Legal Characterizations of Battered% Women and Their Experiences 191

CHAPTER SIX. Domestic Violence and Civil Protective Orders 210

A. Scope of Protection 214
B. Issues of Process 237
C. Enforcement 257
D. Efficacy 269

CHAPTER SEVEN. Domestic Violence and Criminal Justice 274

A. It's a Crime — 275
B. Police and Arrest Policies — 292
C. Prosecution Policies — 314
D. Sentencing — 339
E. Domestic Violence as a Federal Crime — 355

CHAPTER EIGHT. Evidence in Domestic Violence Cases — 373

A. Physical Evidence — 373
B. Statements Made to Law Enforcement — 375
C. Prior Acts and Patterns of Abuse — 391
D. Expert Testimony — 395
E. Spouses and Children as Witnesses — 409
F. Statements Made to Medical Professionals — 416

CHAPTER NINE. Defenses Available to Battered Women Defendants — 423

A. Women's Self–Defense Claims: Gender Bias and the Role of Expert Testimony — 424
B. Battered Criminal Defendants and Alternative Defense Theories — 461
C. Post–Conviction Relief and Clemency — 485

CHAPTER TEN. Domestic Violence and Family Law — 502

A. Divorce and the Distribution of Assets — 504
B. Setting the Scene to Think About Custody — 517
C. Best Interests of the Child — 530
D. Statutes that Create Presumptions Against Awarding Custody to Batterers — 538
E. Joint Custody and Friendly Parent Provisions — 545
F. Visitation — 554
G. Relocation — 564

CHAPTER ELEVEN. Processing Domestic Violence Cases in Family Courts — 598

A. The Role of the Guardian Ad Litem in Cases Involving Domestic Violence — 598
B. Expert Witnesses in Domestic Violence Family Law Cases — 611
C. Mediation in the Context of Abuse — 617
D. Parental Education Programs When There Has Been Domestic Violence — 637

CHAPTER TWELVE.   Domestic Violence and the Child Protective System --- 645

A. The Workings of the Child Welfare System ---------------------------- 653
B. How the System Works Against Battered Women --------------------- 659
C. Constitutional Issues in *Nicholson v. Williams* ------------------- 670
D. Prosecuting Battered Mothers for Failure to Protect ----------------- 673
E. Traditional Tensions and New Collaborations ------------------------- 688

CHAPTER THIRTEEN.   Domestic Violence and Tort Law ----- 697

A. Interspousal Tort Immunity --------------------------------- 698
B. Existing Causes of Action --------------------------------- 703
C. Abusers' Defensive Actions to Tort Suits -------------------- 717
D. The Relationship Between Tort Actions and Divorce Proceedings--- 737

CHAPTER FOURTEEN.   Law Enforcement and Employer Liability for Domestic Violence ----------------------------- 744

A. When Law Enforcement Fails to Protect ------------------------ 745
B. Domestic Violence at the Workplace---------------------------- 785

CHAPTER FIFTEEN.   Domestic Violence, Immigration and Asylum --- 812

A. The Immigrant Victim of Domestic Violence --------------------- 813
B. Asylum --- 829

CHAPTER SIXTEEN.   Domestic Violence as a Violation of Civil Rights --- 849

A. Violence, Equality and Citizenship----------------------------- 851
B. The Civil Rights Remedy Created by the Violence Against Women Act of 1994--- 859
C. State Civil Rights Remedies ----------------------------------- 894

CHAPTER SEVENTEEN.   Domestic Violence as a Violation of International Human Rights --------------------------------- 900

A. Domestic Violence as a Violation of International Human Rights --- 901
B. International Human Rights Documents and Reports on Domestic Violence--- 912
C. Linking the International to the Domestic ------------------------ 936

CHAPTER EIGHTEEN.   Doing the Work------------------------- 942

A. Representing Clients Who Have Been Abused ---------------------- 943
B. Legal Advocacy: A Changed and Changing Landscape -------------- 968

Index -- 991

*

TABLE OF CONTENTS

PREFACE v
ACKNOWLEDGEMENTS vii
TABLE OF CASES xxxix

CHAPTER ONE. Domestic Violence in Historical and Social Context 4
A. Experiences with Domestic Violence 5
    Notes and Questions 7
B. The Pervasiveness of Domestic Violence 8
    Notes and Questions 11
C. Domestic Violence: A Historical Perspective 13
    Bradley v. State 14
    Notes and Questions 15
    Reva B. Siegel, "The Rule of Love": Wife Beating As Prerogative and Privacy 16
    Notes and Questions 18
D. History of the Current Domestic Violence Movement 18
    Susan Schechter, Women and Male Violence: The Visions and Struggles of the Battered Women's Movement (1982) 18
    Elizabeth M. Schneider, Battered Women and Feminist Lawmaking (2000) 20
    Notes and Questions 21
E. Current Controversies 23
    Elizabeth M. Schneider, Battered Women and Feminist Lawmaking (2000) 24
    Emily J. Sack, Battered Women and the State: The Struggle for the Future of Domestic Violence Policy 25
F. The U.S. Supreme Court and Domestic Violence 28
    Planned Parenthood v. Casey 29
    United States v. Morrison 30
    Town of Castle Rock, Colorado v. Gonzales 34
    Notes and Questions 35

CHAPTER TWO. The Dynamics of Abusive Relationships 38
A. Women's Experiences of Abusive Relationships 41
    Angela Browne, Courtship and Early Marriage: From Affection to Assault, When Battered Women Kill (1987) 42
    Notes and Questions 48
    Karla Fischer, Neil Vidmar and Rene Ellis, The Culture of Battering and the Role of Mediation in Domestic Violence Cases ... 49
    Notes and Questions 55
    Lenore Walker, Terrifying Love: Why Battered Women Kill and How Society Responds (1989) 56
    Power and Control and Equality Wheels 58
    Domestic Abuse Intervention Project, Duluth, Minnesota 58
    Notes and Questions 58

A. Women's Experiences of Abusive Relationships—Continued

Sarah M. Buel, Fifty Obstacles to Leaving, *a.k.a.,* Why Abuse Victims Stay 59

Notes and Questions 63

Edward Gondolf with Ellen Fisher, Battered Women as Survivors: An Alternative to Treating Learned Helplessness (1988) 66

Notes and Questions 68

B. Men's Experiences as Abusers 72

Cheryl Hanna, The Paradox of Hope: The Crime and Punishment of Domestic Violence 73

Notes and Questions 77

Lundy Bancroft, Why Does He Do That? Inside the Minds of Angry and Controlling Men (2002) 81

Notes and Questions 83

CHAPTER THREE. Dimensions of the Battering Experience 85

A. Battering in Same–Sex Relationships 86

David Island and Patrick Letellier, The Neighbors Call the Police, Men Who Beat the Men Who Love Them (1991) 86

Notes and Questions 89

State v. Linner 92

Notes and Questions 94

B. Race, Culture, Immigration, Religion and the Experience of Abuse 97

Beth Richie, Compelled to Crime: The Gender Entrapment of Battered Black Women (1996) 98

Notes and Questions 101

Karin Wang, Battered Asian American Women: Community Responses from the Battered Women's Movement and the Asian American Community 101

Michelle Fine, Rosemarie A. Roberts and Lois Weis, Puerto Rican Battered Women Redefining Gender, Sexuality, Culture, Violence, and Resistance, in Domestic Violence at the Margins, (Natalie J. Sokoloff, ed., 2005) 102

Michelle Decasas, Protecting Hispanic Women: The Inadequacy of Domestic Violence Policy 104

Notes and Questions 106

Minnesota v. Vue 109

Notes and Questions 111

Notes and Questions 112

Kimberle Crenshaw, Mapping the Margins: Intersectionality, Identity Politics, and Violence Against Women of Color 115

Notes and Questions 119

Azizah Y. al–Hibri, An Islamic Perspective on Domestic Violence ... 120

Notes and Questions 120

Stacey A. Guthartz, Domestic Violence and the Jewish Community 121

Notes and Questions 122

C. Teens, Elders, and Individuals with Disabilities as Victims of Domestic Violence ----- 127

    Cheryl Hanna, Sex Before Violence: Girls, Dating Violence, and (Perceived) Sexual Autonomy ----- 127

    Cynthia Rodriguez, Cynthia's Story ----- 128

    Notes and Questions ----- 130

    Ken Picard, In Harm's Way: Elder Abuse–Outing the Other Domestic Violence ----- 132

    Notes and Questions ----- 134

    Karen Nutter, Domestic Violence in The Lives Of Women With Disabilities: No (Accessible) Shelter From The Storm ----- 136

    Notes and Questions ----- 138

D. Battered Women and Poverty ----- 140

    Shelby A.D. Moore, Understanding the Connection Between Domestic Violence, Crime, and Poverty: How Welfare Reform May Keep Battered Women From Leaving Abusive Relationships ----- 141

    Notes and Questions ----- 144

    Bouley v. Young–Sabourin ----- 147

    Notes and Questions ----- 149

    Wendy Boka, Domestic Violence in Farming Communities: Overcoming The Unique Problems Posed By The Rural Setting ----- 151

    Notes and Questions ----- 152

CHAPTER FOUR. Domestic Violence, Reproductive Rights and Sexual Autonomy ----- 154

A. Sexual Consent and Marital Rape ----- 155

    State v. Russell ----- 156

    Notes and Questions ----- 161

B. Access to Birth Control and Disease Prevention ----- 164

    Michelle J. Anderson, Marital Immunity, Intimate Relationships, and Improper Inferences: A New Law On Sexual Offenses by Intimates ----- 164

    Notes and Questions ----- 167

C. Reproductive Rights ----- 171

    Planned Parenthood v. Casey ----- 172

    Notes and Questions ----- 176

D. Battering During Pregnancy ----- 178

    Deborah Tuerkheimer, Reconceptualizing Violence Against Pregnant Women ----- 180

    Notes and Questions ----- 183

    People v. Taylor ----- 183

    Notes and Questions ----- 187

CHAPTER FIVE. Legal Characterizations of Battered Women and Their Experiences 191

Connecticut v. Borrelli 195

Notes and Questions 198

People v. Santiago 201

Notes and Questions 205

CHAPTER SIX. Domestic Violence and Civil Protective Orders 210

Barbara Hart, State Codes on Domestic Violence: Analysis, Commentary and Recommendations 212

Notes and Questions 213

A. Scope of Protection 214

  Judith A. Smith, Battered Non–Wives and Unequal Protection Order Coverage: A Call for Reform 216

  Notes and Questions 218

  Peter Finn and Sarah Colson, Civil Protection Orders: Legislation, Current Court Practice, and Enforcement 220

  Notes and Questions 221

  Katsenelenbogen v. Katsenelenbogen 222

  Notes and Questions 226

  Barbara Hart, State Codes on Domestic Violence: Analysis, Commentary and Recommendations 228

  Notes and Questions 231

  Emily J. Sack, Domestic Violence Across State Lines: The Full Faith and Credit Clause, Congressional Power, and Interstate Enforcement of Protective Orders 232

  Notes and Questions 236

B. Issues of Process 237

  Margaret F. Brown, Domestic Violence Advocates' Exposure to Liability for Engaging in the Unauthorized Practice of Law 240

  Notes and Questions 244

  Beverly Balos, Domestic Violence Matters: The Case for Appointed Counsel in Protective Order Proceedings 245

  Notes and Questions 247

  Mitchell v. Mitchell 249

  Notes and Questions 253

  Notes and Questions 257

C. Enforcement 257

  State v. Lucas 258

  Notes and Questions 260

  Notes and Questions 265

D. Efficacy 269

  Beverly Balos, Domestic Violence Matters: The Case for Appointed Counsel in Protective Order Proceedings 270

  Notes and Questions 271

CHAPTER SEVEN. Domestic Violence and Criminal Justice 274

A. It's a Crime 275
  State v. Wright 277
  Notes and Questions 280
  Stalking and Domestic Violence: A Report to Congress 283
  United States Department of Justice, Violence Against Women
    Office, May 2001 283
  Notes and Questions 284

B. Police and Arrest Policies 292
  Georgia v. Randolph 292
  Notes and Questions 297
  Joan Zorza, The Criminal Law of Misdemeanor Domestic Vio-
    lence, 1970–1990 298
  Janell D. Schmidt and Lawrence W. Sherman, Does Arrest Deter
    Domestic Violence? in Do Arrests and Restraining Orders Work?
    (E.S. Buzawa and C.G. Buzawa, eds. 1996) 301
  Notes and Questions 303
  Wade v. Miles 309
  Notes and Questions 312

C. Prosecution Policies 314
  People v. Brown 315
  Notes and Questions 325
  Cheryl Hanna, No Right To Choose: Mandated Victim Partic-
    ipation In Domestic Violence Prosecutions 329
  Notes and Questions 331
  G. Kristian Miccio, A House Divided: Mandatory Arrest, Domestic
    Violence, and the Conservatization of the Battered Women's
    Movement 332
  Notes and Questions 334
  Linda Mills, Killing Her Softly: Intimate Abuse and the Violence
    of State Intervention 335
  Notes and Questions 337

D. Sentencing 339
  Cheryl Hanna, The Paradox of Hope: The Crime and Punishment
    of Domestic Violence 340
  Notes and Questions 341
  Lisa Lightman and Francine Byrne, Addressing the Co–Occur-
    rence of Domestic Violence & Substance Abuse: Lessons from
    Problem–Solving Courts 346
  Notes and Questions 349
  Lawrence W. Sherman, Domestic Violence and Restorative Justice:
    Answering Key Questions 350
  Donna Coker, Enhancing Autonomy for Battered Women: Lessons
    Learned From Navajo Peacemaking 352
  Notes and Questions 355

E. Domestic Violence as a Federal Crime 355
  Michelle W. Easterling, For Better or Worse: The Federalization of
    Domestic Violence 356
  Notes and Questions 358

E. Domestic Violence as a Federal Crime—Continued
   United States v. Page --- 359
   Notes and Questions --- 364
   United States v. Gluzman -- 365
   Michelle Easterling, For Better or Worse: The Federalization of
     Domestic Violence --- 368
   Jamie Gorelick and Harry Litman, Prosecutorial Discretion and
     the Federalization Debate -- 369
   Notes and Questions --- 371

CHAPTER EIGHT. Evidence in Domestic Violence Cases ----- 373
A. Physical Evidence -- 373
   Notes and Questions --- 375
B. Statements Made to Law Enforcement ------------------------------- 375
   Crawford v. Washington -- 375
   Notes and Questions --- 378
   Tom Lininger, Prosecuting Batterers After Crawford ------------ 378
   Notes and Questions --- 380
   *On Writs of Certiorari to the Supreme Courts of Washington and
     Indiana* --- 380
   *Brief of Amici Curiae the National Network to End Domestic
     Violence, Indiana and Washington Coalitions Against Domestic
     Violence, Legal Momentum, et al. in Support of Respondents* 380
   Brief Amicus Curiae of the American Civil Liberties Union ---------- 381
   The ACLU of Washington and the Indiana Civil Liberties Union in
     Support of Petitioners --- 381
   Davis v. Washington -- 382
   Notes and Questions --- 389
C. Prior Acts and Patterns of Abuse --------------------------------------- 391
   State v. Sanders --- 392
   Notes and Questions --- 393
D. Expert Testimony --- 395
   Arcoren v. United States -- 398
   Notes and Questions --- 401
   Ryan v. State --- 404
   Notes and Questions --- 407
E. Spouses and Children as Witnesses ------------------------------------- 409
   State v. Thorton --- 409
   Notes and Questions --- 411
   Rachel L. Melissa, Oregon's Response to the Impact of Domestic
     Violence on Children -- 413
   Notes and Questions --- 415
F. Statements Made to Medical Professionals ------------------------- 416
   United States v. Joe -- 416
   Notes and Questions --- 418

**CHAPTER NINE. Defenses Available to Battered Women
    Defendants** -- 423
A. Women's Self–Defense Claims: Gender Bias and the Role of Expert
   Testimony -- 424
   Elizabeth M. Schneider, Battered Women and Feminist Lawmak-
     ing (2000) -- 424

A. Women's Self–Defense Claims: Gender Bias and the Role of Expert Testimony—Continued

Notes and Questions 427
State of Washington v. Wanrow 430
Notes and Questions 434
State v. Kelly 436
Notes and Questions 442
Elizabeth M. Schneider, Battered Women and Feminist Lawmaking (2000) 446
Notes and Questions 447
People v. Humphrey 448
Notes and Questions 453
State v. Daws 455
Notes and Questions 457
Sarah M. Buel, Effective Assistance of Counsel for Battered Women Defendants: A Normative Construct 458
Notes and Questions 460
B. Battered Criminal Defendants and Alternative Defense Theories ... 461
Shelby A.D. Moore, Understanding the Connection between Domestic Violence, Crime, and Poverty: How Welfare Reform May Keep Battered Women from Leaving Abusive Relationships 461
Notes and Questions 464
Beth I.Z. Boland, Battered Women Who Act Under Duress 465
Notes and Questions 468
People v. Romero 468
Notes and Questions 472
Dunn v. Roberts 475
Notes and Questions 478
Dixon v. United States 479
Notes and Questions 482
C. Post–Conviction Relief and Clemency 485
Elizabeth M. Schneider, Battered Women and Feminist Lawmaking (2000) 485
Notes and Questions 486
Kosmin v. New Jersey State Parole Board 487
Notes and Questions 491
Jane C. Murphy, Lawyering for Social Change: The Power of the Narrative in Domestic Violence Law Reform 494
Notes and Questions 496
Linda L. Ammons, Why Do You Do the Things You Do? Clemency for Battered Incarcerated Women: A Decade's Review 497
Notes and Questions 501

CHAPTER TEN. Domestic Violence and Family Law 502
A. Divorce and the Distribution of Assets 504
Demie Kurz, For Richer For Poorer: Mothers Confront Divorce (1995) 505
Notes and Questions 508

A. Divorce and the Distribution of Assets—Continued

Mehren v. Dargan --- 513

Notes and Questions --- 514

B. Setting the Scene to Think About Custody ------------------------ 517

Paula Sharp, Crows Over A Wheatfield (1996) ----------------- 518

Notes and Questions --- 522

Judith G. Greenberg, Domestic Violence and the Danger of Joint Custody Presumptions --- 522

Notes and Questions --- 524

Joan S. Meier, Domestic Violence, Child Custody, and Child Protection: Understanding Judicial Resistance and Imagining the Solutions -- 524

Notes and Questions --- 530

C. Best Interests of the Child -- 530

Wissink v. Wissink -- 531

Notes and Questions --- 534

D. Statutes that Create Presumptions Against Awarding Custody to Batterers -- 538

Nancy K. D. Lemon, Statutes Creating Rebuttable Presumptions Against Custody to Batterers: How Effective Are They? ----------- 538

Lawrence v. Delkamp -- 539

Notes and Questions --- 542

E. Joint Custody and Friendly Parent Provisions --------------------- 545

Solangel Maldonado, Beyond Economic Fatherhood: Encouraging Divorced Fathers to Parent --- 547

Clare Dalton, When Paradigms Collide: Protecting Battered Parents and Their Children in the Family Court System --------------- 551

Notes and Questions --- 553

F. Visitation -- 554

Karjanis v. Karjanis --- 555

Notes and Questions --- 559

G. Relocation --- 564

Janet M. Bowermaster, Relocation Custody Disputes Involving Domestic Violence --- 566

Notes and Questions --- 568

Janet M. Bowermaster, Relocation Custody Disputes Involving Domestic Violence --- 569

Notes and Questions --- 570

Valentine v. Valentine -- 572

Notes and Questions --- 574

Odom v. Odom --- 577

Notes and Questions --- 580

Notes and Questions --- 581

Deborah M. Goelman, Shelter from the Storm: Using Jurisdictional Statutes to Protect Victims of Domestic Violence after the Violence Against Women Act of 2000 ----------------------------- 585

Notes and Questions --- 587

Olguín v. Santana --- 590

Notes and Questions --- 595

CHAPTER ELEVEN. Processing Domestic Violence Cases in Family Courts 598

A. The Role of the Guardian Ad Litem in Cases Involving Domestic Violence 598

    Notes and Questions 600

    Clark v. Alexander 601

    Notes and Questions 606

    Massachusetts Chapter of the National Association of Social Workers Committee on Domestic Violence and Sexual Assault 609

    Preliminary Report of the Guardian ad Litem Assessment Project ... 609

    Notes and Questions 610

B. Expert Witnesses in Domestic Violence Family Law Cases 611

    Keesee v. Keesee 612

    Notes and Questions 615

C. Mediation in the Context of Abuse 617

    Trina Grillo, The Mediation Alternative: Process Dangers for Women 618

    Karla Fischer, Neil Vidmar and Rene Ellis, The Culture of Battering and the Role of Mediation in Domestic Violence Cases ... 619

    Notes and Questions 624

    Lauri Boxer–Macomber, Revisiting the Impact of California's Mandatory Custody Mediation Program on Victims of Domestic Violence through a Feminist Positionality Lens 626

    Notes and Questions 629

    Carol J. King, Burdening Access to Justice: The Cost of Divorce Mediation on the Cheap 632

    Pearson v. District Court 633

    Notes and Questions 635

D. Parental Education Programs When There Has Been Domestic Violence 637

    Victoria L. Lutz and Cara E. Gady, Necessary Measures and Logistics to Maximize the Safety of Victims of Domestic Violence Attending Parent Education Programs 641

    Notes and Questions 644

CHAPTER TWELVE. Domestic Violence and the Child Protective System 645

Notes and Questions 646

Nicholson v. Williams 648

Notes and Questions 651

A. The Workings of the Child Welfare System 653

    Amy Sinden, "Why Won't Mom Cooperate?": A Critique of Informality in Child Welfare Proceedings 653

    Notes and Questions 656

B. How the System Works Against Battered Women 659

    In Re Glenn G. 659

    Notes and Questions 663

    Nicholson v. Scoppetta 666

    Notes and Questions 668

C. Constitutional Issues in *Nicholson v. Williams* ⸻ 670
D. Prosecuting Battered Mothers for Failure to Protect ⸻ 673
    Campbell v. State ⸻ 674
    Notes and Questions ⸻ 678
    Dorothy E. Roberts, Mothers Who Fail to Protect their Children ⸻ 680
    Notes and Questions ⸻ 685
E. Traditional Tensions and New Collaborations ⸻ 688
    Janet Findlater and Susan Kelly, Child Protective Services and Domestic Violence ⸻ 689
    Linda Spears, Building Bridges Between Domestic Violence Organizations and Child Protective Services ⸻ 689
    Notes and Questions ⸻ 694

CHAPTER THIRTEEN. Domestic Violence and Tort Law ⸻ 697
A. Interspousal Tort Immunity ⸻ 698
    Clare Dalton, Domestic Violence, Domestic Torts, and Divorce: Constraints and Possibilities ⸻ 699
    Notes and Questions ⸻ 700
B. Existing Causes of Action ⸻ 703
    Ira Mark Ellman and Stephen D. Sugarman, Spousal Emotional Abuse as a Tort? ⸻ 706
    Notes and Questions ⸻ 710
    Feltmeier v. Feltmeier ⸻ 711
    Notes and Questions ⸻ 716
C. Abusers' Defensive Actions to Tort Suits ⸻ 717
    Notes and Questions ⸻ 719
    Giovine v. Giovine ⸻ 720
    Nussbaum v. Steinberg ⸻ 721
    Notes and Questions ⸻ 724
    Feltmeier v. Feltmeier ⸻ 726
    Notes and Questions ⸻ 728
    Celley v. Stevens ⸻ 730
    Notes and Questions ⸻ 733
D. The Relationship Between Tort Actions and Divorce Proceedings ⸻ 737
    Twyman v. Twyman ⸻ 737
    Notes and Questions ⸻ 739

CHAPTER FOURTEEN. Law Enforcement and Employer Liability for Domestic Violence ⸻ 744
A. When Law Enforcement Fails to Protect ⸻ 745
    Joan Zorza, The Criminal Law of Misdemeanor Domestic Violence, 1970–1990 ⸻ 745
    Thurman v. City of Torrington ⸻ 748
    Notes and Questions ⸻ 754
    DeShaney v. Winnebago County Dept. of Social Services ⸻ 757
    Notes and Questions ⸻ 761
    Castle Rock v. Gonzales ⸻ 763
    Notes and Questions ⸻ 770
    Massee v. Thompson ⸻ 772

A. When Law Enforcement Fails to Protect—Continued
Notes and Questions -- 777
Donaldson v. City of Seattle -- 780
Notes and Questions -- 785
B. Domestic Violence at the Workplace ------------------------------------- 785
Dildy v. MBW Investments, Inc. -------------------------------------- 788
Notes and Questions -- 791
Carroll v. Shoney's, Inc., d/b/a Captain D's Restaurant -------------- 793
Notes and Questions -- 796
Green v. Bryant -- 799
Notes and Questions -- 802
Fredrica Lehrman, Domestic Violence Practice and Procedure ------- 806
Notes and Questions -- 808

CHAPTER FIFTEEN. Domestic Violence, Immigration and Asylum -- 812
A. The Immigrant Victim of Domestic Violence --------------------------- 813
Julie Dinnerstein, Working with Immigrant Victims of Domestic Violence, in Immigration Remedies for Domestic Violence Victims: VAWA Self–Petitions and Battered Spouse Waivers ---------- 813
Notes and Questions -- 815
Linda Kelly, Stories From the Front: Seeking Refuge for Battered Immigrants in the Violence Against Women Act --------------------- 816
Notes and Questions -- 818
Notes and Questions -- 819
Julie Dinnerstein, Working with Immigrant Victims of Domestic Violence, in Immigration Remedies for Domestic Violence Victims: VAWA Self–Petitions and Battered Spouse Waivers ---------- 822
Notes and Questions -- 823
Jayashri Srikantiah, Perfect Victims and Real Survivors: The Iconic Victim in Domestic Human Trafficking Law ----------------- 825
Notes and Questions -- 827
B. Asylum -- 829
In Re R–A– -- 831
Notes and Questions -- 844

CHAPTER SIXTEEN. Domestic Violence as a Violation of Civil Rights -- 849
A. Violence, Equality and Citizenship -- 851
Isabel Marcus, Reframing Domestic Violence as Terrorism in the Home -- 851
Notes and Questions -- 852
Joyce McConnell, Beyond Metaphor: Battered Women, Involuntary Servitude and the Thirteenth Amendment ----------------------------- 853
Note and Questions -- 855
Robin West, Toward an Abolitionist Interpretation of the Fourteenth Amendment --- 855
Notes and Questions -- 858

B. The Civil Rights Remedy Created by the Violence Against Women
      Act of 1994 --- 859
      Sally Goldfarb, Statement of the NOW Legal Defense and Edu-
        cation Fund on the Violence Against Women Act ------------------- 859
      Notes and Questions --- 865
      Sally F. Goldfarb, Violence Against Women and the Persistence of
        Privacy --- 865
      Notes and Questions --- 869
      Reva B. Siegel, The Rule of Love: Wife Beating as Prerogative ------ 871
      Notes and Questions --- 877
      United States v. Morrison --- 878
      Notes and Questions --- 889
C. State Civil Rights Remedies -- 894
      Julie Goldscheid, The Civil Rights Remedy of the 1994 Violence
        Against Women Act: Struck Down But Not Ruled Out -------------- 894
      Notes and Questions --- 897

**CHAPTER SEVENTEEN. Domestic Violence as a Violation
      of International Human Rights** --------------------------------------- 900
A. Domestic Violence as a Violation of International Human Rights --- 901
      Dorothy Q. Thomas and Michele E. Beasley, Domestic Violence As
        a Human Rights Issue --- 901
      Rhonda Copelon, International Human Rights Dimensions of Inti-
        mate Violence: Another Strand in the Dialectic of Feminist Law
        Making -- 902
      *The Secretary–General's In–Depth Study on All Forms of Violence
        Against Women (2006)* --- 908
      Notes and Questions --- 909
B. International Human Rights Documents and Reports on Domestic
      Violence -- 912
      *The Secretary–General's In–Depth Study on All Forms of Violence
        Against Women (2006)* --- 913
      Harold Hongju Koh, Why America Should Ratify the Women's
        Rights Treaty --- 914
      Notes and Questions --- 915
      General Recommendation No. 19: Violence against Women ----------- 917
      CEDAW Committee, U.N. Doc. A/47/38 (1992) ------------------------ 917
      General Assembly Resolution 48/104 of 20 December 1993 ----------- 919
      Notes and Questions --- 921
      *Preliminary Report of the Special Rapporteur on Violence Against
        Women, Its Causes and Consequences, Radhika Coomaraswamy,
        Commission on Human Rights* --- 923
      Notes and Questions --- 925
      *Report of the Special Rapporteur on Violence Against Women, Its
        Causes and Consequences, Radhika Coomaraswamy, Commis-
        sion on Human Rights* -- 927
      *The Due Diligence Standard as a Tool for the Elimination of
        Violence against Women* --- 930

B. International Human Rights Documents and Reports on Domestic
    Violence—Continued
    *Report of the Special Rapporteur on Violence against Women, its
    Causes and Consequences, Yakin Ertürk, Commission on Hu-
    man Rights* 930
    Notes and Questions 932
    Human Rights Watch 934
    World Report 2000 934
    Notes and Questions 935
C. Linking the International to the Domestic 936
    Elizabeth M. Schneider, Transnational Law as a Domestic Re-
    source: Thoughts on the Case of Women's Rights 936
    Notes and Questions 940

CHAPTER EIGHTEEN. Doing the Work 942
A. Representing Clients Who Have Been Abused 943
    Ann Shalleck, Theory and Experience in Constructing the Rela-
    tionship Between Lawyer and Client: Representing Women Who
    Have Been Abused 943
    Notes and Questions 945
    Ann Shalleck, Theory and Experience in Constructing the Rela-
    tionship between Lawyer and Client: Representing Women Who
    Have Been Abused 946
    Notes and Questions 951
    Judith Lewis Herman, Trauma and Recovery 952
    Notes and Questions 957
    Joan S. Meier, Notes From the Underground: Integrating Psycho-
    logical and Legal Perspectives on Domestic Violence in Theory
    and Practice 958
    Notes and Questions 960
    Lois H. Kanter and V. Pualani Enos, ... 960
    Client–Centered Interviewing and Counseling Skills 960
    Notes and Questions 966
B. Legal Advocacy: A Changed and Changing Landscape 968
    Emily J. Sack, Battered Women and the State: The Struggle for
    the Future of Domestic Violence Policy 968
    Notes and Questions 973
    Sarah M. Buel, Effective Assistance of Counsel for Battered Wom-
    en Defendants: A Normative Construct 975
    Notes and Questions 977
    Ann Jones, Next Time She'll Be Dead: Battering and How to Stop
    It 983
    Notes and Questions 987

INDEX 991

*

TABLE OF CASES

Principal cases are in bold type. Non-principal cases are in roman type. References are to Pages.

Adoption of (see name of party)

Alan FF., In re, 811 N.Y.S.2d 158 (N.Y.A.D. 3 Dept.2006), 669

Alber v. Alber, 2006 WL 399656 (Mich.App. 2006), 516

Aldinger v. Segler, 263 F.Supp.2d 284 (D.Puerto Rico 2003), 596

Allen, Commonwealth v., 506 Pa. 500, 486 A.2d 363 (Pa.1984), 264

Apessos v. Memorial Press Group, 2002 WL 31324115 (Mass.Super.2002), 802

Appleby, Commonwealth v., 380 Mass. 296, 402 N.E.2d 1051 (Mass.1980), 163

Application of (see name of party)

Arab, United States v., 2001 WL 536476 (Army Ct.Crim.App.2001), 164

Arcoren v. United States, 929 F.2d 1235 (8th Cir.1991), **398**

Ayotte v. Planned Parenthood of Northern New England, 546 U.S. 320, 126 S.Ct. 961, 163 L.Ed.2d 812 (2006), 178

Bailey, United States v., 112 F.3d 758 (4th Cir.1997), 365

Balistreri v. Pacifica Police Dept., 901 F.2d 696 (9th Cir.1988), 754

Bambi's Roofing, Inc. v. Moriarty, Dahms & Yarian, 859 N.E.2d 347 (Ind.App.2006), 726

Bates, In re Marriage of, 212 Ill.2d 489, 289 Ill.Dec. 218, 819 N.E.2d 714 (Ill.2004), 608

Bather v. Bather, 170 S.W.3d 487 (Mo.App. W.D.2005), 562

Bechtel v. State, 840 P.2d 1 (Okla.Crim.App. 1992), 457

Belay v. Getachew, 272 F.Supp.2d 553 (D.Md. 2003), 596

Bergeron v. Bergeron, 48 F.Supp.2d 628 (M.D.La.1999), 877

Bhatia v. Debek, 2005 WL 1271709 (Conn.Super.2005), 562

Bishop, Commonwealth v., 416 Mass. 169, 617 N.E.2d 990 (Mass.1993), 163

Blazel v. Bradley, 698 F.Supp. 756 (W.D.Wis. 1988), 238

Blondin v. Dubois, 238 F.3d 153 (2nd Cir. 2001), 596

Blondin v. Dubois, 78 F.Supp.2d 283 (S.D.N.Y.2000), 597

Borrelli, State v., 227 Conn. 153, 629 A.2d 1105 (Conn.1993), **195**

Bouley v. Young–Sabourin, 394 F.Supp.2d 675 (D.Vt.2005), **147**

Boyle v. Boyle, 12 Pa. D. & C.3d 767 (Pa. Com.Pl.1979), 238

Bradley v. State, 1 Miss. 156 (Miss.1824), **14**

Bradwell v. State of Illinois, 83 U.S. 130, 21 L.Ed. 442 (1872), 13

Brennan v. Orban, 145 N.J. 282, 678 A.2d 667 (N.J.1996), 739

Brinkman v. Brinkman, 966 S.W.2d 780 (Tex. App.-San Antonio 1998), 740

Brown v. Bronx Cross County Medical Group, 834 F.Supp. 105 (S.D.N.Y.1993), 798

Brown, In re Marriage of, 187 S.W.3d 143 (Tex.App.-Waco 2006), 515

Brown, People v., 117 Cal.Rptr.2d 738 (Cal.App.Super.2001), **315**

Brunson v. State of Arkansas, 349 Ark. 300, 79 S.W.3d 304 (Ark.2002), 407

Brzonkala v. Virginia Polytechnic Institute & State University, 169 F.3d 820 (4th Cir. 1999), 878

Calloway v. Kinkelaar, 168 Ill.2d 312, 213 Ill.Dec. 675, 659 N.E.2d 1322 (Ill.1995), 778

Campbell v. Campbell, 294 N.J.Super. 18, 682 A.2d 272 (N.J.Super.L.1996), 779

Campbell v. State, 999 P.2d 649 (Wyo. 2000), **674**

Cardell, State v., 318 N.J.Super. 175, 723 A.2d 111 (N.J.Super.A.D.1999), 285

Carroll v. Shoney's, Inc. d/b/a Captain D's Restaurant, 775 So.2d 753 (Ala. 2000), **793**

Carswell, State v., 114 Ohio St.3d 210, 871 N.E.2d 547 (Ohio 2007), 96

Castle Rock v. Gonzales, 545 U.S. 748, 125 S.Ct. 2796, 162 L.Ed.2d 658 (2005), **34, 212,** 265, 688, **763,** 771, 940

C.B.M. Group, Inc., United States and Alvera v., No. 01–857–PA (D. Or. filed June 8, 2001), 149

Celley v. Stevens, 2004 WL 134000 (Mich. App.2004), **730**

Cellini v. City of Sterling Heights, 856 F.Supp. 1215 (E.D.Mich.1994), 754

Chesser v. City of Hammond, 725 N.E.2d 926 (Ind.App.2000), 809

Christians v. Christians, 637 N.W.2d 377 (S.D.2001), 716

Christopher B., In re, 809 N.Y.S.2d 202 (N.Y.A.D. 2 Dept.2006), 669

Ciskie, State v., 110 Wash.2d 263, 751 P.2d 1165 (Wash.1988), 403

Clark v. Alexander, 953 P.2d 145 (Wyo. 1998), **601**

Cole v. Cole, 147 Misc.2d 297, 556 N.Y.S.2d 217 (N.Y.Fam.Ct.1990), 258

Collins v. Pond Creek Mining Co., 468 F.3d 213 (4th Cir.2006), 734

Commonwealth v. _____ (see opposing party)

Cox v. Brazo, 165 Ga.App. 888, 303 S.E.2d 71 (Ga.App.1983), 798

Crawford v. Washington, 541 U.S. 36, 124 S.Ct. 1354, 158 L.Ed.2d 177 (2004), **375**

Cronic, United States v., 466 U.S. 648, 104 S.Ct. 2039, 80 L.Ed.2d 657 (1984), 486

Culberson v. Doan, 65 F.Supp.2d 701 (S.D.Ohio 1999), 877

Custody of Krause, In re, 304 Mont. 202, 19 P.3d 811 (Mont.2001), 608, 611

C.W. v. K.A.W., 774 A.2d 745 (Pa.Super.2001), 600

Daubert v. Merrell Dow Pharmaceuticals, Inc., 509 U.S. 579, 113 S.Ct. 2786, 125 L.Ed.2d 469 (1993), 397

Daulo v. Commonwealth Edison, 938 F.Supp. 1388 (N.D.Ill.1996), 798

Davis v. Monroe County Bd. of Educ., 526 U.S. 629, 119 S.Ct. 1661, 143 L.Ed.2d 839 (1999), 893

Davis v. Remy, 2006 WL 2780114 (Ohio App. 4 Dist.2006), 733

Davis v. Washington, ___ U.S. ___, 126 S.Ct. 2266, 165 L.Ed.2d 224 (2006), 380, **382**

Daws, State v., 104 Ohio App.3d 448, 662 N.E.2d 805 (Ohio App. 2 Dist.1994), **455**

Deacon v. Landers, 68 Ohio App.3d 26, 587 N.E.2d 395 (Ohio App. 4 Dist.1990), 256

Department of Housing & Urban Development v. Rucker, 535 U.S. 125, 122 S.Ct. 1230, 152 L.Ed.2d 258 (2002), 147

DeShaney v. Winnebago County Dept. of Social Services, 489 U.S. 189, 109 S.Ct. 998, 103 L.Ed.2d 249 (1989), 265, 688, **757**

DiDomenico, United States v., 985 F.2d 1159 (2nd Cir.1993), 397

Dildy v. MBW Investments, Inc., 152 N.C.App. 65, 566 S.E.2d 759 (N.C.App. 2002), **788**

Dixon v. United States, ___ U.S. ___, 126 S.Ct. 2437, 165 L.Ed.2d 299 (2006), 198, **479**

Dixon, United States v., 413 F.3d 520 (5th Cir.2005), 396, 473

Dixon, United States v., 509 U.S. 688, 113 S.Ct. 2849, 125 L.Ed.2d 556 (1993), 266

Doe v. Doe, 929 F.Supp. 608 (D.Conn.1996), 877

Doe v. Garcia, 5 F.Supp.2d 767 (D.Ariz.1998), 719

Doe v. Holy See, 793 N.Y.S.2d 565 (N.Y.A.D. 3 Dept.2005), 719

Donaldson v. City of Seattle, 65 Wash. App. 661, 831 P.2d 1098 (Wash.App. Div. 1 1992), **780**

Dowd, State v., 1994 WL 18645 (Ohio App. 9 Dist.1994), 403

Doyal v. Oklahoma Heart, Inc., 213 F.3d 492 (10th Cir.2000), 809

Duchesne v. Sugarman, 566 F.2d 817 (2nd Cir.1977), 672

Dunn v. Roberts, 963 F.2d 308 (10th Cir. 1992), **475**

Duong v. County of Arapahoe, 837 P.2d 226 (Colo.App.1992), 761

Duplechin v. Toce, 497 So.2d 763 (La.App. 3 Cir.1986), 701

Eagleston v. Guido, 41 F.3d 865 (2nd Cir. 1994), 754

Eisenstadt v. Baird, 405 U.S. 438, 92 S.Ct. 1029, 31 L.Ed.2d 349 (1972), 167

Ely, Commonwealth v., 396 Pa.Super. 330, 578 A.2d 540 (Pa.Super.1990), 473

Eryck N., In re, 791 N.Y.S.2d 857 (N.Y.A.D. 3 Dept.2005), 669

Ex parte (see name of party)

Fabre v. Walton, 441 Mass. 9, 802 N.E.2d 1030 (Mass.2004), 735

Fazal–Ur–Raheman–Fazal, United States v., 355 F.3d 40 (1st Cir.2004), 597

Feltmeier v. Feltmeier, 207 Ill.2d 263, 278 Ill.Dec. 228, 798 N.E.2d 75 (Ill.2003), **711, 726**

Flugge v. Flugge, 681 N.W.2d 837 (S.D.2004), 742

Fortin, People v., 184 Misc.2d 10, 706 N.Y.S.2d 611 (N.Y.Co.Ct.2000), 562

Foster v. Cleveland Clinic Foundation, 2004 WL 2914985 (Ohio App. 8 Dist.2004), 792

Franco v. Mudford, 60 Mass.App.Ct. 1112, 802 N.E.2d 129 (Mass.App.Ct.2004), 733, 735

Freeman v. Ferguson, 911 F.2d 52 (8th Cir. 1990), 762

Friedrich v. Friedrich, 78 F.3d 1060 (6th Cir. 1996), 596

Frost, State v., 242 N.J.Super. 601, 577 A.2d 1282 (N.J.Super.A.D.1990), 403

Frye v. United States, 293 F. 1013 (D.C.Cir. 1923), 397

Fuentes v. Shevin, 407 U.S. 67, 92 S.Ct. 1983, 32 L.Ed.2d 556 (1972), 238

Galvin v. Francis, 2003 WL 21696740 (N.Y.Sup.2003), 729

Gates v. Gates, 277 Ga. 175, 587 S.E.2d 32 (Ga.2003), 701, 702

Georgia v. Randolph, 547 U.S. 103, 126 S.Ct. 1515, 164 L.Ed.2d 208 (2006), **292**

Giovine v. Giovine, 284 N.J.Super. 3, 663 A.2d 109 (N.J.Super.A.D.1995), **720, 729**

Glauber v. Glauber, 192 A.D.2d 94, 600 N.Y.S.2d 740 (N.Y.A.D. 2 Dept.1993), 124

Glenn G., In re, 154 Misc.2d 677, 587 N.Y.S.2d 464 (N.Y.Fam.Ct.1992), **659**

Gluzman, United States v., 154 F.3d 49 (2nd Cir.1998), 365

Gluzman, United States v., 953 F.Supp. 84 (S.D.N.Y.1997), 365, **365**

Gonzales v. Carhart, ___ U.S. ___, 127 S.Ct. 1610, 167 L.Ed.2d 480 (2007), 154, 178

Gonzales v. Oregon, 546 U.S. 243, 126 S.Ct. 904, 163 L.Ed.2d 748 (2006), 890

Gonzales v. Raich, 545 U.S. 1, 125 S.Ct. 2195, 162 L.Ed.2d 1 (2005), 890

Green v. Bryant, 887 F.Supp. 798 (E.D.Pa. 1995), **799**

Greenberg v. McCabe, 453 F.Supp. 765 (E.D.Pa.1978), 725

Griffin v. AAA Auto Club South, Inc., 221 Ga.App. 1, 470 S.E.2d 474 (Ga.App.1996), 797

Griswold v. Connecticut, 381 U.S. 479, 85 S.Ct. 1678, 14 L.Ed.2d 510 (1965), 167

Gross v. Gross, 836 N.Y.S.2d 166 (N.Y.A.D. 1 Dept.2007), 508

Grove, Commonwealth v., 363 Pa.Super. 328, 526 A.2d 369 (Pa.Super.1987), 454

Guerrero v. Memorial Medical Center of East Texas, 938 S.W.2d 789 (Tex.App.-Beaumont 1997), 796

Guest, United States v., 383 U.S. 745, 86 S.Ct. 1170, 16 L.Ed.2d 239 (1966), 883

Guillory v. Interstate Gas Station, 653 So.2d 1152 (La.1995), 792

Guinn, State v., 105 Wash.App. 1030 (Wash. App. Div. 2 2001), 164

Hagedorn v. Hagedorn, 584 So.2d 353 (La. App. 3 Cir.1991), 584

Hagerty, State v., 2002 WL 707858 (Tenn. Crim.App.2002), 461

Harris v. State, 71 Miss. 462, 14 So. 266 (Miss.1894), 15

Heacock v. Heacock, 30 Mass.App.Ct. 304, 568 N.E.2d 621 (Mass.App.Ct.1991), 742

Helem, United States v., 186 F.3d 449 (4th Cir.1999), 364

Hemric v. Reed and Prince Mfg. Co., 54 N.C.App. 314, 283 S.E.2d 436 (N.C.App. 1981), 792

Hendricks, State v., 173 Vt. 132, 787 A.2d 1270 (Vt.2001), 393

Hernandez v. Ashcroft, 345 F.3d 824 (9th Cir.2003), 512, 820

Holder v. Polanski, 111 N.J. 344, 544 A.2d 852 (N.J.1988), 571

Hope House, Inc., State ex rel. v. Merrigan, 133 S.W.3d 44 (Mo.2004), 147

Howle, Ex parte, 776 So.2d 133 (Ala.2000), 740

Hugo, Adoption of, 428 Mass. 219, 700 N.E.2d 516 (Mass.1998), 672

Humphrey, People v., 56 Cal.Rptr.2d 142, 921 P.2d 1 (Cal.1996), **448**

Hutcherson v. City of Phoenix, 192 Ariz. 51, 961 P.2d 449 (Ariz.1998), 779

Illinois v. Gaines, 9 Ill.App.3d 589, 292 N.E.2d 500 (Ill.App. 3 Dist.1973), 189

Imes v. City of Asheville, 163 N.C.App. 668, 594 S.E.2d 397 (N.C.App.2004), 802

In re (see name of party)

Ireland v. Ireland, 246 Conn. 413, 717 A.2d 676 (Conn.1998), 571

Jabri v. Qaddura, 108 S.W.3d 404 (Tex.App.-Fort Worth 2003), 123

Jacques v. DiMarzio, Inc., 386 F.3d 192 (2nd Cir.2004), 810

Jaffee v. Redmond, 518 U.S. 1, 116 S.Ct. 1923, 135 L.Ed.2d 337 (1996), 163

Joe, United States v., 8 F.3d 1488 (10th Cir.1993), **416**

Johnson, United States v., 956 F.2d 894 (9th Cir.1992), 472

Jones v. Jones, 242 N.J.Super. 195, 576 A.2d 316 (N.J.Super.A.D.1990), 718

Jones v. Pledger, 363 F.2d 986 (D.C.Cir. 1966), 705

Kargoe v. Mitchell, 785 N.Y.S.2d 557 (N.Y.A.D. 3 Dept.2004), 563

Karjanis v. Karjanis, 2005 WL 1274112 (Conn.Super.2005), **555**

Katsenelenbogen v. Katsenelenbogen, 365 Md. 122, 775 A.2d 1249 (Md.2001), **222**

Keesee v. Keesee, 675 So.2d 655 (Fla.App. 5 Dist.1996), **612**

Kelly, State v., 97 N.J. 178, 478 A.2d 364 (N.J.1984), 397, **436**

Kerans v. Porter Paint Co., 61 Ohio St.3d 486, 575 N.E.2d 428 (Ohio 1991), 798

Kmart Corp. v. Workers' Comp. Bd., 561 Pa. 111, 748 A.2d 660 (Pa.2000), 792

Kosmin v. New Jersey State Parole Bd., 363 N.J.Super. 28, 830 A.2d 914 (N.J.Super.A.D.2003), **487**

Krank v. Krank, 529 N.W.2d 844 (N.D.1995), 545

Kuhn v. Kuhn, 1999 WL 519326 (N.D.Ill. 1999), 877

Kumho Tire Co. v. Carmichael, 526 U.S. 137, 119 S.Ct. 1167, 143 L.Ed.2d 238 (1999), 397

Kurr, People v., 253 Mich.App. 317, 654 N.W.2d 651 (Mich.App.2002), 189

Lamb, Commonwealth v., 365 Mass. 265, 311 N.E.2d 47 (Mass.1974), 608

Lamb v. Lamb, 939 So.2d 918 (Ala.Civ.App. 2006), 535

Lassiter v. Department of Social Services, 452 U.S. 18, 101 S.Ct. 2153, 68 L.Ed.2d 640 (1981), 245

Lawrence v. Delkamp, 658 N.W.2d 758 (N.D. 2003), 542

Lawrence v. Delkamp, 620 N.W.2d 151 (N.D.2000), **539**

Lawrence v. Roberdeau, 665 N.W.2d 719 (N.D.2003), 736

Lawrence v. Texas, 539 U.S. 558, 123 S.Ct. 2472, 156 L.Ed.2d 508 (2003), 95

Lillith, In re, 61 Mass.App.Ct. 132, 807 N.E.2d 237 (Mass.App.Ct.2004), 544

Linner, State v., 77 Ohio Misc.2d 22, 665 N.E.2d 1180 (Ohio Mun.1996), **92**

Lippman, United States v., 369 F.3d 1039 (8th Cir.2004), 346

Lisa B. v. Salim G., 801 N.Y.S.2d 235 (N.Y.Fam.Ct.2005), 562

Lopez, United States v., 514 U.S. 549, 115 S.Ct. 1624, 131 L.Ed.2d 626 (1995), 364, 879

Losinski v. County of Trempealeau, 946 F.2d 544 (7th Cir.1991), 761

Lucas, State v., 100 Ohio St.3d 1, 795 N.E.2d 642 (Ohio 2003), **258**

Lusby v. Lusby, 283 Md. 334, 390 A.2d 77 (Md.1978), 702

Malott v. Her Majesty the Queen, 1 S.CR 123 (1998), 444

Margrabia, Matter of, 695 A.2d 1378 (N.J. 1997), 811

Marriage of (see name of party)

Marsh, State ex rel. Williams v., 626 S.W.2d 223 (Mo.1982), 238

Marshall v. Marshall, 1998 WL 725941 (Ohio App. 3 Dist.1998), 580

Marshall v. Marshall, 117 Ohio App.3d 182, 690 N.E.2d 68 (Ohio App. 3 Dist.1997), 580

Maryland v. Craig, 497 U.S. 836, 110 S.Ct. 3157, 111 L.Ed.2d 666 (1990), 415

Massee v. Thompson, 321 Mont. 210, 90 P.3d 394 (Mont.2004), **772**

Maswai, United States v., 419 F.3d 822 (8th Cir.2005), 824

Mathews v. Eldridge, 424 U.S. 319, 96 S.Ct. 893, 47 L.Ed.2d 18 (1976), 238

Matter of (see name of party)

Matthews v. Pickett County, 996 S.W.2d 162 (Tenn.1999), 779

McAlindin v. County of San Diego, 192 F.3d 1226 (9th Cir.1999), 810

McCulloh v. Drake, 24 P.3d 1162 (Wyo.2001), 739

McKee v. City of Rockwall, 877 F.2d 409 (5th Cir.1989), 754

McLarnon v. Jokisch, 431 Mass. 343, 727 N.E.2d 813 (Mass.2000), 735

Mehren v. Dargan, 13 Cal.Rptr.3d 522 (Cal. App. 4 Dist.2004), **513**

Merrigan, State ex rel. Hope House, Inc. v., 133 S.W.3d 44 (Mo.2004), 147

Meyer v. Nebraska, 262 U.S. 390, 43 S.Ct. 625, 67 L.Ed. 1042 (1923), 671

Michigan v. Christel, 449 Mich. 578, 537 N.W.2d 194 (Mich.1995), 402

Midgette v. Wal–Mart Stores, Inc., 317 F.Supp.2d 550 (E.D.Pa.2004), 797

Mills v. Mills, 939 S.W.2d 72 (Mo.App. W.D. 1997), 601

Minnesota v. Vue, 606 N.W.2d 719 (Minn. App.2000), 83, **109**

Mitchell v. Mitchell, 62 Mass.App.Ct. 769, 821 N.E.2d 79 (Mass.App.Ct.2005), **249**

Moran v. Beyer, 734 F.2d 1245 (7th Cir. 1984), 702, 858

Morrison, United States v., 529 U.S. 598, 120 S.Ct. 1740, 146 L.Ed.2d 658 (2000), **30,** 365, 859, **878**

Morrison, United States v., 449 U.S. 361, 101 S.Ct. 665, 66 L.Ed.2d 564 (1981), 486

Morton County Social Service Bd. v. Schumacher, 674 N.W.2d 505 (N.D.2004), 543

Muhammad, In re Marriage of, 153 Wash.2d 795, 108 P.3d 779 (Wash.2005), 517

Municipality of Anchorage v. Gregg, 101 P.3d 181 (Alaska 2004), 803

Musick, People v., 960 P.2d 89 (Colo.1998), 811

Nearing v. Weaver, 295 Or. 702, 670 P.2d 137 (Or.1983), 777

Neuzil, State v., 589 N.W.2d 708 (Iowa 1999), 285

Nicholson v. Scoppetta, 787 N.Y.S.2d 196, 820 N.E.2d 840 (N.Y.2004), **666**

Nicholson v. Scoppetta, 344 F.3d 154 (2nd Cir.2003), 665, 671

Nicholson v. Williams, 203 F.Supp.2d 153 (E.D.N.Y.2002), **648,** 652, 670

Nixon, State v., 165 Ohio App.3d 178, 845 N.E.2d 544 (Ohio App. 9 Dist.2006), 96

Nobriga, United States v., 408 F.3d 1178 (9th Cir.2005), 346

Nunez–Escudero v. Tice–Menley, 58 F.3d 374 (8th Cir.1995), 596

Nussbaum v. Steinberg, 162 Misc.2d 524, 618 N.Y.S.2d 168 (N.Y.Sup.1994), **721**

Odom v. Odom, 606 So.2d 862 (La.App. 2 Cir.1992), **577**

Ogas v. Texas, 655 S.W.2d 322 (Tex.App.-Amarillo 1983), 189

Ohendalski v. Ohendalski, 203 S.W.3d 910 (Tex.App.-Beaumont 2006), 517

Olguín v. Santana, 2005 WL 67094 (E.D.N.Y.2005), **590**

Oliphant v. Suquamish Indian Tribe, 435 U.S. 191, 98 S.Ct. 1011, 55 L.Ed.2d 209 (1978), 112

Osborne v. County of Riverside, 385 F.Supp.2d 1048 (C.D.Cal.2005), 673

Page, United States v., 167 F.3d 325 (6th Cir.1999), **359**

Panpat v. Owens–Brockway Glass Container, Inc., 188 Or.App. 384, 71 P.3d 553 (Or. App.2003), 797

Paul U., In re, 785 N.Y.S.2d 767 (N.Y.A.D. 3 Dept.2004), 669

Pearson v. District Court, 924 P.2d 512 (Colo.1996), **633**

People v. _____ (see opposing party)

Perales–Cumpean v. Gonzales, 429 F.3d 977 (10th Cir.2005), 513

Petersen v. State of Alaska, 930 P.2d 414 (Alaska App.1996), 286

Petition to Compel Cooperation with Child Abuse Investigation, In re, 875 A.2d 365 (Pa.Super.2005), 673

Pierce v. Society of the Sisters, 268 U.S. 510, 45 S.Ct. 571, 69 L.Ed. 1070 (1925), 671

Pima County Juvenile Delinquency Action No. 102091–01, Matter of, 162 Ariz. 421, 783 P.2d 1213 (Ariz.App. Div. 2 1989), 673

Pinder v. Johnson, 54 F.3d 1169 (4th Cir. 1995), 762

Planned Parenthood v. Casey, 505 U.S. 833, 112 S.Ct. 2791, 120 L.Ed.2d 674 (1992), 1, 9, **29,** 154, **172**

Potter v. Potter, 121 Nev. 613, 119 P.3d 1246 (Nev.2005), 576

Price v. Dyke, 2001 WL 127871 (Ohio App. 2 Dist.2001), 733, 734

Quilloin v. Walcott, 434 U.S. 246, 98 S.Ct. 549, 54 L.Ed.2d 511 (1978), 672

R. v. Lavallee, [1990] 1 S.C.R. 852 (S.C.C. 1990), 444

Racsko v. Racsko, 91 Conn.App. 315, 881 A.2d 460 (Conn.App.2005), 576

Ravern H., In re, 789 N.Y.S.2d 563 (N.Y.A.D. 4 Dept.2005), 668

R.D. v. State, 706 So.2d 770 (Ala.Crim.App. 1997), 147

Reed v. Reed, 189 Misc.2d 734, 734 N.Y.S.2d 806 (N.Y.Sup.2001), 608

Reza v. Leyasi, 95 Conn.App. 562, 897 A.2d 679 (Conn.App.2006), 580

R.H. v. B.F., 39 Mass.App.Ct. 29, 653 N.E.2d 195 (Mass.App.Ct.1995), 538

Riccobene v. Scales, 19 F.Supp.2d 577 (N.D.W.Va.1998), 736

Richard v. Richard, 131 Vt. 98, 300 A.2d 637 (Vt.1973), 701

Richards v. Bruce, 691 A.2d 1223 (Me.1997), 607, 608

Ricketts v. City of Columbia, 36 F.3d 775 (8th Cir.1994), 755, 762

Rideout v. Riendeau, 761 A.2d 291 (Me.2000), 124

Riemers v. Anderson, 680 N.W.2d 280 (N.D. 2004), 736

Riemers v. Peters–Riemers, 684 N.W.2d 619 (N.D.2004), 734, 736

Riley v. Presnell, 409 Mass. 239, 565 N.E.2d 780 (Mass.1991), 725

Riss v. City of New York, 293 N.Y.S.2d 897, 240 N.E.2d 860 (N.Y.1968), 778

Robeson v. International Indem. Co., 248 Ga. 306, 282 S.E.2d 896 (Ga.1981), 702

Robinson v. United States, 769 A.2d 747 (D.C.2001), 349

Robinson, State v., 718 N.W.2d 400 (Minn. 2006), 419

Rodvik v. Rodvik, 151 P.3d 338 (Alaska 2006), 516

Roe v. Wade, 410 U.S. 113, 93 S.Ct. 705, 35 L.Ed.2d 147 (1973), 188

Romer v. Evans, 517 U.S. 620, 116 S.Ct. 1620, 134 L.Ed.2d 855 (1996), 94

Romero, People v., 13 Cal.Rptr.2d 332 (Cal. App. 2 Dist.1992), **468**

Rosenthal v. Maney, 51 Mass.App.Ct. 257, 745 N.E.2d 350 (Mass.App.Ct.2001), 576

Roussel v. Roussel, 2003 WL 22951910 (Va. Cir. Ct.2003), 741

Roy v. City of Everett, 118 Wash.2d 352, 823 P.2d 1084 (Wash.1992), 777

Rupert v. Stienne, 90 Nev. 397, 528 P.2d 1013 (Nev.1974), 701

Russell v. State, 2002 WL 31667313 (2002), **156**

Ryan v. State, 988 P.2d 46 (Wyo.1999), **404**

Sanders, State v., 168 Vt. 60, 716 A.2d 11 (Vt.1998), **392**

Santiago, People v., 2003 WL 21507176 (N.Y.Sup.2003), **201**

Santosky v. Kramer, 455 U.S. 745, 102 S.Ct. 1388, 71 L.Ed.2d 599 (1982), 657

Schestler v. Schestler, 486 N.W.2d 509 (N.D. 1992), 543

Schwartz v. Isaac, 2005 WL 45683 (U.S. 2005), 561

Seaton v. Seaton, 971 F.Supp. 1188 (E.D.Tenn.1997), 877

Silbaugh v. Silbaugh, 543 N.W.2d 639 (Minn. 1996), 571, 581

Simmons v. United States, 805 F.2d 1363 (9th Cir.1986), 725

Simpson v. City of Miami, 700 So.2d 87 (Fla. App. 3 Dist.1997), 778

Smith v. City of Elyria, 857 F.Supp. 1203 (N.D.Ohio 1994), 762

Sorichetti v. City of New York, 492 N.Y.S.2d 591, 482 N.E.2d 70 (N.Y.1985), 778

Sotirescu v. Sotirescu, 52 S.W.3d 1 (Mo.App. E.D.2001), 741

Soto v. Carrasquillo, 878 F.Supp. 324 (D.Puerto Rico 1995), 755

Soto v. Flores, 103 F.3d 1056 (1st Cir.1997), 754

Stanley v. Illinois, 405 U.S. 645, 92 S.Ct. 1208, 31 L.Ed.2d 551 (1972), 671

State v. _____ (see opposing party)

State ex rel. v. _____ (see opposing party and relator)

State in Interest of A.R., 937 P.2d 1037 (Utah App.1997), 673

Stenberg v. Carhart, 530 U.S. 914, 120 S.Ct. 2597, 147 L.Ed.2d 743 (2000), 178

Stevenson v. Stevenson, 314 N.J.Super. 350, 714 A.2d 986 (N.J.Super.Ch.1998), 253

Stone v. Traylor Brothers, 360 S.C. 271, 600 S.E.2d 551 (S.C.App.2004), 792

St. Pierre v. Burrows, 788 N.Y.S.2d 494 (N.Y.A.D. 3 Dept.2005), 563

Strickland v. Washington, 466 U.S. 668, 104 S.Ct. 2052, 80 L.Ed.2d 674 (1984), 487

Stuart v. Stuart, 140 Wis.2d 455, 410 N.W.2d 632 (Wis.App.1987), 741, 742

Sudan v. Sudan, 145 S.W.3d 280 (Tex.App.-Hous. (14 Dist.) 2004), 716

Taylor, People v., 11 Cal.Rptr.3d 510, 86 P.3d 881 (Cal.2004), **183**
Temple v. Denali Princess Lodge, 21 P.3d 813 (Alaska 2001), 792
Thigpen v. State, 248 Ga.App. 301, 546 S.E.2d 60 (Ga.App.2001), 460
Thorndike v. Thorndike, 154 N.H. 443, 910 A.2d 1224 (N.H.2006), 725
Thornton, State v., 119 Wash.2d 578, 835 P.2d 216 (Wash.1992), **409**
Thurman v. City of Torrington, 595 F.Supp. 1521 (D.Conn.1984), **748**
Timm v. Delong, 59 F.Supp.2d 944 (D.Neb. 1998), 877
Torres v. Lancellotti, 257 N.J.Super. 126, 607 A.2d 1375 (N.J.Super.Ch.1992), 254
Torres v. Triangle Handbag Mfg. Co., 13 A.D.2d 559, 211 N.Y.S.2d 992 (N.Y.A.D. 3 Dept.1961), 793
Town of (see name of town)
Townsend v. Townsend, 708 S.W.2d 646 (Mo. 1986), 698
Townsend, People v., 183 Ill.App.3d 268, 131 Ill.Dec. 741, 538 N.E.2d 1297 (Ill.App. 4 Dist.1989), 253
Tripolone, Commonwealth v., 425 Mass. 487, 681 N.E.2d 1216 (Mass.1997), 163
Tropea v. Tropea, 642 N.Y.S.2d 575, 665 N.E.2d 145 (N.Y.1996), 571
Troxel v. Granville, 530 U.S. 57, 120 S.Ct. 2054, 147 L.Ed.2d 49 (2000), 560, 671
Turner v. Frowein, 253 Conn. 312, 752 A.2d 955 (Conn.2000), 597
Twyman v. Twyman, 855 S.W.2d 619 (Tex. 1993), 711, **737**

United States v. _____ (see opposing party)

Valentine v. Valentine, 2005 WL 3096587 (Ohio App. 12 Dist.2005), 574
Valentine v. Valentine, 2005 WL 1131748 (Ohio App. 12 Dist.2005), **572**

Von Foelkel, United States v., 136 F.3d 339 (2nd Cir.1998), 365

Wade v. Hirschman, 903 So.2d 928 (Fla. 2005), 562
Wade v. Miles, 106 Wash.App. 1005 (Wash. App. Div. 1 2001), **309**
Walsh v. Walsh, 221 F.3d 204 (1st Cir.2000), 596
Wanrow, State of Washington v., 88 Wash.2d 221, 559 P.2d 548 (Wash.1977), **430**
Ward v. Ward, 155 Vt. 242, 583 A.2d 577 (Vt.1990), 701
Watt v. Watt, 971 P.2d 608 (Wyo.1999), 571
Weiand v. State, 732 So.2d 1044 (Fla.1999), 429
Whallon v. Lynn, 230 F.3d 450 (1st Cir.2000), 596
Whorton v. Bockting, 549 U.S. ___, 127 S.Ct. 1173, 167 L.Ed.2d 1 (2007), 391
Wild v. Wild, 13 Neb.App. 495, 696 N.W.2d 886 (Neb.App.2005), 575
Williams, State ex rel. v. Marsh, 626 S.W.2d 223 (Mo.1982), 238
Willis, United States v., 38 F.3d 170 (5th Cir.1994), 472
Wilmore v. Gonzales, 455 F.3d 524 (5th Cir. 2006), 513
Wisconsin v. Yoder, 406 U.S. 205, 92 S.Ct. 1526, 32 L.Ed.2d 15 (1972), 671
Wissink v. Wissink, 301 A.D.2d 36, 749 N.Y.S.2d 550 (N.Y.A.D. 2 Dept.2002), **531**
Wright v. Village of Phoenix, 2000 WL 246266 (N.D.Ill.2000), 762
Wright v. Wright, No. Civ. 98–572–A (W.D. Okla. Apr. 27, 1999), 877
Wright, State v., 349 S.C. 310, 563 S.E.2d 311 (S.C.2002), **277**
Wright, United States v., 965 F.Supp. 1307 (D.Neb.1997), 365

Zappaunbulso v. Zappaunbulso, 367 N.J.Super. 216, 842 A.2d 300 (N.J.Super.A.D.2004), 231
Ziegler v. Ziegler, 28 F.Supp.2d 601 (E.D.Wash.1998), 877

DOMESTIC VIOLENCE AND THE LAW:
THEORY AND PRACTICE

*

INTRODUCTION

The first edition of this book, Battered Women and the Law, published in 2001, marked the growing legal recognition of the systemic violence done predominately to women by their intimate partners. In 1992, thirty years after advocates first began organizing efforts on behalf of battered women and their children, the United States Supreme Court recognized the pervasiveness and severity of domestic violence in *Planned Parenthood v. Casey*, 505 U.S. 833 (1992). In 1994 Congress passed the Violence Against Women Act, creating for the first time at the federal level both criminal and civil causes of action addressing domestic violence. State legislatures throughout the country also began developing protections for victims, reforming both the criminal justice and family law systems. These and many other developments were a result of feminist lawmaking that gave name and visibility to harms experienced by women. In particular, feminist lawyers and activists recognized that domestic violence not only threatened women's right to physical integrity, and perhaps even life itself, but also women's liberty, autonomy, and equality. The development of what is often referred to as the "battered women's movement" has been one of the most important contributions of the women's rights struggle. This movement constructed a theoretical framework that linked the "private problem" of battering to the public context in which it occurred. The results of those early approaches, both legal and theoretical, were the focus of the first edition.

The second edition of this book, renamed Domestic Violence and the Law: Theory and Practice, marks the continuation of those early legal and theoretical developments and the controversies generated by them. One could never have predicted the tremendous proliferation of case law, statutes, polices, and other initiatives that followed the publication of the first edition. For example, between 2004 and 2006, the United States Supreme Court heard six cases that directly or indirectly involved victims of domestic violence. The Violence Against Women Act of 1994 has been twice reauthorized, in 2000, and again in 2005, expanding the scope of federal protections and resources on behalf of those abused by intimate partners. As legislatures continue to pass innovative laws, many are now being challenged in the courts. As more scholars and activists enter the discussion as to how to end intimate partner violence, there is a growing theoretical richness and debate over the causes of, and appropriate legal responses to, domestic violence. These current cases and controversies are the focus of the second edition. While this book is primarily intended for specialized law courses on domestic violence, it can also be used as a supplement in a range of courses, including criminal law, family law, constitutional law, torts, civil rights and international human rights. It can also serve as a text for graduate and undergraduate courses in many disciplines.

There are significant changes between the first and second editions. First, and most obviously, the title has changed. In the first edition, the term "battered women" acknowledged the origins of legal activism and legal reform on behalf of those who had been abused. This edition remains committed to the history and the theoretical approaches introduced by the modern battered women's movement. Yet the term "domestic violence" has become the most often used legal characterization to describe and categorize battering relationships. "Domestic violence" also reflects a growing recognition that while women abused by men are still the primary victims of abuse, battering occurs in same-sex relationships, and that, in some cases, men are abused by women. Furthermore, "domestic violence" focuses our attention on the broader social and legal contexts of battering rather than on victims and their individual psychologies. It also includes material that reaches beyond the narrow phenomenon of physical battering to a definition of violence that includes all forms of power and control used by perpetrators, including sexual, financial, and emotional abuse. While we recognize that no single term or title can capture the full range of experiences, we hope this new title reflects the growing recognition of the complex legal and social dynamics involved.

The changes in this new edition go well beyond the title to focus on recent developments in both the case law and legislative policy. Three new chapters explore the relationship between domestic violence, sexual autonomy, and reproduction, evidentiary issues in domestic violence cases and domestic violence, immigration and asylum. There is a new section on the interplay of domestic violence and divorce and asset distribution. Throughout the book there is increased focus on how domestic violence and the law's response to it affects people based on their socio-economic and demographic backgrounds, with new sections on teens, the elderly, and those in different religious communities. This edition also has expanded notes dealing with new topics and areas of law, including a greater emphasis on the rights of those accused of domestic violence. In general, materials have been revised and updated and there is extensive discussion of the implications of the new United States Supreme Court decisions.

This book begins with the history of domestic violence as a legal and social problem. It then incorporates the latest research on the dynamics of abusive relationships, and how the experience of abuse is shaped by race, cultural identity, sexual orientation, economic status, age, religious affiliation, and the physical and mental status of the abused and the abuser. Next, it explores the relationship between sexual autonomy, reproductive rights, and battering, making the explicit link between domestic violence and women's equality more generally. Then we examine how the law has tended to characterize domestic violence and how it often focuses primarily on abuse as a psychological problem rather than recognizing the broader social contexts in which it occurs.

The book then turns to substantive law, with chapters on the civil protection order system, the criminal justice system, evidence, and the use of self-defense and other claims on behalf of battered defendants. In this edition we have moved the materials on the civil protection order system and the criminal justice system ahead of the chapters dealing with the family to emphasize the criminal nature of abuse and to allow students who have often worked with the civil protective system or in prosecutors' offices to encounter material relevant to their work early in the course. The book then examines the substance and process of family law and the child welfare system, with an emphasis on the ways in which the law responds to children who grow up with a parent who is battered or is battering. Next the book examines domestic violence as a basis for tort claims, the potential third-party liability of police and employers, and issues pertinent to immigration and asylum. It then explores claims based on both civil rights and international human rights before concluding with a look at the unique challenges involved in advocacy on behalf of battered clients and some cutting-edge approaches both within and outside the legal system.

This book provides an important starting point for lawyers-in-training who, despite the area of law in which they specialize, will no doubt encounter domestic violence issues in legal practice. We hope it also proves to be a useful resource for lawyers, judges, advocates, and policy-makers who work in this area. As we completed this edition, the breadth and depth of lawmaking that relates to domestic violence was striking to us. On the pages that follow, we analyze these significant developments and explore the many ways in which domestic violence shapes, and is shaped by, the law.

CHAPTER ONE

DOMESTIC VIOLENCE IN HISTORICAL AND SOCIAL CONTEXT

Introduction

Over the last forty years, domestic violence has increasingly been recognized as a phenomenon worthy of serious attention. Of course, violent relationships have always existed. Shakespeare's *Taming of the Shrew* indicates that the Bard was familiar with such relationships centuries ago. Since the 1960s, however, academics from the social sciences and humanities, activists, doctors, and lawyers have begun to focus on what these relationships have in common with each other, how they differ from one another, how they get formed, why they are so hard to end, and what the various professions can do to assist the victims and reduce the level of abuse. In the legal arena, attention was originally placed on the creation of a new form of judicial order—a civil protective order—that would set limits on the abuser's access to the victim, on legally protecting victims who defended themselves with violence, and on criminal law and its potential for making victims' lives safer. More recently, domestic violence advocates have also focused on proceedings in family courts and on victims' vulnerability at work, in housing, and in other aspects of their daily lives. In addition, because many countries have refused to act so as to protect victims from violence at the hands of their intimate partners, many advocates have recently turned to international human rights as a potential source of assistance.

This book focuses on domestic violence in all of these contexts. In order for you to learn to be an effective legal advocate, you must first understand the experience of domestic violence for victims, perpetrators, and families. Clearly, intimate violence has an effect on the psyches of all involved. Similarly, it is terribly frightening to the direct victims and to other non-perpetrators in the family. But, beyond these concerns, we want you to consider the effects of domestic violence on the lives of victims and their families more broadly. Initially, there are questions of who victims of violence are, how their various racial, religious, or other identities affect their experiences and how the presence of battering relationships affects the communities in which they live.

A second set of important issues revolve around the role of abusive relationships in limiting women's opportunities to participate freely in society. The modern movement against domestic violence developed in the late 1960s from the feminist revolution of the same period. Early advocates for battered women saw themselves as trying to improve the status of women because they believed that victims of intimate violence were primarily women. Today, the exclusivity of this connection between abuse at the

4

hands of an intimate and being female has been challenged, as we understand more about same-sex violence, for example. For those who see a gendered dimension to the violence, there are additional questions about the ways in which abusive relationships deprive their victims of liberty and autonomy (including sexual autonomy.) In other words, are abusive relations a mechanism for the subordination of the targets of the abuse? Does battering create a form of slavery in which victims act so as to please the abusers rather than to achieve their own independent goals? How does abuse mold a female victim's ability to mother? What is its effect on victims' capacity to retain a job and thus to achieve economic stability?

A third set of issues that we focus on in this book relates to the law and to law-related policies. Many types of legal actions—including criminal prosecutions, divorces and custody determinations, and tort actions—are important in dealing with domestic violence. In addition, the framework through which the law is viewed is crucial. Is domestic violence an issue of individual or couple psychopathology or is it more of a structural problem that should be handled systemically through the legal system? Should problems of domestic violence be seen through the lens of civil rights? To what extent should the government act to protect victims, even if they do not want to be protected? Should the government have a duty or obligation to protect victims or is that an invasion of privacy? Should the existence of intimate violence be considered in custody actions involving children, even if the child is not the abuser's intended victim? All of these concerns are critical in thinking about domestic violence.

Subsequent chapters will introduce you in detail to problems of domestic violence in the contexts of criminal, family, employment, housing, tort, civil rights, immigration, and international human rights law. This chapter aims to give you an initial impression of the victim's experience of violent relationships, some background on the pervasiveness of domestic violence, an introduction to the recent historical and social settings in which people have focused on domestic violence, and a quick view of the United States Supreme Court's ambivalent and ambiguous approach to the problem.

A.   EXPERIENCES WITH DOMESTIC VIOLENCE

It is important that advocates for victims and for abusers both understand the dynamics of violent relationships. They are not always obvious. Many have seen these relationships as semi-comedic—remember the old cartoons of women chasing their husbands with frying pans. Sometimes these relationships are portrayed as involving obsessional love. In the middle of the last century, people often thought that the victims of violent relationships were masochists who derived sexual pleasure from being abused. Today we tend to understand violent relationships as the result of one partner's effort to dominate and control the other. There may also be varying degrees of psychopathology involved in some violent relationships, but the dominant dynamic in the relationships discussed in this book is usually one of control.

Below are a number of short descriptions of moments in relationships involving violence. As you read them, try to identify the various techniques aside from physical violence that abusers use for maintaining control over their partners. Why do you think victims are often reluctant to tell others about the violence? Why do victims stay in relationships characterized by violence?

He always found something wrong with what I did, even if I did what he asked. No matter what it was. It was never the way he wanted it. I was either too fat, didn't cook the food right.... I think he wanted to hurt me. To hurt me in the sense ... to make me feel like I was nothing. And that I did something wrong, when I didn't do anything wrong....

I can't talk to adults.... I feel like I never had an opinion on politics or on life. I don't know how to interact because he would [always] be going like this to me [mimicking abuser's gesture of drawing a line with his index finger] ... that was his big signal to make me shut up, or he'd be kicking me under the table to shut my mouth. Karla Fischer, Neil Vidmar and Rene Ellis, *The Culture of Battering and the Role of Mediation in Domestic Violence Cases,* 46 S.M.U. L. REV. 2117 (1993).

He felt I was a child. He'd say, "I'm going to teach you a lesson' raise you right." He'd make himself angry, lecturing me. I was always caught off guard by his attacks. They seemed to be mainly dependent on his mood, rather than on things going on around him. He would slap me, hit with his fists, twist my arms behind my back, call me names, and say awful things about—and to—my mother. And then he'd tell me it was for my own good. If I tried to say anything, he'd call that "talking back" and I'd get hit. But if I kept quiet, he'd say I was ignoring him. No matter what I did, it just got worse and worse, once it got started. Karla Fischer, Neil Vidmar and Rene Ellis, *The Culture of Battering and the Role of Mediation in Domestic Violence Cases,* 46 S.M.U. L. REV. 2117 (1993).

[Francine and Mickey moved to a new town where Mickey found a job. He would not allow Francine to work.] He and Francine moved into an apartment over a hardware store nearby. It was a dark, gloomy place with no windows in the back room. Francine ... had no friends to visit, no telephone, no TV, nothing to do except housework....

"I would try to clean everything up, and with him gone, there wasn't anybody to mess things up.... Sometimes I would sit there all day with nothing to do, not daring to go out, for fear he would get jealous...."

One day, on a furtive outing, Francine dropped into a drugstore and bought some nail polish. When Mickey came home he instantly noticed her painted nails. He asked how she had gotten the polish. She told him she had gone for a walk. Mickey said he didn't think she needed to go for walks. Francine began to pour out her unhappiness—how she hated the idleness, the loneliness, the gloomy high-ceilinged apartment. Mickey was unsympathetic. Francine protested she had the right to go for a walk if she chose. The scene ended in a beating. Faith McNulty, THE BURNING BED (1980).

At one moment we were laying [sic] together and kissing and everything seemed fine. And, it was like a second later, he was saying that I stayed out too late, and asked who was there and stuff, and then just ... everything blew up. I know he threw me off the bed. And he told me he was going to beat me to death. And then he said, "I'm going to set the trailer on fire with you and your daughter in it." And then he goes, "well first, bitch, you are going to get me a glass of ice water." Karla Fischer, Neil Vidmar and Rene Ellis, *The Culture of Battering and the Role of Mediation in Domestic Violence Cases,* 46 S.M.U. L. REV. 2137–2138 (1993).

That session in the hospital when I had been married one month, and the nurse came and sat on the bed and said she had heard I didn't care if I went home for Christmas.... The truth was, I couldn't face what I was going home to. I instinctively knew it was very bad to lie about this but I couldn't bear to tell the truth. It was too humiliating. I didn't tell her anything. To my friends, I said I fell down. I did not intend to cover for him but for myself ... for the confusion and humiliation ... for finding myself in this unbelievable position. Martha R. Mahoney, *Legal Images of Battered Women: Redefining the Issue of Separation,* 90 MICH. L. REV. 1 (1991).

[M]y husband is an alcoholic. Things have been really bad these past few years. But we've been married thirteen years. And I have three children. For nine of those years, he was the best husband and father anyone could have asked for.... I may have to leave. But if I do, I'm giving up on a father for the children, and I'm giving up on him.... I can't just throw away those nine years. Martha R. Mahoney, *Legal Images of Battered Women: Redefining the Issue of Separation,* 90 MICH. L. REV. 1 (1991).

NOTES AND QUESTIONS

1. **Forms of Abuse.** Although domestic violence is often thought of as primarily physical, these descriptions involve many means of abuse beyond the physical. Note that abusers commonly combine physical abuse with psychological, financial, or other forms of abuse, such as isolation. How many different types of abuse do you see in the above descriptions? Can behavior that might superficially appear as "caring" be a form of abuse? For example, think about an abuser who will not allow his partner to work, claiming that it is for her own good.

2. **Abuse in Order to Control.** As indicated above, abusers frequently use violence or other abusive tactics to gain control of their partners. Can you see that dynamic above, both in the use of violence and in the use of other forms of abuse? Does the abuse appear to be precipitated by incidents that warrant the abuser's anger? If not, do you think the unpredictability of the abuse makes victims more likely to submit to the abuse?

3. **Minimizing or Denying Abuse.** Not surprisingly, you will find that abusers tend to minimize the effects of their abuse or to deny altogether

that they have been violent. But it might be more surprising to you that victims often do the same as to abuse perpetrated against them. Why would this be the case?

4. **Why Do Victims Stay in Abusive Relationships?** One of the questions that is asked repeatedly is why victims of violence stay in the relationships. The excerpts above do not give you a lot of information with which to respond to this question, but they do provide some. How would you answer the question as to why victims stay? Notice the effect that children may have on victims' willingness to stay in abusive relationships. In some cases, the presence of children may make victims want to give to abuser yet another chance; in other settings the presence of children may encourage the victim to leave. Can you find examples of both of these effects in the excerpts above?

5. **Coercive Control as a Form of Entrapment.** Evan Stark has recently argued that the level of control that abusers exercise over their partners functions to deprive victims of their liberty. They are told what to do when, how to dress, when to go out and where, who to talk to or to see, what to buy, and, generally, how to live their lives. Stark's point is that the violence is less significant in making the victim's life unbearable than are the limits that the abuser imposes on all aspects of the victim's life.

> The women in my practice have repeatedly made clear that what is done to them is less important that what their partners have prevented them from doing for themselves by appropriating their resources; undermining their social support; subverting their rights to privacy, self-respect, and autonomy; and depriving them of substantive equality. These harms highlight ... that coercive control is a liberty crime rather than a crime of assault. Preventing a substantial group of women from freely applying their agency in economic and political life obstructs overall social development. Coercive Control: How Men Entrap Women in Personal Life (2007).

Do you agree with Stark that coercive control in its more extreme forms could be understood as a deprivation of liberty? The Thirteenth Amendment to the U.S. Constitution prohibits slavery from existing in the U.S. Could one argue that the coercive control behind domestic violence runs afoul of the Amendment? Later chapters contain more detailed information on the dynamics of violent relationships and on the viability of civil rights remedies.

B. The Pervasiveness of Domestic Violence

There are few generally accepted statistics about the frequency, severity, or persistence of domestic violence. In part this is because definitions of "domestic violence" differ. Should one just count events reported to the police? Or, should one consider those that are described by participants in survey studies? Does only physical abuse count or should one also consider the economic and psychological forms of abuse noted above? Has domestic violence ended when the physical violence stops even if the victim remains scared of the abuser for years thereafter? The statistics below all come from generally reputable sources, but you should question them all the same. This questioning should force you to think, yet again, about the role of domestic violence in United States.

Our first statistical picture of domestic violence is taken from the Supreme Court's decision in *Planned Parenthood v. Casey*, 505 U.S. 833 (1992). *Casey* is widely known as the decision in which the Supreme Court narrowly upheld constitutional protection for women's right to reproductive choice, not as a case about domestic violence. But the restrictive Pennsylvania abortion statute challenged in *Casey* included a provision that required a pregnant woman to notify her husband before undergoing an abortion. Battered women's advocacy organizations argued that enforcement of this provision would mean that women who lived with violent partners would be unable freely to exercise their reproductive choice because they could not tell their partners that they were pregnant, or that they wanted an abortion, without fear of reprisal. The Court struck down the spousal notification provision as unconstitutional. For now, we want you to focus not on the constitutional considerations in the case, but rather on the statistics on which the Court relied to support its conclusion that domestic violence was a serious and widespread problem with a severe impact on women's reproductive freedom:

> The American Medical Association (AMA) has published a summary of the recent research in this field, which indicates that in an average 12 month period in this country, approximately two million women are victims of severe assaults by their male partners. In a 1985 survey, women reported that nearly one of every eight husbands had assaulted their wives during the past year. The AMA views these figures as "marked underestimates," because the nature of these incidents discourages women from reporting them, and because surveys typically exclude the very poor, those who do not speak English well, and women who are homeless or in institutions or hospitals when the survey is conducted. According to the AMA, "researchers on family violence agree that the true incidence of partner violence is probably *double* the above estimates; or four million severely assaulted women per year. Studies on prevalence suggest that from one-fifth to one-third of all women will be physically assaulted by a partner or ex-partner during their lifetime." Thus on an average day in the United States, nearly 11,000 women are severely assaulted by their male partners. Many of these incidents involve sexual assault. In families where wife beating takes place, moreover, child abuse is often present as well.

Other studies fill in the rest of this troubling picture. Physical violence is only the most visible form of abuse. Psychological abuse, particularly forced social and economic isolation of women, is also common. Many victims of domestic violence remain with their abusers, perhaps because they perceive no superior alternative. Many abused women who find temporary refuge in shelters return to their husbands, in large part because they have no other source of income. Returning to one's abuser can be dangerous. Recent Federal Bureau of

Investigation statistics disclose that 8.8 percent of all homicide victims in the United States are killed by their spouses. Thirty percent of female homicide victims are killed by their male partners. *Id.* at 891–892.

There are an increasing number of sources of data concerning violence against women. Pursuant to the Violence Against Women Act (VAWA) of 1994, the first major federal legislation on domestic violence, the newly created Violence Against Women Office within the United States Department of Justice gathers statistics from federal, state and private sources. The American Bar Association's Commission on Domestic Violence also gathers statistics. Many other federal agencies have also conducted studies and gathered information. Here are some preliminary statistics to consider:

- One in four women in the United States will likely experience domestic violence during her lifetime. Women account for 85% of the victims of domestic violence. The National Institute for Justice and the Centers for Disease Control and Prevention, *Extent, Nature, and Consequences of Intimate Partner Violence* (2000).

- Young women, 16–24 years old, experience the highest rates of domestic violence—16 per 1,000 persons. Bureau of Justice Statistics, U.S. Dep't of Justice, *Reporting Crime to the Police 1992–2000* (March 2003).

- The number one killer of African–American women ages 15 to 34 is homicide at the hands of a current or former intimate partner. Commission on Domestic Violence, American Bar Association, *Survey of Recent Statistics* (2007).

- Females were 84% of spouse abuse victims and 86% of victims of abuse at the hands of a boyfriend or girlfriend. Bureau of Justice Statistics, U.S. Dep't of Justice, *Family Violence Statistics* (June 2005).

- In 2004, 466,600 women were victims of a violent crime committed by an intimate partner. This accounts for 21% of all violent crimes committed against women. By comparison, 11,759 men were victimized by an intimate partner. This accounts for 4% of all violent victimizations committed against men. Bureau of Justice Statistics, U.S. Dep't of Justice, NCJ–210674, *Criminal Victimization in the United States* (2004).

- 11% of lesbians reported violence by their female partner and 15% of gay men who had lived with a male partner reported being victimized by a male partner. Commission on Domestic Violence, American Bar Association, *Survey of Recent Statistics* (2007).

- Studies show that 25–50% of disputed custody cases involve domestic violence. Commission on Domestic Violence, American Bar Association, *10 Myths about Custody and Domestic Violence and How to Counter Them* (2006).

- Each year, an estimated 3.3 million children are exposed to violence by family members against their mothers or female caretakers.

Violence and the Family: *Report of the American Psychological Association Presidential Task Force on Violence and the Family*, 11 (1996).

- Police encounter at least half a million children a year during domestic violence arrests. There is an overlap of 30 to 60 percent between violence against children and violence against women in the same families. Office of Juvenile Justice and Delinquency Prevention, U.S. Dep't of Justice, NCJ–182789 *Safe from the Start: Taking Action on Children Exposed to Violence* (November 2000).

NOTES AND QUESTIONS

1. **Considering the Statistics.** From the statistics above, what can you say about who commits domestic violence, who is likely to be a victim of the violence, and the settings in which it occurs?

2. **Sources of Information.** Studies may have widely varying results depending on the sources of their information. Statistics drawn from criminal justice sources, for example, catch only those instances of violence that are reported to, and recorded by, the police—and that are reported and recorded as incidents of domestic violence. Reporting practices still vary widely from state to state, and even community to community. And many of those who experience violence at the hands of a partner do not report; sometimes out of fear, sometimes because they do not want to set the criminal justice machinery in motion, and sometimes because they do not interpret what has happened to them as a crime. Many social science studies, on the other hand, depend on self-reporting, raising issues about the reliability of the numbers generated. For an interesting analysis of the extent to which reporting by victims matches reporting by perpetrators, and some provocative hypotheses about how to interpret discrepancies, see R. Dobash, R. Emerson Dobash, Kate Cavanaugh and Ruth Lewis, *Separate and Intersecting Realities: A Comparison of Men's and Women's Accounts of Violence Against Women,* 4 VIOLENCE AGAINST WOMEN 382 (1998). At least one commentator has suggested that a reason why domestic violence statistics often show a large percentage of ex-husband or ex-boyfriend perpetrators (as opposed to current husband or boyfriend perpetrators) is that women are more likely to experience the continued stalking, harassment and violence of these men, with whom they have broken off relationships, as criminal. Murray A. Straus, *The Controversy Over Domestic Violence By Women: A Methodological, Theoretical, and Sociology of Science Analysis,* in VIOLENCE IN INTIMATE RELATIONSHIPS, 17 (X.B. Arriaga and S. Oskamp, eds., 1999).

3. **Men Abusing Women or Women Abusing Men?** One of the big controversies in the domestic violence literature is whether, or to what degree, domestic violence has a "male on female" dynamic. The statistics above indicate that women are much more likely than men to be the victims of intimate violence. However, some work of Murray Straus, a major researcher in this field, indicates that women and men are equally likely to use violence against their marital partners. Murray Straus, *Victims and Aggressors in Marital Violence,* 23 AM. BEHAVIORAL SCIENTIST 681 (1980). The claim that men and women are equally violent may be

misleading, however. Straus bases this statement on the Conflict Tactics Scales (CTS) that he developed. This is an interview protocol that asks questions about particular forms of violence and verbal aggression. It has been criticized for asking about violence specifically in the context of marital conflict, thus perhaps missing violent episodes that appear to come out of nowhere. Also, the CTS asks about particular forms of violence without taking the context within which they occur into account. Thus, it might ask about whether either partner has kicked the other without indicating if the kick was directed at a shod foot or a pregnant abdomen. Work by Straus and by others in the field has also indicated that husbands are more likely to use a severe level of violence than wives and that husbands are more likely to respond to their wives' minor violence with serious violence. Finally, the claim that men and women are equally victims of domestic violence is undermined by the facts that women victims of domestic violence are more likely to be seriously injured and that women's violence is often in self-defense or in defense of a child. For more discussion on this topic, *see* Straus, Evan Stark and Anne Flitcraft, *Violence Among Intimates*, in HANDBOOK OF FAMILY VIOLENCE (Van Hasselt *et al.* eds. 1988); Daniel G. Saunders, *Wife Abuse, Husband Abuse, or Mutual Combat?* In FEMINIST PERSPECTIVES ON WIFE ABUSE (Yllö and Bograd eds. 1988).

4. **Using Female Pronouns to Refer to Victims of Intimate Violence.** As the previous note indicates, there is some controversy as to whether only women are the victims of violence or whether men are equally the victims. While it is clear that men are sometimes the victims of domestic violence, we have chosen to use female pronouns to refer to victims so as to emphasize the gendered dimensions of the violence. Although some academics and fathers' rights advocates claim that men and women are violent to each other at equal rates, many statistics continue to show that women are vastly disproportionately the victims of the violence and that women suffer more serious injuries as a result of the violence. Furthermore, men's violence against their female partners often occurs as a result of their anger against women and their effort to control women. Indeed, much of this anger and control occurs when women partners do not perform their traditional gender roles in a manner consistent with the man's expectations. Rebecca Emerson Dobash and Russell P. Dobash, *Violent Men and Violent Contexts*, in RETHINKING VIOLENCE AGAINST WOMEN (Dobash and Dobash eds. 1998). As you work your way through the materials in this book, think about whether you agree that there is a gendered aspect to domestic violence and whether you would have made the same choice of pronouns.

5. **Naming the Violence.** A second issue relating to language choices is what to call the violence that is studied in this book. Initially in the 1970s the term "wife-abuse" was used. We have rejected this term because it is too tied to marital relations. Much violence occurs between non-married couples, whether heterosexual or homosexual, although the term does have the advantage of focusing on the gendered nature of the violence. The term "spouse abuse," is also too focused on marriage and is too gender neutral to suit our understanding of the situation. Similarly, the term "family violence" does not sufficiently take the gendered dynamics into account

and might also imply that the violence comes from the ways that family members interrelate and suggest that all are somewhat at fault. We do sometimes use the phrase "intimate abuse" since the violence primarily targets intimates. This term is also helpful in indicating that the dynamics of child abuse are not covered by these materials. Finally, we also sometimes use the words "domestic violence" since, today, this is the language most commonly used to refer to this phenomenon. Of course, neither "intimate violence" nor "domestic violence" capture the gendered aspects of the violence. In sum, we have not found one term that conveys all of the dimensions of the violence that we will be studying. We will use a variety of terms, recognizing the disadvantages of each.

C.   DOMESTIC VIOLENCE: A HISTORICAL PERSPECTIVE

Over time, the way we have understood the phenomenon of domestic violence has been closely tied to the status and roles of women. When women were viewed as inferior to men, needing to be instructed by men, what we now call domestic violence was simply seen as an appropriate part of that instruction. In a now infamous concurrence in *Bradwell v. State of Illinois*, 83 U.S. 130 (1872), Justice Bradley justified denying a woman, Myra Bradwell, admission to the Illinois state bar on the grounds that women were appropriately subordinate to men and should not seek to overturn the natural order.

> [T]he civil law, as well as nature herself, has always recognized a wide difference in the respective spheres and destinies of man and woman. Man is, or should be, woman's protector and defender. The natural and proper timidity and delicacy which belongs to the female sex evidently unfits it for many of the occupations of civil life. The constitution of the family organization, which is founded in the divine ordinance, as well as in the nature of things, indicates the domestic sphere as that which properly belongs to the domain and functions of womanhood. The harmony, not to say identity, of interest and views which belong, or should belong, to the family institution is repugnant to the idea of a woman adopting a distinct and independent career from that of her husband.... The paramount destiny and mission of woman are to fulfil the noble and benign offices of wife and mother. This is the law of the Creator.

Elizabeth Pleck, a historian, argues that there were three aspects of the ideal of family in America prior to the 20th century that contributed to societal reluctance to intervene in violent families. These are the idea that the family is private, that it gives the husband conjugal rights over the wife, and that it is intended to endure for life. Elizabeth Pleck, DOMESTIC TYRANNY: THE MAKING OF AMERICAN SOCIAL POLICY AGAINST FAMILY VIOLENCE FROM COLONIAL TIMES TO THE PRESENT (1987). These ideas, together with news of the proper sphere for women, as exemplified in Justice Bradley's concurrence, have functioned to limit the protections that society has been willing to offer to women terrorized by family violence. As you read the excerpt below from an early 19th century case, think about how these ideas about women and families influenced the court.

Bradley v. State

Supreme Court of Mississippi, 1824.
1 Miss. 156, Walker 156.

■ HON. POWHATTAN ELLIS.

[The defendant was indicted for assault and battery on his wife Lydia Bradley. At trial, the defendant requested that the jury be instructed that if the victim was the defendant's wife, the defendant could not be held guilty. The court refused the instruction and charged the jury that a husband could commit an assault and battery upon his wife. The jury found the defendant guilty.]

The only question submitted for the consideration of the court, is, whether a husband can commit an assault and battery upon the body of his wife. This, as an abstract proposition, will not admit of doubt. But I am fully persuaded, from the examination I have made, an unlimited license of this kind cannot be sanctioned, either upon principles of law or humanity. It is true, according to the old law, the husband might give his wife moderate correction, because he is answerable for her misbehaviour; hence it was thought reasonable to intrust him with a power necessary to restrain the indiscretions of one for whose conduct he was to be made responsible. . . . I believe it was in a case before Mr. Justice Raymond, when the same doctrine was recognised, with proper limitations and restrictions, well suited to the condition and feelings of those who might think proper to use a whip or rattan, no bigger than my thumb, in order to enforce the salutary restraints of domestic discipline. I think his lordship might have narrowed down the rule in such a manner as to restrain the exercise of the right, within the compass of great moderation, without producing a destruction of the principle itself. If the defendant now before us, could shew from the record in this case, he confined himself within reasonable bounds, when he thought proper to chastise his wife, we would deliberate long before an affirmance of the judgment. . . .

However abhorrent to the feelings of every member of the bench must be the exercise of this remnant of feudal authority, to inflict pain and suffering, when all the finer feelings of the heart should be warmed into devotion, by our most affectionate regards, yet every principle of public policy and expediency, in reference to the domestic relations, would seem to require the establishment of the rule we have laid down, in order to prevent the deplorable spectacle of the exhibition of similar cases in our courts of justice. Family broils and dissentions cannot be investigated before the tribunals of the country, without casting a shade over the character of those who are unfortunately engaged in the controversy. To screen from public reproach those who may be thus unhappily situated, let the husband be permitted to exercise the right of moderate chastisement, in cases of great emergency, and use salutary restraints in every case of misbehaviour, without being subjected to vexatious prosecutions, resulting in the mutual discredit and shame of all parties concerned. Judgment affirmed.

NOTES AND QUESTIONS

1. **The Meaning of *Bradley*.** *Bradley* stands for the proposition that husbands have the right to use "moderate chastisement" against their wives. Today we might consider this to be a form of domestic violence. Which aspects of the idea of family or of the role of women supported the recognition of this right?

One of the rights that feminists at the Seneca Falls Convention demanded in the Declaration of Sentiments in 1848 was the right to be held accountable for one's own crimes. In *Bradley,* the Court had noted that a husband could be held responsible for his wife's "misbehavior." How do you think this connected to the 19th century feminists' desire to be held responsible for their own actions? For a historical accounting of the right to chastise one's wife, see Beirne Stedman, *Right of Husband to Chastise Wife,* 3 VIRGINIA LAW REGISTER 241 (1917).

2. ***Bradley* Overruled.** *Bradley* was overruled in *Harris v. State,* 14 So. 266 (1894). The court held, "The suggestion in the evidence of . . . a fancied right in the husband to chastise the wife in moderation makes it proper for us to say that this brutality found in the ancient common law, though strangely recognized in *Bradley v. State* has never since received countenance; and it is superfluous to now say that the blind adherence shown in that case to revolting precedent has long been utterly repudiated, in the administration of criminal law in our courts."

3. **Connecting Policy on Domestic Violence to Social History.** Historian Linda Gordon contends that domestic violence appears and disappears over time as a public issue in connection with social anxiety about the family. When society is worried that the institution of the family is weakening and that women (or children) are becoming too powerful or autonomous, people tend not to see violence within the family as being a significant issue. Thus, she argues

> [F]amily violence cannot be understood outside the context of the overall politics of the family. Today's anxiety about family issues— divorce, sexual permissiveness, abortion, teenage pregnancy, single mothers, runaway or allegedly stolen children, gay rights—is not unprecedented. For at least 150 years there have been periods of fear that "the family"—meaning a popular image of what families were supposed to be like, by no means a correct recollection of any actual "traditional family"—was in decline; and these fears have tended to escalate in periods of social stress. Anxieties about family life, further-more, have usually expressed socially conservative fears about the increasing power and autonomy of women and children, and the corresponding decline in male, sometimes rendered as fatherly, control of family members. For much of the history of the family-violence concern, moreover, these anxieties have been particularly projected onto lower-class families. Thus an historical analysis of family violence

must include a view of the changing power relations among classes, sexes, and generations. Linda Gordon, HEROES OF THEIR OWN LIVES: THE POLITICS AND HISTORY OF FAMILY VIOLENCE (1988).

4. **A Psychological or Sociological Approach to Understanding Domestic Violence?** Gordon provides a sociological/political understanding of domestic violence. According to her, recognition of the ills of domestic violence is tied to larger social and political concerns about the family. Others, however, see domestic violence as rooted instead in individual psychology. These two explanations are in tension with each other. Gordon's social and political understanding of domestic violence implies that there is a connection between power, abuse, and recognition of the abuse. Those who agree would probably believe that remedies require structural changes in power relations between men and women and within the family. In contrast, those who believe that domestic violence occurs because of individual pathologies would be less likely to think that major social changes are necessary in order to reduce violence among intimates. Instead, they would look to individual therapeutic solutions or perhaps to therapeutic remedies that focus on the specific family as a unit. Although many scholars, particularly feminist scholars, agree with Gordon, the law has tended to adopt a more psychological perspective. This stance is particularly strong in family law, but is also evident in criminal law and other areas.

5. **Legal Efforts to Preserve the Status Quo Through a Transformation of the Law.** The next reading examines the legal history of domestic violence and argues that superficial change can mask a rearguard effort to uphold the status quo.

Reva B. Siegel

"The Rule of Love": Wife Beating As Prerogative and Privacy

105 YALE L.J. 2117 (1996).

The Anglo–American common law originally provided that a husband, as master of his household, could subject his wife to corporal punishment or "chastisement" so long as he did not inflict permanent injury upon her.

The persistence of domestic violence raises important questions about the nature of the legal reforms that abrogated the chastisement prerogative. By examining how regulation of marital violence evolved after the state denied men the privilege of beating their wives, we can learn much about the ways in which civil rights reform changes a body of status law. In the nineteenth century, and again in the twentieth century, the American feminist movement has attempted to reform the law of marriage to secure for wives equality with their husbands. Its efforts in each century have produced significant changes in the law of marriage. The status of married women has improved, but wives still have not attained equality with their husbands—if we measure equality as the dignity and material "goods" associated with the wealth wives control, or the kinds of work they perform, or the degree of physical security they enjoy. Despite the efforts of the feminist movement, the legal system continues to play an important role in perpetuating these status differences, although, over time, the role law plays in enforcing status relations has become increasingly less visible.

Efforts to reform a status regime do bring about change—but not always the kind of change advocates seek. When the legitimacy of a status regime is successfully contested, lawmakers and jurists will both cede and defend status privileges—gradually relinquishing the original rules and justificatory rhetoric of the contested regime and finding new rules and reasons to protect such privileges as they choose to defend. Thus, civil rights reform can breathe new life into a body of status law, by pressuring legal elites to translate it into a more contemporary, and less controversial, social idiom. I call this kind of change in the rules and rhetoric of a status regime "preservation through transformation," and illustrate this modernization dynamic in a case study of domestic assault law as it evolved in rule structure and rationale from a law of marital prerogative to a law of marital privacy.

As the nineteenth-century feminist movement protested a husband's prerogatives, the movement helped bring about the repudiation of chastisement doctrine; but, in so doing, the movement also precipitated changes in the regulation of marital violence that "modernized" this body of status law. A survey of criminal and tort law regulating marital violence during the Reconstruction Era reveals that the American legal system did not simply internalize norms of sex equality espoused by feminist critics of the chastisement prerogative; instead, during the Reconstruction Era, chastisement law was supplanted by a new body of marital violence policies that were premised on a variety of gender-, race-, and class-based assumptions. This new body of common law differed from chastisement doctrine, both in rule structure and rhetoric. Judges no longer insisted that a husband had the legal prerogative to beat his wife; instead, they often asserted that the legal system should not interfere in cases of wife beating, in order to protect the privacy of the marriage relationship and to promote domestic harmony. Judges most often invoked considerations of marital privacy when contemplating the prosecution of middle- and upper-class men for wife beating. Thus, the body of formal and informal immunity rules that sprang up in criminal and tort law during the Reconstruction Era was both gender- and class-salient: It functioned to preserve authority relations between husband and wife, and among men of different social classes as well.

These changes in the rule structure of marital status law were justified in a distinctive rhetoric: one that diverged from the traditional idiom of chastisement doctrine. Instead of reasoning about marriage in the older, hierarchy-based norms of the common law, jurists began to justify the regulation of domestic violence in the language of privacy and love associated with companionate marriage in the industrial era. Jurists reasoning in this discourse of "affective privacy" progressively abandoned tropes of hierarchy and began to employ tropes of interiority to describe the marriage relationship, justifying the new regime of common law immunity rules in languages that invoked the feelings and spaces of domesticity. Once translated from an antiquated to a more contemporary gender idiom, the state's justification for treating wife beating differently from other kinds of assault seemed reasonable in ways the law of chastisement did not.

As the history of domestic violence law illustrates, political opposition to a status regime may bring about changes that improve the welfare of subordinated groups. With the demise of chastisement law, the situation of married women improved—certainly, in dignitary terms, and perhaps materially as well. At the same time, the story of chastisement's demise suggest that there is a price for such dignitary and material gains as civil rights reform may bring. If a reform movement is at all successful in advancing its justice claims, it will bring pressure to bear on lawmakers to rationalize status-enforcing state action in new and less socially controversial terms. This process of adaptation can actually revitalize a body of status law, enhancing its capacity to legitimate social inequalities that remain among status-differentiated groups. Examined from this perspective, the reform of chastisement doctrine can teach us much about the dilemmas confronting movements for social justice in America today.

NOTES AND QUESTIONS

1. **Rethinking *Bradley*.** Do you think *Bradley v. State* supports Siegel's theory? In justifying the refusal to punish the husband who beat his wife, does the court substitute a new notion of family privacy for the earlier status hierarchy?

D.   HISTORY OF THE CURRENT DOMESTIC VIOLENCE MOVEMENT

If we accept Pleck's and Gordon's claims that domestic violence can only be understood within the context of the social and political setting in which it takes place, it is important to understand some of the context in which the recent focus on family violence has occurred. The past 50 years have seen the strengthening (and perhaps weakening) of another feminist period. With this came concerns about women's position in relation to men's, about gender roles, and reproductive autonomy. Not surprisingly, given Siegel's thesis that status changes are often met with political opposition, there has also been some resistance. The readings in this section provide some brief insight into the context in which attention to the problem of domestic violence flourished and an introduction into the controversies generated by this attention.

Susan Schechter
Women and Male Violence: The Visions and Struggles of the Battered Women's Movement (1982)

The Influence of the Anti–Rape Movement

Although many activists in the battered women's movement never did rape crisis work, the battered women's movement maintains a striking and obvious resemblance to the anti-rape movement and owes it several debts. The anti-rape movement articulated that violence is a particular form of domination based on social relationships of unequal power. Through the efforts of the anti-rape movement it became clear that violence is one mechanism for female social control. Today this sounds obvious; ten years ago it was a revelation. The anti-rape movement changed women's consciousness and redefined the parameters of what women would individually and collectively tolerate.

The feminist anti-rape movement has not only laid the foundation to change public consciousness, but also has built organizations and networks of politically sophisticated and active women. The anti-rape movement has unmasked the domination that violence maintains, has torn away a veil of shame, and shown that women can aid one another, transforming individual silence and pain into a social movement. Such work handed ideological tools, collective work structures and political resources to the battered women's movement. Without this precedent, the new movement might have faced far greater resistance and hostility from bureaucracies, legislatures, and the general public. By 1975, it was clear that since rape and battering had the same effects upon their victims and depended upon similar sexist mythology, battering had to be declared socially, not privately, caused.

Ideological and Personal Diversity Within the Movement

Women who started battered women's programs were motivated by diverse ideological and personal experience....

Those who entered the battered women's movement from a woman's rights perspective often came with a social work or legal background. They assumed that equality with men would be gained through reforming the existing social system. While some women's rights activists defined their goals more broadly, most were primarily committed to ending discrimination. Questions of organizational structure and process were secondary: most often hierarchy was the preferred model in order to perform tasks quickly.

Unlike women's rights activists, radical feminists articulated a theory in which specific non-hierarchical organizational forms and self-help methods were a logical outcome of an analysis of violence against women. In many programs, locally and nationally, radical feminists organized first, setting the style and practice that continues to dominate in much of the battered women's movement. Radical feminists believe that historically and structurally the division of labor and power between men and women became the basis for other forms of exploitation, including class, ethnic, racial and religious ones....

Socialist feminists who worked within the battered women's movement joined an analysis of male domination to one of class and race oppression. They grounded women's oppression within material reality: the unequal division of labor between the sexes inside and outside the home, female responsibility for childbearing, and women's work maintaining home and family. For socialist feminists, although male domination predated capitalism, class and race oppression could not be reduced to or explained by patriarchy. Each form of oppression had its unique historical foundations.... Socialist feminists urged an explanation of the changing nature of the family and the state under capitalism, refusing to label all women as one class and asserting that differences among women by class and race were as important as similarities....

In many locations, lesbian feminists were among those initiating battered women's services. Committing themselves to help women and children live free from terror and pain was their goal. As one woman said: "Lesbians were able to look at violence and its political ramifications and not freak out about its meaning for their relationships with men. If you live with men and work with battered women, you have to find a way to deal with anger and rage."...

Third world feminists brought their own diverse experiences and political ideologies to the battered women's movement.... Their unique histories of cultural and racial oppression shaped their politics. The Combahee River Collective—a black feminist group whose members have worked on diverse projects and issues including sterilization abuse, abortion rights, rape, health care, and battered women-defines its goal as developing "a politics that was antiracist, unlike those of white women, and antisexist, unlike those of black and white men...."

Other black feminists had different analyses and different politics. However, almost all third world women with the battered women's movement asserted that their experiences as women were different from those of white women. Some also explained third world male violence in a different way:

> ... This country has systematically discriminated against, humiliated, and degraded certain of its people. These battered people, the poor and powerless, the ethnic minorities, the disenfranchised, are the real abused children of the white patriarchy.... These powerless men inflict violence on women and children, the only people who are even more powerless than themselves.

Feminist ideology and diverse experiences of women in the movement were not all that determined practice. Circumstances influenced the form the battered women's movement took in different locales, and how it expressed its politics. Some rural, more conservative communities translate feminism into "women who just want to break up families." Rural women had to tread even more carefully than their urban counterparts who were forced to exercise substantial caution but who, at least, had more potential allies. It is a stark understatement to suggest that circumstances forced feminists to work in less than ideal environments and to downplay, if not modify, their politics.

Elizabeth M. Schneider
Battered Women and Feminist Lawmaking (2000)

It took the rebirth of feminism in the 1960s for the "rediscovery" of battering. With a new spotlight on intimate violence and the ensuing development of a battered women's movement, many reforms designed to protect women from marital violence have been secured.

In both England and the United States, the focus of feminist consciousness raising about domestic violence was on intimate violence in the context of heterosexual relationships. The term first used to describe the problem was "wife-abuse," which revealed that it was viewed primarily through the lens of a marital relationship. Domestic violence was seen as part of the larger problem of patriarchy within the marital relationship.

Feminist activism around issues of domestic violence was highly diffuse and took many different forms. One focus was the development of battered women's "refuges," "shelters," or "safe houses." These houses, women-run and women-centered, were established to give battered women a place to go when they left a violent home, and to provide safety for them and their children. The idea of temporary residences for battered women was devised by a group of women in London who established a neighborhood center, Chiswick, that offered child care and a refuge for homeless women; many of those who needed the help of the center were women who had been abused. Police, social workers, social service agencies, and doctors wouldn't help them, but Chiswick admitted any woman who wanted to stay. Soon, women began to arrive from all over, and the center received wide publicity. Other shelters were set up around the country....

From the beginning of the battered women's movement in the 1960s, legal work played an important role in activist efforts on battering. Activists saw the law as a necessary and important tool in obtaining safety and protection for battered women....

One of the first and most important legal issues that came to the fore was the failure of police to protect battered women from assault. In the early 1970s, class-action lawsuits were filed in New York City and Oakland, California, which challenged police's failure to arrest batterers. This litigation raised the dramatic notion that domestic violence was criminal, sanctionable activity that was a harm against the "public," the state, not just an individual woman, and should be treated the same as an assault against a stranger.... Development of injunctive remedies to keep the batterer away, known as civil protective or restraining orders, was also an important area of work. These orders were first sought in the late 1960s, and during the late 1960s and early 1970s many states passed statutes to provide for civil protective remedies.

NOTES AND QUESTIONS

1. **Relevance of the Anti–Rape Movement?** What are the connections that Schechter asserts link the anti-rape movement with the anti-domestic violence movement? Again, notice the importance of gendered power relations and of the asserted role of violence in maintaining male power. As you read through the materials in this book, ask yourself whether you agree that domestic violence is a means through which either men in general or some men reinforce their dominance. How do you then account for battering in homosexual relationships?

2. **The Diversity of the Modern Anti–Domestic Violence Movement.** As Schechter indicates, one of the strengths of the late 20th century anti-domestic violence movement was that it brought together advocates from many different political, social, economic and intellectual positions. This had a clear effect on the movement's actions and priorities. In a portion of the book omitted from the above excerpt, Schechter pointed out that the women's advocates who started the earliest shelters were committed to an non-hierarchical organizational arrangement. Thus, women who had been abused worked together to make the shelters successful, without experts or bureaucrats. As you work your way through this book, you will see the clear contributions of academics and activists of color, of those who put material resources first, and of others who owe huge debts to the advocates who came before them.

3. **Women's Physical Security and the Construction of the Battered Woman.** One of the initial concerns of activists in the domestic violence movement was the physical safety of victims of violence. This led to the early establishment of shelters for victims. It also focused attention on the failure of the police to arrest batterers. This, in turn, had the effect of causing people to ask why anyone would stay in a violent relationship. Indeed, there was some sense that relationships could not be as dangerous as claimed if victims did not abandon them immediately and permanently. As Dorileen Loseke says in her study of shelters:

> . . . The collective representation of wife abuse leads to the common sense conclusion that a woman *should* leave such a relationship, and this prescription is part of the collective representation: A woman experiencing wife abuse must leave her relationship. . . .

> . . . [I]f she stays because she does not mind the abuse, indeed, if she stays because she *chooses* to stay for any reason, then claims about the content of this public problem are challenged. THE BATTERED WOMAN AND SHELTERS (1992).

Loseke argues that the result is that women who stay in abusive relationships—battered women—become defined as having particular traits that make them different from other women. We will return throughout this book to the definition of or the image of "battered women." As we do, think about how conceptions of the "battered woman" are connected to an interest in abused women's safety and in trying to account for why they remain in dangerous relationships.

4. **Violence Against Women Act of 1994.** Since the 1980's shelter services for battered women and their children have continued to expand and to gain in legitimacy. A big boost was provided by the Violence Against Women Act of 1994 (VAWA) that authorized the expenditure of federal funds to support shelters. While one priority continues to be increasing the availability of beds, another is to expand the range of services to women and children who for a variety of reasons cannot, or are not willing, or would not be served by, moving into a shelter. These services include support groups for both women and children, individual counseling for women, and a range of advocacy services to secure needed legal relief or public benefits. The Violence Against Women Act of 1994 and the 2000

reauthorization also included provisions to make restraining orders clearly subject to the Constitution's Full Faith and Credit clause and to create protections for immigrants who were dependent on their abusers. These will be discussed in subsequent chapters.

E.   CURRENT CONTROVERSIES

By 2007, there was a virtual explosion in legislation and other policies intended to reduce domestic violence. Not all advocates for battered women have been pleased with the evolution of the law relative to abused women. Those working on behalf of victims of domestic violence come from diverse ideological, social, and demographic backgrounds. As a result, many areas of law reform are controversial.

One area of controversy revolves around how we should understand battering. Is it a function of social structure and political organization or an individualized psychological problem? This is important because if battering is seen as connected to social structure and the subordination of women, it is much less likely that men are the victims of domestic violence. Another related controversy is who should be trusted to describe the experience and dynamics of domestic violence. Is it something that only experts who have studied the problem for many years can explain or an issue with which lay people also are familiar. These two issues are interrelated because the more we think of the problem as a psychological one, the more likely we are to need to rely on experts in the field for diagnoses and remedies. If the question involves the organization of society, then the topic calls for widespread debate about the policies that encourage violence and the possible social solutions.

A second area of current controversy is centered on the question of whether and to what extent the existence of domestic violence requires state intervention in the lives of victims, even against their will. Questions of autonomy and liberty are complicated. Is a victim's autonomy enhanced by letting her decide while enmeshed in a violent relationship that she will be worse off if the state intervenes or is it enhanced by forcing her to separate one way or another from the abuser and then providing the possibility of an independent life? These questions are made even more difficult because what might be best for some victims will not necessarily be best for others. We must remember that victims and their abusers are situated in different communities—racial, ethnic, religious and otherwise—and have different resources at their disposal.

The issue of state involvement is closely tied to the question of whether the state has a responsibility to reduce and remedy domestic violence. Is violence within an intimate setting a public issue or a private one? As you will see, the U.S. response to this is conflicted. In some settings state legislatures appear to have directed local actors to diminish the violence; in others, courts have specifically denied that governmental personnel have this responsibility. This has also been an issue internationally where women's human rights advocates have argued that there is state responsibility for "private violence."

These issues, highlighted in the following two excerpts, are only a few of the current challenges facing those who are concerned about the problems of domestic violence in our society. Keep them in mind as you read the excerpts that follow.

Elizabeth M. Schneider

Battered Women and Feminist Lawmaking (2000)

The battered women's movement defined battering within the larger framework of gender subordination. Domestic violence was linked to women's inferior position within the family, discrimination within the workplace, wage inequity, lack of educational opportunities, the absence of social supports for mothering, and the lack of child care. Traditionally, however, intimate violence had been viewed from a psychological perspective. This approach, which predated the feminist analysis of the 1960s, had been concerned with how violence is linked to specific pathology in the individual's personality traits and psychological disorders.

Significantly, even since the advent of the battered women's movement, this psychological perspective has not focused primarily on the pathology of male batterers. Although violent men are commonly labeled "sick" or "emotionally disturbed," in the public mind this perspective of pathology focuses largely on the woman who is battered. Those who are battered and who remain in battering relationships are regarded as more pathological, more deeply troubled, than the men who batter them. . . .

A second perspective, a sociological approach, rests on the premise that social structures affect people and their behaviors. This approach, which exploded as a focus of research on battering in the early 1980s, focuses on the problem of family violence—the way the institution of the family is set up to allow and even encourage violence among family members. Proponents of this view look at violence as a result of family dysfunction and examine how all participants in the family may be involved in perpetuating the violence.

Research on family violence further deflected attention from the crucial link to gender, and shifted focus onto research tools that deeply challenged feminist approaches. In a review of the family violence literature in 1983, Wini Breines and Linda Gordon perceived the dangers in this approach: "First, all violence must be seen in the context of wider power relations; violence is not necessarily deviant or fundamentally different from other means of exerting power over another person. Thus, violence cannot be accurately viewed as a set of isolated events but must be placed in an entire social context. Second, the social contexts of family violence have gender and generational inequalities at heart. There are patterns to violence between intimates which only an analysis of gender and its centrality to the family can illuminate."

. . . [B]oth psychological and sociological perspectives have done much to shape the context of research and the nature of public views of violence. Evan Stark has observed: "For fifty years or more, the realities have been concealed behind images that alternatively 'pathologize' family violence or else 'normalize' it, making it seem the inevitable byproduct of some combination of predisposition—because the abuser was mistreated as a child, for example—and environmental 'stress.' The use of violence is abstracted from its political context in gender and generational struggles, and its varied meanings in different cultures and classes are simply glossed over. Static conceptions posit aggression as inherent in (male) human nature or as inevitable given poverty, 'violence prone' cultures or personalities, and intergenerational transmission." Advocates of psychological and sociological perspectives recognize the significance of the "alternate" perspective and acknowledge that both psychological and social factors are significant variables. Yet both these approaches minimize the role and the impact of gender and are grounded in gender-neutral explanations. . . .

This politicization of social "knowledge" by "experts" on battering has a long history. In 1983 Evan Stark and Anne Flitcraft identified "the sudden social science concern with family violence in the 1980's" as part of the "same self-righteous puritanism that reappears in the very upper-class campaign to abolish 'sin' (prostitution, alcoholism, 'dirty homes' and wife beating) among the working classes." They argued that "just behind the cycle of concern about abuse lies a new ideological affinity between those who document the evils at the heart of family life, those who 'treat' these evils, and those who, like the ideologues supporting the current Family Protection Act, would unhesitatingly restore traditional patriarchal authority whatever the costs in individual freedom, an alliance between those who locate the principles of violence in 'private' life and those who would leave violence against women to private solutions." Contested sources of knowledge about battering highlight the deeply political nature of the descriptive stakes.

Emily J. Sack

Battered Women and the State: The Struggle for the Future of Domestic Violence Policy

2004 WIS. L. REV. 1657 (2004).

Introduction

In an episode of her television show that focused on domestic violence, Oprah Winfrey started off an interview of women in a battered women's shelter by commenting, "We've only played the women as victims and never asked them to—to ask themselves: What is your role in this?" Oprah asked the battered women to look within themselves and ask, "What have I done to contribute to this situation? Do you feel that you were a part of the sick dance?"

A few months earlier, the New York Times Magazine published an article on domestic violence policy that featured the story of Michael and

Sylvia Wilkes. Michael was physically abusive to Sylvia, beat their daughter with a stick, and assaulted a woman at his job, breaking her eye socket. Nevertheless, Michael was portrayed sympathetically as a man with a bad childhood whom the writer described as "trying hard to shoulder full responsibility for his actions," though he blamed his violent behavior on "[t]he distrust of a woman." Sylvia said that the dynamic of domestic violence was mutual, and that in a prior relationship that had also been violent, "[s]he was defensive and her fuse was short." One commentator supported this characterization of domestic violence, noting that although "[d]omestic violence is construed as one-sided aggression . . . often there is a warped dynamic of intimacy in which both the men and the women are players," and "[i]t is dishonest . . . to stifle conversation about the ways in which women, too, are aggressive and violent."

While this does not represent the predominant view of battered women in current domestic violence policy, it does demonstrate a disturbing strain of criticism of the current policy that recently has been making its way into the popular culture. This critique is in many ways a throwback to a very old conception of domestic violence, and depicts the dynamics of this violence as a psychological problem between two partners, in which the battered woman is as much, or more, to blame for the violence inflicted on her. In just a few decades, we have moved from the centuries-old view that condoned or ignored domestic violence, through a transformation which brought recognition that this violence was a matter of public concern and demanded dramatic changes in public policy to address it, and have now reverted back to the argument that domestic violence is a "family" matter, a "sick dance" that is best addressed outside the legal system.

Many factors have contributed to this recent portrayal of domestic violence in the media. These include disillusionment that the substantial policy changes of the last decades have not proven to be panaceas, as well as the advocacy of men's rights activists who believe the justice system is controlled by women to victimize men, and the popular writings of conservative women terming themselves "feminists," who argue that domestic violence policy has been contorted to serve the rigid view of patriarchy in which mainstream feminists have invested. The ongoing criticism of the "old guard"—actors in the criminal justice system who have continued to resist the changes to more aggressive policies—has also played a part in this negative depiction of battered women, as has journalists' simple need for a hook to grab the attention of readers bored by the same old stories of domestic violence. Of most concern is that this current of criticism is strengthening its position by taking advantage of fundamental tensions over domestic violence criminal justice policies that exist within the battered women's movement itself. The critique offered by these groups, who do not have the interest of battered women at heart, threatens to destroy decades of progress in domestic violence policy. . . .

The Critique from Within: Criticism of Domestic Violence Criminal Justice Policy by Battered Women's Advocates

While battered women's advocates are concerned about the effectiveness of mandatory policies, their fundamental interest is the impact of these policies on the safety and the autonomy of battered women. Although the push for mandatory criminal justice policies came from the battered women's movement, some within that movement argue that women have been revictimized by these policies. These critics argue that when the arresting officer and prosecutor have no discretion, domestic violence victims lose the opportunity to make choices about whether they want the abuser arrested or prosecuted, and they are placed at greater risk. These critics argue that battered women are the best predictors of the severity of risk they face from their abusers, and their desire not to press charges may be motivated by the knowledge that this will aggravate the violence. When victims realize that they have no choice once police and prosecutors get involved, they are less likely to initiate calls for help, and mandatory policies thus have an effect contrary to that which was intended. More broadly, they argue that these policies disempower victims, and some analogize this taking of power and control from the victim to the dynamic of the battering relationship itself.

Critics from within the movement have also argued that certain groups of women, including immigrants and racial minorities, may be particularly harmed by the imposition of these mandatory state policies. For example, if the abuser is an immigrant, he may be subject to deportation if convicted of a domestic violence crime; this can be a powerful disincentive for a woman to pursue criminal charges. African American women may resist calling the police or pursuing prosecution because they are hesitant to expose African American men to a criminal justice system that they perceive as racist. For these reasons, the benefits of mandatory policies may be outweighed by their costs, particularly for poor, immigrant, or minority women.

The battered women's advocates who criticize the mandatory policies have focused on the excesses of police conduct, such as increases in arrests of women or dual arrests; failures to implement the policy correctly; and the indirect consequences of arrest, such as initiation of child neglect proceedings against the battered mother or deportation proceedings. As mandatory arrest and no-drop policies have been implemented, critics within the battered women's movement argue that these policies are affirmatively causing harm to domestic violence victims. While there may be debate over how severe or widespread some of these problems are, there is no question that many of the concerns raised by these critics of the mandatory policies have been borne out.

The Attack on the Changes in Domestic Violence Policy from Outside the
    Battered Women's Movement

. . . Although men's rights proponents and conservative pseudofeminists [those who label themselves feminists, but in fact attack feminists in order to pursue a conservative agenda] have diverse agendas, they agree on several propositions. . . . [B]oth of these groups argue that women have been able to change the justice system so dramatically that they have succeeded in creating a complete focus on the victimization of women and distorted the reality of men's and women's statuses. For both groups, the dramatic changes in domestic violence policy exemplify the worst distortions of the justice system, and an attack on the changes in this area is central to both groups' more general critique of what they consider the state's misguided focus on women.

For the men's rights groups, these changes in policy have meant that men are now the victims of the justice system. This movement, which gains much of its impetus from fathers who have been denied custody rights in family law cases, has expanded to argue that domestic violence policy is biased against men, presumes men to be guilty of violence, and ignores men who are its victims. The men's rights proponents argue that the extent of violence perpetrated by men against women is exaggerated, and that the criminalization of domestic violence has stereotyped all men due to the actions of a few. Central to their argument on current domestic violence policy is that women are the aggressors in half of all domestic violence incidents. Therefore, men have a far from privileged status, and are, in fact, the victims of aggressive and violent women.

The "violent women" theory is also critical to the argument of the pseudofeminists. They argue that these data have been deliberately ignored by mainstream feminists because the results do not fit into their "essential feminist tenet that society is controlled by an all-encompassing patriarchal structure." The pseudofeminists claim simply to be interested in a candid discussion of domestic violence, as opposed to the mainstream feminists who have sacrificed intellectual honesty in exchange for loyalty to their positions.

This attack on recent domestic violence policy is only a part of a far broader assault on feminists and the policies they espouse. The pseudofeminists maintain that they represent the true feminist perspective, rather than the mainstream feminists who have jettisoned the real interests of women (and men) in order to adhere rigidly to their feminist agenda. The pseudofeminists argue that they support equality, fairness, and open opportunity in the tradition of the original feminists who wanted the same rights for women that men enjoyed. It is the " 'Second Wave' " mainstream feminists who have rejected the true feminist tradition, and created a gender war preoccupied with male dominance over women in order to achieve their narrow goals. . . .

F.   THE U.S. SUPREME COURT AND DOMESTIC VIOLENCE

Between 2004 and 2006, the United States Supreme Court heard six cases that directly or indirectly involved victims of domestic violence. Those cases dealt with questions of police liability for failure to enforce restraining orders, the admissibility of evidence in the prosecution of abusers, search and seizure law, legal standards governing duress, and the reproductive rights of teenagers who could have been victims of abuse. Such a wide range of cases in front of the Supreme Court is evidence of the growing importance of legal remedies to domestic violence cases.

Most of these cases, including the three below, are discussed later in this book. Here we want to use very brief excerpts from three of these cases, presented in chronological order, to discuss how the Court has responded to some of the important themes that have been highlighted by this introduction. First, how important is an understanding of the dynamics of violence to the fashioning of legal remedies? Second, is domestic violence a problem of women's subordination in society, with the violence being just one mechanism for denying women their autonomy, equality, or liberty? Finally, what is the role of the state in protecting victims of violence, be they men or women?

Planned Parenthood v. Casey

Supreme Court of the United States, 1992.
505 U.S. 833.

■ JUSTICE O'CONNOR, JUSTICE KENNEDY, and JUSTICE SOUTER delivered the opinion of the Court.

[In this case, the court was asked to decide whether § 3209 of Pennsylvania's abortion law, the section that required wives to notify their husbands before seeking an abortion, was unconstitutional because it placed an undue burden on a woman's right to terminate her pregnancy.]

. . . In well-functioning marriages, spouses discuss important intimate decisions such as whether to bear a child. But there are millions of women in this country who are the victims of regular physical and psychological abuse at the hands of their husbands. Should these women become pregnant, they may have very good reasons for not wishing to inform their husbands of their decision to obtain an abortion. Many may have justifiable fears of physical abuse, but may be no less fearful of the consequences of reporting prior abuse to the Commonwealth of Pennsylvania. Many may have a reasonable fear that notifying their husbands will provoke further instances of child abuse; these women are not exempt from § 3209's notification requirement. Many may fear devastating forms of psychological abuse from their husbands, including verbal harassment, threats of future violence, the destruction of possessions, physical confinement to the home, the withdrawal of financial support, or the disclosure of the abortion to family and friends. These methods of psychological abuse may act as even more of a deterrent to notification than the possibility of physical violence, but women who are the victims of the abuse are not exempt from § 3209's notification requirement. And many women who are pregnant as a result of sexual assaults by their husbands will be unable to avail themselves of the exception for spousal sexual assault, because the exception requires that the woman have notified law enforcement authorities within 90 days of the assault, and her husband will be notified of her report once an investigation begins. If anything in this field is certain, it is that victims of spousal sexual assault are extremely reluctant to report the abuse to the government; hence, a great many spousal rape victims will not be exempt from the notification requirement. . . .

The spousal notification requirement is thus likely to prevent a significant number of women from obtaining an abortion. It does not merely make abortions a little more difficult or expensive to obtain; for many women, it will impose a substantial obstacle. We must not blind ourselves to the fact that the significant number of women who fear for their safety and the safety of their children are likely to be deterred from procuring an abortion as surely as if the Commonwealth had outlawed abortion in all cases....

There was a time, not so long ago, when a different understanding of the family and of the Constitution prevailed.... [and] three members of this Court reaffirmed the common-law principle that "a woman had no legal existence separate from her husband, who was regarded as her head and representative in the social state...."

Section 3209 embodies a view of marriage consonant with the common-law status of married women but repugnant to our present understanding of marriage and of the nature of the rights secured by the Constitution. Women do not lose their constitutionally protected liberty when they marry. The Constitution protects all individuals, male or female, married or unmarried, from the abuse of governmental power, even where that power is employed for the supposed benefit of a member of the individual's family....

■ CHIEF JUSTICE REHNQUIST, with whom JUSTICE WHITE, JUSTICE SCALIA, and JUSTICE THOMAS join, concurring in the judgment in part and dissenting in part.

... In our view, the spousal notice requirement is a rational attempt by the State to improve truthful communication between spouses and encourage collaborative decision-making, and thereby fosters marital integrity. Petitioners argue that the notification requirement does not further any such interest; they assert that the majority of wives already notify their husbands of their abortion decisions, and the remainder have excellent reasons for keeping their decisions a secret. In the first case, they argue, the law is unnecessary, and in the second case it will only serve to foster marital discord and threats of harm. Thus, petitioners see the law as a totally irrational means of furthering whatever legitimate interest the State might have. But, in our view, it is unrealistic to assume that every husband-wife relationship is either (1) so perfect that this type of truthful and important communication will take place as a matter of course, or (2) so imperfect that, upon notice, the husband will react selfishly, violently, or contrary to the best interests of his wife. The spousal notice provision will admittedly be unnecessary in some circumstances, and possibly harmful in others, but "the existence of particular cases in which a feature of a statute performs no function (or is even counterproductive) ordinarily does not render the statute unconstitutional or even constitutionally suspect." The Pennsylvania Legislature was in a position to weigh the likely benefits of the provision against its likely adverse effects, and presumably concluded, on balance, that the provision would be beneficial. Whether this was a wise decision or not, we cannot say that it was irrational.

United States v. Morrison

Supreme Court of the United States, 2000.
529 U.S. 598.

[Christy Brzonkala, a student at Virginia Polytech Institute, alleged that she was raped by two members of the varsity football team, Antonio

Morrison and James Crawford. As well as filing charges against the two under Virginia Tech's Sexual Assault policy, she sued Morrison and Crawford, and Virginia Tech alleging that Morrison and Crawford's attack violated Section 13981 of the Violence Against Women Act. This law allowed victims of gender motivated violence to sue their attackers in federal court, thus creating a civil rights remedy for victims of both domestic violence and sexual assault. Congress claimed authority to pass such a law under both the Commerce Clause and Section 5 of the Fourteenth Amendment. The majority rejected both rationales and found that Congress had exceeded its authority in passing Section 13981.]

■ REHNQUIST, C.J.

II.

[Here the Court considers the argument that violence against women substantially affects interstate commerce, thus justifying Section 13981 under the Commerce Clause.]

 . . . Section 13981 *is* supported by numerous findings regarding the serious impact that gender-motivated violence has on victims and their families. But the existence of congressional findings is not sufficient, by itself, to sustain the constitutionality of Commerce Clause legislation. . . . Congress found that gender-motivated violence affects interstate commerce:

> by deterring potential victims from traveling interstate, from engaging in employment in interstate business, and from transacting with business, and in places involved in interstate commerce . . . by diminishing national productivity, increasing medical and other costs, and decreasing the supply of and the demand for interstate products.

 . . . The reasoning that petitioners advance seeks to follow the but-for causal chain from the initial occurrence of violent crime (the suppression of which has always been the prime object of the States' police power) to every attenuated effect upon interstate commerce. If accepted, petitioners' reasoning would allow Congress to regulate any crime as long as the nationwide, aggregated impact of that crime has substantial effects on employment, production, transit, or consumption. Indeed, if Congress may regulate gender-motivated violence, it would be able to regulate murder or any other type of violence since gender-motivated violence, as a subset of all violent crime, is certain to have lesser economic impacts than the larger class of which it is a part.

 Petitioners' reasoning, moreover, will not limit Congress to regulating violence but may . . . be applied equally as well to family law and other areas of traditional state regulation since the aggregate effect of marriage, divorce, and childrearing on the national economy is undoubtedly significant. . . .

 We accordingly reject the argument that Congress may regulate noneconomic, violent criminal conduct based solely on that conduct's aggregate effect on interstate commerce. The Constitution requires a distinction between what is truly national and what is truly local. . . . In recognizing this fact we preserve one of the few principles that has been consistent since the Clause was adopted.... Indeed, we can think of no better example of the police power, which the Founders denied the National Government and reposed in the States, than the suppression of violent crime and vindication of its victims....

III.

[Here the Court considers and rejects the argument that Section 13981 is a valid exercise of Congressional power under Section 5 of the Fourteenth Amendment.]

Petitioners' § 5 argument is founded on an assertion that there is pervasive bias in various state justice systems against victims of gender-motivated violence. This assertion is supported by a voluminous congressional record. Specifically, Congress received evidence that many participants in state justice systems are perpetuating an array of erroneous stereotypes and assumptions. Congress concluded that these discriminatory stereotypes often result in insufficient investigation and prosecution of gender-motivated crime, inappropriate focus on the behavior and credibility of the victims of that crime, and unacceptably lenient punishments for those who are actually convicted of gender-motivated violence.... Petitioners contend that this bias denies victims of gender-motivated violence the equal protection of the laws and that Congress therefore acted appropriately in enacting a private civil remedy against the perpetrators of gender-motivated violence to both remedy the States' bias and deter future instances of discrimination in the state courts....

However, the language and purpose of the Fourteenth Amendment place certain limitations on the manner in which Congress may attack discriminatory conduct. These limitations are necessary to prevent the Fourteenth Amendment from obliterating the Framers' carefully crafted balance of power between the States and the National Government ... Foremost among these limitations is the time-honored principle that the Fourteenth Amendment, by its very terms, prohibits only state action. The principle has become firmly embedded in our constitutional law that the action inhibited by the first section of the Fourteenth Amendment is only such action as may fairly be said to be that of the States. That Amendment erects no shield against merely private conduct, however discriminatory or wrongful....

... Section 13981 is not aimed at proscribing discrimination by officials which the Fourteenth Amendment might not itself proscribe; it is directed not at any State or state actor, but at individuals who have committed criminal acts motivated by gender bias.

In the present cases, for example, § 13981 visits no consequence whatever on any Virginia public official involved in investigating or prosecuting Brzonkala's assault. The section is, therefore, unlike any of the § 5 remedies that we have previously upheld. For example, in Katzenbach v. Morgan, 384 U.S. 641 (1966), Congress prohibited New York from imposing literacy tests as a prerequisite for voting because it found that such a requirement disenfranchised thousands of Puerto Rican immigrants who had been educated in the Spanish language of their home territory. That law, which we upheld, was directed at New York officials who administered the State's election law and prohibited them from using a provision of that law.... Similarly, in Ex parte Virginia, 100 U.S. 339 (1880), Congress criminally punished state officials who intentionally discriminated in jury selection; again, the remedy was directed to the culpable state official.

Section 13981 is also different from these previously upheld remedies in that it applies uniformly throughout the Nation. Congress' findings indicate that the problem of discrimination against the victims of gender-motivated crimes does not exist in all States, or even most States....

IV.

... If the allegations here are true, no civilized system of justice could fail to provide her a remedy for the conduct of respondent Morrison. But under our federal system that remedy must be provided by the Commonwealth of Virginia, and not by the United States.

■ JUSTICE SOUTER, with whom JUSTICE STEVENS, JUSTICE GINSBURG, and JUSTICE BREYER join, dissenting.

Passage of the [Violence Against Women] Act in 1994 was preceded by four years of hearings, which included testimony from physicians and law professors; from survivors of rape and domestic violence; and from representatives of state law enforcement and private business. The record includes reports on gender bias from task forces in 21 States, and we have the benefit of specific factual findings in the eight separate Reports issued by Congress and its committees over the long course leading to enactment.... [The opinion then recites at least two pages of findings describing the extent of violence against women in the U.S.]

Based on the data thus partially summarized, Congress found that:

crimes of violence motivated by gender have a substantial adverse effect on interstate commerce, by deterring potential victims from traveling interstate, from engaging in employment in interstate business, and from transacting with business, and in places involved, in interstate commerce ... [,] by diminishing national productivity, increasing medical and other costs, and decreasing the supply of and the demand for interstate products....

Congress thereby explicitly stated the predicate for the exercise of its Commerce Clause power. Is its conclusion irrational in view of the data amassed? True, the methodology of particular studies may be challenged, and some of the figures arrived at may be disputed. But the sufficiency of the evidence before Congress to provide a rational basis for the finding cannot seriously be questioned....

While Congress did not, to my knowledge, calculate aggregate dollar values for the nationwide effects of racial discrimination in 1964, in 1994 it did rely on evidence of the harms caused by domestic violence and sexual assault, citing annual costs of $3 billion in 1990, and $5 to $10 billion in 1993. Equally important, though, gender-based violence in the 1990's was shown to operate in a manner similar to racial discrimination in the 1960's in reducing the mobility of employees and their production and consumption of goods shipped in interstate commerce. Like racial discrimination, "gender-based violence bars its most likely targets women from full participation in the national economy. . . ."

■ JUSTICE BREYER, with whom JUSTICE STEVENS joins, . . . dissenting.

. . . The majority adds that Congress found that the problem of inadequacy of state remedies "does not exist in all States, or even most States." But Congress had before it the task force reports of at least 21 States documenting constitutional violations. And it made its own findings about pervasive gender-based stereotypes hampering many state legal systems, sometimes unconstitutionally so. . . . The record nowhere reveals a congressional finding that the problem "does not exist" elsewhere. Why can Congress not take the evidence before it as evidence of a national problem? This Court has not previously held that Congress must document the existence of a problem in every State prior to proposing a national solution. . . .

Town of Castle Rock, Colorado v. Gonzales

Supreme Court of the United States, 2005.
545 U.S. 748.

[Jessica Gonzales had a restraining order against her husband. The order commanded him not to "molest or disturb the peace" of Gonzales or her children, although it did allow him restricted access to the children. One evening, he took his three daughters from outside their home at a time not authorized by the restraining order. Despite Gonzales's repeated calls to the police telling them where her husband was, the police never looked for him. Hours later, her husband began shooting at the police station. The police killed him. The children were founded murdered in the back of his truck. He had killed them earlier that evening. Gonzales sued the police department, claiming that it violated her due process rights when refusing to enforce the restraining order despite having probable cause to believe it had been violated.]

■ SCALIA, J., delivered the opinion of the Court, in which REHNQUIST, C.J., and O'CONNOR, KENNEDY, SOUTER, THOMAS, and BREYER, JJ., joined.

. . . [A] true mandate of police action would require some stronger indication from the Colorado Legislature than "shall use every reasonable means to enforce a restraining order" (or even "shall arrest . . . or . . . seek a warrant"). That language is not perceptibly more mandatory than the Colorado statute which has long told municipal chiefs of police that they "shall pursue and arrest any person fleeing from justice in any part of the state" and that they "shall apprehend any person in the act of committing any offense . . . and, forthwith and without any warrant, bring such person before a . . . competent authority for examination and trial." It is hard to imagine that a Colorado peace officer would not have some discretion to determine that—despite probable cause to believe a restraining order has been violated—the circumstances of the violation or the competing duties of that officer or his agency counsel decisively against enforcement in a particular instance. The practical necessity for discretion is particularly apparent in a case such as this one, where the suspected violator is not actually present and his whereabouts are unknown. . . .

Even if the statute could be said to have made enforcement of restraining orders "mandatory" because of the domestic-violence context of the underlying statute, that would not necessarily mean that state law gave *respondent* an entitlement to *enforcement* of the mandate. Making the actions of government employees obligatory can serve various legitimate ends other than the conferral of a benefit on a specific class of people. The serving of public rather than private ends is the normal course of the criminal law because criminal acts, "besides the injury [they do] to individuals . . . strike at the very being of society; which cannot possibly subsist, where actions of this sort are suffered to escape with impunity." This principle underlies, for example, a Colorado district attorney's discretion to prosecute a domestic assault, even though the victim withdraws her charge. . . .

III.

. . . [T]he benefit that a third party may receive from having someone else arrested for a crime generally does not trigger protections under the Due Process Clause, neither in its procedural nor in its "substantive" manifestations. This result reflects our continuing reluctance to treat the Fourteenth Amendment as " 'a font of tort law,' does not mean States are powerless to provide victims with personally enforceable remedies. Although the framers of the Fourteenth Amendment and the Civil Rights Act of 1871 did not create a system by which police departments are generally held financially accountable for crimes that better policing might have prevented, the people of Colorado are free to craft such a system under state law."

■ JUSTICE STEVENS, with whom JUSTICE GINSBURG joins, dissenting.

Because respondent had a property interest in the enforcement of the restraining order, state officials could not deprive her of that interest without observing fair procedures. Her description of the police behavior in this case and the department's callous policy of failing to respond properly to reports of restraining order violations clearly alleges a due process violation. At the very least, due process requires that the relevant state decision-maker *listen* to the claimant and then *apply the relevant criteria* in reaching his decision. The failure to observe these minimal procedural safeguards creates an unacceptable risk of arbitrary and "erroneous deprivation[s]." According to respondent's complaint—which we must construe liberally at this early stage in the litigation,—the process she was afforded by the police constituted nothing more than a " 'sham or a pretense.' . . ."

NOTES AND QUESTIONS

1. **Victim Safety.** All three cases implicate the safety of the victim. In *Casey*, preserving a woman's safety is essential to the Court's decision. In

Morrison, Congress intends a civil rights remedy to act as a deterrent to future violence concerning the unconstitutionality of spousal notification respecting abortion. In *Castle Rock*, the victim is trying to keep herself and her daughters safe, and she has no ability to do so without protection from the police. As you continue in this course, the safety of victims and their children will be a recurring theme. Think about how safety questions become even more complicated if the abuser and his partner have children in common. It is very likely that the abuser's parenting rights prevented Gonzales and her children from moving away from the children's father. Furthermore, consider how the law helps or hinders victims in seeking safety. Who has the primary responsibility for keeping victims safe? Victims themselves? Their families and communities? The police? State legislators?

2.   **Domestic Violence and Victims' Autonomy.** In *Casey* the Court was very clear about the way in which victims' reproductive autonomy would be limited if the effects of the notification provision on the dynamics of violent relationships were not taken into account. Do you think the Court's decision in *Morrison* will have a similar effect on victims' overall autonomy? Remember that Congress had made findings that domestic violence reduced victims' mobility and thus their ability to cross state lines to work, shop, and otherwise participate in the economy.

3.   **Domestic Violence as a Civil Rights Issue.** In *Morrison*, the Court argued that a federal civil rights remedy was not required because Congress had not found that the states failed to protect victims of gender motivated violence. After having considered what happened in *Castle Rock*, do you think that the states are adequately addressing the needs of victims and their families? When the state refuses to become involved in "private" violence should we consider that to be "state action?" Does finding that domestic violence is primarily a state issue, rather than a federal one, deny the ways in which nation-wide social and legal norms reinforce violence against women?

4.   **Domestic Violence and Women's Equality.** After *Casey*, there was much hope that the Supreme Court would take a leadership role in ending domestic violence, just as it had a generation earlier in ending racial discrimination. In *Casey*, the Court takes seriously the premise that being a victim of domestic violence inhibits one's ability to exercise one's full autonomy in the area of reproductive rights as well as other areas of women's lives. The Court makes explicit mention of prior legal precedent that held that women were property of their husbands and thus had no independent legal rights. The Court makes the broader argument that women's independent legal status requires that they be free from domestic violence and the consequences of it. Yet, after *Casey*, although the Court doesn't necessarily condone domestic violence, it retreats from linking individual violence to the larger legal structures that permit it, and, in *Morrison* in particular, minimizes both its prevalence and its scope. Thus, while in *Casey*, the Court sees domestic violence within the larger framework of women's equality, it retreats from this position in *Morrison* and *Castle Rock*. Domestic violence is then viewed as a personal, individual

problem rather than a systemic one. Why is it that the Court retreats from its original understanding in *Casey*?

Keep in mind that Justice Sandra Day O'Connor was in the majority in all three cases, and thus the answer may not be as simple as pointing to individual justices and their views on women's equality. Are there distinctions to be made between the three cases? Some suggest that even though *Morrison* and *Castle Rock* involve domestic violence, they are fundamentally cases about states' rights.

5. **Domestic Violence, Legal Reforms, and Retrenchment.** Reva Siegel suggested in the excerpt above from *"The Rule of Love,"* that one of the dangers of reform movements that have any success is that they bring pressure to reinforce the prior status regime in ways that are not socially controversial. In many ways, *Casey* represents a success of the women's movement and the anti-domestic violence movement. Do you think the language of federalism and states' rights in *Morrison* and *Castle Rock* represents just the type of retrenchment that Siegel predicted? If so, what are the implications of this for those who argue in favor of relying on legal remedies for the abuses of intimate violence?

6. **State Intervention in Violent Relationships.** One theme that will repeat frequently throughout this book is whether police, prosecutors, doctors, and other professionals who are in a position to assist victims of domestic violence ought to be required to do so. The Court in *Castle Rock* rejects the argument that there is a constitutional duty to protect victims of domestic violence even when they are seeking out the protection. What position does *Casey* take on the state's obligation to protect victims of domestic abuse? Do these cases conflict with each other or not? Which position do you prefer and why?

7. **Why Doesn't She Leave?** One major question we will explore in this book is "why doesn't the victim leave?" Consider that question in light of the Court's holdings in *Casey, Morrison,* and *Castle Rock*. Do the decisions in these cases make it safer or less safe for victims to try to leave abusers?

As you read through the rest of the book, keep these questions about the dynamics of violent relationships, the lives of victims, the desirability of state intervention, and liberty, subordination, and autonomy in mind. They will always be relevant to your study of domestic violence.

CHAPTER TWO

THE DYNAMICS OF ABUSIVE RELATIONSHIPS

Introduction

The previous chapter stressed the "systemic" nature of partner abuse—the ways in which men's abuse of women, through tactics of power and control that include physical violence, is enabled by a cultural context that subordinates women and makes them available for abuse. In part, this arrangement is likely to be supported by public regulation that privileges male status. But in addition, the hierarchy is likely to be enforced by enabling individual men to control individual women, even, in some cases, when that involves inflicting physical injury. It goes without saying that in such a society women will not have the same freedom to exert control over, or exact services from, men.

American society has never been completely tolerant of woman abuse, of course. Throughout American history, when a man killed or injured or sexually assaulted a woman with whom he had no intimate relationship, it was, in the eyes of the law, homicide, or assault, or rape, unless, perhaps, the woman was a slave, and the man her owner. In the period in which husbands were licensed to chastise their wives, men often had a valid defense to homicide. If the relationship was intimate, but not marital, the man's privilege was only informal, operative when law enforcement looked the other way, or witnesses could not be found to testify. That same informal privilege continues to operate today, when the laws on the books prohibit the use of violence even within marriage, and yet enforcement lags behind. The one substantial area of continuing legal privilege for a husband's violence is sexual access, where many states continue to differentiate between a stranger's rape or sexual assault, and a husband's.

If we were to look not at legal sanctions, but social ones, we would find a somewhat similar pattern; clear disapproval of certain extreme forms of violence, but lesser and greater degrees of tolerance in other circumstances, where the man is viewed as having the "right" to exert discipline or insist on sexual access, or as having an excuse for his "loss of control," either because of his relationship with the woman, or because of her behavior towards him.

This chapter continues our inquiry into the three questions we posed at the beginning: What are the experiences of domestic violence; how do those experiences relate to broader social and legal norms that limit women's participation in society; and how might the law then respond? In this chapter, we turn our focus towards the first of these questions—the individual, psychological and emotional dynamics of battering. The abusive relationship will have its own internal dynamic, and the partners will understand the violence as a problematic, or perhaps an unproblematic, aspect of that dynamic. Similarly, many of those with whom the batterer and his partner will interact—family members, friends, neighbors, teachers, pastors, social service providers, law enforcement personnel, lawyers, judges—will see the problem as lodged in the couple's relationship, rather than any larger social or political framework. In this chapter, we introduce contemporary understandings of the internal dynamics of abusive relationships, and some of the controversies currently animating discussions of those dynamics in the sociological and psychological literatures.

Why should lawyers struggle to understand the psychodynamics of abusive relationships? Why is it not enough to take a stand against partner abuse, insist that the legal system eradicate any residual tolerance for abuse or resistance to those who would challenge it, and offer legal assistance to women who seek to hold their batterers accountable? First, unless we understand the subjective experience of battering or being battered, we are unlikely to create laws, or implement them, in ways that serve our clients. Second, if our understanding of the problem is at odds with our clients' understandings, it will be hard to represent them effectively, even within the existing legal system. Third, we will encounter misunderstandings among the social service providers, the law enforcement personnel and the lawyers, judges and jurors who will have power over our clients' lives, and must be able to advocate for our clients in non-legal as well as legal settings.

Most of the readings in this chapter deal explicitly with heterosexual relationships in which the male is most often the abuser, and do not differentiate based on race or culture. The next chapter asks what is the same and what is different if the abusive relationship is between partners of the same sex, and how the particulars of race, culture, or socio-economic or immigrant status, or physical, mental or emotional disability, may influence the experience of abuse. This chapter and the next focus almost exclusively on the batterer and his partner, while later in the book we explore what it means for a woman who is being battered to be a mother of young children, as so many are.

The chapter opens with a look at the behaviors that make a relationship abusive. The focus here is on the whole spectrum of behaviors through which an abusive partner exerts power and control—not all of which involve physical violence. Although the law's concern is largely with violence, violence is only one of many strategies an abuser may use to impose his will on his partner, and the threat of violence alone, or a rare exercise of violence combined with more frequent threats and emotional abuse, may be enough to ensure her subjugation. Abusers can exert financial control, emotionally terrorize, or isolate the victim from friends and family. As advocates for victims, therefore, we need to understand the broader context of abuse within which physical violence plays a part.

There are those who would argue that to call a woman "battered," as if a single adjective summed her up, describes her in an inappropriate manner and limits our understanding of her situation. Unless and until she pays the ultimate price, she is also, and importantly, a survivor. She may be a cellist, a salesperson, a lawyer, secretary or truck driver, or be the most fun mom on the block. She may be a woman others would describe as sexy, or funny, or tough, before they would describe her as battered. Thus, what can we say about how and why women are drawn into relationships that become violent, and why they stay even once the violence has begun, or is escalating to dangerous levels? To understand these dynamics, we have to pay close attention to the distinction between who these women were before their abusive relationships began, who they may become after a period of exposure to the trauma of physical and emotional abuse, and the potential they may have for an entirely different life once the violence ends. There is disagreement within the community of those seeking to understand woman abuse and its consequences. Some members of that community have stressed the debilitating consequences of abuse and the "learned helplessness" of those exposed to random violence over which they seem incapable of exercising control, while others have emphasized the strength and resourcefulness of women seeking to protect themselves and their children from abuse.

The next readings in this chapter address the question of why men become abusers. Is abuse just a caricatured version of "normal" male behavior in this society, as some believe? Is it instead always symptomatic of pathology, as others have argued? Or is the truth somewhere in between?

What makes a relationship abusive? One of the issues that has bedeviled social scientists who attempt to assess the prevalence of domestic violence is the question of what measure to use. Should one look only at physical abuse? Surveys that use a single incidence of physical violence, from a slap or a push to a shooting or stabbing, as a test of abuse may overestimate the number of genuinely abusive relationships, as well as overestimating the abuse of men by women. The same emphasis on incidents of physical violence, independent of the broader context in which they occur, has tended to characterize the legal framework within which crimes of domestic violence are adjudicated. This limited legal focus often results in an underestimation of the danger posed by a batterer, and the imposition of an inadequate sanction, which leaves his partner vulnerable to continued abuse.

Focusing on the relational context of abuse, however, does not automatically produce a more accurate understanding of domestic violence. Another frequent mistake is to understand the relationship as "conflictual," as if the abuse grew out of disagreement, or from the inability of the partners to communicate and resolve their differences by other means. The notion that couples counseling is appropriate for an abuser and his partner often derives from this vision. So does the insistence on the part of family courts that an abuser and his partner can profit by mediating the issues that have brought them to court.

Instead, this text is premised on understanding abusive relationships as relationships in which one partner systematically seeks to exert control over the other through a range of strategies which may well include, but are certainly not limited to, physical abuse. Evan Stark has called this the "coercive control" model of domestic violence, and Karla Fischer, Neil Vidmar and Rene Ellis, in the excerpt below, emphasize the "culture of battering" within which individual incidents of violence occur. Within this culture, an abuser is likely to use a range of behaviors to impose his will—a range suggested both by the "Power and Control Wheel" reproduced below. The control model does not describe all violent relationships—there are certainly some psychotic abusers and couples who do use violence as a means of dispute resolution. The focus of this text, however, is on those relationships in which power and control of one intimate partner by another is the primary relational dynamic.

A. WOMEN'S EXPERIENCES OF ABUSIVE RELATIONSHIPS

In this section, we focus on two key questions: First, how do women become involved in abusive relationships, and second, once they are in one, why do they stay? For many years it was thought that women in battering relationships were masochistic. Some psychologists argued that women were psychologically dependent on abusive treatment; provocative, or self-defeating. Recent studies have found no empirical basis for such claims. The authors of one such study suggested in 1986 that battered women differ from non-battered women only in the extent of violence in their families of origin. Others have suggested that while there is no "personality profile" for the victim of domestic violence, many women are rendered susceptible to abuse both by gender-role socialization that encourages them to adapt and submit to male demands, and by childhood experiences— whether personal or familial—of violence and sexual molestation or assault. If there is no psychological predisposition on the part of a woman to choose an abusive partner, then it becomes important to ask how it is that women find themselves in such relationships. Angela Browne has written movingly about the "courtship" of batterers, recounting stories that illustrate how the most violent partner can appear an ideal suitor at the start of the relationship, when his possessiveness masquerades as attentiveness, and his obsessive focus can be a welcome change from others' seeming careless-ness. An excerpt from her 1987 book WHEN BATTERED WOMEN KILL is included here.

It is equally important to ask why a woman may find it difficult or impossible to leave her abusive relationship—to the extent we think that question is not fully answered by the credible threats of retribution from the batterer, or the intimidating economic and social barriers she faces. This question marches us right into the midst of a lively dispute within the growing academic field of domestic violence studies—the validity, and the usefulness, of the concept of learned helplessness in explaining the behavior and choices of battered women. First, it is necessary to understand what the experience of battering is for those who are in such a relationship. To further that understanding, we include an excerpt from Karla Fischer and her colleagues that describe in detail the experiences of women in abusive relationships. Fischer's descriptions are then followed by a piece by Lenore Walker, in which she describes the cycle of violence that is common for many. The next piece is from Sarah Buel, who describes why women stay in abusive relationships. She focuses both on material and psychological barriers to leaving.

Angela Browne

Courtship and Early Marriage: From Affection to Assault, When Battered Women Kill (1987)

Molly met Jim Johnson in the fall of 1978, when she was twenty-nine. Jim was thirty-five, tall and muscular, and strikingly good-looking. Friends indicated he had had a long string of relationships with women and never wanted to settle down, but with Molly it was different. Jim's interest in Molly began at their first meeting and never abated. He was dependable and attentive, rearranging his schedule to be with her and dropping other activities and even former friends with whom she felt uncomfortable.

In the following months, Jim was with her every moment Molly would allow. He occasionally spent time away from her and went drinking with old friends, but when he came back was as gentle and considerate as ever and he never drank heavily around her. Most of the things they did they did alone together. Jim said Molly was too fragile for his male world, and that he found relief from the daily pressures of life just being around her. And he did seem at peace; his friends said he was the happiest they had ever seen him, and Molly was glad to be a part of that. From what she knew of his past, she felt like he'd had a hard life.

Thinking back on that time, Molly remembers that she just felt fortunate Jim had noticed her. He didn't seem to mind her shyness; wasn't always pushing her to talk more or to party with him, like other men she had dated. And was always attentive and there—something that was important to her, after the long absences of her first husband. In May 1979, Molly married Jim in a quiet ceremony by a justice of the peace with two of Molly's employers in attendance.

There wasn't any abuse during the first few months Molly and Jim were married. Jim was working steadily and was good to Molly. At his urging, Molly quit work and stayed home; she enjoyed setting up a household again. But then Jim quit his job during a fight with his boss and couldn't get another one. He wouldn't hear of Molly going back to work, telling her he had married her and would support her. They stayed in the apartment another month, and then Jim put everything in storage and he and Molly moved into his van. They were living at the coast and would move the camper from rest stop to rest stop. Jim usually left in the truck during the day to look for work; Molly waited for him to come home, then fixed supper on the camp stove and they'd move to another location for the night.

Molly tried hard to be supportive; Jim was a proud man and she knew it was a difficult time for him. He was very quiet and moody, but most of the time they got along alright. The only serious arguments they had were when Molly attempted to persuade him to let her look for work, even if just on a temporary basis. The first time Jim yelled at Molly was over this issue, and Molly never brought it up again. Jim refused to let her go with him into town, and persuaded her not to tell her family and friends where she was until they got themselves settled. Molly knew Jim was embarrassed about the change in his circumstances and complied. It seemed to her that it rained all fall; she read a lot, and tried not to let herself get depressed.

As the weeks went by, Jim began coming back later at night, often drunk. When drinking, Jim was different than Molly had ever seen him— yelling at her, calling her names, accusing her of not loving him or of wanting to leave him. And sometimes, he raped her. Molly didn't think you could call it rape, when it was your own husband, but he was very rough during lovemaking—pinching and biting and treating her with anger. At these times, he was like another person; he didn't seem to know her or realize what he was doing. Molly began to have constant bruises and bite marks. But Jim was always cold sober by morning—quiet and depressed and terribly sorry. He would apologize and stroke her face, and drink less and spend more time with her for the next several days. Molly prayed he'd find work soon. She kept telling herself things would be alright once he got a job and they moved out of that van.

The First Beating

Jim found employment just before Christmas, and they moved from the van to an old house in town. He was gone most of the time now, getting things in order and working overtime to pay back bills. But Molly was ecstatic; so glad to have a home again and to be moving things into shelves and closets. After unpacking, she began fixing the house for Christmas. Jim didn't want her to spend much money, but she put up a tree and made some decorations. She also made a couple of presents for Jim.

When Jim came home from work on Christmas Eve, he seemed alright. But suddenly he became very irritated, angry that she hadn't reminded him to get her a Christmas gift. The more Molly tried to reassure him, the more angry Jim became. He tore the tree down, then began to hit Molly in the head with his fists. Molly attempted to pull away, but Jim grabbed her by the hair and slammed her head back against the wall with all his force. Molly came to with Jim throwing water on her. When he saw that she was conscious, he hit her in the stomach, carried her to the bedroom and had sex with her, and then fell asleep. Molly slipped into the bathroom and cried. Jim had never beaten her like that and she could not understand it. She thought maybe it was because his brother had been killed the month before in Viet Nam.

The next day, Molly had black eyes, a swollen nose, and bruises on her face and stomach. Jim said he was sorry, but added that if she had reminded him to buy her something for Christmas, it wouldn't have happened. He made her put makeup on her face so he wouldn't have to look at the bruises, and while she was doing that, he fixed the tree. But Molly hid the presents, for fear of making him angry again. For the next few weeks, Molly just felt numb, realizing that Jim had hit her. She'd go up to the attic and sit staring out of the window for hours. They had an income and a house. This is when things were supposed to be getting better.

First Impressions

[Browne studied women who had been battered, a group of whom had eventually committed homicide.]

Molly's initial impressions of Jim were similar to those reported by the majority of women in the homicide group about their mates. Women noted that these men were, in the first weeks and months they knew them, the most romantic and attentive lovers they'd ever had. Such characteristics as early and intense interest; a constant concern with the woman's where-abouts and activities; a desire to be with them all the time; wanting to do everything together, often alone; and major changes in the men's life-styles were mentioned over and over again. The women remembered that the men showed a particularly intense concern with what they were thinking and feeling, watching them closely and responding strongly to any per-ceived shifts; and this the women also saw as evidence of sensitivity and love.

The women often perceived these men as unusually communicative and open as well; the men's need for an early commitment and their expressed fears of being hurt seemed endearingly honest and vulnerable. In the early stages of a relationship, with all the attendant insecurities and unknowns, neediness can be a charming quality in a partner. A man who wants you so would never turn around and leave you; a man who cares so deeply and is so aware of your moods seems unlikely to later treat you badly.

One woman, raised in an abusive family, remembered that her partner was "a wonderful man" when she first met him, "very observant and gentlemanly." She did know he "liked women" and that he was used to "stepping out"; she caught him in an affair once and nearly left him. But he was so sorry and so charming; his intensity over her convinced her she was really the one he cared for. He pressed her to move in with him, and then to marry him, and she felt they had worked through their problems. In those early days, he laughed easily and drank lightly; it was three years before she realized he was an alcoholic. His temper started to change in the second year: You could say one thing and he would laugh at it, and then later become angry over the same thing. She learned that much of the time he was lying to her about his past and his activities; he quit his job two months before she found out he wasn't going to work. The third year they were married he began "dating"; the physical abuse started soon after.

Even with some indications of prior trouble, women often believed the men had changed, and they made their commitment to the men as they were when they met them....

Early Warnings

... Typically—in 72 percent to 77 percent of the cases—violence occurs only after a couple has become seriously involved, is engaged, or is living together; rather than in the early, more casual stages of dating. Victims have difficulty interpreting assaultive behavior from someone they thought they knew so well. Violent episodes are attributed to specific circumstances (or even to love . . .), and the relationships continue despite the outburst. Although many respondents report that their relationships worsened or terminated after the violence, in 26 percent to 37 percent of the cases, respondents report that their relationships "improved" or became more committed after an assault. (It is interesting to note that, in at least one study, men were twice as likely as women to say that their relationships improved after the use of violence, whereas women were more likely to say the relationships deteriorated.) The longer the couple is involved and the more serious their commitment, the more likely they are to remain together after a physical attack.

It is sometimes difficult to separate the warning signs of future violence from more typical romantic interactions. Couples newly in love do think primarily of one another, want to spend time together and, in the process, often isolate themselves from other acquaintances. Verbal expressions are intense and emotions easily triggered. Since our romantic tradition is based on gender stereotypes and premises of possession, characteristics of a partner that suggest a potential for future violence are often hidden within behaviors culturally sanctioned as appropriate for men who are in love. A clustering of these behaviors, however, particularly in the areas of intrusion and possessive control, should be carefully evaluated for the history that might underlie their outward expressions.

Intrusion

Many of the behaviors that women in the homicide group initially thought so romantic, over time became the triggers that led to their assault. The men's constant desire to know their whereabouts, for example—which at first made the women feel missed and cared for—stiffened into a requirement that they account for every hour and led to violent reprisals when their partners were not satisfied with their explanations. Women reported being followed to work or to friends' houses, constant phone calls to make sure they were where they said they would be, and sudden appearances to check up on them. The early interest in their activities became confounded with suspicion and distrust, and arriving home a few minutes late could mean a beating.

Isolation

This need for constant knowledge of the woman's whereabouts, combined with a preference for not letting the woman interact with people other than themselves, led in most cases to severe restrictions of the women's activities, especially once a commitment had been established. Men in the homicide group cut their partners off from friends and family, refused to let them work outside the home, and treated activities the women wanted to pursue without them as a personal affront. There had usually been some indication of this tendency to isolate the woman from outside contacts in the early days of the relationships: Women remembered that their partners had often not wanted them around their friends and had shown little interest in, or even expressed jealousy of, the women's friends. In the first stages of the relationships, however, this unwillingness to be a part of a larger network had gone unnoticed in the intensity of being together. Such isolation left the women at great risk once the abuse began, reducing their resources and the chance that others would be aware of their plight or intervene.

Possession

The dynamics of touch and intimacy also changed for these women, from the gentle but persistent persuasion reported as characteristic of the early experiences with the abusers to forceful possession without regard for the women's wishes or well-being. For many women in the homicide group, physical intimacy changed from a joy to the most threatening part of the relationship. They found they were unable to predict when lovemaking would be affectionate and when assaultive; consequently, they felt at risk any time intimate contact was initiated. Now women remembered that, even in the good days, there had been something determined about the way the man guided them through a room at a party or indicated by touch that they were his. In the early days of courtship, this had seemed more protective than controlling.

That the women should be confused about the meanings of touch is not surprising. Possession is an accepted part of romantic interactions between men and women, and many of these behaviors would be hard to distinguish from more normal ways of relating until they began to degenerate over time. In our present culture, even the violent forcing of physical intimacy is frequently seen as an indication of true love: In the popular genre of Harlequin romance novels, for instance, dashing ''heros'' tear women's clothing and leave bruises on the bodies, thus alerting the reader that they really love them and will probably marry them by the end of the tale. Ironically, such unions are presented as a stroke of immense good fortune for the women involved: Marriage to an assaultive man *is* the ''happy ending'' to the story.

Jealousy

Another factor woven throughout our tradition of romantic love is the expression of jealousy. From the ''chivalry'' of dueling to folklore and ballads about crimes of passion, jealousy has been used not only as a yardstick by which to gauge affection, but as a justification for violence. In the homicide group, the men's tendencies toward extremes of jealousy were often masked by an initial emphasis on the positive dimensions of being alone, or were only implicit in their constant inquiries about the women's activities and thoughts. Yet all the women reported that this became a serious problem in their relationships with their abusers. Many violent incidents were triggered by a partner's jealous rage and, in almost all cases, the men's jealous suspicions far exceeded all bounds of possibility by the end of the relationships.

Prone to Anger

Reports of women in both the homicide and comparison groups suggest other warning signs, less confounded with our concepts of romantic love, although still supported by cultural stereotypes for male behavior. Even before their partners became physically assaultive, the women noticed that many of these men seemed easily angered. Their mood could change from laughter to fury without warning, and what might set them off was hard to predict. More importantly, this anger was often completely out of proportion to the circumstance that occasioned it, and it was this pattern that later left women victims of violent attacks for something so minor as forgetting to turn off the oven or leaving the checkbook in the car.

Early outbursts of violence were frequently directed at objects or against pets, rather than against persons. Women reported watching their men rip pictures off walls or smash furniture, when the reasons for their distress were not exactly clear. An aggressive approach to life was frequently displayed in driving behavior as well. Women recounted occasions of recklessness in which the men seemed to deliberately put both their lives in danger, and reported them deliberately running into things such as stop signs or parked cars, or using the car as a weapon or threat. These behaviors demonstrate a man's willingness to do damage. . . .

Unknown Pasts

Many of the women knew almost nothing about the pasts of their men when they first became involved with them, or even at the point at which they made major commitments. Most had spent relatively little time with their partner's friends early in the relationship and few had mutual acquaintances who knew the man well. Thus, their impressions were based almost exclusively on their own interactions and on the sides of the man they were allowed to see. The women were often so blinded by the men's intense interest and desire to know about *their* pasts that they didn't notice how little they knew about the men's.

Such knowledge might have helped them. The majority of men in the homicide group had a history of violent interactions, if not with prior female partners, then with peers or family members. . . .

While other warning signs may be hard to separate from more typical romantic interactions, a prior history of violence is a factor that should not be ignored. Even if prior assaults were not directed at female partners, it is very hard to keep repeated violence compartmentalized in one area of one's life. . . .

Women's Responses to Early Assaults

Women reacted to initial assaults with shock and disbelief; sometimes attempting to discuss the incidents with their partners, often withdrawing into silence and confusion and attempting to avoid any further confrontations while they thought it out on their own. As one woman, who had not had any exposure to physical abuse prior to her marriage, described the sequence of shock and denial: "You wonder if it's something wrong with you that is causing him to behave this way; what the fact that your partner is violent with you says about you. You tell yourself things might be better if he wasn't so unhappy at his job, if you lived in another house, if you weren't working, or if you were. You begin to question if it really is as bad as you are making it out; if you're exaggerating, if you're going crazy. You wonder if anyone would believe you if you told them. But you keep it all inside, so you never do find out how others might judge the situation if they knew. Sometimes you wonder if it ever happened. In an odd way, you attempt to protect your sanity by denying your own reality.''

Most women in the homicide group did not attempt to seek help after the first incidents of violence—or refused outside intervention if it was offered—as a result of their shock, confusion, and shame. Again, this is typical of women's reactions to assault by their intimate partners. A few women attempted to leave the men after the onset of violence.... However, most of these women were talked into returning by the men's assurances that the violence would not occur again, and by their own sense that they should give the relationship another chance. In some cases, even when women made serious escape attempts, the very sources they turned to for help persuaded them to return.

NOTES AND QUESTIONS

1. **The Ease of Attachment.** One of the most striking themes about Molly's story is just how easy it was for her to slip into this relationship, and how the physical abuse began only after many other controlling behaviors. Browne emphasizes the cycle of violence that can happen in these relationships, and the reluctance of women to leave at the first sign of violence. Significantly, Browne highlights the degree to which patterns of control only appear in retrospect. Think back upon your own relationships. Have you been in one which you should have, in hindsight, ended before you actually did? What were the reasons that you stayed in that relationship? Much of the law that you will read assumes that there is something pathological about those who stay in violent relationships. Yet, many of the reasons people stay—love, hope, commitment—are the reasons many of us stay in unfulfilling relationships.

2. **Violence in Relationships.** In *Love and Violence: Gender Paradoxes in Volatile Attachments,* 29 FAMILY PROCESS 343 (1990), the authors, Virginia Goldner, Peggy Penn, Marcia Sheinberg and Gillian Walker, report on a study growing out of their couples counseling with partners whose relationships were marked by violence, but who expressed a desire to stay together. It is very common that abused women will say that what they want is for the violence to stop but that they do not want to end the relationship. In other words, these women want to end the violence in their relationships, but not to end the relationships themselves. Many have been critical of using couples counseling in the context of domestic violence, fearing for the safety of the abused partner, and doubting that the process can be a productive one in the presence of such a disparity of power between the two individuals. The authors of this study felt that with appropriate safeguards, and within a framework in which the abusive partner was asked to take responsibility for his violence, useful work could be done.

As they explored the violent relationships of their clients, they came to understand them as deeply influenced by the assumptions the partners brought to the relationship about gender, and the tensions associated with the partners' contradictory needs to meet traditional expectations associated with their gender, on the one hand, and escape the straightjackets imposed by those expectations, on the other. Among the issues they explore is the one we are discussing here—why it is that women form emotional attachments to violent men, and sometimes have difficulty severing those attachments, even when the relationships become highly dangerous. The next reading delves deeper into the dynamics of these abusive relationships.

Karla Fischer, Neil Vidmar and Rene Ellis
The Culture of Battering and the Role of Mediation in Domestic Violence Cases
46 S. M. U. L. REV. 2117 (1993).

Researchers in the field of domestic violence have not agreed on a uniform definition of what constitutes violence or an abusive relationship. It is important to briefly consider this literature in order to, first, expand the definition of abuse beyond physical assault, and, second, to distinguish relationships that are characterized by a culture of battering from those involving isolated acts of physical assault or other forms of abuse. Acts of assault and abuse occur in many domestic disputes and while they might incur criminal charges, relationships involving a culture of battering are of another order (they are qualitatively and perhaps quantitatively different as well). . . .

As sociologist Liz Kelly has noted, the prevailing stereotype about domestic violence is that assaults are "physical, frequent, and life threatening." Yet, the reality of battered women's lives does not conform solely to this image. Advocates for battered women have long noted that financial abuse and property abuse are forms of emotional abuse inflicted upon women. Abusers frequently restrict women's access to money and destroy their personal property in an effort to gain control over them or keep them in a state of fear. Emotional and sexual abuse may be even more common. Forms of emotional abuse include acts that do not constitute overt threats of injury or violence, such as constant humiliation, insults, degradation, and ridicule. Of course, explicit threats to harm or kill, including those attached to vivid descriptions of the method the abuser would use to carry it out, also have emotional consequences. The abuser may extend threats of harm to the victim's extended family or her children. . . .

Researchers who have investigated the phenomenon find that rates of battered women who have been sexually assaulted consistently fall in the thirty-three percent to sixty percent range. Sexual abuse frequently involves acts that could also be classified as physical assaults, blurring the line between physical and sexual abuse, such as the insertion of objects into the woman's vagina, forced anal or oral sex, bondage, forced sex with others, and sex with animals. Sexual violence sometimes marks the end of a physical abusive incident; for others, the sexual violence begins the assault. Some of the abuse involves the use of pornography, as batterers may force their partners to look at or watch pornographic materials and/or act out pictures or scenes from these materials.

Emotional, familial, and sexual abuse have also been recently labeled as domestic violence because these forms of assault harm women, both psychologically and physically. Some battered women have described psychological degradation and humiliation as the most painful abuse they have experienced. The impact of this kind of abuse can be long lasting and harmful to women's psychological health. Emotional, familial, and sexual abuse may also affect women's physical health. Physical symptoms such as high blood pressure, ulcers, chronic back pain, chronic fatigue, and tension headaches may manifest as a result of physical abuse or as a result of the stress produced by the other forms of violence. Research on the psychological impact of rape suggests that sexual abuse, particularly when the assailant is known to the woman, has deleterious mental health effects including depression, anxiety, suicidal ideation, and a loss of self esteem and self worth. . . .

The Systematic Pattern of Control and Domination

1.   *The Context of Rule–Making*

a.   *The Ruler and the Ruled*

Battered women have frequently reported that abusers are extremely controlling of the everyday activities of the family. This domination can be all encompassing: as one of the batterers from Angela Browne's study was fond of stating, "[y]ou're going to dance to my music ... be the kind of wife I want you to be." Charlotte Fedders' account of the escalating rules imposed by her husband over the course of their seventeen year, extremely violent marriage is particularly illuminating about the range of control that abusers can exert. Her husband insisted that no one (including guests and their toddler children) wear shoes in the house, that the furniture be in the same indentations in the carpet, that the vacuum marks in the carpet be parallel, and that any sand that spilled from the children's sandbox during their play be removed from the surrounding grass. Charlotte was not allowed to write checks from their joint checking account. Any real or perceived infraction of these rules could result in her husband beating her, or at the very least, the expression of his irritation that was frequently a harbinger to a beating.

Typically, battered women talk to the men about the abuse, partly as an attempt to concretize the rules that are connected to the absence of abuse. In turn, many abusers promise to stop the abuse. One abuser in Browne's study formalized such discussions into a written document, where he set forth a list of conditions that his victim was to agree to in exchange for cessation of his violence. These conditions were: 1) the children were to keep their rooms clean without being told; 2) the children could not argue with each other; 3) he was to have absolute freedom to come and go as he wished, and could have a girlfriend if he wanted one; 4) she would perform oral sex on him anytime he requested; and 5) she would have anal sex with him. He enforced this document shortly after she "agreed" to it and continued to sexually assault her until his death. This abuser simply made explicit the rules in the relationship and made it obvious that abuse was the punishment for violating the rules.

In many abusive relationships, however, the rules do not need to be verbally expressed to create a family atmosphere controlled by the batterer. Charlotte Fedders' story is a prototype of a battered woman who becomes very good at reading nonverbal messages from her abuser. She writes of how she restricted the play of her four young boys in order to avoid her husband's increasingly subtle signs of displeasure:

> Eventually ... we just stopped using the living room and the family room because little things out of place would make him angry.... If [the boys'] rooms were a mess, he'd complain to me, so I was reluctant to let them play there. So they pretty much played in the basement.... I'd let them play only in the backyard, not the front, because John was so proud and particular about it. He wanted it perfectly green, and orderly.... He didn't like my putting a swing set up for the kids in the backyard, so it had to go all the way in the back, where no one would see it.

The characteristics of the Fedders' marriage are consistent with accounts reported by other battered women indicating that the violence does not need to be a constant presence for the victims to feel threatened that it could erupt at any point, nor does the explosion always have to be physical. Violence need only symbolize the threat of future abuse in order to keep the victim in fear and control her behavior. For example, [one scholar] has called property abuse "symbolic violence." The following accounts from Fischer's study explain how this could be so:

> When I came back to the apartment, he had smashed every single piece of furniture in the bedroom. On the wall there was the red dress that I had worn to my office Christmas party the week before. It was stuck to the wall with a butcher knife through the heart.

> I saw him standing out in the street with an ax handle over his shoulder, yelling for me to come out, and luckily I was at a house with people and a telephone to get help. So he trashed my car. There was glass all over the street from my car windows that he busted out. And he was walking ... with the ax handle in his hand.... [When I saw the damage] I just fell on my car, I never cried so hard in my life. I could not believe it ... there was glass clear over in this extra yard. And, it wasn't that it was a good car or anything. It was just the fact that it could have been my head....

b.   The Internalization of Rules over Time: The Process of Self–Censorship

As time goes on in a battering relationship, as in the Fedders' case, specific rules and their attached consequences give way to a general climate of increasingly subtle control, where the batterer needs to do less and less to structure his family's behavior. Caught up in the day to day fight for survival, the victims may not even be aware of this censorship process:

> I would do anything for him. I would cook, clean, you know, pick up his shit, whatever. He could have said, drop off the face of the earth, and,

sure, I would have done it.... I was so stressed out that I was scared from one day to the next of what was going to happen with him. When I first moved in things were pretty happy-go-lucky. In the second year I was starting to ... I wouldn't go out, I'd make excuses to people. I got to understanding that he didn't want me telling a lot of people where I lived, who I was seeing ... That started clicking in ... I wouldn't let my family come over to the house because I didn't know what kind of a mood he was going to be in, if he would want company. I was living a lie for two and a half years.

I suppose you might be able to prevent [the abuse] by suppressing so much of yourself, learning to avoid the kind of behaviour that precipitates it. But then that in itself is a form of violence.

What fuels this self censorship process is the responsibility the victim feels, both as a woman socialized into believing that making relationships work is her job, and the responsibility added by the abuser, who blames her for the "failure" of the relationship, as evidenced by the occurrence of abuse. Women are taught in our society to care for others, to make decisions around what is best for other people, even if it denigrates their own needs. Batterers reinforce this societal message by consistently blaming women for everything that goes awry in their lives. The end result is manifested in frantic attempts by the woman to be the perfect wife, mother, and home-maker.

c. The Enforcement of Rules by Punishment

The rules that battered women try desperately to follow become established in a pattern of domination and control by the enforcement mechanism used by the batterer. Batterers may either simply respond with abuse when a rule is broken, or they may make it clear that the abuse is punishment for violations.

He felt I was a child. He'd say, "I'm going to teach you a lesson; raise you right." He'd make himself angry, lecturing me. I was always caught off guard by his attacks. They seemed to be mainly dependent on his mood, rather than on things going on around him. He would slap me, hit with his fists, twist my arms behind my back, call me names, and say awful things about—and to—my mother. And then he'd tell me it was for my own good. If I tried to say anything, he'd call that "talking back" and I'd get hit. But if I kept quiet, he'd say I was ignoring him. No matter what I did, it just got worse and worse, once it got started. He said, "Well, I'm going to take you out to ... I'm gonna take you somewhere and I'm gonna teach you a lesson." ... He turned around and he said to [the child], "Well, you know, ... your mother is nothing but a lying bitch—a lying cold bitch." ... [He] drove us to the next town out on this kind of, like, deserted road. He stopped and I got out of the Jeep, and he got out of the Jeep, and he raised his fist to me a couple of times and each time I'd duck.... [H]e was gonna leave me there to walk and to think things over—like I had really been doing something bad and he was punishing me.

d.   Cementing the Connection Through Fear, Emotional Abuse, and Social Isolation

At the core of these types of systematic control and domination is the fear that battered women have about future violence. This fear can be a result of past beatings or threats of physical or sexual abuse. The fear may also be triggered by any verbal or nonverbal symbol associated with the onset of an abusive incident. In some cases, threats of harm against the victim's extended family or against her children may be as effective in controlling her behavior as physical violence itself.

> [The child] was only about nine months old. She was in her high chair, and I was feeding her cereal. I had to go to the bathroom, something like that, and I asked him to finish feeding her. When I came out of the bathroom he got mad at her for something, and he pushed the bowl of cereal right in her hair. I don't know why he got mad at her. I don't know what made him do that at that instant, but he did do that, unless he was trying to make me mad or something.... There were a few times that she was just walking and he picked her up and heaved her from one side of the room to another. To make me behave.

Control is also maintained, and fear is intensified, through the extensive use of humiliation, ridicule, criticism, and other forms of emotional abuse; financial abuse; and social isolation. It is undoubtedly easier to control someone if they think less of themselves. It is difficult for victims to leave their abusers when they do not have access to money. Similarly, limiting victims' interactions with other people enhances the batterers' domination over the family by both cutting off potential sources of support and by making the boundary between the family culture of battering and the outside world more defined.

2.   Rebellion and Resistance

The pattern of rule-making and rule-enforcing, nested within the control and domination exerted by the batterer over his family, is frequently interspersed with episodes of rebellion by the victims. Expanding on Hannah Arendt's argument that force is only used when power is threatened, Liz Kelly suggested that the victim's resistance strategies force the abuser to make his coercive power explicit. Any threat, however small, to the abuser's authority within the family is likely to be met with violence: "I think because I was sticking up for myself the hidings got harder. I think that's what it was, he wanted to show that he was still my governor." These resistance incidents are not initiated with ignorance on the part of victims, as they are very much aware that any type of challenge to the batterer is likely to result in further, perhaps escalating, violence.

Rebellion can take one of several different forms....

In addition to indirect methods of rebellion, Francine [Hughes'] story includes several episodes where she directly confronted her batterer by simply refusing to do what he ordered her to do. Her husband did not hesitate to abuse her when she declined to fetch a drink for a friend during a party at their home, an obvious and public challenge to his authority in the household. The most poignant instance of Francine's resistance is when she declined to back down when her batterer dictated that she could not visit her mother:

> Francine saw a chance to visit her mother; [her friends] would give her a ride both ways.
>
> Mickey objected. "There's no sense in it. You don't need to go. What do you want to go up to Jackson for?"
>
> "I haven't seen Mom in a long time," Francine said, "I'd just like to see her, that's all. I've got nothing to do here."
>
> Mickey scowled. "You don't need to go to Jackson to look for something to do, and you don't need to see your mom."
>
> Suddenly Francine rebelled. "I just couldn't stand Mickey's eternal domination one more minute. I picked up my coat and started for the door. I said, 'I want to see Mom and I'm going, no matter what you say. I don't care!' That did it! Mickey pulled back his fist and floored me.... Then Mickey beat the living hell out of me. He stayed home from work and we fought all afternoon."

This was the worst beating Francine had yet. Her face and body were covered with bruises.

The noteworthy elements of this piece of Francine's story are the abuse that was a response to her direct verbal confrontation with her abuser as well as the surrounding contextual factors. As with the previous example, her batterer denigrated her needs by forcing his definition of what her needs were through violence. Francine was inevitably abused when she attempted to express her needs for the structure of their relationship. This particular episode of rebellion was threatening to Francine's abuser not only because it was direct, but also because Francine was attempting to break her imposed social isolation by visiting her mother. This challenge to his singular hold over her was probably among the most threatening forms of rebellion. Consequently, it is not surprising that it was met with escalated and serious violence.

It is important to distinguish episodes of rebellion and resistance (of which helpseeking is one example), which depart from the victim's usual active attempts to follow the rules, from the consequences of those episodes. The fact that battered women seek help for the abuse, a process that increases over time, and periodically rebel against their abusers' rule structures does not mean that they escape punishment for doing so. That battered women continue to resist the domination and control asserted against them even in the face of brutality is further evidence of their resilience and courage. As illustrated by the narratives above, they risk further and heightened violence each and every time they resist. Resistance breaks the most fundamental rule in the relationship: do not rebel against any of the rules....

4. Separation Abuse: Heightened Risk for Abuse Following Separation

The most dangerous time for a battered woman is when she separates from her partner. Many attacks are precipitated in retaliation for her leaving, some as part of an escalation of violence following separation. Separation tends to increase, not decrease the violence, and many of the women who are murdered by their partners are killed after separation. As Martha Mahoney has argued, women who leave their partners may commit the ultimate act of rebellion, which triggers the fatal control/domination response from the abuser, the final episode of violence. As separation abuse illustrates, the victim's attempt to end the relationship does not ensure that the control and domination will end; indeed, it may escalate.

Hiding, Denying, and Minimizing the Abuse

This third element of the culture of battering involves the shame and embarrassment battered women feel, particularly when their injuries are visible to others. It is typical for women to remain inside their homes until their bruises and other injuries fade away. . . .

> After a beating Francine instinctively tried to hide the fact. She wore sunglasses and makeup to cover a black eye or stayed out of sight while a split lip healed, and in fact, no one seemed to notice. Friends and neighbors, Mickey's brothers and their wives, studiously ignored any marks on her. Francine felt as though she had an unmentionable affliction from which everyone turned away.

Even when it becomes impossible to hide the abuse from others, battered women may engage in extreme forms of denial or minimize the seriousness of the abuse or the abuser's intent to harm. . . .

. . . The coping strategy of minimization, like denial, allows women to escape temporarily from the pain and trauma of the violence. Women may not identify themselves as battered, citing a lack of physical abuse or examples of women who have been more severely abused. Minimizing the abuse also may involve attending to the positive aspects of the relationship, reducing the impact of the abuse on the victims' lives. As Liz Kelly wrote, minimization is fostered by the cyclical nature of domestic violence: "Where there were long gaps between violent episodes, women tended to minimize the violence by choosing [to] focus on the time when it was not occurring and by hoping that it would not occur in the future."

NOTES AND QUESTIONS

1. **Patterns of Abuse.** In this excerpt, the authors portray distinct patterns of abuse that encompass far more than just violent behavior. The patterns include controlling behavior, followed by the victim responding in such a way as to minimize the violence. These patterns suggest a far more complicated dynamic than just one person getting angry at another, or a couple using violence as a means to resolve conflicts within their relationships. As you read further, think about the ways in which these patterns might affect legal decision-making on the part of all the parties involved— victims and defendants alike. For example, how might the fact that a victim feels shame affect her desire for legal assistance? How might being served with a restraining order impact an abuser?

2.   **The Cycle of Violence.** No account of battering behaviors would be complete without addressing the "cycle of violence;" a pattern of abusive behavior first identified and described by Lenore Walker, an early pioneer in research on battering. Walker initially wrote about the cycle of violence in her 1979 book, THE BATTERED WOMAN, but the account excerpted here comes from a later work, published in 1989. She reported that the cycle of violence occurred in two-thirds of sixteen hundred battering incidents studied; others have suggested that it is characteristic of only some batterers, and caution against assuming that it will be present in all abusive relationships.

Lenore Walker

Terrifying Love: Why Battered Women Kill and How Society Responds (1989)

The Cycle of Violence

I break the Cycle of Violence into three phases: the tension-building phase; the acute battering incident; and the tranquil, loving (or at least non-violent) phase that follows.

During the tension-building phase, minor battering incidents occur; slaps, pinches, controlled verbal abuse, and psychological warfare may all be part of this phase. The women's attempts to calm the batterer can range from a show of kind, nurturing behavior to simply staying out of his way. What really happens in this phase is that she allows herself to be abused in ways that, to her, are comparatively minor. More than anything, she wants to prevent the batterer's violence from growing. This desire, however, proves to be a sort of double-edged sword, because her placatory, docile behavior legitimizes his belief that he has the right to abuse her in the first place. . . .

As the cycle progresses, the battered woman's placatory techniques become less effective. Violence and verbal abuse worsen. Each partner senses the impending loss of control and becomes more desperate, this mutual desperation fueling the tension even more. Many battered women say that the psychological anguish of this phase is its worst aspect. (Some will even provoke an acute incident, just to "get it over with" and, at the cost of grave physical injury, save themselves from real insanity or death.) But, sooner or later, exhausted from the unrelenting stress, the battered woman withdraws emotionally. Angry at her emotional unavailability and, because of that anger, less likely to be placated, the batterer becomes more oppressive and abusive. At some point and often not predictably, the violence spirals out of control, and an acute battering incident occurs.

During the acute phase—set apart from minor battering incidents by its savagery, destructiveness, and uncontrolled nature—the violence has escalated to a point of rampage, injury, brutality, and sometimes death. Although the battered woman sees it as unpredictable, she also feels that the acute battering incident is somehow inevitable. In this phase, she has no control; only the batterer may put an end to the violence. . . . Usually, the battered woman realizes that she cannot reason with him, that resistance will only make things worse. She has a sense of being distant from the attack and from the terrible pain, although she may later remember each detail with great precision. What she is likely to feel most strongly at the time is a sense of being psychologically trapped.

Many battered women don't seek help during an acute battering incident. They often wait for several days afterward before seeking medical attention, if they do so at all. And, like other survivors of trauma and disaster, they may not experience severe depression or emotional collapse until days or even months later....

When the acute battering incident ends, the final phase in the Cycle of Violence begins. In this phase, usually all tension and violence are gone, which both members of the couple experience as a profound relief. This is a tranquil period, during which the batterer may exhibit warm, nurturing, loving behavior toward his spouse. He knows he's been "bad," and tries to atone; he promises never to do it again; he begs her forgiveness.... During the third phase, the battered woman may join with the batterer in sustaining this illusion of bliss. She convinces herself, too, that it will never happen again; her lover can change, she tells herself. This "good" man, who is gentle and sensitive and nurturing toward her now, is the "real" man, the man she married, the man she loves. Many battered women believe that they are the sole support of the batterer's emotional stability and sanity, the one link their men have to the normal world. Sensing the batterer's isolation and despair, they feel responsible for his well-being....

It is in this phase of loving contrition that the battered woman is most thoroughly victimized psychologically. Now the illusion of absolute interdependency is firmly solidified in the woman's psyche, for in this phase battered women and their batterers really are emotionally dependent on one another—she for his caring behavior, he for her forgiveness. Underneath the grim cycle of tension, violence, and forgiveness that make their love truly terrifying, each partner may believe that death is preferable to separation. Neither one may truly feel that she or he is an independent individual, capable of functioning without the other....

Power and Control Wheel

The Power and Control Wheel and the Equality Wheel were first developed by the Domestic Abuse Intervention Project in Duluth, Minnesota, one the earliest and most thoughtful battered women's advocacy organizations in the United States. The wheels are used in professional trainings, in batterer treatment programs, in public education forums, and in a variety of other contexts to help people understand the complicated nature of abusive relationships.

The "power and control wheel" is a particularly helpful tool in understanding the patterns of abusive and violent behaviors used by batterers to establish and maintain control over their partners. Very often, one or more violent incidents are accompanied by an array and range of these other types of abuse, less easily identified, but firmly establishing a regime of intimidation and control. The "equality wheel," by contrast, describes the kinds of "negotiated" relationships in which neither partner tries to control the other.

One point of the wheel is to show that power and control results from a number of techniques, used together. Notice that the wheel shows the various techniques held together by a rim of physical and sexual violence. Do you think that these images are helpful? Which techniques in the spokes can you identify in the stories we have already read? Which can you identify in your own relationships?

Power and Control and Equality Wheels

Domestic Abuse Intervention Project, Duluth, Minnesota

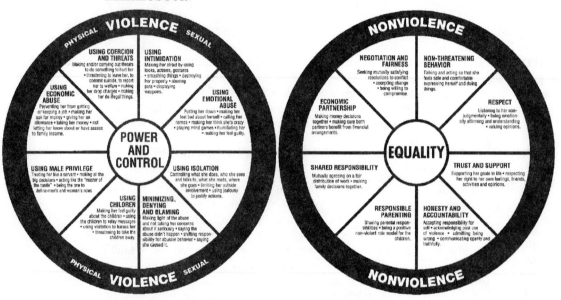

NOTES AND QUESTIONS

1. **Further Paradigms of Abuse.** Much recent social science literature has sought to distinguish among violent relationships, suggesting that no single paradigm or experience captures the multitude of experiences. Michael Johnson, for example, has categorized violence into four subcategories: mutual violent control (in which couples engaged in mutual violence to resolve conflicts); situational couple violence (period episodes triggered by an event), violent resistance (a pattern where one partner uses violence as a way to control a partner), and intimate terrorism (a pattern of abusive and controlling behaviors). While women participate more in those relationships where there is less control of one partner by the other, they are more likely to be victims of the more severe forms of controlling violence. See Michael P. Johnson, *Conflict & Control, Gender Symmetry and Asymmetry in Domestic Violence*, 12 VIOLENCE AGAINST WOMEN 1003 (2006). Evan Stark responds to Johnson's analysis in *Commentary on Johnson's "Conflict & Control: Gender Symmetry and Asymmetry in Domestic Violence,"* 12 VIO-

LENCE AGAINST WOMEN 1019 (2006), and Stark suggests in this article that domestic violence is not an incident-based phenomenon, but a form of systemic subordination and a denial of human rights. See also Evan Stark, COERCIVE CONTROL: HOW MEN ENTRAP WOMEN IN PERSONAL LIFE (2007).

Why Does She Stay?

This next excerpt is from an article by Sarah Buel, a long time battered women's advocate. Buel was once herself in a battering relationship and has written extensively about domestic violence and the legal system's response. In this piece, she lists the many reasons why abuse victims stay. While not all of the fifty reasons she identifies in the full article are included in this excerpt, this list reflects the psychological, physical, and material reasons many victims stay in abusive relationships.

Sarah M. Buel

Fifty Obstacles to Leaving, *a.k.a.*, Why Abuse Victims Stay

28 COLORADO LAWYER 19 (1999).

That abuse victims make many courageous efforts to flee the violence is too often overlooked in the process of judging them for *now* being with the batterer. Regardless of whether I am providing training to legal, law enforcement, medical, mental health, or social service professionals, when people find out I also have been a victim of abuse, some inevitably ask, "How is it you could get a full scholarship to Harvard Law School, but you stayed with a violent husband for three years?" This question has been fueled by those who believe that remaining with a batterer indicates stupidity, masochism, or codependence. Far from being accurate, such labels prove dangerous to victims because they tend to absolve batterers of responsibility for their crimes.

Domestic violence represents serious violent crime; this is *not* codependence, for there is nothing the victim can do to stop the violence, nor is there anything she does to deserve the abuse. Domestic violence victims stay for many valid reasons that must be understood by lawyers, judges, and the legal community if they are to stem the tide of homicides, assaults, and other abusive behavior. The following represents a much-abbreviated, alphabetical list of some reasons I have either witnessed among the thousands of victims with whom I have had the honor of working over the past twenty-two years—or that reflect my own experiences.

FIFTY OBSTACLES TO LEAVING

1. **Advocate:** When the victim lacks a tenacious advocate, she often feels intimidated, discouraged, and, ultimately, hopeless about being able to navigate the complex legal and social service systems needed to escape the batterer. Some well-intentioned advocates engage in dangerous victim-blaming with the assumption that there is *something* about the victim's behavior or past that precipitates the violence....

3. **Believes Threats:** The victim believes the batterer's threats to kill her and the children if she attempts to leave. It is estimated that a

battered woman is 75 percent more likely to be murdered when she tries to flee or has fled, than when she stays. Thus, it is dangerous for counsel to advise a victim to simply leave without ensuring that a trained advocate or attorney has worked with her to conduct extensive safety planning.

4. **Children's Best Interest:** Some victims believe it is in the children's best interest to have both parents in the home, particularly if the abuser does not physically assault the children. The victims—as well as their counsel and the judge—may be unaware of the deleterious impact on children witnessing domestic violence, *whether or not they have been beaten by the abuser* . . . .

7. **Denial:** Some victims are in denial about the danger, instead believing that if they could be better partners, the abuse would stop. Victims, family members, and professionals are clear that violence perpetrated by strangers is wrong and dangerous, yet they seem to adopt a double standard when that same level of abuse is inflicted by an intimate partner. As long as those closest to the victim minimize and deny the level of the victim's danger, we should not be surprised that the victim also adopts an attitude of disbelief about her own degree of harm.

10. **Excuses:** The victim may believe the abuser's excuses to justify the violence, often blaming job stress or substance abuse, in part because she sees no one holding the offender responsible for his crimes. Domestic violence is *not caused by* stress or substance abuse, although they can exacerbate the problem. They should not be used as excuses for violent behavior. In fact, most men when under stress *do not* batter their partners.

12. **Fear of Retaliation:** Victims cite fear of retaliation as a key obstacle to leaving. The acute trauma to which battered women are exposed induces a terror justified by the abuser's behavior. The batterer has already shown his willingness to carry out threats; thus, the wise victim takes seriously the batterer's promises of harming the victim or the children if the victim seeks help or attempts to flee.

14. **Financial Abuse:** Financial abuse is a common tactic of abusers, although it may take different forms, depending on the couple's socio-economic status. The batterer may control estate planning and access to all financial records, as well as make all money decisions. Victims report being forced to sign false tax returns or take part in other unlawful financial transactions. Victims also may be convinced that they are incapable of managing their finances or that they will face prison terms for their part in perpetrating a fraud if they tell someone.

16. **Gratitude:** The victim may feel gratitude toward the batterer because he has helped support and raise her children from a previous relationship. Additionally, a victim who is overweight or has mental health, medical, or other serious problems often appreciates that the abuser professes his love, despite the victim's perceived faults. Many batterers tell a victim, "You are so lucky I put up with you; certainly nobody else would," fueling the victim's low self-esteem and reinforcing her belief that she deserves no better than an abusive partner.

17. **Guilt:** Guilt is common among victims whose batterers have convinced them that, but for the victims' incompetent and faulty behavior, the violence would not occur. Since too many victims rarely encounter anyone who holds the abusers responsible for their actions, they mistakenly assume that the *something* to stop the abuse lies in their hands.

19. **Hope for the Violence to Cease:** A victim's hope for the violence to cease is typically fueled by the batterer's promises of change; pleas from the children; clergy members' admonishments to pray more; the family's advice to save the relationship; and other well-intentioned, but dangerously misguided counsel. Many victims are hopeful because they want so desperately to believe that *this* time the batterer really has seen the error of his ways and intends to change, not realizing that, without serious interventions, chances are slim that the abuse will stop.

21. **Keeping the Family Together:** Wanting to keep the family together motivates many abuse victims to stay, believing that it is in their children's best interest to have their father or a male role model in the family. As they have not been educated about the adverse impact on children of witnessing abuse, victims often cite their desire to make a good home as a key factor in their decision to stay.

27. **Love:** A victim may say she still loves the perpetrator, although she definitely wants the violence to stop. Most people will be in an abusive relationship at some point in their lives, be it with a boss or family member who mistreats them. However, most do not immediately leave the job or stop loving the family member when treated badly; they tend to try harder to please the abuser, whether because they need or love the job or the person, or hope that renewed effort and loyalty will result in cessation of the abuse. Since many batterers are charismatic and charming during the courtship stage, victims fall in love and may have difficulty in immediately altering their feelings with the first sign of a problem.

29. **Medical Problems:** Medical problems, including being HIV-or AIDS-positive, may mean that the victim must remain with the batterer to obtain medical services. If the abuser's insurance covers the family or he is the victim's primary caretaker, the victim knows that without adequate care, her *life* also is imperiled. Past attempts to elicit help from medical providers may have proved fruitless, in part because they often lack adequate training in identification and treatment of domestic violence victims.

33. **No Place to Go:** Victims with no place to go understand the bleak reality that affordable housing is at a premium in virtually every community in this country, including our Tribal Nations. Often, there is *no shelter space,* particularly for victims with children, or the shelter policy dictates that victims must quit their jobs to be admitted. Such misguided policies are based on the premise that abusers will follow victims from their place of employment to the shelter, thus endangering not only the victim, but other residents and staff as well. Instead of financially crippling the victims, intensive safety planning should be conducted with the victim and children, including notice to employers and law enforcement to ensure the perpetrator's arrest if any problems ensue.

34. **No Job Skills:** Victims with no job skills usually have no choice but to work for employers paying minimum wage, with few, if any, medical and other benefits. Thus, any medical emergency or need for prolonged care (*e.g.*, asthma, diabetes, car accident, or problems resulting from the violence) often forces the victim to return to welfare to obtain Medicaid coverage—or to return to the batterer.

35. **No Knowledge of Options:** Victims with no knowledge of the options and resources logically assume that none exist. Few communities use posters, brochures, radio and television public service announcements, and other public education campaigns to apprise victims of available resources. It is no wonder that many victims are surprised to learn that help may be available. Given the array of free and low-cost domestic violence community education materials available, every bar and civic association needs to prioritize their dispensation.

39. **Promises of Change:** The batterer's promises of change may be easy to believe because he sounds so sincere, swearing that he will never drink or hit the victim again. In part because she wants so desperately to give credence to such assertions, the victim may give him another chance, even if such promises have been made repeatedly in the past. Victims are socialized to be forgiving and do not want their marriages or important relationships to fail because they refuse to forgive what has been portrayed as an inconsequential incident.

41. **Rural Victims:** Such victims may be more isolated and simply unable to access services due to lack of transportation, or the needed programs are distant and unable to provide outreach. In smaller communities, where most people know each other and have frequent contact victims may be reluctant to reveal the abuse because such heightened scrutiny can cause them great embarrassment among their family and friends.

46. **Substance Abuse or Alcohol:** Either the victim's or offender's substance abuse or alcoholism may inhibit seeking help, often for fear that the children will be removed, in spite of efforts to get treatment. To make matters worse, it is only the exceptional shelter—such as Tulsa's Domestic Abuse Intervention Program Shelter—that will accept addicted abuse victims.

50. **Undocumented Victims:** Undocumented victims facing complex immigration problems if they leave are often forced to stay with the batterers who may control their Immigration and Naturalization Service ("INS") status. Misguided INS regulations afford too many abusers the power to determine if a victim will be deported. Victims must come up with substantial fees to petition for residency status. Sometimes, because of a victim's lack of financial resources, only the abuser can access an immigration attorney to navigate the convoluted laws; otherwise, the victim could lose custody of her children. Even those abusers without such power are often able to convince foreign-born victims that their residency status lies in the abuser's control.

NOTES AND QUESTIONS

1. **Separation Assaults.** In the readings above from both Fischer, et al. and Buel, there are references to the dangers many victims face when leaving a violent relationship. As Buel notes, a woman is 75% more likely to be murdered when she tries to flee or has fled the relationship. Thus, many women stay in relationships because they believe this is their safest option. The term "separation assault," which captures the risks of leaving abusive relationships, was developed by Martha Mahoney in her article, *Legal Images of Battered Women: Redefining Issues of Separation Assault*, 90 MICH.L.REV. 1 (1991). Mahoney takes on the particular question so often asked of battered women by the legal system: "Why didn't she just leave?" Mahoney describes separation assaults:

> To expose the struggle for control, we should recognize the assault on the woman's separation as a specific type of attack that occurs at or after the moment she decides on a separation or begins to prepare for one. I propose that we call it "separation assault." The varied violent and coercive moves in the process of separation assault can be termed "separation attacks."

> Separation assault is the attack on the woman's body and volition in which her partner seeks to prevent her from leaving, retaliate for the separation, or force her to return. It aims at overbearing her will as to where and with whom she will live, and coercing her in order to enforce connection in a relationship. It is an attempt to gain, retain, or regain power in a relationship, or to punish the woman for ending the relationship. It often takes place over time.

Mahoney further emphasizes that naming separation assault is crucial to a broader understanding of the power and control dynamic, and more accurately captures the experience of leaving that many women face. As we will see later in this book, it is crucial that the legal system recognize that often when a woman stays in abusive relationships, it is because it is her safest option. We will read in later chapters the stories of women who have tried to leave but were killed. Thus, as Buel notes, no one—not lawyers or doctors—should counsel a victim to leave without first ensuring that a trained advocate has worked to conduct an extensive safety plan with her.

2. **Psychological Profiles.** Research suggests that there is no specific type (or personality trait) characteristic of abused women. However, women who have experienced sexual or physical abuse as a child, or other trauma, may be more susceptible to violence. See Michele Harway, *Battered Women: Characteristics & Causes*, in BATTERING AND FAMILY THERAPY: A FEMINIST PERSPECTIVE, (M. Hanson and M. Harway, eds. 1993).

In their work on battered women, Virginia Goldner and her colleagues also suggest that women often stay in abusive relationships in part because they have been socialized into a caretaking role, and that, in part, they may stay to take care of their abusers, whose lives they may perceive as being more fragile than their own. Goldner gives the following example:

> ... The central tenet in all the new work about women is the idea that women form a sense of self, of self-worth, and of feminine identity

through their ability to build and maintain relationships with others. This imperative is passed to daughters from mothers whose view of feminine obligation has been to preserve both family relationships and the family as a whole, no matter what the personal cost. Thus, the daughter, like her mother, eventually comes to measure her self-esteem by the success or failure of her attempts to connect, form relationships, provide care, "reach" the other person.

Sarah, who as a child was beaten (as was her mother) by an alcoholic father, and who now is being battered by her husband Mike, put it like this: "From the time that Mike and I got involved, I got the sense that he was like a hurt child. I felt the best way of working on our relationship was to try to build him up and make him feel better about himself." Thus, even in the context of her own victimization, Sarah, against her own best interests, can humanize her abuser and devote herself to his care.

With this idea alone we have the beginning of a positive re-description of the meanings of staying in a bad relationship. For Sarah or women like her, staying put is not about weak character, morbid dependency, or masochism, but is better understood as an affirmation of the feminine ideal: to hold connections together, to heal and care for another, no matter what the personal cost. . . . Virginia Goldner, Peggy Penn, Marcia Sheinberg and Gillian Walker, *Love and Violence: Gender Paradoxes in Violent Attachments*, 29 Family Process 343 (1990).

3. **Definition of Learned Helplessness.** Throughout our inquiry, we will often come across the concept of "learned helplessness," a concept that is often used to describe battered women's reactions to abuse and "battered women's syndrome," which we will examine in later chapters. Lenore Walker has written that:

> One consequence for those who develop learned helplessness is the loss of their belief that they can reliably predict that a particular response will bring about their safety. This is called a lack of response-outcome contingencies, in behavioral psychology language, and describes the loss of ability to predict normally expected contingent outcomes when a particular response is made. In the case of battered women with learned helplessness, they do not respond with total helplessness or passivity; rather, they narrow their choice of responses, opting for those that have the highest predictability of creating successful out-comes. Even if learned helplessness were another way of labeling the BWS [battered women's syndrome], which it is not, the process does not suggest the alleged helplessness or inherent weakness of battered women. Lenore Walker, *The Battered Women Syndrome is a Psychological Consequence of Abuse,* in Current Controversies on Family Violence (R.J. Gelles and D.R. Loseke, eds. 1993).

Walker further explains that learned helplessness is really a subcategory of post traumatic stress syndrome (PTSD). PTSD is triggered by a traumatic event and can cause a variety of symptoms including anxiety, depression, memory and cognitive distortions, including difficulty to think and reason, intrusive memories, irritability, and even angry responses to interventions.

Cognitive and memory distortions make up the first group of symptoms listed in the PTSD criteria. *Cognitive distortions* take many forms, including difficulty in concentration and confused thinking. The insistence of the batterer that he monopolizes the woman's perceptions may result in her believing his twisting of the truth. The pessimistic thinking style of those who develop learned helplessness ... is another example of a cognitive disorder than can result in poor judgment....

Memory distortions in PTSD can take two major forms: *intrusive* memories of the trauma that frighten the woman and magnify her terror, and *partial psychogenic amnesia* that causes her to forget much of the painful experiences.... Often those battered women who have also been victims of child sexual abuse learn to dissociate from the experience to reduce their ability to feel the pain. Those who dissociate, or split their minds from their bodies, may also develop psychogenic amnesia for parts of the abuse....

Intrusive memories can occur spontaneously, without any conscious thoughts about the abusive incidents. They often occur when the woman is quietly at rest and may cause her to engage in frenetic, hysterical types of activities or obsessive thinking to avoid the frightening spontaneous thoughts. [One researcher] found that the single factor that best predicted female alcohol and drug abusers is whether or not they were abuse victims. He suggests that the chemical substances are used by such women to continue to keep away the intrusive memories that prolong the experience of terror, abuse, and its subsequent pain. The memories can also intrude during the woman's dreams, whether they specifically reenact parts of past battering incidents or re-create her feelings of vulnerability and terror....

High avoidance, depression, and other flight symptoms make up the second set of BWS symptoms that measure avoidance responses and numbing of feelings. They include a variety of ways of avoiding the situation, including physically leaving whenever possible and, when this is not possible, using psychological defense mechanisms, usually unconsciously, to leave the situation mentally. Most battered women are aware that leaving the man does not stop the violence.... Many battered women try to avoid thinking about the violence by conscious efforts not to deal with it other than by keeping the man as calm as possible as well as unconscious attempts through coping strategies such as minimization, denial, repression and dissociation.... Some battered women become so mentally confused that they cannot concentrate on the extent of their fears; others become obsessed about trying to reduce the probability that they will be seriously hurt....

High arousal, anxiety based symptoms, and other fight symptoms make up the third set of symptoms that often develops in women trying to protect themselves from further abuse. *Sleep problems*, such as too little or too much sleep and difficulties in falling asleep and in staying asleep, are common.... Sometimes this pattern has been established by the batterer, who won't let [his partner] go to sleep as he forces her to pay attention to him or else he wakes the sleeping woman when he isn't sleeping.... *Eating problems* are also present, whether the battered woman can't eat because of the high stress or because the man actually controls what kind of food and how much of it she eats....

Irritability and even *angry responses* by a battered woman are also included in this list of high-arousal symptoms. Some have suggested that someone with BWS must behave consistent with the stereotype of the passive and ineffective battered woman, which is not part of the criteria.... [M]any battered women do block th[eir] legitimate angry feelings so that they often come out slowly, in indirect ways, or through irritability at times when it is less dangerous to express such angry feelings....

All of these behaviors may make a woman who has been abused seem less than perfect. She may be, at times, confused, angry, depressed, defiant, and unsure of what she ought to do. She may remember something one day, and forget it the next. These behavioral characteristics can be aggravating and confusing to lawyers and judges. These behaviors can also be frustrating, especially when clients do not follow your advice because of these behaviors. Thus, it is crucial for lawyers and the courts to understand why abused women may act in these ways.

Victims and Survivors

Without denying the potential for abuse to leave emotional scars, Edward Gondolf, in the work excerpted below, suggests the dangers involved in imagining that all battered women respond in similar ways to abuse. He counteracts the stereotype of the "helpless" battered women by documenting the strength and resilience that many victims of abuse bring to their situations. He also asks society to look at the way it responds to victims, and ask some hard questions about whether women who seem trapped in violent relationships are trapped by their own lack of resources, or by the failure of helping institutions and professions to assist them in their efforts to free themselves from violence. While Gondolf's work is now twenty years old, it remains one of the defining texts in how women respond to abuse.

Edward Gondolf with Ellen Fisher

Battered Women as Survivors: An Alternative to Treating Learned Helplessness (1988)

Our assertion that battered women are active survivors raises a fundamental theoretical issue. It appears to contradict the prevailing characterization that battered women suffer from learned helplessness. According to learned helplessness, battered women tend to "give up" in the course of being abused; they suffer psychological paralysis and an underlying masochism that needs to be treated by specialized therapy. Our survivor hypothesis, on the other hand, suggests that women respond to abuse with helpseeking efforts that are largely unmet. What the women most need are the resources and social support that would enable them to become more independent and leave the batterer. . . .

Explanations of Battered Women

It is not surprising, then, that the notion of learned helplessness has become a fixture in the domestic field as well. Battered women, as the theory goes, typically are conditioned to tolerate the abuse as a result of persistent and intermittent reinforcement from the batterer. The community lack of response to the abuse, and frequent accusation that the woman contributed to the abuse, further the helplessness. The cage door is shut, so to speak, and the women have no apparent way out.

Additionally, studies have suggested that learned helplessness may be rooted in childhood exposure to violence. Exposure to violence as a child may, in fact, predispose a woman to an abusive relationship as an adult. . . . She may grow up thinking that abuse is normal, or feel such shame and rejection that she expects and accepts the worst. The relationship between abuse as a child and as an adult may, however, be spurious or inevitable given the amount of violence in and around our homes. . . . Perhaps a more acceptable position is that the batterers appear to be "violence prone," and not battered women. . . .

Another popular explanation for what appears as learned helplessness is the "brainwashing" that a woman experiences in an abusive relationship as an adult. The batterer's manipulation and control of the woman has, in fact, been likened to the tactics used by brainwashers in prisoner-of-war camps. Eventually the captive is psychologically broken down to the point of relinquishing any sense of autonomy and complying to all the wishes of the captor.

Psychologist Donald Dutton and Susan Painter . . . have similarly applied the theory of "traumatic bonding" to battered women. They point out that the abuse leaves the victim emotionally and physically drained and in desperate need of some human support or care. She is therefore likely to respond to the batterer's apologies and affection after the abuse. In this vulnerable state, she may sympathize and over-identify with the batterer, much as some prisoners of war or concentration camps have become sympathetic toward their guards. In essence, the trauma makes the woman prone to a kind of masochism.

Toward a Survivor Theory

The Survivor Hypothesis

The alternative characterization of battered women is that they are active survivors rather than helpless victims. . . . As suggested above, battered women remain in abusive situations not because they have been passive but because they have tried to escape with no avail. We offer, therefore, a survivor hypothesis that contradicts the assumptions of learned helplessness: Battered women increase their helpseeking in the face of increased violence, rather than decrease helpseeking as learned helplessness would suggest. More specifically, we contend that helpseeking is likely to increase as wife abuse, child abuse, and the batterer's antisocial behavior (substance abuse, general violence, and arrests) increase. This helpseeking may be mediated, as current research suggests, by the resources available to the woman, her commitment to the relationship, the number of children she has, and the kinds of abuse she may have experienced as a child.

The fundamental assumption is, however, that women seek assistance in proportion to the realization that they and their children are more and more in danger. They are attempting, in a very logical fashion, to assure themselves and their children protection and therefore survival. Their effort to survive transcends even fearsome danger, depression or guilt, and economic constraints. It supersedes the "giving up and giving in" which occurs according to learned helplessness. In this effort to survive, battered women are, in fact, heroically assertive and persistent.

Redefining the Symptoms

This is not to deny the observations of shelter workers that some battered women do experience severe low self-esteem, guilt, self-blame, depression, vulnerability, and futility—all of which are identified with learned helplessness. Some battered women may even appear to act carelessly and provocatively at times, as the proponents of masochism argue. But cast in another light, these "symptoms" take on a different meaning, as well as a different proportion.

The so-called symptoms of learned helplessness may in fact be part of the adjustment to active helpseeking. They may represent traumatic shock from the abuse, a sense of commitment to the batterer, or separation anxiety amidst an unresponsive community. All of these are quite natural and healthy responses. . . . Not to respond with some doubts, anxiety, or depression would suggest emotional superficiality and denial of the real difficulties faced in helpseeking.

NOTES AND QUESTIONS

1. **Healing Processes.** For a powerful and persuasive account of the ways in which battered women's responses to abuse parallel the responses of other trauma victims, particularly veterans of combat and prisoners of war, see Judith L. Herman, TRAUMA AND RECOVERY (1992). Both Judith Herman and Mary Ann Dutton, in EMPOWERING AND HEALING THE BATTERED WOMAN (1992) offer descriptions of effective clinical interventions with battered women, of the healing process, and of how women's experiences of abuse affect their relationships with mental health providers.

2. **Focus on Strengths.** In an essay written with Angela Browne, Edward Gondolf continues to urge those working with battered women not to overlook their strengths. The authors urge mental health clinicians to conduct a "strengths assessment" with their clients, to use the resulting inventory to assist women in applying their strengths to "difficulties and problems related to past or current abuse," and to "communicate information on the strengths of victims and survivors to other service providers or

referrals as actively as clinicians now communicate information on the negative outcomes of abuse and trauma." At the same time, Gondolf and Browne acknowledge the toll that abuse takes on its victims, and the reality of both post-trauma effects and, in some cases, mental illness that is either precipitated by abuse or a chronic underlying condition. Edward Gondolf with Angela Browne, *Recognizing the Strengths of Battered Women,* in ASSESSING WOMAN BATTERING IN MENTAL HEALTH SERVICES (E. W. Gondolf, ed. 1998).

3. **Women as Abusers.** Certainly women are capable of violence in intimate and family relationships. We know that some women abuse their children, both physically and emotionally; we know that there is abuse in lesbian relationships and we have read highly publicized cases in which women do violence to, or kill, their male partners. In the context of heterosexual relationships, the argument about women's capacity for violence gains intensity from the suspicion that it is politically motivated—by the desire to minimize, or even justify, male violence, and by the desire to undermine women's claims to have used violence in self-defense. For those who see men's use of violence against women partners as an enforcement of patriarchal norms, still to some extent socially condoned, evidence of relationships in which men are abused by women is also theoretically inconvenient.

It is possible, however, to embed male violence towards women in a larger theoretical framework that accommodates a recognition of women's violence without denying the particular susceptibility of women to male violence in a society that has traditionally been, and to some extent still is, governed by patriarchal norms. Such a larger theory would incorporate the psychological factors that drive some but not other individuals to control and abuse those with whom they are in relationship, and the cultural, political and economic factors that render certain groups, and individuals within those groups, more vulnerable to abuse (because more dependent or less socially valued, for example) than others.

In a recent article, Linda Kelly suggests that there are many reasons why female violence has been relatively unexplored despite what she claims is the similarity between men and women in the frequency and severity of violence in their intimate relationships. She acknowledges that male violence produces injury at six times the rate of female violence. Women also suffer greater psychological symptoms than do men who are abused. Nevertheless, she argues that one reason there has not been an acknowledgement of women's violence is that doing so challenges the feminist paradigms of woman abuse:

> Acknowledging the damage differential in the domestic violence used by men and women may seem to end the need to study female violence. Yet does it? A number of important practical and theoretical justifications militate against ignoring female violence. First, notwithstanding the "damage differential," some important normative observations about men and women can be drawn from an acknowledgment of male and female violence. Given the statistical parity in the use of domestic violence, there appears to be no basis for the traditional belief that

women are either born or bred to be less physically aggressive than men. Likewise, the statistics do not bear out the "nagging" wife stereotype. Women are not more prone to engage in verbal abuse than men. Moreover, the recognition of the difference in consequences between male and female violence does not diminish the fact that men and women bear similar intentions in regard to their inclination to engage in intimate violence. In fact, their comparable intent leads to similar results when the physical strength difference between men and women is taken into account. Controlling for the "hand-to-hand" combat advantage of men by relying solely upon statistics measuring injury produced by domestic violence involving a weapon, the rate at which men are injured by women is similar or greater than the rate at which women are injured by men. Put succinctly by one commentator, "[a]pparently, it's just a matter of style"....

The significant decreases in the use and approval of male violence, in drastic contrast to the lack of change in use or approval of female violence, has led researchers to what appears to be a self-evident conclusion. "[S]ocial movements condemning violence against women, legal and institutional reforms, and systemic antiviolence educational efforts can produce major changes in public attitudes about violence and should therefore be expanded." However, even recommending "zero tolerance of violence by both men and women" does not necessitate complete insensitivity to the greater risk of injury which female victims of domestic violence face. Yet an emphasis on the abuse of women by men is far different from demanding an exclusive focus on such abuse to the preclusion of the abuse of men by women. Indeed, even if motivated solely by an interest in ending wife or child abuse, it is still necessary to address the various forms family violence can take—including female violence. The abuse of men by women and the abuse of children by either parent are two forms of family violence which are directly related to any effort to systematically address wife abuse. Consequently, a fourth argument for acknowledging and addressing the abuse of men by women is that it will ultimately work to end the abuse of women by men. Put in blunt utilitarian terms, female violence must be addressed in order to protect women as a man provoked by a violent female has the potential to inflict greater injury. Linda Kelly, *Disabusing the Definition of Domestic Abuse: How Women Batter Men and the Role of the Feminist State* 30 FLA. ST. U.L. REV. 791 (2003).

Do such reasons for exploring women's violence against men intuitively make sense to you? Is there a difference between conflict in relationships which results in physical aggression and battering based on power and control? What role might law and culture play in the recognition of women's violence against men?

4. **Domestic Homicides.** Kelly cites data that found that the rates of severe violence by men against women has been dropping while women's violence has remained steady. This might suggest that increased attention to domestic violence by men seems to have had some social impact.

However, when examining homicide data of intimate partners, a slightly different picture emerges. The number of males killed by their female intimate partners has declined 71% from 1976 to 2002, while the number of females killed by their intimate partners remained relatively steady for two decades. In 1993, it began to decline, although not nearly as steadily as for men. For white women, more were being killed in the mid–1980's. By 2004, the number had returned to 1976 levels. This data suggests that at least when it comes to lethal violence, women's use of lethal violence has declined more relative to men's. In other words, men have benefited more from domestic violence reforms than women, at least when measured by intimate homicides. See *The United States Department of Justice, Bureau of Justice Statistics, Homicide Trends in the United States*, 2006.

5. **Measuring Violence.** All research on domestic violence must overcome methodological shortcomings. There is a concern about the accuracy of measures like the Conflict Tactics Scale, which depend on men's and women's self-reporting to define both the scope and the prevalence of violence. In a study that included 95 couples, researchers discovered significant discrepancies between the accounts of abuse given by the two partners, with men tending to under-report their violence. See Russell P. Dobash, P. Emerson Dobash, Kate Cavanaugh and Ruth Lewis, *Separate and Intersecting Realities: A Comparison of Men's and Women's Accounts of Violence Against Women*, 4 Violence Against Women 382 (1998).

Other measures, which do not depend on self-reporting, show a much less symmetrical pattern of partner abuse. One incontrovertible statistic is that 85% of heterosexual partner violence reported to and recorded by law-enforcement authorities is perpetrated by men. U.S. Department of Justice, Office of Justice Programs, *Bureau of Justice Statistics, Crime Data Brief, Intimate Partner Violence*, 1993–2001 (2003). But any statistic that depends on reports to law enforcement is likely to reflect only the more serious levels of violence or threat, or the behaviors most clearly understood by those against whom they are directed as unlawful. Official reports will also underrepresent any victim constituency reluctant to seek official intervention. It has often been claimed that domestic violence by men is significantly under-reported, although this may be changing as the problem, and the availability of services for victims, become more widely publicized. In a society that stresses male self-reliance, however, it may be even more difficult for a man to call the police to report that his female partner is abusing him. See Murray A. Straus, *Physical Assaults by Wives: A Major Social Problem,* in Current Controversies on Family Violence (R.J. Gelles and Dorileen R. Loseke, eds. 1993).

Supporting the conclusion that serious male violence is much more prevalent than serious female violence are consistent findings that men injure women at much higher rates than women injure men. See, for example, the seven to one ratio reported in J.E. Stets and M.A. Straus, *Gender Differences in Reporting of Marital Violence and Its Medical Consequences*, in Physical Violence in American Families: Risk Factors and Adaptations to Violence in Families (M.A. Straus and R.J. Gelles, eds. 1990).

B.   MEN'S EXPERIENCES AS ABUSERS

Our contemporary attention to, and concern with, the problem of domestic violence grows out of the battered women's movement. That movement, in turn, grew out of the recognition that violence against women in their homes was a much larger problem than had previously been appreciated, and that women, isolated in abusive relationships, lacked any kind of social, legal or emotional support to assist them in ending the violence in their lives. Shelter for women, legal redress for women, counseling services for women—women's safety and independence—these were the movement's goals. Viewed from this perspective, the batterer was not someone on whom attention should be lavished—not someone it was important to understand or help. As Lynn Caesar and Kevin Hamberger say in the preface to their book TREATING MEN WHO BATTER: THEORY, PRACTICE AND PROGRAMS (1989):

> "All of us who have worked with, known, or been battered may question why a man who violates the civil liberties of a woman in a violent, humiliating and dehumanizing fashion should engender empathy, concern, or special attention. To offer help to a man who beats his wife suggests that we will share the problem. Assisting a man who rapes, beats and infringes upon the rights of his female partner arouses strong emotions within anyone who cares enough about the problem of wife battery to get involved. To feel moral outrage when a battered woman reveals her blackened eyes but to contain the anger to get close enough to the batterer to whom the woman may soon return is, at times, an exercise in emotional gymnastics."

To the extent that advocates and activists within the battered women's movement did focus on the batterer, it was to wake the public up to the very real danger he posed to his partner. The goal here was to shift public understanding from the view of the batterer as someone provoked beyond endurance by a shrewish wife, or as someone who occasionally lost control, perhaps after having "one too many," to a view of the batterer as someone who systematically set out to control his partner's every movement and every thought, and would stop at nothing, including extreme physical violence, to achieve that end. To win public funding for battered women's programs, and support for new legal mechanisms of protection, the batterer was portrayed as a monster from whom his partner had to be rescued.

Within the context of the criminal justice system in particular, battered women's advocates sought to ensure that men accused of violence against their intimate partners were treated like other violent criminals. They should be arrested, not merely walked around the block to "cool off." They were rational and instrumental in their use of violence, not mentally ill, and should be prosecuted, not merely diverted into treatment programs without ever standing trial or facing conviction. They should be incarcerated for serious violence, not merely put on probation.

As with any stereotype, this view of the batterer has severe limitations. While to some extent it served as a corrective for earlier myths and misconceptions, it falls far short of explaining who batterers are, what motivates them to behave as they do, and why women make and sustain strong emotional commitments to them. And while this deeper understanding may once have seemed irrelevant for purposes of raising public consciousness about domestic violence, or insisting on its recognition as a crime, there are weighty reasons today to move beyond the "monster" stereotype. First, not all batterers are alike, and the less monstrous any individual man appears to a judge, or an untrained therapist, the less likely they are to appreciate the danger he poses, and to exercise proper caution in their dealings with him. Second, domestic violence is not a problem that could be solved by incarcerating all batterers, even if the criminal justice system were a lot more willing than it is today to invoke that sanction. Thus, while it remains crucial to use the tools currently available to us to keep individual women and their children safe, we must be looking in the long-term to forms of treatment that can help at least some batterers become non-violent partners, and to learn what makes a batterer, so that we can focus on raising non-violent men.

Finally, and perhaps most importantly, women in relationships with abusive men rarely understand them as monsters, pure and simple. Unwittingly, when we portray them as such, we fuel the persistent question "Why did she stay?" When we respond to that question only by stressing the debilitating effects of violence, or the external social and economic constraints which make it hard or impossible to leave, or the fear of retaliatory violence, we deny, and may seem to delegitimate, the ongoing emotional connection that may prompt a woman, for at least some period of time, to endure the violence in the hopes that it can be ended without the relationship itself coming to an end. Ironically, then, increasing our understanding of the batterer may leave us with a greater understanding of, and respect for, the woman he is abusing, and assist us in supporting her without undermining her self-respect.

How the legal system responds to domestic violence is in part informed by the explanations for it. Why men are abusive towards women is a complicated question and often provokes a multitude of responses. The first excerpt, written in 1998, continues to the capture the current state of research on men who batter. It is followed by a series of notes on possible explanatory theories about male violence against women. The next excerpt is from Lundy Bancroft, who has more than fifteen years of experience working with abusive men. He takes a hard look at today's culture to suggest why boys may learn to disrespect and abuse women.

Cheryl Hanna
The Paradox of Hope: The Crime and Punishment of Domestic Violence

39 WM. & MARY L. REV. 1505 (1998).

1. Batterer Typologies

Some of the most promising domestic violence research attempts to differentiate among batterers. Different "types" of batterers emerge from a synthesis of this research. Amy Holtzworth–Munroe and Gregory Stuart recently reviewed nineteen studies on typologies and identified three sub-types of abusive men: family-only batterers; borderline batterers; and generally violent/antisocial batterers. I rely primary on the categories hypothesized by Holtzworth–Monroe and Stuart, but also integrate the research of Edward Gondolf, Donald Dutton, and others. Emerging typologies among different researchers are surprisingly similar: differences lie more in terminology than in concept. Family-only batterers constitute approximately fifty percent of all batterer samples. These men tend to engage in the least severe marital violence, psychological and sexual abuse. Family-only batterers are less impulsive, less likely to use weapons, and more likely to be apologetic after abusive incidents. These men may be the most deterred by the threat of criminal sanctions and the most treatable because of their ability to function normally outside of their relationships.

Borderline batterers constitute approximately twenty-five percent of batterer samples. These men tend to "engage in moderate to severe abuse, including psychological and sexual abuse." Their violence generally is confined to the family, but not always. They may evince borderline personality characteristics and may have problems associated with drugs and alcohol. Batterer treatment, as it is currently structured, is likely to be insufficient to change their behavior because many men in this group may need more intensive treatment.

Generally violent or antisocial batterers engage in moderate to severe violence, including psychological and sexual abuse. Edward Gondolf terms these batterers sociopathic. It is estimated that this group constitutes twenty-five percent of batterer samples. Uniformly, studies have found that generally violent men engage in more severe family violence than family-only men. This finding challenges the myth that abusers are only violent against family members. Generally violent batterers often have extensive criminal histories, including property, drug or alcohol offenses, and violence crimes against nonfamily victims. These men are the most impulsive, the most likely to use weapons, and feel the least amount of empathy towards their victims. Batterer treatment programs for this group are inappropriate given the high degree of danger they pose. Arguably, sociopathic batterers may be untreatable, and, in many cases, ought to be incarcerated if only to protect their potential victims.

All abusive men are not equally dangerous. Some men are frequent and severe batterers; others are not. Dr. Donald Dutton, a psychology professor at the University of British Columbia and director of the Assaultive Husband's Program in Vancouver, focuses his research on personality traits of abusive men. He distinguishes "cyclical" batterers from men who may occasionally be aggressive in their relationships, "like the distinction between a single fender bender and continual head-on collisions." Cyclical batterers constitute a subgroup of men who are violent only in their intimate relationships. They are repeat offenders who injure their partners, both psychologically and physically, until courts intervene, but appear "normal" to the outside world because they direct their violence primarily at their mates. Dutton theorizes that these characteristics are a product of being abandoned by a loved one earlier in life. These men attribute their negative feelings to real or perceived misdeeds by their partners and retaliate. Violence diminishes anxiety about attachment by maintaining control over a partner.

Dutton's distinction between men who are chronically abusive and those who are not has important implications for prosecutorial and sentencing decisions. "If once in his marriage a man happens to push his wife in reaction to situational stresses, he would still be considered abusive.... But, psychologically, that is a very different type of individual than one who repeatedly abuses or beats up his wife or engages in more serious assaults." According to Dutton, only two percent of the total male population are "repeatedly severely assaultive" to women in any given year. Thus, the criminal justice system ought to be cautious before treating every man who engages in intimate violence as a high-risk offender. In fact, Dutton's research suggests that we may be able to identify and focus limited resources on the chronically abusive, similar to other crime control strategies that target career criminals rather than petty offenders.

2. Biomedical Factors

Some researchers have suggested that some violent behavior may correlate to biomedical conditions. For example, one study found that men with previous head injuries were six times as likely to display marital aggression as other men. This research is consistent with findings that there may be a link between head trauma and violent behavior.

Other research has linked aggressive, dominant and antisocial behavior to high testosterone levels and impulsive aggression to low serotonin levels. To date, however, whether testosterone and/or serotonin are potential correlates of family violence remains unclear.

Sociobiologists and evolutionary psychologists might also add to our understanding of violent behavior by men against women, although the application of evolutionary theories is still too new for any valid conclusions to be drawn. From a biologist's perspective, men have an inherited tendency to secrete adrenalin when they believe themselves to be sexually threatened by other males. The label applied to this arousal, however, will be socially determined. Thus, male aggression against females is part of male reproductive strategies geared toward reproducing offspring and ensuring paternity; this sexual aggression is well-documented throughout the primate world and cross-culturally.

Biomedical factors alone cannot account for all abusive behavior. At best, a more complex interaction of social and neurological factors trigger violence in some. Nor is there any evidence suggesting that biological factors should be a legal excuse to violent behavior. Nevertheless, the emerging research on biology and human behavior may provide valuable future insights. Additionally, screening abusers for medical as well as psychological factors might be prudent. Some men might benefit from medical as well as psychological interventions, especially in cases involving substance addictions or patterns of antisocial behavior. At the very least, this research suggests that we need to take a broader view of what "treatment" or other interventions might entail apart from the current feminist-based group therapy models currently in vogue.

3.   External Factors

Although domestic violence occurs across all socioeconomic, ethnic, and age groups, some groups may be at higher risk of violence. For example, children exposed to violence are more likely to become violent or to be victims of violence. Couples in their twenties and thirties and those who cohabitate experience more violence than those who are older and married.

The most severely abusive men are not composed of mere low-income or minority cases, as some batterer stereotypes might suggest. Empirical evidence, however, points to a connection between domestic violence and low family income. Other studies have found that abused women are more likely to live in communities with the highest rates of stranger violence, suggesting a link between domestic violence, general violence, and neighborhoods with fewer economic and social resources.

Multiple interpretations can be made from these findings. First, people in lower socioeconomic groups are more likely to report violence to police, police are more likely to arrest people in poor and middle-class neighborhoods than upper-class ones, and women without economic resources are more likely to seek shelter than those with higher incomes. Those with a lower socioeconomic status are likely to be over-represented in batterer samples.

Second, some have theorized that the relationship between lower socioeconomic status and domestic violence is due, in part, to the existence of a "subculture of violence" that condones violence in general and assaultive behavior towards women in particular. This explanation emerges from theories linking domestic violence to deep-seated cultural acceptance of violence more generally. As William Stacey and Anson Shupe conclude:

> [W]e think there is good reason to believe that a cult of violence is spreading throughout our society and affecting every sector. By "cult" we do not mean that it is an organized movement or conspiracy. Rather, it is a cultural pattern, a trend. The glorification of violence in motion pictures, television, and books, and the electronic media's technical sophistication that shows us violence realistically but makes it exciting, contribute to this cult. But this is not the cause. The cult is an acceptance of violence, learning to expect it, to tolerate it, and to commit it, however much one dreads it. This cult is stimulated by a violent environment that affects each generation of men and women, making them more yet desensitized to the problem.

Those in lower socioeconomic groups might be more susceptible to this "cult of violence" because they have more to gain and less to lose by engaging in violent behavior; in other words, they have no stake in conforming to cultural norms that dictate against violence. "Culture of violence" theories remain highly controversial as they have a tendency to essentialize poor and minority communities as inherently violent. Such theories suggest, however, that violence may be a rational response given certain environmental and social conditions, not pathological or determined behavior.

Just as likely is that those with fewer resources face more stressors. "Indeed, it is generally believed-and certainly makes good clinical sense-that stress in itself does not lead directly to violence, but rather that various other factors exacerbate or buffer the relationship between stress and [domestic] violence." Living in a stressful environment may place some men at higher risk for the use of aggression.

The link between domestic violence and poverty is controversial. Describing domestic violence as "our" problem and not "their" problem is powerful political rhetoric. It facilitates legal reform and avoids stereotyping poor people and people of color as inherently dangerous. Although demographic factors do not predict violence, this research suggests that poverty breeds many ills-domestic violence among them.

NOTES AND QUESTIONS

1. **Additional Risk Factors.** While everyone is capable of engaging in domestic violence, some men may be more at risk for becoming a batterer than others. In particular, men who are under or unemployed, and those who live with children not their own may be more likely to engage in violence.

Recent researchers have found links between domestic violence and unemployment. For example, a recent study of 265 intentionally injured women in the New England Journal of Medicine found that women at greatest risk for injury from domestic violence include those with male partners who abuse alcohol or use drugs, are unemployed or intermittently employed, have less than a high-school education, and are former husbands, estranged husbands, or former boyfriends of the women. Demetrios N. Kyriacou, Deirdre Anglin, Ellen Taliaferro, Susan Stone, Toni Tubb, Judith Linden, Robert Muelleman, Erik Barton and Jess Kraus, *Risk Factors for Injury to Women from Domestic Violence*, 341 NEW ENGLAND J. OF MEDICINE 1892 (1999).

An even more recent study found that unemployment was the most predictive factor in whether a woman would be killed by her intimate partner. Indeed, lack of a job increased the risk of femicide four-fold. The most common household risk factor was the presence of a stepchild in the home. This finding too is consistent with Molly Walker Wilson's analysis, discussed below, that the presence of another man's child in the home increases the risk of sexual jealousy. See Jacquelyn C. Campbell, Daniel Webster, Jane Koziol–McLain, Carolyn Block, Doris Campell, Mary Ann Curry, Faye Gary, Nancy Glass, Judith McFarlane, Carolyn Sachs, Phyllis Sharps, Yvonne Ulrich, Susan Wilt, Jennifer Manganello, Xiao Xu, Janet Schollenberger, Victoria Frey and Kathryn Laughon, *Risk Factors for Femicide in Abusive Relationships*, 93 AMERICAN J. PUBLIC HEALTH 1089 (2003).

2. **Policy Implications.** There are many alternative theories as to why males abuse females. As we have already discussed, feminists often point to a patriarchal legal and social system which approves of male violence. Still others point to more individual psychological experiences. Current researchers are trying to refine their classifications of batterers into different typologies and to dispel some myths about abusers with the hope that more sophisticated typologies can aid in prevention of domestic violence. Consider the conclusions of some recent research:

> A review and synthesis of the literature reveals three types of batterers common across current typology research—a low, moderate, and high-risk offender. Each of these types can be further stereotyped according to the dimensions of severity and frequency of violence, criminal history, and level of psychopathology. Careful examination of these three types demonstrates that most male offenders (those in the low and moderate categories) do not escalate over time from low to high levels of risk. This observation refutes previous claims among researchers and advocates that battering always escalates in frequency and intensity over time. Because there are particular characteristics specific to each type that establishes thresholds distinct to each classification, it is unlikely that an offender will move from one particular type to another. . . .

> Aside from exclusionary criteria such as substance abuse and severe mental illness, current batterer treatment programs employ no other mechanisms through which to match an offender to a specific treatment modality or approach. Assessments are conducted initially, by some programs, to evaluate the severity and lethality of an entering participant. However, very few of these evaluation tools are empirically based, and their reliability and validity varies widely. In addition, little consideration is given as to the offender's suitability regarding the program's content, structure, or approach and the offender's particular treatment needs. This is analogous to treating cases of malaria where quinine is used regardless of the severity of the case. Mary M. Cavanaugh and Richard J. Gelles, *The Utility of Male Domestic Violence Offender Typologies*, 20 JOURNAL OF INTERPERSONAL VIOLENCE 155 (2005).

3. **Evolutionary Perspectives.** Evolutionary psychology looks at the issue of whether domestic violence is triggered by sexual jealousy. A recent article by Molly J. Walker Wilson explains an evolutionary perspective on male violence:

> The fundamental principle upon which evolutionary psychology's theory of male domestic violence is based is paternity assurance. Paternity assurance is the process by which the male of a species guarantees that he is not devoting valuable resources to supporting juveniles who are not genetically his own offspring. The concern over the issue of paternity leads a male to adopt an attitude of proprietariness with respect to his female partner. In homo sapiens, research has demonstrated that men and women exhibit markedly different patterns of sexual jealousy. A human male, like males of other species, has the problem of determining whether his sexual partner's children are also

his offspring. Women do not have similar concerns about their biological relationship to the child. Instead, a woman is primarily concerned with determining that once she has conceived a child with a man, he will stay to support and protect the child. Fundamental biological differences cause men to be particularly concerned about sexual fidelity, whereas women are more concerned with emotional fealty. . . .

Male sexual jealousy can manifest itself in a multitude of ways. One manifestation of male sexual jealousy involves a man's resentment and poor treatment of children from a partner's former marriage. The Reproductive Access Theory suggests that a man may even see a stepchild as a threat to his access to a woman's reproductive resources. Male violence toward women can be viewed as another manifestation of extreme sexual jealousy. Wilson and Daily maintain that "[s]ublethal assaults and threats to kill can be interpreted as coercive tactics that terrorize wives and keep them under their husbands' control." Molly J. Walker Wilson, *An Evolutionary Perspective on Male Domestic Violence: Practical and Policy Implications*, 32 Am. J. Crim. L. 291 (2005).

From an evolutionary perspective, violence against one's intimate partner, at its core, is a strategy to ensure faithfulness and ultimately ensure that any offspring belong to one's self. Is such an explanation consistent with feminist theories of power and control? Does it sound plausible to you that being violent against one's partner leads to a faithful partner? What is the difference between this understanding and a more historic understanding that domestic violence is rooted in a system of patriarchy? Does accepting that men and women may have different strategic goals as a result of evolution undermine feminist arguments that gender differences are socially rather than biologically constructed? Keep these themes in mind when we study domestic violence and sexual autonomy.

One of the problems with using an evolutionary analysis is that people often think that because something exists in nature, then it must be good or desirable. This is often called the naturalistic fallacy. Yet, for most evolutionary biologists, it is just that—a logical fallacy to assume that there is any normative or moral content in describing what happens in nature. Rather, most biologists suggest that while they might describe what happens, it is up to society to make value judgments as to which behaviors are desirable and which are not. Thus, in the context of domestic violence, while biologists may describe the evolutionary basis for male violence against women, they do not advocate that it is desirable or inevitable. Nevertheless, one concern about biological explanations is that they could ultimately be used to excuse male violence against women under the theory that "boys will be boys."

Does the fact that primates also experience "intimate" violence persuade you that such behaviors are strategic rather than pathological? What sort of policy implications would acceptance of a biological paradigm for battering have?

4. **Race, Ethnicity, and Class.** In later chapters, we will explore the proposition that all men are equally at risk for battering. While it is true

that men across race, class, and ethnicity do batter, there is much emerging research to suggest that minorities and the poor are more likely to batter than are white, middle class men. As we examine the subsequent material on batterers, consider why some groups may be more at risk than others and what policy implications such propositions might have.

5. **Individual Factors.** Even given ongoing uncertainty about batterer typologies, the identification of batterers with different behavior profiles may be an important contribution to those who work in the field of domestic violence. It helps us resist stereotypes and easy assumptions about who is and who is not likely to abuse a partner. It may also contribute to the development of more accurate tools for threat and lethality assessment. The next level of question is how boys become batterers of one type or another; what genetic predisposition, what physical or emotional injuries, what societal or familial influences create batterers out of children. The work of Donald Dutton looks at those questions. His work grows out of twenty-five years of experience as both a researcher and a clinician. He suggests that in early childhood, boys develop abusive personalities. Both mothers and fathers can play a key role in the development of abusive men. Brutal fathers and mothers who are not emotionally available to their sons because they are also suffering from abuse may, in turn, create boys who grow up to abuse their own partners. See Donald G. Dutton with Susan K. Golant, THE BATTERER: A PSYCHOLOGICAL PROFILE, THE CREATION OF A CYCLICAL BATTERER (1995).

One of the factors Dutton discusses is that men who have had strong and positive male relationships are less likely to be abusive. What does such a theory suggest about the importance of men to the battered women's movement as well as to the lives of children? Many commentators have suggested that in modern American culture, men, and especially their contributions to the family, have been marginalized. Do you agree?

6. **The Military and Law Enforcement.** Does one's profession make one more likely to batter? Are abusive men more likely to choose a profession that incorporates violence? Recent data suggests that military families experience as much as five times the rate of domestic violence as civilian families. These numbers may, in part, reflect how domestic violence is categorized. But they also may suggest that the stress of military service increases the risk that one will become an abuser. See Jennifer Heintz, *Safe at Home? A Look at the Military's New Approach to Dealing with Domestic Violence on Military Installations*, 48 ST.LOUIS.U.L.J. 277 (2003); Jerri L. Fosnaught, *Domestic Violence in the Armed Forces: Using Restorative Mediation as a Method to Resolve Disputes Between Service Members & Their Significant Others*, 19 OHIO ST. J. ON DISP. RESOL. 1059 (2004). In 2003, Congress passed the *Armed Forces Domestic Security Act*, 10 U.S.C. § 1851a (PL 107–311) (2003). This law gives civil protection orders the same legal effect on military installations as they would have in the issuing state.

Similarly, data also suggests that police officers are more likely to assault their intimate partners than are those in those who work outside law enforcement. See Donald C. Sheehan, *Domestic Violence by Police*

Officers: A Compilation of Papers Submitted to the Domestic Violence by Police Officers Conference, FBI Academy, (2000). One concern about both of these populations is the ready availability of firearms. In 2003, the International Association of Police Chiefs issued policy guidelines to help police departments combat domestic violence by police officers. See The International Association of Police Chiefs, *Domestic Violence by Police Officers, A Policy of the IACO, Police Responses to Violence Against Women Project*, July 2003, available at: http://www.theiacp.org/documents/pdfs/Publications/DomViolenceModelPolicy.pdf

7. **A Culture of Violence.** Although it is tempting to suggest that parents play a large role in raising boys who then engage in violence, culture, and the times in which we live, may also contribute to attitudes about battering. Consider the observations of Lundy Bancroft, a counselor at EMERGE, one of the most respected batterer treatment programs.

Lundy Bancroft

Why Does He Do That? Inside the Minds of Angry and Controlling Men (2002)

● Popular performers both reflect and shape social attitudes.

The white rapper Eminem won a Grammy Award while I was writing this book. At the time of his award, one of his newest popular songs was "Kim," the name of Eminem's wife. The song begins with the singer putting his baby daughter to bed and then preparing to murder his wife for being with another man. He tells his wife, "If you move I'll beat the shit out of you," and informs her that he has already murdered their four-year-old son. He then tells his wife he is going to drive away with her in the car, leaving the baby at home alone, and then will bring her home dead in the trunk. Kim's voice (as performed by Eminem) is audible off and on throughout the song, screaming with terror. At times she pleads with him not to hurt her. He describes to her how he is going to make it look as if she is the one who killed their son and that he killed her in self defense, so that he'll get away with it. Kim screams for help, then is audibly choked to death, as Eminem screams, "Bleed, bitch, bleed! Bleed!" The murder is followed by the sound of a body being dragged across dry leaves, thrown into the trunk of a car, and closed in.

Even more horrible than Eminem's decision to record this song glorifying the murder of a woman and child is the fact that it did not stop him from receiving a Grammy. What is a teen boy or a young man to conclude about our culture from this award? I believe I can safely say that a singer who openly promoted the killing of Jews, or blacks, or people in wheelchairs would be considered ineligible for a Grammy. But not so, unfortunately, for encouraging the brutal and premeditated murder of one's wife and child, complete with a plan for how to escape the consequences for it. . . .

● Pornographic videos, magazines, and web sites are learning grounds.

As a boy enters his teen years, he is likely to encounter another powerful shaper of his outlook on females and how to treat them: pornography. Most pornographic movies, magazines, and web sites can function as training manuals for abusers, whether they intend to or not, teaching that women are unworthy of respect and valuable only as sex objects for men. The Internet has made access to pornography much easier—and free—for teenage boys; a recent study found, for example, that one in four teenage boys has experienced exposure to unwanted sexual material, most commonly through Internet solicitations. A great deal of mainstream pornographic material—not just so-called "hard core"—contains stories and images showing the abuse of both women and children as sexy, sometimes including presentations of rape as erotic. The harm to teens from looking at pornography has little to do with its sexual explicitness and everything to do with the *attitudes* it teaches toward women, relationships, sexual assault, and abuse. Spend some time looking at pornography yourself—if you can stand it—and think about the messages it is sending to young people and especially to boys.

I learned of a recent case in an upper-class suburb involving a group of middle school-aged boys who were in the habit of spending hours each day after school watching pornography on their computers. One day they went from this activity to a party where they succeeded in pressuring several girls—with an average age of twelve—into performing group oral sex on them, inspired by something they had watched at a web site. Parents found out about what happened and a scandal ensued, but the community still did not seem to recognize the critical influence of the images to which the boys were being exposed.

• Boys often learn that they are not responsible for their actions.

Boys' aggressiveness is increasingly being treated as a *medical* problem, particularly in schools, a trend that has led to the diagnosing and medicating of boys whose problem may really be that they have been traumatized and influenced by exposure to violence and abuse at home. Treating these boys as though they have a chemical problem not only overlooks the distress they are in but also reinforces their belief that they are "out of control" or "sick," rather than helping them to recognize that they are making bad choices based on destructive values. I have sometimes heard adults telling girls that they should be flattered by boys' invasive or aggressive behavior "because it means they really like you," an approach that prepares both boys and girls to confuse love with abuse and socializes girls to feel helpless.

In most media coverage of bullying and school violence, including highly publicized school murders such as Columbine, reporters have overlooked the gender issues. Headlines have described these events as "kids killing kids," when close to 100 percent of them have involved *boys* killing kids. In some cases it has been revealed that the killings were related to boys' hostility towards females, including one case in which the two boys who went on a murderous rampage said afterward that they had done it because they were angry that their girlfriends had broken up with them.

But the urgent need to confront the anti-female attitudes among these boys was never mentioned as a strategy for preventing future school violence.

NOTES AND QUESTIONS

1. **The Killing of Girls.** In recent years, there have been many high profile cases in which girls and young women have been the target of mass murders. In one case, Charles Carl Roberts barricaded himself in a one room Amish schoolhouse in Pennsylvania. He bound and shot 11 girls, killing five and wounding the rest, and then killed himself. He had previously told his wife that he had molested young girls in his past and that these were "revenge killings." See Alan Levin, *Grief Travels Through Amish Country*, USA TODAY, October 26, 2006. Just weeks before this incident, a Colorado man took six girls hostage in a high school a short distance from Columbine and killed one before killing himself. These shootings raise memories of the December 1989 shooting at L'École Polytechnique–in–Montreal. The shooter, Marc Lépine, separated the men from the women, telling—the men to leave. Claiming to be "fighting feminism," he killed 13 women students and a female employee before killing himself. These mass killings raise the deeper question of what is it about our culture than can lead to such extreme violence against girls and women in both in intimate relationships and among complete strangers.

In a New York Times op-ed piece just after the Pennsylvania and Amish school killings, columnist Bob Herbert wrote:

> In the widespread coverage that followed these crimes, very little was made of the fact that only girls were targeted. Imagine if a gunman had gone into a school, separated the kids on the basis of race or religion, and then shot only the black kids. Or only the white kids. Or only the Jews.
>
> There would have been thunderous outrage. The country would have first recoiled in horror, and then mobilized in an effort to eradicate that kind of murderous bigotry. There would have been calls for action and reflection. And the attack would have been seen for what it really was: a hate crime.
>
> None of that occurred because there were just girls, and we have become so accustomed to living in a society saturated with misogyny that violence against females is more or less to be expected. . . . The disrespectful, degrading, contemptuous treatment of women is so pervasive and so mainstream that it has just about lost its ability to shock. Bob Herbert, *Why Aren't We Shocked*? N.Y. TIMES, Oct. 16, 2006.

2. **Cultural Excuses.** Is it too easy to blame culture for male abuses against women? Does doing so have the tendency to excuse male violence, and to relieve men of individual responsibility? As we will see in the next chapter, many cultures support male violence against women. The question for the law then becomes when should the law excuse male violence when it is the cultural norm? Consider *State v. Vue*, 606 N.W.2d 719 (Minn.App. 2000), a case we read in the next chapter. The case involved a Hmong

immigrant who had assaulted and raped his girlfriend. There was testimony offered at trial by the prosecution that "male-dominance was fairly universal among the Hmong culture." The evidence was intended to help explain why the victim never sought help, but could have had the unintended consequence of excusing the rape and assault. Can't the same be said about most cultures? Is there anything particularly unique about American culture that might make violence against women more or less prevalent? Under the same reasoning, is there anything about Western culture that makes it more or less likely women will become victims of abuse?

CHAPTER THREE

DIMENSIONS OF THE BATTERING EXPERIENCE

Introduction

In the previous chapter we examined, as the paradigm of an abusive relationship, the relationship between a male abuser and a female target. While we asked whether the roles are sometimes reversed, we did not ask whether partners in same-sex couples are also vulnerable to abuse. We did not ask whether our paradigm couple was white, of color, or interracial; what socio-economic class the partners belonged to; whether they were new immigrants to the United States or came from families who had been in the country for generations; whether English was their primary language; or whether they identified with a particular racial, cultural or religious sub-community.

In this chapter we examine some of these dimensions. We ask five questions:

- Do these dimensions change the subjective experiences of the abusive and abused partners in the relationship?

- Do these dimensions isolate the partners within a community in which support or assistance is not available?

- Do the specific features of the abuser's or the abused's identity affect the willingness or the ability of the partners to reach out for support or assistance to those in the broader society who are in a position to provide it?

- Will identifying characteristics of the abuser or the abused affect the responses of those in the broader society who are either charged with a responsibility to intervene, or who have the capacity to intervene?

- How should law and policy be shaped to account for these dimensions while maintaining a uniform sense of justice throughout the legal system?

Asking these questions broadens our understanding to include the influence of these factors on the experience of partner abuse.

The specific dimensions examined in this chapter include sexual orientation, race, culture and ethnicity, poverty, age, religion and disability. There are two necessary caveats. First, none of these dimensions can be fully isolated for analysis; in the life of any given individual the influence of any one factor is intertwined with the influence of all the others. We need, as Kimberle Crenshaw describes in an excerpt later in this chapter, an "intersectional" understanding of how individuals become vulnerable to abuse, and of how their responses to abuse, and others' responses to them, are conditioned by the particularities of their identity and situation. The second is that this provisional list of influential factors is, and probably always would be, incomplete. In thinking about abuse, we must always keep in mind both the particularity of each person's experience and the ways in which that experience can be generalized.

A.   BATTERING IN SAME-SEX RELATIONSHIPS

We first consider battering that takes place in same-sex couples. Consider some recent data:

> In October of 2004, the National Coalition of Anti–Violence Programs ("NCAVP") released its most recent statistics on the prevalence of same-sex domestic violence. The participating NCAVP member organizations documented a record 6,523 same-sex domestic violence incidents in 2003. This total represented a 13% increase in the number of cases reported by the same agencies in 2002, and included six reported same-sex domestic violence-related deaths.
>
> The NCAVP study demonstrated that same-sex domestic violence cut across gender and racial lines. Of the 6,523 cases reported in 2003, 44% of the victims identified as male, 36% identified as female, 2% identified as transgender and the remaining victims did not self-identify. Although member agencies reported the race/ethnicity of victims in only 42% of cases, those numbers indicated that 44% were white, 25% were Latino, 15% were of African descent, 5% were Asian/Pacific Islander, and 4% were multi-racial.
>
> These statistics reveal that same-sex domestic violence continues to be a significant problem in the United States. In fact, same-sex domestic violence is believed to occur at a rate equal to heterosexual domestic violence, estimated in 25–33 percent of relationships. Some experts have even speculated that gay men's domestic violence occurs more frequently than heterosexual domestic violence. Yet, despite the prevalence of same-sex domestic violence, the issue has traditionally been plagued by invisibility and lack of societal awareness. Tara R. Pfeifer, *Out of the Shadows: The Positive Impact of Lawrence v. Texas on Victims of Same-sex Domestic Violence*, 109 PENN ST. L. REV. 1251 (2005).

Now consider one man's story:

David Island and Patrick Letellier
The Neighbors Call the Police, Men Who Beat the Men Who Love Them (1991)

... He is livid now. The blow to my mouth comes fast and direct-POW! He hits me so hard he cuts both my lip and his knuckle; we are both bleeding. I turn my head quickly to avoid the next punch, and blood is smeared on the wall. We continue to struggle and grapple with each other, and Stephen is

relentlessly punching me, in the face, in the stomach, on the side of my head, in the chest. It is all I can do to defend myself. I know that somehow I have to get out of the apartment. I literally throw him across the room, using every ounce of my strength, and bolt for the front door. Next to the front door is a coat closet and its door is open. As I run for the front door, Stephen pushes me hard from behind, and I land face down in the closet on top of some suitcases with my legs sticking out into the hall.

Instantly Stephen is there behind me, kicking me in the shins. Kicking, kicking, kicking, with all his might, as hard as he can. From where I am I can see his face. For the first time I can see the expression on his face as he batters me ... The intensity, the deliberation, the concentration....

Then, suddenly, it is over. His rage has passed. The shouting and scream- ing that had been going on has stopped, and the apartment is quiet. Stephen walks away, going ... I don't know where. I go into the bathroom and look at my lip. "It's a small cut," I think. "Maybe nobody will notice it." I feel my shins. I know they are bruised and will hurt even more later. And then I remember blood on a wall somewhere. I wet a facecloth, wipe my face and cut lip, and go into the bedroom to look for blood stains. As I'm wiping them off the wall, the doorbell rings. Stephen, looking out of a window, mutters, "Oh my God. There's a police car out front." Then he directs me, "Pull yourself together." Remarkably, he looks worse than I.

I listen from the bedroom as Stephen talks to the police. I hear only fragments. "No, no problems here. We were just having an argument, that's all...." And then I hear the policewoman say something about "not leaving until we see the other party." Stephen politely calls out, "Patrick, will you come here please. They want to see you."

I quickly check my appearance in the mirror (I look okay. "Good enough," I think) and go to the door. "Everything is fine," I hear myself say. "We were just having an argument, that's all...." I smile weakly.

... I stand there, numbly staring at those two officers, wondering if they think I've been beating Stephen, because he looks absolutely terrified right now. I hear them something about intervening, "if it gets physical." They leave....

"Neighbors" ... shows how reluctant a victim may be, even when the opportunity is present, to tell the police the truth about the violence and to file a complaint against the batterer. There are many reasons for victim reluctance. Fear is at the top of the list. Fear of recrimination from the batterer may prevent victims from saying anything to the police, particular- ly in the presence of the batterer. Gay male victims may also be under- standably afraid of homohating police officers. Patrick has no way of knowing what the police may do if he identifies Stephen as a lover who beats him. They may decide the abuse is "mutual combat" and arrest them both. They may ridicule Patrick as a "fag" who deserves to get beaten up. They may tell both Patrick and Stephen that they are "sissies who should learn to fight like real men." (Both of the above scenarios were reported by victims of gay men's domestic violence when the San Francisco police arrived at their homes.) The police may also arrest Stephen and book him on spouse abuse, as they should, but Patrick has no way of knowing what they will do. At such times, victims may believe that silence is their safest option.

The most important lesson of this narrative is about complicity. Patrick has now inadvertently joined Stephen as a "partner in crime." Patrick colluded with Stephen to lie to the police and to "cover up" the violence. They are now joined together as partners in violence against the world "out there," including the police. This act of complicity will make it even more difficult for Patrick to extricate himself from the relationship and much more difficult for him to convince Stephen that he wants no part of the violence. . . .

Reasons gay male victims do not call the police more frequently than they do include their valid fear of retaliation . . . and homophobic or abusive treatment by the police. But those are not the only reasons. An analysis of the American family also supplies a reason.

In a family, such as a gay couple, the members are bound to each other by emotional, economic, and psychological bonds. Solidarity develops, which explains why and how a family rallies to form a united front when a tragedy occurs. Old disputes are put aside and the family functions as "one" to overcome a problem or fight outside forces.

. . . High solidarity means personal closeness in which family members identify with each other and can easily put themselves in each other's shoes, and it means longstanding and strong emotional connections. High solidarity, then, resists family break-up.

Furthermore, in gay relationships solidarity may be abnormally high. Living in a homohating society such as the United States, many gays, cut off from family, church, and other traditional forms of societal support, may place a greater value on their own relationship. Often gay couples hold an "us against the world" view, obviously intensifying the solidarity between the members of the couple. Homophobia may also play a more direct role in increasing solidarity in gay couples. Gay couples with children may understandably fear police involvement and the accompanying hetero-sexist custody laws that may destroy their families. Fear of bigotry and police brutality may unite victims and batterers on one side, as members of an oppressed and hated minority, and police on the other side, as oppressors and gay-haters. For many gay men of color, trusting the police may simply be out of the question. . . .

. . . This discussion of solidarity has important messages for victims. First, it is important for gay victims to understand that their reluctance to turn in their batterers may have its roots in a healthy and normal human phenomenon: high solidarity with family. However, in relationships with violent men, high solidarity can be lethal, inhibiting victims from effective-ly dealing with a life-threatening situation. Victims must acknowledge, then put aside, their feelings of solidarity in order to survive.

Second, a batterer's pathological dependence may have the illusion of solidarity, but much more is involved, and their dependence should be recognized as extremely unhealthy. In fact, acknowledging batterer obsession may help victims put aside their own feelings of solidarity, as they see the disparity between the two forces.

NOTES AND QUESTIONS

1. **Homophobia.** Just as the myth of mutual battering reflects a homophobic assumption that can be exploited by a gay or lesbian batterer, so too can other societal manifestations of homophobia be used by gay or lesbian batterers against their partners:

> Society's fear and hatred of homosexuality causes isolation and increases the vulnerability of gay men and lesbians to domestic abuse. The same-sex batterer frequently uses homophobia as a powerful tool to maintain the control and power imbalance in the relationship in a variety of ways. For example, the batterer may threaten "to out" the victim to family, friends, co-workers and ex-spouses who are not aware of and will not accept his or her sexuality. When forced "out of the closet," victims may lose child custody, prestigious careers, and valued personal relationships. Since there are few positive gay and lesbian role models, batterers may convince "newly out" partners that their relationship is normal and abuse occurs in all gay or lesbian relationships. They may also take advantage of their partners' own internal homophobia and guilt to convince them that they do not deserve any better because they are homosexual. . . .

> A victim's prior unpleasant experiences with members of heterosexual society often lend credibility to batterers' claims. For example: a shelter may have refused to admit or help the gay man; a restraining order clinic advocate may have asked the battered lesbian for her husband's name; the hot line worker may not have believed that the male caller is really a domestic violence victim; or the police officers may have referred to the gay male victim as "she". . . .

> As a result of homophobia, some people believe that gay and lesbian victims are less deserving of assistance and intervention because their lifestyles are immoral. Victims are reluctant to report violence that will only reinforce the homophobic attitudes that all "unnatural relationships" have such problems because gay men and lesbians have worked so hard to validate their relationships to heterosexual society. Other people mistakenly believe that because gay men and lesbians are not as emotionally committed as heterosexual partners, it should be easier to leave the abusive relationship, especially since they are not legally married and usually do not have children. Such beliefs demonstrate a serious lack of understanding about homosexuality and the dynamics of domestic violence.

> In addition to the typical characteristics of a domestic violence situation, "the fact alone of being lesbian or gay tends to increase one's distance from the larger society and from its resources." Gay and lesbian victims often do not have a strong support system, causing them to feel they do not have many options to help them stop the violence. People with AIDS or who are HIV positive particularly may

feel they have no viable alternatives to staying with their abusive partners. If victims are geographically separated from other gay men and lesbians, they may think their partners are the only ones who can understand and accept their sexuality. The gay man or lesbian may be concealing his or her sexual orientation or facing disapproval from other people, including his or her own family. Both gay men and lesbians are less likely than heterosexual women to turn to family members for emotional support. Kathleen Finley Duthu, *Why Doesn't Anyone Talk About Gay and Lesbian Domestic Violence?* 18 T. JEFFERSON L. REV. 23 (1996).

2. **Loss of Community.** Solidarity between the abuser and his or her victim is the theme of this last excerpt. Other important factors increasing the vulnerability of gay and lesbian victims of partner violence are the solidarity within their respective communities, the reluctance to acknowledge abuse, and the reluctance to sanction internally (through ostracism, for example), or to report abusers to external authorities.

In her article *Lavender Bruises: Intra-Lesbian Violence, Law and Lesbian Legal Theory*, 20 GOLDEN GATE U. L. REV. 567 (1990), Ruthann Robson reports the story of one battered lesbian:

> The response of the local lesbian community to the arrest of my former lover was demoralizing. Lesbians were upset—even angry—that I had called the police. "I can see turning in a batterer and calling the cops," said one woman. "But a lover? What does that say about your ability to be intimate with anyone?" . . . Several women put a lot of pressure on me to drop the charges. They said things like: "Oh, come on. Haven't you ever hit a lover? It wasn't all that bad." "You're dragging your lover's name through the mud. It was in the newspapers." "Do you realize that the state could take away her children because of what you have done?" They suggested setting up a meeting between my former lover and me. They volunteered to mediate so we could reach an "agreement."
>
> I can think of few crueler demands on a woman who has been attacked than to insist she sit down with her attacker and talk things out. I would guess that none of the lesbians who wanted me to do that would consider demanding such a thing from a straight woman who had just been attacked by her boyfriend. . . . The lowest blow came when a friend called me the day before a pre-trial hearing. "You should drop the charges," she said. "We in the lesbian community can take care of our own." "But what about me? Who's going to guarantee my safety and see that my house doesn't get trashed?" She had no response.

3. **Lack of Help.** The less able a victim of gay or lesbian violence feels to reach out for support, the more vulnerable he or she will be to ongoing abuse. When homophobic attitudes on the part of law enforcement derail effective intervention, the danger can be acute, or even deadly:

> "He's buck naked. He has been beaten up . . . he is really hurt . . . he needs some help," said concerned neighbors in a telephone call to 911 emergency services, reporting the alarming presence of a young man

on the street. Police officers responding to the call dismissed emergency services personnel from the scene and forcibly returned the young man to the apartment of an older male, who persuaded them that the incident was nothing more than "a homosexual tiff." In a radio report from the scene, the officers laughingly described the result of their cursory investigation of the home: "Intoxicated Asian, naked male, was returned to his sober boyfriend." When one local woman called the police station to protest this casual disregard for the younger man's safety and offered additional information, she was told by another officer, "I can't do anything about somebody's sexual preferences in life." Thirty minutes later, fourteen-year-old Konerak Sinthasomphone became the thirteenth of seventeen young men tortured, killed, mutilated and sometimes eaten by his supposed companion, Jeffrey Dahmer. Nancy E. Murphy, *Queer Justice: Equal Protection for Victims of Same-Sex Domestic Violence,* 30 VAL. U. L. REV. 335 (1995).

According to Sandy Lundy's assessment:

[L]esbian and gay violence is largely unreported, in part because of an expectation of hostile responses from those in authority. When the battered same-sex partner does take the extraordinary step of disclosing her or his situation to persons in authority, s/he is likely to be subjected to a devastating, institutionalized re-victimization. S/he may find, for instance, that s/he is excluded from protection under the state's domestic violence laws. Not all states protect victims of same-sex domestic violence, and the abuse protection laws of several states specifically exclude such victims from their protection. Same-sex victims who are nominally protected by the law may not fare much better. [One commentator] notes that "at every point in the system, [gay men are] more afraid to identify themselves as a victim," and that their pleas for help are often met by police, district attorneys' offices, and even their own attorneys with demeaning, abusive remarks such as, "Why aren't you defending yourself? You're a man. Stand up for yourself." Negative reactions by the police also were overwhelmingly common in one study of lesbians who reported abuse. Often, for example, police failed to take any action once they realized that a domestic dispute involved two women. As one interviewee told Professor Renzetti, "I called the police, but nothing was done about it. I kept thinking, 'No one cares because I'm a lesbian.' The police basically took the attitude, 'So two dykes are trying to kill each other; big deal.'" One gay man reported to Island and Letellier that he was repeatedly referred to as "she" by police officers to whom he reported an incident of domestic violence. Sandra E. Lundy, *Abuse That Dare Not Speak Its Name: Assisting Victims of Lesbian and Gay Domestic Violence in Massachusetts,* 28 NEW ENG. L. REV. 273 (1993).

In the fifteen years since this article was written, there have been increased resources made available to those in the GLBT communities. For one source of the growth of expanded services, see *Lesbian, Gay, Bisexual & Transgender Domestic Violence: 2003 Supplement,* A REPORT BY THE NATIONAL COALITION OF ANTI-VIOLENCE PROGRAMS (2004).

4. **The Dynamics of Abusive Same–Sex Relationships.** In Chapter Two we explored the dynamics in heterosexual relationships. The literature on battering suggests that similar patterns of coercive control exist regardless of the sex of the abused or the abuser. What dynamics do you see in the excerpts from Island and Letellier and Robson, that were present in the instances of heterosexual battering we have already examined? How might those dynamics be different?

5. **Challenges to Domestic Violence Theory.** When domestic violence theory was first formulated within the feminist movement, the premise of why men batter was based on the argument that battering had its roots in patriarchal culture. This paradigm never considered same-sex battering. A recent article by Adele M. Morrison, *Queering Domestic Violence to "Straighten Out" Criminal Law: What Might Happen When Queer Theory and Practice Meet Criminal Law's Conventional Responses to Domestic Violence,* 13 S. CAL. REV. L. & WOMEN'S STUD. 81 (2003), considers the way in which same-sex battering impacts traditional feminist theory and practice. Morrison argues that the law assumes heterosexuality, what she calls "straight laws."

One problem with "straight laws" that Morrison discusses is the issue of how to distinguish the batterer from the victim in an incident of same-sex battering when both parties claim victim status, or both are bruised or scratched. Of course, this problem is not limited to same-sex relationships. However, the problem may well be exacerbated in same-sex relationships, both because the partners may more often be physically matched and because of an assumption that "fighting" or "mutual combat" is a typical, or at least not a surprising, aspect of a gay or lesbian relationship. Those assumptions can be exploited by gay and lesbian batterers:

> ... [S]ame-sex batterers often use the myth of mutual battering to disguise their abuse as mutual, consensual combat; alienate the victim from sources of assistance; reinforce the victim's guilt and self-doubt; and allow the abusive relationship to continue without challenge. The myth of mutual abuse, which at bottom is founded on sexist and heterosexist assumptions about how people behave, thus becomes a potent tool of control in many abusive same-sex relationships. Sandra Lundy, *Abuse That Dare Not Speak Its Name: Assisting Victims of Lesbian and Gay Domestic Violence in Massachusetts,* 28 NEW ENG. L. REV. 273 (1993).

6. **"Straight Laws."** Morrison further notes that the lack of specificity as to gays, lesbians, bisexual and transgendered (GLBT) persons in domestic violence statutes has led to many legal challenges over the question of inclusion. When considering whether domestic violence laws are applicable to same-sex couples, most courts have held that they are. The following case is consistent with most holdings in this area.

State v. Linner

Ohio Municipal Court, 1996.
665 N.E.2d 1180.

■ TIMOTHY BLACK, JUDGE.

This criminal case came on for trial to the court on January 17, 1996 upon the state's charge that defendant Bernice Linner committed the crime of domestic violence ... when she allegedly assaulted her live-in girlfriend, Vickie Birch, on December 24, 1995.

At trial, Birch identified the defendant as her lover, with whom she had been living together for thirteen months in an intimate, lesbian relationship. Per Birch's testimony, the defendant had asked Birch to marry her in March 1995, and they had three children between them, albeit patently from previous relationships. Ironically, the spark of the altercation at issue revolved around an expensive diamond ring which Birch was attempting to give to the defendant for Christmas. The defendant, in turn, rejected the ring as unnecessarily expensive, asserting, *inter alia,* that "we've got three kids [where we can better spend that much money]."

At trial, the evidence and testimony about the parties' physical altercation was extensive and upsetting. The state introduced a set of nine photographs of Birch taken on the night of the brawl, and they evidence a significant assault upon her, including a black eye, numerous bruises, cuts and scratches, several bruised squeeze marks on both arms, and a very badly bitten lip.

The defendant's explanation of the state's evidence sounded in self-defense, Linner testifying that she had acted only as "a calming influence." At six feet, two hundred sixty pounds, the defendant acknowledged her significant physical advantage over Birch.

At the close of trial, defense counsel timely moved for acquittal ... arguing that the state had failed to evidence that the victim was "a family or household member" statutorily entitled to the protection of Ohio's domestic violence laws....

The better-reasoned analysis of the law reflects that Ohio's domestic violence laws apply equally to all persons regardless of their gender. Any person of either sex who can prove that he or she "otherwise is cohabiting" with another person of either sex as a "family or household member" is a person who is entitled to the protection of Ohio's domestic violence laws....

Thus, the domestic violence statutes apply to and protect many persons other than those legally married, including parents, children, aunts, uncles, nephews, and nieces, as well as spouses, former spouses, and "persons living as spouses." Indeed, upon careful review, the statutory definitions do not require the person to be a spouse but merely to function like a spouse. Therefore, even if a person may not legally be a spouse, due to sex or current marital status, he or she is not precluded from proving that he or she is a person functioning like a spouse. Such a person is included within the statutory definition of a "person living as a spouse...."

The legislature was fully aware that members of the same-sex cohabit in the same manner as members of the opposite sex. If the legislature had intended to limit the application of the domestic violence statutes to people of opposite sexes, the legislature would have made specific reference to gender....

Finally, fundamental principles of constitutional law would preclude application of the domestic violence laws only to heterosexuals. A gender-based construction of the statute would render the statute unconstitutional on equal protection grounds. In this regard, "courts must apply all presumptions and pertinent rules of construction so as to uphold, if at all possible, a statute or ordinance assailed as unconstitutional." Accordingly, this court construes R.C. 2919.25(E) so as to avoid an equal protection challenge to the constitutionality of the statute. . . .

In light of these principles of law, and upon the evidence presented at trial in this cause, which evidence satisfies virtually all of the factors indicative of cohabitation, the court concludes that the victim here, Vickie Birch, has proved beyond a reasonable doubt that she is a person who otherwise is cohabiting with the defendant. Thus, the domestic violence statute applies to this same-sex couple. Moreover, upon the evidence of the assault as described above, the court concludes easily that the defendant knowingly caused physical harm to Birch.

NOTES AND QUESTIONS

1.   **Heterosexual Specific Statutes.** Many states, including California, have removed any language from their domestic violence statutes that limit them to heterosexual couples and thus are gender neutral, leaving it to courts to decide the applicability to same-sex couples. Other states, such as Montana and South Carolina, specifically exclude gays and lesbians from protection. Only Hawaii's statute affirmatively includes same-sex couples. See Nat'l Coalition of Anti–Violence Programs, Lesbians, Gays, Bisexual and Transgender Domestic Violence in 2001: A Report of the National Coalition of Anti-Violence Programs (2002). *See also* Tara R. Pfeifer, *Out of the Shadows: The Positive Impact of Lawrence v. Texas on Victims of Same-sex Domestic Violence*, 109 Penn St. L. Rev. 1251 (2005).

2.   **Equal Protection Analysis.** Are statutes that deny same-sex couples the same protections as opposite sex couples constitutional? The issue has never been directly addressed by the United States Supreme Court. Homosexuals have yet to be identified as a suspect class, thus triggering strict scrutiny of laws that discriminate against them. Thus, laws which discriminate on the basis of sexual orientation are reviewed under a rational basis test. Nevertheless, the Court is not always tolerant of discrimination against gays and lesbians. Could *Romer v. Evans,* 517 U.S. 620 (1996) provide the basis for overturning domestic violence legislation that includes only straight couples? Consider the following argument:

> In *Evans v. Romer*, the Colorado Supreme Court reviewed proposed Amendment Two to the Colorado Constitution which explicitly prohibited "all legislative, executive or judicial action at any level of state or local government designed to protect . . . homosexual persons."
>
> The [United States] Court held that the controversial amendment is "born of animosity toward the class of persons affected," thus serving no legitimate government interest. Furthermore, the means proposed by the amendment bore no rational relation to the objective asserted

by the state. In effect, the *Romer* Court established that arbitrary discrimination against homosexuals violates the Equal Protection Clause.

Avoiding the determination of homosexuals as a quasi-suspect or suspect class, coupled with a finding that Amendment Two was unconstitutional, strongly suggests use of a "rational basis with teeth" analysis. Independent of an actual label, commentators are in agreement that the *Romer* Court applied some elevated form of rational basis review.

Under *Romer v. Evans*, domestic violence statutes excluding homosexuals should not be upheld. The Court should apply the same rational basis analysis as applied in Romer and find the statutes unconstitutional. Once a state enacts a domestic violence statute, it must equally apply the provision to everyone. Because the circumstances regarding domestic violence statutes mirror those involving Amendment Two in *Romer v. Evans*, for the same reasons that the Court held Amendment Two unconstitutional, discriminatory domestic violence statutes should be stricken. Pamela M. Jablow, *Victims of Abuse and Discrimination: Protecting Battered Homosexuals Under Domestic Violence Legislation*, 28 HOFSTRA L. REV. 1095 (2000).

Do you think that the circumstances surrounding the passage of domestic violence statutes mirror those in the statute involved in *Romer*? In what ways are they similar or different? How should these laws affect constitutional analysis?

3. **The Impact of *Lawrence v. Texas* on Domestic Violence.** In 2003, in *Lawrence v. Texas,* 539 U.S. 558 (2003), the United States Supreme Court struck down Texas's sodomy statute. This excerpt explores the impact of sodomy statutes on domestic violence and impact Lawrence may have on future laws.

> Until the recent Supreme Court decision in Lawrence v. Texas, an additional factor complicating the problem of gay and lesbian partner abuse was the existence of sodomy statutes on the books in 13 states. These laws served to deter victims from reporting violence at the hands of a same-sex partner, as penalties for violation ranged from fines to 20–year prison terms. . . . Generally, these statutes criminalized oral and anal sex between consenting adults, including in the privacy of their own homes. While criminal enforcement of these statutes has been very rare, they have functioned to stigmatize certain forms of sexuality. Over the years, sodomy statutes have often been cited to the detriment of gays and lesbians in legal cases regarding issues of employment, custody, and marriage, and have provided ammunition for the thriving societal homophobia. . . .
>
> On June 26, 2003, the U.S. Supreme Court, in a 6–3 decision, struck down the Texas [sodomy] law, as well as the laws of three other states, each of which criminalized sodomy among homosexuals. The decision effectively invalidated sodomy laws in nine additional states covering heterosexual and homosexual couples. The Court held that the right to

liberty under the Due Process Clause precludes the government from intruding on the personal and private life of the individual, regardless of sexual orientation. Most significant, in his majority opinion overruling Bowers, Justice Kennedy stated that the central holding of Bowers [a 1986 Supreme Court case upholding the sodomy laws] has been brought into question and "its continuance as precedent demeans the lives of homosexual persons."

It remains to be seen how this decision will affect gay rights laws; nevertheless, it eliminates the major justification for discriminating against gays and lesbians. This decision arguably has profound implications for the future rights of gays in the area of domestic violence, as well as many others including custody, adoption, foster care, employment, and housing. Michelle Aulivola, *Outing Domestic Violence: Affording Appropriate Protections to Gay and Lesbian Victims*, 42 FAM. CT. REV. 162 (2004).

Do you think *Lawrence* will embolden same-sex victims to seek police assistance, or do you think the police will refuse to assist those victims on the grounds that the conduct is private?

4. **Same–Sex Marriage Amendments.** Because only Hawaii specifically covers GLBT victims in its domestic violence statutes, victims have had to rely on courts interpreting statutes to extend the law's protections to them. Recently, however, opponents of same-sex marriage have challenged these rulings. They argue that states that have constitutional amendments or laws defining marriage as only between a man and a woman exclude same-sex and unmarried heterosexual couples from coverage under domestic violence statutes. See, e.g. *State v. Nixon*, 845 N.E.2d 544 (Ohio App. 2006) (rejecting the argument that Ohio's Marriage Amendment nullifies the domestic violence statutes as applied to unmarried couples). In *State v. Carswell* the Ohio Supreme Court became the first state supreme court to consider whether a marriage amendment nullified a domestic violence law that covers those "living together" as spouses. As Marc Spindelman describes the argument before the Ohio Supreme Court:

> ... Carswell's [an unmarried heterosexual male accused of abusing his girlfriend] position can be stated this way: The Marriage Amendment, which seeks to preserve the unique legal status of marriage, bars the state from treating unmarried individuals like married individuals. The state's domestic violence law does just that by extending unmarried individuals legal protections against intimate partner violence on a marriage model. Therefore, the Marriage Amendment invalidates the domestic violence law as applied to married couples. Marc Spindelman, *The Honeymoon's Over*, LEGAL TIMES, June 12, 2006 at 66.

In a 6–1 decision, the justices rejected this argument, holding that the state plays no role in creating cohabitation, but it does have a role in creating marriage. See *State v. Carswell*, 871 N.E.2d 547 (Ohio 2007). This decision is significant in that at least 27 states have marriage amendments.

B.   Race, Culture, Immigration, Religion and the Experience of Abuse

This group of readings addresses partner violence in communities of color, communities with a specific minority ethnic or cultural identity, immigrant communities, and religious communities. Of course, some of the stories we have already read about relationships and violence have been experienced by people of color; not all of the women about whom Angela Browne writes, for example, are white. But now it is time to ask how battering may be experienced differently, and responses to battering may be different, both on the part of those involved in the relationships, and on the part of others in the society, when the batterer and/or his victim is black, or Asian, or Latino/a, or American Indian, or Eastern European. Even to use these labels is to risk minimizing potential differences, and overlooking relevant nuances. We are, after all, talking about women, and men, who are, by birth or family origin, African American, Caribbean, Haitian, Vietnamese, Sri Lankan, Hawaiian, Cuban, Mexican, Portuguese, Romanian, Croatian, Navajo or Sioux, just to name a few possibilities. Moreover, even if they hail from the same country, they may be part of radically different political, cultural or religious subcommunities. They may be new immigrants, or born and raised in the United States.

These few pages cannot do justice to the multitude of issues these differences raise. Instead, we will offer examples of thoughtful writing about some of them, within the framework offered in the introduction to this chapter. We ask, that is to say, how issues of race, culture, ethnicity and immigrant status might affect:

(a) individuals' subjective experiences of abuse;

(b) their own community's understanding of abuse, in the context of community norms about family structure and gender role expectations;

(c) their ability to reach out from their own community to the larger society for assistance; and

(d) the larger society's responses to their abuse—while not losing sight of the ways in which these questions are profoundly interrelated.

The section opens with a look at differences in how women understand or interpret their own experiences of abuse. The first reading is drawn from a book by Beth Richie, Compelled to Crime: The Gender Entrapment of Battered Black Women (1996), in which she reports on a study of women incarcerated on Riker's Island for criminal activity that she discovered was often related, directly or indirectly, to the abuse they suffered at the hands of an intimate partner. Her study included African American battered women, white battered women, and non-battered African American women. In looking at their backgrounds, at their expectations of themselves and their partners, and at their experiences, she uncovered some important and thought-provoking differences among the three groups. This excerpt suggests some ways in which women's subjective experiences of abuse—and of the "gender entrapment," in Richie's words, that results in abuse—may differ in ways that are, if not determined by race, then at least influenced by race.

Richie's study provides a wonderful example of the kind of highly contextual and nuanced inquiry necessary to an understanding of the ways in which numerous aspects of women's lives "intersect" to influence their vulnerability to abuse, how they understand or interpret their abuse, and their responses to it. She is not writing about all African American women, but about a specific subgroup—incarcerated African American women, all of whom come from economically deprived backgrounds. Even within this sample, she is at pains to demonstrate that generalizations about her subjects are misleading; rather, their backgrounds and experiences, while inevitably influenced by race as well as economic status, fall into quite distinct patterns, with important different consequences. This study also serves as a reminder that we should not develop broad, over-reaching stereotypes of people based on their backgrounds.

Beth Richie

Compelled to Crime: The Gender Entrapment of Battered Black Women (1996)

Several features generally characterize all of the families of origin of the three subgroups in this study. Despite slight variations in income level, all of the women's families lived close to the social and economic margin. Even those women who described their lives as "comfortable" experienced their economic status as fragile. Most of the families depended on multiple incomes from unstable jobs to support the family, and even those who accumulated extra material possessions were vulnerable to changes in employment status, health problems, and other unexpected family crises. In both subgroups of African American women, the women's mothers worked outside of the homes, while the white women did so only on occasion. In all of the families, the women were primary caretakers of the children, and all of the women worked in their households, performing routine household tasks that were usually organized around gender. Only the white families were highly organized by generation; in the African American families the distinctions between children and adults were less rigid.

Of the seven themes that emerged about the families, childhood roles, and the construction of female identities, the findings indicated that the three subgroups in this study were distinct. The African American women who were battered were distinguished by their racial/ethnic identity and by their early childhood experiences. . . .

In terms of their positions in their households, the African American battered women described childhoods that were distinguished from other childhoods by more privileges, material possessions and attention. With this elevated status came a symbolic burden on the women to *maintain* the privileged status through emotional, academic, household, and other "*work.*" This unusual position and their efforts to maintain status were the initial circumstance that left the African American battered women vulnerable to gender entrapment.

In contrast, the African American women who were not battered recalled being average children, feeling a sense of commonality with the other children with whom they grew up. As such, they were less concerned with differentiating themselves from others. Of the three groups, the white children typically described childhood experiences that were the most deprived relative to other children in their families. They tended to be scapegoated and ignored, and their burdens were more concrete than emotional in nature. They almost came to expect degrading treatment and recognized it as such.

The second theme that emerged from the data as an important finding for the gender-entrapment theory was the images the women had of adult women and men. The African American battered women recalled a paradoxical relationship with their female caretakers. On the one hand, they tended to idealize them, and, on the other hand, they described feeling distant and, at times, disappointed in their mothers' lack of emotional and physical availability to them as children. The African American battered women adopted their mothers' tendency to feel sorry for men in their lives, tolerating their irresponsibility, their limitations, their indiscretions, and, ultimately, their violence....

The African American women who were not battered had a more realistic sense of who their mothers were. This subgroup tended to identify with their mothers in more ways than the African American battered women, including taking on their mothers' dismissal or disdain for men. Their mothers were less generous with their tolerance and more discounting of men's roles in their lives. In this way, they were significantly less vulnerable to men's violence as adults. The white women were generally more distant from adults as children than the other two groups, and they tended to feel sorry for their mothers and avoid interaction with their fathers. However, as children, the white battered women developed an understanding of the relative power that men and boys held in their families and, indeed, in the world.

The findings from this theme were related to a third theme that emerged from the data as relevant to gender entrapment: the women's experiences and observation of abuse during their childhood. In each subgroup, the women tended to internalize and draw meaning from their mothers' responses to abuse if they observed it. The African American battered women's mothers who were battered themselves tended not to leave abusive relationships, while the African American non-battered women's mothers tended to resist and leave right away. The white women's mothers responded to being abused by planning to leave and attempting to leave. However, in the end, they were not able to stay away permanently for a number of reasons. In each case, the decision to stay or leave was related to the mother's sense of herself in relationship to the man by whom she was abused, as well as the availability of concrete options.

For those women in this study who themselves experienced abuse as children, the effect was significant, albeit different, for each subgroup. The African American battered women were less often physically abused as children, and more often abused sexually, which is a significant element in their gender entrapment. The role of protecting the adults who committed this heinous act was added to the burden of being "special" children.... The African American non-battered women experienced some physical and sexual abuse, but were not targeted as victims any more than other children in their families.... All of the white women in this sample were abused as children, and, like the African American battered women, internalized some of the consequences. For them, the situation was compounded by serious childhood neglect.

As the African American battered women grew up and began to encounter the subtle messages and overt pressures from the social world to conform to "appropriate" gender and racial/ethnic roles, they began to engage in self-limiting behavior in order to more consistently fit within their sense of expected behaviors. The African American battered women were surprised that they did not command the same respect from teachers, employers, and peers that they did from their families, and they began to work even harder to please others rather than themselves. They tended to avoid risks, and some even sabotaged their opportunities for social advancement. Instead, they focused on their domestic relationships, becoming overconfident of their abilities to effect change in the private sphere of their lives.

At the other extreme from the African American battered women, the African American non-battered women in the sample were the most likely to ignore expectations and to take symbolic and concrete risks while they were growing up. When they felt discriminatory treatment in the public or private sphere that limited their choices or constricted their behavior, they defied regulations despite the threat of punishment. The women in this subgroup were much more peer-identified than the other two groups, and they did not censor themselves. Instead, they sometimes acted incautiously and engaged in behaviors that resulted in negative sanctions. The white battered women in the sample tried to avoid rejections, as did the African American battered women, but they had come to expect it and had learned to cope more effectively with it....

The last theme that emerged ... was the importance of racial/ethnic identity and solidarity in the women's overall sense of themselves. As the cases illustrated, the African American women in both groups expressed a keener sense of their racial/ethnic identity than the white battered women. However, for the African American battered women, loyalty was directed to their families and, by implication, to African American men in their families. This factor was a key element in their emotional interest, every-day work, and identities as "Black women trying to create families with Black men," which was changing to "battered women," "victim," or "female offenders." In contrast, the African American women who were not battered constructed their racial/ethnic identities more in terms of the African American community as a whole, including African American women. They consider the contemporary issues that limit women's lives as central and important. Their identities were less gender-bound and relationship-bound. The white battered women did not indicate that race/ethnicity was a critical element of their identities, and it did not overtly influence their behaviors, thoughts, or feelings as much as it did the African American battered women.

NOTES AND QUESTIONS

1. **Richie's Hypothesis.** While we may not have parallel in-depth studies to guide our understanding of how women of other races, ethnicities, cultures and classes may experience abuse, Richie's work demonstrates the need to avoid making assumptions about those experiences, and suggests the kinds of questions we might want to ask to test our starting hypotheses. What sort of questions might you ask? For example, do you think it is possible to separate out the effects of childhood abuse, relations with parents, and race?

2. **Domestic Violence and Women's Incarceration.** It is important to note that Richie interviewed women who were incarcerated for a variety of crimes, yet had backgrounds of domestic violence. Being a victim of domestic violence is a pathway into the criminal justice system for many women. This raises questions about the data of the pervasiveness of domestic violence. There are many women who have experienced domestic violence but these women have not been asked about it. Thus, lawyers ought to screen all of their clients for domestic violence, and assess the relevance of their victimization to their criminal case. We return to this topic in Chapter Nine.

3. **Community Norms.** Richie's account also suggests the power of community norms, often transmitted through families, other community institutions, and peer culture, to shape the experience of abuse. These next readings take up this question of culturally specific community norms that shape understandings of, and responses to, abuse.

Karin Wang

Battered Asian American Women: Community Responses from the Battered Women's Movement and the Asian American Community

3 ASIAN L.J. 151 (1996).

The Importance of Family and Gender Roles

> *"I didn't sense the danger because I was so focused on the shame my daughter's actions would bring in the Cambodian community. And I was thinking about my daughter's children and the importance of their having a family." Kim Leang is remembering her daughter Kim Seng, killed by her abusive husband, Sartout Nom. A week before Kim Seng's murder, Kim Leang had organized a family meeting, where both sides of the family urged the young couple to stay together and asked Nom to*

stop beating Kim Seng. Says Kim Leang, "Sometimes because we value our cultural conditions, we try to get families reunited at whatever cost."

Asian cultures are group-oriented. A person's identity and worth are not measured individually, but are instead reflected by the group as a whole. Consequently, the family is the most important social unit. A person is regarded as an extension of the family and is expected to subjugate individual needs to family interests....

To the extent that individualism does matter in Asian cultures, male individuals are valued over females....

These traditional cultural beliefs about family and gender roles have important implications for battered Asian American women.... First, the group focus of Asian cultures protects family reputation at the expense of the individual. In many Asian cultures, "keeping face" is an important social rule. Because the individual is viewed as an extension of the group, one family member's guilt or shame transfers to the rest of the family. The individual must "keep face" and minimize public attention to her and, by extension, to her family's problems. For a battered Asian American woman, publicly admitting that she is battered would often be "synonymous with condemning herself to isolation and ostracization." The pressure to "keep face" prevents many battered Asian American women from seeking assistance from outsiders or even from other family members. Furthermore, the emphasis on "keeping face" also pressures the batterer and other members in the family to hide any abuse from non-family and non-community members. By avoiding external intervention or public acknowledgment of battering, the battered Asian American woman, her abuser, and their families keep the violence hidden inside the family, which complicates the already frustrating problem of general under reporting of domestic violence incidents.

Michelle Fine, Rosemarie A. Roberts and Lois Weis

Puerto Rican Battered Women Redefining Gender, Sexuality, Culture, Violence, and Resistance, in Domestic Violence at the Margins, (Natalie J. Sokoloff, ed., 2005)

Puerto Rican women grow up understanding that women's tasks sweep across nurturance and feeding of young and old, socialization for subordination to men, learning that they have responsibility for controlling men's anger, self-consciously "over protecting" children (especially daughters), and assuring that the next generation is imbued with a sense of optimism despite the overwhelming evidence to the contrary. Latinas have long had to pick up the pieces of colonialism, economic and state violence, and domestic abuse....

BEATRICE: *I felt that it was my job,* yes. I was raised in the type where ... I cooked everything. But it depends, as a female that was my job. This is why, this is like a *trade school* where I would be taught what to do for the future. So, now I had this man.

DINA: What ... uh, yeah. He was the type that if things did not go his way, he was very dominant. He had to be served. He had to be obeyed like he was some father or god or something, and that's when the beating started.

MUN: His hand was easy, just smacked you?

DINA: He was hitting me when I was pregnant, but I never, never told my mother. Never told her cuz she was hurt by what I did so I said I'm never gonna tell her that he's abusing me.

His mother, she felt what he was doing was right, yes. If I wasn't a *disciplined woman to him and if I had a bad mouth and talked back to him, I deserved to get hit.* Oh yes, you just don't know ... [laugh] ... Yeah, and being the way I was raised and how I have so much respect for older people, how I learned not to act like one of those wild crazy women. I was the type that....

MUN: Quiet?

DINA: Yeah, I just took what hit me ... *I felt like I deserved it anyway.* I put myself in that situation.

MUN: When he hit you?

DINA: Hey, when he hit me, I felt like I didn't deserve to get hit, but I didn't deserve either to make my mother feel the pain I was going through.

The women seem to endure, until the children begin to notice.

MUN: Did at any time, did you call the police?

DINA: *I never called the police on him, only until ... My daughter—* well, my daughter was born and she was in the play pen in the kitchen and I had this ... no, he never touched her until one day, he did touch her, and that's when I practically almost killed him, I picked up the knife, and I said, "This is it."

MUN: He slapped the girl?

DINA: He hit my daughter, but he hit her, not on her face, but he bent over because she started ... she was teething. She had two baby front teeth and she started biting on the kitchen chairs. He bent over and started hitting her. He hit her so hard, like she was three, four, five years old. Boy, I climbed on him like a cat. I scratched his neck and everything, and he threw me against the refrigerator. He took me, and he hit me and I fell to the floor. He kicked me in the stomach. I got up and picked up a knife.

MUN: Did you stab him?

DINA: No, I didn't get to stab him. I was swinging the knife. I said, "Please," I said, "Come over and hit me again. Please come and hit me again."....

As these young women witnessed and endured this betrayal, somewhere, quietly, they tucked away a plan to care for themselves and their children. And yet they kept watching, hoping for a change. Not all leave—with "welfare reform," we would predict painfully that fewer can. But those who leave often do so to "protect the children."

Michelle Decasas

Protecting Hispanic Women: The Inadequacy of Domestic Violence Policy

24 CHICANO-LATINO L. REV. 56 (2003).

Domestic violence research has documented a series of risk factors that have been associated with victimization. Women at greatest risk for injury from domestic violence include those with male partners who abuse alcohol, are unemployed, have less than a high-school education, and have a low socio-economic status. Hispanic women are more exposed to these factors as a whole than are Black and White women. Without an understanding of the economic, social and political factors that impact Hispanic women's lives, an analysis of domestic violence against women is incomplete. The data suggest that the comparatively poor economic and political position of Hispanics place them at a distinct disadvantage, thus causing Hispanics to experience and respond to domestic violence differently than White women.

Alcohol abuse by an intimate male is one factor that increases a woman's chances of being a victim of domestic violence. Heavier drinkers are at increased risk for being perpetrators of intimate partner violence. Based on research conducted by the Substance Abuse and Mental Health Services Administration (SAMHSA), the rate of binge use and/or heavy use of alcohol was higher among Hispanics than Whites or Blacks. According to the 2000–2001 National Household Survey on Drug Abuse, Hispanics represent 24.6 percent of binge drinkers compared to 22.2 percent for Whites and 19.7 percent for Blacks.

In addition, the Survey indicates that males are more than twice as likely to be binge drinkers than are females. From this data we can infer that Hispanic males are more likely than Black or White males to be binge and/or heavy drinkers. Therefore, Hispanic women are more exposed to the risk factor of alcohol abuse by their male partners than are Black or White women.

Unemployment is another key risk factor associated with domestic violence victimization. Men who are unemployed or have recently become unemployed represent a significant percentage of perpetrators of domestic violence. The rate of unemployment for Hispanics is 7.2 percent. This percentage represents the proportion of Hispanics who are unemployed as a percent of those in the labor force. This, however, does not take into consideration Hispanics who are not in the labor force, which is a serious limitation for two reasons. First, given that there is a large Hispanic immigrant population, some of whom may be undocumented, these numbers may not truly represent the current unemployment rate. Illegal immigrants are unlikely to be included in the quantification of the current unemployment situation if the process entails reporting by the employees or employers, for fear of the legal consequences. Second, Hispanic men who fall outside the definition of unemployed and into the definition of those not in the labor force may be considered equivalent, for purposes of this analysis. Both categories of men may equally contribute to the risk of domestic violence victimization of Hispanic women. This second limitation equally applies to Black and White women who, in comparison to Hispanic women, have unemployment rates of 9.7 and 4.8 percent respectively. Keeping in mind the apparent limitations of the statistical data available, Hispanics are exposed to the risk factor of unemployment second only to Black women and more than White women.

Having less than a high school education is yet another factor that is correlated with an increased risk of domestic violence victimization. Over the past four decades, Hispanic males have remained the leading group of high school dropouts.

Accordingly, in 2000 Hispanic males represented 31.8 percent of all dropouts between the ages of 16 and 24. Comparatively, Black men represented 15.3 percent and White men represented only 7.0 percent of dropouts. These statistics are under-inclusive for quantifying less than a high school education because they fail to consider those who attained less than eight years of education. The data on educational attainment only serves to further develop the argument that Hispanics are more likely than Whites or Blacks to attain less than a high school education. Among the total Hispanic population above the age of eighteen, an unfortunate 24.5 percent attain less than an eighth grade education. In comparison, only 3.8 percent of Whites and 5.8 percent of Blacks attain less than an eight grade education. It is clear that Hispanic women are more likely to have a male partner with less than a high school education than are White or Black women.

The final factor considered to increase the risk of domestic violence victimization is low socio-economic status (SES). Research has shown that women living in households with lower annual household incomes experience intimate partner violence at significantly higher rates than women in households with higher annual incomes.

According to the U.S. Census Bureau, 6.7 percent of Hispanic households have an annual income of less than $7,500. This is lower than the percentage of Black men (11.7 percent) and higher than the percentage of White men (4.9 percent). These statistics are problematic because they likely do not include immigrant workers. As asserted previously, immigrant workers are unlikely to participate in a population survey that calculates income distribution. Despite this inadequacy, however, we will assume that based on the data available for analysis Hispanic women are less exposed to low socio-economic men than Black women, but are more exposed than White women. . . .

There exists a large foreign-born population of Hispanics in the United States. In addition to, and somewhat related to, the barriers already discussed, immigrant women face distinctive barriers attributable to their immigration status. Many women emigrate from their native countries dependent on their spouse for financial support, legal status, and/or both. This makes immigrant women particularly vulnerable to domestic violence. Immigrant women refrain from reporting domestic violence for fear that the undocumented spouse on whom they are dependent will be deported. These women commonly come to the United States with no independent financial resources. They are therefore wholly dependent on their husband for financial support. This creates a rationale for remaining in the abusive relationship. . . .

Women fearful of their own deportation are also reluctant to report domestic violence. Immigrant women are often dependent on their U.S. citizen or lawful permanent resident spouse for their legal status. These women desist from reporting their abusive spouse for fear that they will be deported. Abusive husbands can use this reliance to condition sponsorship on staying in the relationship despite the abuse. Even if legal status is no longer dependent on the husband's sponsorship, due to the lack of access to information, women continue to be intimidated by such threats.

In addition to the threat of deportation, immigrant women who are undocumented are not eligible for public assistance. This further deters immigrant women from seeking assistance given that it is limited to church or private groups devoted to providing services to undocumented families.

NOTES AND QUESTIONS

1. **Sameness or Difference?** How much of the experience that is described in the excerpts above is racially or culturally unique, and how much is shared? What do these women have in common? As you begin to think about the multiple dimensions of battering, try to identify what relevance one's cultural or racial heritage may play in how women experience battering and how they respond to it.

2. **Saving Face.** Many of the victims we will read about throughout this book are reluctant to come forward about their situations because they feel shame. Thus, they tolerate abuse to "save face" in their communities. Karin Wang discusses how many Asian women hide abuse from their family members. As we will see later in this chapter, a similar dynamic exists for Jewish women as well. Why do you think women might feel as if they have to "save face?" Do you think it is only minority women who feel as if they must do so? For a discussion of how black women may face similar pressure to keep their families together see, Zanita E. Fenton, *Silence Compounded—The Conjunction of Race and Gender Violence*, 11 AM. U. J. GENDER SOC. POL'Y & L. 271 (2003).

3. **Reluctance to Seek Help.** Another common theme in the literature about battering among racial and ethnic minorities is their reluctance to seek help from outsiders. Many factors compound this reluctance. Language barriers, unfamiliarity with American law, fear of deportation, shame, the fear of being ostracized by their communities, and a belief system that compels them to stay in their relationships regardless of the

abuse all contribute to the reluctance of victims to seek help. How might the legal system make it easier for such victims to seek services? Should each community have its outreach?

4. **Protecting Children.** As Michelle Fine and her co-authors describe in the excerpt about Puerto Rican women, often what compels women to leave is not their own safety, but the safety of their children. We have not yet explored in detail the experience of battered women who are also mothers. Yet, for many women, especially those in poor and minority communities, whether to stay in an abusive relationship is particularly complicated because of children. One factor that is especially important is how state welfare agencies view battered women who are unable to protect their children. We will examine this issue in detail in Chapter Twelve. In thinking about this, it is relevant that African–American families are grossly over-represented in the child welfare system. See Dorothy E. Roberts, *Child Welfare and Civil Rights*, 2003 U. ILL. L.REV. 171 (2003).

5. **Immigration.** As we will see in Chapter Fifteen, and as Michelle Decasas notes above, fear of deportation can be the main reason immigrant women do not seek outside help. This is true among all immigrant communities.

6. **Importing Culture.** Immigrants often import from their native countries cultural, social, and economic conditions to the United States. Thus, it is critical to understand both the problems of and solutions to domestic violence when addressing battering within cultural communities. Consider this explanation of what it is like for Haitian women in the United States:

> The political violence in Haiti not only sets the stage for violence against women, it detracts attention from the magnitude of the problem. Due to the political environment and history of subordination of Haiti, it is extremely difficult for these women to break the cycle of abuse. This environment contributes to the predictors of emotional, physical and domestic violence against women. Studies have identified four domains of predictors: individual, relationship, household and community characteristics. These findings indicate that seven factors consistently increase Haitian women's risk of intimate partner violence, regardless of the form of violence. These factors include women's lack of completion of primary school, violence in women's family of origin, partner's jealousy, partner's need for power, relationship quality, partner's history of intoxication, and female-dominated financial decision-making. Mary Clark, *Domestic Violence in the Haitian Culture and the American Legal Response*, 37 U. MIAMI INTER-AM. L. REV. 297 (2006).

7. **Blaming Culture.** Locating women's vulnerability to violence in particular community norms may be essential to shaping interventions and services that "fit" women's self-definitions, situations and needs. At the same time, we have to use this information with caution. In specifying what it is in "other" cultures that make women targets for abuse, we should not let "mainstream" American culture off the hook, or indeed allow ourselves to fall into unwarranted negative stereotypes about those "other" cultures. Leti Volpp makes this point in the specific context of immigrant cultures,

but what she says has equal applicability to minority community cultures here in the United States:

> Selectively blaming culture leads to the misapprehension that certain . . . cultures are fundamentally different from "our" culture. Ethnic difference is equated with moral difference, with which we must struggle in a multicultural state. Specifically, commentators depict the sex-subordinating practices of certain immigrants as creating an irreconcilable tension between the values of feminism and multiculturalism. The presumed existence of this conflict leads to policy proposals and theoretical conclusions that exaggerate differences between "us" and "them." Such misreadings prevent us from seeing, understanding and struggling against specific relations of power—both within "other" cultures and our own. Leti Volpp, *Blaming Culture for Bad Behavior,* 12 YALE J.L. & HUMAN. 89 (2000).

This tendency to "blame culture," and the conflict it can create between members of the cultural subcommunity and mainstream advocates and activists is well illustrated by reactions to the case of Dong Lu Chen, a Chinese American man sentenced by a New York judge to only five years probation for the murder of his wife. The judge based his decision on testimony that Chen's state of mind at the time of the murder was dictated by traditional Chinese values; Chen had learned of his wife's infidelity and was driven to kill her, he claimed, by culturally specific attitudes about adultery and loss of manhood. While this did not exonerate him, it led to a verdict of manslaughter rather than murder, and permitted the lenient sentence. Although cultural arguments on behalf of criminal defendants have been loosely called "cultural defense" arguments, they are in fact arguments that support other defenses, or support a reduction in the severity of the charges, or in the sentence, as in Chen's case.

Although Asian American community activists and feminists came together briefly to protest the judge's decision, the coalition quickly fell apart. White feminists argued that it was altogether inappropriate to allow defense arguments based on culture. The District Attorney, Elizabeth Holtzman, said: "There should be one standard of justice, not one that depends on the cultural background of the defendant. There may be barbaric customs in various parts of the world, but that cannot excuse criminal conduct here." What outraged Asian American activists about the verdict, by contrast, was the depiction of Chinese culture as tolerating such a killing. Barbara Chang, from the Asian Women's Center in New York, said firmly: "Chinese culture does not give a man permission to kill his wife regardless of what the situation was at home." For the Asian American activists, on the other hand, the argument that culture should be routinely excluded from the courtroom was nonsensical. In the words of Monona Yin of the Committee Against Anti–Asian Violence, "Culture informs everything each person does." For further discussions of the Chen case, and of cultural defense arguments in domestic violence cases more generally, see Karin Wang, *Battered Asian American Women: Community Responses from the Battered Women's Movement and the Asian American Community*, 3 ASIAN L.J. 151 (1996); Leti Volpp, *(Mis)identifying Culture:*

Asian Women and the "Cultural Defense," 17 HARV. WOMEN'S L.J. 57 (1994); Nilda Rimonte, *A Question of Culture: Cultural Approval of Violence Against Women in the Pacific–Asian Community and the Cultural Defense,* 43 STAN. L. REV. 1311 (1991).

8. **Assessing the Credibility of Women of Color.** The challenge for jurors to understand why a victim behaves as she does may be significant when she is a woman of color or part of an immigrant community. This next case examines the admissibility of testimony about specific cultures and the problems that such testimony may present.

Minnesota v. Vue

Court of Appeals of Minnesota, 2000.
606 N.W.2d 719.

Appellant and M.V. are Hmong immigrants who came to the United States from Laos in the late 1970s. They were never legally married, but lived as husband and wife from 1980 through the mid-to-late 1990s, when their relationship deteriorated. In February 1998, M.V. obtained an order for protection against appellant.

On June 5, 1998, M.V. reported appellant to the police, claiming he had raped her four times in four separate incident.... Appellant was arrested and charged with four counts of criminal sexual conduct.

Before jury selection, the court and counsel had a preliminary discussion on the state's plan to introduce expert testimony on Hmong culture. The prosecutor noted that the jury pool's responses to questionnaires showed a poor understanding of Hmong culture. The prosecutor sought to introduce expert testimony to provide context for the jury's determinations of witness credibility.... The prosecutor described the scope of the proposed testimony and added that it could help explain M.V.'s delay in coming forward and rebut the defense theory that the allegations were rooted in M.V.'s jealousy of appellant's second wife. The defense objected to the proposed testimony....

At trial, M.V. testified about the clan structure of Hmong society, the hierarchy of leadership within the clan, and the role of Hmong women in choosing a husband. She said it was inappropriate in Hmong culture for individuals with family or clan-related problems to seek help from outside the clan and that she was being treated as an outcast for having reported her husband to the police. She claimed appellant had been threatening and abusive to her throughout their marriage and had forced her to have sex with him hundreds of times. She said she did not report the rapes earlier because of Hmong social pressure and because appellant said he would kill her if she did.

During a break in the state's case-in-chief, the court held a voir dire examination of the proposed expert witness, a white Minneapolis Park Police officer, and a hearing on the defense motion to exclude his testimony. On direct and cross-examination, the officer described his interest in and personal and professional exposure to Hmong culture.... [The court then allowed the testimony.]

As an example of a conflict between Hmong culture and the American legal system, the officer described a traditional marriage practice in which men "kidnap" young girls. Among other generalized statements, the state's expert testified that Southeast Asian victims are generally reluctant to report crimes. Speaking of Hmong culture, he testified in part:

> Well, as I indicated it is a male-dominated culture, very clearly. It's not the only culture that's male dominated, I might add, but it's very clear in Hmong culture. Women are to be obedient, to be silent, to suffer rather than to tell. Domestic abuse is a very private situation. I'm not even so sure if the abuse is shared with other women. I think it's kept very much internal.

On cross-examination, the officer stated that "male-dominance" was "fairly universal in the Hmong culture." In addition, the defense counsel asked and the expert responded as follows:

> Q: Are you suggesting that what male dominance really means is abuse?
>
> A: I have seen evidence—secondhand, I might add, maybe third-hand, not firsthand or I would have to act as a police officer—of male aggression within the Hmong community to keep the female in her place.
>
> Q: Are you saying that that is a general trait or are you saying that all Hmong traditional males are abusive?
>
> A: I've been around long enough to know that you can never make a statement that says all of anything will happen all of the time. I think there are patterns that can be identified over time and that that pattern is disturbing in the Hmong culture....

Appellant argues the expert testimony was inadmissible cultural stereotyping calculated to appeal to cultural and racial prejudice....

There is little in this record suggesting cultural testimony was necessary. The complainant was a grown woman; she was bilingual and educated; and she had been in the United States for many years. A lay jury would not have had trouble understanding or believing her testimony simply because she was Hmong. It is patronizing to suggest otherwise.... The expert testimony itself confirmed the lack of relevancy to this case and to this victim. The transcription shows the following questions and answers:

> Q: Are you saying then—and this is what I'm leading up to, Lieutenant—that all of the Hmong people in Minnesota are following the same cultural trends?
>
> A: I would not say that all Hmong follow the same cultural trends, but I would say that the Hmong culture that I've observed is slower to change than other cultures that I've observed.
>
> Q: Would you say that language is one reason why, at least in your observations, there has been a slower cultural change?

A: I would strongly agree that, *particularly among older Hmong citizens where English is nonexistent or very difficult at best.* I would say that the isolation that comes from not being able to go to a mall and shop and exchange normal conversation with shopkeepers or other people in society has kept Hmong women, in particular older Hmong women, prisoners in their homes.

(Emphasis added.)

Thus, the "expert's" cultural testimony emphasized the barriers on reporting "among older Hmong citizens where English is nonexistent or very difficult at best." This is not our case.

Further, the credentials of this Minneapolis Park Police officer to give expert opinions on Hmong culture are suspect. The record shows that the officer's contact with Hmong culture arose primarily from personal experience with family friends, that his exposure to Hmong culture as a police officer was limited, and that he had little or no academic training involving Hmong culture.

The "expert" testimony was inherently prejudicial. It went far beyond describing Hmong cultural practices that would help explain the alleged victim's behavior, *if* such testimony was needed. The testimony included generic statements about "male-dominance" in Hmong culture and directly implied a generalized perceived pattern of abuse of Hmong females by Hmong males. . . .

We conclude the prejudicial effect of the expert testimony about Hmong males' tendency to dominate and abuse their wives, and the tendency of Hmong wives not to want to report assaults, far outweighed any probative value. We find the district court abused its discretion in qualifying the expert and admitting his testimony.

NOTES AND QUESTIONS

1. **Understanding or Prejudice?** One of the conundrums in *State v. Vue* is whether some understanding of the victim's culture is necessary to help the jury understand her actions, or whether, by admitting the testimony, the jury might convict the defendant based on prejudice. But this can cut both ways: either culture made me do it, or I am guilty because of my culture. In both instances the court finds cultural evidence inappropriate. How did being Hmong shape the experiences of both the victim and the defendant? Did the testimony in question play on prejudice? Was any of this testimony helpful to the jury?

Native Americans

American Indian history and traditions offer a vision of male-female relationships quite different than the patriarchal model common to European, Asian and Latin American cultures. Here is a collection of testaments to that alternative, taken from the introduction to Gloria Valencia–Weber and Christine P. Zuni, *Domestic Violence and Tribal Protection of Indigenous Women in the United States*, 69 ST. JOHN'S L. REV. 69 (1995):

A man who battered his wife was considered irrational and thus could no longer lead a war party, a hunt, or participate in either. He could not be trusted to behave properly ... He was thought of as contrary to Lakota law and lost many privileges of life and many roles in Lakota society and the societies within the society.

What we do know is that in most Native American societies men's and women's roles were delineated in such a way that violence against women among their own groups did not seem to be a common and regular practice.

We were always taught that women were sacred and that everything in the home belonged to the women. Our extended families used to live together and no one would have ever thought of abusing women and children. It wasn't until families started to move into town or to move away from each other that we started to hear stories about someone beating up his wife.

Further evidence of this comes from the Navajo common law, explained in a piece by James W. Zion and Elsie B. Zion in *Hozho' Sokee'—Stay Together Nicely: Domestic Violence Under Navajo Common Law,* 25 ARIZ. ST. L.J. 407 (1993). They argue that the rise of domestic violence among the Navajo is a consequence of the disruption of traditional norms and practices caused by forced assimilation and the imposition of mainstream values and culture: "it exists in a climate of institutionalized violence, where traditional values of equality and harmony have been broken down, and new forces have caused people to lose hope and replace it with dependence and disharmony." The question posed by these authors is whether sufficient vitality remains in traditional Navajo institutions and cultural norms to promote culturally specific responses to domestic violence.

NOTES AND QUESTIONS

1. **The Severity of the Problem for Native Americans.** Despite cultural histories that stand in direct contrast to cultures premised on male privilege, American Indian and Alaska Native (AI/AN) women and men report higher rates of intimate partner violence than do women and men from other minority backgrounds. According to the United States Department of Justice, 37.5% of AI/AN women and 12.4% of AI/AN men are victimized by intimate partner violence in a lifetime, defined by rape, physical assault or stalking. These are the highest rates for any racial or ethnic groups, and more than twice the rate for white American women. About one in six violent victimizations among American Indians involved an offender who was an intimate or family member to the victim. *American Indians and Crime,* U.S. DEPT. OF JUSTICE, BUREAU OF JUSTICE STATISTICS, NCJ–173386 (February 1999).

2. **Jurisdictional Concerns over Non–Indians.** One of the questions we asked at the beginning of this chapter was whether the identity of the victim or the abuser impacted the availability of legal responses. In *Oliphant v. Suquamish Indian Tribe,* 435 U.S. 191 (1978), the Supreme Court ruled that Indian Nations lacked criminal jurisdiction over non-Indians

committing crimes in Indian Country. Statistics provided by Native American rights advocacy groups state that as many as 70% of reported crimes in Indian Country are committed by Non–Indians. Furthermore, between 1992–96, about 9 in 10 American Indian victims of rape or sexual assault had assailants who were either white or black. This means that tribal courts lack jurisdiction in a significant number of cases involving intimate partner violence against Native American women. Non–Indian misdemeanor crimes may often go unpunished due to a shortage of resources. U.S. Attorneys often focus on the most serious crimes. Additionally, many Native American women committed to tribal revitalization and adherence to tribal approaches may not desire to bring in outside agencies and may mistrust government law enforcement. Under these complex circumstances, crimes involving domestic violence by a Non–Indian perpetrator are unlikely to be prosecuted. Difficulties in prosecution may unfortunately exacerbate the problem of victimization by non-Indian perpetrators. For a discussion of these issues see Amy Radon, *Tribal Jurisdiction and Domestic Violence: The Need for Non–Indian Accountability on the Reservation*, 37 U. MICH. J.L. REFORM 1275 (2004).

The following case demonstrates the way one tribal court has dealt with the lack of criminal jurisdiction in domestic violence cases. In *Whiteagle–Fintak v. Fintak*, a case before the Ho–Chunk Nation Trial Court, the mother, Whiteagle–Fintak, and her daughter were enrolled members of the Ho–Chunk Nation and resided on the Ho–Chunk Nation Trust Land. Her husband, a Non–Indian, also resided on the Ho–Chunk Nation Trust Land. Whiteagle–Fintak filed for a protection order against Fintak and established that Fintak had engaged in a pattern of physical and mental abuse, including intimidation. The Court found that jurisdiction existed over the husband due to his residing on Ho–Chunk Nation Trust land. It found that the traditional laws of the Ho–Chunk Nation require respect between all people. This mandate includes a prohibition against physical violence and intimidation. Case summary available at The Tribal Law and Policy Institute, TRIBAL DOMESTIC VIOLENCE CASE LAW (2005). Case available at: http://Hochunknation.com/government/judicial/opinions/dv9901.htm.

3. **Native American Responses to Domestic Violence.** Several tribes have implemented programs that are viewed as promising by those who acknowledge that distinct cultural components are needed when addressing domestic violence in tribal communities. Such programs typically seek to heal the victim as well as provide legal services and protective shelters. Tribal programs for victims of domestic violence often also strive to provide cultural relevance while strengthening the victim's sense of tribal identity and connection to the tribal community. Providing cultural relevance means interweaving traditional tribal teachings, ceremonies, and native arts in response to domestic violence. Below is a short description of one such program:

> The Victim Services Program of the Sault Ste. Marie Tribe of Chippewa Indians has a very proactive approach to providing services to victims of crime ... Female victims of crime can attend a womens' talking circle, an educational group for victims of domestic violence,

sexual assault, and stalking. Native American teachings are incorporated into the group process. No victim is mandated to participate in ceremonies—however, the program expects all participants in the talking circles to show respect for traditional beliefs and practices. Other cultural activities include arts and crafts, sweat lodge ceremonies, and seasonal women's ceremonies. These activities are essential to the healing process because they help victims stay connected with their identity and community. Often, non-Native American programs cannot provide cultural services due to lack of funding or knowledge. Because of the connections that the Sault Ste. Marie Victim Services Program has in the community, the important needs of victims can be immediately addressed in a culturally competent manner. By using the traditional Chippewa culture, the program deals with the aftereffects of violence and works to help crime victims reintegrate into society. *Promising Practices in Indian Country,* U.S. DEPARTMENT OF JUSTICE, OFFICE FOR VICTIMS OF CRIME, NCJ–207019 (Nov. 2004).

Of course, it is difficult to assess the success of such programs. Because this program addresses only victims, it is important to ask whether programs that do not integrate some programs for the abuser can be successful in reducing violence within communities.

4. **Risk Factors, Including Poverty.** A common theme in many of the excepts you have read is the link between poverty and domestic violence. Think back to Michelle Decasas's article on risk factors for domestic violence among Hispanics. Also, in the materials in Chapter Two, the studies cited find that unemployment is a risk factor among all men, regardless of their race or ethnicity. Native Americans experience some of the most crushing poverty in the United States. A recent study of intimate partner violence among Americans in Oklahoma concluded the following:

Despite the variability in IPV (intimate partner violence) rates observed among studies of Native American women, findings suggest that, across tribes, Native American women experience up to two or three times more IPV than U.S. women in general. Many scholars contend that Western imperialism and its concomitant devaluation, exploitation, and abuse of Native peoples and Native American women, are largely responsible for the present day problem of violence against Native American women. Native peoples in the U.S. have been subject to a long, brutal history of colonization by the U.S. government, resulting in massive loss of lands and resources, and in severe disruption of traditional gender roles and family structures. One legacy of this colonization is that Native Americans have the highest poverty rate (24.5%) of all racial/ethnic groups in the United States.

The severely depressed socioeconomic conditions under which a disproportionate percentage of Native American families live may explain their higher IPV rates. Lorraine Halinka Malcoe, Bonnie M. Duran, and Juliann M. Montgomery, *Socioeconomic Disparities in Intimate Partner Violence Against Native American Women: A Cross–Sectional Study*, 2 BMC MEDICINE 20 (2004).

One of the consistent risk factors in the literature is unemployment or underemployment. The problems of unemployment are profound for Native Americans, especially those on reservations. In thinking about how we can respond to domestic violence, one of the most promising strategies may be to elevate the economic status of both males and females within a community. We now turn to the intersection of race, ethnicity and poverty.

Race and Culture Intersect

The next reading considers whether women are able to reach out from their particular communities to the larger society for assistance in dealing with intimate partner violence, and how the larger society responds to those requests. The author, Kimberle Crenshaw, describes how gender, race and culture intersect to produce contextualized responses to abuse. Crenshaw first developed the concept of "intersectionality" to describe how race and gender interact to shape the employment experiences of Black women. Kimberle Crenshaw, *Demarginalizing the Intersection of Race and Sex: A Black Feminist Critique of Antidiscrimination Doctrine, Feminist Theory and Antiracist Politics,* 1989 U. CHI. LEGAL F. 139 (1989). In the excerpt below, she applies that analysis to the experience of domestic violence.

Kimberle Crenshaw
Mapping the Margins: Intersectionality, Identity Politics, and Violence Against Women of Color

43 STAN. L. REV. 1241 (1991).

Structural Intersectionality and Battering

I observed the dynamics of structural intersectionality during a brief field study of battered women's shelters located in minority communities in Los Angeles.... Many women who seek protection are unemployed or underemployed, and a good number of them are poor. Shelters serving these women cannot afford to address only the violence inflicted by the batterer; they must also confront the other multilayered and routinized forms of domination that often converge in these women's lives, hindering their ability to create alternatives to the abusive relationships that brought them to shelter in the first place. Many women of color, for example, are burdened by poverty, child care responsibilities, and the lack of job skills. These burdens, largely the consequence of gender and class oppression, are then compounded by the racially discriminatory employment and housing practices women of color often face, as well as by the disproportionately high unemployment among people of color that makes battered women of color less able to rely on the support of friends and relatives for temporary shelter.

When systems of race, gender and class domination converge ... interventions based solely on the experiences of women who do not share the same class or race backgrounds will be of limited help to women who because of race and class face different obstacles. ...

Political Intersectionality

The concept of political intersectionality highlights the fact that women of color are situated within at least two subordinated groups that frequently pursue conflicting political agendas. The need to split one's political energies between two sometimes opposing groups is a dimension of intersectional disempowerment that men of color and white women seldom confront. Indeed, their specific race and gendered experiences, although intersectional, often define as well as confine the interests of the entire group. For example, racism as experienced by people of color who are of a particular gender—male—tends to determine the parameters of antiracist strategies, just as sexism as experienced by women who are of a particular race—white—tends to ground the women's movement. The problem is not simply that both discourses fail women of color by not acknowledging the "additional" issue of race or of patriarchy but that the discourses are often inadequate even to the discrete tasks of articulating the full dimensions of racism and sexism. Because women of color experience racism in ways not always the same as those experienced by men of color and sexism in ways not always parallel to experiences of white women, antiracism and feminism are limited, even on their own terms.

. . . The failure of feminism to interrogate race means that the resistance strategies of feminism will often replicate and reinforce the subordination of people of color, and the failure of antiracism to interrogate patriarchy means that antiracism will frequently reproduce the subordination of women. These mutual elisions present a particularly difficult political dilemma for women of color. Adopting either analysis constitutes a denial of a fundamental dimension of our subordination and precludes the development of a political discourse that more fully empowers women of color.

A. The Politicization of Domestic Violence

That the political interests of women of color are obscured and sometimes jeopardized by political strategies that ignore or suppress intersectional issues is illustrated by my experiences in gathering information for this article. I attempted to review Los Angeles Police Department statistics reflecting the rate of domestic violence interventions by precinct because such statistics can provide a rough picture of arrests by racial group, given the degree of racial segregation in Los Angeles. L.A.P.D., however, would not release the statistics. A representative explained that one reason the statistics were not released was that domestic violence activists both within and outside the Department feared that statistics reflecting the extent of domestic violence in minority communities might be selectively interpreted and publicized so as to undermine long-term efforts to force the Department to address domestic violence as a serious problem. I was told that activists were worried that the statistics might permit opponents to dismiss domestic violence as a minority problem and, therefore, not deserving of aggressive action.

The informant also claimed that representatives from various minority communities opposed the release of the statistics. They were concerned, apparently, that the data would unfairly represent Black and Brown communities as unusually violent, potentially reinforcing stereotypes that might be used in attempts to justify oppressive police tactics and other discriminatory practices. These misgivings are based on the familiar and not unfounded premise that certain minority groups—especially Black men—have already been stereotyped as uncontrollably violent. Some worry that attempts to make domestic violence an object of political action may only serve to confirm such stereotypes and undermine efforts to combat negative beliefs about the Black community.

1. Domestic violence and antiracist politics.

Within communities of color, efforts to stem the politicization of domestic violence are often grounded in attempts to maintain the integrity of the community. The articulation of this perspective takes different forms. Some critics allege that feminism has no place within communities of color, that the issues are internally divisive, and that they represent the migration of white women's concerns into a context in which they are not only irrelevant but also harmful. At its most extreme, this rhetoric denies that gender violence is a problem in the community and characterizes any effort to politicize gender subordination as itself a community problem....

... People of color often must weigh their interests in avoiding issues that might reinforce distorted public perceptions against the need to acknowledge and address intracommunity problems. Yet the cost of suppression is seldom recognized in part because the failure to discuss the issue shapes perceptions of how serious the problem is in the first place....

The political imperatives of a narrowly focused antiracist strategy support other practices that isolate women of color. For example, activists who have attempted to provide support services to Asian-and African–American women report intense resistance from those communities. At other times, cultural and social factors contribute to suppression. Nilda Rimonte, director of Everywoman's Shelter in Los Angeles, points out that in the Asian community, saving the honor of the family from shame is a priority. Unfortunately, this priority tends to be interpreted as obliging women not to scream rather than obliging men not to hit.

Race and culture contribute to the suppression of domestic violence in other ways as well. Women of color are often reluctant to call the police, a hesitancy likely due to a general unwillingness among people of color to subject their private lives to the scrutiny and control of a police force that is frequently hostile. There is also a more generalized community ethic against public intervention, the product of a desire to create a private world free from the diverse assaults on the public lives of racially subordinated people. The home ... may ... function as a safe haven from the indignities of life in a racist society. However, but for this "safe haven" in many cases, women of color victimized by violence might otherwise seek help.

There is also a general tendency within antiracist discourse to regard the problem of violence against women of color as just another manifestation of racism. In this sense, the relevance of gender domination within the community is reconfigured as a consequence of discrimination against men. Of course, it is probably true that racism contributes to the cycle of violence, given the stress that men of color experience in dominant society. It is therefore more than reasonable to explore the links between racism and domestic violence. But the chain of violence is more complex and extends beyond this single link. Racism is linked to patriarchy to the extent that racism denies men of color the power and privilege that dominant men enjoy. When violence is understood as an acting-out of being denied male power in other spheres, it seems counterproductive to embrace constructs that implicitly link the solution to domestic violence to the acquisition of greater male power.... [W]hile understanding links between racism and domestic violence is an important component of any effective intervention strategy, it is also clear that women of color need not await the ultimate triumph over racism before they can expect to live violence-free lives.

2.   Race and the domestic violence lobby.

   ... Efforts to politicize the issue of violence against women challenge beliefs that violence occurs only in the homes of "others." While it is unlikely that advocates and others who adopt this rhetorical strategy intend to exclude or ignore the needs of poor and colored women, the underlying premise of this seemingly universalistic appeal is to keep the sensibilities of dominant social groups focused on the experiences of those groups. Indeed, as subtly suggested by the opening comments of Senator David Boren (D.Okla.) in support of the Violence Against Women Act of 1991, the displacement of the "other" as the presumed victim of domestic violence works primarily as a political appeal to rally white elites. Boren said:

> Violent crimes against women are not limited to the streets of the inner cities, but also occur in homes in the urban and rural areas across the country.
>
> Violence against women affects not only those who are actually beaten and brutalized, but indirectly affects all women. Today, our wives, mothers, daughters, sisters, and colleagues are held captive by fear generated from these violent crimes—held captive not for what they do or who they are, but solely because of gender.

Rather than focusing on and illuminating how violence is disregarded when the home is "othered," the strategy implicit in Senator Boren's remarks functions instead to politicize the problem only in the dominant community.... The experience of violence by minority women is ignored, except to the extent it gains white support for domestic violence programs in the white community.

   ... The point here is not that the Violence Against Women Act is particularistic on its own terms, but that unless the Senators and other policymakers ask why violence remained insignificant as long as it was understood as a minority problem, it is unlikely that women of color will share equally in the distribution of resources and concern.... As long as attempts to politicize domestic violence focus on convincing whites that this is not a "minority" problem but their problem, any authentic and sensitive attention to the experiences of Black and other minority women probably will continue to be regarded as jeopardizing the movement.

NOTES AND QUESTIONS

1. **Reluctance to Summon the Police.** The reluctance on the part of women from immigrant or minority communities to summon police to their homes in response to domestic violence is widely documented. In part that reluctance may have to do with community norms of honor and shame, but distrust of law enforcement is another strong and widely held sentiment. These issues are further discussed in the Chapter Seven.

2. **Reluctance to Seek Services.** Just as language and cultural barriers may play a part in the failure of women to seek police assistance, so too, may they prevent women from seeking other services. Shelters may not have multilingual capacity, and may offer living or eating arrangements that are culturally alien, or violate cultural or religious norms. An Orthodox Jewish woman, to give just one example, may not be able to keep kosher in the shelter. Common shelter rules that preclude women from having contact with anyone outside the shelter for an initial period (often 72 hours) may leave a woman whose sense of herself is embedded in extended family and community more thoroughly disoriented and traumatized than did the violent incident that brought her to shelter. Mainstream American culture is a good deal more conversant and comfortable with the therapeutic paradigm than other cultures, which may depend more heavily on informal support networks. Ironically, of course, taking advantage of those informal networks may require staying within the community, and not "betraying" it, or the abuser, by disclosing abuse to the authorities.

    Can you identify other possible ways in which language and cultural barriers might impede access to medical and legal assistance as well as to public benefits?

Religion

People's lives are shaped by a multitude of experiences, including their personal spiritual beliefs and their participation in religious communities. Each religion, in both its spiritual texts and its teachings, will often have messages about the role of women and its tolerance of domestic violence. The problem with examining religious text, be it the Bible, the Qur'an, or some other sacred document, is that language is open to a multitude of interpretations, and thus can be used to justify whatever position one takes. This is true whether one practices a traditional religion, such as Christianity or Judaism, or whether one practices a non-traditional religion, such as Hatian Vodou, described in a note below.

Our inquiry focuses on how one's religious beliefs and associations with religious communities impact one's experiences with domestic violence. Just as Puerto Rican women are influenced by their culture, their culture is also shaped by religious beliefs. In turn, religion may itself isolate victims, or be a source of resistance. Thus, when answering the questions, "why doesn't she leave?" it is imperative to ask both what religious beliefs, and what cultural and legal expressions of those believes further complicate already complicated lives.

The readings highlight two questions. First, how does discrimination against a religious community affect the internal dynamics within that community relative to domestic violence? Could it be that the stress of discrimination makes intimate violence more likely? Second, how do internal religious beliefs and customs act as both a source of oppression and as a source of resistance? In the following excerpt, Azizha al-Hibri discusses the impact of discrimination against American Muslims.

Azizah Y. al–Hibri
An Islamic Perspective on Domestic Violence
27 FORDHAM INT'L L.J. 195 (2003).

The impact of September 11, 2001, on the American Muslim community has been both severe and multi-faceted. It ranged from sadness regarding mass deaths to civil rights concerns that caused a significant number of immigrants to leave the United States altogether. The threat of sudden raids at home and at work, detentions, the use of secret evidence, profiling, and registration under the National Security Entry–Exit Registration System ("NSEERS") program, are only some of the recent developments that gave rise to these concerns. In the raids, which took place in Northern Virginia in the spring of 2002, women whose homes and offices were raided suffered severe trauma, and some sought counseling to overcome the ordeal.

American Muslim men suffered greater trauma because they suddenly became suspects. For example, the NSEERS program was directed at men from several Muslim countries between the ages of sixteen and forty-five. This registration program resulted in an unexpectedly large number of arrests based usually on no more than technical violations of immigration law that rendered the registrant "out of status." These arrests led to detentions, separation of family members, and a great deal of anxiety. The freezing of Muslim charities' bank accounts and the arrest of leading, as well as obscure Muslim men around the country, only served to increase communal insecurity, especially among the male Muslim population.

These mass communal problems have trickled down to impact the American Muslim family. Generally, Muslim men and women closed ranks in these difficult times and concentrated on constructively addressing their familial and communal affairs. As a result, the American Muslim community has experienced a new awakening and a determination to become an active part of the American democratic process. In some cases, however, the cumulative effect of fear, frustration, experiences of discrimination, and job insecurity, bled into the Muslim family. Where latent problems of domestic violence already existed, the new pressures made the situation worse.

NOTES AND QUESTIONS

1. **The Impact of Discrimination.** How does discrimination against religious minorities impact communities? Al–Hibri suggests discrimination

against males in a community may thus lead to more pressures at home, making domestic violence more likely. Similarly, within Jewish culture, there can be an "us v. them" mentality which can isolate victims.

> Some Jews, especially observant Jews, possess an "us versus them" mentality with regard to the secular world. Years of general anti-Semitic thoughts and feelings foster a belief that Jews should stick together and keep what happens to Jews within their own communities at all costs. The need to band together against the outsider led to the development of a society that attempts to maintain the pretenses of having no internal strife or dissention. Stacey A. Guthartz, *Domestic Violence and the Jewish Community,* 11 MICH.GENDER & L. 27 (2004).

Gutharz raises an interesting question as to the impact that discrimination from the dominant culture may have on minority communities with regard to their intimate relationships. Gutharz suggests that when Jews feel oppressed, they may be less likely to acknowledge the presence of domestic violence in their homes. In this next excerpt, she explains how shame can also isolate abused Jewish women. As you read this excerpt, think back to Karin Wang's description of how Asian women strive to "keep face."

Stacey A. Guthartz
Domestic Violence and the Jewish Community
11 MICH. J. GENDER & L. 27 (2004).

. . . Another concept that contributes to abused women's isolation is shondeh, a disgrace. Both secular and Jewish women often experience a sense of shame from being abused. "The Jewish community reinforces battered women's embarrassment and self-blame by calling abuse a shanda, blaming women for causing or not preventing it in their own home." Shame as a Jewish concept is explained by Lipshutz, Kaufman and Setel:

> The issue of shame in the Jewish community is a complicated one. So vulnerable to the random violence of surrounding cultures for so long, Jews still have the fear of looking "bad" to others. Throughout our history, Jews have often dealt with community dysfunction by flatly denying that problems such as spousal abuse, addiction and incest even existed. We idealized our homes as refuges from a hostile, anti-Semitic world. For generations of Jewish women and children, the abuse suffered within those families was hidden or even viewed as acceptable. Now that victims and survivors have demanded these issues no longer be ignored, they are sometimes blamed for "airing dirty laundry" or bringing shame on the community. Sadly, women victims often have a similar experience: When they take the courageous step of leaving an abusive relationship, they may be perceived as betraying the Jewish ideals of family and marital fidelity.

The notion of "airing dirty laundry" remains present today in such a force that it can work to sabotage domestic violence agencies and outreach centers' efforts to combat domestic abuse. One agency attempted to reach abused Jewish women by hanging posters at the mikveh. The posters were consistently torn down by individuals who do not want domestic violence discussed in the open.

A woman may not keep silent for her shame alone, as children are affected by the shondeh of domestic violence as well. These women know that exposing flaws comes with a certain amount of danger, including jeopardizing the children's chances of marriage.

[I]n some cultures, such as the Orthodox community where marriages are initiated by a shidduch (matchmaking) a young man or woman from a home where there was known to be abuse may not be considered favorable for a shidduch. Knowledge in the community of significant discord within the home may stigmatize the children, hence the penchant for secrecy....

Statistics show that Jewish women stay in abusive relationships longer than non-Jewish women. This difference is not surprising considering the religious traditions and mythology surrounding Jews and Jewish women in particular. A Jewish woman who seeks to divorce her husband may further entrap herself in the cycle of abuse, since according to Jewish law, a halachically valid marriage can generally only be dissolved in two ways: through the documented death of one of the partners, or by the husband issuing a get to his wife. The get, a document of divorce, releases the woman from the man. A wife cannot deliver the get to her husband, and much controversy exists as to whether a beit din, religious court, may terminate, dissolve, or annul a marriage. Though the wife must consent to a divorce, the get must be initiated by the husband. When a husband refuses to give his wife a get, or, if he is presumed dead but there is no proof of his death, the wife becomes an agunah.

An agunah is a "bound" woman: chained or anchored to the husband to whom she no longer wishes to be married. Agunot are not permitted to remarry under Jewish law. If an agunah were to remarry or cohabitate with another man, it would be considered an adulterous relationship. Any children born of such a relationship are mamzerim. Mamzerim, loosely translated as illegitimate, are severely stigmatized under Jewish law. For example, a mamzer is generally permitted to marry only another mamzer.

Often a husband will agree to a get in exchange for the woman giving up her rights to custody of the children, alimony, child support, the family home, etc. Because Jewish law does not recognize civil marriage or civil divorce, the woman is at the mercy of her husband and his extortive measures if she wants a religious end to her marriage....

NOTES AND QUESTIONS

1. **Further Readings.** In 1995, Beverly Horsburgh wrote one of the first articles discussing domestic violence in the Jewish community. She argued that battering was largely ignored in the Jewish community despite its prevalence. She called for an end to what she termed "intragroup oppression" that manifested in culture that fosters the mistreatment of women. See Beverly Horsburgh, *Lifting the Veil of Secrecy: Domestic Violence in the*

Jewish Community, 18 Harv. Women's L.J. 171 (1995). A decade later, in her analysis of attitudes and awareness among Jews in Austin, Texas, Lydia Belzer found that while many had come to acknowledge the problem, few knew of resources that were available. She suggests that the challenge is to continue raising awareness. Lydia M. Belzer, *Toward True Shalom Bayit: Acknowledging Domestic Abuse in the Jewish Community and What to Do About It,* 11 Cardozo Women's L.J. 241 (2005).

2.   **Comparative Perspectives.** Because many Arab and Muslim women are recent immigrants to the United States, it is helpful to understand the cultures from which they have come. For an excellent article on comparative domestic violence law see, Lisa Hajjar, *Religion, State Power, and Domestic Violence in Muslim Societies: A Framework for Comparative Analysis,* 29 Law & Soc. Inquiry 1 (2004). Hajjar points out that in many Muslim countries, there is resistance to accepting any international human rights norms that would expand women's rights. The belief that women's rights are anti-Islam resonates throughout the Muslim world.

3.   **Parting Ways.** Stacey Guthartz explains how Jewish women can enter marriages with the understanding that those marriages can only be dissolved according to Jewish law. The same issue can exist for Muslim women who, as Azizah Y. al-Hibri puts it, seek to part ways with their husbands. Many Muslim women who reside in the United States believe that divorce is the right of a man, not a woman. Further, many reject the idea that abuse is grounds for divorce. Many Muslim women do not believe in divorce, nor do they see it as their right.

Even for those wishing a divorce, one complication Muslim women may face in leaving an abusive relationship is the use of arbitration agreements, which are often entered into by the parties at the start of a marriage, similar to a prenuptial contract. In an effort to accommodate religious beliefs in the family law context, pre-marital arbitration agreements that provide for the settlement of any disagreements by an arbiter (chosen by the parties) who is familiar with the traditions of Sharia Law are sometimes entered into by Muslim citizens of the United States or Canada. These are similar to the ones Jewish enter into as a means of insuring that marital relationships and family matters conform to their religious doctrine.

Such "voluntary" agreements have been upheld by courts. For example, in *Jabri v. Qaddura,* a Texas court indicated that an arbitration agreement providing for the resolution of the disputes, including the divorce itself and child custody, by a "Texas Islamic Court" with a panel of appointed Islamic arbiters, was valid and binding. *Jabri v. Qaddura,* 108 S.W.3d 404 (Tex. App. 2003). In this case, the court showed particularly high deference to the arbitration agreement. States and provinces within the United States and Canada typically allow the resolution of civil matters through private contractual arbitration agreements.

Since the constitutions of the United States and Canada protect both freedom of religion and equality rights of all residents from infringements by the state, there may be considerable tension when applying Islamic laws, which may not be found to protect the state's interest in certain family law situations or the equality rights of women, especially in the context of divorce proceedings. Generally, arbitration agreements are allowed to accommodate religious diversity, nevertheless, constitutional protections offered to minorities and federal statutory protections have usually taken precedence over arbitration agreements if the agreements do not offer the full protections provided for by constitutional provisions and federal statutory law. For examples of how a balancing test is typically applied in the family law context when dealing with binding arbitration agreements, state interests, and religious freedoms see, *Glauber v. Glauber*, 600 N.Y.S.2d 740 (N.Y.A.D. 2nd Dept. 1993) and, *Rideout v. Riendeau*, 761 A.2d 291 (Me. 2000). While courts will usually not uphold provisions that are contrary to public policy, the deference given to arbitration agreements is determined by individual state/provincial law and the individual interpretations of family law judges. In the *Jabri* case, the Texas court opted to not review the provisions even though it encompassed issues of the high state interest including child custody and the best interests of the children. Instead, the court gave full deference to the arbitration agreement within the family law context, as long as the agreement covered the arising dispute in unambiguous language and "a meeting of the minds" occurred at the time the agreement was entered into.

Consider the potential problems that may occur as a result of such high deference for arbitration agreements in the context of ensuring a woman's rights and interests are adequately protected, especially in cases involving domestic violence. In Natasha Bakht's article, *Family Arbitration Using Sharia Law: Examining Ontario's Arbitration Act and its Impact on Women*, 1 MUSLIM WORLD JOURNAL OF HUMAN RIGHTS (2004), she raises the concerns that due to the private nature of arbitration, courts will not be aware of provisions that do not meet legal standards unless a case is brought for review. Furthermore, Bakht stresses that challenging a binding arbitration agreement may be the source of tremendous personal conflict for an Islamic woman who may lack financial resources and perhaps, even more significantly, feel under tremendous pressure to abide by the terms of the agreement, believing she must do so in order to honor her religious beliefs.

Arbitration agreements may afford Islamic women far less protection than they would be offered under either state or federal law. There is also concern regarding the "meeting of the minds" that presumably must occur for an arbitration agreement to be held valid. In situations where an arbitration agreement will govern the marital relationship it is important to consider whether most Islamic women entering into such agreements receive sound legal advice beforehand, especially if their relationship was abusive from the beginning.

Finally, will Islamic women who enter into arbitration agreements have adequate access to a fair divorce? Consider the type of limitations that may arise from the existence of an arbitration agreement and the type of pressure Islamic women may face within their faith community and from spiritual leaders to conform to Islamic law even if their mental or physical well-being are endangered. Conversely, consider the benefits of accommodating religious practices and allowing for expressions of communal values. Many societies do not emphasize individual rights to an extent or in a manner that conforms to American notions of liberty and personal freedom. Some societies choose to emphasize adherence to spiritual doctrine and focus upon the well-being and preservation of the community and communal values. Is there room for women with strong religious convictions to put their faith above their own personal needs? For a discussion of arbitration sessions, see Nooria Faizi, *Domestic Violence in the Muslim Community*, 10 TEX. J. WOMEN & L. 209 (2001).

4. **Help for Abused Women from the Muslim Community.** As is the case for Jewish women and other women in tight-knit communities, many fear gossip or that they will bring shame to both the family and to Islam when seeking help for abuse. This problem may be even greater for Muslim women, who often see the help available to them as incompatible with their Islamic beliefs. Such feelings may be even stronger after September 11, 2001, where fear of American authorities may be even greater than the fear of intimate violence. The following excerpt describes one program that addresses these concerns:

> Atlanta has an impressive program established to help battered Muslim women. The Baitul Salaam [House of Peace] Network has existed for more than four years. The network includes a shelter and counseling services and provides referral services for women across the country. The program is funded by grants from private foundations, private donors, and a work program with the Aramark Corporation. The women provide temporary labor as concession stand workers at Turner Field, home of the Atlanta Braves, and Baitul Salaam receives a flat rate fee per worker for their services.
>
> General safety planning is conducted with all women, and neither confidentiality nor safety has been a problem to date. The shelter maintains close contacts with the Imams in the area, and male Muslim volunteers assist in checking the premises periodically. The major differences between non-Muslim shelters and the Baitul Salaam shelter are accommodations for prayer, privacy, and dietary requirements. At the Baitul Salaam shelter, basic Islamic guidelines are enforced. Women who come to the shelter are informed that prayers are established, but no one is forced to participate. There is a curfew of 9:00 p.m., but some accommodations are made for those whose jobs require them to stay past that time. The women are given the freedom to practice their religion as they deem appropriate. Baitul Salaam has an open-door policy, and about twenty percent of the women who have accessed the shelter have been non-Muslims. However, these women understand that none of the rules will be compromised because of them. Nooria Faizi, *Domestic Violence in the Muslim Community*, 10 TEX. J. WOMEN & L. 209 (2001).

We have read about many different groups who may have particular needs and concerns. One question to consider is whether each of those groups should have their own shelters. How might shelters in communities such as religious communities provide a change in the general culture of acceptance for abuse? Do we need a specific shelter for every minority group, or is there some value in having women from different backgrounds identify their common struggles? Does providing shelter then require women to flee? Why should not the abuser be the one to leave the home?

5. **Progressive Religious Movements.** In her article, *What's God Got to Do with It? Church and State Collaboration in the Subordination of Women and Domestic Violence*, 51 RUTGERS L. REV. 1207 (1999) Linda Ammons is particularly concerned about the ways in which Judeo–Christian teachings sought to control women's sexuality through sanctions, including violence, and is critical of how religion has often been used to justify violence against women. However, many clergy and religious communities actively work to end domestic violence against women. Consider the thoughts of one feminist theologian:

> The Church must teach clearly and consistently, and the average person must understand what the Church is teaching: that there is absolutely no Biblical or theological justification for domestic abuse. The Church must stress that enforced dominance and subordination in intimate relationships stands in fundamental opposition to the vision of creation presented in both the Hebrew Scriptures and the Christian New Testament. Only then will significant progress be made toward changing the moral climate that condones abuse. Reverend Katherine Hancock Ragsdale, *The Role of Religious Institutions in Responding to the Domestic Violence Crisis*, 58 ALB. L. REV. 1149 (1995).

6. **Religious Resistance to Violence in Other Countries.** Earlier in this chapter you read an excerpt about domestic violence in Haiti. Now consider how religion in that country is being used to combat the problem and think about how such religious-based strategies can be implemented in the United States among immigrant communities.

> Haitian Vodou is a religious tradition that grew in part as a resistance to slavery, with the core understanding that every person has worth and dignity. Vodouisants acknowledge one creator God who becomes known to people through the spirits, lwa, each of whom manifest a different attribute of God or the world. The teachings of Vodou are centered around relationships where the lwa are part of the community through ceremonies in which they possess their devotees. Priests (Houngan) and priestesses (Mambo) are central to inviting the spirits into the community life and serve as interpreters of spiritual meaning. The central belief permeating all of Vodou theology is that God creates all people equal. Women play important roles of expression in Vodou, and serve as spiritual leaders.

> The fundamental beliefs in Vodou theology run counter to the misogynist culture in Haiti. The core beliefs that people are created equal are antithetical to domestic violence because violence denies the relationship each individual person has with the spirits and their value within the community. Religious and community leaders are beginning grassroots movements to spread this message throughout Haiti. For example, female spirits in Vodou have begun to tell the stories of women's lives from their point of view, and thus address issues of

violence. However, spreading this message is challenging given that Vodou has no governing structure and over half the population of Haiti cannot read or write. Therefore, the impact of individual leaders' rejection of domestic violence has been extremely localized. Mary Clark, *Domestic Violence in the Haitian Culture and the American Legal Response,* U. Miami Inter-Am. L. Rev. 297 (2006).

7. **Religious Attitudes and Attendance at Services.** Does being religious make it more or less likely one will become a victim or perpetrator of domestic violence? Some research suggests that men who hold much more conservative ideological views than their partners are especially likely to perpetuate domestic violence. Yet, women who attend regular religious services are less likely to self-report domestic violence, and men who attend religious services on a weekly basis also appear less likely to be abusive. See Christopher G. Ellison, John Barthowski and Kristen L. Anderson, *Are There Religious Variations in Domestic Violence?*, 20 J. of Family Issues 87 (1999); Christopher G. Ellison and Kristin L. Anderson, *Religious Involvement and Domestic Violence Among U.S. Couples,* 40 Journal for the Scientific Study of Religion 269 (2001).

C.   Teens, Elders, and Individuals with Disabilities as Victims of Domestic Violence

Age and intimate violence

In this next section we explore how domestic violence affects people throughout their lives. What is the relationship between domestic violence, age, and battering? The following excerpt begins to explore that question.

Cheryl Hanna
Sex Before Violence: Girls, Dating Violence, and (Perceived) Sexual Autonomy

33 Fordham Urb. L.J. 437 (2006).

Throughout [a woman's] life, as long as one is in an intimate relationship, one is always at some risk of domestic violence. Whether someone is fourteen or eighty years old, the primary reason one engages in verbal, physical, or sexual abuse against an intimate partner is a desire for control. Violence is often triggered by sexual conflict, sexual jealousy, or a fear that the relationship is changing or will end. The context for domestic violence is intimacy—both sexual and emotional. Yet, one of the reasons we often "miss" the young and the elderly in our analysis of domestic violence is that our culture denies that the young and the elderly engage in the kinds of romantic or sexual relationships that can lead to violence.

We often misconstrue violence by young people as being something other than domestic violence. We may attribute violence in dating relationships to individual social problems, or we may minimize it as innocent horseplay. It is telling that among the volumes of legal academic literature on domestic violence, for example, few articles focus specifically on adolescent dating relationships.

Similarly, there is a popular misunderstanding that violence among the elderly is triggered by "caregiver" stress. When abuse happens in the context of an intimate relationship, however, it is almost always an outgrowth of domestic violence. Once an elderly couple reaches a certain age, we label it "elder abuse" when, in fact, it is the similar pattern of domestic abuse that we see among younger couples. The overall pattern of behavior in violent relationships is similar regardless of the age of the abuser or the victim.

One might speculate that older women experience more violence than younger women, because older women are likely to take less advantage of the available legal and social interventions and to maintain more traditional views of domestic violence as a private family matter. Their spouses, too, would arguably be more likely to have come of age in a time when it was considered acceptable, or at least not punishable, to batter one's spouse. Yet, violent crime data shows that the young are more likely to engage in violence, including domestic violence. Data from the Federal Bureau of Investigation Uniform Crime Reports shows that, between 1996 and 2001, there were 5,148 incidents of domestic abuse perpetrated by a significant other against someone over age sixty-five. In contrast, there were 47,000 domestic violence incidents perpetrated by a significant other against someone under the age of eighteen. This suggests that the older one gets without experiencing violence, the less likely he or she will become a victim of it.

The earlier in her life a woman is exposed to violence or becomes violent, the more likely she is to continue those patterns of abuse throughout her life, and the more likely she is to experience a host of other social problems, including an increased likelihood of ending up in the criminal justice system. Yet, most of our legal and social strategies have focused almost exclusively on adults. By the time these adults end up in the criminal justice system, they may already have long histories of violence within their relationships. Thus, early intervention could be an effective strategy for reducing intimate violence both by and against women. In turn, such intervention could reduce women's exposure to the criminal justice system.

Teen Dating Violence

The next reading looks at one teen's experience with violence in a dating relationship.

Cynthia Rodriguez
Cynthia's Story

3 WHITTIER J. CHILD & FAM. ADVOC. 123 (2003).

My name is Cynthia Rodriguez and I am a client of Break the Cycle. I want to share my story with you. It is a story about surviving dating violence and finding a future of hope. I think it's important to share this story because so many people are blindfolded and don't realize that this abuse is life-threatening and very common. But those things are all true.

I never imagined this could happen to me. I remember how my health teacher talked to my class about domestic violence, but I was just like "Okay, what does this have to do with me? That's never going to happen to me." But it did happen.

I met a guy in my high school and we started dating. Things were great in the beginning. He was my first boyfriend and I thought that nothing could go wrong. He was so perfect, or so I thought. He would follow me around everywhere like a puppy. He would never let me leave his sight. I thought it was so cute.

But slowly he isolated me from everyone. He started telling me sweetly that he felt uncomfortable for me to be talking to other guys at school. He wanted me to be with him and only him. I wasn't allowed to talk to anyone or have any friends because he would tell me that they were bad people.

He would also verbally abuse me by calling me names that made me feel bad. He abused me emotionally by making me believe that I was the one to blame for his behavior. I was the one that made him do those awful things to me. It was all my fault. When I would try to break up with him he would beg for my forgiveness, promise me that he would never hit me again. He always told me that I was the only one that he had in his life, that his family didn't care for him, that only I could help him and change him to become a better person. And I would give into him, and didn't leave him.

His behavior towards me became physically violent and out of control. He would hurt me by hitting me. He would also pick me up and force me down on concrete benches at school. He would push me, and then jerk me back by my ponytail.

It seemed to me that he had a double personality. He had the loving caring side and he also had the scary demonic side that I feared so much. I never knew which one was going to be with me every time he was around. I would always try my hardest to keep the nice one around by doing everything right, not looking up, always looking down, never talking to people and of course always wearing baggy clothes, always doing what he said because I wanted to be a perfect girlfriend, and keep the nice guy around. But I always seemed to say or do something wrong that brought out the demon and I got slapped, or my hair got pulled because I was the bad one. He always told me I was the one who forced him to do this to me.

So many times I lied to my friends telling them that everything was good and how wonderful my boyfriend was because I was so embarrassed to tell them otherwise. We were one of the cutest couples at school and I didn't want anyone to think otherwise. Every time I got the strength inside of me to stand up to him and leave him he would cry and say that I was the only thing he had, that without me he was nothing, that he would kill himself or that he would kill me. He would get on his knees begging for me to please stay. From crying he would go to screaming and being violent. He would use all in his power to change my mind not to leave him. I was so scared for him and of what he would do to himself or to me. Sometimes I didn't feel like I wanted to be alive.

We had been going out for one year and two months when I realized that I couldn't take it anymore and that the demon had built a fence around me. He wanted me to believe that I was his property and without him I was nothing. I was tired of believing that. My body couldn't take the abuse anymore and my mind couldn't take the manipulation.

He started to sense that I was planning on leaving him. It seemed like he could sense it so he became more violent. I remember on one occasion I refused to say I love you to him so he pulled my hair and slapped me and threw me against a wall and he grabbed me by my neck. My feet were off the ground. I couldn't breathe at all. In his eyes I could see an anger that terrified me. Suddenly he let me go. I was on the floor trying to breathe. He started to cry saying he was sorry. But I was tired of it. I saw myself in the mirror. My cheek was cut and bleeding from when he threw me against the wall and my eyes were so red. That's when I realized that enough was enough.

By this point, he was stalking me, walking around my school trying to keep an eye on me, coming after school to interrogate me—why have I not answered his phone calls, why was I acting like I didn't care for him anymore? He came to my house and wouldn't leave until I went outside and talked to him, or else he would make a scene. I didn't want my mom and neighbors to hear him screaming at me and calling me names, so I would talk to him. Everywhere that I went, he was there. He would seem to find me anywhere that I would go or try to run away from him.

I remembered my nice health teacher, and she had talked to us about domestic violence. So I immediately looked for her on my school campus and I found her and told her everything that had happened to me, and she helped me a lot and gave me the number for Break the Cycle. I called the same day and met an attorney at Break the Cycle. She helped me get a domestic violence restraining order, and helped me through the process and made me feel really comforted. She really gave me a lot of strength to go through with the restraining order. Another attorney there gave me support too. I'm really thankful that I met both of them because without them I would still be suffering the violence and probably wouldn't be alive right now. I wouldn't be alive now to tell you that Break the Cycle helped me to break the cycle of being abused. And I'm thankful that this organization is there to support people that get abused because this organization really does make a difference. It saved my life and I'm sure it has saved and will save many more.

NOTES AND QUESTIONS

1. **Prevalence of Teen Dating Violence.** Cynthia's story is not unique. Consider a review of recent studies on teen dating violence:

Most studies of intimate violence have not included non-residential dating relationships or teenagers. Thus, there is limited data on the extent to which teens experience aggression within their earliest relationships. It is particularly difficult to measure whether teenagers face more violence today than a generation ago, since very little data from before the 1990s exists on this issue. Nevertheless, the research that does exist suggests that violence in heterosexual teenage relationships is fairly common.

In recent literature, Carolyn Tucker Halpern used data from the National Longitudinal Study of Adolescent Health ("Add Health") to determine the extent of dating violence. Add Health contains the most comprehensive data to date on the health-related behaviors of adolescents in the seventh to twelfth grades, with more than 90,000 adolescents completing questionnaires. In analyzing a sample from this data, Halpern and her colleagues found that thirty-two percent of respondents reported experiencing aggression within a heterosexual romantic relationship. Most of the aggressive behaviors reported were psychological—particularly swearing. Approximately twelve percent of those surveyed reported being the victim of physical violence.

These estimates are consistent with other recent studies both in the United States and in other Anglo countries. The Commonwealth Fund Survey of the Health of Adolescent Girls found that twenty-six percent of American girls surveyed said that they had been either sexually and/or physically abused by a date or boyfriend. A survey of Massachusetts high school students found that one in five females had experienced physical or sexual violence from dating partners. A similar survey of New Zealand teens found that about one-fifth of females had been physically hurt in a dating relationship. In a qualitative study of Canadian teens aged fourteen to nineteen, Francine Lavoie and her colleagues also found a wide variety of adolescent dating violence, including death threats, sexual and psychological abuse, and what some of the teens considered "consensual" rough sex. Cheryl Hanna, *Sex Before Violence: Girls, Dating Violence, and (Perceived) Sexual Autonomy*, 33 Fordham Urb. L.J. 437 (2006).

Do such numbers surprise you? Think back to your own experiences in high school. Did you know anyone who was in an abusive relationship? What was the culture at your school relative to girls and violence? What might you have done had Cynthia shared with you her story? Is there something about teen culture today that might make intimate violence even more prevalent than it was a generation ago? Think back to Chapter Two, to Lundy Bancroft's observations about the prevalence of pornography among teens, for example. Does popular culture today promote misogyny?

2. **Interventions on Behalf of Teens.** There are an increasing number of legal interventions geared towards teens, including expanding the availability of restraining orders for teens, expanding warrantless arrest statutes to cover teens, holding schools liable for failure to intervene when they know a teen is a victim of violence at school, and, to a lesser extent, holding

teens criminally liable for their abuse. One of the most innovative programs in the country is in Santa Clara County, which has a specialized juvenile court for domestic offenders. The Court was started after it was found that most of the county's domestic violence related homicides happened in relationships that began when the victim was underage. The program offers services to both the abuser and the victim with the hope of breaking the cycle of violence early in their lives. For a description of the program see Inger Sagatun–Edwards, Hon. Eugene M. Hyman, Tracy Lafontaine and Erin Nelson–Serrano, *The Santa Clara County Juvenile Domestic and Family Violence Court*, 4 J. Center For Families, Child. & Cts. 91 (2003).

3.   **Programs Addressing Teen Dating Violence.** Very few teens eventually access the legal system to end a violent dating relationship. Rather, most turn only to friends for help, making peers the first line of defense against teen dating violence. To ensure that teens have proper information about healthy dating relationships, some schools have implemented programs addressing teen violence. In 1993 Massachusetts became the first state to implement a statewide strategy to combat teen dating violence. One of the most successful programs to date has been the Safe Dates Program in North Carolina. For a program description, see Vangie A. Foshee, G. Fletcher Linder, Karl E. Bauman, Stacey A. Langwick, Ximena B. Arriaga, Janet L. Heath, Pamela M. McMahan and Shrihant Bangdiwala, *The Safe Dates Project: Theoretical Basis, Evaluation Design, and Selected Baseline Findings*, 12 Am. J. Preventive Med. 39 (1996).

Domestic Abuse of the Elderly

We next turn to an examination of domestic violence among the elderly. As noted above, while there is a common perception that violence in senior relationships is usually a result of caretaker stress or some other ailment related to aging or illness, much of what we term elder abuse is simply domestic violence grown old. We tend to label it elder abuse, yet the patterns of controlling behavior are quite similar to those patterns in the young. Thus, many legal scholars and advocates for women are reframing their understanding of elder abuse to recognize that it follows the same patterns and reflects the same dynamics of domestic violence among the young. Yet, just as teens face challenges because of their age, so too do the elderly often face challenges responding to these relationships, such as increased frailty, changing mental capacity, and financial and physical dependency issues.

Ken Picard

In Harm's Way: Elder Abuse–Outing the Other Domestic Violence

Seven Days, (Burlington, Vermont) June 9, 2004.

Nora was widowed at the age of 77. By 82, her health was in decline. With her family living far away, Nora felt isolated, lonely and depressed. Then at 85, she met a man named Ray, who was married to a woman living across the street. As Jane recalls, Nora initially found Ray to be "obnoxious, overbearing and constantly needing to be the center of attention."

Then Ray's wife died in early June 1997, and within a month he began courting Nora heavily, taking her to church, dinner, movies and concerts. By the end of July, the two were together constantly; by September, Jane recalls her mother was giddily in love. A month later, Nora announced that she and Ray were to be married in November.

"My mother was not impulsive. This was out of character," Jane explains. But at her advanced age, Nora had found a renewed zest for life and her children didn't object. And Ray seemed to treat their mother like a queen, doting on her constantly and showering her with new clothes and expensive jewelry.

The first warning sign, Jane says, came at the wedding. Ray, then 82, didn't stop talking about his sexual prowess. Nora's family was initially amused, but his incessant boasting soon became offensive. The family didn't want to spoil their mother's joyous weekend, however, so they made the best of the situation.

After the wedding, things seemed to go well for the newlyweds. The family learned to tolerate Ray's eccentricities, though Jane soon noticed that her mother often seemed irritated with him. Soon, Nora stopped talking altogether whenever Ray was in the room. Eventually, Nora and her family began catching Ray in little lies.

It wasn't long before Ray began to isolate Nora from her friends and family. As soon as he moved into Nora's duplex, he forbade her children and grandchildren from staying in the house when they visited. Nora was also not allowed to eat lunch with her friends at the village clubhouse, as she had done for the previous 12 years. Within months, Nora was virtually cut off from her entire support network.

Ray had a bad temper, Jane remembers, and would often fly into an inexplicable rage. His behavior grew even more erratic at about the same time that Nora's health deteriorated in ways her doctors couldn't explain. Her Parkinson's worsened, but the symptoms didn't seem to fit the disease's normal profile. Then Nora started having panic attacks at night, sleeping all day and pacing the floor at night. "This was a woman who could barely walk 20 or 30 feet without having to sit down," Jane notes.

In March 2002, Nora suffered another stroke and seemed to give up on life. Although she later recovered, Nora said she wouldn't need her family furniture anymore, and asked her children to take it all away—a request her children found strange. A few months later, Jane's sister flew down to see their mother and pick up the family heirlooms. It was during this visit, Jane says, that Nora finally disclosed her horrifying secret.

"What Ray was doing was, he was terrorizing her. He was raping her and sodomizing her daily," Jane says. "He would start at about two or three o'clock in the afternoon, telling her—and this is a quote from her— 'I'm going to get you tonight. You don't know when or how, but I'm going to get you.'

"We had no idea how to process this. We'd never been through this before," Jane adds. "Thank God I live in Vermont. Living in a small state has its advantages." Jane immediately sought help from Women Helping

Battered Women in Burlington and Vermont Legal Aid. Both agencies put her in touch with similar advocacy groups in her mother's state.

Within days, the family had removed Nora from her home and hired a lawyer experienced with elder abuse. Within a week, Nora had filed for a legal separation and given her children power of attorney over her financial affairs. Then, to the surprise of her children, she asked to move back to Vermont and told Ray she never wanted to see him again.

"As soon as we came on the scene and said, 'Mom, we're going to protect you. Nothing's going to happen to you.' that's when she began talking about the abuse," Jane says. Lest there be any doubt about Nora's mental competency or the veracity of her allegations, the nurses who examined her documented that she was indeed the victim of repeated sexual assaults.

Only after Nora was safely out of the abusive setting was her family able to piece together the various tactics Ray had used to manipulate and control her. Jane discovered, for example, that Ray had been tampering with her hearing aids so that she couldn't talk on the phone with her children or grandchildren. More seriously, he had increased the dosage of her Parkinson's medication in order to pacify her at night so that he could more easily have his way with her. "It's a wonder she didn't die," Jane notes.

Ray also depleted Nora's bank account, cleaned out her safe-deposit box and sold off her engagement ring and family jewelry. Nora's friends later told the family that while she was still in the hospital; Ray was already making overtures towards other single women in their retirement complex, apparently setting sights on his next victim. A search of their apartment uncovered drawers full of sexual-enhancement drugs, books, videos and, as Jane puts it, "other pornographic material of the grossest sort."

Ray was eventually evicted from the senior-housing complex, but at Nora's request, no further legal action was taken against him. "If he weren't so old, I would have done it in a minute," Jane says. To quell her ethical concern that Ray might try to victimize another women, however, Jane wrote a letter to his family outlining his aberrant behavior and criminal tendencies.

NOTES AND QUESTIONS

1. **Patterns of Abuse.** What is striking about both Cynthia's and Nora's stories are that the patterns of abuse are very much the same as they are for most of the victims about whom we have read. All these women have been victims of a pattern of power and control. Yet, depending on one's age, the tools of control vary. Think back over these two readings and identify the ways in which age did impact the experience of abuse.

Age can also impact the options for available for victims. One of the major problems for the elderly, for example, is the need for care-taking and the desire to stay in one's home. It is not easy for the elderly to leave and seek shelter, especially if they are dependent on their abuser for physical care-taking. Teens usually live with their parents and can't simply leave their homes. Teens may not be eligible for legal remedies, such as restraining orders, which are often not available to teens in dating relationships.

2. **Representing Abused Elderly Clients.** Assume that you represent a client like Nora, who has been abused by her partner. Whether elderly clients are competent is central to representation. Consider the following information:

> If, at the conclusion of the first interview, an elderly client appears incompetent, it should be determined if his or her competency has been questioned in the past. Has the diagnosis of incompetence occurred since the client has been in a living arrangement with a potentially abusive individual? . . . If there is a history of questioned or documented incompetence, this history should be assessed as to whether it is credible. Has the diagnosis occurred seemingly quickly without a new medical condition to explain its rapid appearance (e.g., minor stroke)? Or has its rapid onset occurred since the client's living arrangement has included a person who may be an abuser?

> If it is determined that there is some reason to question the client's competence, the professional should conduct a second and third follow-up interview. The second interview of the client takes place without the suspected abuser present. The client should be well rested and have received proper food and, if applicable, medications. Some clients experience what is known as "sundowner syndrome," the tendency among persons with dementia for the memory to become more disjointed or impaired at the end of the day. In such cases, mid to late morning meetings are often preferable. . . .

> Even in cases where there are suspicions that the client is legally incompetent, investigating allegations of abuse independently should be considered. It is not uncommon for an abusive family member or caretaker to strongly state that alleged abuse is a result of the client's incompetence. Often caregiver stress will be used to justify abusive behavior. It is important to realize that providing support to the abuser will not protect the safety of the client. Competency issues are important in forming a decision on the illegality of certain actions against the client, but regardless of mental status, the safety of the client must be considered foremost in all decisions. . . . Bonnie Brandl and Tess Meuer, *Domestic Abuse in Later Life*, 8 Elder L. J. 297 (2000).

3. **Mandatory Reporting.** Many attorneys may be required to report elder abuse to the state, even if they learn of that abuse through a confidential communication. Is this the best way to ensure elder victims have adequate legal protection, or does it undermine their autonomy, and possibly place them at greater risk? Most mandatory reporting laws don't require the elderly to be legally incompetent for the purposes of reporting. What is the difference between elderly victims and younger ones? Should the law make such distinctions? Should there be similar laws for teen victims of abuse?

4. **Other Abusers.** The elderly are not just abused by their spouses. Adult children constitute the greatest segment of those who abuse the elderly. While domestic abuse by non-intimate partners is beyond the scope of this book, it is important to note that many of the dynamics and hence interventions on behalf of the elderly are likely to be the same regardless of who is perpetrating the abuse. For a discussion of these issues, see Sande L. Buhai and James W. Gilliam, Jr., *Honor thy Mother and Father: Preventing Elder Abuse Through Education and Litigation*, 36 LOY. L.A. L. REV. 565 (2003).

Women with Disabilities

It has been only very recently that the domestic violence community has paid separate and special attention to the particular vulnerability of abused women who suffer from physical, mental or emotional disabilities. The elderly may or may not fall within this group. New studies document the ways in which women with disabilities are more vulnerable to abuse by their partners than other women, and new documentation of the incidence of abuse in this population confirms that increased vulnerability.

At the same time, the abuse of women with disabilities raises at least two important new questions. First, when such a woman is abused by her partner, are we seeing the by now familiar "power and control" dynamic at work, or might there be a competing interpretation—could the abuse be the result of "caregiver stress," as is often argued when the abuser is not a partner, but a parent, or child, or other caregiver? If the disability is itself the consequence of prior abuse, the question may be easy to answer. But if the disability predates the abuse, or its origins are distinct from the abuse, the question may take a little more investigation. Once we have answered it, we need then to determine how our answer affects our response to the situation, and what legal remedies we would want to see available.

The second question is whether, in this context, our definition of "domestic" violence should expand to include non-family members, either in those cases in which we see "coercive control" as the motivation for abuse, or more generally. Individuals with disabilities often have expanded "families" of caregivers, who have the kind of intimate access usually reserved for partners or other family members. Should the restraining order mechanism, to take one very concrete example, be available to an individual who claims that she, or he, is being abused by an unrelated caregiver? Illinois is the one state to have comprehensively revised its abuse protection legislation to cover this situation. In other states, coverage may depend on such arbitrary factors as whether the caregiver is living in the same household as the abused individual.

Karen Nutter

Domestic Violence in The Lives Of Women With Disabilities: No (Accessible) Shelter From The Storm

13 S. CAL. REV. L. & WOMEN'S STUD. 329 (2004).

Women with disabilities are not abused; it is just too low and cowardly to assault or threaten someone who cannot fight back. And because women with disabilities are not sexual and do not form intimate relationships in the first place, they certainly cannot be victims of domestic violence. Even if they do experience the occasional act of abuse, the men who care for them deserve a little leeway; it is too much to expect that a man with such a difficult job—a martyr, really—not vent his frustration once in a while. Besides, women with disabilities are child-like, and their accusations should not be believed. After all, if women with disabilities were really being abused, wouldn't they call domestic violence shelters for help? Wouldn't the Violence Against Women Act of 1994 and a major national report on violence against women at least have mentioned them?

With the exception of the omission of women with disabilities from the Act and report, all of the above are myths. Women with disabilities can and do form intimate relationships, and too many of them experience real physical and emotional abuse at the hands of their partners. Indeed, researchers agree that these women face a higher risk of being abused than do women without disabilities. At the same time, researchers also agree that the provisions of protective orders and crisis shelters—conventional ways of escape used by battered women—are grossly inadequate to serve the needs of women with disabilities. . . .

B.   Domestic Violence: The Experience of Women With Disabilities

In addition to the "traditional" types of domestic violence . . . women with disabilities face additional types of abuse. A batterer may take away or dismantle a wheelchair or other assistive device, disconnect the telephone or otherwise put it out of her reach, withhold food, or, if the woman has a visual impairment, put something dangerous in her path. He may withhold her medication, give her too much or too little medication, refuse to help her dress, leave her unclothed, refuse to turn her if she is at risk of pressure sores, refuse to help her use the toilet, or leave her in the bathtub for several days.

An accurate number of women with disabilities who have experienced domestic violence is difficult to ascertain. One study conducted by the Center for Research on Women with Disabilities found that women with disabilities were not more likely than women without disabilities to experience emotional or physical abuse at the hands of their husbands, although women with disabilities reported longer durations of physical or sexual abuse. This study also found that women with disabilities were also more likely to have been abused by attendants or health care workers. Another commonly cited statistic is that people with disabilities are one-and-one-half times more likely to experience a single incident of abuse than people without disabilities of their same age and gender, and two to five times more likely to experience abuse when multiple incidents against the same victim are considered.

Regardless of the percentage of women with disabilities who experience domestic violence, there are many reasons why they may find it more difficult to leave their batterers than do women without disabilities. In the first place, a woman, particularly if she has a developmental disability, may not know that what she is experiencing is abuse. If her batterer has kept her isolated from peers who enjoy loving relationships, she may accept the abuse as an inevitable part of the life of a person with a disability. This is especially true in situations in which the woman has been given few opportunities in the past to make decisions about how she lives her life.

Even a woman who recognizes the abuse may feel that she can do little to escape. Obviously, women with mobility or visual impairments may not be able to physically flee from their abusers, and women who cannot drive may depend on transportation services that require them to call in advance for a ride. In addition, women who, due to disabilities, grew up in protected atmospheres or were otherwise isolated from general activities may not feel that they can make decisions on their own. Further, women who have lived under the supervision of health practitioners or institutional personnel may be inclined to passively accept the dictates of authority figures, making them particularly attractive to men who seek vulnerable women to control. Moreover, general social prejudice against women with disabilities, including the notion that they are "asexual," may make the women feel that they should appreciate any kind of intimate attention, even if it is abusive. A woman may then be prone to believing her batterer when he calls her names or tells her that without his care, she would be in an institution, that no other man would want her. . . .

NOTES AND QUESTIONS

1. **Vulnerabilities.** Girls and women with disabilities may in addition be particularly vulnerable to sexual abuse, and to forming relationships with men who abuse them sexually:

> When a young woman reaches dating age, she may have fewer opportunities because of her difference, to experience a healthy process of learning what she likes and dislikes sexually, and how to set boundaries that are pleasing for her; she may not have dates, go to parties, or engage in any sexual activity appropriate to people her own age. Rejection may be her education, leaving her to first encounter sexual experience at a later age than her able bodied friends. Delaying the pleasure of progressive intimacy may cause her to be confused when the opportunity for any sort of sexual relationship arises. There are questions: Is this sexual activity suitable even though I am not enjoying it? Should I do what my partner demands because that person knows more about sex than I do? Should I do whatever s/he wants, because sex, pleasant or not, makes me feel more "normal"? Should I go along with it because *I have no idea* how to begin a relationship?
>
> . . . If we use the example of the disabled woman who is naive about sexuality and has no experience with courtship, but is now confronted with a real situation, in addition to the fear of the unknown, she may also be excited by the attention. Her desire to be a "normal" woman, means she must repress that fear and let her partner lead her into unfamiliar territory. If she is lucky, that person will be caring and sensitive to her needs . . . or instead may do what s/he pleases. This may not be the beginning of emotional battering, but unwillingness to

pay attention to the woman's concerns can set up an unhealthy model that can lead to physical abuse if that person is inclined to such behavior. If she frees herself from this person, she may be left with the belief that only people who want to control her or to hurt her are those ... whom she will be able to have as sexual partners. She may feel she is left with one choice: celibacy or potentially violent sexual encounters.... Chris Womendez and Karen Schneiderman, *Escaping from Abuse: Unique Issues for Women with Disabilities,* 9 SEXUALITY AND DISABILITY 273 (1991).

2. **Ignorance about Women with Disabilities.** The vulnerabilities women with disabilities suffer within their intimate relationships are compounded by the difficulties they face accessing services to assist them in escaping from abuse. A woman with a communication or physical impairment may be unable, without assistance, to contact police or find her way to a shelter. Appropriate and affordable transportation may not be available. At the shelter, she may find that the physical facilities do not meet her needs, or that shelter workers lack the training and sensitivity to help her manage those needs. Many courthouses are old and architecturally inaccessible. Although TDDs are more widely available than they used to be, few shelters, courts or law enforcement agencies have them, or are trained to use them effectively. The absence of sign language interpreters in shelters, hospitals and police stations prevents Deaf individuals from communicating with service providers. Personal assistance for completing forms, complaints or affidavits may not be readily available to a person who because of an intellectual disability or vision impairment cannot read or write.

Beyond these practical limitations, however, are others produced by society's continuing ignorance about, and prejudice against, individuals with disabilities. A 1995 report by L'Institut Roeher, *Harm's Way: The Many Faces of Violence and Abuse Against People with Disabilities,* documents the attitude that individuals with disabilities "are stupid and can be taken advantage of," and that they are "lesser beings." Along with these negative assumptions come others about the unreliability of individuals with disabilities, and a tendency to "doubt their story or blame them" for alleged incidents of abuse. Speech impairments, hearing impairments, mental, physical and other disabilities may all reduce the credibility of victims in the eyes of police, judges, attorneys, juries and the community at large.

3. **Shelters for Victims with Disabilities.** Domestic violence shelters are covered under Title III of the Americans with Disabilities Act. Yet, many shelters are not equipped to handle victims with special needs, in large part because of lack of funding.

Recently, the first shelter for women with hearing disabilities opened in Seattle, Washington. A Place of Our Own has specially designed facilities and staff, and is being replicated throughout the country. See Molly M. Ginty, *Women's Silent Pleas Are Heard By Seattle Facility,* Women's eNews, Nov. 20, 2006. See also Abused Deaf Women's Services at http://www.adwas.org/.

4. **State Responses to Individuals with Disabilities.** Several states have responded to the barriers to access faced by individuals with disabilities seeking legal protection from abuse. The most common provision is one allowing a third party to apply for a protection or restraining order on behalf of a person prevented by physical or mental capacity from taken that step themselves. See, for example, ARIZ. REV. STAT. ANN. § 13–3602 (1989 & Supp. 1997); W. VA. CODE § 48–2A–4 (1996). In addition, some states allow hearings to be scheduled by telephone in order to accommodate a disability (see, e.g., WASH. REV. CODE ANN. § 26.50.050 (1997)), or require court appointment of an interpreter for an individual who has a hearing or speech impairment (WASH. REV. CODE ANN. § 26.50.055 (1997)). Should there be similar laws for the caretakers of teens?

5. **Caregivers.** What do you think is the practical impact of making restraining orders available against caregivers who are not otherwise family or household members? How else might an individual with a disability take action against, for example, a neglectful caregiver, or one who was exploiting the individual financially? Does your assessment of the utility of the restraining order mechanism depend on the range of relief it authorizes? For a more detailed look at the remedies authorized under state restraining order legislation, see Chapter Six.

6. **Financial Exploitation.** Many statutes covering both the elderly and the disabled make it a crime to financially exploit them. Do you have concerns about stretching the definition of domestic violence to cover financial exploitation of an individual by a paid caregiver? How would you articulate those concerns? Are they concerns for the conceptual integrity of the legislation, or for the potential political consequences of extending the protective reach of the statute? What might those consequences be, do you think? Are they more likely to be negative than positive?

D.   BATTERED WOMEN AND POVERTY

Are poor women more battered than other women? Does battering make or keep women poor? Does being poor hold women more firmly in abusive relationships? Are poor men more likely to inflict domestic violence than men with more economic resources at their disposal? In the political climate of the battered women's movement of the seventies and eighties these questions were out of bounds; activists and advocates alike stressed the universality of abuse, and its origins in gender, not class, oppression. Today, these questions are of renewed interest both because of changes in welfare policy over the last decade and because of emerging research that shows a strong link between socio-economic status and battering.

For many battered women, leaving or ending an abusive relationship exposes them to greater financial hardship. In an attempt to address the economic vulnerability of many victims of domestic violence, Donna Coker has argued that every intervention for domestic violence should be subject to a material resources test. As she describes it:

> Domestic violence laws and policies may directly provide women with
> material resources such as housing, food, clothing, or money, or they

may increase resources indirectly through the availability of services such as job training, childcare, and transportation. The material resources test requires first that priority be given to those programs, laws, or policies that provide women with direct aid. Second, even when the primary goal of an intervention strategy is not the allocation of material resources, we should prefer methods of implementation that are likely to, directly or indirectly, improve women's access to material resources. Further, we should usually prefer local assessment of the impact of law and policy on women's material resources over universal assessments because the impact of a policy will always be mediated by the particular conditions facing women in a given locale. We should always prefer assessment that is informed by the circumstances of those women who are in the greatest need. In most circumstances this will be poor women of color who are sandwiched by their heightened vulnerability to battering, on the one hand, and their heightened vulnerability to intrusive state control, on the other. Strategies that increase material resources for poor women of color are likely to benefit—or at least not harm—other battered women in the same locale. Donna Coker, *Shifting Power for Battered Women: Law, Material Resources, and Poor Women of Color*, 33 U.C. DAVIS L. REV. 1009 (2000).

What might be the outcome if we in fact, first considered economic security rather than physical safety in shaping our responses to domestic violence? Would increasing women's material wealth make it less likely that they would become victims of abuse? Would improving the material wealth of men make it less likely that they would become abusive? These are among the questions that we explore in this section.

The first issue we focus on is a practical one—how do victims who need public assistance fare under current welfare law. There were major reforms of the welfare system in the 1990's. Advocates for battered women worried that these reforms would make it harder for women to leave abusive relationships. This in turn has led to the recognition that in fact poor women *are* more likely to be battered than their wealthier counterparts, and that poor men *are* more likely to abuse their partners than their wealthier counterparts. See Jody Raphael, SAVING BERNICE: BATTERED WOMEN, WELFARE AND POVERTY (2000). The next reading addresses the relationship between welfare reform and domestic abuse.

Shelby A.D. Moore
Understanding the Connection Between Domestic Violence, Crime, and Poverty: How Welfare Reform May Keep Battered Women From Leaving Abusive Relationships

12 TEX J. WOMEN & L. 451 (2003).

Funding for AFDC [Aid for Families with Dependent Children] was reduced in the 1980s and 1990s, and a further stigma attached to its recipients. By 1996, the fate of poor battered women was in the hands of those who desired to abolish AFDC. AFDC and similar programs had long been the subject of conservative rhetoric depicting their recipients as people who refused to work and who were dependent on government handouts and critics believed that the money could be best used for other causes. Public perception was also that the program fostered a "pathological, lifelong dependence."

With the history of the perception that federally-funded social programs were being abused by lazy, no-good recipients, President Bill Clinton enacted the Personal Responsibility and Work Opportunity Reconciliation Act (PRWORA) of 1996. The Act abolished AFDC, replacing it with the Temporary Assistance for Needy Families (TANF) program. The provisions of TANF differ from those of AFDC in three primary ways. First, under the PRWORA, there is no longer an entitlement to receive benefits as was the case under AFDC for qualified recipients. Next, it established a maximum life-time benefit of five years, whether or not they were received consecutively. Finally, the Act establishes a work requirement for all recipients, leaving the states to design and administer their own program.

The stated goals of the PRWORA are to increase state flexibility while ending the dependence of needy parents on government benefits by promoting job preparation, work, and marriage. Another goal is to encourage the formulation and maintenance of two-parent families. For some women, however, it may be impossible to realize these goals. Instead, these goals present a conflict "between a battered woman seeking assistance and the welfare system from which she is seeking it." Indeed, while society often criticizes a woman who remains in an abusive relationship, the PRWORA encourages her to stay.

As one commentator notes, mandatory work requirements may force a woman to choose between the welfare funds her family needs, and the physical safety of both herself and her children.

Women who manage to leave abusive relationships often have no transportation, no house, no bank account, and no job. They may not have family and friends who can assist them. Even if such sources of support are available, battered women may still need welfare benefits in order to fully escape their abusers. And in cases where women have had to go "underground," changing their identity as well as their children's, they cannot readily work to become self-sustaining. In this instance, welfare may be the only option. If government assistance is not available, many battered women would be forced to remain in, or return to, dangerous or life-threatening situations.

4.   PRWORA: The Family Violence Option

Recognizing that battered women often have difficulty complying with the work requirements established by PRWORA, Congress included the Family Violence Option (FVO). Under the FVO, battered women who meet the criteria are exempt from work requirements and lifetime benefit limits. The provision applies where compliance would make it more difficult to escape domestic violence, would penalize battered or once battered women, or would endanger battered women. The provision is optional, yet thirty-nine states have adopted the FVO. However, these states are required to develop their own procedures for screening, referring women to counseling, and, ultimately, granting waivers.

Commentators and advocates for battered women argue that the FVO is inadequate for several reasons. First, it is not clear how many domestic violence exemptions can be granted. Next, the block-grant funding system discourages the use of FVO exemptions. Finally, "bonus awards encourage states to compete with each other by moving recipients off welfare." In addition, the PRWORA includes a cap, permitting states to exempt up to twenty percent of their total caseloads from the five-year lifetime limit on benefits and from work requirements based on "hardship" or domestic violence. Debates have arisen over whether domestic violence victims are to be counted within the "hardship" exception's twenty percent exemption. There are also concerns about whether states would be penalized if granting waivers pushed their targets over federal work or five-year limit quotas.

Although the PRWORA was enacted in 1996, it was not until 1999 that the U.S. Department of Health and Human Services (HHS) adopted regulations interpreting the FVO. The regulation established that good cause waivers certified under the FVO guidelines are considered outside of the twenty percent waiver established by the hardship exemption. This means that states are required to follow the guidelines for waiver certification and reporting. Further, they must still meet federal targets for work requirements and time limits. Simply put, "[a] state must meet its work participation and time requirements and not have more than 20% of its recipients within the hardship exemption before counting domestic violence waivers." But it has been argued that despite the alternative reading indicated by the HHS regulations, the PRWORA by its terms states that there is a twenty percent cap on exemptions. The HHS regulation, which expressly excludes domestic violence victims, seems to directly contradict the statute, which expressly includes them.

Battered women also face other impediments, including substance abuse and poor health, which make it more difficult to maintain gainful employment. Approximately twenty to thirty percent of women enrolled in TANF are presently involved in violent relationships. Two-thirds have experienced domestic violence as adults and may be suffering the effects of long-term abuse. These statistics indicate that a twenty percent exemption is inadequate to cover domestic violence victims, let alone all hardship cases combined.

5. Problems with Implementing the FVO

A recent state-by-state survey of state implementation of the FVO found that the chief hurdle preventing domestic violence services from reaching their intended beneficiaries is the lack of information. Many TANF recipients do not know they have a right to request a waiver, nor do they understand the impact domestic violence has on their receiving TANF benefits. In some states, over seventy percent of applicants were not screened for domestic violence and where they did reveal that they were victims of abuse, seventy-five percent were not told how to obtain support services. Clearly, since battered women must weigh and bear the risk of every alternative, they need all available information to make such decisions.

Even where states have effectively apprised women of the benefits available to them, the PRWORA's funding structure discourages incentives for providing exemptions.... The effect is that "states have a strong incentive to offer no exemptions, or to define exemptions very narrowly."....

A final problem is that states compete with each other to receive annual High Performance Bonuses. Established by the federal government, these bonuses are awarded to states that achieve the highest levels in given categories, including job entry and retention rates. "These bonuses are harmful to battered women because they encourage states to compete with each other. Taken in tandem with the increasingly disproportionate number of battered women on welfare rolls ... the bonuses will encourage competition among states to move those with the most barriers into employment the fastest." The result is that battered women are forced into the workforce before they are ready, impeding their chances of successfully leaving their batterers. For some, it may mean a return to their abusers for economic security. The bottom line is that because of the number of barriers battered women face, they cannot fully benefit from the PRWORA.

NOTES AND QUESTIONS

1. **Domestic Violence and Welfare Reform.** Moore's article details the complicated regulations governing access to public assistance. She describes only access to aid—yet victims who rely on their abuser for support may also need access to child care, health care, disability benefits and other resources. As Moore points out, lack of information may be the greatest hurdle.

Nevertheless, the implementation of the Family Violence Option under the Temporary Assistance for Needy Families program is a significant development. Historically, the poverty movement and the battered women's movement were disconnected. Welfare "reform" culminating in the federal Personal Responsibility and Work Opportunity Reconciliation Act of 1996, brought the poverty movement and the battered women's movement together, and stimulated some important learning on both sides. Below Joan Meier discusses these developments:

At the heart of the disconnection between progressive discussions of poverty and feminist discussions of domestic violence is a fundamental clash of ideologies and philosophies between the domestic violence and anti-poverty movements, one which parallels the clash between the ideologies of conservative reformers and poverty activists in the welfare reform debate. On the poverty side, the feminists' emphasis on the values and attitudes which lead to abuse and the need for moral education of perpetrators in order to change their beliefs and behavior, is anathema to anti-poverty activists who preach the structural and socioeconomic causes of the ills of the poor and who see any talk of moral or dysfunctional behavior of the poor as a form of blaming the victim. On the domestic violence side, battered women's activists have strenuously avoided discussing battering as a problem related to poverty in order to avoid its marginalization and to further the understanding that domestic violence is a reflection of fairly universal norms of a sexist society.... At first glance, the perspectives are quite incompatible. This potential clash has caused even feminist poverty analysts to separate out the domestic violence issue and pigeonhole it as a "feminist"—but not particularly a "poverty" issue....

... Recognition that battering is intentional and goal-oriented, aimed at keeping its victim under the perpetrator's control and possession, is the most profound and radical element of the battered women's movement, for it demonstrates that battering is simply the logical extension of the sexist belief that men have the right to dominate women.... Thus, treating battering as an outgrowth of poverty rather than a behavior motivated by malevolence and sexism, allows anti-poverty advocates to remain morally engaged with their clients and cause. Sadly, it also contributes to the deep denial about the nature of battering which still seems to exist in poor communities of color, and sacrifices women and children in the name of "enlightened" dedication to the poor. Joan Meier, *Domestic Violence, Character, and Social Change in the Welfare Reform Debate*, 19 LAW AND POL'Y 205 (1997).

Meier highlights what is a fundamental tension between advocates for the poor and advocates for battered women. Can these tensions be reconciled? Think back to our materials in Chapter Two about the relationship between men who batter and unemployment. Remember also the excerpts on Hispanic and Native American communities and the link between poverty and battering in those communities. While it is true that poverty does not cause battering, it is important to consider how it affects the experience of battering. See also Jody Raphael, *Battering Through the Lens of Class*, 11 AM. U. J. GENDER SOC. POL'Y & L. 367 (2003).

2.   **Domestic Violence Among the Privileged.** As we will see in examples throughout this book, economic security does not protect one from either being an abuser or being abused. In SHATTERED DREAMS (1987), Charlotte Fedders, with Laura Elliot, tells the story of her marriage to John Fedders, who was chief of Enforcement at the Securities and Exchange Commission under President Ronald Reagan. During their 17–year marriage, she was severely beaten by him. Even after her father, who is a doctor, counseled her to leave, she stayed, out of obligation to her family as well as shame and humiliation. What is striking about her account is that the dynamics of the relationship reflect the same dynamics that we discussed in Chapter Two. She too suffered from insecurity and self-doubt, and left only after she saw the effects of the abuse on her five children. The main difference between someone like Charlotte Fedders and women who lack economic resources is that she had the economic means to seek a lawyer and sue for divorce. It was only after her husband bitterly contested

the divorce did she testify about the abuse in court. The Wall Street Journal then chronicled her story.

As Sarah Buel writes in *Fifty Obstacles to Leaving*:

#2: **Batterer:** If the batterer is wealthy, a politician, famous, a popular athlete, or otherwise a powerful player in his community, he can generally afford to hire private counsel and pressure the decision-makers to view his case with leniency. Some wealthy abusers not only hire private detectives to stalk, terrorize, and frivolously sue their partners, but the advocates who assist them as well. Sarah M. Buel, *Fifty Obstacles to Leaving, a.k.a. Why Abuse Victims Stay*, 28 COLO. LAW. 19 (1999).

3. **Homelessness.** Although it is difficult to know how many women are homeless as a result of domestic violence, it is fair to suggest that among women and children, domestic violence is a leading cause of homelessness as women try to leave relationships but have no where to go. During hearings for the Violence Against Women Act, the Senate Judiciary Committee estimated that half of all homeless women and children were fleeing a domestic violence situation. In December of 2001, the U.S. Conference of Mayors found that domestic violence was the major cause of homelessness in eight American cities. For a discussion of these issues see Eliza Hurst, *The Housing Crisis for Victims of Domestic Violence: Disparate Impact Claims and Other Housing Protection for Victims of Domestic Violence*, 10 GEO. J. ON POVERTY L. & POL'Y 131 (2003); Lenora M. Lapidus, *Doubly Victimized: Housing Discrimination Against Victims of Domestic Violence*, 11 AM. U. J. GENDER SOC. POL'Y & L. 377 (2003).

The problem of homelessness is compounded by the fact that the approximately 1200 shelters for battered women cannot accommodate demand and thus many battered women and their children have to seek shelter at homeless shelters, which are not equipped to adequately protect them or provide them needed services. In addition, because of the lack of both transitional and low income housing, many battered women are forced to stay in relationships or find themselves on the street. See Veronica L. Zoltowski, *Zero Tolerance Policies: Fighting Drugs or Punishing Domestic Violence Victims*, 37 NEW ENG. L. REV. 1231 (2003).

4. **Shelters and Confidentiality.** Shelters for victims of domestic violence operate under the strictest of confidentiality, often keeping their locations secret and relying on police and advocates for referrals. In addition, many of the communications between shelter workers and victims of domestic violence are considered privileged communications under some states' evidence codes. In particular some states have extended the privileged communications between patients and therapists to include shelter workers. This prevents the shelter and its employees and volunteers from being forced to testify at trial about their communications with victims. Often, attorneys will subpoena shelter records in cases involving recantation, battered women's self-defense, and allegations of sexual assault. This can be an incredibly important safeguard as many victims may fear what they say to counselors could be used against them in future divorce, custody, or criminal cases. Alabama's statute is a good example of a statute that covers volunteers as well as employees of domestic violence shelters. See ALA. CODE § 15–23–42 (1987).

Other states have extended this privilege via case law. See e.g. *State ex rel. Hope House, Inc. v. Merrigan*, 133 S.W.3d 44, 2004 WL 771724 (Mo. 2004) (statutory confidentiality requirements with respect to information concerning residents of domestic violence shelters apply to all shelter workers or volunteers and are not contingent upon a shelter worker having any contact or communication with the resident); *R.D. v. State*, 706 So.2d 770 (Ala. Crim. App.1997) (records of victim services counselor were protected from discovery in sexual abuse prosecution by statute granting confidential communication privilege to victim counselors, even though counselor was not licensed).

Recently, however, there have been some concerns that such strict confidentiality could be eroded due to federal regulations which require all homeless shelters, including those which provide services to victims of domestic violence, to share client information with the Department of Urban and Housing Development in its effort to track homelessness in America. For an overview of this policy and its implications for battered women, see D. Marisa Black, *Working Outside the HMIS Box: HUD Funding, Domestic Violence Shelters, and Approaches to Protect Domestic Violence Client Confidentiality*, 8 J.L. & FAM. STUD. 203 (2006).

5. **Public Housing.** Another housing issue confronting poor battered women revolves around public housing. Under the Anti–Abuse Drug Act of 1988, all public housing leases contain language allowing for eviction due to drug or criminal activity, regardless of whether or not the tenant knew, should have known, or tried to prevent the criminal activity. This means that tenants are strictly liable for what happens in their homes. Many domestic violence victims are thus evicted when their abusers engage in wrongdoing, such as dealing drugs or even assaulting the victim herself. For a discussion of these issues, see Veronica L. Zoltowski, *Zero Tolerance Policies: Fighting Drugs or Punishing Domestic Violence Victims?*, 37 NEW ENG. L. REV. 1231 (2003).

The United States Supreme Court has yet to hear a case involving a local public housing authority evicting a victim of domestic violence when it was her abuser who engaged in criminal activity such drug dealing, for example. However, the Court has upheld the zero tolerance policy of evicting tenants who are not at fault for the underlying criminal activity. See *Department of Housing & Urban Development v. Rucker*, 535 U.S. 125 (2002).

This case is the first in which a court, in denying a motion for summary judgment, held that discrimination against victims of domestic violence within the housing context could constitute sex discrimination under the Fair Housing Act.

Bouley v. Young–Sabourin

United States District Court for Vermont, 2005.
394 F.Supp.2d 675.

■ MURTHA, DISTRICT JUDGE.

Background

Upon review of the documentation in the record, and solely for the purpose of deciding the pending motions, the Court sets forth the following.

On August 1, 2003, plaintiff Quinn Bouley, her husband, Daniel Swedo, and their two children, rented the apartment upstairs from defendant Jacqueline Young–Sabourin. . . .

On October 15, 2003, at approximately 8:00 p.m., the plaintiff's husband, Daniel Swedo, criminally attacked her. The plaintiff called the police and fled the apartment. St. Albans police arrested her husband and, that night, the plaintiff applied for a restraining order. Swedo eventually pled guilty to several criminal charges related to the incident, including assault.

On the morning of October 18, 2003, the defendant visited the plaintiff's apartment. . . . Later that day, the defendant wrote the following letter, in which she asked the plaintiff to leave the premises by November 30, 2003:

Dear Quinn,

The purpose of my visit this morning was to try and work things out between you, your agreement in your lease, and the other tenants in the building. I felt very disappointed in the fact that you started to holler and scream, and threaten me, in my efforts to help you. This could only lead me to believe that the violence that has been happening in your unit would continue and that I must give you a 30 day notice to leave the premises. . . .

Discussion

The Fair Housing Act makes it unlawful, *inter alia,* "[t]o refuse to sell or rent after the making of a bona fide offer, or to otherwise refuse to negotiate for the sale or rental of, or otherwise make unavailable or deny, a dwelling to any person because of race, color, religion, sex, familial status, or national origin." The plaintiff alleges the defendant unlawfully terminated her lease on the basis of sex. . . . [S]he claims the termination was initiated because she was a victim of domestic violence. . . . These claims, if proven, could constitute unlawful discrimination under the Fair Housing Act.

Claims of housing discrimination are evaluated using the *McDonnell Douglas* burden-shifting framework. "Accordingly, once a plaintiff has established a prima facie case of discrimination, the burden shifts to the defendant to assert a legitimate, nondiscriminatory rationale for the challenged decision. . . . If the defendant makes such a showing, the burden shifts back to the plaintiff to demonstrate that discrimination was the real reason for the defendant's action. . . . Summary judgment is appropriate [only] if no reasonable jury could find that the defendant's actions were motivated by discrimination."

The plaintiff has demonstrated a prima facie case. It is undisputed that, less than 72 hours after the plaintiff's husband assaulted her, the defendant attempted to evict her. . . .

In response, the defendant has presented little evidence of preexisting problems with the plaintiff, as a tenant. In addition, the timing of the eviction, as well as reasonable inferences which a jury could draw from some of the statements in the eviction letter, could lead a reasonable jury to conclude that the real reason for the defendant's actions was unlawful discrimination.

NOTES AND QUESTIONS

1. **Aftermath.** The court found that discriminating against domestic violence victims could constitute sex discrimination, and thus the defendant in the case agreed to a settlement. In a press release following the case, the ACLU, which represented Quinn Bouley, suggested that this ruling would protect women who fear that they might be evicted if their landlords find out about their abuse. It noted that women who lived in rented housing are three times as likely to be abused as women who own their own homes.

2. **Private and Public Landlords and Sex Discrimination.** *In United States and Alvera v. C.B.M. Group, Inc.*, No. 01–857–PA (D. Or. filed June 8, 2001), the question was whether applying a housing complex's "zero tolerance for violence" policy by threatening a person with eviction for having been the victim of domestic violence unlawfully discriminates on the basis of sex.

Tiffanie Alvera, a resident of a low-income apartment complex in Portland, Oregon, was served with a 24–hour notice terminating her tenancy after she informed her landlord that she received an order of protection against her husband for assault. The landlord served this notice to Ms. Alvera claiming to have a policy of evicting any tenant who commits an act of violence or who controls another who commits an act of violence.

Ms. Alvera filed a complaint against her landlord and others with the United States Department of Housing and Urban Development (HUD). The Secretary of HUD issued a charge of discrimination finding that the defendants had discriminated against Ms. Alvera on the basis of sex in violation of the Fair Housing Act.

In a consent decree settling the lawsuit, the C.B.M. Group, the managers of Alvera's apartment complex, agreed not to "evict, or otherwise discriminate against tenants because they have been victims of violence, including domestic violence" and to revise all employee manuals with respect to current eviction proceedings. The agreement requires C.B.M. Group employees to participate in education about discrimination and fair housing laws. The federal government will monitor the company to ensure that it is complying with the terms of the consent decree, which is in effect for five years. C.B.M. Group agreed to pay compensatory damages to Ms. Alvera, and the court awarded payment of her attorney's fees and costs.

3. **State Statutes Protecting Abused Women Within the Housing Context.** Washington State is one of a few states that prohibits discrimination in housing based on a person's status as a victim of domestic violence, sexual assault, or stalking. *See, e.g.* WASH. REV. CODE § 59.18.580 (2006).

While some victims of domestic violence feel trapped in their relationships for fear of being evicted, others fear leaving because they have a long-term lease. Some states, including Oregon and Washington, provide some additional protections for victims of domestic violence in these situations by requiring landlords to allow for early lease terminations without financial penalties when the victim gives proper notice and provides evidence of the abuse. See e.g. WASH. CODE § 59.18.575 (2006). Because most states do not have such protections, lawyers have to rely upon litigation to either help women get out of their long-term leases, or fight evictions which are a result of domestic violence. For an overview of these issues see Naomi Stern, *Early Lease Terminations By Battered Tenants*, 10 DOMESTIC VIO-LENCE REPORT 33 (2005).

4. **The Right to Call the Police or Other Emergency Services.** According to the American Bar Association Commission on Domestic Violence, landlords frequently cite a victim's call to police or emergency services—or the "noise" that results from such calls (such as sirens)—as a basis for an eviction or other punitive action against a tenant. Several states have responded to this practice by passing laws that prohibit lease provisions that waive or limit a tenant's right to seek emergency assistance in response to domestic violence and that ban penalties against tenants for exercising their right to seek such assistance. As of January 2007, Arizona, Colorado, Minnesota, and Texas had such laws.

Additionally, the District of Columbia has passed a bill that is pending Congressional approval. Even in the absence of a specific law on point, if a public housing provider or a local law or ordinance penalizes a tenant for seeking to obtain emergency services, this may violate her First Amendment right to petition the government for redress of grievances.

Additionally, many states also have laws that allow victims to change their own locks or to have a landlord change them within a short period of time. This is important as many victims need to change their locks in order to stay safe. See Emily J. Martin and Deborah A. Widiss, *Using Federal Law and State Laws to Secure Safe Housing for Survivors of Domestic Violence,* THE ABA COMMISSION ON DOMESTIC VIOLENCE QUARTERLY E–LETTER, Winter 2007.

5. **The Violence Against Women Act of 2005.** The Violence Against Women Act of 2005 includes new provisions to protect victims of domestic violence from housing discrimination. Local housing authorities and landlords who participate in the federal § 8 low income housing program are required to comply. VAWA clarifies that an individual's status as a victim of domestic violence, dating violence, or stalking is not an appropriate basis for denial of housing admission or denial of housing assistance. VAWA also establishes an exception to the federal "one-strike" drug and criminal activity eviction rule for tenants who are victims. The relevant federal housing statutes now explicitly provide that an incident of actual or threatened domestic violence, dating violence, or stalking does not qualify as a serious or repeated violation of the lease or good cause for terminating the assistance, tenancy, or occupancy rights of a victim. For an overview of these new provisions see, Naomi S. Stern, *Housing Rights Under VAWA*

2005, THE ABA COMMISSION ON DOMESTIC VIOLENCE QUARTERLY E–LETTER, Winter 2007.

Domestic Violence in Rural Communities

There has been very little attention paid to the plight of domestic violence victims in rural communities. Yet, as emerging research and scholarship suggest, rural victims face many challenges that differ from victims who live in urban settings, and may even be at higher risk for experiencing violence. In rural areas, there are extremely high rates of poverty, a lack of employment opportunities, high rates of alcoholism, and very little housing. In addition, there are very few shelters for abused women located in rural areas, making the problems of homelessness even more profound. These problems can be exacerbated for same-sex partners, immigrants, and other minorities who fear discrimination or unwanted legal interventions. Isolation is perhaps the most pressing problem for rural women. Consider the following excerpt:

Wendy Boka

Domestic Violence in Farming Communities: Overcoming The Unique Problems Posed By The Rural Setting

9 DRAKE J. AGRIC. L. 389 (2004).

. . . Isolation may be the most important ingredient in the formation and continuation of abusive relationships, as "[t]he literature on domestic violence almost universally mentions isolation as a factor in the severity of violence and in the inability of women to leave abusive relationships." Clearly, this issue is a much more significant problem in rural communities where "[t]here are no neighbors to hear screams and no doors to knock upon for immediate help." The proximity to neighbors directly corresponds to the likelihood of third-party reporting of domestic abuse; where there is nobody close enough to hear or see a violent episode, there is nobody to call the police.

Rural women face isolation in their daily lives that can also prevent them from seeking help between the attacks. In a rural county in Wisconsin, "[t]hirty percent of the victims [surveyed at a domestic violence shelter] reported having no phone. This is in great contrast to the general population, in which it was reported that only four percent were without a phone." Perhaps more significantly, "[f]orty-seven percent of the victims reported having no access to a vehicle," usually because their abusive partner had control of the family's only vehicle. This would mean that, unless fleeing on foot, a woman would only be able to leave when the family vehicle—and her abusive partner—was home.

The lack of transportation options, both private and public, often means that rural women in abusive relationships must seek the help of others in order to leave their partners. As previously discussed, most batterers isolate their victims from family and friends, making this option less viable. In addition, the physical isolation that defines rural areas often makes escape more difficult—in the aforementioned rural Wisconsin county, for example, "[f]orty-five percent of the victims reported no family nearby and thirty-five [percent] reported no supportive neighbors." . . .

The immediate resource needed by victims is domestic violence shelters. Unfortunately, this is the resource that is most likely to be inaccessible or simply nonexistent in rural areas. While "[n]ationwide, there are four times more shelters for animals than there are for [battered] women," the scarcity of emergency shelters is particularly apparent in rural areas. As one counselor at a women's resource center in Canada stated, "we are still a rural community and don't have a lot of resources in terms of social justice compared to bigger areas. We have [fewer] follow-up services."

Rural Texas provides perhaps the most striking example of the lack of domestic violence resources in rural areas. Of the 196 rural counties in Texas, only twenty have a family violence center. One advocate described how, prior to the building of a county shelter, "[o]ne [abused] woman ran four miles in her bare feet . . . in the middle of the night through the woods . . . at 3 a.m." to the victim's [sic] home for help. Despite their scarcity in rural areas, the importance of such services cannot be underestimated. One young, battered woman, who was fortunate enough to live in one of the rural Texas counties with a family violence center, arrived at the shelter with bruises on her face, a broken nose, and a ruptured uterus. She stated, "If it hadn't been for [the shelter] . . . I would have stayed."

NOTES AND QUESTIONS

1. **Lack of Responsiveness from Authorities.** In one recent study of domestic violence in rural Texas, the authors found that domestic violence victims expressed concerns about inadequate legal protections, discourteous treatment by the police, and a lack of information about their legal options. Criminal justice workers were reluctant to make arrests, tended to impose lenient sanctions, often disbelieved the victim, and held many victim-blaming attitudes. The authors suggest that part of the problem in rural areas is an ideology of rural patriarchy that seems largely unchallenged by grassroots advocacy. Nikki R. Van Hightower and Joe Gorton, *A Case Study Of Community–Based Responses to Rural Woman Battering*, 8 VIOLENCE AGAINST WOMEN 845 (2002).

2. **Strategies in Rural Areas.** One innovative program geared at helping rural victims is *Have Justice Will Travel*, a service located throughout rural Vermont. Its founder, Wynona Ward, grew up in an abusive household in a rural community, and understands the unique challenges rural victims face. The program seeks to end the generational cycle of abuse in rural families by bridging the legal, cultural, geographical, psychological, and economic gaps that exist for victims of domestic abuse. As well as providing legal and supportive services for battered, low-income women and their children, *Have Justice Will Travel* provides in home legal consultations as well as transportation to all court appearances, doctor's visits,

women's support groups, and other important obligations. For more information on this program see http://www.havejusticewilltravel.org.

How successful do you think such a program will be given the abusers strategies of control and isolation? What will it need to do to be of real assistance to immobile elderly or disabled, immigrants, or members of minority communities?

CHAPTER FOUR

Domestic Violence, Reproductive Rights and Sexual Autonomy

Introduction

So far we have focused on the ways in which domestic violence impacts the lives of women as both individuals and as members of their broader communities. We have examined how race, class, age, and poverty can affect a woman's experience in a violent intimate relationship. We will look at other issues of equality later, such as in the family law system and in the workplace. We now turn to the ways in which domestic violence impacts women's sexual autonomy, from controlling their own fertility, to having, or not having, children, to finding other partners, and to being free from unwanted sexual activity. Domestic violence is about control, and abusers often aim to control their partner's sexuality. This holds true whether we are talking about same or opposite sex couples. Thus, by exploring the ways in which abusers control a victim's sexuality as part of a larger pattern of coercion, we gain a deeper understanding of the experience of domestic violence. Sexual autonomy and reproductive rights are central to question of women's equality within broader legal and social norms.

In Chapter One, we explored the connection between historically condoned violence against women and women's subordination. As we will see in this chapter, laws that allow husbands to have sex with their wives without consent, and laws that prohibit the ability of women to make their own reproductive choices deny women full citizenship. In a recent Supreme Court case, *Gonzales v. Carhart*, 550 U.S. ___, 127 S.Ct. 1610 (2007), Justice Ruth Bader Ginsburg articulates this point. She dissents from the 5–4 majority decision upheld a federal ban on a late-term abortion procedure. While the case does not implicate domestic violence, it does retreat from some of the central reasoning of *Planned Parenthood v. Casey*, 505 U.S. 833 (1992) which was excerpted in Chapter One and is more fully discussed in this chapter. For now, consider Justice Ginsburg's argument about reproductive freedom and women's equality:

> As *Casey* comprehended, at stake in cases challenging abortion restrictions is a woman's "control over her [own] destiny." "There was a time, not so long ago," when women were "regarded as the center of home and family life, with attendant special responsibilities that precluded full and independent legal status under the Constitution." Those views, this Court made clear in *Casey*, "are no longer consistent with our understanding of the family, the individual, or the Constitution." Women, it is now acknowledged, have the talent, capacity, and

right "to participate equally in the economic and social life of the Nation." Their ability to realize their full potential, the Court recognized, is intimately connected to "their ability to control their reproductive lives." Thus, legal challenges to undue restrictions on abortion procedures do not seek to vindicate some generalized notion of privacy; rather, they center on a woman's autonomy to determine her life's course, and thus to enjoy equal citizenship stature....

... [T]he Court deprives women of the right to make an autonomous choice, even at the expense of their safety. ...

This way of thinking reflects ancient notions about women's place in the family and under the Constitution—ideas that have long since been discredited. *Carhart v. Gonzales*, 550 U.S. __, 127 S.Ct. 1610 (2007) (Ginsburg, J. dissenting).

When domestic violence impacts the ability of women to control their sexuality and reproduction, it also hinders their right to full autonomy. To that end, we first look at sexual consent, particularly as related to issues of marital rape. We then examine questions of reproductive rights, including access to birth control and abortion, and we conclude with the relationship between battering and pregnancy. Each of these topics requires us to ask how law and public policy should respond. As you read the material, keep some questions in mind. Consider the ways in which the law, in seeking to help and protect women (and men) from domestic violence, may actually be undermining their sexual autonomy by either enforcing sexual norms which may discriminate against certain groups, or by subordinating the interests of women to the interests of protecting unborn children. These questions suggest that domestic violence is both an individual phenomenon and one that has vast implications for gender equality throughout society.

A.   SEXUAL CONSENT AND MARITAL RAPE

The right to be free from unwanted sexual contact is crucial to maintaining both one's sexual autonomy and controlling one's reproduction. Yet, victims in abusive relationships lose their ability to control their own sexuality and reproduction. The Department of Justice estimates that as many as 62% of all adult rapes are committed by current or former husbands, or boyfriends. Patricia Tjaden and Nancy Thoennes, *National Institute of Justice Research Report: Full Report of the Prevalence, Incidence, and Consequences of Violence Against Women: Findings from the National Violence Against Women Survey* (2000). As we saw in Chapter Two, and, and as is illustrated in the *State v. Russell* excerpt that follows, sexual assaults and rape are often part of a pattern of abuse that includes physical violence as well. This phenomenon is supported, in part, by laws that still allow husbands to have sex with their wives without first gaining full and knowing consent.

In thinking about the facts presented in *State v. Russell*, what do you think the relationship is between sexual assault and domestic violence? How does domestic violence impact a woman's sexual autonomy as well as her physical safety? Why do abusers feel as if they have a "right" to engage in sexual intercourse with their partners and what role does the law play in reinforcing that view?

State v. Russell

Court of Appeals of Alaska, 2002.
2002 WL 31667313.

■ MANNHEIMER, JUDGE.

In 1994, Dan L. Russell was convicted of first-degree sexual assault upon his estranged wife, T.R. We affirmed his conviction on appeal. In 1998, Russell filed a petition for post-conviction relief. He asserted that his trial attorney, Assistant Public Defender David Seid, had not investigated or prepared his case properly. After a lengthy evidentiary hearing, the superior court denied Russell's petition for post-conviction relief. Russell now appeals that decision.

Generally speaking, Russell's claims of ineffective assistance of counsel rest on the assertion that his trial attorney failed to anticipate, and then failed to adequately investigate and rebut, the State's evidence that Russell had assaulted T.R. in the past and that T.R. was a "battered woman"—i.e., a woman who, having been physically abused by her husband, voluntarily returned to him and was physically abused again. Russell contends that, if his defense attorney had competently prepared the case, the attorney would have discovered evidence to convincingly rebut, or at least seriously under-cut, the State's allegations of prior marital assaults and the State's assertion that T.R. was a battered woman. . . .

Russell was accused of raping T.R., his estranged wife, while the two of them were alone in Russell's hotel room in Ketchikan on July 1, 1994.

Russell and T.R. had separated four months earlier, in March. After the separation, Russell and T.R. began marital counseling with Susan Jordan at the Gateway Center, but Russell stopped attending after several sessions. T.R. continued to see Jordan by herself.

In early May, Russell left town to work on Prince of Wales Island. T.R. obtained dissolution papers from the court and sent them to Russell, but he refused to sign them.

Also in May, T.R. obtained a domestic violence restraining order against Russell. In the ensuing weeks, Russell repeatedly violated this restraining order. He telephoned T.R. and he wrote her dozens of letters and cards—approximately sixty letters and cards between May and early July. In most of Russell's letters and cards to T.R., he pleaded with her not to divorce him, begged her for another chance, and told her how much he loved and needed her.

For instance, in a letter dated May 13, 1994, Russell begged T.R. not to divorce him and also begged her not to turn him in for violating the restraining order. The next day, May 14th, Russell sent a letter asking T.R. to love him still, and reminding her of all the good times they had shared, including "excellent love-making". On May 16th, Russell wrote T.R. three times. He sent her a letter in which he said that he didn't want to live alone, and he begged T.R. to give him her love. Russell also sent T.R. a card. This card depicted two polar bear faces, which Russell had labeled "Dan" and "[T.R.]". The accompanying caption read, "Polar bears making love in an Alaskan snow storm." On the back of the card, Russell wrote, "I sure wish we could do this again." Russell also sent a postcard that day, saying that he loved T.R. and needed her. . . .

[The Court then outlines a number of letters Russell sent to T.R. which included many sexual references.]

On June 28th, Russell wrote T.R. a letter on the back of a sexual harassment flyer. He told her that this was the only paper he could find. He apologized for putting so much pressure on T.R., and he assured her that the pressure would stop "if you could only tell me that you love me."

One of this series of letters, dated June 20, 1994, received special attention at Russell's trial. In this letter, Russell wrote:

[T.R.], you told me that you liked me to take matters into my own hands. So I guess I will, even if it means raping you. I do need you and want you.

T.R. and Russell did not see each other face to face until July 1st, eleven days after this letter. . . .

After the two unsuccessful phone calls [to a shelter seeking T.R.], Russell left a note for T.R. on the shelter door, asking her to call him at his hotel. He then set up watch across the street from the shelter. By coincidence, T.R. and her twelve-year-old son, Jeffrey, were walking near the shelter, and Russell saw them.

Russell, T.R., and Jeffrey went to McDonald's together to talk. Russell kept trying to kiss T.R., but she was reluctant; she covered up her face. Finally, she gave Russell a "peck". After the meal, Russell insisted on accompanying T.R. and Jeffrey on their errands. When T.R. could not dissuade him from this plan, she offered to walk Russell back to his hotel, then take her son home and call Russell later.

When the three of them got to the hotel, Russell gave Jeffrey some money to go play video games in the hotel's arcade, so that Russell and T.R. could be alone in Russell's room. At this point, T.R.'s and Russell's accounts of events diverge radically.

T.R. testified that Russell pulled her toward him and started to kiss her. She pushed away and tried to leave the room, but Russell blocked her way to the door. T.R. stated that Russell then pulled his penis out of his pants and pushed her to her knees so that she could perform fellatio on him, but T.R. stood up and told him that she wanted to leave. In response, Russell picked T.R. up, carried her to the bed, and started to undo her pants. T.R. testified that she fought, but Russell succeeded in pulling her pants down to her knees. Then he pushed her legs up toward her shoulders and raped her.

While this was happening, Jeffrey returned to the room and knocked on the door. When T.R. turned her head to answer, Russell placed his hand over her mouth. Eventually, Jeffrey went away, but he came back some minutes later and knocked again. By this time, the rape was over; T.R. spoke to her son, saying that she would be out in a minute.

(Jeffrey testified that, when he heard his mother's voice through the door, it sounded like she had been crying. And when his mother came out of the room and joined him in the video arcade, she looked as if she had been crying; "her eyes were all red".)

As T.R. was getting ready to leave the room, Russell began telling T.R. that he was sorry for forcing her to have sex, and that he loved her. T.R. told the jury that "[it] seemed like [Russell] was really hurt for what he had done. And he just said that he was ashamed and that he was sorry . . . [and] that he knew [that] he had blew everything."

Russell, for his part, did not agree that his encounter with T.R. and Jeffrey was accidental. According to Russell, when he met T.R. and her son on the street near the women's shelter, T.R. told him that she had been trying to find him. They went to McDonald's, where Russell and T.R. talked about their relationship, and Russell gave T.R. some jewelry that he had purchased for her. Then they walked back to Russell's hotel.

Russell testified that when they got inside the room, T.R. stood staring out the window. Russell came up behind her, put his arms around her, and kissed her on the neck. In response, T.R. "kind of moved in a romantic way, with [Russell's] arms around her, looking out the window." . . . .

After Jeffrey was gone, Russell held T.R. and kissed her, and then he unzipped his pants and exposed his penis to her. According to Russell, T.R. said, "Oh, darn, why do you do this to me? You know I melt every time I get around you." Then T.R. willingly gave Russell oral sex.

But after a while, T.R. stopped and told Russell, "That's all you get." When Russell replied, "That's not fair; you['ve] got to do something to me. Why can't I do something to you?" T.R. said "Okay."

At this point, Russell carried T.R. to the bed, where they fondled each other. Russell testified that T.R. said, "You know, Dan, we shouldn't be doing this, because my counselors don't want me to have any contact with you." Finally, after more foreplay, T.R. told him, "Okay, but this is going to be our little secret. You['ve] got to promise me [that] nobody is going to find out about this—that I'm having sex with you." Then they had consensual sex.

Russell said that when the sexual intercourse was over, T.R. started crying. When Russell asked T.R. what was wrong; she replied that she had promised her counselors that this would not happen—that she would be strong and not make love to Russell. Russell assured her that everything would be okay, and he handed her a tissue. As they parted, Russell told T.R. that he loved her. T.R. answered, "I know you love me, Dan. I love you too."

The parties agreed, in large part, on what happened following T.R.'s departure from the hotel. T.R. called Russell at his hotel two or three times that evening. And, the next day (July 2nd), T.R. went down to the ferry terminal to see Russell off. At their farewell meeting, Russell gave T.R. one hundred dollars, which she used to make a payment on her wedding ring.

A few days later, the women's shelter notified T.R. that they had received a card addressed to her. The card was from Russell. He wrote:

[T.R.]—

Thank you so much for seeing me. I am so sorry, if you know what I mean. Honest, I told myself years ago [that] I would never ever really force you. I'm so ashamed for what I did. Don't hate me for it. I thought maybe you might have liked it. I did. Don't hate me, please.

T.R. did not tell anyone that she had been raped until July 4th. However, T.R.'s friend, Connie Taylor, testified that T.R.'s demeanor changed noticeably during the first few days of July....

The State's first witness was T.R. We have already described her testimony regarding her encounter with Russell on July 1, 1994. In addition, T.R. described two prior incidents in which Russell used violence against her.

The first was the incident that occurred in August 1993, when she and Russell were living in Coffman Cove (a small community on the eastern shore of Prince of Wales Island, about halfway between Ketchikan and Petersburg). T.R. testified that, during an argument, Russell hit her with his hands, struck her with a coffee table, and choked her. As a consequence, T.R. lost consciousness, had to be revived twice, and was ultimately medivacked to Ketchikan.

Based on this Coffman Cove incident, the State charged Russell with felony assault. However (as T.R. told the jurors at Russell's trial), when T.R. appeared before the grand jury in 1993, she testified that she was the one at fault; she told the grand jurors that her injuries had been self-inflicted and that Russell was innocent. In her testimony at Russell's trial, T.R. declared that her grand jury testimony had been false—that she lied to protect Russell because she loved him and because she did not want him to go to prison.

The second incident occurred one month later (September 1993) in Ketchikan. T.R. went out for the evening with a girlfriend. They were in a bar, playing darts and socializing. Russell was present as well, and he got jealous. He pushed T.R., and then he left the bar. Later, after T.R. and her friend left the bar, Russell confronted them on the street (actually, in the tunnel near downtown Ketchikan). Holding a checkbook in his hand, Russell punched T.R. in the chest and called her names. Afterwards, T.R. went to the hospital for treatment. She suffered a bruise to her chest....

In his defense summation, Seid told the jury that they should not be confused by the evidence of Russell's prior assaults on T.R. He conceded that Russell "has a history of being bad." Russell had acknowledged assaulting T.R. in August 1993, and the State had introduced evidence of another assault in September 1993. But Seid told the jury that Russell's past acts were not a proper basis for convicting him of sexual assault in the present case:

> That's not what this case is about. This was a consensual sexual encounter. It wasn't a sexual assault; it wasn't a rape. What happened on July 1st was the last time they lived as husband and wife; they made love.

Seid argued that T.R. had significant motives for lying about what happened in the hotel room. First, she was angry at Russell for the way he had treated her in the past, and for the times he had neglected his family responsibilities while they were living together. Second, she was arguably angry at herself for allowing Russell to seduce her—for even though she still loved him, she was also trying to establish her independence of him. Third, T.R. had begun a new sexual relationship with another man—an old friend of Russell's.

Seid pointed out that many of the undisputed events of July 1st were consistent with the conclusion that T.R. and Russell had engaged in consensual sex. T.R. and her son went to McDonald's with Russell. They walked back to Russell's hotel together. T.R. and Russell took the elevator by themselves while Jeffrey took the stairs. Afterwards, when T.R. emerged from Russell's room, she and her son went shopping at a video store. That night, T.R. did not telephone the police or the women's shelter or her friend Connie Taylor. Rather, T.R. telephoned Russell. The next day, she went to the ferry terminal to see Russell off. She accepted money from him and then went to make a payment on her wedding ring.

Seid pointed out that T.R. did not report the rape . . .

Seid urged the jurors to consider Russell's explanation of the apology letter—the explanation that Russell was ashamed for having "persuaded [T.R.] to have sex [with him] when he didn't feel that she really wanted to do this at first." Seid asked the jurors to consider: if Russell truly had intended to apologize to T.R. for raping her, would he have sent his apology to the women's shelter, where anyone could potentially read it?

When he concluded his remarks, Seid reminded the jurors:

> [The] issue [is not] whether [T.R.] is a sympathetic person. Because, in a lot of ways, she is. [The issue is] not . . . whether Dan's a good partner or a good father, or whether he ever assaulted her before. The issue is whether or not a sexual encounter on July 1st was consensual. And I suggest to you that the evidence shows otherwise.

> You can leave this courtroom and you can say, "I don't like Dan Russell." You can leave this courtroom [and say], "I have a lot of sympathy for [T.R.]." You can leave this courtroom and say, "This was a really bad marriage." But I suggest to you that you cannot convict Dan Russell, on this evidence that you've heard . . ., of sexual assault in the first degree. . . .

Russell asserts that evidence of his prior assaults on T.R. played a major role in the State's case, and he is right. As described above, the prosecutor relied on these prior assaults to support the argument that T.R. was afraid of Russell—thus explaining why she wanted to accompany Russell back to his hotel (rather than having Russell walk her home and find out where she lived), and also explaining why she did not offer much physical resistance to the rape....

During pre-trial preparation, Russell repeatedly told Seid that he had never struck a woman. But Seid testified that he did not believe that his client was telling him the truth on this point....

Even leaving aside Russell's trial testimony, the state trooper investigative report on the Coffman Cove incident contained detailed statements from a number of independent witnesses—witnesses who presumably would have been called by the State if Seid had requested a continuance to attack the Coffman Cove assault allegation....

Given all of this evidence available to the State, even if Seid had used the inconsistent statements in the medical records to attack T.R.'s credibility, Seid could reasonably conclude that he would be unable to convince a jury that T.R. had fabricated these prior assaults. For these reasons, we uphold Judge Jahnke's ruling that Seid acted competently when he chose to proceed to trial, and to argue that the prior assaults did not prove the current rape, rather than asking for more time to challenge the State's assertions that Russell assaulted T.R. in August and September 1993....

NOTES AND QUESTIONS

1. **The Impact of Prior Abuse on Sexual Assault Victims.** Was the evidence of the prior assaults relevant to the sexual assault charge? After all, assault is a different crime than rape and prior bad acts evidence is usually inadmissible. The Court points out that the evidence of prior assaults on T.R. helped to explain, in part, why T.R. accompanied Russell after the alleged rape, and why she did not resist further. Absent this evidence, the jury may not have understood the context in which the rape happened. Thus, the court, through its evidentiary rulings, allows the prosecution to locate the rape within the larger framework of violence.

2. **The History of Marital Rape Laws.** All states now allow for the prosecution of a husband who has raped his wife, but this has not always been the case. First consider the history of such laws.

In the late 1600s, the Chief Justice in England, Lord Matthew Hale, articulated what would become the most popular justification in modern jurisprudence for the marital rape exemption. Hale understood marriage as granting a wife's ongoing consent to sexual intercourse. He wrote, "the husband cannot be guilty of a rape committed by himself upon his lawful wife, for by their mutual matrimonial consent and contract the wife hath given up herself in this kind unto her husband, which she cannot retract." A man could not, however, force his wife to have sex with a third party: "for tho she hath given her body to her husband, she is not to be prostituted by him to another." By giving "her body" sexually to her husband, a woman thereby gave her ongoing contractual consent to conjugal relations with him in the future. This ongoing consent ideology permeates rape law even today. Michelle J. Anderson, *Marital Immunity, Intimate Relationships, and Improper Inferences: A New Law On Sexual Offenses By Intimates*, 54 HASTINGS L. J. 1465 (2003).

Michelle Anderson argues that this belief that men have the right to rape their partners continues today and is manifested in laws that provide immunity for married spouses. In analyzing current rape statutes, she finds the following:

> Many people believe that reformers won the battle against the marital rape exemption. This belief is, unfortunately, incorrect. The good news is that twenty-four states and the District of Columbia have abolished marital immunity for sexual offenses. The bad news is that twenty-six states retain marital immunity in one form or another. Although in some of these twenty-six states marital immunity for the specific crime of forcible rape is dead, immunity for other sexual offenses thrives. For example, twenty states grant marital immunity for sex with a wife who is incapacitated or unconscious and cannot consent. Fifteen states grant marital immunity for sexual offenses unless requirements such as prompt complaint, extra force, separation, or divorce are met. The law in more than half the states today makes it harder to convict men of sexual offenses committed against their wives. In so doing, the law in these jurisdictions degrades married women and affords men who sexually assault their wives an unwarranted status preference. *Id*.

3. **Evidence of Consent.** Despite rape shield laws that protect the defendant from probing into the victim's sexual past, the fact that the victim consented to sex with the defendant in the past can be used as evidence that she consented to the current sexual encounter. See, e.g. Federal Rule of Evidence 412.

Does this rule create an assumption that if the victim consented to sexual relations in the past, she could have done so again on this occasion? Note that this rule makes it much harder to prosecute cases of sexual assault when the parties have been involved in a prior sexual relationship. For a discussion of these issues, see Michelle J. Anderson, *From Chastity Requirement to Sexual License: Sexual Consent and a New Rape Shield Law*, 70 GEO.WASH.L.REV. 51 (2002).

4. **Confidentiality of Victim's Counseling Records.** In many cases involving allegations of sexual assault, attorneys seek to discover the victim's counseling records. Attorneys often hope that such records will contain information that will undermine the victim's credibility. Fear that counseling records may be used often chills the victim's willingness to come forward, and thus interferes with her ability to hold her abuser accountable.

All states currently afford a testimonial privilege between patients and psychotherapists, but many victims of domestic violence receive counseling from social workers, shelter counselors, or other service providers, particularly those funded through some public assistance. Thus, many states now

provide for the patient-psychotherapist privilege to extend to other professionals, in part under the rationale that it is unfair to distinguish between
costly psychotherapists and those who provide services to those whose
resources are limited.

There are three types of laws that protect the confidentiality between
counselor and victim. The first are laws like those in Florida and Pennsylvania, which absolutely forbid the release of confidential communications
without the victim's consent. The second are those that forbid the disclosure of confidential communications except when it is in the public interest
to do so. The most common situations that courts have found to involve the
public interest and thus require disclosure are situations involving allegations of child abuse or neglect. The third type requires disclosure when the
court finds it necessary given the facts of the case. In these cases, courts
generally engage in a balancing test, weighing the defendant's rights
against the victim's need to keep the information confidential. Most states,
including California, have such laws. In these cases, the court often reviews
the counseling records *in camera* before making a decision.

Some states have been less willing to allow for absolute privileges. In
Massachusetts, for example, the Supreme Judicial Court has found that in
some cases, defendants must have the right to see counseling records in
order to have a fair trial. In these cases, the court will weigh the privacy
interests of the victim with the defendant's constitutional rights. See,
Commonwealth v. Bishop, 617 N.E.2d 990 (Mass. 1993); *Commonwealth v.
Tripolone,* 681 N.E.2d 1216 (Mass. Sup. Ct. 1997).

In 1996, the Supreme Court, for the first time, recognized the patient-
counselor privilege in *Jaffee v. Redmond,* 518 U.S. 1 (1996). The Court
extended the privilege to a clinical social worker. This ruling has had a
positive impact on the ways in which state courts are interpreting the
privilege. For an excellent review of this issue see Dep't. of Justice, *Privacy
of Victims' Counseling Communications, Legal Series Bulletin #8,* November 2002, at http://www.ojp.usdoj.gov/ovc/publications/bulletins/legalseries/
bulletin8/2.html.

5. **The Interplay of Sex and Violence.** In many cases of domestic
violence, sexual assault is just one of many means by which the abuser
controls his victim. However, there are also some cases in which the sex
itself is violent, especially in those instances in which there is a claim that
the parties were involved in sadomasochistic sex. Under the law, physical
violence is treated differently than is sex. While consent can be a complete
defense to a sexual assault, consent is not a defense to physical assault. See,
e.g., *Commonwealth v. Appleby,* 402 N.E.2d 1051 (1980). Thus, as a matter
of legal doctrine, traditionally, there has been no defense of consent when
someone is physically injured in the course of a sexual encounter. See
Cheryl Hanna, *Sex Is Not A Sport: Consent and Violence In The Criminal
Law,* 42 B.C.L. Rev. 239 (2001).

However, as noted in Chapter Three, the Supreme Court has held in
Lawrence v. Texas that private, consensual adult relationships are protected by the Constitution. Does this mean that the traditional rule that rejects
consent as a defense to physical injuries occurring in sexual contexts is no

longer constitutional? What effect might this have on domestic violence prosecutions? See, Monica Pa, *Beyond the Pleasure Principle: The Criminalization of Consensual Sadomasochistic Sex*, 11 TEX.J. WOM. & L. 51 (2001).

6. **Rape and Assault Charges.** One issue that often arises in domestic violence cases is that defendants are charged with both assault and rape or some other sexual offense. Historically, courts have treated these charges separately and have disallowed the consent defense to go forward in a rape case even though the violence took place within the sexual context. See e.g. *State of Washington v. Guinn,* 105 Wash.App. 1030 (March 30, 2001) (unpublished opinion); *U.S. v. Arab,* 55 M.J. 508 (2001). In many of these cases, the courts avoid the legal question of whether consent could be a defense to sexual violence, but rather have found that, given the facts, no person could have honestly and reasonably believed that the victim was consenting to the assaults given the nature of the crime and the extent of the injury.

B.   ACCESS TO BIRTH CONTROL AND DISEASE PREVENTION

One consequence of rape and sexual assault in intimate relationships is that the victim's sexual autonomy and sexual health are threatened when being forced to engage in unwanted sexual acts. In the following article, Michelle Anderson explores some of the effects of marital rape on women. As you read it, consider how the question of consent not only affects one's sexual autonomy, but also impacts the ability to control one's fertility and stay healthy.

Michelle J. Anderson
Marital Immunity, Intimate Relationships, and Improper Inferences: A New Law On Sexual Offenses by Intimates

54 HASTINGS L.J. 1465 (2003).

. . . [A] number of scholars have argued that the "generalized consent" that marriage grants a husband should extend to circumstances in which the wife is mentally incapacitated or unconscious and cannot consent. The related notion is that incapacitated or unconscious rape by a spouse is not harmful enough for the justice system to recognize. In a number of states, men even enjoy immunity when they themselves drug their wives, rendering them unable to consent.

As a preliminary matter, it is important to note that drugging a wife to have sex with her is not an uncommon weapon in a batterer's arsenal. In one case, for example, a man laced his wife's food with half a bottle of antidepressants, rendering her unconscious. While she was unconscious, he orally and digitally penetrated her as he videotaped the episode. The use of drugs is analogous to the use of physical force to render a woman incapacitated. Some men beat or choke their wives to render them unconscious before raping them. As one victim in a study on wife rape described:

> [My husband] would try to choke me, and then I would pass out. Then he would rape me. He would put me to sleep and then rape me. Sometimes when we were out somewhere, and he didn't like something I did, he would say, "You wanna go to sleep?" and laugh like it was real funny. It was like a punishment.

> Although most states would recognize the choking here as force that makes the sexual offense rape, too many states would not recognize drugging a wife for the identical purpose as force that makes the sexual offense rape.

Distinct from the issue of deliberate drugging on the part of the husband, in twenty states men enjoy immunity when they simply take advantage of their wives' mental incapacity or unconsciousness to have sex with them without their consent. Some scholars roundly dismiss the potential harm of this kind of invasion. [Donald] Dripps argues that it should not be criminal for a man to penetrate his wife when she is passed out. The problems with this position are both principled and practical.

As a matter of principle, the argument in favor of the marital exemption for mental incapacitation or unconscious rape ignores or greatly undervalues a married woman's sexual autonomy—her freedom to decide whether and when to engage in intercourse. A woman has the right to reserve her body for her own ends and not to be used as an object for someone else's ends. Affording married women this right is crucial to their dignity and equality under the law. It is this right that rape laws should be designed to protect.

[Michael] Hilf argues, however, "A married person has, to some extent, a lesser expectation of personal autonomy; therefore, the affront to one's autonomy is less in the case of spousal rape than in the case of ordinary rape." While married individuals may have lesser expectations of certain kinds of autonomy, it does not follow that in the sexual realm, a woman's autonomy must bow to the demands of her husband's interest in obtaining sex. A man's desire for an orgasm simply does not outweigh his wife's interest in avoiding the invasion of unwanted intercourse. A married woman's expectation of sexual autonomy should be no less than a single person's.

As a practical matter, the argument that incapacitated and unconscious rape are not harmful reveals ignorance about the perils of sexual penetration for a woman. A man who penetrates a woman when she is unconscious denies her the power to negotiate the use of contraceptives and other protection to prevent pregnancy and disease. In [an] 1921 Alabama case, for example, when the wife withdrew from sexual relations in order to stop having children, her husband proceeded to force her to have sex against her will. If she had been drugged and he had taken advantage of her unconscious state and made her pregnant as a result, the primary injury she sought to avoid—unwanted pregnancy—would have been the same. Unwanted pregnancy and disease are serious injuries for both unmarried and married women.

Even if the man does not make his unconscious wife pregnant against her will or give her a sexually transmitted disease, he has profoundly degraded her bodily integrity. Women's dry orifices are not permeable. To penetrate them takes force that may bruise, tear, and otherwise damage tissue. Physical and psychological pain will likely greet the woman when she regains consciousness. These injuries and this suffering matter. Sexual injury and suffering are what rape laws should be designed to prevent. Because incapacitated and unconscious rape denies sexual autonomy and causes harm, the twenty states that currently provide immunity for it should abolish that immunity.

Third, a number of scholars have argued that spousal sexual offenses in general are not harmful enough for the justice system to criminalize. It is this argument that underlies the general downgrading of spousal sexual offenses, subjecting them to lesser penalties and requiring prompt complaints in seven states. Interestingly, it is the ongoing consent in marriage that supposedly makes spousal sexual assaults less harmful ... Senator Denton argued that the "character of the voluntary association of a husband and wife ... could be thought to mitigate the nature of the harm resulting from the unwanted intercourse." The implicit position is that stranger sexual offenses are injurious to victims, but, because of ongoing consent, spousal sexual offenses are not.

The research, however, indicates that wife rape is as harmful to victims as stranger rape. Marital sexual attacks are more likely than stranger sexual attacks to end in completed rapes rather than attempted rapes. Wife rape victims are more likely than victims of acquaintances or strangers to be raped orally and anally. Contrary to popular opinion, wife rapes tend to be more violent than stranger rapes. Men have raped their wives with wooden batons, fists, dogs, and loaded firearms. The physical consequences of wife rape can, therefore, be painful and dangerous:

> The physical effects of marital rape may include injuries to the vaginal and anal areas, lacerations, soreness, bruising, torn muscles, fatigue and vomiting. Women who have been battered and raped by their husbands may suffer other physical consequences including broken bones, black eyes, bloody noses, and knife wounds that occur during the sexual violence. [Researchers] report that one half of the marital rape survivors in their sample were kicked, hit or burned during sex. Specific gynecological consequences of marital rape include vaginal stretching, miscarriages, stillbirths, bladder infections, infertility and the potential contraction of sexually transmitted diseases, including HIV.

Despite the serious physical consequences of wife rape, the psychological consequences are usually more devastating. Short-term psychological effects of wife rape may include "anxiety, shock, intense fear, depression, suicidal ideation, and post-traumatic stress disorder." Long-term psychological effects may include "disordered eating, sleep problems, depression, problems establishing trusting relationships, and increased negative feelings about themselves" as well as "flash-backs, sexual dysfunction, and emotional pain for years after the violence." In one study of raped wives, "[m]ore than half of the women mentioned considering or attempting suicide at some point."

One reason that wife rapes are so traumatic is that victims are less likely to tell family members, rape crisis counselors, or police officers about their experiences, and they are less likely to receive support when they do. In her groundbreaking study on wife rape, Diana Russell concluded:

> [W]ife rape can be as terrifying and life threatening to the victim as stranger rape. In addition, it often evokes a powerful sense of betrayal, deep disillusionment, and total isolation. Women often receive very poor treatment by friends, relatives, and professional services when they are raped by strangers. This isolation can be even more extreme for victims of wife rape. And just as they are more likely to be blamed, they are more likely to blame themselves.

In addition to feeling betrayed, isolated, and blamed, victims of wife rape are also more likely than victims of stranger rape to endure multiple offenses from their attackers and to suffer from persistent terror. In their follow-up study on marital rape, David Finkelhor and Kersti Yllo reported that fifty percent of the women in their study had been sexually assaulted twenty times or more. The negative physical and mental consequences of such repeated sexual attacks include chronic injury and trauma. Given the serious physical and psychological harm of wife rape, the seven states that currently maintain such unfair requirements should not downgrade it, subject it to lesser penalties, or refuse to prosecute it without a prompt complaint.

At a bare minimum, twenty-six states must abolish the remaining marital immunity for sexual offenses. They need to treat marital and non-marital sexual assault the same and repeal the laws that require separation or divorce, extra force, or prompt complaint, as well as the provisions that downgrade spousal sexual offenses or exempt incapacitated or unconscious rape from legal condemnation.

Formal neutrality as to the marital status of the parties in sexual offense statutes is, at this point, long overdue. Although legal scholars have not until now specifically analyzed and challenged the provisions that remain in statutes today, some have argued generally for the deletion of marital exemptions or for new provisions that authorize the prosecution of wife rape. By eliminating the provisions that evince bias against married women and favoritism toward sexually abusive men, these proposals would achieve formal neutrality on the question of the marital status of the parties in sexual offense statutes.

NOTES AND QUESTIONS

1. **Birth Control Options and the Risk of Sabotage.** In *Griswold v. Connecticut*, 381 U.S. 479 (1965) and then in *Eisenstadt v. Baird*, 405 U.S. 438 (1972), the United States Supreme Court recognized the right of

privacy encompassed the right to use birth control for both married and unmarried women. This right to control one's fertility is seen as central to women's overall equality. Being the victim of domestic violence, however, arguably undermines the ability of women to control their own fertility. The following excerpt explores the relationship between abuse and birth control.

Women who experience violence in their current intimate relationships are also at a much higher risk of experiencing unintended pregnancies and are therefore more likely to face legal restrictions on their ability to make decisions about their pregnancy. Women who experience physical, sexual or psychological abuse during their relationships are more likely to use contraception less frequently, to have their partner restrict their ability to use contraception, and to have their partner refuse to use contraception themselves, all factors which may increase the likelihood of an unintended pregnancy.

Research suggests that women in abusive relationships tend to feel they lack the ability to prevent an unintended pregnancy. This may be due to a number of reasons which stem from the abuser's ability to dominate and control his victim. One study of the effects of abuse on African American women's ability to negotiate contraceptive use with their partners found that those women that reported abuse within their relationships were far more likely to report that their partners never used condoms (71% of abused women compared to 43% of nonabused women). The report found that women in abusive relationships were verbally abused, threatened with abuse, or threatened with abandonment when they requested that their partners use contraception at significantly higher rates than those not in abusive relationships. As a result, these women report feeling more fearful of asking their partner to use contraceptives and more isolated in being in their ability to access contraceptive services.

Abusers are reported to use a variety of techniques to control their partner's ability to use contraception and make decisions about pregnancy. One study of young mothers in Chicago found that abusers use both verbal and behavioral coercion to interfere with the woman's ability to control contraceptive use, terming the interference "birth control sabotage". That study found that 66% of those who reported violence in their relationship also reported some form of birth control sabotage, compared with 34% of those who did not report experiencing violence. Among those who reported birth control sabotage, 62% reported experiencing verbal sabotage, while 22% reported experiencing behavioral sabotage. For purposes of this study, verbal sabotage included statements such as "you want to use birth control so you can sleep around," "if you have a baby, you'll never have to worry that I'll leave," and "you would have my baby if you loved me." Behavioral sabotage included actual restriction on the use of contraceptives or forced sexual contact while unprotected. Accounts reported by the victims in that study ranged from birth control pills being flushed down the toilet by the abuser to black eyes after the abuser discovered the woman was using contraception.

In addition to finding a high correlation between domestic violence and birth control sabotage, the study also found that as the severity of the violence in the relationship increased, so did the severity of birth control sabotage, resulting in a greater risk of unintended pregnancy in especially violent relationships. To avoid confrontation about the issue of birth control, many young women stated they had attempted to get Depo-Provera shots from clinics because it was easier to conceal from their boyfriends. Of the women who were able to get the Depo-Provera shot, those who were caught by their partner were often physically abused as a result of her deception. This problem raises a concern about the availability of contraceptive options for women who live in violent relationships. There is a need for safe, reliable and affordable options which do not require a woman to make frequent visits to a health care clinic risking her safety. The issue is one which victim advocates and health care providers should be aware of when they are assisting a victim in making choices about her situation. When the victim finds that she cannot or will not leave a violent relationship, those providing services to the victim should advise her on contraceptive options which may keep her from increased physical harm. Kimberly D. Perdue, *The Impact of Violence on Reproductive Decision–Making* (2006) (unpublished research paper on file with the authors). See also: *Domestic Violence and Birth Control Sabotage: A Report from the Teen Parent Project, Center for Impact Research* (Feb. 2000); Mary Ellsberg and Barbara Shane. *Violence Against Women: Effects on Reproductive Health*, 20 Outlook 1 (2002); Gina Wingwood and Ralph DiClemente, *The Effects of an Abusive Primary Partner on Condom Use and Sexual Negotiation Practices of African American Women*, 87 Am. J. P.H. 1016 (1997).

2. **Sexual Health.** Emerging research suggests that abused women are at much greater risk for contracting sexually transmitted diseases, including HIV and AIDS, than are non-abused women. Furthermore, women in violent relationships are three times more likely to have a gynecological health problem, such as sexually transmitted diseases, vaginal bleeding or infections, fibroids, urinary tract infections, pelvic pain, genital irritation and decreased sexual pleasure. Jacquelyn C. Campbell, *Health Consequences of Intimate Partner Violence*, 359 The Lancet 9314 (2002). Similar patterns of health consequences exist for same-sex couples in violent relationships. For a recent study examining these, see Pauline Freedberg, *Health Care Barriers and Same–Sex Intimate Partner Violence: A Review of the Literature*, 2 J. Forensic Nursing 15 (2006).

3. **Health Professionals and Domestic Violence.** While the legal profession has taken a lead in combating domestic violence, lawyers are not the only group of professionals who participate in domestic violence intervention, prevention and education. Many other professionals are integrating the assessment and treatment of domestic violence into the specific missions and responsibilities unique to their areas of expertise. In the

1990's several groups within the healthcare professions formulated policies and guidelines acknowledging the need to address domestic violence, and establishing an agenda for action. In 1993, for example, the American Medical Association (AMA) sponsored the National Coalition of Physicians Against Family Violence. Then, in 1996, the AMA adopted a resolution in support of the education of medical students and residents in domestic violence by advocating that:

> . . . medical schools and graduate medical education programs educate students and resident physicians to sensitively inquire about family abuse with all patients, when appropriate and as part of a comprehensive history and physical examination, and provide information about the available community resources for the management of the patient. AMA Resolution HB 295.912 (1996).

The American Psychological Association (APA) published a *Resolution on Male Violence Against Women* in 1999, and sponsors the APA Presidential Task Force on Violence in the Family, which was convened to bring psychological research and clinical experience to bear on the problems of family violence, including partner abuse. The American Nurses Association (ANA) sponsors the Family Violence Protection Fund, which is involved in efforts to promote routine screening of every woman who is hospitalized or comes to a nurse practitioner's or doctor's office. Patricia Underwood, PhD, RN, at Media Briefing on ANA Family Violence Protection Fund (Oct. 14, 1999). Finally, the American Academy of Pediatrics issued a pediatric guide, *Diagnostic and Treatment Guidelines on Domestic Violence*, in 1996, and in 1998 issued a resolution on *The Role of the Pediatrician in Recognizing and Intervening on Behalf of Abused Women*, in which they recognized that "the abuse of women is a pediatric issue." American Academy of Pediatrics, Policy Statement R–9748 (June, 1998). Nor are these domestic violence initiatives limited to the health care professions. The National Education Association, for example, urges school districts and communities to provide preventive training and educational programs for education employees, students, and parents/guardians/care givers. National Education Association, Resolution C–8: Family/Domestic Violence (1999). They also encourage ongoing communications regarding domestic violence issues between social service agencies and education employees.

4. **Mandatory Reporting of Domestic Violence by Health Professionals.** If a medical professional suspects that a patient has been a victim of domestic violence, should she report her suspicions to legal authorities? Does mandatory reporting erode the relationship between the patient and her doctor? Does it undermine her autonomy? Although the reporting of child, elderly and incompetent adult abuse is mandated in all 50 states, reporting competent adult abuse remains a controversial topic. The laws requiring reporting vary dramatically from state to state. California and Kentucky have the most expansive statutes, requiring health care providers to report any suspected domestic abuse. A handful of other states require the reporting of intentionally inflicted injuries. The majority of states require the reporting of injuries that are also criminal offenses such as

stabbing or gun shot wounds. All states protect physicians from civil liability if they do report in good faith. Consider the following argument:

> Recently, the American medical community has recognized domestic violence as a public health issue and has taken steps to develop effective responses to domestic violence. The American Medical Association has stated that intimate violence is a "public health problem that has reached epidemic proportions." Domestic-violence-related injuries to women account for more injuries to women than rapes, muggings, and car accidents combined. Moreover, the U.S. Department of Justice reported that "37% of all women treated in hospital emergency rooms for violence-related injuries in 1994 were harmed by their former or current partners." The fact that the health care system sees and treats so many victims and potential victims makes it a logical place for domestic violence intervention....
>
> The mandatory reporting statutes are "[b]ased on statistics that suggest that battered women are much more likely to visit a physician than to call the police following an incident of domestic violence," and the goal that requiring medical professionals to report injuries to law enforcement will provide law enforcement with greater access to victims and allow for more arrests or other police intervention. Those who support adoption of mandatory reporting laws argue that this policy ensures state intervention in a violent relationship at the earliest possible point. However, proponents of these laws fail to realize that victims seeking medical attention may not want the police to be involved.... Additionally, the American Medical Association (AMA), though identifying valid arguments on both sides of the controversy, rejected mandatory reporting laws as conflicting with patient's rights and physician's responsibilities. The official AMA policy states: "The American Medical Association opposes the adoption of mandatory reporting laws for physicians treating competent adult victims of domestic violence if the required reports identify victims. Such laws violate the basic tenets of medical ethics and are of unproven value."

Nichole Miras Mordini, *Mandatory State Interventions for Domestic Abuse Cases: An Examination of the Effects on Victim Autonomy & Safety*, 52 DRAKE L. REV. 295 (2004).

For further discussion of these issues, see Karen West, Lisa Bledsoe, Joni Jenkins and Lois Margaret Nora, *The Mandatory Reporting of Adult Victims of Violence: Perspectives from the Field*, 90 KY. L.J. 1071 (2002); Ariella Hyman, Dean Schillinger and Bernard Lo, *Laws Mandating Reporting of Domestic Violence, Do They Promote Patient Well–Being?* 273 JAMA 1781 (1995); Ariella Hyman and Ronald Chez, *Mandatory Reporting of Domestic Violence by Health Care Providers: A Misguided Approach*, WOMEN'S HEALTH ISSUES, Winter 1995.

C. REPRODUCTIVE RIGHTS

In the first chapter, we briefly discussed *Planned Parenthood v. Casey*, the first case in which the United States Supreme Court acknowledged the harms of domestic violence and drew the connection between intimate violence and reproductive rights. What follows are the relevant portions of the case in which, by a narrow majority, the Court struck down the portion of the Pennsylvania statute which required women to notify their spouses before obtaining an abortion.

Planned Parenthood v. Casey

United States Supreme Court, 1992.
505 U.S. 833.

■ JUSTICE O'CONNOR, JUSTICE KENNEDY, and JUSTICE SOUTER delivered the opinion of the Court.

Section 3209 of Pennsylvania's abortion law provides, except in cases of medical emergency, that no physician shall perform an abortion on a married woman without receiving a signed statement from the woman that she has notified her spouse that she is about to undergo an abortion. The woman has the option of providing an alternative signed statement certifying that her husband is not the man who impregnated her; that her husband could not be located; that the pregnancy is the result of spousal sexual assault which she has reported; or that the woman believes that notifying her husband will cause him or someone else to inflict bodily injury upon her. A physician who performs an abortion on a married woman without receiving the appropriate signed statement will have his or her license revoked, and is liable to the husband for damages.

The District Court heard the testimony of numerous expert witnesses, and made detailed findings of fact regarding the effect of this statute. [After the Court set forth in detail statistics supporting that domestic violence was a widespread problem and negatively impacts on women's reproductive choices, the Court concluded:]

This information and the District Court's findings reinforce what common sense would suggest. In well-functioning marriages, spouses discuss important intimate decisions such as whether to bear a child. But there are millions of women in this country who are the victims of regular physical and psychological abuse at the hands of their husbands. Should these women become pregnant, they may have very good reasons for not wishing to inform their husbands of their decision to obtain an abortion. Many may have justifiable fears of physical abuse, but may be no less fearful of the consequences of reporting prior abuse to the Commonwealth of Pennsylvania. Many may have a reasonable fear that notifying their husbands will provoke further instances of child abuse; these women are not exempt from § 3209's notification requirement. Many may fear devastating forms of psychological abuse from their husbands, including verbal harassment, threats of future violence, the destruction of possessions, physical confinement to the home, the withdrawal of financial support, or the disclosure of the abortion to family and friends. These methods of psychological abuse may act as even more of a deterrent to notification than the possibility of physical violence, but women who are the victims of the abuse are not exempt from § 3209's notification requirement. And many women who are pregnant as a result of sexual assaults by their husbands will be unable to avail themselves of the exception for spousal sexual assault, § 3209(b)(3), because the exception requires that the woman have notified law enforcement authorities within 90 days of the assault, and her husband will be notified of her report once an investigation begins, § 3128(c). If anything in this field is certain, it is that victims of spousal sexual assault are extremely reluctant to report the abuse to the government; hence, a great many spousal rape victims will not be exempt from the notification requirement imposed by § 3209.

The spousal notification requirement is thus likely to prevent a significant number of women from obtaining an abortion. It does not merely make abortions a little more difficult or expensive to obtain; for many women, it will impose a substantial obstacle. We must not blind ourselves to the fact that the significant number of women who fear for their safety and the safety of their children are likely to be deterred from procuring an abortion as surely as if the Commonwealth had outlawed abortion in all cases. . . .

. . . The unfortunate yet persisting conditions we document above will mean that in a large fraction of the cases in which § 3209 is relevant, it will operate as a substantial obstacle to a woman's choice to undergo an abortion. It is an undue burden, and therefore invalid.

This conclusion is in no way inconsistent with our decisions upholding parental notification or consent requirements. Those enactments, and our judgment that they are constitutional, are based on the quite reasonable assumption that minors will benefit from consultation with their parents and that children will often not realize that their parents have their best interests at heart. We cannot adopt a parallel assumption about adult women.

We recognize that a husband has a "deep and proper concern and interest . . . in his wife's pregnancy and in the growth and development of the fetus she is carrying." With regard to the children he has fathered and raised, the Court has recognized his "cognizable and substantial" interest in their custody. If these cases concerned a State's ability to require the mother to notify the father before taking some action with respect to a living child raised by both, therefore, it would be reasonable to conclude as a general matter that the father's interest in the welfare of the child and the mother's interest are equal.

Before birth, however, the issue takes on a very different cast. It is an inescapable biological fact that state regulation with respect to the child a woman is carrying will have a far greater impact on the mother's liberty than on the father's. The effect of state regulation on a woman's protected liberty is doubly deserving of scrutiny in such a case, as the State has touched not only upon the private sphere of the family but upon the very bodily integrity of the pregnant woman. The Court has held that "when the wife and the husband disagree on this decision, the view of only one of the two marriage partners can prevail. Inasmuch as it is the woman who physically bears the child and who is the more directly and immediately affected by the pregnancy, as between the two, the balance weighs in her favor." This conclusion rests upon the basic nature of marriage and the nature of our Constitution: "[T]he marital couple is not an independent entity with a mind and heart of its own, but an association of two individuals each with a separate intellectual and emotional makeup. If the right of privacy means anything, it is the right of the individual, married or single, to be free from unwarranted governmental intrusion into matters so fundamentally affecting a person as the decision whether to bear or beget a child." The Constitution protects individuals, men and women alike, from unjustified state interference, even when that interference is enacted into law for the benefit of their spouses.

There was a time, not so long ago, when a different understanding of the family and of the Constitution prevailed. In *Bradwell v. State,* three Members of this Court reaffirmed the common-law principle that "a woman had no legal existence separate from her husband, who was regarded as her head and representative in the social state; and, notwithstanding some recent modifications of this civil status, many of the special rules of law flowing from and dependent upon this cardinal principle still exist in full force in most States." Only one generation has passed since this Court observed that "woman is still regarded as the center of home and family life," with attendant "special responsibilities" that precluded full and independent legal status under the Constitution. These views, of course, are no longer consistent with our understanding of the family, the individual, or the Constitution.

In keeping with our rejection of the common-law understanding of a woman's role within the family, the Court held in *Danforth* that the Constitution does not permit a State to require a married woman to obtain her husband's consent before undergoing an abortion. The principles that guided the Court in *Danforth* should be our guides today. For the great many women who are victims of abuse inflicted by their husbands, or whose children are the victims of such abuse, a spousal notice requirement enables the husband to wield an effective veto over his wife's decision. Whether the prospect of notification itself deters such women from seeking abortions, or whether the husband, through physical force or psychological pressure or economic coercion, prevents his wife from obtaining an abortion until it is too late, the notice requirement will often be tantamount to the veto found unconstitutional in *Danforth.* The women most affected by this law—those who most reasonably fear the consequences of notifying their husbands that they are pregnant—are in the gravest danger.

The husband's interest in the life of the child his wife is carrying does not permit the State to empower him with this troubling degree of authority over his wife. The contrary view leads to consequences reminiscent of the common law. A husband has no enforceable right to require a wife to advise him before she exercises her personal choices. If a husband's interest in the potential life of the child outweighs a wife's liberty, the State could require a married woman to notify her husband before she uses a postfertilization contraceptive. Perhaps next in line would be a statute requiring pregnant married women to notify their husbands before engaging in conduct causing risks to the fetus. After all, if the husband's interest in the fetus' safety is a sufficient predicate for state regulation, the State could reasonably conclude that pregnant wives should notify their husbands before drinking alcohol or smoking. Perhaps married women should notify their husbands before using contraceptives or before undergoing any type of surgery that may have complications affecting the husband's interest in his wife's reproductive organs. And if a husband's interest justifies notice in any of these cases, one might reasonably argue that it justifies exactly what the *Danforth* Court held it did not justify—a requirement of the husband's consent as well. A State may not give to a man the kind of dominion over his wife that parents exercise over their children.

Section 3209 embodies a view of marriage consonant with the common-law status of married women but repugnant to our present understanding of marriage and of the nature of the rights secured by the Constitution. Women do not lose their constitutionally protected liberty when they marry. The Constitution protects all individuals, male or female, married or unmarried, from the abuse of governmental power, even where that power is employed for the supposed benefit of a member of the individual's family. These considerations confirm our conclusion that § 3209 is invalid.

■ Chief Justice Rehnquist, with whom Justice White, Justice Scalia, and Justice Thomas join, concurring in the judgment in part and dissenting in part.

The question before us is therefore whether the spousal notification requirement rationally furthers any legitimate state interests. We conclude that it does. First, a husband's interests in procreation within marriage and in the potential life of his unborn child are certainly substantial ones. The State itself has legitimate interests both in protecting these interests of the father and in protecting the potential life of the fetus, and the spousal notification requirement is reasonably related to advancing those state interests. By providing that a husband will usually know of his spouse's intent to have an abortion, the provision makes it more likely that the husband will participate in deciding the fate of his unborn child, a possibility that might otherwise have been denied him. This participation might in some cases result in a decision to proceed with the pregnancy. As Judge Alito observed in his dissent below, "[t]he Pennsylvania legislature could have rationally believed that some married women are initially inclined to obtain an abortion without their husbands' knowledge because of perceived problems—such as economic constraints, future plans, or the husbands' previously expressed opposition—that may be obviated by discussion prior to the abortion."

The State also has a legitimate interest in promoting "the integrity of the marital relationship." This Court has previously recognized "the importance of the marital relationship in our society." In our view, the spousal notice requirement is a rational attempt by the State to improve truthful communication between spouses and encourage collaborative decisionmaking, and thereby fosters marital integrity. Petitioners argue that the notification requirement does not further any such interest; they assert that the majority of wives already notify their husbands of their abortion decisions, and the remainder have excellent reasons for keeping their decisions a secret. In the first case, they argue, the law is unnecessary, and in the second case it will only serve to foster marital discord and threats of harm. Thus, petitioners see the law as a totally irrational means of furthering whatever legitimate interest the State might have. But, in our view, it is unrealistic to assume that every husband-wife relationship is either (1) so perfect that this type of truthful and important communication will take place as a matter of course, or (2) so imperfect that, upon notice, the husband will react selfishly, violently, or contrary to the best interests of his wife. The spousal notice provision will admittedly be unnecessary in some circumstances, and possibly harmful in others, but "the existence of particular cases in which a feature of a statute performs no function (or is even counterproductive) ordinarily does not render the statute unconstitutional or even constitutionally suspect." The Pennsylvania Legislature was in a position to weigh the likely benefits of the provision against its likely adverse effects, and presumably concluded, on balance, that the provision would be beneficial. Whether this was a wise decision or not, we cannot say that it was irrational. We therefore conclude that the spousal notice provision comports with the Constitution.

NOTES AND QUESTIONS

1. **Changes on the Court.** Since 1992, new justices have been appointed to the Court. Most notably, Sandra Day O'Connor retired in 2005 and was replaced by Samuel Alito during the Court's 2005–2006 term. As noted in the dissent above, Justice Alito voted to uphold the spousal notification provision while he was on the Third Circuit Court of Appeals. Given the current composition of the Court, do you think spousal notification laws would be upheld today?

2. **Differing Views of Marriage.** Note the different ways in which the majority and the dissent view marriage. For the majority, a woman's sexual autonomy and safety are paramount concerns. For the dissent, women compromise some of their sexual autonomy in marriage. Do these themes echo the discussion above on marital rape? Do they remind you of the husband's right to chastise his wife in *Bradley* from Chapter One?

3. **Father's Rights?** As noted in the decision, the vast majority of women who have abortions are unmarried. So too are the vast majority of victims of domestic abuse. If what the dissent is really concerned about is the rights of the father, then wouldn't it stand to reason that all biological fathers, married or unmarried, should be notified before terminating a pregnancy?

4. **Mandatory Waiting Periods.** In *Casey*, the Court upheld a mandatory 24–hour waiting period before a woman can obtain an abortion. Consider how such laws may impact victims of domestic violence:

> Despite the Supreme Court's recognition of the problems relating to the effect of a spousal notification requirement in abusive relationships, the Court failed to apply the same logic to the effects that a mandatory waiting period would have. By upholding these laws, the Court, to use its own words, enabled the states to wield an effective

veto over many women's decisions to terminate their pregnancies. Currently, 22 states require a woman seeking an abortion to obtain counseling followed by an average 24–hour waiting period, requiring the woman to make two separate trips to the facility. If one considers that 87% of the counties in the U.S. have no abortion provider and women living in those areas must drive at least one hour, usually more, to the nearest abortion provider, a 24–hour waiting period act prevents many women from carrying out their decision to terminate her pregnancy for fear that they will be caught by their abusive partners. For those women in abusive relationships who chose to go through with a decision to have an abortion despite the risk of being discovered, a waiting period puts them at a much greater risk of abuse or death because of the amount of time they will spend before the procedure. Although the Court in *Casey* considered the district court's finding that the waiting period would be "particularly burdensome" to "those women that have difficulty explaining their whereabouts, such as battered women," it found that this did not amount to a substantial obstacle. As a result of this decision many women who face abuse within their relationships on a daily basis will not be able to make safe decisions for themselves and their families. Waiting periods create a burden on battered women equal to that of spousal notification requirements and should likewise be found unconstitutional. If the Court continued its focus of inquiry on the impact of further restrictions on an abused woman's ability to terminate her pregnancy, as it did for the spousal notification requirements in *Casey*, these restrictions would likely be found unconstitutional. Kimberly D. Perdue, *The Impact of Violence on Reproductive Decision–Making* (2006) (unpublished research paper on file with the authors).

5. **Parental Consent Statutes.** The court in *Casey* also upheld the portion of the Pennsylvania statute that required minors to seek consent from one parent before obtaining an abortion. The law provided that except in a medical emergency, an unemancipated young woman under 18 may not obtain an abortion unless she and one of her parents (or guardian) provide informed consent. If neither a parent nor a guardian provides consent, a court may authorize the performance of an abortion upon a determination that the young woman is mature and capable of giving informed consent and has in fact given her informed consent, or that an abortion would be in her best interests. The Court had previously upheld such statutes provided that there was an adequate judicial bypass procedure. In 2006, forty-four states had either parental notification or consent statutes for teens, thirty-six of which were in effect. Think back to Chapter Three and our discussion of the prevalence of teen dating violence. For many teens, sexual coercion is part of a larger pattern of violence within these young relationships. How might parental notification and consent statutes affect teen victims of dating violence? Should the Court in *Casey* have applied a similar analysis as to whether such laws create an undue burden on abused teens? Think of instances not only where a girl becomes pregnant as a result of teen dating violence, but the common situation in which her mother is in an abusive relationship. In later chapters we will

consider the impact of domestic violence on children, but for now pause to consider how domestic violence might impact teens whose parents are victims of abuse.

6. **The Controversy over Judicial Bypass and Health Exceptions.** In 2003, the New Hampshire legislature passed a statute that required parental notification for minors seeking an abortion. Under the statute, an abortion could only be performed without notification if the minor's life was in danger. While the law provided for a judicial bypass, it did not provide for the possibility that a medical professional could perform an abortion without notification or a judicial bypass if the minor's health was in danger. In *Ayotte v. Planned Parenthood of Northern New England*, 546 U.S. 320 (2006), the Supreme Court was asked to consider the consequence of not having an emergency health exception. In a very limited unanimous holding, the Court remanded the case to the lower Court, although Justice Sandra Day O'Connor reiterated that it was not revisiting its prior holdings, which had mandated that the absence of an emergency health exception created an undue burden on a minor's reproductive rights. New Hampshire subsequently repealed its parental notification statute.

Currently, states may not impose restrictions on abortion that create an undue burden. In *Stenberg v. Carhart*, 530 U.S. 914 (2000) the Court held that every abortion restriction must contain a health exception that allows an abortion when "necessary, in appropriate medical judgment, for the preservation of the life or health of the mother." Opponents of the health exception argue that it is too vague and allows for terminating a pregnancy for mental as well as physical health reasons. Yet in *Gonzales v. Carhart*, 550 U.S. ___, 127 S.Ct. 1610 (2007) the Court upheld a federal ban on a late-term abortion procedure, sometimes called a "partial birth abortion," which did not contain a health exception. This decision calls into question whether the health exception for abortion restrictions is still constitutionally mandated.

Consider why a victim of abuse might seek an abortion and how the availability of a health exception may affect her decisions. Why would such an exception be important for both minors and adults? Conversely, should abused women be able to terminate a pregnancy at any stage? Even in the case of rape by one's partner, for example, should the state's interest in the child's potential life outweigh, at some point, concerns the woman might have for her own safety?

D.   BATTERING DURING PREGNANCY

While some abusers interfere with their partner's sexual autonomy by sabotaging their birth control or preventing them from terminating an unwanted pregnancy, others interfere with a woman's pregnancy by forcing her to terminate a wanted pregnancy or being violent towards her while she is pregnant. Restricting a woman's right to carry a child to term undermines her sexual autonomy just as increasing her risk of an unintended pregnancy or prohibiting her from seeking a medically safe abortion does. A woman's ability to choose if, and when, to have a child is at the core of women's equality.

It is impossible to know just how many women are coerced or forced into having an abortion as a result of being in an abusive relationship or living in a home where there is domestic abuse. Each year approximately 1.3 million pregnancies end in abortion. Of those, 13,000, or approximately 1% result from rape or incest. A recent study by the Guttmacher Institute found that of 1209 abortion patients surveyed, fewer than 1% said that their partners' or their parents' desire for them to have an abortion was the most important reason they did so. A much higher percentage (48%) cited relationship problems or fear of being a single mother as a primary motivating factor, although specific questions relative to domestic violence were not part of the study. See Lawrence Finer, Lori Frohwirth, Lindsay Dauphinee, Susheela Singh and Ann Moore, *Reasons U.S. Women Have Abortions: Quantitative and Qualitative Perspectives*, 37 PERSPECTIVES ON SEXUAL AND REPRODUCTIVE HEALTH 110 (2005).

There is much research in the United States, Canada, and Great Britain that documents the high rates of domestic violence among women who seek abortions. A recent study of Canadian women found those seeking a third abortion are 2.5 times more likely to report a history of physical abuse by their partner and sexual abuse and violence than women seeking a first abortion. William A. Fisher, Sukhbir S. Singh, Paul A. Shuper, Mark Carey, Felicia Otchet, Deborah MacLean–Brine, Diane Dal Bello and Jennifer Gunter, *Characteristics of Women Undergoing Repeat Induced Abortion*, 172 CANADIAN MEDICAL ASS. J. 637 (2005). For further research on the relationship between abortion and domestic violence, see Gigi Evins and Nancy Chesheir, *Prevalence of Domestic Violence Among Women Seeking Abortion Services*, 6 WOMEN'S HEALTH ISSUES 204 (1996) (finding that 31.4% of the abortion seekers reported a lifetime history of physical or sexual abuse; 21.6% of these women had been abused in the prior calendar year and 7.8% had experienced abuse during the current pregnancy (none for the first time). 54.5% of women with a self-reported lifetime history of abuse had witnessed domestic violence in their family of origin and 36.4% had been abused as a child.) These studies, along with others, suggest that domestic violence may be correlated to the decision to terminate a pregnancy, and that women in abusive relationships might often decide to terminate their pregnancies as a last resort, as their life circumstances preclude safe and positive parenting. These findings have led many doctors to suggest that patients seeking abortion should be routinely screened for domestic violence in order to help them with safety planning and acquiring needed support. See Ellen R. Wiebe and Patricia Janssen, *Universal Screening for Domestic Violence in Abortion*, 11 WOMEN'S HEALTH ISSUES 436 (2001).

As we will see throughout this book, addressing domestic violence in women's lives does not fall neatly into any political or theoretical paradigm. Just as advocates for battered women resisted restrictions on abortion at issue in *Planned Parenthood v. Casey*, so too have advocates who oppose abortion sought legislation intended to protect abused women from coerced abortions. For example, in 2006, lawmakers in the Michigan House of Representatives passed the Coercive Abortion Protection Act. The bill makes it illegal for anyone to intimidate or coerce a woman or girl into having an abortion, requires abortion providers to screen for intimidation or coercion, imposes a twenty-four hour waiting period if there is evidence of either coercion or intimidation and requires specific information to be given to the patient about domestic violence shelters, her right to sue the person who intimidated her for damages for emotional distress, and mandates a referral to authorities for minors. The bill was supported by groups such as Feminists for Life and the National Right to Life Coalition. These groups argue that the bill is intended to aid and protect the reproductive autonomy of victims of domestic violence. The bill was opposed by both the National Organization for Women and the American Civil Liberties Union. These groups criticized the bill as yet another way to restrict women's access to abortion. A similar bill, called the Elizabeth Cady Stanton Act, was introduced in the United States Congress in 2005. It too is supported mainly by advocates who oppose abortion and is not supported by advocates for reproductive rights.

One fundamental question to consider is whether the availability of legal abortions thus makes women more vulnerable to coercion to end a pregnancy. It remains unclear as to whether the absence of legal abortions would simply be replaced by illegal, "back-alley" abortions, creating further risks for victims of abuse who are coerced or intimidated into ending their pregnancies.

It is important to recognize that the early feminists understood that an individual woman's freedom and equality would be compromised by exposure to violence, her lack of material resources, and her lack of support from the father of her child. Thus, questions of choice and consent, the foundation of one's ability to exercise control over one's reproductive life, are complicated by the existence of intimate violence in a woman's life.

Deborah Tuerkheimer
Reconceptualizing Violence Against Pregnant Women
81 IND.L.J. 667 (2006).

Predictably, given the dialectical nature of the relationship between law and social change, the topic of pregnancy battering has been largely absent from both legal and extralegal discourse on domestic violence and pregnancy. Social scientists have recently begun to address violence during pregnancy, focusing largely on the question of prevalence.

Studies have varied widely in their findings on the frequency with which pregnancy battering occurs. Yet a general consensus among researchers seems to have emerged that pregnancy battering is "a serious public health problem." In the largest meta-analysis of first-generation research on abuse during pregnancy, the authors found that, on average, from 3.9% to 8.3% of pregnant women experienced violence during pregnancy. If this range is, "reasonably accurate and the estimates ... [are]

applied to the four million women who deliver liveborn infants each year in the United States, one would expect approximately 156,000 to 332,000 of these women to experience violence during pregnancy." In all likelihood, however, since they are derived from prevalence ranges that are themselves subject to challenge as misleadingly low, these figures grossly underestimate the number of women victimized by violence during pregnancy. Importantly, the two studies reviewed in the meta-analysis that found a prevalence rate of around 20% relied on "detailed in-person interviews ... that included several questions related to violence, and both included all 3 trimesters of the pregnancy," which would tend to suggest greater accuracy.

Researchers have reached divergent conclusions regarding the onset of abuse of pregnant women. While at least one study determined that violence most often begins during pregnancy, many have found that the strongest predictor of violence during pregnancy is prior abuse, which may become more frequent or severe as a woman's pregnancy progresses. As a means of accommodating this divide, one researcher has suggested the likelihood that "[two] patterns of violence occur. In [one] pattern, violence is a chronic problem for women who experience violence periodically or regularly; in the other pattern, violence is acute among women who had not experienced violence previously."

Abuse during pregnancy is frequently recurrent. In one study, 60% of abused pregnant women reported two or more episodes of violence by the perpetrator. And pregnancy battering is often lethal: an analysis of pregnancy-associated mortality revealed that the leading cause of death among pregnant women was homicide.

In the vast majority of cases, violence against pregnant women is perpetrated by an intimate. While little has been written about victims' perceptions of their abuse, researchers have recognized that "all abuse against women is intentional and is aimed at power and control by the perpetrator."

Many adverse fetal outcomes, including miscarriage, stillborn birth, preterm labor and delivery, direct fetal injury, fetal hemorrhage, and placental abruption, are directly attributable to physical trauma. Studies have also found an association between violence during pregnancy and other significant risks to maternal and fetal health. For instance, violence during pregnancy has been associated with maternal substance abuse, smoking, unhealthy diet, low weight gain, delayed entry into prenatal care, and low birth weight.

Existing scientific literature on violence during pregnancy leaves important questions unanswered, suggesting an agenda for future inquiry. Given the extent to which abuse during pregnancy impacts other aspects of women's and children's lives, this next generation of research might be fruitfully integrated with research in related areas.

B. Glimpses from Case Law

Although the particularities of pregnant, battered women's experiences differ, common patterns tend to characterize the context in which episodic physical violence occurs. Violence during pregnancy, like other violence between intimates, can best be understood as expressing the batterer's need for control. But a victim of domestic violence likely experiences the power of her batterer differently if she is pregnant. What distinguishes pregnant victims from other domestic violence victims is a unique vulnerability that derives from the status of pregnancy.

Within law, because the definition of crime is framed so as largely to obscure context, accounts of these dynamics—and even, in cases, the very occurrence of pregnancy battering—must be found in what I have called the "fissures of appellate decisions." Opinions that reference battering during pregnancy generally fall into one of two categories: those that do so incidentally, either while detailing a "prior history" of abuse or simply to complete the event narrative; and those in which the fact of pregnancy is relevant to the charge or charges, most often because a "fetal victim" has been injured. In none of these cases is the full measure of the woman's suffering reflected or remedied. Indeed, the extent of the defendant's control over her may be barely glimpsed among even brief appellate recitations of "relevant" facts. The following cases illustrate this point.

One defendant was convicted of punching his wife—six months pregnant at the time—shoving her body against a dresser, and chasing her as she attempted to escape to a neighbor's house. The next day he tried breaking into the house by prying open the window. After his arrest, the defendant called his wife from jail with threats to "get her." At trial, the victim testified to the defendant's prior history of violence that included numerous threats and assaults, including a recent incident in which the defendant kicked his wife in the hip while she was pregnant, and an attack during a previous pregnancy in which the defendant kicked her in the stomach.

Another defendant was convicted of punching his girlfriend—three months pregnant at the time—in the face and stomach, and kicking her in the stomach. Prior to the incident, a history of abuse had led her to obtain a restraining order against the defendant, but it had expired at the time of the assault. When a police officer suggested to the victim that she apply for another order of protection, she "cried out in fear, 'he's out there, he's going to get me, you can't make me go out there.'" ...

One defendant repeatedly threatened to kill the mother of his child and to "take her daughter away." A prior history of violence included an incident in which the defendant kicked the victim in the stomach while she was pregnant (after which she miscarried), another beating so severe that the victim was hospitalized, and an attack on her eye that left the victim with permanent scarring.

Yet another defendant kicked the stomach of his live-in girlfriend, who was four months pregnant, after she failed to answer a question quickly enough. At the time of the incident, the victim had been "pondering how she was going to keep her appointment with a lady from Choices, a domestic violence shelter, later that night." ...

For every reported appellate decision containing similar facts, there are, of course, far more cases that never result in a written opinion and countless stories of pregnancy battering that never even penetrate the boundaries of law.

NOTES AND QUESTIONS

1. **Reasons for Battering During Pregnancy.** Tuerkheimer suggests that power and control are the primary reasons abusers batter during pregnancy. Note that in the cases Turkheimer discusses, the batterer targeted the abdomen. What is it about being pregnant that may heighten the risk of abuse? Some evolutionary theorists suggest that battering during pregnancy results when the male feels jealous and suspects infidelity, fearing that the child is not his. Evolutionary psychologists predict that battering, especially during pregnancy, will be highest in communities where there are low marriage rates, high rates of single motherhood, and more sexual promiscuity. All these factors contribute to the likelihood that a male may fear that a child claimed to be his is really that of another. For further references on battering during pregnancy and evolutionary theory, see Lee Ellis and Anthony Walsh, *Gene–Based Evolutionary Theories in Criminology,* 35 CRIMINOLOGY 229 (1997).

2. **The Law's Response to Battering During Pregnancy.** How does the law respond when a pregnant woman is battered? Should the fetus be considered a separate victim, or should the law focus solely on the woman and the harm she suffers? Consider the following case involving the unintentional killing of a fetus by a woman's former boyfriend.

People v. Taylor

Supreme Court of California, 2004.
86 P.3d 881.

■ BROWN, J.

A defendant shoots a woman, killing her. As a result, her fetus also dies. In the absence of evidence the defendant knew the woman was pregnant, may the defendant be held liable for the second degree implied malice murder of the fetus? We conclude he may, and therefore reverse the judgment of the Court of Appeal.

FACTS AND PROCEDURAL BACKGROUND

The following facts are taken largely from the Court of Appeal opinion. Defendant Harold Wayne Taylor and the victim, Ms. Patty Fansler, met in the spring of 1997. They dated and then lived together along with Fansler's three children. In July 1998 Fansler moved out. Defendant was heard threatening to kill Fansler and anyone close to her if she left him. Defendant wanted to "get back" with Fansler, and told one of her friends he could not handle the breakup, and if he could not have her, "nobody else could."

Defendant and Fansler spent New Year's Eve 1998 together. On January 1, 1999, a police officer responded to a call regarding a woman screaming in a motel room. In the room he found defendant and Fansler. Fansler was "upset and crying," and said defendant had raped her. Defendant was arrested, and shortly thereafter Fansler obtained a restraining order against him.

After the first of the year, Fansler asked her employer to alter her shifts so defendant would not know when she was working. In January 1999, defendant followed Fansler and her ex-husband in a car at high speeds for a mile or so, and on two other occasions tailgated her.

On March 9, 1999, defendant entered Fansler's apartment through a ruse, and after an apparent struggle, shot and killed Fansler. Fansler's son Robert, who heard his mother's muffled screams, but was unable to enter the apartment, pounded on Fansler's window outside the bedroom in which she was being attacked, and yelled "Goddamn it, you better not hurt her." Defendant was seen leaving the apartment, and Robert and a friend, John, Jr., chased but did not catch him.

Back in the apartment Fansler was found by her boyfriend John Benback, his son, John, Jr., and Robert. John Benback, Sr., testified, "She was lying on her back on the bed. The room had been pretty well trashed. There was blood everywhere."

Fansler died of a single gunshot wound to the head. (A subsequent search of the room revealed a second bullet had penetrated and exited the nightstand, and a fragment of this bullet was found near the nightstand.) Fansler also suffered a laceration on the back of her head that penetrated to her skull and chipped the bone, and bruising on her neck, legs, and elbows.

The autopsy revealed that Fansler was pregnant. The fetus was a male between 11 and 13 weeks old who died as a result of his mother's death. The examining pathologist could not discern that Fansler, who weighed approximately 200 pounds, was pregnant just by observing her on the examination table.

The prosecution proceeded on a theory of second degree implied malice murder as to the fetus. The jury convicted defendant of two counts of second degree murder, and found true attendant firearm enhancements. He was sentenced to 65–years-to-life in prison.

The Court of Appeal reversed defendant's second degree murder conviction based on the fetus's death. The court concluded there was evidence to support the physical, but not the mental, component of implied malice murder. "There is not an iota of evidence that [defendant] knew his conduct endangered fetal life and acted with disregard of that fetal life. It is undisputed that the fetus was [11] to 13 weeks old; the pregnancy was not yet visible and [defendant] did not know Ms. Fansler was pregnant." In contrast to "the classic example of indiscriminate shooting/implied malice" of a person firing a bullet through a window not knowing or caring if anyone is behind it, "[t]he undetectable early pregnancy [here] was too latent and remote a risk factor to bear on [defendant's] liability or the gravity of his offense." [T]he risk to unknown fetal life is latent and indeterminate, something the average person would not be aware of or consciously disregard. Were we to adopt the People's position, we would dispense with the subjective mental component of implied malice. Where is the evidence that [defendant] acted with knowledge of the danger to, and conscious disregard for, fetal life? There is none. This is dispositive.

We granted the Attorney General's petition for review.

II. DISCUSSION

Murder is the unlawful killing of a human being, or a fetus, with malice aforethought. [V]iability is not an element of fetal homicide ... but the state must demonstrate that the fetus has progressed beyond the embryonic stage of seven to eight weeks.

Malice may be either express or implied. It is express when the defendant manifests "a deliberate intention unlawfully to take away the life of a fellow creature." It is implied ... "when the killing results from an intentional act, the natural consequences of which are dangerous to life, which act was deliberately performed by a person who knows that his conduct endangers the life of another and who acts with conscious disregard for life". For convenience, we shall refer to this mental state as "conscious disregard for life." [I]mplied malice has both a physical and a mental component, the physical component being the performance of an act, the natural consequences of which are dangerous to life, and the mental component being the requirement that the defendant knows that his conduct endangers the life of another and ... acts with a conscious disregard for life....

Here, as the Attorney General notes, defendant "knowingly put human life at grave risk when he fired his gun twice in an occupied apartment building." As the Attorney General observed during oral argument, if a gunman simply walked down the hall of an apartment building and fired through the closed doors, he would be liable for the murder of all the victims struck by his bullets—including a fetus of one of his anonymous victims who happened to be pregnant. Likewise, defense counsel conceded at oral argument that defendant would be guilty of implied malice murder if one of his bullets had struck an infant concealed by the bed covers. On this point, both counsel are right. Had one of Fansler's other children died during defendant's assault, there would be no inquiry into whether defendant knew the child was present for implied malice murder liability to attach. Similarly, there is no principled basis on which to require defendant to know Fansler was pregnant to justify an implied malice murder conviction as to her fetus.

In battering and shooting Fansler, defendant acted with knowledge of the danger to and conscious disregard for life in general. That is all that is required for implied malice murder. He did not need to be specifically aware how many potential victims his conscious disregard for life endangered....

The judgment of the Court of Appeal is reversed, and the case remanded for proceedings consistent with this opinion.

■ Dissenting Opinion by Kennard, J.

A man who shoots a woman, unlawfully and intentionally causing her death, is guilty of the woman's murder, of course. If the woman is some 12 weeks pregnant, and the fetus also dies, is the man also guilty of murdering the fetus even though he did not intend to kill the fetus and did not even know of its existence?

A person may be convicted of murder of another human being on a theory of implied malice, which requires only proof of causing the victim's death by an intentional act, the natural consequences of which were dangerous to human life, with knowledge of that danger. The majority asserts, however, that for a conviction of implied malice murder of a fetus, it is sufficient that the person acted with conscious disregard "for life in general." I disagree.

The Legislature has carefully defined murder in terms of two distinct classes of victims—human beings and fetuses. The majority's reasoning effectively abrogates this important distinction by the manner in which it defines the mental state requirements for implied malice fetal murder. Instead of requiring proof of implied malice toward a particular fetus or fetuses in general, the majority requires only proof of implied malice toward "life in general." In my view, however, a defendant is guilty of murdering a fetus on an implied malice theory only if the fetus's death resulted from the defendant's intentional act, the natural consequences of which were dangerous to fetal life, with knowledge of that particular danger. . . .

Fetal murder is a relatively new crime in California. Beginning in 1850, our law defined murder as "the unlawful killing of a human being, with malice aforethought." In 1970, the Legislature amended that statutory definition by including "a fetus" in the definition of murder. . . .

. . . At the same time, the Legislature rejected a proposal to add the killing of a fetus to the definition of manslaughter. Thus, California does not recognize a crime of fetal manslaughter; "only the unlawful killing of a human being can constitute manslaughter." . . .

"When a killer intentionally but unlawfully kills in a sudden quarrel or heat of passion, the killer lacks malice and is guilty only of voluntary manslaughter." The effect of omitting a crime of fetal manslaughter is evident in the following scenario: A man comes home and finds his wife in bed with another man. Grabbing a handgun from the nightstand, he shoots his wife, killing her, unaware that his wife is nine weeks pregnant. Her death causes the death of the fetus. He is charged with the murders of his wife and the fetus. At trial he presents a defense of having acted in the heat of passion. The jury believes him, finding him guilty of the lesser offense of manslaughter for his wife's death. With respect to the dead fetus, the jury, having been instructed by the trial court that California has no crime of fetal manslaughter, and having found that defendant acted with provocation, which negates malice, cannot legally convict defendant of murder. Nor can it legally convict him of a lesser offense of manslaughter, because there is no crime of fetal manslaughter. Thus the killer, despite his mental state of conscious disregard for life in general, is liable only for the death of his wife (manslaughter) but not for the death of the fetus (no crime).

The lack of parallel punishment for killing a human being and killing a fetus suggests that the Legislature did not intend the crime of fetal murder to parallel that of murder of a human being. To the extent California's homicide law "attempts to sort killings according to the culpability they reflect" the fact that the same murderous conduct is punished differently depending upon the type of victim, either a human being or a fetus, implies that the Legislature intended to treat fetal murders differently. If murder of a fetus is not the same crime as murder of a human being, is the mental state for murder of a fetus different from the mental state required for murder of a human being? After much thought and considerable research, I cannot answer the question. The Legislature has given no clue what it intended in this regard.

In attempting to answer the question just posed, one must recognize the biological fact that for a considerable time a fetus's presence in its mother's womb may not be readily apparent to others. What, then, is the required mental state when one kills the fetus of a woman who shows no outward signs of pregnancy, and the killer's conduct or expressions of intent do not permit the inference that he acted with express malice toward the fetus? Those are the cases that are difficult to grapple with. . . .

When interpreting a law defining a crime, and the statutory language is susceptible to two equally reasonable constructions, it is the policy in this state to construe the statute in the defendant's favor lest defendants not have fair warning of what conduct is prohibited. Absent some clear indication of what mental state the Legislature intended for implied malice murder of a fetus, I would hold that a defendant who neither knows nor has reason to suspect that his female victim is pregnant, is not liable for the implied malice murder of a fetus who dies as a result of a murderous attack on the fetus's mother.

I would affirm the Court of Appeal's judgment reversing defendant's conviction for the second degree murder of Fansler's fetus.

NOTES AND QUESTIONS

1. **The Context of Domestic Violence.** Note that in *People v. Taylor,* the fetus was killed in the context of a domestic violence assault. This was true in most of the cases cited in the opinion. Apart from those involving driving accidents injuring pregnant women, the vast majority of fetal injury or death happens when a boyfriend, former boyfriend, husband, or ex-husband is battering the pregnant woman. Yet it is striking to note that the court makes no real mention of the implications that might have for the law. What is the consequence of such a lack of recognition about the relationship between domestic violence and the injuring or killing of a fetus?

2. **Should Defendants be Liable for "Unknowing" Killings?** In *People v. Taylor*, the dissent argues that allowing culpability for killing that happens with malice, but no knowledge, makes an assailant liable for hurting or killing a fetus even if he doesn't know of its existence. Does this seem unfair to you, or is this an appropriate consequence for anyone who harms a woman of child-bearing years if they act with the kind of reckless disregard for human life as was the case here? Keep in mind that in many states, second degree murder can result in life in prison, and in many states, first degree murder is a capital offense. In this case, the punishment "fits the crime" in that both the mother and the fetus died. What about cases in which the mother lives, relatively unharmed, but the fetus is killed? Should this situation result in a first or second degree murder charge? Does it matter whether the defendant intended to kill the fetus?

3. **Laws Regulating Fetal Injury and Feticide.** Each state determines the circumstances under which someone is criminally liable for injuring or killing a fetus. At least 31 states have laws either explicitly or implicitly recognizing the fetus as victim. Other states follow the common law rule, that the defendant is not guilty of murder unless the child was "born alive." Other states consider it a killing only if the fetus is "viable," somewhere around 20–22 weeks of gestation. Still other states criminalize the killing of a "quickened" fetus. This is when the mother begins to feel movement, somewhere between 16 and 18 weeks of pregnancy. Finally, others set the line at twelve weeks. California is among the states that penalize harm between six and eight weeks, while at least seven states penalize harm to a fetus beginning at conception. A few states also criminalize the injuring of a pregnant woman that causes her to miscarry or have a stillbirth, and a few others have enhanced penalties for injuring or killing a pregnant woman. All of these laws are considered to be constitutional and not in conflict with *Roe v. Wade,* 410 U.S. 113 (1973).

In 2004, the Federal Government passed the Unborn Victims of Violence Act, otherwise known as "Laci and Conner's Law," named after Laci Peterson who was murdered just before Christmas in 2002. At the time, she was eight months pregnant with a son whom she had named Conner. Her husband, Scott Peterson, was convicted of both Laci and Connor's murder. The law makes it a crime to injure or kill an "unborn" child during the commission of the crime against the mother. The law exempts the mother herself. It defines "unborn" child as "a child in utero, [which] means a member of the species homo sapiens, at any stage of development, who is carried in the womb." The law applies only in those places, such as Indian reservations, which are subject to federal law, and contains language exempting legal abortions. This legislation is intended to encourage the states to pass similar laws.

4. **Fetal Rights v. Women's Rights.** Many have taken issue with both the Unborn Victims of Violence Act and similar state statutes that purport to protect abused women, arguing that these laws are merely a way in which to undermine a woman's reproductive rights by granting independent legal status to the fetus separate and apart from the mother. Consider Deborah Tuerkheimer's analysis:

Despite the spread of laws ostensibly directed at violence during pregnancy, existing statutory frameworks fail to capture the harm of pregnancy battering. By granting fetuses victim status, the UVV [Unborn Victims of Violence Act] and similar state laws sever the interests of fetus and pregnant woman, ultimately furthering an agenda of control over women's bodies and lives. Redefining the fetus as a victim—to the exclusion of the pregnant woman—the law obscures the injury that has been inflicted on the woman. It does so in a manner that, by removing her from consideration altogether, effectively precludes an account of the nature of her suffering, or even recognition of her existence as a person who has been harmed. The suffering of pregnant victims of domestic violence is thus rendered invisible, leaving real injuries to women unremedied. Deborah Tuerkheimer, *Reconceptualizing Violence Against Pregnant Women*, 81 IND.L.J. 667 (2006).

As an alternative to the Unborn Victims of Violence Act, some in Congress introduced the Motherhood Protection Act, which would have provided additional punishment when someone injures a woman in such a way as to cause an "interruption in the normal course" of a pregnancy. Would such a law have been more consistent with protecting battered women while preserving reproductive rights? Consider the response of Serrin M. Foster, President, Feminists for Life of America.

An "interruption?" That implies something temporary, as if it were possible for the victim's pregnancy to start back up again. Dare we ask: mother of whom? Motherhood is neither protected nor honored through the proposed Motherhood Protection Act. Instead, it tells grieving mothers that their lost children don't count. It ignores these mothers' cries for recognition of their loss and for justice. It is a step backward in efforts to reduce violence against women. *Committee on the Judiciary, U.S. House of Representatives, Hearing on H.R. 1997, The Unborn Victims of Violence Act,* July 8, 2003.

5. **Woman's Right to Defend Her Fetus.** Another controversial issue is whether a woman has the right to kill her abuser to protect her fetus. Chapter Nine will examine legal questions of self-defense for battered women in cases where they assault or kill their abusers, acting to save their own lives. But when can a person kill to defend a fetus? In *Illinois v. Gaines,* 292 N.E.2d 500 (Ill. App. Ct. 1973) the court rejected an argument by a woman who had been battered by her husband that she had a right to kill him to protect her five-month fetus, which she eventually lost to a miscarriage. The court reasoned that in order to claim defense of a fetus, the defendant had to be protecting herself as well. See also *Ogas v. Texas,* 655 S.W.2d 322 (Tex.App. 1983) which rejected a similar claim by a woman who also had a history of being abused by her partner. In neither case did the woman claim that she feared for her own life, only the life of her fetus. Both of these cases were decided before courts recognized claims of self-defense by battered women.

In a more recent case, *People v. Kurr,* 654 N.W.2d 651 (Mich. Ct. App. 2002), the Michigan Court of Appeals held that the state's fetal protection statute allowed a woman to kill another person to protect her fetus even if her own life was not in danger. The Court was very sympathetic to the defendant, who presented evidence of past abuse by the victim.

Is the outcome in *Kurr* desirable? At least one commentator finds *Kurr* to violate fundamental principles of liberalism:

> The *Kurr* strategy reflects not only an illicit preference for pregnant women; it also privileges harm to the fetus over harm to its mother. In denying Kurr's claim to self-defense, a jury found that her response was unnecessary and/or excessive. The jury accordingly denied her authority to judge the magnitude of an attack that she faced. In sustaining her claim of defense of others, on the other hand, the jury affirmed her authority to judge the magnitude of force with which her fetuses were threatened. Yet, as an epistemic matter, a jury ought to place more confidence in a woman's assessment of the threat an attack poses to her than it places in her assessment of the threat posed to her fetus. After all, she comes to the former assessment by way of immediate sense-perceptions, the most reliable source of information, while she can arrive at the latter only through a process of conjecture that even science is without resources to support. Indeed, given the dearth of scientific evidence on the subject of the consequences to the fetus of blows to its mother's stomach, it is clear that a jury's rejection of self-defense and finding of justified defense of others cannot be based on any factual determination about the threat the fetus faced relative to that faced by its mother. Instead, such a jury's verdict can only be read as a statement expressing a belief that fetuses deserve more protection than the women who carry them. Amy J. Sepinwall, *Defense of Others & Defenseless "Others,"* 17 YALE J. L. & FEMINISM 327 (2005).

6. **Protectionism or Paternalism?** Think back to Chapter One and Emily Sack's article about the ongoing conflict between advocates of state interventions on behalf of battered women and those who believe that women must remain free from too much state intervention in order to preserve their autonomy. In some respects, debates over fetal rights become trapped in the same controversial paradigm. On the one hand, granting abused women greater legal options to protect their pregnancies as well as recognizing the actual harms they suffer when they are battered during pregnancy would seem, to some at least, a desirable state intervention. This might be especially true given that historically courts denied women protections from abusive husbands and, at common law, did not recognize the loss of a pregnancy when it resulted from battering. On the other hand, laws that seek to "protect" women can be said to actually control them, as well as rob them of choices. Recognizing the harm to the fetus may be another step down the road to restricting women's reproductive choices in other contexts. Furthermore, it robs women of the "right" to be treated as equal citizens by over-emphasizing their victim status.

As we proceed throughout the book, we will examine these tensions in other contexts, such as in the arrest and prosecution of batterers against the wishes of the victim. For now, begin to think about how you might resolve some of these conflicts and how notions of fairness, justice, safety, and equality embedded in legal doctrines and policies.

CHAPTER FIVE

Legal Characterizations of Battered Women and Their Experiences

Introduction

As you have seen thus far, there are many differing perspectives on battering. When abuse is presented in legal cases, these differing perspectives are reflected in legal argumentation, in the admission of evidence, and in judicial decision-making, as well as in the framing of legal remedies. This chapter is intended to introduce you to some generic issues concerning the way that battering—what it is, and what it does—is presented and reflected in law and in legal cases We address these issues here because they pervade all the different legal contexts in which issues of domestic violence are implicated—criminal law, family law, civil orders of protection, tort and employment law—just to mention a few. In this sense, this chapter is a bridge between the previous chapters, which have presented the historical and social context of domestic violence, the dynamics and dimensions of abuse, and the link between domestic violence, gender equality, sexual autonomy and reproductive rights, and the chapters that follow, which examine in concrete contexts and in considerable detail the various ways in which domestic violence is understood and treated by the legal system.

Characterizations of battering by feminists early in the development of the battered women's movement explicitly articulated a broad view—of violence as a "moment" in, or part of, a relationship of power and control. Yet the legal system has historically denied or minimized abuse in intimate relationships, and focused on single incidents of violence rather than grappling with the broader context in which these incidents occur. To put it simply, domestic violence has been invisible or distorted in many cases in which it is relevant. To remedy these problems, academics and activists who have studied domestic violence have sought to "explain" abuse and describe it more broadly to the legal profession, the lawyers who will argue cases to the courts and the judges who will decide them or instruct the juries who will decide them.

In Chapter Two, you have already seen some of these various explanatory approaches. For example, Evan Stark emphasizes the batterer's pattern of coercion and control rather than his violent acts or their effect on the psyche of the victim. Evan Stark, *Re–Presenting Woman Battering: From Battered Women Syndrome to Coercive Control*, 58 Alb. L. Rev. 973 (1995). Stark's description draws on the traditional feminist interpretation of intimate violence: "The coercive control framework shifts the basis of women's justice claims from stigmatizing psychological assessment of traumatization to the links between structural inequality, the systemic nature of women's oppression in a particular relationship and the harms associated with domination and resistance as it has been lived". The framework emphasizes "restrictions on 'liberty', highlighting a class of harms that extends beyond psychological or physical suffering to fundamental human rights." Deprivation of liberty results from a process of ongoing, intimidation, isolation and control.

In an approach with a different emphasis, Martha Mahoney takes on the particular question so often asked of battered women by the legal system: "Why didn't she just leave?" Mahoney describes battering in terms of the concept of "separation assault," the way the woman's effort to assert her independence and separate from her abuser triggers battering, and often an escalation of violence. Martha Mahoney, *Legal Images of Battered Women: Redefining the Issue of Separation*, 90 MICH. L. REV. 1 (1990). Mahoney maintains that the struggle for power and control is at the heart of the battering relationship. At the moment of separation or attempted separation—for many women the first encounter with the authority of law—the batterer's quest for control often becomes acutely violent and potentially lethal. Separation assault is "the particular assault on a woman's body and volition that seeks to block her from leaving, retaliate for her departure, or forcibly end the separation." Mahoney emphasizes that naming "separation assault" as the harm is crucial to a broader understanding of power and control:

> As with other assaults on women that were not cognizable until the feminist movement named and explained them, separation assault must be identified before women can recognize our own experience and before we can develop legal rules to deal with this particular sort of violence. Naming the particular aspect of the violence then illuminates the rest. For example, the very concept of "acquaintance rape" moves consciousness away from the stereotype of rape (assault by a stranger) and toward a focus on the woman's volition (violation of her will, "consent"). Similarly, by emphasizing the urgent control moves that seek to prevent the woman from ending the relationship, the concept of separation assault raises questions that inevitably focus additional attention on the ongoing struggle for power and control in the relationship.

In the chapters you have already read, you have considered multiple understandings of domestic violence and the context of abuse. Whether the issue is understanding what battering is, or what it does to the victim—the strategies it forces them to deploy in order to survive, and the emotional toll it takes—lawyers need to be familiar with these various approaches. First, they may be necessary to help them understand the domestic violence case on which they are working. Second, they may need to present evidence to explain battering in court and make the experience of abuse visible.

For those who represent battered women in court, the problem of making abuse visible through the introduction of evidence has three distinct aspects. First, the abuse must be understood as relevant to the proceedings—evidence of abuse will not be admitted unless it bears on the legal issues in the case. For example in cases involving battered women's claims of self-defense when they are charged with homicide or assault against their batterer, often called battered women's self-defense cases, a restrictive definition of self-defense might, and indeed often did, prevent the battered woman defendant from introducing evidence of any incident prior to the one in which she killed her batterer. Yet without understanding the background of her relationship with her batterer, a jury could not find her fear credible or her actions to defend herself reasonable. In custody cases, as long as a father's behavior toward his partner was felt to be legally irrelevant to the quality of his fathering, his partner abuse was irrelevant to the question of whether he should be granted sole or joint custody of his children.

Second, evidence of the abuse must become a part of the case. Storytelling—using the "stories" of clients as the factual matrix of the case—has always been an essential part of good lawyering. But a lawyer's ability to tell a battered woman's story in court assumes that the lawyer is capable of listening and hearing battered women's experiences and then translating them into law. Bias and ignorance have impacted the way many lawyers have understood and presented arguments based on battered women's experiences. Although intimate partner violence is a widespread problem that affects almost every aspect of legal practice, most lawyers are unfamiliar with its dynamics. They have not been adequately trained to consider this issue or to deal with clients who may have been abused. Many women who have been battered have been reluctant to talk about their experiences, particularly to lawyers, and many lawyers do not know how to pick up signals concerning possible battering. Moreover, lawyers may have been personally involved in violence and have ethical conflicts in representation.

As a result, in almost every field, cases continue to proliferate in which battering may be an issue but is not made visible in either the factual development or the legal argumentation in the case—because the client did not tell the lawyer, because the lawyer did not ask, or because the lawyer was not aware of how abuse might affect the particular legal issue that might need resolution. Lawyers who are sensitive to issues of abuse or have experience representing battered women frequently discover that a case on which they are working involves issues of abuse that were not raised by prior counsel. Often it is too late to raise them.

Third, the evidence that is presented must be sufficient to support the weight of the argument it has been introduced to bolster. Sometimes that means supplementing the testimony of the battered woman herself with the testimony of others; she may be too traumatized to be able to testify or to testify credibly; she may have been terrorized by her batterer into staying silent or recanting an earlier incriminating statement; she may on prior occasions have lied to medical or social workers so that there is no corroboration of her claims; she may have been too isolated to confide in friends or family. In some cases there will be other witnesses; neighbors, friends, doctors or emergency medical technicians, or police. But in other cases there may be none.

There may be many sources of evidence that are used by lawyers in legal cases involving abuse. These different types of evidence will be more fully described in Chapter Eight. But because expert testimony is often used in court to explain abuse and often shapes the way in which the law characterizes abuse, we focus here on expert testimony. Expert testimony by a psychologist or social worker or other professional knowledgeable about domestic violence, was developed first in battered women's self defense cases, but then in a variety of other legal contexts, to address each of these three aspects of making domestic violence visible to law. First, it was designed to assist judges in understanding the relevance of abuse to the legal issues raised by the case. Second, expert witnesses can work with (often less expert) lawyers to ensure that the client's story of abuse and its implications for her case are fully understood and presented. Third, expert testimony can supplement the testimony of the woman herself and shore up her credibility: reassuring the jury that her experiences, which might seem outlandish, were in fact not unusual within the context of battering relationships; or explaining why she might have complained to the police on one occasion, but then refused to press charges; or even why she might have never sought relief from her batterer's abuse in ten years of marriage, but raise it for the first time in the context of a divorce, in which the custody of her children was at issue.

Since the early cases in which expert testimony on battering and its effects was first proffered, state and federal courts have wrestled with the question of its admissibility. In most states those issues have been dealt with under existing case law and legislation, but in a handful of states special legislation has been adopted. We will explore in further detail evidentiary issues relative to admissibility of expert testimony in Chapter Eight. For now we focus on broader questions concerning this testimony, because it highlights important tensions in how domestic violence is "explained" and "characterized" in the law.

With the benefit of hindsight we can acknowledge that the first framework developed for the introduction of expert testimony on battering—battered women's syndrome—was perhaps unfortunate. On the one hand, it allowed psychologists specializing in domestic violence, like Lenore Walker, to claim that the growing body of knowledge about abuse and its impact met standards of scientific credibility, and allowed them to qualify as experts in that recognized field. On the other hand, it exacerbated the tension between describing women's responses to violence as rational reactions to the extreme demands of an abusive relationship, and describing them in psychological terms that imply abnormality and illness. This tension has been particularly acute in the legal context, where the difference between "reasonable" behavior and behavior that is excusable but based on "impaired" judgment can have important legal consequences. You have already seen this tension in Chapter Two and you will see it surface again in many legal contexts in the chapters that follow. In criminal cases involving claims of self-defense, for example, it can mean the difference between a verdict of justifiable homicide, and a manslaughter conviction based on diminished capacity. But in other contexts too, a defense that is understood as a "state of mind" defense may have more limited application than a defense asserting the reasonableness of the defendant's conduct.

The first case in this section demonstrates the use of what has been called "battered women's syndrome" testimony to explain the victim's recantation of a statement she made supporting the prosecution of her abuser. The Supreme Court of Connecticut demonstrates a sound understanding of both the nature and the purposes of the testimony. In particular, the court resists the defendant's efforts to define the testimony in purely psychological terms, but accepts it as helpful in understanding a range of otherwise puzzling behaviors battered women deploy in response to violence, including apparent inconsistency in their efforts to invoke the criminal justice system. The second case, *People v. Santiago*, reflects more recent understanding of the dynamics of abusive relationships by judges and the value of the past thirty years of research on domestic abuse in aiding that understanding. Both of these cases deal with the admissibility of evidence introduced by the prosecution to explain why a victim is acting as she is, and, in particular, why she denies the abuse happened despite overwhelming evidence to the contrary. In contrast, in *Dixon v. United States,* discussed in the notes following *Borrelli*, the Fifth Circuit refuses to admit expert testimony on behalf of a victim charged with receiving a firearm and making false statements. In this case, expert testimony on "battered women's syndrome" was intended to bolster the defendant's credibility in explaining that she committed the alleged offenses in the context of an abusive relationship. For now, our focus is exploring how explanations of battering by social scientists and psychologists are then translated into legal decision-making, and how these translations often fail to capture the full range of experiences and factual circumstances that we saw in the previous chapters.

Connecticut v. Borrelli

Supreme Court of Connecticut, 1993.
629 A.2d 1105.

■ BERDON, J.

The defendant was charged in an information with kidnapping in the first degree ..., assault in the second degree ..., criminal mischief in the third degree, ... unlawful restraint in the first degree, ... and threatening.... He was also charged with breach of the peace.... The defendant pleaded not guilty to all charges and elected a jury trial. Prior to trial, the defendant filed a motion to dismiss all charges, except for the breach of the peace charge, on the ground that there was insufficient evidence. The trial court denied the motion after a full evidentiary hearing and consolidated all charges for trial. After a jury verdict of guilty on all charges, the defendant was sentenced to an effective term of imprisonment of twenty years, suspended after ten years, with five years probation. The defendant appealed to this court.... We affirm the judgment of the trial court.

The following evidence was presented at trial. On December 30, 1990, the victim, the wife of the defendant, accompanied by three of her children, went to the Torrington police department in the evening hours and spoke to police officer Dale Olofson. She gave Olofson a written statement alleging that the defendant had physically abused and detained her the previous evening. She read and signed the statement. Her statement reveals the following: The defendant smoked some cocaine in the late evening hours of December 29, 1990, and then began accusing her of cheating on him. He cut up her clothing, underwear, driver's license and social security card with a knife. He held a pillow over her face so she could not breathe, and then tied her hands and feet together with rope behind her back. While she was bound, he threw a knife into the bedroom walls a number of times. He repeatedly threatened to kill her and members of her family, cut her lips with a knife, and held a cigarette lighter near her genital area. At approximately 6 a.m., he released her by cutting the ropes with a knife, and ordered her to give him a ride to Waterbury to buy drugs. They returned at 9 or 9:30 in the morning. She was tired but he would not let her sleep. He also would not let her cancel dinner plans they had made, so she began cooking.[1]

At the hearing on the motion to dismiss, the victim testified that the events alleged in her statement had not happened. At trial, she again recanted. During cross-examination by the defendant at trial, she testified for the first time that it was actually she who had tied up and physically abused the defendant. She also testified that she had made up her initial story in the hopes that the defendant would be arrested and given drug treatment. . . .

II.   The defendant next claims that the trial court improperly admitted the testimony of an expert witness concerning battered woman's syndrome. The state in its case-in-chief offered into evidence the expert testimony of Evan Stark, a sociologist, on the subject of that syndrome. The evidence was offered for the purpose of providing a possible explanation for the victim's recantation and to impeach her subsequent testimony that she had lied in the statement to get the defendant drug counseling. After a preliminary examination of Stark outside of the presence of the jury and briefing and argument by counsel, the trial court allowed the testimony over the defendant's objection. . . .

Not only was Stark qualified to testify, but his testimony focused on a subject that is beyond the knowledge and experience of the average juror. . . . Commentators have noted that "the research data indicates that potential jurors may hold beliefs and attitudes about abused women at variance with the views of experts who have studied or had experience with abused women. In particular, males are likely to be skeptical about the fear

---

1. The following evidence was presented in support of the breach of the peace charge. A neighbor of the victim's testified that an April 9, 1991, he looked out his window and saw the victim and the defendant arguing loudly on the street. When he was not looking, he heard a woman yell for help and called 911. He looked out the window again and saw the defendant block the victim as she tried to get into her car. He then saw the defendant push the victim up against another car, with his hands around her face and neck area. Police officers arrested the defendant, who was crouching down behind the stairs leading into the house. Both officers testified that the victim had red marks on her neck.

the woman feels in an abusive relationship and about her inability to leave a setting in which abuse is threatened.''

In the present case, Stark presented a general description of battered woman's syndrome, based on his experience with battered women and research and study in the area of domestic violence. Stark defined the term "battered woman's syndrome" as referring "to the behavioral and psychological consequences that many victims, but by no means all victims, experience as a consequence of living in domestic violence situations."

Stark explained that there are certain characteristics that are commonly found in relationships involving domestic violence. First, there is the "cycle of violence," in which "there's a period of tension build up in the relationship and then there's what we call the abusive episode where the batterer explodes and there's violence maybe combined with other forms of force and harassment ... and it's at that point or soon after that point that the battered woman may be quite clear about her danger and quite forthright in seeking help. But the next phase is what we call the honeymoon phase or where the batterer either says he'll never do it again or ... enters some kind of treatment program.... And she doesn't want the relationship to end, she wants violence to end. And she believes maybe this time it will be different. So at that point she's likely to believe that, in fact, it won't happen again. And she may at that point then either change her story or try to ... do what she needs to do ... in order to survive and to feel safe in the relationship."

Stark testified that some battered women develop a "learned helplessness" from repeated failures to take control of the relationship. The result of such learned helplessness is that battered women fail to take advantage of subsequent opportunities to seek help and escape the battering situation.

Stark also testified: "Now, the battered woman's syndrome includes a lot of behaviors which don't make any sense when you understand them as an outsider, but only make sense when you understand them from the standpoint of survival and safety;" Stark testified that battered women may stay in a relationship with an abuser despite the abuse. Battered women commonly fail to report their problems or delay reporting them to the authorities or others. Such women, who have suffered extraordinary harm, commonly minimize or even deny the harm that they have suffered. Finally, there is the "paradoxical situation ... where a woman will come in on one occasion and present a very clear and concise picture of danger that she's in, either explaining it to her health provider or to a police officer, and then a week later completely change her story." Stark testified that this last pattern "is one of the most common things that we see in the field."

Stark's testimony was consistent with the theory of battered woman's syndrome as it has been presented and discussed in scholarly commentary. Moreover, expert testimony concerning battered woman's syndrome has been accepted by many courts when the testimony was offered by a criminal defendant to bolster a claim of self-defense.... Such expert testimony has also been accepted if offered by the prosecution to explain the recantation of the complaining witness; and if offered to explain the victim's delay in reporting the abuse and remaining with the defendant after the abuse. We conclude that the subject of battered woman's syndrome is "beyond the ken of the average juror," and therefore meets the threshold test for admissibility of expert testimony in this state. . . .

Finally, Stark's expert testimony in this case was helpful to the jury. The most important issue in this case was the credibility of the victim. Her written, signed statement alleged that she had been the victim of egregious abuse. Before the jury, the victim testified that she had not been abused and that indeed it was she who had tied up the defendant and abused him. The defendant, through cross-examination of Olofson, questioned the credibility of the victim's written statement in view of her eighteen hour delay in making the complaint. The victim testified that she had made up the statement in order to get her husband into drug treatment. The state offered a different explanation, one beyond the knowledge and understanding of the average juror—that the statement was true, and the victim's recantation was a pattern of typical behavior consistent with battered woman's syndrome. . . .

NOTES AND QUESTIONS

1. **"Helpful" to the Jury.** One of the key points raised by the court in *Borrelli* is that expert testimony is admissible when it is helpful to the jury. This legal standard comes from Federal Rules of Evidence 702. All the states follow this rationale to some degree. We will return to these issues later in the chapter on Evidence Chapter Eight. For now, however, consider the underlying premise that jurors can benefit from some greater understanding about the dynamics of abusive relationships because it is likely outside the realm of their own experiences. Given what we know about domestic violence and its prevalence, do you believe that this is true? Do you think jurors might have some misconceptions about domestic violence? Since you have been studying this subject, what preconceived ideas did you have about the nature of abusive relationships that have now been challenged?

2. **The Relevance of Expert Testimony.** The issues that arise with respect to the admission of expert testimony differ with the context, as well as differing from state to state. The threshold issue is whether such testimony is relevant to the case. While courts have been willing to admit such testimony to explain why battered witnesses may then minimize or recant prior statements implicating their abusers, they have been somewhat reluctant to admit such evidence when offered by battered defendants to bolster their credibility. Take, for example, *Dixon v. United States*, 548 U.S. ___, 126 S.Ct. 2437 (2006). The defendant, Keshia Dixon, purchased multiple firearms at a gun show, and provided false addresses in doing so. She was charged and convicted for the illegal possession of a firearm and for making false statements in obtaining a firearm while she had another indictment pending. She raised a duress defense, claiming her boyfriend threatened to kill or hurt her and her two daughters did she not do so. The Supreme Court reviewed the issue of the proper burden of proof in duress

cases and we will consider this aspect of the case in detail on that issue in Chapter Nine. At the trial, Dixon attempted to introduce an expert witness who would have testified that she suffered from "battered women's syndrome" to explain why she acted the way she did. The trial court refused to admit that evidence, and the Supreme Court did not review on that issue. The Fifth Circuit did, however. Below is an excerpt from the Fifth Circuit's ruling:

> Dixon testified that she had been abused by Wright, who allegedly beat her on a regular basis and threatened her children. Her description of the relationship was largely corroborated by the testimony of her two daughters. Dixon further testified that she was afraid that, if she did not buy the guns for Wright, he would harm or even kill her or her daughters.
>
> In support of her duress defense, Dixon attempted to introduce the testimony of Dr. Toby Myers, a domestic violence expert, regarding the reactions of battered women to their abusers. The court held that Dr. Myers's testimony addressed Dixon's subjective state of mind and was therefore inadmissible to show duress. Dixon also attempted to introduce the testimony of Kelly Oates, an agent with the Bureau of Alcohol, Tobacco and Firearms, concerning an out-of-court statement by Wright that he gave Dixon $115 to purchase a gun for him. The district court excluded Oates's testimony as inadmissible hearsay....
>
> The narrow question raised by Dixon is whether the district court abused its discretion in holding that Dr. Myers's testimony would not have assisted the jury in making a determination as to a material fact.
>
> Dixon sought to introduce Dr. Myers's expert testimony in support of a defense of duress. Duress is an affirmative defense that has been developed through the common law and adopted by the federal courts....
>
> In short, the duress defense requires an objective inquiry into whether a defendant's conduct, although illegal, represented her only reasonable alternative to serious bodily injury or death.
>
> Most of the expert testimony proffered in this case ... dealt with the defendant's subjective vulnerability to coercion. [E]xpert testimony that a defendant "suffers from the battered woman's syndrome" is "inherently subjective" and therefore inadmissible to support a defense of duress. In the case at bar, although Myers carefully avoided using the term "battered woman's syndrome,", she nonetheless explained that Dixon was "more vulnerable because she had lost her job" and that Dixon "didn't think [calling the police] would do any good.". Dr. Myers concluded that, as a result of Wright's threats and repeated battery, Dixon believed "in her heart and mind [that] she didn't have a choice" as to whether to buy the guns. In short, this testimony clearly focuses on Dr. Myers's opinions as to Dixon's individual state of mind.
>
> To the extent that Dr. Myers's proffered testimony described Dixon's subjective perceptions of danger, it was not relevant to the inquiry at hand—that is, to whether such perceptions were "well-grounded" or

objectively reasonable under the circumstances. As such, it could not have "assist[ed] the trier of fact" in making any determination of material fact. Thus, we hold that the district court did not err in excluding this portion of Dr. Myers's testimony. [Footnote 2: Furthermore, Dr. Myers's assertion that Dixon's fears were reasonable does not redeem her testimony. Whether a defendant's apprehension of harm is reasonable under the circumstances is ultimately a question for the jury. Although it is certainly possible that expert testimony might shed light on the reasonableness of a given type of conduct by describing typical reactions to unusual circumstances, such was not the case here. Instead, at the prompting of counsel, Dr. Myers offered the wholly conclusory assertions (1) that Dixon's fear of Wright was "well grounded" and (2) that her decision not to leave Wright was not "reckless or negligent".] ... *United States v. Dixon*, 413 F.3d 520 (5th Cir.2005).

In *Borrelli*, the Connecticut Supreme Court found that expert testimony was relevant to helping the jury evaluate the victim's recanted testimony. In contrast, the Fifth Circuit finds that testimony bolstering the defendant's testimony wasn't helpful to the jury because the jury must decide whether Dixon's conduct was reasonable. In both cases, however, would the jury have had difficulty in determining whether the person acted reasonably under the circumstances? If the general public needs some education from experts on the dynamics of abusive relationships, then shouldn't such testimony be admissible in both cases? In *Dixon*, the assumption was that the jury could decide on its own whether Dixon could have resisted the threats of her abuser. In *Borrelli*, the court allows the testimony of the expert to explain why she doesn't leave, and why she may not resist those threats. Thus, at the heart of both cases is "Why doesn't she leave?" The jury, with the aid of expert testimony, understands why the victim in *Borrelli* did not. In *Dixon*, absent that aid, the jury finds that she should have resisted. Do these results seem consistent to you? Are they fair?

3. **More Sophisticated Legal Understandings of Abuse.** In the next case, the Court court acknowledges the difference between a domestic and a stranger-to-stranger case of violence. The Court held that domestic violence cases must be viewed differently and rules of evidence should be applied based upon what decades of research and evidence have revealed about battered women and domestic violence. The following excerpt provides Judge Atlas' reasoning on allowing the witness's prior testimony despite her unwillingness to continue with prosecution. An expert witness also testified at the trial, bolstering the argument as to why the witness would recant because of the nature of her relationship. The witness had testified to a grand jury in a closed court session regarding the episodes of violence at the hands of her intimate partner and then later recanted. The judge's statements regarding public policy and domestic violence cases also reflect some of the progress made in understanding the dynamics and complexity of domestic violence cases. They also highlight a strategy by prosecutors to focus beyond a single incidence of abuse to the broader pattern of coercive control. Not all courts are so sophisticated in the their understanding of

abuse, and, as the notes following suggest, it remains unclear as to what legal policies courts should implement in light of that understanding.

People v. Santiago

New York Supreme Court, 2003.
2003 WL 21507176.

■ Jeffrey M. Atlas, J.

The defendant is charged with Aggravated Criminal Contempt and two counts of Criminal Contempt in the First Degree based on Angela R.'s allegations that he violated an Order of Protection which was issued to protect her. She and the defendant have lived together for many years, and as happens frequently in cases of this kind, prior to trial, Angela R. declared that she no longer wished to press charges, that she would decline to testify at trial, and that if she were made to testify she would declare that all the allegations she previously made to the police, prosecutor, and Grand Jury were fabricated by the police and the District Attorney. In view of that, the People moved for an order permitting them to use Angela R.'s Grand Jury testimony and her other out of court statements during the presentation of their direct case against the defendant. The People's theory is that the defendant's longstanding pattern of physical and emotional abuse toward Angela R. effectively forced her to become unavailable as a witness for the People at trial. The defendant opposes this motion, arguing that Angela R. is available and willing to testify at trial, and that her credibility is a matter for the jury. For the reasons which follow, the People's motion is granted. . . .

In addition to providing information about Battered Women's Syndrome"battered women's syndrome", Dr. [Anne Wolbert] Burgess reviewed all of the data collected by the police and District Attorney pertaining to the many complaints made by Angela R. against the defendant, and she discussed with the prosecutor the complainant's current position regarding further prosecution of the defendant. Dr. Burgess reviewed Angela R.'s hearing testimony and she attempted to interview Angela R., but the complainant refused to speak with Dr. Burgess.

Dr. Burgess testified that, in her expert opinion, the relationship between Angela R. and the defendant is a classic example of a domestic violence relationship and that Angela R. is an abused woman whose current behavior is explained by Battered Women's Syndrome"battered women's syndrome". In support of her opinion, Dr. Burgess noted that over a period of years, in a relationship marked by episodes of violence, Angela R. regularly called the police when attacked, obtained orders of protection from the court, then recanted her allegations and refused to prosecute. Dr. Burgess also noted evidence of the defendant's use of psychological abuse to control the complainant. He threatened to kill her, he blamed her for things that she had not done, he took things that were precious to her, he destroyed things that were important to her, and he acted in ways that enhanced her dependence upon him. While noting that their domestic violence cycle has entered the so-called honeymoon phase, Dr. Burgess also observed that while the defendant is in prison, Angela R. has been placed under tremendous pressure to not testify against him. Dr. Burgess testified that, given the amount of recent contact between the defendant and Angela R., the defendant has played a major role in her recantation and willingness to perjure herself. Dr. Burgess concluded that Angela R.'s behavior as a reluctant witness, her willingness to tell patent lies in court, to rationalize the defendant's behavior, and to accept blame for her current predicament reflects her imposed lack of self esteem and her level of desperation. This, according to the expert, can only be attributed to the coercion inherent in the honeymoon phase of the cycle of violence and the tremendous pressure that the defendant has placed on Angela R. to relieve him of his current confinement. . . .

I am convinced that Angela R. has been physically and emotionally abused by the defendant for many years, and her suffering has gone unchecked and untreated since, at least, 1996. The credible evidence at this hearing makes very clear that Angela R.'s current attitude toward testifying is a classic example of a battered woman's reaction to what has been described as the honeymoon phase of the abusive relationship. Angela R. is frightened that separation will leave her isolated and without help in caring for her child and her home. The evidence shows that in the past she has feared, and she continues to fear, that the defendant's violent behavior will be directed toward her again and conceivably toward her child. The evidence establishes the defendant's contribution to the complainant's low self-esteem and sense of helplessness. Her interaction with those seeking to help her demonstrates her lack of confidence in herself and her inability to speak up in her own defense. The evidence shows that in the past the defendant had taken steps to isolate Angela R. from those who tried to assist her and that he prevented her from having access to social support agencies. The evidence reveals that the defendant threatened to hurt her if she sought help, he intercepted phone calls from a counselor and he took her Order of Protection (one of many), leaving the complainant to believe that she could not get the help of the police without it. In general, the defendant's behavior toward Angela R. has been abusive, demeaning and humiliating. According to the testimony, the complainant sought help quite often, but only when she was in acute distress, hurt or terrified. However, the testimony also establishes that she is unwilling to follow through when people try to help her because her feelings of shame and humiliation prevent her from discussing her plight publicly. The record also shows Angela R.'s repeated withdrawal of her complaints to law enforcement. In every case that she initiates, she eventually recants and she takes the blame for incidents in which she has been the wounded party. Indeed, the hearing evidence establishes in this case the defendant's contribution toward the complainant's sense of guilt for the predicament she currently finds herself in. Over time, the defendant has violated one court Order of Protection after another with impunity because, as he testified, the complainant never testifies against him.

Once again, Angela R. has declined to testify against the defendant. However, in this instance there is clear and convincing evidence that her unwillingness to continue with the prosecution comes after persistent efforts by the defendant to reconcile with the complainant and convince her to do what is necessary to get him out of jail. The defendant, in over 100 conversations with her (each of which seems to have constituted another violation of an Order of Protection), has used the complainant's desires for a normal and loving relationship to his own end. Angela R. fears that continued prosecution will make the defendant suffer in prison, hurt their relationship, and likely lead to additional acts of violence. Obviously, the avoidance of any jail time is a tremendous incentive for the defendant to place extraordinary pressure upon the complainant. Indeed, the defendant testified that he has regularly discussed with Angela R. his urgent desire to be out of jail, and his view that it is up to her to get him out of jail and home to her. . . .

Conclusions

Nonetheless, the defense contends that the defendant did not explicitly threaten the complaining witness during those 100 phone calls and that the complainant's current reluctance to testify is not as a result of any misconduct committed by him since the inception of this case. The defendant argues that this distinguishes this case from others in which a witness's prior statements were properly admitted because the defendant's misconduct, committed between the inception of the case and the date of trial, was found sufficiently threatening to have caused the witness's unavailability. Moreover, implicit in the defendant's argument is the notion that I should treat the complainant's current effort to withdraw the charge with no greater concern than I might have toward efforts to withdraw in other kinds of cases. The defense argument in this case suggests that no matter how frustrating, I should simply accept this as a failed prosecution. In this respect the defense argument implies that I view the withdrawal of complaints in domestic violence cases in the same way that I have viewed the occasional attempts to withdraw prosecutions in other kinds of cases where the complainant and defendant were strangers to each other. Except where proof existed that the witness became unavailable because of the wrongdoing of the defendant, in other kinds of cases we have often taken for granted that a complainant's desire to withdraw from the prosecution was based on the simple unwillingness to get involved in the process, or give up the time it takes to follow through on the complaint, or because of the witness's unsubstantiated fears of reprisal from some unspecified source. We have frequently not looked beyond those excuses in such cases where no proof was immediately available that a particular and recent act of misconduct by the defendant had brought about the witness's unavailability.

However, I do not believe domestic violence cases are of the same character as other kinds of cases and I am unable to be indifferent about the effort of this complainant to withdraw her complaint. Moreover, I do not believe that the cases admitting prior testimony of an unavailable witness should be read to hold that prior evidence given by an unavailable witness is admissible only when the defendant's misconduct causing the unavailability occurs between the defendant's arrest and the date of trial.

While that may occur in the usual case, domestic violence matters are of such a different character as to justify a broader application of the rule.

Expert studies and our experience in the criminal process have taught us that there is a difference between the dynamics of domestic violence and other types of assault cases adjudicated by our courts. Countless Judges have presided in courts through which the devastated victims of domestic violence have come, first to seek protection but later to withdraw their complaints even though it was clear from prior experience that they were likely to be the victims of violence again at the hands of their partners. There was a time when domestic violence cases were taken less seriously than other cases because of the routine withdrawal of such complaints and the frequent inability to prosecute these cases notwithstanding the serious injuries suffered by the complainants. Over the years we threw up our hands in surrender and tolerated domestic violence because we did not have a method by which these cases could be prosecuted over the complainants' objections.

We are now aware that domestic violence cases brought by complainants with a long standing history of abuse are to be viewed differently from other crimes of violence which come through our courts. We are accustomed to injured victims seeking retribution, punishment and protection from society. That, without a doubt, is the norm. It is fair to say that we now recognize that in domestic violence cases repeated abuse followed by repeated withdrawal of prosecution and the repeated grant of forgiveness to the abuser make such cases very different from the norm.

What is evident is that domestic violence cases are different because of the complainant's desire for a stable relationship and the exploitation of that desire by the defendant. The hallmark of such cases is the hope for a brighter future with the abuser held by the complainant who is weakened by past abuse and seduced by untrustworthy gestures of love but, whose expectations are eventually met with repeated abuse to the perverse satisfaction of the abuser. In other kinds of cases there has been little, if any, intimate interaction between the parties and generally there is no expectation of a future relationship. As I have noted, in the vast majority of cases victims pursue their complaints seeking retribution and safety from the process provided by the police and courts. Such complainants, although sometimes apprehensive, follow through because they have the strength, the will and the need to do so. Victims of domestic violence do not have the will to follow through. They lack the self esteem and strength to seek retribution or permanent safety from their attackers. This is so not only because of the psychological damage done by repeated abuse but, also because there lurks in the mind of such complainants the fear of physical retaliation to themselves and their children at the hands of an offender whose past behavior toward the complainant makes it highly probable that such abuse will occur again. In short, the defendant's pattern of behavior causes the victim of domestic abuse to succumb to the offender's importuning in ways that others might not. Thus, attempts to become unavailable as a prosecuting witness cannot be viewed as we might see voluntary withdrawal in a case where the complainant and the defendant are strangers to one another. Nor, can such withdrawal be viewed as having been made without the misconduct of the defendant....

Clearly, the nature of this syndrome and the cost to the families involved, the police, medical professionals, the courts and society in general cry out for a solution. It is simply unacceptable for our process to turn a blind eye to the dangers of such abuse by shrugging our shoulders and saying that nothing can be done within the framework of existing law....

NOTES AND QUESTIONS

1. **Angela R.** It is interesting to note that the judge used only the victim's first name to spare her further embarrassment. Courts may sometimes protect the identity of victims in cases involving sexual assault but do not usually do so in cases of domestic violence. Was it appropriate for the judge to do this? Should all victims of domestic violence have their names withheld? Does being abused require a victim to feel shame? Does having one's name withheld suggest that shame is appropriate, or is it protective of the victim?

2. **Is Domestic Violence Really Different**? The judge suggested domestic violence is different from other kinds of cases involving non-intimate partners. If it is, why is that?

3. **Paternalism or Protection?** Some scholars have not viewed the *Santiago* decision in completely favorable terms. In a news article, Emily Jane Goodman, *Prosecuting The Batterer Without The Victim's Approval*, GOTHAM GAZETTE, June 18, 2003, Elizabeth Schneider called the *Santiago* decision very valuable in the specific facts of this case, but notes that "doing anything that is not what the victim wants is a problem." The issue, she says, is "whether you go with the woman's wishes or the evidence that she is recanting only out of fear or threats." However, Carlin Meyer acknowledged that "hitters don't hit just one woman," and that therefore society—not just Angela R.—needs to be protected, and adds, "but the state is never going to protect her." Meyer also stated that "No one walks in the victim's shoes and she should be allowed to assess the potential danger to herself, the benefits and burdens, that flow from going forward with a complaint. The state (and the prosecutors who act for it) can't know if she's better off with her batterer working and not in jail. It's paternalistic for the state to force her to testify and act as if it knows better." She points to the possibility of a "slippery slope" where hearings might be skipped, experts disallowed and the rights of both parties might be jeopardized. After evaluating the criticism provided by Schneider and Meyer, do you think the state was being unduly paternalistic in the *Santiago* case? What options did the court have? Should it have dismissed the case when Angela R. refused to testify? We will return to the question of when the state should proceed without the victim's consent in subsequent chapters, but for now consider the value of a richer understanding of the dynamics of abuse for lawyers and the legal system.

4. **Admitting Evidence of Battered Women's Experiences.** In her work, Mary Ann Dutton is careful to point out that not all women respond

to battering in the same way. She emphasizes the importance of focusing on evidence of "battered women's experiences" instead of "battered woman syndrome:"

> First, descriptive references should be made to "expert testimony concerning battered women's experiences," rather than to "battered woman syndrome" per se. Second, the scope of the testimony concerning battered women's experiences should be framed within the overall social context that is essential for explaining battered women's responses to violence. Third, evaluation and testimony concerning battered women's psychological reactions to violence should incorporate the diverse range of traumatic reactions described in the scientific literature, and should not be limited to an examination of learned helplessness, PTSD, or any other single reaction or "profile." Mary Ann Dutton, *Understanding Women's Responses to Domestic Violence: A Redefinition of Battered Women's Syndrome*, 21 Hofstra L. Rev. 1191 (1993).

Dutton is responding to the tendency of judges to understand battered woman syndrome testimony as offering a "profile" that will fit all women who have suffered from abuse. One danger with this approach is that the "stereotypical" battered woman will be defined as both helpless and impaired. In the words of Elizabeth Schneider:

> "[B]attered woman syndrome" carries with it stereotypes of individual incapacity and inferiority which lawyers and judges may respond to precisely because they correspond to stereotypes of women which the lawyers and judges already hold. Battered woman syndrome does not mean, but can be heard as reinforcing stereotypes of women as passive, sick, powerless and victimized. Elizabeth M. Schneider, *Describing and Changing: Women's Self–Defense Work and the Problem of Expert Testimony on Battering*, 9 Wmns. Rts. L. Rptr. 195 (1986).

Dutton's account undercuts this stereotype in part by insisting that looking at women's experiences with abuse must include looking at the strategies they have used, as well as the ones they have not, to cope with, or contain, the violence.

In 1996, the U.S. Departments of Justice and Health and Human Services issued a report on *The Validity and Use of Evidence Concerning Battering and Its Effects in Criminal Trials*, under a mandate contained in the 1994 Violence Against Women Act. Report Responding to § 40507 of the Violence Against Women Act, NCJ–160972 (May 1996). One aspect of the report was a summary of the current "state of play" with respect to expert testimony. The summary was based on a study of state and federal court decisions, as well as state legislation. The report found that judges, prosecutors, and defense attorneys interviewed concerning the impact of such evidence in criminal trials said that, within the courtroom, it has increased recognition of the broader problem of domestic violence and that its introduction can assist judges and juries to better understand the issues and/or dispel myths and stereotypes related to battered women.

However, the reports' authors cautioned in strong terms against using the label "battered woman syndrome" to describe expert testimony. Confirming the analysis of Mary Ann Dutton, who was one of the report's principal researchers and writers, and whose work you have just read, the forward of this report states:

> Among the most notable findings was the strong consensus among the researchers, and also among the judges, prosecutors, and defense attorneys interviewed for the assessment, that the term "battered woman syndrome" does not adequately reflect the breadth or the nature of the scientific knowledge now available concerning battering and its effects. There were also concerns that the word "syndrome" carried implications of a malady or psychological impairment and, moreover, suggested that there was a single pattern of response to battering.

5. **Who Counts as a Battered Woman?** As even these few examples illustrate, counsel and judges continue to struggle with the appropriate nature and scope of expert testimony on battering. The case law is convoluted, and becomes only more so as the testimony is used in the wide variety of legal contexts that you will read about in the chapters that follow. One disquieting judicial tendency is for courts to impose order through a new formalism—the development of rigid requirements about who "counts" as battered, and what symptoms "count" as legitimate reactions to abuse. We will examine this issue more thoroughly in other contexts including claims of self-defense and other defenses when the abused has been charged with a crime.

6. **Capturing Battered Women's Diverse Experiences.** Another aspect of this inappropriate focus on "syndrome" is that women who do not fit the stereotype of the passive and powerless battered woman may be denied the benefit of expert testimony; since they do not appear to be suffering from the "syndrome," testimony about the "syndrome" is surely not relevant to their cases. We saw in Chapter Three that there are some common aspects but also many diverse experiences of abuse. Problems of stereotyping concerning "battered woman syndrome" are particularly rife in these contexts. This point has been made with particular poignancy in the context of African American women's self-defense claims, since the "battered woman" stereotype contradicts other cultural stereotypes about the "tough" black woman:

> The looking glass experience of black women is one of being trapped between sub- and super-human imagery and expectations. In addition to the negative stereotypes African–American women encounter, [even] attributes that in their truest sense should be considered positive, when applied to black women, can be detrimental. For example, ... African–American women have been characterized as strong and independent. They are blamed for the breakup of their families. Often the strength of black women to survive and progress despite the almost insurmountable obstacles and odds is labeled as pathological at one extreme and disloyal at the other. Sociologist Calvin Herton attributes the black woman's drive (a character flaw) to the historical treatment

of African–American women. If these stereotypes can affect public policy, routine transactions, and normal discourse, to what extent is the African–American female defendant at a disadvantage when she is brought to trial for a violent crime—even if she claims that she acted in self-defense because she was being battered? Linda L. Ammons, *Mules, Madonnas, Babies, Bathwater, Racial Imagery and Stereotypes: The African–American Woman and the Battered Woman Syndrome*, 1995 WISC. L. REV. 1003 (1995).

The negative stereotypes against which African–American women must defend themselves include "the hostile Sapphire, the wanton Jezebel, and the strong and assertive Sojourner Truth." Sharon Angella Allard, *Rethinking Battered Woman Syndrome: A Black Feminist Perspective*, 1 UCLA WMNS. L. REV. 191 (1991). As Lenore Walker acknowledged in her 1984 book TERRIFYING LOVE: WHY BATTERED WOMEN KILL AND HOW SOCIETY RESPONDS:

> The ratio of Black women to white women convicted of killing their abusers is nearly two to one in one of my studies. My feeling is that this is the result of our society's misperceptions of Black people in general, of women in general, and of Black women in particular. The "angry Black woman" is a common stereotype in many white minds; subtly, but no less powerfully, white society in America fears "Black anger."

Ammons makes the indisputable argument that battered African–American defendants are entitled to "no less" than their white counterparts, when it comes to recognizing the impact of the abuse they suffer at the hands of their partners. Another commentator, Shelby Moore, makes the slightly different point that all women ultimately suffer from having to conform to a "victim" stereotype, and that all women must therefore struggle against the gender essentialism embodied in that stereotype, while acknowledging that African–American women have paid a particularly high price for not conforming, or not being viewed as conforming, to the stereotype. Shelby Moore, *Battered Woman Syndrome: Selling the Shadow to Support the Substance*, 38 HOWARD L.J. 297 (1995). Adele Morrison has recently made the argument that the victim focus in domestic violence advocacy and law is largely shaped by white women's experiences, and that domestic violence discourse and legal argumentation must move from the notion of white victim to multi-cultural survivor. Adele M. Morrison, *Changing the Domestic Violence (Dis)course: Moving From White Victim to Multi–Cultural Survivor*, 39 U.C. DAVIS L. REV. 1061 (2006).

7. **Why Doesn't She or He Leave?** If you were a lawyer, how would you try to capture the experiences of violence in same-sex relationships in court? Would these characterizations distort or simplify those experiences? Given that there is a gendered nature to these characterizations, would introducing expert testimony, for example, work against male victims in particular? For an article exploring the admissibility of expert testimony in cases involving same-sex relationships, see Denise Bricker, *Fatal Defense: An Analysis of Battered Women's Syndrome Expert Testimony For Gays and Lesbians Who Kill Abusive Partners*, 58 BROOK. L. REV. 1379 (1993).

8. **Disempowerment?** The focus on expert testimony should not distract us from the other ways in which women can tell their stories of abuse in courtrooms. In some circumstances, it is necessary for expert testimony to provide a framework to establish the relevance of the woman's story, to fill gaps in the evidence, or to enhance the woman's credibility. Nonetheless, lawyers who represent battered women, battered women's advocates and feminist legal theorists worry that reliance on expert testimony can be just one more way of disempowering women, and robbing women of their own voices. As you will see in Chapter Eight, there are many different ways to document abuse. This tension concerning disempowerment is one to keep in mind as we move now to consider the various legal arenas in which stories of abuse are told.

CHAPTER SIX

DOMESTIC VIOLENCE AND CIVIL PROTECTIVE ORDERS

Introduction

For many battered women, going to court for a restraining order (RO), sometimes also called a temporary restraining order (TRO), protective order (PO) or civil protective order (CPO), is the first legal step towards ending the abuse in their relationships or separating from their abusers. As the names imply, these orders are first and foremost about "restraining" the batterer, and "protecting" the partner who is the target of abuse, but today it is a rare order that simply commands an abusive partner not to abuse. Rather, state legislatures have authorized a wide variety of protective provisions, ranging from "stay away" or "no-contact" orders which require the abusive partner to stay away from his victim's home, place of work, or other neighborhood locations, or a fixed distance from her at all times, through temporary custody and support orders designed to regulate the legal consequences of a separation on an interim basis, to miscellaneous but often crucial provisions such as giving up weapons or keys. Some legislation even authorizes the imposition of restitutionary payments for injuries or property damage.

The entire body of law governing these protective or restraining orders has grown up since the 1970s. Until then, battered women had to initiate divorce proceedings before requesting an order, and until 1976, only two states had restraining order legislation specifically designed for battered women. However, passage of the Pennsylvania Protection from Abuse Act in 1976 marked a turning point, and by 1980 forty-five states and the District of Columbia had implemented similar legislation. At this point every state in the union offers customized relief to victims of partner abuse. Many states have by now revised their legislation several times to expand and refine the relief offered.

Another turning point came in 1994 with the passage of the Violence Against Women Act, which contains two provisions designed to strengthen the protections offered by state protective orders. The first provides that states must offer full faith and credit to protection orders issued in foreign states or tribal courts, as long as due process requirements are met at the time the order issues. The second makes the crossing of state lines to violate a protective order, or interstate violation of a protective order (as where a batterer kidnaps his partner and transports her across state lines in violation of an order), a federal crime, with penalties substantially more severe than those that would attach under state law. Also, the Violent Crime Control and Law Enforcement Act of 1994, prohibits the possession of a firearm or ammunition by any person subject to a court ordered restraining order. A violation of this provision is punishable by up to ten years in prison. While many exceptions apply to 18 U.S.C. § 922(g) (2006), its intent is to protect victims of domestic violence from subsequent violence in which the abuser might use a firearm.

The sections that follow cover numerous aspects of the civil protective order process. They look at the question of who is entitled to relief, at the range of relief offered, at issues of process, and at the mechanics of enforcement. They explore the "federalization" of protective orders through the Violence Against Women Act. They address the constitutional challenges that have been raised, and largely answered, with respect to both state and federal legislation.

Since every state now offers victims of partner abuse orders of protection, since the federal government has thrown its weight behind this mechanism, and since judges around the country have largely endorsed its constitutionality, it is tempting to interpret this history as a success story. However, the story would not be complete without at least three cautionary footnotes.

First, while there is some statistical evidence that restraining orders are an effective mechanism for curbing partner violence, the data we have does not allow us to predict with confidence when they will work, when they are likely to be ineffective, or when they may actually put battered woman at greater risk. Those who work with battered women have individual success stories to share, but all of us who read the papers also know the stories of women who have died at the hands of their abusers despite, and sometimes apparently because of, the restraining orders they secured. The final section of the chapter explores the social science research about the effect of restraining orders on the behavior of abusers.

Second, defendants, those who represent them, and some law enforcement personnel have not passively accepted developing restraining order legislation and practice. Although efforts to have governing legislation declared unconstitutional have been largely unsuccessful, other strategies have proved more effective. Police officers resentful of new mandatory arrest policies have sometimes responded to incidents in which it appears that both parties have used physical force by arresting both, and recommending the issuance of mutual restraining orders, rather than seeking to determine who is the primary perpetrator. Defendants and their counsel have also sought mutual orders, or even preempted the abused partner's application for an order by filing first. The real difficulties presented by mutual orders are addressed later in this chapter. Additionally, some judges and prosecutors have attempted to charge the victim with crimes such as aiding and abetting a restraining order violation when she acts inconsistently by allowing the defendant back into the home, for example.

Another battle is currently being waged around protective order databases that are increasingly maintained by states. Defendants argue that *ex parte* orders which are not converted into permanent orders should be immediately expunged from the system, while advocates argue that because of the many reasons victims do not return to court for permanent orders, including intimidation by their abusers, *ex parte* orders should remain in the system for some reasonable period of time. Defendants bolster their arguments with allegations that *ex parte,* and even permanent, orders are issued too readily and on scant evidence, and provide no trustworthy evidence of abuse. Although these arguments have not been accepted by the many judges who have upheld the constitutionality of restraining order legislation against attacks based on due process, they have found some resonance with state legislators who, for example, have been unwilling to allow the existence of a restraining order, by itself, to provide evidence of abuse in the family law context. Judges and those who work in the courts with victims of abuse can best address these allegations by avoiding shortcuts, and ensuring that convincing testimony supports every restraining order that issues.

Finally, in 2005 the United States Supreme Court in *Castle Rock v. Gonzales,* 545 U.S. 748 (2005) held that when the police fail to enforce a protective order, and either the victim or her children are harmed as a result, she cannot sue under the theory that the police violated her due process rights. This case, along with other Supreme Court cases which impose no duty on the government to protect citizens from private harm, has effectively foreclosed federal constitutional claims for victims of domestic violence to have their restraining orders enforced by the police. While some states have created tort remedies for victims, discussed in Chapter Fourteen, many advocates for domestic violence victims warn that after *Castle Rock,* a restraining order is just a piece of paper that victims should not rely upon too heavily for their safety.

This first reading provides some history into the protective order system.

Barbara Hart

State Codes on Domestic Violence: Analysis, Commentary and Recommendations

43 JUV. & FAM. CT. J. 34 (1992).

In the late 1960's, women's centers across the country became inundated with pleas from battered women for safe shelter and protections from violence and terrorism. With no place to refer abused women, volunteers at the centers opened up their own homes to women fleeing from violence. The demand quickly became so great that volunteers in the safe home networks concluded that shelter facilities for battered women were essential. So they went about the task of organizing their communities to open domestic violence shelters.

Advocates quickly determined that laws and social service systems offered little assistance to abused women. Contemporaneously, legal services attorneys were discovering that many of the women seeking domestic relations representation were abused by their husbands or partners. It was apparent to both advocates and legal services practitioners that short-term housing was an inadequate remedy for women whose husbands were committed to violence as a method of control and coercion, both during and after marriage.

A new remedy was needed. One that would enjoin the perpetrator from future abuse. One that would not displace the abused woman from her home but could compel relocation of the abuser. One that could constrain the abusing husband from interfering with and disrupting the life of the abused woman and children. One that could provide stability and predictability in the lives of women and children. One that would give the mother authority to act as primary caretaker of her children; limiting the risk of abduction by the father to coerce reconciliation or to penalize the abused woman for revealing the violence or terminating the relationship. One that could afford economic support so that the abused woman would not be compelled to return to the abuser to feed, clothe and house her children. One that would sharply limit the power of the battering husband or partner to coerce reconciliation. One that would advance the autonomy and independence of the battered woman from the abuser. Civil protection orders were this new remedy.

Women's advocates and their allies crafting the statutes were clear that domestic violence was intentional, instrumental behavior dedicated to control of the family. They understood that domestic violence is not impulsive, abnormal, anger-driven bursts of violence that dissipate with a short period of "cooling off" or that disappear if wives accommodate husbands' demands perfectly. They also understood that battered women may be at the most acute risk of lethal retaliation from the moment they decide to separate from the perpetrator until the time that the abuser decides not to further retaliate against the battered woman for leaving the relationship or the abuser concludes that he no longer is interested in relationship with or control over the abused woman. This period of elevated danger may last for several years. Legislators also recognized that husbands or male partners would not readily give up power accorded by their violence. Thus, the drafters of civil protection orders produced vehicles designed to provide comprehensive relief to facilitate batterer desistance and victim autonomy.

Protection order codes have proven to be tools that can significantly facilitate the achievement of the goals of safety and autonomy for abused women and children and the goals of constraint and deterrence of abusing men. The utility of protection orders depends both on the specificity of the relief ordered and the enforcement practices of the police and the courts. For orders to be effective, they must be comprehensive; crafted to the particular safety needs of the victim in each case. Providing precise conditions of relief makes the offender aware of the specific behavior prohibited. "A high degree of specificity also makes it easier for police officers and other judges to determine later whether the (perpetrator) has violated the order." Data suggest that civil protective orders increase police responsiveness to the requests of battered women for assistance.

NOTES AND QUESTIONS

1. **Legislative Efforts to Increase Police Protection.** Barbara Hart suggests that police are more likely to respond to domestic violence when

there is a restraining order in place. This is not merely an unanticipated side benefit of the process, but was in fact one of the goals motivating those who worked for the passage of protective order legislation. At a time when police were both nonchalant about domestic incidents, and encouraged by official policy to respond more as social workers than as law enforcement representatives, it was felt that a restraining order would signal both the seriousness of the threat to the victim, and the need for a more forceful intervention. It was also hoped that if police failed to assist victims specifically designated for protection by restraining orders, they would be vulnerable to suit (under state tort law or federal or state civil rights legislation), and not able to argue that they were simply exercising appropriate discretion in situations in which the need for their services outweighed the resources they had to commit. As we will see in Chapter Fourteen, courts have foreclosed any constitutional remedy, and only a few states provide for a tort remedy. For more detailed discussion of police failure to protect victims of domestic violence and efforts to hold police accountable, see Chapter Fourteen.

A. SCOPE OF PROTECTION

There are four dimensions to the scope of protection offered by state protective order legislation. The first important question is whom the legislation protects against—in what kinds of relationship the legislature has authorized this particular intervention. In the original drafting of protective order legislation, and in subsequent amendments, interesting assumptions are revealed about who is vulnerable to abuse, and who deserves specific protection. Early statutes were often quite limited. They saw the problem of "domestic" violence as essentially a problem of "marital," "family" or "household" violence, and some even limited relief to presently married partners on the entirely erroneous assumption that divorce would end the abuse. Failure to extend relief to cohabiting partners may have rested on the assumption that victims of abuse who were not tied to their abusers by marriage would be free to set limits without the additional assistance of a restraining order, even if they were sharing a household. Failure to include "dating" relationships may have rested on the same assumption. Alternatively, it may have been based on a failure to appreciate how early patterns of abuse can be established in intimate relationships, even among very young people, or on a reluctance to introduce such a heavy-handed tool into what were regarded as somewhat superficial relationships. The failure to include same-sex partnerships may have been the result of the relative "invisibility" of abuse in same-sex relationships when protective order legislation was first passed, or of homophobia on the part of legislators, and fears on the part of lobbyists that linking the legislation to the protection of gays and lesbians would reduce its chances of passage.

Different questions arise around whether legislation that was primarily intended to address abuse between intimate partners can be utilized by others who find themselves in power and control relationships with abusers who are not sexual partners. A piece of the answer has been that the statutes, which often talk about "household" or "family" members, or about those related by blood or marriage to their abusers, have been interpreted to include in their coverage protection for children abused by parents, parents abused by children, siblings abused by siblings, and any family member abused by another family member (a grandparent or uncle, for example, or a cousin), when the parties share the same living space. When the issue is a child being abused by a parent, questions may arise about the relationship between the protective order process and the separate mechanisms that exist for addressing child abuse, or the relationship between the protective order process and family law process around issues of custody and visitation. But in a household in which one parent poses an immediate threat both to the other parent and to the children, it may be critically important either to include the children in the protective order obtained by the adult victim, or to allow them their own orders.

Questions have also been raised about whether those who are vulnerable to abuse by caretakers, on whom they depend because they are elderly and infirm, or because of a disability, should be able to take advantage of the protective order process. If a caretaker "lives in," he or she may qualify as a "household member" under the governing statute, but this raises interesting policy questions. Should the availability of relief really depend on a criterion (co-residence) which may have no direct relevance to the vulnerability of the victim or the responsibility of the perpetrator? Is the dynamic of caretaker abuse similar enough to the dynamics of power and control in family and intimate relationships that similar mechanisms of protection should be available? Will a blanket decision to allow this vulnerable constituency to use existing mechanisms really offer meaningful protection, without further legislation which addresses the particular difficulties those with disabilities may face in enforcing their rights? These issues were discussed in greater detail in Chapter Three.

Another category of people who may need protection, but may not qualify under existing legislation, are those who are exposed to the violence of the abuser because of their relationships with his present or former partner. Abusers, as we have seen, routinely threaten violence to other members of their partners' families, or to friends or others with whom their partners have contact. The threats may stem from the abuser's conviction that these relationships challenge his control over his partner; they may be used to coerce his partner into complying with his demands, or they may be triggered by concrete assistance others are offering to support the partner in her efforts to end the violence in her relationship, or to end the relationship itself. While legislatures may be unwilling to extend the protection offered by the extraordinary mechanism of the protective order so far, in some cases it may not be possible to challenge the batterer's regime of intimidation effectively without doing so.

A second way of thinking about the "scope" of protective order legislation is to examine the behavior against which it protects. What level of violence, attempted violence or threatened violence by a defendant will support the claim that a protective order should issue? How soon after the incident must the person hurt or threatened with harm seek the court's protection? If an abuser has refrained from violence or threats for the duration of an order, can it be extended on the basis of old injuries or fears, rather than new ones?

A third measure of a statute's scope is the relief it authorizes through the protective order mechanism. Some legislation is quite limited, some provides detailed and imaginative categories of relief, and some articulates only a limited range of relief, but gives judges broad residual authority to provide other "appropriate" relief as circumstances warrant. Judges tend to be wary of exercising this kind of unrestricted discretion, and somewhat unimaginative in their use of it, so that the legislature can perform a valuable educative function by providing a more detailed list of possibilities. A more generous catalog of available relief can also serve as a useful checklist for advocates and lawyers, as they think with their clients about what set of conditions will best secure their safety, and the safety of others threatened by the abuser's behavior.

The final question with respect to scope is the geographic reach of a protective order. Traditionally this has been a problem for women fleeing their abusers, but two relatively recent developments have made a positive difference. Even a move within the state from which the order issued traditionally necessitated alerting police in the new location to the existence and terms of the order, and more often than not victims of domestic violence were themselves responsible for supplying copies of the order to the new police precinct. As more states work to maintain computerized databases of all restraining orders issued within the state, however, it is becoming more common for police to be able to verify the existence and terms of an order, based only on the victim's name. An even larger problem, historically, was the fact that an order issued in one state was usually not enforceable in another, leaving victims with the difficult choice of either keeping their location secret and losing the protection afforded by the order, or applying for a new order in the new state, but with the consequence that the abuser would be notified of his partner's new general location, if not her specific address. This has changed with the passage of the Violence Against Women Act, under the terms of which an order issued in one state, if it meets due process requirements, will be valid in any other, and enforceable as if it had issued in the state in which it is violated.

The following excerpts expand upon these four aspects of the scope of a protective order.

Against Whom Will an Order Issue?

Judith A. Smith
Battered Non–Wives and Unequal Protection Order Coverage: A Call for Reform
23 YALE L. & POL'Y REV. 93 (2005).

The Relationship Requirement

To qualify for a domestic violence civil protection order, the petitioner must establish her relationship with the respondent. In 1995, thirty-three states limited the availability of civil protection orders to individuals who were married, related by blood, shared a child, or were living with the respondent. Since then, several states have amended their statutes to make protection orders more broadly available. Now, all fifty permit victims related to their abusers by blood or marriage to seek domestic violence orders of protection. The Subsections that follow survey the states on how they handle couples who share a child, those who cohabit, those where in intimate relationships, those who are pregnant, and those who are in same-sex relationships.

1.   Parents of a Common Child

As late as 1993, only forty-one states provided for the protection of parents of a common child. Today, forty-nine states provide protection. This includes two states that do not directly provide for co-parents, but effectively allow for protective orders by allowing coverage for members of past or current dating relationships. The remaining state, Louisiana, provides protection only if the two parents cohabitate, and it limits this protection to cohabitants of the opposite sex.

2.   Cohabitation

Today, forty-seven states protect cohabitants, and two of the remaining three protect dating cohabitants. This leaves only New York as the only state without any protection at all. Of the states that expressly protect cohabitants, all but Delaware, include both current and past cohabitants. Five states deny protection to cohabitants of the same sex.

3.   Dating, Sexual and Intimate Relationships

In 1995, fifteen states authorized domestic violence civil protection orders based solely on a dating relationship. Today, a total of thirty-six states provide protection to members of some form of dating relationship. Some states require that the relationship be sexual in order for the participants to receive protection, but most merely require something more than a platonic relationship. Also, most states that offer the protection to members of dating relationships do so without regard to the age of the people involved. However, some limit the protection to adults. Of these states, two limit protection to members of a current relationship. Two others require the relationship to have taken place within a certain time frame.

4.   Pregnancy

Three states, Arizona, Minnesota, and Utah, specifically allow victims who are pregnant with the respondent's child to obtain domestic violence civil protection orders. Most victims would be entitled to protection under the dating relationship protection offered in Minnesota and thirty-three other states. However, in states like New York where the jurisdiction of the courts to provide civil protection orders is limited, women who are pregnant with their abusers' children may be denied protection.

5. Same–Sex Relationships

As of 1993, ten states specifically denied protection to couples in same-sex relationships. Several other states had statutes open to interpretation. Today, that number has been cut in half. Five states still limit protection to persons in heterosexual relationships.

Until 2000, many states did not provide coverage to couples in dating relationships, provided coverage only to cohabiting couples living "as spouses," or had statutory ambiguities that brought their coverage of same-sex couples into question. Since then, policymakers in all but five of these states have either added coverage for dating couples, regardless of their genders, or courts in these states have interpreted statutes as applying to same-sex couples.

6. No Relationship Requirement

A few states have removed their relationship requirements entirely. These states allow anyone to obtain civil protection without demonstrating a specific relation to the abuser; however, orders without relationship requirements do not typically confer the same benefits as domestic violence protection orders.

7. Summary

In ten years, the coverage of domestic violence civil protection orders has increased dramatically. The number of states offering protection to members of dating relationships has more than tripled. Only twelve states still restrict coverage of domestic violence civil protection orders to circumstances where a woman is or was married or related to her abuser, shares a child with him, or has cohabited with him. Three states have amended statutes to allow victims who are pregnant to petition for protection orders against the fathers of their unborn children. Remaining states, save one, also permit victims who are dating their abusers to obtain civil protection orders.

In states where victims fall outside statutory relationship definitions, they are unable to obtain domestic violence civil protection orders. In such situations, individuals must rely on criminal courts or creative civil courts to obtain protection. It can be difficult and expensive, and the remedies provided under civil protection order statutes may not be otherwise available. Neither may the criminal system suffice; there may not be evidence to sustain proof beyond a reasonable doubt, or the government may simply be unwilling to prosecute.

NOTES AND QUESTIONS

1. **Lying for Protection.** In her article, Judith Smith recounts the following case about the effects of the inadequacy of restraining orders:

> In 1988, Linda White was working in a supermarket to support herself and her family, including her disabled brother. It was there that she met John Strouble. The two quickly fell in love, and John moved in

with Linda a month after they met. But before long, John began to abuse Linda. He would tie her up when he left their home. He savagely beat her and often raped her, once using a broken broomstick. On several occasions, once after threatening to throw her from the roof of their apartment building, he would fire his gun in the air, then hold it to her temple and pull the trigger on an empty chamber, forcing her into a dangerous game of Russian roulette.

In 1989, Linda looked to the Family Court in Brooklyn, New York, for help. She wanted a civil order of protection. The first clerk she talked to told her that she was not entitled to an order of protection against her abuser because they were not married, nor did they have a child together. She went to the next window and told a lie she thought would save her life: "I had to lie and say I was married with kids so that I could get my order of protection, even with a black eye." After telling this lie to the clerk she was finally given her order of protection. One month later, claiming self-defense, Linda White shot John Trouble. At trial, the district attorney used Linda's lie as evidence against her. The jury convicted Linda of murder in the second degree and she was sentenced to seventeen years to life in prison.

As of 2007, under New York's civil order of protection, Linda would still have to lie to obtain a civil protection order. New York's legislature has yet to expand the definition of "family or household" to include cohabitants and dating relationships. Smith argues that the reason for New York's restrictive law is that, historically, domestic violence was treated as a private family matter, attempting to keep families together. She argues that more contemporary goals of criminalizing violence and raising public awareness dictates a change in the law. Judith A. Smith, *Battered Non–Wives and the Unequal Protection–Order Coverage: A Call for Reform*, 23 YALE L. & POL'Y REV. 93 (2005).

What other reasons might a legislator in New York give for failing to expand the law, especially given that 49 other states would cover Linda under their statutes? Is the fear that too many victims will seek orders of protection? Would such laws interfere with property rights of cohabitants?

2. **Privileging Marriage**. As noted in Chapter Three, many states do not provide protection orders to teens who are in violent dating relationships. Others do not extend protections to same-sex couples. Why do you think there might be resistance to do so? Are there reasons why legislatures may be hesitant to provide this remedy? Ruth Colker argues that these and other deficiencies in the law are a result of the legal preference for marriage over other relationships. She is highly critical of this marriage bias as it continues to subordinate women and discriminates against gays and lesbians. See Ruth Colker, *Marriage Mimicry: The Law of Domestic Violence*, 47 WM. & MARY L. REV. 1841 (2006).

3. **Orders of Protection for Pets.** New York, Maine, Vermont, and most recently Connecticut, permit courts to issue orders of protection for pets owned or kept by victims of violence, harassment or stalking. Numerous studies have documented the high correlation between animal abuse and domestic violence. Many abusers will harm or threaten to harm pets to

further abuse victims. Many victims also fear their pets will be harmed if they leave the family home without them. Orders for protection for pets are one way in which states can provide additional protection both for animals and their abused caretakers. See Jennifer Robbins, *Recognizing the Relationship Between Domestic Violence and Animal Abuse: Recommendations for Change to the Texas Legislature*, 16 TEX. J. WOMEN & L. 129 (2006); Janet Mickish & Kathleen Schoen, *Protection Orders & Animal Abuse in Family Violence*, 35–Sep. COLO. LAW. 105 (2006); *Animal Cruelty and Domestic Violence Fact Sheet*, The Humane Society of the United States, available at http://www.hsus.org/acf/cruelty/publiced/animal_cruelty_and_family_violence_making_the_connection/cruelty_domestic_violence_fact_sheet.html.

For What Behavior?

This next excerpt overviews the behaviors which can trigger an order of protection and some of the difficulties statutory definitions can present.

Peter Finn and Sarah Colson

Civil Protection Orders: Legislation, Current Court Practice, and Enforcement

National Institute of Justice, 1990.

Some judges are reluctant to exercise their authority to issue an order when threats are alleged but no actual battery has occurred. For example, a judge in a state that authorized protection orders on the basis of threats grants orders only if there have been several threats and the abuser has the ability to carry out his menaces. This reluctance may in part reflect judges' uncertainty about the extent of their authority when the statutory language regarding "threat" is couched in terms of intimidating the victim. For example, the Maine statute provides that "Abuse" includes "attempting to place or placing another in fear of imminent bodily injury." Like other issues of credibility, of course, the finding of whether a threat has actually occurred is within the discretion of the court.

Statutes in many states specifically include sexual assault of an adult as a ground for providing relief. For example, Oregon's statute includes "causing another to engage in involuntary sexual relations by force, threat of force or duress" within the definition of abuse. Sexual assault of a child is expressly included in the definition of abuse in [many] statutes. Moreover, in *Lucke v. Lucke*, 300 N.W.2d 231 (N.D. 1980), the North Dakota Supreme Court ruled that, although the state statute did not expressly include sexual abuse as a ground for issuing an order, the law defining abuse should be interpreted to allow relief for sexual assault.

A number of states define domestic violence to include "malicious damage to the personal property of the abused party" (Tennessee's wording). The Washington State statute provides that "Domestic violence includes but is not limited to any of the following crimes when committed by one family or household member against another'':

—assault in the first, second, third, or fourth degree

—reckless endangerment

—coercion

—burglary in the first and second degree

—malicious mischief in the first, second, or third degree

—unlawful imprisonment.

Most state statutes do not require a victim to petition for a protection order within any specified time limit, nor is there any automatic disqualification due to prolonged delay. However, although of dubious legality, many judges establish their own guidelines in this matter. For example, one judge interviewed will not issue an order unless the most recent incident occurred within the past 48 hours. That stringent a limitation does not appear to have widespread acceptance; many judges reported that they found that victims often need several days or even weeks after the incident to learn about the availability of civil protection orders; to seek encouragement from family, friends, or victim advocates to initiate legal action; and to reach an invariably difficult decision to petition for an order. As a result, judges in other jurisdictions grant orders as long as the incident did not take place more than a month before the petition was filed. Courts in Oregon are permitted by statute to consider women eligible who have been abused any time in the preceding 180 days.

NOTES AND QUESTIONS

1. **Stalking and Harassment.** An increasing number of states provide orders of protection for stalking and harassment as well. We examine the substantive crimes of stalking and harassment in Chapter Seven.

2. **Restraining Orders as Evidence of Abuse.** Despite claims on the part of defendants, those who represent them, and fathers' rights organizations, that restraining orders are not "real evidence" of abuse, the few empirical studies that have looked in depth at what prompts women to seek restraining orders have found otherwise. One study documented that 56% of the 355 women who sought orders had sustained physical injuries, and that first aid, medical attention, or hospitalization was necessary for 39% of those injured. 55% had suffered severe violence—being punched, choked or strangled, beat up, hurt with a weapon, run down with a car or forced to have sex, and 71% had been subjected to violence of other kinds, including 13% whose children were hurt or taken by the abuser. 31% of women had been threatened with death. Adele Harrell and Barbara E. Smith, *Effects of Restraining Orders on Domestic Violence Victims*, Do ARRESTS AND RESTRAINING ORDERS WORK? 214 (E.S. Buzawa and C.G. Buzawa, eds. 1996). In another study of 663 restraining orders, 64.4% were based on physical assaults on the victim, and in another third of the cases the abuser had threatened to kill or otherwise harm the complainant, her children, or

another relative. The perpetrator was arrested in 10% of the incidents which gave rise to these orders. Andrew R. Klein, *Re–Abuse in a Population of Court–Restrained Male Batterers: Why Restraining Orders Don't Work*, DO ARRESTS AND RESTRAINING ORDERS WORK? 192 (E.S. Buzawa and C.G. Buzawa, eds. 1996).

3.   **Criminal Investigation of Abusive Conduct.** In order to receive a restraining order, the victim must allege that the defendant engaged in some prohibited conduct. In most cases, the conduct alleged in the affidavit is criminal. Pushing, shoving, threatening to kill, destroying property, cruelty to animals, and imprisoning someone is illegal conduct. Yet, judges rarely refer cases to the prosecutor for a criminal investigation, even if the facts alleged in the abuse prevention petition are horrific. Should judges refer cases to the prosecutor? Would doing so encourage or discourage victims from seeking orders of protection? What if the victim only wants the abuser to leave her alone, not to go to jail? In the next chapter, we will examine state intervention on behalf of battered women even in cases in which they express disagreement.

4.   **The Standard of Proof.** What standard of proof should judges use in deciding whether to issue a restraining order? In civil cases, the burden of proof is lower than in criminal cases, usually a preponderance of the evidence, or clear and convincing evidence. In most instances, the only proof of the alleged conduct will be the victim's own testimony. Is this sufficient for issuing a restraining order? Consider the following case:

Katsenelenbogen v. Katsenelenbogen

Court of Appeals of Maryland, 2001.
775 A.2d 1249.

Background

The parties had been married since 1986 and had three children, ages 8, 9, and 12. They lived in a single family home in Potomac. Respondent husband is employed full-time as an engineer; petitioner wife is a nurse who, because of a back problem, was able to work only three days—24 hours—a week. As a further consequence of her back problem, wife hired a live-in nanny to help with the children and various household chores.

By the time of the altercation on New Year's Day, the marriage was obviously in deep trouble. Both parties agree that wife had asked husband to leave the home. Husband said that, in December, his wife admitted to him that, while he was away on a business trip, she had brought another man into the home and had sexual intercourse with him, that she had consulted an attorney, and that she intended to divorce him. Wife denied the affair but acknowledged that she had informed her husband that the marriage was over. She said that she wanted him to leave because "he was disruptive to the children" and was "behaving inappropriately in front of them."

The genesis of the January 1 incident was husband's instruction to the nanny that she was fired and would have to leave the home at once.

Husband said that, in light of his wife's confession of infidelity, he was unwilling to continue occupying the marital bedroom and that he needed the nanny's room. Whether he truly needed the room she was occupying was one of the matters in dispute. When informed by the nanny of her discharge, wife called her attorney and was advised that, as wife had hired and was paying the nanny, husband had no right to discharge her and force her to leave the marital home.

With the benefit of that advice, wife confronted her husband in their bedroom and informed him that the nanny was going to stay, which led to an argument over the matter. Husband picked up their cordless telephone and began walking down the stairs. Wife followed him and continued to follow him despite his request that she "get away from him." Wife said that he was calling the police and that she wanted to hear what he was saying. She overheard him say that he had an employee in the house whom he had fired but who was refusing to leave, and that he wanted the police to come and remove her from the house. She heard him add, "Please come quickly because the situation could escalate, and there could be some possible violence." Wife said that she took that to be a threat.

When the pair reached the foyer, their nine-year old son, Alexander, joined them. Husband, still on the telephone, exited the house. Wife continued to follow him down the driveway, demanding that he give her the telephone. He said that he would give it to her when he was finished. At the time, she claimed, he was shouting profanities at her. When he completed his call to the police, he made another call, apparently to his mother, and began speaking in Russian, which wife did not understand. She continued to demand that he give her the telephone. At that point, according to wife, husband, holding the phone in his right hand, put his left hand on her shoulder and shoved her, which "set her off balance." Alexander then "dove in between us," she said, and husband shoved him out of the way. With Alexander, wife ran to a neighbor's house and called the police. After the police arrived and interviewed the witnesses, wife packed some clothing and she and the children went to stay, temporarily, with her mother. There is no evidence that wife, or Alexander, required any medical treatment. She said that she felt faint at one point and was offered an ambulance, but she declined.

Two days later, wife filed in the Circuit Court for Montgomery County a petition for protection from domestic violence, alleging some of the facts as set forth above. The court entered an immediate *ex parte* order in which it found reasonable grounds to believe that (1) wife was a person eligible for relief, (2) husband committed an act that placed her in fear of imminent serious bodily harm, and (3) the act having that effect was that "Respondent shoved petitioner." Upon those findings, the court directed husband to vacate the marital home and to refrain from abusing or contacting wife, [and] awarded custody of the children to wife. Pursuant to that order, wife resumed occupancy of the marital home.

Through the checking of boxes on the pre-printed petition form, wife contended that the acts of abuse perpetrated against her consisted of shoving, threats of violence, and mental injury of a child. She asked for a panoply of relief, including continued possession of the marital home, to the exclusion of husband, emergency maintenance to be paid by husband, and an order that husband have no contact with her or the children. At the hearing on January 10, wife acknowledged that husband had not struck her prior to the incident on January 1. Nor did she present any evidence that he had ever attempted or threatened to strike her. She stated that he had "displayed violent behavior and anger control problems" in the past, however, and described one incident in which, in a failed attempt to kick the family dog, he put a hole in the wall. Without explaining the specific circumstances of their creation, she added that there were "several holes in the wall." She stated further that husband had used profanity in front of the children and that he had "exhibited anger and threatened to throw things against the wall in front of the children." Finally, she said that, at the time of the January 1 incident, respondent's breath was "reeking" from alcohol. Husband denied having shoved his wife and son, and he also denied that he had been drinking. Although Alexander was apparently brought to the courthouse, he was not called to testify.

On this evidence, supplemented by evidence of the parties' respective financial situations, the court found that "there is a volatile situation here," although it did not know the cause of that situation—whether "it is the extra-marital affair or if it is the alcoholic consumption"—and that "these folks should be separated." The court was "convinced" that wife was shoved and decided, therefore, to grant the protective order. The order, which ran for the better part of a year ... afforded nearly all of the relief requested by wife. Among other things, it directed that husband vacate the family home and not return, that he not contact wife in any way, except for visitation with the children, that he not abuse or threaten to abuse the wife, and that he pay emergency family maintenance to wife in the amount of $2,000/month. The order awarded sole custody of the three children to wife, subject to liberal visitation "without consumption of alcohol," and awarded her as well exclusive use and possession of one of the two family cars.

Obviously anticipating further litigation regarding the dissolution of the marriage, which it suggested be "filed immediately," the court stated:

> "This has no bearing on the final outcome of this case whatsoever. This is merely a band-aid attempt to separate these folks so nobody gets hurt, but it is not a situation where Mr. Katsenelenbogen is going to lose everything or whatever as a result of this hearing because I am going to put on here that it is without prejudice and should not have any bearing on the ultimate decision as to the merits hearing, both on the monetary and the award of custody."

In the actual protective order, the court stated, as part of the visitation provision, that "[t]his is without prejudice to respondent to seek custody of children."

Husband appealed from the order, arguing to the Court of Special Appeals that (1) wife had failed to prove "abuse," within the meaning of the domestic violence law, and (2) if there was abuse, it was limited to the one "isolated and relatively non-serious" incident and that the court erred in granting, as a remedy, the maximum relief affordable under the statute.

[On appeal, the Court of Special Appeals held that on the aspect of abuse, the fear must not only be actual, it must also be reasonable, finding that an objective standard be used. Questioning whether the trial court had applied a reasonable standard, it vacated the order and remanded the case to "whether an order is now appropriate, and, if so, its terms."]

Discussion

[The protective order had expired by the time that the Court of Appeals heard the case, and thus the controversy between the two parties was moot. However, the legal clinic at the House of Ruth, an advocacy organization for victims of domestic violence, which represented the wife, pursued the case. The wife argued that the intermediate appellate court decision "suggests that certain types of domestic violence are permissible" and thus "will endanger victims and encourage abuse," that, in contravention of the statute, it has imposed potential harm to respondents as a "new substantive policy consideration in protective order cases," that it incorrectly analyzed both the order issued by the Circuit Court and the applicable law, and that its definition of the "reasonable person" standard to determine the reasonableness of the victim's fear is inadequate.]

Wife ... takes issue with the conclusion of the Court of Special Appeals that, when the abuse triggering a protective order is the commission of an act that places the victim "in fear of imminent serious bodily harm," the fear must be reasonable and that the standard for reasonableness is whether the conduct was "such as to cause a reasonable person under the same or similar circumstances to fear serious bodily harm." That standard, she urges, "is deeply confusing and in need of clarification by this Court." She agrees that the standard should not be an entirely subjective one, but she rejects as well a generalized objective standard—whether the conduct would cause the mythical reasonable person to have such fear. The proper standard, she urges is an individualized objective one—"a reasonable petitioner in that litigant's shoes."

We agree with wife that the proper standard is an individualized objective one—one that looks at the situation in the light of the circumstances as would be perceived by a reasonable person in the petitioner's position—although we see no confusion on that point in the opinion of the Court of Special Appeals. We dealt with this kind of issue recently in *State v. Marr,* 362 Md. 467, 765 A.2d 645 (2001), involving the standard to be applied in determining whether a criminal defendant offering the defense of self-defense had reasonable grounds to believe himself or herself in apparent or immediate danger of death or serious bodily harm. We held that an objective standard was to be applied in determining the reasonableness of the defendant's asserted belief, but we made clear as well:

> "The objective standard does not require the jury to ignore the defendant's perceptions in determining the reasonableness of his or her conduct. In making that determination, the facts or circumstances *must* be taken as perceived by the defendant, even if they were not the

true facts or circumstances, *so long as a reasonable person in the defendant's position could also reasonably perceive the facts or circumstances in that way."* (emphasis in original).

We added in *Marr* that a belief as to imminent danger "is necessarily founded upon the defendant's sensory and ideational perception of the situation that he or she confronts, often shaded by knowledge or perceptions of ancillary or antecedent events." The issue, we said, was not whether those perceptions were right or wrong, but whether a reasonable person with that background could perceive the situation in the same way.

We believe that to be the proper test to be applied in this context as well. A person who has been subjected to the kind of abuse defined in § 4–501(b) may well be sensitive to non-verbal signals or code words that have proved threatening in the past to that victim but which someone else, not having that experience, would not perceive to be threatening. The reasonableness of an asserted fear emanating from that kind of conduct or communication must be viewed from the perspective of the particular victim. Any special vulnerability or dependence by the victim, by virtue of physical, mental, or emotional condition or impairment, also must be taken into account.

Because the protective order at issue has expired and the case is moot, there is no need for us to determine the validity of the order under the principles stated in this opinion. We shall therefore vacate the judgment of the Court of Special Appeals and remand the case to that court with instructions to dismiss the appeal as moot.

NOTES AND QUESTIONS

1. **Applying the Reasonable Person Standard.** This opinion clarifies the legal standard for issuance of a restraining order. Given this standard, do you think the Circuit Court was correct in issuing the protective order? If you were a judge in the case, what facts would you want to know in making your decision? Is this a case in which an order of protection is appropriate? From the facts before you, would you be convinced that the wife was reasonably fearful for her safety? Does the reasonable person standard discriminate against women, who are most often the victims of domestic violence? Are judges likely to see battered women as reasonable? See Elizabeth M. Schneider, Battered Women and Feminist Lawmaking (2000).

2. **Possible Prejudicial Effects of a Restraining Order**. On appeal to the Court of Special Appeals, the husband also argued that the Circuit Court should have taken into consideration the effect that the protective order will have in subsequent litigation concerning their divorce, suggesting that the remedies provided by the trial court were overly broad and prejudicial. The Court of Special Appeals agreed, holding, "In our view, the circuit court did not attempt to tailor the order to the perceived harm, thereby inducing the parties to address separation and divorce issues in a separate action, but granted maximum relief for the maximum duration on the ground that it would be 'without prejudice.' Such an order would

almost always have the effect, although unintended by the court, of giving an unfair advantage to a party in a subsequent divorce, support, or custody action. The court should carefully consider the terms and duration of the order to ensure that the resulting prejudice is justified.''

The Court of Appeals disagreed and made clear that once the trial court finds that abuse has occurred and that there is need for protection, the court must fashion a remedy that provides the victim with the most protection, regardless of any prejudicial effect remedies such as granting custody and visitation rights, may have on subsequent litigation.

Does this result seem fair? In cases in which the parties are anticipating divorce, should an order of protection give the victim such broad remedies, including child support and visitation rights, which will ultimately be decided in family court? Some defense lawyers complain that one divorcing party will seek an order of protection in order to gain the upperhand in a divorce. Is that what happened here?

3. **Children as Witnesses.** In this case, the couple's nine-year old son was witness to the event that gave rise to the protection order. He did come to court, but didn't testify. Should children be asked to provide further evidence supporting the allegations of abuse? Should the court look to child witnesses to substantiate the petitioner's claims? Given that most statutes allow the court to determine custody and visitation as part of a protection order, should the court be required to interview the children to determine what's best for them? We take up these issues further in Chapters Eight and Ten.

4. **Inadequate Fact–Finding.** Ann Freedman argues that a high proportion of domestic violence situations are "murky and difficult" and need far better fact-finding to protect the children involved, as well as to provide the appropriate protection and support to the victim. Yet, given that many litigants are *pro se*, there is often little to no discovery, and in many cases before the court, judges are incapable of making well-informed decisions. Because of the inadequacy of fact-finding, she argues, "Serious cases of domestic violence are missed, relatively minor incidents are subject to overreaction, appropriate remedies are not ordered, custodial arrangements that are impractical and disruptive to children are adopted by way of compromise, and judges, parties and advocates are likely to become cynical or disheartened." Ann E. Freedman, *Fact–Finding in Civil Domestic Violence Cases: Secondary Traumatic Stress and the Need for Compassionate Witnesses*, 11 AM. U. J. GENDER SOC. POL'Y & L. 567 (2003). Do you agree? How might courts undertake more extensive fact-finding? Would such a process be too long and cumbersome? Would it be too expensive?

Available Relief

The next article outlines the forms of relief that are available to through protective orders. Many states have since expanded relief available to victims, but this excerpt provides a comprehensive overview of the general statutory schemes involved.

Barbara Hart

State Codes on Domestic Violence: Analysis, Commentary and Recommendations

43 JUV. & FAM. CT. J. 3 (1992).

The New Jersey code enumerates the most comprehensive potential relief, including any or all of the following:

—an order restraining the defendant from subjecting the victim to domestic violence;

—an order granting exclusive possession to the plaintiff of the residence or household regardless of whether the residence or household is jointly or solely owned or leased by the parties, but if it is not possible for the victim to remain in the residence;

—an order that the defendant pay the victim's rent at a residence other than the one previously shared by the parties if the defendant has a duty to support the victim;

—an order requiring the defendant to pay monetary compensation for losses suffered by the victim as a direct result of the act of domestic violence, with compensatory losses to include, but not be limited to, loss of earnings or other support, out-of pocket losses for injuries sustained, cost or repair or replacement of real or personal property damaged or destroyed or taken, cost of counseling for the victim, moving or other travel expenses, reasonable attorney's fees, court costs, and compensation for pain and suffering; an award for punitive damages, where appropriate;

—an order requiring the defendant to receive professional domestic violence counseling from a private source or a source appointed by the court and, in that event, at the court's discretion requiring the defendant to provide the court at specified intervals with documentation of attendance at the professional counseling, for which the defendant may be ordered to pay;

—an order restraining the defendant from entering the residence, property, school, or place of employment of the victim or of other family or household members of the victim and requiring the defendant to stay away from any specified place that is named in the order and is frequented regularly by the victim or other family or household members;

—an order restraining the defendant from making any communication likely to cause annoyance or alarm including but not limited to, personal, written or telephone contact with the victim or other family members, or their employers, employees, or fellow workers, or others with whom communication would be likely to cause annoyance or alarm to the victim;

—an order requiring that the defendant make rent or mortgage payments on the residence occupied by the victim if the defendant has a duty to support the victim or other dependent household members, providing this issue has not been resolved or is not being litigated between the parties in another action;

—an order granting either party temporary possession of specified personal property, such as an automobile, checkbook, documentation of health insurance, an identification document, a key and other personal effects;

—an order awarding emergency monetary relief to the victim and other dependents, if any;

—an order awarding temporary custody of a minor child (and the court shall presume that the best interests of the child are served by an award of custody to the non-abusive parent);

—an order that a law enforcement officer accompany either party to the residence to supervise the removal of personal belongings in order to ensure the personal safety of the plaintiff when a restraining order has been issued, provided the order for accompaniment is time-limited;

—an order which permits the victim and the defendant to occupy the same premises but limits the defendant's use of the premises but only if the plaintiff specifically and voluntarily requests such an order and the judge determines the request is voluntary and informed, the order conditions the defendant's access, and explicitly sets out penalties for noncompliance;

—an order granting any other appropriate relief for the plaintiff and dependent children as long as the plaintiff consents to the relief;

—an order that requires the defendant to report to the intake unit of the family court for monitoring; and

—an order prohibiting the defendant from possessing any firearm or other weapon enumerated in the code.

More typically, protection order codes authorize orders restraining the defendant from future acts of domestic violence, orders granting exclusive possession of the victim's residence to the victim and/or eviction of the perpetrator, orders awarding temporary custody to the nonabusing parent, orders for spousal or child support and stay-away or no-contact orders.

In forty-nine of the fifty-one jurisdictions, codes include injunctions against further violence. In fifty jurisdictions, codes permit exclusive use of a residence or eviction of a perpetrator from the victim's household. Awards of custody or visitation are authorized in forty-three jurisdictions. Twenty-three jurisdictions authorize the payment of child or spousal support in protection orders. Half of the codes provide for awards of attorneys' fees and/or costs. About one-quarter of the state statutes permit monetary compensation other than attorneys fees and costs, which may include out-of-pocket expenses occasioned by the abuse, replacement of destroyed property, relocation expenses and/or mortgage or rental payments. Half of the codes provide that a no-contact or no-harassment order may be granted after notice and hearing. The statutes in more than forty jurisdictions allow the court to order any additional relief, as appropriate, with direction typically that the relief should be directed at protecting the victim or bringing about a cessation of the violence.

Custody and visitation orders. Apparently noting the enhanced risk posed to children by perpetrators of domestic violence in the context of visitation, several codes have included protective provisions to safeguard children. The New Jersey code pays careful attention to visitation awards issued in protection orders and specifically directs that the order "shall protect the safety and well-being of the plaintiff and minor children and shall specify the place and frequency of visitation. Visitation arrangements shall not compromise any other remedy provided by the court by requiring or encouraging contact between the plaintiff and defendant. Orders for visitation may include a designation of a place of visitation away from the plaintiff, the participation of a third party or supervised visitation. (And, further) the court shall consider a request by the plaintiff for an investigation or evaluation by the appropriate agency to assess the risk of harm to the child prior to the entry of a visitation order. Any denial of such a request must be on the record and shall only be made if the judge finds the request to be arbitrary or capricious. . . . The court shall consider suspension of the visitation order and hold an emergency hearing upon an application made by the plaintiff certifying under oath that the defendant's access to the child pursuant to the visitation order has threatened the safety and well-being of the child."

The Pennsylvania code is more modest but provides that a defendant shall not be granted custody or unsupervised visitation where "the court finds after a hearing . . . that the defendant abused the minor children of the parties or where the defendant has been convicted of (interference with the custody of children) within two calendar years prior to the filing of the petition . . . The court shall consider, and may impose on a custody award, conditions necessary to assure the safety of the plaintiff and minor children from abuse."

The Vermont code requires that if visitation rights are awarded and the court finds that visitation will result in abuse, the court must specify conditions on visitation to prevent further abuse.

Property orders. The Missouri code, among others, articulates that the court may order that "the petitioner be given temporary possession of specified personal property, such as automobiles, checkbooks, keys and other personal effects." The respondent may be prohibited "from transferring, incumbering or otherwise disposing of specified property mutually owned or leased by the parties" and that the respondent be ordered "to pay a reasonable fee for housing and other services that have been provided or that are being provided to the petitioner by a shelter for victims of domestic violence."

Electronic monitoring. The Washington code uniquely authorizes the court to require the defendant in a protection order proceeding to submit to electronic monitoring, restricting the movement of the perpetrator. The order for electronic monitoring must specify the provider of this service and the terms under which monitoring will be performed, which may include a requirement that the abuser pay the costs thereof.

NOTES AND QUESTIONS

1. **Firearm Prohibitions.** Federal law, known as the Lautenberg Amendment, makes it a federal crime to possess a firearm if one is subject to a domestic violence order of protection. Rather than providing remedial relief, this law is intended to be preventive. However, 18 U.S.C § 922(g)(8) is rarely enforced. By 2002, seven years after the law had been in effect, only 58 cases had been filed by the Office of the United States Attorney, despite estimates that more than 40,000 people violate the law each year. See Tom Lininger, *A Better Way to Disarm Batterers*, 54 HASTINGS L.J. 525 (2003).

Soon after the passage of the law, many constitutional challenges were raised, including that it violated the commerce clause as it exceeded Congressional authority by creating a nationwide firearms disability for batterers; that it violated defendants' due process rights because there was no notice received of the gun ban, and that it was a constitutional infringement on the right to bear arms. All of these arguments have been rejected. Nevertheless, the law remains vastly under-utilized by law enforcement. We examine the Lautenberg Amendment in greater detail in Chapter Seven.

2. **Moving Out of the Neighborhood.** May a trial court order a defendant, who is already subject to a restraining order, to move out of a house in the victim's neighborhood? In *Zappaunbulso v. Zappaunbulso*, 842 A.2d 300 (N.J. Super. 2004), the defendant rented a house close to his wife even though he was subjected to a restraining order that prohibited him from harassing or stalking the victim. The court concluded that he moved into the neighborhood to harass her and exert further control over her life. The court ordered him to move, finding that doing so was within its power to grant "any relief necessary to prevent further abuse."

3. **Lack of Due Process Protections.** Although these laws provide a wide range of relief to the victims, they may also circumvent the important constitutional principle of due process. Looking at New Jersey's Prevention of Domestic Violence Act as an example, it allows a person to file a complaint in family court and seek a temporary restraining order. Within ten days, a summary hearing is held to determine whether the allegations in the complaint occurred. If the court determines they have occurred, it may grant any relief necessary to prevent further abuse, including giving the plaintiff exclusive possession of the marital home, requiring the defendant to pay rent or mortgage payments, giving temporary custody of a minor to the plaintiff, suspension of parenting time opportunities for the defendant, prohibiting the defendant from possessing firearms and awarding temporary custody of personal property like checkbooks and cars to the plaintiff. If the defendant violates any of these orders, it may result in a charge of contempt of court and jail time. The name of the defendant will also be added to New Jersey's Domestic Violence Central Registry. Some argue that one problem with this procedure is that it turns a criminal accusation into a civil proceeding. In doing this, it prevents the defendant from the right to free counsel, right to a jury trial, and a right to a full evidentiary hearing. A defendant may go through the proceedings with no

legal counsel and no idea of what is at stake, with only ten days to prepare a defense and then he could lose his house, his car, and his right to parent. David Heleniak gives some examples of where this type of law has gone wrong. One example is from Massachusetts, where a divorced father of two walked his child to the front door and opened it to let him in, and is now serving a six month sentence. Another father of three was arrested and ordered into a batterers program because he got out of his car to pet the family dog while picking his kids up for a visit. Is this fair? Is this what women's advocates intended a domestic violence prevention law to do? How could the law be rewritten in order to prevent this injustice from happening? See David N. Heleniak, *The New Star Chamber: The New Jersey Family Court and the Prevention of Domestic Violence Act*, 57 RUTGERS L. REV. 1009 (2005).

Geographic Scope

Another legal issue of importance is the geographic scope of restraining orders. This is particularly important when victims seek to move across state lines. The Violence Against Women Act requires states to give full faith and credit to orders issued in other states. This next excerpt examines this issue in more detail.

Emily J. Sack

Domestic Violence Across State Lines: The Full Faith and Credit Clause, Congressional Power, and Interstate Enforcement of Protective Orders

98 Nw.U.L.Rev. 827 (2004).

Every state [must] grant full faith and credit to protection orders from all other states, as part of the Violence Against Women Act of 1994 ("VAWA"). Under the VAWA full faith and credit provision, a state must recognize a valid protection order issued by another state and enforce it just as if it were issued in-state. If the order is valid under the terms of the issuing state, the forum state must enforce it, even if it contains terms or includes parties that would be beyond the scope of an order in the forum state. This provision was designed to provide greater protection to women who have fled their abusers and to avoid re-victimizing women who have already been victims of violence....

Implementation of the Violence Against Women Act's Full Faith and Credit Provision

The implementation of the broad language in the VAWA full faith and credit provision proved to be difficult. Protection orders typically must be enforced in emergency situations when a violation is alleged and victims may be subject to or threatened with physical danger. Most frequently it is a law enforcement officer on the scene of a domestic violence incident who must make the first decision about the validity of an out-of-state protection order in order to decide whether there is probable cause to make an arrest based on violation of the order. If an arrest is made and the defendant charged, then a court, frequently at an early stage of the case, must make a finding about the order's validity. Therefore, in very short time frames, enforcing states are faced with several issues. Questions include the expiration date of the order, its validity under the laws of the issuing state, and whether the defendant has been served with the order.

When VAWA was passed, very few states had any infrastructure in place to quickly determine the answers to these and other related questions. There were no procedures for communicating with courts in the issuing jurisdiction, particularly after business hours. Few, if any, states had computerized registries of protection orders, and no national registry existed that law enforcement or court personnel from the enforcing state could access to obtain information about out-of-state orders. Law enforcement officers, faced with an order on an unfamiliar form and of unclear validity, were concerned about making an arrest that could subject them to civil liability if the order later proved invalid. Not only was enforcement of in-state orders problematic, enforcement of out-of-state orders added other layers of difficulty.

Since VAWA's passage, states have moved toward more effective enforcement of the full faith and credit provision. This has included such strategies as the creation of state protection order registries, development of more uniform order forms both within and between states, and enactment of state laws granting immunity to law enforcement officers who make arrests in good faith based on protection orders that later turn out to be invalid. The federal government has worked to facilitate interstate enforcement in a number of ways. In May 1997, the government created a national protection order registry that is part of the National Crime Information Center ("NCIC") database run by the FBI. State protection order registries transmit their information to the national database at NCIC, and law enforcement across the country can access the NCIC database to obtain information on out-of-state orders. Though not all states are transmitting their information to NCIC, a growing number of orders are contained in the national registry. In addition, the federal government has developed several training and technical assistance programs to support interstate enforcement of protection orders. It has funded numerous training materials for those involved in implementing the VAWA provision and a series of regional full faith and credit conferences to encourage communication between key personnel responsible for interstate enforcement of protection orders. Since 1996, the federal government has also funded the National Center on Full Faith and Credit to provide technical assistance to states implementing the VAWA provision.

1. State–Enabling Legislation.—One strategy in the implementation of the full faith and credit provision has been the movement in each state to pass enabling legislation. While this is not required under VAWA, it has the practical purpose in each state of informing state actors—law enforcement, judges, and court personnel—of the requirements of the federal provision and providing more specific guidance on how to enforce out-of-state orders. Within a few years after VAWA's passage, states began to pass such legislation. Currently all fifty states, the District of Columbia, and the U.S. Commonwealth of the Northern Mariana Islands have some legislation involving enforcement of out-of-state orders.

As the movement for passage of state laws was underway, however, it became clear that some states were developing legislation that was in direct conflict or inconsistent with the VAWA full faith and credit provision.... Utah's statute is one that directly contradicts the VAWA provision by stating that full faith and credit will be given to a protection order issued by another state only if the foreign order is similar to an order issued in Utah. Iowa also defines a foreign protection order that is subject to enforcement in the state as one that would be a protection order, order of release, or sentencing condition if it had been entered in Iowa. This violates the central requirement that an enforcing state must give full faith and credit to an out-of-state order if it is valid in the issuing state, even if it involves parties or contains any terms that would not be valid under the enforcing state's law.

Alaska, Kentucky, Louisiana, and the Northern Mariana Islands require that an out-of-state order be filed in a court in the enforcing state in order to be accorded full faith and credit. Filing was never required under the original VAWA provision, and VAWA 2000 explicitly states that no filing or registration is required to trigger full faith and credit.

This is not a trivial difference. Many victims of domestic violence will be unaware of this requirement when they move to a new state. If a domestic violence incident occurs in the new state, the police will not be able to enforce the out-of-state order if it has not been registered. Even if victims are aware of the need to file in the enforcing state, they may not be able to meet the state law's technical requirements, which may mandate multiple copies of the order certified from the issuing state or a notarized statement by the petitioner of the validity of the order. Such a procedure may be appropriate for the registration of typical foreign judgments, usually done by parties with legal representation and in situations that are not emergencies. The typical domestic violence victim, however, is not represented by a lawyer, is frequently in physical danger, and is not in a position to obtain the paperwork that these procedures require. In addition, a victim who does know of the requirement may be fearful of registering the order, because it may become a public record and accessible to her abuser. Thus, a state's filing requirement undermines a central purpose of VAWA....

Some states vary other components of the VAWA provision. For example, Mississippi's statute states that, when no expiration date appears on the face of the order, it shall be deemed to have expired one year from the date of issuance. While filing of a foreign order is not required for enforcement in Tennessee, it is permitted. The state statute requires a foreign order filed without a specified expiration date to expire one year from the date it was first presented to the Tennessee court. However, VAWA requires that the enforcing state recognize out-of-state orders as valid for the length of time that they would be valid in the issuing state. In many states, protection orders may last far longer than one year. If an expiration date is not clear from the face of the order, the enforcing state has a responsibility to ascertain from the issuing state what the expiration date actually is, rather than simply plugging in a term arbitrarily.

The development of a uniform act on the subject by the National Conference of Commissioners on Uniform State Laws ("NCCUSL") has also impacted the progress of state implementation of the VAWA provision. While NCCUSL's involvement has likely encouraged additional states to pass enabling legislation, inconsistencies between the VAWA provision and the NCCUSL uniform act have complicated the process and ultimately increased the number of states that are out of compliance with federal law.

In 2000, NCCUSL passed the Uniform Interstate Enforcement of Domestic Violence Protection Orders Act ("UIEDVPOA"). Acknowledging that states have not consistently or effectively enforced out-of-state orders, UIEDVPOA was designed to "establish uniform procedures" for effective interstate enforcement. The preface to UIEDVPOA noted that many states had already passed enabling legislation, but that they were "either silent or ambiguous" on several important questions regarding enforcement. UIED-VPOA also made general reference to the VAWA provision, but commented that "this legislation is also silent or ambiguous regarding these important questions." The comment to UIEDVPOA also expressed concern that parts of the VAWA full faith and credit provision may be held unconstitutional. While not expressing a position on the constitutionality of the VAWA provision, NCCUSL's purpose is to encourage states to pass legislation on interstate enforcement and therefore "exercise their independent authority to recognize and enforce foreign orders that they would not otherwise be required to enforce under the Constitution." According to this view, although states may not be required by the Constitution to adhere to the VAWA provision, by passing state full faith and credit legislation, they will voluntarily take on the responsibility to recognize out-of-state protection orders....

Alabama, California, Delaware, Idaho, Indiana, Montana, Nebraska, North Dakota, South Dakota, Texas, West Virginia, and the District of Columbia each have passed versions of UIEDVPOA so that these states are now inconsistent with the federal law. In addition, some jurisdictions have made modifications to UIEDVPOA, meaning that even the states using it are not uniform. Many of the states that enacted UIEDVPOA prior to the 2002 amendments have not updated their laws to make them consistent with the amended act, and even some of the states that passed UIEDVPOA more recently relied on its unamended version. All of these factors have created even greater variations among state-enabling laws. While NCCUSL was no doubt well-intentioned in its effort to encourage interstate enforcement of protection orders, the promulgation of an act that is inconsistent in important ways from the federal law has the ironic effect of making interstate recognition and enforcement of protection orders less uniform. While a stated goal of UIEDVPOA was to increase effectiveness and consistency in the enforcement of protection orders across state lines, its divergence from federal law now creates less predictability, more confusion, and greater inefficiencies.

The Violence Against Women Act of 2000

Congress passed the Violence Against Women Act of 2000 ("VAWA 2000") as part of the Victims of Trafficking and Violence Protection Act.

The House Conference Report on the bill stated that, in addition to re-authorizing several key programs, VAWA 2000 made "some targeted improvements that our experience with the original Act has shown to be necessary." Listed among these targeted changes was the improvement of full faith and credit enforcement.

Several provisions in VAWA 2000 were aimed at addressing problems in implementation of the original Act's full faith and credit provision. Section 2265 was amended to add a provision that prohibited the court in the enforcing state from notifying or requiring notification of the party against whom a protection order had been issued that the protection order had been registered in that enforcing state, unless requested to do so by the protected party. In addition, VAWA 2000 made clear that registration in the new jurisdiction was not required for enforcement, notwithstanding any state law to the contrary. The House Conference Report stated that these provisions were designed to help courts improve interstate enforcement of protection orders as required by the original Violence Against Women Act of 1994.

One of the original Act's central grants programs was renamed to expressly include enforcement of protection orders as a focus for grant program funds and add, as a grant purpose, the provision of technical assistance, computers, and other equipment for enforcing orders. VAWA 2000 also required, as a condition of funding, that recipients of state block grants and direct federal grants going to states and governmental units certify that their laws, practices, and policies do not require victims to pay filing or service costs related to protection orders in both civil and criminal cases. VAWA 2000 made the development and enhancement of data collection and sharing systems to promote enforcement of protection orders a funding priority under the grant program and instructed the Department of Justice to identify and make available information on promising practices in protection order enforcement. Furthermore, VAWA 2000 amended the definition of protection order in section 2266 to clarify which support and custody orders were entitled to full faith and credit under the VAWA provision.

Despite VAWA 2000's attempts to encourage greater state compliance with the full faith and credit provision, it has not impacted the states whose laws do not meet the federal law's requirements. The reason for the various states' noncompliance remains unclear. It may be lack of clarity or ignorance about the mandates of the federal law. It may be that legislators enacted either UIEDVPOA or adopted the Uniform Enforcement of Foreign Judgments Act without recognizing the differences in VAWA and in the domestic violence context. For some states, it may be an intentional decision to differ from the federal law due to policy disagreements.

NOTES AND QUESTIONS

1. **Stay-away Orders.** The new interstate enforceability of protective orders guaranteed by VAWA, under 18 U.S.C.A. § 2265, is something for

lawyers and advocates to keep in mind as they assist clients in determining what relief to ask for. A request that the defendant stay away from specific locations loses its usefulness if the petitioner is no longer at those locations, but wants equivalent protection elsewhere, without alerting her abuser as to her new whereabouts. The most "transportable" form of stay-away order will be the one that requires the defendant to stay a certain distance away from the petitioner at all times. Another alternative might be to frame the stay-away portion of the order so that it requires the defendant to stay away from the petitioner's current residence, which should be identified, for ease of enforceability, if it is already known to the defendant, but in addition from any other place where she might reside during the term of the order. Similar provisions could be crafted to cover schools attended by the children, or the petitioner's workplace.

2. **Constitutionality of the Full Faith and Credit Act.** In her article, Emily Sack asks whether states are constitutionally required to comply with the Full Faith and Credit provisions under VAWA. She argues that while domestic violence protection orders do raise several questions in the unsettled law of full faith and credit, the states are still required to comply as Congress may legislate in absence of guidance from the court of this issue. Thus, states may not constitutionally resist and must bring themselves into compliance. Emily J. Sack, *Domestic Violence Across State Lines: The Full Faith and Credit Clause, Congressional Power, and Interstate Enforcement of Protective Orders*, 98 Nw.U.L.Rev. 827 (2004).

3. **The Violence Against Women Act of 2005**. Section 106 expands the scope of VAWA's Full Faith and Credit provisions by requiring states to recognize and enforce custody, visitation, and support orders contained in protective orders. It also prohibits states from publishing information about victims on the Internet.

4. **Orders Issued by Tribal Courts.** Assume that you are an attorney in New Mexico. A woman who has a restraining order against her abusive boyfriend comes to you asking whether the order, which was issued by a tribal court, is enforceable in state courts. Under VAWA, orders issued by tribal courts are enforceable by state courts. See Kelly Stoner and Richard A. Orona, *Full Faith and Credit, Comity, or Federal Mandate? A Path that Leads to Recognition and Enforcement of Tribal Court Orders, Tribal Protection Orders and Tribal Child Custody Orders*, 34 N.M.L. Rev. 381 (2004).

B. ISSUES OF PROCESS

To some extent, the restraining order process mirrors the process prescribed for any other civil matter. A petition is filed in an appropriate court, a hearing date is set, and personal jurisdiction is obtained over the defendant by service of process within a specified time limit. In almost all jurisdictions the hearing is also governed by the usual civil standard of proof, requiring the complainant to demonstrate by a preponderance of the evidence that she qualifies for relief. However, in almost every respect the restraining order process is tailored to the situation it seeks to address in ways that make it unique.

Emergency, Ex Parte and Permanent Orders

Because of the emergency nature of most restraining order cases, all jurisdictions provide for temporary orders to be issued on an *ex parte* basis to complainants who come into court seeking immediate relief. For an *ex parte* order to issue, the complainant must usually submit, with her application, an affidavit which details the violence, attempted violence, or threats on which the application is based. The judge will often question her further in a brief *ex parte* hearing, although it is notable that the statutory provisions governing these hearings do not explicitly demand the presence of the petitioner. To qualify for *ex parte* relief, a petitioner must substantiate the immediacy of her need, by showing, for example, "immediate and present danger" of domestic violence, or "substantial likelihood of immediate danger," or that "irreparable injury is likely or could occur." If the *ex parte* order is issued, it will generally stay in effect only until the date set for the full hearing, which will determine whether a "permanent" order will issue. The term permanent is somewhat misleading, since very few jurisdictions provide for orders of unlimited duration. Permanent, in this context, means an order for any period up to the maximum authorized by the governing legislation. The defendant will receive notice of the *ex parte* order along with notice of the hearing date for the permanent order. Many jurisdictions limit the range of relief granted in this preliminary order, focusing on immediate issues of safety, but not issues such as custody or support.

In the early days of protective order legislation, constitutional challenges were brought against statutes that permitted a defendant to be excluded from a residence owned or leased by him on the basis of an *ex parte* order supported by testimony that he had no opportunity to rebut. Courts were unanimous, however, in ruling that defendants were not, in this situation, deprived of property without due process of law. In *Boyle v. Boyle*, 12 Pa. D. & C. 3d 767 (Pa. 1979), for example, the Pennsylvania Supreme Court, relying on the U. S. Supreme Court's decision in *Fuentes v. Shevin*, 407 U.S. 67 (1972), found that it was constitutionally permissible to subordinate the respondent's interest in the uninterrupted possession of the residence to the victim's right to immediate protection against abuse. Similarly, in *State ex rel. Williams v. Marsh*, 626 S.W.2d 223 (Mo. 1982), the Missouri Supreme Court applied the balancing test articulated in the U.S. Supreme Court's decision in *Mathews v. Eldridge*, 424 U.S. 319 (1976), and concluded that although the uninterrupted possession of one's own home was a significant private interest, the high incidence and severity of domestic violence made the governmental interest in preventing that violence weightier.

The Missouri court also found that the *ex parte* provisions were a reasonable means to achieve the state's legitimate goal of preventing domestic violence, and afforded adequate procedural safeguards before and after any deprivation of rights. In *Blazel v. Bradley*, 698 F.Supp. 756 (W.D.

Wis.1988), a case challenging the *ex parte* provisions of the Wisconsin statute, the court made a similar reference to the adequacy of the procedural safeguards built into the statute, noting that: "It is explicit in the statute that judicial participation and a verified petition containing detailed allegations are required before an ex parte order may issue, and that a prompt post-deprivation hearing must be provided."

Even the *ex parte* process is not always adequate to protect a victim who requires immediate assistance during evening or weekend hours when the court is not open. A substantial number of jurisdictions have responded to this gap in service through an emergency response system. In Massachusetts, for example, police work with a designated emergency judge, who is authorized to issue orders over the phone after hearing testimony from both the responding police officer and the complainant. The complainant must then go into court the next day it is open to apply for a regular *ex parte* order, and receive a hearing date for the permanent order.

Different statutory schemes allocate the responsibility of converting an *ex parte* order into a permanent order differently. In some statutes, a defendant desiring relief from an emergency order must affirmatively request a hearing. In Oregon, for example, if the defendant does not respond to the notice that an *ex parte* order has issued by requesting a hearing, the original order will remain in effect for the maximum time permitted under statute (one year), or for whatever shorter period has been designated by the court. More commonly, however, the statutory scheme provides that the court must schedule the full hearing, or the complainant must request it, as soon as the *ex parte* order is issued. Even this full process is an expedited one; in most states the hearing is scheduled to take place within ten to twenty days after the initial application. In these states, if the defendant has been properly served but does not appear to contest the order (a not uncommon situation), the court may enter a default judgment, and issue a permanent order, with the full range of relief authorized by the statute. But if the hearing does not take place, which might be because the complainant fails to return to court, because the defendant has not been properly served, or because of administrative difficulties, the *ex parte* order will automatically expire. This can create a situation in which the complainant is forced to return several times to court, spending several hours there each time, to seek extensions of her *ex parte* order while she waits, for example, for her partner to be served. The danger inherent in this system is that the abusive partner, by avoiding service, can place his victim's employment in jeopardy or wreak havoc with her child care arrangements, and may even be able to manipulate the process so that her order expires, leaving her once more unprotected.

The obvious question is why, given the disadvantages of this system, more states do not employ the Oregon model, under which the complainant is protected unless and until the defendant appears to contest the order. One reason may be a fear that such a scheme, by laying such a heavy burden on the defendant, is vulnerable to the charge that it violates due process. Another practical disadvantage is that the defendant who never appears in court may be less likely to comply with the terms of the order—

although even the defendant who receives notice of a hearing date may choose not to appear, and suffer a default judgment which he may also be inclined to ignore. A final difficulty is that even if the statute's service requirements have been met at a technical level, a defendant who has not in fact received notice may be able to invalidate the terms of the order in a subsequent challenge.

Assistance for the Victim

It is fundamental to the protective order regime that it provide victims of domestic violence with easy (and inexpensive) access to the judicial process. To that end, many protective order statutes have specifically provided for *pro se* petitioning. However, most reports on the functioning of the protective order process have emphasized that victims who approach the court without competent assistance fare less well—both in securing orders, and in securing orders containing the full range of available and appropriate relief—than those who have help. Help can come from a variety of sources; from the court clerks who serve as gatekeepers to the process, from victim witness advocates attached to the prosecutor's office, from lay advocates, or from lawyers. Lay advocates may be employed by the court or by social service or shelter organizations or they may be volunteers. Some are currently being funded by the U.S. Department of Justice, under grants authorized by the Violence Against Women Act. Among the volunteers are many law students working in clinical programs or with student-run advocacy projects. Lawyers may be retained by individual victims, employed by a legal services program or prosecutor's office, or members of a volunteer project organized by committed individuals, law firms or local bar organizations.

The following excerpt discusses the use of lay advocates in assisting victims of domestic violence and the potential liability they may face for the unauthorized practice of law. Many of these lay advocates are law students working in connection with a law school-sponsored clinic. Consider whether using lay advocates is an effective strategy for assistance, or whether only attorneys should take responsibility for representing victims.

Margaret F. Brown

Domestic Violence Advocates' Exposure to Liability for Engaging in the Unauthorized Practice of Law

34 COLUM. J.L. & SOC. PROBS. 279 (2001).

Courtroom advocates are nonlawyers who are trained to provide information and support to individuals who are seeking legal protection from abuse by intimate partners. Characteristic responsibilities include explaining the court's procedures for obtaining a protective order and discussing available legal remedies, providing emotional support throughout the process, assisting with safety planning, and providing referrals for shelters and other emergency services. Advocates work for a variety of organizations.

Some volunteer their time and others are compensated by the organization with which they are affiliated....

Batterers have taken legal action against domestic violence advocates. Currently, advocates run the risk of being sued by perpetrators of domestic violence for engaging in the unauthorized practice of law. An advocate in Houston, Texas reported that her agency was forced to discontinue assisting a domestic violence victim because the agency lacked the resources to defend the repeated lawsuits instituted against it by the alleged abuser. In North Dakota, the husband in a divorce proceeding brought third-party complaints alleging unauthorized practice of law against the domestic violence advocates who had assisted his wife in a prior abuse proceeding. The judge dismissed the complaints because they were unrelated to the divorce action, but indicated that the dismissals would not bar the husband from bringing separate actions against the advocates in the future. Recently, the attorney for an alleged abuser filed a complaint claiming unauthorized practice of law against a domestic violence advocate with the North Carolina State Bar. The Unauthorized Practice of Law Committee of the state bar determined that the advocate did act as an attorney by going to a judge's home to get an inaccurately worded protective order corrected and the committee issued the advocate a cautionary letter.

Advocates are often supervised by attorneys and those attorneys are vulnerable to discipline for assisting in the unauthorized practice of law in violation of Rule 5.5(b) of the Model Rules of Professional Conduct. The Model Rules were formulated by the American Bar Association ("ABA") and have been adopted in some form by approximately four-fifths of the states and the District of Columbia. They have the force of law in most jurisdictions that have adopted them. While the Model Rules are intended to provide standards for attorney discipline, many courts also rely upon the rules in determining civil liability. An attorney who assists a nonlawyer in the unauthorized practice of law may be subject to censure, suspension or even disbarment by his or her bar association....

Many victims of domestic violence are financially dependent on their abusers and cannot afford an attorney. The majority of victims who seek orders of protection are pro se petitioners who are typically unfamiliar with the court system and who will likely receive little assistance and even less understanding from judges and other court personnel. A number of studies have revealed that "court clerks offer victims very limited assistance, and that a substantial number actually discourage petitioners from filing for protective orders, much less inform them of additional remedies to pursue." Evidence suggests that "many judges find it frustrating to deal with pro se litigants" and that some judges are biased against women, which is particularly detrimental to petitioners given that "judges' attitudes toward victims of domestic violence can deter women from seeking judicial remedies."

The emotional support provided by domestic violence advocates throughout the judicial process clearly benefits domestic violence victims faced with judges and clerks who lack a basic understanding of domestic violence. Court personnel who are not familiar with the dynamics of abusive relationships might blame the victim for not leaving the relationship sooner or assume that she will never leave. Without the support of an advocate, domestic violence victims are more likely to be deterred from seeking legal redress and less likely to follow through with proceedings if they are initiated. When a petitioner is represented by legal counsel, an advocate may still be able to provide valuable assistance that the attorney often lacks the time to offer. A 1990 study sponsored by the National Institute of Justice found that:

> [V]ictim advocates can often assist petitioners in ways that most attorneys cannot. Advocates may have a better understanding of the emotional and social impact of domestic violence and a greater ability to communicate with victims than most attorneys. They may also have more familiarity with the practical impact of common provisions in protection orders than attorneys who handle only one or two cases a year.

Even where judges and court personnel are enlightened about domestic violence issues and sympathetic to the plight of petitioners, the realities of crowded dockets and the requirements of judicial neutrality limit the amount of assistance court personnel are able to provide. One Family Court judge in Manhattan commented that the cooperative relationship between the court and a nonprofit domestic violence advocacy organization "has demonstrated that the Family Court can provide for value added services to litigants while remaining faithful to its role as neutral adjudicator."

The ABA has recognized the need for lay advocates in order to ensure a meaningful right of access to the courts, yet the ABA Model Rules of Professional Conduct maintain a broad prohibition on assisting the unauthorized practice of law. This ban potentially deters judges and attorneys from cooperating with nonlawyers in finding ways to broaden access to the courts. . . .

The stated purpose of the unauthorized practice ban is to "protect the public against rendition of legal services by unqualified persons." Harm could conceivably arise in three ways. First, an individual might believe that the domestic violence advocate is a lawyer by virtue of the fact that the advocate is providing assistance with a legal matter. In addition to the inherent harm of false representation, the individual might mistakenly believe that she has retained the services of a licensed attorney or that her communications with the advocate are confidential. Second, an individual might suffer serious consequences if a lay advocate provides erroneous information. This danger is especially acute in domestic violence cases where the victim's personal safety is frequently at stake. Finally, because nonlawyers are not subject to court sanction as are members of the bar, an important safeguard and avenue of redress will be unavailable to an injured party. . . .

While the concerns underlying the ban on unauthorized practice of law are valid, they may be addressed through procedural safeguards without jeopardizing the viability of advocacy programs. Domestic violence advocates receive thorough training from their sponsoring organization in court procedure, relevant law, and emotional and practical issues relating to domestic violence. Advocates are instructed to inform each person they assist that the advocate is not an attorney and that communications will not be held confidential. Proper training ensures that advocates are equipped to handle their responsibilities and that the individuals receiving assistance do not mistakenly believe that they are being represented by an attorney. . . .

Another potential oversight mechanism is a limited licensing procedure. States could develop certification requirements and maintain a registry of certified advocates. A bill introduced in the California State Senate in 1997 proposed the creation of a state registry within the Department of Consumer Affairs for nonlawyers who provide self-help legal services. The registry was intended to clarify the role of nonlawyers, allowing them "to help consumers on 'relatively routine legal matters' without running afoul of the state prohibition against unauthorized practice of law." The bill also aimed to protect consumers of legal services by gathering information about legal service providers and subjecting nonlawyers to the same ethical standards as members of the bar. The bill failed to pass within the requisite time and was not enacted. Nevertheless, an advocate registry could help to ensure that advocates are sufficiently qualified and accountable. . . .

The ABA undertook a comprehensive study of nonlawyer activity in 1995. The resulting report recognized the need for the valuable services performed by lay advocates in attaining the ABA's objective of broadening access to the courts. The ABA report recommended that the states, and particularly the state supreme courts, take action to resolve the inherent conflict involved in relying upon nonlawyers to increase the availability of legal assistance.

The Supreme Court of Minnesota had taken action in this area before the ABA's recommendation was made. In 1991, it issued an order authorizing domestic violence advocates to "assist victims of domestic violence in the preparation of petitions for protection orders" and to attend court proceedings, declaring that, "[w]hen they assist victims of domestic violence as specified in this order, domestic abuse advocates are not engaging in the unauthorized practice of law." The Illinois state legislature has adopted a similar provision.

In 1995, the Attorney General of Maryland outlined the types of assistance domestic violence advocates may and may not provide in order to comply with the state's unauthorized practice prohibition and the Maryland Rules of Professional Conduct. Domestic violence advocates are permitted to provide basic information about legal rights and remedies, explain court procedures, and assist in preparing pleadings or other form documents. With the judge's permission, the advocate may sit with the victim during the proceedings. Unless acting under attorney supervision, advocates may not provide legal advice as to which legal remedy to seek, explain "legal aspects of judicial proceedings, such as how to present a case, call witnesses, present evidence, and the like," prepare pleadings using the advocate's own words as opposed to the victim's, or advocate on behalf of an individual victim before a governmental representative.

NOTES AND QUESTIONS

1. **Treatment of Battered Women in the Courthouse.** A 1990 report commissioned by the National Institute for Justice highlights best practices among judges, courts and law enforcement personnel in the administration of the restraining order process, and encourages their emulation by others around the country. The report singles out court clerks for explicit criticism. Peter Finn and Sarah Colson, *Civil Protection Orders: Legislation, Current Practice, & Enforcement*, NAT'L INST. OF JUST., 1990.

However, in many courthouses there is a messier story to be told about the relationships among the constituencies to whom battered women look for support in obtaining their restraining orders, and about the level of support available. For example, in many overworked prosecutors' offices, victims of domestic violence receive assistance with restraining orders, whether from prosecutors or victim advocates, only if they are simultaneously proceeding with criminal complaints against their abusers. To the extent the prosecutor's office is intent upon encouraging prosecution, linking prosecution with other assistance provides a powerful incentive to women to cooperate, but can be quite coercive. Even where prosecutors' offices genuinely lack the resources to assist all those who are seeking protective orders, they have not always welcomed an infusion of resources from other sources, leading others to question their good faith.

Tension between lay advocates working in the courthouse and personnel in the prosecutor's office is commonplace. Sometimes it focuses on disagreements about the extent to which women should be encouraged to cooperate with prosecutors—with accusations that prosecutors are overly aggressive in promoting prosecution, and insufficiently attentive to safety. Sometimes it focuses on concerns that prosecutors are insufficiently experienced or aggressive, and unwilling to commit the resources necessary to build strong cases against dangerous defendants. Similar tensions exist between lay advocates and court clerks, who would often rather labor under an overload of work than have their practices open to scrutiny and criticism by advocates who may bring more experience and commitment to issues of domestic violence, but can also be insufficiently understanding of the constraints involved in working within the courthouse bureaucracy. Judges may be willing in principle to welcome advocacy programs into the courthouse, but unwilling to mediate the conflicts that arise, or even to ensure that advocates are provided with access to the clients they have come to serve.

2. **Interpreters.** As we saw in Chapter Three, immigrant and non-English speaking victims often have difficulty accessing the legal system. One strategy states have employed to combat this problem is to mandate the use of interpreters. Many states require that interpreters be available in all civil proceedings, and both California and North Carolina provide for interpreters specifically in domestic violence cases. The state pays for interpreters when the clients are indigent. For an overview of this issue, see Nancy K. D. Lemon, *Access to Justice: Can Domestic Violence Courts Better Address the Needs of Non–English Speaking Victims of Domestic Violence?* 21 BERKELEY J. GENDER L. & JUST. 38 (2006).

3. **Appointment of Counsel for Victims of Abuse.** Should courts appoint attorneys for victims seeking a restraining order? The following excerpt argues that they should.

Beverly Balos

Domestic Violence Matters: The Case for Appointed Counsel in Protective Order Proceedings

15 TEMP. POL. & CIV. RTS. L. REV. 557 (2006).

The trend over the last decade has been increasing numbers of unrepresented litigants filing cases and appearing in court, particularly in family law, landlord tenant, and small-claims cases. Lack of legal representation is overwhelmingly the condition of parties seeking and defending requests for protective orders. One study found that in Lake County, Illinois, neither party was represented in 83.4% of order for protection cases. This figure is consistent with other studies. In a recent study of 300 order for protection hearings in an urban setting, only twenty percent of the petitioners and twenty percent of the respondents had counsel. Additional confirmation of the overwhelming lack of representation is found in another study that examined three different jurisdictions and found that victims of domestic violence seeking orders for protection often appeared unrepresented; pro se appearances were reported at eighty percent, 80.3 percent and 65.8 percent in the three jurisdictions considered. . . .

The empirical studies examining protective order procedures paint a disturbing picture. Victims of domestic violence seek court protection only after experiencing serious abuse for an extended period of time. Accessing the judicial system presents unique complexities for victims because of the inherent difficulties of a system in which one must confront one's abuser who is also an intimate partner. The nature of that intimate relationship means that the victim is at greater risk and more vulnerable to violence and intimidation. Yet, research tells us that the parties most at risk and potentially most intimidated who seek protection from violence are highly unlikely to have legal representation to help them navigate the intricacies of the process and to advocate on their behalf. Research also tells us that lawyers matter; parties who have legal representation are significantly more likely to obtain protective orders and to obtain comprehensive relief in those orders. . . .

As [*Lassiter v. Dep't of Social Services*, 452 U.S. 18 (1981)], explained, it is the person's interest in personal freedom that triggers the right to appointed counsel. In protective order cases, the target of domestic violence is seeking access to the court because her physical integrity and personal freedom are at stake. While physical liberty may not be at stake in the conventional sense of incarceration, victims of domestic violence experience violence and threats perpetrated by an intimate partner who is exerting control over the victim's life and constraining her freedom and autonomy. Even if this exercise of violence and control does not amount to a deprivation of physical liberty, the private interests at stake and the likelihood of erroneous decisions substantially outweigh the state's pecuniary interest in denying appointed counsel and rebut the presumption articulated in *Lassiter*.

A. Private Interest at Stake

1. Domestic Violence Limits the Fundamental Liberty Interest in Bodily Integrity and Autonomy

In addition to its targets suffering a dignitary harm, domestic violence restricts the most basic aspects of liberty—the right to bodily integrity and to move freely without restraint. Acts of domestic violence pose an immediate and present danger to the physical survival of victims. In addition, in many instances of domestic violence, the victim's freedom of movement is controlled by the abuser. Not only is the victim constrained at home by monitoring of phone calls, visits, and violence or threats of violence, but outside movement is restricted or only allowed when accompanied by the abuser.

At its most basic, liberty means the right to be secure and to move freely. These most basic rights are denied to targets of domestic violence who, because of a lack of security and violence-free movement, are denied fundamental rights of citizenship and are unable to participate as equal citizens in the life of the community. While the constraints on the liberty interest have not been precisely defined, the interest includes the right to be free from bodily restraint. The party seeking relief from the court in a protective order proceeding has a protected liberty interest in personal freedom and security. This interest in personal security is not simply a private, individualized interest. Personal security and the right to be free from domestic violence also encompass a governmental or public interest. As one state supreme court has found, "the general public has an extraordinary interest in a society free from violence, especially where vulnerable persons are at risk."

In withholding appointed counsel from the petitioner in *Lassiter*, the Court relied on a limited definition of physical liberty. The Court cited selected cases which implied that, for due process purposes, the deprivation of one's physical liberty and personal freedom is generally associated with instances of incarceration or civil commitment. However, a different line of jurisprudence that has developed since *Lassiter* defines physical liberty more broadly.

In *Washington v. Glucksberg*, a case in which three terminally ill patients, four physicians, and a nonprofit organization brought an action against the state of Washington for a declaratory judgment that the statute banning assisted suicide violated the Due Process Clause, the citizens argued that "the liberty protected by the Due Process Clause includes basic and intimate exercises of personal autonomy." The citizens based much of their argument on the precedent of *Planned Parenthood of Southeastern Pennsylvania v. Casey*, which specifically addressed a woman's constitutional interest in physical liberty, and asserted that "one aspect of this liberty is a right to bodily integrity, a right to control one's person." In reaffirming that a woman has a constitutionally protected interest in terminating a pregnancy, the Court discussed the constitutional protection afforded to personal decisions involving marriage, family relationships, and reproduction, stating that such matters, involving "choices central to personal dignity and autonomy, are central to the liberty protected by the Fourteenth Amendment."

These choices, as well as physical safety, are precisely what are at stake in order for protection cases. Individuals seeking protective orders will continue to be at risk of losing physical liberty and personal freedom if they fail to obtain a protective order. Many victims of domestic violence seek protective orders as a last resort to reclaim "what the abuse has systematically stripped from them: their control over their activities, their bodies, and their lives." Research on domestic violence patterns shows that "the struggle to control the woman ... lies at the heart of battering." Women seeking protective orders may even be risking their lives in choosing to look to the courts for protection. Additionally, the rights to marry and to divorce may be implicated in cases of domestic violence. For some women, seeking an order for protection is a signal that a marriage or relationship is ending. Retaliatory violence by the abuser further threatens a domestic violence victim's bodily integrity and personal autonomy.

The nature of the private interest at issue in protective order proceedings encompasses both personal freedom and bodily integrity. If we take the *Lassiter* case at face value and apply the notion that fundamental fairness requires the appointment of counsel when physical liberty is at stake, then cases of domestic violence meet that standard. When petitioners in domestic violence cases request the protection of the court, they are petitioning the court to remedy their current experience of violence and constraint, but they are also risking future deprivation of liberty and continuing violence if they lose.

NOTES AND QUESTIONS

1. **Protective Orders and the Indigent.** As Beverly Balos notes, the vast majority of those seeking restraining orders are not represented by counsel. Is this because, for those who lack economic resources, seeking a protective order is one of the few low-cost legal remedies available? Balos further noted that those who are represented by attorneys are more likely to have their requests granted. Does this mean that the legal system discriminates against the poor and others who lack assess to an attorney?

2. **Laws Requiring the Appointment of Counsel.** In 2005, Illinois amended its civil protection order statute. It now provides that the court may appoint counsel to represent the petitioner seeking an order of protection if the respondent is represented by counsel. 740 Ill. Comp. Stat. § 22/204.3 (2005). The legislature found that "providing legal representation to the indigent party in domestic relations cases has a great potential for efficiently reducing the volume of matters which burden the court system in this State." 705 Ill. Comp. Stat. 130/5 (2005). Thus, the state pays for the appointment of counsel in cases where the defendant is

represented by counsel. Do you agree that the state has an interest in providing counsel in these cases?

3. **Should Counsel be Appointed for Defendants?** Illinois provides attorneys for victims when defendants are presented by counsel. Should the state also provide counsel for the defendant? Given that violations of restraining orders can result in criminal charges, do you think defendants have a constitutional right to counsel?

4. **The Effect of *Castle Rock*.** You read an excerpt of *Castle Rock v. Gonzales* in Chapter One, and will study it in more detail in Chapter Fourteen. In that case, the Supreme Court held that failure of the police to enforce a restraining order was not a violation of the 14th Amendment's due process clause. What effect, if any, do you think that opinion would have on the argument that victims have the right to an attorney in civil protection order hearings because of the due process interests involved?

Service of Process

Civil actions are typically commenced by service of process on the defendant; a formal delivery of papers that will detail the nature of the case, the next step to be taken (usually an answer is required from the defendant) and the timing of that next step. The plaintiff initiating the action can personally serve the defendant, or hire a professional process server to do the job. The special nature of the protective order process affects service in a number of ways. First, in the common situation in which the complainant has already received an *ex parte* order, serving the defendant is his notice that he is already subject to a court order constraining his access to his partner, as well as notification that he must defend the issuance of a permanent order. Second, because of the expedited nature of the process, the "next step" is the hearing on the permanent order, which will in most cases take place within one to three weeks of the time the *ex parte* order was granted. Third, although the restraining order is a civil mechanism, its hybrid civil/criminal status is evident in the practice of requiring law enforcement officers to serve the defendant. There are serious safety issues involved in asking the complainant to take responsibility for serving the partner she is accusing of abuse, although this is unfortunately not uncommon, and hiring professional process servers would be beyond the means of most domestic violence victims, so that the use of police is at one level a practical necessity. At the same time, it serves as a useful reminder that although the protective order is a civil remedy, its violation is in most states a criminal offense, and that any incidents of violence that have precipitated its issuance or that are incurred in its violation are themselves criminal offenses.

In the Harrell and Smith study cited previously, which looked at 355 restraining orders issued between January and September of 1991 in a single state, 40% of women did not return to court for a full hearing and a permanent order after their emergency order issued. Of these, more than 40% attributed their failure to follow through to the difficulties they experienced getting the emergency order served. Adele Harrell and Barbara E. Smith, *Effects of Restraining Orders on Domestic Violence Victims,* in DO ARRESTS AND RESTRAINING ORDERS WORK? (E.S. Buzawa and C.G. Buzawa, eds. 1996).

Duration, Extension and Withdrawal or Dismissal of Orders

The duration of a restraining order varies from state to state. A "permanent" order may be in effect only for a specified period of time. For example Pennsylvania's orders last for 18 months, with the option to extend. 23 Pa. Cons. Stat. Ann. § 6108(10)(d)–(e) (West 2001). In contrast, New Jersey provides that a final order will last indefinitely. N.J. Stat. Ann. § 2C:25–29 (West 1995).

When can an order be vacated? This next case examines the standard of review when the defendant seeks to have the order amended or vacated.

Mitchell v. Mitchell

Massachusetts Court of Appeals, 2005.
821 N.E.2d 79.

Six months after Mary Mitchell obtained a G.L. c. 209A abuse prevention order against her husband, James Mitchell, a judge of the Probate Court vacated the order on the husband's motion seeking to reconsider or vacate it. We consider in this appeal by the wife the appropriate standard for deciding a motion to reconsider or vacate a c. 209A order, and whether the husband's evidence was sufficient to support the judge's decision. We conclude that it was not and, therefore, that it was error to vacate the order.

1. *Background.* After suffering from more than ten years of verbal and physical abuse inflicted by the husband, the wife, filed a complaint for protection from abuse under c. 209A, supported by her affidavit and three police reports. An ex parte abuse prevention order was issued that same day directing the husband to (among other things) refrain from abusing or contacting the wife. The husband appeared pro se at a hearing ... on which the initial order was fixed to expire, and after hearing, the order was extended for one year. The husband did not appeal from the extended order.

We accept as fact the wife's averments in her affidavit, including that the husband had kicked and hit her, pulled her hair, and threatened to kill her if she attempted to "get anything" through separation or divorce or if she divulged to the court certain information concerning the parties' finances, and that she was terrified of the husband and feared for her life. This is because there were no contrary findings made in connection with the issuance of the c. 209A order, which ordered the husband (1) not to abuse the wife; (2) to have no contact with the wife, in person, by telephone, in writing, or otherwise, and to stay at least fifty yards away from her "even if the [wife] seems to allow or request contact"; and (3) to surrender any guns or licenses to the local police department because "[t]here is a substantial likelihood of immediate danger of abuse."

The husband filed a verified motion requesting the court "to reconsider or vacate" the order dated January 3, 2002; in the motion he stated that the wife had contacted him repeatedly by telephone since the issuance of the order and had spent time with him in Los Angeles while attending the funeral of his mother. In the husband's view, the wife's repeated "contact[s]" with him and her "successful requests" to spend time alone with him while they were in Los Angeles "clearly indicate that she does not fear physical or verbal abuse from [him] and did not fear such abuse in the past." The husband requested that the abuse prevention order be vacated retroactive to January 3, 2002.

More specifically, the husband averred that he and the wife had engaged in numerous conversations which included both "chit chat" and discussions concerning the parties' pets (all of whom were in the husband's care and needed medical attention) and various civil litigation matters in which the parties were involved. The husband also averred that following the death of his mother in Los Angeles, the wife asked him if she could attend the funeral and proposed that they fly to California together; while in Los Angeles, he and the wife spent time alone (attending a movie and riding in an automobile) and with others (including at his mother's memorial service, burial, and a reception), often at the wife's request; he had dinner with the wife and his sister.

A hearing, at which no testimony was taken, was conducted by the same judge who had issued the [original] order. The judge had before her the husband's affidavit, the wife's verified opposition to the husband's motion, and an affidavit of the husband's sister filed by the wife which, in large part, corroborated the wife's description of events and statements concerning her fear of the husband.

In her opposition, the wife denied or otherwise challenged the husband's averments or his characterizations of events and stated that she continued to be in fear of him. She said, among other things, that she had not voluntarily initiated contact with the husband other than to check on the medical condition of the parties' pets. As for the trip to Los Angeles following the death of the husband's mother, the wife stated that upon receiving an invitation from the husband to attend the services, she consulted with the husband's sister, brother-in-law, and father, who invited her to attend, as they considered her to be part of the family. The husband's family also assured the wife that steps would be taken to ensure her safety. This included paying for a separate flight for her to attend the funeral; arranging for the husband to stay at a hotel while she stayed with members of the husband's family; and attempting to keep the parties separated as much as possible within the circumstances of attending the funeral and related family events. Continuing, the wife stated that there were only two occasions when she was physically alone with the husband (at a movie she had planned to attend with the husband's sister, who backed out at the last moment, and during an automobile ride after the husband's sister sent the husband to pick her up) and that on neither occasion did she choose to be alone with him. The wife said that she was in fear of the husband during the movie and was afraid that the husband would harm her during the automobile ride because he blamed her for getting lost, drove at high rates of speed, and raised his voice at her.

In her affidavit, the husband's sister stated that the wife did not wish to be alone with the husband when she arrived in Los Angeles, that the wife asked that the husband be put up in a hotel so that he would not be in the same home with her, that the wife was "shaken" and "upset" after the two instances she was alone with the husband, and that she (the husband's sister) made sure that the wife was not alone with the husband during the remainder of the wife's stay. In addition, the husband's sister stated that, in her view, the wife's fears for her safety if the restraining order were lifted were "not unfounded."

The motion to reconsider or vacate was marked "allowed" in the margin. No written findings were made, nor was any oral explanation given at the hearing. This appeal followed.

During the hearing the judge posed the following questions, which may provide some insight into the bases for the judge's decision: "What does [the wife] say about the California trip?" and "Did she in fact go out to dinner with him and to the movies?"....

(a) *Request to vacate c. 209A order retroactively.* ... We think that a motion that seeks to vacate retroactively an order issued under c. 209A "on the ground of newly discovered evidence cannot properly be granted unless it is found that the evidence relied on was not available to the party seeking [relief] for introduction at the original trial by the exercise of reasonable diligence, and that such evidence is material not only in the sense that it is relevant and admissible but also in the sense that it is important evidence of such a nature" that it likely would have affected the result had it been available at the time.

Here, even if we were to assume that the wife's conduct subsequent to the issuance of the order somehow constitutes newly discovered evidence (a doubtful proposition), that evidence served only as an after the fact challenge to the wife's credibility at the hearing. It is settled that "a new trial will not ordinarily be granted on the ground of newly-discovered evidence which goes only to impeach the credibility of a witness at trial." There is nothing in the record before us to support a departure from this general rule. Nor, as we shall discuss more fully, was the husband's "new evidence"—of sporadic contacts with the wife during the pendency of the c. 209A order—such that it would likely have affected the result. The order to vacate was not justified on the basis of the husband's claim of newly discovered evidence....

(b) *Request for relief from prospective application of the order.* The husband's motion construed as a request for relief from prospective application of the abuse prevention order calls for a somewhat different analysis. Such a request falls generally into that category of cases invoking the court's power to modify or prospectively to terminate an abuse prevention order ... In determining the appropriate standard applicable to such determinations, we look to cases interpreting the statute and also seek guidance from the rules of procedure and statutes and decisions in related areas of the law.

We have said that "[i]n deciding whether to modify or renew an abuse prevention order, a judge's discretion is 'broad.'" ...

Statutes governing divorce and children born out of wedlock provide that certain orders, including those pertaining to alimony and custody, may be modified upon a showing respectively, of a "substantial" or a "material and substantial" change in circumstances (and, in certain child-related matters, upon an additional finding that the modification will be in the child's best interests). . . .

Historically, a court in equity had the power to modify its decree (more often than not with regard to injunctions) in light of changed conditions or circumstances.

[The court then analyzes the standards by which courts have modified other orders, such as consent decrees.]

We draw on the foregoing principles to reach our conclusion that the standard for determining whether prospective relief from a c. 209A order is warranted must be a flexible one. The level of impact on the underlying risk from harm that a c. 209A order seeks to protect against will vary from case to case; a flexible approach that incorporates the "continuum" paradigm . . . is necessary to enable a court to deal effectively with the myriad circumstances that may arise during the pendency of an abuse prevention order. A request to modify a provision of the order that bears only tangentially on the safety of the protected party (e.g., certain orders for visitation or support) will fall at one end of the continuum, whereas a defendant's request to terminate an abuse prevention order *in its entirety* will fall at the other end. The greater the likelihood that the safety of the protected party may be put at risk by a modification, the more substantial the showing the party seeking relief must make.

Thus, for example, an order might in appropriate circumstances be changed to provide for visitation that was not initially provided for, or for adjustments to a visitation schedule necessitated by changed circumstances. In other circumstances, even a request to alter the distance that a defendant was required to stay away from the plaintiff may pose such a level of risk to the plaintiff as to warrant denial.

Here, the husband suggested that ongoing litigation involving the parties necessitated continued contact with the wife by telephone. Had he substantiated that concern in the context of a request to modify the order by permitting telephone contact, the judge would have been authorized to consider the request and to weigh it against any increased risk to the wife's safety or experience of fear that might result from a change in the order.

In deciding whether to grant or deny a party's request for relief, the basis on which the order was initially issued is not subject to review or attack. Rather, the court must consider the nature of the relief sought keeping in mind the primary purpose of a c. 209A order: to protect a party from harm or the fear of imminent serious harm.

The husband's claims amounted to a collateral attack on an abuse prevention order that, at least for the one-year period of its duration, was final. Such an abuse prevention order, entered after a hearing that satisfies due process requirements, should be set aside only in the most extraordinary circumstances and where it has been clearly and convincingly established that the order is no longer needed to protect the victim from harm or the reasonable fear of serious harm. Furthermore, if the judge determines that it is appropriate to allow a motion to vacate or terminate a c. 209A order, the decision should be supported by findings of fact. . . .

Taking as true the admissible averments of fact in the husband's verified motion, the evidence that the wife might have acquiesced in some contact with the husband (occasioned, in large part, by the unusual circumstance of the husband's mother's funeral) does not suffice to meet the husband's heavy burden of demonstrating that the order was no longer needed to protect the wife. Whether measured against a clear and convincing standard of proof, or proof by some lesser standard, the evidence was insufficient to establish that the order was no longer needed to protect the former wife from harm or reasonable fear of serious harm, and it was therefore error to terminate the order. . . .

Although our analysis indicates that a lesser burden may be imposed upon a defendant seeking to modify certain provisions of an abuse prevention order rather than to have it terminated, we do not intend to suggest that such applications to modify should be routine. While we recognize that some situations may warrant adjustments to the order due to changed circumstances, the opportunity to modify an order may not be abused. Unwarranted requests to modify may themselves be a form of abuse and create a burden on the courts as well as on the opposing party.

NOTES AND QUESTIONS

1. **When Defendants Request Orders be Vacated.** In *Mitchell*, the court suggests that modifications of orders should be treated differently than complete removals, but then notes that seeking modifications can be a form of abuse. At what point should courts sanction defendants for filing modifications? Would doing so violate the defendant's due process rights? Should defendants be required to pay attorneys' fees when they continually file unfounded motions to modify or vacate orders?

2. **When Victims Request Orders be Vacated.** In most jurisdictions, legislation specifically provides that the complainant may seek to vacate the order or have it dismissed. Some statutes require the consent of all the parties, and some require a hearing before an existing order can be dismissed. The New Jersey statute is an example of legislation that seems to permit the court to deny a complainant's motion to dismiss, since the court is required to review the full record of previous hearings before ruling. In *Stevenson v. Stevenson*, 714 A.2d 986 (N.J. Super. Ct. Ch. Div. 1998), a New Jersey court interpreted the legislation in this way; denying a plaintiff's motion to dismiss. The court concluded that a "reasonable, objective, and independent determination of the facts leads to the inescapable conclusion that a real threat of recurrence of domestic violence by the defendant upon his battered wife will exist if the Final Restraining Order is dissolved," and declined to be "an accomplice to further violence by this defendant." In practice, dismissal is generally without prejudice, but the governing legislation does not mandate this result. See also *People v.*

Townsend, 538 N.E.2d 1297 (Ill. App. Ct. 1989). New Jersey has also modified its pre–1990 stance, ruling in *Torres v. Lancellotti*, 607 A.2d 1375 (N.J. Super Ct. Ch. Div. 1992), that a court may not vacate a protection order on the basis of the parties' reunification without determining whether a true reconciliation occurred, and whether there is an ongoing need for protection. Attempted reconciliations of short duration do not amount to true reconciliations. For a discussion of whether courts should assess if victims have been coerced into vacating restraining orders, see Tamara L. Kuennen, *Analyzing the Impact of Coercion on Domestic Violence Victims: How Much is Too Much?* 22 BERKELEY J. GENDER L. & JUST. 2 (2007).

The central issue in these situations is whether the complainant is seeking to have the order vacated voluntarily, or because of pressure exerted by her partner or his family, friends or other allies. It is enormously frustrating for advocates and judges to see a woman whom they believe to be at risk for physical and emotional abuse seeking to have an order vacated. It is even more frustrating, perhaps, when there are children whose wellbeing may also be affected if the order is vacated. In this context it makes good sense to impose a process which allows for careful inquiry into the petitioner's motivation in making the request, and her appreciation of the consequences, which might include, for example, the intervention of child protective services on behalf of children who will be exposed to the defendant's abuse if the protective order is lifted. For an overview of the legal questions involved when courts refuse to lift an order at the victim's request, see Tamara L. Kuennen, *"No-Drop" Civil Protection Orders: Exploring the Bounds of Judicial Intervention in the Lives of Domestic Violence Victims*, 16 UCLA WOMEN'S L.J. 39 (2007).

Mutual Orders of Protection

Imagine these three increasingly common scenarios:

(1) Police arrive at the scene of a domestic incident, having been called by a neighbor. They find a couple, both showing signs of a recent physical altercation. The woman has swelling around one eye, and bruising on her arms; the man has scratches on his face and arms. The woman complains that the man was "beating her up" accusing her of flirting with another man; the man complains that he was yelling at her, but that she "came flying at him" and he hurt her only in trying to get her to "lay off." She alleges the reverse; that he punched her in the eye when she argued with him, and she tried to defend herself. They are both very angry, swearing at one another, using provocative language, and resisting the interventions of the police. Under recent revisions in the state's abuse prevention legislation, the police have a positive responsibility to arrest anyone whom they have probable cause to believe has perpetrated domestic violence. They arrest both parties. Before long they are standing in front of a judge, who must decide whether to release them, and, if so, under what conditions. The police report indicates that each party was violent toward, and inflicted injuries on, the other.

(2) A woman obtains an *ex parte* order on the basis of an affidavit detailing an incident in which her partner threatened her with a knife.

When she and her partner both appear at the hearing for the permanent order, he alleges that the violence in the relationship is mutual, and that he too needs the protection of an order.

(3) A man is arrested at the scene of a domestic incident, but later released without the imposition of any conditions, and without a restraining order being issued. The next day he appears in court and obtains an *ex parte* order on the basis of an affidavit which describes the same incident, but attributes the violence to his partner. At the hearing for the permanent order, his partner alleges that she has consistently been the target of his aggression, and that she is the one in need of a protective order.

What all of these scenarios have in common is that they provide a temptation to busy law enforcement personnel and judges to issue mutual restraining orders, on the grounds that since it is clearly best for the parties to stay out of one another's way, that goal can be accomplished as readily by two orders as by one, without the time and effort needed to sort out whether the relationship involves one perpetrator or two. However, the practice is highly problematic. First, it contributes to the arguments of those who allege that restraining orders are issued so casually that they should be given no probative value in other legal contexts. Victims of domestic violence can ill afford this "cheapening of the currency." Second, to the extent the orders are given weight in other contexts, they may unfairly prejudice the party against whom an order has issued as a matter of convenience rather than evidence. Third, mutual orders create the potential for confusion when police or the criminal justice system are later asked to enforce the orders or address violations, and may put victims of domestic violence at increased risk. Finally, the perpetrator who is successful in obtaining an order against his victim is reinforced in his tendency to place the blame for his violence on her, and deny his own responsibility.

A few state legislatures have explicitly addressed the issue of mutual protection orders. Some statutes prohibit the entry of a mutual order unless both parties have properly filed written petitions and service has been made on both parties. California has adopted language that permits mutual orders only if both parties personally appear and each party presents evidence of actionable domestic abuse. Recognizing that mutual orders of protection often leave law enforcement uncertain about enforcement, some statutes explicitly require that if a mutual order is issued, it must be "sufficiently specific to apprise any law officer as to which party has violated the order, if the parties are in or appear to be in violation of the order." Some state statutes have also addressed the problem of the perpetrator who files first, by authorizing the court to realign the designation of the parties when the court concludes that the original petitioner is the perpetrator of domestic violence.

The federal Violence Against Women Act lends its support to those concerned about the impact of mutual orders. As described in the previous section, the Act provides in general that orders issued in one state shall be given full faith and credit in every other, so that for the first time an order issued in one state can be fully enforced in another. Where a state court has issued mutual orders, however, only the petitioner's order is accorded full faith and credit, unless the defendant has filed a separate petition or pleading seeking an order, and the court has made specific findings that the defendant, as well as the petitioner, is entitled to an order. 18 U.S.C. § 2265.

Even without the assistance of specific state or federal statutory provisions, judges at the state level can resist the demand for mutual orders by simply insisting that every protective order meet the substantive and procedural requirements laid out in the governing statute. For example, in *Deacon v. Landers*, 587 N.E.2d 395 (Ohio App. 1990), the court found that it must allow for the presentation of evidence when one party contests the issuance of an order. At a hearing on issuing a final protective order, the defendant, who was unrepresented, requested that he receive a protection order as well. In ascertaining whether such an order was necessary, consider the relevant portion of the transcript: Mr. Landers was the defendant in the case, and Ms. Kowieski the attorney for the petitioner.

"MR. LANDERS: I would also like for the same protection for me, that she stay away from me. Even after I've been served this petition, she's still gone and found out where I'm at and we've had lunch together and things like that. * * * I'd also like for the same protection.

"THE COURT: I'm going to have to go back to the statute. I'm not sure that this statute permits that kind of, that kind of order, although I think under the same section of the statute which grants the Court authority to grant other equitable relief, the Court would have the authority to provide for restraint against Ms. Deacon from any harassment or molestation. I don't say this, Ms. Deacon, by way of pointing a finger or agreeing with Mr. Landers, but so long as you both understand that you're just not to have any contact. Your—

"MS. KOWIESKI: Your Honor, I would object at this time to granting Mr. Landers some kind of restraining order without so much as an affidavit on his part indicating the evidence—

"THE COURT: What's the problem? You certainly don't want your client associating with him, and he doesn't want her associating with him, and I think that the bare statement is sufficient to grant restraint. I don't think it's going to be necessary, but I don't see any reason why it hurts anything. Nobody's mad at your client, Ms. Kowieski. We're just trying to be fair about this and saying that neither party should have anything to do with the other. It's a very simple matter.

"MS. KOWIESKI: No, I agree with that, Your Honor. I believe that is, would be accomplished by the—

"THE COURT: It will be accomplished by restraining your client from any contact with Mr. Landers and that will also be in the order * * *."

The court ruled, "It is manifestly clear from this exchange that appellant was denied an opportunity to cross-examine appellee and to present rebuttal evidence. Accordingly, we hold that appellant was neither given a 'full hearing' . . . nor afforded an opportunity to be heard or defend herself consistent with due process of law."

NOTES AND QUESTIONS

1. **Full Hearings v. Opportunity to be Heard.** In *Deacon v. Landers*, the court never requires that there be a full hearing, only that the court base its decision on sufficient evidence in order to meet the full requirements of due process. Do you think the kind of back-and-forth questioning between the judge, the attorney, and the defendant was sufficient? What sort of hearing should courts hold in these cases?

2. **Good Faith Claims.** If it were the case that defendant's request was made in good faith, a proposition that was in no way tested by the trial judge, can you think of a way of responding to it without issuing a restraining order against the petitioner? Is it appropriate for judges to "warn" victims not to have any contact with the defendant, for example?

What legal remedies do victims and their lawyers have when defendants continue to file bad faith motions? Attorneys' fees? Motions for other legal outcomes. For a discussion of these and other strategies see Rana Fuller, *How to Effectively Advocate for Battered Women When Systems Fail*, 33 WM. MITCHELL L. REV. 939 (2007).

C. ENFORCEMENT

Enforcement is the Achilles heel of the civil protection process, because an order without enforcement at best offers scant protection, and at worst increases the victim's danger by creating a false sense of security. Offenders may routinely violate orders, if they believe there is no real risk of being arrested. For enforcement to work, the courts need to monitor compliance, victims must report violations, and, most of all, police, prosecutors, and judges should respond sternly to violations that are reported. Peter Finn and Sarah Colson, CIVIL PROTECTION ORDERS: LEGISLATION, CURRENT COURT PRACTICE, AND ENFORCEMENT (National Institute of Justice, 1990).

Any departure by the defendant from the terms of the restraining order is a violation, regardless of whether it involves actual violence, and regardless of whether the conduct would be criminal in its own right. Thus, a single telephone call may violate a no-contact provision, and the defendant's presence within 100 feet of the petitioner's place of work may violate the "safety zone" created by the order. If the order establishes the defendant's visitation schedule, and he returns the children an hour later than the order dictates, that too is a violation. Although this seems obvious enough, police are often reluctant to enforce the order, and particularly reluctant to exercise their arrest powers, unless the defendant's conduct is independently criminal—even when the governing legislation makes violation a criminal misdemeanor, or authorizes enforcement through criminal contempt proceedings.

Once a victim applies for and receives a restraining order against her abuser, most states, either by statute or case law, do not allow the victim to waive, nullify, or modify the order herself. Rather, only the court can order any legal changes. Thus, even if the victim voluntarily contacts the abuser and the two reconcile, he can still be found liable for violating the order. See, e.g. *Cole v. Cole*, 556 N.Y.S.2d 217 (N.Y. Fam. Ct. 1990). This policy is intended to protect the victim even during periods in which she may have some reason for contacting the abuser or attempts to reunite, and to make clear that it is the defendant's responsibility to obey the order, and that the state, not the victim, is in control. Furthermore, it removes the defense of invitation, or perceived invitation, when an order is violated.

But what happens when a victim calls the defendant to fix the furnace, invites him to their child's play, or decides to give the relationship one more try without asking the court to modify the order? Traditionally, the victim was not subject to any legal reprimand for doing so. However, in recent years, some prosecutors have tried to charge victims with complicity to violate the order, or some other charge such as aiding and abetting a violation. A few courts have grown frustrated when victims have initiated contact with their abusers when a restraining order is in effect, and, in some cases, have charged fines, or even jailed them. See Emily J. Sack, *Battered Women and the State: The Struggle for Domestic Violence Policy*, 2004 WIS.L.REV. 1657. Should a victim be liable for allowing or encouraging a defendant to violate an order? Consider the following case:

State v. Lucas

Supreme Court of Ohio, 2003.
795 N.E.2d 642.

Factual and Procedural Background

On May 23, 2001, defendant-appellant, Betty S. Lucas, was charged with one count of domestic violence and one count of complicity to violate a protection order. She had been granted a protection order against Joseph Lucas, her ex-husband, on October 4, 2000. The charges against appellant arose from an incident at her home on May 10, 2001. On that day, appellant had invited her ex-husband into her home for the birthday celebration of one of their children. Appellant and Joseph Lucas consumed alcohol together there, and later had an argument that led to a physical altercation. Joseph Lucas sustained a fractured and dislocated elbow and head injuries and was treated at a hospital. Appellant suffered a bruised nose. Police charged Joseph Lucas with a violation of the protection order. Appellant was charged with complicity to violate a protection order, as well as with domestic violence.

[Betty Lucas plead guilty to the domestic violence charge and no contest to the complicity charge. The trial court found her guilty of both offenses and sentenced her to 90 days in jail on each charge, but suspended the time and placed her on probation for two years.]

Appellant appealed from the conviction on the complicity charge. Appellant argued that a person sheltered by a protection order is the victim of any violation of that order and that as a victim, she is a member of a protected class. Therefore, she maintained, prosecuting the victim runs counter to the intent of the General Assembly. The court of appeals rejected appellant's arguments and affirmed the trial court. The appellate court eschewed public-policy analysis and found that appellant's behavior went beyond what ... the complicity statute requires to show that someone aided or abetted another in the commission of a crime....

Law and Analysis

The United States Supreme Court was faced with an analogous question in construing the Mann Act in *Gebardi v. United States* (1932), 287 U.S. 112, 53 S.Ct. 35, 77 L.Ed. 206. Under the Mann Act, it was a felony for any person to "transport or cause to be transported, or aid or assist in obtaining transportation for, or in transporting, in interstate or foreign commerce, ... any woman or girl for the purpose of prostitution or debauchery ..." In *Gebardi*, the court addressed the issue of whether a female willingly transported across state lines could be convicted of conspiracy to violate the Mann Act.

The court recognized that "the statute is drawn to include those cases in which the woman consents to her own transportation" and first looked at whether the Mann Act itself punished acquiescing women. The court found that punishment of transported women was not a focus of the statute

. . .

The *Gebardi* decision has some roots in the English common law. In *The Queen v. Tyrell* (1893), 1 Q.B. 710, the court held that an underage female cannot aid and abet a male in having "unlawful carnal knowledge" of her. The court noted that by legislative design, females were omitted from the operation of the statute and potential criminal liability....

A more recent case, the court in *In re Meagan R.* (1996), 42 Cal. App.4th 17, 49 Cal.Rptr.2d 325, considered the issue of whether a victim of statutory rape can be charged with aiding and abetting that crime. The court held that "where the Legislature has dealt with crimes which necessarily involve the joint action of two or more persons, and where no punishment at all is provided for the conduct, or misconduct, of one of the participants, the party whose participation is not denounced by statute cannot be charged with criminal conduct on either a conspiracy or aiding and abetting theory."

Although we are dealing with a different statute in this case and a charge of aiding and abetting rather than conspiracy, *Gebardi* is especially instructive. As was the case with the Mann Act, Ohio's protection-order statutes fail to criminalize a protected party's activities in inviting or acquiescing in a violation of the statutes.

In the language of R.C. 3113.31, the General Assembly evinces its recognition that in some instances of violations of protection orders, the protected party invites the violation. R.C. 3113.31(E)(7)(a) provides:

> "If a protection order issued * * * under this section includes a requirement that the respondent ... refrain from entering the residence, school, business, or place of employment of the petitioner or a family or household member, the order or agreement shall state clearly

that *the order or agreement cannot be waived or nullified by an invitation to the respondent from the petitioner* or other family or household member to enter the residence, school, business, or place of employment or by the respondent's entry into one of those places otherwise upon the consent of the petitioner or other family or household member." (Emphasis added.)

The General Assembly both recognizes and addresses the potential problem of a protected party's acquiescence in the violation of a protection order. The General Assembly demonstrates its cognizance of the volatile and mercurial nature of certain interpersonal relationships and insulates protection orders from the heat and chill of shifting emotions. It removes the excuse of an invitation, a perceived invitation, or a concocted invitation from affecting the power of a protection order. The General Assembly has made the issue of an invitation entirely irrelevant as to the culpability of a respondent's violation of a protection order.

Thus, like the *Gebardi* court, we must construe a statute that recognizes that a protected party can participate in the violation of the very statute that affords protection but provides no punishment for the protected party's activity . . .

The practical application of Ohio's protection-order statutes demands this result. If petitioners for protection orders were liable for criminal prosecution, a violator of a protection order could create a real chill on the reporting of the violation by simply threatening to claim that an illegal visit was the result of an illegal invitation.

Finally, this case is different from most. Had Betty Lucas not gotten the better of her husband, this case would probably not be here. In most instances of an invited violation of a protection order, police are not called until the violence starts. In those cases, the protected party receives the brunt of the injuries. If we were to find against appellant in this case, we would also be finding against those other protected parties. We would be, in effect, allowing abused women to be charged with complicity. That is a prospect neither intended by the General Assembly nor acceptable as a matter of public policy.

The General Assembly has made an invitation by the petitioner for the respondent to violate the terms of a protection order irrelevant to a respondent's guilt. Protection orders are about the behavior of the respondent and nothing else. How or why a respondent finds himself at the petitioner's doorstep is irrelevant. To find appellant guilty of complicity would be to criminalize an irrelevancy.

NOTES AND QUESTIONS

1. **Betty's Sentence.** The trial court sentenced Betty Lucas to two years probation and a ninety-day suspended sentence for aiding and abetting the violation of the restraining order, while her husband received only a $100 fine. See Adam Liptak, *Ohio Case Considers Whether Abuse Victim Can Violate Own Restraining Order*, N.Y. Times, May 30, 2003 at A18.

2. **The Victim's Responsibilities.** The court in *State v. Lucas* analogizes victims of domestic violence to minors who have sex in violation of statutory rape laws. Are these appropriate analogies? With statutory rape laws, we assume that those protected are too young to consent to sex. Adult victims of domestic violence arguably have some degree of autonomy. Is it fair to only hold abusers accountable if the victim willingly accepts him back? What responsibilities should victims have in following through with restraining orders they have requested? How realistic is it that the victim will return to court to have a restraining order removed before she has contact with the defendant again?

3. **Motivations Behind the Victim's Actions.** The court writes that: "The General Assembly demonstrates its cognizance of the volatile and mercurial nature of certain interpersonal relationships and insulates protection orders from the heat and chill of shifting emotions." Does this seem correct to you after what you have learned about the dynamics of abusive relationships? Are people always acting on "shifting emotions" when they decide to invite their child's father to a birthday party? What other possible reasons might Betty Lucas have had for inviting over her ex-husband?

4. **Dynamics in an Abusive Relationship.** In this case, Joseph Lucas was injured far more severely than was Betty Lucas. Furthermore, the two had been drinking before the violence occurred. What do the facts of this case suggest about the dynamics of abuse? What do you think is an appropriate legal response given the situation? Do you think restraining orders are effective? Would holding Betty Lucas accountable for complicity in violating the order make them more effective? Was this a case of an overzealous prosecutor taking mandatory enforcement policies too far, or a reasonable response to the problems encountered when victims act inconsistently?

5. **Violating the Order as a Victim.** Several states, including Maine and Minnesota, confirm by statute what has become the working understanding in many jurisdictions, that a petitioner cannot be found in violation of her own order, even if she invites the defendant to ignore its terms. MINN. STAT. ANN. § 5158B.01(14)(g) (West 1993).

But assume this case had come out differently and the court held that Betty Lucas could be charged with complicity in aiding and abetting her husband to violate the order. As an attorney representing victims of domestic violence, what advice would you give a client seeking to obtain a restraining order against her abuser? Should she carefully document all contact? Should she refrain from inviting him to her child's graduation?

Monitoring Compliance

In general, if a civil court order is to be enforced, the person who originally applied for the order must return to court to complain of a violation. In most jurisdictions, this is also true for orders of protection. However, in the domestic violence context there are good reasons to encourage other actors to play a role in monitoring compliance. First, many victims negotiate the restraining order process *pro se*, and may emerge with an order in hand, but with no clear understanding of how to enforce it, beyond calling the police to respond to a violation. Second, many victims suffer violations which they are afraid to report, without encouragement and support from those who can work with them to ensure their safety as they challenge the defendant's continuing violence. Third, many defendants are skilled in manipulating the system, and will engage in behaviors that appear to evade the direct prohibitions of the order, so that victims may need assistance in framing defendants' conduct as violative of the order. Finally, if society has a stake in making the protective order system credible in order to maximize its deterrent effect, and if it is clear that orders will routinely go un-enforced if their enforcement depends on victim initiative, then others need to get involved.

In their 1990 report for the National Institute of Justice, Peter Finn and Sarah Colson suggest that courts take responsibility for monitoring compliance with orders of protection, delegating that task to other appropriate agencies. The example they provide is Duluth, Minnesota:

> [J]udges in Duluth have an arrangement with the Domestic Abuse Intervention Project, which provides a counseling and education program for batterers, to monitor the behavior of respondents who are ordered into the program by the court. Monitoring occurs in three ways. Project staff review police records each day and inform the court if an incident involving a protection order violation has occurred. Project staff also contact each victim once a month to learn of any renewed violence. Finally, if an offender fails to attend counseling sessions or reports new abuses or violations, project staff request a court hearing. If the offender is found in contempt of court, he is usually sentenced to jail, but (for a first violation), given the option of completing the program while serving a probated sentence.
>
> Judges also inform victims that they should contact the Intervention Project if the defendant violates the order. To assist in this aspect of monitoring, the Duluth Women's Coalition maintains contact with victims who have used the Coalition's services, asking them to discuss any problems or violations of the order. When violations are reported during Coalition education group meetings for victims, advocates talk to victims about reporting the violation and provide support and information to do so. Peter Finn and Sarah Colson, CIVIL PROTECTION ORDERS: LEGISLATION, CURRENT COURT PRACTICE, AND ENFORCEMENT (National Institute of Justice, 1990).

If the defendant is also on probation, whether for abuse-related or other crimes, the probation-department may be another source of information, particularly if probation officers are working collaboratively with batterers' intervention programs, and if the probation department has a victim-contact policy in place.

Is there a tension here between monitoring by outside parties and victim autonomy? If external monitoring appears to be necessary to prevent under-enforcement, how do actors within the system deal with the situation where enforcement goes against the wishes of the petitioner? Should they override her desires on the theory that the order is between the defendant and the court? Or should external monitoring be used only to ensure that enforcement is accomplished in any case where it is helpful to, and desired by, the victim? These issues will be treated in much greater depth in the next chapter, in the context of criminal prosecution.

Alternative Mechanisms of Enforcement

Traditionally, civil court orders are enforced through contempt proceedings. Criminal contempt proceedings seek to punish the defendant for flouting the authority of the court, while civil contempt proceedings seek to secure future compliance. In line with this tradition, many states offer civil and/or criminal contempt mechanisms for the enforcement of protective orders. However, the primary means of enforcing a protective order today is to charge the defendant with a criminal misdemeanor. In many jurisdictions police are mandated, or authorized, to arrest the defendant whom they find at the scene of a violation, or whom they have probable cause to believe has violated an order, whether the arrest is for a criminal offense or for criminal contempt. If the defendant's behavior would be criminal in and of itself, regardless of whether it violated an order of protection, then a final option is to charge the defendant with that underlying crime.

As Catherine Klein and Leslye Orloff report, "[t]he statutory trend in recent years is to augment contempt enforcement with misdemeanor charges, and to heighten the criminal classification for a violation of a protection order." Catherine F. Klein and Leslye E. Orloff, *Providing Legal Protection for Battered Women: An Analysis of State Statutes and Case Law*, 21 HOFSTRA L. REV. 801 (1993). This trend reflects the conviction that only by classifying a protective order violation as a crime can society demonstrate its commitment to the protective order process, ensure adequate police response to violations, and impose sufficient sanctions. However, as the next section suggests, the reality of how violations are processed through the criminal justice system threatens to undercut both the message conveyed by criminalization, and its practical advantages. If most violations do not produce arrests, most arrests do not result in prosecutions, and most prosecutions result in minimal sanctions, rarely including incarceration, defendants have little reason to fear the consequences of continuing to abuse their partners. If defendants are routinely released pending trial, and trials are delayed, women remain at risk during a time of particular vulnerability, and the immediacy of the connection between the defendant's conduct and his being called to account for it is lost.

Clearly, much remains to be done to ensure that the criminalization strategy lives up to its potential. But the difficulty of changing entrenched practices and attitudes, and the need to respect the rights of defendants, which increase with the severity of the charge brought and penalty sought, suggest that other enforcement strategies should not be abandoned. In particular, the criminal contempt process may have more to recommend it than generally understood. The major disadvantages of criminal contempt as an enforcement strategy have been thought to be two. First, the maximum sentence for criminal contempt, a petty offense, is usually no more than six months. Second, police have often not been willing, even if authorized, to arrest for criminal contempt.

Since the vast majority of defendants convicted of the misdemeanor of violating a protective order do not serve as much as six months of jail time, the first concern evaporates in light of the reality of enforcement practice. In addition, separate acts of contempt can be consolidated for hearing, and elicit separate penalties which can be aggregated without triggering a higher level of due process for the defendant or the requirement for a jury trial. The second concern can be met by expressly incorporating the arrest power into legislation establishing criminal contempt as an appropriate remedy for a protective order violation, and then ensuring that police are trained to exercise that power when responding to violations. Alternatively, police training could address the extent of the arrest power authorized for criminal contempt by general legislation, and establish protocols for its use in enforcing restraining order violations.

The major advantages of criminal contempt proceedings are the speed with which they can be initiated and concluded, the simplicity of a bench rather than a jury trial, and the possibility in many jurisdictions for victims to initiate their own contempt proceedings, if the state is slow or reluctant to prosecute. For this possibility of private action to offer real advantages, of course, victims must be able to find competent and affordable representation. Although defendants in criminal contempt proceedings enjoy all the same due process rights as criminal defendants, neither the absence of a jury trial, nor pretrial detention violates those rights. On the legitimacy of pretrial detention see, for example, *Commonwealth v. Allen*, 486 A.2d 363 (Pa. 1984), cert. denied, 474 U.S. 842 (1985).

One commentator has made the interesting argument that criminal contempt proceedings can also be preferable to criminal prosecution for a violation because they bring the defendant back, promptly, before the very same court, and possibly even the same judge who issued the order the defendant violated:

> Granting a speedy hearing is essential because batterers are more likely to respond to a fast contempt mechanism than a slower criminal prosecution, because deterrence is generally more potent when a quick punishment follows an infraction. From a batterer's unique psychological perspective, however, contempt also offers distinct advantages. Batterers are manipulative individuals who think they can talk their way out of trouble or evade the constraints that society imposes on individual behavior. Also, because they tend to conceive relationships in terms of power, they tend to respond only to a specific threat from an identifiable person whom they perceive as more powerful. A directive from a family court judge that he or she will lock up the batterer for contempt, which is then followed by a contempt hearing before the same judge, is therefore more effective than the general threat of criminal prosecution—especially since many batterers do not regard their behavior as criminal. David M. Zlotnick, *Empowering the Battered Woman: The Use of Criminal Contempt Sanctions to Enforce Civil Protection Orders*, 56 OHIO ST. L. J. 1153 (1995).

Zlotnick also argues that it may be easier for police and judges to "get behind" contempt proceedings, where the focus is on the defendant's flouting the authority of the court, rather than on his behavior towards his victim: "Judges simply do not like being disobeyed, particularly when they have issued a direct order to someone, and studies suggest that judicial behavior can have profound effects on the outcome of domestic violence cases." Id. at 1204–05.

The potential inherent in the creative use of criminal contempt proceedings does not mean that contempt should be the sole enforcement mechanism. Holding a defendant in contempt is perfectly compatible with also prosecuting him for the crime of violating the order of protection, or for the underlying crimes involved in that violation. In cases in which a restraining order violation involves serious violence, it may be that a contempt proceeding would secure the victim's safety by imposing immediate pre-trial detention and a jail sentence of short duration, while the state prepared to prosecute the criminal charges—which might well be felonies rather than misdemeanors. The extent to which these combined strategies raise issues of double jeopardy is the topic of the next section.

Police Enforcement of Restraining Orders

When an abuser violates a restraining order, victims often call the police and ask that the order be enforced. In many jurisdictions, the police are mandated to arrest the abuser if there is probable cause to believe that he has violated the order in some way. See, e.g. N.J. Stat. Ann. § 2C:25–31 (West 1995) ("*Where a law enforcement officer finds that there is probable cause that a defendant has committed contempt of an order ... the defendant shall be arrested and taken into custody by a law enforcement officer.*") (*emphasis added*). Cal. Penal Code § 13701 (West 1996) ("These policies shall require the arrest of an offender, absent exigent circumstances, if there is probable cause that a protective order ... has been violated.") These provisions mirror mandatory or preferred arrest provisions in the criminal enforcement of domestic violence crimes discussed in Chapter Seven. Such provisions arguably check police discretion in enforcing these orders and provide victims with greater assurance that their orders are enforced.

But what happens when the police ignore or refuse the victim's request to have the order enforced? In 2005, in *Castle Rock v. Gonzales*, 545 U.S. 748 (2005) the United States Supreme Court ruled that a person who has obtained a restraining order has no protected property in having the police enforce the order, and thus cannot sue the police under the theory that their constitutional *procedural* Due Process rights were violated. *Castle Rock* follows a 1989 case, *DeShaney v. Winnebago County Dept. of Social Servs.*, 489 U.S. 189 (1989), in which the Court held that there was no *substantive* component of the Due Process Clause of the 14th Amendment that requires the state to protect people from harms caused by private actors. Together, these two cases effectively foreclose any Federal constitutional remedy for victims whose orders are not enforced.

NOTES AND QUESTIONS

1. **The Value of a Restraining Order.** In *Castle Rock,* the Court of Appeals concluded that unless the police had a constitutional duty to

enforce these orders, it "would render domestic abuse restraining orders utterly valueless." Was the Circuit Court correct that unless victims are entitled to enforcement, restraining orders are effectively valueless? Advocates often warn victims that restraining orders are "just a piece of paper" and encourage them to have alternative safety plans. What should the police have done in this case? Issue a warrant for Mr. Gonzales's arrest? Would having done so have saved the lives of the daughters? Would holding the police liable under a due process theory make any difference?

2. **State Law Remedies.** As Justice Scalia notes in *Castle Rock*, nothing in the decision forecloses states with providing victims with personally enforceable remedies under the state law tort system. Thus, after *Castle Rock*, the only remedy for domestic violence victims who "have suffered harm as a result of police failure to enforce an existing order will lie in state negligence law." In Chapter Fourteen, we explore in more detail third party liability, including police liability, for domestic violence.

3. **Double Jeopardy.** There are several ways in which double jeopardy issues can arise when legal proceedings are initiated in the context of domestic violence. One occurs when a complainant seeks a protective order on the basis of an abusive incident for which the state is also seeking to prosecute the perpetrator. Another occurs when a defendant violates a protective order and faces contempt proceedings, but is also subject to prosecution by the state for the underlying crimes that constituted the violation. A third situation, in which the defendant is prosecuted both for the crime of violating the order and the underlying crimes that constituted the violation is less likely to trigger a double jeopardy challenge, because the prosecutions are likely to be brought together.

In 1993, the United States Supreme Court issued its first decision ever in a domestic violence case, and the issue raised was double jeopardy. In *U.S. v. Dixon*, 509 U.S. 688 (1993), the Court ruled that double jeopardy would not bar a battered woman from enforcing her civil protection order through criminal contempt while the state proceeds against her batterer criminally for his crime, as long as the contempt proceeding and the criminal prosecution each require proof of additional elements. This ruling assures that battered women with civil protection orders will no longer be forced to choose between criminal prosecution and proceeding to enforce civil protection orders through criminal contempt when civil protection order respondents commit new crimes against petitioners. See Catherine F. Klein and Leslye J. Orloff, *Providing Legal Protection for Battered Women: An Analysis of State Statutes and Case Law*, 21 Hofstra L. Rev. 801 (1993). Klein and Orloff offer this further analysis:

> In those few remaining criminal assault cases where double jeopardy *may* pose a bar to the subsequent criminal action if the contempt motion goes forward before the criminal action, the court and petitioner's counsel should first determine whether the contempt action can be decided in such a fashion so as to avoid double jeopardy issues. For example, after hearing the evidence in the case, instead of finding that the respondent assaulted his wife, the trial judge could have found in *Dixon* that respondent approached petitioner in violation of the stay

away provisions of the civil protection order, grabbed her, and threw her against a parked car. . . .

[T]here is a continuing need for cooperation and coordination between domestic violence victims bringing contempt motions and state prosecutors. Coordination will prevent poorly worded contempt findings from unwittingly precluding criminal prosecutions in some cases, as occurred on one count in *Dixon*.

Does it seem at all troubling that the constitutional protections of the Double Jeopardy Clause can, in this view, be neutralized by choosing words to describe what the defendant has done to violate the protective order that avoid labeling his conduct as a criminal offense? Whose interests are at stake when deciding these double jeopardy claims?

4. **The Right to a Jury Trial?** Should defendants have the right to a jury trial in either the issuance of a protective order or in criminal contempt proceedings? Consider the following criticism of New Jersey's system:

> Similarly, from the perspective of going to bed worrying about whether he did "the right thing," a judge has much to lose and little to gain from ruling in favor of the defendant. Only a jury, composed of one-time actors in the justice system, immune from political pressures, can protect a defendant from judicial concerns over job security. And only by amending the Prevention of Domestic Violence Act to spread the responsibility for guessing whether something bad will happen if the TRO is lifted amongst the members of a jury deliberating as a group could the New Jersey Legislature ever hope to provide a defendant with an objective factfinder as opposed to one tending to "err on the side of caution." . . . Question: Where, in TRO hearings, is there a check against the court's exercise of arbitrary power? Answer: There is none. See David N. Heleniak, *The New Star Chamber: The New Jersey Family Court and the Prevention of Domestic Violence Act*, 57 RUTGERS L. REV. 1009 (2005).

Do you agree that the system fails to provide for checks and balances? Are judges more likely to find that an order needs to be issued, or that the defendant violated the order than a jury? Is expediency a good reason to dispose of jury trials?

5. **Sanctions.** What are the appropriate sanctions when a restraining order is violated? Jail time? Counseling? Fines? Paying the victim restitution? Judges often have many options in sentencing violators. In 1990, Peter Finn and Sarah Colson reviewed the sanctions judges imposed when a restraining order was violated. They found that in many cases, judges did in fact order jail for first-time offenders. Peter Finn and Sarah Colson, *Civil Protection Orders: Legislation, Current Court Practice, and Enforcement*, (National Institute of Justice, 1990). Most state statutes limit the amount of prison time that can imposed, anywhere from six months to three years in most jurisdictions. Some states impose graduated sanctions for multiple violates of orders. In Ohio, for example, the third conviction for violating a restraining order is a felony. Judges can also order violators to attend

mandatory counseling programs and be subject to other probationary measures. Finn and Colson also found:

> Several judges reported on the need to consider the victim's safety between the time of the violation and the offender's appearance in court for a violation hearing. As a result, batterers arrested in Portland, Oregon, are not granted release on their own recognizance. . . . This position is reflected in the Pennsylvania statute: bail is usually set at $5,000. In Denver, domestic violence has been taken off the bond schedule so that suspects must stay in jail from a few hours to three days until the next court business day. In Duluth, violators are usually held overnight, allowing time for shelter advocates to contact the victim and help her obtain any assistance she needs before the batterer is released. Minnesota's statute allows jailers to hold an assailant arrested under the probable cause arrest statute for thirty-six hours if the jailer believes the assailant is likely to be a danger to the victim. Id.

Under the Violence Against Women Act, restitution, including the payment of medical expenses, physical therapy, transportation, housing, child care expenses, lost income, attorneys' fees, and other losses, is mandatory. 18 U.S.C. § 2264(b)(3). The court cannot waive restitution because of the perpetrator's economic circumstances, or because the victim can claim insurance benefits for her injuries. The defendant's economic means can be taken into consideration only in setting a payment schedule. 18 U.S.C. § 2264(b)(4). The restitution order must be enforced "by all available and reasonable means" by the U.S. Attorney, but can also be enforced civilly, by the victim. 18 U.S.C. § 2264(b)(1)(B), (b)(2). Many states also require restitution to the victim.

6. **Punishing Possession of a Firearm by an Abuser.** In addition to making interstate violation of a protection order a federal offense, VAWA criminalizes the possession of a firearm by anyone who is subject to a protective order. The maximum penalty for violating this provision is ten years in prison, a $250,000 fine, or both. 18 U.S.C. § 924(a)(2).

Predictably, this provision has triggered reactions ranging from consternation to outrage among law enforcement and private security personnel whose livelihoods depend on their capacity to carry a firearm. This is one context in which the gravity of a finding that the defendant has perpetrated or is credibly threatening to perpetrate domestic violence becomes inescapably clear. Despite the fact that the federal provisions are written to guarantee the perpetrator notice of the protective order hearing and an opportunity to defend against the charges, and to limit the requirement that the perpetrator relinquish any firearm in his possession to cases in which the physical safety of a partner or child is demonstrably at risk, they have provoked widespread criticism. Protesters challenge the integrity of the restraining order process, and assert, albeit without supporting data, that restraining orders are issued on evidence insufficient to warrant potential loss of employment by defendants. Despite the many constitutional challenges to the provision, it has survived scrutiny in all but a very few cases, and has been uniformly upheld by those circuit courts of appeal asked to review it.

Anecdotal reports from domestic violence advocates around the country suggest that in some cases judges are choosing not to issue restraining orders solely to avoid putting defendants' jobs on the line, despite the obvious risks created by leaving domestic violence victims unprotected. In some situations the victims themselves are also choosing not to apply for restraining orders where they know the likely consequence for their partners, and are either afraid of retaliation, or are economically dependent on their partners and afraid that loss of employment by their partners will create a greater risk to the wellbeing of their children or themselves than the risk of future violence. Domestic violence advocates who lobbied for these provisions are now being forced to reassess whether their net impact has been positive. This issue is examined in further detail in Chapter Seven.

D.   EFFICACY

There is no single answer to the apparently simple question, "Do restraining orders work?" One obvious measure is recidivism—does the defendant subject to a restraining order commit further abuse? But even here we have to ask what level of recidivism is small enough for us to decide that the protective order mechanism is a useful one—if forty percent of women who obtain restraining orders live free of violence for the duration of those orders, is that success, or failure? How does it compare with the experience of women who do not obtain protective orders in the aftermath of a violent incident?

A different measure of the efficacy of restraining orders is consumer satisfaction. Do women who obtain orders feel that they have gained by doing so? Here, while freedom from violence at the hands of a partner or former partner may be the ultimate goal, women may be more realistic than many social scientists about that probability, at least in the short term, and more ready to settle for less exacting definitions of success. In the Harrell and Smith study, for example:

> Many women thought the temporary restraining order was helpful in documenting that the abuse occurred: 86% said it was "very" helpful in this regard; 79% said it was "very" or "somewhat" helpful in sending her partner a message that his actions were wrong; and 62% said the order was "very" or "somewhat" helpful in punishing her partner for abusing her. . . . Also, 88% credited the judge with "doing the right thing" for her and her children. . . . Combined, these findings strongly suggest that the women saw the restraining order as worthwhile in significant ways. Adele Harrell and Barbara E. Smith, *Effects of Restraining Orders on Domestic Violence Victims,* DO ARRESTS AND RESTRAINING ORDERS WORK? 214 (E.S. Buzawa and C.G. Buzawa, eds. 1996). Incredibly, women had these positive reactions even though fewer than half thought the man believed that he had to obey the order.

Yet another measure of the efficacy of restraining orders is whether they are in fact enforced as the governing legislation suggests they can and should be. A high rate of violations, combined with the paucity of follow-up by the criminal justice system, is what led Andrew Klein to conclude that restraining orders "don't work." Andrew R. Klein, *Re–Abuse in a Population of Court–Restrained Male Batterers: Why Restraining Orders Don't Work,* Do ARRESTS AND RESTRAINING ORDERS WORK? 192 (E.S. Buzawa and C.G. Buzawa, eds. 1996). On the other hand, it seems to be the case that simply issuing a restraining order has some deterrent effect on some abusers. Thus, even though we might, with Klein, urge that enforcement be given a higher priority, we might not want to make a blanket judgment that the efficacy of an order depends, in all cases, on its enforcement.

Even if a restraining order works in stopping the violence against one victim, abusers may simply move on to another relationship. For example, in Massachusetts, the Office of the Commissioner of Probation reported that from 1992 to 1998, 23.3% of offenders had two different restraining orders issued against them by different victims, with some having as many as eight different victims. See Ann Charon Harrington, *Commonwealth v. Finase: The Scope of the Massachusetts Abuse Prevention Order Prosecution and Efficacy,* 29 N.E. J. ON CRIM. & CIV. CONFINEMENT 193 (2003). Thus, it may be that restraining orders do little to reduce violence overall, but may simply be the impetus for an abuser to replace one victim with another.

The following excerpt briefly describes the current research on the efficacy of restraining orders. While earlier studies raised doubts as to whether those who sought restraining orders were safer, current research suggests that restraining orders do correlate to substantially decreased risks of future violence.

Beverly Balos

Domestic Violence Matters: The Case for Appointed Counsel in Protective Order Proceedings

15 TEMP. POL. & CIV. RTS. L. REV. 557 (2006).

When women seek a protection order it is often after serious violence. Research also suggests that an order is not sought after the first incident of violence but rather is sought after repeated violence. In requesting this intervention from the court, victims of domestic violence seek to have the state vindicate their right to bodily integrity. This request is not undertaken lightly given the threats and retaliatory violence experienced by many who seek the state's help. The serious level of violence and the duration of the abuse experienced by victims before seeking a protective order confirm the danger and potential lethality of the violence in the lives of victims who decide to seek protective orders.

Protective orders have proven to be effective in reducing violence against women. Studies have shown that women report "lower levels of intimate partner violence for up to two years after seeking assistance." In another study seeking to measure the effectiveness of protection orders to prevent future violence, researchers found that a permanent protection order was associated with a significant decrease in subsequent police-reported physical violence. Contact with the court system in requesting a protective order, regardless of whether the protective order is actually granted, also seems to result in decreased violence. Another study of 150 women who applied for and were qualified to obtain a protective order found significant reductions in "threats of abuse, physical abuse, stalking, and worksite harassment" during the subsequent eighteen months. These studies have limitations in terms of sample size and method of reporting later violence. They are consistent, however, in finding lower levels of subsequent violence when victims of domestic abuse seek protective orders. While admittedly "even those studies ostensibly showing success of protective orders report a 20% to 40% violation rate," it must be acknowledged that accessing protective orders is associated with reduced subsequent violence.

NOTES AND QUESTIONS

1. **Sources.** Beverly Balos finds that current research reflects that restraining orders are associated with lower levels of recidivism. Here are her sources: Julia Henderson Gist et al., *Protection Orders and Assault Charges: Do Justice Interventions Reduce Violence Against Women?*, 15 AM. J. FAM. L. 59 (2001); Victoria L. Holt, Mary A. Kernic, Thomas Lumley, Marsha E. Wolf and Frederick P. Rivara, *Civil Protection Orders and Risk of Subsequent Police–Reported Violence*, 288 J. AM. MED. ASSOC. 589 (2002); Judith McFarlane, Ann Malecha, Julia Gist, Kathy Watson, Elizabeth Batten, Iva Hall and Sheila Smith, *Protection Orders and Intimate Partner Violence: An 18–Month Study of 150 Black, Hispanic, and White Women*, 94 AM. J. PUB. HEALTH 613 (2004); Carol E. Jordan, *Intimate Partner Violence and the Justice System: An Examination of the Interface*, 19 J. INTERPERSONAL VIOLENCE 1412 (2004). See also Victoria Holt, Mary A. Kernic, Marsha E. Wolf and Frederick P. Rivara, *Do Protection Orders Affect the Likelihood of Future Partner Violence and Injury?* 24 AMER.J. OF PREVENTIVE MEDICINE 16 (2003).

2. **Effects of Restraining Orders on Psychological Abuse.** One of the most interesting findings in the two studies reported by Harrell and Smith, and by Klein, is that in many respects the level of repeat violence experienced by women who initiated the protective order process was the same regardless of whether they (a) got an *ex parte* order but did not return to court for a permanent order; (b) got a permanent order but returned to court to dismiss it before its expiration date, or (c) kept the permanent order in place until it expired. However, the Harrell and Smith study suggests that having and maintaining a permanent order did correlate with a lower incidence of psychological abuse:

> Having a permanent order did not appear to deter most types of abuse. Statistical tests showed no significant differences in the three most serious types of abuse—severe violence, other forms of physical violence, and threats or property damage—between the 212 women who had a permanent restraining order and the 143 women who did not.... The existence of a permanent order did significantly reduce

the likelihood of acts of psychological abuse. The women with permanent orders were just over half as likely to experience psychological abuse.... Adele Harrell and Barbara E. Smith, *Effects of Restraining Orders on Domestic Violence Victims,* in Do Arrest & Restraining Orders Really Work? (E.S. Buzawa and C.G. Buzawa, eds. 1996).

3.   **Increasing the Risk of Homicide?** Stories of women who are injured or killed after they take out restraining orders make it legitimate to ask whether obtaining an order is counterproductive—creating more danger than it prevents. While that is certainly true in some cases, it is not true as a generalization. While separation assault can happen, as we saw in Chapter Two, there is no empirical evidence to support the proposition that seeking a restraining order will trigger death. However, researchers have found that those seeking restraining orders often experience threats or actual retaliation for seeking an order. Most women seek restraining orders only after repeated violence. Thus, the combination of serious violence and the act of resistance remains a danger for women seeking help. Carol E. Jordan, *Intimate Partner Violence and the Justice System: An Examination of the Interface,* 19 J. Interpersonal Violence 1412 (2004).

4.   **Trying to Predict Recidivism.** Another important question is whether recidivism can be predicted, allowing victims to determine whether taking out an order is likely to protect them, and encouraging both victims and policy makers to think about supplemental or separate strategies that might work in cases where a restraining order is unlikely, by itself, to deter further violence. The studies offer some useful information.

Harrell and Smith and Klein report that the severity of the "presenting incident"—in other words, the incident that prompted the victim to seek an order—provides no basis for predicting reabuse. Harrell and Smith hypothesize that: "Possibly, the incidents reported to the court represent merely 'the straw that broke the camel's back' and occur at the point at which the women decide to seek protection, regardless of the severity of what happened." Klein found that abusers with criminal records, whether for abuse or for alcohol or drug related crimes or crimes against the person, were more likely to reabuse than those with no criminal records. Furthermore, the more extensive the criminal record, the greater the rate of reabuse.

Klein also noted that younger abusers, who were less likely to be married to their victims, were more likely to reabuse. Harrell and Smith also reported that abusers who were living with their victims at the time of the order were less likely to reabuse than abusers who had already separated from their victims, or had never lived with them. Women with children, although their overall experience of reabuse was not higher than that of women without children, were especially vulnerable to violent acts of the less severe kind (70% more likely), and to threats and property damage (50% more likely). Harrell and Smith hypothesize that "these types of abuse occurred around visitation and might be indicative of a need for supervised visitation in some cases."

5.   **Relationship Between Efficacy and Enforcement.** Klein's study was conducted in a jurisdiction nationally recognized for its programs to

stop domestic violence, and one in which violation of a restraining order is a criminal misdemeanor. Nonetheless, he criticizes the criminal justice system's response to violations of the restraining orders. Although 34% of the 663 defendants were later arrested on abuse-related charges, many if not most of which must have included charges of violating the restraining order, almost 33% of the cases were then dismissed outright, and another 10% diverted without any guilty finding. More than 25% of the defendants received probation, and only 18% (42 or 43) were incarcerated for any period of time. In the Harrell and Smith study, 290 of 355 women with restraining orders sought police response to a violation, but despite a mandatory arrest provision in the relevant state law, only 59 arrests were made (20%). Very few women then went back to court to seek a violation hearing, some because they feared the defendant's retaliation, some because they thought it would not help, some because they thought the abuse would stop without court intervention, and some because they did not realize they could return to court.

Klein, noting that the population of abusers in his study "look like criminals, act like criminals, and reabuse like criminals" in no small measure because many *are* in fact criminals with prior records, suggests that it would be naive to expect that restraining orders, standing alone, would have a significant deterrent effect. This population, he points out, is "as high risk for repeat criminal behavior as any offenders generally allowed to be released to the community on probation." If restraining orders are to be effective in containing abuse, he concludes, they must be supported by "vigorous prosecution and significant sanctioning of abusers." Subsequent studies should test the proposition that responding more aggressively to restraining order violations will keep more women safe.

6. **Faith in the System.** Whether or not restraining orders always have the desired effect, it is interesting to note that those seeking orders often have tremendous faith in them. In one study that interviewed women outside courthouses as to why they were seeking a restraining order, the authors found that ninety-two percent of the women were asking for orders because they were tired of the abuse and, for seventy-five percent seeking an order for protection was a last resort after other requests for help had failed. The women surveyed also expressed faith in the justice system to protect them, as ninety-five percent felt that the police would respond quickly to violations of the order. Thus, the court was seen as a protector of the women and their children. The researchers concluded that access to the court was also seen as a tool to reclaim "what abuse has systematically stripped from them: their control over their activities, their bodies, and their lives." Karla Fischer and Mary Rose, *When "Enough is Enough": Battered Women's Decision Making Around Court Orders of Protection*, 41 CRIME & DELINQ. 414 (1995). Given what you have read thus far, do you think some of that faith in the system is misplaced? Or do these perceptions reflect a growing sense that the legal system is responsive to domestic violence? Keep this question in mind as we turn to how the criminal justice system responds to partner abuse.

CHAPTER SEVEN

DOMESTIC VIOLENCE AND CRIMINAL JUSTICE

Introduction

Historically, the criminal justice system has been characterized by its chronic inattention to domestic violence. As we saw in Chapter One, at one time the law allowed a husband to chastise his wife. Crimes committed between spouses were private family matters that dictated against state intervention. Thus, when we ask the question "why doesn't she leave?" we have to remind ourselves that often victims had no assistance from the state in holding the abuser accountable for his actions.

In the last thirty years, however, the criminal justice system has re-examined its approach to domestic violence. Legislatures have passed a series of laws criminalizing domestic violence; police departments have implemented arrest policies, often referred to as preferred or mandatory arrest, that reversed previous policies that simply made abusers "take a walk around the block"; and prosecutors have begun to implement far more aggressive strategies to convict abusers, including prosecuting cases despite the victim's desire not to proceed. We have already examined two such cases, *Connecticut v. Borrelli*, and *People v. Santiago*, in Chapter Five. While in many jurisdictions victims still do not receive adequate protection from law enforcement, the overall trend has been towards more state intervention in domestic violence cases.

These laws and policies have been among the most controversial, both from within the battered women's advocacy community and from outside critics. First, many of these policies call into question what the role of the victim ought to be in deciding her fate as well as the fate of her abuser, who may also be the father of her children, the primary breadwinner for her family, and the person that she most loves despite the abuse. Yet, if we accept the premise that the primary dynamic in domestic violence is the abuser exercising power and control over the victim, it then follows that the victim is relatively powerless to stop the abuse on her own. These policies thus call into question how we promote the autonomy of victims while at the same time keeping them safe. Do we do so by intervening, even against her wishes, under the theory that failure to do so undermines her autonomy and condones the violence against her, or do we respect her wishes, and hence enhance her autonomy, when she wants no part of state intervention? A related problem is that minorities, immigrants and other disenfranchised victims may mistrust the criminal justice system more than they distrust their abusers. As we saw in Chapter Three, there are many dimensions to battering that are influenced by demographics, age, sexual orientation, religion, and socio-economic status, and thus not every victim will experience criminal intervention the same way.

A further related question is what the purpose of criminal intervention is. Is it to keep the victim safe? Is it to keep potential future victims safe? Is it to keep the public safe? Is it to punish the abuser? Is it to rehabilitate him in some way? In that vein, given what we know about abusers, does treatment work? Furthermore, whenever the criminal justice system is involved, we must balance the rights of defendants against the needs of the greater society. One of the tensions that we explore is how we balance those rights while also protecting victims.

We start with the basic issue of what crimes are committed when one engages in domestic violence, and whether there ought to be a specific offense of domestic violence, or whether current laws suffice. We then specifically examine stalking, one of the newer offenses to address the behavior of batterers. We then turn to arrest and prosecution policies, with a particular emphasis on the question of aggressive policies. We then look at issues of punishment, with a particular focus on batterer treatment programs. We conclude with a discussion of the federalization of domestic violence laws.

A.   It's a Crime

It seems sensible to open this chapter with a reminder that many of the abusive behaviors by which one partner exerts power and control over another do indeed fit the definition of traditional crimes under state law. The list provided to advocates-in-training by the Harvard Law School's Battered Women's Advocacy Project, based on the criminal law of Massachusetts, for example, includes:

- Assault (an attempted battery, where the perpetrator intends a harmful or unpermitted touching, takes an overt step towards accomplishing that intent, comes reasonably close to accomplishing it, and causes the intended victim reasonable fear that a battery is imminent)

- Assault and Battery (the perpetrator intentionally touches the victim, without any right to do so, and does it either without consent or in a fashion that is actually or potentially harmful)

- Assault and Battery on An Officer (the same elements as an assault and battery, but where the victim is an officer on duty, and the perpetrator knows that s/he is. This offense would apply where an officer responding to a domestic incident is attacked by the abusive partner)

- Assault or Assault and Battery with a Dangerous Weapon (the same elements as an assault or an assault and battery, but where the attempt, or the actual touching, is done with a dangerous weapon)

- Attempt to Commit a Crime (the perpetrator has a specific intent to commit a crime, engages in an overt act towards that end and comes reasonably close to committing the crime, but doesn't complete the crime)

- Breaking and Entering (the perpetrator breaks into the building, residential unit or vehicle of another, and enters it with an intent to commit a misdemeanor or a felony therein)

- Criminal Trespass (the perpetrator enters into or remains in or on the building, residential unit, vehicle or land of another, either without the right or the permission to be there, or after permission has been withdrawn by the person who has legal control over the space)

- Disorderly Conduct (frightening, threatening or violent behavior, involving actions that are reasonably likely to affect the public, and which cause public inconvenience, annoyance or alarm, or recklessly create that risk)

- Disturbing the Peace (conduct which most people would find unreasonably disruptive, which is intentional, and which did in fact annoy at least one person)

- Willful and Malicious Destruction of Property (self-explanatory)

- Harassing Phone Calls (the perpetrator makes phone calls to the victim, or causes phone calls to be made to the victim, on two or more occasions, with the sole purpose of harassing, annoying or molesting the victim)

- Violation of a Restraining Order (as discussed in Chapter Six; where a court has issued an order of protection prohibiting the defendant from engaging in certain behavior, the order is in effect on the date the defendant engages in that prohibited behavior, and the defendant had notice of the order and its terms)

- Intimidation of a Witness (a willful endeavor through gift, offer, promise, misrepresentation, intimidation, force or threats of force to impede, obstruct, delay or interfere with any witness or informant in a criminal proceeding or investigation. This would apply whether the perpetrator was intimidating his partner, or another potential witness). See, RESOURCE AND TRAINING MANUAL, Harvard Law School Battered Women's Advocacy Project (1996).

To this already lengthy list should be added at least the crimes of kidnapping, attempted homicide and homicide, rape and sexual assault, and the new crime of stalking. And as you have already seen in Chapter Four, crimes of marital rape and sexual assault may also be involved.

Partner Abuse as a Distinct Offense

In its efforts to change law enforcement attitudes and practices with respect to domestic violence, many states have amended their criminal code to target partner abuse as a specific crime, making it a felony rather than the more typical domestic violence misdemeanor. These specific laws are intended to emphasize the criminal nature of abuse, despite the fact that existing laws make no distinction between the abused and the abuser. The following case examines the constitutionality of such a statute.

State v. Wright

Supreme Court of South Carolina, 2002.
563 S.E.2d 311.

■ WALLER, JUSTICE:

Todd William Wright was convicted of criminal domestic violence of a high and aggravated nature (CDVHAN) and sentenced to 10 years imprisonment, suspended upon service of 8 years, and 5 years probation. We affirm.

FACTS

Wright, 6″ tall and weighing 216 lbs., beat and kicked his wife Wendy on the evening of February 16, 1999. Her injuries were so severe that two of her ribs were fractured and her spleen had to be removed. Wright was indicted for criminal domestic violence of a high and aggravated nature.[1] The aggravating factors alleged in the indictment were "a difference in the sexes of the victim and the defendant" and/or that "the defendant did inflict serious bodily harm upon the victim by kicking her in the mid-section requiring her to seek medical attention."

Wright objected to the judge's charge on the aggravating circumstance of "a difference of the sexes," contending it violated equal protection. The objection was overruled; Wright was found guilty as charged.

ISSUE

Does the aggravating circumstance of a "difference in the sexes" violate equal protection?

DISCUSSION

Wright contends the judge's charge on the aggravating circumstance of a "difference in the sexes" violated his right to equal protection. We disagree.

The equal protection clause prevents only irrational and unjustified classifications, not all classifications. For a gender-based classification to pass constitutional muster, it must serve an important governmental objective and be substantially related to the achievement of that objective. A law will be upheld where the gender classification realistically reflects the fact that the sexes are not similarly situated in certain circumstances. "The

---

1. The offense of CDVHAN incorporates the elements of ABHAN (assault and battery of a high and aggravated nature) S.C.Code § 16–25–65 (Supp. 2000). The elements of ABHAN are 1) the unlawful act of violent injury to another, accompanied by circumstances of aggravation. Circumstances of aggravation include the use of a deadly weapon, the intent to commit a felony, infliction of serious bodily injury, great disparity in the ages or physical conditions of the parties, a difference in gender, the purposeful infliction of shame and disgrace, taking indecent liberties or familiarities with a female, and resistance to lawful authority. . . .

relevant inquiry . . . is not whether the statute is drawn as precisely as it might have been, but whether the line chosen by the [legislature] is within constitutional limitations.''

In *Michael M., (1981),* Justice Stewart wrote:

[In] [certain narrow] circumstances, a gender classification based on clear differences between the sexes in [sic] not invidious, and a legislative classification realistically based upon those differences is not unconstitutional . . . When men and women are not in fact similarly situated in the area covered by the legislation in question, the Equal Protection Clause does not mean that the physiological differences between men and women must be disregarded. While those differences must never be permitted to become a pretext for invidious discrimination, no such discrimination is presented by this case. The Constitution surely does not require a State to pretend that demonstrable differences between men and women do not really exist.

In *State v. Gurganus* (1979), the North Carolina Supreme Court upheld a statute enhancing the punishment for males convicted of assault on a female, stating, "We base our decision instead upon the demonstrable and observable fact that the average adult male is taller, heavier and possesses greater body strength than the average female." We take judicial notice of these physiological facts, and think that the General Assembly was also entitled to take note of the differing physical sizes and strengths of the sexes. Having noted such facts, the General Assembly could reasonably conclude that assaults and batteries without deadly weapons by physically larger and stronger males are likely to cause greater physical injury and risk of death than similar assaults by females. Having so concluded, the General Assembly could choose to provide greater punishment for these offenses, which it found created greater danger to life and limb, without violating the Fourteenth Amendment. We recognize that classifications based upon average physical differences between the sexes could be invalid in certain situations involving equal employment opportunity, participation in sports and other areas. . . . We believe that an analytical approach taking into account such average differences is an entirely valid approach, however, when distinguishing classes of direct physical violence. This is particularly true where, as here, the acts of violence classified are all criminal when engaged in by any person whatsoever and have no arguably productive end. Certainly some individual females are larger, stronger and more violent than many males. The General Assembly is not, however, required by the Fourteenth Amendment to modify criminal statutes which have met the test of time in order to make specific provisions for any such individuals. The Constitution of the United States has not altered certain virtually immutable facts of nature, and the General Assembly of North Carolina is not required to undertake to alter those facts. [The North Carolina statute] establishes classifications by gender which serve important governmental objectives and are substantially related to achievement of those objectives. Therefore, we hold that the statute does not deny males equal protection of law in violation of the Fourteenth Amendment to the Constitution of the United States.

We find that the "difference in gender" aggravator is legitimately based upon realistic physiological size and strength differences of men and women such that it does not violate equal protection. We therefore affirm Wright's convictions.

■ TOAL, CHIEF JUSTICE, concurring in result only.

While I concur with the majority's decision to affirm Wright's CDVHAN conviction, I disagree with the majority's conclusion that the "difference in the sexes" aggravating circumstance does not violate equal protection. I believe the "difference in the sexes" aggravating circumstance, as a gender-based classification, violates equal protection. However, the violation is harmless in this instance because the jury found another aggravating circumstance, infliction of serious bodily injury, which does not violate equal protection.

I agree with the majority that the "difference in the sexes" aggravator is inherently gender-based, but would find that it does not satisfy the second prong of the analysis employed by the majority. As explained by the majority, to pass constitutional muster, a gender-based classification must (1) serve an important governmental objective and (2) be substantially related to the achievement of that objective. The burden rests on the state to make this showing. Although the "difference in the sexes" classification is presumably intended to serve the governmental objective of preventing domestic violence, I would find it is not substantially related to achieving this objective.

The CDVHAN statute was designed to address violence in the home; it applies when any person harms any member of their household. The statute then is designed to prevent domestic violence against men, women, and children by perpetrators of both sexes. Having an aggravating circumstance based solely on gender does not substantially further this objective or the narrower objective of protecting women from domestic abuse. In *In the Interest of Joseph T.,* this Court held a statute criminalizing communication of indecent messages to females violated Equal Protection. Although the Court recognized that some gender-based classifications which realistically reflect that men and women are not similarly situated can withstand equal protection scrutiny on occasion, it clarified that distinctions in the law which were based on "old notions" that women should be afforded "special protection" could no longer withstand equal protection scrutiny.

In my opinion, this "difference in gender" aggravating circumstance is a distinction that perpetuates these "old notions." There is no logical purpose for it except to protect physically inferior women from stronger men; a purpose based on out-dated generalizations of the sexes no longer favored in legal analysis. . . .

Deterring domestic violence is more efficiently and appropriately accomplished through other aggravators, such as the "great disparity in ages or physical conditions of the parties" and "infliction of serious bodily injury" aggravators. In many cases, there may be a great disparity in strength between a male and a female, but if there is not, there is no reason why a difference in gender should serve as an aggravating circumstance to "protect" women to the detriment of men. Therefore, I would find that the "difference in the sexes" aggravating circumstance violates equal protection because it fails to substantially relate to the government objective of preventing domestic violence. However, I would affirm Wright's conviction because the jury also found a permissible, gender-neutral aggravating circumstance: infliction of serious bodily injury.

Accordingly, I respectfully concur in result only.

NOTES AND QUESTIONS

1. **Gender Discrimination.** The courts have routinely upheld statutes that specifically target domestic violence. Yet, South Carolina already had an assault and battery statute that would have criminalized the defendant's conduct. Should a man be penalized more for assaulting a household member than for assaulting a male stranger? Should the fact that a man assaults a woman be considered an aggravating circumstance? Do such laws really protect women or do they reinforce gendered stereotypes? One way to think about this issue is to consider whether gender-specific laws correct for past historical discrimination, or whether they merely reinforce gender differences. Another issue to consider is whether it is more harmful to society when one assaults someone in the context of an intimate relationship. Does hurting someone you claim to love warrant greater punishment? How do we assess the relative moral harm of such behavior?

2. **A Moment in Time.** As Evan Stark has noted, the physical violence experienced in the context of a battering relationship captures only a "moment in time." The criminal law tends to focus on a specific and isolated incident—a slap, a stabbing, a sexual assault—but it isn't able to capture the ongoing patterns of behavior that we explored in Chapter Two. In Chapter Thirteen, we will look at the notion of "continuing tort" that captures the ongoing nature of abuse. There isn't a similar concept in the criminal law. Some commentators have suggested that there ought to be a separate crime of domestic violence that captures the kind of ongoing coercion that battered women experience. For example, Deborah Tuerkheimer has argued that the criminal law fails to account for the experience of battering within a larger context. She proposes a new crime of battering:

> The application of existing legal structures to domestic violence represents tremendous progress in the development of criminal law. And yet, for the reasons we have been discussing, new structures are needed to account for truths antithetical to existing criminal law paradigms. A course of conduct crime of battering represents the next stage in the evolution of law's growing responsiveness to harms suffered by women.

A battering statute might read as follows:

A person is guilty of battering when:

He or she intentionally engages in a course of conduct directed at a family or household member; and

He or she knows or reasonably should know that such conduct is likely to result in substantial power or control over the family or household member; and

At least two acts comprising the course of conduct constitute a crime in this jurisdiction.

Definitions

"Family or household member," means spouses, former spouses, adults related by consanguinity or affinity, an adult with whom the actor is or has been in a continuing relationship of a sexual or otherwise intimate nature, and adults who have a child in common regardless of whether they have been married or have resided together at any time.

"Course of conduct" means a pattern of conduct comprised of a series of acts over a period of time, however short, evidencing a continuity of purpose.

"Crime" means a misdemeanor or a felony. Note how criminalizing domestic violence as a course of conduct refocuses the lens through which evidence is filtered. Context is now relevant, as is relationship. Physical manifestations of power are no longer understood as the sole incidents of battering. What were seemingly disconnected events become woven together by the thread of control. Battering is described accurately by the legislative language which purports to criminalize it. Deborah Tuerkheimer, *Recognizing and Remedying the Harm of Battering: A Call to Criminalize Domestic Violence*, 94 J. Crim. L. & Criminology 959 (2004). See also Alafair S. Burke, *Domestic Violence as a Crime of Pattern & Intent: An Alternative Reconceptualization*, 75 Geo. Wash. L. Rev. 552 (2007).

Burke expands upon Tuerkheimer's theory by proposing a "coercive domestic violence statute" which focuses on the defendant's motivations rather than on the harm to the victim. Do you think such a statute is necessary? What arguments can be made in support of such a scheme? What arguments can you think of to oppose it?

3. **Federal Law.** Other specific domestic violence crimes have been created at the federal level by the Violence Against Women Act of 1994, which makes both the interstate commission of domestic violence and the interstate violation of a restraining order federal offenses, with potentially stiffer sanctions than those typically imposed under state law, except for the most serious felony offenses. These are discussed later in this chapter. Many have taken offense at the gendered name of the law, which is entitled "Violence Against Women," and its focus on violence against Warren even though provisions of the law apply to both genders equally.

4. **Felonies v. Misdemeanors.** The assault in *State v. Wright* is quite horrific, which is one reason why the defendant was charged with a felony. However, the vast majority of domestic violence cases are classified as misdemeanors. Misdemeanors carry shorter sentences and are often disposed of through plea agreements. This, as we shall see later in this chapter, makes it highly unlikely the defendant will receive jail time. Yet, in many cases, the conduct does rise to the level of a felony, suggesting that

prosecutors may under-charge in order to obtain plea deals and avoid the problems of going to trial.

Stalking

In 1990, California became the first state to pass legislation making stalking a crime. Since then all the states, as well as the District of Columbia, have enacted anti-stalking laws, and in 1996 a federal law was passed making it a crime for stalkers to travel across state lines in pursuit of their targets. While the most publicized cases prompting these legislative initiatives have usually involved celebrities rather than victims of domestic violence, battered women's advocates have heralded the new legislation as one more tool in the arsenal of those seeking to hold batterers accountable for their tactics of intimidation.

This development in the law has been crucial for victims of domestic violence. Stalking behavior directly addresses the question of "why doesn't she leave." As we will see in this section, just as we saw in Chapter Two, many victims attempt to leave their relationships, only to be stalked and harassed by their abusers. Stalking also highlights the dangers of separation assault, and why leaving may actually increase the danger to the victim.

What is stalking? As defined in *Stalking and Domestic Violence: The Third Annual Report to Congress under the Violence Against Women Act*, published by the U.S. Department of Justice in 1998, it is:

> harassing or threatening behavior that an individual engages in repeatedly, such as following a person, appearing at a person's home or place of business, making harassing phone calls, leaving written messages or objects, or vandalizing a person's property. These actions may or may not be accompanied by a credible threat of serious crime, and they may or may not be precursors to an assault or murder.

The National Violence Against Women Survey, jointly sponsored by the National Institute of Justice and the Centers for Disease Control and Prevention and summarized in the same *Third Annual Report*, is based on interviews with 8,000 American women and 8,000 American men. Extrapolating from this sample, the researchers, Pat Tjaden and Nancy Thoennes of the Center for Policy Research, conclude that at least one million women and 370,000 men are stalked annually—almost five times as many as previously estimated. (The definition of stalking used in the survey required the victim to fear bodily harm from his or her stalker.) Ninety-four percent of the stalkers identified by women victims and 60% of the stalkers identified by men were men, so that 87% of stalkers overall were men. The average stalking lasted more than eighteen months, and all but six percent of victims were forced to alter their lives significantly in response to their stalkers' tactics. 59% of women victims, compared with 30% of male victims, were stalked by current or former husbands, cohabiting partners or former dates or boy or girlfriends rather than by strangers. Interestingly, 21% of women victims reported that the stalking had occurred before the relationship ended, while 43% said it started only after the relationship ended, and 36% said it occurred both during and after the relationship ended. Others have estimated that as many as 90% of women murdered by present or ex-boyfriends or husbands have been stalked prior to their deaths.

Prosecutions for stalking have been increasing since new laws have been put in place. In the most recent report to Congress on stalking and domestic violence, the Justice Department found that jurisdictions were increasingly taking stalking crimes seriously, with more than 80% of jurisdictions providing special training on stalking and more than 57% of police departments having special protocols. See *Stalking and Domestic Violence: A Report to Congress*, U.S. Department of Justice, Violence Against Women Office, (May 2001).

One of the most important developments has been the use of federal law in this context. Under the Violence Against Women Act, 18 U.S.C.A. § 2261A provides:

> Whoever travels across a State line or within the special maritime and territorial jurisdiction of the United States with the intent to injure or harass another person, and in the course of, or as a result of, such travel places that person in reasonable fear of the death of, or serious bodily injury ... to, that person or a member of that person's immediate family ... shall be punished as provided in Section 2261 of this Title. P.L. 104–201, Div. A, Title X, Subtitle F, § 1069(a), 110 Stat. 2655 (September 23, 1996).

It is notable that federal legislation outlaws even a single instance of stalking, in contrast to legislation in many states that requires a pattern or course of conduct, or repeated instances of nonconsensual contact. At the same time the federal sentencing guidelines, by imposing increased penalties on repeat offenders, adopt a strategy similar to that adopted by those states in which a second offense is a more serious crime, with correspondingly stiffer sanctions.

What is crucial about federal law is that many stalking cases cross jurisdictional boundaries. The following are examples of cases that have been prosecuted under the federal interstate stalking statute. As you read these summaries, keep in mind the issues of separation assault that we studied in Chapter Two. As these cases suggest, even when victims leave their abusers, they are often subject to ongoing abuse, and a heightened risk of death.

Stalking and Domestic Violence: A Report to Congress
United States Department of Justice, Violence Against Women Office, May 2001

[The United States Attorney's Office] for the Western District of Texas prosecuted a defendant who traveled from Alabama to Texas, where he terrorized his ex-wife and three grown sons. The defendant, who had been in Federal custody in Alabama for making interstate threatening phone calls to another ex-wife, traveled to Texas after he lost custody of a minor child. At sentencing, the court considered the defendant's lengthy history of abusing the 4 stalking victims—a history that included beatings, torture, abandonment, threats to kill, stabbing, and burning—and departed upward from the sentencing guidelines to impose the maximum sentence of 20 years.

In a case prosecuted in the Eastern District of North Carolina, the defendant, who previously had been verbally abusive toward his wife, assaulted and threatened to kill her while she was visiting him in the State where he was studying to receive a license to practice medicine. When she returned to their home State, he continued to threaten her over the telephone, and he arrived at her home one day after threatening to kill her. He was sentenced to 22 months and was ordered to pay the victim $7,000 in restitution.

In another case, the defendant had been convicted in Nevada of assaulting his wife and had served a 6–month sentence for the offense. After his release from prison, he called the victim in California and threatened that he would come after her and would destroy her car. While subject to a protection order in Nevada, he traveled to California and set fire to his wife's car. He was sentenced to 60 months of incarceration and 3 years of supervised release.

Another defendant, who had been abusing his wife for several years, threatened to kill her sister, who was a police officer in a neighboring State. He also threatened to kill a man whom he accused of being involved with his wife. The day after he made these threats, the defendant was found approximately a quarter mile from the home of his wife's sister, armed with a revolver and an automatic weapon. He has been convicted of interstate stalking and awaits sentencing. In a case prosecuted in the District of Maine, the defendant, after losing custody of his children, traveled to the State where his wife, from whom he was separated, was living. An accomplice lured his wife's brother and boyfriend out of the house, and the defendant killed them both. He and his accomplice then kidnapped his wife and drove her to New York where they were found in a motel room. The defendant was convicted of interstate domestic violence, interstate stalking, kidnapping, and interstate violation of a protection order. He received a life sentence.

Another defendant forced his wife to travel from Florida to Kentucky, where he and an accomplice sexually assaulted her. He also harassed his wife, obtained false arrest warrants for her, and posted signs seeking information on her whereabouts and offering a reward for any such information. The defendant was convicted at trial of interstate domestic violence, interstate violation of a protection order, and interstate stalking. At sentencing, the judge departed upward and sentenced the defendant to 87 months in prison and 3 years of supervised release.

NOTES AND QUESTIONS

1. **Varying Definitions of Stalking.** Although all fifty states and the federal government have laws which outlaw stalking, the definition of the offense varies widely. Some states have very specific definitions which list

the prohibited conduct, while others are more vague. For example, Michigan's statute is among the most specific:

See, e.g., MICH. COMP. LAWS § 750.411h(1)(e) (2004). "Unconsented contact" is defined, in Michigan and elsewhere, as:

any contact with another individual that is initiated or continued without that individual's consent or in disregard of that individual's expressed desire that the contact be avoided or discontinued. Unconsented contact includes, but is not limited to, any of the following:

(i) Following or appearing within the sight of that individual.

(ii) Approaching or confronting that individual in a public place or on private property.

(iii) Appearing at that individual's workplace or residence.

(iv) Entering onto or remaining on property owned, leased, or occupied by that individual.

(v) Contacting that individual by telephone.

(vi) Sending mail or electronic communications to that individual.

(vii) Placing an object on, or delivering an object to, property owned, leased, or occupied by that individual.

Other states use much narrower definitions. Connecticut, in contrast, defines stalking only as "following or lying in wait." CONN. GEN. STAT. §§ 53a–181d, –181e (2005).

Another element of stalking crimes involves intent. When many of these laws were first passed, they required that the defendant have the specific intent to cause the victim to fear for her safety. Yet, determining the intent of stalkers can be hard as many former intimate partners could argue that his intent was to reunite, not to cause harm. As a result, many states have amended their statutes only to require general intent to engage in the prohibited acts—that the defendant know or should have known that his conduct would cause fear in the victim. Courts have upheld stalking statutes with general intent. See *State* v. *Neuzil*, 589 N.W.2d 708 (Iowa 1999); *State* v. *Cardell*, 723 A.2d 111 (N.J. Super. A.D. 1999).

For a review of stalking laws and issues related to definitions, see Strengthening Antistalking Laws, Dep't of Justice, Legal Series Bulletin, January 2002, available at http://www.ojp.usdoj.gov/ovc/publications/bulletins/legalseries/bulletin1/1.html.

2. **Cyberstalking.** Many victims are stalked via email and instant messaging, raising a host of concerns for law enforcement. There are many ways in which a victim can be stalked via the internet. The harasser may post comments intended to cause distress to the victim or intended to make the victim subject to harassment by others. The victim may receive a constant stream of emails. The harasser can pose as the victim and send out offensive messages to family friends, significant others, or coworkers. He could hack into the victim's email account and take it over entirely. The harasser may sign the victim up for spam, porn sites and questionable offers. Harassers can also follow victims into chat rooms and discussion

boards and post lies and hateful messages about the victim, or post sexually explicit images on websites. All of these behaviors can be threatening to a victim, and are other ways in which batterers exert power and control. At least 44 states now include electronic communications within the definition of harassment or stalking. For complete list, see The National Conference of State Legislatures, http://www.ncsl.org/programs/lis/cip/stalk99.htm.

In a recent report to Congress, the Justice Department found that cyberstalking has been greatly increasing over the years, and that law enforcement often lacks the training and experience to investigate and prosecute such cases. One of the difficulties with cyberstalkers is anonymity. Simply identifying who the stalker is can pose enormous difficulties for law enforcement. As we saw in Chapter Six, many states now include cyberstalking in the conduct that can serve as the basis for an order of protection.

3. **Constitutionality of Stalking Laws.** There have been some constitutional challenges to stalking laws. Some have been challenges as unconstitutionally vague, overbroad, or both. For example in *Petersen et al. v. State of Alaska,* 930 P.2d 414 (Alaska Ct. App.1996) the Court of Appeals of Alaska consolidated three cases involving three quite different stalking scenarios. The statute at issue, ALASKA STAT. § 11.41.270, defines stalking, in Subsection (a), as: "knowingly engag[ing] in a course of conduct that recklessly places another person in fear of death or physical injury, or in fear of the death or physical injury of a family member. Subsections (b)(1) and (b)(3) of the statute further define 'course of conduct' as 'repeated acts of nonconsensual contact involving the victim or a family member'," and define nonconsensual contact in the same language as that used in the Michigan statute cited above. The court upheld the statute over the defendants' concerns that they were engaged in protected first amendment conduct. The Court suggested, for example, that there might be borderline cases in which political protesters might be captured under the statute's definition. Yet, given the conduct of the defendants, the Court held:

> The constitutional arguments raised by the defendants are not trivial. As we noted at the beginning of this section, the stalking statutes' definition of "nonconsensual contact" covers a wide spectrum of social interaction. This definition is undoubtedly the Alaska Legislature's most comprehensive codification of a person's right to be free from unwanted contact. Yet even though our society values and protects individual autonomy and privacy, our society at the same time recognizes a person's right to engage in uncomfortable, distasteful, and annoying contacts—even abrasive confrontations—with other citizens. Such interactions are not merely tolerated; they are explicitly protected by our Constitution.

> However, the Constitution does not guarantee a right to threaten other people. When a person's words or actions constitute an assault—when they cause other people to reasonably fear for their own safety or the safety of those close to them—the Constitution no longer provides a refuge. *Id.*

In those states in which the courts have found statutes unconstitutionally vague or overbroad, the legislatures of those states have often amended their laws to address the court's concerns. For a summary, see Strengthening Antistalking Statutes, Dep't of Justice, Legal Series Bulletin, January 2002, available at http://www.ojp.usdoj.gov/ovc/publications/bulletins/legalseries/bulletin1/1.html.

4. **Evidentiary Problems.** Prosecutors from both Dover, New Hampshire and Cook County, Illinois, have noted that they had difficulty getting "prior acts" into evidence in stalking cases. If the statute requires "repeated" behaviors, or a "course of conduct," then evidence of a sequence of events, some more recent than others, is essential, and it is hard to see how a judge could rule that evidence inadmissible. However, if the prosecution is trying instead to introduce evidence of past abuse, rather than stalking, then it is easier to understand how a judge might find that the evidence was highly prejudicial to the defendant, and be inclined to exclude it, just as judges routinely used to exclude evidence of past abuse in cases where women who killed their batterers argued that they had acted in self-defense. In both situations, however, the evidence is in fact highly relevant, and often essential. Only by introducing the fact-finder to the defendant's prior abuse of the victim can the prosecution demonstrate that the defendant's most recent conduct made the victim fearful, and that her fear was reasonable. In the stalking context, evidence of prior abuse will also support the claim that the defendant had reason to know he was frightening the victim, even in the absence of explicit threats. We examine the issue of admissibility of evidence of prior bad acts in the next chapter.

5. **Supervision.** In any time period following an arrest when a stalker is not detained, whether because he has been released pre-trial, released between conviction and sentencing, or sentenced to probation, the target of his stalking may be particularly vulnerable. Every stage is a dangerous time. In the pre-trial period, or the period between conviction and sentencing, the offender may feel that he is looking at his last window of opportunity to plead his case with, or settle his score with, his victim. After conviction, the stalker who is put on probation without any initial period of incarceration, and without a suspended sentence hanging over his head, may receive the message that his behavior, if not entirely condoned, is not regarded as seriously problematic, and may interpret that as a license to reoffend. That message is dramatically reinforced if subsequent offenses again bring no sanction more onerous than probation. The management and disposition of stalking cases must therefore take into account not just offender accountability, but also victim safety. Supervision of the offender is a critical factor in this equation.

One means of facilitating supervision is for law enforcement to encourage the stalking victim to obtain a restraining order with clear no-contact provisions as soon as the criminal process is initiated, if she has not already done so. A violation of this order will then provide additional mechanisms for policing the stalker, including warrantless arrest powers. There are two problems with this approach. The first is that the onus for reporting violations rests entirely with the victim; law enforcement personnel are not offering surveillance, but only, at most, an enhanced response to reported conduct in violation of the order. The second is that a simplified restraining order mechanism will only be available to victims who have been in family, household or intimate relationships with their stalkers under the definitions provided by state restraining order legislation. In this regard individuals who are stalked by strangers have fewer protections available to them.

The other means of supervising stalkers during and after the disposition of their cases involves the imposition of conditions on their bail, presentence or post-conviction release. Again, imposing conditions is of limited assistance if there is no surveillance mechanism attached, but if compliance with those conditions is supervised by the probation department, some of the burden is shifted from the victim to the criminal justice system, although supervision will be most effective if they work together. Once there has been a conviction there is no legal impediment to attaching conditions to the offender's release; the difficulties lie in crafting an effective set of constraints, and monitoring the offender's compliance. Prior to conviction, however, any conditions imposed on the offender must be attached to bail, which raises a different set of questions.

Enforcement Issues

For women who have been physically abused, the problem has not been that their partners' behavior falls outside accepted categories of criminal conduct. Rather, the issue has been that the criminal justice system—from police and prosecutors to judges and probation officers—has turned a blind eye, refusing to respond to or take seriously criminal violations by intimate partners. A walk through the process by which a crime is identified and prosecuted, and a defendant convicted and sentenced, reveals the numerous points at which the victim may receive the message that the system is or is not concerned for her safety, and the abuser may receive the message that he will or will not be held accountable for his behavior.

When violence erupts in an intimate relationship, the first question is whether it will come to the attention of law enforcement authorities. If the victim or another witness responds by calling the police, it will, although if there is then no police response, or the police respond without ever filing a report on the incident, it will almost immediately disappear from official view. If the police are not called at the time of the incident, there is still an opportunity for the victim to instigate an official response by going to the police and filing a subsequent report. The victim will generally only do this if she is interested in prosecution, and is using the police report as her "passport" into the prosecutor's office. One further possibility is that the victim will respond to the incident by seeking a protective order, and through that process will come to the attention of the prosecutor's office. This is perhaps most likely to happen if the court where she goes for her order is one in which victim witness advocates working in the prosecutor's office are assigned to assist women with restraining orders, or one in which lay advocates working on restraining orders maintain close relationships with the prosecutor's office. However, it is also possible for the judge who issues the restraining order to bring the precipitating incident to the attention of the prosecutor, if she is concerned for the victim's safety.

If the police respond to a call, and appear at the scene of a domestic violence incident, their behavior will have an important impact on the ultimate outcome. One crucial aspect of police intervention is the writing and filing of a report. As suggested above, if police fail to enter a report, the incident will disappear from official memory, and provide no support for more aggressive intervention the next time violence is reported. It is also critical that the report be complete, detailed, and free of bias, so that it can be put to effective use in any subsequent prosecution. At the policy level, it is also important that the report carry a marker identifying the incident as one involving partner abuse, so that the state has an accurate measure of the incidence of domestic violence to justify expenditures on training or services, and any necessary substantive or procedural reforms.

A second crucial police choice is whether to arrest the perpetrator, if he is still on the premises and state law mandates or permits arrest without a warrant, or, in cases in which he has already left, whether to seek a warrant for his arrest. A related choice is whether to issue a citation, commanding the offender's later appearance in court to answer charges, but without arresting him. Finally, police response to the victim and her children—the level of immediate support provided, and the identification of other resources for the family—can dramatically affect the victim's ability and willingness to cooperate in holding her abuser accountable for his violence.

If the perpetrator is arrested, and removed from the scene, the next set of choices have to do with whether, and how, criminal charges are brought, and whether, and for how long, the perpetrator will be held before being released back into the community. If the arrest is regarded simply as a warning, and an independent decision is made by the authorities not to press charges, then the perpetrator will be released almost immediately. If the victim has chosen to obtain a restraining order, then her only ongoing protection will be the terms of that order, and the possibility of enforcing any violation. A slightly different scenario would involve the prosecutor's office consulting with the victim about the desirability of pursuing criminal action, but again, the decision not to press charges will result in the perpetrator's release, and the victim's exclusive reliance on a protective order to secure her future safety. The victim could be, but is often not, given advance notice of her perpetrator's release, so that she can take proper precautions, whether those involve moving into a shelter, staying away from her home temporarily, or simply taking whatever steps she can to secure her home against his intrusion.

If, after an arrest, a decision is made to pursue criminal charges, then the perpetrator will be detained for some period of time until he can be arraigned, a bail hearing held, and a trial date set. Although the primary purpose of bail proceedings is to ensure that the defendant shows up at trial, in many jurisdictions pre-trial detention can also be justified, albeit sparingly, on the grounds that the defendant poses an identifiable and serious risk to himself or others. It is also available to the hearing officer to condition release not only on the provision of a bond, but also on the defendant's consent to a protective order, or to conditions with the same effect. In volatile situations the victim's safety, or at a minimum her continued cooperation with the prosecutor, may be entirely dependent on the defendant's continuing detention, or on the conscientious and careful imposition and enforcement of conditions that keep the defendant away from her pending his trial. Again, it should be, but is not, standard practice to notify the victim before her abuser is released. If felony charges have been brought, then a grand jury proceeding will be initiated, either before or after the arraignment, and the case will proceed only on the grand jury's finding of probable cause.

The most debated issues of prosecutorial policy have been the standards governing whether or not to prosecute, and whether prosecutors should be required to prosecute domestic violence cases under "no-drop" policies even in situations where the victim is not cooperative. But another crucial choice the prosecutor has to make is how to frame the charge. Should the focus be on the violation of a restraining order? This crime is often relatively easy to prove, but may underemphasize the level of violence involved, and result in a slap on the wrist rather than a more meaningful sanction. Should the choice be to pursue one or more criminal misdemeanor charges, which may produce a speedier resolution, or to go after felony charges which will carry more significant penalties, but will also move more slowly, and require a greater investment of prosecutorial resources, perhaps at the expense of other victims?

Even after a decision has been made to bring charges, the case may still be disposed of without a trial. If the victim proves uncooperative, and if the prosecutor's office has no expertise in or enthusiasm for presenting the case without her testimony, the charges may still be dropped. Alternatively, if the defendant or his counsel are willing to cooperate with the prosecutor, the charges may be dropped on condition that the defendant agree to the terms of a protective order, or agree to participate in a batterer's treatment program, or provide restitution, or some combination of these or other conditions. Another critical choice for prosecutors is whether to offer these "pre-trial diversion" programs, which will leave the defendant with no criminal record, or whether to insist that any such "diversion" depend on a plea-bargain which will result in a conviction, although for a lesser offense than the defendant was originally charged with. Obtaining a conviction has the advantage that the defendant can then be sentenced, with the sentence being suspended as long as he is in compliance with the terms of the "diversion" agreement. This greatly simplifies the task of holding the defendant accountable for any violation of his agreement.

These choices can in theory be made at any point between the initial charging and the trial, and often are negotiated between the prosecutor and the defendant's attorney without any judicial input. They may, on the other hand, be influenced by the judge's reaction to the case at the pretrial conference, which will usually be scheduled shortly before the trial date. Even on the day the trial is scheduled to begin, the judge, under pressure to dispose of cases as quickly as possible, may make a final effort to secure a negotiated disposition, rather than see the case go to trial.

At trial, there is, of course, always the possibility that the defendant will be acquitted. Alternatively, the case may be continued without a finding, with the threat that the trial will resume if the defendant violates the terms of the probation to which he is assigned, and the promise that if he completes the probationary period without a violation, the case will be dismissed. This poses similar risks to those created by pre-trial diversion. It will be more difficult to obtain a conviction on the original charges once any significant time has elapsed, and if the case is ultimately dismissed, there is nothing in the defendant's record to warn of his propensity for violence. Finally, if the defendant is convicted, while incarceration is increasingly a possibility, the likelihood is still that he will instead be assigned to probation, and required to comply with the terms of a protective order, as well as completing one or more treatment programs (commonly programs for alcohol and substance abuse, in addition to a batterer's treatment program). A suspended sentence may also be imposed to increase the defendant's motivation to comply with the terms of his probation.

Specialized Courts

One effective justice system response to domestic violence is the specialized domestic violence court. In the early 1980s, Cook County Illinois established the first such court to hear all domestic violence misdemeanor cases, and since then a number of other jurisdictions have followed suit. Funding under the Violence Against Women Act has supported the development of specialized courts or court sessions throughout the country.

These specialized courts vary in the extent of their jurisdiction. Some deal only with protective orders, or only with criminal misdemeanor cases, others combine both, and the most comprehensive also have jurisdiction over related civil matters, such as paternity, child support, custody, visitation and divorce. Among the most common, and effective, features of specialized courts are their specialized intake units, which provide a range of services to victims; the allocation of dedicated calendars and specialized judges to expedite hearings and provide consistency; and integrated adjudication of abuse-related proceedings to avoid duplication and potentially inconsistent rulings from different courts.

The next three sections take up issues raised by police responses to domestic violence, prosecutorial policy, and sentencing, including the role of batterers' treatment programs. Although it may seem inappropriate to address a mental health intervention like batterers' treatment in the context of a chapter on the criminal justice system, the vast majority of batterers who attend counseling focused on their abusive behavior do so because a court order has mandated their attendance, or because they have agreed to participate to avoid a criminal record or a stiffer sanction. In this respect, batterers' treatment is an integral aspect of the criminal justice system's response to domestic violence. We also explore alternatives to traditional sanctions.

B.   POLICE AND ARREST POLICIES

In 2006, the United States Supreme Court debated the impact that arrest policies and procedures might potentially have on domestic violence victims. *Georgia v. Randolph* is a good example of how far the law has progressed relative to domestic violence. Even in a case that does not involve a domestic violence law *per se*, the nation's highest court considers how allowing co-occupants to consent to searches will affect victims of domestic violence. At the heart of the discussion is whether victims of domestic violence need special protection, or whether, by so doing, we reinforce gender stereotypes. These same tensions were at play in *State v. Wright*, above.

Georgia v. Randolph

United States Supreme Court, 2006.
547 U.S. 103.

■ JUSTICE SOUTER delivered the opinion of the Court.

The Fourth Amendment recognizes a valid warrantless entry and search of premises when police obtain the voluntary consent of an occupant who shares, or is reasonably believed to share, authority over the area in common with a co-occupant who later objects to the use of evidence so obtained. The question here is whether such an evidentiary seizure is likewise lawful with the permission of one occupant when the other, who later seeks to suppress the evidence, is present at the scene and expressly refuses to consent. We hold that, in the circumstances here at issue, a physically present co-occupant's stated refusal to permit entry prevails, rendering the warrantless search unreasonable and invalid as to him.

Respondent Scott Randolph and his wife, Janet, separated in late May 2001, when she left the marital residence in Americus, Georgia, and went to stay with her parents in Canada, taking their son and some belongings. In July, she returned to the Americus house with the child, though the record does not reveal whether her object was reconciliation or retrieval of remaining possessions.

On the morning of July 6, she complained to the police that after a domestic dispute her husband took their son away, and when officers reached the house she told them that her husband was a cocaine user whose habit had caused financial troubles. She mentioned the marital problems and said that she and their son had only recently returned after a stay of several weeks with her parents. Shortly after the police arrived, Scott Randolph returned and explained that he had removed the child to a neighbor's house out of concern that his wife might take the boy out of the country again; he denied cocaine use, and countered that it was in fact his wife who abused drugs and alcohol.

One of the officers, Sergeant Murray, went with Janet Randolph to reclaim the child, and when they returned she not only renewed her complaints about her husband's drug use, but also volunteered that there were " 'items of drug evidence' " in the house. Sergeant Murray asked Scott Randolph for permission to search the house, which he unequivocally refused.

The sergeant turned to Janet Randolph for consent to search, which she readily gave. She led the officer upstairs to a bedroom that she identified as Scott's, where the sergeant noticed a section of a drinking straw with a powdery residue he suspected was cocaine. He then left the house to get an evidence bag from his car and to call the district attorney's office, which instructed him to stop the search and apply for a warrant. When Sergeant Murray returned to the house, Janet Randolph withdrew her consent. The police took the straw to the police station, along with the Randolphs. After getting a search warrant, they returned to the house and seized further evidence of drug use, on the basis of which Scott Randolph was indicted for possession of cocaine. . . .

Since the co-tenant wishing to open the door to a third party has no recognized authority in law or social practice to prevail over a present and objecting co-tenant, his disputed invitation, without more, gives a police officer no better claim to reasonableness in entering than the officer would have in the absence of any consent at all. Accordingly, in the balancing of competing individual and governmental interests entailed by the bar to unreasonable searches, the cooperative occupant's invitation adds nothing to the government's side to counter the force of an objecting individual's claim to security against the government's intrusion into his dwelling place. Since we hold to the "centuries-old principle of respect for the privacy of the home," "it is beyond dispute that the home is entitled to special protection as the center of the private lives of our people." We have, after all, lived our whole national history with an understanding of "the ancient adage that a man's home is his castle [to the point that t]he poorest man may in his cottage bid defiance to all the forces of the Crown." . . .

Nor should this established policy of Fourth Amendment law be undermined by the principal dissent's claim that it shields spousal abusers and other violent co-tenants who will refuse to allow the police to enter a dwelling when their victims ask the police for help. It is not that the dissent exaggerates violence in the home; we recognize that domestic abuse is a serious problem in the United States.

But this case has no bearing on the capacity of the police to protect domestic victims. The dissent's argument rests on the failure to distinguish two different issues: when the police may enter without committing a trespass, and when the police may enter to search for evidence. No question has been raised, or reasonably could be, about the authority of the police to enter a dwelling to protect a resident from domestic violence; so long as they have good reason to believe such a threat exists, it would be silly to suggest that the police would commit a tort by entering, say, to give a complaining tenant the opportunity to collect belongings and get out safely, or to determine whether violence (or threat of violence) has just occurred or is about to (or soon will) occur, however much a spouse or other co-tenant objected. (And since the police would then be lawfully in the premises, there is no question that they could seize any evidence in plain view or take further action supported by any consequent probable cause.) Thus, the question whether the police might lawfully enter over objection in order to provide any protection that might be reasonable is easily answered yes. . . . The undoubted right of the police to enter in order to protect a victim, however, has nothing to do with the question in this case, whether a search with the consent of one co-tenant is good against another, standing at the door and expressly refusing consent.[7] . . .

The dissent's red herring aside, we know, of course, that alternatives to disputed consent will not always open the door to search for evidence that the police suspect is inside. The consenting tenant may simply not disclose enough information, or information factual enough, to add up to a showing of probable cause, and there may be no exigency to justify fast action. But nothing in social custom or its reflection in private law argues for placing a higher value on delving into private premises to search for evidence in the face of disputed consent, than on requiring clear justification before the government searches private living quarters over a resident's objection. We therefore hold that a warrantless search of a shared dwelling for evidence over the express refusal of consent by a physically present resident cannot be justified as reasonable as to him on the basis of consent given to the police by another resident.

■ JUSTICE STEVENS, concurring.

In the 18th century, when the Fourth Amendment was adopted, the advice would have been quite different from what is appropriate today. Given the then-prevailing dramatic differences between the property rights of the husband and the far lesser rights of the wife, only the consent of the husband would matter. Whether "the master of the house" consented or objected, his decision would control. Thus if "original understanding" were to govern the outcome of this case, the search was clearly invalid because the husband did not consent. History, however, is not dispositive because it is now clear, as a matter of constitutional law, that the male and the female are equal partners.

In today's world the only advice that an officer could properly give should make it clear that each of the partners has a constitutional right that he or she may independently assert or waive. Assuming that both spouses are competent, neither one is a master possessing the power to override the other's constitutional right to deny entry to their castle . . .

---

7. We understand the possibility that a battered individual will be afraid to express fear candidly, but this does not seem to be a reason to think such a person would invite the police into the dwelling to search for evidence against another. Hence, if a rule crediting consent over denial of consent were built on hoping to protect household victims, it would distort the Fourth Amendment with little, if any, constructive effect on domestic abuse investigations.

■ JUSTICE BREYER, concurring.

... [T]he risk of an ongoing crime or other exigent circumstance can make a critical difference. Consider, for example, instances of domestic abuse. "Family disturbance calls ... constitute the largest single category of calls received by police departments each year." And, law enforcement officers must be able to respond effectively when confronted with the possibility of abuse.

If a possible abuse victim invites a responding officer to enter a home or consents to the officer's entry request, that invitation (or consent) itself could reflect the victim's fear about being left alone with an abuser. It could also indicate the availability of evidence, in the form of an immediate willingness to speak, that might not otherwise exist. In that context, an invitation (or consent) would provide a special reason for immediate, rather than later, police entry. And, entry following invitation or consent by one party ordinarily would be reasonable even in the face of direct objection by the other. That being so, contrary to the THE CHIEF JUSTICE's suggestion, today's decision will not adversely affect ordinary law enforcement practices.

■ CHIEF JUSTICE ROBERTS, with whom JUSTICE SCALIA joins, dissenting.

Perhaps the most serious consequence of the majority's rule is its operation in domestic abuse situations, a context in which the present question often arises. While people living together might typically be accommodating to the wishes of their cotenants, requests for police assistance may well come from coinhabitants who are having a disagreement. The Court concludes that because "no sensible person would go inside" in the face of disputed consent, and the consenting cotenant thus has "no recognized authority" to insist on the guest's admission, a "police officer [has] no better claim to reasonableness in entering than the officer would have in the absence of any consent at all." But the police officer's superior claim to enter is obvious: Mrs. Randolph did not invite the police to join her for dessert and coffee; the officer's precise purpose in knocking on the door was to assist with a dispute between the Randolphs—one in which Mrs. Randolph felt the need for the protective presence of the police. The majority's rule apparently forbids police from entering to assist with a domestic dispute if the abuser whose behavior prompted the request for police assistance objects.[2]

The majority acknowledges these concerns, but dismisses them on the ground that its rule can be expected to give rise to exigent situations, and police can then rely on an exigent circumstances exception to justify entry. This is a strange way to justify a rule, and the fact that alternative

---

2. In response to this concern, the majority asserts that its rule applies "merely [to] evidentiary searches." But the fundamental premise of the majority's argument is that an inviting co-occupant has "no recognized authority" to "open the door" over a co-occupant's objection.... The point is that the majority's rule transforms what may have begun as a request for consent to conduct an evidentiary search into something else altogether, by giving veto power over the consenting co-occupant's wishes to an occupant who would exclude the police from *entry*. The majority would afford the now quite vulnerable consenting co-occupant sufficient time to gather her belongings and leave, apparently putting to one side the fact that it is her castle, too.

justifications for entry might arise does not show that entry pursuant to consent is unreasonable. In addition, it is far from clear that an exception for emergency entries suffices to protect the safety of occupants in domestic disputes.

Rather than give effect to a consenting spouse's authority to permit entry into her house to avoid such situations, the majority again alters established Fourth Amendment rules to defend giving veto power to the objecting spouse. In response to the concern that police might be turned away under its rule before entry can be justified based on exigency, the majority creates a new rule: A "good reason" to enter, coupled with one occupant's consent, will ensure that a police officer is "lawfully in the premises." As support for this "consent plus a good reason" rule, the majority cites a treatise, which itself refers only to *emergency* entries. For the sake of defending what it concedes are fine, formalistic lines, the majority spins out an entirely new framework for analyzing exigent circumstances. Police may now enter with a "good reason" to believe that "violence (or threat of violence) has just occurred or is about to (or soon will) occur." And apparently a key factor allowing entry with a "good reason" short of exigency is the very consent of one co-occupant the majority finds so inadequate in the first place....

Our third-party consent cases have recognized that a person who shares common areas with others "assume[s] the risk that one of their number might permit the common area to be searched." The majority reminds us, in high tones, that a man's home is his castle, but even under the majority's rule, it is not his castle if he happens to be absent, asleep in the keep, or otherwise engaged when the constable arrives at the gate. Then it is his co-owner's castle. And, of course, it is not his castle if he wants to consent to entry, but his co-owner objects. Rather than constitutionalize such an arbitrary rule, we should acknowledge that a decision to share a private place, like a decision to share a secret or a confidential document, necessarily entails the risk that those with whom we share may in turn choose to share—for their own protection or for other reasons— with the police.

■ JUSTICE SCALIA, dissenting.

■ I join the dissent of THE CHIEF JUSTICE, but add these few words in response to JUSTICE STEVENS' concurrence.

... Justice STEVENS' panegyric to the *equal* rights of women under modern property law does not support his conclusion that "[a]ssuming ... both spouses are competent, neither one is a master possessing the power to override the other's constitutional right to deny entry to their castle." The issue at hand is what to do when there is a *conflict* between two equals. Now that women have authority to consent, as Justice STEVENS claims men alone once did, it does not follow that the spouse who *refuses* consent should be the winner of the contest. Justice STEVENS could just as well have followed the same historical developments to the opposite conclusion: Now that "the male and the female are equal partners," and women can consent to a search of their property, men can no longer obstruct their wishes. Men and women are no more "equal" in the majority's regime, where both sexes can veto each other's consent, than on the dissent's view, where both sexes cannot.

Finally, I must express grave doubt that today's decision deserves Justice STEVENS' celebration as part of the forward march of women's equality. Given the usual patterns of domestic violence, how often can police be expected to encounter the situation in which a man urges them to enter the home while a woman simultaneously demands that they stay out? The most common practical effect of today's decision, insofar as the contest between the sexes is concerned, is to give men the power to stop women from allowing police into their homes—which is, curiously enough, *precisely* the power that Justice STEVENS disapprovingly presumes men had in 1791.

NOTES AND QUESTIONS

1. **Concern for Victims of Domestic Violence.** Do you think the justices were genuinely interested in protecting victims of domestic violence or do you think they used the issue of domestic violence as a means to make their arguments? Note that Justice Ruth Bader Ginsburg, the only woman on the Court when the decision was rendered, did not separately author an opinion.

2. **Formal v. Contextual Equality.** The majority, particularly Justice Stevens, views men and women equally situated in domestic relationships and thus gives the individual autonomy to make decisions only on behalf of him or herself. In contrast, the dissenters, particularly Justice Scalia, do not adopt this formal equality viewpoint, but consider the context in which domestic violence may take place. Which side do you think is correct? As you read the subsequent material, consider how you might have ruled in this case.

3. **Rights of Criminal Defendants v. Concern for Victims:** How are courts to balance the constitutional rights of defendants with concern for victims who have very few constitutional rights? One of the interesting aspects of *Georgia v. Randolph* is that the Court privileges the privacy of the potential defendant, reinforcing the private nature of home and family life. This was the first time in many years that the Supreme Court actually expanded the privacy rights of criminal defendants under the Fourth Amendment. Thus, we might view the decision as privatizing the family relationship by reinforcing the lack of state intervention into conflicted family relationships. Or, we might celebrate the decision as protecting individual rights for all citizens.

4. **Widely Held Social Expectations v. Assumption of Risk.** There is a fundamental difference in the case about what standard ought to govern third party consents. Justice Souter relies on the notion of "widely held social expectations" that co-occupants do not speak for each other, while Chief Justice Roberts suggests that co-occupants assume the risk that those with whom we share our premises may turn to the police. What are the "widely held social expectations" about how couples operate, and do those expectations hold true in the context of an abusive relationship? Think

back to Chapter Two and how abusers use power and control over their victims. Does empowering the victim to consent even when her abuser refuses to do so give her a way to break the cycle of violence?

Justice Souter points out that the police can still intervene in cases where there are exigent circumstances even when the co-occupant refuses to consent to a search. Yet, as Chief Justice Roberts notes, that burden may be too high in domestic situations where there is no immediate threat of violence. For example, the abuser may have an illegal firearm in the home that the victim wants the police to confiscate. If she consents to a search of her home, but the abuser objects, the police would then be forced to obtain a warrant. Does the Court's holding unnecessarily tie the hands of law enforcement in domestic violence situations? The impact of *Georgia v. Randolph* in domestic violence cases has yet to be seen. For a criticism of the Court's approach to understanding exigency in domestic violence cases see Deborah Tuerkheimer, *Exigency*, 49 ARIZ.L.REV. ___ (forthcoming 2007).

Background: Police Response to Domestic Violence

Assume a victim calls the police to her home following an incident in which her abuser has assaulted her. When the police arrive, what should they do? Historically, in these situations, as Joan Zorza describes in the excerpt below, the police would often tell the abuser to take a walk around the block, but would not arrest him. Below Zorza describes such policies.

Joan Zorza

The Criminal Law of Misdemeanor Domestic Violence, 1970–1990

83 J. CRIM. L. & CRIMINOLOGY 46 (1992).

... [T]hose police departments that had policies on handling domestic calls in the 1970s had a clear non-arrest policy. The Oakland Police Department's *1975 Training Bulletin on Techniques of Dispute Intervention* explicitly described:

> [t]he police role in a dispute situation [as] more often that of a mediator and peacemaker than enforcer of the law.... [T]he possibility that ... arrest will only aggravate the dispute or create a serious danger for the arresting officers due to possible efforts to resist arrest ... is most likely when a husband or father is arrested in his home.... Normally, officers should adhere to the policy that arrests shall be avoided ... but when one of the parties demands arrest, you should attempt to explain the ramifications of such action (e.g. loss of wages, bail procedures, court appearances) and encourage the parties to reason with each other.

Detroit Police commander James Bannon, in his address to the 1975 American Bar Association convention, described the manner in which his police officers respond to domestic violence calls. According to Bannon, the dispatcher would screen calls from battered women to respond only to those women who appeared in the most imminent danger. If the woman had only minor injuries when they arrived, the police became angry and would not respond quickly the next time. Women often learned to report that a stranger was attacking them or that their abuser had a gun. While such a desperate ploy might have worked once for a woman, police simply declared her not credible if they found no serious injuries. Lacking credibility, she was deemed unworthy of police protection if she called again. Police treated poor women and women of color with less concern than they did middle class and white women, even when they were severely injured....

In this light, it is hardly surprising that the police who did respond to domestic violence calls almost always took the man's side. And because abusers, when they did not or could not deny their abuse, tried to shift the blame onto others, especially their victims, the police frequently joined in blaming the victim. The responding officer often admonished the woman to be a better wife or asked, or at least wondered, why she did not leave. Some officers concluded that she must enjoy the beatings, or at least not mind them. These officers conveniently ignored the fact that their failure to protect the woman, her lack of money, and the far greater risk of being beaten or killed if she tried to separate herself from her abuser all combined to make her decision logical....

Pro–Arrest and Mandatory Arrest Policies

Criticism of police response to domestic violence has been based not only on the argument that it is inadequate, exposing victims to an unwarranted and unnecessary degree of danger, but also on the argument that it is discriminatory. Most commonly, the argument is that stranger assault is treated differently by police than domestic assault, and that since domestic assaults reported to the police disproportionately involve women victims and male perpetrators, this different treatment discriminates against women. Others have countered that police respond "situationally" to all assaults, and that what determines police response is not whether the assault is domestic, but the totality of circumstances involved in the assault. A study published in 1996, looking at one police department's responses to assaults in 1986 and 1987, set out to test that proposition, and found that even once all the surrounding circumstances were taken into account, there was evidence of discrimination against victims of domestic violence. Eve S. Buzawa, Thomas L. Austin and Carl G. Buzawa, *The Role of Arrest in Domestic Versus Stranger Assault: Is There a Difference?*, in DO ARRESTS AND RESTRAINING ORDERS WORK? (E.S. Buzawa and C.G. Buzawa, eds. 1996).

Much has changed since 1987. Beginning in the 1970s, the battered women's movement adopted as one of its top priorities increasing the responsiveness of the police to domestic violence assaults. In 1976, two groups of attorneys filed class action complaints, one in the Northern District of California, and the other in the Supreme Court of New York, alleging the failure of the police to provide protection to battered women, and seeking declaratory and injunctive relief.

As a result of these cases, many police departments agreed to change their policies and practices with respect to domestic violence voluntarily, before similar suits were brought against them, and before they found themselves liable for attorneys' fees, or even civil damages. This vulnerability was made even more real by the case of *Thurman v. City of Torrington, Connecticut*, 595 F. Supp. 1521 (1984) in which a federal jury awarded Tracey Thurman $2.3 million in damages for negligence, in compensation for the devastating injuries inflicted by her abusive husband while the police stood by and watched, after ignoring her repeated requests for protection.

Court challenges to police inaction on constitutional grounds, including the *Thurman* case, are the topic of a later chapter. Here they illustrate just one strategy among several by which battered women's advocates sought to change police policy and practice. Another strategy, as already suggested, was to use the leverage generated by success in these cases to persuade each individual police department to develop a progressive domestic violence policy. Another more ambitious strategy was to persuade state legislatures to change the laws governing arrest to facilitate a more aggressive response. As Joan Zorza reports:

> While officers could arrest when they had probable cause to believe that a felony offense had been committed, in most, but not all, jurisdictions police could not make an arrest for a misdemeanor assault unless the assault occurred in the police officer's presence. Because most police charge domestic violence offenses only as misdemeanors, the law, in order to enable an officer to arrest the abuser when the offense was not committed in the officer's presence, has to permit the arrest without a warrant.

Joan Zorza, *The Criminal Law of Misdemeanor Domestic Violence, 1970–1990*, 83 J. CRIM. LAW & CRIMINOLOGY 46 (1992). By 1983 police arrest powers in domestic violence cases had been expanded in thirty-three states. Twenty-eight states authorized arrest without a warrant where the officer had probable cause to believe that a domestic violence misdemeanor had been committed, nineteen states permitted arrest without a warrant if there was probable cause to believe a protective order had been violated, and fourteen states permitted warrantless arrest in both these situations. *Id.*

A different approach was taken in Oregon, where the state Coalition Against Domestic and Sexual Violence proposed, and the legislature in 1977 adopted, the first "mandatory arrest" law, requiring police to arrest when there was probable cause to believe that someone had committed an assault, or put a victim with a restraining order in fear of imminent serious physical injury. OR. REV. STAT. § 133.055(2), § 133.310(3) (1989). Originally the statute provided that police need not arrest if the victim objected, but this provision was eliminated in 1981 because it was being used by police to undermine the mandatory arrest provisions. By 1982, five states required police to arrest where probable cause existed to believe that a misdemeanor had been committed or a restraining order violated, and by 1992 fifteen states had adopted mandatory arrest for domestic violence misdemeanors, and nineteen for protective order violations.

What accounts for this flurry of legislative activity reversing well-established policing policy? In no small measure, the widespread adoption of mandatory arrest provisions can be attributed to a single highly influential study, conducted by Lawrence Sherman and Richard Berk, and publish-ed in 1984. Called the Minneapolis Domestic Violence Experiment, it was the first controlled, randomized test of the effectiveness of arrest for any offense, and the results showed that arrest cut in half the risk of future assaults against the same domestic violence victim during a 6 month follow up period, when measured against either separating the couple, or mediat-ing between the partners. This study was then highlighted by the U.S. Attorney General's Task Force on Family Violence, in a 1984 report which stressed the importance of treating family violence as a criminal activity. Although the authors of the Minneapolis study themselves recommended against the adoption of mandatory arrest policies until further studies had been conducted, the momentum of these early findings overrode caution.

In 1986 and 1987, the National Institute for Justice funded six replica-tion experiments, although none were identical to the original Minneapolis experiment. The results of these newer studies have significantly clouded the issue, to the point where Lawrence Sherman, co-author of the original study, has urged that mandatory arrest laws be repealed. What follows are findings and recommendations from their research in 1996.

Janell D. Schmidt and Lawrence W. Sherman
Does Arrest Deter Domestic Violence? in Do ARRESTS AND RESTRAINING ORDERS WORK? (E.S. Buzawa and C.G. Buzawa, eds. 1996)

Choosing between the lesser of two evils is best guided by the following summary of the facts and dilemmas gleaned from the domestic violence research published to date....

1. *Arrest reduces domestic violence in some cities but increases it in others.* It is not clear from current research how officials in any city can know which effect arrest is likely to have in their city. Cities that do not adopt an arrest policy may pass up an opportunity to help victims of domestic violence. But cities that do adopt arrest policies—or have them imposed by state law—may catalyze more domestic violence than would otherwise occur. Either choice entails a possible moral wrong.

2. *Arrest reduces domestic violence among employed people but in-creases it among unemployed people.* Mandatory arrest policies may thus protect working-class women but cause greater harm to those who are poor. Conversely, not making arrests may hurt working women but reduce violence against economically poor women. Similar trade-offs may exist on the basis of race, marriage, education and neighborhood. Thus, even in cities where arrest reduces domestic violence overall, as an unintended side effect it may increase violence against the poorest victims.

3. *Arrest reduces domestic violence in the short run but may increase it in the long run.* Three-hour arrests in Milwaukee reduced the 7% chance that a victim would be battered as soon as the police left to a 2% chance of being battered when the spouse returned from jail. But over the course of 1 year, those arrests doubled the rate of violence by the same suspects. No

arrest means more danger to the victim now, whereas making an arrest may mean more danger of violence later for the same victim or for someone else. . . .

To some, the choice between two wrongs invokes despair and inaction. Yet, policing domestic violence may not be hopeless. Careful review of the policy implications, combined with the freedom to test alternative policies, can lead to more effective solutions. Use of the best information . . . to date guides the following five policy recommendations:

1. *Repeal mandatory arrest laws.* The most compelling implication of these findings is to challenge the wisdom of mandatory arrest. States and cities that have enacted such laws should repeal them, especially if they have substantial ghetto poverty populations with high unemployment rates. These are the settings in which mandatory arrest policies are most likely to backfire. It remains possible but unlikely that mandatory arrest creates a general deterrent effect among the wider public not arrested. Even if it does, however, increased violence among unemployed persons who are arrested is a serious moral stain on the benefits of general deterrence. The argument that arrest expresses the moral outrage of the state also appears weak if the price of that outrage is increased violence against the same victims.

2. *Substitute structured police discretion.* Instead of mandating arrest in cases of misdemeanor domestic violence, state legislatures should mandate that each police agency develop its own list of approved options to be exercised at the discretion of the officer. Legislatures might also mandate 1 day of training each year to ensure that discretion is fully informed by the latest research available. The options could include allowing victims to decide whether their assailants should be arrested, transporting victims to shelters, or taking the suspects to an alcohol detoxification center.

3. *Allow warrantless arrests.* Whereas mandatory arrest has become the major issue in some states, warrantless arrest remains an issue in others. . . . The success of arrest in some cities suggests that every state should add this option to the police tool kit. Deciding when to use it can then become a matter of police policy based on continuing research and clinical experience, rather than on the massive effort required to change state law.

4. *Encourage issuance of arrest warrants for absent offenders.* The landmark Omaha experiment suggests that more domestic violence could be prevented by this policy than by any offender-present policy. The kinds of people who flee the scene might be more deterrable than those who stay. A prosecutor willing to issue warrants and a police agency willing to serve them can capitalize on that greater deterrability. If the Omaha warrant experiment can be replicated in other cities—a very big if—then the warrant policy might actually deter more violence than do arrests of suspects who are still present. Because it will likely be years before more research on the question is done, such policies should be adopted now. They can easily be discarded later if they are found to be harmful or ineffective.

NOTES AND QUESTIONS

1. **Recent Research.** The most recent data on mandatory arrest policies suggest that they can deter subsequent violence. Findings from a study of the National Institute of Justice's Spouse Assault Replication Program (SARP), using pooled data from previous studies and addressing some methodological problems from earlier research, show that mandatory arrest policies may deter subsequent violence. In particular, the study found that there was no association between arresting the offender and an increased risk of subsequent aggression against women. Thus, the study concludes that arresting male batterers may reduce subsequent violence. But consider another conclusion they reached:

> [O]ur research showed that a majority of suspects discontinued their aggressive behaviors even without an arrest. This suggests that policies requiring arrest for all suspects may unnecessarily take a community's resources away from identifying and responding to the worst offenders and victims most at risk ... Although there may be other benefits from policies requiring arrest that this research has not measured (including general deterrence), there are also likely costs of using arrests every time the police respond to an incident of partner violence. Further research in this area needs to assess the benefits and costs of arresting all suspects before there can be a systematic conclusion or preferred or mandatory arrest policies.... Christopher D. Maxwell, Joel H. Garner and Jeffrey A. Fagan, *The Effects of Arrest on Intimate Partner Violence: New Evidence From the Spouse Assault Replication Program*, NATIONAL INSTITUTE OF JUSTICE (2001).

This most recent research is consistent with the research on batterers that we read in Chapter Two, suggesting that all men are not equally abusive, and may not present the same risks of recidivism. However, it can be very difficult for the police to ascertain who is the most dangerous and under what circumstances.

2. **The Purpose of Arrest.** Studies on the effects of arrest have dealt almost exclusively with whether or not arrest reduces recidivism. However, there may be other reasons for arresting abusers, including, as noted above, general deterrence. There have been no studies to date that have measured whether the risk of arrest reduces violence against women overall. Such studies would be difficult to conduct as it is hard to isolate arrest as a causal factor in light of the general social and cultural shift to treat domestic violence as a more serious crime.

3. **Differences Among Abusers.** In the 1990s, researchers found that arrest is more likely to deter the employed. Why might this be? Is it that middle and working class men have more to lose by being arrested than those men who are already marginalized by society? Does the fact that arrest is less likely to deter the unemployed increase the risks of ongoing violence for their partners? Yet, if we were to have different policies for different groups, wouldn't that undermine the law's effectiveness and legitimacy overall? Keep these questions in mind as we explore both prosecution and punishment issues later in this chapter.

4. **Warrantless Arrest Statutes.** One of the recommendations from Buzawa, Austin and Buzawa, cited above, was that states adopt warrantless arrest statutes. Because most acts of domestic violence are generally simple assault and battery, a misdemeanor, officers had no authority to arrest unless the offense took place in their presence. This meant that most abusers were never arrested. Beginning in the mid–1980's, states began passing laws allowing for warrantless arrests in domestic violence situations when the police have probable cause that a domestic assault took place. By 2000, all states adopted warrantless arrest statutes.

5. **Police Discretion and Factors in Arrest.** Despite Buzawa, Austin & Buzawa's recommendation to repeal mandatory arrest laws, jurisdictions continue to implement preferred and mandatory arrest policies. The goal of these policies is to remove discretion from the police when deciding whether to make an arrest.

Subsequent studies have suggested that police are more likely to make an arrest of the abuser when someone other than the victim called the police. This is arguably because when bystanders become involved, the violence is no longer a private family matter but now a public disturbance. The presence of weapons, injuries, and children also increase the likelihood that the batterer will be arrested. See, Eve S. Buzawa and Carl G. Buzawa, *Factors Affecting Police Response*, in DOMESTIC VIOLENCE: THE CRIMINAL JUSTICE RESPONSE (2003).

6. **Victim's Role in Arrest.** In the choice between mandatory and pro-arrest policies, one important consideration is whether victim choice should be considered in the decision whether to arrest. Given what we have studied about the dynamics of abusive relationships and the complicated nature of victims' lives, it is understandable that a victim may not want her abuser arrested. Some commentators argue that, despite concerns about victim safety, victim preferences should be honored in arrest decisions, in part because victims themselves have a better sense of what will keep them safe then do the police. See Eve S. Buzawa and Carl G. Buzawa, *Arrest is No Panacea*, in CURRENT CONTROVERSIES ON FAMILY VIOLENCE (R.G. Gelles and D.R. Loseke eds. 1993). Buzawa and Buzawa also look at material reasons arrest may not be preferable, including the loss of family income, the social stigma of arrest, and the mistrust of the police, especially among minority communities.

7. **Empowerment or Disempowerment?** On the question of whether mandatory arrest ultimately disempowers women in abusive relationships, opinions even within the battered women's movement are divided. As you have seen, Joan Zorza, an experienced advocate for battered women in both family and criminal law contexts, supports mandatory arrest. Others oppose both mandatory arrest and no-drop prosecution policies. Evan Stark acknowledges the "dilemma" posed by mandatory arrest, and yet concludes that the advantages of mandatory arrest outweigh the costs:

> The conflicting realities of coercive control and empowerment through victim preference raise what is undoubtedly the most difficult dilemma about mandatory arrest. Too often in women's lives, the question of who speaks in their name has been dealt with fatuously. For battered

women, in particular, there is no more important issue in recovery than the restoration of "voice"; the essence of empowerment, we like to say, is allowing women to make the *wrong* decision. At the same time, and although all choices are constrained by an implicit calculus of costs and benefits to a certain extent, for women who are seriously injured or for those whose decisions reflect ignorance of their danger or psychological, material, economic, or racial deprivation, it is hard to see how the benefits of individual choice outweigh the social interest in stopping the use of illegitimate power. Only in situations where there are no injuries and where there is an expressed desire *not* to arrest despite probable cause to believe an assault has taken place is it likely that the arrest decision will be experienced as demeaning. Because this profile may describe the *most* as well as the least dangerous situations, I would prefer to mandate arrest than leave assessment to police. Evan Stark, *Mandatory Arrest of Batterers: A Reply to Its Critics*, in DO ARRESTS AND RESTRAINING ORDERS WORK? (E.S. Buzawa and C.G. Buzawa eds. 1996).

8. **Gay and Lesbian Battering and Mandatory Arrest.** It is important to keep in mind that most studies of arrest policies focus exclusively on heterosexual couples. How might mandatory arrest policies affect same-sex couples? Consider the following critiques:

As with all marginalized groups, such as the queer community, one must seek legal protection through other avenues when one has been alienated by the legal community such as access to police services.

However, abused lesbians find it difficult to rely on the police because of the history of police misconduct within the queer community. It is not unreasonable for the victim to decide not to report the abuse because she assumes that law enforcement will be unsympathetic, or even hostile, to her abusive situation. In addition, the battered lesbian fears the possibility of exposing herself to further victimization and harassment from the legal community because of her sexual identity. For instance, "[o]ne woman ... reported ... that when she told police officers, and later the assistant district attorney, about her partner's abusive behavior, they 'drooled' and 'snickered' when they heard that she was a lesbian." "Another woman reported that her own attorney seemed more interested in the details of 'what two women did in bed' than in knowing and presenting the facts of the abuse." Moreover, the batterer may use the inadequacies of the legal system's response to same-sex abuse as a weapon of isolation, telling her victim that it is futile to turn to the police and courts for help. The reservations that the abused already has in seeking assistance from the legal community and the batterer capitalizing on the legal deficiencies in providing support to the battered lesbian both play an integral role in whether the abused will seek help from the police. Marnie J. Franklin, *The Closet Becomes Darker for the Abused: A Perspective on Lesbian Partner Abuse*, 9 CARDOZO WOMEN'S L.J. 299 (2003).

9. **Class and Arrest.** Another critic, Peter Manning, offers a class analysis of proarrest policies, arguing that they reflect an increasingly

"market-driven" conception of policing, and play to a middle-class audience, while targeting lower-class groups. While his assessment of the older conception of policing is consistent with Ferraro and Pope's account of policing in the context of a culture of power, he argues that this framework is under attack. Manning's critique also incorporates an extreme skepticism about any claimed deterrent effect for arrest.

> ... Growth in the demand for "law enforcement," and the transition of policing to a demand-focused "service" industry rationing its "services," is revealed in the police response to the movement to criminalize domestic conflict. Police are under pressure, some of it self-created, to make explicit their market strategy, how they differentially serve target groups and "submarkets," and manage demand. The police are moving away from an explicit egalitarian allocational and distributional function and toward a rationing, market-based corporate strategy that assumes a distributional bias. This strategy entails explicit service goals, sets differential levels of response, and seeks to manage demand. This strategy creates tensions and contradictions because the public position of 24–hour available response coupled with secret, private, discretionary rationing decisions is being replaced with reduced service, public statements of priorities, and explicit policies that ration police services. Quantitative measures of efficiency and effectiveness can become reified and be used to rationalize differentially serving needy and demanding groups. Peter K. Manning, *The Preventive Conceit: The Black Box in Market Context,* in DO ARRESTS AND RESTRAINING ORDERS WORK? (E.S. Buzawa and C.G. Buzawa eds. 1996).

10. **Mandatory Arrest and Race.** Barbara Fedders, a former volunteer of a community-based organization for battered women, once lobbied for mandatory arrest policies on the belief that arrests would have both a deterrent effect and express social condemnation of domestic violence. She reflected upon her position in the following excerpt.

> Illustrating the particular difficulties posed by the intersection of race and sex, many Black women active in domestic violence research, policy advocacy, and organizing have warned battered women against allowing themselves to be "guilt-tripped" by abusive men who accuse them of racism and betrayal for reporting them to the police. One scholar argues, "We have paid our dues, and black men must be held responsible for every injury they cause." Another activist asserts : "It's a copout for brothers to use the issue of racism to make us feel bad."
>
> Women must have the right to receive effective police assistance when they are suffering abuse, no matter from whom. This is particularly important for Black women, who face a historic presumption by police that their race predisposes them to enjoy violence. My argument is not that arrest for domestic violence in communities of color is always an inappropriate response. Rather, I am arguing that a mandatory arrest policy presents unique problems for women of color and poor women that have been largely overlooked by mandatory-arrest advocates. Barbara Fedders, *Lobbying for Mandatory–Arrest Policies: Race, Class,*

and the Politics of the Battered Women's Movement, 23 N.Y.U. REV. L. & SOC. CHANGE 281 (1997).

Jennifer Nash also criticizes the lack of "intersectionality" when analyzing the impact of domestic violence arrest policies. She is particularly concerned about the lack of privacy for black women. For white feminists, relinquishing privacy for safety may be a rational trade-off, but for black women who have little privacy to begin with, mandatory arrest laws may exacerbate their lack of rights. She argues:

> The black body is subject to an array of cultural, social, discursive, and legal forces which operate to hyper-survey and regulate it. Numerous theorists have examined the simultaneous hyper-visibility and invisibility of the black body in our cultural moment, rendering black subjects invisible from a panoply of cultural institutions and hyper-visible in the cultural association of blackness with criminality, poverty, and deviance. The hyper-visibility of the black body is most apparent in the fact that the black body is a critical subject of cultural and political discourse. That is, the black body is always public, a site of debate, concern, and scrutiny, because of its perceived link to "social ills" including crime, teenage pregnancy, and drugs, and because of the presumed "dysfunctionality" of the black subject....

> Because the black body is already seen as a public site, a space which is subject to cultural and legal hyper-regulation and hyper-surveillance, some theorists have asserted that the private is a site of particular importance for black subjects. That is, the home becomes a site where black subjects can seek refuge from the simultaneity of racism and sexism. The home also functions as a locus of safety and community-building, a space where black subjects can safely gather without the threat of racism. The importance of this radical conception of the private must be grappled with if feminists are to fully understand the consequences and repercussions of the blanket problematization of the private. In situating the private as a potentially radical site, it becomes apparent that feminists need to cultivate new, nuanced conceptions of the private, which simultaneously problematize the legacy of separate spheres ideology and its harm to female subjects as well as critique the generalized and simplified framing of the private as a site of singular and monolithic meaning. Jennifer C. Nash, *From Lavender to Purple: Privacy, Black Women, and Feminist Legal Theory*, 11 CARDOZO WOMEN'S L.J. 303 (2005).

11. **Stereotyping.** Nash and Fedders both make convincing arguments that advocates for battered women, who have largely been white and middle class, have not thoroughly understood the impact of aggressive arrest policies can have on women of color and poor women. Fedder suggests that this narrow perspective grows from the concern that linking race to either a batterer's propensity or a woman's experience with victimization, could perpetuate racist stereotypes. Do mandatory arrest policies evince a "white" bias? Would failure to arrest suggest that the criminal justice system is unwilling to protect poor women and women of color? How do mandatory arrest policies affect other communities? The following

readings examine further complications in deciding what police policy is best, and for whom.

12. **Immigrant Women and Arrest.** Consider how aggressive arrest statutes impact on immigrant women:

> Battered immigrant women's lack of trust in the system and its officers intersects with many other fears: fear of deportation, fear of retribution by abusers, fear of being the one arrested and separated from children, and fear of future economic, social and/or employability repercussions. These issues preclude many battered immigrant women from requesting the help they need to counter the domestic violence they experience in their lives. These barriers become even more pronounced when the batterer is a U.S. citizen and the victim is a non-citizen. Police officers are more likely to believe the citizen batterer when he contradicts the battered immigrant woman's accusations of violence. In many instances, the fact that battered immigrant women have no legal immigration status or documentation in the U.S. is a result of the batterer's use of the victim's immigration status as a weapon of abuse.

> In certain instances, the police in effect act as the gatekeepers to the judicial system. Their discretion is the determining factor in deciding whether immigrant victims will gain access to the system and be able to find protection from the violence perpetrated against them in their homes. In many cases, unfortunately, the most difficult hurdle for battered immigrant women is that of police indifference and inaction. This inaction can act as an almost impassable barrier for many battered immigrant women to overcome, leaving them trapped and without any legal remedies. Leslye E. Orloff, Mary Ann Dutton, Giselle Aguilar Hass, and Nawal Ammar, *Battered Immigrant Women's Willingness to Call for Help and Police Response*, 13 UCLA WOMEN'S L.J. 43 (2003).

Given these issues, Leslye Orloff and her colleagues conducted a study of the police response to battered immigrant Latina women and found that immigrant women did not call the police for help unless they had previously spoken to someone about the abuse. The authors suggest that this underscores the importance of community education and outreach to victims of domestic violence. They also note the grave need to increase bilingual staff and to train law enforcement and attorneys about immigration issues. Furthermore, immigrant women may fear arrest because of the consequences to their immigrant status. For a discussion of this issue, see Hannah R. Shapiro, *Battered Immigrant Women Caught in the Intersection of U.S. and Criminal or Immigration Laws: Consequences & Remedies*, 16 TEMP. INT'L & COMP. L.J. 27 (2002). The effect of immigration laws on immigrant women who experience domestic violence is discussed in Chapter Fifteen.

Dual Arrests

When the police do arrive at the scene, they must have probable cause to believe that a misdemeanor has been committed or a restraining order violated. Several commentators have suggested that police are less willing to find probable cause in the domestic violence context than in the context of other violent crimes. And, to the extent that police resent the reduction in discretion intended by mandatory arrest policies, some may find ways to subvert their implementation, or simply misunderstand the law's intent. One such strategy is the "dual arrest," where police claim to be unable to determine, on the scene, which party has been the aggressor, or whether one party has used force only in self-defense. Preferred and mandatory arrest policies certainly had the intended consequence of increasing domestic violence arrests overall. They also had the of the unintended consequences of increase in the number of "dual arrests." In California, for example, mandatory arrest policies increased arrests of men by 37%, and increased arrests of women by 446%. Overall, about 25% of those arrested for a domestic offense are women. The result of dual arrests is that many victims will be afraid to call the police for fear that they too will be arrested. At least twenty-four states have felt it necessary to respond to this development by enacting legislation specifically directing police to arrest only the primary physical aggressor or the party not responding in self-defense. Officers are required to take into account the relative injury of each party, their fear, and any history of abuse that can be ascertained when making an arrest. The Department of Justice, in making grants to states, has also a stated preference for laws which discourage dual arrests.

The issue of dual arrests raises a more fundamental issue we have already examined in other contexts: one of the unintended consequences of formal equality for women is that they may, in fact, be treated more harshly given the context of abuse. Dual arrest statutes at least attempt to adjust for that unintended consequence by requiring police to determine who is the primary aggressor rather than arrest both parties. On the other hand, these statutes may also reinforce notions of gender stereotyping—that women are weak and men aggressive, when, in fact, as we have seen, the gendered dynamics between intimate partners can be far more complicated.

The following case examines some of the underlying dynamics that happen during an arrest and raises the question of gender stereotyping and defendant's rights, questioning whether aggressive arrest statutes can go too far.

Wade v. Miles

Court of Appeals of Washington, 2001.
106 Wash. App. 1005.

Joel Wade appeals the summary dismissal of his claims against Deputy Michael Miles and King County for false arrest, false imprisonment, malicious prosecution and violation of civil rights under 42 U.S.C. § 1983. The claims arise from his arrest following an altercation with his wife. Because Deputy Miles had probable cause to arrest Wade and the deputy was entitled to qualified immunity and statutory immunity from suit, the trial court properly dismissed the claims. We affirm.

In July 1996, Deputy Michael Miles and Deputy Curt Lysen of the King County Sheriff's Office each drove to the home of Joel and Sandra Wade. They were responding to a 911 dispatch to investigate a domestic violence report. Deputy Miles was informed that Sandra had called 911 and reported that her husband Joel had assaulted her. Deputy Miles arrived at the Wade home first. Upon arrival, Deputy Miles got out of his car and Joel walked up to him. According to Deputy Miles, Joel then told him that Sandra had hit him with her car. Joel denies the conversation ever took place. When Deputy Lysen arrived a short time later, Deputy Miles told Joel to stay with Deputy Lysen as he wanted to speak to Sandra separately.

Deputy Miles found Sandra Wade sitting in the front seat of her car with Alena Lomax, a 15–year old babysitter, seated next to her on the passenger side. Sandra appeared emotional and distraught, and Deputy Miles observed that she had fresh scratch marks on the upper part of her chest. Sandra then told Deputy Miles what had precipitated her 911 call. Deputy Miles testified that he could not remember everything Sandra told him. But he did recall that she said her husband had struck her in the face through the open car window and grabbed her on the chest. Deputy Miles also asked Sandra whether she had run her husband over with her car to which she replied that she had not.

Deputy Miles next spoke to Lomax. When asked by Deputy Miles whether Sandra had run over Joel with her car, Lomax responded no. Lomax also confirmed that Joel had grabbed Sandra and caused the scratch marks on her chest. Deputy Miles then walked over to where Deputy Lysen was and told him to arrest Joel. Deputy Lysen was reluctant to do so and tried to explain to Deputy Miles that Joel was "a good guy" and that Sandra was "crazy." Deputy Miles then handcuffed Joel himself and placed him in Deputy Lysen's police car. During this time, Deputy Lysen spoke with Sandra and Lomax. Based on that conversation, Deputy Lysen agreed that Joel's arrest was warranted and then drove off with Joel in his police car. After Deputy Lysen and Joel left, Deputy Miles took formal statements from Sandra and Lomax separately. Both confirmed their earlier statements that Joel struck Sandra in the face and grabbed her on her chest, leaving scratch marks.

The State charged Joel with fourth degree assault. A jury acquitted him, finding that he had used lawful force in self-defense to try to stop Sandra from driving away while his right arm was stuck inside the car. Joel then commenced this action against King County, former Sheriff James Montgomery, Deputy Miles, and Sandra Wade. He alleges various causes of action. The pertinent ones for this appeal include false arrest, false imprisonment, malicious prosecution, and violation of civil rights ... The trial court granted certain defendants' motion for summary judgment, dismissing Joel's claims against all parties except Sandra on grounds of probable cause, qualified immunity, and statutory immunity....

Joel appeals.

Probable Cause

Joel first argues that the trial court erred as a matter of law in concluding that Deputy Miles had probable cause to arrest him because

Deputy Miles failed to investigate his version of the events leading to his arrest. There was probable cause to arrest Joel Wade. . . .

Police officers have a statutory duty . . . to take a suspect into custody if they have probable cause to believe the suspect committed an assault against a household or family member.

False arrest or false imprisonment is the unlawful violation of a person's right of liberty or the restraint of that person without legal authority. The existence of probable cause to arrest is a complete defense to an action for false arrest, false imprisonment, and malicious prosecution. Probable cause for warrantless arrests exists when an officer has reasonably trustworthy information sufficient to permit a person of reasonable caution to believe that an offense has been or is being committed. It is a reasonableness test, considering the time, place, and circumstances, and the officer's special expertise in identifying criminal behavior. Probability, not a prima facie showing of criminal activity, is the standard for probable cause. The question of whether a police officer had probable cause to arrest is generally one of fact. However, when the evidence conclusively establishes that the officer had probable cause to arrest, the court need not submit the issue to a jury and can make a determination as a matter of law.

The material facts concerning the arrest here are undisputed. Thus, for purposes of summary judgment, the legal question is whether Deputy Miles and the others are entitled to judgment as a matter of law.

Here, Deputy Miles was dispatched to the Wade home after being informed that Sandra had called 911 to report that her husband had assaulted her. Upon arrival, Deputy Miles observed that Joel was not injured while Sandra had fresh, red scratch marks below her neck. Both Sandra and Lomax stated that Joel had reached in the car and hit Sandra and both denied that Sandra had tried to hit Joel with the car. Under these circumstances, Deputy Miles had probable cause to believe that this was a domestic dispute in which Joel had assaulted Sandra. That necessitated Joel's arrest. . . . The trial court's determination of probable cause was proper.

Joel claims that Deputy Miles' alleged failure to interview Joel and listen to his version of the events precluded a determination that he was the "primary physical aggressor" . . . First, while it may be advisable for an officer to do so, the governing statute neither expressly nor implicitly requires that the officer interview each participant in a domestic dispute. Second, even if there was a requirement for an officer to interview each participant in a domestic dispute, express statutory factors support the deputy's decision that Joel was the primary physical aggressor in this case. In determining the primary physical aggressor, a police officer should consider:

(i)[t]he intent to protect victims of domestic violence under RCW 10.99.010; (ii) the comparative extent of injuries inflicted or serious threats creating fear of physical injury; and (iii) the history of domestic violence between the persons involved.

Here, factor (iii) is neutral. Deputy Miles had never met Sandra or Joel before, and there is no allegation of a history of domestic violence between them. But factors (i) and (ii) support the deputy's decision that Joel was the primary physical aggressor given that Sandra, rather than Joel, sustained physical injuries and appeared emotional and distraught. In short, she appeared to be the victim of domestic violence and entitled to the protection that the statute mandates—the arrest of Joel. . . .

NOTES AND QUESTIONS

1. **Determining the Primary Aggressor.** Police often have difficulty determining which party is the primary aggressor in these cases. In *Wade v. Miles*, the two responding police officers even seemed to disagree about what happened. What do you think might have happened were there not a primary aggressor statute? Would it have been inappropriate for the police to arrest both parties? Keep in mind that the jury acquitted Joel Wade, finding that he was not guilty. Do you think Joel was arrested primarily because he was a male? Should this sort of gender stereotyping be grounds for a civil rights action?

2. **Dual Arrests and Police Training for Same–Sex Couples.** Many police officers receive training to help them determine which party is the primary aggressor. The following is an example of how some police departments are dealing with the problems of dual arrests in same-sex relationships:

> As a result of the inability to readily discern which party is the aggressor in gay and lesbian domestic abuse situations, police often react by either arresting both parties or arresting neither, and courts often issue mutual restraining orders. This presents grave consequences to the victims of domestic violence in that it perpetuates the belief that the abuse involves mutual combat in addition to undermining the attempts made by the victim in seeking out legal protections.

> Recent efforts have been made in many large cities to raise awareness of the intricacies involved in same-sex domestic violence cases by local police departments. San Diego's City Attorney's Domestic Violence Unit is one good example. San Diego is at the forefront of same-sex domestic violence prosecution and currently employs one full-time prosecutor and one part-time advocate who are solely assigned to handle these types of cases. In addition, it is not uncommon for prosecutors in the City Attorney's Office to ride along with law enforcement personnel responding to domestic violence calls in areas with large gay and lesbian populations to see these issues firsthand. In addition, the City of San Diego has recently completed production of a training video on the issue of gay and lesbian domestic violence, which will be viewed by the entire patrol force of the San Diego Police Department. Likewise, in cities such as New York, Los Angeles, and Seattle, police are trained in a similar manner. Michelle Aulivola, *Outing Domestic Violence: Affording Appropriate Protections to Gay and Lesbian Victims*, 42 FAM. CT. REV. 162 (2004).

3. **Police Immunity.** Washington is one of many states that grant police officers immunity from civil liability for actions resulting from responding to a domestic violence incident. Consider if Sandra Wade had been arrested along with Miles. Should she be able to sue the police for a violation of her civil rights if they fail to determine the primary aggressor? We will take up this subject in more detail in Chapter Fourteen, but for now, contemplate what recourse a victim should have if she is arrested even though she may have been acting in self-defense.

4. **Tort Actions by Abusers.** Keep in mind that in *Wade v. Miles*, Joel Wade is also suing Sandra Wade for false arrest. The court did not dismiss that lawsuit and thus allowed that claim to proceed to trial. We will take up the question of tort law relative to domestic violence incidents in Chapter Thirteen.

5. **Police Investigation of Domestic Violence Incidents.** Another crucial police function is the investigation and reporting of incidents of domestic violence, even in cases where the perpetrator is not arrested or prosecuted. Unless an incident is reported, the victim has no back-up for any subsequent assertion that she was abused, and the city, county or state has no way to document the incidence of domestic violence, or determine what priority it should be accorded in the allocation of resources. Unless an incident is thoroughly investigated, and the report made is as detailed and complete as possible, the prosecutor's task is made significantly more difficult, especially in cases where the victim is afraid to testify, or her abuser strongly contests her testimony.

Jurisdictions that have worked to develop model criminal justice responses to domestic violence have been attentive to this aspect of the police function. San Diego was among the first and most aggressive jurisdictions in investigating domestic violence.

Law enforcement protocols which address the need for comprehensive guidelines covering initial police response, preliminary investigation, evidence gathering, follow-up investigation, training, and advocacy are slowly emerging. According to Casey Gwinn and Anne O'Dell, the most effective approach appears to focus on two questions: (1) can we prove this case without the participation of the victim; and (2) if not, will the victim participate with law enforcement by testifying truthfully. This approach allows officers to focus on how to create a case even if the victim is too frightened and confused to cooperate, while not forgetting the importance of victim advocacy. The minimum investigation must include interviewing all children and adult witnesses, recording all statements of the victim, documenting all prior incidents, and taking photographs in order to allow prosecution to proceed even if the victim later becomes uncooperative. Casey G. Gwinn and Sgt. Anne O'Dell, *Stopping the Violence: The Role of the Police Officer and the Prosecutor*, 20 W. St. U. L. Rev. 297 (1993).

6. **Criminal Protective Orders.** After an abuser is arrested, he will be arraigned. If he is to be released either on bail or his own recognizance, the court can impose certain conditions of release, such as requiring that the defendant stay away from the victim until the trial. Unlike civil protection orders, which a court can impose at the victim's request, criminal protec-

tion orders are issued even if the victim does not want one. Violations of these orders can then result in new criminal charges against the defendant. Jeannie Suk, in *Criminal Law Comes Home*, 116 YALE L.J. 2 (2006), is highly critical of court-imposed protection orders, suggesting that they undermine victim autonomy and give the state far too much control over the dynamics of personal relationships. What troubles Suk most is that defendants face criminal penalties merely for "going home." For a response to Suk's article, see Cheryl Hanna, *Because Breaking Up is Hard to Do*, 116 YALE L.J. POCKET PART 92 (2006). Hanna argues that such orders are necessary, if only to give the victim some breathing room to decide what it is that she wants to do. She emphasizes that in times of crisis, none of us are clear about what we want, and thus victim safety and long-term autonomy are paramount. We will see these tensions again when discussing no-drop policies in the next section.

7. **Legislative Reform.** Assume that you are a state legislator who wants to draft a statute ensuring that victims of domestic violence receive adequate protection. What kind of policy would you implement? Would you consider a mandatory arrest policy or leave arrests to police discretion? What kind of training should your officers be given? How would you deal with the problems of dual arrest, especially in gay and lesbian and immigrant communities? In crafting this legislation, whose input would you seek?

C. PROSECUTION POLICIES

Introduction

Prosecutors often failed to initiate charges or follow through with prosecution, in large part because victims did not want to proceed for many of the same reasons that victims did not want their abusers arrested. Once proactive arrest policies were in place, however, prosecutors faced increasing pressure not to simply drop these cases when the victim was reluctant to proceed. Further, the media began following domestic violence cases more closely, especially after the murder of Nicole Brown Simpson in 1994, and the subsequent trial of her husband, football star O.J. Simpson. See Elizabeth M. Schneider, *What Happened to Public Education About Domestic Violence?* in POSTMORTEM: THE O.J. SIMPSON CASE (J. Abramson, ed. 1996). There was a growing sense among the public and prosecutors that it was preferable to intervene early in domestic violence cases, rather than wait for a homicide to occur. In addition, federal legislation, including the Violence Against Women Act of 1994, encouraged more aggressive prosecutions. Finally, and perhaps most importantly, an ever increasing number of women graduated from law school and became district attorneys. This generation of women brought with them different perspectives of women's concerns, and often were the leaders prompting internal change within their offices.

The most important, and controversial, change in prosecution policies involves the question of whether to proceed in a case when the victim is reluctant or refuses to proceed. Many jurisdictions began implementing more progressive approaches to domestic violence, including implementing evidence-based prosecutions in which the victim's testimony was no longer the sole or primary source of evidence, and thus proceeding regardless of the victim's wishes. This section focuses primarily on these approaches to prosecuting domestic violence and the controversies surrounding them.

The first case in this section is atypical as it involves another football star, Jim Brown, who was accused of abusing his wife. Yet, in many respects, it also represents the more typical case as it involved misdemeanor, not felony charges, and the state decided to proceed despite Monique Brown's resistance to go forward. It is also a good example of an evidence-based prosecution and highlights many of the tensions of aggressive approaches to prosecution.

People v. Brown

Appellate Department, Superior Court of California, 2001.
117 Cal.Rptr.2d 738.

■ LEE, J.

On July 1, 1999, appellant was charged in a misdemeanor complaint with violating Penal Code sections 422 (terrorist threat-count I) and 594, subdivision (a) (vandalism-count II). Appellant pled not guilty to both charges.

After a jury trial lasting approximately three weeks, the jury acquitted appellant of the terrorist threat charge, but convicted him of vandalism. Appellant was thereafter initially sentenced to three years' summary probation under various terms and conditions, including completing a 12–month batterer's counseling program and paying $1,500 to a battered women's shelter. Appellant rejected the terms of probation, however, and was then sentenced to six months in jail and a restitution fine of $100. Appellant's driver's license was also suspended for one year. This appeal timely followed. . . .

Prosecution's Case–in–Chief

Prior to the prosecution's first witness being called to the stand on August 31, 1999, the tape of Monique Brown's 911 telephone call on June 15, 1999, a transcript of the tape, and a computer printout that accompanied the tape, were received into evidence. The tape was played for the jury.

1.   Fernando Montes De Oca.

The prosecution then called its first witness, Fernando Montes De Oca. He testified that he was an officer with the Los Angeles Police Department assigned to the Hollywood Division. He was on patrol with his partner, Officer Lauraine Arellano, on June 15, 1999, about 5:15 p.m., when he responded to a domestic violence call ... The dispatch information also reported that there was a gun inside the location, the suspect had vandalized a car with the shovel, the "suspect threatened to kill" the woman, and that there was a "history of domestic violence."

... As they drove up, the woman, Monique Brown (hereafter Monique), accompanied by a dog, came outside the gate of the residence to meet them. She appeared visibly upset, had obviously been crying, and was nervous and shaken. She told the officers that she and her husband, James Nathaniel Brown (hereafter appellant), had become involved in a verbal dispute about the latter's infidelity. The argument took place in their bedroom and became very heated. As she was about to leave, appellant told her that he was going to kill her by snapping her neck. She stated that she then left the house and went to their garage. Appellant followed her into the garage. He picked up a shovel and began to strike her vehicle. Afraid for her safety, Monique left and went to the neighbors ... to call 911.

Montes De Oca stated that during the 15 to 20 minutes he spoke with Monique at the scene, she was upset, teary, and fearful, but very cooperative, rational, and coherent. Monique asked that the officers stand by while she went to retrieve some personal items of clothing. She stated she wanted to go back to New York.

Monique also recounted to the officers her history of domestic abuse with appellant, stating there had been prior domestic violence incidents involving physical confrontations during their two-year marriage that she had never reported to the police. The officer stated, over defense counsel's objection, that in his opinion, Monique was credible.

Montes De Oca stated that he asked Monique if there were any weapons in the house. She answered that a handgun was kept in a drawer next to the bed. She also stated that appellant had been drinking. The officer then informed Monique that the police could not simply stand by while she retrieved clothing, and that since a crime had been committed, they could not just leave. Upon being given this information, Monique did not change any part of her earlier statements to the police.

The officer stated that nine units showed up on this domestic violence call, which was customary given the nature of the call, namely, a domestic violence dispute with a gun and a threat to kill the victim reported in the broadcast. Montes De Oca stated he did not know the husband was Jim Brown, the celebrity, until about 15 minutes after he arrived.

Montes De Oca testified the officers devised a plan to call appellant and have him step outside his home, without anything in his hands, and walk up the driveway of his residence at 1851 Sunset Plaza Drive, at which time he would be taken into custody. When they made the telephone call, however, no one answered the telephone. Fearing a possible worst-case scenario, the officers stationed themselves outside the residence for a potential barricade situation. The lieutenant in charge at the scene, however, decided to simply go up to the front door and knock on it. A total of six officers went to the door, including Montes De Oca and his partner, Arellano.

Appellant answered the knock at the door. He was advised of the situation by the officers, told to turn around, and arrested. Appellant was very calm and cooperative. Montes De Oca and Arellano then went into the bedroom to locate and retrieve the gun. They located the gun where Monique had stated, namely, inside the drawer, and it was loaded, with one round in the chamber. Next to the gun were two knives and a box of ammunition.

Montes De Oca also testified that he observed Monique's car that evening. He stated it was a white Honda, located in the garage, and all the windows were "busted out." There were also dents all over the vehicle. Next to the car on the floor of the garage was a shovel. He then identified for the jury the shovel that he had seen that night in the garage. He also identified a photograph of the car's license plate, as well as several photographs showing the damage to the car. All the foregoing items were received into evidence. Montes De Oca stated that he did verify that evening that the car belonged to Monique, through a Department of Motor Vehicles printout reflecting the owner as Latifa Gunthrop, which was Monique's maiden name.

On cross-examination, Montes De Oca testified that Monique told him that appellant never swung, or threatened to swing, the shovel at her. He also acknowledged that Monique did not want to sign a complaint that day against appellant, and that appellant was arrested for a felony. When shown a photograph of the car taken on the day of the incident, the officer acknowledged that the front window was not broken.

2.   Jerry Janecek.

. . . When they arrived at the station, Monique and the dog were taken into the captain's office. The captain was on vacation at the time, and his office was the only place big enough for Monique and the dog. Detective Brian Gasparian came in and began to interview Monique. Monique cried periodically and answered his questions quietly and in a cooperative manner. Janecek was in and out of the office, sometimes getting water for Monique and her dog, another time getting tissues after Monique began to cry. Janecek's job was to take care of the dog. While he was in the office, he observed Monique answering questions freely and cooperatively.

When she told Gasparian about prior incidents of violence, she would cry periodically, but she did not appear reluctant to discuss these matters. After the interview was concluded, Janecek went to get an emergency protective order for Monique, a customary police procedure in a domestic violence call. Although the officer stated that the emergency protective order was not mandatory, he felt that it was necessary in light of appellant's threat to kill his wife. Monique was then taken back to her house. The officer stated when the subject of a shelter or some other place to go came up, Monique stated she had only one place to go.

The officers took Monique back to her house and stood by while she packed up a few things to take to a hotel. While she was packing her things, the officers talked with appellant's daughter. After Monique finished, she got her keys to the white Honda and put her things into the car. She then got into the car and drove away. The officers followed her down to Sunset. They did not know which hotel Monique was going to.

[The prosecution then called three other witnesses. Officer Lauraine Arellano, who was the first officer to respond to the scene. Based on her experience responding to hundreds of domestic violence calls, she found Monique Brown to be coherent and rational. The next witness authenticated a videotape of the scene of the incident. The third witness, Lieutenant Michael Albanese, responded to the scene to ensure that proper procedures were followed.]

6.   Monique Brown.

The prosecution called Monique as its next witness. She stated her true name was Latifa Monique Brown, and that her birth name was Latifa Monique Gunthrop. She testified that she had been married to appellant for two years. She was 23 years old when she married appellant, who was then 61 years old. Her occupation was director of operations for Ameri–Can Program, Inc., as well as the secretary/treasurer for the Ameri–Can Foundation for Social Change. Ameri–Can Program, Inc., is a corporation solely owned by appellant. Ameri–Can's office is in their home at 1851 Sunset Plaza Drive. Since her marriage, appellant provided for Monique financially, which included a monthly salary working for Ameri–Can. She was in her third year at Santa Monica Community College.

She stated that on June 15, 1999, she made a 911 call from a neighbor's house located at 1825 Sunset Plaza Drive. She did not recall the neighbor's name, in that this was the first time they had met. She stated that she told the 911 operator her husband was inside the house and had broken the car windows with a shovel. She said she told the operator that she had not been hit. She remembered telling the operator to "[p]lease be respectful. There is no danger there. I am fine." She claimed she made this statement at the end of the call. When asked if it would refresh her recollection if the prosecutor played the tape, she replied, "No, it would not because it's not on the tape." Shortly thereafter, however, she stated this language was on that portion of the tape that the transcript labeled "inaudible." She stated that although she felt free to answer the telephone operator's questions, the operator was leading her and "the tone was being set." Monique testified that immediately after she completed the 911 call, she called her home to speak with appellant, but no one answered.

Monique stated that she had an argument with appellant that day because she suspected him of having an affair. The matter had been building up for six months, and she confronted him. When asked by the prosecutor if she told Detective Gasparian that the argument was also about her inviting a male friend from school named Jack to stay in the residence and problems had been brewing for a few days, Monique stated that she did not recall. She did say that she invited Jack, a friend from Ohio, to spend a weekend in the house because he needed to take a test at the police academy that weekend. Monique stated she thought that she did tell Gasparian that the actual argument started on June 13, 1999, over Jack's staying the weekend, but she had also said the incident had been building up since appellant's best friend, George Hughley, died in February. She told Gasparian that appellant had been withdrawn, depressed, crying, and drinking. She stated that she did not tell Gasparian that appellant had tried to start a fight with her that morning over Jack's staying at the house.

Monique testified that she had an argument with appellant on June 13, 1999, when she returned from rollerblading at Venice Beach with Jack. When she returned, she found appellant in bed crying. Appellant was angry, not because she had been rollerblading with Jack, but because she had left the house in the middle of their argument, which he deemed disrespectful. She stated that she did not tell Gasparian that appellant had thrown things or broken things, or that appellant had grabbed a cane and began beating the bed with the cane. When asked later if she had told Gasparian that appellant became angry in the argument and took the cane and began beating the bed, she acknowledged that she had said "something to that effect, but I don't remember exactly." Although he was beating the bed with the cane yelling at her, it did not scare her. She stated that although she told the detective that it scared her and appellant was yelling, "[H]ow dare you bring another man into the house," such statements were not true.

She had testified that she did not remember telling Gasparian that appellant told her that he had to pray to God so he would not kill her and Jack, but she remembered saying something to the effect that he said he had to pray to find peace "because of the things I had been coming at him with." She did admit telling Gasparian that appellant had told her that he had to drink to pass out so he could avoid killing her and Jack, but this statement to Gasparian was not true. Although appellant had been drinking that day, she had never seen him drink except socially, until this one incident. Monique stated appellant had to drink "to find peace to calm his mind because I had been coming at him with all these crazy accusations. . . ."

She acknowledged that appellant did tell her on the evening of June 13 that the marriage was over. She did not recall if appellant told her to go back to Buffalo. She stated her only blood relative in Los Angeles was a 12–year–old niece. Monique testified that although she stayed at a hotel that night, she did not have to.

She stated that she returned from the hotel on June 14, 1999. Later that day she told appellant that she had reserved a flight to Buffalo. He responded that she did not have to go, and she spent the night at the house. The next day, however, on Tuesday, June 15, she told appellant that she was not going to take it anymore and the marriage was over. She felt that appellant was having an affair, while appellant felt that it was disrespectful to have another man in the house. She felt, however, that Jack was just a "scapegoat" and an "excuse."

She then testified that the argument was really about appellant's plan to go to Miami, which is where she thought the other woman was. This was the final straw, according to Monique, because she thought he had been carrying on a relationship with this woman for six months. She stated that although appellant had been drinking on June 13, he was not drinking on June 15. Appellant was on the bed in the bedroom watching television, and during the argument his emotional demeanor was indifference; he was extremely passive.

She became very angry, and she called him names and yelled at him. Appellant shifted the conversation away from his alleged infidelity to Monique's rollerblading with Jack, which he felt was a sign of disrespect to appellant. Appellant continued to lie on the bed; he did not get angry and only slightly raised his voice. Monique told appellant, "[F]uck this, I'm not taking this shit," all in an effort to provoke some type of response. She told him that she was leaving. Appellant continued to watch television, so she picked up the remote and turned the set off.

Monique said that appellant never threatened to kill her by snapping her neck. Also, she stated she never went to her car; rather, she and her dog, Cruiser, walked up the driveway. About 30 to 40 seconds after she left the house, she heard the front door open, and she turned and saw appellant. He was yelling and appeared angry and upset. He yelled, "[W]hat the hell is wrong with you? Get out." He looked at Monique and said, "I'm going to break out these fucking car windows." Appellant went to the side entrance of the garage. Monique stated that she yelled at him, "[G]o ahead, you son of a bitch," and "it's your car, I don't give a shit, you're going to have to pay for it." She testified that the white Honda was not her car. She initially stated that she did see appellant breaking windows, but then immediately changed her testimony and asserted that she never saw him breaking windows. When shown the registration which listed her as the registered owner of the white Honda, she acknowledged that it did, in fact, list her as the registered owner.

Monique testified that she went immediately to a neighbor's house from the driveway. She knew to tell the 911 operator that appellant beat her car with a shovel because, as she was walking up the hill, she saw him reaching for the shovel. Therefore, she assumed he used the shovel. She stated that the shovel was not inside the garage by the white Honda. When asked if she thought she had a choice when appellant told her he was going to break her "fucking windows," Monique stated that he never threatened to break out the windows of her car, and that she did not care if he broke out windows. She stated, "I gave him permission because any type of reaction, I felt, would get him to the level of where he would admit to his affair." Although appellant had come out of the house angry and yelling, and had threatened to break out the windows of the car, Monique was never afraid. . . .

Monique testified that, in fact, there had never been any incidents of domestic violence.

She did acknowledge that there was one prior occasion where she left the house and went to a neighbor's and called a friend, "but not out of any fear." She stated that on that occasion she and appellant had argued about their business and how it should be run. When she got to the neighbor's house, she called George and Shirley Hughley, who came and took her to their home. She spent the night at the Hughley house and returned home after a day or so. The Hughleys acted like mediators between her and appellant. . . .

Monique was then cross-examined by appellant's counsel. She stated that the white Honda belonged to the corporation and was used to transport children, but because they did not want the company to become liable if there were any accidents, the car was transferred to her name. She identified a certificate of title showing the car was owned by the corporation in 1994. She stated that for insurance purposes title was transferred to her before she married appellant.

When asked why she told appellant he could break the windows on the car, she stated she was very frustrated and it was "like a dare." When he told her he intended to break the windows, she gave him permission. She stated that the money to repair the car came from the corporation. She stated she had been trying to provoke appellant the entire day of June 15, because he was not taking her seriously.

Because her yelling and telling him to break the windows had not worked, Monique stated that she felt desperate, hurt, and humiliated. She wanted appellant to feel the pain that she was feeling. She stated that she loved and respected her husband, but she would never let him abuse her.

Monique testified that she met her husband on a television show where she was doing some modeling. She became an employee of the Ameri–Can corporation. The Ameri–Can Education Program is a 15–chapter life management skills curriculum that deals with the responsibility of self-determination. She acted as a facilitator or teacher of the Ameri–Can Program while she was doing commercial modeling and working in a law firm as a legal secretary. Monique stated that while appellant provided the vision for Ameri–Can, she actually ran the corporation.

She stated that she was the person in the house who broke things. For months she had been confronting her husband about her suspicion of his infidelity, but she would back off periodically because of concerns about his grief for his friend. Appellant would ask her not to take advantage of his grieving. At one point Monique got angry when he left the house, and she threw glasses against the wall and broke a lamp. She also broke some other things in the bedroom. The incidents occurred probably a few weeks before the June 15 incident. Appellant was not present when she broke these items.

Monique stated that she was never scared during their arguments, even though he was larger than she was, because he had never laid a hand on her and she had no reason to think he ever would. Around June 15, she was worried about appellant's infidelity so she mentioned Jack to "push his buttons," to upset and provoke him. She stated that she knew that going rollerblading with Jack on June 13 would upset appellant. When she heard on June 15 that he was going to Miami, she "just snapped. . . ."

On redirect, Monique stated that she told Gasparian that she gave appellant permission to strike her car. She stated that the first time she publicly stated she gave such permission was on Larry King Live on August 14, 1999, and before that she and appellant had held various press conferences in their home. When asked by the prosecutor if it was correct that she never mentioned allegedly giving appellant permission to strike her Honda on Geraldo Live on July 12, 1999, Monique answered "Yes, that's correct." She acknowledged that she had stated on that television show that one of the reasons she had acted as she had that day, was due to premenstrual syndrome (hereafter PMS). Her own counsel elicited further information on her PMS medical ailment, to the effect that she becomes more sensitive and emotional in this condition. She testified that she would take certain vitamins and stay away from certain foods to help this condition, but she was not taking such steps on June 15....

[The prosecution also called other witnesses, including an expert who testified about the dynamics of abusive relationships and why Monique might be minimizing her testimony.]

Defense Case

1.   Kimberly Brown.

The first witness for appellant was Kimberly Brown, appellant's teenage daughter. She testified that on June 15, 1999, she heard Monique yelling and cursing at appellant. Kimberly went upstairs and looked out the window. From the window she observed appellant walking into the garage and Monique walking down the driveway with her dog. Kimberly next heard appellant talking to himself and glass breaking. She stated that Monique had lived with appellant and her for approximately five years, and during that time she had never seen Monique with a black eye or choke marks on her neck. She testified that she had never seen appellant standing over Monique with a metal spear and that there were no metal spears in the house. She never saw appellant commit or threaten violence upon Monique, and never heard Monique complain of such violence or threats of violence....

6.   Helene McDonald.

Helene McDonald, a medical doctor and licensed psychiatrist, was appellant's next trial witness. She testified that she conducted a psychiatric evaluation of Monique, which spanned 12 hours over the course of three days, and had reviewed various items, including the 911 tape, appellant's interview with the police, certain medical records, the crime scene report, and follow-up reports by Gasparian and McNeal. Her conclusion was that Monique met the criteria for a borderline personality disorder. People suffering from this condition cannot tolerate being alone, rejected, or abandoned. In relationships, they tend to continuously repeat a cycle of idealizing their mate, getting scared of intimacy, and then devaluing the person and rejecting him or her before being rejected first. Persons with borderline personality disorder have terrible mood swings and are irritable, impulsive, and lack reasoning and judgment when in an enraged state. Often they will take steps, sometimes unconsciously, to hurt or humiliate the man or woman in their lives because they fear abandonment.

McDonald stated that when appellant was grieving and withdrawn over the death of his friend, Monique felt abandoned and rejected. Monique told McDonald that she invited Jack to go rollerblading to make appellant angry and jealous. Later she called 911 because she felt bad and wanted appellant to feel the way she did. She also told McDonald that when appellant said he was going to break the car windows, she stated "go ahead," happy to finally get a reaction out of him. Later at the police station, Monique believed that appellant would certainly divorce her at this point, so she "created a scenario" to make it appear appellant had been abusive to her in the past. McDonald stated that, in her opinion, Monique's condition of borderline personality disorder had a very large and important impact on the events of June 15, and Monique was not faking a borderline personality disorder.

At the conclusion of McDonald's testimony, appellant rested. . . .

The jury began deliberations on September 9, 1999, at 9:00 a.m. At approximately 3:30 p.m. on September 10, 1999, the jury returned with a verdict finding appellant not guilty of count I (terrorist threat) and guilty of count II (vandalism).

Once the trial court indicated that it would impose domestic violence counseling as a mandatory probationary term, appellant's counsel stated that there was no need to discuss the other probationary terms. After appellant's rejection of probation, the court imposed the following sentence: six months in jail, a $100 restitution fine, and a suspension of his driver's license for one year.

Discussion

. . . Appellant contends that during the initial sentencing, the trial court abused its discretion by imposing "unauthorized" and "illegal" probationary terms. . . .

The trial court apparently gave some credence to appellant's "the car is the victim" contention and concluded domestic violence conditions were not mandatory, but rather only discretionary. We conclude, however, that the $200 payment and domestic violence counseling were mandatory probationary terms in this case. The position that the car was the victim, rather than appellant's wife, is inconsistent with common sense, as well as the language and purpose of the relevant statutes. No one would reasonably contend, for example, that if a person steals a wallet off a table, the wallet is the victim, not the owner of the wallet.

Even if appellant's version of the facts were accepted as true, appellant smashed out most of the windows in the car immediately after a domestic argument because he was "frustrated," and his wife was walking away at the time and heard the sound of glass breaking. The only reasonable inference from this evidence is that appellant's wife was a victim of the vandalism in a domestic violence setting. . . .

In summary, we conclude that the probationary terms requiring the $200 payment and attendance at domestic violence counseling were mandatory. Even if not mandatory, these provisions, as well as the other probationary terms, were well within the court's discretion. . . .

Finally, appellant contends that the trial court abused its discretion in imposing the maximum custody term of six months as "punishment" for his rejection of probation. It is settled that a criminal defendant has the right to refuse probation and undergo a sentence. . . .

Upon review of the record, it is clear that the trial court considered appellant's crime to be serious, in light of the evidence at trial, and one deserving of six months in jail. On January 5, 2000, counsel and the court had an in-chambers conference that was reported. When asked by appellant's counsel how much time appellant would receive if he rejected probation, and immediately after the prosecutor interjected that she would request the maximum sentence, the court stated: "Long before I heard the people's recommendation, long before anything came up in this case, after I heard the evidence, that was what I concluded an appropriate nonprobationary sentence would be. . . ."

Thus, the court had previously determined, after viewing the evidence and before appellant's possible rejection of probation ever came up, that six months in jail was appropriate. In later proceedings that day in open court, the court spoke further on the issue of an appropriate sentence, as follows:

"It's difficult for me to evaluate how to sentence a defendant who does refuse to accept probation. The first consideration is the nature of the crimes, and although the defense has repeatedly minimized this particular crime of vandalism as compared to others, in fact the contrary is true.

"I have not seen a crime of vandalism which compared to this. As I indicated, most crimes of vandalism are more properly described as malicious mischief, young people spray painting on a wall. This is a crime of extreme violence. In most cases, the monetary damage is minimal.

"There was a tremendous degree of violence involved, as I said. The crime was committed whether with rage, or mere frustration as Mr. Brown said, in my view, with the intent to have an impact on the victim. I don't know how anyone could conclude otherwise. It's beyond the mere property damage which occurred and which apparently was quickly fixed.

"There's also been a lack of acknowledgement that the conduct was even wrong. I mean we repeatedly hear that it was in a garage and nobody saw it and there wasn't really a victim and it was only a broken window and it was either his anyway or theirs or Mrs. Brown consented.

"That after the fact Mr. Graysen argued to me that Mr. Brown recognized he was angry and should have stepped back does not change the situation.

"The fact that Mr. Brown is refusing to accept help with the anger and violence which was my much-preferred approach to this case only indicates to me the necessity for a significant punishment."

As the record reflects, the trial court did not impose a retaliatory sentence, but rather analyzed the necessary factors in determining the appropriate sentence to carry out its objectives. These factors include " 'the nature and circumstances of the offense, the defendant's appreciation of and attitude toward the offense, or his traits of character as evidenced by his behavior and demeanor at the trial.' " The custody sentence by the trial court was manifestly not an abuse of discretion.

The judgment and sentence are affirmed.

NOTES AND QUESTIONS

1. **Police Response.** Just before the trial, Monique and Jim Brown, a member of the National Football League Hall of Fame, appeared on the Larry King Live show to discuss the case. The show also included experts on domestic violence. Consider the following comments by Dr. Donald Dutton, a psychologist who has done extensive research on abusive men:

> [T]here was a point back in the 1970's when you couldn't even get the police out to handle domestic calls, and now, I mean, 15 cars actually show up for this? We did police training for years, and we used to kind of teach the zen of intervention, that is you can under-respond and you can over-respond. If you over-respond, you can trigger a reaction from people that's just as bad as if you under-respond and 15 cars showed up; that's an over-response.

Now consider the comments of Charlotte Watson of the New York Governor's Office for the Prevention of Domestic Violence:

> [W]e have a long way to go yet before we've swung too far out of control. It was even in the 1990's that we couldn't get police officers to in some jurisdictions to make arrests. Even today, there are some women who claim that the police don't take their claims seriously, although in large part the police are making a stronger response.

Given what you have studied thus far, do you think that the police response here was appropriate? How are police supposed to gauge the seriousness of a situation?

2. **African–American Men and the Criminal Justice System.** Although Jim Brown did not testify at trial, he did appear on Larry King Live with his wife. Brown admitted to having hit women in the past, but denied that he had engaged in any violent behavior since 1988. Consider his explanation for the police reaction:

> I don't want to play the race card. I don't want to play the independent black man. I don't want to play that particular game. But it is a fact that in this country policeman have been killing people for having screwdrivers in their hands. There has been brutality in New York. There are cases all over this country wherein African–Americans and Latinos are being harassed. I'm not blatantly saying that every policeman is against me or the black community. I am saying that the community have no trust in law enforcement.

Of course, given Brown's fame, this is hardly a typical case. Yet, many commentators have suggested that mandatory arrests have a negative impact on minorities, especially African–American men. Consider the following perspectives on aggressive criminal responses and black incarceration rates.

> On any given day, nearly one-third of black men in their twenties are under the supervision of the criminal justice system—either behind

bars, on probation, or on parole. The gap between black and white incarceration rates, moreover, has deepened along with rising inmate numbers. African Americans experience a uniquely astronomical rate of imprisonment, and the social effects of imprisonment are concentrated in their communities. Thus, the transformation of prison policy at the turn of the twenty-first century is most accurately characterized as the mass incarceration of African Americans. . . .

This distrust of law enforcement has had a profound impact on strategies for combating domestic violence in African American communities. Feminist scholars increasingly question the wisdom of relying on criminal justice remedies for domestic abuse, especially in minority communities. Given the history of police brutality against blacks, many black women are reluctant to enlist law enforcement to protect them. Dorothy E. Roberts, *The Social and Moral Cost of Mass Incarceration in African American Communities*, 56 STAN. L. REV. 1271 (2004).

In this next excerpt, Sarah Buel discusses some data that shows how minorities are over-represented in the criminal justice system in one community.

As people of color and the poor continue to experience disproportionate rates of arrest, prosecution and sentencing, the academy—and certainly feminist legal scholars—ought to be teaching racialist law reform. For example, as is typical in many jurisdictions, Milwaukee County, Wisconsin, reports that although African–Americans constitute just 24% of the population, they represent 66% of the domestic violence arrests that find their way to the district attorney's office. Whites are 62% of the populace, but surface in just 32% of the domestic violence cases reviewed by prosecutors. To its credit, Milwaukee County has established a Judicial Oversight Initiative Committee ("JOIC") to address the disparity, in part by studying the city versus suburban police responses. In the more white suburbs, the JOIC found batterers were often issued municipal citations and paid fines, while those of color in the City of Milwaukee tended to be arrested, charged with state crimes and prosecuted. The JOIC Report states that, "The problem lies in the fact that it appears that some people in our community, depending on where they live, their race, ethnicity, income or occupation, are not being held to the same standard of accountability." Sarah M. Buel, *The Pedagogy of Domestic Violence Law: Situating Domestic Violence Work in Law Schools, Adding the Lenses of Race & Class*, 11 AM. U. J. GENDER SOC. POL'Y & L. 309 (2003).

3. **Women and Autonomy.** Both on Larry King Live and in her testimony, Monique Brown minimized the incident and placed a great deal of blame for the incident on herself. What reasons might she have had for doing so? Could her relatively young age and financial dependence on her husband have influenced her response? Was this a case of police and prosecutor over-reaction, or was law enforcement trying to be sensitive to the complex situation in which Monique found herself? Given all the

circumstances, what would have been the appropriate response? Consider Linda Mills' analysis of the *Brown* case:

> Jim Brown's wife, Monique, journeyed through the criminal justice system and faced all the challenges and paradoxes of a mandatory system. Mrs. Brown had two options: she could protect herself by testifying against her husband, or she could protect her husband by not testifying against him. Mrs. Brown made the decision that most women make: she chose to protect her husband. By doing this, she rendered ineffective the prosecutor's efforts to hold Jim responsible for the domestic violence crimes he allegedly committed. Jim Brown was eventually acquitted of "threatening to kill" his wife and therefore was convicted of a less significant crime. It was Los Angeles's mandatory prosecution policy that helped Brown escape the more serious charges. Through these policies, the prosecutor was forced to bring the case to trial rather than to find a middle ground with Monique Brown that may have held her husband more accountable for the intimate violence he committed in ways that addressed the violence rather than judged it. Linda Mills, INSULT TO INJURY: RETHINKING OUR RESPONSES TO INTIMATE ABUSE (2003).

What other options might the prosecution have pursued given Monique's dilemma, as Mills describes it? Since her husband refused to accept counseling, was there another option short of dismissing the case? Should both Monique and Jim have been offered marriage counseling, or some other therapeutic, as opposed to a punitive response? Consider these questions later in the chapter.

4. **Sentencing.** Jim Brown ultimately served prison time. This was in part because he refused to accept a plea deal. Was sending him to prison the best outcome? Do you think short prison sentences are likely to deter future violence? If Brown had accepted treatment, should he still have done jail time? What alternatives to treatment might have been available?

5. **Coordinated Approaches with Victim Advocates.** It is not clear whether Monique Brown had an advocate to help her through the criminal trial, but many victims find this very helpful. However, there is some debate as to whether to locate victim support services inside or outside the prosecutor's office. There is a possibility that external programs can maintain a more exclusive focus on the needs of victims, where internal programs will have additional responsibilities to prosecutors, including providing investigative and litigation support. There are just as likely to be situations in which victim support personnel hired by the prosecutor actually experience conflict between the needs of the office and the needs of individual victims. This is especially problematic when the victim is disinclined to cooperate with the prosecution, and wants to receive counseling and support in securing her safety by other means. Another argument for locating victim advocates outside the prosecutor's office, therefore, is that independent advocates will be freer to provide a full range of information and support, unconstrained by any competing loyalty to the prosecutorial agenda. The ideal may be to have advocates both inside and outside the

prosecutor's office, and to accept that while they will often be able to work together, on occasion those working relationships will be strained.

6. **Victims of Domestic Violence and their Pets.** While it may seem odd that Monique Brown brought her dog with her to the police station, one of the many reasons that victims do not want to leave abusive relationships, or stay at a shelter, is out of concern for what will happen to their pets. As previously discussed in Chapter Six many abusers also can be cruel to animals as a way of exerting power and control over the victim and there is a high correlation between animal abuse and domestic violence. Even if the abuser has not hurt the family pet, the victim may fear what will happen if she can't keep that pet with her. In response to these concerns, some communities have established support programs for pets of victims of domestic violence. For example, in Anne Arundel County, Maryland, law enforcement officials and the Humane Society have teamed up to provide temporary safe shelters and foster families for pets and larger animals, such as horses. This allows the victim to make decisions about her own safety knowing her animals are safe. For information on this and other programs, see http://www.aacounty.org/AnimalControl/domesticViolence.cfm.

7. **No–Drop Policies.** Like mandatory arrest provisions, no-drop policies take control of the process away from the victim. The justification is that the perpetrator should know that he has committed a crime against the state, rather than "merely" violated his partner, that the state insists his wrong be addressed, and that he lacks the power to avoid criminal sanctions by bullying his partner into dropping charges. As participants in San Diego's innovative prosecutorial program have observed:

> In San Diego, we learned a number of years ago that abusers would become more violent and aggressive toward the victim when they learned that she controlled the outcome of the criminal prosecution. By definition, most batterers have the power in violent relationships. Thus, when the system demanded that the victim act in the role of prosecutor, in reality the batterer was being given control of the criminal case. The batterer's control over the victim is generally so complete that he was able to dictate whether she talked to the prosecutor, what she said, and whether she appeared in court.

> The solution to this vexing issue was to take the responsibility out of the hands of the victim and place it with the State where it belongs. The police officer is paid to be the police officer. The prosecutor is paid to be the prosecutor. The victim of a crime is neither trained nor emotionally able to act in the role of cop or prosecutor. Once prosecutors and police officers stop asking victims whether they want to press charges, they quickly find that victims stop asking to press charges or drop charges. The victim is able to be the victim and address her pressing issues of safety for herself and her children and the system is able to focus on the one who broke the law. Casey G. Gwinn and Sgt. Anne O'Dell, *Stopping the Violence: The Role of the Police Officer and the Prosecutor*, 20 W.St.U. L.Rev. 297 (1993).

Nonetheless, some battered women's advocates argue that there are cases in which the victim has good reason to fear the consequences of going through with a prosecution. They express concern that in some cases women who know a no-drop policy is in effect will be deterred from seeking police assistance for fear of what may follow. They also worry that prosecutors will rely on no-drop policies to coerce victims into cooperation, rather than working to ensure that victims feel sufficiently supported by the criminal justice system, and sufficiently safe, to cooperate voluntarily. The specter of an abused woman being terrorized by her partner into withholding her cooperation, only to be jailed on contempt charges, is a haunting one. Finally, no-drop policies will backfire if they result in prosecutors taking weak cases into court, only to have them dismissed by irate judges who feel that their time is being wasted. No prosecutor likes to build a record of losses, and it is tempting then both to blame the victim for the loss, and to avoid similar cases in the future, regardless of official policy. In more than one high profile case, the reluctant victim, compelled to testify on threat of imprisonment for contempt if she fails to appear, has changed her story and even blamed herself for the violence rather than risk the consequences of her abuser being convicted. When this results in an acquittal, the prosecutor and judge are likely to have all their victim-blaming tendencies reinforced, and the abuser still gets the message that he can control the criminal justice process just as he controls his partner. Ultimately, the argument is not as simple as whether or not to adopt, or advocate for, a no-drop prosecution policy. No-drop policies are in reality an amalgam of policies and practices which together dictate how prosecutors will pursue domestic violence cases. Within the mix there is plenty of room to maneuver in an attempt to reap the advantages of the no-drop strategy, without putting victims of domestic violence in greater danger of private abuse, or making them newly vulnerable to abuse at the hands of the state. Various "model" programs around the country illustrate a variety of promising approaches. Nonetheless, the question of whether a victim should be required to participate in the (perhaps rare) prosecution which cannot be won without her contribution is a question which will undoubtedly continue to be a subject of dispute among battered women's advocates. The theoretical dilemmas it poses are the topic of the next reading. The author, Cheryl Hanna, acknowledges the force of arguments against mandated participation and their grounding in feminist theory, but comes out in its favor, arguing that pragmatically, in the current context, battered women have more to gain than to lose from aggressive prosecution.

Cheryl Hanna

No Right To Choose: Mandated Victim Participation In Domestic Violence Prosecutions

109 HARV. L. REV. 1849 (1996).

C.   *Agency/Victimization and the Tendency to Blame*

One difficulty in discussing mandated participation is distinguishing between victim-blaming arguments and arguments that call on women to overcome their victim status. In domestic violence work, this tension is often known as the "agency/victimization" dichotomy. Elizabeth Schneider explains:

> We now alternate between visions of the battered woman as agent—as cause or provocateur of the battering—and the battered woman as helpless victim. And we go back and forth between these two images without any real public engagement on the problems underlying battering. However, portraying women solely as victims or solely as agents is neither accurate nor adequate to explain the complex realities of women's lives.

> The question of what the battered women's role in the prosecution process ought to be often masks an ambivalence about what her role in the abusive relationship is. Women who want to follow through with prosecution are seen either as true victims of domestic violence or as manipulators with an agenda. Women who do not want to proceed are characterized either as agents in the battering—allowing it to continue because of their lack of cooperation with the state—or as true victims who have "learned helplessness."

> ... If we reject mandated participation because it would be "revictimizing," we neither account for women's strength and resilience nor acknowledge the political and social context in which battering occurs. If we rationalize mandated participation on the assumption that the battered woman cannot assess her situation realistically, we reinforce her helplessness. In either case the policy can be criticized as paternalistic....

> At this point in history, however, the long-term benefits of mandated participation outweigh the short-term costs—costs that can be greatly diminished if we examine the issue in a pragmatic context. In particular, we need to examine the influence that mandated participation has on the effectiveness of the criminal justice system as well as the impact of such a policy on individual women....

> ... [W]e should be cautious not to treat victims of domestic violence differently than we would treat victims of other crimes. Most crime victims distrust the system.... Domestic violence cases are sometimes similar to other cases in which victims may believe that they have more to lose than to gain by testifying. For example, organized crime, gang- and drug-related offenses, and rape often involve witnesses who face intimidation or perceive that they will be in danger if they testify. Yet rather than allow these crimes to go unprosecuted, prosecutors have developed realistic strategies to respond to witness reluctance. Similarly, prosecutors should develop strategies for domestic violence cases that address the victim's concerns, but should never allow the victim's level of cooperation to be the sole or primary factor in deciding whether to prosecute. This approach is consistent with the criminal justice system's approach in other areas and preserves the integrity of the state's response. It is also far less paternalistic and sexist than dismissing cases based on the victim's wishes in the domestic violence context while refusing to do so in other contexts. Requiring mandated participation places domestic violence on the same level as all violent crimes and ensures the equal protection of law enforcement for

women who are victimized by their intimate partners as well as for women who are victimized by strangers.

No-drop policies that do not compel victim cooperation lack credibility. When a batterer and his defense counsel know that a victim's failure to cooperate may result in case dismissal, they control the judicial process. If participation is mandated, the state takes away the batterer's ability to influence the victim's actions. Basing prosecutorial decisionmaking on witness cooperation in domestic violence cases ultimately places the victim in more danger....

In my experience as a prosecutor, the fact that the state was not likely to request a body attachment for victims who failed to appear for trial traveled very quickly by word of mouth. Defense attorneys often informed women that if they did not appear in court, they would probably not be arrested. Day after day, women would not appear and defense attorneys would request dismissals. Many times I could not locate the victim by phone or mail and did not know if the batterer or his attorney had ensured her absence. Judges rarely allowed me to postpone the case unless I had an explanation for the victim's absence.... My example illustrates that prosecutors must be willing—in at least some instances—to mandate participation, including having women picked up by police officers and brought to court if they refuse to appear. Otherwise, the state response to domestic violence is unacceptably undermined....

A prosecutor's lack of resolve also corrupts other parts of the system. When cases are dismissed because the prosecutor fails to mandate participation, police officers and other criminal justice personnel may question the legitimacy of the trial preparation process.

Tremendous progress has been made in instituting preferred and mandatory arrest policies.... When police do make an appropriate arrest, only to see the case dismissed at trial because the victim did not want to proceed, their decreased confidence in the value of arrest can undermine their diligence when policing domestic violence....

NOTES AND QUESTIONS

1. **Sensitivity to Victim Concerns.** San Diego has implemented a policy that is consistent with Hanna's recommendations, and yet sensitive to the issue of revictimization:

> Our official policy is that we will request arrest warrants for victims who are subpoenaed and fail to appear in court. This is widely publicized in our community. The actual enforcement of the policy, however, is much more complicated. If a victim fails to appear on the day of trial for which she has been subpoenaed, a specially trained Domestic Violence Unit prosecutor will decide how to proceed. The initiative does not come from the judge or from a prosecutor insensitive to domestic violence issues. The prosecutor's decision will be impacted by whether we can prove the case without the victim's cooperation. About 60% of our cases are provable without the victim based on 911

tapes, photographs, medical records, spontaneous declarations by the victim to the officers, admissions by the defendant, neighbors' testimony, relatives' testimony, and general police officer testimony related to the case and the subsequent investigation. If the case can be proved without the victim, we will proceed to trial without requesting a warrant for the victim's arrest.

For cases that cannot be proven without the victim, the prosecutor may request a continuance and a bench warrant. This, however, is not always the case. The prosecutor may conclude the case does not merit the risk of jailing the victim. We now have legislation in California that allows us to refile the case after we locate the victim. If the prosecutor does ask for a continuance and a bench warrant, we do not let the warrant simply go into the system. We attempt to locate the victim immediately and bring her to court. In some cases, we may ask the judge to hold the warrant and continue the case for a week while we notify the victim of the pending risk of arrest. This often results in the victim contacting our victim assistance staff and agreeing to come to court. Casey G. Gwinn and Sgt. Anne O'Dell, *Stopping the Violence: The Role of the Police Officer and the Prosecutor,* 20 W. ST. U. L. REV. 297 (1993).

2. **The Politics of Aggressive Policies.** When Hanna wrote this article in 1996, few jurisdictions had implemented such aggressive policies. In the decade that followed, many jurisdictions experimented with such policies. As a result of those experiments, and continued theoretical inquiry into the pros and cons of aggressive prosecution, many have come to see such policies as inherently conservative as opposed to progressive. Below is a critique of Hanna's position. As you read it, consider whether mandated approaches are as conservative and as misplaced as the author suggests.

G. Kristian Miccio

A House Divided: Mandatory Arrest, Domestic Violence, and the Conservatization of the Battered Women's Movement

42 HOUS. L. REV. 237 (2005).

The current discourse on mandatory practices implicates two distinct ideological positions. The Protagonists view mandatory practices as a necessity in making women safe. A dominant and troubling theme that has emerged within the Protagonist bloc is that such practices are necessary because battered women are incapable of making a ''rational'' choice while being traumatized by the violence. Mandatory practices then serve as a necessary shield—not just from the violence of individual males, but from what is perceived as survivor powerlessness. While not characteristic of the entire battered women's movement, this position correlates with a conservative element within the movement that has achieved both political and social ascendancy. The conservative position is problematic because it dislocates mandatory practices from their historical moorings while reifying the cultural stereotypes of the incapacitated and irrational woman—stereotypes that confine women to, rather than liberate women from, oppressive home. . . .

And while the Protagonists do not represent the entire battered women's movement, their influence is far-reaching and affects how we view male intimate violence and women survivors. An underlying assumption of the Protagonist position is that the societal benefits of mandatory state intervention outweigh the short-term costs to women's autonomy. According to Cheryl Hanna, former prosecutor and law professor, the social benefits of mandatory state intervention are punishing criminal conduct, deterring future violence, and sending a message that—in the case of male intimate violence—such conduct will not be condoned. Additionally, sacrificing women's autonomy by forced participation through mandatory arrest and prosecution becomes necessary to "protect women overall." Although Hanna's insights into the criminal justice system are powerful, her trust in law enforcement as remedy is misplaced, and her willingness to sacrifice women's autonomy to the state is alarming. . . .

In attempting to reconcile the tension in prosecuting male intimate violence cases, the Protagonists have come up with a simplistic answer: Mandatory state intervention is required because all battered women are incapable of rational choice in trauma. Professor Hanna's reconstruction of the Beverly Johnson case illustrates this point.

While in the Baltimore City State Attorney's Office, Hanna handled a case involving a woman, Beverly Johnson, beaten by her boyfriend. Although Ms. Johnson had called the police and the offender was later arrested, she decided not to prosecute because she was dying from AIDS and did not "want a criminal case to interfere with [her] life." Johnson also claimed that the glare of prosecution would reveal her condition to her family who, up to that point, was unaware of it.

Although Hanna begged Johnson to prosecute, Johnson refused. Hanna pulled the case but not before warning Johnson that the case would be reopened if "her boyfriend laid a finger on her." Professor Hanna ends this account by claiming she should have pursued the case. She believed she wrongfully arrived at a decision because she attempted to "preserve [Johnson's] privacy rather than . . . pursue a law enforcement objective."

However, this case was not about Johnson's privacy, it was about her safety. Johnson claimed that by continuing the prosecution her life was getting "worse, not better." Johnson made the decision to cease prosecution to preserve her health and her relationships—not only with her boyfriend but also with her family. Here, safety was associated with Johnson's conditions particular to AIDS and not the violence perpetrated by the boyfriend.

Johnson's decision was strategic. It may not have been the one that Hanna or another survivor of violence with AIDS would have chosen, but it was not irrational nor did it evince incapability. It was a decision based on the conditions that shaped Johnson's environment, with AIDS taking center stage. Finally, there was no guarantee that prosecution would have been the better alternative. In fact, the opposite may have been true because in this case prosecution would have been the equivalent of severing a relationship with her boyfriend and her family at a time when she perceived a need for their support.

There is, however, another consequence of the Protagonist ideology: It constructs a set of false dichotomies. The first involves conceptions of authenticity. By authenticity, I am referring to social notions concerning legitimate claims of violence and how the genuineness of a claim is judged by whether the survivor leaves or stays. Both law and popular culture equate existence of violence with separation from the relationship. Staying becomes a socially suspect choice undermining the woman's claim of abuse. Leaving, on the other hand, validates her assertion of harm. If we listen to women survivors, we learn that they stay for myriad reasons—fear of reprisal, fear of losing their children, economic concerns, emotional ties to the batterer or his family, lack of social or familial support, and lack of a place to go. Yet the Protagonists have collapsed a complex set of interactions into narrow categories that fail to adequately describe the conditions that frame her life, her choices, and her conduct.

NOTES AND QUESTIONS

1. **Victim Cooperation.** To maximize the effectiveness of law enforcement while reducing the risks of mandated participation to individual women, Hanna, like other commentators, recommends two concurrent strategies. First, that prosecutors seek to create an environment in which women will voluntarily cooperate, both because they feel they can do so in relative safety, and because they have confidence that the prosecution will be successful, and meet their needs. Second, that prosecutors rely where possible not on the victim's testimony, but on other available sources of testimony. She argues that more effort needs to be put into gathering physical evidence, and into persuading courts to admit less traditional forms of evidence.

2. **Achieving Equality.** Is it inconsistent for battered women's advocates to argue *both* that prosecutors should not discriminate against victims of domestic violence, *and* that they should allow victims of domestic violence to exercise more control over prosecutorial decisions than victims of other crimes are traditionally permitted? Is this a fair characterization of advocates' demands of the system? Can an analogy be made to women's demands in the workplace—where they have sought both equal opportunity, and changes in workplace practices to accommodate needs more commonly experienced by women than by men?

3. **Victimless Prosecutions.** What happens when a victim refuses to cooperate regardless of all the support she receives? In the article from which the next reading is drawn, the authors advocate strongly for an approach which proceeds without her:

> A recent training book for prosecutors and defense attorneys (written by a defense attorney) included this statement: "In domestic violence cases, the abused spouse is the main source of the evidence." This is

exactly what the defense bar wants prosecutors to believe and this is how prosecutors have functioned for too long. As long as the investigation and the prosecution focus on the victim, cases will be inadequately investigated and prosecutors will fail to win convictions in large numbers of cases. Casey G. Gwinn and Sgt. Anne O'Dell, *Stopping the Violence: The Role of the Police Officer and the Prosecutor*, 20 W. St. U. L. Rev. 297 (1993).

4. **Resistance to Aggressive Approaches.** Not all advocates for battered women agree that approaches like the one in San Diego are appropriate. In the following excerpt, Linda Mills, one of the most outspoken critics of mandatory interventions argues that such approaches have the effect of victimizing the victim. She suggests that criminal justice interventions be based in a clinical understanding of the dynamics of abuse. She is vehemently against proceeding when the victim does not wish to go forward.

Linda Mills

Killing Her Softly: Intimate Abuse and the Violence of State Intervention

113 Harv. L. Rev. 550 (1999).

From the accumulated evidence, a dynamic between the state and the battered woman emerges that distinctly mimics the violent dynamic in the battering relationship. Three correlative themes are the most problematic. First, mandatory interventions reinforce the battered woman's psychic injury and encourage feelings of guilt, low self-esteem, and dependency. Mandatory interventions are predicated on the assumption that state actors are incapable of distinguishing between battered women who are truly suffering from "learned helplessness" and battered women who are capable of making reasoned decisions about which healing strategies to pursue. As we have seen, this disinterest, or even laziness, on the part of the state in developing a person-by-person approach to domestic violence intervention causes the state to replicate unwittingly the behavior of the batterer in some cases.

Second, mandatory interventions may have the ironic effect of realigning the battered woman with the batterer. Some studies suggest and numerous authors have surmised that when the battered woman has a negative interaction with the state, she is less likely to rely on governmental assistance in the future. Indeed, some have argued, as I am arguing, that if a battered woman is given the choice between abuse by the batterer, which is familiar, and abuse by state actors, which is unfamiliar, she is likely to choose the abuse she knows best.

Finally, mandatory interventions deny the battered woman an important opportunity to partner with the state to help ensure her future safety.

IV.   Survivor–Centered Model

. . . Many of the recommendations of the Survivor–Centered Model rely on the ability of police officers or prosecutors to perform clinically sensitive interviews and to develop survivor-centered strategies and plans. Training is therefore necessary both to improve how state actors relate to victims and to assess the capacity of these state actors to perform services. If it is revealed that police officers and prosecutors or even their designated representatives such as victim assistance support staff (who work in close proximity to law enforcement personnel) are incapable of providing these services, then it might be necessary to restructure the system more radically so that it directly involves trained clinicians. . . .

2. Respect.—A respectful response to a battered woman is meant to counteract the destructive dynamic of "degradation." State actors can foster a respectful dynamic by a number of means. . . .

[P]rosecutors can respect battered women by subpoenaing them only at their request. As with the element of acceptance, respecting the battered woman involves knowing her individual needs and responding to them accordingly. By providing a requested subpoena, prosecutors both respect the victims' desires and allow victims to tell their batterers that they are required to testify—and tell the truth about the abuse—or else be prosecuted for perjury. In contrast, by subpoenaing them against their will, prosecutors may make battered women recant; battered women feel compelled to tell a "version" of the events. The state can avoid encouraging battered women to testify on behalf of their batterers by strategizing with victims who have expressed interest in prosecution on how best to address their role at trial. When a battered woman is adamantly opposed to prosecuting the batterer, the trial should not occur. . . .

3. Reassurance.—Reassurance by state actors should help alleviate the fear and anxiety that women feel when in an abusive relationship; it should act to help the battered woman feel cared for, heard, and understood. For example, reassurance may involve planning for her safety and documenting an inventory of social support services available to her in the event of a subsequent emergency. In addition, state actors should consider the possibility that arrest and prosecution may not be the safest option for a battered woman to pursue and may actually be destructive to her healing process. . . .

4. Engagement.—The state's effort to engage the battered woman should be designed to counteract the social isolation experienced in the battering relationship. [R]econnection is key to the survivor's healing. State actors, especially law enforcement officers and prosecutors, should reject abusive patterns of relating and counteract their own frustration with the victim's choices. . . .

5. Resocialization.—The state could also help resocialize, rather than missocialize, by countering the alienation from friends and family that battered women so often experience. Resocialization involves helping the survivor to reconnect with lost social networks and to reengage in activities outside her relationship with the batterer. . . .

6. Empowerment.—Empowerment is the single most critical element in promoting a dynamic in which state actors let battered women direct how an intervention unfolds. Several battered women's advocates have

argued that mandatory interventions, as they are currently formulated, promote "empowerment" because they free the battered woman from making the decision to arrest or prosecute the batterer. Because the police and prosecutor make the decision for her, she cannot be blamed for the batterer's arrest and prosecution. This attitude assumes that the sole reason battered women avoid pursuing arrest and prosecution is that they fear repercussions from the abuser. . . .

7.   Emotional Responsiveness.—State actors should be emotionally responsive to the battered woman to compensate for the lack of emotional support that so often harms the battered woman. Instead of withholding support from the battered woman, state actors should respond in emotionally affirmative ways that indicate their understanding of her particular circumstances. Emotional responsiveness can take many forms, including listening, affirming, and discussing her options. When the battered woman feels heard, she is much more likely to cooperate with the state and to become involved in the arrest and prosecution of the batterer.

8.   Liberation.—State actors can counteract the "close confinement" evident in some abusive relationships by providing the battered woman with opportunities to escape her confinement. A battered woman should, assuming state actors have employed these other survivor-centered strategies, feel safe enough to discuss openly how best to liberate herself from the violence she endures. . . .

This approach raises a critical question: Should the battered woman, under all circumstances, direct the decision-making process? In certain limited situations, battered women may suffer from an identifiable mental illness that prevents them from making decisions on their own behalf. Lawyers or other advocates should not assume, however, that all battered women have such an illness. Only a trained clinician can distinguish those battered women who can navigate the healing process on their own from those who need the aid of others. The purpose of this assessment should not be to interfere with battered women's agency, or to label them as mentally ill, but rather to develop responses that respect their individual needs and interests. . . .

NOTES AND QUESTIONS

1.   **Softening No–Drop Polices.** As prosecutors become more familiar and successful with "victimless prosecutions" it is becoming increasingly apparent that for some victims, the reassurance that the case can be won without their testimony turns them from hostile witnesses to allies in the prosecution. Victimless prosecution allows them to disavow in public their interest in seeing their abuser sanctioned, while assisting the prosecutor in private. If victimless prosecution is pursued as a strategy for winning victim cooperation, it can be a crucial means of "softening" an otherwise tough no-drop policy. Obviously there is a world of difference between pursuing a no-drop policy by coercing the reluctant testimony of a victim, to the point of threatening her with incarceration if she refuses, and pursuing it by winning the case without ever asking her to take the stand.

At the same time, even within the range of strategies open to the prosecutor who plans a victimless prosecution, some may be more protective of the victim than others. Using the victim's excited utterance, for example, still involves the victim's condemnation of her abuser, albeit less directly than if she were to repeat her accusation at trial. Using the independent testimony of police and neighbors, along with medical reports, goes further in distancing the victim from the prosecution. Evidentiary issues are examined in detail in Chapter Eight.

2. **When Should the Victim Decide?** Cheryl Hanna and Linda Mills have very different views of the role of the prosecutor. For Hanna, the primary role is to enforce the law, while for Mills, the primary role is to help the victim. Are these positions incompatible with each other? Mills suggests that prosecutors be trained in the clinical aspects of violence. Is this an appropriate role for the prosecutor to play? What resources should be devoted to the approach Mills suggests? Should domestic violence units employ trained psychologists or battered women's advocates to help prosecutors make the determination whether or not to proceed?

3. **Prosecution and Race.** As with arrest policies, there remains the question as to whether aggressive prosecution hurts or helps victims of color. For example, do African–American women prefer their abusive partners to be prosecuted? It isn't entirely clear. In a recent study, the authors found that 65% of women wanted their abusers prosecuted, and that those who experienced abuse for a longer period of time, were more seriously injured or who were already separated from their partner were more likely to favor prosecution. So too were those women whose abuser had drug and alcohol problems. See Arlene N. Weisz, *Prosecution of Batterers: Views of African American Battered Women*, 17 VIOLENCE & VICTIMS 19 (2002).

4. **Defendant's Rights.** Consider Deborah Epstein's general concern that the increasing attention the legal system has paid to domestic violence has had the consequence of undermining the rights of the defendant. She is particularly concerned with the ways in which abusers may not have a voice in the criminal justice system, and hence, may be less likely to comply with court orders. She also opposes mandatory policies in favor of those which preference victim's choices. See Deborah Epstein, *Procedural Justice: Tempering the State's Response to Domestic Violence*, 43 WM. & MARY L. REV. 1843 (2002).

5. **Representing Batterers.** Until now, we have focused primarily on the role of the prosecutor in the criminal justice system. However, defense counsel plays an equally important role in ensuring that, within its zealousness, the state does not violate the rights of the defendant. It is notable that very little has been written about the dilemma many defense lawyers may face in representing defendants whom they believe to be an ongoing risk to the victim. Assume for example, that the victim calls her abuser's defense attorney and asks what will happen if she simply doesn't show up for a scheduled trial? Does she have an ethical duty to her to inform the victim that, absent her testimony, the state will likely drop the charges?

Does she have a duty to the court to tell the victim that she is under subpoena and must appear? There are no clear answers to these questions.

Another issue that can arise is simply how to prepare a defense to a domestic violence charge. In an interview, public defender Marion Gaston suggests that defense attorneys let defendants testify if they are manipulative or addicts, and that in "he-said/she said" cases, they insist on witnesses who can corroborate the defendant's testimony. Renee Harrison, *Representing Defendants in Domestic Violence Prosecutions*, 11 J. CONTEMP.LEGAL ISSUES 63 (2000). We will return to issues of representation of batterers in the last chapter. For now, consider how the availability of treatment might impact whether defense attorneys request a plea agreement.

D.   SENTENCING

Previous sections of this chapter have already suggested that another important variable in the management of domestic violence cases within the criminal justice system is the sentence finally imposed on a convicted offender. This decision will be driven in part by the charges the prosecutor chooses to bring, in part by applicable statutory or regulatory sentencing guidelines, in part by the type and level of resources available within the system, and in part on judicial discretion. Where the sentence involves alternatives to incarceration—notably probation and treatment—it will also depend on the discretion and resources of those in charge of supervising the offender conditionally released into the community.

Provocative hypotheses have been put forward by observers discouraged at the extent to which convicted domestic violence offenders continue to serve only minimal prison sentences, or to avoid incarceration altogether. One such hypothesis is that the criminal justice system continues to discriminate against victims of domestic violence, and covertly condone the behavior of perpetrators, by imposing more lenient sentences in these cases than in parallel stranger violence cases. Another is that the system's atypical commitment to a "treatment" paradigm in domestic violence cases reflects a continuing conviction that domestic violence is more "private" than "public," and more about "illness" than about "crime." The readings that follow acknowledge the basis for these critiques, but at the same time cast doubt on these and other easy explanations for current sentencing practices.

Discussions of sentencing in domestic violence cases must ultimately be framed by our broader understanding of the role we want criminal sanctions to play, and what experience teaches us about their efficacy. Are we trying to rehabilitate offenders? Do we know whether treatment is more effective in reshaping the attitudes and behaviors of offenders than incarceration? If we are more modest in our goals, and simply want to deter convicted abusers from reoffending, rather than rehabilitate them, do we know whether treatment, supervised probation without treatment, or incarceration is the most effective specific deterrent? Is a longer period of incarceration more effective as a deterrent than a shorter one? If our goal is even more modest, and we are simply out to "incapacitate" the offender—to deprive him of the opportunity for further violations, do we know if we can effectively do that without locking him up? Furthermore, since we do know that except in the most exceptional of circumstances he will not remain behind bars indefinitely, do we know what to predict when he is released? If we include among our goals reducing the amount of partner abuse in the society at large, and are using the criminal justice system in part as a force for public education and general deterrence, do we know whether those goals are served better by some sentencing practices than others? Finally, are batterers homogeneous enough as a group that we can assume a uniform response to different enforcement strategies, or should we be tailoring our responses to take account of important differences among categories of offender?

The first reading provides an overview of sentencing practices, one that casts doubt on the assertion that perpetrators of domestic violence are treated more leniently by the system than other violent offenders, but confirms the bias towards treatment rather than incarceration. The notes that follow highlight a series of issues relative to batterer treatment programs. In particular, there is still no reliable data that suggest that batterer treatment programs, as they currently exist, are effective at reducing recidivism.

Cheryl Hanna

The Paradox of Hope: The Crime and Punishment of Domestic Violence

39 WM. AND MARY L. REVIEW 1505 (1998).

. . . Despite increased attention to domestic violence, there is still a deep reluctance to incarcerate domestic violence offenders. Rather, most receive probation with mandated treatment regardless of the severity of the offense or their past violent histories. This trend continues despite empirical research that questions whether there is any direct causal link between participation in a batterer treatment program and recidivism. . . .

Unfortunately, we know surprisingly little about the outcomes of all violent crimes. Few studies compare the outcome of domestic violence with other violent offenses. Furthermore, sparse data exists on the number of domestic violence cases that arrive in the criminal justice system and what happens to them once they get there. The federal government and a majority of the states collect statistics on domestic violence, but there are wide variations in how each jurisdiction defines offenses, determines what is counted, and measures or reports incidents. . . .

Prosecutors and judges have numerous disposition options once a domestic violence case enters the system: outright dismissal; pretrial diversion; postconviction probation with conditions, including fines; batterer treatment and/or substance abuse counseling; or incarceration. Prosecution policies nationwide are becoming more rigorous, with many jurisdictions forming specialized prosecution units and implementing "no-drop" policies. The available data, however, suggests that most of these cases still end with arrest ... Of those cases that are prosecuted, many are charged or pled down to misdemeanors despite facts that suggest the conduct constituted a felony.

When prosecutors decide to go forward, the final disposition is often a period of probation, either pre- or postconviction, contingent upon completion of a batterer treatment program. For example, in Sussex County, New Jersey, counseling and other social services for both the victim and the abuser, rather than jail time, is the preferred sentence as a matter of jurisdictional policy. There is little evidence, however, that probation departments follow up on these orders, allowing many abusers to slip through the cracks.

NOTES AND QUESTIONS

1. **A Typical Case?** Hanna opens her article with a harrowing story of a woman killed by her abusive partner after multiple interventions by the criminal justice system:

> In 1995, a Chicago district court judge allowed Samuel Gutierrez to enroll in a batterer treatment program in exchange for pleading guilty to choking his girlfriend Kelly Gonzalez. This was one of nine incidents of abuse documented by Chicago police reports.
>
> Then, in August 1996, after failing to appear for a status hearing, the police again arrested Gutierrez for beating Gonzalez. Five days later, the judge imposed, then stayed, a 120 day sentence, again ordering Gutierrez to enroll in treatment. One month later, in September 1996, the same judge continued the case. For the third time, Gutierrez was told to get counseling or face jail. In February 1997, Kelly Gonzalez's body was found; Gutierrez admitted to killing and hiding her body back in September 1996. If Gutierrez is telling the truth, then he killed Gonzalez when he should have been in treatment. Cheryl Hanna, *The Paradox of Hope: The Crime and Punishment of Domestic Violence*, 39 WM. & MARY L. REV. 1505 (1998).

Hanna writes: "[t]he criminal justice system arguably 'did the right thing' in this case. The defendant was arrested, prosecuted, and sentenced to a batterer treatment program intended to aid him in unlearning his violent behavior. A probation officer even followed up to ensure that Gutierrez met his conditions of release." Do you agree that the criminal justice system's response to Gutierrez was appropriate? Was probation with counseling an appropriate sentence at his initial conviction, given the nine violent incidents documented by the Chicago police? Was it appropriate, at his second conviction, to suspend his sentence and again order him to enroll in treatment, when his prior referral to treatment had not prevented him from re-offending? When a month later he was still not enrolled in a treatment program, was it appropriate to offer him yet another warning, rather than revoking his probation and incarcerating him? This level of leniency in sentencing can only fuel suspicions that judges are either minimizing the seriousness of domestic violence offenses, or dramatically underestimating the danger posed by many domestic violence offenders. It seems further that treatment, under these circumstances, is imposed not because of any real hope that it will serve a rehabilitative function, but because it serves to legitimate the choice of probation over incarceration. Responding to these kinds of concerns, the National Council of Juvenile and Family Court Judges has recommended that: "[d]iversion should only occur in extraordinary cases, and then only after an admission before a judicial officer has been entered." Diversion is inappropriate, according to the Council, when "it is used as a calendar management tool, when first offenders are long term abusers, when the required treatment is only of brief duration and has not been monitored, and perhaps most important, when the use of diversion is perceived as a less than serious response to the crime."

2. **Recent Data on Sentencing.** The New York District Attorney's office is one of the most aggressive in the nation in prosecuting domestic violence cases. In a recent study comparing case outcomes between domestic violence and non-domestic violence misdemeanor cases, researchers found that only about one-third of domestic cases resulted in a conviction, compared with over half of non-domestic cases. Domestic violence cases were twice as likely as non-domestic violence cases to be dismissed. Of those cases prosecuted resulting in conviction, 72% of domestic violence cases resulted in some conditional discharge, including participation in a batterer treatment program or drug and alcohol treatment, compared with 47% of non-domestic cases. Only 17% of domestic violence defendants received a sentence that included jail, as opposed to 45% of the non-domestic cases. Richard R. Peterson, *Combating Domestic Violence in New York City: A Study of Domestic Violence Cases in the Criminal Courts*, New York City Criminal Justice Agency (2003). This data suggests that there still remain differences in how domestic violence cases are handled in the criminal justice system and that there remains a strong preference for treatment over more conventional forms of punishment.

3. **Preferred Disposition.** In 1984, the Attorney General's Task Force on Family Violence threw its significant weight behind court-mandated batterers' treatment as an appropriate response to domestic violence crimes, except for the most serious. Whether that recommendation was sound remains an open question. Knowing what these programs purport to deliver is a precondition both to assessing their efficacy and to evaluating them as an alternative to other criminal justice responses.

4. **Treatment Models.** Hanna notes that "most court-ordered treatment programs today treat only men," because of the extent to which couples therapy in the context of domestic violence has been "discredited." Similarly, she notes that "[m]ental health programs that focus on psychotherapy, stress management, anger control, and conflict resolution," criticized by feminists as inattentive to the gender dynamics at work in abusive relationships, "are also becoming less common." The dominant paradigm in court-ordered programs is the pro-feminist model, as practiced in Duluth, Minnesota, and elsewhere:

The Duluth model philosophy is: "Batterers, like those who intervene to help them, have been immersed in a culture that supports relationships of dominance. This cultural acceptance of dominance is rooted in the assumption that, based on differences, some people have the legitimate right to master others." The curriculum uses an educational and counseling approach, as opposed to anger-control intervention. It focuses on the use of violence by the batterer to establish power and control over his partner. Men meet in weekly groups run by a facilitator. The facilitator is not necessarily a mental health professional but is a trained lay person. Participants engage in exercises geared towards confronting their violent behavior. For example, each participant maintains a "control log" or diary that identifies their abusive behavior. Role plays based on individual experiences are used to build nonviolent skills. Videotapes, such as Profile of an Assailant, are shown to prompt discussion. Skills such as taking timeouts and recognizing women's anger are also taught. Most of these exercises preclude discussion of the particular relationship, instead focusing on the underlying issues of power and control.

EMERGE in Boston is another popular feminist-inspired treatment model. The program considers itself a "collective" of men working to end violence against women. Although trained counselors run the program, sessions are conducted as supervised self-help groups. EMERGE considers itself to be part of a movement organizing men to challenge sexism in society. Battered women's shelters established other programs, like the House of Ruth in Baltimore and the Domestic Violence Project in Ann Arbor, Michigan. Shelter staff attempt to monitor both sides of the relationship and oversee both parties involved. Most programs charge the abuser a fee; many will not accept an abuser into their program unless he pleads guilty and acknowledges the underlying abusive behavior. Cheryl Hanna, *The Paradox of Hope: The Crime and Punishment of Domestic Violence*, 39 WM. & MARY L. REV. 1505 (1998).

Some of the common elements of treatment models require that participants be violence-free, not use alcohol or drugs, and confront their "sexist attitude." See Juliet Austin and Juergen Dankwort, *A Review of Standards for Batterer Intervention Programs*, National Electronic Network on Violence Against Women, Applied Research Forum (August 1998).

5. **Efficacy of Batterer Treatment Programs.** In 2003, the National Institute of Justice conducted evaluations of programs in Broward County, Florida and Brooklyn, New York. The study used rigorous research methods, overcoming many of the problems of previous studies. Nevertheless, it found that these programs had little or no effect on offenders' attitudes, beliefs, or behaviors. It concludes, "The stakes for women's safety are simply too high to rely on batterer intervention programs without stronger empirical evidence that they work." Shelly Jackson, Lynette Feder, David R. Forde, Robert C. Davis, Christopher D. Maxwell and Bruce G. Taylor, *Batterer Intervention Programs: Where Do We Go From Here?*, NATIONAL INSTITUTE OF JUSTICE (2003). These findings are consistent with other

studies. See e.g. Jill A. Gordon and Laura J. Moriarty, *The Effects of Domestic Violence Batterer Treatment on Domestic Violence Recidivism*, 30 CRIMINAL JUSTICE AND BEHAVIOR 118 (2003); Melissa Labriola, Michael Rempel, Chris O'Sullivan and Phyllis Frank with Jim McDowell and Rachel Finkelstein, *Court Responses to Batterer Program Noncompliance: A National Perspective*, CENTER FOR COURT INNOVATION (March 2007). This study confirms that there is still no evidence that batterer treatment programs reduce recidivism.

6. **Rethinking Why Men Batter.** Many have been critical of feminist explanations for battering and responses to it. Consider the following excerpt:

> The scientifically unsupported and tautological beliefs of profeminist advocates have resulted in substituting advocacy for science. Advocates' near stranglehold on the field of DV and their adamant refusal to allow for alternative explanations as to why men act out violently in their intimate relationships has stilted and stifled the development of the field—possibly putting the victim at more risk for violence. For example, Gondolf and Fisher found that the single best predictor of whether, after a shelter stay, a woman would return to a violent partner was that the batterer sought treatment. Mary M. Cavanaugh and Richard J. Gelles, *The Utility of Male Domestic Violence Offender Typologies, New Directions for Research, Policy, and Practice*, 20 J. INTERPERSONAL VIOLENCE 155 (2005).

Think back to the research on batterer typologies. Could classifying someone as a low, moderate, or high risk offender have implications for treatment? Should we be treating all abusers the same? Cavanaugh and Gelles suggest that the ability to identify types of offenders may lead to more accurate interventions. Why have domestic violence advocates resisted rethinking batterer intervention programs? It may be because advocates have much vested in these programs, both materially and theoretically. If sexism isn't the primary reason men batter, then what implications does acknowledging that have on domestic violence policy and practice more generally?

7. **Racial and Cultural Issues.** Regardless of whether a batterer's intervention program emphasizes the profeminist approach to treatment exemplified by the Duluth and EMERGE programs or another more nuanced approach, a separate question that arises is the suitability of treatment programs for men from different racial or cultural backgrounds. Fernando Mederos, a founder of "Common Purpose," another Boston-based batterers' treatment organization, is working to develop "culturally competent" curricula for men of color. He writes:

> Physically abusive men of color often claim that those who confront them are trying to destroy their culture or deprive them of their manhood. This is no more true for them than it is for European American offenders; to challenge someone's abusive behavior is not to destroy their culture. Instead, you can say (just as we do with Anglo batterers) that violence and abuse are never justified, and there is no

way of getting off the hook about this issue. This is a legitimate cross-cultural or universal value.

... [T]here is a danger that this extended discussion of culture and domestic violence emphasizes only the parts of European American and other cultures which give people permission to be violent or encourage them to tolerate violence. This perspective pathologizes culture in general.... It is profoundly inaccurate. The reality is that all cultures have elements—values and traditions—which are protective against the use of violence and which offenders can use to shape a non-abusive identity. In European American culture, batterer intervention programs use the ideal of equality—a resonant, if not perfectly practiced value—to help men shape their change process. In Hispanic culture, the corresponding value is respect (respeto) which is also a highly resonant and not always practiced ideal. Fernando Mederos, *Domestic Violence and Culture: Moving Toward More Sophisticated Encounters* (unpublished paper, 1998).

This perspective suggests that while men of color may face different challenges, culture should not be an excuse in batterer treatment programs, but rather a source of strength and transformation.

8. **Gun Confiscation and the Lautenberg Amendment.** One important issue to consider in sentencing batterers is whether they have firearms. On September 30, 1996, as an amendment to the Crime Control Act of 1968, President Clinton signed the Lautenberg Amendment into law. The Amendment provides that: "[i]t shall be unlawful for any person ... who has been convicted in any court of a misdemeanor crime of domestic violence, to ship or transport in interstate or foreign commerce, or possess in or affecting commerce, any firearm or ammunition; or to receive any firearm or ammunition which has been shipped or transported in interstate or foreign commerce." 18 U.S.C. § 922(g)(9) (Supp. III 1997). The logic of the Amendment, as articulated by its sponsor, is that: "[d]omestic violence, no matter how it is labeled, leads to more domestic violence, and guns in the hands of convicted wife beaters leads to death." 142 Cong. Rec. S10378 (1996) (statement of Sen. Lautenberg). See also Maria Kelly, *Domestic Violence and Guns: Seizing Weapons before the Court Has Made a Finding of Abuse*, 23 VT. L. REV. 349 (1998).

Under the Amendment an automatic sanction attaching to all domestic violence misdemeanor convictions is the requirement that the offender surrender all firearms, and presumably his license to carry arms, since the ban is permanent. The offender does not have to be charged with a crime specifically defined as a domestic violence offense; it is enough that the crime occur in a domestic violence context. This was the first time in the history of Congressional gun control legislation that no exemption was provided for police, military personnel, or government officials.

The impact on offenders whose employment depends on their ability to carry a firearm has been one rallying point for critics. See e.g. Lisa D. May, *The Backfiring of the Domestic Violence Firearm Bans*, 14 COLUM. J. GENDER & L. 1 (2005). Others have sought, unsuccessfully, to challenge the legislation as an unconstitutional exercise of power under the Commerce Clause.

To date, none of these challenges have been successful. See, e.g. *United States v. Nobriga*, 408 F.3d 1178 (9th Cir. 2005); *United States v. Lippman*, 369 F.3d 1039 (8th Cir. 2004).

In a recent article, Tom Lininger, a former Assistant United States Attorney, argues that while there are a growing number of prosecutions under the Lautenberg Amendment, it is still under-utilized by federal prosecutors. He suggests that since its constitutionality has been settled, it is time to revise the amendment's language to make it easier for prosecutors to ensure that those convicted of a domestic violence offense do not have guns. See Tom Lininger, *A Better Way to Disarm Batterers*, 54 HASTINGS L.J. 525 (2003).

Substance Abuse

A criticism often leveled at sentencing practices in the past was that when defendants appeared to have substance abuse problems, judges frequently assigned them to treatment programs addressing these problems rather than their abusive behavior. The misguided premise behind such dispositions was that the violence is a product of the drinking or the drugs, rather than the drinking or drugs being an accompaniment to or occasionally a facilitator of that violence, but not its root cause. On the other hand, it is unlikely that a perpetrator will be able to take advantage of a batterers' treatment program unless his substance abuse is being or has been addressed. Many batterers' treatment programs make it a condition of enrollment that a batterer be able to show that he has no such problem, or that he is in treatment for it. Today it is more common for substance-abusing perpetrators of domestic violence to be assigned by courts simultaneously to drug or alcohol treatment and to batterers' treatment, where both resources are available. The following excerpt discusses new models for dealing with domestic offenders.

Lisa Lightman and Francine Byrne
Addressing the Co–Occurrence of Domestic Violence & Substance Abuse: Lessons from Problem–Solving Courts

6 J. CENTER FOR FAMILIES, CHILD. & THE CTS. 53 (2005).

High rates of co-occurring substance use and domestic violence are well established. A recent study found that fully 92 percent of domestic violence perpetrators had used alcohol or drugs on the day of a domestic violence assault, and 72 percent had a record of prior arrests related to substance use. Other studies have shown that between one-fourth and one-half of men who commit acts of domestic violence are addicted to alcohol or other drugs. Research also shows that alcohol and drug abuse are related to an increased risk of violent death in the home. Early onset of drug-and alcohol-related problems is strongly correlated to domestic violence. In addition, alcohol and drug use has been associated with greater severity of injuries and increased lethality rates when present in conjunction with domestic violence. Although neither alcohol use nor drug use has, by itself, been proven to cause domestic violence, and though the cessation of alcohol or substance abuse is no guarantee that batterers will change their abusive behavior, research does suggest that, overall, domestic violence is reduced through the treatment of alcohol abuse.

Despite this research, the criminal justice system and community-based services do not routinely recognize or contend with the frequent co-occurrence of these problems in cases that may present solely as domestic violence or as substance abuse. Domestic violence convictions that do not result in incarceration generally lead to batterers' intervention programs, with substance abuse treatment being ordered only for offenders with obvious substance addiction issues. Similarly, battering behavior in defendants charged with substance abuse is rarely identified or acted on ... Moreover, failure to address domestic violence can affect recovery from drug addiction. Judge Finlay referred to research indicating that "unless you address both of the issues—substance abuse as well as violent behaviors—neither gets any better. In fact both can get worse." She noted that in "[e]very single failure that I look at, with rare exception, on the probation revocation calendar, a person who cannot do the domestic violence program, it's because of alcohol or other drug issues."

Because of the different causes and behaviors associated with domestic violence and substance abuse, a single type of service intervention will never be adequate to address both problems. As Patti Bland, statewide training coordinator for the Alaska Network on Domestic Violence and Sexual Assault, explained, "Substance abuse treatment can help make it possible for batterers to recover from alcohol and other drug dependence but does not adequately address domestic violence and cannot be substituted for batterer accountability or intervention programs designed to stop violence." The question then becomes how best to approach the coexistence of these issues. Specialized problem-solving courts could provide the judicial attention and service coordination necessary to address the co-occurrence of substance abuse and domestic violence. . . .

In recent years, policymakers, courts, and practitioners have supported the development of problem-solving courts as a response to increasing caseloads and the growing frustration of "business-as-usual" case processing. These innovative court models evolved from a recognition that the legal system, in its inability to stem the tide of drug usage or stop the violence, is "doomed if it remains static." As New York State Chief Judge Judith S. Kaye has written, "In many of today's cases, the traditional approach yields unsatisfying results. The addict arrested for drug dealing is adjudicated, does time, then goes right back to dealing on the street. The battered wife obtains a protective order, goes home and is beaten again. Every legal right of the litigants is protected, all procedures followed, yet we aren't making a dent in the underlying problem."

Instead of simply moving cases through the system, problem-solving courts focus on strong collaborations with service providers and legal partners to address the underlying issues in these cases. Judicial leadership is critical to promote defendant compliance and to ensure effective relationships among the court and its partners, including prosecutors, defense attorneys, law enforcement and probation officials, and service providers in a variety of community-based agencies. Judicial oversight appears to have significant impact in motivating behavioral change, thereby improving outcomes for victims and defendants while increasing public safety. The positive results of specialized courts have resulted in public and political recognition of their efficacy and an increase in financial support to the courts from executive agencies, legislators, and county governments. As we enter the second decade of problem-solving courts, and as our knowledge and sophistication about the complexities of comprehensive interventions grow, the justice system will continue to refine and expand these innovative initiatives. Drug courts and domestic violence courts are well positioned to consider new methods that advance the coordination of substance abuse and domestic violence interventions. . . .

Fundamental differences can be noted in the philosophy and goals of drug courts and domestic violence courts that reflect the distinct causes and dynamics of substance abuse and domestic violence as well as appropriate interventions for them. Drug courts generally rely on a medical model of treatment—approaching the addiction as a disease—and though they require accountability, they operate on the assumption that relapse is a natural part of recovery. Drug courts typically handle only nonviolent offenders and focus on their rehabilitation, an achievable goal because successful methods of promoting recovery from substance abuse are well established. Defendants voluntarily opt to have their cases heard in drug court by agreeing to accept both a plea and the conditions of treatment that the court and clinical staff have identified as necessary for successful completion after an initial assessment. Once the defendant is participating in drug court, the court, the prosecutor, and the defense attorney are all focused on the defendant's success, so they adopt a "team approach" to handling issues that arise. Drug courts promote a supportive atmosphere where participants are applauded and rewarded for good behavior and progress in treatment.

In contrast, domestic violence courts focus on violent perpetrators who have hurt their targeted victims. These courts see domestic violence not as an illness but as a learned and voluntary behavior, making an illness and treatment model inapplicable. "Relapse" in domestic violence is not tolerated. Moreover, unlike treatment programs for substance abuse, batterers' intervention programs are largely untested, and no approach has clearly proven successful in reducing long-term battering behavior. For practitioners familiar with the dynamics of domestic violence, the concepts of rehabilitation and being powerless over addiction, familiar ideas in drug courts, are inappropriate in domestic violence courts.

Instead, the highest priority of domestic violence courts is victim safety, and therefore the court focuses on procedures and outcomes that will promote it. The court emphasizes victim services, which are voluntary and centered on assisting the victim and the children to achieve safety both in the short and long term. These services can include links to shelter and food, counseling, safety planning, health care, and job training. For the defendant, the court's focus is on accountability and punishment rather than rehabilitation. The court routinely imposes criminal sentences, including incarceration and intensive probation supervision. . . .

A deep philosophical divide separates the approaches to substance abuse and domestic violence that dictate the distinct goals and practices of drug courts and domestic violence courts, as well as their varying service interventions. It may never be possible, or even appropriate, to attempt to merge these practices into a single approach to both issues. But it may be feasible to identify the primary issue before the court and maintain the procedures suited to that problem while also recognizing and addressing other existing problems. The development of such a coordinated approach to the co-occurrence of substance abuse and domestic violence would be a sensitive and complex project, yet it deserves further consideration.

NOTES AND QUESTIONS

1. **Specialized Courts and Gender Discrimination.** The specialized court described above is a very unique model, taking a far more integrated approach. Other specialized courts simply hear only domestic violence cases. Do specialized courts that exclusively handle domestic violence cases violate the due process and equal protection rights of defendants? In *Robinson v. United States*, 769 A.2d 747 (D.C. Cir.2001) the defendant argued that a Domestic Violence Unit established in Washington D.C. to deal specifically with these cases was unconstitutional. In particular, he argued that the arrest policy of the police, the prosecution policy of the U.S. Attorney's Office, and the trial defendants in a domestic violence court that handled both civil and criminal cases resulted in, "prejudice against men and the automatic assumption that men are violent." The Court rejected his claims. Are there particular risks or benefits to handling both civil and criminal cases together? Do we undermine the criminal wrong-doing of domestic violence when we use integrated approaches, or are we more likely to provide better solutions to victims and their families?

2. **Child Abuse and Specialized Courts.** Not all commentators applaud the move to specialized courts. For example Deborah Epstein argues that specialized courts may increase tensions between those communities which are primarily concerned with domestic violence and those communities which are primarily concerned with child abuse and neglect. She finds:

> An integrated court system creates an environment in which victims with children are more likely to have extensive contact with government attorneys and paralegals. This, in turn, means that government workers are more likely to hear about abuse that occurred in the presence of children or where children themselves actually were harmed. In the District of Columbia, this has led to an increase (albeit a small one) in the rate of government reports to Child Protective Service. Deborah Epstein, *Effective Intervention in Domestic Violence Cases: Rethinking the Roles of Prosecutors, Judges, and the Court System*, 11 YALE J.L. & FEMINISM 3 (1999).

What other risks might there be for victims who have their cases heard in specialized courts? Does the focus solely on providing treatment for the defendant really help the victim, or might she need services herself? In the next section, we consider responses to domestic violence that are not based on traditional criminal models of arrest, prosecution, and sentencing.

3. **Noncompliance.** Whether or not a defendant is sentenced to treatment, drug or alcohol counseling, or a program via a specialized court, he or she must comply with the conditions of his or her probation, or risk jail. Even though there is no evidence that batterer treatment programs reduce recidivism, there is some evidence that they can increase batterer accountability, particularly in those jurisdictions that have graduated sanctions for failure to attend treatment. Few courts, however, have a system of monitoring noncompliance. See Melissa Labriola, et al., *Court Responses to Batterer Program Noncompliance: A National Perspective*, CENTER FOR COURT INNOVATION (March 2007).

Alternatives to Criminal Sanctions

Although there continue to be innovations and research in the sentencing and treatment of domestic violence offenders, many commentators have questioned whether a punitive response to domestic violence is the best or whether there ought to be a more "therapeutic" response. Below are excerpts from two articles exploring alternatives to the criminal justice system. The first excerpt focuses on a restorative justice model, a model for punishment that is quite different from the American model. The second model is drawn from Navajo Peacemaking.

Lawrence W. Sherman

Domestic Violence and Restorative Justice: Answering Key Questions

8 VA. J. SOC. POL'Y & L. 263 (2000).

One major alternative to incarceration may be loosely described as "restorative justice." The term most often describes responses to crime that involve reparations rather than incarceration, although a broad definition of this form of jurisprudence may include certain activities (such as apologies) associated with imprisonment and even execution. Over the past decade, this approach has become increasingly popular for juvenile offenses throughout Anglo–American legal systems, as well as for certain adult offenses. This approach, however, has rarely been considered in relation to domestic violence. . . .

Retribution is generally absent in standard criminal justice since the vast majority of all offenses leading to arrest never result in punishment. For example, in Milwaukee in the late 1980's, less than 5% of arrests for domestic violence resulted in a prosecution. Of the 14 million or more arrests each year in the U.S., fewer than 500,000–4 percent—result in time served in prison. In Canberra, Australia, in contrast, violent offenders sent to restorative justice paid higher amounts of money to charity than the amounts of fines paid by violent offenders sent to court.

Restorative justice is thus different from both "retributive" justice, which is more punitive than most American courts, and "standard"—or low probability of punishment—justice. The differences between restorative and standard justice are found in the following dimensions: repairing harm, listening to victims, deliberative democracy, egalitarian procedures, and informal social control. Neither retributive nor standard justice employ any of these features. While not all innovations in justice that are labeled "restorative" employ all of these features, many of them do. The Canberra, Australia experiments, which provide the most detailed evidence to date on the effects of such procedures for various crimes (not including domestic violence), employ all of these features.

A. The Goal of Repairing Harm.

The most basic feature of restorative justice is that it restores the state of affairs prior to the commission of a crime, at least to the extent possible. The restorative justice approach aims for this restoration of pre-crime status in different ways—for victims and their loved ones, for communities, and for offenders and their loved ones.

1. Restoring the Victims

For victims, restorative justice seeks both physical and emotional restoration. This is typically attempted through the creation of goods for victims rather than through the infliction of pain on offenders. While some might argue that it is emotionally restorative for a rape victim to see her offender executed, the premise of restorative justice—and the distinction from retributive justice—is that something of positive value should be given to the victim. By definition, restorative jurisprudence does not consider infliction of pain or death on the offender to be of positive value.

Certain kinds of harm are clearly irreparable, and beyond any meaningful exchange of value. This may even be more true of emotional harm than of physical harm. A victim who loses a kidney in an assault can accept an offender's donation of a kidney (under certain medical conditions), and be restored to the state of having two kidneys. But the system cannot restore the victim's absence of fear about death or serious disability that would result from the loss of a kidney. In cases of domestic violence, once a man hits a woman who loves him, there can never be the same level of trust and security that there was prior to that first assault. No matter how much positive value might be offered in compensation for the physical pain, the experience of fear can never be erased.

Thus, restoration of victims is a goal of restorative justice rather than a guarantee. It is the attempt to achieve this goal, rather than its full accomplishment, that defines a restorative justice process. In contrast to standard justice, restorative justice is distinct in merely pursuing this goal. However weak or incomplete the attempts to restore victims may be, they are likely to be more substantial than the consequences of standard and retributive justice procedures that bypass restoration altogether.

2. Repairing Society

Restorative justice also recognizes the ripple effects of crime, mapped across the social networks of victims' families and friends. These effects are mostly emotional, but they can also be financial. When a family is dependent upon the victim's earnings and earnings are disrupted by the results of domestic violence, the material harm of crime can clearly be restored—when offenders have enough money to do so. Victim's families may also participate in a ceremony in which offenders accept full responsibility for the harm they have caused, apologize for their actions, and commit themselves to repairing the harm in order to restore emotional harm. As recent surveys of citizens in New England have shown, there is a high level of interest in providing opportunities for such encounters. These encounters may provide far more satisfaction that offenders take responsibility for their actions than a brief appearance in court. . . .

3. Restoring Offenders

Restoring offenders is the most controversial aspect of restorative justice. In retributive terms, an offender has no right to be restored to their position in society prior to committing a crime. That is the logic for depriving felons of voting rights, and banning them from certain kinds of employment. The restorative approach, however, assumes that the greatest good to the community would result from a full restoration of the offender to a law-abiding citizen. Unlike traditional "rehabilitation," there is no medical model for how this should occur. The various theories of restoring offenders, as described in answer to the next question, assume that offenders can become law-abiding through acts and relationships rather than through a personality change or "treatment." Repairing the harm to victims, victims' loved ones, and the community is the most important kind of act offenders can commit to restore themselves. Such repair allows them to repay their moral debts to all these parties, or at least to come closer to that goal than would be the case under "standard" justice. This community also includes offenders' own loved ones, since the pain they suffer is also a net loss for the community. . . .

Donna Coker

Enhancing Autonomy for Battered Women: Lessons Learned From Navajo Peacemaking

47 UCLA L. REV. 1 (1999).

Navajo Peacemaking is a process in which a Naat'aanii (peacemaker), familiar with Navajo common law and traditional Navajo stories, guides disputing parties to develop a resolution. A Peacemaking session includes members of the extended families of the disputants and may also include community members with relevant expertise (e.g., alcohol treatment counselors and social workers). Peacemakers understand Peacemaking as a spiritual process in which the primary purpose is the restoration of hózhó, roughly (but inadequately) translated as "harmony. . . ."

Many feminist anti-domestic violence scholars and activists have been understandably skeptical of the use of informal processes such as Peacemaking in domestic violence cases. The concerns are that informal methods of adjudication may ignore domestic power hierarchies and thus facilitate the batterer's ongoing violence against the victim, resulting in unfair and coerced "agreements." Informal processes may create an occasion for the batterer, his family, and perhaps even the victim's family, to blame the victim for the batterer's anger, violence, or both. Further, a focus on the particular needs of individual victims and batterers may fail to represent society's substantial interest in preventing domestic violence.

The debate between advocates of formal and informal methods of intervention in domestic violence cases fails to address some of the concerns that are of greatest importance to many battered women. These concerns illuminate Peacemaking's potential benefits for some battered women. The most important of these concerns is the ability of domestic violence intervention strategies to realize change in the material and social conditions that foster battering. Material conditions are implicated both in women's vulnerability to battering and in understanding why some men batter women they purport to love. . . .

Peacemaking is structured around procedural steps. It begins with an opening prayer in both Navajo and English. After the peacemaker has explained the rules, the petitioner is allowed to explain his or her complaint. The respondent is then asked to respond to the petitioner's complaint. Next, the peacemaker provides a "[b]rief overview of the problem as presented by the disputants." Family members and other participants, including traditional teachers, may then join the discussion, providing their description or explanation of the problem(s).

The peacemaker, usually chosen by his or her chapter, is a respected person with a demonstrated knowledge of traditional Navajo stories. He or she must be someone who possesses the power of persuasion, because peacemakers do not judge or decide cases. Their power lies in their words and their influence. Peacemakers "show a lot of love, they use encouraging words, [when you] use [Navajo] teaching to lift [participants] up you can accomplish a lot, [if you] are very patient. . . ."

Peacemaking is a formal part of the Navajo legal system, developed and overseen by the Navajo Nation judiciary. There are two primary routes by which cases reach Peacemaking: court referral and self-referral. Criminal cases may be referred by the court as the result of diversion or as a condition of probation. The Domestic Abuse Protection Act creates special rules for domestic violence protection order cases: A referral to Peacemaking must be approved by the petitioner, and the peacemaker must have received special domestic violence training. In all other civil cases, the rules allow courts to refer cases to Peacemaking over a party's objection, but in practice judges seldom refer civil cases involving allegations of domestic violence unless both parties agree to the referral. In addition to court referral, Peacemaking may be initiated by a petitioner on a claim that he or she has been "injured, hurt or aggrieved by the actions of another." Self-referred cases make up the majority of Peacemaking cases. In a self-referred case, the peacemaker liaison seeks authorization from the district court to subpoena the respondent and all other necessary parties identified by the petitioner....

In a case involving family violence, a young man related his excuses, exhibiting denial, minimilization and externalization. One of the people who listened was the young man's sister. She listened to his story and confronted him by saying, "you know very well you have a drinking problem." She then related the times she had seen him drunk and abusive.... [S]he told her brother she loved him very much and was willing to help him if only he would admit his problems. He did.

Bluehouse described this confrontational aspect of Peacemaking:

[T]here may be issues of domestic violence where there's some denial, the victimizer may be intellectualizing which becomes very obvious in Peacemaking, because family members will know. [They will say,] "this doesn't sound like you...." [Family members may say,] "Uncle, I can't understand why you are talking to your family like this [in Peacemaking]; is this another side of you? We like this side of you, we'd like to see more of this side of you. We've seen you ... deal with your wife in a cruel and inhuman [manner], so why all of a sudden in a Peacemaking room with a person from the outside [do you behave this way]?" Families cannot always be counted on to confront an abusive family member, however. Family members may deny, minimize, and blame the victim for the batterer's violence. Peacemakers note that parents in particular are prone to cover for their son and blame his partner. Thus, peacemakers must confront familial or parental denial in order to confront the batterer's denial. "[I]f there is a lot of denial you have to confront the person with respect and love, but you have to cut through [the denial], and you have to confront them."

Denial and familial solidarity are not the only impediments to families confronting batterers. Family members—his or hers—may be too afraid of the batterer to confront him or too focused on hiding the past or current violence in their own households. In such cases, if the batterer is confronted, it must be by the peacemaker.

Peacemaking also provides a forum for the victim's family to intervene on her behalf. For example, in one case an uncle was a copetitioner with his niece. The uncle expressed concern that his niece's daughters took her husband's side in arguments and that both the father and the daughters verbally and physically abused the mother.

In addition to encouraging family participation, Peacemaking may also provide a mechanism for transferring material resources to the victim, thus lessening her economic and social vulnerability. This could occur in three ways. First, the abuser or his family or both may agree to provide nalyeeh (reparations) in the form of money, goods, or personal services for the victim. Nalyeeh is a concrete recognition that the harm of battering is real and that responsibility for it extends beyond the individual batterer. In addition, both abuser and victim are likely to be referred to social service providers and to traditional healing ceremonies. The assistance given by agencies and by traditional healers often results in increased community and governmental material support. Finally, the victim's family may overcome past estrangement from the victim and agree to provide her with assistance.

NOTES AND QUESTIONS

1. **Alternative Approaches to Punishment.** In Lawrence Sherman's description of restorative justice, he focuses on repairing harm to both the victim and the community. These are similar goals to Navajo Peacemaking as described by Donna Coker. In each of these systems, there is emphasis placed on healing the victim, both psychologically and materially. Others have suggested similar alternative approaches. For example, Linda Mills suggests that the criminal justice system adopt The Intimate Abuse Circle (IAC) process. Similar to both restorative justice and Navajo Peacemaking, IAC includes the couple's community in the healing process. It emphasizes "narrative theory"—and the importance of understanding each individual's experience with abuse. For a description see Linda G. Mills, FROM INSULT TO INJURY: RETHINKING OUR RESPONSES TO INTIMATE ABUSE (2003). To date, only a few jurisdictions have implemented such alternatives.

E.   DOMESTIC VIOLENCE AS A FEDERAL CRIME

Introduction

We have already examined the role the Federal government plays in combating domestic violence. The Violence Against Women Act of 1994, part of the larger Violent Crime Control and Law Enforcement Act of 1994, Pub. L. No. 103–322, 108 Stat. 1796 (codified as amended in scattered sections of 42 U.S.C.), federalized the enforcement of restraining orders by requiring that states provide full faith and credit to orders issued by sister states, but also criminalized interstate violations of restraining orders. In addition, the act made "interstate domestic violence" a federal crime. The definition of "interstate domestic violence" will be explored further in this section. As the first section of this chapter described, interstate stalking was added to the list of federal domestic violence crimes in 1996. 18 U.S.C. § 2261A. Finally, offenses relating to the transportation or possession of firearms by state and federal domestic violence offenders are incorporated both in the original Violence Against Women Act, for those subject to valid restraining orders, 18 U.S.C. § 922(g)(8), and in the later and more controversial Lautenberg Amendment, for those convicted of a domestic violence misdemeanor, 18 U.S.C. § 922(g)(9). Gun confiscation was also discussed earlier.

The Violence Against Women Act was reauthorized in 2000, and again in 2005. In those authorizations, Congress strengthened the interstate stalking provisions discussed by surveillance and intimidation to the list of proscribed offenses. It also doubled penalties for repeat domestic violence and stalking offenders, and added "dating partners" to its definition of domestic violence. In addition, more funds were appropriated for states to combat teen dating violence, provide victims with services, and engage men and boys in programs aimed at preventing domestic violence.

The criminal provisions of VAWA have faced robust challenges on constitutional and policy grounds, not only by defendants anxious to escape the consequences of federal prosecution, but by scholars and participant observers who worry about the growing role of federal law enforcement in areas traditionally left to the states. This section opens with an excerpt that introduces the interstate domestic violence provision, and also provides a reminder of how the criminal provisions of the Violence Against Women Act fit into the broader context of that legislation. The next readings address interpretive issues arising out of the interstate domestic violence provision. Next, the section addresses the (predominantly unsuccessful) constitutional challenges brought against the criminal provisions. The section closes with arguments for and against the creation of federal crimes from a policy, rather than a constitutional, perspective.

Michelle W. Easterling

For Better or Worse: The Federalization of Domestic Violence

98 W. Va. L. Rev. 933 (1996).

On December 1, 1994, Christopher Jarett Bailey carried his comatose wife Sonya into a Corbin, Kentucky emergency room. The Kentucky physicians discovered a large open wound on Sonya's forehead, two black eyes, bruises on her neck, chin, and forearms, as well as signs of rope burns on her wrists and ankles. Upon inspection of the couple's car, police discovered that the trunk lid was dented on the inside, there were scratch marks around the lock, and there was a pool of blood and urine. The couple had last been seen arguing in a bar on November 25, 1994. Bailey had beaten his wife into unconsciousness at their home in St. Albans, West Virginia. Bailey then began an aimless six-day drive in and out of West Virginia and Kentucky. Sonya had spent at least part of that journey in the trunk. When Bailey finally carried Sonya into a Kentucky hospital, doctors discovered that she had suffered a severe head injury and was near death from the loss of blood, fluids and oxygen. Sonya Bailey's doctors predict that she will spend the remainder of a normal life expectancy comatose in a nursing home. Christopher Bailey, convicted of kidnapping and interstate domestic violence, will spend the remainder of his life in a federal prison. On May 23, 1995, after only two and one-half hours of deliberations, Bailey became the first person convicted under ... the Federal Violence Against Women Act of 1994.

The [Act] ... created two new federal criminal offenses: interstate domestic violence and interstate violation of a protective order....

[The] new [interstate domestic violence] offense allows for the federal prosecution of a person who travels across a state line with the intent to injure, harass, or intimidate his or her spouse, and who intentionally commits a crime of violence causing bodily injury to that spouse. One is also subject to federal prosecution if he or she, like Bailey, causes a spouse to cross a state line by force, coercion, duress, or fraud and in the course or as a result of that conduct intentionally commits a crime of violence causing injury to his or her spouse. The Act calls for the defendants convicted of interstate domestic violence to be sentenced as according to the extent of injuries to the victim. If the victim dies, the offender can be sentenced to life or any term of years. If permanent disfigurement or life threatening bodily injury results, the offender may be sentenced to a maximum of twenty years in prison. If the victim suffers serious bodily injury, or if the offender uses a dangerous weapon when committing the offense, imprisonment can not exceed ten years. Otherwise, sentencing is allowed ... for not more than five years. The VAWA also directs the court to order restitution to be paid to the victim.... Other provisions of the VAWA call for law enforcement and prosecution grants to aid in the reduction of violent crimes against women. Section 2263 allows the victim of domestic violence an opportunity to be heard about the danger posed by the defendant when determining pre-trial release conditions....

The Violence Against Women Act ... was only enacted after extensive congressional hearings concerning domestic violence statistics and testimonials about domestic abuse. The resulting Act was intended to be a comprehensive piece of legislation in order to prevent, punish, and deter spousal abusers....

Congress, alarmed by the startling statistics, was apparently convinced that the states were not solving the domestic violence problem, and that the federal government's involvement was needed. Senator Kennedy said that "the bill provides funds to train and educate police, prosecutors and judges so that violence within the family will be taken seriously and treated as the crime that it is." Representative Moakley urged the House that "(d)omestic violence is no longer an issue that we, in society, can ignore or simply dismiss as a lover's quarrel...."

Perhaps the most straightforward remarks were made by Representative Schumer from New York:

> (t)here is a dirty little secret hidden here, and that secret is that our legal system is all too indifferent to this violence. Our legal system looks the other way, tolerating the daily battering and abuse of women ... A woman is raped; she goes to the police and is told, "You aren't really hurt. Just try and forget about it." Another victim is told by the prosecutor, "I won't bring this case because you were wearing a short skirt." A woman has her nose broken by her husband. When the police finally come they say, "You two work out your problems together." A woman goes before a judge asking for a protection order from a husband she has tried to leave, and the judge says, "Why are you two wasting our time with marital squabbles?"

... Congress responded to the terrifying testimonials and statistics with the VAWA. The Act was intended to be a comprehensive arsenal to fight a war against gender-motivated violence. The VAWA was designed to deter, punish and rehabilitate offenders in order to prevent domestic abuse. Senator Biden explained that the bill would make women substantially safer because of the increased number of battered women's shelters, the education of prosecutors and judges, and the creation of both criminal and civil causes of actions. Grants were included to train and educate police, prosecutors and judges so that domestic violence "would be taken seriously." Funds were also allotted to assist law enforcement, support counselors and shelters, and restore a national toll-free domestic violence hotline.

As passed, the VAWA provided for $1.62 billion to be given to the states over the next six years for funding community programs to battle violence against women and provide battered women with support. Each state was to receive $500,000 a year, with additional funds to be provided to states with higher populations. In 1995, Congress allotted $426,000 for each state. After the states submitted plans to the Department of Justice, the government planned to release the remainder of the funds. For example, West Virginia's general plan includes training and cross-training between law enforcement, courts, and those who provide direct services to abuse victims. The plan also contains more legal advocates to aid victims and a computerized system to allow officers to track protective orders across county lines. It extends direct services to all fifty-five West Virginia counties and provides awareness about local resources which would help women in abusive situations.

Finally, the VAWA also called for several studies to be conducted by various branches of government to examine gender bias in courts, campus sexual assaults, battered women's syndrome, the confidentiality of victims' addresses, and domestic violence related recordkeeping. These studies were designed to gain a clear understanding of the origins and extent of women's issues and to provide recommendations for further reform.

NOTES AND QUESTIONS

1. **Statutory Language.** Although Easterling uses the word "spouse" in her account of the interstate domestic violence provision, the language of the statute actually encompasses all "intimate partners" as well as "dating partners," a provision that was added in 2005. Also, penalties for repeat offenders were doubled.

2. **Interpretive Issues.** One of the issues the federal courts have faced is what conduct constitutes a violation of the offense. In *United States v. Page*, below, the defendant objected that his violence toward his girlfriend had ended before he caused her to cross a state line, and that § 2261(a)(2) did not properly apply. The defendant was convicted in the District Court for the Southern District of Ohio after a jury trial. On appeal the Sixth Circuit reversed and remanded. The United States then obtained a rehearing en banc, and when the sixteen members of the plenary panel were equally divided in their vote, the defendant's conviction and sentence were restored. A petition for certiorari was denied. The following excerpts from opinions in the case both supporting and opposing the conviction address the interpretive question raised.

United States v. Page

United States Court of Appeals for the Sixth Circuit, 1999.
167 F.3d 325.

■ KAREN NELSON MOORE, CIRCUIT JUDGE, concurring in the order.

Derek Page, the defendant in this case, was convicted under 18 U.S.C. § 2261(a)(2)....

On appeal, he raises the questions whether physical violence that occurs before interstate travel begins can satisfy the "in the course ... of that conduct" requirement of § 2261(a)(2) and whether a threat of violence that results in the aggravation of pre-existing injuries can be a "crime of violence" causing "bodily injury" for purposes of the statute. I would answer both questions in the affirmative and conclude that there was sufficient evidence for the jury to convict Page under either theory....

I. BACKGROUND

The facts of this case are not unlike the stories of many women who attempt to leave abusive relationships. Carla Scrivens's relationship with Page started out on fairly blissful terms. Yet, Page soon became controlling, possessive, and even physically abusive, demanding that Scrivens stop associating with her friends and family, controlling what she could wear and eat, and on one occasion even punishing her disobedience with a stun gun and mace. In light of the deterioration of their relationship, after less than three months together, Scrivens told Page that she was moving out and ending their relationship.

The planned attack against Scrivens took place when she attempted to retrieve her belongings, all of which were still in Page's condominium in Columbus, Ohio. Upon Scrivens's arrival, Page pushed her down, dragged her away from the door when she attempted to leave, and tried to spray her with mace. He then beat her with his fists, a claw hammer, and a pipe wrench over the course of several hours. Scrivens also testified that Page used a stun gun during the assault. After the beating, Page carried his victim, who could not walk on her battered feet and legs, and who had fallen into unconsciousness several times during the attack, and placed her into his car under threat of further violence from his stun gun. Page then drove around for approximately four hours, crossing state lines through West Virginia into Pennsylvania and intentionally passing several local hospitals on the way even though Scrivens pleaded with him to stop for medical treatment at either Riverside or Ohio State University, two hospitals in the Columbus area. During this time, Scrivens continued to bleed, and painful swelling from her injuries increased. Page eventually left her at a hospital in Washington, Pennsylvania, where, after she realized that Page would not return, Scrivens told emergency room personnel that Page had attacked her, and agreed to report the incident to the police.

II. STATUTORY SCOPE

Page's conduct, as presented to the jury, falls within the scope of § 2261(a)(2) under at least two theories of liability. The evidence showed that he committed interstate domestic violence both: (1) when, by beating his ex-girlfriend into a state of semi-consciousness over the course of several hours, he was enabled to and did force her across state lines against her will in an attempt to evade the law, and (2) when he forced her to travel interstate under threat of violence, intentionally preventing her from obtaining medical treatment, thereby causing aggravation of her pre-existing injuries.

A.   *"In the Course of": Infliction of Bodily Injury Integrally Related to the Forcible Transportation of a Victim Across State Lines*

In order to escape liability under § 2261(a)(2), Page argues that "in the course ... of that conduct" as used in the statute refers to the narrow act of "crossing a State line" rather than to all conduct involved in "causing a spouse or intimate partner to cross a State line ... by force, coercion, duress, or fraud...." This construction not only distorts the plain language of the statute but also makes little sense given the reality of the crime and the very reasons why Congress believed federal involvement was necessary in this area that has traditionally been left to the states.

The crime of violence that took place inside Page's condominium—the beating and the use of a stun gun and mace—is precisely what enabled Page to force Scrivens to travel across state lines. The beating subdued his victim, rendered her in no condition to resist him physically as she was being placed into his car, and frightened her so severely that she agreed not to make any "commotion" that might attract attention and aid from others once they left his condominium. The attack also allowed Page to retain control over Scrivens during the forcible transportation. Not surprisingly, a person who has just been beaten in the manner Scrivens had been is far less capable physically and emotionally of attempting an escape, formulating a method of escape, or eliciting aid from others. The beating was an integral part of the forcible transportation since it enabled Page to force Scrivens on an unwilling four-hour journey the destination of which was not revealed to Scrivens until much later. Consequently, the beating that took place inside Page's condominium clearly occurred "in the course" of Page forcibly "causing" Scrivens "to cross a State line."

Furthermore, evidence presented to the jury showed that Page removed Scrivens from the local area precisely because he feared the consequences of his having harmed her and knew that interstate travel would make it more difficult for police authorities to hold him liable for his crime. It is difficult to believe that Congress intended to exclude from this statute's purview the beating of an intimate partner by a batterer who then forcibly transports his victim across state lines under threat of further violence in order to avoid detection from the law. Gaps and inadequacies of state law enforcement were among the main reasons for which federal legislation dealing with domestic violence was thought to be necessary. The VAWA was intended to deal with the problem of batterers who make their crimes more difficult to discover and prosecute by carrying or forcing their intimate partners across state lines. Those who enacted the VAWA's interstate domestic violence provision recognized that batterers were using interstate travel as a loophole in the system of state law enforcement and that such crimes, "because of their interstate nature, transcend the abilities of State law enforcement agencies." When batterers take their victims across state lines, local prosecutors often encounter difficulties subpoenaing hospital documents and witnesses from other states. Multi-state jurisdiction is also valuable during the investigative stage, in which local police officers encounter similar barriers.... As it has often done, Congress used the VAWA "to 'come to the aid of the states in detecting and punishing criminals whose offenses are complete under state law, but who utilize the channels of interstate commerce to make a successful getaway and thus make the state's detecting and punitive processes impotent.'" ... Page's crabbed interpretation would prevent the statute from reaching precisely the type of situation for which a federal domestic violence statute would be needed and that § 2261(a)(2) was intended to cover.

... To assume that Congress intended to criminalize only those beatings occurring precisely during travel but not those occurring inside a home that are integrally related to forcible interstate travel would be to suggest that Congress somehow missed the boat.

The text of § 2261(a)(2) refers to violence that occurs in a course of "conduct." Its neighboring statutes demonstrate that Congress knew how to say in the course of "travel" when it wanted to. In addition to interstate domestic violence, Congress has created the federal crimes of interstate stalking and interstate violation of a protection order. All three of these statutes require interstate travel as an element of the crime, but only § 2261(a)(2) and § 2262(a)(2) involve forcing another person to cross state lines. Sections 2261 and 2262 are parallel, prohibiting interstate domestic violence and interstate violation of a protection order, respectively. Subsection (a)(1) of each section prohibits interstate travel with the intent to commit domestic violence or violate a protection order, respectively. In these provisions—and in § 2261A, which prohibits travel with the intent to harass—coverage is clearly limited to violence or harassment that occurs during or after interstate travel: the statutes refer to actions that occur "subsequent[]" to interstate travel or "in the course of or as a result of such travel." See 18 U.S.C. §§ 2261(a)(1), 2261A, 2262(a)(1)(B). In contrast, subsection (a)(2) of both § 2261 and § 2262 specifically addresses violations that involve forcing another person to travel, and only these two subsections, of all the VAWA crimes, refer to "that conduct." This is a sensible distinction that should not be read out of the statute.

B.   "In the Course of": Aggravation of Injuries During Forced Interstate Travel

The government argues that Page's threats during the trip to Pennsylvania resulted in "bodily injury" to the extent that they kept Scrivens from receiving medical treatment sooner and aggravated her preexisting wounds. I agree that threats can be a "crime of violence," that aggravation of preexisting injuries can be "bodily injury," and that there was sufficient evidence to convict Page under this theory.

A "crime of violence" includes "an offense that has as an element the use, attempted use, or threatened use of physical force against the person or property of another." 18 U.S.C. § 16(a). It may also be an offense "that is a felony and that, by its nature, involves a substantial risk that physical force against the person or property of another may be used in the course of committing the offense." 18 U.S.C. § 16(b). To meet this definition, the government was required to prove that Page committed some state or federal "offense" and that this offense was of a type described in § 6(a) or (b). The two offenses that the jury considered were kidnapping and assault. . . .

In addition to proving that Page committed a kidnapping or an assault during the actual travel, in order to obtain a conviction under its aggravation-of-injury theory, the government had to prove that the kidnapping or assault caused Scrivens to suffer bodily injury. . . .

Nowhere does the statute suggest that the bodily injury must be an injury newly inflicted, completely distinct from the prior criminal actions of the batterer. Such a limitation would make little sense. If we were to require that an injury be "fresh" in order to satisfy the statute, Page's actions would not constitute a crime of interstate domestic violence even if Scrivens had bled to death or gone into shock during and as a result of the forcible transportation. Page's interpretation would also prevent the statute from reaching the conduct at issue in *United States v. Bailey*, 112 F.3d 758 (4th Cir.), cert. denied, 522 U.S. 896 (1997). The defendant in *Bailey* severely injured his wife, put her in a car, and drove around West Virginia and Kentucky for five days before taking her to a hospital. The victim suffered further injuries—including blood loss, which led to permanent brain damage, and dehydration, which led to renal failure—due to the defendant's failure to obtain medical care or provide adequate food and water. There was no question in *Bailey* that the statute applied. Yet, there is no relevant distinction between a person who forcibly prevents his intimate partner from obtaining medical care, causing her to bleed to death; a person who forcibly prevents his diabetic intimate partner from obtaining insulin shots, causing her to fall into a coma; and a person who forcibly prevents his intimate partner from obtaining food and water for several days, causing her to suffer renal failure. Any prior criminal actions of these batterers should in no way weaken or negate the observation that these three situations are analogous and that in all of these scenarios the batterer has committed a crime of violence causing bodily harm.

■ KENNEDY, CIRCUIT JUDGE, dissenting in the order.

Preceded by a descriptive caption, one sentence containing four separate elements defines the federal domestic violence crime in question:

Causing the crossing of a State line.—A person who [1] *causes* a spouse or intimate partner *to cross a State line* . . . [2] *and, in the course or as a result of that conduct*, [3] intentionally commits a crime of violence [4] *and thereby causes bodily injury* to the person's spouse or intimate partner, shall be punished as provided in subsection (b).

A literal or precise reading of the words of the sentence, and the sequence of elements described there, requires me to find that Page should not be punished under this statute for the criminal assault that occurred before he began to cause Scrivens to cross a state line. That result is necessary because an offender is covered by the statute only if he "causes" the victim "to cross a state line" by force, coercion, duress, or fraud, and "causes bodily injury" to the victim "in the course . . . of that conduct;" that conduct of causing the victim "to cross a state line" by force, coercion, duress, or fraud. The literal meaning of the words does not allow punishment of a man who beats a woman before the journey begins *unless of course his purpose in inflicting bodily injury is to cause her to cross state lines*. The provision therefore criminalizes an act of domestic violence that occurs before interstate travel actually begins only if the violence is the same "force" that the attacker employs to cause his victim to cross state lines against her will *and* the attacker's purpose at the time he inflicts the injury is to transport his victim across state lines.

The construction I have described above appears to be the obvious meaning of the statute. . . .

Judge Moore concludes that because Scrivens was completely incapacitated by the attack, she was under Page's control continuously from the time she entered the condominium until she crossed state lines, and that this somehow permitted the jury to find that the injuries she suffered in the attack in the condominium were inflicted in the course of causing her to cross state lines. While I agree that injuries inflicted before any travel begins can be found to be a part of "that conduct" if inflicted to cause the victim to cross state lines, there is no evidence here that such intent caused any of the injuries Scrivens sustained before she was placed in the car.

Were the evidence in this case such that the jury could conclude that the *severity* of the attack was to enable Page to take Scrivens across state lines to a distant hospital, then I could agree that conduct was covered by the statute. . . .

If there were some evidence that any of the *particular injuries* inflicted on Scrivens were inflicted not merely to prevent her escape from the condominium, but specifically in order to make it easier to transport her across state lines, . . . I could then agree that Page's attack is covered by the statute. While causing someone to cross state lines encompasses broader conduct than simply traveling across state lines, still there must be some evidence from which the jury could find the connection between the earlier violence and "causing" the victim to travel. . . .

In sum, the plain language of section 2261(a)(2) shows that Congress did not intend the statute to apply to those attacks where, after the fact, the defendant decides to use interstate travel to conceal his wrongdoing. By no means do I suggest that Congress should not have criminalized such conduct . . . As enacted by Congress, however, the Act requires the attacker to intend to cause interstate travel. The provision at issue applies to situations where "force, coercion, duress or fraud" on the part of the defendant triggers the interstate travel, and then sometime in the course or as a result of *causing* the victim to travel, the defendant commits a crime of violence and inflicts bodily injury on the victim. Sadly, Congress simply did not draft the statute to cover the situation in which an attacker first beats an intimate partner, and only later develops the intent to transport her across state lines in order to hamstring law enforcement efforts or conceal evidence. If Congress intends to criminalize such conduct, Congress should state so clearly. Accordingly, I would reverse the judgment and the conviction.

I agree with Judge Moore that the evidence would permit the jury to find that the further injuries Scrivens suffered while the defendant was causing her to cross state lines would sustain a guilty verdict. However, the case was neither argued to the jury nor submitted on instructions on that theory. I would, therefore remand the case for a new trial on that theory.

NOTES AND QUESTIONS

1. **Interstate Domestic Violence.** In *United States v. Helem,* 186 F.3d 449 (4th Cir. 1999), the Fourth Circuit followed the reasoning of Circuit Judge Moore in the *Page* case, upholding the defendant's conviction in District court in a case very similar to *Page*. The defendant viciously assaulted his wife in their Maryland apartment, as she was packing to leave him, and then drove her through Virginia to North Carolina. Eventually he took her to a hospital, where he "hovered over her" and told medical personnel she had been in a car accident. She was able to communicate what had happened to her, and the defendant was arrested. The court concluded:

> The evidence showed that Helem committed interstate domestic violence both (1) when, by beating his wife into a state of semi-consciousness, he was enabled to and did force her across state lines against her will in an attempt to evade the law, and (2) when he forced her to travel across state lines under threat of violence, intentionally preventing her from obtaining medical treatment, thereby exacerbating her injuries.

On November 15, 1999 the Supreme Court denied certiorari in *Page,* 520 U.S. 1003 (1999). If the Court had granted certiorari, which party do you think would have had the stronger argument on this issue?

Constitutional Challenges

The criminal provisions of the Violence Against Women Act rest on Congress's authority to regulate interstate commerce under the Commerce Clause. Historically, this power has been far reaching. The Supreme Court has traditionally upheld federal statutes demonstrating only the most tenuous links to interstate commerce, and for decades those convicted of federal crimes have been unsuccessful in challenging, under the Commerce Clause, the criminal statutes on which their convictions were based.

However, with its decision in *United States v. Lopez,* 514 U.S. 549 (1995), the Supreme Court signaled its willingness to reconsider its interpretation of congressional Commerce Clause authority. The defendant in *Lopez* successfully challenged a provision of the Gun–Free School Zone Act (GFSZA) of 1990, on the grounds that the prohibited conduct—knowingly possessing a firearm within 1,000 feet of a school—had an insufficient connection to interstate commerce. In the years since *Lopez* was decided, litigation has tested the new limits on congressional authority, only to discover that the changes heralded by *Lopez* were less than many imagined they might be.

On the strength of *Lopez*, defendants in cases brought under VAWA's criminal provisions challenged Congress's authority to regulate interstate domestic violence (and interstate violations of restraining orders) under the Commerce Clause. With one exception, *United States v. Wright*, 965 F.Supp. 1307 (D. Neb. 1997), rev'd on appeal, 128 F.3d 1274 (8th Cir. 1997), the courts have distinguished *Lopez* and the GFSZA, and upheld the validity of both § 2261 and § 2262.

It is notable that, even after *United States v. Morrison,* 529 U.S. 598 (2000) discussed in Chapter One, and then later in Chapter Sixteen, in which the Supreme Court struck down the civil rights remedy in VAWA, the courts continued to uphold VAWA's criminal provisions. A thorough analysis is provided by the Southern District of New York, in *United States v. Gluzman,* 953 F.Supp. 84 (S.D.N.Y. 1997), in an opinion adopted wholesale by the Second Circuit, which described the analysis as "admirable." *United States v. Gluzman,* 154 F.3d 49 (2d Cir. 1998). For another Circuit Court of Appeals decision upholding the interstate domestic violence provision of VAWA, see *United States v. Bailey,* 112 F.3d 758 (4th Cir. 1997), and for a parallel decision upholding the interstate violation of a restraining order provision see *United States v. Von Foelkel,* 136 F.3d 339 (2d Cir. 1998).

United States v. Gluzman

United States District Court for the Southern District of New York, 1997.
953 F.Supp. 84.

■ PARKER, DISTRICT JUDGE.

On April 25, 1996, defendant Rita Gluzman ... was indicted for conspiring to commit interstate domestic violence and for committing interstate domestic violence in violation of 18 U.S.C. § 2261 (1996). Gluzman moves to dismiss the indictment on the ground that Congress, when it enacted section 2261, exceeded its authority under the Commerce Clause. See U.S. Const., Art. I, § 8, cl. 3. For the reasons stated below, I find the challenged provision to be a constitutional exercise of Congress' power to regulate interstate commerce. Accordingly, the motion to dismiss is denied....

Gluzman argues ... that the legislative history of 18 U.S.C. § 2261 fails to indicate that the statute as finally enacted was based on any findings in that history that the interstate travel in furtherance of spousal abuse was activity that affected interstate commerce. She further contends that section 2261 neither regulates a commercial activity nor contains a requirement that the activity in question be connected to interstate commerce, and therefore its enactment exceeded the authority of Congress to legislate under the Commerce Clause.

The challenged statutory provision arose in an area in which Congressional power is exceedingly broad....

Review of the legislative history of the section, although sparse, indicates that Congress had a rational basis for concluding that the regulation of interstate domestic violence was "reasonably adapted to [an] end permitted by the Constitution...." Congress, in enacting section 2261, alluded to the substantial toll of domestic violence on the physical and economic welfare of individuals directly affected by such violence as well as the public generally.... Although gender-based violence, particularly when it is targeted against women, was clearly of primary concern to Congress, it was not the exclusive motive for the VAWA in its entirety. As previously noted, when addressing section 2261, the Committee considered, in nongender specific terms, "the health care, criminal justice, and other social costs of domestic violence, ..." and crafted what it believed to be an "appropriate response to the problem[s] of domestic violence which, because of their interstate nature, transcend the abilities of State law enforcement agencies...."

Having determined that a rational basis exists, "the only remaining question for judicial inquiry is whether the 'means chosen by [Congress] [are] reasonably adapted to the end permitted by the Constitution.'" ... Gluzman suggests that the Supreme Court's recent decision in *United States v. Lopez*, ... compels the conclusion that they are not.

... In defining the contours of the Commerce Clause, the *Lopez* Court identified three broad categories of activity that Congress may regulate under its commerce power: (1) the use of the channels of interstate commerce; (2) the instrumentalities of interstate commerce or persons or things in interstate commerce, even though the threat comes only from intrastate activity; and (3) intrastate activities that have a substantial relation to interstate commerce.... *Lopez*, however, was concerned only with the third category of activity, and did not purport to affect Congress' exercise of its commerce power with regard to the regulation of the use of the channels or instrumentalities of commerce.

Unlike the statute at issue in *Lopez*, section 2261 does not regulate purely local activity, but, instead, is an exercise of Congress' power under the first category of cases articulated by the *Lopez* Court—the authority to regulate the use of channels of commerce. Furthermore, the statute clearly requires an identifiable interstate nexus, namely, the crossing of a state line with the criminal intent to commit domestic violence against one's spouse and the actual commission of such violence. Section 2261 therefore avoids the constitutional deficiencies identified in Lopez where the interstate nexus was non-existent and the activity to be regulated was purely local. Thus, whatever limitation Lopez may have recognized with respect to congressional power over intrastate activities that may affect commerce, the decision did not speak to the broad power of Congress to regulate the channels of interstate commerce, an area occupied by section 2261 as well as numerous other criminal statutes.

Congress' authority "to keep the channels of interstate commerce free from immoral or injurious uses has been frequently sustained, and is no longer open to question...." Thus, courts consistently have upheld federal criminal statutes that regulate the crossing of state lines by persons or things in a manner incident to some criminal activity. . . .

Gluzman contends, nonetheless, that Congress exceeded the scope of its authority under the Commerce Clause by attempting to regulate an activity that was not commercial. According to the defendant, for statutory enactments under *Lopez* categories one and two to pass constitutional muster, such regulations must involve "economic activity" or must expressly require movement "in interstate commerce" as grounds for jurisdiction. In other words, in order to affect the channels of interstate commerce as a basis for regulation, the conduct sought to be criminalized must involve the transportation of something—e.g. pornography or goods—from state to state or at a minimum some other commercial activity that has a clearly identifiable connection with commerce.

While these contentions might carry some weight if the analysis concerns whether local activities substantially affect interstate commerce, they are wide of the mark where, as here, the statute regulates conduct in interstate commerce. Five days after *Lopez* was decided, in *United States v. Robertson*, 514 U.S. 669 . . . (1995) (per curiam), the Supreme Court reaffirmed the distinction between activities in interstate commerce and local activities that substantially affect interstate commerce. There, the Court concluded that it was not necessary to prove that an Alaskan gold mine "affect[ed]" interstate commerce to bring it under the Racketeer Influenced and Corrupt Organizations Act (RICO); it was sufficient merely to prove that the gold mine was an "enterprise . . . engaged in . . . interstate or foreign commerce." . . . The Court made clear that "[t]he 'affecting commerce' test was developed [] to define the extent of Congress' power over purely *intra* state commercial activities that nonetheless have substantial *inter* state effect. . . ."

As the Ninth Circuit recently stated, the Supreme Court in Robertson "explained that the[] three bases of congressional authority [identified in *Lopez*] are analytically distinct. . . ." Thus, to the extent that Congress seeks to regulate persons or things in interstate commerce—as opposed to local activities that affect interstate commerce—its power to do so was not changed by *Lopez*.

It has long been established that Congress can not only regulate activities that involve interstate or international transportation of goods and people, but it can do so "regardless of whether the transportation is motivated by a 'commercial purpose.' " . . . Congress has long exercised the authority to keep the channels of interstate commerce free from injurious noncommercial uses, including, among others, the transportation of firearms for private use, . . . pornography for private use, . . . liquor for private use, . . . and obscene materials for private use. . . . The Court has also upheld the Mann Act's application to interstate transportation of persons for an immoral purpose—polygamy—on the ground that the statute, "while primarily aimed at the use of interstate commerce for the purpose of commercialized sex, is not restricted to that end. . . ."

Moreover, this Court cannot glean, as Gluzman urges, any principled distinction between Congress' power to prohibit one from transporting an article or another person and its power to prohibit the use of commerce by the illegal actor herself. Indeed, statutes regulating persons who cross state lines harboring the intent to commit an unlawful activity have consistently been upheld as within Congress' authority under the commerce clause. . . .

Section 2261 has the requisite relation to interstate commerce as defined under controlling law since it is triggered only if an individual crosses a state line with the intent to injure, harass, or intimidate his or her spouse or intimate partner, and that travel actually results in the intentional commission of a crime of violence that causes bodily injury to such spouse or intimate partner. See 18 U.S.C. § 2261. As was previously noted, it is a "well settled principle that Congress may impose relevant conditions and requirements on those who use the channels of interstate commerce in order that those channels will not become the means of promoting or spreading evil, whether physical, moral, or economic in nature. . . ."

Broader Federalization Concerns

Sections 2261 and 2262 continue to survive constitutional challenges based on the scope of the powers accorded to Congress under the Commerce Clause, as the prior analysis suggests. Nonetheless, there are those who oppose the creation of these, and many other, federal crimes, on broader policy grounds. The following two excerpts provide a concise summary of these objections, and of the arguments mounted by those with a more positive view of the federal role in this and other arenas. The authors of the second piece were, at the time they delivered their remarks at a symposium at Hastings College of Law, the Deputy Attorney General and a Deputy Assistant Attorney General, respectively, with the U.S. Department of Justice.

Michelle Easterling
For Better or Worse: The Federalization of Domestic Violence
98 W. VA. L. REV. 933 (1996).

The primary argument against the federalization of criminal offenses is that it would swell the federal judicial docket. The increased workload is said to reduce the quality of adjudication by decreasing the time and attention judges spend on each individual case. Expanding the federal docket with cases that can be handled effectively by the states is considered a misallocation of resources. Many of these problems are blamed on the Speedy Trial Act requirements, which are accused of pushing "civil cases off the docket altogether" or causing "such severe backlogs as to result in dismissals of serious criminal cases." With more than 3,000 federal crimes now on the books, many of those sharing jurisdiction with nearly identical state crimes, the concern for overwhelming the federal courts is widespread. . . .

Another prevalent de-federalization argument is that the federalization of criminal statutes is a blatant usurpation of states' rights. The states traditionally were left with primary jurisdiction over criminal problems because they were largely of local interest and impact. As Congress creates more and more federal criminal offenses, it shows less and less regard for the states. For example, by enacting the death penalty for dozens of federal crimes, Congress has encroached upon the will of several states and the District of Columbia which have banned capital punishment.

One reason proffered for federalization is that it achieves uniformity in the law. This uniformity ordinarily involves stiffer sentencing, often ten to twenty times higher. However, criminal offenders committing identical crimes can now receive radically different treatment depending on who prosecutes them. For example, Christopher Bailey, convicted of kidnapping and interstate domestic violence, received life in prison and cannot seek parole for thirty-five years (when he reaches age 70). If he had been prosecuted and convicted for his crimes against Sonya by the state of West Virginia, he would have been sentenced to between two and ten years in prison for malicious assault. Even more alarming than the sentencing disparity is that in some cases double jeopardy does not bar an offender being tried by both federal and state prosecutors.

The primary problem with the stiffer sentencing is the arbitrariness by which a defendant is subjected to federal criminal prosecution, so arbitrary in fact that it has been called "a cruel lottery." While the United States Attorney's manual contains general guidelines to aid in the decision of whether to prosecute, the manual does not mandate that the federal prosecutors try the case. The lack of set guidelines has given rise to unusual forms of prosecutorial discretion such as "Federal Day" in the Southern District of New York. "Federal Day" is one random day each week on which all street-level drug offenders apprehended by police are tried in federal court, with the stiffer federal penalties, in an attempt to create a Russian–Roulette type of deterrence. Much of the prosecutorial discretion in federal cases is exercised with a similar motive....

After being convicted in federal court, the offenders have no equal protection challenge to the disparity in sentencing, even if the prosecutor's decision to try the case was motivated by the harsher sentence itself. Those opposed to federalization note that the sentencing disparity between identical federal and state crimes is contrary to federal sentencing policy. The Sentencing Reform Act of 1984 states that one of the factors to be considered in sentencing is the avoidance of disparities among similar defendants with similar records found guilty of similar conduct. In some cases, rather than promoting uniformity, prosecutors have seized the disparity and used the tougher federal sentence as a threat so that a defendant will take a plea bargain and sentence from state court. The disparate treatment of offenders, as well as the arbitrariness in choosing a forum, lead many to criticize the federalization of criminal law.

Jamie Gorelick and Harry Litman
Prosecutorial Discretion and the Federalization Debate

46 HASTINGS L.J. 967 (1995).

... [P]roposals for the creation of new federal crimes have drawn fire on a number of grounds. Some claim that the continuing federalization of crime will swamp the federal courts with "local" crimes, thereby preventing them from fulfilling a traditional role of adjudicating distinctively federal matters. Other critics believe that some of the recently enacted federal crimes inappropriately infringe on federalism interests by taking matters traditionally of local concern out of the hands of local officials. Still others believe that the new federal criminal laws are political gimmicks that will do nothing to address the nation's real crime problems. . . .

At least two ideas animate such proposals. The first is that the federal courts are a scarce resource with specialized functions that cannot be fully performed in the state courts. The second is that matters of public concern can be neatly divided into fixed spheres of federal and of state responsibility so that it is possible and useful to divide criminal jurisdiction generally into "inherently state areas" and "inherently federal areas."

The Department wholeheartedly subscribes to the first of these two ideas: for a number of well-known reasons, the federal courts must be viewed as a scarce resource whose specialized functions should be carefully safeguarded.

For these reasons, we agree that it is vital to identify where the potential lies for a distinctively federal contribution to the fight against crime and to ensure that, as in other areas of the law, the federal government's role is designed to exploit its peculiar advantages.

But [we do] not agree that the principle for identifying a distinctively federal contribution should—or can—be framed in terms of fixed spheres of federal and state activity. . . . That approach has significant failings.

First, such a limiting principle cannot be squared with the historical development of the federal courts' jurisdiction. Large sections of the federal criminal code—including offenses that today are universally accepted as core federal court matters—originally represented an extension of the federal law into areas traditionally and concurrently subject to state jurisdiction. . . . Even civil rights offenses—often cited as the paradigm of proper federal criminal jurisdiction—are clearly appropriate for prosecution under state law. Indeed, a strict application of the "fixed-spheres" approach would leave no room for the Department to respond to state prosecutions that leave compelling federal interests unvindicated, as in the Rodney King or Crown Heights cases. . . .

. . . [C]ases in which a state is completely unable to prosecute because of, for example, jurisdictional problems or the inability of the state to protect witnesses are only the most extreme examples of cases in which the federal government has a demonstrable advantage in dealing with certain aspects of a crime problem. . . . [A] federal response may [also] be needed to secure full justice in other cases. Federal legal and investigative advantages in some instances permit the federal government to undertake a complete and efficient prosecution where a state could not. But such full justice will not be possible unless the federal government is able to assert a concurrent jurisdiction over the kind of criminal conduct at issue. . . .

Our view on the scope of federal criminal jurisdiction is that it is appropriate for Congress to provide for federal involvement in a particular criminal area where: (1) there is a pressing problem of national concern; (2) state criminal jurisdiction is inadequate to solve significant aspects of the problem; and (3) the federal government—by virtue of its investigative, prosecutorial or legal resources—is positioned to make a qualitative difference to the solution of the problem....

... It is exceedingly difficult to draft a statute in a way that includes only those crimes that are sophisticated, inter-jurisdictional, or sensitive enough to require a federal solution. In order to allow sufficient flexibility to bring a federal prosecution when an aspect of a law enforcement problem requires it, federal criminal jurisdiction will inevitably have to be overinclusive. It will have to be drafted in a way that includes criminal activities that state and local criminal justice systems can handle, as well as activities that they cannot.

... The exercise of prosecutorial discretion, then, becomes the most important and effective brake on the federalization of crime....

The Department's prosecutorial policy emphasizes two elements: (1) allocation of criminal justice resources according to the comparative advantage of the federal, state, and local governments; and (2) cooperation between federal and state or local law enforcement officials to promote the most efficient use of criminal justice resources.

The comparative advantage approach rests on the idea that each agency or level of government should handle those aspects of a law enforcement problem that it is best equipped to handle. The federal government's advantages may vary according to the case, but they typically include inter-jurisdictional investigative capabilities, victim- and witness-assistance programs, expertise in traditionally federal areas of law such as organized crime or environmental crime, and favorable procedures, such as preventive detention. The availability of stiffer penalties in the federal system is also a potential comparative advantage, particularly in multiple-offender cases, where the prospect of a long sentence may induce a low-level figure to plead guilty and cooperate in the prosecution of the most culpable offenders.

The comparative advantage approach does not imply that a federal prosecution should be brought whenever the federal government has a comparative advantage. Rather, federal law enforcement resources should be deployed in the way that federal, state, and local actors jointly believe would be most effective. For example, federal investigative resources or witness- and victim-protection programs can be made available to state authorities in cases in which a state prosecution is brought. This approach can maximize the effectiveness of state and federal criminal justice resources.

NOTES AND QUESTIONS

1. **Federal v. State Responses.** Gorelick and Litman argue that the availability in the federal system of preventive detention, or a longer sentence, can be a legitimate reason for a federal as opposed to a state

prosecution. Steven Clymer, on the other hand, lists these two features of the federal system along with three others—less access to pretrial discovery; fewer opportunities to suppress evidence, and lack of parole eligibility—that he argues make federal prosecution decisions vulnerable on equal protection grounds:

> The federalization of substantive criminal law and the disparity between treatment received in federal and state criminal justice systems have created . . . a "cruel lottery," in which some unfortunate offenders are subject to dramatically harsher treatment than similarly situated others. Equal protection, which requires that government actors have a rational basis for imposing differential treatment—even in contexts in which there is far less at stake than in the criminal justice system—should impose the same obligations on prosecutors. It compels federal prosecutors, whose selection decisions can mean the difference between pretrial release and detention, dismissal and conviction, or a slap on the wrist and a lengthy prison term, to use principled methods of determining which eligible offenders will be subject to federal rather than state prosecution. To ensure rational charging decisions, the Department of Justice should amend its "Principles of Federal Prosecution" to require that federal prosecutors not only avoid bad reasons for making charging decisions, but that they have good ones for treating federally prosecuted offenders differently than those charged in state court.

> If faced with evidence that arbitrary selection is routine and unchecked by administrative policy, courts should reconsider their reluctance to review charging decisions absent proof of improper discrimination. Considerations that counsel judicial restraint are not convincing barriers to limited judicial oversight of the rationality of federal prosecutors' decisions to bring charges under duplicative federal statutes. Although such review would rarely result in a finding of an equal protection violation and the need to grant a remedy, it would prompt federal prosecutors to make principled selection decisions. Steven D. Clymer, *Unequal Justice: The Federalization of Criminal Law,* 70 S. CAL. L. REV. 643 (1997).

2. **Equal Protection Concerns.** Using Gorelick and Litman's guidelines, when do you think federal prosecutors should become involved in interstate domestic violence, or interstate violation of restraining order cases? Are you confident that the criteria you have settled on would survive an equal protection scrutiny of the kind suggested by Clymer?

3. **Further Discussion.** For further information on the impact of federal laws on domestic violence see Myrna S. Raeder, *Domestic Violence in Federal Court: Abused Women as Victims, Survivors, and Offenders,* 19 FEDERAL SENTENCING REPORTER 91 (Dec. 2006); Myrna S. Raeder, *Gender-related Issues in a Post–Booker Federal Guidelines World,* 37 McGEORGE L.REV. 691 (2006).

CHAPTER EIGHT

EVIDENCE IN DOMESTIC VIOLENCE CASES

In both civil and criminal cases, proving domestic violence can be difficult. Often the victim and possibly her children are the only witnesses to the abuse. Victims may be reluctant or refuse to testify, or they may refuse to allow their children to testify. Even if the victim does testify, she may minimize what happened. And in many cases, even despite her testimony, juries and judges may fail to find a victim's testimony credible. These problems can be compounded in cases involving same-sex relationships or minorities, and in cases in which the victim has a drug or alcohol problem, or doesn't meet the stereotype of the "perfect battered woman." Thus, prosecutors and civil attorneys representing victims of domestic violence must be able to prove the alleged incident using as much evidence as is available. This can involve introducing the following: physical evidence, such as photographs of injuries or ripped and bloodied clothing; statements made by the victim to 911 operators or the police; evidence of past abuse; expert testimony; testimony by children, neighbors or other witnesses; and testimony by doctors or other medical professionals.

In recent years, legislatures and courts have both helped and hindered efforts to introduce evidence documenting domestic violence. In particular, courts have shown a growing concern for the rights of criminal defendants when the reliability of the evidence introduced is questionable. In this chapter, we will review some of the legal strategies attorneys have used to introduce evidence in these cases, as well as some of the legal responses to them. The chapter is organized to reflect the ways in which attorneys prepare for cases. Physical evidence, for example, is often far more persuasive then testimonial evidence, so we begin with this. After physical evidence, we examine testimony by victims, witnesses, and experts. As you read this chapter, consider how one might mount a case proving domestic violence, whether there ought to be special evidentiary laws governing domestic violence cases, and how one balances the rights of the defendant with the need to protect the victim.

A. PHYSICAL EVIDENCE

There is often far more physical evidence of domestic abuse than one might think. Assume the police arrive to a home in which the victim claims she was physically assaulted by her partner. The police may find plenty of physical evidence to corroborate her story, such as broken glasses, a bloodied shirt, a smashed cell phone, or a hole punched into a wall. All of this helps to provide context for the abuse. Police should, and in many jurisdictions routinely do, gather this kind of evidence at the scene.

One of the most effective ways to prove a domestic violence incident is to introduce photographs of the victim's injuries. In order to secure such photographs, police must be trained in how to obtain them. For example, bruises may not set in until two or three days after an incident, requiring the police to take follow-up photographs. Police must also have the proper equipment. In the 1990s the Polaroid Company developed cameras specifically to photograph domestic violence victims and their injuries. There are many benefits to using instant photographs. District attorneys have immediate evidence from arraignment, the photos are tamper resistant, and police have to take fewer shots because they can immediately see the results. According to the Polaroid Corporation, more than 50,000 police officers have used Polaroid cameras to document domestic violence injuries. See Polaroid Fact Sheet: Domestic Violence Documentation, http://www.policeone.com/police-products/investigation/forensic-supplies/press-releases/86106/. As well as taking close-up photos of the victim's injuries, officers can also photograph evidence of past abuse, such as scars or cluster bruises. They can document defense injuries, such as cuts on a person's forearms. They can photograph smashed furniture, broken mirrors, and other evidence of violence. They can photograph evidence of drug or alcohol use. They can also capture evidence of violence against children, and images of the abuser. When photographs are taken, conviction rates increase dramatically. In San Diego, for example, photographs documenting the abuse resulted in a 95% conviction rate. Perhaps most importantly, evidence-based prosecutions dramatically reduce the need for the victim's testimony.

Many police departments are now turning to digital photography rather than using Polaroid cameras. Crystal Garcia, Sheila Suess Kennedy and Barbara Lawrence discuss a project in the Marion and Hamilton County (Indiana) Prosecutors' offices in which officers were equipped with digital cameras. Digital cameras were cost effective. Also, given that both jurisdictions had adopted no-drop policies, it was important to have as much evidence as possible in violence cases. The major advantage to digital photography is that it produces higher quality photographs. They found:

> After controlling for confounding variables such as whether the victim needed medical assistance, charge type, and prior criminal history, the study concluded that digital photography used by the officers first responding to a domestic violence call can quadruple the likelihood of conviction—mostly through plea bargains—even in cases where the victim refused to testify. In cases where there was digital photographic evidence, "Defendants were six times more likely to plead guilty, four and one-half times more likely to be convicted, and five times more likely to be sentenced to some time in custody." Crystal A. Garcia, Sheila Suess Kennedy and Barbara Lawrence, *Picturing Powerlessness: Digital Photography, Domestic Violence, and the Fight over Victim Autonomy,* 25 HAMLINE J. PUB. L. & POL'Y 1 (2003).

NOTES AND QUESTIONS

1. **Victim Autonomy.** The use of photographs is particularly important in jurisdictions that have adopted mandatory or no-drop prosecution policies. As we saw in the previous chapter, such policies are often opposed by victim advocates, who believe the choice of whether to proceed with a prosecution should be solely the victim's decision. How does the use of photographs inform that debate? Does the fact that photographs increase the likelihood of a plea bargain help or hurt victims who would rather not proceed? Does taking a photograph of the victim against her wishes otherwise undermine her autonomy?

2. **Concerns about Authentication.** In order for a photograph to be admitted, *anyone* familiar with what is in the image can testify that the image is what the party offering it purports it to be. Yet, given how easily digital photographs can be altered, there is some concern that having them admitted may be more difficult if police departments do not institute a system whereby the original images are saved onto an unalterable format, such as an unwritable CD. Increasingly, police departments are adopting procedures to ensure the authenticity of digital photographs. Do you think it is likely that police would alter the photographs of victims to make them look more injured? What might motivate the police to alter digital photographs?

B. STATEMENTS MADE TO LAW ENFORCEMENT

Victims will often refuse to testify or recant their testimony for a variety of reasons, including fear of retaliation from the defendant, a general mistrust of the criminal justice system, fear that the defendant will be jailed, or a desire to reconcile. In these cases, prosecutors often try to introduce statements that victims have made to the police after the incident occurred. These out-of-court statements offered for the truth of what they assert are considered hearsay and are generally inadmissible to prove the charges against the defendant. Prosecutors had been successful in arguing that these statements are "firmly rooted hearsay exceptions" such as excited utterances or then existing mental, physical, or emotional state of mind, or statements that bear a "particularized guarantee of trustworthiness." Then in 2004, the United States Supreme Court, in the unanimous opinion of *Crawford v. Washington*, limited the use of such out-of-court statements.

Crawford v. Washington

United States Supreme Court, 2004.
541 U.S. 36.

■ JUSTICE SCALIA delivered the opinion for the court:

On August 5, 1999, Kenneth Lee was stabbed at his apartment. Police arrested petitioner later that night. After giving petitioner and his wife *Miranda* warnings, detectives interrogated each of them twice. Petitioner eventually confessed that he and Sylvia had gone in search of Lee because he was upset over an earlier incident in which Lee had tried to rape her. The two had found Lee at his apartment, and a fight ensued in which Lee was stabbed in the torso and petitioner's hand was cut.

Petitioner gave the following account of the fight:

"Q. Okay. Did you ever see anything in [Lee's] hands?

"A. I think so, but I'm not positive.

"Q. Okay, when you think so, what do you mean by that?

"A. I could a swore I seen him goin' for somethin' before, right before everything happened. He was like reachin', fiddlin' around down here and stuff ... and I just ... I don't know, I think, this is just a possibility, but I think, I think that he pulled somethin' out and I grabbed for it and that's how I got cut ... but I'm not positive. I, I, my mind goes blank when things like this happen. I mean, I just, I remember things wrong, I remember things that just doesn't, don't make sense to me later." App. 155 (punctuation added).

Sylvia generally corroborated petitioner's story about the events leading up to the fight, but her account of the fight itself was arguably different-particularly with respect to whether Lee had drawn a weapon before petitioner assaulted him:

"Q. Did Kenny do anything to fight back from this assault?

"A. (pausing) I know he reached into his pocket ... or somethin' ... I don't know what.

"Q. After he was stabbed?

"A. He saw Michael coming up. He lifted his hand ... his chest open, he might [have] went to go strike his hand out or something and then (inaudible).

"Q. Okay, you, you gotta speak up.

"A. Okay, he lifted his hand over his head maybe to strike Michael's hand down or something and then he put his hands in his ... put his right hand in his right pocket ... took a step back ... Michael proceeded to stab him ... then his hands were like ... how do you explain this ... open arms ... with his hands open and he fell down ... and we ran (describing subject holding hands open, palms toward assailant).

"Q. Okay, when he's standing there with his open hands, you're talking about Kenny, correct?

"A. Yeah, after, after the fact, yes.

"Q. Did you see anything in his hands at that point?

"A. (pausing) um um (no)."

The State charged petitioner with assault and attempted murder. At trial, he claimed self-defense. Sylvia did not testify because of the state marital privilege, which generally bars a spouse from testifying without the other spouse's consent. In Washington, this privilege does not extend to a spouse's out-of-court statements admissible under a hearsay exception, so the State sought to introduce Sylvia's tape-recorded statements to the police as evidence that the stabbing was not in self-defense. Noting that Sylvia had admitted she led petitioner to Lee's apartment and thus had facilitated the assault, the State invoked the hearsay exception for statements against penal interest.

Petitioner countered that, state law notwithstanding, admitting the evidence would violate his federal constitutional right to be "confronted with the witnesses against him...."

The Sixth Amendment's Confrontation Clause provides that, "[i]n all criminal prosecutions, the accused shall enjoy the right ... to be confronted with the witnesses against him." We have held that this bedrock procedural guarantee applies to both federal and state prosecutions.... *Roberts v. Ohio* says that an unavailable witness's out-of-court statement may be admitted so long as it has adequate indicia of reliability—*i.e.,* falls within a "firmly rooted hearsay exception" or bears "particularized guarantees of trustworthiness." Petitioner argues that this test strays from the original meaning of the Confrontation Clause and urges us to reconsider it.

[After surveying the historical background of the Confrontation Clause, from Roman times to the mid–1800's, the Court made the following conclusions:]

Where testimonial statements are involved, we do not think the Framers meant to leave the Sixth Amendment's protection to the vagaries of the rules of evidence, much less to amorphous notions of "reliability." Certainly none of the authorities discussed above acknowledges any general reliability exception to the common-law rule. Admitting statements deemed reliable by a judge is fundamentally at odds with the right of confrontation. To be sure, the Clause's ultimate goal is to ensure reliability of evidence, but it is a procedural rather than a substantive guarantee. It commands, not that evidence be reliable, but that reliability be assessed in a particular manner: by testing in the crucible of cross-examination. The Clause thus reflects a judgment, not only about the desirability of reliable evidence (a point on which there could be little dissent), but about how reliability can best be determined....

The State Supreme Court gave dispositive weight to the interlocking nature of the two statements—that they were both ambiguous as to when and whether Lee had a weapon. The court's claim that the two statements were *equally* ambiguous is hard to accept. Petitioner's statement is ambiguous only in the sense that he had lingering doubts about his recollection: "A. I could a swore I seen him goin' for somethin' before, right before everything happened ... [B]ut I'm not positive." Sylvia's statement, on the other hand, is truly inscrutable, since the key timing detail was simply assumed in the leading question she was asked: "Q. Did Kenny do anything to fight back from this assault?" Moreover, Sylvia specifically said Lee had nothing in his hands after he was stabbed, while petitioner was not asked about that.

The prosecutor obviously did not share the court's view that Sylvia's statement was ambiguous—he called it "damning evidence" that "completely refutes [petitioner's] claim of self-defense." We have no way of knowing whether the jury agreed with the prosecutor or the court. Far from obviating the need for cross-examination, the "interlocking" ambiguity of the two statements made it all the more imperative that they be tested to tease out the truth. . . .

We have no doubt that the courts below were acting in utmost good faith when they found reliability. The Framers, however, would not have been content to indulge this assumption. They knew that judges, like other government officers, could not always be trusted to safeguard the rights of the people. . . . They were loath to leave too much discretion in judicial hands. By replacing categorical constitutional guarantees with open-ended balancing tests, we do violence to their design. Vague standards are manipulable, and, while that might be a small concern in run-of-the-mill assault prosecutions like this one, the Framers had an eye toward politically charged cases like Raleigh's—great state trials where the impartiality of even those at the highest levels of the judiciary might not be so clear. . . .

Where nontestimonial hearsay is at issue, it is wholly consistent with the Framers' design to afford the States flexibility in their development of hearsay law . . . Where testimonial evidence is at issue . . . the Sixth Amendment demands what the common law required: unavailability and a prior opportunity for cross-examination. We leave for another day any effort to spell out a comprehensive definition of "testimonial." Whatever else the term covers, it applies at a minimum to prior testimony at a preliminary hearing, before a grand jury, or at a former trial; and to police interrogations. These are the modern practices with closest kinship to the abuses at which the Confrontation Clause was directed.

NOTES AND QUESTIONS

1. **Post–Crawford.** The crux of *Crawford* is that statements to law enforcement officers cannot be trusted unless the defendant had the right to cross-examine the witness at the time the statement was made. The Court discussed at length the problem of *ex parte* communications to state officials, and the problems associated with the manipulation of out-of-court testimony by law enforcement. The Court left open the question of what constituted "testimonial" evidence. Thus, although *Crawford* did not involve domestic violence, it called into question the admissibility of evidence in domestic violence prosecutions. Below is an excerpt that describes the post-*Crawford* landscape for the prosecution of batterers.

Tom Lininger
Prosecuting Batterers After Crawford
91 VA. L. REV. 747 (2005).

Three cases decided in the summer of 2004 illustrate the dramatic impact of *Crawford v. Washington*, a United States Supreme Court ruling that restricts the use of hearsay evidence in criminal trials when the declarant is unavailable for cross-examination. In *State v. Courtney*, the defendant appealed his conviction for domestic assault. The evidence indicated that he had choked his former girlfriend until she lost consciousness. He had beaten her so severely that her blood splattered on the bedroom walls. She woke up with her head in a toilet. Her six-year-old daughter described the assault in an interview conducted by a child-protection worker. The trial court admitted a videotape of this interview. Citing *Crawford*, the appellate court reversed the defendant's conviction because the daughter was not available for cross-examination at trial.

In *People v. Adams*, the defendant appealed his conviction for inflicting corporal injury upon a cohabitant. The prosecution's evidence showed that the defendant had battered his pregnant girlfriend, forced her to the floor, and pushed his knee down on her abdomen while she pleaded with him to spare her baby's life. The victim gave a statement to police on the day of the incident, but the prosecution was not able to subpoena her as a trial witness. The prosecution introduced her hearsay statements to the police in lieu of her live testimony at trial. The appellate court vacated the defendant's conviction, holding that the admission of the victim's hearsay statements violated *Crawford*.

In *People v. Kilday*, the jury found the defendant guilty of battering and torturing his girlfriend. Evidence introduced at trial showed that the defendant had cut the victim repeatedly with pieces of glass. He had also burned her with an iron on several occasions. She gave a statement to the police on the day of the defendant's arrest, but she later refused to cooperate with the prosecution, indicating that the defendant had threatened to retaliate against her. The prosecution relied on her hearsay statements to police, and the appellate court vacated the conviction under *Crawford*.

These three cases are not isolated examples of *Crawford's* effect on domestic violence prosecutions. Indeed, within days—even hours—of the *Crawford* decision, prosecutors were dismissing or losing hundreds of domestic violence cases that would have presented little difficulty in the past. For example, during the summer of 2004, half of the domestic violence cases set for trial in Dallas County, Texas, were dismissed because of evidentiary problems under *Crawford*.

In a survey of over 60 prosecutors' offices in California, Oregon, and Washington, 63 percent of respondents reported the *Crawford* decision has significantly impeded prosecutions of domestic violence. Seventy-six percent indicated that after *Crawford*, their offices are more likely to drop domestic violence charges when the victims recant or refuse to cooperate. Alarmingly, 65 percent of respondents reported that victims of domestic violence are less safe in their jurisdictions than during the era preceding the *Crawford* decision.

Why is *Crawford* creating such a burden for prosecutions of domestic violence? There is nothing intrinsically wrong with the *Crawford* decision. Its reasoning is difficult to refute, and its fealty to early constitutional history is admirable. *Crawford's* deleterious effect cannot be blamed on its doctrinal analysis, but is primarily a consequence of the Supreme Court's abrupt departure from recent jurisprudence under the Confrontation Clause. *Crawford* represents a sudden shift in the constitutional fault lines underlying the statutory framework of the states' evidence codes. Statutory hearsay law is now misaligned with constitutional confrontation law, and the incongruities are more problematic in domestic violence prosecutions than in any other context.

NOTES AND QUESTIONS

1. **911 Calls and Statement to Police Officers at the Scene.** Prior to the decision in *Crawford*, prosecutors routinely introduced 911 calls to police as evidence of what happened on a particular occasion. These calls were generally admitted under the theory that 911 calls qualify as "excited utterances" under the rules of evidence. As such, prosecutors had to show that the declarant was under the stress of excitement caused by an external event sufficient to still the declarant's reflective faculties, thereby preventing opportunity for deliberation which might lead the declarant to be untruthful. See, e.g. FRE 803 (2). In 911 calls, one can often hear the terror in the voice of the victim, the defendant shouting at or threatening the victim, or actual physical violence taking place. Some estimate that at least a third of domestic violence 911 calls to police are made by children. Hearing what happened is often the most powerful evidence in these cases. After *Crawford*, however, the admissibility of such tapes was in doubt.

The admissibility of statements made to police officers at the scene, which often qualified as excited utterances, also was in doubt. These statements had been routinely admitted when the officer testified that the victim was upset and crying and then shared how she was injured.

To clear up this confusion, in 2006, the United States Supreme Court agreed to hear two cases, consolidated in *Davis v. Washington*, 547 U.S. ___, 126 S.Ct. 2266 (2006), involving domestic violence prosecutions in which both a 911 call and a statement to the police were at issue. First consider the arguments made in *amici curiae* briefs by the National Coalition for Battered Women and the American Civil Liberties Union. Then decide whether the Court made the right decision.

Brief Amici Curiae of the National Network to End Domestic Violence, Indiana and Washington Coalitions Against Domestic Violence, Legal Momentum, et al. in Support of Respondents

These cases present an opportunity to clarify the uncertainty created by *Crawford v. Washington*, which has led many prosecutors to drop domestic violence charges or seek to compel victims of abuse to testify under extreme duress. Adhering to the original meaning of the Confrontation Clause does not require this Court to ignore the brutal reality of domestic violence or permit batterers to evade prosecution by wielding the Clause as a sword against their victims.

Domestic violence is a pervasive problem with its roots in centuries of legal and social norms sanctioning men's use of violence in the family. Due to the judicial system's historic reluctance to prosecute these crimes and its inability to protect victims from the weapons of control available to batterers, many abused women are unwilling or unable to testify in criminal proceedings. Over time, the criminal justice system has recognized the forces that work to prevent victims from testifying and established alternative means to obtain reliable evidence. The resulting practice of "evidence-based" prosecution ensures that violent abusers are held accountable when their own conduct makes the victim's testimony impossible to obtain. In the short time since *Crawford* was decided, however, many prosecutors and courts have responded by dropping or dismissing charges in a disturbing range of cases. Adoption of a broad definition of "testimonial" will unquestionably further cripple the potential for evidence-based prosecution.

The Confrontation Clause addressed a specific evil identified by the Framers: unchecked State inquisitorial power designed to use out-of-court testimony from a witness in order to deprive the defendant of his opportunity to confront his accuser in court. In domestic violence prosecutions, a different evil exists: here, the defendant, not the State, seeks to silence the key witness. In adopting the Confrontation Clause, the Framers did not and could not have fully anticipated this result, in which the only or key witness is subject to the control and coercion of the accused.

Determining the application of the Confrontation Clause to domestic violence—a phenomenon that was widespread at the time the Clause was adopted and whose effects on the judicial process were unexamined—necessarily involves "some degree of estimation." Nonetheless, a definition of "testimonial" that is faithful to the original purpose of the Confrontation Clause will continue to allow some forms of evidence-based prosecution of domestic violence cases while protecting constitutional safeguards and preserving the integrity of the adversary process.

Brief Amicus Curiae of the American Civil Liberties Union

The ACLU of Washington and the Indiana Civil Liberties Union in Support of Petitioners

The present cases involve the relationship between two vital concerns. First, criminal trials must be conducted fairly and in accordance with the Sixth Amendment's Confrontation Clause. Second, violence against women, and domestic violence in particular, is a significant social problem that has too often failed to receive the attention it deserves from the criminal justice system. These concerns cannot and should not be treated as mutually incompatible. Victims of domestic violence have a right to expect that laws designed for their protection will be enforced against their abusers, and those accused of domestic violence have a right to cross-examine the witnesses against them in any criminal proceeding.

If the victim is willing to testify, the solution is simple. In many cases, however, domestic violence victims are unwilling to testify for various reasons, including the fear of further victimization. Many prosecutors in the past used that reluctance as an excuse to abandon prosecutions they were not enthusiastic about in the first instance. That, in turn, produced a public backlash that forced the law enforcement community to treat domestic violence more seriously. In response, prosecutors have increasingly sought to overcome the problem of reluctant domestic violence witnesses by employing what is sometimes called an "evidence-based prosecution" or "victimless prosecution," where the victim's out-of-court description of the crime is entered into evidence in lieu of live testimony from the witness. Unfortunately, that has merely replaced one problem with another.

As this Court explained in *Crawford*, the Confrontation Clause prohibits the use of testimonial evidence that has not been subject to cross-examination even if there are indicia of reliability that would otherwise satisfy the rules of evidence governing hearsay. That is because the Confrontation Clause serves a broader purpose than the hearsay rules. Among other things, the framers of the Constitution were well aware that the reliance on ex parte evidence undermines the credibility of the judicial process regardless of how reliable the evidence might be in particular cases. By its very nature, such ex parte evidence is also more susceptible to manipulation.

Davis v. Washington

United States Supreme Court, 2006.
547 U.S. ___, 126 S.Ct. 2266.

■ JUSTICE SCALIA delivered the opinion of the Court.

These cases require us to determine when statements made to law enforcement personnel during a 911 call or at a crime scene are "testimonial" and thus subject to the requirements of the Sixth Amendment's Confrontation Clause.

The relevant statements in *Davis v. Washington,* were made to a 911 emergency operator on February 1, 2001. When the operator answered the initial call, the connection terminated before anyone spoke. She reversed the call, and Michelle McCottry answered. In the ensuing conversation, the operator ascertained that McCottry was involved in a domestic disturbance with her former boyfriend Adrian Davis, the petitioner in this case:

"911 Operator: Hello.

"Complainant: Hello.

"911 Operator: What's going on?

"Complainant: He's here jumpin' on me again.

"911 Operator: Okay. Listen to me carefully. Are you in a house or an apartment?

"Complainant: I'm in a house.

"911 Operator: Are there any weapons?

"Complainant: No. He's usin' his fists.

"911 Operator: Okay. Has he been drinking?

"Complainant: No.

"911 Operator: Okay, sweetie. I've got help started. Stay on the line with me, okay?

"Complainant: I'm on the line.

"911 Operator: Listen to me carefully. Do you know his last name?

"Complainant: It's Davis.

"911 Operator: Davis? Okay, what's his first name?

"Complainant: Adrian

"911 Operator: What is it?

"Complainant: Adrian.

"911 Operator: Adrian?

"Complainant: Yeah.

"911 Operator: Okay. What's his middle initial?

"Complainant: Martell. He's runnin' now."

As the conversation continued, the operator learned that Davis had "just r[un] out the door" after hitting McCottry, and that he was leaving in a car with someone else. McCottry started talking, but the operator cut her off, saying, "Stop talking and answer my questions." She then gathered more information about Davis (including his birthday), and learned that Davis had told McCottry that his purpose in coming to the house was "to get his stuff," since McCottry was moving. McCottry described the context of the assault, after which the operator told her that the police were on their way. "They're gonna check the area for him first," the operator said, "and then they're gonna come talk to you."

The police arrived within four minutes of the 911 call and observed McCottry's shaken state, the "fresh injuries on her forearm and her face," and her "frantic efforts to gather her belongings and her children so that they could leave the residence."

The State charged Davis with felony violation of a domestic no-contact order. "The State's only witnesses were the two police officers who responded to the 911 call. Both officers testified that McCottry exhibited injuries that appeared to be recent, but neither officer could testify as to the cause of the injuries." McCottry presumably could have testified as to whether Davis was her assailant, but she did not appear. Over Davis's objection, based on the Confrontation Clause of the Sixth Amendment, the trial court admitted the recording of her exchange with the 911 operator, and the jury convicted him . . . .

In *Hammon v. Indiana,* police responded late on the night of February 26, 2003, to a "reported domestic disturbance" at the home of Hershel and Amy Hammon. They found Amy alone on the front porch, appearing " 'somewhat frightened,' " but she told them that " 'nothing was the matter.' " She gave them permission to enter the house, where an officer saw "a gas heating unit in the corner of the living room" that had "flames coming out of the . . . partial glass front. There were pieces of glass on the ground in front of it and there was flame emitting from the front of the heating unit."

Hershel, meanwhile, was in the kitchen. He told the police "that he and his wife had 'been in an argument' but 'everything was fine now' and the argument 'never became physical.' " By this point Amy had come back inside. One of the officers remained with Hershel; the other went to the living room to talk with Amy, and "again asked [her] what had occurred." Hershel made several attempts to participate in Amy's conversation with the police, but was rebuffed. The officer later testified that Hershel "became angry when I insisted that [he] stay separated from Mrs. Hammon so that we can investigate what had happened." After hearing Amy's account, the officer "had her fill out and sign a battery affidavit." Amy handwrote the following: "Broke our Furnace & shoved me down on the floor into the broken glass. Hit me in the chest and threw me down. Broke our lamps & phone. Tore up my van where I couldn't leave the house. Attacked my daughter."

The State charged Hershel with domestic battery and with violating his probation. Amy was subpoenaed, but she did not appear at his subsequent bench trial. The State called the officer who had questioned Amy, and asked him to recount what Amy told him and to authenticate the affidavit. Hershel's counsel repeatedly objected to the admission of this evidence. At one point, after hearing the prosecutor defend the affidavit because it was made "under oath," defense counsel said, "That doesn't give us the opportunity to cross examine [the] person who allegedly drafted it. Makes me mad." Nonetheless, the trial court admitted the affidavit as a "present sense impression," and Amy's statements as "excited utterances" that "are expressly permitted in these kinds of cases even if the declarant is not available to testify." The officer thus testified that Amy "informed me that she and Hershel had been in an argument." That he became irrate [sic] over the fact of their daughter going to a boyfriend's house. The argument became . . . physical after being verbal and she informed me that Mr. Hammon, during the verbal part of the argument was breaking things in the living room and I believe she stated he broke the phone, broke the lamp, broke the front of the heater. When it became physical he threw her down into the glass of the heater. . . .

"She informed me Mr. Hammon had pushed her onto the ground, had shoved her head into the broken glass of the heater and that he had punched her in the chest twice I believe."

The trial judge found Hershel guilty on both charges, and the Indiana Court of Appeals affirmed in relevant part. The Indiana Supreme Court also affirmed.

The Confrontation Clause of the Sixth Amendment provides: "In all criminal prosecutions, the accused shall enjoy the right ... to be confronted with the witnesses against him." In *Crawford v. Washington* we held that this provision bars "admission of testimonial statements of a witness who did not appear at trial unless he was unavailable to testify, and the defendant had had a prior opportunity for cross-examination." A critical portion of this holding, and the portion central to resolution of the two cases now before us, is the phrase "testimonial statements." Only statements of this sort cause the declarant to be a "witness" within the meaning of the Confrontation Clause. It is the testimonial character of the statement that separates it from other hearsay that, while subject to traditional limitations upon hearsay evidence, is not subject to the Confrontation Clause. . . .

Without attempting to produce an exhaustive classification of all conceivable statements—or even all conceivable statements in response to police interrogation—as either testimonial or nontestimonial, it suffices to decide the present cases to hold as follows: Statements are nontestimonial when made in the course of police interrogation under circumstances objectively indicating that the primary purpose of the interrogation is to enable police assistance to meet an ongoing emergency. They are testimonial when the circumstances objectively indicate that there is no such ongoing emergency, and that the primary purpose of the interrogation is to establish or prove past events potentially relevant to later criminal prosecution.

In *Crawford,* the facts ... spared us the need to define what we meant by "interrogations." The *Davis* case today does not permit us this luxury of indecision. The inquiries of a police operator in the course of a 911 call[2] are an interrogation in one sense, but not in a sense that "qualifies under any conceivable definition." We must decide, therefore, whether the Confrontation Clause applies only to testimonial hearsay; and, if so, whether the recording of a 911 call qualifies. . . .

... When we said in *Crawford,* that "interrogations by law enforcement officers fall squarely within [the] class" of testimonial hearsay, we had immediately in mind (for that was the case before us) interrogations solely directed at establishing the facts of a past crime, in order to identify (or provide evidence to convict) the perpetrator. The product of such interrogation, whether reduced to a writing signed by the declarant or embedded in the memory (and perhaps notes) of the interrogating officer, is testimonial. It is, in the terms of the 1828 American dictionary quoted in *Crawford,* " '[a] solemn declaration or affirmation made for the purpose of establishing or proving some fact'". . . . A 911 call, on the other hand, and at least the initial interrogation conducted in connection with a 911 call, is

---

2. If 911 operators are not themselves law enforcement officers, they may at least be agents of law enforcement when they conduct interrogations of 911 callers. For purposes of this opinion (and without deciding the point), we consider their acts to be acts of the police.

As in *Crawford v. Washington,* therefore, our holding today makes it unnecessary to consider whether and when statements made to someone other than law enforcement personnel are "testimonial."

ordinarily not designed primarily to "establis[h] or prov[e]" some past fact, but to describe current circumstances requiring police assistance.

The difference between the interrogation in *Davis* and the one in *Crawford* is apparent on the face of things. In *Davis,* McCottry was speaking about events *as they were actually happening,* rather than "describ[ing] past events." Sylvia Crawford's interrogation, on the other hand, took place hours after the events she described had occurred. Moreover, any reasonable listener would recognize that McCottry (unlike Sylvia Crawford) was facing an ongoing emergency. Although one *might* call 911 to provide a narrative report of a crime absent any imminent danger, McCottry's call was plainly a call for help against bona fide physical threat. Third, the nature of what was asked and answered in *Davis,* again viewed objectively, was such that the elicited statements were necessary to be able to *resolve* the present emergency, rather than simply to learn (as in *Crawford*) what had happened in the past. That is true even of the operator's effort to establish the identity of the assailant, so that the dispatched officers might know whether they would be encountering a violent felon. And finally, the difference in the level of formality between the two interviews is striking. *Crawford* was responding calmly, at the station house, to a series of questions, with the officer-interrogator taping and making notes of her answers; McCottry's frantic answers were provided over the phone, in an environment that was not tranquil, or even (as far as any reasonable 911 operator could make out) safe.

We conclude from all this that the circumstances of McCottry's interrogation objectively indicate its primary purpose was to enable police assistance to meet an ongoing emergency. She simply was not acting as a *witness;* she was not *testifying* ... No "witness" goes into court to proclaim an emergency and seek help. . . .

This is not to say that a conversation which begins as an interrogation to determine the need for emergency assistance cannot, as the Indiana Supreme Court put it, "evolve into testimonial statements," once that purpose has been achieved. In this case, for example, after the operator gained the information needed to address the exigency of the moment, the emergency appears to have ended (when Davis drove away from the premises). The operator then told McCottry to be quiet, and proceeded to pose a battery of questions. It could readily be maintained that, from that point on, McCottry's statements were testimonial, not unlike the "structured police questioning" that occurred in *Crawford*. This presents no great problem. Just as, for Fifth Amendment purposes, "police officers can and will distinguish almost instinctively between questions necessary to secure their own safety or the safety of the public and questions designed solely to elicit testimonial evidence from a suspect," trial courts will recognize the point at which, for Sixth Amendment purposes, statements in response to interrogations become testimonial. Through *in limine* procedure, they should redact or exclude the portions of any statement that have become testimonial, as they do, for example, with unduly prejudicial portions of otherwise admissible evidence. Davis's jury did not hear the *complete* 911 call, although it may well have heard some testimonial portions. We were asked to classify only McCottry's early statements identifying Davis as her assailant, and we agree with the Washington Supreme Court that they were not testimonial. That court also concluded that, even if later parts of the call were testimonial, their admission was harmless beyond a reasonable doubt. Davis does not challenge that holding, and we therefore assume it to be correct.

Determining the testimonial or nontestimonial character of the statements that were the product of the interrogation in *Hammon* is a much easier task, since they were not much different from the statements we found to be testimonial in *Crawford*. It is entirely clear from the circumstances that the interrogation was part of an investigation into possibly criminal past conduct—as, indeed, the testifying officer expressly acknowledged. There was no emergency in progress; the interrogating officer testified that he had heard no arguments or crashing and saw no one throw or break anything. When the officers first arrived, Amy told them that things were fine, and there was no immediate threat to her person. When the officer questioned Amy for the second time, and elicited the challenged statements, he was not seeking to determine (as in *Davis*) "what is happening," but rather "what happened." Objectively viewed, the primary, if not indeed the sole, purpose of the interrogation was to investigate a possible crime—which is, of course, precisely what the officer *should* have done.

It is true that the *Crawford* interrogation was more formal. It followed a *Miranda* warning, was tape-recorded, and took place at the station house. While these features certainly strengthened the statements' testimonial aspect-made it more objectively apparent, that is, that the purpose of the exercise was to nail down the truth about past criminal events—none was essential to the point. It was formal enough that Amy's interrogation was conducted in a separate room, away from her husband (who tried to intervene), with the officer receiving her replies for use in his "investigat[ion]." What we called the "striking resemblance" of the *Crawford* statement to civil-law *ex parte* examinations, is shared by Amy's statement here. Both declarants were actively separated from the defendant–officers forcibly prevented Hershel from participating in the interrogation. Both statements deliberately recounted, in response to police questioning, how potentially criminal past events began and progressed. And both took place some time after the events described were over. Such statements under official interrogation are an obvious substitute for live testimony, because they do precisely *what a witness does* on direct examination; they are inherently testimonial. . . .

Respondents in both cases, joined by a number of their *amici*, contend that the nature of the offenses charged in these two cases—domestic violence—requires greater flexibility in the use of testimonial evidence. This particular type of crime is notoriously susceptible to intimidation or coercion of the victim to ensure that she does not testify at trial. When this occurs, the Confrontation Clause gives the criminal a windfall. We may not, however, vitiate constitutional guarantees when they have the effect of allowing the guilty to go free. But when defendants seek to undermine the judicial process by procuring or coercing silence from witnesses and victims, the Sixth Amendment does not require courts to acquiesce. While defendants have no duty to assist the State in proving their guilt, they *do* have the duty to refrain from acting in ways that destroy the integrity of the criminal-trial system. We reiterate what we said in *Crawford:* that "the rule of forfeiture by wrongdoing ... extinguishes confrontation claims on essentially equitable grounds." That is, one who obtains the absence of a witness by wrongdoing forfeits the constitutional right to confrontation.

We have determined that, absent a finding of forfeiture by wrongdoing, the Sixth Amendment operates to exclude Amy Hammon's affidavit. The Indiana courts may (if they are asked) determine on remand whether such a claim of forfeiture is properly raised and, if so, whether it is meritorious.

■ JUSTICE THOMAS, concurring in the judgment in part and dissenting in part.

In *Crawford v. Washington,* we abandoned the general reliability inquiry we had long employed to judge the admissibility of hearsay evidence under the Confrontation Clause, describing that inquiry as "*inherently,* and therefore *permanently,* unpredictable." Today, a mere two years after the Court decided *Crawford,* it adopts an equally unpredictable test, under which district courts are charged with divining the "primary purpose" of police interrogations. Besides being difficult for courts to apply, this test characterizes as "testimonial," and therefore inadmissible, evidence that bears little resemblance to what we have recognized as the evidence targeted by the Confrontation Clause. Because neither of the cases before the Court today would implicate the Confrontation Clause under an appropriately targeted standard, I concur only in the judgment in *Davis v. Washington,* and dissent from the Court's resolution of *Hammon v. Indiana,* ...

Neither the 911 call at issue in *Davis* nor the police questioning at issue in *Hammon* is testimonial under the appropriate framework. Neither the call nor the questioning is itself a formalized dialogue ... [T]he statements were neither Mirandized nor custodial, nor accompanied by any similar indicia of formality. Finally, there is no suggestion that the prosecution attempted to offer the women's hearsay evidence at trial in order to evade confrontation. Accordingly, the statements at issue in both cases are nontestimonial and admissible under the Confrontation Clause....

The Court draws a line between the two cases based on its explanation that *Hammon* involves "no emergency in progress," but instead, mere questioning as "part of an investigation into possibly criminal past conduct," and its explanation that *Davis* involves questioning for the "primary purpose" of "enabl[ing] police assistance to meet an ongoing emergency". But the fact that the officer in *Hammon* was investigating Mr. Hammon's past conduct does not foreclose the possibility that the primary purpose of his inquiry was to assess whether Mr. Hammon constituted a continuing danger to his wife, requiring further police presence or action. It is hardly remarkable that Hammon did not act abusively towards his wife in the presence of the officers, and his good judgment to refrain from criminal behavior in the presence of police sheds little, if any, light on whether his violence would have resumed had the police left without further questioning, transforming what the Court dismisses as "past conduct" back into an "ongoing emergency." Nor does the mere fact that McCottry needed emergency aid shed light on whether the "primary purpose" of gathering, for example, the name of her assailant was to protect the police, to protect the victim, or to gather information for prosecution. In both of the cases before the Court, like many similar cases, pronouncement of the "primary" motive behind the interrogation calls for nothing more than a guess by courts.

NOTES AND QUESTIONS

1. **The Difference Between 911 Calls and Statements to the Police.** *Davis* appears to at least begin to clear up some of the confusion as to what statements qualify as testimonial. The Court based its reasoning on determining the objective purpose of the statement. Does this reasoning make sense? Is Justice Thomas correct in that such a standard creates more confusion by determining statements on a case-by-case basis? What are the primary differences between 911 calls and statements to the police? How do you think *Davis* will now impact domestic violence prosecutions? For an overview of the impact of *Davis* on future domestic violence prosecutions, see Tom Lininger, *Reconceptualizing Confrontation After Davis*, 85 TEX. L. REV. 271 (2006).

2. **Whose Rights?** Does it surprise you that the ACLU would argue against the admissibility of 911 calls and statements to the police? Are they correct in arguing that there is no inherent conflict between the rights of criminal defendants and the rights of victims? The ACLU concludes its brief by arguing the following:

> In addition, while domestic violence is a crime deserving vigorous enforcement and punishment, the number of defendants convicted is not the only, or even the most important, measure of success in the struggle against domestic violence. Helping domestic violence victims address their immediate needs for housing, financial support, physical safety, and the like indirectly increases the probability victims will cooperate with prosecution; far more importantly, however, such assistance directly increases the likelihood victims of violence will be able to end violent relationships and protect themselves in the long term. Safety and autonomy for victims of violence is the ultimate goal of domestic violence policy. While criminal law enforcement is an important piece of such efforts, standing alone it cannot achieve these goals. Communities will be most successful in eradicating domestic violence when they mount a broad response to the problem.

Do you agree? What is the importance of criminal justice prosecutions in combating domestic violence?

3. **Police Trustworthiness.** *Crawford* and the Sixth Amendment are premised upon the assumption that state actors cannot always be trusted to be truthful. Rather, *Crawford* acts as a firm check on the power of the police to fabricate evidence. *Davis* reinforces that concern by disallowing

certain statements made to police officers at the scene. Given what we have studied about law enforcement and its response to domestic violence, do you think it is likely that the police would fabricate, or even exaggerate the statements victims make to them concerning a domestic violence incident? Do the police lie to ensure that they receive a conviction in these cases?

4. **Victim Autonomy.** *Crawford* and *Davis* will not generally impede prosecution where the victim willingly testifies to a full version of the events. They do, however, make it significantly harder in the majority of cases in which the victim refuses to testify, recants her testimony, or minimizes what happens. Some commentators have celebrated *Crawford* as empowering victims who do not want to proceed with prosecution. Do you think *Crawford* empowers victims, or does it make them even more vulnerable to threats and intimidation by the defendant?

5. **Forfeiture by Wrongdoing.** What if a defendant threatens or intimidates a victim not to testify? Federal Rule of Evidence 804 (b)(6) allows out-of-court statements to be admitted "against a party who has engaged or acquiesced in wrongdoing that was intended to, and did, procure the unavailability of the declarant as a witness." In other words, if a defendant engages in wrongful conduct, he forfeits his constitutional rights. This doctrine of forfeiture by wrongdoing has only been adopted by a few states, despite the fact that most states otherwise conform to the Federal Rules of Evidence. Some commentators have suggested that all states adopt this rule, which will overcome many of the hurdles presented by *Crawford*, see Tom Lininger, *Prosecuting Batterers After Crawford*, 91 VA. L. REV 747 (2005). Note that the Court in *Davis* leaves the Federal forfeiture rule clearly intact as a remedy to deal with defendants who try to obstruct the proceedings. For more on this topic see, Andrew King–Ries, *Forfeiture by Wrongdoing: A Panacea for Victimless Domestic Violence Prosecutions*, 39 CREIGHTON L. REV. 441 (2006); Deborah Tuerkheimer, *Crawford's Triangle: Domestic Violence and the Right of Confrontation*, 85 N.C.L. REV. 1 (2006); James F. Flanagan, *Confrontation, Equity, & the Misnamed Exception of "Forfeiture" by Wrongdoing*, 14 WM. & MARY BILL RTS. J. 1193 (2006).

6. **Statutes Directed at Domestic Violence:** Some states, such as Oregon and California, allow statements made by victims of domestic violence to be admitted even though they would otherwise fall outside the hearsay exceptions. California allows statements made near or at the time of the incident describing the incident to be admitted if the witness then becomes unavailable. Oregon allows for even a broader exception with statements made up to 24 hours later whether or not the victim is available to testify. For a discussion of the impact of the *Crawford* decision on these special statutes, see Myrna Raeder, *Remember the Ladies and Children Too: Crawford's Impact on Domestic Violence and Child Abuse Cases*, 71 BROOK. L. REV. 311 (2005). How will *Crawford* and *Davis* affect the constitutionality of such statutes?

7. **Prior Inconsistent Statements.** In only a few states, prior inconsistent statements of witnesses can be admitted for substantive evidence. Thus, if the victim first tells a police officer she has been abused by her husband, and then testifies that she fell down the stairs, her prior state-

ment can be admitted for the truth of what it asserts. However, under FRE 801(d)(1)(a), and in the vast majority of jurisdictions, only those prior statements that were made under oath are admissible for substantive purposes. In the example above, in a federal rules jurisdiction, the statement could only be admitted to impeach her testimony. One commentator, Andrew King–Ries, has argued that FRE 801(D)(1)(A) should be revised to admit any prior statements as substantive evidence. See Andrew King–Ries, *An Argument for Original Intent: Restoring Rule 801(D)(1)(A) to Protect Domestic Violence Victims in a Post–Crawford World*, 27 PACE L. REV. 199 (2007).

8.   **The Difficulty of Cross–Examination.** As Tom Lininger discusses in *Bearing the Cross*, 74 FORDHAM L. REV. 1353 (2005), *Crawford* makes it far more likely that victims will have to testify at trial, and thus will be subject to cross-examination. He notes:

> Any discussion of accusers' ordeals during cross-examination must emphasize the heavy-handed tactics used by lawyers. The conventional wisdom in the defense bar is that harsh cross-examination of accusers offers the best—and perhaps the only—means of exonerating the accused. Prosecutors also have treated accusers in a callous manner. As the prosecutor mentioned to the rape victim in the movie *The Accused*, "I'm not a rape counselor. I'm a prosecutor." Many prosecutors, fearing the victims' potential recusal, come to regard accusers as saboteurs. Few other categories of accusers have such unpleasant relations with both prosecutors and defense attorneys.

Lininger suggests a number of reforms that could protect accusers from harsh and unnecessary cross-examinations, including bringing one's own attorney to trial. Given what you know about the criminal justice system, what concerns do you think accusers might have about cross-examination at trial? What ways can you think of to minimize the impact of cross-examinations? See also Myrna S. Raeder, *Domestic Violence Cases After Davis: Is the Glass Half Empty or Half Full?*, 15 J. L. & POL'Y 759 (2007).

9.   **Retroactivity.** In 2007, *Whorton v. Bockting*, 549 U.S. ___, 127 S.Ct. 1173 (2007), the Supreme Court held that the rule in *Crawford* did not announce a "watershed" of criminal procedure and therefore could not be applied retroactively on collateral review.

C.   PRIOR ACTS AND PATTERNS OF ABUSE

Except under very limited exceptions, both the Federal Rules of Evidence and all 50 states generally forbid the introduction of prior conduct to prove that the defendant acted in conformity with his or her character, sometimes referred to as "propensity evidence." See FRE 404(a). The courts are particularly skeptical of evidence that may lead the jury to conclude "if he did it before, he'll do it again." However, such evidence may be admissible for some other purpose, such as to prove motive or intent. See, e.g. FRE 404(b). In the following case, the state sought to introduce evidence of the defendant's prior assaults on the victim. Consider what such evidence proves and why it is relevant.

State v. Sanders

Vermont Supreme Court, 1998.
716 A.2d 11.

■ MORSE, JUSTICE.

Defendant appeals his jury conviction of aggravated domestic assault, claiming that the court erred by ... admitting evidence that defendant had assaulted the victim on prior occasions. We affirm.

The assault charge stemmed from a confrontation on March 31, 1996, in Burlington. The victim, defendant's live-in girlfriend, came home that evening with a friend, Jodi Bell. She was surprised to find defendant home because he had told her earlier that day he was moving out due to problems in their relationship. As the victim and her friend were getting ready to go out for the night, they heard defendant breaking glass and smashing things around the house. Frightened, the women locked themselves in the bathroom. Bell then ran next door to call the police, and when she returned, she found defendant and the victim standing in the kitchen. Bell, to protect the victim, inserted herself in between them. Defendant then picked up a knife and said "someone is going to die ... who's it gonna be?" The State charged defendant with aggravated domestic assault for being armed with a deadly weapon and threatening to use that weapon on a household member.

Over two months prior to trial, the State sent defense counsel a letter listing several "prior bad acts" they intended to introduce at trial. Defendant brought a motion *in limine* to exclude the evidence, but the judge allowed the State to introduce two of the prior bad acts to go to the issue of intent. The first was an incident that occurred on December 30, 1995, in which the victim asked defendant to leave the apartment. In response to her request, he choked her and threw her across the room, giving her a bloody nose. The second was an incident that occurred on January 6, 1996, when defendant took victim's car without permission and screamed threats at her, saying he would never leave without a fight. During trial, it was revealed that these incidents actually occurred on February 10, 1996, and February 18, 1996, respectively. However, on the stand, the victim recanted most of the substantive facts of these prior sworn statements. . . .

Defendant ... argues that the court erred by admitting evidence that defendant had assaulted the victim on prior occasions. Defendant claims that the State is merely using this evidence to show his propensity for criminal behavior, and therefore it should be excluded under V.R.E. 404(b) and 403. The State argues that the evidence was offered to show why the victim was afraid of defendant and to prove that defendant had the requisite intent ... to "threaten" the victim with the knife.

In reviewing the trial court's admission of evidence under 404(b), we must decide whether the evidence was both relevant and material to the subject cause of action ... and if so, whether the trial court abused its discretion in deciding that the introduction of such evidence was more probative than prejudicial.

Here, we need not decide whether the prior bad acts may be admissible solely to show fear or intent because the evidence was relevant also to portray the history surrounding the abusive relationship, providing the needed context for the behavior in issue. The purpose of establishing defendant's history of abusing the victim is not to show his general character for such abuse, but to provide the jury with an understanding of defendant's actions on the date in question.

Allegations of a single act of domestic violence, taken out of its situational context, are likely to seem "incongruous and incredible" to a jury. Without knowing the history of the relationship between the defendant and the victim, jurors may not believe the victim was actually abused, since domestic violence is "learned, ... controlling behavior aimed at gaining another's compliance" through multiple incidents. The prior occasions tend to prove that defendant meant to threaten and intimidate his friend when he raised the knife and said "someone is going to die." Therefore, the evidence was admissible.

Previous incidents of domestic abuse are also relevant to put the victim's recantation of prior statements into context for the jury. Victims of domestic abuse are likely to change their stories out of fear of retribution, or even out of misguided affection. This prior history of abuse gives the jury an understanding of why the victim is less than candid in her testimony and allows them to decide more accurately which of the victim's statements more reliably reflect reality.

These considerations compel us to find that the trial court did not err by admitting the prior bad acts evidence. . . .

NOTES AND QUESTIONS

1. **The Relevance of Prior Bad Acts.** In *Sanders*, the victim recanted her testimony. Should prior acts of domestic violence only be admitted in order to explain why the victim recanted her testimony? In a subsequent case, *State v. Hendricks*, 787 A.2d 1270 (Vt.2001), the Vermont Supreme Court clarified that prior bad acts are admissible in domestic violence cases even where the victim has not recanted her testimony. Rather, the court reasoned that the evidence was relevant to establish the context in which the abuse took place. The court further emphasized that its ruling only applied to domestic violence cases, and not other types of crimes. This opinion is consistent with those in most states, which allow for the introduction of prior acts only if offered to show something other than propensity, such as the history of the relationship, or to show that the defendant did in fact intend to harm the victim. See Andrea M. Kovach, *Prosecutorial Use of Other Acts of Domestic Violence for Propensity Purposes: A Brief Look at its Past, Present, & Future*, 2003 U. ILL. L. REV. 1115 (2003).

2. **Special Rules of Evidence for Domestic Violence Cases?** In a concurring opinion in *State v. Hendricks*, one of the justices urged the Vermont legislature to pass a specific exception to its rules of evidence that would allow for prior bad acts in these cases to prove context. Should there be special rules of evidence governing domestic violence cases? What is the difference between someone who engages in intimate violence and someone who sells drugs or robs convenience stores? Won't such evidence lead the jury to conclude that the defendant is an abuser, precisely the conclusion the rules of evidence are deigned to prohibit? Doesn't proof of past abuse show a tendency to abuse? Will such laws unnecessarily hurt the rights of criminal defendants?

3. **Propensity Evidence in Sexual Assault and Child Molestation Cases.** Under rules enacted by Congress in 1994, Federal Rules of Evidence, 413–415 now allow for introduction of character evidence in cases in which the defendant is accused of sexual assault, child molestation, or in civil cases predicated on the party's commission of an offense involving sexual assault or child molestation. Other states, including California and Michigan, have passed similar laws. The prior acts need not have resulted in a conviction, or even have been reported to the police. These rules are a significant departure from the general ban on character evidence. In such cases, it is entirely proper for the jury to conclude, "if he did it before, he'll do it again." Congress and state legislatures have been persuaded to pass such rules in part because of the argument that sexual offenders have a propensity, or compulsion, to continue to offend. Given what we have learned about domestic violence abusers, do you think a similar argument could be made about their "compulsion" to abuse? What is the difference between someone who, for example, molests children, and someone who abuses his partner?

4. **Modern Trends in Evidence.** At least two states, California and Arizona, have passed statutes that allow for the introduction of prior abuse in domestic violence cases to prove a propensity to abuse. See Cal. Evid. Code § 1109 (1997) & Alaska R. Evid. § 404(b)(4) (2002). In both states, prosecutors may introduce in their case-in-chief prior acts of domestic violence against either the same or a different victim, regardless of whether that conduct resulted in a conviction or a report to the police. Consider the rationale for such laws:

> As in sex offense cases, the use of character evidence in domestic violence cases is more justified than in a murder case or a forgery case. The legislative history of section 1109, which recognizes the special nature of domestic violence crime, supports this point: "The propensity inference is particularly appropriate in the area of domestic violence because on-going violence and abuse is the norm in domestic violence cases. Not only is there a great likelihood that any one battering episode is part of a larger scheme of dominance and control, that scheme usually escalates in frequency and severity. Without the propensity inference, the escalating nature of domestic violence is likewise masked. If we fail to address the very essence of domestic violence, we will continue to see cases where perpetrators of this violence will beat

their partners, even kill them, and go on to beat or kill the next intimate partner. Since criminal prosecution is one of the few factors which may interrupt the escalating pattern of domestic violence, we must be willing to look at that pattern during the criminal prosecution, or we will miss the opportunity to address this problem at all." *People v. Hoover*, 92 Cal.Rptr.2d 208 (Cal. Ct. App. 2000).

How does this reasoning differ from the reasoning in *State v. Sanders*? In both cases, the courts conclude that there is something unique about domestic violence cases that make prior bad acts relevant. The question remains how evidence of prior abuse is relevant for purposes other than proving propensity? *Sanders* focuses on context, *Hoover* on further violence. Is there a difference? Are these cases just an end-run around the propensity rule? If so, why should domestic violence cases be treated differently than other kinds of cases?

D. EXPERT TESTIMONY

As we saw in Chapter Five, and as we will examine in more detail in subsequent chapters, lawyers often seek to have experts testify in a range of cases involving domestic violence. Prosecutors may seek to introduce expert testimony to show why a victim might be recanting her testimony. Defense attorneys may seek to introduce such testimony to prove why a woman who killed her abuser was reasonable in believing that she had to act in self-defense. A family lawyer might seek to have an expert explain why a battered mother is acting in her children's best interests when insisting upon supervised visitation. Sarah Buel explains the use of experts in representing defendants in criminal cases who have been battered:

> [T]he expert will likely need to correlate the escalating violence with the abused person's inability to identify and use resources. In the alternative, an expert can explain why existing options were unavailable to a specific victim—perhaps because she lacked transportation, job skills, and childcare, or did not speak English, drive, or was not permitted to leave the home. In forensic cases, expert testimony may describe abuse victims' sequelae, the general nature of domestic violence, the rationale for what seems to be illogical behavior, and the ways in which this client is not a "typical" abuse victim.

> An expert might also explain the frequency, severity, and nature of the abuse suffered by the battered defendant to the jury. In some cases, the client is able to convey this information with the necessary level of clarity and detail. However, some survivors are too traumatized, depressed, angry, catatonic, inarticulate, or ashamed to present the facts sufficiently. They may have trouble remembering the horrific events or be grief-stricken from killing a partner they loved. The survivor's reactions to the abuse often meet some or all of the criteria for Post–Traumatic Stress Disorder (PTSD). It thus may be necessary to supplement the survivor's testimony with that of an expert ... Sarah M.

Buel, *Effective Assistance of Counsel for Battered Women Defendants: A Normative Construct*, 26 HARV. WOMEN'S L.J. 217 (2003).

What Buel describes above is not the kind of narrow psychological testimony that we saw at play in Chapter Five. Rather, she suggests that expert testimony on battering can provide a broad context for the jury, rather than narrowly defining those who have been abused as suffering from a "syndrome." This picks up on themes that we discussed in Chapter Five concerning the difference between testimony on "battered woman syndrome" and expert testimony on battering generally. Thus, when discussing expert testimony on battering, we put "battered women's syndrome" in quotes to express skepticism about the accuracy or the usefulness of expert testimony when it is focused on purely psychological constructs. Although such testimony may have proved helpful in specific cases, the overall history of "battered women's syndrome" has been troublesome. As we will see in this chapter, not only does testimony on "battered women's syndrome" distort the experiences of victims, but it is also lacks scientific integrity, even though it has been widely accepted by the courts. One irony is that courts have tended to reject scientific fact and embraced stereotypes about battered victims, something the rules of evidence were designed to protect against.

There are three evidentiary issues that govern the admissibility of expert testimony. The first is that the expert's testimony must be relevant to the case. Relevance under FRE 401 is defined as "having any tendency to make the existence of a fact that is of consequence to the determination of the action more probable or less probable than it would be without the evidence." Whether expert testimony is relevant is based on the underlying substantive legal issues involved. For example, in *United States v. Dixon*, 413 F.3d 520 (5th Cir. 2005), discussed in Chapter Five, the court refused to allow expert testimony in a case where the victim claimed that she acted under the duress of her abusive boyfriend. The court reasoned that expert testimony on the victim's subjective vulnerability to abuse and coercion did not help the jury decide whether she acted reasonably, and therefore the expert testimony was not relevant. Thus, lawyers must argue why expert testimony is relevant in a particular case. When a court rules expert testimony is not admissible, it is almost always because the court finds such testimony to be irrelevant given the specific facts and substantive law of the particular case.

The second and related issue to relevance is whether the testimony is "helpful" to the jury. Under Federal Rule of Evidence 702, expert testimony is admissible if it will "assist the trier of act to understand evidence or to determine a fact in issue." The issue for courts has been whether the jury could not otherwise make sense of the victim's behavior absent some additional testimony on the dynamics of abusive relationships. Thus, testimony on battering is introduced to give the jury some broader context in which to understand the victim's actions. Yet, the testimony cannot substitute for the jury's role as fact-finder. Thus, in many cases, experts are prohibited from drawing conclusions, such as whether a victim recanted her testimony because she was in fear, or whether a defendant did, in fact, kill in self-defense.

The third issue is whether the expert's opinion is based on reliable information. Prior to 1993, in order for scientific evidence to be admitted, it had to be generally accepted within the scientific community. This was known as the Frye test, from *Frye v. United States*, 293 F. 1013 (D.C.Cir. 1923). Then, in *Daubert v. Merrell Dow Pharmaceuticals, Inc.*, 509 U.S. 579 (1993), the United States Supreme Court charged trial judges with the responsibility of acting as gatekeepers to exclude unreliable expert testimony based in science. Subsequently, in *Kumho Tire Co. v. Carmichael*, 526 U.S. 137 (1999), the Court extended *Daubert* to all expert testimony. *Daubert* sets forth a list of non-exclusive factors for judges to consider when deciding whether expert testimony is reliable. Those factors include whether the theory has been subject to peer review, whether the theory is generally accepted in the community, and whether the theory is based on reliable principles and methodology. Expert testimony about domestic violence relationships, as well as testimony about "battered women's syndrome", is based on social science. In these cases, courts have been less demanding of the kind of scientific rigor they can sometimes demand of the "hard" sciences. See *United States v. DiDomenico*, 985 F.2d 1159 (2d Cir. 1993), *cert. denied* 519 U.S. 1006 (1996). *Daubert* and its progeny provide for fairly wide latitude for litigants to introduce expert testimony.

In the 1980s, when expert testimony on battering and its psychological effects, often referred to as "battered women's syndrome", was first introduced, some courts rejected the evidence as not having a sufficient scientific basis. We will see an example of this in *State v. Kelly*, 478 A.2d 364 (N.J.1984), excerpted in Chapter Nine. However, over time, courts began accepting the scientific reliability of theories on battering, either in the context of "battered women's syndrome," or the more general diagnosis of post-traumatic stress disorder. The liberalizing of legal standards after *Daubert* certainly facilitated the admissibility of such evidence.

While the majority of states have adopted FRE 702, many use varying standards for the admissibility of expert testimony. Not all states adhere to *Daubert*. Some still use the Frye test or a variation of it. Nevertheless, by the mid 1990s expert testimony on battering was rarely excluded under the theory that it was unreliable. Thus, expert testimony on battering and its effects has been admitted in every state as well as in federal court.

The following case is the first in which a federal court admits testimony on "battered women's syndrome." Federal law on the admissibility of expert testimony often guides state court rulings on these matters. As you read it, focus on the first two issues discussed above—is the expert testimony relevant and is it helpful to the jury? Also, think back to the discussion in Chapter Five and the problems of characterizing abused women as suffering from a "syndrome." Do such characterizations oversimplify the complex nature of battering and how it affects its victims? Also, think about the possibilities for discussing battering beyond the narrow characterization of psychological evidence.

Arcoren v. United States

Eighth Circuit Court of Appeals, 1991.
929 F.2d 1235.

■ FRIEDMAN, SENIOR CIRCUIT JUDGE.

Arcoren's convictions stem from events occurring on September 17, 1989 at his apartment in St. Francis, South Dakota, which is on the Rosebud Indian Reservation. Viewing the facts most favorably to the government, which is the standard on appeal from criminal convictions, there was evidence from which the jury could have found the following:

After attending a dance and doing some drinking, Arcoren, an American Indian, returned to his apartment around 3:00 a.m., accompanied by his nephew, brother, and four young girls—including Charlene Bordeaux (Bordeaux), Arcoren's wife's fifteen-year-old niece. Arcoren's pregnant wife, Brenda Brave Bird (Brave Bird), from whom he had separated two days before, was not in the apartment. Arcoren and Bordeaux went into the bedroom while the others remained in the living room, where they drank beer and played the stereo.

At approximately 5:00 a.m., Brave Bird arrived at the apartment and, after a brief argument with Arcoren, left. Arcoren returned to the bedroom and had consensual sexual intercourse with Bordeaux. Brave Bird later returned to the apartment, discovering Arcoren and Bordeaux in the bedroom. Arcoren forcefully pulled Brave Bird into the bedroom; verbally and physically abused her; prevented Brave Bird and Bordeaux from leaving the bedroom; and, for the next several hours, forced both women to have sexual intercourse with him.

Later in the morning, while Arcoren slept, Brave Bird left the apartment in Arcoren's car, flagged down a police officer, John Two Eagle, and reported the assaults. At his instruction, Brave Bird then went to the hospital for medical treatment, where she told a nurse and attending physician about the beatings and rapes. At the hospital, Brave Bird also described the assaults to Phillip Charles, a criminal investigator with the Bureau of Indian Affairs.

Three days later, Brave Bird testified before a South Dakota federal grand jury, describing in detail Arcoren's violent sexual and physical assaults of both herself and Bordeaux. . . .

At trial, Bordeaux testified that she and Arcoren had voluntary intercourse; that after Brave Bird arrived, Arcoren verbally abused and beat Brave Bird, and then forced both herself and Brave Bird to have sexual intercourse with him as the other watched. John Two Eagle, the police officer, testified that when Brave Bird stopped him on the morning of September 17th, she had a swollen face with a cut on the bridge of her nose, blood on her clothing, and was "really upset." According to Two Eagle, Brave Bird stated that Arcoren "had assaulted her most of the night, forced her to stay at the apartment there on the east side of town and raped her and that there was another girl there that was being forced to stay at the apartment by [Arcoren] and that he raped her, too."

Carol Edwards, the receiving nurse at the hospital emergency room, testified that upon arrival, Brave Bird was "crying and upset" and told her that she had been "beaten up twice and she had been raped twice...." Dr. Teresa Mareska, the treating physician at the hospital, testified that Brave Bird reported being "assaulted by an individual named Tim" and "forced in some sexual activities." Phillip Charles, the Bureau of Indian Affairs criminal investigator who interviewed Brave Bird at the emergency room, testified in great detail about Brave Bird's account of the violent physical and sexual assaults by Arcoren upon Brave Bird and Bordeaux.

When the government called Brave Bird as a witness, she recanted her prior grand jury testimony and denied that Arcoren had beaten and raped her.

After using Brave Bird's grand jury testimony to impeach her trial testimony, the government introduced portions of the grand jury testimony, which were read aloud to the jury by the court reporter, as "substantive evidence...."

Finally, Arcoren testified on his own behalf. He stated that although he had argued that night with Brave Bird over Bordeaux—during which time Brave Bird's nose was accidentally bloodied—they later made up and then had voluntary intercourse while Bordeaux was asleep. He also testified that the two women were free to leave at any time, and that he "did not make any sexual contact with Charlene [Bordeaux] whatsoever."

As noted, at trial Brave Bird recanted her grand jury testimony. She denied Arcoren raped her, denied that she had seen Arcoren and Bordeaux have sexual intercourse, and stated that the cuts and bruises on her body resulted from an earlier motorbike wreck. When the government confronted her with her contradictory grand jury testimony, Brave Bird stated that she could not remember making the statements or that, where she did recall making them, they were incorrect. She stated that when she made the statements on September 17th accusing Arcoren of raping her, she was angry with Arcoren because "he was with another woman" and not "because he raped [her]."

The government then called an expert witness, Carol Maicky, to testify regarding "battered woman syndrome." She was a psychologist who had worked with battered women for 10 years and with rape victims for 14 years. The government gave the following reasons for offering the evidence:

> Your Honor, there are certain facts which the jury has before it from the testimony which we contend will go unnoticed by a lay jury unless put into a perspective by an expert. We're offering her opinion under Rule 702 to show that these particular facts, while [they] may seem insignificant by themselves when put together against a battered women syndrome would allow the jury to determine the credibility of her in court testimony ... and help them determine which of the two diametrically opposed sworn statements of Brenda Brave Bird to believe.

After hearing Maicky's proffered testimony in chambers, the court, over defense counsel's objection, admitted the evidence. The court ruled that the evidence was admissible under Rule 702 of the Federal Rules of Evidence because it was "scientific, technical or other specialized knowledge [that] will assist the [jury] to understand the evidence or to determine a fact in issue" and that "the evidence would be more probative than prejudicial." The court, however, warned that Maicky could not "testify as to the ultimate fact that a particular party in this case, not the defendant, the party actually suffers from battered women syndrome. This determination must be left to the trier of fact."

In her testimony before the jury, Maicky generally described the battered woman syndrome. According to her testimony, which was based on her knowledge of the literature dealing with the subject and her professional experience, a "battered woman" is one who assumes responsibility for a cycle of violence occurring in a relationship, where the abuser (a husband or boyfriend) has told her that the first violent episode was her fault. Maicky described the syndrome's general characteristics to include (1) the belief that violence to the woman is her fault; (2) an inability to place responsibility for the violence elsewhere; (3) a fear for her life and the lives of her children; and (4) an irrational belief that the abuser is omnipresent and omniscient. According to Ms. Maicky, a battered woman develops coping mechanisms to deal with the ever-present violence, believing that by doing just one more thing she can stop the violence.

In accordance with the court's direction, Maicky expressed no opinion whether Brave Bird suffered from or displayed symptoms of the syndrome. . . .

The jury in the present case was faced with a bizarre situation. Immediately after the rapes and assaults, Brave Bird had described them to the police officer whose car she flagged down, to the nurse and the doctor at the hospital where she had gone for treatment, and to a criminal investigator from the Bureau of Indian Affairs. Three days later, she described the rapes and assaults in detail in sworn testimony before the grand jury.

Four months later, at Arcoren's trial, she recanted her grand jury testimony. There she stated that she either did not remember statements to the grand jury or that, if she did remember them, the statements were incorrect and that some of them were things she had "made up." At trial, she also changed her explanation for the injuries to her leg she had suffered on September 18, 1989. Although she told the police officer, the nurse and doctors at the hospital, and the criminal investigator that Arcoren had inflicted those injuries when he beat her, at trial she testified that the injuries resulted from a motorbike wreck. She also testified that the reason she stopped the police officer after leaving Arcoren's apartment was because she had been driving 70 miles per hour.

A jury naturally would be puzzled at the complete about-face she made, and would have great difficulty in determining which version of Brave Bird's testimony it should believe. If there were some explanation for Brave Bird's changed statements, such explanation would aid the jury in deciding which statements were credible.

Maicky's expert testimony regarding the battered woman syndrome provided that explanation to the jury. As the witness told the jury, the syndrome is a psychological condition, which leads a female victim of physical abuse to accept her beatings because she believes that she is responsible for them, and hopes that by accepting one more beating, the pattern will stop. Maicky's testimony provided the jury with information that would help it to determine which of Brave Bird's testimony to credit. If the jury concluded that Brave Bird suffered from battered woman syndrome, that would explain her change in testimony—her unwillingness to say something damaging against her husband....

Arcoren also challenges the admission of Maicky's testimony on the ground that "the jury was in a better position than the government's expert to judge the credibility of Brave Bird." Maicky, however, expressed no opinion on whether Brave Bird suffered from battered woman syndrome or which of her conflicting statements were more credible. Maicky merely provided expert information to aid the jury in evaluating the evidence. Maicky's testimony did not interfere with or impinge upon the jury's role in determining the credibility of witnesses.

The decision whether to admit expert testimony ordinarily lies within the discretion of the trial court and will not be reversed unless there has been an abuse of discretion. In the unusual circumstances of this case, the district court did not abuse its discretion in admitting Maicky's expert testimony regarding battered woman syndrome.

NOTES AND QUESTIONS

1. **Use of Expert Testimony to Bolster Witness Credibility.** In *Arcoren*, do you think the jury needed the expert testimony in order to decide whether the victim was being truthful? The benefits of using such testimony are obvious when the victim later recants. But could the use of such testimony backfire? Consider Laurie S. Kohn, *Barriers to Reliable Credibility Assessments: Domestic Violence Victim–Witnesses*, 11 Am. U. J. Gender Soc. Pol'y & L. 733 (2003):

> What are the additional risks that we as advocates run by advocating the use of expert testimony in domestic violence cases, and are those risks worth taking?
>
> One detrimental by-product of the use of expert witnesses is that it may reinforce stereotypes and enhance women's subordination. Replacing one set of assumptions about appropriate behavior for a woman with another set of expectations hardly improves the chances of future women being judged on the basis of their testimony alone, absent gender stereotypes. In addition, permitting an expert to pathologize a woman's behavior and interpret it for the court in a way that is "reasonable" may tend to further undermine a woman's credibility. Some argue that experts rob women of their agency.

Kohn goes on to argue that these risks are lessened when, rather than using evidence of "battered women's syndrome," which sometimes suggests that all women act the same way when abused, expert testimony is based on rigorous social science that accounts for the complex reactions victims have towards battering. She suggests that such evidence is particularly helpful when victims do not react with the stereotypical fear and shame many jurors might think they should.

In *Arcoren*, the victim acted as a "victim" in the sense that she recanted her testimony. Now consider whether expert testimony is relevant when a victim does testify but is portrayed as less than credible by the defense. In *Michigan v. Christel*, 537 N.W.2d 194 (Mich. 1995) the defendant was charged with beating and raping his girlfriend. At trial, the victim testified that the relationship deteriorated over time, with the defendant becoming increasingly jealous. This jealousy turned to rage, which then turned to physical and sexual violence. The defense portrayed the victim as a liar. The prosecution introduced expert testimony to bolster the victim's credibility. The Michigan Supreme Court recognized the admissibility of expert testimony on "battered woman syndrome" but qualified its holding, emphasizing "that the admissibility of syndrome evidence is limited to a description of the uniqueness of a specific behavior brought out at trial." Here the court found the victim did not possess that uniqueness.

> ... We find the necessary factual underpinnings for admission of expert testimony lacking. Certainly there may have been a question why complainant tolerated prolonged abuse without reporting it to authorities or friends. However, defendant never denied that some [of the prior] abuse occurred. Furthermore, complainant testified that the relationship ended one month before the assault and did not attempt to hide or deny the instant sexual assault. Moreover, complainant did not delay reporting this incident, but, instead, immediately sought medical attention with accompanying discussions with police.... Complainant also never recanted that the assault occurred.... [W]e reject the prosecution's contention that the battered woman syndrome was relevant in this case.

While the court ultimately found the error harmless, consider the long-term implications of this reasoning. Must victims fit certain "stereotypes" before such evidence can be admitted? What role does such testimony play when the victim acts as the jury would hope that she would act? Shouldn't the jury be able to decide when a witness is credible?

2. **The Scientific Reliability of "Battered Women's Syndrome."** *Arcoren* was decided before *Daubert*. The *Frye* test, used prior to *Daubert*, required that the expert's theory be "generally accepted" within the scientific community. The *Arcoren* court found that "the theory underlying the battered woman syndrome is beyond the experimental stage and has gained a substantial enough scientific acceptance to warrant admissibility." 929 F.2d at 1241. Since *Arcoren*, courts have generally not questioned the reliability of expert testimony on "battered women's syndrome."

However, some commentators have been very critical of Lenore Walker's original research and question the validity of "battered women's syndrome". For example, David L. Faigman and Amy J. Wright in *The Battered Woman Syndrome in the Age of Science*, 39 ARIZ. L. REV. 67 (1997) argue that the "battered women's syndrome" never had a basis in science, but rather is a political theory about gender roles that conforms to a political agenda. The result, they argue, has been bad for battered women and bad for science. In particular, they are highly critical of Lenore Walker's research on both the cycle of violence and the concept of learned helplessness. Although the authors predicted that after *Daubert*, courts and advocates would abandon the syndrome, expert testimony on "battered women's syndrome" continues to be admitted despite its methodological and evidentiary shortcomings. See also Alafair S. Burke, *Rational Actors, Self–Defense, and Duress: Making Sense, Not Syndromes, Out of the Battered Woman*, 81 N.C. L. Rev. 211 (2002).

For a discussion about the nuances of the scientific validity of "battered women's syndrome" and its relationship to women's equality, see Erica Beecher–Monas, *Domestic Violence: Competing Conceptions of Equality in the Law of Evidence*, 47 Loy. L. Rev. 81 (2001).

3. **Evidence on Battering as Propensity Evidence.** In 1988, the Washington Supreme Court was the first to uphold the admission of "battered women's syndrome" testimony on behalf of the prosecution. *State v. Ciskie*, 751 P.2d 1165 (Wash. 1988). See also *State v. Frost*, 577 A.2d 1282 (N.J. Super. Ct. App. Div. 1990). Since then, the vast majority of state courts have allowed prosecutors to introduce expert evidence on battering to explain why a victim minimized or recanted her testimony, although some states have rejected this approach. For example, in *State v. Dowd*, 1994 WL 18645 (Ohio App. 9 Dist. 1994) the trial court refused to introduce testimony by a psychologist that would have explained why an abused victim might recant her testimony. The appellate court agreed, arguing that such testimony could create a potentially prejudicial inference by the jury that if the defendant had beaten the victim before, he did so on this occasion. This would impact the defendant's right to a fair trial.

4. **Stereotypes and Native Americans.** In *Arcoren*, both the defendant and the victims were Native American. What stereotypes or assumptions, if any, do you think might have influenced the jury in deciding whether Brave Bird was telling the truth just after the incident or in court? As we saw in Chapter Three, Native American women experience all forms of violence, including domestic violence, at twice the rates of white women. One study found that domestic violence occurred in 15.5% of Indian marriages, with 7.2% reporting severe violence (as opposed to 14.8% and 5.3% of white couples.) Other studies have suggested that Native American women are at greatest risk for being victims of intimate violence. Why might this be the case? See Sumayyah Waheed, *Domestic Violence on the Reservation: Imperfect Laws, Imperfect Solution*, 19 Berkeley Women's L.J. 287 (2004). Did expert testimony in this case help combat some of those stereotypes?

5. **Who Qualifies as an Expert?** Federal Rule 702 defines experts by knowledge, skill, experience, training, or education. Thus, many people who work with domestic violence victims can be used as experts including social workers, counselors, shelter workers, and even the police. To lay the foundation for such witnesses, the attorney should focus on the background and experience of the witness. Consider one attorney's advice:

Deciding whom to utilize as an expert must be done on a case-by-case basis. Whether a credentialed professional (usually a Ph.D. psychologist or M.D. psychiatrist), law enforcement officer, nurse, experienced domestic violence advocate, minister, or other professional will be the most effective expert is highly case specific. Often, the doctorate level professionals cost far more than the survivor can afford or than the court will allow for an indigent defendant. As a result, counsel must carefully select other professionals in the community who have the requisite expertise for a specific case. Whom the attorney chooses should also depend on what testimony is needed for the specific case. I have often qualified certain law enforcement officers as experts to describe the typicality of victims returning to their batterers, to repudiate offender behavior, and to voice a deep desire for offenders to obtain treatment. Sarah M. Buel, *Effective Assistance of Counsel for Battered Women Defendants: A Normative Construct*, 26 HARV. WOMEN'S L.J. 217 (2003).

See also Lauren Zykorie, *Can a Domestic Violence Advocate Testify as an Expert Witness? Follow the ABC's of Expert Testimony Standards in Texas Courts*, 11 TEX. J. WOMEN & L. 275 (2002); Anna Farber Conrad, *The Use of Victim Advocates & Expert Witnesses in Battered Women's Cases*, 30 DEC. COLO. LAW. 43 (2001).

6. **Batterer Profiling.** Lenore Walker was at one time retained by O.J. Simpson's defense team during his trial for allegedly murdering his wife Nicole Brown Simpson and her friend Ronald Goldman. Although never ultimately called to testify, Walker had suggested that O.J. Simpson might not have fit the "profile" of batterers who then go on to murder their wives. See Scott Sleek, *Walker Defends Right to Testify for O.J.*, AMERICAN PSYCHOLOGICAL ASSOCIATION MONITOR (1995) (available at http://www.dpi.bnu.edu.cn/apa/monitor/apr95/lenore.html). Walker's willingness to testify on behalf of O.J. Simpson caused much controversy among battered women's advocates, who felt as if Walker was somehow being disloyal. Walker never took the stand, so we don't know if the court would have admitted her testimony. However, the admissibility of such testimony does raise significant questions for the law. In particular, can the defendant claim "I'm Not a Batterer Defense"? See Myrna Raeder, *The Better Way: The Role of Batterers' Profiles and Expert "Social Framework" Background in Cases Implicating Domestic Violence*, 68 U. COLO. L. REV. 147 (1997).

There have been some cases in which the prosecution has attempted to introduce general information about batterers to prove that it was the defendant who committed the alleged act. Thus, the admissibility of expert testimony is arguably relevant to prove the defendant's behavior. Below is one of the most frequently cited cases that has dealt with this issue.

Ryan v. State

Supreme Court of Wyoming, 1999.
988 P.2d 46.

■ KALOKATHIS, DISTRICT JUDGE.

Convicted of murdering his wife, Appellant alleges numerous errors deprived him of his right to a fair trial. While we find that Appellant was impermissibly profiled by expert testimony, the error was harmless beyond a reasonable doubt. As none of Appellant's other contentions are meritorious, we affirm. . . .

Ryan and Keri had a turbulent marriage punctuated by Ryan's physical abuse of his wife, which he admitted at trial. An exhaustive list of friends, neighbors, and coworkers testified to Ryan's physical, mental, and emotional abuse of Keri throughout the course of their marriage. The State produced witnesses who testified to several incidents where Ryan punched and kicked Keri in fits of rage. Additionally, the State produced witnesses who stated that Ryan controlled and isolated Keri. Ryan would not allow Keri to go anywhere without his permission, and he demanded to know where she was and who she was with at all times. According to Keri's coworkers, Ryan called her at work ten times or more during her shifts to check up on her. There was testimony that Ryan had attempted to commit suicide in Keri's presence on one occasion. There was testimony that Ryan emotionally abused Keri through constant criticism. There was extensive testimony about Ryan's excessive jealousy. He often accused Keri of having extramarital affairs with the customers she spoke with at work, and on more than one occasion he assaulted men who spoke with Keri.

Keri left Ryan in early November of 1996 and had a family violence protection order issued against Ryan on November 5, 1996. That order was subsequently dismissed at Keri's request. During the separation period, Keri expressed her desire to return to school; she began dating another man and suggested that Ryan begin dating other women. For his part, Ryan did not handle the separation well. He became depressed and had noticeable weight loss.

[One evening, Ryan killed Keri and then unsuccessfully turned the gun on himself.]

1. SEPARATION VIOLENCE—THE BRATTON TESTIMONY

Rosemary Bratton has extensive experience working with both battered and battering spouses and has previously testified as an expert on the subject of Battered Woman Syndrome (BWS). BWS experts generally attempt to explain the irrational behavior of battered spouses, such as seeking withdrawal of a protective order or continually returning to an abusive spouse. Here, however, the State made known to defense counsel that Bratton would also testify about the characteristics of batterers and the kind of conduct they tend to exhibit. Ryan objected to that portion of the Bratton testimony pertaining to anything he might have done. While the trial judge admitted that he was having trouble determining the relevancy of Bratton's testimony concerning Ryan's actual or possible actions; ultimately, she was allowed to testify.

At trial, Bratton began by explaining the now familiar characteristics of BWS to the jury. She explained the cyclical pattern of violence often present in abusive relationships and then went on to describe a phenomena termed, "separation violence":

Q.   Now, is there any particular phase of this cycle of violence which tends to be more dangerous than another?

A.   Yes. And we actually term it now as separation violence. What I know from my experience and what we know from the literature and the research that has been done is that the time that the victim is planning to leave or has left this relationship is the time of the greatest danger. That's the time more homicides are committed, that's the time when there's greater physical injury, and it happens because perpetrators of domestic violence who need to maintain power and control over their partner become extremely upset, nervous, agitated when they feel that they are losing that control. When they feel that that person is actually going to leave them, then it becomes far more dangerous for the victim, because the violence will escalate to whatever it takes to prevent this person from actually leaving. They are losing control, they are losing access to this individual, and it's a very very dangerous time for victims.

Q.   Now, this separation violence is what you've termed this; is that correct?

A.   That's correct.

Q.   And have there been any studies done here in Wyoming on that issue?

A.   Yes, there have. There's a study that our coalition sponsored. We started this study in the early '90s, and we went back to 1985 and looked at those incidents of domestic homicides in our state, and one of the interesting facts that we learned was that of the—of the 38 individuals that—that are a part of our research, 16 of those had actually left the relationship.

Bratton added that the majority of the women involved in the study were killed with guns. She then described those characteristics exhibited by batterers. She testified that batterers tend to control and isolate their spouses by such means as constant calls to their place of employment, demanding to know where they are, who they are with, and when they will return. Bratton stated that batterers will often threaten to commit suicide in order to force their partner to remain in the relationship. She testified that batterers tend to abuse their spouses emotionally through constant criticism. She also testified that batterers tend to exhibit pathological jealousy often accusing their spouses of having adulterous affairs with random strangers. . . .

At the outset, we must determine whether separation violence evidence falls within the emerging field of "social framework and syndrome" evidence. In general, BWS and other syndrome evidence is considered a proper subject for expert testimony, and does not implicate the proscription against character evidence.

Usually framework and syndrome evidence *is offered by prosecutors and relates to the victim,* as in sexual assault and child abuse trials. But sometimes it is offered by the defense and relates to defendants, as in the setting of homicide trials of women charged with killing husbands or intimate companions. And typical patterns of usage do not always hold true, for defendants sometimes offer evidence that patterns of behavior or attitudes in the alleged victim did not fit the syndrome and *prosecutors sometimes offer evidence of battered women syndrome in trials of men to explain the victim's behavior....*

When such evidence is raised by the prosecution in its case-in-chief and *relates to the defendant,* however, the testimony "draws close to commenting directly on what likely happened" and "looks like character evidence after all...."

Expert testimony on BWS which relates to the victim is entirely proper. Evidence concerning the defendant's involvement, however, demands close scrutiny under the character evidence rules. This is so even if reference to the defendant may only be inferred from the testimony.

Bratton did not say that because Ryan was possessed of a violent character he acted in conformity therewith on the night of the murder. She was more subtle, but the effect was the same. After showing that the subjects of the study tended to commit homicide when faced with the prospect of separation, she impliedly invited the jury to group Ryan among those subjects and by this method determine conduct.

Finding guilt by reference to common characteristics of a class of individuals to which one belongs raises the specter of profile evidence. Profile or syndrome evidence is developed through expert testimony and tends to classify people by their shared physical, emotional, or mental characteristics.

Translated into the battering spouse context, a profile is a compilation of characteristics repeatedly seen in those who batter their spouses. While our research has not disclosed any case dealing specifically with battering spouses, other jurisdictions in different contexts have dealt with similar attempts to construct a criminal profile for the purpose of proving conduct in conformity therewith. Those jurisdictions that have considered profiles of battering parents, pedophiles, rapists, and drug couriers unanimously agree that the prosecution may not offer such evidence in its case-in-chief as substantive evidence of guilt....

A criminal trial is by its very nature an individualized adjudication of a defendant's guilt or legal innocence. Testimony regarding a criminal profile is nothing more than an expert's opinion as to certain characteristics which are common to some or most of the individuals who commit particular crimes....

NOTES AND QUESTIONS

1. **Case Involving Risk Factors.** In a similar case involving a husband who murdered his estranged wife, *Brunson v. State of Arkansas*, 79 S.W.3d 304 (Ark. 2002), the prosecution introduced testimony by an expert that the defendant exhibited "risk" factors for homicide. He too had an extensive history of abusing and stalking his wife. The Supreme Court of Arkansas, relying on the reasoning from *Ryan,* also ruled that such

testimony was inadmissible as it placed the batterer in the category of potential murderers, which was unduly prejudicial, and ordered a new trial.

2.   **Common Patterns of Behavior.** In both *Ryan* and *Brunson*, noted above, the defendants' behavior followed a similar pattern. After separation, they stalked their partners, and were fueled, to some extent, by sexual jealousy. Is expert testimony on these common patterns of behavior helpful to jurors? Or can jurors understand this dynamic without the aid of expert testimony? "Separation-assault" often explains why women stay. Does the fact that women leave these relationships provide motive as to why their partners then kill them? In *Ryan*, the court ruled that the testimony should not have been admitted, but found that the error was harmless and upheld the conviction.

3.   **Defendant's Rights.** In both *Brunson* and *Ryan*, the courts are particularly concerned with the rights of criminal defendants. "Profiling" evidence allows the jury to over-rely on expert testimony rather than letting the jury decide from the facts themselves whether the defendant is guilty. Isn't protecting the rights of criminal defendants crucial in this regard? Note, however, that the right of defendants does not necessarily extend to cases involving battered women as criminal defendants. We take up this problem in Chapter Nine.

4.   **Batterer Profile Evidence as a Mitigating Factor.** One of the difficulties in admitting evidence of "batterer profiles" is that there is no common agreement concerning what that profile entails. Nevertheless, there have been cases in which defendants have attempted to introduce evidence that their "batterer profile" should mitigate their punishment. Myrna Raeder describes one such case:

> The classic case of *People v. Berry,* 556 P.2d 777 (Cal. 1976), which reversed a lower court judge's refusal to instruct the jury on manslaughter because the defendant waited twenty hours for his wife to come home, employed this type of mitigating defense. Berry's psychiatrist testified that the defendant had been emotionally victimized by numerous women, and had been convicted for stabbing his previous wife. He also portrayed the defendant's long wait as the result of pent-up passion, not premeditation. In other words, the defense employed a batterer's profile to portray Berry as a man who chose or gravitated toward women who provoked him to violence. The psychiatrist testified: "We have this pattern of enormous dependency on these women and then rupture of the relationship with tremendous rage, almost uncontrollable." This tactic transformed a factor that established the intentionality of his act into one that emphasized his rage and lack of malice, thereby blaming the victim for the batterer's repeated failure to come to grips with his assaultive personality. Sadly, the court did not understand the dynamics of domestic violence well enough to recognize that it was not the victim's previous sexual behavior, but her attempt to leave the defendant that provoked him to violence.

> Generally, there is no easy way to resolve the conflict between the determinism that underpins syndrome and profile evidence and society's overriding belief in free will. However, pure determinism has no

place in our criminal justice system. No advocate of batterer's profiles has claimed that an individual who fits one of these profiles is preordained to commit a crime. Personality profile evidence should not lessen the batterer's blame for his actions. Much like alcoholics who drive after drinking, most domestic violence defendants are aware that their actions are wrong. Myrna Raeder, *The Better Way: The Role of Batterers' Profiles and Expert "Social Framework" Background in Cases Implicating Domestic Violence*, 68 U. COLO. L. REV. 147 (1997).

Can the same be said for victims of domestic violence who, for example, are coerced by their abusers to commit crimes? What is the relationship between free will and determinism, or as Elizabeth Schneider has phrased it, between "agency and victimization"? Elizabeth M. Schneider, BATTERED WOMEN AND FEMINIST LAWMAKING (2000).

5.   **Expert Testimony on Battering in Civil Cases.** While the focus of this Chapter has primarily been on criminal cases, civil attorneys also introduce expert testimony on battering in divorce, custody, child welfare, tort and other civil matters. For an overview of these issues, see Jane H. Aiken & Jane C. Murphy, *Evidence Issues in Domestic Violence Civil Cases,* 34 FAM. L.Q. 43 (2000). We discuss these issues of expert testimony in civil cases in later chapters.

E.   SPOUSES AND CHILDREN AS WITNESSES

Spousal Privileges

At common law spousal privileges were intended to protect marriages by disallowing spouses to give adverse testimony. There are two kinds of spousal privileges in common law. The first is spousal disqualification, or spousal incompetency privilege. In these cases, a spouse may testify against a defendant spouse without his or her consent, but cannot be forced to do so. The second is a marital communications privilege, sometimes referred to as the "pillow-talk" privilege. This privilege protects private communications that took place between the husband and wife during a marriage. In these cases the defendant spouse can prohibit his spouse from testifying. How do such privileges affect domestic violence cases? Consider the following case:

State v. Thorton

Supreme Court of Washington, 1992.
835 P.2d 216.

We are asked to decide if a wife can testify against her husband (the defendant) in a prosecution for burglary of her home. At issue is the scope of the exception to the spousal incompetency rule which applies when one spouse commits a crime against the other.

Defendant, Robert Thornton, is married to Arlene Thornton. On July 11, 1990, a no-contact order was entered in Renton Municipal Court against defendant. The certificate of probable cause filed by the prosecuting attorney's office contains the following description of the relevant facts:

On August 3, 1990 at approximately 11 a.m., while Ms. Thornton was at work, the defendant entered her home without permission, breaking a window to gain entry. Inside the residence, the defendant slashed his wife's waterbed with a butcher knife, and stole her suitcase.

The defendant was observed inside Ms. Thornton's residence by a neighbor, who called the police. The defendant fled before the police arrived, but his automobile was seen in the area. Defendant was charged with residential burglary.

Defendant moved to exclude his wife's testimony. The State conceded, and the trial court acknowledged, that Washington appellate cases which would not allow her testimony were binding upon the trial court. Accordingly, the trial court granted the motion and dismissed the charge without prejudice, and the State appeals. We overrule previous cases which interpret RCW 5.60.060(1) in a manner inconsistent with this opinion, and we therefore reverse and remand for further proceedings.

RCW 5.60.060(1) provides:

A husband shall not be examined for or against his wife, without the consent of the wife, nor a wife for or against her husband without the consent of the husband. . . .

The privilege is often referred to as the rule of spousal incompetency because it operates to entirely preclude a witness's testimony. The statute contains several exceptions to the rule. One of these is that the privilege does not apply "to a criminal action or proceeding for a crime committed by one [spouse] against the other".

Under the plain language of the statute, defendant here cannot preclude his wife's testimony. The victim of the burglary was the defendant's spouse; thus, the spousal incompetency rule does not apply on its face. However, this exception has been interpreted in earlier cases of this court as applying only to crimes of *personal violence* by one spouse against the other.

The leading case in this regard is *Kephart,* decided in 1910. There, the trial court allowed a wife to testify against her husband in a prosecution for arson involving a barn which belonged to her. This court rejected the State's argument that the statute should be construed literally, and instead held that the privilege could be abrogated only in crimes involving personal violence against the spouse. The court declined to adhere to the plain language of the statute, holding that the statute was "declaratory of the common law." The significance of spousal incompetency was explained as follows:

Public policy, as at present defined, demands, on the one hand, that the sanctity and harmony of the marital relation be preserved; and on the other, it insists that one spouse shall not maintain a suit . . . by the testimony of the other. Experience has taught us that in most cases where the testimony of the husband or wife is taken for or against the other, the truth is obscured and justice hoodwinked. There is nothing more dangerous to truth than testimony prompted by conjugal affection, unless it be the echoes of a shattered home where love has flown and hatred broods expectant for the fray. These are the reasons underlying the common law rule....

Recently, the United States Supreme Court pointed out that the spousal immunity rule has its origins in the English common law:

> This spousal disqualification sprang from two canons of medieval jurisprudence: first, the rule that an accused was not permitted to testify in his own behalf because of his interest in the proceeding; second, the concept that husband and wife were one, and that since the woman had no recognized separate legal existence, the husband was that one. From those two now long-abandoned doctrines, it followed that what was inadmissible from the lips of the defendant-husband was also inadmissible from his wife.

We conclude that the policy reasons set out in *Kephart* are based on a view of the marriage relationship which is no longer accepted. It is hard to conceive of any credible justification for preventing an injured spouse from testifying in a criminal proceeding against the perpetrator. Certainly, the marital relationship has already been damaged, and if criminal activity is occurring, no legitimate purpose is served by refusing the victim of the crime the opportunity to testify against the person who committed it. The "sanctity of the marital relation" should not be preserved at the expense of one spouse's safety or peace of mind. As the Supreme Court stated in *Trammel:*

> The ancient foundations for so sweeping a privilege have long since disappeared. Nowhere in the common-law world—indeed in any modern society—is a woman regarded as chattel or demeaned by denial of a separate legal identity and the dignity associated with recognition as a whole human being....

The contemporary justification for affording an accused such a privilege is also unpersuasive. When one spouse is willing to testify against the other in a criminal proceeding—whatever the motivation—their relationship is almost certainly in disrepair; there is probably little in the way of marital harmony for the privilege to preserve. In these circumstances, a rule of evidence that permits an accused to prevent adverse spousal testimony seems far more likely to frustrate justice than to foster family peace.

We reverse the trial court and remand for further proceedings.

NOTES AND QUESTIONS

1. **Spousal Immunity and Domestic Violence.** In *Thorton*, the wife wanted to testify against her husband and, as the Court notes, in this situation, there seems to be little reason to prohibit her from doing so. Yet, what would happen if Mrs. Thorton refused to testify against her husband? Under the traditional law of spousal testimonial privilege, one spouse could

not be compelled to testify against the other spouse. By the 1990's many advocates lobbied to have these privileges abolished out of concern that spouses who were abused were then intimidated by their abusers not to testify. By 2005, all states had an exception to spousal testimonial privilege. Now, a victim of domestic violence cannot refuse to testify against her spouse on the grounds that they are married. Is that a good idea? Should a wife be compelled to testify against her husband even if she doesn't want to do so? Do such laws undermine her autonomy?

2. **Has Removing the Privilege Gone Too Far?** Given that spouses can no longer invoke privilege in many domestic violence cases, some have now resorted to taking the Fifth Amendment to avoid testifying against their spouse. Consider the following observation:

> Victims of domestic violence and sexual assault sometimes wish to "take the Fifth" for a variety of reasons: They fear that their inconsistent statements over time may subject them to prosecution for perjury; they fear that their own violence against their assailants may amount to criminal conduct; or they have no valid basis for the privilege and are simply seeking to avoid testifying on a particular issue. Lately, victims find it more difficult to invoke the privilege against self-incrimination. In 2004, the Supreme Court tightened the test for determining whether statements are truly self-incriminating. The new test requires a closer nexus between the statement and the potential criminal liability of the speaker. Further, prosecutors are immunizing an increasing number of witnesses who would otherwise take refuge under the Fifth Amendment. Prosecutors realize that immunizing these witnesses may be the only way to meet *Crawford*'s new confrontation requirements. Thus the privilege against self-incrimination currently offers less solace to victims than it has in the past. Tom Lininger, *Bearing the Cross*, 74 FORDHAM L. REV. 1353 (2005).

3. **What are Domestic Violence Crimes?** While all fifty states and the Federal Government can mandate that a victim testify in cases in which she is the victim of a physical assault, questions remain as to what type of crimes are covered. In *Thorton*, the court expanded the statutory definition to include burglary. What about crimes such as disorderly conduct that result from domestic violence? Or when an abusive spouse retaliates against his estranged partner by killing her new boyfriend? For an overview of these issues, see Malinda Seymore, *Isn't It a Crime: Feminist Perspectives on Spousal Immunity and Spousal Violence*, 90 NW U. L. REV. 1032 (1996).

Child Witnesses

As we will examine in Chapters Ten, Eleven, and Twelve, children who witness domestic violence, or are themselves abused, are affected by those experiences in a multitude of ways. There is much controversy as to whether children who witness domestic violence should be called to testify at trial. Children are not entitled to any special privileges that would protect them from testifying. As long as they are competent to testify, generally understood as having the ability to testify truthfully, they can be called to do so. Thus, the attorney in each case must decide whether a child's testimony is relevant, reliable, and necessary. These questions become even more difficult when the defendant is charged with an offense that criminalizes an assault in the presence of children. This next excerpt considers whether children should be called to testify.

Rachel L. Melissa
Oregon's Response to the Impact of Domestic Violence on Children

82 OR. L. REV. 1125 (2003).

A.   *The Effects of Testifying on Child Witnesses*

Researchers and commentators are clearly divided on the issue of whether, and to what degree, testifying has a negative impact on the child witness. Many believe that testifying can be stressful and even traumatic for children, which can result in revictimization of an already emotionally traumatized child. Others, however, do not believe that testifying against a parent or loved one is always a negative experience for a child. Lucy Berliner, Director of the Center for Sexual Assault and Traumatic Stress at Harborview Medical Center, has found no evidence to suggest that testifying is traumatic for children in a lasting way. Instead, some professionals have found that testifying is actually an empowering experience for a child who has been helpless in protecting the victim of abuse for so long. In some instances, children may actually become angry if they are not permitted to testify. Other researchers have noted that, while the immediate effects of testifying can be adverse, over a period of approximately three months children's behavioral adjustments improve to a point that makes children who testify indistinguishable from children who did not have to testify.

Despite the diverging opinions among professionals in this field, a review of the research has revealed that four primary factors contribute to trauma resulting from testimony in criminal trials, particularly in the domestic violence context. These factors include: (1) fear of the abuser; (2) fear of the legal process and the physical courtroom environment; (3) number of times the child has to testify and length of the trial; and (4) presence of maternal support. Not only do these factors jeopardize the child testifier's emotional well-being, but they also could potentially compromise the veracity of the child's testimony.

1.   Fear of the Abuser

The first of these four factors—fear of the abuser—is particularly relevant in a domestic violence context, as the child has already witnessed the deleterious results of the offending parent's uncontrolled anger. Certainly, a child witness of domestic violence would not want to anger the abusive parent and submit himself—or the non-offending parent—to further physical abuse. "Children who witness domestic violence are often terrified of the abuser. They know and have seen the violence this individual has inflicted and thus, are likely to fear the consequences of their testimony." Regardless of whether the child fears future retaliation by the defendant, "[s]imply being in the same room as the defendant can be incredibly traumatic." These fears relating to the accused perpetrator of domestic violence may contribute to further trauma experienced by the child as a result of testifying.

2.   Fear of the Legal Process and the Courtroom Environment

In addition to fearing the presence of the perpetrator, the appearance of the courtroom and judge can be enough to frighten a child in any testimony situation, let alone one in which the child's parent may be sent to prison. "Many children naturally express fear upon seeing the defendant, meeting the judge, speaking in front of an audience, and being cross-examined." This fear largely stems from a lack of understanding of the legal system and the ramifications of testifying:

> Children have little idea of what to expect from court; what little they do know comes from the media and television and often causes intense fear and anxiety. They believe that they could go to jail for giving a wrong answer or that the defendant will be permitted to "get" them or yell at them.

Furthermore, the discomfort and possible trauma a child experiences can be exacerbated on cross-examination by a defense attorney who is inexperienced at working with child witnesses. Alternatively, defense attorneys may purposefully try to confuse a child by using complicated words and double negatives, though this technique intuitively seems counterproductive, as the jury would likely empathize with the child's discomfort and scorn the malevolent tactics of the defense attorney.

3.   Number of Times Testifying and Length of Trial

According to a study performed by Gail S. Goodman, an expert in the field of children's testimony, "[t]estifying multiple times appeared to be a stressor and was more likely to be required of children who were already experiencing other forms of trauma in their lives." Goodman tailored a study "to determine whether and under what conditions courtroom testimony is associated with child witnesses' emotional distress." The team of researchers assessed the behavioral adjustment of child testifiers at three and seven month intervals after testifying at a preliminary hearing, and at the conclusion of the case. The results indicated that, after three months, the behavioral adjustment of the child testifiers improved similarly to the behavioral adjustment of the children who did not testify. However, the follow-up seven months later demonstrated that child testifiers experienced greater disturbance than those who did not testify. To account for the conflicting results, Goodman noted that "[o]ne possible reason is that, by the 7–month test, more of the children had testified at trial. Perhaps trial testimony produces an increase in behavioral disturbance, especially if the case does not close quickly."

4.   Presence of Maternal Support

Perhaps the most crucial determinant of a child testifier's emotional well-being is the presence—or absence—of support by the child's mother, particularly in a domestic violence case where the mother was the victim of the abuse. One cannot dispute that testifying against a parent or loved one—an act that may result in a prison sentence for the offender—requires emotional strength. If the child's mother does not have the strength to support her child, the child will most likely lack the necessary strength as well. A devastating situation could well arise in a situation where a mother, as a result of her fear of the perpetrator's rage upon the conclusion of the case and her desire to prevent the perpetrator from going to prison, encourages her child to lie about the incident, thereby extinguishing the child's critical support-base needed to testify successfully. A child in this predicament would have the unfortunate decision of choosing whether to jeopardize the safety of his mother and send his father to prison by complying with the wishes of the prosecutor, or perjuring himself. However, in a case where the mother shows support not only for her child's testimony but also for the criminal justice system in general, the child will more likely escape the injurious effects that can otherwise occur.

NOTES AND QUESTIONS

1. **One–Way Closed Circuit Television.** Attorneys do have other options available to them rather than calling children to the stand. The first is to use one-way closed circuit television. The United States Supreme Court addressed the Constitutional issues that arise when using this technique in *Maryland v. Craig*, 497 U.S. 836 (1990). The case involved a six year old victim of child abuse. In upholding the Maryland statute that allowed for the use of one-way closed circuit television in child abuse and molestation cases, the court held:

> [W]here necessary to protect a child witness from trauma that would be caused by testifying in the physical presence of the defendant, at least where such trauma would impair the child's ability to communicate, the Confrontation Clause does not prohibit use of a procedure that, despite the absence of face-to-face confrontation, ensures the reliability of the evidence by subjecting it to rigorous adversarial testing and thereby preserves the essence of effective confrontation. Because there is no dispute that the child witnesses in this case testified under oath, were subject to full cross-examination, and were able to be observed by the judge, jury, and defendant as they testified, we conclude that, to the extent that a proper finding of necessity has been made, the admission of such testimony would be consonant with the Confrontation Clause.

Could such a rationale be extended beyond the child abuse context to domestic violence cases? How would one make such an argument? Think about how you might draft special legislation allowing for the use of closed circuit television in domestic violence cases when using child witnesses.

2. **Crawford and Child Testimony.** It remains unclear the effect that *Crawford* and *Davis* will have on statements by children to law enforcement. After all, if the Court uses an objective standard to determine

admissibility, would children reasonably know their statements could be used in an adversarial process?

F.   STATEMENTS MADE TO MEDICAL PROFESSIONALS

The final evidentiary issue we examine involves statements victims make to medical professionals concerning who inflicted their injuries. Under FRE 803(4), statements made to medical professionals for the purposes of diagnosis or treatment are generally admissible under the theory that such statements are inherently reliable. However, statements as to fault are generally inadmissible hearsay statements. Consider how one court has examined this issue.

United States v. Joe

United States Court of Appeals, 10th Circuit, 1993.
8 F.3d 1488.

Melvin Joe and Julia Joe were married in November 1980. Ms. Joe filed a petition for divorce in August 1991 and the couple separated. The Joes had four young children who continued to reside with Ms. Joe in Sanostee, New Mexico, a small, rural village located within the Navajo Indian Reservation.

On February 23, 1992, Melvin and his brother, Wallace Joe, drank beer continually throughout the morning and afternoon and Melvin passed out in Wallace's truck at approximately two o'clock. Sometime after six o'clock, Melvin drove a Chevrolet blazer belonging to his mother, Edith Joe, to his wife's residence. He knocked on the front door. When no one answered, he kicked open the door and entered the home brandishing an unloaded .22 caliber rifle. Melvin and Julia Joe fought and Melvin became physically abusive. Eventually, with the help of a neighbor, Matilda Washburn, Julia was able to get Melvin to leave the house.

Fearful that Melvin would return, Julia, Ms. Washburn, and one of the Joe children decided to leave the house and go to Ms. Washburn's home. As they exited, they noticed that Melvin had returned to the Blazer and was circling Julia's house. They stood next to the house for protection. The child, Jessica Joe, eventually ran to Ms. Washburn's house without interference. When Julia and Ms. Washburn tried to run, however, Melvin altered his circular pattern and drove straight at the fleeing Ms. Joe, striking her with the truck. Ms. Washburn went to the aid of the injured and screaming Julia Joe, helping her to the anticipated shelter of a nearby truck bed located in the field between the two houses. The truck bed, which had been completely removed from its frame, rested on four short wooden stumps.

Melvin apparently was undeterred by this new obstacle. He turned the Blazer in the direction of the truck bed, and, from a distance of approximately fifty feet, accelerated toward the truck bed, ramming the end of it opposite where the two women were standing. Upon impact, Melvin continued to accelerate, knocking the truck bed off the wooden stumps and pushing it over and onto Julia and Ms. Washburn. Still accelerating, Melvin pushed the truck bed forward another fifty feet, running over the two women.

Julia Joe and Ms. Washburn both died of multiple internal and external injuries caused by blunt force. After kicking Julia's body several times, Melvin put it in the Blazer and drove to a hilly area three miles from the crime scene. Officers later recovered the abandoned Blazer with the keys in the ignition and Julia's body still inside. Two days later, on February 25, 1992, Melvin Joe turned himself in. Joe was indicted for two counts of first degree murder . . . .

B.   Dr. Smoker's Testimony

At trial, defense counsel conceded that Melvin Joe had killed the two women. Mr. Joe's defense was that at the time of the killings he was intoxicated and enraged over the pending divorce, thus negating the requisite specific intent to sustain a conviction for first degree murder. With respect to Joe's intent, the government presented two types of evidence: the circumstances surrounding the murders and the testimony of Dr. Brett Smoker regarding statements made to him by Julia Joe. Dr. Smoker, an Indian Health Service family physician, testified that, eight days before Ms. Joe was killed, he treated her for an alleged rape and that she had identified her assailant as the defendant, Mr. Joe. (We will refer to Ms. Joe's comments regarding the alleged rape and her assailant as the "rape statement.") Dr. Smoker further testified that Ms. Joe stated she was "afraid sometimes" because Mr. Joe suspected her of having an extramarital affair and had threatened to kill her if he caught her with another man. (We will refer to Ms. Joe's comments regarding her fear and the basis for her fear as the "threat statement".)

1.   The rape statement

a.   Rule 803(4)

Rule 803(4) excepts from the hearsay bar "[s]tatements made for purposes of medical diagnosis or treatment and describing medical history, or past or present symptoms, pain, or sensations, or the inception or general character of the cause or external source thereof insofar as reasonably pertinent to diagnosis or treatment." The Rule 803(4) exception to the hearsay rule is founded on a theory of reliability that emanates from the patient's own selfish motive-her understanding "that the effectiveness of the treatment received will depend upon the accuracy of the information provided to the physician." The Supreme Court has noted that "statements made in the course of receiving medical care . . . are made in contexts that provide substantial guarantees of their trustworthiness."

While this guaranty of trustworthiness extends to statements of causation, it does not ordinarily extend to statements regarding fault. Thus, a declarant's statement relating the *identity* of the person allegedly responsible for her injuries is not ordinarily admissible under Rule 803(4) because statements of identity are not normally thought necessary to promote effective treatment.

Nevertheless, the Fourth, Eighth and Ninth Circuits have held that statements made by a child to a physician which identify the sexual abuser as a member of the family or household are "reasonably pertinent to diagnosis or treatment" and may therefore be admissible. Statements revealing the identity of the child abuser are "reasonably pertinent" to treatment because the physician must be attentive to treating the child's emotional and psychological injuries, the exact nature and extent of which often depend on the identity of the abuser. Moreover, physicians often have an obligation under state law to prevent an abused child from being returned to an abusive environment. As a result, where the abuser is a member of the family or household, the abuser's identity is especially pertinent to the physician's recommendation regarding an appropriate course of treatment, which may include removing the child from the home.

Unlike the victims in the cases cited above, Ms. Joe was not a child but rather the estranged wife of the alleged sexual abuser. However, the identity of the abuser is reasonably pertinent to treatment in virtually every domestic sexual assault case, even those not involving children. All victims of domestic sexual abuse suffer emotional and psychological injuries, the exact nature and extent of which depend on the identity of the abuser. The physician generally must know who the abuser was in order to render proper treatment because the physician's treatment will necessarily differ when the abuser is a member of the victim's family or household. In the domestic sexual abuse case, for example, the treating physician may recommend special therapy or counseling and instruct the victim to remove herself from the dangerous environment by leaving the home and seeking shelter elsewhere. In short, the domestic sexual abuser's identity is admissible under Rule 803(4) where the abuser has such an intimate relationship with the victim that the abuser's identity becomes "reasonably pertinent" to the victim's proper treatment.

The facts of this case underscore the point. After performing a rape kit test on Ms. Joe, Dr. Smoker asked her several questions relating to her injuries. In answering these questions, Ms. Joe identified her husband, Melvin Joe, as her sexual abuser. Dr. Smoker testified that the identity of the sexual assailant was important for his recommendation regarding Ms. Joe's after-care, including appropriate counseling. Moreover, after discovering her assailant's identity, Dr. Smoker specifically recommended that Ms. Joe seek protection, offering her the number of the Navajo Police Department and referring her to the women's shelter in Shiprock, New Mexico. It is abundantly clear that the statement made by Ms. Joe revealing the identity of her alleged abuser was "reasonably pertinent" to her proper treatment by Dr. Smoker. Thus, we conclude that Dr. Smoker's testimony regarding Ms. Joe's rape statement, which identified Mr. Joe as her assailant, is admissible under Fed.R.Evid. 803(4).

NOTES AND QUESTIONS

1. **The Future of Statements Made to Physicians and the Hearsay Exceptions.** As Myrna Raeder has suggested, the key issue after the

Crawford decision is whether statements made for the purpose of medical diagnosis and treatment, if those statements include statements as to the identity of the abuser, are testimonial. *Davis* suggests that such statements would not be considered testimonial because they are not made with the purpose of aiding law enforcement. For a discussion of this issue see Myrna Raeder, *Remember the Ladies and the Children Too: Crawford's Impact on Domestic Violence and Child Abuse Cases*, 71 Brook. L. Rev. 311 (2005). However, as Raeder points out, if doctors are mandated to report abuse, as discussed in Chapter Four, then arguably the statements made to them concerning the identity of the abuser could be considered testimonial.

2.   **When Statements to Medical Professionals are not Admissible.** Not all courts have followed the reasoning in *United States v. Joe.* For example in *State v. Robinson*, 718 N.W.2d 400 (Minn. 2006), the Minnesota Supreme Court rejected the argument that a victim's statement to a nurse identifying the defendant as the one who slapped her was admissible. The Court reasoned:

> We are not able to determine, by judicial notice or general knowledge, whether the notion that the identification of the perpetrator of domestic violence is reasonably pertinent to medical diagnosis and treatment is generally accepted in the medical profession. To this extent, the medical exception to the hearsay rules depends, in the first instance, on the views of the medical profession, not on the views of the courts. We can speculate that the medical profession may have evolved to recognize the importance of treating the whole person of a victim of domestic violence, including the emotional and psychological effects of past violence and the potential of future violence. But we can do no more than speculate. The record before us contains no medical expert testimony on the scope of the customary treatment of a victim of domestic violence or whether the identity of the domestic abuser is reasonably pertinent to that treatment. *Id.* at 406.

The Court did not foreclose the possibility that it could, in the future, rule statements as to fault in domestic violence cases would be admissible. Rather, it suggested that a special hearing be scheduled in which expert testimony could be introduced. Do you agree with the reasoning in *Joe* or in *Robinson*? Do you think these cases are distinguishable on the grounds that doctors prescribe different therapies for rape by an intimate partner than for rape by a stranger, but are unlikely to treat slaps differently depending on the perpetrator's identity? Or does the fact that the American Medical Association suggests that all patients be screened for domestic violence mean that the identity of the abuser is reasonably pertinent to medical diagnosis or treatment? Should it be courts who decide? The medical profession? The legislature?

3.   **Training Doctors to Better Document Abuse.** As well as introducing the doctor's testimony as to what the victim said, medical records can also be very useful evidence. In a study of how doctors document abuse, Nancy E. Isaac and Pualani Enos found that doctors did not always understand how to document domestic abuse, and often failed to provide detailed information that would assist lawyers in a litigation context. Also,

few doctors included photographs in their medical records. The authors recommend a variety of reforms, particularly providing physicians and other medical professionals better training. See Nancy E. Isaac and Pualani Enos, *Medical Records as Legal Evidence of Domestic Violence*, National Institute of Justice (May 2000).

This research also identified some relatively minor changes in documentation practices that would be likely to improve the usefulness of abused women's medical records in legal contexts. Such changes may help health care providers to "work smarter, not harder" on behalf of their abused patients. Some recommended changes for clinicians include the following:

- Clinicians should, when at all feasible, take photographs of injuries that are known or suspected to have resulted from interpersonal violence. Optimally, there should be at least one photo each of the full body, the injury itself, and the patient's face.

- Clinicians should stay away from words that imply doubt about the patient's reliability ("patient claims ...," "patient alleges ..."). Alleges is a legal term. It implies the statement following it is unproven and may not have occurred. Providers should instead use quotes around statements made by the patient. If the clinician's direct observations are in conflict with the patient's description of events, the clinician's reasons for doubt should be stated explicitly.

- Clinicians should not use legal terms such as "alleged perpetrator," "assailant," "assault," etc. All legal terms are defined with great detail by federal or state statute and case law. Typically, such terms are used by lay persons to mean something more ambiguous or larger in scope. By using legal terms, providers may convey an unintended meaning. For example, assault is defined as an attempt to cause an unwanted touching, whether or not the touching actually occurred. Naming the person who has injured the patient as her "assailant" or "perpetrator" after the patient has identified the person who has hurt her as a husband, boyfriend, father of her child or by name, is likely to be interpreted in a legal setting as the provider's doubting the patient's credibility. These terms are used regularly by attorneys seeking to raise doubt as to who committed an act.

- Placing the term "domestic violence" or abbreviations such as "DV" in the diagnosis fields of medical records is of no benefit to the patient in legal contexts. This practice should be reconsidered unless there are other clear benefits with respect to medical treatment.

- Clinicians should include words that describe a patient's demeanor, such as: crying, shaking, upset, calm, angry, agitated, happy. Clinicians should describe what they observe, even if they find the demeanor to be confusing given statements of abuse.

- Clinicians should record the time of day in their record, and (ideally) some indication of how much time has passed since the incident (e.g., "patient states that *early this morning* her boyfriend, Robert Jones, hit her . . .").

Though these changes would go a long way to improve medical documentation of abuse, the research findings also imply that changes will be needed at the institutional level if the use of medical records in domestic violence cases is to improve. Specifically it appears that:

- The importance of photographing traumatic injuries needs to be reemphasized in training programs on medical response to domestic violence. Research should determine the most common barriers to taking photographs. Interventions that aim at increasing the frequency of taking photographs should be developed and evaluated.

- Medical units that handle abuse cases routinely (e.g., emergency medicine, social work) should have cameras stored in a secure but easy to access location. Resources should be allocated to buy cameras and film, and to train providers in their use. Each institution's policy on response to domestic violence should include details on where the camera can be found, how to photograph injuries, where to store photographs, and how to document the existence and location of these photographs in the medical record.

- Non-clinical health professionals (medical records managers, administrators, risk managers) should work with domestic violence legal and clinical experts to examine changes that might facilitate the accessibility of medical records for legal use without compromising patient confidentiality.

- Training regarding current health care response to domestic violence should be provided to judges who hear domestic violence cases regularly.

- Domestic violence training programs and materials for health care providers should clarify that a failure to document domestic violence completely when treating an abused patient does not constitute taking a "neutral" stance about the incident. It will almost always convey a legal advantage to the abuser. In medical terms, it constitutes poor preventive medicine.

4. **The Best Way to Document Abuse.** The recommendation that physicians not hesitate to record patient demeanor reflects the discovery of an important rift between health care providers and lawyers. Health care providers had assumed that it was more helpful to bolster their patients' credibility by *not* revealing that they were "upset" "shaking" or "hysterical." Lawyers, on the other hand, recognized that it was exactly these descriptions of emotional state that might qualify patient statements as "excited utterances," and allow them to be introduced as evidence despite the hearsay rule. Can you find other examples of documentation practice that reflect medical providers' mistaken assumptions about legal matters? When clinicians hedge their descriptions with language like: "the patient claims . . ." or "the alleged assailant . . ." are they perhaps worrying about their own vulnerability to a defamation suit by the perpetrator? Is that a real worry or one that good legal advice would help set to rest?

5. **Levels of Detail.** Do you find yourself surprised by the level of detail the researchers' feel it is necessary to include in a documentation policy? Would it be realistic to expect a healthcare institution to generate a policy that detailed without input from "outsiders" whether those "outsiders" are lawyers, or battered women's advocates?

6. **Physician Liability for Failure to Report.** Assume that Beatrice is a 25 year-old woman who has repeatedly seen her family practice doctor for a variety of injuries, including a broken arm, bruised ribs, a black eye, and the loss of hearing in one ear. She suffers from depression, for which her doctor prescribed anti-depressants. Her doctor suspects that Beatrice is being abused by her husband and has asked her about this. Beatrice has acknowledged that they are having marital problems, but has been reluctant to say much more than that. Her doctor never refers her to any services or provides her with any information on domestic violence. Three weeks after Beatrice sees her doctor for a cracked jaw, she is found murdered in her home. Her husband beat her in the head until she died and then killed himself. Assume Beatrice's sister, who is now the guardian of her ten year-old son, wants to sue the doctor for failure to report the domestic violence to the authorities and for failure to properly diagnose and treat Beatrice. Should the doctor be liable for failure to act? Does it matter whether or not the state has a mandatory reporting law specifically for domestic violence? For a discussion of these issues, see James T.R. Jones, *Battered Spouses' Damage Actions Against Non–Reporting Physicians*, 45 DEPAUL L. REV. 191 (1996).

CHAPTER NINE

DEFENSES AVAILABLE TO BATTERED WOMEN DEFENDANTS

Introduction

This chapter deals with the legal problems that face battered women as criminal defendants. The first section addresses cases in which women have killed their abusers. Relatively few women actually kill their abusers. In fact, the number of males killed by their female intimate partners has declined 71% from 1976 to 2002. In 1976, 1,384 men were killed by an intimate partner. By 2004, only 385 men were killed. By comparison, in 1976, 1,596 women were killed by an intimate partner. In 2004, 1,159 women were killed. Bureau of Justice Statistics, U.S. Dep't of Justice, *Bureau of Justice Statistics, Homicide Trends in the United States*, 2006. This suggests that the legal reforms that we are studying throughout this book may have reduced male homicides. Access to shelters and other resources, increased police intervention, more aggressive prosecutions, and the availability of civil restraining orders make it less likely today that a battered partner will be in a situation in which resorting to homicide in self-defense is her only option to live.

Even though fewer women face charges for murdering their partners than they once did, the history and current state of self-defense law remains crucial to our broader understanding of legal responses to partner abuse. The first set of materials examines early cases in which judges were persuaded to put women's violence into the specific social and psychological context of violence *against* women, and to allow lawyers to educate juries about the nature of battering relationships before they addressed the question of whether any particular woman had acted reasonably in defending herself against her batterer. It also explains the form this reform movement took, dealing especially with arguments about the need for expert testimony, and addressing precisely how that expert testimony was supposed to help decision-makers apply the law of self-defense accurately and fairly to battered women's cases. Finally, it analyzes the limitations of this strategy, limitations that have become more apparent over time. Unfortunately, those limitations are apparent not only in judicial decisions, but also in some of the special legislation that has been introduced at the state level to ensure the admissibility of expert testimony about battering in cases in which it may be relevant to women's criminal defenses. This section also presents some more recent and hopeful material, suggesting that both policy makers and judges are developing a more sophisticated understanding of the dynamics of battering relationships and of the functions that can be served by expert testimony.

The next set of materials carry the analysis beyond self defense, into other criminal cases in which battered women defendants seek to use evidence of their abuse to eliminate or mitigate their responsibility for the crimes for which they are charged. While relatively few women kill their abusers, a significant number of women who commit crimes are in a battering relationship and often commit crimes under duress or while aiding and abetting an abusive partner. We explore both the success and challenges lawyers for battered defendants face in these other contexts.

The final section takes us beyond the moment at which a battered woman is convicted of the crime with which she is charged, and asks whether, and how, that conviction can be challenged, in circumstances in which her trial was tainted by the failure of her lawyer to address her situation as a battered woman, or by the failure of the criminal process more generally to incorporate that perspective into her trial. The issues addressed here are not whether a successful appeal can be brought, but whether the battered woman defendant can argue ineffective assistance of counsel, convince a parole board to release her, or step outside the criminal justice system to seek clemency.

A.   WOMEN'S SELF-DEFENSE CLAIMS: GENDER BIAS AND THE ROLE OF EXPERT TESTIMONY

Elizabeth M. Schneider
Battered Women and Feminist Lawmaking (2000)

The Problem of Equal Rights to Trial

The insight that first generated legal work on this issue was that, for a variety of reasons, women who were battered and faced criminal charges for homicide or assault of their assailant were likely to be denied equal rights to trial—that is, equal rights to present the circumstances of their acts within the framework of the criminal law. The equal-rights problem in this context flows from an equal-rights problem in criminal law generally: what Stephen Schulhofer has described as the fact that "the criminal justice system is dominated (incontrovertibly so) by a preoccupation with men and male perspectives."

The equal-rights problem for battered women who kill has many sources: widespread views of women who act violently, particularly against intimates, as "monsters"; commonly held misconceptions about battered women (that they "ask for" or provoke the violence, for example); gender bias in the concept of reasonableness; societal misconceptions about self-defense and application of the legal standards of imminent danger and proportionality; and deeply held cultural attitudes that pathologize women generally and battered women particularly. Moreover, the law has traditionally viewed husband-killing as a special crime that strikes at the root of all civil government, threatening basic conceptions of traditional society. Long ago, William Blackstone observed that a woman who killed her husband was committing "treason": "If the baron kills his feme it is the same as if he had killed a stranger, or any other person; but if the feme kills her baron, it is regarded by the laws as a much more atrocious crime, as she not only breaks through the restraints of humanity and conjugal affection, but throws off all subjection to the authority of her husband. And therefore, the law denominates her crime a species of treason, and condemns her to the same punishment as if she had killed the king. And for every species of treason ... the sentence of women was to be drawn and burnt alive." Based on the confluence of these factors, the equal-rights argument holds that battered women who kill are more likely to be viewed as crazy than reasonable; thus they are likely to face substantial hurdles in asserting self-defense and to be limited in the range of defense options available at trial.

The goal of this work has been to expand defense options in order to equalize women's rights to trial and afford women equal opportunity to present an effective defense. It has not rested on the claim that all battered women are entitled to self-defense, or that there should be a special defense for battered women, either as self-defense or as a special "battered woman defense." To the contrary, the argument is that battered women, like all criminal defendants, had to be included within the traditional framework of the criminal law in order to guarantee their equal rights to trial.

Those insights have generated much legal scholarship, case law, and statutory reform. Nevertheless, much of this work is premised on a fundamental misunderstanding of the original arguments, and is based on the assumption that pleas of self-defense or a special "battered woman defense" are appropriate in all cases of battered women who kill their assailants. These efforts miss the crucial insight that has shaped this work: that the particular facts and circumstances of each case must be evaluated in light of the general problem of gender bias in order to ensure an individual woman's equal right to trial. . . .

With respect to battered women who kill, gender bias pervades the entire criminal process. It permeates perceptions of appropriate self-defense and the legal standard of self-defense, the broader problem of choice of defense, and the need for expert testimony on battering, all of which are interrelated. Lawyers' failure to appreciate the problem of gender bias in the law of self-defense and in judicial application of the law of self-defense can lead to problematic judgments concerning the choice of defense in any particular case, as well as all decisions that flow from this (such as expert testimony that might be proffered in support of that defense), since the defense necessarily shapes the content of all testimony at trial. . . .

The Legal Framework

Homicide is generally divided into first- and second-degree murder, manslaughter, and justifiable or excusable homicide. If a homicide is justifiable or excusable, it is because special circumstances exist that the law recognizes as justifying or excusing the defendant's acts from criminal liability. Proof that a killing occurred in a sudden, provoked "heat of passion"—upon provocation that would cause a "reasonable man to lose his self-control"—is considered in most jurisdictions to indicate manslaughter. Manslaughter is an "intermediate" crime between murder and justifiable homicide; it means that the homicidal act is not "justifiable" but, because of the circumstances of the individual, is "understandable" or "excusable" and therefore deserving of some mitigation in punishment. Alternatively, where a defendant's belief in the need to use force to defend herself is "reasonable," and she is not the initial aggressor, self-defense is a "complete" defense and results in acquittal. Where a defendant's belief is found to be honest but "unreasonable," some jurisdictions recognize "imperfect" self-defense, permitting a reduction from murder to manslaughter.

Although the law of self-defense is purportedly universally applicable, it is widely recognized that social concepts of justification have been shaped by male experience. Familiar images of self-defense are a soldier; a man protecting his home, his family, or the chastity of his wife; or a man fighting off an assailant. Yet the circumstances in which women kill in self-defense are usually related to physical or sexual abuse by an intimate, not to the conventional barroom brawl or fist fight with a stranger that shapes male experience with self-defense. Society, through its prosecutors, juries, and judges, has more readily excused a man for killing his wife's lover than a woman for killing a rapist. The acts of men and women are subject to a different set of legal expectations and standards. The man's act, while not always legally condoned, is viewed sympathetically. He is not forgiven, but his motivation is understood by those sitting in judgment. The law, however, has never protected a wife who killed her husband after finding him with another woman. A woman's husband simply does not belong to her in the same way that she belongs to him.

The man who kills his wife after finding her with another man is the paradigmatic example of provocation; his conduct is widely perceived to deserve more lenient treatment than other kinds of killings under the law. In a Maryland case involving a man who shot and killed his wife four hours after coming home and finding her in bed with another man, the judge sentenced the man to only eighteen months in a work release program, stating that he could imagine nothing that would provoke "an uncontrollable rage greater than this: for someone who is happily married to be betrayed in your personal life, when you're out working to support the spouse.... I seriously wonder how many men married five, four years ... would have the strength to walk away without inflicting some corporal punishment." Although many homicides of women committed by men are now recognized as occurring in a context of domestic violence, men's killings of their wives are, as Donna Coker has put it, "seldom recognized as belonging to the universe of 'domestic violence' killings." Conversely, women who have killed their husbands in response to battering have raised considerable controversy and are perceived to deserve harsher treatment under the law.

Consequently, it is not generally acknowledged that women defendants face substantial hurdles in pleading self-defense. Battered women defendants experience serious problems in meeting the judicial application of the standard of reasonableness and elements of the law of self-defense; the requirement of temporal proximity of the danger perceived by the defendant; the requirement of equal proportionality of force used by the defendant to that used against her by the batterer; and the duty to retreat.

Alternatives to self-defense are the insanity defense and the range of partial responsibility or impaired mental state defenses, which vary among jurisdictions. If a defendant pleads insanity, she claims that, owing to her mental condition at the time of the act, she is not guilty because she either did not know what she was doing or did not know that it was wrong. The insanity defense is usually a "complete" defense, in the sense that the defendant is not legally responsible for the act committed. However, a finding of not guilty by reason of insanity most often results in institutionalization for an indefinite period of time. Some, but not all, jurisdictions recognize partial responsibility or impaired mental state defenses, such as heat-of-passion and intoxication, where a successful defense will mitigate the act and reduce a charge from murder to manslaughter.

The Goals of Equal Rights to Trial

 . . . [T]he crux of self-defense is the concept of reasonableness. In order for a defense lawyer to believe that a battered woman has a credible claim of self-defense, the lawyer will first have to overcome sex-based stereotypes of reasonableness, understand enough about the experiences of battered women to be able to consider whether the woman's actions are reasonable, and, in a manner sensitive to the problems of gender-bias, be able to listen to the woman's experiences. Early work on women's self-defense asserted that in many cases of women charged with homicide, particularly battered women, self-defense was likely to be overlooked by defense counsel, but might be appropriate and should be considered. The goal was to ensure that the full range of defenses were available and explored for battered women defendants, just as they should be available for all other criminal defendants.

The next step was to make sure that battered women's experiences were heard—first by defense lawyers in the process of representation and choice of defense, and then in the courtroom—regardless of what defense was chosen. Admission of evidence on battering was considered crucial, first from the woman and others who might have observed or known about the violence, and then from experts who might be able to explain those experiences and assist fact finders to overcome misconceptions that might impede their determination. Evidence concerning the history and experience of abuse was not only relevant, but essential to determining guilt. The goal was not to have every battered woman on trial plead self-defense, but to improve the rationality of the fact-finding process. . . .

NOTES AND QUESTIONS

1. **Historical Understanding of Intimate Homicide.** Historically, have women who have killed their husbands been treated more harshly

than men who kill their wives? Carolyn B. Ramsey examined homicide data from 1880–1920 in both New York and Colorado. She writes:

> Nineteenth-century feminists assumed that juries routinely exonerated men of passion killings but proved reluctant to do so when women stood trial. Similarly, in recent decades, feminist scholars have complained that in the criminal law, and especially the heat-of-passion and self-defense doctrines, justify or excuse men's aggression. A number of histories of wife-beating exist, but there are few academic studies of the legal history of intimate homicide and, except for this article, no multi-state analyses of the topic that rigorously explore public responses to both men's and women's cases. The relative lack of historical research on intimate violence, as opposed to non-lethal wife-beating, has generated incomplete and even erroneous views of the way gender norms affected public responses to violence among lovers, spouses, and other family members. The hasty assumption that, in the past, female defendants received severe punishments for avenging infidelity or defending themselves against abuse, whereas men were given a virtual license to kill, remains common. . . .
>
> The exemplary punishment of men who failed to keep their passions in check contrasted with the relatively lenient treatment of female murder defendants, almost all of whom were either exonerated or convicted of lesser-included offenses. Paternalistic sympathy for women often came in the form of insanity acquittals. But the willingness of courts and juries to consider evidence of past abuse also meant that a woman's trial might focus on the history of an intimate relationship scarred by terrifying violence and a protracted struggle for power, rather than simply on the lethal moment when she killed the deceased. Hence, some female defendants prevailed or received mitigation on grounds of perfect or imperfect self-defense; their options were not limited to insanity claims. Indeed, retaining a modicum of control over their trials, many women took the witness stand in their own defense and thus helped construct the narratives designed to spare them.

Carolyn B. Ramsey, *Intimate Homicide: Gender and Crime Control*, 1880–1920, 77 U.COLO.L.REV. 101 (2006).

Does this data suggest that the criminal justice system operated with gender bias? Does it suggest that absent legal theories about battering, judges and juries were often able to reach just conclusions in these cases? Have advocates for battered women been too hasty in assuming that the legal system operated to privilege males, or were women treated with a "paternalistic kind of passion" as Ramsey suggests?

2. **Gender Bias.** How specifically might gender bias interact with self-defense doctrine to prejudice battered women defendants? In BATTERED WOMEN & FEMINIST LAWMAKING, Elizabeth Schneider mentions four specific areas. One is the "reasonableness" of the defendant's determination that force was necessary, and the extent to which a reasoned judgment can draw on the defendant's experiences as a woman, or a battered woman. This theme is amply elaborated on in the pages that follow.

A second is the "temporal proximity" between the threat against the defendant and her use of violence to deflect it. Some jurisdictions require that the threat be "imminent," while others use "immediacy," which in general requires closer proximity, as the standard. Whichever standard is used, the critical issue for battered women is whether the jury will be invited to look at the question of proximate threat from the perspective of someone who has suffered abuse from this perpetrator before, and reads the signals of impending violence differently from someone with no prior exposure.

A third is the "proportionality" of the violence threatened, and the violence used in self-defense. For women, this sometimes raises the question of when their smaller stature, or lack of physical training, permits them to use a weapon, when it would not be appropriate for a man to use one in similar circumstances. This was part of the court's analysis in the *Wanrow* case, which follows. But "proportionality" also involves assessing the level of threat posed by the assailant who is then injured or killed by his intended victim, and here again the question will be whether the woman can share with the jury her experience with her abuser, which informs her assessment.

A fourth relevant aspect of the doctrine of self-defense is the so-called duty to retreat, by which some, but not all, jurisdictions require a person threatened by violence to retreat rather than counterattack *if they can safely do so*. Traditionally, jurisdictions that did impose such a duty (it was more common in Northeastern states than in the frontier territories of the South and West) created an exemption, permitting individuals to stand their ground when they were threatened in their own homes. However, some of these jurisdictions then limited the exemption, holding that it would not apply in situations in which the attacker was a cohabitant, or in which the person claiming self defense had struck the first blow. The "cohabitant" rule limits the use of self defense by those attacked in their homes by intimate partners, and therefore has a clearly disparate impact on women and children, who more often than men bear the brunt of those attacks. More generally, however, there is a danger that judges and juries will confuse the question of whether the defendant had a duty to retreat in the specific incident which led to her prosecution with the more general question of why she did not leave her abuser. They may then blame her for putting herself in the way of violence rather than avoiding it, in ways that prejudice their conclusions about the case, even if they do not technically decide that she has violated a duty to retreat. For a case in this area see *Weiand v. State*, 732 So.2d 1044 (Fla. 1999), in which the Florida Supreme Court retreated from a 1982 decision imposing a duty to retreat on co-occupants. The court based its change of heart on increased knowledge about domestic violence, and an evolution in the public policy of the state. The new standard adopted by the court still requires retreat within the home, to the extent reasonably possible without increasing the danger, but does not require an attacked co-occupant to flee the residence before resorting to force in self defense.

3.   **Justification v. Excuse.** Many have criticized self-defense claims as being an excuse for the killing rather than a justification. For example, Anne M. Coughlin in *Excusing Women,* 82 CAL.L.REV. 1 (1994), argues that "battered women's syndrome" is a mental disorder which excuses women for their wrongdoing. She argues that because the defense defines women as a collection of mental symptoms, it reinforces negative gender-stereotypes about women as lacking the mental capacity to choose lawful means to end their relationships. This, in turn, reinforces the notion that women are less responsible than men. Do you agree with this criticism? Do self-defense claims on behalf of battered women reinforce the concept that women aren't capable of acting on their own behalf? Do they undermine women's legal and social autonomy?

More recently, Alan Dershowitz is among many critics of the use of expert testimony on battering. "I think in a great many cases it simply gives the jury a hook on which to hang their hat, he deserved to die, he was a batterer, he had it coming, we're not going to put anybody in jail for killing this son of a bitch," Dershowitz is quoted as saying. Lenore Walker recalled that in one of the first cases she worked on, the prosecutor argued that allowing her to testify about battered woman syndrome would mean an "open season on killing men." Denise Lavoie, *Abuse Defense Rarely Gets Acquittals,* Associated Press, June 2, 2007.

Do you think evidence of the psychological effects of battering creates an "abuse excuse?" Do you think that it encourages women to kill their abusers rather than seek help? Dershowitz notes that the vast majority of abused women do not kill their abusers. Does this fact strengthen or weaken the "abuse excuse" argument?

4.   **The Doctrine of Self Defense.** Yvonne Wanrow did not kill her batterer. Rather, she killed a man whom she barely knew, but whom she perceived as dangerous, and who appeared to be threatening her. Decided in 1977, the case provides a valuable introduction to issues of potential gender bias in the application of self-defense doctrine.

State of Washington v. Wanrow

Supreme Court of Washington, 1977.
559 P.2d 548.

■ UTTER, JUDGE.

On the afternoon of August 11, 1972, defendant's (respondent's) two children were staying at the home of Ms. Hooper, a friend of defendant. Defendant's son was playing in the neighborhood and came back to Ms. Hooper's house and told her that a man tried to pull him off his bicycle and drag him into a house. Some months earlier, Ms. Hooper's 7–year–old daughter had developed a rash on her body which was diagnosed as venereal disease. Ms. Hooper had been unable to persuade her daughter to tell her who had molested her. It was not until the night of the shooting that Ms. Hooper discovered it was William Wesler (decedent) who allegedly had violated her daughter. A few minutes after the defendant's son related his story to Ms. Hooper about the man who tried to detain him, Mr. Wesler appeared on the porch of the Hooper house and stated through the door, "I didn't touch the kid, I didn't touch the kid." At that moment, the Hooper girl, seeing Wesler at the door, indicated to her mother that Wesler was the man who had molested her. Joseph Fah, Ms. Hooper's landlord, saw Wesler as he was leaving and informed Shirley Hooper that Wesler had tried to molest a young boy who had earlier lived in the same house, and that Wesler had previously been committed to the Eastern State Hospital for the mentally ill. Immediately after this revelation from Mr. Fah, Ms. Hooper called the police who, upon their arrival at the Hooper residence, were informed of all the events which had transpired that day. Ms. Hooper requested that Wesler be arrested then and there, but the police stated, "We can't, until Monday morning." Ms. Hooper was urged by the police officer to go to the police station Monday morning and "swear out a warrant." Ms. Hooper's landlord, who was present during the conversation, suggested that Ms. Hooper get a baseball bat located at the corner of the house and "conk him over the head" should Wesler try to enter the house uninvited during the weekend. To this suggestion, the policeman replied, "Yes, but wait until he gets in the house." (A week before this incident Shirley Hooper had noticed someone prowling around her house at night. Two days before the shooting someone had attempted to get into Ms. Hooper's bedroom and had slashed the window screen. She suspected that such person was Wesler.)

That evening, Ms. Hooper called the defendant and asked her to spend the night with her in the Hooper house. At that time she related to Ms. Wanrow the facts we have previously set forth. The defendant arrived sometime after 6 p.m. with a pistol in her handbag. The two women ultimately determined that they were too afraid to stay alone and decided to ask some friends to come over for added protection. The two women then called the defendant's sister and brother-in-law, Angie and Chuck Michel. The four adults did not go to bed that evening, but remained awake talking and watching for any possible prowlers. There were eight young children in the house with them. At around 5 a.m., Chuck Michel, without the knowledge of the women in the house, went to Wesler's house, carrying a baseball bat. Upon arriving at the Wesler residence, Mr. Michel accused Wesler of molesting little children. Mr. Wesler then suggested that they go over to the Hooper residence and get the whole thing straightened out. Another man, one David Kelly, was also present, and together the three men went over to the Hooper house. Mr. Michel and Mr. Kelly remained outside while Wesler entered the residence.

The testimony as to what next took place is considerably less precise. It appears that Wesler, a large man who was visibly intoxicated, entered the home and when told to leave declined to do so. A good deal of shouting and confusion then arose, and a young child, asleep on the couch, awoke crying. The testimony indicates that Wesler then approached this child, stating, "My what a cute little boy," or words to that effect, and that the child's mother, Ms. Michel, stepped between Wesler and the child. By this time Hooper was screaming for Wesler to get out. Ms. Wanrow, a 5–foot 4–inch woman who at the time had a broken leg and was using a crutch, testified that she then went to the front door to enlist the aid of Chuck Michel. She stated that she shouted for him and, upon turning around to reenter the living room, found Wesler standing directly behind her. She testified to being gravely startled by this situation and to having then shot Wesler in what amounted to a reflex action.

After Wesler was shot, Ms. Hooper called the police via a Spokane crime check emergency phone number, stating, "There's a guy broke in, and my girlfriend shot him." The defendant later took the phone and engaged in a conversation with the police operator. . . .

Reversal of respondent's conviction is required by a . . . serious error committed by the trial court . . . setting forth the law of self-defense, incorrectly limited the jury's consideration of acts and circumstances pertinent to respondent's perception of the alleged threat to her person. An examination of the record of the testimony and of the colloquys which took place with regard to the instructions on self-defense indicate the critical importance of these instructions to the respondent's theory of the case. Based upon the evidence we have already set out, it is obviously crucial that the jury be precisely instructed as to the defense of justification.

In the opening paragraph of instruction No. 10, the jury, in evaluating the gravity of the danger to the respondent, was directed to consider only those acts and circumstances occurring "at or immediately before the killing. . . ."[1] This is not now, and never has been, the law of self-defense in Washington. On the contrary, the justification of self-defense is to be evaluated in light of all the facts and circumstances known to the defendant, including those known substantially before the killing. . . .

The State attempts to minimize this deficiency in instruction No. 10 by invoking the rule that an instruction is "sufficient" if counsel may satisfactorily argue his or her theory of the case. This is a mistaken application of the rule and will cause widespread mischief in civil as well as criminal cases if adopted here. . . . [T]he test of an instruction's sufficiency is an additional safeguard to be applied only where the instruction given is first found to be an accurate statement of the law. Furthermore, it would be illogical to apply such a test to erroneous instructions—of what significance is it that counsel may or may not be able to argue his theory to the jury when the jury has been misinformed about the law to be applied? . . .

---

1. Instruction No. 10 reads:

"To justify killing in self-defense, there need be no actual or real danger to the life or person of the party killing, but there must be, or reasonably appear to be, at or immediately before the killing, some overt act, or some circumstances which would reasonably indicate to the party killing that the person slain, is, at the time, endeavoring to kill him or inflict upon him great bodily harm.

"However, when there is no reasonable ground for the person attacked to believe that his person is in imminent danger of death or great bodily harm, and it appears to him that only an ordinary battery is all that is intended, and all that he has reasonable grounds to fear from his assailant, he has a right to stand his ground and repel such threatened assault, yet he has no right to repel a threatened assault with naked hands, by the use of a deadly weapon in a deadly manner, unless he believes, and has reasonable grounds to believe, that he is in imminent danger of death or great bodily harm."

[I]nstruction No. 10 erred in limiting the acts and circumstances which the jury could consider in evaluating the nature of the threat of harm as perceived by respondent. Under the well-established rule, this error is presumed to have been prejudicial. Moreover, far from affirmatively showing that the error was harmless, the record demonstrates the limitation to circumstances "at or immediately before the killing" was of crucial importance in the present case. Respondent's knowledge of the victim's reputation for aggressive acts was gained many hours before the killing and was based upon events which occurred over a period of years. Under the law of this state, the jury should have been allowed to consider this information in making the critical determination of the " 'degree of force which ... a reasonable person in the same situation ... seeing what [s]he sees and knowing what [s]he knows, then would believe to be necessary.' ..."

The second paragraph of instruction No. 10 contains an equally erroneous and prejudicial statement of the law. That portion of the instruction reads:

> However, when there is no reasonable ground for the person attacked to believe that his person is in imminent danger of death or great bodily harm, and it appears to him that only an ordinary battery is all that is intended, and all that he has reasonable grounds to fear from his assailant, he has a right to stand his ground and repel such threatened assault, yet he has no right to repel a threatened assault with naked hands, by the use of a deadly weapon in a deadly manner, unless he believes, and has reasonable grounds to believe, that he is in imminent danger of death or great bodily harm.

In our society women suffer from a conspicuous lack of access to training in and the means of developing those skills necessary to effectively repel a male assailant without resorting to the use of deadly weapons. Instruction No. 12 does indicate that the "relative size and strength of the persons involved" may be considered; however, it does not make clear that the defendant's actions are to be judged against her own subjective impressions and not those which a detached jury might determine to be objectively reasonable....

The second paragraph of instruction No. 10 not only establishes an objective standard, but through the persistent use of the masculine gender leaves the jury with the impression the objective standard to be applied is that applicable to an altercation between two men. The impression created—that a 5–foot 4–inch woman with a cast on her leg and using a crutch must, under the law, somehow repel an assault by a 6–foot 2–inch intoxicated man without employing weapons in her defense, unless the jury finds her determination of the degree of danger to be objectively reasonable—constitutes a separate and distinct misstatement of the law and, in the context of this case, violates the respondent's right to equal protection of the law. The respondent was entitled to have the jury consider her actions in the light of her own perceptions of the situation, including those perceptions which were the product of our nation's "long and unfortunate history of sex discrimination." Until such time as the effects of that history are eradicated, care must be taken to assure that our self-defense instructions afford women the right to have their conduct judged in light of the individual physical handicaps which are the product of sex discrimination. To fail to do so is to deny the right of the individual woman involved to trial by the same rules which are applicable to male defendants.... The portion of the instruction above quoted misstates our law in creating an objective standard of "reasonableness." It then compounds that error by utilizing language suggesting that the respondent's conduct must be measured against that of a reasonable male individual finding himself in the same circumstances. We conclude that the instruction here in question contains an improper statement of the law on a vital issue in the case, is inconsistent, misleading, and prejudicial when read in conjunction with other instructions pertaining to the same issue, and therefore is a proper basis for a finding of reversible error....

In light of the errors in admission of evidence and instruction of the jury, the decision of the Court of Appeals is affirmed, the conviction reversed, and the case remanded for a new trial.

NOTES AND QUESTIONS

1. **Reasonableness Standard.** The arguments first raised in *Wanrow* and accepted by a plurality of the Washington Supreme Court rest on several assumptions that have gradually won wider and wider acceptance: first that women act in self-defense under different circumstances and in different ways than men; second, that the traditional law of self-defense, as applied, incorporates sex bias; and third, that sex-based stereotypes of women generally, and battered or raped women specifically, interfere with jurors' assessments of women's claims of self-defense. *Wanrow* and the substantial work on women's self-defense that followed it resulted from efforts to have the reasonableness standard of self-defense expand to include women's different experience.

On the level of practice, *Wanrow* and subsequent women's self-defense work sought to expand the legal options available to women defending against charges of homicide or assault for killing men who battered or raped them. Through explanations of the circumstances in which women acted to save their own lives, women's acts that had previously been viewed as outside the purview of self-defense but appropriate for insanity, diminished capacity or heat of passion defenses could now be seen as legitimately within the province of self-defense. Violence used in self-defense is justified violence; justification rests on a determination that the act was right because of its circumstances. In contrast, violence prompted by insanity, diminished capacity or the heat of passion is still wrong, although we may excuse it (and treat it less harshly) because of the actor's particular characteristics or state of mind. Traditionally, women's acts of violence were not understood as reasonable, and could not, therefore, be justified. Instead, the inquiry shifted to excuse. Women's self-defense work, beginning with *Wanrow*, has attempted to redraw the lines between justification and excuse, and to challenge the stereotypes that might prevent women's acts from being seen as justified.

2. **The Standard for Reasonableness.** The value of the decision in *Wanrow* to other women seeking to develop self-defense claims was limited in one important respect. Washington State had a standard of self-defense that facilitated an arguably subjective interpretation of reasonableness. Yvonne Wanrow was required to prove was that she honestly believed in the necessity of using lethal force to protect herself. In fact, of course, the proof Wanrow and her counsel offered went further than that. The content of the individualized perspective that *Wanrow* illuminated was not simply psychological, but clearly social; Yvonne Wanrow's individual perspective was shaped by her experience as a woman within the collective and historical experience of sex discrimination. Elizabeth Schneider, who was co-counsel in the *Wanrow* case, comments that "[a]t the time, it seemed difficult enough to convince a jury that the woman might be reasonable even when applying a standard emphasizing the woman's own perspective. It was even more difficult to imagine arguing that the woman's experience was objectively reasonable." Elizabeth M. Schneider, BATTERED WOMEN AND FEMINIST LAWMAKING (2000). Nonetheless, the self-defense standard in most jurisdictions requires a showing not only that the defendant honestly believed that force was necessary, but also that the use of force was objectively reasonable under the circumstances in which the defendant found him or herself. Lawyers representing battered women who killed in self-defense therefore had, in most cases, to take on the harder task of showing that the defendant's violence met an objective standard of reasonableness.

3. **Early Cases Using Expert Testimony.** The next case, *State v. Kelly*, provides an early example of the use of expert testimony to support a defendant's claim that her use of violence was objectively reasonable. At the same time, the case demonstrates some of the dangers inherent in this strategy, and particularly in the use of the label "battered woman's syndrome" to describe the content of the expert testimony.

The question of the admissibility of expert testimony on battering has been the primary legal issue that appellate courts have addressed in the area of women's self-defense work. There are several reasons for this. First, most women's self-defense cases have involved battered women. The Women's Self–Defense Law Project, a joint project of the Center for Constitutional Rights and the National Jury Project founded in 1978. which began legal work in this field, see WOMEN'S SELF-DEFENSE CASES: THEORY AND PRACTICE (Elizabeth Bochnak, ed. 1981), had stressed the particular utility of expert testimony in this context, depending on the facts of the case. Many lawyers defending women have sought to introduce expert testimony on battering at trial. Today The National Clearinghouse for the Defense of Battered Women in Philadelphia is an important resource to assist attorneys.

As we learned in Chapters Five and Eight, the question of the admissibility of expert testimony has frequently become the major issue on appeal. As a consequence, the question of expert testimony has received a great deal of attention from courts and commentators. Significantly, the majority of appellate courts that have ruled on the trial court's exclusion of expert testimony have determined that expert testimony on battering or "battered woman's syndrome" is relevant to a claim of self-defense. Moreover, even if the trial court admits the expert testimony proffered by the defense, the prosecution may be permitted to have an expert testify to counter the assertion that the woman is battered or that the experience affected her in a particular way.

Expert testimony on battering has had a substantial impact on the criminal process. At this point it has been admitted in cases involving battered women defendants in all fifty states and the District of Columbia, and not only in those involving claims of self-defense. Defense lawyers have also proffered it in response to other criminal charges, and at other stages of the criminal process, such as before the grand jury, on motions to dismiss, and at sentencing. Where expert testimony on battering has been held inadmissible, courts have largely ruled simply that there was an insufficient basis on which to find it admissible in the particular context or on the facts presented. These cases have demonstrated judicial recognition of the depth and severity of the problems of sex stereotyping in the criminal process for battered women.

State v. Kelly

Supreme Court of New Jersey, 1984.
478 A.2d 364.

■ WILENTZ, C.S.

The central issue before us is whether expert testimony about the battered-woman's syndrome is admissible to help establish a claim of self-defense in a homicide case. The question is one of first impression in this state. We hold, based on the limited record before us (the State not having had a full opportunity to prove the contrary), that the battered-woman's syndrome is an appropriate subject for expert testimony; that the experts' conclusions, despite the relative newness of the field, are sufficiently reliable under New Jersey's standards for scientific testimony; and that defendant's expert was sufficiently qualified. Accordingly, we reverse and remand for a new trial. If on retrial after a full examination of these issues the evidence continues to support these conclusions, the expert's testimony on the battered-woman's syndrome shall be admitted as relevant to the honesty and reasonableness of defendant's belief that deadly force was necessary to protect her against death or serious bodily harm. . . .

II.

The Kellys had a stormy marriage. Some of the details of their relationship, especially the stabbing, are disputed. The following is Ms. Kelly's version of what happened—a version that the jury could have accepted and, if they had, a version that would make the proffered expert testimony not only relevant, but critical.

The day after the marriage, Mr. Kelly got drunk and knocked Ms. Kelly down. Although a period of calm followed the initial attack, the next seven years were accompanied by periodic and frequent beatings, sometimes as often as once a week. During the attacks, which generally occurred when Mr. Kelly was drunk, he threatened to kill Ms. Kelly and to cut off parts of her body if she tried to leave him. Mr. Kelly often moved out of the house after an attack, later returning with a promise that he would change his ways. Until the day of the homicide, only one of the attacks had taken place in public.

The day before the stabbing, Gladys and Ernest went shopping. They did not have enough money to buy food for the entire week, so Ernest said he would give his wife more money the next day.

The following morning he left for work. Ms. Kelly next saw her husband late that afternoon at a friend's house. She had gone there with her daughter, Annette, to ask Ernest for money to buy food. He told her to wait until they got home, and shortly thereafter the Kellys left. After walking past several houses, Mr. Kelly, who was drunk, angrily asked "What the hell did you come around here for?" He then grabbed the collar of her dress, and the two fell to the ground. He choked her by pushing his fingers against her throat, punched or hit her face, and bit her leg.

A crowd gathered on the street. Two men from the crowd separated them, just as Gladys felt that she was "passing out" from being choked. Fearing that Annette had been pushed around in the crowd, Gladys then left to look for her. Upon finding Annette, defendant noticed that Annette had defendant's pocketbook. Gladys had dropped it during the fight. Annette had retrieved it and gave her mother the pocketbook.

After finding her daughter, Ms. Kelly then observed Mr. Kelly running toward her with his hands raised. Within seconds he was right next to her. Unsure of whether he had armed himself while she was looking for their daughter, and thinking that he had come back to kill her, she grabbed a pair of scissors from her pocketbook. She tried to scare him away, but instead stabbed him.[3]

III.

The central question in this case is whether the trial court erred in its exclusion of expert testimony on the battered-woman's syndrome. That testimony was intended to explain defendant's state of mind and bolster her claim of self-defense. . . .

Some popular misconceptions about battered women include the beliefs that they are masochistic and actually enjoy their beatings, that they purposely provoke their husbands into violent behavior, and, most critically, as we shall soon see, that women who remain in battering relationships are free to leave their abusers at any time.

---

3. This version of the homicide—with a drunk Mr. Kelly as the aggressor both in pushing Ms. Kelly to the ground and again in rushing at her with his hands in a threatening position after the two had been separated—is sharply disputed by the State. The prosecution presented testimony intended to show that the initial scuffle was started by Gladys; that upon disentanglement, while she was restrained by bystanders, she stated that she intended to kill Ernest; that she then chased after him, and upon catching up with him stabbed him with a pair of scissors taken from her pocketbook.

As these cases so tragically suggest, not only do many women suffer physical abuse at the hands of their mates, but a significant number of women kill (or are killed by) their husbands. . . .

As the problem of battered women has begun to receive more attention, sociologists and psychologists have begun to focus on the effects a sustained pattern of physical and psychological abuse can have on a woman. The effects of such abuse are what some scientific observers have termed "the battered-woman's syndrome," a series of common characteristics that appear in women who are abused physically and psychologically over an extended period of time by the dominant male figure in their lives. . . .

[The judge then described the "tension-building," "acute battering incident" and "contrition" phases of the "cycle of violence," as presented in Lenore Walker's early work.]

Dr. Veronen described the various psychological tests and examinations she had performed in connection with her independent research. These tests and their methodology, including their interpretation, are, according to Dr. Veronen, widely accepted by clinical psychologists. Applying this methodology to defendant (who was subjected to all of the tests, including a five-hour interview), Dr. Veronen concluded that defendant was a battered woman and subject to the battered-woman's syndrome.

In addition, Dr. Veronen was prepared to testify as to how, as a battered woman, Gladys Kelly perceived her situation at the time of the stabbing, and why, in her opinion, defendant did not leave her husband despite the constant beatings she endured. . . .

V.

Gladys Kelly claims that she stabbed her husband in self-defense, believing he was about to kill her. The gist of the State's case was that Gladys Kelly was the aggressor, that she consciously intended to kill her husband, and that she certainly was not acting in self-defense.

The credibility of Gladys Kelly is a critical issue in this case. If the jury does not believe Gladys Kelly's account, it cannot find she acted in self-defense. The expert testimony offered was directly relevant to one of the critical elements of that account, namely, what Gladys Kelly believed at the time of the stabbing, and was thus material to establish the honesty of her stated belief that she was in imminent danger of death.

The State argues that there is no need to bolster defendant's credibility with expert testimony concerning the battering because the State did not attempt to undermine defendant's testimony concerning her prior mistreatment at the hands of her husband. The State's claim is simply untrue. In her summation, the prosecutor suggested that had Ernest Kelly lived, he might have told a different story from the one Gladys told. (In its brief, the State argues that evidence in the case suggests that Gladys Kelly's claims of abuse could have been contradicted by her husband.) This is obviously a direct attempt to undermine defendant's testimony about her prior mistreatment.

Moreover, defendant's credibility was also attacked in other ways. Gladys Kelly's prior conviction for conspiracy to commit robbery was admitted into evidence for the express purpose of impeachment, even though this conviction had occurred nine years before the stabbing. Other questions, about Gladys Kelly's use of alcohol and drugs and about her premarital sexual conduct, were clearly efforts to impeach credibility.

As can be seen from our discussion of the expert testimony, Dr. Veronen would have bolstered Gladys Kelly's credibility. Specifically, by showing that her experience, although concededly difficult to comprehend, was common to that of other women who had been in similarly abusive relationships, Dr. Veronen would have helped the jury understand that Gladys Kelly could have honestly feared that she would suffer serious bodily harm from her husband's attacks, yet still remain with him. This, in turn, would support Ms. Kelly's testimony about her state of mind (that is, that she honestly feared serious bodily harm) at the time of the stabbing.

On the facts in this case, we find that the expert testimony was relevant to Gladys Kelly's state of mind, namely, it was admissible to show she honestly believed she was in imminent danger of death.... Moreover, we find that because this testimony was central to the defendant's claim of self-defense, its exclusion, if otherwise admissible, cannot be held to be harmless error.

We also find the expert testimony relevant to the reasonableness of defendant's belief that she was in imminent danger of death or serious injury. We do not mean that the expert's testimony could be used to show that it was understandable that a battered woman might believe that her life was in danger when indeed it was not and when a reasonable person would not have so believed.... Expert testimony in that direction would be relevant solely to the honesty of defendant's belief, not its objective reasonableness. Rather, our conclusion is that the expert's testimony, if accepted by the jury, would have aided it in determining whether, under the circumstances, a reasonable person would have believed there was imminent danger to her life.

At the heart of the claim of self-defense was defendant's story that she had been repeatedly subjected to "beatings" over the course of her marriage. While defendant's testimony was somewhat lacking in detail, a juror could infer from the use of the word "beatings," as well as the detail given concerning some of these events (the choking, the biting, the use of fists), that these physical assaults posed a risk of serious injury or death. When that regular pattern of serious physical abuse is combined with defendant's claim that the decedent sometimes threatened to kill her, defendant's statement that on this occasion she thought she might be killed when she saw Mr. Kelly running toward her could be found to reflect a reasonable fear; that is, it could so be found if the jury believed Gladys Kelly's story of the prior beatings, if it believed her story of the prior threats, and, of course, if it believed her story of the events of that particular day.

The crucial issue of fact on which this expert's testimony would bear is why, given such allegedly severe and constant beatings, combined with threats to kill, defendant had not long ago left decedent. Whether raised by the prosecutor as a factual issue or not, our own common knowledge tells us that most of us, including the ordinary juror, would ask himself or herself just such a question. And our knowledge is bolstered by the experts' knowledge, for the experts point out that one of the common myths, apparently believed by most people, is that battered wives are free to leave. To some, this misconception is followed by the observation that the battered wife is masochistic, proven by her refusal to leave despite the severe beatings; to others, however, the fact that the battered wife stays on unquestionably suggests that the "beatings" could not have been too bad for if they had been, she certainly would have left. The expert could clear up these myths, by explaining that one of the common characteristics of a battered wife is her inability to leave despite such constant beatings; her "learned helplessness"; her lack of anywhere to go; her feeling that if she tried to leave, she would be subjected to even more merciless treatment; her belief in the omnipotence of her battering husband; and sometimes her hope that her husband will change his ways.

Unfortunately, in this case the State reinforced the myths about battered women. On cross-examination, when discussing an occasion when Mr. Kelly temporarily moved out of the house, the State repeatedly asked Ms. Kelly: "You wanted him back, didn't you?" The implication was clear: domestic life could not have been too bad if she wanted him back. In its closing argument, the State trivialized the severity of the beatings, saying: I'm not going to say they happened or they didn't happen, but life isn't pretty. Life is not a bowl of cherries. We each and every person who takes a breath has problems. Defense counsel says bruised and battered. Is there any one of us who hasn't been battered by life in some manner or means?

Even had the State not taken this approach, however, expert testimony would be essential to rebut the general misconceptions regarding battered women.

The difficulty with the expert's testimony is that it sounds as if an expert is giving knowledge to a jury about something the jury knows as well as anyone else, namely, the reasonableness of a person's fear of imminent serious danger. That is not at all, however, what this testimony is directly aimed at. It is aimed at an area where the purported common knowledge of the jury may be very much mistaken, an area where jurors' logic, drawn from their own experience, may lead to a wholly incorrect conclusion, an area where expert knowledge would enable the jurors to disregard their prior conclusions as being common myths rather than common knowledge. After hearing the expert, instead of saying Gladys Kelly could not have been beaten up so badly for if she had, she certainly would have left, the jury could conclude that her failure to leave was very much part and parcel of her life as a battered wife. The jury could conclude that instead of casting doubt on the accuracy of her testimony about the severity and frequency of prior beatings, her failure to leave actually reinforced her credibility.

Since a retrial is necessary, we think it advisable to indicate the limit of the expert's testimony on this issue of reasonableness. . . . No expert is needed . . . to tell the jury the logical conclusion, namely, that a person who has in fact been severely and continuously beaten might very well reasonably fear that the imminent beating she was about to suffer could be either life-threatening or pose a risk of serious injury. What the expert could state was that defendant had the battered-woman's syndrome, and could explain that syndrome in detail, relating its characteristics to defendant, but only to enable the jury better to determine the honesty and reasonableness of defendant's belief. Depending on its content, the expert's testimony might also enable the jury to find that the battered wife, because of the prior beatings, numerous beatings, as often as once a week, for seven years, from the day they were married to the day he died, is particularly able to predict accurately the likely extent of violence in any attack on her. That conclusion could significantly affect the jury's evaluation of the reasonableness of defendant's fear for her life.[4]

VI.[5]

. . . [T]he record before us reveals that the battered woman's syndrome has a sufficient scientific basis to produce uniform and reasonably reliable results. . . . The numerous books, articles and papers referred to earlier indicate the presence of a growing field of study and research about the battered woman's syndrome and recognition of the syndrome in the scientific field. However, while the record before us could require such a ruling, we refrain from conclusively ruling that Dr. Veronen's proffered testimony about the battered-woman's syndrome would satisfy New Jersey's standard of acceptability for scientific evidence. This is because the State was not given a full opportunity in the trial court to question Dr. Veronen's methodology in studying battered women or her implicit assertion that the battered-woman's syndrome has been accepted by the relevant scientific community.

. . .

We have concluded that the appropriate disposal of this appeal is to reverse and remand for a new trial. . . .

■ HANDLER, JUDGE, concurring in part and dissenting in part.

The Court in this case takes a major stride in recognizing the scientific authenticity of the "battered women's syndrome" and its legal and factual

---

4. . . . Defendant's counsel at oral argument made it clear that defendant's basic contention was that her belief in the immediate need to use deadly force was both honest and reasonable; and that the evidence concerning the battered-woman's syndrome was being offered solely on that issue. We therefore are not faced with any claim that a battered woman's honest belief in the need to use deadly force, even if objectively unreasonable, constitutes justification so long as its unreasonableness results from the psychological impact of the beatings. . . .

5. Of course, expert testimony that meets these three criteria is still subject to

other rules of evidence. For example, the probative value of the testimony must not be substantially outweighed by the risk that its admission would necessitate undue consumption of time or create substantial danger of undue prejudice or of confusing the issues or of misleading the jury. . . . The danger of undue prejudice would be only slightly greater if expert testimony on the battered-woman's syndrome is introduced than without it, however, because the jury, even without it, will certainly hear about the past beatings from lay witnesses.

significance in the trial of certain criminal cases. My difference with the Court is quite narrow. I believe that defendant Gladys Kelly has demonstrated at her trial by sufficient expert evidence her entitlement to the use of the "battered women's syndrome" in connection with her defense of self-defense. I would therefore not require this issue—the admissibility of the "battered women's syndrome"—to be tried again. . . .

NOTES AND QUESTIONS

1. **Kelly's Retrial.** On remand, Gladys Kelly was convicted, and the expert testimony of Dr. Veronen was again excluded, this time on the basis that "battered woman's syndrome" lacked the necessary level of acceptance in the relevant scientific community. Today, every state has accepted the scientific validity of expert testimony on battering either in specific terms of "battered woman's syndrome" or some other framework. For discussion of the litigation in *Kelly*, by one of the lawyers who argued the case in the New Jersey Supreme Court, see Elizabeth M. Schneider, *Describing and Changing: Women's Self–Defense Work and the Problem of Expert Testimony on Battering,* 9 WOMEN'S RTS. L. REP. 195 (1986).

2. **The Impact of Testimony on Battering.** It is important to remember that even when battered women defendants are successful in introducing expert testimony in their trials, that testimony by no means guarantees their acquittal. As noted in Chapter Five, one of the most comprehensive surveys in 1995 looked at the appeals of 152 battered women defendants in state courts. It found that 63 percent resulted in affirmance of the woman's conviction or sentence, even though expert testimony was admitted or found admissible in 71 percent of the affirmances. *The Validity and Use of Evidence Concerning Battering and Its Effects in Criminal Trials,* REPORT RESPONDING TO SECTION 40507 OF THE VIOLENCE AGAINST WOMEN ACT, NCJ–160972, *Overview and Highlights* (May 1996).

In the decade since that report, there has been no comprehensive study examining the impact of testimony on battering and self-defense. However, consider these observations:

> Experts and advocates say evoking battered woman syndrome in self-defense rarely gets women off completely. The strategy works best when the defendant is a white, middle-class woman who has done what people have asked her to do, from getting a restraining order to trying to get into a shelter, said Sarah Buel, a clinical professor at the University of Texas School of Law. . . . "It doesn't work as well in pretty much any other case," said Buel, who has worked with battered women for three decades. . . . In Massachusetts, there have been only about a half-dozen criminal cases over the last two decades in which women claimed they specifically suffered from the syndrome. Only one of those women who went to trial was acquitted by reason of insanity, a Bridgewater woman who admitted killing her boyfriend by plunging steak knives into his eyes as he slept. The rest were found guilty of murder or manslaughter. Denise Lavoie, *Abuse Defense Rarely Gets Acquittals,* Associated Press, June 2, 2007.

Despite continued emphasis on battering or "battered women's syndrome" as a separate defense, there is in fact no separate defense. Furthermore, keep in mind that an insanity defense is different than self-defense. A verdict of insanity is likely to result in the defendant being committed to a secure mental health facility, sometimes indefinitely. In contrast, if a jury finds that a defendant acts in self-defense, the defendant is acquitted. Imperfect self-defense mitigates the charge from first or second degree murder to manslaughter or negligent homicide. What do you believe would be the impact of using testimony on battering in today's political climate? Do you think jurors are more educated now about domestic violence than they were in 1984, when Kelly's case was argued?

3.   **Why Didn't She Leave?** If Gladys Kelly had not been married to the man she killed, do you think she would have had difficulty establishing that she acted in self-defense, assuming the jury accepted her version of the events leading up to the killing? What is it precisely about her prior relationship with the decedent that makes the self-defense claim so problematic, and suggests the necessity for expert testimony? Is it the "imminence" requirement; the requirement that the force she use be proportional to the level of threat against her; her motivation for the killing, or more than one of these elements that might be affected by her relationship? Justice Wilentz suggests that the most important function of the expert testimony may be to explain to the jury why Gladys Kelly had not walked out on Ernest before the events that led to his death. Why is that, do you suppose?

In his own explanation of why Gladys Kelly, or any other battered woman, might not leave her batterer, even though she was subjected to serious abuse, and afraid for her safety or even her life, Wilentz mentions both internal and external factors. On the one hand, he talks about the "psychological paralysis" women can sink into; their tendency to believe that their husbands are omnipotent, and that attempts to escape will be futile; and their capacity to be "trapped by their own fear." On the other, he talks about the practical difficulties encountered by women who lack the material and social resources to support themselves and their children; the social stigma attached to women who abandon their children, and the real prospect that leaving will provoke increased violence. Unfortunately, as you have discovered earlier in this book, lumping all these factors together under the heading "battered woman's syndrome" frequently leads to judicial emphasis on the "internal" rather than the "external" factors. The term "syndrome" also calls into question whether the defendant's "state of mind" is indeed reasonable, so that her violence is justified, or whether instead her violence is "excusable," on the basis that her state of mind is disordered, for reasons that lead us to conclude she should be not be held fully accountable for her actions. Although Justice Wilentz himself emphasizes the value of the testimony as offering grounds for the conclusion that the defendant acted reasonably, it is easy to see how other less careful interpreters of the testimony (both lawyers and judges) have been led in a different direction. The description of the battered women that too many courts are hearing and to which they are responding is that of damaged women, not of women who perceive themselves to be, and in fact are, acting competently and rationally in light of the alternatives.

4. **Rational Actors.** At another point in his opinion, Wilentz offers a different analysis, one that is consistent with a view of women as competent, rational, and capable of exercising sound judgment about the need to use force in self defense. He notes that the battered partner in a relationship may, because of her prior experience with her partner, be more sensitive to his signals of impending or escalating violence, and better able than an outsider "to predict the likely extent of violence in any attack on her." If the jury were to draw this conclusion about a defendant's knowledge of her abusive partner, Wilentz goes on to say, it could clearly influence the jury's evaluation of the reasonableness of defendant's fear for her life. In this analysis the defendant is essentially presented as an "expert" in her partner's violence, rather than someone's whose perceptions have been distorted by her experience. The contrast between the image of the woman as damaged, on the one hand, and acting as an "expert" on the other is quite stark. How do you reconcile these two images? Which best captures the experiences of those who have been battered? How should the jury reconcile these two images?

5. **Dangers of Stereotyping.** There is a danger that "battered woman's syndrome" testimony is operating to create a new stereotype, fostering the view that the "real" battered woman is one who is dependent, passive, psychologically as well as physically damaged by the abuse, and helpless. This stereotype is crowding out the competing image of the battered woman who saves her own life by making a reasonable and informed judgment that she has no alternative but to use violence against her abuser. This in turn creates the risk that women who do not conform to the helpless stereotype may be unable to benefit from expert testimony about battering, and may even be precluded from arguing that they acted in self-defense, even though their decisions to use violence are indistinguishable from the decisions made by those who defend themselves against the violence of strangers.

This issue is tackled head on by Judge L'Heureux Dubé of Canada's Supreme Court, in *Malott v. Her Majesty the Queen*, [1998] 1 S.C.R. 123. The *Lavallee* case discussed by Dubé is an earlier decision in which the court recognized the importance of admitting expert testimony in battered women's self-defense cases. *R. v. Lavallee*, [1990] 1 S.C.R. 852. In *Malott*, Judge Dubé commented:

> It is possible that those women who are unable to fit themselves within the stereotype of a victimized, passive, helpless, dependent, battered woman will not have their claims to self-defence fairly decided. For instance, women who have demonstrated too much strength or initiative, women of colour, women who are professionals, or women who might have fought back against their abusers on previous occasions, should not be penalized for failing to accord with the stereotypical image of the archetypal battered women.... Needless to say, women with these characteristics are still entitled to have their claims of self-defence fairly adjudicated, and they are also still entitled to have their

experiences as battered women inform the analysis. Professor Grant ... warns against allowing the law to develop such that a woman accused of killing her abuser must either have been "reasonable 'like a man' or reasonable 'like a battered women'." I agree that this must be avoided. The "reasonable woman" must not be forgotten in the analysis, and deserves to be as much a part of the objective standard of the reasonable person as does the "reasonable man."

How should the courts combat the "syndromization" of battered women who act in self-defense? The legal inquiry into the moral culpability of a woman who is, for instance, claiming self-defence must focus on the *reasonableness* of her actions in the context of her personal experiences, and her experiences as a woman, not on her status as a battered woman and her entitlement to claim that she is suffering from "battered woman syndrome." ... By emphasizing a woman's "learned helplessness," her dependence, her victimization, and her low self-esteem, in order to establish that she suffers from "battered woman syndrome" the legal debate shifts from the objective rationality of her actions to preserve her own life to those personal inadequacies which apparently explain her failure to flee from her abuser. Such an emphasis comports too well with society's stereotypes about women. Therefore, it should be scrupulously avoided because it only serves to undermine the important advancements achieved by the decision in *Lavallee*.

There are other elements of a women's social context which help to explain her inability to leave her abuser, and which do not focus on those characteristics most consistent with traditional stereotypes. As Wilson J. herself recognized in *Lavallee*, ... "environmental factors may also impair the woman's ability to leave—lack of job skills, the presence of children to care for, fear of retaliation by the man, etc. may each have a role to play in some cases." To this list of factors I would add a woman's need to protect her children from abuse, a fear of losing custody of her children, pressures to keep the family together, weaknesses of social and financial support for battered women, and no guarantee that the violence would cease simply because she left. The considerations necessarily inform the reasonableness of a woman's beliefs or perceptions of, for instance, her lack of an alternative to the use of deadly force to preserve herself from death or grievous bodily harm.

How should these principles be given practical effect in the context of a jury trial of a woman accused of murdering her abuser? To fully accord with the spirit of Lavallee, where the reasonableness of a battered woman's belief is at issue in a criminal case, a judge and jury should be made to appreciate that a battered woman's experiences are both individualized, based on her own history and relationships, as well as shared with other women, within the context of a society and a legal system which has historically undervalued women's experiences. A judge and jury should be told that a battered woman's experiences are generally outside the common understanding of the average judge and juror, and that they should seek to understand the evidence being presented to them in order to overcome the myths and stereotypes which we all share. Finally, all of this should be presented in such a way as to focus on the reasonableness of the woman's actions, without relying on old or new stereotypes about battered women.

In this opinion, Judge L'Heureux Dubé ties together the need for expert testimony to address reasonableness, the interplay between the individual and the social, and the hurdles of "syndromization." She highlights the possibilities and dilemmas of expert testimony on battering, details the obstacles to fair consideration, and illuminates the profound challenge that feminist lawmaking poses to judges.

6. **Special Legislation v. Judicial Action.** While many states initially admitted expert testimony about battered women's experiences, by judicial decision, and have allowed the standards for admissibility to evolve in the same way, other jurisdictions chose to address the issue through special legislation. At least 15 states now allow for the admissibility of expert testimony in self-defense cases. However, the legislative route has its problems, as the following excerpt suggests.

Elizabeth M. Schneider
Battered Women and Feminist Lawmaking (2000)

... Statutes that focus exclusively on battered women, largely centering around admissibility of expert testimony, are problematic for several reasons. First, they tend to single out problems of battered women as though they are "special" and should not be understood within the general framework of the criminal law. For example, a statute that makes evidence of battered woman syndrome admissible suggests that this evidence would not otherwise be admissible. Second, it is questionable whether wholesale legislative reforms are the best solution to the problem of unequal treatment of battered woman defendants, since many problems result from unequal application of the law. Third, experience demonstrates that the language used in these statutes may be too limiting and will restrict their utility.

Two examples are a Maryland statute that permits evidence of abuse of the defendant and expert testimony on "battered spouse syndrome," and two Ohio statutes that authorize expert testimony on "battered-woman syndrome" in self-defense and insanity defenses. The Ohio statutes permit the introduction of expert testimony only to support either the imminence element of a self-defense claim or "to establish the requisite impairment of the Defendant's reason necessary for finding that the Defendant is not guilty by reason of insanity." Both the Ohio statutes and the Maryland statute assume that this evidence would not be otherwise admissible. This assumption can create the impression that a separate defense for battered women has been codified.

The need for special legislation concerning battering may also be questioned on other grounds. Depending on the particular state, it may be the legal standard of self-defense or the law governing the admissibility of evidence of battering that is problematic and needs reform, or it may be simply that judges apply these laws in gender-biased fashion. In many states, special legislation has been rushed through as a "quick fix" to the problem of domestic violence, without careful analysis of the particular state's criminal-law statutory scheme and of case law on procedural issues, such as burden of proof on self-defense.

If special legislation to admit expert testimony is developed, it is important that the statutory language be as inclusive as possible to admit evidence of battering generally. One example is a Texas statute which states that, in all prosecutions for murder, the defendant shall be permitted to offer "relevant evidence that the defendant had been the victim of acts of family violence committed by the deceased and relevant expert testimony regarding the condition of [her] mind ... [including] relevant facts and circumstances relating to family violence that are the basis of experts' opinions." Similarly, in Louisiana, the relevant statute does not refer at all to "battered woman syndrome" but provides simply that "an expert's opinion as to the effects of the prior assaultive acts on the accused's state of mind is admissible." A Massachusetts statute provides for admissibility of evidence "that the defendant is or has been the victim of acts of physical, sexual or psychological harm or abuse" in a wide range of circumstances, including self-defense, defense of another, duress or coercion, or "accidental harm."

NOTES AND QUESTIONS

1. **Limiting Admissibility by Statute.** Half of the twelve statutory provisions in place by 1995 referred specifically to expert testimony on "battered woman syndrome," or "battered spouse syndrome," while the other half used more generic language, referring to the nature and effects of domestic violence, family violence or physical, sexual or psychological abuse on the beliefs, perceptions and behaviors of the person being abused. *The Validity and Use of Evidence Concerning Battering and Its Effects in Criminal Trials,* REPORT RESPONDING TO SECTION 40507 OF THE VIOLENCE AGAINST WOMEN ACT, NCJ–160972, *Trend Analysis* (May 1996). In Missouri as well as Ohio, the statutory provisions have been interpreted as limiting the admissibility of expert testimony to self-defense cases, even though they do not expressly preclude introduction of relevant expert testimony in other cases involving battered women. In eight of the states the statutes use mandatory language, while in four (Georgia, Maryland, Ohio and Wyoming) the language is permissive.

2. **Critiques of Targeted Legislation.** One scholar who has been critical of targeted legislation governing the admissibility of expert testimony on battering is Holly Maguigan. In *Battered Women and Self–Defense: Myths and Misconceptions in Current Reform Proposals,* 140 U. PA. L. REV. 379 (1991), Maguigan argues that the problems faced by battered women criminal defendants in the courts have more to do with biased application of the rules than with deficiencies in the rules themselves. If judicial bias or ignorance is the real problem, then supplementing the body of law judges are required to interpret and apply is a strategy as likely to backfire as to produce real change. In addition, Maguigan worries that many legislative

initiatives in this area are incorporating restrictions that add, rather than remove, barriers to the admission of relevant expert testimony and will make it available to only a small percentage of battered women. Maguigan further argues that legislative efforts have been based on the misguided assumption that most battered women do not kill in circumstances defined as "non-confrontational." Her review of data suggests that more than 70% of battered women who kill do so in the context of an ongoing attack or imminent threat. Further, she argues that traditional self-defense law applied correctly, can account for battered women who kill in self-defense.

Yet, not all courts have adhered to traditional self-defense law in cases involving battered defendants.

The following case contains both the majority's account of how testimony on battering can, in general terms, be relevant to the issue of reasonableness, and a concurring judge's detailed analysis of the relevance of the testimony in this particular case. As you read it, consider whether the court's reasoning is sound.

People v. Humphrey

Supreme Court of California, 1996.
921 P.2d 1.

■ CHIN, JUDGE.

Defendant claimed she shot Hampton in self-defense. To support the claim, the defense presented first expert testimony and then nonexpert testimony, including that of defendant herself.

1. Expert Testimony

Dr. Lee Bowker testified as an expert on "battered women's syndrome". The syndrome, he testified, "is not just a psychological construction, but it's a term for a wide variety of controlling mechanisms that the man or it can be a woman, but in general for this syndrome it's a man, uses against the woman, and for the effect that those control mechanisms have." ...

Dr. Bowker interviewed defendant for a full day. He believed she suffered not only from "battered women's syndrome", but also from being the child of an alcoholic and an incest victim. He testified that all three of defendant's partners before Hampton were abusive and significantly older than she.

Dr. Bowker described defendant's relationship with Hampton. Hampton was a 49–year–old man who weighed almost twice as much as defendant. The two had a battering relationship that Dr. Bowker characterized as a "traditional cycle of violence." The cycle included phases of tension building, violence, and then forgiveness-seeking in which Hampton would promise not to batter defendant any more and she would believe him. During this period, there would be occasional good times. For example, defendant told Dr. Bowker that Hampton would give her a rose. "That's one of the things that hooks people in. Intermittent reinforcement is the key." But after a while, the violence would begin again. The violence would recur because "basically ... the woman doesn't perfectly obey. That's the bottom line." For example, defendant would talk to another man, or fail to clean house "just so."

The situation worsened over time, especially when Hampton got off parole shortly before his death. He became more physically and emotionally abusive, repeatedly threatened defendant's life, and even shot at her the night before his death. Hampton often allowed defendant to go out, but she was afraid to flee because she felt he would find her as he had in the past. "He enforced her belief that she can never escape him." Dr. Bowker testified that unless her injuries were so severe that "something absolutely had to be treated," he would not expect her to seek medical treatment. "That's the pattern of her life...."

Dr. Bowker believed defendant's description of her experiences. In his opinion, she suffered from "battered women's syndrome" in "about as extreme a pattern as you could find."

2.   Nonexpert Testimony

Defendant confirmed many of the details of her life and relationship with Hampton underlying Dr. Bowker's opinion. She testified that her father forcefully molested her from the time she was seven years old until she was fifteen. She described her relationship with another abusive man as being like "Nightmare on Elm Street." Regarding Hampton, she testified that they often argued and that he beat her regularly. Both were heavy drinkers. Hampton once threw a can of beer at her face, breaking her nose. Her dental plates hurt because Hampton hit her so often. He often kicked her, but usually hit her in the back of the head because, he told her, it "won't leave bruises." Hampton sometimes threatened to kill her, and often said she "would live to regret it." Matters got worse towards the end.

The evening before the shooting, March 27, 1992, Hampton arrived home "very drunk." He yelled at her and called her names. At one point when she was standing by the bedroom window, he fired his .357 magnum revolver at her. She testified, "He didn't miss me by much either." She was "real scared."

The next day, the two drove into the mountains. They argued, and Hampton continually hit her. While returning, he said that their location would be a good place to kill her because "they wouldn't find [her] for a while." She took it as a joke, although she feared him. When they returned, the arguing continued. He hit her again, then entered the kitchen. He threatened, "This time, bitch, when I shoot at you, I won't miss." He came from the kitchen and reached for the gun on the living room table. She grabbed it first, pointed it at him, and told him "that he wasn't going to hit [her]." She backed Hampton into the kitchen. He was saying something, but she did not know what. He reached for her hand and she shot him. She believed he was reaching for the gun and was going to shoot her.

Several other witnesses testified about defendant's relationship with Hampton, his abusive conduct in general, and his physical abuse of, and threats to, defendant in particular. This testimony generally corroborated defendant's. A neighbor testified that the night before the shooting, she heard a gunshot. The next morning, defendant told the neighbor that Hampton had shot at her, and that she was afraid of him. After the shooting, investigators found a bullet hole through the frame of the bedroom window and a bullet embedded in a tree in line with the window. Another neighbor testified that shortly before hearing the shot that killed Hampton, she heard defendant say, "Stop it, Albert. Stop it." ...

C. Procedural History

... The court instructed the jury on second degree murder and both voluntary and involuntary manslaughter. It also instructed on self-defense, explaining that an actual and reasonable belief that the killing was necessary was a complete defense; an actual but unreasonable belief was a defense to murder, but not to voluntary manslaughter. In determining reasonableness, the jury was to consider what "would appear to be necessary to a reasonable person in a similar situation and with similar knowledge."

The court also instructed:

"Evidence regarding Battered Women's Syndrome has been introduced in this case. Such evidence, if believed, may be considered by you only for the purpose of determining whether or not the defendant held the necessary subjective honest [belief] which is a requirement for both perfect and imperfect self-defense. However, that same evidence regarding Battered Women's Syndrome may not be considered or used by you in evaluating the objective reasonableness requirement for perfect self-defense.

"Battered Women's Syndrome seeks to describe and explain common reactions of women to that experience. Thus, you may consider the evidence concerning the syndrome and its effects only for the limited purpose of showing, if it does show, that the defendant's reactions, as demonstrated by the evidence, are not inconsistent with her having been physically abused or the beliefs, perceptions, or behavior of victims of domestic violence."

During deliberations, the jury asked for and received clarification of the terms "subjectively honest and objectively unreasonable." It found defendant guilty of voluntary manslaughter with personal use of a firearm. The court sentenced defendant to prison for eight years, consisting of the lower term of three years for manslaughter, plus the upper term of five years for firearm use. The Court of Appeal remanded for resentencing on the use enhancement, but otherwise affirmed the judgment.

We granted defendant's petition for review.

II. Discussion[6]

... [Prior cases] too narrowly interpreted the reasonableness element [and] failed to consider that the jury, in determining objective reasonable-

---

6. We use the term "battered women's syndrome" because Evidence Code section 1107 and the cases use that term. We note, however, that according to amici curiae Cali-

ness, must view the situation from the defendant's perspective. Here, for example, Dr. Bowker testified that the violence can escalate and that a battered woman can become increasingly sensitive to the abuser's behavior, testimony relevant to determining whether defendant reasonably believed when she fired the gun that this time the threat to her life was imminent. Indeed, the prosecutor argued that, "from an objective, reasonable man's standard, there was no reason for her to go get that gun. This threat that she says he made was like so many threats before. There was no reason for her to react that way." Dr. Bowker's testimony supplied a response that the jury might not otherwise receive. As violence increases over time, and threats gain credibility, a battered person might become sensitized and thus able reasonably to discern when danger is real and when it is not....

[W]e are not changing the standard from objective to subjective, or replacing the reasonable "person" standard with a reasonable "battered woman" standard. Our decision would not, in another context, compel adoption of a " 'reasonable gang member' standard." The jury must consider defendant's situation and knowledge, which makes the evidence relevant, but the ultimate question is whether a reasonable person, not a reasonable battered woman, would believe in the need to kill to prevent imminent harm. Moreover, it is the jury, not the expert, that determines whether defendant's belief and, ultimately, her actions, were objectively reasonable....

We do not hold that Dr. Bowker's entire testimony was relevant to both prongs of perfect self-defense. Just as many types of evidence may be relevant to some disputed issues but not all, some of the expert evidence was no doubt relevant only to the subjective existence of defendant's belief. Evidence merely showing that a person's use of deadly force is scientifically explainable or empirically common does not, in itself, show it was objectively reasonable. To dispel any possible confusion, it might be appropriate for the court, on request, to clarify that, in assessing reasonableness, the question is whether a reasonable person in the defendant's circumstances would have perceived a threat of imminent injury or death, and not whether killing the abuser was reasonable in the sense of being an understandable response to ongoing abuse; and that, therefore, in making that assessment, the jury may not consider evidence merely showing that an abused person's use of force against the abuser is understandable.[7]

fornia Alliance Against Domestic Violence et al., "... the preferred term among many experts today is 'expert testimony on battering and its effects' or 'expert testimony on battered women's experiences.' Domestic violence experts have critiqued the phrase 'battered women's syndrome' because (1) it implies that there is one syndrome which all battered women develop, (2) it has pathological connotations which suggest that battered women suffer from some sort of sickness, (3) expert testimony on domestic violence refers to more than women's psychological reactions to violence, (4) it focuses attention on the battered woman rather than on the batterer's coercive and controlling behavior and (5) it creates an image of battered women as suffering victims rather than as active survivors." (Fns. omitted.)

7. If the prosecution offers the battered women's syndrome evidence, an additional limiting instruction might also be appropriate on request, given the statutory prohibition against use of this evidence "to prove the occurrence of the act or acts of abuse which

We also emphasize that, as with any evidence, the jury may give this testimony whatever weight it deems appropriate in light of the evidence as a whole. The ultimate judgment of reasonableness is solely for the jury. We simply hold that evidence of "battered women's syndrome" is generally relevant to the reasonableness, as well as the subjective existence, of defendant's belief in the need to defend, and, to the extent it is relevant, the jury may consider it in deciding both questions. The court's contrary instruction was erroneous. . . .

■ BROWN, JUDGE, concurring in the order.

. . . Turning to the facts of this case, for the most part defendant's account of events leading to the shooting did not require the filter of an expert's opinion to assist in determining the question of reasonableness. She presented a relatively straightforward claim of self-defense the jury could either accept or reject as such. According to defendant, Hampton had been physically and verbally abusive for most of the year they lived together. His threats and acts of violence had been increasing for several weeks prior to the fateful evening. Although he liked guns and owned several, he had never shot at her until the previous night. On the way home from the mountains the next day, he pointed out what he thought would be a good place to kill her because no one would find the body for awhile. Just minutes before the shooting with the gun lying within easy reach, he told her "[t]his time" he would not miss. She then grabbed the weapon as he appeared about to do the same. While she was holding him at bay, he reached for her arm at which point she apparently shot him. On their face, nothing in these facts lies beyond the experience of the average reasonable person or the ken of the average juror.

At the same time, defendant also testified to facts implicating characteristics of BWS that correspond to the objective element of self-defense. Consistent with his threats, Hampton began hitting her more frequently when he got off parole. The night before, he was "getting crazy" asking for the gun, which he then shot in her direction narrowly missing her. At that moment, he had a "look on his face" that defendant had seen before "but not this bad"; he "wasn't the same person." As to events surrounding Hampton's death, defendant related that shortly before she grabbed the gun, the two were screaming and arguing; "then all of a sudden, he got quiet for a minute or two, and, then, he just snapped." A few moments later, he moved from the kitchen toward the gun saying, "This time, bitch, when I shoot at you, I won't miss." At this point, she "knew he would shoot me" and was "scared to death" not only because of Hampton's threats and prior violence but also because of his "very, very heavy" walk indicating he was "mad." She had no doubt he would kill her if she did not kill him first. As they confronted each other in the kitchen, he "looked crazy." She assumed he was going for the gun when he reached for her arm and shot him.

form the basis of the criminal charge." (Evid. Code, § 1107, subd. (a); see CALJIC No. 9.35.01 (1996 new) (5th ed. Supp.).)

As relevant to this testimony, Dr. Bowker explained generally that with the cycles of violence typifying BWS the "severity tends to escalate over time." Battered women develop a heightened awareness of this escalation as threats and physical abuse become increasingly menacing. A sense of the batterer's omnipotence due to his dominance may augment this hypervigilance, causing the woman to believe all the more he will act on his threats of violence.

Bowker also discussed some specifics arguably relating to defendant's objective perception of imminent harm: "[T]he escalation had been such, particularly the night before, where [Hampton] actually shot at her that it would be pretty hard to doubt the seriousness." "A difference, I think, [between Hampton's last threat and previous ones] is that [defendant] felt for the first time that he really intended to do it and, you know, my experience with battered women who kill in self-defense their abusers, it's always related to their perceived change of what's going on in a relationship. They become very sensitive to what sets off batterers. They watch for this stuff very carefully. Anybody who is abused over a period of time becomes sensitive to the abuser's behavior and when she sees a change acceleration begin in that behavior, it tells them something is going to happen and usually the abuser said things specifically like 'I'm really going to kill you this time,' and, you know, they don't admit to that something happens that there's a label put on it by the abuser which was certainly true in Albert's case and that's intensification or an acceleration of the process is what leads to some self-defensive action which is beyond anything that the woman has ever done before."

This testimony could assist the jury in determining whether a reasonable person in defendant's situation would have perceived from the totality of the circumstances imminent peril of serious bodily injury or death. Absent the expert's explanation, the average juror might be unduly skeptical that a look, footstep, or tone of voice could in fact signal impending grave harm or that a reasonable person would be able accurately to assess the need to take self-defensive action on that basis. Accordingly, the trial court erred in categorically precluding consideration of evidence relevant to this purpose rather than giving a properly worded limiting instruction.

NOTES AND QUESTIONS

1. **What Standard of Reasonableness?** Critics of battered women's self-defense often argue that cases such as *Humphrey* depart from traditional self-defense law by creating a special defense for battered women, thereby excusing the killing. However, Kit Kinports suggests that when courts allow in evidence of battering they are not creating a "reasonable battered woman" standard, but rather are adhering to traditional self-defense doctrine. Consider her criticism of *Humphrey*:

> [T]he so-called "reasonable battered woman" standard adopted by some courts is just a short-hand description for the conventional "reasonable person under the circumstances" standard that courts apply in all self-defense cases. Thus, it makes no sense for the Califor-

nia Supreme Court to take the position it articulates in *People v. Humphrey*, where it disclaims any intent to "replace the reasonable 'person' standard with a reasonable 'battered woman' standard"— reasoning that "the ultimate question is whether a reasonable person, not a reasonable battered woman, would believe in the need to kill to prevent imminent harm"—but then goes on to hold that "the jury, in determining objective reasonableness, must view the situation from the defendant's perspective" and "must consider all of the relevant circumstances in which defendant found herself." The court acknowledges, as it must, that the defendant's history of abuse is one of "the relevant circumstances" to be considered, and it does not deny that her experience as a battered woman must have colored her "perspective." Thus, the objective standard it adopts seems not much different from the one it purports to reject. Kit Kinports, *So Much Activity, So Little Change: A Reply to the Critics of Battered Women's Self–Defense*, 23 St. Louis U. Pub. L. Rev. 155 (2004).

Do you agree that the court merely applied a reasonable person standard in *Humphrey*? Or did it create a special category of defense for battered defendants?

2. **Imminence and Terrorism.** While courts have been willing to admit expert testimony on battering in cases in which defendants kill in traditional self-defense scenarios, they have been less likely to admit such evidence when the killing is done during a lull in the violence. For example, in *Commonwealth v. Grove*, 526 A.2d 369 (Pa. Super.1987), a Pennsylvania court held that it was not an error to exclude evidence of a 22 year history of abuse when the wife killed her drunk and sleeping husband.

In an article, Jane Campbell Moriarty suggests that courts should take an expanded view of imminence by looking to the theory of the preemption doctrine in the context of unilateral strikes on aggressors. She compares anticipatory self defense (ASD) in the domestic violence context to the military policy of using ASD for national security. Comparing abusers to terrorists, she argues:

> But whether sleeping, turned away, or physically distant, the threat of a domestic violence terrorist does not disappear after he has made the threat. There is a more sensible approach than to watch the clock for objective evidence of an imminent threat. Rather, the more reasoned view is to consider the situation with a view toward the totality of the circumstances: Did the decedent make lethal threats? Were there prior incidents of physical abuse? How serious were they? Did the decedent tell other people of his intent to harm the defendant? Did the decedent have access to a weapon? Was the decedent intoxicated by drugs or alcohol at the time he threatened to kill the defendant? By considering these factors, the factfinder is in a much better position to evaluate whether the killing was rational and necessary.

> Pursuant to international law, ASD may be legitimately invoked if a targeted country has been victimized by prior attacks and learns more attacks are planned. When a prior aggressor threatens to commit

future violence, international law treats that threat as real. So should domestic criminal law.

We would think it foolhardy if the U.S. Department of Defense evaluated the threat of a terrorist attack on any given day in 2005 based only on the immediate circumstances of that given day, much less hour or minute. Rather, there is a lucid understanding in the international terrorism context that the determination of legitimate self-defense must be made through a rational evaluation of the totality of the circumstances, which may include a more elastic consideration of the time period to judge the threat. Similarly, in the domestic violence context, we should not separate the moment of killing from context and past behavior to determine whether the threat was "imminent" or "immediate" and whether the use of force was appropriate. Jane Campbell Moriarty, *While Dangers Gather: The Bush Preemption Doctrine, Battered Women, Imminence, and Anticipatory Self-Defense*, 30 N.Y.U. REV. L. & SOC. CHANGE 1 (2005).

Do you agree that battered defendants must wait for an imminent attack before responding? What would be the consequence of an ASD doctrine for battered defendants, or for others who kill anticipating a credible and likely future attack? For another perspective analogizing self-defense of battered women and military theory, see Kimberly Kessler Ferzan, *Defending Imminence: From Battered Women to Iraq*, 46 ARIZ.L.REV. 213 (2004).

3. **Jury Instructions.** As you have already seen in several cases, jury instructions often provide the basis for the appeals brought by battered women who have killed their batterers when they are convicted at the trial level. *Wanrow* involved the issue of jury instructions and in *Humphrey* it was the jury instruction that provided an opportunity for the California Supreme Court to clarify its self-defense standard. Jury instructions must track both the theory of the defense in the particular case, and the governing law; they provide an opportunity to educate the jury about the law and its potential application to the facts of the case. The next case demonstrates the perils involved in shaping appropriate jury instructions in this complex and evolving area of law. Note that the substantive self-defense standard in Ohio is a more subjective one, like the Washington standard that governed *Wanrow*.

State v. Daws

Court of Appeals of Ohio, 1994.
662 N.E.2d 805.

■ WOLFF, JUDGE.

I.   THE TRIAL COURT ERRED IN INSTRUCTING THE JURY.

In this assignment of error, Susan asserts that the trial court erred in failing to instruct the jury on the battered woman syndrome. Given the extensive testimony on the battered woman syndrome during trial, Susan contends that a jury instruction tailored to the syndrome was essential to assist the jury in applying that evidence to her claim of self-defense.

In response, the State argues that ... the failure to give the instruction presented by defense counsel was neither prejudicial nor plain error because the instruction requested was not a correct statement of the law and because the trial court's instruction on self-defense was sufficient....

Susan's proffered instructions were as follows:

[1] You have heard evidence that the Defendant suffers from Battered Woman Syndrome. In determining if this is true you must consider the following factors:

    a. The nature and length of her relationship with the deceased;

    b. The history of physical abuse between the couple including, but not limited to, previous reports to the police, physicians, counselors, family or friends; and

    c. The status of the Defendant that is, did she have small children to care for, the psychological assessment of her by the experts who testified in this case.

[2] If you find from all of your deliberations that evidence presented shows the Defendant suffered from Battered Woman syndrome, you must consider that fact in assessing her state of mind at the time of the homicide.

[3] If you find from all of your deliberations that she did not so suffer then you must not consider that fact in assessing her state of mind at time of the homicide.

[4] A person is justified in the use of force when and to the extent that she reasonably believes that such conduct is necessary to defend herself against the imminent use of force.

[5] However, a person is justified in the use of (sic) which is intended or likely to cause death or great bodily harm only if she reasonably believes as a Battered Woman that such force is necessary to prevent imminent death or great bodily harm to herself or the commission of a forcible felony.

[6] A person who suffers from the Battered Woman syndrome may reasonably believe such force is necessary at a threshold lower than that which a person (sic) does not so suffer would consider reasonable.

[7] You have heard evidence that the victim in this case has committed certain violent acts against the Defendant. If, after your consideration of the evidence, you believe this to be true, you must consider that fact in assessing whether the Defendant was in fear at the time of the homicide.

Our review of these proposed jury instructions indicates that they are improper for several reasons. First, paragraph one mandates that the jury consider three factors in determining whether Susan was a battered woman. However, this list of factors is not exhaustive of the factors relevant to this determination nor are the factors given necessarily the most important considerations in determining whether Susan was a battered woman. Thus, this instruction incorrectly highlights certain evidentiary factors to the jury and improperly limits the jury's deliberation to those factors. Second, paragraphs four and five, which attempt to explain the law of self-defense, were also improper in this case. Paragraph four explains when the use of force against another is justified. However, it does not explain when the use of deadly force is justified and is thus not relevant to a homicide case in which the accused claims that she acted in self-defense. Paragraph five, on the other hand, does contain the pertinent law of this case and explains to the jury what circumstances justify the use of deadly force. However, in instructing the jury to consider what Susan "reasonably believes as a Battered Woman," paragraph five implies that Susan's status as a battered woman could justify her use of force. Thus, this instruction tends to elevate the battered woman syndrome to the level of an independent affirmative defense, rather than informing the jury that evidence of the syndrome is merely one factor to consider in evaluating Susan's self-defense claim. Therefore, paragraph five does not accurately inform the jury as to the proper use of evidence relating to the battered woman syndrome.... Finally, paragraph six is misleading in informing the jury that a battered woman may reasonably believe that force is necessary at a threshold lower than others who do not suffer from the syndrome. As stated supra, Ohio has a subjective test in self-defense cases. Therefore, the reasonableness of the accused's beliefs and actions are determined on a case by case basis, and there are no objective "thresholds" or "reasonable person" standard. A woman's status as a battered woman does not alter her evidentiary burden in establishing her self-defense claim. Any instruction suggesting otherwise would be improper. Although paragraph six, taken in isolation, may be a correct abstract statement, it tends to invite the jury to excuse unreasonable behavior.

However, we do believe that given the complexity of the syndrome itself and its limited applicability to the defense, some specific instruction with respect to the battered woman syndrome would have been appropriate. For instance, the jury should have been instructed that the battered woman syndrome is not a defense in and of itself and that evidence of it is only offered to assist the jury in determining whether the defendant acted out of a reasonable belief that she was in imminent danger of death or great bodily harm and that the use of force was her only means of escaping that danger. Additionally, the jury should have been instructed that it could only consider the evidence of the battered woman syndrome if it found that the Defendant was a battered woman.

Accordingly, we agree with Susan that an instruction tailored to the battered woman syndrome was warranted in this case. However, as discussed supra, the proposed jury instructions were not limited to matters of law and did not accurately reflect the law of Ohio. Therefore, we must conclude that the trial court did not err in refusing to accept them.

NOTES AND QUESTIONS

1. **Jury Instructions.** In *Daws*, the court ultimately concludes that while an instruction on "battered women's syndrome" was warranted, it was not required by law. In contrast, some states have required special jury instructions in these cases. In *Bechtel v. State*, 840 P.2d 1 (Okla. Crim. App. 1992),

the Oklahoma Court of Criminal Appeals adopted a special jury instruction for battered women's self-defense cases that struck the pattern jury instruction's reference to "a reasonable person" and instead advised the jury to consider whether "a person, in the circumstances and from the viewpoint of the defendant, would reasonably have believed that she was in imminent danger of death or great bodily harm." How would you write a self-defense instruction that would have satisfied the court in the *Daws* case? How would you then adapt that instruction for use in the larger number of jurisdictions that use an objective standard of reasonableness?

2. **Voir Dire.** Focusing on instructions to the jury leads to a question about who the jurors will be, and what control the defendant may be able to exercise over their selection. Voir dire is the process by which attorneys elicit information from prospective jurors in order to determine how their attitudes, experiences and personality are likely to influence their reactions to the evidence, witnesses, and testimony in the case on trial. Voir dire is also an opportunity for attorneys to begin to educate jurors about the law and their duties and responsibilities. In preparation for trial, attorneys formulate voir dire questions in language that is easy for laypersons to understand, and design them to reveal attitudes and experiences that are relevant to the theory of the case. Areas for voir dire questions of particular import for battered women's self-defense cases include the ability to accept the legal concept of self-defense, jurors' exposure to violence, exposure to pretrial publicity about the case or media coverage about domestic violence more generally, attitudes about women's roles in society, racism, attitudes about psychological opinions, possible responses to gruesome evidence, and attitudes about unflattering facts that may come out about the defendant at trial, such as use of drugs or alcohol, or possession or use of a weapon. The following excerpt discusses the use of voir dire questions when representing battered defendants in self-defense cases and when battered defendants have been charged with other crimes as well.

Sarah M. Buel

Effective Assistance of Counsel for Battered Women Defendants: A Normative Construct

26 Harv. Women's L.J. 217 (2003).

As a prosecutor conducting voir dire in domestic violence cases, I was astonished how often jurors would admit their biases if asked directly how they felt. I routinely asked, "How many of you think that if a husband hits his wife, she must have deserved it?" I expected that perhaps elder members of the venire might respond in the affirmative, yet, time and again, without even hearing the facts of the case, venire members of all ages answered "yes." Further probing with those jurors almost always revealed deep-seated biases, including blaming battered women for abuse and being unable to hold the offender as accountable as they would have in a stranger assault.

If the battered defendant is a person of color or low-income, counsel should also ask specific questions relating to jurors' possible misconceptions and biases concerning race and socio-economic status. It is an error to assume that jurors who share the same race, ethnicity, or socio-economic status as the battered client will necessarily sympathize with her. In one case, an African American woman told me that the Haitian battered woman defendant should have stayed in her own country and not brought her problems to the United States. On another occasion, a Chinese man stated that he would not reward a Chinese battered woman for disclosing family problems to the public and bringing shame on him and his community. A low-income Irish woman said essentially that all men are violent sometimes and that she saw potential jury duty as a waste of time on behalf of an Irish battered woman who just needed to accept abuse as an unchangeable reality with poor men. These examples illustrate the import of counsel being careful to identify cultural biases among jurors and not assume their biases from her own stereotypes about how potential jurors will react to the plight of her client.

Since it may be important for jurors to understand why the victim did not leave her abuser after the first assault, counsel must be prepared to question jurors on all relevant aspects of this phenomenon. Questions can include: "How many of you are aware that a family of three in Texas receives just $208 per month on welfare?"; "How many of you are aware that the number one reason battered women return to their abusers is a lack of money?"; "How many of you think that a battered woman with few job skills might feel forced to return to her batterer?"; "How many of you think that a mother and two children can survive on one minimum wage job?"; "How many of you know that with a minimum wage job you would take home about $200 per week, gross?"; and "How many of you are aware that childcare for a four-year-old in our area averages about $90 per week?" It may be beyond the ken of the average juror to comprehend the economic realities some victims face. Thus, such detailed questions should be permitted by the court as they address biases that jurors may hold regarding how easy it is for victims to leave violent relationships.

I consulted on a case in which a Chicano law enforcement officer murdered his wife after years of battering her. His defense was that in Mexico she was a compliant and good wife, but that when she got to Texas she became "tart-tongued," wanted to go to school, and wore short skirts. Although the prosecutors assumed that the all-Hispanic jury would certainly find such a defense ludicrous, the defendant was acquitted. Fortunately, the case was overturned on appeal for technical errors, and the killer was convicted after the second trial. This case taught my fellow prosecutors and me to routinely ask questions such as, "How many of you think that an Hispanic woman should obey her husband's wishes about what she can wear and whether she can work outside the home?" or "How many of you think that Hispanic men are just more violent than other men and their wives should understand?" Counsel should make these questions case specific, depending on the race, culture, or ethnicity of the litigants.

Similarly, if counsel is representing a gay or lesbian battered client, it will be necessary to ask questions specific to potential jurors' homophobia. In *Burdine*, a case which involved a gay male charged with a non-domestic violence offense, defense counsel not only failed to inquire about possible juror bias against gay men, but also did not introduce any evidence regarding how the partner abuse impacted Burdine.

Just as it is necessary to address possible juror homophobia, counsel must also identify potential bias against female substance-abusers. Counsel may ask, "How many of you admire Betty Ford for acknowledging that she had a drinking problem and doing something about it?" In my experience, many jurors will respond affirmatively, prompting follow-up questions, such as, "How many of you are aware that it took Mrs. Ford some time to acknowledge she had a problem and then get help?"; "How many of you think that if a woman is getting beaten up by her partner, she might drink to dull the pain?"; and "How many of you think that if a woman gets drunk, she deserves to get beaten up?" Surprisingly, a few of the venire will concede such biases, allowing counsel to remove them from the pool and increase the likelihood of a fair trial.

NOTES AND QUESTIONS

1. **Identifying Bias.** Buel suggests ways in which voir dire can uncover jury biases. Yet, she notes that potential jurors do not always admit them. How should lawyers deal with this problem? Does expert testimony on battering help to implicitly confront some of those biases?

2. **Credibility and Medication in Prison.** In CONVICTED SURVIVORS: THE IMPRISONMENT OF BATTERED WOMEN WHO KILL (2002), Elizabeth Leonard examines the plight of more than 40 women in California who are serving prison sentences for killing their abusers. Among her many findings is that while in jail, these women often received psychotropic drugs to treat their depression and anxiety. This medication made it very difficult for women to recall what happened and to present themselves well to the jury. What is the obligation of defense counsel in these situations? How does a client's depression and fear during trial translate to the jury?

3. **The Changing Social Context.** As legal remedies and other social services become available to those in abusive relationships, what do you think the future of expert testimony on battering will be in self-defense cases? In the 1970s and 1980s, when most of the cases defining the scope of defenses to battered defendants were argued, fewer legal remedies, such as restraining orders, were available in comparison to today. Will courts or juries reject claims of self-defense, for example, when a defendant has obtained a restraining order? In *Thigpen v. State*, 546 S.E.2d 60 (Ga. Ct. App. 2001), the Georgia Court of Appeals rejected an ineffective assistance of counsel claim when the attorney failed to introduce expert testimony on battering in a case in which a wife shot and killed her ex-husband, allegedly in self-defense. The defendant had previously sought a restraining order and an arrest warrant. In rejecting the ineffective assistance of counsel claim, the court reasoned, "Not only was there no evidence of a pattern of physical abuse over an extended period of time, Thigpen's swift response in seeking a restraining order and warrant for her ex-husband's arrest falls far short of demonstrating the 'psychological paralysis' that is the hallmark of the battered woman syndrome." Should the court consider attempts to legally end the abuse as a factor mitigating against the introduction of evidence on battering? Or should it allow testimony on efforts to leave the

relationship so as to show why self-defense was a reasonable option after pursing legal remedies failed?

In contrast, what if the defendant had never sought a restraining order or called the police? Does the failure to seek legal help mean that the defendant voluntarily stayed in a violent relationship and thus loses her right to have expert testimony admitted on self-defense? Does failure to seek help imply premeditation? See *State v. Hagerty,* 2002 WL 707858 (Tenn. Crim. App. 2002).

Keep in mind the double bind of seeking help that battered defendants might face as we explore other crimes and possible defenses.

B.   BATTERED CRIMINAL DEFENDANTS AND ALTERNATIVE DEFENSE THEORIES

The materials you have just read highlighted the issue of self-defense for battered women who kill their assailants. But there are other contexts in which battered women face criminal charges that may be related to the abuse they have experienced. Women frequently find themselves involved in other criminal activity because they are coerced by their batterers to engage in criminal conduct, forced to participate *with* their batterers in criminal conduct, or witness their batterers' criminal conduct without attempting to intervene, leave the scene, or alert law enforcement. These crimes are not committed against their abusers, but against third parties. Unlike when women kill their abusers, courts have been far more reluctant to admit expert testimony on battering in these contexts. As you read this section, ask yourself what the relationship between battering and crime is, and how the law ought to respond to crimes committed by battered defendants who claim defenses such as duress.

Battering and Crime

Beth Richie, in her book COMPELLED TO CRIME: THE GENDER ENTRAPMENT OF BATTERED BLACK WOMEN (1996), reports that in her study of women incarcerated for a variety of criminal offenses, African American women's criminal activity (whether illegal drug use, illegal sex work, or economic or even violent crime) was particularly likely to grow out of their entrapment in violent relationships. The next excerpt further explores the relationship between battering and crime.

Shelby A.D. Moore
Understanding the Connection between Domestic Violence, Crime, and Poverty: How Welfare Reform May Keep Battered Women from Leaving Abusive Relationships

12 TEX. J. WOMEN & L. 451 (2003).

Women, in general, commit crimes for a number of reasons. Notably, recent studies indicate that as many as forty percent of women in prison have been victims of domestic violence. Scholars and those engaged in battered women's defense work are beginning to document that many battered women are accused of crimes relating directly or indirectly to an abusive relationship. . . .

B.   Drug Offenses and Family Violence

There is a dearth of information concerning battered women who abuse drugs or commit drug offenses. The reason, quite simply, is that lawyers and legal scholars have given little attention to the connection between domestic violence and the prosecution of women for the use or sale of narcotics. Few articles have been written about the legal attempts to prosecute crack-addicted mothers who give birth to drug-addicted babies. A small number of other writings analyze the disparate impact of federal and state sentencing guidelines, especially on women trapped in violent relationships with drug-dealing men. Even fewer legal commentators and lawyers examine the complexities of the situations of female criminals in the context of women who sell or use crack cocaine, particularly women who have been abused. However, recent statistics indicate that the percentage of women arrested and prosecuted for drug offenses has dramatically increased above all other crimes. They are being imprisoned in both the state and federal systems for drug offenses at an alarming rate, most often for drug possession.

Attention has been given, however, to domestic violence and substance abuse as it relates to child welfare. Indeed, some scholars indicate that there is clearly a nexus between substance abuse and domestic violence. Where domestic violence is present in the home, battered women self-medicate—resorting to drug and alcohol abuse to cope with their depression, pain, and fear. These substances impair battered women's ability to care for either themselves or their children. Accordingly, they make "particularly unsympathetic parties in abuse and neglect proceedings."

For some time, social scientists have recognized that abused women either sell or use drugs as a means of psychological and physical escape. Beth E. Richie has detailed stories of battered women who were incarcerated for drug offenses. In one case, she presents the story of a twenty-one year old woman detained for drug use. She had been battered by her boyfriend for four years prior to her arrest.

> I would be in serious pain and couldn't stop screaming. At first I denied and tried to hide the abuse, but he would beat me to keep me quiet! But sometimes I'd have broken bones, so I couldn't just be quiet. He would go out and come home with "medicine," which I think was initially legit, and I fell for his acting like he was taking care of me. He'd shoot me up with it. He started buying morphine on the street. It really helped the physical pain and the emotional pain. And soon I needed more and more to numb the pain of broken bones that weren't set, including a broken arm. Now I try to get it on my own even when he isn't beating me because I am addicted. . . .

They are not always immobilized by their own drug addiction, however. Instead, they may sell drugs as a means of getting money to escape the abuse. The following story demonstrates the measures women may take to leave their batterer:

> There is one and only one reason I am here ... I sold drugs to try to get an apartment. The undercovers who busted me knew that I was not an addict, but I guess they didn't care. They need a certain number of arrests before they can go home. I had lots of drugs on me, and I was about to cop lots of money.... That's all they needed to know. I tried working, but my husband found out, beat me up, and took my money. There were lots of drugs in our neighborhood, and so it wasn't hard to find customers and suppliers. I never had an identity as a dealer, but I was starting to save enough to move out. No one, so far, has believed me that I only did it as a way to get away from him.

By recognizing that battered women sell or use drugs, we do not have to endorse these activities. But we must understand the full range of and the circumstances surrounding the crimes they commit. One commentator notes, "If we are going to advocate an end to violence against women, we must understand more about all types of violence women experience as well as the range of coping mechanisms women develop." Further, if we cannot envision that it is even plausible that battered women engage in the sale or use of narcotics as a means of coping with or escaping violent relationships, it is difficult to see how we can effectively represent them. We, quite simply, cannot provide complete or adequate representation.

C.   Property Crimes and Domestic Violence

   ... In addition to detailing the burdens faced by battered women prosecuted for narcotics offenses, Beth E. Richie has also given thoughtful attention to women who commit property crimes, including arson, burglary, and theft. She presents the stories of abused women incarcerated in Rikers Island for crimes they committed or are alleged to have committed as a result of abusive relationships. She recounts the story of a woman charged with arson for an accidental fire started while fending off a beating by her husband. Her neighbors heard her threatening to kill her husband if he did not stop beating her. Police used this information to arrest her for arson after she and her husband knocked over a candle during the struggle. She did not intend to start a fire. And although she and her husband escaped the apartment without injury, the police arrested her, even after observing her black eyes and scarred face.

   Richie also tells the story of a woman trapped in a violent marriage for seven years. She was detained for burglary after stealing from her employer for whom she worked as a maid. She states:

> The abuse got so bad that it was getting hard for me to keep going to work. Since we needed the money, this only made him more upset, and I was getting really desperate. I started working for a white family who had more than enough things, so I started lifting food and clothes. They would just leave money around, and once he came there to finish an attack he started the night before and he saw the money and took it and some jewelry. He said he had no respect for me for being a maid and all, and that he'd think more of me if I put my "slave work" to use

for us. So I began to move from job to job every few months to steal stuff. He'd sell it and keep the money. He was beating me and harassing me and teasing me all the while, unless I made a good boost. It was like we were working together for the first time. The only time I felt really good was when he was spotting for me. It was like he was acting like a real husband for the first time, and I got sucked into feeling protected and taken care of. Since I was the one stealing, I've served time twice before for possession of stolen property and burglary. But he was the one who set it up. He was the one who beat me if I didn't get the goods.

This scenario is not presented to suggest that all battered women commit crimes because their abusers compelled them to do so. As one scholar states, there are times when the situation is more complicated, including when the abused woman engages in crime with her abuser because it presents an opportunity for mutuality and shared power. Indeed, she notes, "The more complicated the facts, the more difficult it becomes for us to decipher where the abuse creates entry into criminal activity and where the battered woman's own agency has taken over." This is a particularly difficult question, yet it cannot erase those circumstances where battered women commit crimes in the company of or in fear of their batterers. It is a question which must be explored, not only by feminist legal theorists, but also by defense attorneys who have undertaken the onerous task of representing battered women defendants who commit crimes other than homicide or related offenses.

NOTES AND QUESTIONS

1. **Battered Women and Crime.** Shelby Moore describes some of the crimes battered women commit. Consider further data:

> [Beth] Richie's findings are further substantiated by a recent, in-depth study of women being held in the Cook County Jail of Chicago that revealed inmates had been victims of child abuse, sexual assault, and domestic violence at rates two and three times the national average. At the time of their arrest, the majority of the women were homeless, with just eight percent able to list a residence to which they could go upon their release. Many of the women also had histories of substance abuse and mental illness, often associated with their past abuse having gone untreated. Thirty-four percent of the women interviewed were sex workers, some to obtain food or shelter and others to satisfy their addictions. Those involved in prostitution had a greater likelihood of being intimate violence survivors and were subjected to higher rates of detention. Twenty-nine percent of the women had either been terminated from or denied public assistance within the twelve months preceding their arrests, with missing an appointment the most frequently cited reason for not being able to obtain government assistance. One arrestee said, "If I was getting the benefits that I needed, I wouldn't have been in the situation to commit the crimes." Sarah M.

Buel, *Effective Assistance of Counsel for Battered Women Defendants: A Normative Construct*, 26 HARV. WOMEN'S L.J. 217 (2003).

Buel notes that we often fail to make the link between sex work and domestic violence. She also notes that Latina and African–American women are disproportionately prosecuted for drug offenses, prostitution, theft, and the failure to protect their children.

Think back to Chapter Three and the relationship between poverty, racism, and domestic violence. More than 180,000 women are incarcerated in prisons and local jail cells. Between 1990 and 2005, the number of women in prison has more than doubled. African–American and Latina women are incarcerated at a disproportionate rate. Of those women who are incarcerated, 80% are mothers. What do you think the link is between domestic violence and these data? Is the rate of domestic violence among those communities in poverty one of the reasons so many women are now being incarcerated?

2. **Why Battering May be Relevant.** One of the primary reasons that the link between women's criminality and domestic violence is often missed is that defense attorneys do not regularly screen for it, and, even when they do, they aren't always sure how prior abuse is relevant to any possible defenses. What do you think attorneys should ask their clients? How might evidence of abuse be legally relevant in a drug charge, for example? A perfect or imperfect defense? The mitigation of a sentence?

Duress

Most commonly, the defense to which battering is relevant is duress, because duress expresses the law's understanding that a defendant should not, as a general matter, be responsible for an action that is not chosen, but is coerced. The law has traditionally defined duress very narrowly. At present, the legal doctrine of duress may not, even with the introduction of expert testimony, capture the full range of coercive behaviors that prompt abused women to crime. Second, even before we introduce the complexities of battering and expert testimony, there is disagreement about the precise nature of the duress defense; whether it "wipes the slate clean" by depriving the defendant of the intent that is a necessary element of the crime, or whether instead it acts as an "affirmative defense," justifying or excusing the conduct even though it is criminal. If the question is whether duress can eliminate intent, the answer may depend on what level of intent is required for the crime in question. If we are choosing between duress as justifying criminal conduct, and duress as excusing criminal conduct, what is the distinction? Consider the following article.

Beth I.Z. Boland
Battered Women Who Act Under Duress
28 NEW ENG. L.REV. 603 (1994).

To establish a *prima facie* defense of duress under the common law, the defendant charged with a crime other than murder must introduce evidence sufficient to prove that she reasonably believed the only way to avoid imminent death or serious bodily injury to herself or another person was to engage in criminal conduct, and that the unlawful threat legally "caused" her to engage in that conduct. As in claims of self-defense, duress at common law requires a "present, immediate and impending threat" of such a nature as to induce a well-founded fear of death or serious bodily injury. Similarly, a claim of duress requires that the circumstances be such that the actor has no reasonable chance of escape.

A significant minority of states have adopted in whole or in substantial part the Model Penal Code (MPC) definition of duress, which applies to a defendant who committed a crime "because he was coerced to do so by the use of, or a threat to use, unlawful force ... that a person of reasonable firmness in his situation would have been unable to resist." The MPC differs from the common-law rule in several key respects: (1) it eliminates the requirement of imminency; (2) it eliminates the requirement of deadly force; (3) it is available as a defense even to homicide; and (4) it covers cases where the defendant was "brainwashed" upon the coercer's *prior* use of force.

Scholars have also debated whether duress acts as an excuse or as a justification for otherwise criminal activity. If considered a justification, the defense's success depends upon whether the harm avoided (i.e., the harm threatened by the batterer) is greater than the harm committed (i.e., the criminal activity). If seen as an excuse, the defendant ostensibly need only show that her free will was overcome such that she was not acting voluntarily, regardless of the heinousness of the crime committed while under duress.

Whether utilizing the common law or the MPC standard, or whether viewing duress as an excuse or as a justification, in each case the defendant's credibility and her state of mind—including whether she honestly and reasonably believed she was in imminent danger from her batterer—will be placed directly before the jury. In addition, the jurors must also make a moral judgment regarding the defendant's blameworthiness, whether in the context of determining that the threats "caused" the criminal activity (under the common law), or whether the defendant maintained "reasonable firmness" in the face of the threats (under the MPC).

In any event, evidence of past abuse should be relevant and admissible on the issues of the defendant's state of mind and her credibility in order to allow the jury to make a reasoned and informed decision about the defendant's culpability. In fact, the inquiry into the defendant's apprehension of danger in the context of a duress claim is virtually identical to that used for self-defense. A woman who views her circumstances through the eyes of one who has already suffered abuse at the hands of the coercer may see imminent danger even though some time may pass between the threat and her subsequent criminal act, and even though others may see no serious threat at all. There is no reason why the defendant's perception, altered through a cycle of battering, of the imminence of the threat should be any less informative in a case of coerced conduct than where the defendant acted in self-defense. And, in the same way that evidence of past abuse may affect the jury's perception of the defendant's credibility in cases of self-defense, so, too, does it apply in duress cases.

Finally, evidence of past abuse is relevant in assessing the blameworthiness of the defendant's decision to engage in criminal activity rather than to risk the physical abuse she faces. As noted above, the defendant's precise mental state at the hands of her coercer can be viewed in one of two ways: either the defendant's free will was overcome by the threat of harm to her, so that she had no criminal intent, or she voluntarily acted to avoid what she perceived to be the lesser of two evils (i.e., committing the unlawful act versus being beaten), so that she should be excused from criminal culpability. In either event, the relevance of evidence of past abuse seems clear.

In the former inquiry, the strength of the defendant's will in the face of her batterer's threats is in large part a function of the level of abuse— and particularly the level of physical and psychological abuse—that she suffered in the past. Expert testimony regarding the effect of a seemingly minimal level of threats upon a woman who has been "beaten down" over long periods of time would undoubtedly go far in educating the jury as to the point at which the defendant's will may be overcome. Thus, to the extent the defendant can show, through her own testimony and/or that of an expert, that her ability to resist the batterer was precipitously low to begin with, the greater the chances are that the jury will conclude that it was overcome by the particular threats at issue....

2. Proportionality and Fault—The Lack of an "In–Kind" Response to the Batterer's Threats, and the "Innocent Victim" Problem

In the case of self-defense, proportionality is maintained by the requirement that lethal force can only be used when one is threatened with like force, and only against the person initially making such a threat. When translated to the defense of duress, however, the equation changes dramatically: not only is the threat of physical force not always met with physical force in return, but the defendant's activities are directed away from the batterer and onto an innocent third party. The question then becomes whether the admission of evidence of past abuse to support a claim of duress unfairly shifts the balance on behalf of the defendant further than is desirable.

The beauty and simplicity of a self-defense claim lies in the apparent symmetry with which the defendant responds to the threat presented to her: the defendant is threatened by her batterer with physical force and responds directly in kind against her batterer with physical force. As such, self-defense appears to maintain the boundaries of communication and interaction within the relationship: the woman injures her batterer, and her response travels in the same medium and in the same direction as the threat.

By contrast, a defendant claiming duress requests forgiveness for an act (which may or may not involve physical violence) against an innocent third party.... If the jury accepts the reasonableness of the defendant's trade-off, it must also conclude that it was reasonable for her to put her self-interest ahead of that of an innocent third party, and to do so in a way that bears little direct relation to the threat she perceives to herself. Thus, duress on the surface raises far more troubling questions of proportionality and fault for the jury....

NOTES AND QUESTIONS

1. **Model Penal Code.** Model Penal Code § 2.09 reads, in relevant part, as follows:

> (1) It is an affirmative defense that the actor engaged in the conduct charged to constitute an offense because he was coerced to do so by the use of, or a threat to use, unlawful force against his person or the person of another, which a person of reasonable firmness in his situation would have been unable to resist.

> (2) The defense provided by this Section is unavailable if the actor recklessly placed himself in a situation in which it was probable that he would be subjected to duress. The defense is also unavailable if he was negligent in placing himself in such a situation, whenever negligence suffices to establish culpability for the offense charged.

2. **Common Law.** At common law, a wife who could show that her husband commanded her to commit a crime was entitled to a presumption of duress. The modern view, embraced by the Model Penal Code, is that coercion of a wife by a husband should be treated no differently than coercion in any other situation. Model Penal Code § 2.09(3). Some jurisdictions follow the lead of the Model Penal Code in accepting threats against a person other than the defendant as part of a duress claim, especially family members.

3. **Relevance of Expert Testimony in Duress Cases.** In the next case, a California appeals court considered the relevance of expert testimony about battered women's experiences to a duress defense, and determined that defense counsel's failure to offer such testimony amounted to ineffective assistance of counsel. As you read it, focus on the court's reasoning in light of self-defense claims.

People v. Romero

Court of Appeal of California, Second Appellate District, 1992.
13 Cal.Rptr.2d 332.

Debra Romero and Terrance Romero were both charged with one count of second degree robbery and four counts of attempted robbery. Debra's defense was duress. She admitted the crimes but claimed she participated because she was afraid Terrance would kill her if she didn't do as he demanded. The jury apparently didn't believe Debra and she was convicted as charged. She now petitions for a writ of habeas corpus, contending her lawyer was ineffective because he failed to present expert testimony explaining Battered Woman Syndrome. We agree.

FACTS

Debra and Terrance are not married but they began living together (with Terrance's two minor children and his father) in March 1989. About six weeks after Debra moved in, Terrance began hitting her if she didn't get money when he told her to do so (they are both cocaine addicts and he needed the money to support his habit) and, from that point on, he hit her "almost every day." Debra left Terrance on several occasions but he would always find her and persuade her to return. When he became angry, he would rip screens off windows, throw things out of windows and, when she would try to leave, he would threaten her, telling her that he would kill her and that, "If I can't have you, nobody else can." At one point, Debra's father obtained a restraining order against Terrance because he had been throwing things through her father's windows. On another occasion, Debra was hospitalized after she attempted to jump through a window to get away from Terrance. The window fell on her and she was badly cut (she required 23 stitches). Debra did not tell the police about Terrance's beatings.

[The court then outlined four prior instances of robbery.]

On July 23, 1989, James Stratton was stopped at a light on Pacific Coast Highway when Debra approached the passenger side of his van and said she had been beaten and robbed. She appeared hysterical and had her hand over her left eye. She tried the door handle, found it was locked, then reached through the open window, opened the door, and got into the van. Her face was bruised and puffy and she looked as though she had been hit. At that point, Terrance drove up on the left side of Stratton's van and pointed a gun at Stratton. Debra grabbed the key to turn off Stratton's engine and Terrance told Stratton to give his money to Debra. Debra said, "He has a gun. Give him all the money." Stratton panicked, knocked Debra's hand off the ignition key and drove off, followed by Terrance. Debra screamed at him, pleading to be let out of the car. Stratton eventually stopped, when he could no longer see Terrance in his rear view mirror, and Debra got out.[9] Debra and Terrance were charged with one count of second degree robbery and four counts of attempted robbery. Enhancement allegations charged Terrance with the personal use of a handgun and Debra with participating in crimes in which a principal was armed with a handgun. They both pleaded not guilty and were able to make bail. While they were awaiting trial, Debra continued to see Terrance and he continued to beat her.

At trial, Debra testified to the facts stated above, agreeing with the victims' testimony and simply adding her explanation for why she did what she did. Terrance also testified on his own behalf, telling the jury that he met Debra when he picked her up on a street corner and offered her money for sex and that she moved in with him about a year later. Not withstanding that he was identified by all [the] victims (not to mention Debra's testimony), Terrance said he was not involved in any of the incidents and

---

9. The officer who arrested Debra that night testified that she appeared to have been beaten. Although he could not recall prior contacts with her, his report for July 23 notes that "on each of these occasions and during this arrest, [Debra] had showed [sic] severe beating on her face with her eyes swollen and was bruising much [sic] on her face."

never saw any of the victims prior to the court proceedings. Terrance also testified that he is "very much in love" with Debra, he has never threatened her and he has never hit her. On the night she tried to jump out the window, it was because he was trying to stop her from going out to buy more cocaine. Debra wrote to him while he was incarcerated and her letters expressed her love.

Debra was convicted of all five charges....

DISCUSSION

Debra contends she was denied the effective assistance of counsel because her trial attorney failed to present expert testimony about Battered Woman Syndrome to corroborate her duress defense. As indicated at the outset, we agree....

If "battered women's syndrome" testimony is relevant to credibility when a woman kills her batterer, it is a fortiori relevant to her credibility when she participates in robberies at her batterer's insistence....[10] Such evidence would have assisted the jury in objectively analyzing [Debra's] claim of [duress] by dispelling many of the commonly held misconceptions about battered women. As the record reflects, the prosecutor [and Terrance] exploited several of these misconceptions in urging the jury to reject [Debra's duress] claim....

" 'Expert testimony on the battered woman syndrome would help dispel the ordinary lay person's perception that a woman in a battering relationship is free to leave at any time. The expert evidence would counter any 'common sense' conclusions by the jury that if the beatings were really that bad the woman would have left her [batterer] much earlier. Popular misconceptions about battered women would be put to rest, including the beliefs the women are masochistic and enjoy the beatings and that they intentionally provoke their [batterers] into fits of rage.' "

As relevant to this case, the defense of duress is the same as self-defense—in both, the key issue is whether the defendant reasonably and honestly believed she was in imminent danger of great bodily harm or death. To establish duress, a defendant must raise a reasonable doubt that she acted in the exercise of her free will ... by showing she committed the charged crime under threats or menaces sufficient to create a good faith, objectively reasonable belief that there was an imminent threat of danger

---

10. Debra was tried in 1990. In 1991, the Legislature added section 1107 to the Evidence Code, to provide that, "[i]n a criminal action, expert testimony is admissible by either the prosecution or the defense regarding battered women's syndrome, including the physical, emotional, or mental effects upon the beliefs, perceptions, or behavior of victims of domestic violence, except when offered against a criminal defendant to prove the occurrence of the act or acts of abuse which form the basis of the criminal charge." (Stats. 1991, ch. 812, § 1.) There is nothing in the language of the statute suggesting a legislative intent to limit its application to cases involving a claim of self-defense. To the contrary, section 1107 appears to make expert testimony admissible in *any* criminal case, regardless of the charges or defenses, except a case in which the batterer is prosecuted for his acts of abuse and the evidence is offered to prove that he committed those acts.

to her life. Fear of great bodily harm is sufficient and, except as to homicide, duress is available as a defense to any crime. . . .

With the two defenses thus juxtaposed, it is clear that a rule permitting expert testimony about BWS in a self-defense case must necessarily permit it in a case where duress is claimed as a defense. In both cases, the evidence is relevant to the woman's credibility and to support her testimony that she entertained a good faith objectively reasonable and honest belief that her act was necessary to prevent an imminent threat of greater harm. . . .

. . . This is not a case in which there can be any doubt about whether trial counsel's failure to conduct a careful investigation withdrew an obviously crucial defense from his client's case. Berger admitted to Anyon that he recognized the possibility that Debra suffered from BWS and considered offering BWS evidence to support Debra's duress defense. Indeed, he obtained the name of a BWS expert who could evaluate Debra and testify at trial. But that's all he did. When he was unable to reach the expert before trial, he simply dropped the ball and his failure to provide a declaration explaining his conduct (notwithstanding several requests from Anyon) permits us to presume the absence of a satisfactory explanation. . . . At the risk of understating the obvious, we conclude that Berger neither carefully nor sufficiently investigated an obviously crucial defense. . . . We agree with Debra that there is a reasonable probability that presentation of expert testimony about BWS would have bolstered her credibility and persuaded the jury to accept the defense of duress. . . .

Debra admitted that she committed all of the charged offenses and her sole defense was duress. Although substantial evidence established that Debra was frequently and severely beaten by Terrance and that he threatened her with further harm and even death if she left or did not do what he wanted her to do . . . there was no mention at all of BWS. There was no explanation for Debra's failure simply to walk away from Terrance or for her continued participation in the robberies or for her apparently inconsistent behavior after they were arrested, when she wrote loving letters to him while he was still incarcerated.

Evidence of BWS would have explained a behavior pattern that might otherwise (and obviously did) appear unreasonable to the jurors. Evidence of BWS not only explains how a battered woman might think, react, or behave, it also places the behavior in an understandable light. "One of the most commonly made argument[s] by prosecutors in urging rejection of a defense is that the person's behavior is inconsistent with that defense. . . . Jurors are told to evaluate and react to evidence by what a reasonable person would do or not do. Frequently, conduct appears unreasonable to those who have not been exposed to the same circumstances. . . . It is only natural that people might speculate as to how they would react and yet be totally wrong about how most people in fact react."

That is precisely what happened here. The prosecutor argued that, assuming Debra wasn't lying about the whole thing, she could have run away and that she was not really in any imminent danger. An expert could have helped persuade the jury that Debra was not lying and also could have explained that battered women are afraid to run away because they are convinced their batterers will find them and beat them again or even kill them. An expert could have explained that Terrance's threat—"If I can't have you, nobody else can"—is the threat most commonly made by battering males. An expert could have explained a battered woman's heightened awareness of danger and the jury could have considered that circumstance in deciding whether Debra believed she was in imminent danger. And Terrance's lawyer's suggestion that Debra would have reported the beatings to the police or to her family if, in fact, they had really occurred could have been met with an expert's explanation that only about one in ten incidents of battering are reported because shame and fear of reprisals frequently keep battered women from calling the police. . . .

Expert testimony explaining BWS would have given the jurors an ability to understand why a battered woman acts as she does and, with that information, the jury could have fairly decided the ultimate questions about whether Debra was, in fact, suffering from BWS and, if so, whether she was acting under duress. Since the presentation of BWS evidence would have given Debra's attorney something affirmative to argue while at the same time eliminating much of the prosecutor's ability to attack her defense, the conclusion is unavoidable that the failure to present this evidence was prejudicial. . . .

[*The California Supreme Court reversed the appeal court's decision in* Romero, *but on grounds unrelated to the admission of expert testimony, in* People v. Romero, *8 Cal. 4th 728, 883 P.2d 388 (Cal. 1994).*]

NOTES AND QUESTIONS

1. **Evidence of Battering in Other Cases.** Other courts have not followed the reasoning in *Romero.* In *United States v. Johnson*, 956 F.2d 894 (9th Cir. 1992), for example, female defendants appealed their convictions of low-level activity in a drug ring operated by a "violent drug lord." The defendants offered evidence that they were battered by their intimate partners, and that their response of acquiescence to the threats and abuse of the drug lord was therefore reasonable. The Ninth Circuit held that evidence of battering was not relevant to duress, because the "reasonable firmness" test imposed an objective standard. The evidence was considered relevant, however, under the Federal Sentencing Guidelines, for a downward departure at sentencing. The court therefore remanded the women's cases for reconsideration of their sentences.

In *United States v. Willis*, 38 F.3d 170 (5th Cir. 1994), the Fifth Circuit held that evidence of battering was not relevant to a duress defense. Kathy Evelyn Willis appealed her conviction for carrying a firearm during and in relation to the commission of a drug trafficking crime, based on the trial court's exclusion of expert testimony on battering she offered at trial as relevant to her defense of duress, on an erroneous jury instruction on duress, and on ineffective assistance of counsel.

The court laid out the four traditional common law requirements for a complete duress defense: (i) present, imminent, and impending threat inducing a well-grounded apprehension of death or great bodily injury, (ii) that the defendant did not recklessly or negligently place herself in a situation where she was likely to be coerced into criminal acts, (iii) that the defendant had no opportunity to escape or other reasonable opportunity to avoid the threatened harm, and (iv) a direct causal relationship between the criminal act and the avoidance of the threatened harm. Although the court articulated each requirement of the law of duress as though it were at least to some degree a subjective test, it then went on to say that this formulation of the law of duress is "in harmony with the analysis of duress in the Model Penal Code which ... [states that] 'a person of reasonable firmness in his [or her] situation would have been unable to resist.'" The court then concluded, citing *Johnson*, that evidence of battering is not relevant to the objective test for the law of duress:

> [e]vidence that the defendant is suffering from the battered woman's syndrome is inherently subjective ... such evidence is usually consulted to explain why this particular defendant succumbed when a reasonable person without a background of being battered might not have. Specifically, battered woman's syndrome evidence seeks to establish that, because of her psychological condition, the defendant is unusually susceptible to the coercion.

More recently, in *United States v. Dixon*, 413 F.3d 520 (5th Cir. 2005), discussed in Chapter Five, as well as later in this Chapter, the Fifth Circuit refused to admit expert testimony in a case in which the defendant bought a handgun, allegedly at the command of her abusive boyfriend. The court reasoned that expert testimony only would have explained the defendant's subjective vulnerability to coercion. It would not have explained why her behavior was reasonable. At the trial both defendant and her daughters testified as to the abuse, but absent expert testimony, it is unclear whether the jury believed the defendant or whether, despite believing that she was abused, did not believe that she acted reasonably. The Supreme Court did not review the Fifth Circuit's decision on this issue.

Duress cases involving battered women also appear at the state level. In some states, evidence of battering has been held to be relevant to duress. It would seem that battered women might fare better in states that have, following the Model Penal Code, eliminated the requirement that the defendant be subject to an "imminent" threat. However, in Pennsylvania, the absence of an imminence requirement persuaded at least one court that testimony about battering was entirely irrelevant to a duress defense. In *Commonwealth v. Ely*, 578 A.2d 540 (Pa. Super. Ct.1990) a developmentally disabled woman appealed her conviction in a bench trial of endangering the welfare of children, indecent assault, indecent exposure, incest, and corruption of minors, based on ineffective assistance of counsel. The court, in denying her appeal, noted that:

> the controversial aspect of the battered woman's syndrome theory of self-defense case is not controversial in duress cases. The stumbling block in battered woman's syndrome self-defense cases is the legislative requirement that there be an immediate or imminent threat of serious bodily injury when the deadly force was used; the battered

woman's syndrome theory of self-defense (even if accepted) merely establishes that the accused reasonably perceived an immediate or imminent threat which did not actually exist ... Immediacy or imminence is not a requirement of duress, as it is of self-defense. Consequently, acceptance of the battered woman's syndrome theory of self-defense in Pennsylvania would add little, if anything, to the existing law that the existence of duress is to be determined by considering whether under the totality of the circumstances ... the threat ... or use of force was such that a person of reasonable firmness would have been unable to resist.

Furthermore, many states have limited the admissibility of expert testimony on battering by statute. Some states, such as Ohio and Missouri, only allow such testimony in certain instances, removing from the trial judge the discretion to admit such evidence on a case-by-case basis. In these cases, the statutes that we discussed earlier in the chapter often limit such evidence only in cases involving self-defense, thereby effectively precluding such evidence in duress cases. Other states, such as Massachusetts, allow expert testimony in cases "charging the use of force against another where the issue of defense of self or another, defense of duress or coercion, or accidental harm is asserted." Mass. Ann. Laws ch. 233, § 23F (Law Co-op. 2000).

2. **The Distinction between Self–Defense and Duress.** In *Romero*, the court argues that if expert testimony on battering is admissible in self-defense cases, it must also be admissible in duress cases. Yet, many courts have rejected this view. Is this because of the differences in legal doctrine, or an unstated policy judgment that women can act in self-defense against their abusers because this seems just, but that their inability to resist their abuser should not harm third parties? Consider one commentator's analysis:

> Like the standard for duress, the traditional approach to self-defense also requires an objective standard, asking whether a reasonable person would have perceived a threat. Accordingly, an advocate of the objective-subjective distinction as a basis for rejecting battered woman syndrome evidence in the duress context should conclude, as I do, that the evidence is equally inapplicable to an objective standard of self-defense. Nevertheless, when a battered woman kills her batterer and claims self-defense, courts have permitted evidence of the battered woman syndrome not only to support the defendant's subjective perception of her situation, but also to determine the objective reasonableness of her perception and response.

With no convincing basis upon which to admit battered woman syndrome evidence in the self-defense context and exclude it in the duress context, courts that draw this distinction ultimately appear satisfied with the unexplained, policy-based conclusion that the extension of such evidence to the duress context would be "unwise." ...

If we truly believed that the battered women syndrome accurately described the characteristics of domestic violence victims, the discrepancy between the acceptance of the syndrome in the self-defense and duress contexts is unexplainable. One might argue that the reluctance to expand the defense of duress is attributable to the moral ambivalence already surrounding the traditional scope of the defense. Because the duress doctrine excuses crimes committed against innocent third parties, it may simply be a less favored defense generally than self-defense. For example, the common law rule that duress could never excuse an intentional homicide certainly reflects a preference for defensive force over coerced force. However, the preferential treatment of the justification of self-defense over the excuse of duress explains only the ultimate result in these cases, i.e., that battered women who kill in self-defense are shown more sympathy and are more likely to get requested jury instructions, be acquitted, or successfully appeal their convictions than battered women who act under duress against third parties. This preference does not explain the differential acceptance of the theory of battered woman syndrome itself in the two contexts. Alafair S. Burke, *Rational Actors, Self–Defense, & Duress: Making Sense Not Syndromes Out of the Battered Woman,* 81 N.C.L.Rev. 211 (2002).

Do you agree that courts admit evidence in one context but not another because they are result oriented? Do you think this distinction undermines the over-all reliability of evidence on battering? Is there an alternative approach courts could take? Part of the distinction between self-defense and duress is the requirement of imminence. Could it be that society insists on holding battered women morally culpable for their actions unless the threat to themselves or their children is imminent?

3. **Aiding and Abetting a Boyfriend.** Another case that raises the more difficult question of when a woman's behavior should be excused is *Dunn v. Roberts*, excerpted below. Lisa Dunn was convicted of aiding and abetting her former boyfriend, Daniel Remeta, in a crime spree that included kidnapping, murder, and armed robbery. After consistently high academic performance in high school, Lisa began to have troubles at home and in school at the age of 15, including problems with drugs and alcohol. At 17, she left home and was raped in Florida. Because she did not cooperate with the district attorney, her rapists were never prosecuted. Shortly after returning home to a stormy relationship with her parents, she met Remeta. When he decided to jump bail for a charge of breaking into a car, she went with him to Florida, taking with her one of her father's guns.

Dunn v. Roberts

Tenth Circuit Court of Appeals, 1992.
963 F.2d 308.

■ McKay, Chief Judge.

The sole question we address is whether the state trial court denied Petitioner due process when it refused Petitioner's request for funds to employ a psychiatric expert to assist in her defense.

Petitioner is an inmate at the Kansas Correctional Institute. She was convicted as an aider and abettor in 1985 of two counts of felony murder, two counts of aggravated kidnaping, one count of aggravated battery on a law enforcement officer, one count of aggravated robbery, and one count of aggravated battery....

Petitioner was eighteen years old when she met Daniel Remeta in Michigan in December of 1984. In January of 1985, Daniel Remeta, Petitioner, and another individual decided to travel to Florida. Before leaving Michigan, Petitioner took a .357 magnum pistol from her father's gun collection at Daniel Remeta's request.

According to Petitioner's trial testimony, she first became aware of Daniel Remeta's prison record and cruel nature during the drive to Florida. Petitioner stated that when she expressed a desire to return home to Michigan, Daniel Remeta threatened her with the .357 magnum. Petitioner testified that, as the trio continued their travels from Florida to Kansas, Daniel Remeta repeatedly threatened to harm Petitioner or her family if she left him. Daniel Remeta testified that Petitioner had no choice regarding her whereabouts and affirmed that he would have carried out his threats had Petitioner attempted to leave him. Petitioner testified further that Daniel Remeta's erratic and violent behavior intensified and he exerted more and more control over her as the trip continued.

On February 13, 1985, the trio picked up a hitchhiker north of Wichita, Kansas. Shortly thereafter, Daniel Remeta verbally threatened the hitchhiker and fired shots out of the car window. Near Levant, Kansas, the group was stopped by a sheriff driving a patrol car. Daniel Remeta exited his vehicle and shot the sheriff a number of times.

The group then drove to a grain elevator in Levant. At the grain elevator, Daniel Remeta forced two individuals into the back of a pickup truck at gunpoint. Daniel Remeta also shot and wounded another individual who was attempting to call the police. The group then drove in the pickup truck to a point near Colby, Kansas. Here Daniel Remeta shot the two hostages with the .357 magnum and left their bodies by the side of the road. Shortly thereafter, the group was captured after a gun battle. Petitioner was charged with a number of crimes relating to the events discussed above.

Prior to trial, Petitioner moved the court ... for $1800 to employ a psychological expert to assist in developing her defense. At the hearing, Petitioner's counsel presented the testimony of a jail chaplain who had spent approximately fourteen hours talking with Petitioner. The chaplain testified that Petitioner had told him that Daniel Remeta had threatened her with a gun, had choked her and had repeatedly threatened to kill her family if she left him or didn't do what he wanted her to do....

Petitioner's counsel then discussed statements Daniel Remeta had made to the media regarding his abusive treatment of Petitioner. Petitioner's counsel related Daniel Remeta's admissions that he had threatened to kill Petitioner many times, that he had subjected her to Russian Roulette with the .357 magnum, and that he had advised her that her family or other innocent parties would be in danger if she contemplated leaving him....

Petitioner's counsel stated that he had discussed the case with both a Michigan psychologist who had evaluated Daniel Remeta and a forensic psychiatrist from the Menninger Foundation.... Counsel said that both had suggested he investigate whether Petitioner suffered from battered woman's syndrome and dissociative response when she was with Daniel Remeta. Counsel related his belief that such evidence was relevant to Petitioner's mental state at the time the crimes were committed.... He explained that such evidence would be important because the state's case cast Petitioner as an aider and abettor of Daniel Remeta's crimes and that specific intent to assist, rather than mere presence, was a necessary element of the crime of aiding and abetting.... Counsel stated that he was not competent to investigate and develop such evidence....

In requesting the funds, Petitioner's counsel explicitly stated that the assistance sought did not relate to the defense of compulsion but, rather, lack of intent....

The trial court rejected Petitioner's request, stating basically that Petitioner would have to convince the jury of her lack of intent without the assistance of an expert.... Petitioner renewed her request twice more, but the trial court denied each motion.

At trial, witnesses for the state and the defense offered conflicting evidence concerning Petitioner's participation in the crimes. None of the witnesses identified Petitioner as having a weapon or personally engaging in violence at any time. The only evidence offered of any direct participation by Petitioner was the testimony of four witnesses who said they saw Petitioner or someone with Petitioner's hair color driving the pickup after the elevator robbery. Daniel Remeta, the hitchhiker, and Petitioner all testified that Petitioner did not drive the truck. Another witness testified that she had seen another member of the group driving the truck. Thus, the State's principal arguments in support if its aiding and abetting theory relied heavily on Petitioner's presence with Daniel Remeta at the time the crimes were committed.

The jury found Petitioner guilty of aiding and abetting Daniel Remeta's crimes ... Petitioner was originally sentenced to four consecutive terms of 15 years to life. These terms were later modified to be served concurrently....

The record indicates that the state trial judge was made aware in general terms of Daniel Remeta's threats against and physical abuse of Petitioner and that evidence of battered woman's syndrome would likely have bearing on whether Petitioner had the state of mind necessary to commit the crime of aiding and abetting. Petitioner's counsel explained clearly that the state's case against Petitioner rested heavily on an aiding and abetting theory; that specific intent to assist, rather than mere presence, is a necessary element of the crime of aiding and abetting; that Petitioner's case rested on her ability to show that she lacked the requisite intent; and that Petitioner could not develop an effective rebuttal of that element without the assistance of an expert....

... Because specific intent is an essential element of the offense for which Petitioner was tried, the state was required to prove beyond a reasonable doubt that Petitioner entertained a specific mental objective to assist Daniel Remeta in committing the crimes. If the jury found that Petitioner, for any reason, did not entertain that particular mental state, it could not convict Petitioner of that crime. Thus, Petitioner's mental condition was squarely at issue in this case.

The state's theory of aiding and abetting rested heavily on Petitioner's presence with Daniel Remeta at the time the crimes were committed. From Petitioner's presence, the jury was asked to infer that Petitioner specifically intended to participate in Daniel Remeta's crimes. In light of the state's overwhelming emphasis on Petitioner's presence, it is clear that an expert would have aided Petitioner in her defense by supporting her assertion that she did not have the required specific intent.

The mystery in this case, as in all battered woman cases, is why Petitioner remained with Daniel Remeta despite repeated abuse. An expert could have explained to the jury the nature of battered woman's syndrome and given an opinion on whether Petitioner suffered from the syndrome. This is an area where expert opinion is particularly useful and oftentimes necessary to interpret for the jury a situation beyond average experience and common understanding. The effect of the expert testimony would be to explain why a defendant suffering from the battered woman syndrome wouldn't leave her batterer. ... Thus, such evidence could have provided an alternative reason for Petitioner's continued presence with Daniel Remeta. We agree with the District Court that this evidence should have been "considered by the jury in evaluating whether Petitioner had the requisite intent to participate in the crimes of which she was charged." This would not be the first case in which psychiatric testimony was considered crucial to the issue of intent. ... By refusing Petitioner the funds for expert assistance, the state trial court effectively prohibited Petitioner from presenting relevant information directly bearing on an essential element of the crime of which she was convicted. Without that assistance, Petitioner was deprived of the fair trial due process demands. ...

For the foregoing reasons, we conclude that Petitioner is entitled to a new trial with the assistance of an expert in the preparation and presentation of her defense.

NOTES AND QUESTIONS

1. **Funds for Expert Witnesses.** On the specific issue before the court in *Dunn*—whether the trial court should have provided funding for an expert to testify—the Tenth Circuit's decision is unusual. In at least five states—Georgia, Kansas, Mississippi, Montana and Tennessee—state courts have determined that no violation of due process involved resulted from the denial of such funds. It was the Kansas decision that was successfully appealed in *Dunn*. Ironically, Tennessee has also found counsel ineffective for not presenting expert testimony in battered women's cases, suggesting

a "Catch–22" when counsel cannot obtain funding for an indigent client to have the testimony to which they are entitled. *The Validity and Use of Evidence Concerning Battering and Its Effects in Criminal Trials,* REPORT RESPONDING TO SECTION 40507 OF THE VIOLENCE AGAINST WOMEN ACT, NCJ–160972, *Trend Analysis* (May 1996).

2. **Battering as Evidence to Negate Mens Rea.** Dunn's counsel argued that the testimony was relevant, not to a claim of duress, but to a claim of lack of intent. Why did the lawyer take that approach? Do you agree that the case is not one of duress? Why did the Kansas Supreme Court decide that Dunn was not entitled to raise a defense based on duress, or compulsion? What is the crime with which Lisa Dunn is charged, and what level of intent does it require? Did her counsel want to argue (a) that she was psychologically impaired, and incapable of forming the necessary intent, or (b) that she participated in her abuser's crime spree only under compulsion, or (c) that the testimony would simply suggest that she had no intent to assist or encourage him, but that there was an alternative explanation for her accompanying him? What consequences might flow from choosing one or another of these theories?

3. **Burden of Proof in Duress Cases.** The following case, *Dixon v. United States,* examines the burden of proof in federal cases involving duress. We have looked at the Fifth Circuit decision in this case in Chapter Five, in which the court ruled expert testimony on battering was not relevant to the duress claim. The other issue in the case involved which party has the burden of proof. This was the only issue the United States Supreme Court addressed. As you read the case, consider why who bears the burden of proof might make a difference in the outcome of a case.

Dixon v. United States

United States Supreme Court, 2006.
548 U.S. ___, 126 S.Ct. 2437.

■ JUSTICE STEVENS delivered the opinion of the Court.

In January 2003, petitioner Keshia Dixon purchased multiple firearms at two gun shows, during the course of which she provided an incorrect address and falsely stated that she was not under indictment for a felony. As a result of these illegal acts, petitioner was indicted and convicted on one count of receiving a firearm while under indictment in violation of 18 U.S.C. § 922(n) and eight counts of making false statements in connection with the acquisition of a firearm in violation of § 922(a)(6). At trial, petitioner admitted that she knew she was under indictment when she made the purchases and that she knew doing so was a crime; her defense was that she acted under duress because her boyfriend threatened to kill her or hurt her daughters if she did not buy the guns for him.

Petitioner contends that the trial judge's instructions to the jury erroneously required her to prove duress by a preponderance of the evidence instead of requiring the Government to prove beyond a reasonable doubt that she did not act under duress. The Court of Appeals rejected petitioner's contention; given contrary treatment of the issue by other federal courts, we granted certiorari.

I

At trial, in her request for jury instructions on her defense of duress, petitioner contended that she "should have the burden of production, and then that the Government should be required to disprove beyond a reasonable doubt the duress." Petitioner admitted that this request was contrary to Fifth Circuit precedent, and the trial court, correctly finding itself bound by Circuit precedent, denied petitioner's request. Instead, the judge's instructions to the jury defined the elements of the duress defense and stated that petitioner has "the burden of proof to establish the defense of duress by a preponderance of the evidence."[11]

Petitioner argues here, as she did in the District Court and the Court of Appeals, that federal law requires the Government to bear the burden of disproving her defense beyond a reasonable doubt and that the trial court's erroneous instruction on this point entitles her to a new trial. There are two aspects to petitioner's argument in support of her proposed instruction that merit separate discussion. First, petitioner contends that her defense "controverted the *mens rea* required for conviction" and therefore that the Due Process Clause requires the Government to retain the burden of persuasion on that element. Second, petitioner argues that Fifth Circuit's rule is "contrary to modern common law."

II

The crimes for which petitioner was convicted require that she have acted "knowingly," § 922(a)(6), or "willfully." As we have explained, "unless the text of the statute dictates a different result, the term 'knowingly' merely requires proof of knowledge of the facts that constitute the offense." And the term "willfully" in § 924(a)(1)(D) requires a defendant to have "acted with knowledge that his conduct was unlawful." In this case, then, the Government bore the burden of proving beyond a reasonable doubt that petitioner knew she was making false statements in connection with the acquisition of firearms and that she knew she was breaking the law when she acquired a firearm while under indictment. Although the Government may have proved these elements in other ways, it clearly met its burden when petitioner testified that she knowingly committed certain acts—she put a false address on the forms she completed

---

11. There is no federal statute defining the elements of the duress defense. We have not specified the elements of the defense, and need not do so today. Instead, we presume the accuracy of the District Court's description of these elements: (1) The defendant was under an unlawful and imminent threat of such a nature as to induce a well-grounded apprehension of death or serious bodily injury; (2) the defendant had not recklessly or negligently placed herself in a situation in which it was probable that she would be forced to perform the criminal conduct; (3) the defendant had no reasonable, legal alternative to violating the law, that is, a chance both to refuse to perform the criminal act and also to avoid the threatened harm; and, (4) that a direct causal relationship may be reasonably anticipated between the criminal act and the avoidance of the threatened harm.

to purchase the firearms, falsely claimed that she was the actual buyer of the firearms, and falsely stated that she was not under indictment at the time of the purchase—and when she testified that she knew she was breaking the law when, as an individual under indictment at the time, she purchased a firearm.

Petitioner contends, however, that she cannot have formed the necessary *mens rea* for these crimes because she did not freely choose to commit the acts in question. But even if we assume that petitioner's will was overborne by the threats made against her and her daughters, she still *knew* that she was making false statements and *knew* that she was breaking the law by buying a firearm. The duress defense . . . may excuse conduct that would otherwise be punishable, but the existence of duress normally does not controvert any of the elements of the offense itself. . . . Like the defense of necessity, the defense of duress does not negate a defendant's criminal state of mind when the applicable offense requires a defendant to have acted knowingly or willfully; instead, it allows the defendant to "avoid liability . . . because coercive conditions or necessity negates a conclusion of guilt even though the necessary *mens rea* was present." . . .

IV

Congress can, if it chooses, enact a duress defense that places the burden on the Government to disprove duress beyond a reasonable doubt. In light of Congress' silence on the issue, however, it is up to the federal courts to effectuate the affirmative defense of duress as Congress "may have contemplated" it in an offense-specific context. In the context of the firearms offenses at issue—as will usually be the case, given the long-established common-law rule—we presume that Congress intended the petitioner to bear the burden of proving the defense of duress by a preponderance of the evidence. Accordingly, the judgment of the Court of Appeals is affirmed.

■ Justice Breyer, with whom Justice Souter joins, dissenting.

[S]everal factors favor placing the burden on the prosecution. For one thing, in certain respects the question of duress resembles that of *mens rea,* an issue that is always for the prosecution to prove beyond a reasonable doubt. The questions are not the same. The defendant's criminal activity here was voluntary; no external principle, such as the wind, propelled her when she acted. Moreover, her actions were intentional. Whether she wanted to buy the guns or not, and whether she wanted to lie while doing so or not, she decided to do these things and knew that she was doing them. Indeed, her action was willful in the sense that she knew that to do them was to break the law.

Nonetheless, where a defendant acts under duress, she lacks any semblance of a meaningful choice. In that sense her choice is not free. As Blackstone wrote, the criminal law punishes "abuse[s] of th[e] free will"; hence "it is highly just and equitable that a man should be excused for those acts, which are done through unavoidable force and compulsion."

And it is in this "force and compulsion," acting upon the will, that the resemblance to lack of *mens rea* lies. . . .

Further, while I concede the logic of the Government's practical argument—that defendants have superior access to the evidence—I remain uncertain of the argument's strength. After all, "[i]n every criminal case the defendant has at least an equal familiarity with the facts and in most a greater familiarity with them than the prosecution." And the strict contours of the duress defense, as well as the defendant's burden of production, already substantially narrow the circumstances under which the defense may be used. A defendant may find it difficult, for example, to show duress where the relevant conduct took place too long before the criminal act. That is because the defendant must show that he had no alternative to breaking the law. More important, the need to prove *mens rea* can easily present precisely the same practical difficulties of proof for the prosecutor. Suppose for example the defendant claims that an old lady told him that the white powder he transported across the border was medicine for her dying son.

It is particularly difficult to see a practical distinction between this affirmative defense and, say, self-defense. The Government says that the prosecution may "be unable to call the witness most likely to have information bearing on the point," namely, the defendant. But what is the difference in this respect between the defendant here, who says her boyfriend threatened to kill her, and a battered woman who says that she killed her husband in self-defense, where the husband's evidence is certainly unavailable Regardless, unless the defendant testifies, it could prove difficult to satisfy the defendant's burden of *production;* and, of course, once the defendant testifies, cross-examination is possible. . . .

For these reasons I believe that, in the absence of an indication of congressional intent to the contrary, federal criminal law should place the burden of persuasion in respect to the duress defense upon the prosecution, which, as is now common in respect to many affirmative defenses, it must prove beyond a reasonable doubt. With respect, I dissent.

NOTES AND QUESTIONS

1. **The Right to be Held Accountable for Crimes.** One of the criticisms of the duress defense is that it takes responsibility away from women for their own choices. For example, one could argue that Keshia Dixon made her own choices when helping her boyfriend and whether she had an "evil" will or not is materially irrelevant to the criminal law. Does it matter if those choices take place within the context of an abusive relationship? The early feminists at the Seneca Falls Convention in 1848 wrote a Declaration of Sentiments which included the following: "He has made her, morally, an irresponsible being, as she can commit many crimes with impunity, provided they be done in the presence of her husband." In 1848, had Dixon been married to her boyfriend, she would not have been morally or criminally culpable for her actions, something that America's first feminists found to be a violation of women's rights. Should women be held

accountable for their crimes even if they were committed under the influence of their partners? For a discussion of social ambivalence concerning this issue see Cheryl Hanna, *Everything Old is New Again: A Foreword to the Tenth Anniversary Edition of the Duke Journal of Gender Law, & Policy*, 10 DUKE J. GENDER L. & POL'Y (2003).

2. **Why the Burden of Proof Matters.** *Dixon* might at first seem to be about a case of legal technicalities, but, in fact, who bears the burden of persuasion can have enormous impact on whether defendants can prove that they acted under duress. Had the Court rejected the Fifth Circuit's minority rule and placed the burden of persuasion with the prosecution, it would make it much easier for a criminal defendant to prove duress. Once she introduces some evidence of duress (such as the testimony by *Dixon* and her daughters as to her boyfriend's abusive behavior), the prosecution would then have the ultimate responsibility of proving beyond a reasonable doubt that she did not act under duress. However, now, after *Dixon*, in Federal cases, she must persuade the jury she acted under duress— something that can be very difficult to do, especially if expert testimony on "battered women's syndrome" is disallowed.

There are some practical considerations to consider, as is illustrated in the amicus brief submitted by the National Clearinghouse for the Defense of Battered Women and the National Association of Criminal Defense Attorneys. They feared that there would be too many different standards for the jury to remember if the Court placed the burden on the defendant, as the defendant would have to prove by a preponderance of the evidence that duress did exist, while the government would have to prove beyond a reasonable doubt that the defendant met all the elements of the offense. The risk of the jury convicting the defendant based on the failure of defense evidence, as opposed to the strength of the government's case, is simply too great, and requires a single standard of beyond a reasonable doubt that the government must satisfy. See THE BRIEF OF THE NATIONAL ASSOCIATION OF CRIMINAL DEFENSE LAWYERS AND THE NATIONAL CLEARINGHOUSE FOR THE DEFENSE OF BATTERED WOMEN AS AMICI CURIAE IN SUPPORT OF PETITIONER.

In contrast, the government argued that the defendant will likely have more access to information supporting the duress defense. Many of the events that provide the basis for the duress claim occurred before the events that caused the government to become involved with the case, and thus it may be fairer to place the burden on the party with easier access to the necessary information. Second, in most cases involving a duress defense, the government will be unable to call as a witness the person most likely to have information about the events leading to the claim, the person alleged to have coerced the defendant into committing the illegal act. Because most of the coercive conduct involved in a duress defense constitutes a criminal defense, the person alleged to have made the threat will assert his Fifth Amendment right against self-incrimination. Once the person alleges his Fifth Amendment rights, the government will not be able to question him about the events surrounding the duress defense, making it nearly impossible for them to prove beyond a reasonable doubt that duress did not exist. Third, placing the burden on the defendant will prevent false or frivolous affirmative defenses such as duress. Since the duress defense excuses a defendant from criminal liability, the threat of fraudulent claims and the potential for abuse require courts to establish strict rules for its use, including requiring the defendant to prove that duress existed. Finally, requiring the government to prove that duress existed presents high social costs, as the reasonable doubt standard would overprotect defendants while jeopardizing important interests in punishing those who violate the law. See THE BRIEF FOR THE GOVERNMENT OF THE UNITED STATES.

Which arguments do you find most persuasive? Should it be Dixon's responsibility to prove to the jury that she acted under duress?

3. **Expert Testimony and African–American Defendants.** As noted above, Keshia Dixon wanted to introduce expert testimony to support her duress defense. Would such testimony have helped her or does our current conceptualization of battered women exclude African–American women and other minorities who do not embody the stereotypical battered woman? For a discussion of this issue see Linda Ammons, *Mules, Madonnas, Babies, Bathwater, Racial Imagery & Stereotypes: The African–American Woman and the Battered Woman Syndrome*, 1995 WIS. L.REV. 1003 (1995). Arguably, expert testimony might have helped bolster Dixon's credibility. Ammons also suggests that expert testimony might specifically address myths and stereotypes jurors might have about minority defendants in particular. This might have been very helpful to Dixon given that she already had a criminal record.

4. **Plea Bargaining and Battered Defendants.** Most criminal cases are disposed of by plea bargaining. Yet, as Peter Margulies notes, the current plea bargaining system may disadvantage battered defendants.

> Unfortunately, the current plea bargaining system forces survivor-defendants to accept inequitable consequences. For example, a survivor who, on behalf of the abuser, acts as a courier in a drug transaction can end up with a sentence of up to twenty-five years without a meaningful opportunity to mitigate punishment. In fact, survivors can end up with charges and sentences higher than those for their abusers, even when the abuser's culpability seems demonstrably greater. Survivors who kill their abusers in self-defense often receive sentences higher than those for abusers who kill. . . .
>
> The remedy for such problems requires leveraging the multilateral dimension of plea bargaining to help rather than harm survivor-defendants. In order to do this, four steps are crucial. First, the Federal Sentencing Guidelines should incorporate a new Domestic Violence Departure, which accords a defendant meaningful relief in her sentence upon a showing that an abuser-kingpin in a criminal enterprise has subjected her to a pattern of physical abuse. Second, prosecutors should have an affirmative duty to hand over to defense counsel any and all evidence of intimate abuse committed by a cooperating defendant against another defendant from the same criminal enterprise. Third, each prosecutor's office should have an official and public policy on plea bargaining and survivors of domestic violence. Fourth, courts

should liberalize opportunities for survivor-defendants to withdraw or collaterally attack pleas when such pleas stem from express or implied threats by an abuser-kingpin, a survivor's psychological denial of domestic violence, or defense counsel's failure to research, investigate or assert a defense or mitigation claim related to domestic violence issues. Peter Margulies, *Battered Bargaining: Domestic Violence and Plea Negotiation in the Criminal Justice System*, 11 S.CAL. REV. L. & WOMEN'S STUD. 153 (2001).

How might plea bargaining help battered defendants? Should there be a downward departure for battering, as Marguiles argues? Would such a system excuse the behavior of battered defendants or would it result it fairer outcomes? What about plea bargaining for batterers? Should past childhood abuse, for example, be a mitigating factor? At what point does determinism end and free will begin?

5. **Legislative Reform.** In *Dixon*, the Court suggests that Congress is always free to amend the law to be clear about which party bears the burden of persuasion. Congress could also authorize, for example, the admissibility of expert testimony in duress claims, or downward departures for battered defendants. Assume you are a Senator from your home state. What type of bill might you introduce to address some aspects of the current law you find troubling? What political issues do you think might arise when advocating for those changes?

C.   POST-CONVICTION RELIEF AND CLEMENCY

This final section addresses three ways in which defendants convicted of crimes can receive some post-conviction relief. We focus on three areas: ineffective assistance of counsel claims, parole, and clemency. Each of these options provides further opportunities for battered defendants to present information and evidence about the role domestic abuse played in their crimes.

Ineffective Assistance of Counsel

One avenue of post-conviction relief is claiming ineffective assistance of counsel. Elizabeth Schneider explains this legal remedy and its hurdles in the following excerpt.

Elizabeth M. Schneider
Battered Women and Feminist Lawmaking (2000)

Over the past several years, battered women defendants have initiated post-conviction efforts to claim ineffective assistance of counsel against lawyers who represented them at trial. These cases are notoriously difficult to win, for the standard for ineffectiveness set by the Supreme Court requires egregious error resulting in prejudice to the defendant; at trial the defendant has the burden of proof to show such error, and anything that may be characterized as a tactical decision by the trial attorney is non-reviewable.

Of the many claims of ineffective assistance of counsel that have been brought by battered women who have been convicted at trial, a majority tend to fall into the category of claimed attorney error that courts rarely review, particularly if they are based on an attorney's failure to interview possible defense witnesses, or to otherwise investigate sources of information which could possibly be helpful to the defense. Among cases involving battered women defendants where ineffective assistance of counsel claims have been successful, the most common ground appears to be faulty advice, either in the plea-bargaining process or regarding whether the defendant should testify. Courts have also found ineffective assistance based on the attorney's failure to adduce evidence or examine witnesses at trial. Generally, the attorney's failure in either of these areas has resulted in no evidence of battering being offered at trial from such sources as medical reports, lay witnesses, family members, or the defendant's own testimony, or in no expert testimony on battering being offered.

From the number of claims of ineffective assistance of counsel based on faulty advice regarding plea bargains or the defendant testifying, and on attorney failure to present evidence and testimony that could have assisted the jury to understand and eradicate the very same misconceptions apparently held by counsel, it is apparent that attorneys are susceptible to misconceptions about battered women. Cases involving claims of ineffective assistance based on counsel's failure to offer jury instructions on battering suggest that many attorneys lack knowledge about the particular complexities of representing battered women. Nevertheless, because many of the judges who rule on ineffective assistance of counsel claims also lack knowledge about domestic violence, and have not been sensitive to the complex issues of choice of defense and admission of evidence, they may not be particularly thoughtful or rigorous in evaluating these claims.

NOTES AND QUESTIONS

1. **Legal Issues in Ineffective Assistance of Counsel Cases.** The *Romero* case above has already introduced you to claims of ineffective assistance of counsel in the domestic violence context. The Sixth Amendment guarantees the right of criminal defendants "to have the assistance of counsel for [their] defence." U.S. Const. Am. VI. This right has been understood to function to "assure fairness in the adversary process." *U.S. v. Cronic*, 466 U.S. 648 (1984) [citing *U.S. v. Morrison*, 449 U.S. 361, 364 (1981)]. Thus, the rights of the accused have not been met where either interference by the state in the form of court orders or statutes, or the defense attorney's own actions or omissions, cause the trial process to lose "its character as a confrontation between adversaries." Since the function of the right to counsel is to "assure fairness in the adversary process," when a criminal defendant is not represented by her attorney in a manner that subjects the prosecution's case to the "crucible of meaningful adver-

sary testing," she has received ineffective assistance of counsel, and her Sixth Amendment rights have been violated. As Sarah Buel explains:

> [*Strickland v. Washington*, 466 U.S. 668 (1984)] provides a two-prong test for determining whether the effective assistance of counsel standard has been met. Bearing the burden of proof to reverse a conviction, the defendant must first establish that the lawyer's mistakes were serious enough to practically deny the Sixth Amendment right to counsel. The second prong requires the defendant to show that counsel's errors compromised the defense. Declining to provide much specificity in its guidelines, the Court stated only that counsel should afford "reasonably effective assistance," based on "prevailing professional norms." *Strickland* also cautioned that evenhanded review of a lawyer's conduct must avoid "the distorting effects of hindsight," thus protecting counsel from sanctions if the case strategy seemed sound at the time. Here, attorneys' unfamiliarity with domestic violence is highly problematic to the client because *Strickland* refuses to question critical decisions made by counsel without the benefit of essential information. Sarah M. Buel, *Effective Assistance of Counsel for Battered Women Defendants: A Normative Construct*, 26 HARV. WOMEN'S L.J. 217 (2003).

Parole

While states do not keep statistics on the number of women imprisoned for killing their abusers, current estimates place the number between 2,000 and 4,000. Most of these women will be eligible for parole at some point during their incarceration. Parole boards consider many factors in deciding whether to grant early release, including whether the detainee has been a model citizen, whether she is likely to re-offend, and what the views of the victims and their families are. If the parole board denies the request, judicial review is usually available, but courts will only overturn decisions that are arbitrary and unreasonable, or those which fail to follow statutory law. Prisoners may also challenge parole board decisions if they violate their constitutional rights under 42 U.S.C. § 1983.

The following case deals with one woman's petition to receive parole. As you read it, consider some of the obstacles facing women convicted of killing their abusers after they have been sentenced.

Kosmin v. New Jersey State Parole Board

New Jersey Superior Court, Appellate Division, 2003.
830 A.2d 914.

■ PRESSLER, P.J.A.D.

Kosmin pleaded guilty in 1994 to aggravated manslaughter ... Her parole eligibility date was December 27, 2001.

The gravamen of appellant's crimes, in which she was aided by her accomplice, her friend Tammy Molewicz, was the shooting murder of William Kelly and their attempt to cover up the crime by burning the car in which they had transported his body to the woods. Appellant's motive for the murder was undisputed. After many years of severe physical, psychological and sexual abuse by Kelly, with whom she lived during two different periods of her life and who had fathered her daughter, she had apparently concluded that only his death would free her and her daughter from him and from the terror to which he had reduced her life.

The fact of the abuse and its severity were acknowledged by the trial judge at sentencing. . . .

[The court then detailed the appellant's history and attempts to leave the abusive relationship with Kelly.]

According to the record before us, appellant has been a model prisoner since her incarceration. Not only had she been infraction-free for seven years, but she also availed herself of a wide variety of programs, including NA/AA. As the panel eventually noted, "Your parole records abound with certificates for participating in programs too numerous to mention in this notice. The Board panel has reviewed a bound set of documents entitled 'Institutional Program Certificates of Achievement and Recognition.' The Board Panel has also reviewed your Special Activities Reports and your Progress Report both outlining your program involvement."

More to the point, the psychological evaluation dated July 30, 2002, inexplicably eight months after her initial two-member panel hearing in November 2001, can only be regarded as inordinately supportive of release on parole. The report noted that appellant had no prior criminal history, that her institutional adjustment had been above average, that her interview behavior had been entirely appropriate and that she had been substance-free for nine years. The evaluation included the following clinical impression:

> She continues to present as an intelligent, articulate woman who has completed numerous programs and courses during the nine years that she has been incarcerated. She continues to admit to committing the present offense and to trying to cover up the offense by lighting her car on fire. She also admitted to being under the influence of vodka and xanax at the time of her crime. The inmate was a child of an alcoholic who was physically abusive to his wife and mentally abusive to the inmate and her siblings. The victim of the present offense was reportedly physically and sexually abusive to the inmate from the ages of 13–18-1/2 years old. She was able to escape from him for about 14 years when he finally found her and proceeded to terrorize her and her family for the next 18 months. The inmate continues to express insight into the factors which contribute to and maintain domestic violence relationships. She expressed remorse about the crime and an intention to speak to other women about battered relationships. She does not appear to be an imminent risk of violence to self or others.

The evaluation also included the notation that appellant's judgment, impulse control, insight, institutional adjustment, and institutional programming were all "Good," and concluded with an "above-average" prognosis for successful completion of parole.

The July 30, 2002, evaluation was followed by an "In–Depth Psychological Evaluation" dated January 24, 2003. That evaluation reports that it was done on referral from the Parole Board in view of the Board's opinion that appellant "takes no responsibility for the current offense and attempts to answer questions in an elusive and manipulative manner. She portrays herself as a victim." The evaluation contains the following Summary/Conclusions section: . . .

> Likelihood of Acting Out/Risk Behavior: Low Risk factors for re-offending include: No psychiatric commitment or major and/or acute psychiatric disorder. No known prior offenses of a violent nature, one victim of violence, violence not planned for the future. She expresses guilt over the aggressive behavior and remorse for the death of the victim as well as admitting to having the desire to kill another human being and being responsible for his death. She is not overtly hostile and has no disciplinary charges involving aggression or acting out. There is no thought disorder present and she is not prescribed psychotropic medication. She has been involved in individual counseling and is aware of the need for further psychotherapeutic treatment to assist in healing herself further as well as in her relationships with her daughter, father, step-father and her ex-husband (who has re-established a relationship with his adoptive daughter, Ms. Kosmin). Ms. Kosmin has participated in drug/alcohol abuse programs as well as other self-improvement, vocational skills building and educational programs. Ms. Kosmin presents as a low-risk for re-offending and having a solid plan for re-uniting with the community with a sound support system. . . .

The reasons stated for the denial were the multiple crimes of which appellant was convicted and her continued denial that she was the shooter, circumstances the Panel equated with denial of the crime. The Panel therefore concluded that "a substantial likelihood exists that you would commit a new crime if released on parole." . . .

The dispositive issue governing the parole decision is whether the rehabilitative aspect of the sentence has been satisfied, and the basic test thereof is whether there is a substantial likelihood that the defendant will commit another crime if released on parole. . . .

The question then before us is whether the record supports by a preponderance of the evidence the Board's conclusion that if released on parole appellant will be substantially likely to commit another offense. . . . Since the statute creates a presumption of release on the parole eligibility date, the decision not to release must be regarded as arbitrary if it is not supported by a preponderance of evidence in the record.

We have carefully scrutinized this record. The preponderance of the evidence cannot support a finding of any likelihood, to say nothing of a substantial likelihood, that appellant would commit another crime if released. To the contrary, the preponderance of the evidence impels exactly the opposite prediction. First, we reject the Board's justification for disregarding the psychological evaluations that conclude that appellant presents a low risk of recidivism. The evaluations were done by professionals whose business it is to evaluate self-reported statements. Indeed, self-reported statements would appear to us to be what an interview with a psychiatrist is all about.

We also are of the view that the Parole Board cannot insist that appellant's insight into her criminal behavior is impaired by reason of the fact that she will not admit that she was the actual shooter. The fact of the matter is that appellant has admitted full responsibility for the crime and that the identity of the shooter, she or Molewicz, was never established. A defendant who refuses to admit an established or adjudicated fact is one thing. It is altogether another to refuse to admit a fact that may not be true when there is no reasonable way of knowing whether it is true or not. The identity of the shooter is, simply, neither objectively determined nor determinable. We further note in this regard the Panel's finding that it was incredible that a mere friend of appellant who had not herself been the subject of Kelly's abuse would actually have pulled the trigger. We see nothing in logic or common sense to make that act any more incredible than any other aspect of Molewicz's acknowledged participation in the crime.

The Board is also apparently troubled by appellant regarding herself as a victim. We do not intend to minimize appellant's crime in any way or to depreciate its seriousness. She took a life, and she has paid the penalty. But to deny her victim status is to ignore the dynamics of the relationship that led her to her extreme action. She was a victim. She was cruelly brutalized over an extended period of time by a man who can be realistically said to have virtually destroyed her life. The Board also makes much of appellant's asserted inability to recite the NA/AA steps, concluding that she thereby demonstrated "lack of articulable insight regarding her criminal behavior despite years of attending counseling sessions." In context, we regard that conclusion as a non-sequitur. The Board also viewed as significant the multiple crimes of which appellant was convicted. As we have noted, however, all were part of the same ongoing event, and in the context of this defendant and her background and this crime, we do not perceive how the attempted cover-up of the shooting makes it more likely that appellant will commit another crime if released.

The final conclusion of the Board was that while appellant "did immerse herself in counseling while incarcerated," the "Adult Panel was unable to deem from the record established at the Panel hearing an indication that she had sufficiently addressed the underlying causes of her criminal behavior...." We have difficulty in understanding just what the Board meant by this statement. The underlying cause of appellant's criminal behavior was her brutalization by Kelly. Beyond that, the Adult Panel might well have perceived the indication it was looking for had it considered the psychological evaluations it had ordered but then chose to ignore.

We do not lightly reverse a parole-denial decision by the Parole Board. Nevertheless, its implicit conclusion that appellant did not cooperate in her rehabilitation and its expressed conclusion that there is a substantial likelihood that she will commit another crime if released are so far off the mark and so fundamentally contradicted by the record as to compel us to do so here.

The final decision of the Parole Board denying Margaret Kosmin parole is reversed. The Parole Board having approved appellant's parole release plan, we direct that she be released on parole forthwith.

NOTES AND QUESTIONS

1. **Parole Denials.** Kosmin's case is unusual. It is difficult to prove denial of parole was unreasonable given the discretion that parole boards have in making these decisions. Furthermore, there was nothing in the record to indicate that the deceased's family protested Kosmin's release. Yet, in many cases, the wishes of family members are considered crucial in the parole boards decisions. For a discussion of the use of protest letters in parole decisions involving battered women defendants see Jennifer S. Bales, *Equal Protection and the Use of Protest Letters in Parole Proceedings, A Particular Dilemma for Battered Women Inmates*, 27 Seton Hall L. Rev. 33 (1996).

Some states, including California, direct their parole boards to take histories of domestic violence into account when considering parole petitions. Yet, even when parole boards decide to grant early release, governors in Oklahoma, Maryland, and California have the power to overturn those decisions. In California, for example, during almost six years in office, Governor Davis granted parole to only seven of 261 homicide convicts recommended by the board. Three of those who were paroled were women had been convicted of killing their abusive spouses. The California Supreme Court has upheld the executive power of the governor to deny parole. See Jill E. Adams, *Unlocking Liberty: Is California's Habeas Law the Key to Freeing Unjustly Imprisoned Battered Women?*, 19 Berkeley Women's L.J. 217 (2004).

In 2004, California enacted a statute that allows individuals convicted of violent crimes before 1996 who can prove their abusers coerced them into committing a crime, or those convicted of killing an intimate partner, who were denied evidence of battering and its effects to have their cases re-examined. Sandy Corbin, *Law Gives Battered Inmates in California New Hope*, Women's E-News, Sept. 23, 2004, available at http://www.womensenews.org/article.cfm/dyn/aid/1999.

2. **Support Programs for Battered Women in Prison.** Despite the number of battered women defendants who are incarcerated, there exist few support programs for them. This is in part because male correctional institutions often receive more support and funding. For an overview of this issue, see Haegyung Cho, *Incarcerated Women and Abuse: The Crime Connection and the Lack of Treatment in Correctional Facilities*, 14 S. Cal. Rev. L. & Women's Stud. 137 (2004).

Clemency for Battered Defendants

The first national recognition of what has since been named the "clemency movement" occurred in October, 1990, when the former Governor of Ohio, Richard Celeste, just before he left office, granted clemency to twenty-five battered women who had been convicted of killing or assaulting their batterers. For background reading about the clemency movement see Patricia Gagne, BATTERED WOMEN'S JUSTICE: THE MOVEMENT FOR CLEMENCY AND THE POLITICS OF SELF-DEFENSE (1998); Leslie Friedman Goldstein, CONTEMPORARY CASES IN WOMEN'S RIGHTS 276 (1994), and Linda L. Ammons, *Discretionary Justice: A Legal and Policy Analysis of a Governor's Use of the Clemency Power in the Cases of Incarcerated Battered Women,* 3 J. L. & POL'Y 1 (1994). The experience of women incarcerated in Maryland for killing their abusers is captured in the 1990 documentary film *A Plea for Justice,* and both the film and the women's subsequent petition for clemency are discussed in Jane C. Murphy, *Lawyering for Social Change: The Power of the Narrative in Domestic Violence Law Reform,* 21 HOFSTRA L. REV. 1243 (1993).

Executive clemency is the power of the executive branch of government (the President or Governor) to mitigate the consequence of a sentence. It is a remedy that is grounded in the United States Constitution, but it also exists in some form in every major nation but China. Comments of Cookie Ridolfi in *Courtroom, Code and Clemency: Reform in Self Defense Jurisprudence for Battered Women* (panel discussion), 23 GOLDEN GATE U. L. REV. 829 (1994). A major criticism of clemency is that it violates the principle of separation of powers because it appears to allow the executive branch to interfere with and override decisions about criminal liability and punishment properly made by the judicial and legislative branches of government. However, the Federalist Papers make clear that the power was specifically included in the constitution to balance and complement the other two powers in the area of criminal law. Because no justice system can predict every case that may come before it, no system can mete out perfect justice. There will always be cases in which the rules say a person is guilty and must be punished, even though most people would agree that this is an unjust result.

Cookie Ridolfi, a defense attorney who has represented many battered women and contributed to women's self-defense work, says there are essentially three types of situations where clemency is appropriate: 1. situations where the convicted person is factually innocent; 2. situations in which the convicted person is technically guilty, but mitigating factors exist which argue for leniency; and 3. situations in which the convicted person is technically guilty, but morally innocent. The third case is frequently the most accurate description of what has happened to a formerly battered woman who fought back against her batterer. Essentially, the argument goes that but for imperfections in the law as it existed at the time of her trial, or as it currently exists, or trial factors such as jury bias or improper jury instructions, the person would have not have been convicted. This third case is strongest when the law has changed, since the defendant was convicted and it is unlikely the defendant would be convicted again if retried under contemporary standards. It is easier, that is to say, for the executive branch to challenge decisions that either the legislative or judicial branch of government has already acknowledged were based on a flawed vision of justice.

Clemency may take the form of commutation, pardon, reprieve, or amnesty. A pardon implies forgiveness or acknowledgement of the convicted person's actual or moral innocence. Generally, pardon restores rights lost by being convicted of a crime, such as the right to vote or to serve on a jury. It may be granted after release from prison and/or after parole supervision has ended. It may be conditional. A reprieve suspends execution of sentence, usually to allow time for further investigation or an appeal. Reprieves are most common in death penalty cases. Amnesty excuses groups of convicted persons, usually where the crimes with which they were charged were political acts.

Finally, commutation is the substitution of a less severe punishment than the one imposed by the court at sentencing. It usually implies not that the person is actually or morally innocent, but that the punishment is overly harsh, given the circumstances of crime, some inequity in the law, or circumstances that have occurred since sentencing (being diagnosed with a terminal illness, for example, so that a five year sentence becomes a de facto life sentence, or a subsequent change in the law so that the defendant might well not be found guilty if retried under the new regime). It may lead to parole and does not restore civil rights. Commutation may reduce a death sentence to life imprisonment, shorten a sentence of imprisonment, reduce the minimum sentence so that the parole eligibility date is advanced, or reduce the maximum sentence (either shortening probation time after parole or reducing the time served in prison). A commutation to time served will make the defendant eligible for immediate release. Even when a person is granted a commutation, he or she may still need to apply for and be granted parole. Commutation is the appropriate form of clemency in most cases of battered women who kill their assailants, because they are usually not facing a death penalty, have usually not been released, and are not considered political prisoners.

Executive clemency is at the discretion of the governor or president. An advisory board, usually the Parole Board, may be authorized to advise and make recommendations to the executive officer. Typically, executive officers follow the recommendations of their advisory boards. Therefore, appeals to this body are an important part of the clemency process. Generally, the petitioner must exhaust all administrative remedies before applying for commutation. Usually, the clemency process involves several levels. First, the petition must meet basic requirements or be changed to comply with such requirements. Second, an investigation is conducted into the petitioner's criminal, social, and institutional histories. Third, the advisory or parole board makes a recommendation to the executive officer, based upon which the officer makes her determination. Finally, where commutation is granted, there is usually a review conducted under the auspices of the executive officer, sometimes including another hearing. Because executive officers, as well as many executive advisory or parole board members, are elected to office, they are particularly susceptible to public opinion. Community education about battering and identifying support by the community are therefore also very important parts of the clemency process.

There is a connection between clemency and "special" legislation. Policy makers often think that legislation making expert testimony admissible in the trials of battered women who kill their batterers is the key to battered women staying out of prison. For this reason, they may focus their efforts on creating "special" legislation for battered women. Along with other problems associated with special treatment (including pathologizing women or presenting them as passive victims), such measures can obstruct the possibility of clemency for women by creating the illusion that clemency is no longer necessary. "A statute allowing Battered Woman Syndrome evidence is not necessarily going to prevent convictions, but policy makers may feel that there is no longer a problem." Comments of Rebecca Isaacs in *Courtroom, Code and Clemency: Reform in Self Defense Jurisprudence for Battered Women* (panel discussion), 23 GOLDEN GATE U. L. REV. 829, 833 (1994). Moreover, the absence of "special" statutes is often cited in support of clemency. In Ohio, for example, Governor Celeste justified clemency for battered women on the grounds that a state Supreme Court decision specifically barred expert testimony about battering until 1990. In Maryland, clemency activism was also based on the inadmissibility of evidence of battering. Finally, and perhaps problematically, in Florida the parole board has adopted a rule making "battered women's syndrome" a criterion for consideration of clemency. Rita Thaemert, *Till Violence Do Us Part,* STATE LEGISLATURES (March 1993).

The role of public education in creating a climate within which elected officials can grant clemency to convicted "killers" without fearing adverse political consequences is captured in the following reading, which describes efforts by a coalition of battered women's advocates in Maryland to change the context within which battered women's self-defense claims were heard and understood.

Jane C. Murphy

Lawyering for Social Change: The Power of the Narrative in Domestic Violence Law Reform

21 HOFSTRA L. REV. 1243 (1993).

... Creative new strategies were needed. The coalition shifted the focus [away from litigation and legislation] to storytelling—having victims who had killed or attempted to kill their abusers tell the grim stories of their lives with their abusers—in a variety of ways, to a number of audiences.... First, the Domestic Violence Task Force arranged for the financing and production of a videotape, *A Plea for Justice.* The objective of the videotape was to have victims tell their stories to a wide audience....

In May 1990, the thirty-minute videotape, one of the first of its kind, was completed and premiered to a large audience in Baltimore. Representatives from the coalition interviewed thirty women who had killed or attempted to kill their abusers and were serving time at Maryland's only women's prison, the Maryland Correctional Institution for Women (the "MCIW"). From these interviews, the stories of four Baltimore women—

serving sentences ranging from fifteen years to life for killing their partners—were selected to feature in the film. With the exception of the narrator, a battered woman herself, and brief statements from psychologist Lenore Walker and former Attorney General Benjamin Civiletti, the voices in the film are those of the women telling their stories.

The stories were classic examples of domestic violence. All of the women were the product of abusive homes, and all had initially sought a haven within their relationships. The batterers began as "intense" and "passionate" partners. Later, this passion turned to violence and isolation, making the women totally dependent upon their abusers. The details of the stories vary, yet paint a horrifying picture of lives that led these women to believe that killing their abusers was their only chance to live. . . .

The targeted audience for the film included: the Governor of Maryland, who could grant clemency or recommend parole to the Parole Commission; the Parole Commission; the Maryland Legislature, which in 1990 had rejected a bill that would have required the admission of battered spouse syndrome testimony, and would consider another version of the bill in 1991; the Maryland Congressional Delegation; and the general public.

The Governor of Maryland, William Donald Schaefer, was one of the first legal decisionmakers targeted. During his sixteen years as Mayor of the City of Baltimore and his first four-year term as Governor, Schaefer had never actively supported legislation or policies designed to improve the plight of domestic violence victims. The Governor viewed the film with key members of his staff. Moved by what he saw, he asked to meet with the women in the film. He met with those women and others for over two hours at the MCIW, and he listened to their stories. When Governor Schaefer emerged from that meeting, he told reporters how the experience had changed his understanding of the plight of battered women:

> You read a newspaper: "Mary Jones shot her husband." When you see Mary Jones and understand how she got there, it is a little different. . . . [The women told] stories of a lack of self-esteem, abuse, hoping things get better, things don't get better, and finally a point where the women break.

Later, testifying before a congressional subcommittee that was considering legislation intended to strengthen training for judges who deal with domestic violence and to encourage the enactment of state laws allowing the introduction of testimony of abuse and battered spouse syndrome, Schaefer commented:

> I never focused on the issue of domestic violence until two years ago. I had no interest in it at all and I started off unsympathetic. After hearing the women's stories I decided they should be given a chance to say how they were treated.

The third and final piece of the storytelling campaign was the filing in January, 1991, of a 300–page petition seeking clemency on behalf of twelve inmates at the MCIW who were serving sentences from fifteen years to life for killing or attempting to kill their abusers. The petition, entitled *Twice Imprisoned*, described the components of battered spouse syndrome, analyzed the law in Maryland and around the country with regard to the admissibility and use of this testimony, and described the clemency options available to the Governor. At the heart of the petition, however, are the stories of the four women featured in the videotape, and the stories of eight other women as well. The stories, called *Inmate Profiles*, included a careful review of the development of domestic violence in each relationship, a discussion of the specific circumstances surrounding the crime, a review of the woman's institutional record and achievements, a commentary on her family and educational background, and a brief summary of the woman's plans if released. Most, if not all, of this information was not before the court at trial or at sentencing, nor was it in the inmates' institutional parole files.

As a result of the storytelling in all its forms, in February, 1991, the Governor signed executive orders commuting the sentences of eight women.... Although the women became eligible for immediate release, they would be subject to supervised probation for the balance of their sentences. In announcing this decision, the governor's press secretary noted that the governor had met with several of the women and was "very impressed by the circumstances that led to their imprisonment," and "sympathize[d] with the difficulty they have had in the courts trying to explain their circumstances that led to the crime...." It was a historic and dramatic conclusion to the first phase of a successful campaign in which storytelling had played a central role.

NOTES AND QUESTIONS

1. **The Status of the Clemency Movement.** According to the National Clearinghouse for the Defense of Battered Women, at least 124 women from 23 states have received clemency since 1978, most of them since 1990. *Nat'l Clearinghouse for the Defense of Battered Women, Battered Women Who Have Received Clemency* (2002), available at *http://www.ncdbw.org/ index.htm*. See also Carol Jacobsen, Kammy Mizga and Lynn D'Orio, *Battered Women, Homicide Convictions, & Sentencing: The Case for Clemency*, 18 HASTINGS WOMEN'S L. J. 31 (2007), Bridget B. Romero, Jennifer Collins, Carrie Johnson, Jennifer Merrigan, Lynne Perkins, Judith Sznyter and Lisa Dale May, *The Missouri Battered Women's Clemency Coalition: A Collaborative Effort in Justice for Eleven Missouri Women*, 23 ST. LOUIS U. PUB.L.REV. 193 (2004).

2. **Ineffective Assistance of Counsel.** If counsel is ineffective at trial, that can have implications for women seeking clemency. As Mary Becker explains,

> In the clemency cases I've worked on for poor women, the major problem was that they were inadequately represented by counsel, they had defense counsel who did not have investigative resources, sometimes they had defense counsel who were not ethical, or were just plain incompetent, and I will give just one example. In one of our cases, our client who had only one arm, killed her partner when he was attacking her. She said that he had consumed a thousand dollars worth of

cocaine that weekend and that he had a crazy look in his eyes. Her public defender told her that the autopsy showed no cocaine, and she had better plead guilty. She did. She got forty years. Our students took the autopsy report to a doctor, and the doctor said "Yeah, there's no cocaine in his system. There's a lot of the substance that cocaine breaks down to when it's in the human body." There is no solution for this, the major problem facing battered women in prison, without providing adequate representation for all defendants in criminal cases. It's one thing to have caseloads for prosecutors that are so heavy that they have to plea bargain most cases. It is quite another thing to have that true for defense attorneys who as a result pressure their clients, who have no other options into pleading guilty, when they are not. Mary Becker, *Domestic Violence and Victimizing the Victim: Relief, Results, Reform*, 23 N. Ill. U. L. Rev. 477 (2003).

For further discussion of clemency for battered women see Mary Becker, *Access to Justice for Battered Women*, 12 Wash. U. J.L. & Pol'y 63 (2003).

3.   **The Politics of Granting Clemency.** What are the politics involved in granting battered defendants clemency? In this final excerpt, Linda Ammons explores some of the reasons why governors have granted clemency to battered defendants.

Linda L. Ammons

Why Do You Do the Things You Do? Clemency for Battered Incarcerated Women: A Decade's Review

11 Am. U. J. Gender Soc. Pol'y & L. 533 (2003).

A decade ago, Richard F. Celeste, the governor of a large Mid-western state, used his Constitutional power to grant clemency to twenty-eight incarcerated women who petitioned for relief. These women were in prison because they killed their abusive intimates. When the Ohio women were granted clemency, most of the state-wide and national newspaper response was positive. Predictably, prosecutors were among the most vocal detractors. There were also media critics who questioned the morality and integrity of the governor. Andy Rooney, the CBS Sixty Minutes commentator, stated that the governor had given all women the license to kill their abusive partners. Rooney's column included the following statement, "In releasing these women, Celeste effectively declared open season on husbands in his state."

When a case involves a homicide, the political stakes are high, and the scrutiny by media and others can be intense. A politician smeared with being soft on crime either by the media or by his or her political opponents is not considered to be worthy of holding office. During the 2000 Presidential primary season, then Governor George W. Bush of Texas, the Republican contender, was faced with the decision of whether he would intervene in the case of sixty-two-year-old Betty Lou Beets, a woman given the death penalty for killing her husband. Her appeals lawyers argued that she had been a victim of domestic abuse. When asked by a reporter how he would review the case, Bush answered, "We've had a lot of controversial cases come across my desk, and each time, I've asked the question of innocence and guilt, and each time, I've asked the question, has the person had full access to the courts? And so, I'm going to wait to see what the ... Board of Pardons and Parole says first ... before I make a decision on this case." Beets died by lethal injection on February 24, 2000, and became the second woman from Texas to be executed since the Supreme Court allowed state executions to resume and the fourth woman in the United States to be executed. Bush stated his reason for not reducing her sentence, "After careful review of the evidence of the case, I concur with the jury that Betty Lou Beets is guilty of this murder." ...

Probing the mind of a governor for his or her rationale in making a clemency decision is not an easy task. There may be various motivations for action or inaction ranging from self-interest (in re-election or a legacy) to a conviction that is based on personal moral or ethical considerations. The chief executive may also take on an initiative because of a belief in what is best for the constituency. One of the most important aspects of having a plan successfully implemented is the strategic spin that is crafted for the media and, subsequently, the citizens in that jurisdiction. It is often important that the official tell the story first, as opposed to letting the story be told by those who may not fully understand the issue or have some ulterior motives for not getting the facts straight. Governors hold press conferences, make themselves available to the media, or release official statements when they want to ensure that their point of view is accurately articulated.

I decided to inquire into the stated reasons why other governors granted clemency to incarcerated battered women during the past decade. In Ohio, governors are required by law to report to the legislature on their clemency grants. Although one cannot always be certain that the stated position is the reason for political action, the released statements of the official are the most reliable documentation. When this information is not readily available, newspaper accounts can serve as records.

Shortly after the Celeste commutations, Governor William Schaefer of Maryland commuted the sentences of eight women. Schaefer gave this explanation to the press: "First of all you think: They committed murder. And as a lawyer you think: All the evidence was there; what else could happen?" However, Schaefer also concluded that because the evidence of abuse was not admissible as a mitigating factor in their criminal trials, "the women have served enough time." When Missouri Governor (now U.S. Attorney General) John Ashcroft reduced the sentences of two battered women in 1992, he said, "In both of these women's cases, the law prohibited juries from hearing about the severe abuse and trauma they had endured.... In the interest of justice, I am commuting the sentences to life with the possibility of parole." Governor Terry Brandstad of Iowa also commuted the sentence of a battered woman in 1992. His reason was to the point. He stated, "I have concluded that Katherine Sallis was an abused woman who feared her husband." Governor Pete Wilson of California granted clemency to Frances Mary Caccavale and Brenda Aris. Wilson released Caccavale because of her age (seventy-eight years old), medical condition, and because she had been battered for over fifty years before she stabbed and killed her husband. Wilson stated that "he felt compassion for the 'pain and terror' she endured from her husband over the years." Brenda Aris' sentence was reduced from "fifteen years to life" to "twelve years minimum." While the law in California changed because of Aris' case, she did not benefit from it. She was paroled a year and a half before her sentence would have been completed. When commuting the sentence of Jeanette Crawford, a third battered woman, Governor Wilson made it clear that his decision was not based on "battered women's syndrome," but on "ineffective assistance of counsel." He was presented with several other cases of battered women, but he declined their requests. Wilson told the press that in making his decision:

> The question is not whether victims of domestic violence have suffered . . . The question is whether it is the function of either the criminal law or the clemency process to absolve them of personal responsibility if they choose to take a human life—even the life of a vicious abuser— when there is available the option of taking another course to escape the abuse.

Wilson further elaborated:

> The test of whether clemency should be considered in cases where the request is based on [battered women syndrome] must be: Did the petitioner have the option to leave her abuser, or was the homicide realistically her only chance to escape? The test is a narrow one . . . and must be . . . to avoid the manipulation of [battered women syndrome] as a rationalization for cold-blooded, premeditated murder.

Governor William Weld of Massachusetts commuted the sentence of Eugenia Moore, one of the "Framingham Eight," in 1993. Speaking on behalf of the governor, Weld's chief counsel, Robert Cordy, said that Weld made his decision because the pardon board had voted unanimously in her case and because "the evidence supporting her was strong and clear cut." Governor Romer of Colorado provided relief for four women: Gertrude Reed, Debra Muniz, Hope Gudowski, and Catherine Laughlin. Explaining his power to commute, Romer commented "it allows us to consider mercy for those women trapped in abusive and life-threatening relationships who reasonably believed they had no way out." When Florida Governor Lawton Chiles commuted the sentence of Kimberly Soubielle, the first battered woman in his administration to receive clemency, he asserted, "This action is a recognition that battering of women is a tragic reality that affects women in every walk of life. And the circumstances of this particular case indicate it played a considerable role in the actions of Kimberly Soubielle." Chiles was also clear that he was not promoting self-help: "We certainly don't condone acts or crimes of violence, just as we do not condone crimes of domestic violence." Chiles' general counsel stated that the governor did "recognize the syndrome could be a significant factor . . . it's a very complex one." In 1996, Governor Brereton Jones of Kentucky explained to a national television audience that he had commuted the sentences of nine

Kentucky women because "[t]hese people were unjustly incarcerated." That same year New Hampshire Governor Steve Merrill granted June Briand a conditional pardon and remarked: "She's a different person than she was when she committed the crime." He also noted, "There is sufficient evidence of physical and emotional abuse to constitute a finding of what is commonly known as 'battered women's syndrome.'" Two days before Christmas of the same year, Governor George Pataki of New York shortened the sentence of Charlene Brundidge from "fifteen years to life" to the ten years she had already served. Pataki's remarks included the following: "The extraordinary powers of clemency allow me to exercise compassion and to recognize that Charlene Brundidge's crime was an aberrant act in an otherwise law abiding and productive life, an act that was a direct response to her history of domestic abuse." Governor Jim Edgar of Illinois granted clemency to Guinevere Garcia, a battered woman who was to be executed. Edgar reduced her sentence to life in prison without parole and insisted, "I have concluded that the punishment decreed for her was not typical ... Horrible as was her crime, it is an offense comparable to those that judges and jurors have determined over and over again should not be punishable by death." In the case of another woman who had been convicted of plotting to kill an abusive husband, who admitted that he had battered her for over a decade, Edgar commented through his press office that the woman "had served enough time." Before leaving office, Oregon Governor Barbara Roberts commuted the sentence of one woman and told the legislature that the prisoner was a battered woman, who had a dual diagnosis of post-traumatic stress disorder and battered woman syndrome.

Most of the governors (nine) characterized their actions as a response to women who were trapped in relationships because of a mental deficiency, a "syndrome." The second largest category (four) was an admission that the women were unable to get the full story of abuse before a jury. Those governors indicated that "justice" required them to act. Two governors cited mercy and/or compassion and three felt that the punishment was either too severe (a proportionality concept) or that the women had served enough time. The majority of the reported reasons for clemency were linked to excusing the actions of the women because of their circumstances (a psycho-social explanation) and a failure of the legal system to properly hear or weigh the factors involved that led to the commission of the act for which the women were incarcerated. The closest public admission by a governor that battered women were not just excused, but perhaps justified in protecting themselves from imminent danger of death or bodily harm, the legal standard for self-defense, came from Governor Jones of Kentucky.

No reasonable person would suggest that criminal behavior should not be sanctioned and deterred. However, it is not a crime to protect oneself within the boundaries of the law. The question is not simply whether victims who strike back should be held to a legal standard of reasonableness. The first issue for a battered woman, who has fought to protect herself, is how the law will be applied to her case in such a way that the mere fact that she is a battered woman is not a proxy for unreasonableness. The second dilemma is, if the criminal justice system fails to fully appreciate the circumstances of a battered woman and she is incarcerated must the last legal and political forum of appeal (i.e. the governor) be blind and turn a deaf ear because of political inconvenience?

Despite the fact that governors may be morally, legally and politically justified in providing the requested relief, no governor wants to make the mistake of setting free a person who is likely to kill again. There is no guarantee that a released offender will never fall from grace. . . .

NOTES AND QUESTIONS

1. **Reasons for Clemency.** Given what you have learned, if you were governor of your state, what factors would you consider before granting clemency to a battered defendant? Do you think that there is increased public sympathy for battered defendants? Or is there a growing frustration with the inability of other legal remedies to curb domestic violence? What political constituencies do you think would support clemency for battered defendants? Note that Governor Pete Wilson focused exclusively on the question of whether the defendant had the opportunity to leave the relationship. Does this focus obscure the broader problems faced by battered defendants, or is it the only just criteria for evaluating such claims? Thinking back to the notion of an equal trial, if the system fails battered defendants, should it be the governor's duty to remedy that?

CHAPTER TEN

DOMESTIC VIOLENCE AND FAMILY LAW

Introduction

We turn now from the responses of the criminal law system to domestic violence to the responses of the family law system. These are two different systems, with different objectives and different understandings of how the world operates. Whereas judges and others involved in criminal prosecutions are used to thinking in terms of victims and "perpetrators," family law courts have a strong bias in favor of keeping families as intact as possible. As Clare Dalton has noted, "the prevailing ideology of family courts . . . emphasizes the mediated resolution of conflict, the desirability of minor children continuing to have significant relationships with both parents, and the development of stable post-divorce relationships between parents in the interests of children." *Domestic Violence, Domestic Torts and Divorce*, 31 NEW ENG. L. REV. 319 (1997); see *also* Elizabeth S. Scott, *Parental Autonomy and Children's Welfare*, 11 WM. & MARY BILL RTS. J. 1071 (2003). Furthermore, family law judges and their staffs have often acted as if they do not have to be particularly concerned about domestic violence. There are probably two additional reasons for this. First, most divorces today are granted on no-fault grounds, making the domestic violence in the relationship legally irrelevant to the divorce action. Secondly, judges and court personnel often believe that the violence will abate after the divorce since the couple will then be separated. Given our earlier discussions of "separation assault", this is an assumption that we now know is not only unwarranted, but, in many cases, the opposite of the truth. Martha R. Mahoney, *Legal Images of Battered Women: Redefining the Issue of Separation* 90 MICH. L. REV. 1 (1991). Thus, perhaps it should not surprise us that long after restraining orders were widely accepted, and long after expert testimony on battering was held to be admissible in a variety of criminal cases, family law courts are still reluctant to admit that domestic violence has occurred or that it should influence the outcome of custody cases.

The no-fault revolution of the 1970s changed the landscape in terms of divorce and its economic effects. In the space of little over a decade, we moved from a system in which one could not obtain a divorce without a showing of fault to one in which the vast majority of divorces are granted without any discussion of fault. Commentators have debated whether this change in the law ended up injuring women. Very little has been written about its effect on intimate partners who have been abused.

Most of the academic attention and advocacy work on family law and domestic violence has been directed at looking at the effect of domestic violence on children. Those who work with families in which there has been violence understood relatively quickly the deleterious effect that violence could have on children. In the past two decades, there has been a tremendous amount of research that has demonstrated the seriousness of these effects on children. The question now is how to integrate this understanding into the law. Advocates of victims of domestic violence argue that parents who have abused their partners should be assumed to be bad parents because of the negative effects that their violence may have on the kids. This presumption should exist, advocates argue, even if abusers have not physically abused the children.

While victims' advocates contend that abusive parents should be disfavored in custody battles, advocates of noncustodial parents (usually fathers' rights advocates) argue that it is important for children to maintain significant contact with both parents. These fathers' rights advocates do not address domestic violence cases in particular, but because of the prevalence of domestic violence in litigated custody cases, they often end up advocating sustained contact in situations which most probably involve violence.

The result has been a series of legislative and judicial reforms of both substantive and procedural custody issues. Since the middle of the last century, courts have used the "best interests" standard to determine custody. Clearly, different judges can interpret this standard differently. Since family law courts do not use juries, the judge's understanding of the child's "best interests" is crucial. Those who are concerned about the effects of domestic violence have argued that the violence should be taken into account in determining a child's best interests. On the other hand, fathers' advocates have argued for reforms that encourage significant contact between the child and both parents. Often these two reform urges conflict with one another: if one parent's abuse of the other is to be taken into account in determining a child's best interests for custody purposes, it is likely to diminish, not increase, the amount of time that the child spends with the abusive parent.

These issues show up again in the context of parental mobility. Sometimes parents want to move from where they have been living with the abuser. They may want to do this to escape the abuser or merely to get on with their lives with a new partner, new job, or something similar. A custody order, if there is one, is likely to limit a custodial parent's ability to move with the children. Such provisions are seen as protecting the noncustodial parent's access to the children. Once again, the victimized parent may claim that it is better for her and for the children to be elsewhere. Similarly, a parent may want to move with the children before there is a custody order or to flee without them. Regardless of the timing and the circumstances, the family court will have to resolve conflicting claims of safety and the children's well-being with claims of the importance of continuing contact with both parents.

The materials that follow discuss these issues. They begin with materials on no-fault divorce and the distribution of assets. Then they turn to the much more heavily studied issue of custody. The three readings in the introduction to the custody readings are aimed at providing some background and context for your consideration of the judicial and legislative policies that follow. The first two readings focus on the connection between domestic violence and injury to children. The opening reading, from Paula Sharp's 1996 novel CROWS OVER A WHEATFIELD, offers a poignant example of the risk that those who abuse their partners will also abuse their children. Although studies show somewhat varying results, it is probably accurate to say that approximately 50% of those who abuse their intimate partners also abuse their children, Clare Dalton, Susan Carbon and Nancy Olesen, *High Conflict Divorce, Violence, and Abuse*, 54 JUV. & FAM.CT.J. 11 (2003). In reading this excerpt, think about the dynamic that precipitates physical or sexual abuse of a child in a post-divorce situation like the one in the novel. How is it tied up with the dynamics of abuse and control?

The second reading, from an article by Judith Greenberg, catalogues the variety of ways that domestic violence can be injurious to children, including emotional damage, academic problems, behavioral "acting out," and physical injury. In addition to providing relevant information, reading this article should again raise for you questions concerning the role of social science research in lawyering. Is the research useful only to provide a context for the lawyers? Can it be used in litigation? How would a lawyer question the results of the research? The third excerpt, by Joan Meier, discusses the question of why family courts have been so slow to credit women's accounts of violence despite the fact that criminal courts have come to accept the widespread nature of intimate abuse. Thinking about this subject will help you to identify differences in the ideology and processes of the family and criminal courts.

The rest of the chapter looks at substantive custody law and how the law affects families in which there is domestic violence. We look first at modern approaches to best interests analysis and statutory presumptions against giving custody to a batterer. Both of these require explicit consideration of violence against a spouse or intimate partner in deciding custody; they have been advocated by those concerned about the victims of family violence. Then the readings turn to reform proposals on the side of fathers' advocates. These include a preference for joint custody and for "friendly" parents who will work to facilitate the other parent's continued access to the child. As you assess these proposals, and the possibility of allowing the abuser visitation with the child, you will need to consider how harmful you think continued contact with an abuser is for a child and under what circumstances it is harmful. You will also need to consider how beneficial (if at all) a sustained relationship with the abuser is for the child and how that can be accomplished. These sections are followed by materials on visitation and relocation.

A.   DIVORCE AND THE DISTRIBUTION OF ASSETS

Through the 1960s, divorce was available only if one party could prove that the other had acted wrongfully. For example, adultery, cruelty, and abandonment have traditionally justified divorce. In 1969, California adopted the first "no-fault" divorce statute, quickly followed by a majority of the other states. As of 2005, 32 states had added "no-fault" grounds to their traditional fault-based grounds for divorce. The remaining states had substituted "no-fault" grounds for the original fault-based grounds. Linda D. Elrod and Robert G. Spector, *A Review of the Year in Family Law: Parentage and Assisted Reproduction Problems Take Center Stage*, 39 FAM. L. Q. 879 (2006). No-fault divorce takes many different forms. In most states, unilateral divorce is possible. That is, if one spouse claims the marriage is definitely broken, the court then has authority to divorce the parties. In some states, like New York, no-fault divorce requires the parties to agree on the terms of the divorce. This means that no-fault divorce is available only with the consent of both parties. Finally, in some states, fault is also irrelevant in terms of the distribution of assets, alimony, or child custody. In others, the grounds for the divorce may not take fault into account, but fault may be considered in dividing property, ordering spousal support, or awarding custody.

The concept of no-fault divorce was popular in part because the fault-based system required one party to present evidence in court of the other party's misdeeds. Some thought that this resulted in a public display of facts that were really private; others objected because it encouraged collusion and, even, perjury; additional critics argued that it emphasized "matrimonial misconduct that might have little to do with the personal dynamics of the relationship," focusing on particular incidents instead of on the way that the parties had simply grown apart. Herma Hill Kay, *Equality and Difference: A Perspective on No–Fault Divorce and its Aftermath*, 56 U.CIN. L. REV. 1 (1987).

Academics began criticizing no-fault divorce almost right away. By 1985, Lenore Weitzman had published a landmark study indicating that no-fault divorce often resulted in the impoverishment of women and their children. Lenore Weitzman, THE DIVORCE REVOLUTION (1985). Furthermore, some commentators blamed no-fault divorce laws for the increase in divorce rates that coincided with the enacting of the no-fault divorce laws. Lynn D. Wardle, *No–Fault Divorce and the Divorce Conundrum*, 1991 B.Y.U. L. REV. 79. Our concern here is less with these global questions surrounding the move to no-fault divorce than it is with the questions of what effect, if any, that move has had on people caught in violent marital relations and what divorce strategies victims of violence can employ.

It is clear that domestic violence is one reason why people get divorced. The following reading illustrates this with stories. As you read, consider what role ideas of fault play in women's descriptions of why they divorce after violent marriages.

Demie Kurz

For Richer For Poorer: Mothers Confront Divorce (1995)

Although the home is spoken of as [the] site of love and caring, we know now that the prevalence of violence is alarmingly high in contemporary marriages. In a given year, anywhere from 10 to 20 percent of women are beaten by a male intimate, and a quarter to a half of all women will experience violence at the hands of a male intimate in their lifetime. Some are even beaten during pregnancy. At least four women in the United States are killed every day by male partners. The National Centers for Disease Control reports that in emergency rooms, more women are treated for injuries from battering than from (nonmarital) rapes, muggings, and traffic accidents combined. Children who witness domestic violence are believed to be at risk for emotional and developmental problems....

In this sample [of randomly selected mothers who were divorced by the Philadelphia Family Court in 1986], 70 percent of women of all classes and races experienced violence at the hands of their husbands at least once. Fifty percent of women experienced violence at least two to three times....

I will first discuss the experiences of the 19 percent of women in the sample who said they left their marriages because of violence ... The accounts of these women resonate with fear and pain. One can easily imagine how the children who witnessed this violence were very fearful and deeply saddened. At the same time, a quiet courage runs through the accounts of these women as they assessed the costs and benefits of staying in their marriages.

While many women in the sample experienced violence, those who stated that they separated because of the violence had experienced much more serious physical violence than women who gave other reasons for separating. Many of these women stated that they left their husbands after a particularly serious fight. Some women, such as this 41–year–old white working-class mother of two, felt that their lives could have been in danger.

> It took a year for the separation to come through. I filed. We separated for the last time after he beat me up. It was Mother's Day. He beat me up in front of the kids and his parents. I was really scared then. I thought, "if he'll do this in front of them, what could he do next?" I had to get a protection order at the time and that cost $300.
>
> We had been going to a counselor.... The therapist called me one night and said to come right over. He said, "Your husband doesn't know right from wrong. He only thinks he is right. You'd better get away. He could kill you." I now believe that. At the time I thought he would still change....

Some women left when the violence affected their children. One woman left when her husband sexually assaulted her son by a former marriage. She filed a criminal charge against her ex-husband, who is now serving time in prison for this crime. This poverty-level black woman left because of the effect of the violence on her children and on herself.

> All the violence was hard on my son. He saw me injured when he was two years old. He saw blood, he saw a lot. It's affected my son. He's mixed up.

I left because I was afraid of what this was doing for my son. I left because of what it was doing to me. I realized I could have shot my ex-husband. But I couldn't do that for my son's sake.

I finally realized the marriage wasn't working. I really wanted a marriage. I wanted that marriage to work. But I finally realized it just wasn't working. [28–year old black woman living at the poverty-level, mother of one, married six years]

As will be described below, some women also watched their husbands destroy property and found this frightening. This 33–year–old white middle-class mother of two, who owned and ran a business with her husband, described his violence:

I was the one who left. My ex-husband had a terrible temper. He used violence a lot. He didn't hurt me physically very much but he destroyed property a lot.

He flew off the handle a lot. He was also an alcoholic. He had an explosive angry temper.

In conclusion, many of the divorced women in this sample were "battered women." We rarely think of divorce and battering together, instead viewing "battered women" and "divorced women" as two different categories. We must incorporate an understanding of violence into our portrayal of all aspects of family life, including divorce.... The problem is, because we do little to alleviate the hardships of divorce for women, we make them pay a heavy price for leaving marriages because of domestic violence.

Grounds for Divorce

The availability in most states of both fault-based and no-fault grounds for divorce means that often victims of marital violence will be able to choose which basis they want for their divorces. As an attorney for such a victim, what considerations would you want to discuss with your client? Certainly one consideration is that a recounting of the violence may play important roles in aiding the legal system to reach better outcomes, maintaining client integrity, and assisting in client healing. A lot has been written on how clients' stories affect these goals. See, e.g., Anthony V. Alfieri, *Reconstructive Poverty Law Practice*, 100 YALE L.J. 2107 (1991) and Leslie G. Espinoza, *Legal Narratives, Therapeutic Narrative*, 95 MICH. L. REV. 901 (1997). To the extent that these are important objectives for your client, you might want to consider pleading fault-based grounds in the petition.

Another consideration for an attorney in this situation is whether the abuse of your client qualifies as "cruelty" under your state's divorce statute. Not surprisingly, different states define cruelty in very different ways. In Maryland, the Court of Special Appeals found that there was cruelty in a case in which the wife testified that the husband, "[made] me stay up all night in order to listen to him, [and isolated] me from my friends and from my family...." In addition, she testified that he hit and pinched her and pulled her hair. She had obtained a protective order against him, but the stress of the marriage had brought on health problems, including a cardiac arrhythmia. The Court, after reviewing a series of previous Maryland cases dealing with cruelty said

> [M]ost are quite old and give victims little relief from their aggressive partners by modern standards. . . . Verbal and physical abuse may have been tolerated in another era, and our predecessors at bar may have placed the continuity of the marital bond above the well-being of individual participants, but our values are different today. . . . *Das v. Das*, 754 A.2d 441 (2000).

In contrast, in New York, in a very recent case, the Appellate Division decided that the conduct against the plaintiff-wife did not constitute cruelty under the divorce statute. In this case, the plaintiff had testified that her husband had once "forced himself on her sexually," adding that it was the only time he had really hurt her. In that incident he had "[r]ammed [her] up against the [bathroom] wall." She also testified that on many other occasions he had grabbed her, pulled her down the hall, blocked her so she could not leave the room, thrown her onto the bed, and pushed her against the wall. She said she had been injured as a result of his conduct, although the opinion does not describe the injuries. *Gross v. Gross*, 836 N.Y.S.2d 166 (N.Y.A.D. 1st Dept. 2007). The Court denied that the husband's conduct provided grounds for a divorce on the basis of cruelty:

> To obtain a divorce on the ground of cruel and inhuman treatment, the plaintiff must show serious misconduct, not mere incompatibility, i.e., a course of conduct by the defendant that is harmful to the plaintiff's physical or mental health and makes cohabitation unsafe or improper. Moreover, in a marriage of long duration a high degree of proof of cruel and inhuman treatment is required. . . . Reprehensible and highly offensive behavior, however, is not necessarily sufficient to establish the cruel-and-inhuman-treatment ground for divorce. Plaintiff's uncorroborated testimony regarding unwanted physical contact was vague and general, and no evidence was adduced from plaintiff regarding the effects, if any, of defendant's conduct on her physical or mental well-being. . . . [P]laintiff presented no evidence regarding the effects, if any, on her mental well-being of defendant's conduct in entering the bathroom of their residence while plaintiff was showering. . . . The absence of medical evidence here is particularly telling in light of plaintiff's failure to offer any other evidence tending to demonstrate that defendant's conduct was harmful to the plaintiff's physical or mental health and makes cohabitation unsafe or improper. At bottom, we are left to speculate as to the effects, if any, of defendant's conduct on plaintiff's physical and mental well-being. *Gross v. Gross*, 836 N.Y.S. 2d 166 (N.Y.A.D. 1st Dept. 2007).

NOTES AND QUESTIONS

1. **The Legal Meaning of Cruelty.** Think about the short histories of abuse captured in the excerpt from Kurz's book, above. Do you think the victims would qualify for a divorce on the basis of cruelty in Maryland? In New York? Do you agree with the court in *Gross* that the cruelty standard

should be more demanding in a long marriage than in a short one? What might be the rationale behind such a rule? Would it have made sense at one time as an effort to protect non-employed women from the economic ruin that might come from a divorce if their husbands were able to argue that small affronts by the wives against the husbands constituted cruelty? In *Gross*, the parties had been married for more than 37 years. Do you think the plaintiff in *Gross* claimed "enough" abuse that a reasonable person would see the abuse as the cause for the end of the marriage or do you think the abuse should be discounted as part of the "accepted" texture of that long marriage?

2. **Waiting Periods.** Many states require that couples seeking divorces on no-fault grounds wait for some period of time after the filing of the complaint or the service on the defendant. These waiting periods vary from a matter of days, e.g. Ga. Code § 19–5–3 (30 days), to years, e.g. 23 Pa. C.S.A. § 3301 (2 years). Might these waiting periods, especially the longer ones, influence some victims of abuse to seek their divorces on fault-based grounds that have no waiting periods?

3. **Proving Cruelty.** Can you imagine reasons why a victim of domestic violence might choose not to try to prove the fact of the violence but instead sue on no-fault grounds? What evidence is necessary to show cruelty? Are there reasons why that evidence might not be readily available? Furthermore, might some victims of domestic violence reasonably worry that suing on fault-based grounds will be more dangerous to them than suing on no-fault grounds?

4. **No–Fault Divorce and Marital Privacy.** One of the impulses behind the adoption of no-fault divorce is the idea that divorce should be a private matter between the members of a divorcing couple. Only they know if their marriage is irreparably broken. Lynn D. Wardle, *No–Fault Divorce and the Divorce Conundrum*, 1991 B.Y.U. L. Rev. 79. Recently, in a no-fault divorce case, the Massachusetts Supreme Judicial Court adopted a similar position:

> [A]n irretrievable breakdown of the marriage is inherently subjective and . . . need not be objectively documented, tested and proven. . . . [I]t is sufficient that a party or parties subjectively decide that their marriage is over and there is no hope of reconciliation. In adopting no-fault divorce, the Legislature implicitly recognized that the parties to a marriage should be able to make personal and unavoidably subjective decisions about marriage and divorce free from overwhelming state control. *Caffyn v. Caffyn*, 806 N.E.2d 415 (Mass. 2004).

Familial privacy has, as you have seen, often been an argument used against the recognition of domestic violence. Do you think no-fault divorce downplays the significance of domestic violence as a cause of divorce? If you were a legislator would this be a reason for you to vote against including a no-fault grounds in your state's divorce statute? Would it be a reason why you would not want no-fault to be the sole grounds for divorce in your state? If you had a client who was suing for divorce and had been the victim of domestic violence, should no-fault's diminution of the importance of violence in the demise of the relationship affect your readiness to assert no-fault as the basis for the divorce?

5. **The Effect of No–Fault Divorce Laws on Divorce Rates.** There is a significant literature on the effects of no-fault divorce laws on the divorce rate. Some studies have found that the institution of no-fault divorce caused an increase in divorce rates in the short run, but no longer term effect. Justin Wolfers, *Did Unilateral Divorce Laws Raise Divorce Rates?* 96 AM. ECON. REV. 1802 (2006). In contrast, others have found that divorce rates are positively correlated with no-fault divorce laws when the no-fault divorce laws considered are those that do not take fault into account either in the grounds for divorce or in the award of assets or alimony. Margaret F. Brinig and F.H. Buckley, *No–Fault Laws and At–Fault People*, 18 INT'L. REV. L. & ECON. 325 (1998). These studies try to answer the question of whether there is Coasian bargaining among the parties to a marriage. A fault-based regime for divorce empowers the party who does not want the divorce; no divorce will occur unless he or she agrees to the filing of a divorce based on fault. In contrast, a unilateral no-fault regime empowers the party who wants to leave the marriage. The legal regime alone should not determine whether or not the parties divorce. Instead, regardless of the assignment of legal rights, Coasian theory implies that the parties will bargain among themselves for the most efficient outcome. For example, if the law only allows fault-based divorces and one party desperately wants to get out of the marriage, she or he will "bribe" the other party to end the marriage.

For our purposes, the general questions about the effects of no-fault divorce on divorce rates are not crucial. Our interest here is in what effect these legal changes may have had on levels of domestic violence. Once again, academics have taken opposing positions. One study, by Betsey Stevenson and Justin Wolfers, argues that unilateral no-fault divorce laws have the effect of empowering those who most want to leave the marriage and that victims of abuse are likely to be among those wanting to leave. Furthermore, Stevenson and Wolfers posit that the mere threat of divorce may sufficiently empower the victimized partner so as to prevent or reduce future abuse. Stevenson and Wolfers found that states that instituted unilateral no-fault divorce laws also showed drops in their domestic violence rates by approximately one-third. Furthermore, there was also a 10% reduction in the numbers of women murdered by their partners and a drop in female suicide rates, although it was not clear if the latter was due to the change in divorce laws or to other factors. Betsey Stevenson and Justin Wolfers *Bargaining in the Shadow of the Law: Divorce Laws and Family Distress*, 121 Q. J. ECON. 267 (2006). These are significant changes in the levels of domestic violence coincident with changes in the law of divorce, but, as with many social science studies, these findings do not prove a causal relationship. Can you think of an explanation as to why there might be a causal relationship? Or, can you identify other variables that may be affecting the rates of domestic violence during this period?

In contrast, Lynn Wardle argues that marriage is "the safest environment for women when it comes to risk of domestic violence." Lynn D. Wardle, *Marriage and Domestic Violence in the United States: New Perspectives about Legal Strategies to Combat Domestic Violence*, 15 ST. THOMAS L. REV. 791 (2003). Wardle argues that those who are divorced or separated are the subjects of the highest rates of domestic violence. He also argues that marriage functions to protect the parties to a marriage because marriage requires a significant investment in the relationship, married people are more likely to be integrated into community and family than those who are not married, and married people have more to lose if the relationship dissolves. All of this means that married partners are most likely to limit their aggressive tendencies and to resolve their difficulties in a peaceful manner.

Given what you already know about the dynamics of violent relationships, which of these studies of divorce rules and domestic violence sounds more credible to you and why? Do you agree that marriage is protective? Do you think that no-fault rules might provide an abused spouse with more power with which to bargain for changes in the dynamic within the marriage?

6.   **Divorce and Immigration Law.** Many people enter the country or seek to adjust their immigration status after their marriage to current U.S. citizens or legal permanent residents. When the marriage has occurred within 2 years of the entry or adjustment in status, the spouse seeking to enter or obtain a new immigrant status is given conditional residency. The conditional status will be removed and legal permanent residency awarded if the marriage is shown to be bona fide and the parties are still married after two years. This is part of an effort by the Congress and the U.S. Citizen and Immigration Service (USCIS) to ensure that the marriage was not just a ruse for entering the U.S. Thus, the petition to remove the condition must normally be filed jointly by the petitioner and the citizen or legal permanent resident spouse. A petitioning spouse who divorces before the condition is removed may lose conditional residency status and be subject to deportation.

This requirement can be extremely problematic for victims of domestic violence. These victims, who are likely to be isolated from their own families and friends by the fact of immigration and from others in the United States by language and cultural barriers, may feel like they cannot leave their abusers until the petition is filed and legal permanent residency status is conferred. Not surprisingly, abusers often use this process as yet another means of maintaining control over their wives.

The 1994 Violence Against Women Act created a "self-petitioning" option for victims of family violence with conditional residencies. In order to self-petition successfully, the abused spouse must be able to show that she or he lived with the citizen or legal permanent resident spouse in the U.S., that the marriage was a bona fide marriage, that the marriage ended in divorce within two years of the petition because of abuse, and that the abuse survivor is a person of good moral character who was either battered or subject to extreme cruelty during the marriage by her or his spouse. Each of these requirements may be difficult for a survivor of domestic violence. First, the abused spouse must be able to show that she or he actually lived with the abusive spouse in the U.S. This may not be the case if the abuser had another sexual partner elsewhere with whom he or she lived or if the abuser simply maintained a separate residence for purposes of freedom. Lauri J. Owen, *Forced Through the Cracks: Deprivation of the Violence Against Women Act's Immigration Relief in San Francisco Bay Area Immigrant Domestic Violence Survivors' Cases,* 21 BERKELEY J. GENDER L. & JUST. 13 (2006). It may also be difficult to prove that the marriage was a bona fide marriage. The USCIS requires extensive evidence and documentation to show that the marriage took place and that the parties' lives have been commingled. Unfortunately, even obtaining the basic documentation may be difficult if the wedding occurred in a country that does not keep good or easily accessible records. Furthermore, the victim's ability to obtain the records may be compromised by her distance from the country where they are, her illiteracy, her poverty, or her isolation. To show that their lives have been commingled, parties often try to prove that they socialize together as husband and wife and that they have joint bank accounts. Given what you know about the dynamics of violent relationships, can you explain why these ways of proving a bona fide marriage might not be available to victims of domestic violence?

In order to be able to self-petition successfully, the abused spouse must also be able to show that the marriage ended in divorce within two years because of the abuse and that the self-petitioning spouse is a person of good moral character who has either been battered or subjected to extreme cruelty. Showing that the marriage ended within two years of the marriage requires that the divorce have been finalized. Given the crowded calendars in many family courts and the ability of most litigants to delay, this too may be a problem. If the divorce is a no-fault divorce, it will be even more difficult to show that it was caused by abuse. This would require the petitioner to litigate in the immigration proceedings the very issues that the move to no-fault divorce tried to avoid. The self-petitioning spouse will also need to show that she is of good moral character. USCIS usually considers that petitioners with criminal records do not meet the good moral character requirement. Why might victims of intimate violence themselves have criminal records that would disqualify them? Congress recognized this problem and, in the Violence Against Women Act amendments of 2000, gave the Attorney General authority to waive the barring effect of certain acts or convictions if they were connected to the alien's having been abused. The final requirement to qualify to self-petition is that the petitioner have been either battered or subjected to extreme cruelty. How would you prove this? How likely do you think it is that an immigrant would have a full set of police and medical records proving the abuse? Another problem is that, given the dynamics of violent relationships, the violence may have taken place outside the U.S., with only threats, demeaning comments, or even contrition within the U.S. Advocates for victims of violence have argued that since these are a well-known aspect of how abusers maintain dominance and their abusive power, these actions should qualify even without physical violence. Lauri J. Owen, *Forced Through the Cracks: Deprivation of the Violence Against Women Act's Immigration Relief in San Francisco Bay Area Immigrant Domestic Violence Survivors' Cases,* 21 BERKELEY J. GENDER L. & JUST. 13, 22 (2006). The Courts of Appeals have been divided on the question of whether they could reverse a lower decision that did not see such actions as qualifying as "extreme cruelty." *Hernandez v. Ashcroft*, 345 F.3d 824 (9th Cir. 2003) (reversal appropriate); *Wilmore v. Gonzales*, 455 F.3d 524 (5th Cir. 2006) and *Perales–Cumpean v. Gonzales*, 429 F.3d 977 (10th Cir. 2005) (reversal not appropriate.)

For additional sources on these issues, see Nicole Lawrence Ezer, *The Intersection of Immigration Law and Family Law*, 40 Fam. L.Q. 339 (2006) and Laura L. Lichter, *Nuts and Bolts of Family–Based Immigration*, Am. L. Inst.-A.B.A. Cont. L. Educ. (April 26–27, 2007). We will further discuss problems facing immigrant battered women in Chapter Fifteen.

Division of Assets

Most states require that the parties' marital or community assets be divided "equitably;" a few require an equal division. An equitable division of assets need not be an equal division. What is equitable is usually determined by consideration of the parties' contributions to the marriage and by taking into account the parties' need and their other available resources.

One important question from our viewpoint is whether fault should be taken into account in determining the division of marital assets. In the majority of states, only conduct which has an economic impact on the parties may be considered in determining the division of assets. In a sizable minority of states, however, non-economic fault may be taken into account. Brett R. Turner, *The Role of Marital Misconduct in Dividing Property Upon Divorce,* 15 Divorce Litig. 117 (2003). In a small number of states, like California as illustrated in the case below, neither economic nor non-economic fault can be taken into account in dividing the assets.

The following case involves a post-marital agreement, a type of contract between the parties that is ordinarily enforceable if consideration can be shown. In many cases involving post-marital agreements the consideration is the promise to reconcile or to remain together if separation was imminent. Do you think that the agreement in the following case should have been enforceable? Although the case below does not involve domestic violence, can you imagine the parties making a similar agreement in which the husband promised to refrain from being violent in return for the wife's promise to reconcile? Should such an agreement be enforceable?

Mehren v. Dargan

California Court of Appeal, 2004.
13 Cal.Rptr.3d 522.

■ Rylaarsdam, J.

. . . Christopher Dargan (husband) appealed from an order . . . upholding the validity of a postmarital agreement. In the agreement he promised to grant respondent Monica Mehren (wife) all of his interest in certain of the parties' community property should he use illicit drugs. We conclude that such an agreement is unenforceable because it violates the public policy favoring no-fault divorce. We therefore order the trial court to vacate its order and enter a new order providing that the agreement is unenforceable....

Husband has suffered an off-and-on addiction to cocaine for many years. It is not necessary for us to relate his unsuccessful attempts to free himself from his addiction other than to note that several years after their marriage, the parties separated after another episode resulting from husband's use of cocaine. Months later, the parties agreed that husband would return to the family home. Subsequently, the parties entered into an "Agreement re Transfer of Property." The agreement recited that wife "consented to the resumption of marital relations on the condition that [husband] abstain from the deliberate, intentional use or ingestion of any mind altering chemical or substance excluding such use that may be prescribed or approved by a medical doctor. In the event of such deliberate, intentional use or ingestion of mind altering chemicals or substances by [husband], [husband] agrees that he will forfeit all of his right, title and interest in [described property]." Husband and wife signed the document before a notary public.

Unfortunately, husband did not keep his promise. Thereafter wife filed for divorce, asking that the property described in the agreement be confirmed to her as her separate property. The trial court concluded in a pretrial proceeding that the agreement did not violate public policy....

As far as we and the parties were able to determine, the specific issue before us is a novel one.... [W]e must decide whether the statutory regulations pertaining to marriage would be frustrated were we to enforce the agreement. We answer this query in the affirmative. Because the conduct of one spouse would affect the division of community property, the agreement frustrates the statutory policy favoring no-fault divorce....

[T]he agreement attempts to avoid the no-fault provisions of Family Code section 2310 [providing no-fault grounds for divorce]. As such, its objective is illegal ... [because] a contract [is] unlawful if it is 1. [c]ontrary to an express provision of law; 2. [c]ontrary to the policy of express law, ... or, 3. [o]therwise contrary to good morals. ... Further, the very issue determining whether she was entitled to the property would necessarily involve a judicial determination concerning husband's drug use, a factual adjudication of fault that the no-fault statute seeks to avoid....

The trial court is ordered to vacate its order ... and to enter a new order providing that the postmarital agreement between the parties is unenforceable....

NOTES AND QUESTIONS

1. **Is Fault a Relevant Consideration in the Division of Assets?** The Uniform Marriage and Divorce Act (UMDA), section 307, specifically provides that assets are to be divided on dissolution of the marriage "without regard to marital misconduct." One commentator notes,

> Clearly, the drafters believed that consideration of fault in divorce cases—whether the issue was grounds, property division, or spousal

support—was "unproductive," and that the process would be more "productive" if fault were not considered. As any divorce practitioner knows, consideration of fault tends to bog the court down into considering emotionally charged factual issues which are often more relevant to the parties themselves than to the attorneys or the court. The drafters of the UMDA believed that the property division process would be more efficient, and would focus better upon the real economic issues at stake, if fault were not considered. Brett R. Turner, *The Role of Marital Misconduct in Dividing Property Upon Divorce,* 15 DIVORCE LITIG. 117 (2003).

Do you think the drafters of the UMDA had the dynamics of violent relationships in mind when they decided that fault should not be a consideration in determining the allocation of assets? Should it matter that one form of abuse may have been to isolate the target of the violence so as to limit her ability to earn money or to accrue assets? Could this conduct also have had the effect of reducing the total amount of the familial assets? Should it matter that lack of economic resources sometimes forces victims of violence to remain with or return to a batterer? Do you think that, regardless of these issues, the victim of the violence should get a disproportionate share of the assets merely because the abuser was responsible for the break-down of the marriage? Is this last suggestion inconsistent with using a no-fault basis for obtaining the divorce? Cheryl J. Lee, *Escaping the Lion's Den and Going Back for your Hat—Why Domestic Violence Should be Considered in the Distribution of Marital Property Upon Dissolution of Marriage,* 23 PACE L. REV. 273 (2002).

2. **If Fault is to Be Considered, to What Extent Should it Affect the Distribution of Assets?** Here are summaries of three recent cases that discuss a range of options in terms of how a court might divide marital assets in a situation in which the marriage dissolved because of the wrongful actions of one party. Do you think that any of these courts got it right?

In re Marriage of Brown, 187 S.W.3d 143 (Tex. App. 2006). The Court specifically held that a trial court should have the discretion to consider "proven" fault in dividing the community property on divorce. The trial court had awarded all of the property to the wife, in part on the grounds that the incarcerated husband would simply waste any property awarded to him. At the time of trial he had served only 3 years on a 50 year sentence for child molestation. The Court of Appeals reversed and remanded for further proceedings. It thought there was an inadequate listing of the community assets and their value. Do you think the size of the marital estate should be taken into account in determining what percentage goes to the party who is not at fault in the break-up of the marriage? If the husband is to be in prison for the rest of his life, should all community assets go to the wife? Should the amounts expended from community property for his criminal defense be taken into account in distributing the assets? Is there any reason not to award all of the assets to the "innocent" spouse? Would your answers to any of these questions change if the husband had been in prison for abuse of his wife or for molesting one of his own children?

Alber v. Alber, 2006 WL 399656 (Mich. App.). In this case the trial court had divided the marital estate of approximately $170,000 equally, except that it gave the wife an extra $20,000. The wife received this extra $20,000 in part on account of pension benefits accrued during the marriage, but also in part because the husband had kicked her in the knee, causing an injury. The Court of Appeals does not provide much information about the violence between the parties, but it did uphold the award of the extra $20,000 to the wife saying there was "ample evidence and testimony concerning defendant's physical assaults of plaintiff, and his alleged controlling and violent behavior involving plaintiff and her three children.... Testimony and other evidence, including plaintiff's hospitalization record, supported the court's findings with regard to plaintiff's knee injury. Plaintiff testified that the knee injury affected her ability to work, resulting in lost wages. Further, because of the injury, she would likely be able to work only two more years and would have been able to work longer had she not been injured." Do you think that the evidence about the effects of the violence on the wife's ability to work subsequently should be crucial? Should a victim of intimate violence be able to recover a disproportionate share of the assets merely because of the violence, even if it did not affect future earning power? Should the amount that the victim recovers be tied to the resulting reduction in her or his annual earnings or should it be a percentage of the total marital assets? If the latter, what percentage? Was the Court here really recognizing that the husband had committed an intentional tort against his wife and awarding damages for that tort? For details on the complicated relationship between torts and divorce, see Chapter Thirteen.

Rodvik v. Rodvik, 151 P.3d 338 (Alaska 2006). This case involved a divorce that the court called "contentious." During the period when the divorce was being litigated, the wife obtained four different protective orders against the husband. The first were granted on the grounds that he "deprived her of sleep, prevented her from leaving, was verbally abusive, drank heavily, struck the children, pushed [her], butted her with his shoulder, and grabbed her." The other orders involved similar conduct on his part; at one point the court specifically found that the husband posed a threat to the wife's and the children's physical safety. The trial court awarded approximately $158,000 in marital assets to the wife and $146,000 to the husband, justifying this slight inequality on the grounds that the wife would have responsibility for caring for the children. On appeal, the Alaska Supreme Court said that an equal division of assets was "presumptively" the equitable way to divide them. As a result, the Court rejected the slightly unequal division unless the trial court could explain why the children's needs could not be met through an award of child support. The Supreme Court did uphold an award of the couple's gun collection to the wife because, under federal law, it would be unlawful for the husband to possess firearms, given the restraining orders against him. Notice that the Court did not even discuss the possibility of considering the husband's domestic violence as a basis for an unequal division. Do you think the husband's violence should be taken into account in dividing the assets? Do you think that the court considered the violence here to be insufficiently serious to take into account? Why didn't the existence of four protective orders mean something to the Court in terms of the seriousness of the violence?

As you think about these cases, consider whether you think evidence of domestic violence without evidence about its effect on the victim's earning capacity should justify an unequal division of assets. See also *Ohendalski v. Ohendalski*, 203 S.W.3d 910 (Tex. App. 2006) (specifically recognizing fault as a factor to be considered in dividing the community assets, upholding an award of 81% of the assets to the wife, and considering not only the husband's cruelty to her, but also the abusive husband's higher earning potential, higher level of education, wasteful expenditures on an extramarital affair, and her contribution of separate assets to the community estate.) If domestic violence does justify that the victim receive a disproportionate amount of the assets, how injurious or destructive must the violence be? Do you think there is some level of violence that would not justify a deviation from a norm of equal distribution?

3. **What Counts as Fault?** Fault comes in many different forms. So far, we have focused on domestic violence as fault. Traditionally, adultery was an important consideration in thinking about whether a party was at fault in a divorce. Similarly, as the notes above and the introduction to this section indicate, fault can also found in the dissipation of marital or community assets. But advocates for domestic violence victims should take care in arguing in favor of the consideration of fault that has an effect on the community's economic resources. In one recent divorce case, a trial court gave the abusive husband a disproportionate amount of the marital resources. The wife had obtained a protective order against the husband after he threatened her with a gun and he had then lost his job as a deputy sheriff. The trial judge said, "She ... should have known ... that if she proceeded with this protective order ... he was not going to have a job ... and he wasn't going to be able to pay his debts.... [I]f she felt she really needed the protection order, then she had to proceed with that. But then I think if that's the situation, she has to recognize the consequences.... Those consequences have been taken into consideration in terms of trying to make the distribution somewhat equitable." *In the Matter of the Marriage of Muhammad*, 108 P.3d 779 (Wash. 2005). The Washington Supreme Court overturned the consideration of the protective order as fault on the wife's part because the state statute specifically forbade the consideration of fault. How do you think this would have come out if fault had been an appropriate factor to consider in the division of marital property? Do you think that courts that are not well educated about the dynamics of violent relationships are likely to see victims' efforts to protect themselves as being at fault in destroying either the marriage or the couple's economic stability?

B. SETTING THE SCENE TO THINK ABOUT CUSTODY

The following excerpt comes from a novel that describes the continuing dynamics of abusive after separation and that shows how abusers often use children as a way of showing their former partners that they are still in a position to harm them.

Paula Sharp

Crows Over A Wheatfield (1996)

[Ben is the child of Mildred and Daniel. Daniel has been abusive toward Mildred who has recently separated from him. The narrator is Melanie, a friend of Mildred's. Melanie has volunteered to drive Ben to and from his mandated visits with his father. The others in the story are also friends of Mildred's.]

At nine o'clock I knocked on Daniel's door, but he refused to answer. I returned to the van, warmed up the motor, and played the radio loudly. . . .

At ten Daniel came outside. He put Ben down in the snow in front of the blue house and returned inside, without speaking. Ben stayed where he was, looking at his feet. I picked him up, and he did not fight or hug me. I belted him in the back seat. On the ride home Ben at first eluded every attempt I made to talk with him.

"Ben, did you have a good time?"

"I don't know."

"What did you do?"

"I don't know."

"Did you play checkers?"

"No."

"Did you go outside?"

"No."

"Did you stay inside?"

"No."

"Did you eat lunch?"

"No."

"Do you like saying no?"

"Yes," Ben answered, and tilted his head back against his seat. He looked weary, like an adult after a long week.

"Matt and Stretch Rockefeller made you icicles out of Kool–Aid," I said. "They hung a can from a hot-water pipe on the roof, and it dripped down Kool–Aid all night."

"Will it give me chicken pops?"

"You can't get chicken pox from things," I said.

"Daddy says all the presents will give me chicken pops."

"Daddy made a mistake. You can't get chicken pox from things. Believe me, I know. I've had chicken pox, and worse."

Ben didn't answer.

"The icicles are green and purple," I said. "Everybody missed you. You were gone so long."

"Daddy took away my sword," Ben said miserably.

When I looked in the rearview mirror, Ben was crying quietly. His head tilted forward and he whimpered. "Oh, oh, oh!" he said. "Oh, oh, oh."

I pulled over the car. I crawled in the back and put Ben on my lap. His clothes smelt like stale urine, and his hair was acrid. "What's wrong, honey? What is it?"

Ben kept sobbing, in that way children have, where their chests convulse and they hiccough as they cry. I could not help him stop. After a while he exhausted himself and curled sideways in my lap. I stroked his hair and felt his forehead. It was hot and soaked with tears. I held him until he relaxed in my arms, and then I drove him home.

When I carried him into the Steck's, Mrs. Shove was there. . . . She wore an auburn pantsuit and a new hairstyle that made me think of a bantam.

Mildred rushed to the door, lifted Ben, and said, "Sugarbeet, you're back." She whispered to me, "He smells like an old drunk."

He roused, pressed his face into her shoulder, and said, "I do not!"

"He feels a little hot," I said.

Mrs. Shove walked over to Mildred and touched Ben's cheek. "It's not really a fever," she told me. "He's probably just overtired. It seems like ninety-nine or a hundred. I used to give my boys a sponge bath when they were like that."

"That's just what I'll do," Mildred told her. "This boy needs fumigating." She kissed Ben's hair.

"Well, let me help," Mrs. Shove said. She followed Mildred up the stairs, to the bathroom, talking. I heard Ben cry out, and Mrs. Shove say, "Why, his pants look like he pooped in them a day ago. Look at this rash!"

I reached the top of the stairs as Mildred was settling Ben into the bathtub.

"Hey you," Mildred was saying. "Hey you, hey you."

Mrs. Shove sat on the toilet lid and poured bubble bath into the tub. I picked up Ben's soiled pants and ran them under the sink tap. They reeked. I reached under the sink for soap, filled the basin with soapy water, and scrubbed at them.

"Try this, Sugarbeet," Mildred said, and handed Ben two orange aspirin tablets.

"They taste like candy," Ben said.

"How was the interview?" I asked her.

"I don't know," Mildred answered. "It was awkward. The doctor is sort of full of himself. He's not going to ask to see Ben. Don't you think that's strange? That he wouldn't want to see how Ben acts around Daniel?"

"What did that Munk man do, run him around in those wet clothes?" Mrs. Shove asked, peering at the sink.

"Do you have a penis?" Ben asked Mrs. Shove.

Mrs. Shove raised one plucked eyebrow and answered, "Not that I know of."

Ben looked at the bubbles rising around him, and said, "I took a bath last night."

"Well, it looks like you need another one," Mildred told him.

"Daddy made me take a bath, and then he made me sleep in dirty clothes!"

John poked his head inside the bathroom. "How's it going up here?"

"Oh, we ladies are having a to-do," Mrs. Shove answered.

"Everyone's in the bathroom!" Ben said.

"Matt and Stretch Rockefeller sent Ben this," John said, holding up a long icicle, striped green and purple. "It's lime and grape flavored."

"You can't come in!" Ben told him. "There's no more room in the bathtub."

"I'm not getting in the bathtub," John said. "I'm just handing you your icicle."

Ben reached for the icicle and said "It's hot!" and withdrew his hand.

"I'll take it," Mrs. Shove said, and wrapped a washcloth around the base. "Hold it here, honey." John's footsteps receded down the stairs.

"Daddy made me take a bath with him, too."

"Daddy took a bath with you?" Mildred asked.

"Why, he's too big for that! There wouldn't be enough room," Mrs. Shove said.

Ben took the icicle, stirred the bubbles with his free hand to clear a circle in the water, and stuck the icicle's point into it. "It turns the water purple," he said.

"It's melting," Mrs. Shove told him.

"Do you have a penis?" Ben asked Mildred.

"No, sweetheart," she answered. "I'm a lady, so I don't have a penis."

"*I* have a penis. Daddy has a big penis. A big penis that gets bigger when you touch it."

Mrs. Shove frowned. I stopped wringing the clothes in the sink.

Mildred drew a breath and asked, "Did Daddy let you touch his big old penis?"

Ben looked at his mother's face, puzzled, and said, "I don't know."

"Christ," I said.

"He got into the bathtub with me!" Ben answered.

"He did?" Mildred asked.

"It was my bathtub!" Ben said. "I hit him with my sword."

"You had your sword in the bathtub?" I said.

Ben smiled. "Yes." Then he frowned. "He took my sword! He hit me back with it."

"He did? Which sword?" Mildred asked. "The wood one with the red handle?"

Ben nodded. "It's my sword," he said.

"Where did he hit you?"

"He smattered the side of my head."

"Did he hit you on the head?"

"He *smattered* it. It made noise right through my neck." Ben touched his ear. Then he repeated, "It's my sword." Almost as an afterthought, he added, "And then he punched me on the side."

Mildred wiped the bubbles from Ben's shoulders and pulled his hands up.

"Show me where," she said.

"Here," Ben answered, touching the fold of his upper arm. And then we all saw it, on the right side of his rib cage, high up, a yellow bruise like an enamel rose on china.

Mildred would not release Ben for further visitation. "Daniel found something that would force me to keep Ben away. Now he'll accuse me of interfering with visitation," Mildred said. "His lawyer will use this to argue that I shouldn't have custody, won't he? And it won't matter to the judge that Daniel hit Ben, or did anything else to him, will it?"

When Mildred asked me this, she was seated in Ottilie's peacock-blue armchair. The hair in Mildred's braid had unwoven in feathery tufts, as if she had been pulling on it out of nervousness. Her flannel shirt was buttoned wrong, the collar slanting on the left side to meet a low button-hole. Ben lay asleep in her lap. After the Saturday visit Ben clung to her as if he feared she would disappear if he strayed so far as another room by himself.

Vogelsang had filed a new petition in court the Monday after Ben's overnight visit, asking to terminate unsupervised visitation and attaching affidavits from all of us, and a letter from Ben's pediatrician. ("I assured the mother that there is no evidence of a concussion," he wrote, "and the hearing is intact. But the bruises on the upper torso and behind the ear are large.") Judge Bracken sat on the papers. He did not want extra work, and set the return date for the new petition on the same day he had originally scheduled for us to appear in court.

Even before this result, I thought the judge would merely find the further suggestion of Daniel's lack of sexual boundaries with his son distasteful, and shun our papers, and dismiss the evidence of Daniel's violence. Daniel was too hard to assemble into a picture, and an understanding of Daniel's motives would never be within the grasp of Judge Bracken's court: Daniel's love of brinksmanship, his desire to know that he could get away with anything. Even now it is unnerving for me to remember how effectively a man like Daniel, who subverted every code, fit the law into his hand like a well-worn tool. It was as though the law had been designed specifically for him all along.

NOTES AND QUESTIONS

1. **Child Abuse in the Context of Partner Abuse.** Daniel's abuse of Ben has several dimensions. In part, it appears that Daniel is seeking to punish Mildred for separating from him, by abusing and neglecting their son in ways that he knows will be intolerable to her. In part he is also showing her that he still has the power to control her, through her attachment to Ben, even though she has sought to break free of his control. In addition, however, it seems that his physical and sexual abuse of Ben demonstrates an inability or unwillingness to respect boundaries in his relationships; he treats others as instruments to his own ends. Finally, it may be that his need to control is as strong in his relationship with his son as it was in his relationship with his partner. Notice how aspects of the abusive relationship that you have already seen reappear in this context.

2. **How Real is This Excerpt?** If Mildred's and Melanie's fears about how the legal system will respond to Daniel's abuse of Ben seem farfetched, you may decide after reading the materials in this and the following chapters that truth is stranger than fiction. CROWS OVER A WHEATFIELD is a damning but not unrealistic indictment of the family law system, showing how three factors combine to put mothers and children at risk: judicial lack of understanding of battering relationships and batterers; judicial distrust of women's testimony and motives; and abusers' abilities to manipulate the system (witnesses as well as judges) to serve their own ends.

Judith G. Greenberg

Domestic Violence and the Danger of Joint Custody Presumptions

25 N. Ill. U. L. Rev. 403 (2005).

... Children do not thrive when their mothers are caught in violent relationships. There is considerable evidence that it is the violence and the controlling relationship that develops as a result that is injurious, not just the conflict between the parents that often accompanies divorce. Children who grow up in families in which there is domestic violence experience a number of behavioral, psychological, and educational difficulties. Studies show that over 85% of children in families in which there is domestic violence have been witnesses to it. Studies also show that children witness about half of the incidents of domestic violence. Even more children are "exposed" to the abuse because they see broken objects, bruises on the victim, or watch the abuser's arrest.

Children who have been exposed to domestic violence often act in socially unacceptable ways. They are likely to be aggressive and destructive toward other children, to be more oppositional in their behavior, to be cruel to animals, and to use drugs and alcohol. These children also have troubled friendships. They are less likely than other children to have close friends and yet they are more likely to worry about their friends. They are also likely to suffer from depression, to tend toward suicide, to have low self-esteem, and to experience somatic symptoms like headaches, insomnia or bedwetting. In addition, they often show signs of post traumatic stress disorder, including nightmares, flashbacks, and hyper-vigilance. Recent research shows that some of this may even be due to changes in the children's brain structures. Although these last may be irreversible, there is also some evidence that at least some of the behavioral and psychological problems improve if the children are removed from their father's presence.

As a result of these difficulties, children exposed to domestic violence also have difficulty in school. Their hypervigilance makes it hard for them to concentrate on schoolwork. They have difficulty reflecting or focusing on their own work. Indeed, there are unusually high rates of attention deficit hyperactivity disorder among these children. Children from families in which there is intimate partner abuse also often have problems relating to other people, both their peers and adults. If they engage in fights with or bullying behavior toward other children, they will constantly be in trouble in school. One legal services organization has reported that many of the clients who need representation because they have been suspended or expelled from school turn out to be children traumatized by domestic violence. Children who have been traumatized in their homes may perceive the world as dangerous and unpredictable. This attitude makes it hard for them to trust either their teachers or their school to keep them safe.

Domestic violence, whether between cohabiting parents or separated parents, is also deleterious for children because the children frequently get caught up in the violence. This can happen in one of two ways. First, those who abuse their partners are also likely to be abusive toward their children. Clare Dalton, Susan Carbon and Nancy Olesen note that studies have found that almost half of those who abuse their intimate partners also abuse their children, whereas only 7% of non-batterers abuse their children. Dalton, Carbon and Olesen also point to studies that show that mothers of incest victims are likely to be battered by the child's abuser. Another study found that approximately one quarter of batterers kidnapped or threatened to kidnap their children during times when they had access to them. Children may also get caught up in the violence in other ways. Sometimes children are emotionally torn by the situation, trying to maintain some loyalty to each parent. In other cases, however, children are physically injured by the domestic violence. One recent study found that a quarter of the women responding said that their children were "physically involved" in the battering incident. Sometimes this physical involvement occurs because the children have intervened in the abusive incident in an effort to protect their mothers. Other times the children are injured because the batterer's assaults on the children's mother put the nearby children at risk. Zoe Hilton describes the incidents that were reported to her as follows:

> One man threatened, while driving with his wife and children in the car, to crash the car and kill them all. Some men pushed, hit, and squeezed women with babies in their arms. One man tried to pull a child away from his separated wife during an unofficial access visit....

Whether or not the father intends to injure the child, it is dangerous for a child to be in a setting in which there is violence against the child's mother.

NOTES AND QUESTIONS

1. **Process.** The effects of violence on children may be relevant in two somewhat different settings. First, victims of violence, on first separating from their abusive partner, may want an order of custody, with or without visitation by the abuser. Remember that in many states victims petitioning for protective orders can also ask for custody. These temporary orders of custody are likely to be heard in a crisis setting. Another time when the effects of the violence on the children are significant is when the judge makes a final decision on custody. In many cases this does not occur until months (or years) after the parties have separated. The level of violence may even have changed during that period. As an advocate for either party, how might the setting (immediate crisis v. long-term custody decision) affect your argument about the effects of domestic violence on children?

2. **Heterogeneity of Response.** Not surprisingly, children respond very differently from one another to the presence of partner abuse in their homes. Some children are unaffected by the violence, while others may find reservoirs of strength insides themselves to deal with it. Even for those children who have negative reactions to the violence, the reactions vary by their age, sex, whether they are living in a shelter, the types, length and severity of the violence, and their mothers' responses and adjustment to the violence, to name just a few of the factors. DOMESTIC VIOLENCE IN THE LIVES OF CHILDREN (Sandra Graham–Bermann and Jeffrey Edleson, eds., 2001); CHILDREN EXPOSED TO MARITAL VIOLENCE (George Holden, Robert Geffner and Ernest N. Jouriles, eds., 1998). If children's reactions are so variable, how would knowledge about the studies of the effects of violence on children be useful to an advocate?

Joan S. Meier
Domestic Violence, Child Custody, and Child Protection: Understanding Judicial Resistance and Imagining the Solutions
11 AM. U. J. GENDER SOC. POL'Y & L. 657 (2003).

. . .

II.   Judicial Schizophrenia in Responses to Domestic Violence

While significant progress has been achieved in many state courts concerning basic understandings of domestic violence [in the restraining order context] . . . there has been a striking insulation of custody/visitation adjudications from this new "enlightenment." Despite the widespread acceptance of the growing body of evidence that adult domestic violence is detrimental to children, both courts and lawyers commonly separate the issue of domestic violence from custody/visitation, and even sometimes excuse it in a divorce context. More notably, sympathy and concern to an adult battering victim can be transformed into an attitude of disdain and outright hostility when the battered woman seeks to limit the abuser's access to his child. This disjunction can even occur within a single case, heard by a single judge. . . . [T]his judicial attitude all too often inures to the profound detriment of the children involved.

A.   Changes in Courts' Understanding of Domestic Violence

If we consider domestic violence proceedings which are not focused on children, e.g., protection order cases, it is fair to say that a battle has been fought and at least partially won, regarding the seriousness with which domestic violence is taken by the courts. . . . Many courts have instituted dedicated domestic violence dockets or courts, and in a growing number of jurisdictions it is no longer acceptable conventional practice, at least in protection order or criminal cases, to treat domestic violence allegations as implausible or trivial. . . . But it is these very improvements in the handling of domestic violence cases that have made the lack of such respect for battering claims in custody/visitation cases within the same court so striking.

B.   Limits of the "New Enlightenment": Custody and Visitation Determinations

Thus, in [one case which the author litigated in the new District of Columbia] Domestic Violence Court, the judge's very demeanor switched from being objective and basically respectful regarding the domestic violence allegations (which were related to the claim of contempt of the protection order), to hostile and demeaning when the subject of child visitation was addressed (as part of the abuser's motion to modify the CPO). In response to my argument that the batterer should not receive visitation pending the next court date in two months, the judge snarlingly dismissed my description of the child's destructive behaviors because it came from "the mother" (who was standing right next to me). The judge's hostility toward the abused mother's claim of risk to the child was in marked contrast to his receptivity to the abuser's claim that the mother's new boyfriend was abusing the child. In fact, the court ordered a child abuse investigation of the mother and her boyfriend, but not the batterer. It is important to bear in mind that this judge, although known to have quite a temper, was generally considered fairly enlightened on domestic violence. Moreover, he has since been elevated to a significant administrative position, was previously credited as one of the more effective judges in the Domestic Violence Court, and has generally expressed a fair degree of openness to the concerns of domestic violence advocates....

This sense that many family judges seem to retain a mental "bifurcation" between "custody/visitation" matters and "domestic violence" matters was crystallized during planning discussions in 2002 for the new Family Court in the District of Columbia. While the new court does not encompass the existing Domestic Violence Unit, where protection orders and criminal cases are handled, it adjudicates all other family law cases. When the question arose of how domestic violence would be handled in the new Family Court, both the judges and attorneys involved in the planning stated that this court would not be handling "domestic violence cases," as though domestic violence is not an issue in divorce and custody cases....

III. Why and How Courts Resist Domestic Violence Claims in Custody Cases

It can generally be assumed that judges and forensic evaluators who react negatively to battered mothers' claims in custody/visitation contests do not (with some notable exceptions) consciously do so out of sexism. Rather, they often rely on apparently gender-neutral rationales, which undercut the likelihood that a battered mother is truly seeking to protect her children.... [O]ne sometimes unspoken but extremely powerful "gender-neutral" norm which pervasively influences courts adjudicating custody and visitation, and militates against serious consideration of domestic violence [is] the emphasis on parental equality, which more specifically takes the form of a focus on fathers. It is my sense that the desire for greater parental involvement is exerting a magnetic pull in these cases which impels courts to avoid full consideration of domestic violence....

A. Parental Equality at all Costs

... [T]he equality principle is ... powerfully driven by substantive values. Such values derive most obviously from the powerful (although incomplete) gender revolution of the 1960s, which ushered in the rejection of explicitly gendered standards in family law, in particular, the tender years presumption as a means of determining the best interest of the child. One thing has been clear since "women's liberation": mothers are no longer supposed to be considered the pre-eminent parent.... [S]ome form of joint custody has increasingly become not just an aspiration, invitation, or even a preference, but an absolute ideal. Buttressing the notion of co-equal parenting as the highest good for children and the only fair resolution for parents has been the rapid adoption of a series of other legislative and judicial policies ... Both of these notions reflect and further the seductive assumptions that any parent who does not support co-equal parenting (typically mothers) is by definition a deficient parent, and that any parent who advocates joint parenting (typically fathers) is inherently virtuous....

[W]hat is important for present purposes is the recognition of and reasons for the remarkably powerful hold of these "equal parenting" principles on the courts. It appears that these principles, which seek to ensure more access by fathers to children, fall on fertile ground. In essence, they tap into a widespread, deeply felt lack of fathering throughout our culture and courts. Anyone who has litigated custody knows that it is an unspoken "given" in most custody courts that fathers' involvement with their children is both rare and very important. A concomitant assumption is the implicit sense that mothers start with an unfair advantage, presumably because they fit our intuitive image of "parent," and are assumed to be primary and/or "natural" parents. The combined effect of these unspoken assumptions is that custody courts, while believing they are merely furthering parental "equality," not infrequently give fathers' claims and requests greater weight than mothers'.

In short, the judicial emphasis on both parental equality and father involvement in custody is powerfully driven ... by ... norms, which fuel resistance to considering domestic violence as determinative of custody or visitation....

B. Discounting the Credibility of Domestic Violence Accusations

The gulf between domestic violence advocates and those (predominantly judges and court-appointed forensic evaluators) who resist the characterization of fathers as batterers who are dangerous to their children, is defined in large part by advocates' willingness to believe women's claims (both about risk to themselves and to the children), and the courts' skepticism toward those same claims. These fundamentally contradictory starting perspectives are fueled by differing attitudes toward three core elements of factual assessment which shape the players' judgments in these cases: (i) the meaning of neutrality, (ii) gender bias, and (iii) demeanors of victims and perpetrators.

1. The Meaning of Neutrality

[I]nstead of genuine neutrality, which is receptive to information, many judges and evaluators actually exhibit skepticism or disbelief toward abuse allegations.... Both existing statistics and qualitative knowledge about domestic violence offer some objective guidance.... [W]e know empirically that domestic violence is surprisingly widespread and that it is perpetrated most often by males against females. Further, we know that domestic violence is more prevalent in the relationships of parties who are divorcing, and still more common—with estimates of up to 75%—among couples in conflict over visitation or custody.

Moreover, contrary to the assumptions of many evaluators and judges, ... fabricated claims of abuse are rare.... On the contrary, women tend to minimize and deny abuse while understating the amount and severity of abuse. Women's reluctance to reveal that they have been abused is widely recognized. This uncontroversial truth is hard to square with the belief prevalent in the legal system that women in litigation (whether as plaintiffs or defendants) frequently fabricate such claims. In short, much of the skepticism toward women's claims of domestic violence and child abuse appears to be based on an inaccurate understanding of the real prevalence of domestic violence among couples engaged in contested custody litigation.

Finally, when not dismissing domestic violence claims altogether, courts and evaluators often reject such claims as exaggerated or insufficient. However, in many cases, the view that abuse is merely "minor" or "exaggerated" ignores both the better-documented phenomenon of minimization and denial, and the reality that domestic abuse spans a wide spectrum of behaviors (and that victims often reveal lesser incidents before they disclose the most traumatic ones). Not all domestic violence results in bruises or broken bones. Some forms of abuse are predominantly sexual. Yet the hallmarks of an abusive relationship, namely the power, control, domination and state of fear, even without much severe physical violence, may still be profoundly damaging.

While courts are quick to discount mothers' claims of battering, they tend implicitly to over-value fathers' claims of desire for custody. It is now well-established that many batterers seek custody primarily as an extension of their power and control over and abuse of the mother. The American Psychological Association found that batterers are twice as likely to contest custody as non-batterers, and are more likely to contest custody of sons. In addition to seeking to impose their rigid views of gender roles on their children, many batterers see winning custody over the mother as a powerful means of vindicating their moral and functional superiority....

The net effect of the courts' unwarranted skepticism toward mothers' claims of battering and excessive deference toward accused fathers, then, is that it is highly unusual for a battered woman in private litigation to be recognized by a court to be sincerely advocating for her children's safety. Rather, her very status as a litigant, a mother, and battered, seems to ensure that she will be viewed as, at best, merely self-interested, and at worst, not credible. Conversely, men's demands for access to their children are typically met with a presumption of good faith, even when those men are adjudicated batterers. Notably, this type of resistance to battered mothers' veracity in litigation over the children can co-exist with the court's basic acceptance of her claims for purposes of the non-child-centered aspects of the case. In other words, the mere presence of children as a "stake" in the litigation can profoundly shift the culture of a case.

2.   Gender Bias

Given what is known about domestic violence and batterers, the courts' insistence on "neutrality" or "objectivity" leads us inescapably back to the question of gender bias.... In fact, strikingly, many courts themselves (through appointed commissions) have identified dynamics of gender bias in custody and/or domestic violence adjudications. The Massachusetts Gender Bias study of 2100 disputed custody cases found that courts consistently held mothers to higher standards of proof than fathers, a finding that it stated "directly contradicts the popular misconception that if gender bias does exist in child custody cases, it is in favor of mothers." Karen Czapanskiy has found that states' gender bias studies consistently indicate that the "credibility accorded women litigants is less than that accorded men litigants" in domestic violence cases. For instance:

> These responses reveal a strong perception by both the bar and the judiciary that, at least in rape and in domestic violence cases, a female comes to court in Georgia bearing a credibility burden, a burden based on a stereotypic view of gender that does not affect males in the same

way. The effect of such undue skepticism frequently places female litigants in a position where they must offer more evidence than do male litigants. . . .

3. Demeanor Differences between Perpetrators and Victims of Abuse

Battered women, and especially battered mothers, may be disbelieved for another, and arguably more "appropriate," reason: the parties' respective demeanors. Judges (and arguably, evaluators) are in the business of assessing credibility. Unfortunately, many common assumptions about witness credibility backfire when applied to victims and perpetrators of domestic violence.

While courts often find batterers to be sympathetic and convincing in their denials, these credibility assessments are often incorrect. Many who work in batterers' counseling attest that a common characteristic of batterers is their passionate and eloquent denial of the abuse and the impact of their own conduct on others. As Bancroft and Silverman succinctly state, "it is common for our clients to be skillfully dishonest. . . ." Batterers convince not only other people, but also themselves that they are "right" and their accusers are wrong and unworthy. Their denials are especially believable by courts in cases where the allegations of physical violence can be perceived as minor.

Many batterers also exhibit a smooth and charming persona in public and when it is in their interest. . . .

In contrast, battered women, particularly those who have made it to court, are often angry or emotional. While this is a perfectly understandable reaction to domestic abuse and contests over custody, these demeanors do not enhance women's credibility in the eyes of a judge or other evaluator. Moreover, many battered women in court are experiencing some stage of post-traumatic-stress-disorder ("PTSD"), which may distort their affect. In particular, PTSD can cause victims to over-react to ostensibly trivial issues, to display a strange lack of affect when discussing the violence, or to giggle inappropriately. . . .

Thus, judges and evaluators lacking in-depth knowledge about domestic violence and PTSD may easily be misled into trusting the calm, sincere-sounding accused's veracity more than the "strange" or emotional purported victim's.

C. Insistence on Mutual Blame or Blamelessness

For all the reasons discussed above, courts' first line of defense against domestic violence allegations is often disbelief. However, many courts also marginalize or neutralize such allegations without overtly taking a stand against the mother, merely by hewing firmly to the "neutral" role and treating both parents "equally." Thus a common response to the difficulty in evaluating the truth in these cases is to blame both parties for the "mess," and abdicate the duty to find the facts: the judge or evaluator simply says that the contradictions of the two parties make neither one credible. Judges' resistance to finding the facts is signaled when they characterize the dispute over abuse as "mudslinging" . . . or, more politely, a "swearing contest." . . .

I believe this view—that domestic violence, like all other relationship issues, is a mutual problem—is, consistent with the equality principle, at the root of many courts' unsatisfactory responses to domestic violence allegations in custody cases. In particular, the belief in mutuality appears often to guide many mental health professionals involved in evaluations in such cases. . . .

Conclusion

These [claims describe] the entrenched attitudes of [family] courts that prevent them from taking seriously battered mothers' claims, and that lead them repeatedly and disturbingly to place children (and women) at unnecessary risk. . . .

NOTES AND QUESTIONS

1. **Is Skepticism about Victims Specific to Family Law?** Victims of intimate violence often do not come across as very credible. We have explored similar problems already in the context of criminal law; as you saw in Chapters Five and Eight, sometimes expert testimony is used to explain the victim's conduct. Which of the reasons offered by Meier for family law judges' skepticism about claims of domestic violence are specific to family law proceedings and which reflect a larger social reluctance to believe victims of violence?

2. **More on Family Courts' Disbelief of Victims.** Clare Dalton offers yet another reason to consider why family law courts may be even less willing to credit claims of violence than criminal courts or those dealing with protective orders: "When a woman asks a court for a restraining order, she is usually either wearing the marks of violence or telling a story so detailed and so immediate that her credibility is readily established. In other proceedings, however, a victim may disclose abuse for the first time in the context of a separation, divorce, or custody dispute. There may be no precipitating act of violence, and the stories may be heard as an effort to perpetuate the conflict that has poisoned the relationship or to gain leverage in the contest over money and children. In this context, credibility is harder to earn," Clare Dalton, *When Paradigms Collide: Protecting Battered Parents and Their Children in the Family Court System*, 37 FAM. & CONCIL. CTS. REV. 273 (1999).

C.   BEST INTERESTS OF THE CHILD

One of the most important questions in a divorce case is how to provide for custody of the children of the marriage. Until the second half of the 20th century, courts usually gave custody of any children to the mother on the theory that children needed their mother in order to develop properly. However, if the divorce was granted because of the mother's "fault," then she might not get custody of the children. Once states began to adopt no-fault grounds for divorce, once the Fourteenth Amendment's Equal Protection clause began to be extended to cover discrimination on the basis of sex, and once fathers began to argue that they too could raise children, states turned to a "best interests" standard for determining child custody, see Barbara Bennett Woodhouse, *Child Custody in the Age of Children's Rights*, 33 FAM. L. Q. 815, 817–820 (1999). This standard asks what custody arrangement would be in the child's best interests. Today, all states use some form of the "best interests" standard in deciding custody cases.

Some state statutes explicitly identify a number of factors that judges must consider in order to determine a child's best interests but others do not. Most of the states do not allocate particular weights to specific factors. Instead, the weighing of the factors is usually left up to the judge in light of the unique facts of each case. Not surprisingly, this makes it hard to predict how any particular case will be decided. It also allows a judge's own biases to affect the outcome, or, at least, it allows a losing litigant to believe that is what happened.

The lack of direction is particularly a problem when domestic violence is involved. Some judges might see domestic violence as a relevant factor in determining custody while others might think that the abuse was irrelevant since it was not directed at the children, see Sarah M. Buel, *Domestic Violence and the Law*, 33 FAM. L. Q. 719 (1999). Even where domestic violence is explicitly enumerated in the statute as a factor to be considered in determining a child's best interests, some judges might give it a lot of weight while others give it very little. As the studies previously described indicate, domestic violence, even when not aimed at the child, is often injurious to the child. As you read the following case, think about how the trial court and the Appellate Division weighed the various factors that they considered relevant. Given cases like *Wissink*, do you think it is desirable to maintain the best interests standard or would you favor moving to a rule that prevents abusers from obtaining custody?

Wissink v. Wissink

New York Supreme Court, Appellate Division, 2002.
749 N.Y.S.2d 550 (2nd Dept.)

■ S. MILLER, J.

This appeal presents a vexing custody dispute over a teenaged girl who has expressed a clear preference to live with her father. While both parents are seemingly fit custodians, the father has a history of domestic violence directed at the mother; yet he has never posed a direct threat to the child. . . .

The child in controversy, Andrea, born June 21, 1986, is the biological child of the mother and father; the mother also has a daughter, Karin, by a prior marriage. The parties have had a tumultuous relationship marked by

numerous episodes of heated arguments, physical violence, police intervention and Family Court orders of protection. . . .

The parties have lived apart at various times during their marriage,
and separated most recently in 1999 following yet another physical altercation. The mother commenced a family offense proceeding and a proceeding
for custody of Andrea. The father cross-petitioned for custody. The Family
Court assigned a law guardian and ordered a mental health study which
was clearly deficient. A hearing was held at which the parties, Karin, and
other witnesses testified, and the court examined Andrea in camera; she
downplayed the father's culpability and expressed her clear preference for
living with him.

The order appealed from awarded custody to the father. . . .

Andrea's preference for her father and her closely bonded relationship
to him were confirmed by her law guardian and the "mental health
professional" social worker who interviewed her. Indeed, putting aside the
established fact of his abusive conduct toward her mother, Andrea's father
appears a truly model parent. He is significantly involved in her school
work and her extracurricular activities. They enjoy many pleasurable
activities, including movies, shopping, building a barn, and horseback
riding. He provides her with material benefits—a television set, clothing, a
horse, a trip to Europe. He is loving and affectionate. She is his "princess,"
his "best girl." In contrast, Andrea's mother has not been significantly
involved in her school work or her extracurricular activities, and Andrea
does not enjoy her company or their relationship.

Were it not for the documented history of domestic violence confirmed
by the court after a hearing, we would have unanimously affirmed the
Family Court's award of custody to the father in accordance with Andrea's
expressed preference and the evidence documenting their positive relationship. However, the fact of domestic violence should have been considered
more than superficially, particularly in this case where Andrea expressed
her unequivocal preference for the abuser, while denying the very existence
of the domestic violence that the court found she witnessed.

The record is replete with incidents of domestic violence reported by
the mother, and by evidence supporting her testimony. The earliest incident that the mother reported was perpetrated when Andrea was merely an
infant in 1986. In a fit of anger the father hit and kicked the mother and
pulled out chunks of her hair. In the course of the attack she heard him
say, "Oh well, she's going to die." On Super Bowl Sunday in 1995, he
attacked her, throwing her on the floor, kicking, hitting, and choking her.
She sustained marks on her neck and a sore throat causing pain while
speaking and inhibiting her ability to swallow.

In March 1995, she obtained an order of protection from the Village
Court of Montgomery. In the fall of that year the father allegedly held a
knife, approximately 8 to 10 inches long, to the mother's throat while
Andrea, then nine, sat on her lap. In February 1996 the mother again
obtained an order of protection from the Village Court of Montgomery.

In 1997, the father attacked the mother, hit and kicked her, resulting in her obtaining a permanent order of protection from the Orange County Family Court. The severity of her injuries are documented by a photograph, entered in evidence, showing a large black and blue bruise on her left hip.

In June 1999, the mother left the marital home with Andrea and moved into a shelter where they remained for five days. Upon their return home the father blocked her car in the driveway, yelled at the mother and punched her.

On June 24, 1999, a few days after her return from the shelter, during a dispute over tax returns, the father tried to wrest papers the mother held in her teeth by squeezing her face in his hands, leaving marks and even enlisting the assistance of Andrea; he allegedly directed the child to "hold [the mother's] nose so she can't breathe."

On December 20, 1999, while Andrea was at home, the father attacked the mother, choking her. She had marks on her neck for days.

The latter two incidents were the subjects of the mother's most recent Family Offense petition, which the court sustained. In doing so, the Family Court also noted that a final order of protection had been entered in 1997, stating "based upon the proceeding [of 1997] as well as the succeeding [incidents] ... Mr. Wissink is guilty of incidents of domestic violence occurring on June 24, [1999] and December 20, [1999]."

Domestic Relations Law § 240(1) provides that in any action concerning custody or visitation where domestic violence is alleged, "the court must consider" the effect of such domestic violence upon the best interest of the child, together with other factors and circumstances as the court deems relevant in making an award of custody. In this case the Family Court did not entirely ignore that legislative mandate, and specifically noted that it had considered the effect of domestic violence in rendering its custody determination. However, the "consideration" afforded the effect of domestic violence in this case was, in our view, sorely inadequate.

The court-ordered mental health evaluation consisted of the social worker's interview of Andrea on two occasions (about 45 minutes each) and each parent once (about one hour each). These interviews resulted in the social worker's clearly foreseeable conclusion that Andrea was far more comfortable and involved with her father than her mother, that she did not relate well to her mother, and that she preferred living with her father.

In a case such as this, where the record reveals years of domestic violence, which is denied by the child who witnessed it, and the child has expressed her preference to live with the abuser, the court should have ordered a comprehensive psychological evaluation. Such an evaluation would likely include a clinical evaluation, psychological testing, and review of records and information from collateral sources. The forensic evaluator would be concerned with such issues as the nature of the psychopathology of the abuser and of the victim; whether the child might be in danger of becoming a future victim, or a witness to the abuse of some other victim; the child's developmental needs given the fact that she has lived in the polluted environment of domestic violence all of her life and the remedial efforts that should be undertaken in regard to all parties concerned.

The devastating consequences of domestic violence have been recognized by our courts, by law enforcement, and by society as a whole. The effect of such violence on children exposed to it has also been established. There is overwhelming authority that a child living in a home where there has been abuse between the adults becomes a secondary victim and is likely to suffer psychological injury.

Moreover, that child learns a dangerous and morally depraved lesson that abusive behavior is not only acceptable, but may even be rewarded.

In many states a rebuttable presumption that perpetrators of domestic violence should not be eligible for legal or physical custody has been accepted and the courts of those states are required to specify why custody should be granted to an offender and how such an order is in the best interest of the child. We in New York have not gone that far, but the legislature, in enacting Domestic Relations Law § 240, has recognized that domestic violence is a factor which the court must consider among others in awarding custody or visitation.

Moreover, the court also erred in limiting the mother's inquiry regarding the father's failure to comply with child support obligations and in finding financial consideration "not relevant at all" to the custody proceeding. The Family Court was required to consider the parties' support obligations and their compliance with court orders and to evaluate each party's ability to support the child. If, as the mother alleged, the father violated the child support order, and if he terminated the telephone and electrical services in the marital residence after he had been ordered to stay away pursuant to an order of protection, these facts would clearly be relevant to the court's custody determination.

Only after considering the complex nature of the issues and the relative merits and deficiencies of the alternatives can the court attempt to determine the difficult issue of the best interest of the child in a case such as this.

For the above reasons we thus reverse the custody order and direct a new custody hearing to be conducted after completion of a comprehensive psychological evaluation of the parties and the child. However, we stay Andrea's return to her mother, permitting her continued residence with her father, pending a final custody determination.

NOTES AND QUESTIONS

1. **Further Information Needed?** Do you agree with the Appellate Division that this case should have been remanded for further information? What do you think the requested psychological evaluations are likely to show? How likely do you think it is that the trial court will award custody to the mother on remand?

2. **Best Interests Factors.** The New York statute applicable in the *Wissink* case required the court to determine the child's best interests by

considering allegations of domestic violence proven by a preponderance of the evidence and any other factors the court thought were relevant. What "other factors" did the trial court deem relevant in *Wissink*? If you had been the trial judge, how would you have weighed the factors in this case?

In considering the factors relevant to a child's best interests, should the court also take into account that, as we saw above, there are different types of batterers and differing motivations for violence among intimate partners? For an argument that these differences are important in considering custody, see Nancy Ver Steegh, *Differentiating Types of Domestic Violence: Implications for Child Custody*, 65 LA. L. REV. 1379 (2005).

3. **Balancing Abuse of an Intimate Partner Against Absence of Abuse of the Child.** Historically, many courts believed that if the child who was the subject of the custody action had never been abused, then abuse of the child's parent was not relevant. Some courts continue to take that position. In *Lamb v. Lamb*, 939 So.2d 918 (Ala. Civ. App. 2006) the Court awarded custody to the father despite significant evidence of his abuse of the child's mother. The Court noted that although there was evidence that the father had abused his wife (the child's mother) and at least one of her children from a previous relationship, he had never abused this child. Furthermore, the wife's other children sometimes looked unkempt and had contracted head lice, the husband was employed but the wife was not, and the wife had suffered a mental break-down with hospitalization as a result of the abuse. Do you agree that, weighing all the evidence, the child's best interests would be served by awarding custody to the father? Do you think the trial court's determination on behalf of the father should have been overturned on appeal given that the standard of review allows a reversal only if the trial judge has abused his discretion?

4. **Parenting and Domestic Violence.** Since victims of domestic violence often experience depression, lowered self-esteem, post-traumatic stress, and other types of psychological injury, it is possible that Mrs. Wissink's inability to connect with her daughter was due to the abuse she had suffered. This raises a series of important questions for a judge deciding a custody case. First, are victims of abuse likely to be worse parents? Second, should an abusive parent be "rewarded" with custody of the child if the abuse is the reason for the other parent's diminished ability to parent? And, third, how long will the effects of the abuse continue to affect the victimized parent's ability to parent? If the victimized parent can recover at least some of the parenting skills within months of a divorce (assuming the violence actually ends) should custody be given to that parent or should she or he have to move for a modification of custody subsequently when parenting abilities have improved?

Research to date shows that women who are victims of domestic violence are very similar to non-battered mothers in many aspects of their parenting and disciplinary styles. (There are no rigorous studies of the parenting of men who are victims of violence.) Although early studies found that women who were in battered women's shelters tended to be inconsistent in their parenting and aggressive toward their children, subsequent studies attributed much of this to poverty, not abuse. More recent studies have found that there is little difference on average between battered women and a comparison group's abilities to provide warmth to their children, be emotionally available, or positively reinforce their children. Similarly, there is little difference in the rate of corporal punishment of the children. Although a greater percentage of battered women report using physically aggressive behavior toward their children, at a 6–month follow-up, the abused women no longer parented more aggressively than the control group. See George W. Holden, Joshua D. Stein, Kathy L. Ritchie, Susan D. Harris and Ernest N. Jouriles, *Parenting Behaviors and Beliefs of Battered Women*, in CHILDREN EXPOSED TO MARITAL VIOLENCE 289 (G. W. Holden, R. Geffner, and E. N. Jouriles, eds., 1998); Donna J. Hitchens and Patricia Van Horne, *The Court's Role in Supporting and Protecting Children Exposed to Domestic Violence,* 6 J. CENTER FOR FAMILIES, CHILD. & CTS. 31 (2005).

Of course, this is not to say that domestic violence never affects an individual woman's parenting. Bancroft and Silverman, in their important study of batterers, note that batterers often deliberately undermine a mother's authority with the children by overruling the mother's decisions in relation to the child, belittling or demeaning the mother in front of the child, rewarding children's disrespectful behavior toward the mother, or using other similar tactics. Lundy Bancroft and Jay G. Silverman, THE BATTERER AS PARENT 57–64 (2002). Another recent study tried to identify the specific mechanisms through which domestic violence affects a victim's parenting ability and the factors that may mediate or moderate these effects. It showed that both physical and psychological abuse have a significant effect on maternal warmth, with psychological abuse having an even more damaging effect than physical abuse. Although the mechanism by which abuse affects parenting is not clear, the study's authors speculated that the experience of chronic abuse [may] deplete[] one of the ability to give emotional support to others, including one's children. Alytia Levendosky and Sandra Graham–Bermann, *Behavioral Observations of Parenting in Battered Women*, 14 J. FAM. PSYCH. 80 (2000). The same study noted that mothers' experiences of psychological abuse correlated with antisocial behavior on the part of their children. Again, the exact connection was unclear, but the authors noted that children, at least by "middle childhood" appear to identify with the aggressors and to act in hostile ways toward their mothers. This is consistent with Bancroft and Silverman's observation that batterers often encourage such hostile behavior as a means of undermining the mother's authority.

If domestic violence affects some aspects of some mothers' parenting ability, the next question is how long these effects can be expected to last. One study found significant improvement in affected mothers' parenting within 6 months of leaving a domestic violence shelter. George W. Holden, Joshua D. Stein, Kathy L. Ritchie, Susan D. Harris and Ernest N. Jouriles, *Parenting Behaviors and Beliefs of Battered Women*, in CHILDREN EXPOSED TO MARITAL VIOLENCE 289 (G. W. Holden, R. Geffner and E. N. Jouriles, eds., 1998). Another study found that 7% of women were permanently disabled as mothers by the violence that they had experienced, while 37% were only temporarily disabled, Lorraine Radford and Marianne Hester, *Overcoming*

Mother Blaming? in Domestic Violence in the Lives of Children 143 (Sandra A. Graham–Bermann and Jeffrey L. Edleson, eds., 2001).

How, if at all, would these studies be helpful to you as an advocate for a victim of domestic violence in a custody proceeding like *Wissink*? If you were the attorney for the father in a case like *Wissink*, what arguments would you use to try to convince the judge not to rely on these studies? As academics studying this topic, what additional kinds of studies would you look for?

5. **Why Children Choose to Live with Battering Parents.** *Wissink* also raises the question of why a child would choose to be in the custody of the abusive parent instead of the non-abusive parent. Notice that in *Wissink* the child told the judge that the father was a great father, that she wanted to live with him, and that he had not been violent toward her mother (despite what the evidence showed).

Initially a child's desire to live with a batterer may be taken as evidence that the battering did not actually occur or was not serious. However, there are a number of reasons why a child may align himself or herself with the abuser. Two long time advocates for battered women have speculated as to some of the reasons why this may occur:

First, the child might have identified with the abuser and actually want to live with him. The child may see the abuser as the "winner" and have absorbed his corrupt belief system. Due to the father's successful debasement of the mother, the child may believe it was the mother's "misbehavior" that caused the violence and blame the mother for the family's problems. As Justice Miller expressed it: the child "learns a dangerous and morally depraved lesson that abusive behavior is not only acceptable, but may even be rewarded." Second, fear might cause the child to express a preference to live with the batterer, as contradictory as this seems. While one might naturally assume that a child who fears one parent would prefer to live with the other, such an assumption underestimates the effects of domestic terror on its victims. The child may have a well-founded fear that the abusive father will harm the mother, if custody is awarded to the mother, or that the father will retaliate against the child if he finds out the child wants to live with the mother. This engulfing fear could prompt a child to plead with the court to be allowed to live with the abusive parent, believing that granting custody to the father will keep both the child and the mother safe. Third, the child may believe a decision to live with the abusive parent will put an end to the fighting. Sadly, this belief may not be accurate, since batterers often use court actions to continue the abuse once the parties are apart, and even winning the custody battle probably will not end the father's abusive tactics. [Fourth] [t]he child may also understand that the mother will forgive the child's decision to live with the father, while the father will withdraw his affection if the child chooses the mother. [Finally,] [w]here the mother has steadfastly insisted on a separation from the abusive father, the child may even hope a decision to live with the father will cause the mother to want to reconcile, so they can all be a family again. Any one of these beliefs could cause a child to minimize the past abuse, or even to "forget" it happened. Recollection of past abuse, already survived, may be overshadowed by fear that denying the father the custody he wants would bring on unknown, possibly fatal, danger in the future. Judith M. Reichler and Nancy S. Erickson, *Custody, Domestic Violence and a Child's Preference*, N.Y.L.J., April 24, 2003.

There are at least two additional reasons why a child might choose the abusive parent as the custodial parent. Some children feel responsible for the batterer's well-being and might, for this reason, choose to live with the batterer. They may believe that only they can keep the batterer from "losing his temper" or "feeling completely isolated in the world." *R.H. v. B.F.*, 653 N.E.2d 195, 200 (Mass. App. Ct. 1995), *aff'd. sub nom Custody of Vaughn*, 664 N.E.2d 434 (Mass. 1996) (psychologist testified that the 11–year old boy had an "excessive sense of personal responsibility" for his abusive father.)

Finally, it is also possible that the daughter in *Wissink* may have chosen to live with her father because she blamed her mother for the violence. A recent study of mother-child relationships in families in which there was domestic violence found that children blamed the mother even when they knew on a rational level that the mother's actions made no difference. Some children interpreted their mother's refusal to accommodate the batterer as evidence that she bore some responsibility for the subsequent violence while others saw their mother's decisions to do what the batterer demanded as indications of a willingness to be victimized. In addition, there were children who thought that their mothers were at fault when they returned to an abuser after leaving, even if they realized that the mother was returning for the sake of the children, Audrey Mullender, Gill Hague, Umme Imman, Liz Kelly, Ellen Malos and Linda Regan, CHILDREN'S PERSPECTIVES ON DOMESTIC VIOLENCE (2002).

Given this information, if you were the trial judge on remand in *Wissink* and the child still wanted to live with her father, how much weight would you give her preference? Remember, this girl is approximately 16 years old and may vote with her feet if the judge does not award custody in the way that the child wants.

D.   STATUTES THAT CREATE PRESUMPTIONS AGAINST AWARDING CUSTODY TO BATTERERS

Nancy K. D. Lemon

Statutes Creating Rebuttable Presumptions Against Custody to Batterers: How Effective Are They?

28 WM. MITCHELL L. REV. 601 (2001).

By the 1980's, the domestic violence movement had become a vocal presence, and was developing some sophistication in terms of changing entrenched policies. Advocates began to call for legislators and courts to protect children from batterers. Feminists stressed the harmful effects of exposure to domestic violence on children, and stated that it is not actually possible to be a violent husband and a good father. At the same time, there was a strong trend toward trying to keep fathers close to their children. Father's rights groups pushed for, and succeeded in getting, legislation stressing the importance of joint custody. Families were no longer seen as "broken," but instead were "in transition," with the goal being that both parents were still involved in their children's lives. . . .

In all too many cases, these two trends worked at cross-purposes. Given the high rates of domestic violence in the U.S., especially among divorcing couples, there were many cases in which courts were presented with one parent arguing for joint custody and the other parent arguing that the history of domestic violence should preclude such a decision. Starting in 1991, some states resolved this conflict by enacting statutes creating a presumption against custody to batterers. . . .

There were several bases for this new trend [including a U.S. House of Representatives resolution and statements by the National Council of Juvenile and Family Court Judges and by the American Bar Association.] . . . In 1994, the ABA published a report to its president suggesting the adoption of statutes creating a presumption against custody to batterers. . . . Another reason statutes establishing a presumption against custody to batterers were enacted was the growing body of social science literature showing the often severe and long-lasting effects of domestic violence on children. This literature also argued that joint custody was contraindicated when there has been family violence. . . . Furthermore, studies and articles started to show that when fathers in general or batterers in particular fought for custody, they usually won. There are also many cases in which mothers initially or eventually lost custody due to their inability to get along with the fathers. In some of these, in which there were no allegations of partner abuse, the court first awarded joint custody, [and] then found after awhile that this was unworkable due to continued conflict between the parents.

In other cases, there was extensive evidence of partner abuse. The fact that a formerly battered mother and her former batterer are not able to co-parent effectively is not at all surprising. However, it is very unfortunate that many courts are still so unaware of how domestic violence dynamics enter into custody cases. One wonders why the court ever expected people in this situation to suddenly be able to cooperate. . . .

In response to the growing body of policy statements, studies, articles and cases, states started to adopt statutes establishing a rebuttable presumption against custody to batterers. As of January 2001, there were sixteen states plus the District of Columbia which had adopted such statutes.

Lawrence v. Delkamp

Supreme Court of North Dakota, 2000.
620 N.W.2d 151.

■ VANDE WALLE, CHIEF JUSTICE.

John Daniel Lawrence appealed from an order, dated February 2, 2000, restricting visitation with his son. . . .

I

Although Lawrence and Delkamp were never married to each other, they had a son who was born in August 1992. Through a series of amended judgments and orders, Delkamp was awarded custody of the child with visitation for Lawrence.... The court ... found Lawrence had committed domestic violence, and the court restricted Lawrence's visitations with the child to supervised visits at the Family Safety Center in Bismarck. On appeal, Lawrence claims the trial court's finding of domestic violence is clearly erroneous and requests a reversal and redetermination of visitation.

In awarding custody in the best interests of the child, the court must consider the factors listed under N.D.C.C. § 14–09–06.2. In the hierarchy of factors to be considered, domestic violence predominates when there is credible evidence of it.... Section 14–09–06.2(1)(j) provides in relevant part:

> In awarding custody or granting rights of visitation, the court shall consider evidence of domestic violence. If the court finds credible evidence that domestic violence has occurred, and there exists one incident of domestic violence which resulted in serious bodily injury or involved the use of a dangerous weapon or there exists a pattern of domestic violence within a reasonable time proximate to the proceeding, this combination creates a rebuttable presumption that a parent who has perpetrated domestic violence may not be awarded sole or joint custody of a child. This presumption may be overcome only by clear and convincing evidence that the best interests of the child require that parent's participation as a custodial parent. The court shall cite specific findings of fact to show that the custody or visitation arrangement best protects the child and the parent or other family or household member who is the victim of domestic violence....

Section 14–07.1–01(2), N.D.C.C., defines domestic violence:

> *"Domestic violence" includes* physical harm, bodily injury, sexual activity compelled by physical force, assault, or *the infliction of fear of imminent physical harm,* bodily injury, sexual activity compelled by physical force, or assault, not committed in self-defense, on the complaining family or household members.

> (Emphasis added)....

In this case, the trial court made the following specific finding regarding domestic violence:

> 1. *Domestic violence.* On one occasion John Daniel Lawrence ("Dan") told Tina Lucille Delkamp ("Tina") he would have his girlfriend "beat the crap out" of Tina if Tina pursued the issue of child support. On another occasion, Dan told Tina he could "eliminate" Rylan [their son] in a boating accident. Dan told Tina she would not be seeing Rylan once Dan got him. Dan also told Tina on one occasion he would not return Rylan to Tina after a visitation unless she agreed to let Dan

claim Rylan as an exemption on Dan's tax return. Most of these incidents occurred more than two years ago but during Rylan's life. . . . Dan has perpetrated domestic violence. Moreover, he engaged in a pattern of conduct within a reasonable time proximate to the proceedings just completed to create a rebuttable presumption that Dan should not have joint or sole custody of Rylan. . . . State law requires any visitation arrangement under such circumstances must be designed to protect Rylan and Tina from further domestic violence.

The trial court made no finding that Lawrence has ever committed physical harm or bodily injury to Rylan or Delkamp. Nor is there any evidence in the record to support such a finding. The court's finding of domestic violence rests solely upon threats made by Lawrence. Under our domestic violence statutes, threats can only constitute domestic violence for purposes of creating a rebuttable presumption against custody and for restriction of visitation, if they constitute "the infliction of fear of imminent physical harm." . . .

The record supports the trial court's finding that Lawrence made threats to Delkamp. The record shows that Lawrence threatened he would have a girlfriend "beat" Delkamp if she pursued child support, that Lawrence said he could "eliminate" Rylan in a boating accident, and that Lawrence said he would not return Rylan after a visitation unless Delkamp agreed to a specific tax exemption for Lawrence. These threats are serious and reprehensible, and we do not dismiss their relevance. The trial court can certainly consider Lawrence's threatening behavior in deciding custody and visitation issues. Under N.D.C.C. § 14–09–06.2 Lawrence's threats are relevant to the court's consideration of such factors as the capacity and disposition of the parents to give the child love, affection, and guidance, the moral fitness of the parents, and the mental and physical health of the parents. However, the specific issue before us in this appeal is whether Lawrence's threats constitute domestic violence, as that term is defined under the statute, for purposes of imposing restricted visitation.

The threats made by Lawrence are clearly distinguishable from the threats made in *Lovcik v. Ellingson* [569 N.W.2d 697 (N.D. 1997)], which the trial court found were domestic violence. In *Lovcik*, a protection order had been entered against the father for committing violent physical acts of aggression against the mother, including pushing her against a wall, choking her while she was holding one of the children, and pushing her to the ground. During the evening after the parties had attended a court hearing on custody and child support modification, the father became very angry and made a series of telephone calls to the mother. During those calls, the father used harassing language toward the mother and called her derogatory names. The series of angry threatening calls made the mother immediately fear for her safety. She "became nauseated and shook from fear," and she immediately locked all doors and windows of the home and called the police to request protection. The trial court found the father's harassing calls caused the mother to have fear of imminent physical harm and also found that her fear was reasonable because of her past experience of having been physically abused by the perpetrator. This Court affirmed the trial court's finding of domestic violence, concluding, under those circumstances, the threats constituted an infliction of fear of imminent physical harm.

Unlike the circumstances in *Lovcik,* there is no history shown on this record of physical assault or violence by Lawrence toward Delkamp or the child. The threats made by Lawrence, while objectionable, were qualified threats of possible future conduct conditioned upon the occurrence of certain actions or responses by Delkamp. There was no finding by the trial court that at the time Lawrence made the threats Delkamp was put in fear of immediate or soon to be inflicted physical harm. . . .

The threats the court found Lawrence made in this case ... were of future conduct and did not denote immediacy so as to place Delkamp in fear of harm occurring without delay. Under this interpretation ... Lawrence's threats did not constitute domestic violence ... and the trial court's finding of domestic violence is clearly erroneous. In establishing visitation for Lawrence with Rylan the trial court erred in considering Lawrence's conduct to be domestic violence requiring visitation restrictions. We remand for the trial court to redetermine appropriate visitation.

NOTES AND QUESTIONS

1. **Result on Remand.** On remand, the trial court again gave custody to the mother and gave the father supervised visitation. This time the trial court considered the father's threats in its analysis of what was in the child's best interests. Its decision was upheld in *Lawrence v. Delkamp,* 658 N.W.2d 758 (N.D. 2003).

2. **Defining Domestic Violence.** Like the protective order statutes, statutes that create a presumption against awarding custody to a partner who has engaged in domestic violence must define "domestic violence." The North Dakota statute's definition of domestic violence as an act that causes bodily harm, fear of imminent bodily harm, or coerced sexual activity is a common definition. Some states define domestic violence for the purposes of the presumption statute by cross-reference either to their criminal statutes or to their protective order statutes. Minn. Stat. § 518.17 (2006). Others create a presumption against giving custody to a batterer only if the batterer has actually been convicted of particular crimes involving domestic violence. Fla. Stat. § 61.13 (2005) (requiring conviction of a felony in the 3d degree or higher that involves domestic violence.) What are the advantages and disadvantages of each approach? In order for the presumption to attach, the North Dakota statute requires not only that an act of domestic violence have occurred, but also that there have been either "one incident of domestic violence which resulted in serious bodily injury or involved the use of a dangerous weapon" or that there be "a pattern of domestic violence within a reasonable time proximate to the proceeding." N.D. St. § 14–09–06.2 (2005). What function does this requirement serve? For a comprehensive discussion of the statutes creating a presumption against awarding custody to a batterer, see Nancy K.D.

Lemon, *Statutes Creating Rebuttable Presumptions Against Custody to Batterers: How Effective are They?* 28 WM. MITCHELL L. REV. 601 (2001).

3. **Victims' Credibility and Definitions of Domestic Violence.** Of course, no definition of domestic violence will protect against bad custody decisions if the court does not believe the victim's claims of abuse. In *Morton County Social Service Board v. Schumacher*, 674 N.W.2d 505 (N.D.2004), the North Dakota Supreme Court upheld a trial court's finding that there was no "domestic violence" under the statute in a case in which the mother claimed two separate incidents of domestic violence. In the first, when she was pregnant with the child, the irate father destroyed a computer with an axe and told her he would have used the axe on her if she had not been pregnant. He was arrested for disorderly conduct. In the second incident, the mother and a third party claimed that, as part of some game, the father grabbed the mother, dragged her down some stairs and injured her neck. The court found neither of these incidents constituted occurrences of domestic violence. In the first, the court did not think that the mother was ever threatened. The court did not believe the testimony as to the second because the mother did not seek immediate treatment for the alleged injury. The trial court awarded custody of the child to the father. The father's request for custody had come as a counterclaim in an action in which he was originally sued for child support. Do you think this case might illustrate the points that Joan Meier was making in *Domestic Violence, Child Custody, and Child Protection*, excerpted above? It is not unusual for fathers to request custody in response to mothers' suits for child support.

4. **Standards of Proof for Triggering and Rebutting the Presumption.** Under the North Dakota statute the presumption against awarding custody to a batterer comes into existence if there is "credible" evidence and can be rebutted only by "clear and convincing" evidence. This high standard for rebutting the presumption was enacted after a 1992 case in which the N.D. Supreme Court upheld a trial court determination that the presumption had been overcome by evidence that the father's violence had never been directed at the children, that the father had a more stable home environment, and that there was more love and affection between the father and the children than between the mother and the children. *Schestler v. Schestler*, 486 N.W.2d 509 (N.D.1992). Do you think the current North Dakota statute sets the evidentiary burden in the right place? In Massachusetts, the presumption is both created and rebutted by a preponderance of evidence. M.G.L. 208 § 31A (2006). If you were drafting a statute, what standard of proof would you require to create the presumption and what standard to rebut it? What are the advantages and disadvantages of lower evidentiary requirements for the creation of the presumption? For rebutting it?

5. **Time Lapse Between the Violence and the Custody Proceeding.** The North Dakota statute requires that the domestic violence have occurred "within a reasonable time proximate to the proceeding." Why would a state impose such a requirement? Should "proximate" be interpreted more generously in cases involving violence that might cause serious bodily

injury? For example, is evidence that the father backed his car into the mother and "planted her in a snow pile" six years before the custody proceeding sufficiently important to be considered in establishing a presumption against the father? Suppose he then pleaded guilty to assault with a dangerous weapon and served 30 days in jail? What about evidence that before backing up into her, he had smashed her head into the car's windshield, fracturing her skull? *In re Lillith*, 807 N.E.2d 237 (Mass. App. Ct. 2004).

6. **Rebutting the Presumption.** What type of evidence is sufficient to overcome the presumption? Some statutes specify what the court should consider. For example, in California, the statute directs the court to consider all of the following: the best interests of the child, successful completion of a batterer's treatment program, successful completion of a parenting class if appropriate, compliance with any probation or parole terms, compliance with the terms of an applicable restraining order, and commission of any further acts of domestic violence. West's Ann. Cal. Fam. Code § 3044(b) (West 2006). Many statutes do not specify what information would rebut the presumption. In such a state, would you want to introduce information of a type not referred to by the California statute? Given what you learned about the effectiveness of batterers' programs, should evidence that an abuser has completed a program for batterers be sufficient? What about evidence of the completion of alcohol or drug abuse programs? See, Kristina C. Evans, *Can a Leopard Change His Spots?*, 11 DUKE J. GENDER L. & POL'Y 121 (2004). Should it be easier to rebut the presumption if the victim of the violence, for whatever reason (e.g., mental illness, death), is unable to be the custodial parent?

7. **Protective Orders and Presumptions Against Awarding Custody to Batterers.** In some states, like Massachusetts, the presumption statute specifically states that the existence of a protective order against one parent is not to be considered as evidence of domestic violence on the part of that parent. M.G.L. ch. 208 § 31A. Provisions like this appear to be based on a fear that courts grant protective orders to complainants without sufficient review of the evidence. However, if you are inclined to think that protective orders against a parent ought to be taken into account in determining if a parent is an abuser, remember that batterers may obtain protective orders against their victims for strategic or harassment purposes, Nina W. Tarr, *The Cost to Children When Batterers Misuse Order for Protection Statutes in Child Custody Cases*, 13 S. CAL. REV. L. & WOMEN'S STUD. 35 (2003). Given what you now know about the protective order process, do you think the existence of a protective order should be allowed as evidence of abuse in custody proceedings? Should seeking but not receiving or seeking but dropping a protective order weigh against the petitioning parent in a custody battle? Or, would that backfire against true victims of family violence? If you were drafting a statute with a presumption against giving custody to a batterer, what, if any, weight would you allow to be placed on previous orders of protection?

8. **Credibility of Claims of Intimate Violence in Custody Cases.** In addition to arguing that protective orders are granted too easily, fathers'

rights advocates often complain that inaccurate allegations of domestic violence are frequently made in custody disputes as a strategic ploy. A 1999 California statewide study reviewed approximately 18,000 child custody cases that were seen by family court services and found allegations of domestic violence against fathers in 26% of the cases and against mothers in 9% of the cases, but it did not indicate what proportion of these were substantiated. More recently, studies have found that between 40% and 75% of allegations of domestic violence made against fathers during custody disputes have been substantiated, Janet R. Johnston, Soyoung Lee, Nancy W. Olesen and Marjorie G. Walters, *Allegations and Substantiations of Abuse in Custody–Disputing Families*, 43 FAM. CT. REV. 283 (2005). How do you interpret these statistics? Do they show that such allegations should be taken seriously or that they are likely to be strategic? If an allegation turns out not to be substantiated, does that mean it was made in bad faith and that no abuse occurred?

9. **Allegations of Mutual Abuse.** We have already discussed mutual battering in the context of protective orders and arrests. Allegations of mutual battering are also significant in determining which parent has engaged in domestic violence so as to trigger a statutory presumption against him or her in a custody proceeding. How should the statutes deal with claims of mutual battering? Should such allegations raise presumptions against both parents? Should the presumption drop out of existence as soon as mutual allegations are raised? The North Dakota statute says nothing specific about how to handle claims of mutual abuse, but the North Dakota Supreme Court has said that when there are claims of mutual abuse the trial court should attempt to determine which parent is the primary abuser. The presumption applies against that person. If the parties have perpetrated approximately equal amounts of abuse toward each other, the presumption drops out. *Krank v. Krank*, 529 N.W.2d 844 (1995). Louisiana, in contrast, requires the following: "If the court finds that both parents have a history of perpetrating family violence, custody shall be awarded solely to the parent who is less likely to continue to perpetrate family violence." La. Rev. Stat. § 9:364 (2004).

In thinking about mutual abuse, it is also important to keep in mind that not all violence between intimate partners involves the assertion of power and control. Some may occur as a result of transient anger against the partner, while some may be an effort at self-defense. Should the presumption against giving custody to a batterer apply in situations involving violence that is not linked to power and control? For further discussion of these issues, see Clare Dalton, *When Paradigms Collide: Protecting Battered Parents and Their Children in the Family Court System*, 37 FAM. & CONCIL. CTS. REV. 273 (1999); Linda C. Neilson, *Assessing Mutual Partner–Abuse Claims in Child Custody and Access Cases*, 42 FAM. CT. REV. 411 (2004).

E. JOINT CUSTODY AND FRIENDLY PARENT PROVISIONS

While advocates for victims of domestic violence were focusing on convincing judges and legislatures that the violence was injurious to children and should be considered in custody determinations, others were arguing that the goal of custody determinations in general should be to maintain the family in a position that resembled the pre-divorce family or that maximized the child's contact with both parents. These advocates of ensuring post-divorce family stability and large blocks of time with each parent often support joint custody and friendly parent provisions. Advocates of joint custody and friendly parent provisions promote them for divorcing families in general. They are not specifically aimed at families in which there is domestic violence. The materials that follow explore how these more general reforms interact with the needs of families in which there has been violence. As you will see, it is difficult to implement these reforms while simultaneously ensuring the safety of adult and child victims of domestic violence.

Before we start that exploration, it is important to understand the various meanings of joint custody and of friendly parent provisions. Joint custody may mean either joint legal custody or joint physical custody. Joint legal custody gives both parents the right and responsibility to participate in making major decisions about a child's life. In most jurisdictions, this includes decisions about the child's education, health care, and religious or moral training. Joint legal custody implies nothing about a child's physical residence; the parents could be awarded joint legal custody with the child's residence being solely with one parent. In contrast, joint physical custody gives each parent the right and the responsibility for the child's physical care. Contrary to what some people may think, however, this does not mean that the parents necessarily split their time with the child fifty-fifty. Joint physical custody arrangements frequently involve a 60%–40% (or even 35%–65%) split of the child's residential time.

Friendly parent provisions require a court to give positive weight in a custody determination to the parent who is most likely to facilitate the child's relationship with the other parent. For example, Florida requires a judge, in determining a child's best interests, to consider both "[t]he parent who is more likely to allow the child frequent and continuing contact with the nonresidential parent" and "[t]he willingness and ability of each parent to facilitate and encourage a close and continuing parent-child relationship between the child and the other parent." Fla. St. § 61.13(3)(a) and (j)(2004). Both joint custody and friendly parent provisions involve serious risks for victims of domestic violence.

In reading the materials that follow and that discuss efforts to maintain the child's contact with both parents, you should consider a number of issues. First, think about the reasons that are articulated for maintaining such contact. Is it better for the children? What do the studies say? Or, do advocates of joint custody and friendly parent provisions think a child should have a continuing relationship with both parents for ideological reasons? These might include the belief that such contact makes the parents more equal or an attachment to the notion of a two-parent family. Second, how do the authors whose work you are reading think about family dynamics? Do they tend to see disputes as merely conflicts between equals or do they see them as part of a continuing abusive interaction? If they understand the conflict to be part of a continuing abusive relationship, how important and how common do they think the presence of abuse is?

Solangel Maldonado

Beyond Economic Fatherhood: Encouraging Divorced Fathers to Parent

153 U. PA. L. REV. 921 (2005).

Introduction

"[F]atherhood is in vogue." Married fathers are dedicating more time to their children than ever before.... When one compares this new generation of married fathers to divorced fathers, however, the contrast is rather bleak. There are approximately 1.1 million divorces in the United States each year. About half of these divorcing couples have minor children, resulting in approximately one million children each year experiencing their parents' separation or divorce. Within three years of divorce, fifty percent of fathers have either ceased contact with their children or see them quite infrequently.

Absent fathers are frequently blamed for many of their children's social, emotional, and behavioral problems. Commentators have argued that children who grow up without fathers are more likely than children who grow up in marital families with both of their biological parents to use drugs, perform poorly in school, drop out of high school, become teen parents, be idle (out of work and school), engage in antisocial or criminal activity, get divorced themselves, or commit or attempt suicide....

Child development experts and social scientists, however, debate whether the absence of a father is a significant cause of these negative outcomes. In contrast to the studies relied upon by fathers' advocates, some studies have found no correlation between paternal involvement and children's well-being. When studies have found a positive correlation between paternal absence and an increased risk of behavioral, mental, and social problems among children, some commentators have argued that such correlation results from fathers' failure to pay child support, not father absence per se.... Accordingly, these scholars advocate stronger enforcement of child support awards and governmental support of children and mothers to prevent poverty after divorce.

Even if it is true that what matters is economic support and not paternal involvement per se, absent fathers are still a cause for concern because fathers who maintain significant contact with their children after divorce are more likely to pay child support than fathers who do not maintain contact.... Thus, society and the government may wish to consider encouraging paternal involvement as it may lead to the payment of child support.... In light of the evidence suggesting that paternal disengagement is harmful to children, I argue that it is crucial that fathers not abandon their children after divorce.

In recent years, legal scholars have produced a significant body of scholarship devoted to the law's effect on social norms. Norms theorists have argued that the law can and does influence social norms of marriage and divorce, [and] parenting.... This Article uses social norms theory to explore how the law ... can and should facilitate a norm of involved fatherhood, thereby encouraging nonresidential fathers to remain actively involved in their children's upbringing....

C.   Paternal Involvement and Children's Development

Many Americans firmly believe that children benefit from maintaining significant contact with both parents after divorce. Many social scientists agree.... Studies have found a strong correlation between nonresidential fathers' frequent visitation and children's adjustment to the divorce. Children who have regular contact with their fathers tend to have higher self-esteem and fewer behavioral problems than children who have little or no contact with their fathers. Studies have also found that children adapt better to divorce when their parents share social and financial responsibility for their care than when one parent bears these responsibilities alone. Researchers have cautioned, however, that when parents do not cooperate with each other and visitation takes place in a high-conflict setting, the benefits to the child can be minimal or nonexistent. Not surprisingly, children are unlikely to benefit from a relationship with the nonresidential parent if the parents are unable to interact and communicate in a civilized manner, and the children are caught in the middle of their battles.

1.   Educational and Societal Benefits

Aside from children's "smoother" emotional adjustment to divorce when both parents remain a part of their lives, there may be educational and social benefits derived from paternal involvement. Researchers have found a positive correlation between paternal involvement and both higher IQ and better school performance. They have also found that children with absent fathers tend to have lower grades, higher truancy and high-school dropout rates, and lower college attendance rates than children who grew up with both parents.

Researchers have also found a positive correlation between paternal absence and delinquent behavior and drug abuse. Even after controlling for family income, boys from father-absent homes have much higher delinquency rates than boys growing up with two parents.... [T]eenage pregnancy rates in the United States sample were still five times higher among early father-absent girls than father-present girls. Notably, teenage girls whose fathers were present were less likely to become pregnant even where risk factors such as poverty, inadequate parental supervision, stressful life events, and defiant behavior in grade school existed.

Some scholars argue that father-absent children's lower academic performance and increased behavioral and social problems stem from poverty rather than father absence per se. Thus, they argue that the main problem for father-absent families "is not the absence of a male but rather the lack of income produced by a male." Many studies, however, are "adjusted for differences ... such as race, parents' education, number of siblings, and residential location." Thus, "socioeconomic status [alone] cannot explain why children from one-parent families are doing worse" than children from two-parent families. Although it is not possible to conclusively establish a causal link between paternal presence and children's educational and social outcomes, the persistence of these differences between father-absent and father-present children after controlling for socioeconomic factors suggests that fathers may have a substantial impact on their children's educational and social success independent of their economic contributions....

2.   Emotional and Psychological Benefits

There are reasons for encouraging paternal involvement independent of its likely positive effect on children's educational and social development. First, children want to see their fathers, and they feel rejected when contact with their fathers is infrequent. Indeed, children at "every developmental level experience sadness and even severe depression" when contact with the nonresidential parent is infrequent.... Interestingly, children whose relationships with their fathers terminate as a result of paternal disengagement following divorce do worse than children whose parents die when they are young. Children can understand and accept death, but they cannot accept rejection and abandonment by their fathers....

3.   Child Support

Although studies analyzing the effects of frequent paternal visitation on children's adjustment after divorce are conflicting, it is well established that children whose fathers pay child support tend to experience fewer behavioral and social problems and to perform better in school than children whose fathers do not. Furthermore, even when the parents' relationship with each other is highly conflictual, studies have shown that "the positive effects of child support for child well-being outweigh[] the negative effects of parental conflict." For instance, children whose fathers pay child support do better academically and socially, even if their parents are always fighting, than children whose fathers do not pay child support.... Interestingly, children do better when their fathers pay child support regardless of the amount paid. Thus, a number of researchers have suggested that the payment of child support is important in and of itself, independent of the amount. Regardless of the reasons children experience fewer behavioral and social problems when their fathers pay child support, it is undisputed that children benefit from their fathers' economic support even when it is minimal, and they are more likely to receive support if their fathers are involved in their upbringing.

III.   Reasons for Paternal Disengagement

... Many divorced fathers believe child custody laws are biased against them in favor of mothers. Given that approximately eighty percent of children living with only one parent reside with their mothers, fathers' perception of bias is not surprising....

Even when there is little or no evidence of gender bias, there is a widespread perception among nonresidential fathers that the prevalence of maternal residential custody can only be explained by gender bias. This is inaccurate. In reality, mothers' greater likelihood of obtaining custody is a result of their significantly greater involvement in their children's upbringing during the marriage.... In their initial consultations, divorce attorneys frequently warn fathers who are considering seeking sole or joint custody that mothers obtain residential custody in eighty-five percent of all cases. In reality, however, judges decide only five percent of custody disputes. Thus, parents, not judges, are agreeing to grant mothers sole legal and residential custody. In the relatively small number of cases where parents litigate custody, fathers are awarded sole or joint custody in fifty to sixty-five percent of cases even where the mother was the child's primary caretaker....

IV.   Changing the Norm: Encouraging Paternal Engagement

... In the twenty-five years since California adopted the first joint custody statute in the country, joint legal custody has become quite common.... Under my proposal, only if the parent opposed to sharing legal custody with the other parent rebuts the presumption [in favor of joint legal custody] by showing that the other parent is unfit would the court consider another custodial arrangement, e.g., sole maternal or sole paternal custody ... For example, evidence of domestic violence, mental illness, alcohol or drug abuse, or historical lack of parental interest in the child would be highly relevant and possibly determinative....

Given the inconclusive evidence that joint legal custody leads to greater paternal engagement, why should courts adopt a presumption of joint legal custody? First and foremost, a presumption of joint legal custody serves an important symbolic function. Even if fathers with joint legal custody do not spend more time with their children than sole maternal custody fathers, a presumption of joint legal custody signals to fathers that the law and society respect their rights and responsibilities as parents and sends a message that fathers are important and should be involved in their children's upbringing. Some social scientists have recommended a presumption of joint legal custody because it affirms that both mothers and fathers have rights and responsibilities vis-à-vis their children after divorce. Thus, the primary benefit of joint legal custody may be its symbolic value....

Many fathers reject joint legal custody in favor of joint physical custody, arguing that the former does not provide them greater access to their children because the children still live with the mother in most cases, and the father has only visitation. Thus, they argue, joint legal custody is, in effect, no different from sole maternal custody with paternal visitation, and the law should recognize fathers' equal role in their children's upbringing by awarding them joint physical custody. Given all [this], why do I instead recommend joint legal custody?

First, joint physical custody is difficult to implement logistically.... Second, and more importantly, the law is effective in influencing social norms where there already is some consensus in the community that the norm the legal rule is seeking to establish is legitimate and desirable. In California, possibly the state most supportive of joint custody, the majority of couples who shared physical custody reverted to a traditional maternal residence (or paternal residence in some cases) within two years of divorce. Even with a joint physical custody decree, most parents reverted to maternal residential custody after a short period of time. How can the law enforce joint physical custody if both parents ignore the decree and, in effect, choose maternal residential custody? As Professor Scott has observed, "reforms favoring joint physical custody failed to influence behavior because they were apparently inconsistent with the private preferences of parents regarding custodial arrangements." Thus, so long as parents and society in general are opposed to joint physical custody, it is unlikely that the law can create a norm of shared physical custody. In contrast, Americans believe that both parents should share decision-making authority and both should spend significant periods of time with their children, thereby making it more likely that society will accept a presumption of joint legal custody. . . .

Clare Dalton

When Paradigms Collide: Protecting Battered Parents and Their Children in the Family Court System

37 FAM. & CONCIL. CTS. REV. 273 (1999).

At the level of research and theory, there are at least three separate bodies of learning that describe problematic intimate relationships, test hypotheses about the sources of the problems, and suggest, or measure the efficacy of, specific interventions. One set of literature deals with conflict, another with violence, and a third with abuse. A prime source of tension between specialists in partner abuse and the majority of mental health professionals who work within the family court system is that where the former see abuse, the latter tend to see conflict. . . . [A]buse specialists will always suspect that violence in a relationship indicates the presence of a power and control dynamic, whereas the mental health professional is quicker to associate violence with conflict between relatively evenly matched partners. . . .

The 1970s saw increasing divorce rates, a growing fathers' rights movement, a new body of popular literature favoring shared parenting, and a new body of social science research assessing the impact of divorce on children. The literature and the data on which it relied either asserted or was interpreted to assert two propositions, one negative and one positive. The negative proposition was that children who lose contact with their noncustodial parents after divorce are likely to experience problems. The positive proposition was that children resist the negative emotional fallout of their parents' divorces most successfully when they have generous ongoing access to both parents. On the strength of these propositions, state legislatures and family courts mobilized to support shared parenting through joint custody, "friendly parent" provisions, and generous visitation for noncustodial parents.

Joint custody and friendly parent provisions are intimately related. Joint custody legislation has taken a variety of forms. The weakest form simply makes it explicit that joint custody is an option for judges to consider. A much stronger form authorizes joint custody when either party requests it, even if the other parent is opposed. A third variety authorizes joint custody only when both parents are in agreement but makes the willingness of one parent to accept joint custody a factor in determining which parent should receive sole custody. This disadvantages the "un-friendly" parent, the one who was unwilling to share custody. Some legislation creates a presumption in favor of joint custody, and while parental disagreement may rebut the presumption, the legislation may then favor awarding sole custody to the "friendly" parent who is willing to share.

According to the Family Violence Project of the National Council of Juvenile and Family Court Judges, in 1995, 10 child custody statutes included a public policy statement concerning a parent's ability to allow the child an open, loving, and frequent relationship with the other parent. Eighteen states included such provisions in the list of factors a court must consider when determining the best interest of the child. Even in states without joint custody or friendly parent language in their statutes, many judges act on the belief that shared access is best for children and sole custody is best awarded to the parent most willing to share the child.

In this context, if judges, mediators, or family service officers interpret abuse as conflict and attribute violence to conflict rather than to abuse, they may well conclude that shared parenting is still both feasible and desirable. The parents just need to set aside their own issues and hostilities and focus on the best interests of their children. Mediators, guardians ad litem, custody evaluators, and judges confusing abuse with conflict may also conclude that the parents who oppose shared parenting are acting vindictively and subordinating the interests of the children to their own rather than expressing their legitimate anxieties about their own and their children's ongoing safety. Ironically, within the friendly parent framework, a mother's proper concern about her abusive partner's fitness to parent will negatively affect her chance to win custody, not his. At the same time, the abuser's willingness to share the children, which assures his ongoing access to his partner and allows him to continue to manipulate and intimidate her, will, within the same framework, make him appear the more attractive candidate for custody.

New research is eroding the basis on which joint custody provisions rest. Earlier studies of shared parenting, which tended to reach positive conclusions, used samples composed of couples who were highly motivated and committed to making joint custody work for their children. Beginning in the early 1980s, and swelling in volume as the decade progressed, new studies have emphasized the limitations of those early findings and have raised a series of questions. The most recent studies conclude that there is no convincing evidence that joint custody is either more or less beneficial than sole custody for most children. More important, from the perspective of this article, is the finding that shared parenting is contraindicated if the relationship between the parents is characterized by ongoing conflict. As Janet Johnston summarizes this research,

> Substantial amounts of access to both parents ... and frequent transitions between parents are generally associated with poorer children's adjustment in ... those divorced families where there is ongoing high conflict and continual disputes over the children. Where there has been a history of repeated physical violence between parents, these children are likely to be the most seriously disturbed.

NOTES AND QUESTIONS

1. **Joint Legal or Joint Physical Custody?** Does Maldonado argue in favor of the adoption of a presumption of joint legal custody or joint physical custody? Why does she support one but not the other?

One very common custodial outcome is for the parents to have joint legal custody with the mother having physical custody of the child. One commentator has said,

> I would suggest that fathers who favor joint legal custody are actually seeking more rights and control without a corresponding increase in responsibility for their children. It is also significant that fathers' rights groups are demanding that the courts pay more attention to "parents' rights" (otherwise known as men's rights) rather than focusing on such things as support obligations and enforcement. Emphasis on men's custody rights increases men's power, while emphasis on support enforcement, of course, requires men to be responsive to the economic needs of women and children.... Joint legal custody does not provide a mechanism to ensure equal sharing of the rights and responsibilities of child rearing. In contrast to joint physical custody, where the duties of childrearing are supposedly shared, joint legal custody gives legal decision-making power to parents without corresponding responsibility for physical care of children. This physical care is most often left to the mother. Anne Marie Delorey, *Joint Legal Custody*, quoted in Herma Hill Kay, *No–Fault Divorce and Child Custody: Chilling Out the Gender Wars*, 36 Fam. L. Q. 27 (2002).

How do you think Maldonado would respond to this? Do you agree with her?

2. **Joint Legal Custody and Abusive Relationships.** As Maldonado notes, the studies do not give a clear answer to the question of whether joint legal custody with primary residential custody in only one parent produces increased involvement by the noncustodial parent. In part, this is because not all the studies control for socio-economic factors. In part it is because many of the studies involve large numbers of families who opted on their own for joint legal custody instead of having it imposed on them by the courts. One would expect very different results in families that have determined that joint legal custody will be good for them than in families that are doubtful that they can make it work. However, the studies are quite clear that whatever advantages there may be to joint legal custody are likely to evaporate in families in which there has been domestic violence.

The Dalton article reminds us that family courts are likely to understand the violence to be a result of conflict as opposed to the result of systematic abuse. Why is this an important distinction? According to Dalton, how does it affect the outcome of cases?

Even if family courts were to recognize the difference between abuse and conflict, it is questionable whether they would be able to identify most cases in which there has been domestic violence. Judith Greenberg argues that the tendency of victims and abusers to deny and minimize the presence of violence, victims' fear of disclosing violence, and society's reluctance to admit the pervasiveness of violence all make it unlikely that violence within a relationship will be identified. In addition,

> There are also significant reporting issues for women in various minority communities. Some women of color may be reluctant to report abuse by men of their community because they believe that the police and society in general are already frequently abusive toward the men. Reporting domestic violence may simply be seen as a way of "piling on" when the men are already devalued and belittled. Other women from minority communities may be unwilling to report the abuse because they believe it will make the entire family, or even the entire community, look bad. Similarly, victims of gay or lesbian domestic violence may be unwilling to report it for all of the above reasons and also because of a fear of being "outed." Judith B. Greenberg, *Domestic Violence and the Danger of Joint Custody Presumptions*, 25 N. ILL. U.L. REV. 403 (2005).

Most statutory presumptions in favor of joint custody have exceptions for relationships that have involved domestic violence. D.C. Code Ann. § 16–914(a)(2) (2003) (presumption is rebuttable if there is evidence of an intrafamily offense.) If victims are reluctant to disclose abuse, how effective do you think these exceptions will be in preventing the presumption from being extended to cases in which there has been domestic violence? Does Maldonado take into account the potential destructiveness of joint legal custody for families in which there has been domestic violence?

F.   VISITATION

For the parent who is given neither sole nor joint physical custody of a child in the aftermath of separation or divorce, a visitation order is the mechanism through which to seek some level of ongoing contact with the child. Like custody determinations, orders of visitation are legally governed by a "best interests of the child" standard, but heavily influenced by two other factors. The first of these is an assumption that parents have a "right" to some relationship with their minor children except in the most extreme situations. The second is the conviction, discussed above, that in the overwhelming majority of cases, children will do better if they have access to both parents rather than one. This conviction often guides the recommendations of custody evaluators and guardians ad litem, and the decisions of judges, even in cases in which recent research would suggest that shared access is contraindicated because of intractable conflict or violence between the parents.

Judges have broad discretion to structure visitation, and impose conditions on its exercise so as to protect the best interests of the child. It has sometimes been argued that judges do not have the authority to limit or condition visitation solely for the purpose of protecting the custodial parent, rather than the child. The argument favoring such limits is that they will protect the child's best interests. Placing the custodial parent at physical or emotional risk, after a court has already decided that this individual is the most appropriate caretaker for the child, inevitably adversely affects the child's best interests. To clarify this, the National Council of Family and Juvenile Court Judges recommends explicitly that judicial authority be expanded to take into account "the safety and well-being of the . . . parent who is the victim of domestic or family violence" in making custody and visitation decisions. Model Code on Domestic and Family Violence, Section 402.

In structuring visitation, judges routinely consider both the frequency and length of visits between children and nonresidential parents. Many courts have regular visitation schedules that they routinely assign for children of particular ages. For example, they may provide that visitation for infants and toddlers (up to the age of 2 or 3 years) be frequent and short. As the children age into early elementary school, judges may begin to allow one afternoon or evening of visitation and, perhaps, every second weekend. At this age, many judges consider it appropriate to order overnight visits with the nonresidential parent. These patterned schedules are frequently completely inappropriate in situations involving a history of domestic violence. In domestic violence cases, judges may need to go far beyond routine visitation orders in order to set requirements that ensure the safety of the child and the residential parent. Among the tools that courts have used to protect children in visitation are requiring the nonresidential parent to attend or complete a batterers (or other) program, to abstain from using alcohol or drugs for a set period of time preceding the visit, or to post a bond for the return and safety of the child. Similarly, a court may refuse to permit overnight visitations, may require visitations or exchange of the child to be in a public place or supervised by a third party, or may limit the activities in which the child and nonresidential parent may engage together. In short, the judge can (and should) use his or her discretion to mold the visitation in such a way as to protect the child and the residential parent, both physically and emotionally.

The case below and the notes that follow it are intended to encourage you to rethink whether nonresidential parents should routinely be granted visitation. They also introduce you to the concept of supervised visitation and the practical issues that it raises.

Karjanis v. Karjanis

Superior Court of Connecticut, 2005.
2005 WL 1274112.

■ Patricia Lilly Harleston, Judge.

This is an action instituted by Gina Marie Karjanis against Steven M. Karjanis, Sr., seeking a dissolution of their marriage. . . . The parties were married on July 27, 1996 in Branford, Connecticut. The parties have two children who are issue of the marriage: Thaddeus Aristotle Karjanis, born January 13, 1999; and Steven Michael Karjanis, born August 18, 1997.... The marriage between the parties has broken down irretrievably, there is no reasonable hope of reconciliation, and judgment will enter dissolving the marriage on this ground....

The plaintiff, whose birth name is Gina Marie Lolelli, is 41 years old and is in good health.... She returned to work in 2000 as a floor nurse and occasional building supervisor at Laurel Woods, a rehabilitation subacute facility. She left that position in December 2004 and is now employed as a floor nurse at the Veteran's Administration. She went to work at the Veteran's Administration to obtain benefits for the children, as she could not afford to pay the insurance costs at Laurel Woods. The plaintiff works a forty-hour week and employs a woman, Ms. Beauregard, who lives in the home and provides care for the children.... The plaintiff lives in the marital residence with her two children. The defendant's son from his previous marriage, Chris, stays at the house three or four nights per week; and his daughter, Jessica, is a full-time college student living in the dormitory, but returns to this residence as her home when not in school.

The defendant, Steven Karjanis, is 48 years old and in good health. He has been a Social Worker for the Bridgeport school system for more than nine years....

He and the plaintiff met in 1995. They began living together approximately 3–4 months after meeting. Mr. Karjanis was divorced from his first wife in 1992. He has two children from that marriage: Christopher and Jessica Karjanis. The children were seven and eight years old at the time; and lived with him after the divorce. The plaintiff helped the defendant raise these two children. When the plaintiff and defendant got married, they agreed that she would stop working when she had their first child. The plaintiff testified that they both wanted children. The defendant testified that he wanted to wait a year, but his wife wanted to have children right away.

The Court believes that the primary issues which lead to the breakdown of this marriage are the defendant's lack of support to the plaintiff after the birth of the children; his basically shutting her out; his very controlling personality; his rigid viewpoints regarding the running of the house and raising of the children; and his infidelity. The plaintiff testified that after the birth of their second child, her husband was not supportive of her. He took vacations by himself and with his friends. When the plaintiff would ask if they could go away together, he would reply that she wanted the kids, so she had to stay home and take care of them. Mr. Karjanis went to Europe for two weeks with a friend on his and his wife's anniversary. In 2000 the defendant effectively "disappeared" from the house. He was working two part-time jobs and was basically never home.

When the defendant and plaintiff married, Mrs. Karjanis was working, making $95,000 per year. The day she stopped working and making

$95,000 per year, even though they agreed that she would stay home and take care of the children, she lost all say in her marriage and her life. After they got married, the defendant immediately cut up all of the plaintiff's credit cards without her permission. The defendant had full control of the household budget. He did not permit the plaintiff to spend any money. He did basically all of the grocery shopping. If she bought the children clothes or shoes when they needed them, he would argue with her and chastise her for doing so. The plaintiff wanted a dishwasher and clothes dryer. The defendant refused to allow her to purchase them, saying that he did not believe in using these things and they didn't need one. They were a family of six with a pool and she was forbidden from getting a clothes dryer.

He continuously criticized her for anything she did. He would inspect the grocery bags when she went shopping and yell at her if he didn't approve of her purchases. Defendant, on the other hand, testified that plaintiff couldn't adequately run the household and care for the children; that she was tired and under stress from all the work keeping the house and raising the children. He stated that he and his two kids all had to "pitch in" to help plaintiff take care of the babies and house; that she was suffering from PTSD and on medication for depression; and that the psychiatrist advised her to go back to work. However, when plaintiff repeatedly asked defendant to purchase a clothes dryer and a dishwasher— which certainly would have helped her—he refused because he didn't believe in using those things. This is illogical, inconsiderate and narcissistic thinking on the part of the defendant, and has more to do with his being able to control the plaintiff than with the best interests of the plaintiff or the children.

When they got married, plaintiff was driving a BMW. The defendant took her car from her use and gave her a station wagon which was rusted on the exterior and roof and which broke down on occasion leaving her and the children stranded. He testified that it wasn't feasible for her to use the BMW with all of the children. He told her it was important that he drive the BMW because he was the one making the money and supporting the household. Plaintiff testified that he later sold her BMW to his son and kept the proceeds.

When plaintiff got married she had a retirement account and some savings. The defendant did not have any savings. When he wanted a pool for the house, they used her retirement account of approximately $25,000 to install an in-ground pool in 2001. His retirement account had $25,000 which he kept. In addition, defendant used the plaintiff's $35,000 savings to make a balloon payment to his ex-wife.

When plaintiff wanted to get breast implants to, in her mind, improve her appearance, the defendant "forbade" her from doing so and threatened to leave her if she did. This was basically the last straw for plaintiff of any hope that she could continue in the marriage to her husband.

On December 29, 2003 Mrs. Karjanis was granted a restraining order against her husband as the result of an incident during which he attacked her in the bathroom in the presence of the kids.... Before he was removed from the home, the defendant had been paying all the bills, according to him, i.e., the mortgage, utilities and bills. When he left the house, he stopped paying everything. . . .

Since the filing of this dissolution action, the defendant has had at least thirteen motions for contempt or for immediate hearing [against him] alleging that he is in violation of court orders that he pay the mortgage and expenses for the marital residence ... claiming violation of court orders regarding him going to the marital residence, and regarding his visitation with the children; and one alleging that he was liquidating assets and incurring excessive debt in violation of the Automatic Orders. Defendant has been held in contempt by this court on [numerous occasions.]

The plaintiff testified on July 28, 2004, that defendant told her that if she did not reconcile with him, he was going to give her as difficult a time as he could; that she could expect him not to go by any court orders; he wasn't going to pay anything; that she couldn't live in the house—she had to move out because she couldn't afford it—and that if she wanted to be divorced from him then she would have to leave. It is abundantly clear by the defendant's actions during these proceedings that he meant to do just that. . . .

With regard to the defendant's relationship with his children, this father did not see his children from December 29, 2003 to June 2004. He did visit the children from June 9, 2004 to July 2, 2004. On July 2, 2004, he walked out of the house because his five-year old son couldn't find his shoes fast enough. He drove off and left his son in the driveway crying "Poppi come back." They called him on his cell phone and asked him to please come back. He never came back and never called the five-year old. The six-year old child then refused to go with him that entire week, because she said Poppi keeps saying Mommy is the devil. He has not had any contact with the children since that date.

When he was visiting the children, he would tell them over and over that their mother was the devil. This is emotionally abusive and psychologically damaging to the children. Defendant has claimed throughout these proceedings that his children are the most important thing to him and that he just wants to see and have a relationship with them. Defendant testified on July 28, 2004, however, that unless he could move back into the house he was not going to have contact with his children; that he was not going to be reduced to a visitor. The marriage between this mother and father is being dissolved; and the father will no longer be living in the same house with his children or their mother. This is an unfortunate consequence of divorce, and if the parties love their children, they will make every effort to assure that the children maintain a loving relationship with each parent and suffer as little as possible under the circumstances.

On July 28, 2004, Judge Abery–Wetstone found that the defendant's emotional state was detrimental to the best interests of the children and ordered that he have supervised visitations with them. Based on the behavior that Mr. Karjanis has exhibited and continues to exhibit in this case, this court is also of the opinion that it would be best for the children that supervised visitation continue until such time as the court is convinced that the defendant can be with his children and not let his feelings against his ex-wife hurt them.

The court will further order that a Guardian ad Litem be appointed for the children to assist the court in monitoring the situation and in determining when the defendant will be able to have a healthy, positive relationship with his children. The court strongly believes that these children need the love and involvement of both their parents in their lives, and is hopeful that the father will move on and allow himself to be the father to these children that he so adamantly claims he wants to be....

ORDERS....

2.   Custody and Visitation

a.   The mother shall have sole legal custody of the minor children.... The father shall have supervised visitation with the minor children as arranged by and with Marie Karjanis or Charles Karjanis as the supervisor.

b.   The defendant shall only enter the plaintiff's property to pick up the children for visitation.

c.   The visits shall occur off the premises.

d.   The children shall be allowed to call their father if they wish.

e.   The defendant shall not make any disparaging remarks about the plaintiff to the children, e.g., referring to her as the devil. Neither party shall do anything which may estrange the children from the other party nor injure the opinion of the children as to the other party nor act in such a way as to hamper the free and natural development of the children's love and respect for the other party. There shall be no arguing, screaming, rude, threatening or otherwise abusive behavior by the parents in the children's presence....

NOTES AND QUESTIONS

1.   **Visitation and Studies about the Effects of Paternal Involvement after Divorce.** There are many studies about the advantages to children of having two parents involved in their routine activities. See *e.g.,* Paul R. Amato and Joan G. Gilbreth, *Nonresident Fathers and Children's Well–Being*, 61 J. MARRIAGE & FAM. 557 (1999). One theory of child development focuses on the quality of the child's attachments to his or her parents as significant in the child's overall development and in the child's ability to form relationships and to separate from the parents. These studies usually claim that children build secure attachments by having both parents involved in actual child care responsibilities, as opposed to merely visiting with the children for a couple of hours. The issue is not so much the amount of time spent with the child as the activities in which the parent and child engage. Activities that are said to facilitate attachment include bathing, feeding, chauffering, and assisting with homework, discipline, and bedtime, Michael E. Lamb, *Placing Children's Interests First: Developing Appropriate Parenting Plans*, 10 VA. J. SOC. POL'Y & L. 98 (2002). However, others argue that child development research has not yet been able to

identify the nature and quantity of contacts necessary to create secure attachments. For example, it is well-known that children in traditional two-parent families can form very secure attachments with parents who fulfill the traditional male role of full-time breadwinner and are only occasional parents, Nancy S. Weinfield, *Comments on Lamb's "Placing Children's Interests First,"* 10 VA. J. SOC. POL'Y & L. 120 (2002).

2. **Does a Nonresidential Parent Have a Constitutional Right to Visitation**? Some fathers' rights advocates claim that fathers have a fundamental constitutional right to joint legal and joint physical custody of their children, *see, e.g.,* The Children's Rights Council website, *www.gocrc.com/constitution.html*. These advocates argue that the Supreme Court has frequently recognized the right to raise one's child, see *Troxel v. Granville,* 530 U.S. 57 (2000) (recognizing the importance of a parent's autonomy in raising a child in a suit for grandparent visitation). According to this position, limitations on this fundamental right, whether through a denial of joint custody or, more dramatically, serious restrictions or a denial of visitation constitute an infringement of this right. Such an infringement can only be justified by a compelling state interest and, even so, the infringement must be as narrowly drawn as possible. The advocates of a constitutional right to raise one's own children argue that this is, after all, basic constitutional theory.

Is this argument convincing to you? First, you might want to consider exactly what *Troxel* says about parental rights. *Troxel* is a case in which paternal grandparents sought additional visitation with their grandchildren over the mother's objections. The father was dead. After calling the mother's right to "care, custody and control" of the child one of the "fundamental liberty interests," the Court said that there is a "presumption" that fit parents act in their children's best interests. It also said that the problem with the lower court's decision ordering visitation was that it had given "no special weight at all" to the mother's position. Finally, the Court gave significant import to the fact that the mother had not entirely cut off the grandparents' visitation with the children. What level of scrutiny was the Court using in reviewing the decision? The main opinion in *Troxel* is a plurality opinion written by Justice O'Connor and joined by Chief Justice Rehnquist, Justice Ginsburg, and Justice Breyer. Justice Thomas wrote a concurring opinion in which he said that strict scrutiny should be used, and Justice Souter concurred on other grounds.

If the Court were to adopt strict scrutiny as the appropriate level of review in due process cases in which one parent gets visitation instead of joint physical custody, could you argue that there was a compelling reason for restricting an abusive parent's rights in relation to his or her children? Would the presence of domestic violence and the literature on the effects of domestic violence on children be relevant to your argument? How would you respond to the literature about the benefits of joint custody to children?

Was it constitutional for the *Karjanis* court to order supervised visitation as opposed to unsupervised visitation? Why or why not? Would it have been constitutional in *Karjanis* for the court to have refused the father all visitation? What would the mother's attorney have had to show in order for that to have been constitutional?

In a petition for writ of certiorari to *Schwartz v. Isaac*, 2005 WL 45683, the petitioner argued that because of the weighty interests at stake in denying him significant visitation, he was entitled to a fuller hearing than he had received. The U.S. Supreme Court denied certiorari, 543 U.S. 1153 (2005).

3. **Parental Alienation.** Some children adamantly refuse to have anything to do with one parent. In 1985, Richard Gardner developed the concept of Parental Alienation Syndrome (PAS) to describe situations involving false claims of abuse of the child by the noncustodial parent, an extreme negative reaction to the noncustodial parent by the child, and in which that reaction is caused by the custodial parent's having influenced (some say "brainwashed") the child. In the most severe cases, Gardner recommends that custody of the child be changed from the favored parent to the disfavored one. In domestic violence cases, claims of PAS may surface because a child is reluctant to visit with the abusive parent. Can you explain why, other than as a result of PAS, a child might be reluctant?

The existence of PAS has been hotly debated by the legal and psychological community. No one questions that some children show a clear and powerful aversion to one of their parents. In strongly contested custody fights, as many as 20% of the children may show such a reaction. Janet Johnston, one of the foremost experts on highly conflicted divorces, believes however that this rejection of one parent is not necessarily due to the actions and influences of the custodial parent. Other factors likely to be significant, according to her, are the behavior of the noncustodial parent, the child's level of development, and the specific facts and context of the divorce. Others argue that PAS should not be accepted because it shifts the focus from the claim of abuse by the disfavored parent to the actions of the custodial parent. Still others argue that the alienation is just a part of a natural developmental stage given the experience of the divorce and that, if left alone, the children will reconcile with the rejected parent eventually.

Most commentators on the subject agree that rigorous studies of the area are needed before the idea of PAS can be accepted either scientifically or in litigation. As of now, there are insufficient studies to show that different evaluators would agree on a diagnosis of PAS in the same cases. Furthermore, the efficacy of the suggested therapy of removing the child from the security of the custodial parent also needs to be proven by large scale studies. As a result, many courts have refused to make findings of PAS although others have recognized PAS and have even changed custody as a result. Do you think it is possible to imagine children who are alienated from one parent for any of a variety of reasons without adopting the idea of a syndrome in which the custodial parent is necessarily the cause of the syndrome? What might be the reasons for such alienation?

For further information on this vigorously debated topic, see Richard Gardner, *Commentary on Kelly and Johnston's "The Alienated Child,"* 42 FAM. CT. REV. 611 (2004); Janet R. Johnston, *Children of Divorce Who Reject a Parent and Refuse Visitation*, 38 FAM. L. Q. 757 (2005); Richard A.

Warshak, *Bringing Sense to Parental Alienation,* 37 FAM. L. Q. 273 (2003); Carol S. Bruch, *Parental Alienation Syndrome and Parental Alienation,* 35 FAM. L. Q. 527 (2001). For examples of cases on the topic, see *People v. Fortin,* 706 N.Y.S.2d 611 (N.Y.Crim. Ct. 2000) (criminal case in which the court rejected PAS as not generally accepted in scientific community); *Wade v. Hirschman,* 903 So.2d 928 (Fla. 2005) (rotating custody arrangement changed to sole custody in father based in part on child's alienation).

4. **What is Supervised Visitation?** Supervised visitation, i.e., visitation under the supervision of a third party, grew up to serve families involved in care and protection proceedings. In that context, supervised visitation provides a place for a parent to see and interact with the child while minimizing risks to the child because the visitation is conducted under the watchful eye of a third person. The supervision may be conducted by an individual in a private setting or at a center established for the purpose. Supervised visitation may be ordered for families in which there has been domestic violence. The objective in these cases is to provide visitation opportunities in a setting that will be safe for the child and for the abused parent. Supervised visitation may also be ordered if the court believes that one parent is alienating the child from the other. Some programs also have custody exchange services. These provide a public place for the exchange of the child. Sometimes they also require staggered arrival and departure of the parents so that the abuser cannot follow or accost the victimized parent during the exchange process, Jerry H. Dunn, Barbara Flory, Marla Berg–Weger, *An Exploratory Study of Supervised Access and Custody Exchange Services,* 42 FAM. CT. REV. 60 (2004). Studies have shown that noncustodial parents increase the time they spend with their children while they are participating in a supervised visitation program. The programs also are associated with decreased amounts of conflict (both verbal and physical) between the parents while they are using the service. So far, however, the studies are insufficient to indicate whether these advances are maintained after the families stop using the service.

5. **When Is a Court Likely to Order Supervised Visitation?** What factors in *Karjanis* were important in the court's decision to order supervised visitation? How important was the father's physical, emotional, or financial abuse of the mother? In other cases, courts have ordered supervised visitation because of the noncustodial parent's inability to communicate with the child without undermining the child's relationship with the custodial parent or without expressing anger at the child, *Bhatia v. Debek,* 2005 WL 1271709 (Conn. Super.) or because of the noncustodial parent's threat to flee with the child, *Lisa B. v. Salim G.,* 801 N.Y.S. 2d 235 (N.Y.Fam.Ct.2005). Sometimes supervised visitation is used as a means to protect the supervised parent from the custodial parent's allegations of wrong-doing during supervision or as a means to reestablish a relationship between a noncustodial parent and a child, *Bather v. Bather,* 170 S.W.3d 487 (Mo.App. W.D.2005) Since the terms of visitation depend on the child's "best interests," supervised visitation is often ordered independent of the presence of domestic violence. In contrast, supervised exchanges at visitation are most commonly used in domestic violence cases.

6. **Who Serves as Supervisor When Visitation is Supervised?** If visitation is not to be done at a visitation center that provides supervision, courts often look to a "neutral" third party to supervise—a family member or friend, for example. However, as two commentators have noted, "Even if a family member or friend agrees to supervise visits, he or she may be vulnerable to the noncustodial parent's demands and threats, rendering the supervision ineffective. There is also a risk that the volunteer may simply not believe the allegations made about the visiting parent and may decide to only loosely monitor the visit, further endangering the child." Nat Stern and Karen Oehme, *The Troubling Admission of Supervised Visitation Records in Custody Proceedings*, 75 TEMPLE L. REV. 271 (2002). It is, of course, significantly cheaper to have a family member or friend do the supervising rather than have the supervision performed at a visitation center. In *Karjanis*, the court ordered that Marie and Charles Karjanis supervise the visitation. It seems likely that these are relatives of the father's, perhaps his parents. Is this a good idea?

What qualities should a judge look for in a supervisor? In one case, the law guardian recommended that the court consider the noncustodial father's current wife to supervise his visitation with the children, *In the Matter of St. Pierre v. Burrows*, 788 N.Y.S.2d 494 (App. Div. 3d Dept. 2005). What do you think of this suggestion? Should the court require the proposed supervisor to appear in court before issuing an order for supervised visitation? *In the Matter of Kargoe v. Mitchell*, 785 N.Y.S.2d 557 (App. Div. 3d Dept. 2004). If so, what questions should the court ask the proposed supervisor?

Some states have statutes directing the development of uniform standards for providers of supervised visitation, *see, e.g.*, Cal. Fam. Code § 3200 (2005), but others do not. If you were drawing up standards, what would you put in them? Would you require supervisors to be certified or trained in any particular manner? For an example of guidelines drawn up by the Supervised Visitation Network, *see www.svnetwork.net/StandardsAnd Guidelines.html*.

7. **Use of Supervised Visitation Records in Custody Trials.** Most visitation centers require that the supervisor keep records of the supervised session. These are likely to include the name of the child and of the noncustodial parent; the name of the supervisor; the date, time, and length of the supervised visit; and, some summary of the visit. If the supervised visitation has gone uneventfully, the noncustodial parent may want to use the reports of the visitation in court when he or she moves for unsupervised visitation. Do you think that uneventful supervised visitation is an indicator that the noncustodial parent should be granted unsupervised visitation? Suppose the record of the visitation session contains accounts of loving statements between the noncustodial parent and the child. Are these admissible as evidence of such a relationship? For example, imagine that the supervisor's report states that when the session was over the child said to the father, "Good-bye. I love you, dad." Would the report with this statement be admissible as evidence of a loving relationship between the father and child or are there hearsay problems with its admission? Suppose

the father's attorney were to call the supervisor as a witness to testify to the fact that the father and child appeared to have a loving relationship? Would that be permissible? Aside from potential hearsay problems what other objections might the custodial parent's attorney voice to the admission of the supervised visitation records? For much more detail on the admissibility of supervised visitation records, see Nat Stern and Karen Oehme, *The Troubling Admission of Supervised Visitation Records in Custody Proceedings,* 75 TEMPLE L. REV. 271 (2002). Intake records may also contain information that the abused parent would be reluctant to give to the abuser. Nat Stern and Karen Oehme, *Increasing Safety for Battered Women and Their Children: Creating a Privilege for Supervised Visitation Intake Records,* 41 U. RICH. L. REV. 499 (2007). If you were asked to make recommendations to the supervised visitation center about what information should be kept in their records, how would these issues affect those recommendations?

8. **Pro Se Litigants, Domestic Violence, and Custody Litigation.** In the *Karjanis* case, the father had no lawyer. The father appeared *pro se* although the mother was represented by an attorney. It is very common in domestic relations cases for one or the other (or both) of the parties to be unrepresented. Russell Engler, *Out of Sight and Out of Line,* 85 CAL. L. REV. 79 (1997). Unlike in *Karjanis,* it is more common for women to be unrepresented in family law cases than men. Russell Engler, *And Justice for All—Including the Unrepresented Poor: Revisiting the Roles of Judges, Mediators and Clerks,* 67 FORDHAM L. REV. 1987 (1999). Since custody cases invariably involve strong emotions and high stakes, unrepresented litigants are likely to be particularly vulnerable to threats and bluffs by the other party's attorney. In addition, unrepresented parties may turn to unwilling court personnel or the other party's attorney for information. Given the facts of *Karjanis,* do you think the father was at a disadvantage for not having had an attorney? Should the mother's attorney have modified his or her behavior because the father was not represented?

G.   RELOCATION

Introduction

One way to seek safety from an abusive partner is to move. If the move is distant enough, it may deter further harassment and abuse, even if the batterer still knows where to find his former partner. For some women, on the other hand, only "disappearing" will end the abuse. In cases like this, women may need to go to extraordinary lengths to conceal their new locations; adopting new names, applying for new social security numbers, changing their appearances, and avoiding any careless contact with former friends or family members who might be pressured into disclosing their whereabouts. Despite the enormous social and economic disruptions involved, despite losing jobs and family and social supports, women make these moves in order to live free of fear.

But when women share young children with their abusers, moving becomes even more difficult, if not impossible, to accomplish. Imagine first the situation where a married couple has not formally separated or initiated divorce proceedings, but the violence is escalating, and the woman decides that she must leave. One possibility, if the man is not abusive toward the children, is to leave them with him, at least as a temporary measure. If the woman eventually wants to regain custody of the children, however, she will have to risk the ongoing contact with her abuser that a divorce and custody action requires, and she will have to hope that the jurisdiction in which she brings her action is one in which she will not be penalized for "abandoning" the children when she fled.

If instead she takes the children with her, then she is depriving her partner of his "share" in them, with consequences in both the family law and criminal justice arenas. Under family law, her partner can take his complaint into family court, with a request that because of his partner's abduction of the children he be granted sole custody. If his partner does not respond to the court's summons, which she may not, either because she is unaware of it, or because she is afraid to return, or because she is in a shelter with rules against allowing residents to respond to legal proceedings, then he will in all probability be awarded custody in her absence, she will be ordered to return the children to him, and she will be vulnerable to contempt charges for failing to do so. The combined effect of the federal Parental Kidnapping Prevention Act and state adoption of the Uniform Child Custody Jurisdiction Act makes it very unlikely that she will be able to persuade a court in her new location to take jurisdiction of the case. Only by returning with her children and submitting to the jurisdiction of the "home state" court, thereby making herself vulnerable to her abuser once more, can she hope to retain custody. Under the criminal law she is likely to be guilty of child kidnapping, either at the moment when she deprives her partner of his inherent right to access as a natural parent, or at the latest when she violates the court order awarding him custody. She will avoid these criminal charges only if the law in the state from which she flees recognizes flight from domestic violence as a defense against kidnapping charges, and even if such a defense is available to her, she may be subject to arrest and prosecution at the urging of her abuser, and have to establish her defense in the course of criminal proceedings.

If there has already been a formal separation or divorce and the parents' access to the children has been regulated through custody and visitation orders, the parent who feels that her own or her children's safety is being compromised by those orders has two choices. One is to seek modification of the orders to end the abuser's access to her and the children, and the other is simply to flee, in disregard of the orders. Modification is not an easy route, given judicial reluctance to deprive a parent of access; it becomes harder if the custodial parent wants to take the children out of the state, and harder yet if the idea is to give the abusive parent no information about the family's new location. Furthermore, the period during which the custodial parent has signaled to her abuser that she is trying to escape his control and is processing her request through the courts, a period which is likely to be protracted, is also likely to be a period of increased danger.

On the other hand, fleeing with the children will put the custodial parent in legal jeopardy. She will be in violation of one or more court orders, without even the possibility of arguing that she was unaware of their existence, since they predated her departure. In these circumstances it is not uncommon for courts to transfer custody to the parent left behind, as a way of punishing the departing parent for flouting the authority of the court, despite the fact that custody determinations are legally governed solely by a "best interests of the child" analysis. And again, the departing parent will be vulnerable to child kidnapping charges.

This section explores many of these topics, highlighting the perils involved both in seeking to use the legal process to establish distance from an abuser, and in using the "self-help" remedy of flight in disregard of the legal process. Initially it deals with "flight" in the domestic U.S. context; the final portion of the section deals with "flight" internationally. The section opens with an excerpt from an article which, in its entirety, provides an excellent discussion of the problems of relocation within the U.S.

Working Within the System

Janet M. Bowermaster

Relocation Custody Disputes Involving Domestic Violence

46 U. KAN. L. REV. 433 (1998).

Consider the case of Deb C. Her husband beat her and sexually and verbally abused her. In December 1993, when he beat her in front of their four-year-old son, Deb called 911. Two sheriff's officers responded to the call. Her husband violently resisted the officers. He injured one of the officers so severely that the officer was taken to the hospital and was unable to work for three weeks. The authorities removed Deb's husband from the home and arrested him for two counts of battery against police officers, resisting arrest, battery against Deb, and domestic violence without a weapon. Deb filed for divorce ten days later and believed the horrors were behind her.

In March 1994, Deb's husband was convicted of violently resisting his December arrest. The other charges, including the charge of battery against Deb, were dropped. In April 1994, he attacked her at her bank and was arrested again. Frightened at having been attacked in public, Deb asked the court's permission to remove a restraint that prevented her from leaving the state with her son. She wanted to take her family to Florida where her parents and her brother and his wife were living. She had a job offer there starting at $42,000 a year. She had no friends or family in California, no job, and she lived in constant fear for her life. Her eighteen-year-old daughter from a prior marriage was so frightened she neither slept in her own room nor stayed in the house alone. Deb's now ex-husband had informed her daughter that he had peeked in her windows. He also had broken into their home on many occasions.

In November 1994, Deb's ex-husband pled "no contest" to the battery of Deb at the bank. But arrests, restraining orders, and incarceration were no deterrent to his bizarre, violent behavior. He was subsequently arrested for felony stalking, peeping, violation of a court order, annoying telephone calls, trespass, and felony terrorist threats. Deb and her children were chosen to participate in Sacramento County's AWARE program. The program involves an alarm system provided to "high risk" families who are considered to be in clear and present danger for their lives. In November 1995, Deb's ex-husband pled guilty to stalking and was sentenced to jail.

During this time, Deb was unable to work because of her ex-husband's death threats, batteries, and stalking. She could leave her home only when someone was with her. Because of these circumstances, her only means of support was through Aid to Families with Dependent Children (AFDC).

Pursuant to a court order, Deb's son continued to have "supervised" visits with his father. The boy's mental health suffered to the point that, at age five, he entered weekly therapy that lasted for a year and a half. The son's therapist strongly recommended he be allowed to leave the state with his mother.

During the many months that Deb feared for her life, she went to Family Court Services three different times for court-ordered mediation and still was not allowed to remove her son from the state. A psychological evaluation was ordered, which cost $6,000. The psychologist recommended Deb be allowed to take her son to Florida as soon as possible with only minimal visitation by his father. When her husband challenged the evaluation, two more follow-up evaluations were ordered. Deb's evaluation fees now totaled nearly $15,000. Each evaluator recommended Deb be allowed to take her son to Florida.

Because Deb and her ex-husband could not agree on custody, a hearing was set for November 2, 1995. Witnesses were subpoenaed and Deb's parents flew to California from Florida. On the morning of the hearing, Deb was informed that neither a courtroom nor a judge was available, and the next available trial date would be January 12, 1996. Meanwhile, Deb was not allowed to move. A representative from the District Attorney's office advised her that if she took her son to Florida without the court's approval, she would be prosecuted for federal kidnapping, and her son would be returned to California and placed in his father's custody. When Deb, her parents, and her other witnesses appeared on January 12, 1996, there was another shortage of judges and courtrooms. The hearing was rescheduled again, this time for April 4, 1996. This hearing went forward as scheduled. A week later, the State of California granted Deb's request to remove her son from the state. On May 22, 1996, after a thirty-day stay, the court allowed Deb and her son to fly to safety in Florida. This finally occurred two-and-a-half years after Deb filed for divorce from her violent husband.

When Deb filed for divorce she was a successful business woman, she now owes her family law attorney $50,000, owes her parents $50,000, and has filed for bankruptcy. Yet, she considers herself fortunate to have made it out alive and with her child.

People confronted with stories like Deb's ask how such things can happen. The pervasiveness of domestic violence and its high social costs are well known. Progress in combating domestic violence has been made in many areas. In the family courts, however, stopping violence is not a priority.

NOTES AND QUESTIONS

1. **Domestic Violence, Family Courts and Criminal Courts.** It would be hard to disagree with Bowermaster's conclusion that family courts often do not give priority to stopping violence, or even to recognizing it. Remember the excerpt from Joan Meier's article at the beginning of this chapter. However, in the situation Bowermaster describes, the criminal justice system also seems to have let Deb C. down, in allowing the initial charges of domestic violence to be dropped. The violent incident reflected in these charges was what prompted Deb C. to file for divorce, and yet when she first asked the family court for permission to leave the state, her former partner had no record of criminal convictions for domestic violence. He attacked her again in April of 1994, but then was permitted to plead "no contest" to that battery after a seven-month period during which he was free to continue his harassment. He was not incarcerated until he had been arrested, in addition, on charges of felony stalking, peeping, violation of a court order, annoying telephone calls, trespass, and felony terrorist threats. It took almost two years after his first arrest on domestic violence charges for him to be incarcerated, despite a continuous history of domestic violence offenses throughout that two year period.

Family courts, which have less direct experience with violence, often look to criminal courts for guidance, and assume that if the criminal system has failed to convict or incarcerate a batterer, it must be because he does not pose any serious risk to his victim or their children. This assumption is often unwarranted.

2. **Relocation Requests and Traditional Notions of Patriarchy.** Bowermaster claims that family courts' unwillingness to allow custodial parents to relocate is part of an older legal tradition which accorded the husband and father the right to choose the family domicile. Conceding that "today's laws no longer give husbands the explicit right to choose their wives' domicile," she argues that "the husband's prerogative to control where his wife and children live is still embedded in the American culture." That persistent cultural assumption also underlies current judicial decisions, she suggests, even though judges talk instead about "the best interests of children after separation or divorce and the importance of keeping both parents involved in their children's lives." See in addition, Carol S. Bruch and Janet M. Bowermaster, *The Relocation of Children and Custodial Parents: Public Policy, Past and Present,* 30 F.L.Q. 245 (1996).

In the following excerpt, Bowermaster demonstrates the inconsistency between the arguments contemporary judges use, and the consequences of their decisions. She also notes, however, that a new trend, offering more protection for the custodial family unit, may be beginning to emerge.

Janet M. Bowermaster
Relocation Custody Disputes Involving Domestic Violence

46 U. KAN. L. REV. 433 (1998).

Some courts have advanced the notion that restricting custodial parents' mobility serves children's best interests by preserving their environmental stability. While changing homes, schools, and neighborhoods is stressful for children, it seems clear that the normal incidents of moving are not at the heart of relocation disputes. Acceptable moveaway distances of 50, 100, or 150 miles specified in statutes, judgments, and separation agreements support the notion that it is not the disruptive effect of moving that is the problem in relocation disputes. Children who move even 50 miles must change homes, schools, churches, doctors, dentists, neighbors, and friends. Distance limitations protect only the ability of noncustodial parents to have convenient access to their children. Similarly, cases in which custodial parents have already resettled with their children in new communities and are ordered back to where the noncustodial parents live also belie the stated concern for the child's environmental stability.

When intact families move with their children, it is assumed that the parents have made the decision to move with the best interests of their children in mind. The only difference when a divorced, custodial parent moves with the children is that the move takes the children away from the noncustodial parent. It is the increased distance between the noncustodial parent and the child that is at the heart of relocation custody disputes.

The most widely-accepted rationale for restricting the movement of custodial parents is that children's interests are best served by ensuring frequent and continuing contact with both parents after divorce. This rationale is unconvincing for several reasons. First, the enormous sacrifices some jurisdictions require from custodial parents to keep children near noncustodial parents for visitation does not comport with the failure of those same jurisdictions to require noncustodial parents to actually exercise their visitation. Second, if the goal of frequent and continuing contact is important enough to restrict the mobility of custodial parents, it should support similar restrictions on noncustodial parents. Yet, noncustodial parents in every jurisdiction are free to relocate at will. Third, geographic restrictions do not achieve frequent and continuing contact with both parents in cases where custodial parents are unable or unwilling to remain. Custodial parents cannot constitutionally be prohibited from moving. Rather, courts try to coerce them into "voluntarily" remaining in the jurisdiction by threatening them with loss of custody if they move. When that coercion fails, changing custody does not preserve the child's frequent and continuing contact with both parents. It simply preserves the child's relationship with the noncustodial parent at the expense of the child's primary relationship with the custodial parent. Cases in which custodial parents lose custody by moving suggest that the real goal of relocation restrictions is not to ensure contact with both parents, but to protect the rights of noncustodial parents.

Why is there so much focus on noncustodial fathers' frequent visitation with and proximity to their children, sometimes in stunning disregard of the consequences to custodial mothers and their children? If the openly articulated rationales do not adequately support geographic restrictions on custodial parents, deeper unspoken influences must be at work. At least one of these influences is the cultural residue of traditional marriage laws in which unquestioned deference to the husband's choice of domicile was the law of the land.

Trend Toward Allowing Relocation

Like many other areas of family law, relocation custody law is in transition. Social science research has shed new light on children's best interests in moveaway cases. Simply put, the research literature has convincingly demonstrated the centrality of the primary caretaking relationship to the child's well-being, while finding no similar support for the visiting relationship. . . .

Noted sociologists Frank Furstenberg and Andrew Cherlin conducted a comprehensive multi-disciplinary review of large-scale national research to assess post-divorce problems. The essence of their analyses and recommendations is that because children's welfare strongly depends on the financial and emotional well-being of the custodial parent and data does not establish a comparable link between visitation and the child's well-being, support for the custodial family unit takes precedence over maintaining any particular pattern of visitation with the noncustodial parent. This means that in relocation cases in which the primary caretaker's needs conflict with the noncustodial parent's desires for more frequent visitation, the conflict should be decided in a way that supports the custodial parent's life choices, including relocation. Other prominent social science researchers have reported findings that support these conclusions.

The policy implications of this research are beginning to be recognized in the legal arena. Courts are beginning to back away from the untoward solicitude for fathers' rights that has characterized many relocation custody cases in the past. A distinct trend has emerged in recent state supreme court decisions towards more protection for the custodial family unit. While still careful to provide for noncustodial parents' access to their children, courts are making it easier for custodial parents to decide where they will live without losing custody of their children.

NOTES AND QUESTIONS

1. **Recent Research.** The research by Furstenberg and Cherlin to which Bowermaster refers, and which affirms the importance of supporting the

custodial family unit, is Frank F. Furstenberg and Andrew J. Cherlin, DIVIDED FAMILIES: WHAT HAPPENS TO CHILDREN WHEN PARENTS PART (1991). More recently, Sanford Braver and some colleagues published a study of approximately 600 students whose parents were divorced. These students, who were chosen because they were enrolled in an introductory psychology class at Arizona State University, filled out questionnaires about themselves and their families. The researchers found a "preponderance of negative effects" correlated with either parent's move away from the child, including distress related to the divorce, hostility in interpersonal relations, and reduced perceptions of their parents as role models. In addition, moves of either parent resulted in considerably less financial support for the college students. Braver and his colleagues conclude from this that moves by either parent should be discouraged and that courts should give serious consideration to ordering a change of custody if the custodial parent is going to move with the child. Sanford L. Braver, Ira Mark Ellman, and William V. Fabricius, *Relocation of Children After Divorce and Children's Best Interests*, 17 J. FAMILY PSYCH. 206 (2003). The study was reported with emotion by some newspapers such as USA TODAY which headlined, *Stay Close By, for the Sake of the Kids*. USA TODAY, (July 7, 2003) at D7.

The Braver study, however, has been criticized by a number of other scholars. Some of the study's findings undercut the authors' conclusions that permitting mothers to relocate with their children is damaging to the children. On many important measures—emotional adjustment, substance abuse, platonic friendship patterns, dating behavior, and general life satisfaction—there was no significant difference between those children who moved with the mother and those who remained in a community with both parents. Furthermore, the children in the study who showed the most negative adjustment were those who had either moved with their fathers or who had remained with their fathers while their mothers moved. In addition, like other studies of its kind, the Braver study merely identifies correlations; it makes no claims as to causation. For example, it is possible that relocation cases represent cases in which the divorce occurred when the children were younger. It is also possible that a large percentage of relocation cases are cases in which there was abuse in the parents' relationship. For critiques of the Braver study, see Robert Pasahow, *A Critical Analysis of the First Empirical Research Study on Child Relocation*, 19 J. AM. ACAD. MATRIM. LAW. 321 (2005); *Judith Wallerstein, Comments*, avail. at www.thelizlibrary.org/liz/braver-wallerstein.html; Norval Glenn and David Blankenhorn, *Does Moving After Divorce Damage Kids?* available at www.thelizlibrary.org/liz/braver-wallerstein.html; Carol S. Bruch, *Sound Research or Wishful Thinking in Child Custody Cases? Lessons from Relocation Law*, 40 FAM. L.Q. 281 (2006).

2.   **Case Examples.** For examples of the trend toward greater respect for the custodial unit, see *Silbaugh v. Silbaugh*, 543 N.W.2d 639 (Minn. 1996); *Holder v. Polanski*, 544 A.2d 852 (N.J. 1988); *Tropea v. Tropea*, 665 N.E.2d 145 (N.Y. 1996); *Watt v. Watt*, 971 P.2d 608 (Wyo. 1999); *Ireland v. Ireland*, 717 A.2d 676 (Conn. 1998). Some states have accomplished the same thing by statute, see, e.g., Tenn. Code Ann. § 36–6–108(d) (allows relocation unless no reasonable purpose, harmful to child, or vindicative).

Not all battered women seeking to relocate with their children reap the advantages of this developing trend, however. The following is a recent case in which the mother's petition to relocate may have contributed to her loss of custody.

Valentine v. Valentine

Court of Appeals of Ohio, 2005.
2005 WL 1131748.

■ WALSH, J.

Plaintiff-appellant, Ann M. Valentine, appeals a judgment of the [Trial Court].... denying her request to relocate her children out of state.

Appellant and defendant-appellee, Charles E. Valentine, were married on September 24, 1996. Two children were born issue of the marriage.... The [2003 divorce] decree names appellant the sole residential parent and grants appellee parenting time....

[T]he Decree states: "[Appellee] shall have the right to reasonable telephone contact with the children.... [Appellant] shall make the children available for the telephone calls, shall encourage their participation, and shall not interfere in any way with the telephone calls."

The record on appeal reveals that both parties have continually disagreed, fought, and argued with each other over the children and appellee's right to parenting time. Accordingly, on October 20, 2003, subsequent to one of their numerous disputes, appellee filed a motion for contempt against appellant, and a request for a change of circumstances hearing. In that motion, appellee alleged that appellant denied him the right to phone contact with his children on October 8 and October 15, 2003, and he requested that the court modify the current parenting time schedule, or designate him the residential parent.

In response, on November 21, 2003, appellant, in conjunction with a notice of intent to relocate, filed a motion to modify parental rights and responsibilities. In that motion, appellant asked the court to allow her to relocate with the children to the state of New Jersey....

[At the] hearing on appellee's motion for contempt ... appellee offered evidence that he attempted to call his children at the appointed time on October 8, but the line was busy. He also offered evidence that on October 15, 2003, he called appellant's home and no one answered....

Appellant then presented her own testimony, and testimony from Steve Messer, a friend of appellant's present with her on the dates in question. Both testified that appellant's phone did not ring on October 8, 2003, between 6:30 and 7:30 p.m. They also testified that on October 15, 2003, appellant had car trouble and was not able to be at home between 6:30 and 7:30 p.m.

Appellant then presented evidence in support of her request to relocate. She testified that the move would provide the children a more healthy environment, as well as provide her with a healthy support system. She also testified that she was afraid of appellee, that he was stalking her, and that she would feel safer if she were living in New Jersey. . . .

[A]ppellee testified that if the children were to relocate to New Jersey he would not be able to maintain a meaningful relationship with them. He also testified that he believed part of the reason for appellant seeking the move was to interfere with his ability to see his children.

At the conclusion of the January 21, 2004 hearing, the court rendered the following decision: Appellant was found in contempt for violating appellee's right to phone contact . . . and sentenced to one day in jail; appellant's request to relocate her children to New Jersey was denied; if appellant does choose to relocate by herself, the children will remain in Ohio with appellee as the residential parent. . . .

[Given the evidence] we cannot say the trial court's decision to find appellant in contempt for failing to facilitate phone contact was unreasonable, or grossly violative of fact and logic. . . .

The record reveals that appellant and appellee have been before the same trial court in a long string of contentious and tumultuous proceedings related to their divorce. The contempt motion that is the subject of this appeal was the second granted in appellee's favor.

The trial court has repeatedly commented on the record about the parties continual fighting and lack of cooperation, and has on more than one occasion made comments such as "[t]he parties have never been able to cooperate or have a civil relationship, and . . . both parties behave immaturely." . . . [W]e are inclined to agree. . . .

The record reveals that appellant moved for modification of parental rights and responsibilities in conjunction with a notice of intent to relocate. . . .

R.C. 3109.04(E)(1)(a) governs the modification of a previous order allocating parental rights and responsibilities, and states:

> The court shall not modify a prior decree allocating parental rights and responsibilities for the care of children unless it finds, based on facts that have arisen since the prior decree or that were unknown to the court at the time of the prior decree, that a change has occurred in the circumstances of the child, his residential parent, or either of the parents subject to a shared parenting decree, and that the modification is necessary to serve the best interest of the child. . . .

As noted by the trial court, a relocation, by itself, does not constitute a change of circumstances. A proposed move along with a finding that the move will harm the welfare of the children involved, however, can constitute a change of circumstances.

In the instant case, the trial court determined that appellant's proposed move would have a negative impact on the children by virtually severing their relationship with appellee. Accordingly, the trial court determined that appellant's proposed relocation of the children to New Jersey would constitute a change of circumstances. Upon reviewing the record, we find that the court did not abuse its discretion in reaching this conclusion.

Once the threshold requirement of a change of circumstances has been met, a court must determine whether the proposed modification to the parental rights and responsibilities is in the best interest of the child. . . .

In its findings of fact and conclusions of law, the trial court set forth, in detail, its consideration [of the children's best interests]:

> Both children have significant relationships and interaction with both parents. The children are adjusted to their present environment in Ohio and have a regular schedule with each parent. The court also found appellant's statements that she needs to move to stop appellee from stalking her to be completely lacking in credibility. Finally, the court determined that appellant sought the move, in part, to thwart appellee's attempts to maintain a relationship with his children.

Upon making the foregoing findings, the court concluded that it would not be in the children's best interest to relocate to New Jersey.

The court's best interest findings were substantially based upon testimony from appellant and appellee. As discussed above, the weight given to the testimony of a witness is an issue primarily for the trier of fact; we will not substitute our judgment concerning the credibility of a witness for that of the trial court. Accordingly, we cannot say the court abused its discretion in concluding it would be in the children's best interest to remain in Ohio. . . .

NOTES AND QUESTIONS

1. **Did the Court Miss the Presence of Domestic Violence in *Valentine v. Valentine*?** The trial court made its decision in the *Valentine* case on January 21, 2004. By June of 2004 (before the above appeal was decided), Mr. Valentine was back in court with a motion for a change of custody based on the changed circumstances of Ms. Valentine's having requested to relocate with the children. The trial court found a change of circumstances and then found that the children's best interests justified a change of custody to Mr. Valentine. In the intermediate appeals court decision on change of custody, the court said, "It is apparent from the record that these parents have found little common ground upon which they can agree and have expressed their animosity toward each other through post-decree motions and proceedings. . . . In addition to involving the trial court with motions, both parents have asked police officers to intercede in disputes that have arisen at the police department where the visitation exchange takes place." This appellate court also noted that the trial court had found Mr. Valentine would be more likely to facilitate his former wife's parenting time with the children than she had been to facilitate his parenting time. In addition, the trial court had found that Mr. Valentine was in arrears in his child support payments. Finally, the trial court noted that the parties had brought numerous domestic violence allegations against the other, both in Ohio and New Jersey. *Valentine v. Valentine*, 2005 WL 3096587. In the opinion excerpted above, the Court of Appeals referred to Ms. Valentine's claims that she was afraid of Mr. Valentine and that he was stalking her.

The facts given above indicate that there may have been continuing domestic violence in this relationship. Given the facts, should the trial and appellate courts have done more than they did, and, if so, what? Is it the responsibility of the court to identify and raise the issue of domestic violence if counsel does not do so? If Ms. Valentine's attorney thought there was a possibility that the relationship was abusive, what type of evidence should she have looked for? Do the relative responsibilities of counsel and court change if Ms. Valentine, like so many litigants in family court, had to represent herself? Issues of representation will be taken up again in Chapter Eleven. See also Merle H. Weiner, *Inertia and Inequality: Reconceptualizing Disputes over Parental Relocation*, 40 U.C. Davis L. Rev. 1747 (2007).

2. **Changing Custody as a Result of a Motion to Relocate.** One of the most troubling aspects of this litigation is the court's determination ultimately to change the award of custody from Ms. Valentine to Mr. Valentine. It is hard to avoid thinking that this was done, at least in part, because of her claims that he was violent against her and of the trial court's reluctance to believe those claims. Instead, the trial court saw him as the "friendly" parent in terms of allowing her access to the children. This is a case in which the young children had been in Ms. Valentine's custody since the divorce two years earlier. Furthermore, the guardian ad litem had recommended in favor of leaving custody with Ms. Valentine.

This result is consistent with recent findings. The Leadership Council on Child Abuse and Interpersonal Violence has recently concluded that "raising allegations of abuse [child abuse or spousal abuse] may harm a protective parent more than the alleged abuser. . . . [W]omen who inform custody mediators that they are victims of domestic violence often receive less favorable custody awards than those who do not." Stephanie J. Dallam and Joyanna L. Silberg, *Myths That Place Children at Risk During Custody Disputes*, 9 Sexual Assault Report 33 (Jan./Feb. 2006).

3. **Standards for Determining Relocation Disputes.** As discussed above, a number of states today recognize the importance of maintaining custodial stability despite the custodial parent's desire to relocate. These states often create a presumption or preference in favor of allowing relocation. But, many other states use other standards. One commentator has noted, "Courts often display a rather stunning jingoism to deny what appear to be reasonable requests to relocate. As trial lawyers advising how to oppose a custodial move have put it, 'Do not overlook your home court advantage. Present your case with the presumption that the judge will take some pride in the place he or she has chosen to live.' " Lucy S. McGough, *Starting Over*, 77 St. John's L. Rev. 291 (2003).

Many states review the question of the child's best interests when a custodial parent seeks to relocate, often putting the burden of proof on the custodial parent. For example, Nebraska requires the custodial parent to show both a legitimate reason for leaving and that relocation would be in the child's best interests. *Wild v. Wild*, 696 N.W.2d 886 (Neb. App. 2005) (denying relocation of child). Other states, like Massachusetts, require the custodial parent to show that there is a "real advantage" to the move. If that can be shown, the non-custodial parent's motion to change custody is decided by the usual "substantial change in circumstances" standard. *Rosenthal v. Maney*, 745 N.E.2d 350 (Mass. App. 2001). Consider how rules that place the burden to show a legitimate reason for leaving, a real advantage, or even the child's best interests will function if the custodial parent wants to relocate because of domestic violence (or child abuse) that the court has not recognized. Remember that there are many scenarios under which there might be unrecognized domestic violence.

4. **Relocations in Initial Custody Situations or in Situations in Which the Parents Have Joint Custody.** If neither parent has sole custody, but instead an award of custody has yet to be made, most courts inquire as to the child's best interests. In cases in which the parents have joint custody, courts often require the parent wanting to relocate to bear the burden of filing for a change in custody and showing a substantial change in circumstances. *Potter v. Potter*, 119 P.3d 1246 (Nev. 2005). In these cases also, a court may fail to recognize domestic violence as a basis for allowing the child to relocate with the parent. For example, in *Racsko v. Racsko*, 881 A.2d 460 (Conn. App. 2005), the court held that relocation would not be in the child's best interests despite considerable evidence of domestic violence. In this initial custody determination, the mother had voiced her desire to get away from the father. Despite this and despite the evidence of domestic violence, the court did not allow the relocation of the child.

Leaving Without the Children: Is It Abandonment?

There are many reasons why an abused parent might leave without the children. If the flight is an emergency response to life-threatening violence, there may simply be no time to organize a group departure. Alternatively, the parent who leaves may lack the resources to care for her children, even in the short term. She may not be sure of finding space for her family in a shelter, and may not have the funds for food, housing, or necessary childcare. Then again, she may fear that if she takes the children, she will intensify her batterer's determination to track her down, and put herself and her children at greater risk.

Recognizing the danger that parents who leave their children behind when they flee will be accused of having abandoned them, and may be disadvantaged in any subsequent custody dispute, the National Council of Juvenile and Family Court Judges provides, in its Model Code on Domestic and Family Violence, that:

> If a parent is absent or relocates because of an act of domestic or family violence by the other parent, the absence or relocation is not a factor that weighs against the parent in determining custody or visitation.

MODEL CODE ON DOMESTIC AND FAMILY VIOLENCE, § 402(3) (1994). Several states have followed the Model Code, and enacted similar provisions. See, for example, COLO. REV. STAT. ANN. § 14–10–124 (West 1994); KY. REV. STAT. ANN. § 403.270 (Michie 1994); ME. REV. STAT. ANN. Tit. 15, Secs. 214, 581, 752 (West 1994).

Leaving With the Children and Without the Court's Permission: Civil Consequences

When battered women leave with their children, they may do so either before any formal court proceedings, or in contravention of existing court orders regarding custody and visitation. However, even where no family law proceeding has been initiated prior to the flight, it is common for the abusive partner to seek custody immediately, and to win a default custody judgment when the abused partner does not appear to defend the action. That judgment then becomes the basis for bringing the wife and children back to the "home state" for further proceedings in family court. In this context, courts—particularly trial courts—take very seriously the abused partner's apparent disregard for the authority of the court, and are frequently tempted to "punish" this disregard by awarding custody to the abusive parent, even when the governing statute is clear that this is an inappropriate basis for an award. Courts of Appeal quite routinely overturn these decisions, determining that they represent abuses of judicial discretion. The following case illustrates this pattern.

Odom v. Odom

Court of Appeal of Louisiana 1992.
606 So.2d 862.

■ LINDSAY, JUDGE.

The plaintiff in rule, Katherine Leigh Odom, appeals from a trial court judgment denying her request for change of custody and granting her former husband, Mark W. Odom, continuing custody of their two minor children. For the reasons assigned below, we reverse and remand.

FACTS

The parties were ... married in August, 1987. Of this [marriage], two children were born: Gary ... and Miranda....

On April 4, 1990, Mrs. Odom left the matrimonial domicile in Logansport, taking the children with her. They entered a shelter run by the YWCA Family Violence Program in Shreveport. Witnesses who saw Mrs. Odom upon her entry to the shelter observed that she had a black eye and was bruised and battered. Eight month old Miranda also had a bruise on her head; Mrs. Odom informed the social workers at the shelter that, while trying to hit her, Mr. Odom had struck the child.

On April 19, 1990, Mr. Odom filed a petition for separation, alleging abandonment and cruel treatment by Mrs. Odom. He also sought custody of the children....

On October 29, 1990, [in an uncontested proceeding] ... sole custody of the children was granted to Mr. Odom and the marriage was annulled. (No transcript of this proceeding is found in the appellate record.) ...

On January 23, 1991, Mrs. Odom filed a petition to change custody. She alleged several specific instances of physical abuse against her by Mr. Odom. She also alleged that on June 23, 1990, Mr. Odom attacked her roommate while she was holding Miranda. She asserted that she fled the state because of reliable information that Mr. Odom was planning to kidnap the children. . . .

On August 14, 1991, a hearing was held on the rule to change custody. The parties stipulated and the trial court agreed that joint custody was not in the best interest of the children. Witnesses presented by Mrs. Odom included social workers who had seen her battered and bruised condition when she entered the family violence shelter the day she left her husband. . . .

At the conclusion of the evidence, the trial court found that neither party was psychologically unfit to have custody. Based upon the home studies ordered by the court, it also found that both parents could provide a suitable physical environment. The court characterized both parents as "shakey [sic], emotionally," noting that in the opinion of the psychiatrist appointed to examine the parties any problems they had were intertwined with the court proceedings. The court stated its belief that the relationship between the parents was so hostile that an award of sole custody to either one would effectively terminate the other's parental rights.

The trial court ruled that the best interest of the children required that the prior award of sole custody to Mr. Odom be continued, but it granted "reasonable visitation" to Mrs. Odom. . . .

DETERMINATION OF CUSTODY

The evidence presented at the hearing on the rule to change custody showed that Mr. Odom is a self employed accountant. . . . Mr. Odom began attending the Methodist church in January, 1991, and is active in such activities as choir. Previously, he belonged to a congregation of Jehovah's Witnesses but left because he was facing discipline for allegedly beating Mrs. Odom.

Mr. Odom generally denied Mrs. Odom's charges of physical abuse, but admitted slapping her once while fighting off her sexual advances, as well as an altercation over an unpaid phone bill. He claimed that Mrs. Odom was "insane" and a liar. . . .

Mrs. Odom testified that she was attending community college in Kansas City to earn an associate degree in business and that she planned to work towards a university bachelor degree in business. . . . She was still receiving AFDC aid. . . .

Mrs. Odom also testified as to numerous beatings inflicted upon her by Mr. Odom during their marriage, often in the presence of the children, including the one that caused her to flee the matrimonial domicile in April, 1990. . . .

Two social workers associated with the family violence program verified Mrs. Odom's battered condition when she entered the program in April, 1990, as well as the bruise on Miranda's head. (Mr. Odom claimed that the child was injured because of Mrs. Odom's inattention.) They both testified that Mrs. Odom took excellent care of her children while she was residing at the shelter. . . .

In addition to the testimony presented at the hearing, the trial court also ordered home studies on each of the parents. We have examined these studies in some detail. Although the trial court found that they would support an award of custody to either parent, we disagree.

Mrs. Odom's home study was very complimentary. The social worker found her to be cooperative and open.... The social worker compiling the report found that she could make an "excellent home" for her children, was totally dedicated to her children, and had shown great strength in dealing with a stressful situation.

However, we are at a loss to understand how the trial court could characterize Mr. Odom's home study as being favorable. Although the social worker stated that she did not doubt "Mr. Odom's sincere desire to be a good father and a good person," she evaluated him as being "a controlling person" who becomes "disturbed" by his inability to control the people in his life. The social worker further believed that he had "the potential for violence, but this would most likely be limited to domestic violence, as his position in the community seems important to him." When initially contacted for the home study, Mr. Odom was extremely belligerent. The social worker described him as "a very angry person with a quality of hysteria" whose accusations against the social worker had "a ring of paranoia."

Furthermore, the social worker stated that if Mr. Odom were to be awarded custody of the children, she thought it unlikely "even under the best of circumstances" that he would allow them to have "any positive feelings or attachments" to Mrs. Odom because of his intense anger towards her....

One of the most important factors to be considered in awarding custody is which parent will be the most willing to foster communication between the children and the noncustodial parent. Based upon the record before us, it is abundantly clear that Mr. Odom will not allow the children to have any sort of relationship with their mother. His deep and bitter hatred of Mrs. Odom, which is obviously shared by his mother, is replete throughout the record in both the home studies and the testimony. (In particular, we note his sarcastic and hostile comments on cross examination.) Furthermore, he has repeatedly made accusations of child abuse against her which have not stood up to serious scrutiny by the authorities.

These factors weigh heavily against Mr. Odom. The evidence in this record indicates that Mr. Odom is a manipulative and vindictive person who will not hesitate to use his children to punish his former wife....

Although Mrs. Odom admittedly fled the jurisdiction of the court with the children, she did so because of her great fear of Mr. Odom. (Although the trial court made no findings on this issue, we find that the preponderance of evidence in the record demonstrates that Mr. Odom physically abused Mrs. Odom.) While we cannot condone this flight or completely ignore it, we can understand it in the context of this case. Furthermore, our purpose here is to determine what is best for these children, not to use custody as a means by which to punish a parent for past misconduct.

Additionally, Mrs. Odom has expressed a willingness to allow the children to develop a relationship with their father, a courtesy he obviously would not extend to her.

We are also favorably impressed by Mrs. Odom's efforts to rebuild her life and improve her financial situation by obtaining a higher education. There is no competent evidence in the record that indicates that the children would be anything but well cared for and loved in their mother's custody.

Based on the foregoing, we find that Mrs. Odom has carried her burden of proof and that the trial court judgment maintaining custody in Mr. Odom is manifestly erroneous....

CONCLUSION

The judgment of the trial court is reversed. Sole custody of the two minor children is awarded to the appellant, Mrs. Odom, subject to the reasonable visitation of the appellee, Mr. Odom....

NOTES AND QUESTIONS

1. **Visitation?** Although the Appeals Court did recognize that Mrs. Odom had only left the state with the children because she feared for her own and their safety, it appears to have forgotten just how angry Mr. Odom was at Mrs. Odom. By awarding unspecified "reasonable visitation," instead of limited, supervised visitation, the Appeals Court left Mrs. Odom with the burden of continued interaction with a man who had abused her and whom the court saw as still infuriated at her.

2. **Punishing Survivors of Abuse Who Flee With Their Children.** For another example of an Appeals Court that overturned a trial court's custody decision on the basis that the trial court had inappropriately punished a survivor of violence for leaving the state and failing to return, see *Marshall v. Marshall*, 690 N.E.2d 68 (Ohio App. 1997) and 1998 WL 725941 (Ohio App.) For a case in which the survivor of the violence fled and the trial court did not punish her with a loss of custody, see *Reza v. Leyasi*, 897 A.2d 679 (Conn. App. 2006).

The Model Code on Domestic and Family Violence (1994) provides that relocation because of an act of domestic violence will not be a factor that weighs against the parent in determining custody or visitation (§ 402(3)), and further creates a rebuttable presumption that "it is in the best interest of the child to reside with the parent who is not a perpetrator of domestic or family violence *in the location of that parent's choice, within or outside the state*" (emphasis supplied). Id. § 403. The adoption of the Model Code approach at the state level would do much to enable abused parents to relocate without fearing that they will lose custody of their children.

However, as Janet Bowermaster points out, even protective provisions like these will not prevent abusive parents from using "the right to contest proposed relocations as a tool for continued abuse." Janet Bowermaster, *Relocation Custody Disputes Involving Domestic Violence*, 46 U. KAN. L. REV.

433 (1998). Bowermaster advocates the adoption of state statutes creating a presumption in favor of allowing the custodial parent to relocate with the children. Minnesota has adopted such a presumption, *Silbaugh v. Silbaugh*, 543 N.W.2d 639 (Minn. 1996).

Leaving With the Children and Without the Court's Permission: Child Kidnapping

Removal of a child from a parent who has custodial or visitation rights can constitute the crimes of child kidnapping, child abduction, interference with custodial rights, or unlawful restraint. The conduct may be criminal even if the rights interfered with are limited in nature, and even if the "removal" is effected by someone, most commonly the other parent, who also has custodial rights to the child. These state statutes create real peril for the parent who flees abuse at the hands of a current or former partner and, by taking the children, prevents the abuser from exercising custodial or visitation rights. As state legislatures have become more responsive to domestic violence, many have enacted new statutes or new provisions focusing specifically on kidnapping within the familial setting and on the protection of adult and child victims. The Nevada statute below is an example.

NEVADA REVISED STATUTES SECTION 200.359 (2006)

1.   A person having a limited right of custody to a child by operation of law or pursuant to an order, judgment or decree of any court . . . or any parent having no right of custody to the child, who:

> (a) In violation of an order, judgment or decree of any court willfully detains, conceals or removes the child from a parent, guardian or other person having lawful custody or a right of visitation of the child; or

> (b) In the case of an order, judgment or decree of any court that does not specify when the right to physical custody or visitation is to be exercised, removes the child from the jurisdiction of the court without the consent of either the court or all persons who have the right to custody or visitation, is guilty of a category D felony. . . .

8.   This section does not apply to a person who detains, conceals, or removes a child to protect the child from the imminent danger of abuse or neglect or to protect himself from imminent physical harm, and reported the detention, concealment or removal to a law enforcement agency or an agency which provides child welfare services within 24 hours after detaining, concealing or removing the child, or as soon as the circumstances allowed.

NOTES AND QUESTIONS

1. **Traditional Defenses to Kidnapping Charges.** Older legislation often provided an affirmative defense either in situations in which the kidnapping parent was protecting the welfare of the child, or where the defendant acted with reasonable cause. In a significant number of jurisdic-

tions these are still the frameworks within which battered women must justify a "kidnapping" prompted by domestic violence. For an example of the "welfare of the child" framework see Colo. Rev. Stat. § 18–3–304(3) (2004). For an example of the "reasonable cause" framework see Mont. Code. § 45–5–633 (2005). Such defenses may be helpful to abused parents who flee with the children, so long as children's welfare is understood to include their emotional as well as physical well-being. Similarly, our growing knowledge about the impact on children of witnessing abuse, and about the ways in which abusive parents use children as pawns in their struggles to control their partners, supports the determination that "abductions" prompted by domestic violence are "reasonable cause" abductions. Unless the children have been the direct victims of abuse by their mother's abuser, proving these defenses could require the introduction of the effects of domestic violence on children.

The common law also permitted the defense of necessity to any criminal prosecution. A parent wanting to invoke this defense would need to show that there were no reasonable, legal alternatives to the illegal flight with the child. As Catherine Klein and her colleagues note,

> [I]t is conceivable that a battered woman, who flees the state with her children without having first attempted to contact the police or secure an order of protection, may find the defense of necessity unavailable. A survivor's genuine fear that involving law enforcement or seeking a protective order in the courts of the jurisdiction from which she fled may result in further retaliation by the batterer may thus go unrecognized by a court. Catherine F. Klein, Leslye E. Orloff and Hema Sarangapani, *Border Crossings: Understanding the Civil, Criminal and Immigration Implications for Battered Women Fleeing Across State Lines with Their Children*, 39 FAM. L. Q. 109 (2005).

2. **New Defenses to Kidnapping Charges.** As awareness of the connection between domestic violence and flight with a child has widened, some states have added new defenses to their kidnapping statutes. The Nevada statute excerpted above is indicative of these. First, § 4 provides that a court can only issue an arrest warrant for violation of the statute after determining that the rights of the parties could not be effectively enforced, and the best interests of the child could not be served, through a court order issued in a civil proceeding. Second, the crime can be prosecuted as a misdemeanor rather than a felony, if either: "[T]he defendant has no prior conviction for this offense and the child has suffered no substantial harm as a result . . . ," or "[T]he interests of justice require that the defendant be punished as for a misdemeanor." Finally, 200.359.8 provides a defense to a person who flees with a child in order to protect the child or him or herself from imminent physical abuse or, in the case of the child, neglect. Notice that the fleeing person must report within a very short period of time to law enforcement or protective services.

New Jersey law also provides an affirmative defense to a criminal prosecution if the custodial parent fleeing with the child "reasonably believed he was fleeing from imminent physical danger from the other parent, provided that the parent having custody, as soon as reasonably practicable . . . [g]ives notice of the child's location to the police department of the municipality where the child resided, the office of the county prosecutor in the county where the child resided, or the Division of Youth and Family Services in the Department of Human Services, or . . . [c]ommences an action affecting custody in an appropriate court." N.J.S.A. 2C:13–4 (2005). What do you see as the important differences between the Nevada and the New Jersey defenses? For another example of a statute that provides an affirmative defense for a fleeing custodial parent, see Cal. Penal Code § 278.7 (2006).

3.   **Problems With the New Defenses.** There are two primary difficulties with the approach taken by jurisdictions such as Nevada, New Jersey, and California. The first is that the victim of domestic violence who flees and is unaware of her obligation to file a report or commence a custody proceeding, or is too afraid to do so in the immediate aftermath of the violent incident that prompted her flight, will be deprived of a defense to the child kidnapping charge brought against her. In recognition of this problem, some states simply create an unconditional affirmative defense in situations where the "kidnapping" parent is fleeing domestic violence. Pennsylvania, for example, provides that:

> A person who removes a child from the child's known place of residence with the intent to conceal the child's whereabouts from the child's parent or guardian, unless concealment is authorized by court order or is a reasonable response to domestic violence or child abuse, commits a felony of the third degree. 18 PA.C.S.A.ST. § 2909 (2000)

This more generous approach strikes a different balance between the interests of victims of domestic violence, the interests of parents who have been denied both access to their children and an opportunity to protest that deprivation, and the courts whose authority has been sidestepped.

The second difficulty with the defenses provided by states like Nevada, New Jersey, and California is that states which require fleeing parents to initiate custody proceedings in a court of competent jurisdiction, or an "appropriate" court, are demanding either that the proceeding be initiated in the jurisdiction from which the parent is fleeing, which is difficult enough, or that the proceeding be initiated in the jurisdiction to which the parent flees, which will immediately alert her partner to her new whereabouts.

The Impact of the UCCJA, PKPA, and the UCCJEA

Criminal prosecution of child kidnappers is strictly a matter for the states, and the preceding section illustrates the significant variety of approaches states have taken in addressing the problem. However, to the extent that abductions have been prompted by the desire of parents to relitigate issues of custody and visitation in a new forum, it has long been recognized that coordination among the states to prevent such relitigation might in turn diminish the appeal of abduction, and that the federal government might also have a legitimate role to play in limiting relitigation by clarifying the application of full faith and credit principles in this arena.

In 1968, the National Conference of Commissioners of Uniform State Laws drafted and recommended the Uniform Child Custody Jurisdiction Act (UCCJA). The UCCJA was intended to be a model statute that the states could all adopt and that, once universally adopted, would provide a uniform way for states to handle the problem of parents who crossed state lines with their children in search of new custody rulings. The problem of domestic violence was not foremost in the Commissioners' minds when this was drafted.

The UCCJA provides that in order for a state to have jurisdiction to entertain a motion for custody, one of the following must be the case:

1.   The state is the home state of the child, with home state defined as the state in which the child had lived for the six months immediately preceding the filing of the petition;

2.   It is in the best interests of the child that the state assume jurisdiction and the child and one parent have a significant connection with the state and there is substantial evidence concerning the child in the state;

3.   The child is present in the state and the state must assume jurisdiction because of an emergency in which the child is threatened with abandonment, abuse or neglect.

4.   No other state has jurisdiction and it is in the child's best interests that the state assume jurisdiction. UCCJA § 3.

Unfortunately, since these were alternative bases for assuming jurisdiction, it remained possible that under the UCCJA more than one state would have jurisdiction over custody of the child. For example, one state might have home state jurisdiction, but another state in which the child had lived previously and in which one parent still lived might have significant connection jurisdiction. This meant that if a victim of violence fled with a child and managed to establish home state jurisdiction in the new state, the original state of residence might still have jurisdiction also. Furthermore, the narrow language of the emergency jurisdiction provision could be found not to cover domestic violence cases in which only the parent, not the child, had been threatened. *Hagedorn v. Hagedorn*, 584 So.2d 353 (La. App. 1991).

Although a significant majority of the states had adopted some version of the UCCJA by 1980, jurisdictional conflicts between the states on child custody matters remained. In 1980, Congress adopted the Parental Kidnapping Prevention Act (PKPA). The PKPA had two major provisions. First, it required that a state decree that met its requirements be given full faith and credit, and second, it gave priority to custody decrees based on home state jurisdiction. 28 U.S.C.A. § 1738A (2000). For more on the interplay between these two statutes, see Kate Lee Sullivan Feeney, *The Jurisdictional Juggle of Child Custody: An Analysis of the UCCJA, PKPA, UMEA, and Massachusetts Law*, 16 MASS. FAM. L.J. 35 (1998).

In 1997 the National Conference of Commissioners of Uniform State Laws recommended that states adopt its new proposed statute, the Uniform Child Custody and Jurisdiction Enforcement Act (UCCJEA). This act was intended to overcome the problems of conflicting jurisdiction created by the UCCJA and to bring state jurisdictional law on child custody into accord with the PKPA. Advocates for victims of domestic violence were active in lobbying the drafters of the UCCJEA to consider the victims' problems as they rewrote the statute. By 2006, forty states had adopted the Uniform Child Custody Jurisdiction and Enforcement Act. The following excerpt highlights the drafters' attention to issues of domestic violence.

Deborah M. Goelman
Shelter from the Storm: Using Jurisdictional Statutes to Protect Victims of Domestic Violence after the Violence Against Women Act of 2000

13 COLUM. J. GENDER & L. 101 (2004).

. . . The UCCJEA was promulgated by NCCUSL in 1997 to update the UCCJA. Unlike the UCCJA, the UCCJEA was drafted with domestic violence concerns in mind, in large part because domestic violence victim advocacy organizations participated in the drafting process. The UCCJEA reflects an understanding that when interstate custody disputes arise, domestic violence often is a causal factor. As a result, the UCCJEA contains explicit provisions that courts can utilize to protect victims of domestic violence and to prevent abusers from manipulating the courts in interstate custody cases. The UCCJEA also was designed to harmonize child custody jurisdiction law, given the changes that had been enacted by the PKPA, state domestic violence statutes, and the VAWA.

1.   Jurisdictional Bases

Like the UCCJA, the UCCJEA sets forth four potential bases of jurisdiction: home state, significant connection, last resort, and emergency jurisdiction. The UCCJEA, however, prioritizes home state jurisdiction over the other jurisdictional bases. . . .

When the UCCJEA was being drafted, victim advocacy organizations recommended that in cases in which victims fled across state lines, the refuge state should have preferred jurisdiction by attaching home state jurisdiction to the state to which the victim fled for safety reasons. The Drafting Committee ultimately rejected this proposal. The Committee was concerned about eroding the traditional concept of home state jurisdiction and hypothesized that the home state often would be the state with better access to evidence.

The UCCJEA elevates the home state. Besides having jurisdiction over initial custody determinations, the home state retains exclusive, continuing jurisdiction. This lasts until the home state determines that relevant persons do not have a significant connection with the state and that substantial evidence is no longer available in the state, or that relevant persons no longer reside in the home state. Similarly, the home state retains jurisdiction to modify custody determinations as long as it has exclusive, continuing jurisdiction. Centralizing power in the home state has particular implications for domestic violence victims who flee across state lines to refuge states in which they have greater support.

2.   Emergency Jurisdiction

One of the most prominent changes in the UCCJEA was the expansion of emergency jurisdiction to cases in which a sibling or parent of the child is subjected to or threatened with mistreatment or abuse. The provision was intended to codify common practice under the UCCJA and the PKPA. The comment to the UCCJEA acknowledges that protection order proceedings often are the procedural vehicles through which a court assumes emergency jurisdiction.

Courts may exercise emergency jurisdiction under the UCCJEA to protect victims who flee across state lines even when the children have not been abused. The UCCJEA simply institutionalized the growing trend in case law and state-adopted versions of the UCCJA. It permits courts to exercise emergency jurisdiction when an abused parent flees across state lines and seeks legal relief.

The UCCJEA limits the parameters of emergency jurisdiction by restricting it to temporary orders. The purpose of the temporary order is to protect the child until a state that has initial jurisdiction, exclusive, continuing jurisdiction, or jurisdiction to modify an existing custody order enters an order. This limitation poses a danger to victims who have fled from the home state because the home state retains jurisdiction over the long-term custody proceeding. . . .

3.   Inconvenient Forum

The limits on emergency jurisdiction pose a danger to victims. This danger is addressed in part through the UCCJEA's inconvenient forum provision, which allows a court in the state with preferred jurisdiction to decline to exercise jurisdiction if it determines that it is an inconvenient forum and that there is another more appropriate forum. The UCCJEA mandates that the court consider all relevant factors, including "whether domestic violence has occurred and is likely to continue in the future and which State could best protect the parties and the child."

This mandate to consider domestic violence as a factor in inconvenient forum decisions is a new jurisdictional tool for courts. The UCCJEA instructs a court to determine whether the parties are located in different states because one party is a victim of domestic violence or child abuse. It also requires the court to consider which state can best protect the victim from further violence or abuse. . . .

The issue of inconvenient forum may be raised upon motion of a party, the court's own motion, or request of another court. This flexibility may be critical in domestic violence cases in which victims are unrepresented, as the refuge court could make a request of the home state court where necessary. Although underutilized by family law attorneys and judges, the UCCJEA's inconvenient forum provision was expanded specifically to cover domestic violence cases and could enhance victim safety if courts used this tool consistently.

4. Declining Jurisdiction by Reason of Conduct

The UCCJEA also requires a court to decline to exercise its jurisdiction when a person seeking to invoke its jurisdiction has engaged in unjustifiable conduct. The "clean hands doctrine" is designed to ensure that abducting parents will not benefit from their unjustifiable conduct. Unlike the drafters of the UCCJA, the drafters of the UCCJEA envisioned that the doctrine would restrict those domestic violence offenders seeking to manipulate the court system. For example, an abusive parent who seizes the child and flees to another state to establish jurisdiction has engaged in unjustifiable conduct and the new state must decline to exercise jurisdiction. Domestic violence perpetrators commonly abduct their children, and courts can discourage such behavior by declining jurisdiction based on the perpetrator's conduct.

In the past, domestic violence victims have been penalized for fleeing across state lines with children. The UCCJEA, however, exempts cases covered under the emergency jurisdiction provision of the Act from the "clean hands" provision. Thus, when a victim of domestic violence flees across state lines, as long as the standards for emergency jurisdiction have been satisfied, the refuge state court may not decline jurisdiction by reason of the victim's conduct. . . .

Thus, if a parent flees with a child to escape domestic violence and violates an existing custody decree in doing so, the case should not be dismissed automatically. . . . Rather, the court must determine whether the flight was justifiable under the circumstances of the case. Courts can use this new jurisdictional tool to provide relief to victims who are forced to flee across state lines with their children. . . .

NOTES AND QUESTIONS

1. **Additional Protective Measures in the UCCJEA.** Other respects in which the legislation responds to the needs of victims of domestic violence and their children include the following:

> a) The definition of a "child custody proceeding" (Section 102(4)), the initiation of which will preclude another state from making a custody determination, includes proceedings for "protection from domestic violence, in which the issue may appear."

> b) Section 209(a), which details information to be submitted to the court, makes the disclosure requirements "[s]ubject to local law providing for the confidentiality of procedures, addresses, and other identifying information." The comments make explicit that this provision was drafted to incorporate protections found in state domestic violence legislation, and designed to prevent abusers from tracking down their victims. Where no such protective legislation exists, Section 209(e) provides a different route for information to be sealed, on the basis of "an affidavit or a pleading under oath" alleging that disclosure would jeopardize the health, safety or liberty of a party or child. The information can then be disclosed only after a hearing in which the court

decides that disclosure is in the interest of justice, even after taking into consideration the concerns alleged.

2. **Programs to Maintain Address Confidentiality.** By 2006, at least nineteen states and the federal government had passed statutes authorizing address confidentiality programs for victims of abuse as well as for battered women's shelters. Washington was the first state to create a program in 1991. The programs are similar in most of the states. Some states run their address confidentiality programs through their Attorney General's office while others place it in the Secretary of State's office. Survivors of domestic violence or sexual assault apply for the program. The state entity running the program then assigns them a "dummy" address or an address at the state office. The entity then forwards mail to the program participant's actual physical address. Most states with address confidentiality programs have created procedures to address court summonses, service of process, and other official mail. They also have provisions for confidentiality of other personal information, including voter registration. In most states, program participants vote by absentee ballot and their addresses are exempt from publication with state voter registry records. Information on these programs can be found at the National Conference of State Legislators, http://www.ncsl.org/programs/cyf/dvsurvive.htm.

3. **Notice Requirements and Disclosure.** Unfortunately, securing the confidentiality of present and recent addresses goes only part of the way toward protecting the battered woman who has moved out of state, and is seeking to conceal her whereabouts, and the whereabouts of her children, from her abuser. The inevitable due process requirement, whether the governing legislation is the UCCJA, the PKPA, or the UCCJEA, that she provide notice of any proceedings she files in itself gives her abuser valuable information about her location. It immediately lets him know which state, and probably which county or district within the state, his partner has moved to, even if she is successful in keeping her actual address confidential. This may be an argument for her to litigate in the state from which she has fled, despite the obvious inconvenience and possible risks.

A different issue arises for the woman who is fleeing one state and who fears that her abuser may then initiate legal proceedings of which she will not receive notice, with the result that he obtains a default judgment. Section 5 of the UCCJA, like Section 108 of the UCCJEA, governs notice, and both recognize that publication, in lieu of actual notice, may be the only option when a party's whereabouts are concealed, even though there is no guarantee that publication will reach the intended recipient. If it does not, the result may be a default judgment against the fleeing mother. One remedy might be to develop a system that allowed the fleeing parent to provide confidential address information to the clerk of the court. This information could then be used to notify her of any filing by the abusive spouse. Safeguards would have to be instituted to ensure that the information was not carelessly, or deliberately disclosed, a problem that has plagued courts in those states which have instituted confidentiality mechanisms, only to have them undermined at the level of practice.

International Relocations: The Hague Convention on the Civil Aspects of International Child Abduction

The Hague Convention on the Civil Aspects of International Child Abduction (Hague Convention) is the primary legal mechanism for dealing with the abduction of a child from one country to another. As of 2005, at least 76 countries were either signatories or had ratified the Convention. In order for the procedures of the Convention to be meaningful, both the country from which the child has been taken and the country to which he or she is taken must be members. The vast majority of countries in North and South America and Europe are members; many countries in Africa, Southeast Asia, and the Middle East are not.

The Hague Convention was written on the premise that parents who absconded with children were looking for a more favorable custody determination than they would have received in their home country. This was a species of forum shopping and one of the main goals of the Convention was to prevent forum shopping. To do this, the Convention provides that a child who has been "wrongfully removed" from a country in which he or she "habitually" resides is to be returned "forthwith." Articles 4 & 12. The country to which the child is taken is not to make a substantive custody determination, but rather is to return the child to her or his home country where the custody determination can be made. The defenses available under the Convention to prevent the return of the child are very limited. One parent's violence against the other—violence that might have caused one parent to flee with the child—is not mentioned as a defense. The defense most relevant for our purposes is a defense that relieves the country to which the child was taken of the need to return the child if "there is a grave risk that his or her return would expose the child to physical or psychological harm or otherwise place the child in an intolerable situation." Article 13(b).

Although the Hague Convention was written on the assumption that most parents who fled with their children were doing so to obtain a substantive advantage in a custody dispute, it turns out that a very significant number of abductors are women, fleeing domestic violence with their children. One commentator found that "seven of the nine cases decided by the United States courts of appeal between July 2000 and January 2001 involved an abductor who alleged that she was a victim of domestic violence." Merle H. Weiner, *Navigating the Road Between Uniformity and Progress: The Need for Purposive Analysis of the Hague Convention on the Civil Aspects of International Child Abduction*, 33 COLUM. HUM. RTS. L. REV. 275 (2002). The fact that many fleeing parents are victims of domestic violence has caused some commentators to question the Convention's requirement that a child be returned to the country of his or her habitual residence "forthwith." Merle H. Weiner, *International Child Abduction and the Escape from Domestic Violence*, 69 FORDHAM L. REV. 593 (2000). For more on this subject, see Merle H. Weiner, *The Potential and Challenges of Transnational Litigation for Feminists Concerned about Domestic Violence Here and Abroad*, 11 AM. U. J. GENDER SOC. POL'Y & L. 749 (2003).

Olguín v. Santana

United States District Court, Eastern District of New York, 2005.
2005 WL 67094.

■ GLEESON, J.

Petitioner Noel Stalin Reyes Olguín petitions for the return of his children, Sergio ... and Raul ... pursuant to the Hague Convention on the Civil Aspects of International Child Abduction.... On August 5, 2004, I denied the motion by Respondent María del Carmen Cruz Santana to dismiss, finding that Olguín had proved by a preponderance of the evidence that the removal of Sergio and Raul was wrongful under the Convention. I also found, however, that Olguín had physically abused Santana throughout the course of their relationship, often beating her in front of the children. Because of this abuse, I scheduled a hearing to determine whether sending the children back to Mexico would subject them to a grave risk of physical or psychological harm within the meaning of Article 13(b) of the Convention, and if so, whether any ameliorative measures could be taken that would minimize such a risk....

BACKGROUND

... Olguín and Santana, who never married, began living together in December 1996, shortly after Sergio was born. They lived with Olguín's parents, in the rural town of Jilotepec, Mexico. From the outset, their relationship was rocky. Olguín abused alcohol, physically abused Santana, and spent most of the time when he was not working carousing with friends and girlfriends. Olguín frequently beat Santana, often in front of Sergio (and later in front of Raul), and once in front of his father, Sergio Raul Reyes Olvera ("Reyes"). When Santana became pregnant after Sergio was born [in 1996], Olguín forced her to have an abortion. When Santana again became pregnant (with Raul) [in 1998], Olguín again insisted that she have another abortion. This time Santana refused; Olguín then beat her in an attempt to cause an abortion, frequently kicking her in the stomach and pushing her down stairs. At one point, Olguín, indicating a gun that was kept in the house, threatened to kill Santana.

Olguín's parents did nothing to protect Santana or the boys from Olguín's abuse. Instead, they covered up for Olguín. Sergio stated, for example, that his grandparents would take the boys downstairs while Olguín beat his mother. On occasions when visitors saw Santana's bruises, her mother-in-law would say that Santana was "stupid and fell down."

Although Olguín's physical abuse was mostly directed at Santana, both boys stated in their interviews with Dr. Stephanie Brandt, a child psychiatrist, that Olguín would hit them as well....

The difficulties between Olguín and Santana reached a crescendo on July 19, 2001. On that date, in the presence of Raul, Olguín choked Santana and tried to throw her down the stairs in their home.... Santana reported the beating to Mexican police and went to live with her parents for the next two months. After that two-month period, Santana took the children to New York. After approximately eight months, Olguín ...

showed up at the home in the Bronx where Santana was living with Sergio and Raul [and] promised that everything would change if Santana returned to Mexico. . . .

Santana and the boys returned to Jilotepec in April, 2002. For the first couple of months, Olguín acted differently than he had before the July 2001 incident. He soon reverted, however, to his old habits of beating Santana, abusing alcohol, and carousing at night with other women. Fearful of additional physical abuse, Santana took the boys once again and left Olguín in May 2003, arriving in New York in early June of that year. In February 2004, Olguín filed his claim under the Hague Convention to have the boys returned to Mexico. . . .

A. Psychological Status

Dr. Brandt testified at the December 1, 2004 hearing about Sergio and Raul's emotional status, and the likely psychological impact of sending the boys back to Mexico. . . .

1. Sergio

Dr. Brandt found that Sergio suffers from post traumatic stress disorder ("PTSD") as a result of Olguín's abuse, and that if Sergio is returned to Mexico, he would be at risk of severe psychological damage. . . . [T]his outcome could not be mitigated by any measures that could be put into place to try to protect him.

Dr. Brandt found that Sergio and Raul had experienced many years of extremely severe domestic violence. Santana was repeatedly beaten by Olguín, often in front of the boys, in a house where Olguín's parents tolerated and covered up their son's abusive behavior. Though Olguín hit both Sergio and Raul, the brunt of his physical abuse was directed at their mother. Brandt explained, though, that watching their mother being abused was as traumatic as being abused themselves. . . .

Brandt testified that Sergio was seriously traumatized by Olguín's violent behavior, finding that he was highly defensive, with poor impulse control and near psychotic thinking, and he had a history of suicidal thought and highly aggressive fantasy. When Sergio first arrived in New York, he had recurring nightmares of his father coming after him. He also acted out in school, trying to beat up other children. . . .

Dr. Brandt testified, however, that in recent months Sergio's behavior has apparently improved, especially at school. . . .

When Brandt asked Sergio about returning to Mexico, Sergio stated that he would "kill himself." While such statements from children should not always be taken at face value, Brandt found that Sergio was at risk of committing suicide or some other act of violence. . . .

Dr. Brandt was unequivocal about the likely consequences of returning Sergio to Mexico: "I believe that [Sergio] would suffer a very significant exacerbation or relapse if returned to Mexico." Further, Dr. Brandt found that uprooting Sergio at all from his current, stable living situation would put him at great risk of psychological harm: "If [Sergio] were taken away from this basic security, especially if he feels that his relationship with his mother, or her safety, is jeopardized, it is my professional opinion that Sergio would likely destabilize dramatically."

Brandt stated that Sergio will need ongoing mental health treatment, and noted in her report that there are numerous clinics and social service organizations in New York City through which Sergio can get appropriate and affordable treatment.

2.   Raul

Dr. Brandt found that Raul would also be at risk of severe psychological damage if repatriated to Mexico.... Though Dr. Brandt found no evidence that Raul currently suffers from any psychological disturbance, she believes that Raul's sense of well-being is entirely dependent on his knowledge that his mother is safe. Further, Dr. Brandt stated that if Raul (or Sergio) were separated from Santana, it would be highly traumatic, causing extreme and irreversible psychological damage, "regardless of what environmental supports were put in place."

B.   Social Services Available in Jilotepec

1.   Ziaurriz's testimony

On behalf of Santana, Teresa Ulloa Ziaurriz [an expert in gender violence] submitted a report regarding the availability of social services for victims of domestic violence in rural towns such as Jilotepec.... Ziaurriz explained that in Jilotepec, a poor municipality in the State of Mexico, there are insufficient resources to support defense, shelter and counseling services for victims of domestic violence.... Ziaurriz explained that in addition to having insufficient social and medical resources, the rights of women and children in such municipalities are neglected; local courts are often reluctant to prosecute batterers, or even to issue restraining orders, in part because of culturally ingrained attitudes that favor men. Ziaurriz concluded that there is no doubt that if Santana and the boys were forced to return to Mexico, the boys would be in great danger of suffering mistreatment and "will not receive social services necessary to help victims of domestic abuse." ...

DISCUSSION

The purpose of the Hague Convention is to protect children internationally from the harmful effects of their wrongful removal or retention and to establish procedures to ensure their prompt return to the State of their habitual residence. The Convention is intended to address the situation where parents involved in custody disputes wrongfully take their children across international borders in search of a more sympathetic court....

Once a petitioner establishes that removal was wrongful, the child must be returned to the country of his habitual residence unless the respondent can establish one of the four "narrow" exceptions to repatriation.... Specifically, the question is whether returning the boys to Mexico will expose them to a grave risk of psychological harm within the meaning of Article 13(b) of the Convention.

A. Grave Risk of Harm

Under Article 13(b), "a court may decline to repatriate a child if the party opposing repatriation establishes by clear and convincing evidence that repatriation would create a grave risk of physical or psychological harm to the child." Before a court may decline repatriation, however, it must first determine whether there are any ameliorative measures that could be taken to mitigate this risk and enable a child to return safely to his home country. . . .

Here, there is uncontroverted expert testimony that the children are at great risk of severe psychological damage if they are returned to Mexico. . . . I give great weight to Dr. Brandt's findings, which are consistent with all of the evidence that has been presented in this case. . . .

Olguín, for his part, has not contested Dr. Brandt's diagnoses. . . . Although he does not dispute that Sergio suffers from Post Traumatic Stress Disorder, Olguín has suggested other possible sources of the disorder, such as the boys' separation from their father or grandparents, or their experiences while escaping to the United States. I reject these suggestions. Dr. Brandt ruled out any other source for the PTSD except for Olguín's violent behavior. . . . I credit her conclusion. . . .

As part of the grave-risk analysis under Article 13(b), courts may consider, as non-dispositive factors, whether the child is settled into his new environment, and what the child's own views on repatriation are, taking into account the child's age and degree of maturity. . . .

1. The degree to which the boys are well-settled

Courts have considered a variety of factors in determining how settled a child is in his new environment, including the child's age; the stability of the child's current residence; whether the child attends school or church regularly; the stability of the mother's employment; and whether the child has friends or relatives in the new area.

Sergio and Raul have lived with their mother in New York for more than eighteen months. As the GAL report makes clear, they are settling into a stable routine. . . .

The GAL concluded that "[a]ny disruption to Sergio's identification as an American would be an additional source of stress for Sergio and may impede his recovery from the psychological trauma caused by his exposure to domestic violence."

I find that Sergio and Raul have become well-settled in New York. This factor, while not dispositive, militates against repatriation. Wrenching the boys from their current stable environment, when they are only now beginning to recover from the trauma inflicted by Olguín in Mexico, could only increase the likelihood and severity of harm of their repatriation. . . .

2. The boys' views

After meeting several times with the boys, the GAL, in consultation with its psychiatric expert, concluded that Sergio appeared to be mature enough to have his views taken into account. . . .

Both Sergio and Raul told Dr. Brandt and the GAL that they wanted to remain in the United States, and both expressed fear of returning to Mexico. . . .

The GAL spent significant time with the boys, and I give great weight to the guardian's assessment of the boys' views and maturity level. I find that Sergio is mature enough that his opposition to returning to Mexico should be considered in the Article 13 calculus. . . .

In sum, I find by clear and convincing evidence that repatriation to Mexico would present a grave risk that Sergio and Raul would suffer severe, perhaps cataclysmic harm and would place them in an intolerable situation within the meaning of Article 13(b) of the Convention. While I would have reached this conclusion based solely on Dr. Brandt's testimony and report, my conclusion is buttressed by my finding that the boys, who have now lived in the United States for more than eighteen months, are well-settled in New York and that Sergio's desire to stay in the United States (and severe anxiety at the mere thought of returning to Mexico) deserve consideration.

B. Ameliorative Measures

Before a court may deny repatriation on the ground that a grave risk of harm exists under Article 13(b), it must examine whether any ameliorative measures might mitigate the risk of harm to the child and allow him to return safely pending a final adjudication of custody. This inquiry is necessary because a court must make every effort to simultaneously honor two core mandates of the Convention: (1) to return wrongfully abducted children to their home countries for custody adjudication; while (2) safeguarding those children from grave risk of harm. A court may decline to repatriate a child, however, where it finds that there are no ameliorative measures that could be put in place that would significantly mitigate the grave risk to the child. . . .

Thus, the preliminary question here is whether there are any ameliorative measures that exist that would mitigate the grave risk of harm to Sergio and Raul if repatriated. I find that no such measures present themselves here.

Dr. Brandt testified that, regardless of what arrangements might be made to safeguard Sergio, he would be exposed to severe psychological harm if returned to Mexico because the repatriation in and of itself would trigger a relapse or exacerbation of the PTSD. Dr. Brandt found that Sergio's psychological state is so tenuous that uprooting him in any fashion from his current, stable lifestyle would be traumatic. . . .

I find therefore that there are no ameliorative measures that could diminish the risk to the point where Sergio would no longer be exposed to a grave risk of psychological harm. As discussed above, separating Sergio and

Raul, which no party has proposed, would in itself expose both children to harm. Accordingly, I would deny repatriation on this basis alone.

Even if there were some protective measures that in the abstract could mitigate the risk of harm to the children, no evidence has been presented that such measures would be available in this case. . . .

[A]lthough Olguín testified that he contacted several private doctors, it is not clear that any of them are trained to work with victims of domestic violence; certainly there was no testimony that these doctors had any experience treating PTSD. Instead, it appears that these doctors provide family counseling to prisoners. . . .

Further . . . Olguín has not offered to take any action that might help reduce the risks of repatriation. Here, Olguín, who has not disputed the psychological diagnoses of his children, only their bases, has made no representations regarding any actions that he could take to mitigate the risk to the children.

Finally, I note that Olguín has provided no evidence that he has taken steps to address his own abusive behavior. After Santana first came to New York with the boys, Olguín . . . convinced Santana to return, promising the boys new toys and bicycles. Within months, though, Olguín had reverted to his earlier habits of abusing alcohol and beating Santana. There is no reason to think that if the children were repatriated this time, Olguín would not resume his abusive behavior towards Santana and the boys. Accordingly, I find that there are no significant ameliorative measures available under the circumstances of this case that would mitigate the grave risk that the children would be exposed to psychological harm if repatriated. . . .

In order to protect these children, which is the ultimate aim of the Convention, I will not force them to return to a country under circumstances where they will be exposed to severe psychological harm.

In sum, I find by clear and convincing evidence that (1) there is a grave risk that returning Sergio and Raul to Mexico will expose them to psychological harm or otherwise place them in an intolerable situation; (2) this grave risk will be present regardless of any ameliorative measures that might be put into place; and (3) even if, in the abstract, arrangements existed for children such as Sergio and Raul that could mitigate the risk of repatriation, no such measures will be available in the place which petitioner seeks their return. Accordingly, I find that Santana has established, by clear and convincing evidence, the exception under Article 13(b) to the general rule that children who are wrongfully removed must be repatriated under the Hague Convention, and thus I decline to order the return of Sergio and Raul to Mexico. . . .

NOTES AND QUESTIONS

1. **What Constitutes a "Grave Risk?"** Until relatively recently, courts did not recognize domestic violence directed at the child's mother as constituting a grave risk of harm to the child. To be successful in invoking

Article 13(b) in a case involving abuse, courts required that the physical or sexual abuse be targeted at the child. The courts saw this as consistent with the narrow interpretation of the 13(b) defense required by The Hague Convention's emphasis on having the actual custody decision made by the country of habitual residence. *Friedrich v. Friedrich*, 78 F.3d 1060 (6th Cir. 1996). For example, in *Whallon v. Lynn*, 230 F.3d 450 (1st Cir. 2000), the mother had fled with the child from Mexico to the U.S., claiming domestic violence. The Court found that the 13(b) defense did not bar return of the child to Mexico. The Court specifically noted that the mother had only claimed domestic violence against herself and "had never alleged that [the father] abused [the child], either physically or psychologically." For similar cases, see *Aldinger v. Segler*, 263 F.Supp.2d 284 (D. P.R. 2003), *Belay v. Getachew*, 272 F.Supp.2d 553 (D. Md. 2003) and *Nunez–Escudero v. Tice–Menley*, 58 F.3d 374 (8th Cir. 1995).

Of course, in many cases in which there is domestic violence, there has also been some abuse of the child. More recently, a few courts, like *Reyes Olguín*, have recognized that serious domestic violence directed at the child's mother is also injurious to the child. The U.S. Courts of Appeals for the First and Second Circuits have both upheld the use of 13(b) defenses in this context. *Blondin v. Dubois*, 238 F.3d 153 (2d Cir. 2001); *Walsh v. Walsh*, 221 F.3d 204 (1st Cir. 2000).

Does recognition of the damaging effects that one parent's violence toward the other can have on the children undermine the Hague Convention's focus on having custody determined by the country of habitual residence? Linda Silberman argues that cases like *Reyes Olguín* are troubling because familial domestic violence and corporal punishment of children are so common. As a result they can be asserted in many Hague Convention cases—so many that she worries "the exception will begin to swallow the rule." Linda Silberman, *The Hague Child Abduction Convention Turns Twenty*, 33 N.Y. U. J. INT'L L. & POL'Y 221, 241 (2000), quoting *Matter of LL. Children*, N.Y.L.J., May 22, 2000. Silberman is also concerned that the use of post traumatic stress disorder expert testimony will transform a Hague Convention hearing from a jurisdictional hearing into something similar to a full-blown custody proceeding. Linda Silberman, *Patching Up the Abduction Convention*, 38 TEX. INT'L L.J. 41 (2003). Do you agree with either of these concerns?

2. **Ameliorative Conditions and Undertakings.** Since the objective of the Hague Convention is to ensure that custody is determined by the country of habitual residence, which should have the most information about the child and the family, courts sometimes try to impose conditions on the child's return to make what would otherwise be a risky return safer. These conditions can be private undertakings on the part of the petitioner or they can be actions or agreements made by public agencies or courts in the petitioner's home country. For example, in the much litigated *Blondin* case, the petitioner agreed to pay not only for the children's return airfare, but also for his ex-wife to accompany them back to France. He also agreed to pay for her and the children to stay in a "one-star hotel," while applying for government assistance. In addition, Blondin said that he would not

enforce an existing custody order that would have returned the children to his care until a French judge had an opportunity to rule on a modification petition. Beyond that, the French Ministry of Justice arranged for free legal assistance for Dubois, the mother who had fled with the children claiming domestic violence. Finally, the Office of the Public Prosecutor in France had stated that, if Dubois were to return with the children, it would not prosecute her for having abducted the children or for having forged Blondin's name on the children's passport applications. *Blondin v. Dubois*, 78 F.Supp.2d 283, 289 (S.D.N.Y. 2000). For another example of a case in which the appellate court required the trial court to consider ameliorative measures after finding that return posed a grave risk of harm to the child, see *Turner v. Frowein*, 752 A.2d 955 (Conn. 2000). Notice that state courts also have jurisdiction over Hague petition cases.

To what extent can protective orders issued in the U.S. be helpful in protecting a child who is to be returned to the country of his or her habitual residence? What should a court make of a petitioner's undertaking to comply with a U.S. protective order? Should it matter if the petitioner has previously violated protective orders issued in his home country? How willing should a U.S. court be to rely on "mirror" orders issued by the country of habitual residence and duplicating protective orders issued in the U.S.? Roxanne Hoegger, *What If She Leaves? Domestic Violence Cases under The Hague Convention and the Insufficiency of the Undertakings Remedy,* 18 Berkeley Women's L.J. 181 (2003).

3. **International Kidnapping.** Many countries are not signatories of the Hague Convention and thus are not bound by its procedures. In that case, a parent whose children are removed from their home and taken to a foreign country by the other parent may fall back on domestic criminal law for a remedy. In the U.S., one relevant statute is the International Parental Kidnapping Crime Act (IPKCA), 18 U.S.C. §§ 1204 and 2511(1)(a). The statute makes it a felony to remove a child from the U.S. with the intent to obstruct the "lawful exercise of parental rights." It does not require that there be a pre-existing custody order nor does it require that the conduct be criminal under state law. *U.S. v. Fazal–Ur–Raheman–Fazal*, 355 F.3d 40 (1st Cir. 2004). What difficulties do you foresee for a left-behind parent whose prime recourse is through the IPKCA and not the Hague Convention?

CHAPTER ELEVEN

Processing Domestic Violence Cases in Family Courts

Introduction

Judges in family law cases often rely heavily on experts from other, non-legal disciplines. There are two reasons for this reliance. First, family law reformers have long felt that family courts would be more efficient and effective if they could provide more information to judges about the emotional and relational aspects of the cases. Similarly, the courts' efficiency and effectiveness will be enhanced, reformers argue, if they are in a position to provide additional services to clients. Today, most courts handling family law cases rely on mediators, psychologists, psychiatrists, social workers, and experts in child development to help them make their decisions and to move the processing of the case forward. In addition, judges often turn to guardians ad litem for recommendations as to how a case involving the placement of children should be decided. Modern family courts also often offer or mandate participation in non-adjudicatory services such as mediation and parent education programs.

This chapter will focus on the interplay between these non-legal services and experts and the legal process. We will discuss first the role of "experts" who have two different, but often closely related, functions in the court: the guardian ad litem and the expert witness. Then we will turn to two programs intended to provide additional services to clients and also, simultaneously, to make the process more efficient. These are mediation (often mandatory) and parent education. These non-legal experts, as expected, tend to focus on the family as a unit and the ways the members relate to one another. They are less concerned with—and sometimes not trained to recognize—the family members' individual rights. As you read through the materials, think about whether the focus on families as a unit, instead of on individuals, is desirable. Consider also the advantages and disadvantages of courts' reliance on various experts. Finally, you should be asking yourself whether non-adversary procedures, such as mediation, are better for meeting the needs of victims of family violence than the adversary system.

A. The Role of the Guardian Ad Litem in Cases Involving Domestic Violence

We have already talked about the part played by judges and lawyers in the disposition of custody and visitation cases where partner abuse is at issue. There is, however, another significant player in many of these cases;

the guardian ad litem (GAL) appointed as an officer of the court to assist in the case. The GAL will deliver a report, with or without explicit recommendations as to outcome, to guide the judge's decision. In some states guardians ad litem function more like lawyers for the child; in others their job is to determine what is in the child's best interests, regardless of whether of not the child agrees. In fulfilling his or her role, the guardian ad litem must establish procedures which will protect the confidentiality and the safety of those she or he interviews; sort out truth from fiction, particularly in the stories told by the two parents; listen attentively to what is said by children, while being sensitive to the dynamics which may inhibit their truth-telling; and decide how reliably to supplement the information supplied by the key players.

The GAL is a particularly important player in custody and other proceedings involving children. One study found that judges accept the GAL's recommendation in custody cases approximately 80% of the time, often with very little or no additional investigation. Mary Grams, *Guardians ad Litem and the Cycle of Domestic* Violence, 22 Law & Ineq. 105 (2004). Thus, the GAL's sensitivity to and understanding of the dynamics and risks of violent relationships is particularly important. The GAL's capacity to negotiate this difficult terrain will lay the basis for either a sound or an unsound decision and for safety or danger for children and their victimized parents. Frequently GALs are discouragingly uninformed about the dynamics and effects of domestic violence. The following excerpt describes the unfortunate results in such a case:

> Lorie suffered years of severe violence at the hands of her husband, Noah. He pulled out her hair, slapped her, tore her clothing, and threatened her life. He hit her in the face with his head so hard that he broke her tooth. Lorie and Noah's children lived with the ongoing abuse and often witnessed the violence. During one incident, Lorie was holding their baby in her arms when Noah picked up a butcher knife. "Put the kid down," he said, "I'm going to kill you now."
>
> When litigation began over custody of their children, Lorie was prepared with evidence of the abuse, including dental records documenting her broken tooth and written statements of observers who witnessed the abuse and her injuries. The guardian ad litem appointed to her case, however, refused to look at any of the documentation she offered. Furthermore, during the investigation he said to Lorie, "I know you lied to me [about the abuse]. You better tell the truth now, because I'm getting phone calls from people and they can tell me the truth."
>
> Ignoring the trauma of the abuse Lorie suffered, the guardian ad litem's report to the judge described Lorie as "irrationally angry" and "overly emotional," citing her tendency to burst into tears. The guardian ad litem also discredited Lorie's reports of domestic violence to the court, despite his own acknowledgement that he found Noah to be controlling, domineering, and dishonest. The court ultimately granted Noah full custody of the children. The judge never saw Lorie's extensive documentation, and thus could not consider the impact of

Noah's abusive behavior on the children. Cynthia Grover Hastings, *Letting Down Their Guard*, 24 B.C. Third World L.J. 283 (2004).

Guardians ad litem are frequently appointed in cases in which the future placement of a child is at issue. These include paternity, termination of parental rights, adoption, abuse and neglect, and custody cases. These materials will focus on GALs in the context of contested custody cases. Commentators have noted that GALs are particularly important in contested custody cases because the parents and their lawyers are necessarily focused on the parents' desires. Since the child is not the client of either lawyer, the child's interests may not be highlighted for the court. See Linda D. Elrod, *Reforming the System to Protect Children in High Conflict Custody Cases*, 28 Wm. Mitchell L. Rev. 495 (2001).

As of 2004, judges in every state and the District of Columbia had the power to appoint a guardian ad litem or attorney for the child in a custody case if the judge thought it was necessary. A.B.A. Child Custody and Adoption Pro Bono Project, Chart on Appointment Laws in Divorce Cases, Aug. 12, 2004, available at www.abanet.org/legalservices/probono/divorce chart with role.pdf. Only Wisconsin mandates the appointment of a GAL in contested custody cases. Wisc. Stat. § 767.045 (2001). A half dozen states require the appointment of a GAL or similar official if there are allegations of child abuse or neglect. In contrast, at least one court has intimated that the appointment of a GAL is not necessary in a contested custody case because "in custody cases involving natural parents, despite the bitterness of each party towards each other, both parties are focused on the best interests of the child. Moreover, in a custody case, the trial court is obliged to ascertain the child's best interest. Since both parties and the trial court are focused on the child's best interests, it appears that the appointment of a guardian ad litem would not be proper. . . ." *C.W. v. K.A.W.*, 774 A.2d 745 (Pa. Super. 2001).

As the excerpt above describing Laurie and Noah's custody case indicates, GAL reports are not always complete. However, in the best of all possible worlds, the GAL would impartially investigate the case in a way that ensures the safety of the parties, children, witnesses, and others involved; obtain information directly from the parties, the children, the children's teachers, therapists, and other third parties; conduct home visits when appropriate; and review documentary sources of information including previous court and criminal records. The report should be written in such a way as to be useful to the court given the legal issues involved, but clearly separating facts from any conclusions or recommendations. Probate and Family Court Dept., Massachusetts, Standards for Category F Guardian Ad Litem Investigators, 1/24/2005.

NOTES AND QUESTIONS

1. **When Should a GAL Be Appointed?** Do you agree with the dicta in *C.W. v. K.A.W.* that it is not necessary to appoint a GAL in a contested custody case since both the court and the parties will be looking out for the child's best interests?

In *Mills v. Mills*, 939 S.W.2d 72 (Mo. App. 1997), the Court of Appeals upheld the trial court's decision not to appoint a GAL in a contested custody case in which the mother claimed that she had been beaten up and abused by the husband's family just a few days prior to the trial at which she appeared *pro se*. Missouri law requires the appointment of a GAL if child abuse or neglect is alleged, but merely permits the court to appoint a GAL if custody is contested. Do you think the trial court made the correct decision in not appointing a GAL? What facts aside from the contested nature of the case would you have stressed if you had been the attorney for the wife? Do you think that statutes around the country should be amended to require the appointment of GALs in all contested custody cases involving partner abuse?

2. **Content of the GAL Report.** In the vast majority of states, domestic violence is a factor that the courts must consider in determining custody. Should a GAL report be required to investigate and comment on the presence or absence of domestic violence? Remember that a very large percentage of contested custody cases involve domestic violence. Do you think that a report that fails to discuss whether there has been domestic violence undercuts the requirement that domestic violence be considered as a factor? Would the failure to discuss domestic violence in the report be even more serious if the state has a presumption against awarding custody to an abuser? Cynthia Grover Hastings, *Letting Down their Guard*, 24 B.C. THIRD WORLD L.J. 283 (2004).

The Role of a GAL

GALs can be appointed to serve a variety of different functions. In most states, they serve the investigative role described above. An investigative GAL's job is generally to recommend to the court which solution would be in the child's best interests. In contrast, approximately half of the states allow the appointment of an attorney for the child, either in addition to or in place of the investigative GAL. Theoretically, an attorney for a child, like any other attorney, should advocate for the client's objectives even if the attorney thinks they are wrong-headed or not conducive to the child's best interests. Some states allow for the appointment of a GAL whose role is a mixture of these two.

Clark v. Alexander

Supreme Court of Wyoming, 1998.
953 P.2d 145.

■ TAYLOR, CHIEF JUSTICE.

.... Appellant, K.C. Clark (Mother), and appellee, Clifford Graham Alexander (Father), married in 1981 and had three children. On February 2, 1993, the district court granted a divorce ... with Father having residential custody....

On October 11, 1994, Mother filed a "Verified Petition for Modification of Child Custody," alleging a change of circumstances engendered by Father's relocation with the two younger children to a trailer home and the oldest child residing with "grandfather" in a house on the same property. Mother's petition was accompanied by a request for the appointment of a guardian ad litem.

An order appointing the guardian ad litem was entered January 8, 1996.... The guardian ad litem visited the children in person and by telephone, conducted in-home visits and interviews with both parents, stepfather, and grandfather, and interviewed other family members, teachers, neighbors, and clergy.

... Father's attorney telephoned the guardian ad litem and stated Father had inadvertently taped a conversation between Mother and the two younger children on September 23, 1995. On the tape recording ... the child was urged to telephone the guardian ad litem to report that Father often left the children unsupervised, that the delay was upsetting, and to convey her preference for residing with her mother.

Shortly after listening to the tape recording, the guardian ad litem told Mother's attorney of the tape recording's existence and recommended Mother refrain from involving the children in the custody dispute. The guardian ad litem also consented, without informing Mother, to the continued taping of Mother's conversations due to concerns that Mother would further involve the children during telephone visits. Father proceeded to record Mother's telephone conversations with the children, but only two subsequent conversations, one on October 8, 1995 and one on October 28, 1995, were submitted to the guardian ad litem....

At the modification hearing, Father called the guardian ad litem as his first witness. Through her testimony, the tapes recorded September 23, 1995 and October 8, 1995 were received into evidence, as well as ... the guardian ad litem reports....

At the close of the proceeding, the district judge ... granted Father continued sole custody.... The district court further ordered that the parties not disclose to the children the testimony at trial nor the fact that their conversations with Mother had been taped, and would continue to be taped for six months.... This timely appeal followed....

ROLE OF GUARDIAN AD LITEM

The role of the attorney/guardian ad litem during the proceedings is central to the disposition of this case. Mother claims that because the guardian ad litem actively participated as the children's attorney, it was improper to allow her to testify at the modification hearing....

"[T]he definition of the precise roles of the attorney and the guardian ad litem for children is still evolving and not without difficulty."[2] In Wyoming, the role of an attorney or guardian ad litem in custody cases is not addressed by statute, and like many jurisdictions, case law has failed to clearly delineate the parameters of the duties incumbent upon appoint-

---

2. Our decision here does not address many areas of chronic confusion in the appointment of a guardian ad litem, e.g., when an appointment is necessary, the necessary qualifications to serve as guardian ad litem, and the timeliness of the court's communication of the specific duties expected by the court....

ment. Moreover, the juxtaposition of the separate roles of attorney and guardian ad litem into one "attorney/guardian ad litem," appears especially problematic. Given the lack of clear direction provided to those who must fulfill this role in Wyoming, and our certainty that the issues in this case will reappear in the future, we speak to those issues here. In providing guidance to the role of an attorney appointed to represent a child while at the same time acting as guardian ad litem, we do not intend to usurp the role of the district court in appointing individuals to act solely as an attorney or as guardian ad litem. It is imperative, however, that the appointee request clarification from the appointing court if questions regarding the duties arise.

The guardian ad litem's role has been characterized as investigator, monitor, and champion for the child. The traditional role of a guardian ad litem in custody proceedings has been described as follows:

> [I]n custody matters, the guardian ad litem has traditionally been viewed as functioning as an agent or arm of the court, to which it owes its principal duty of allegiance, and not strictly as legal counsel to a child client.... In essence, the guardian ad litem role fills a void inherent in the procedures required for the adjudication of custody disputes. Absent the assistance of a guardian ad litem, the trial court, charged with rendering a decision in the "best interests of the child," has no practical or effective means to assure itself that all of the requisite information bearing on the question will be brought before it untainted by the parochial interests of the parents. Unhampered by the ex parte and other restrictions that prevent the court from conducting its own investigation of the facts, the guardian ad litem essentially functions as the court's investigative agent, charged with the same ultimate standard that must ultimately govern the court's decision—i.e., the "best interests of the child." Although the child's preferences may, and often should, be considered by the guardian ad litem in performing this traditional role, such preferences are but one fact to be investigated and are not considered binding on the guardian.... Thus, the obligations of a guardian ad litem necessarily impose a higher degree of objectivity on a guardian ad litem than is imposed on an attorney for an adult....

In contrast, the traditional role of an attorney is that of advisor, advocate, negotiator and intermediary. Counsel appointed to represent a child must, as far as reasonably possible, maintain a normal client-lawyer relationship with the child and "abide by a client's decisions concerning the objectives of representation...." Thus, counsel for a child is not free to independently determine and advocate the child's "best interests" if contrary to the preferences of the child.

Wyo. Stat. § 14–3–211 (1997), addressing the appointment of counsel to represent children in abuse and neglect proceedings, distinguishes the role of guardian ad litem from the role of "counsel for the child," but combines the two if no guardian ad litem is appointed. Although the statute does not address custody proceedings, we [previously] applied the statutory language regarding "representation" of the child to custody cases, and held that an attorney appointed as guardian ad litem may not engage in ex parte communications with the trial court. We stated that the attorney/guardian ad litem acts as an advocate for the child and "has the same ethical responsibilities in the proceeding as any other attorney."

Our [previous] decision ..., however, did not address other situations where the attorney's ethical duties under the Rules of Professional Conduct may not coincide with the duties expected of the guardian ad litem. The circumstances of this case clearly illustrate several examples of the problems which may arise. Here, the attorney/guardian ad litem represented three siblings, two of whom expressed conflicting preferences regarding custody. A guardian ad litem, not bound by the expressed preferences of the child, has no conflict in this situation. On the other hand, the Rules of Professional Conduct require the attorney to zealously represent the client's interests. Therefore, the attorney must discontinue representation when two clients' interests, and thereby the attorney's duty, diverge. Similarly, a conflict is present when the attorney/guardian ad litem does not believe the child's expressed interest is in the child's best interest.

The guardian ad litem is also required to inform the court of all relevant information. This expectation may often collide with [the Wyoming Rules of Professional Conduct], which require the attorney to maintain confidentiality unless the client consents to disclosure. In this case, Father's recording of the children's conversations with Mother also included a recording of one child's telephone call to the guardian ad litem. The attorney/guardian ad litem allowed this conversation to be admitted into evidence without objection and without the consent of the child.

Finally, the attorney/guardian ad litem is expected to actively participate as legal counsel for the children, i.e., presenting opening and closing statements and examining witnesses. In contrast, [the Wyoming Rules of Professional Conduct] prohibit an attorney from participating as an advocate in a case where it is likely that he or she will be called to testify to a matter of import at the proceeding. In this case, the attorney/guardian ad litem not only testified regarding the ultimate issue in the case, but was the vehicle through which the taped conversations were admitted.

In those cases where the facts relevant to the children's best interests may not be otherwise presented to the court, the traditional role of guardian ad litem is essential. It is equally apparent that the skills of a legal advocate are invaluable to the child caught within a contentious custody dispute. With counsel, the child has an unbiased adult who can explain the process, inform the court of the child's viewpoint, and ensure an expeditious resolution.

While some jurisdictions have required the separation of these roles, a number of courts have declared the role a "hybrid," which necessarily excuses strict adherence to some rules of professional conduct. We believe that the costs attending the appointment of both an attorney and a guardian ad litem would often be prohibitive and would in every case conscript family resources better directed to the children's needs outside the litigation process. Thus, we too acknowledge the "hybrid" nature of the role of attorney/guardian ad litem which necessitates a modified application of the Rules of Professional Conduct.

Contrary to the ethical rules, the attorney/guardian ad litem is not bound by the client's expressed preferences, but by the client's best interests. If the attorney/guardian ad litem determines that the child's expressed preference is not in the best interests of the child, both the child's wishes and the basis for the attorney/guardian ad litem's disagreement must be presented to the court.

In the same light, the confidentiality normally required in the attorney-client relationship must be modified to the extent that relevant information provided by the child may be brought to the district court's attention. While it is always best to seek consent prior to divulging otherwise confidential information, an attorney/guardian ad litem is not prohibited from disclosure of client communications absent the child's consent. As legal counsel to the child, the attorney/guardian ad litem is obligated to explain to the child, if possible, that the attorney/guardian ad litem is charged with protecting the child's best interest and that information may be provided to the court which would otherwise be protected by the attorney-client relationship.

We recognize that in some instances a child may be too young to understand the purpose of the proceedings or the role of the attorney/guardian ad litem. However, in most cases, the information may be conveyed in an age-appropriate manner.

Although the above rules require compromise in order to effect the dual roles of attorney and guardian ad litem, we do not find the same need applies to [all aspects of the Rules of Professional Conduct.] Our [previous] holding ... clearly mandates that the attorney/guardian ad litem is to be an advocate for the best interests of the child and actively participate at the proceedings. As counsel, the attorney/guardian ad litem has the opportunity and the obligation to conduct all necessary pretrial preparation and present all relevant information through the evidence offered at trial. Recommendations can be made to the court through closing argument based on the evidence received. It is, therefore, unnecessary to allow the attorney/guardian ad litem to place his or her own credibility at issue. Consequently, we join those jurisdictions which hold that an attorney/guardian ad litem may not be a fact witness at a custody hearing.

This is not to say that the attorney/guardian ad litem may not submit a written report to the parties. A detailed report which timely informs the parties of the relevant facts and the basis of the guardian ad litem's recommendation may facilitate agreement prior to trial. If the parties so stipulate, the report may be presented to the court. However, the report should not be filed with the court or received into evidence without the express agreement of the parties. To the extent that prior Wyoming cases may conflict with this holding, they are here overruled.

We find that the district court erred in admitting the testimony of the attorney/guardian ad litem. In turn, all evidence presented through this witness was also erroneously before the district court....

CONCLUSION

The district court erred in admitting the testimony of the attorney/guardian ad litem. The error, however, does not warrant reversal of the district court's determination that Mother failed to show a change in circumstances which justified modification of custody. . . .

NOTES AND QUESTIONS

1. **Possible GAL Roles.** As *Clark v. Alexander* makes clear, a GAL can be appointed to investigate facts relating to what is in the child's best interests. The GAL's report to the court may or may not include recommendations. A GAL might also act as an attorney for the child, advocating for whatever the child determines. Hybrid versions are also possible. It is also possible to see the GAL as an agent of the court, and, in some courts a GAL might be expected to evaluate the children's psychiatric condition. As indicated in *Clark*, some actions are appropriate to one role and some to another. For example, the Court noted that if the GAL was serving as an attorney, he or she would not normally be allowed to represent two children with conflicting desires for custody. On the other hand, a "best interests" GAL might investigate the best interests of more than one child without any ethical problems. Is the court in *Clark* clear about what the role of the GAL is in Wyoming?

2. **Investigative GAL v. Attorney for the Child.** In contrast to an investigative GAL, a court could appoint an attorney for the child. An attorney would be expected to advocate zealously for the client-child's wishes, regardless of whether the attorney agreed that the child's position was in the child's best interests. There are innumerable stories of children who feel that they knew even at very young ages what was in their best interests and that the court ignored their wishes. One 16–year old wrote about her experience:

> My parents separated when I was 5 years old, sparking a custody battle that lasted nine years. I never doubted that I wanted to be with my mother. My father . . . is an abuser, and living with him was a mental and physical hell and definitely not in my best interests. Yet, in . . . Family Court, that seemed to be irrelevant. My family court experience consisted of lawyers, judges, evaluators and social workers who turned their backs on their consciences and their professional oaths. They worked contrary to not only my best interests, but to my health and safety. Alanna Krause, *Letting Children Speak for Themselves*, SAN FRANCISCO DAILY JOURNAL FORUM (July 17, 2000).

One advantage of appointing an attorney instead of a best interests GAL for a child—even a small child—is that the child may benefit from feeling that he or she has a voice in the eventual custody decision, even if it is not what the child would have wanted. Another advantage is that an attorney may be able to force the disputing parents and the court to take the child's needs seriously. A court can, of course, appoint both an attorney and a GAL for a child, although this would be costly. Barbara Ann Atwood,

Representing Children: The Ongoing Search for Clear and Workable Standards, 19 J. AM. ACAD. MATRIM. L. 183 (2005).

New York uses law guardians in custody disputes. Their role is more like that of an attorney for the child than a guardian ad litem. Law guardians, unlike investigative GALs, are generally not supposed to submit reports to the court. Instead, like other attorneys, they make arguments based on the evidence. This makes the role of a law guardian for a very young child difficult. Nancy S. Erickson, *The Role of the Law Guardian in a Custody Case involving Domestic Violence*, 27 FORDHAM URB. L.J. 817 (2000).

3.   **The Uniform Marriage and Divorce Act and GAL Roles.** It is not always easy to discern from a statute which role the GAL should play. For example, the Uniform Marriage and Divorce Act provides that the court "may appoint an attorney to represent the interests of a minor...." UMDA § 310. The official comment says "The attorney is not a guardian ad litem for the child, but an advocate whose role is to represent the child's interests." On first reading, this appears to indicate that the role is one of an attorney whose job is to advocate for the child's goals. However, as Barbara Ann Atwood indicates, it is not so simple:

> The drafters of the UMDA knew to use "child's wishes" when that was their intent. Moreover, by stating that the attorney is not a guardian ad litem, the drafters could have been clarifying that the representative was supposed to function as a lawyer rather than as a witness. Thus, appointments that simply incorporate the language of the UMDA could certainly give rise to confusion. *Representing Children: The Ongoing Search for Clear and Workable Standards*, 19 J. AM. ACAD. MATRIM. LAW 183 (2005).

If you were an attorney appointed to represent a child in a state like Washington that has adopted this provision of the UMDA, what would you do if the child wanted a custody arrangement that you thought was not in his or her best interests?

4.   **GAL as Witness.** *Clark* held that the GAL should not have been allowed to serve as a witness and give testimony at trial. This is at least in part because of the hybrid nature of the attorney/GAL role in that case. The court suggested that instead of testifying as a witness, the attorney/GAL could make recommendations to the court in his or her closing argument. Wyoming is by no means alone in giving the GAL a special status different from a witness. Michigan law permits the GAL to file a written report and recommendation that the court may read, but the court is not permitted to admit the report into evidence unless the parties so stipulate. M.C.L.A. § 722.24(3) (2006). In Maine, the notes that the GAL used in preparation of his or her report are not available to the parties for review. The Court supported this ruling on the grounds that the GAL's informants had been assured of confidentiality in order to get them to speak openly. *Richards v. Bruce*, 691 A.2d 1223 (Me. 1997). Do you think the solution in *Clark* adequately protects the rights of the party against whom the attorney/GAL is recommending? Are either the Michigan or the Maine results adequately protective? Why have these states adopted these unusual procedures?

On the other hand, there are some states that treat the GAL and the GAL's report as they would treat any other witness and pieces of evidence. The Illinois Supreme Court held a statute unconstitutional because it prohibited the child's representative from being called as a witness. The Court held that this deprived the opposing party of due process. *In re Marriage of Bates*, 819 N.E.2d 714 (2004). In Montana, the statute requires that the GAL's report and underlying data be made available to the parties. *In re Custody of Krause*, 19 P.3d 811 (Mont. 2001). Similarly, in Massachusetts, the Probate Courts' Standards subject the GAL to deposition and subpoena. Do you agree that not allowing the opposing party access to the GAL and to the underlying information violates the due process clause? If a legislator asked you which approach should be embodied in the statutes, what would you say?

5. **Confidentiality and the Role of the GAL.** Confidentiality is an important and problematic concern for a GAL. One issue is whether a GAL should be able to promise confidentiality to his or her sources. Some states, like Maine have opted to protect the confidentiality of sources on the grounds that such a policy will result in a better report. *Richards v. Bruce*, 691 A.2d 1223 (Me. 1997). Other states allow the GAL to be examined as to the sources used in the report. Probate and Family Court Department, Commonwealth of Massachusetts, *Standards for Category F Guardian Ad Litem Investigators* (Jan. 24, 2005). For many participants in custody disputes, the most important information gathered by the GAL may be the information on the child's own wishes as to the custodial arrangement. In *Clark v. Alexander*, the Wyoming Supreme Court indicated that the GAL should disclose the child's wishes to the court if they differ from the GAL's own recommendation as to the child's best interests. This is not an uncommon position for states to take. Barbara Ann Atwood, *Representing Children: The Ongoing Search for Clear and Workable Standards*, 19 J. AM. ACAD. MATRIM. LAW 183 (2005). However, some courts have recognized the difficulties for children in being forced to choose openly between their parents. *Reed v. Reed*, 189 Misc.2d 734 (Sup. Ct. N.Y. 2001). The anxieties in doing this are likely to be particularly acute for children in families in which there has been domestic violence. Why is this? If you were a law clerk to a judge faced with a motion to require a GAL to disclose the child's preferences in a case involving domestic violence, what would you recommend that the judge do? If information is going to be subject to disclosure, should the GAL be required to so inform his or her sources before they begin to talk? *Commonwealth v. Lamb*, 311 N.E.2d 47 (Mass. 1974).

The issue of confidentiality is also important in relation to GALs because they often need to talk with therapists, social workers, and others whose conversations with the child may be privileged. The practice in many states is now to appoint special GALs to waive therapeutic privileges for the child. Barbara Trader, *Child Counsel: Caught Betwixt and Between*, MD. B.J. (May/June 2006); Probate and Family Court Department, Commonwealth of Massachusetts, *Standards for Category F Guardian Ad Litem Investigators* 4.6.2 (Jan. 24, 2005). Why is the appointment of a special GAL desirable?

Training for GALs

Massachusetts Chapter of the National Association of Social Workers Committee on Domestic Violence and Sexual Assault

Preliminary Report of the Guardian ad Litem Assessment Project

January 1998.

Executive Summary

Respondents believe that GALs do not possess an adequate understanding of the issue (e.g., do not view domestic violence as serious, do not understand the implications for couples' counseling, do not realize how the courts can be used as a mechanism of control and do not understand the effects of domestic violence on victims and their parenting skills). They also agreed that a GAL's understanding of the issue affects his/her approach to working with battered women (e.g., pathologizing victims, minimizing the importance of domestic violence). Participants also felt that GALs do not always possess the clinical training that would prepare them to assess and respond to developmental and trauma issues among children they interview. They also expressed concern that the safety issues of mothers are not always considered in making recommendations for visitation and custody.... Despite participants' reported concerns about unsafe practices of GALs, few make formal complaints due to fear of retribution from the GAL or the Judge who appointed him/her. Typical issues of concern included perceived bias against the woman, manipulation of the GAL by batterers, unsafe interviewing practices with children, and recommendations without sufficiently considering the impact of violence on women and children.

Participants identified preliminary recommendations to address some of these issues. These include mandatory training for GALs on domestic violence, standardization and professionalization of the GAL role, and clarification and standardization of fee and payment arrangements....

Preliminary Recommendations: Training

Respondents felt that the current level of insight among GALs regarding the extent to which control, manipulation and intimidation are involved in battering relationships is insufficient to evaluate family dynamics accurately. When qualifying numerical responses regarding practice issues, participants made a distinction between "recognizing" or "considering" domestic violence and "understanding" how dynamics of power and control affect all family members. One respondent emphasized the need to address the subtleties of domestic violence and "how broad the coercion is, and how subtle it can be."

"Charm, cooperation and manipulation" were cited by participants as means by which batterers turn GALs and other court officials into allies, portray their former partners as villains rather than victims, deflect even substantiated charges of the physical and/or sexual abuse they have perpetrated. Participants expressed frustration when speaking about the way in which batterers' behaviors invariably sway court officials and outcomes. One respondent stated, "Men who are abusive are often charming and manipulative and successfully shift the focus of the investigation to something other than the abuse."

Most participants expressed concern regarding GALs' limited understanding of how the dynamics of intimidation and control affect children who have witnessed domestic violence. It is difficult to assess and convey children's real thoughts and experiences in a report. Interviewing children may expose them to an abuser's retribution. Limited understanding regarding the fear and control that batterers perpetuate within their families ultimately may result in poorly made recommendations for custody and visitation. One participant called "talking to children" a "minefield." One respondent noted that GALs must be sensitive to the fact that children are "always a source of the batterer's control."

In the stories participants told, visitation exposed children to repeated threats of violence and often made them messengers of these threats to their mothers. In one example, a batterer used visitation as an opportunity to coerce his child into telling the child's mother that he (the batterer) was going to kill her. Given how frequently participants cited similar occurrences, it seems unlikely that all GALs fully recognize the damage visitation may do to a child's psychological and physical well-being.

Many participants reported that battered women often lose custody of their children. Incomplete understanding of the degree of control batterers' hold over their children may lead to the misinterpretation of family dynamics and an award of custody to abusive men. As one participant explained, GALs often observe children interacting with each of their parents as a part of their investigation. Because children may be afraid and, therefore, better-behaved with the batterer, GALs mistakenly conclude that the batterer is the more capable parent. Many participants attributed misguided recommendations to GALs' limited understanding of child development as well as domestic violence.

GALs should also be trained in identifying and intervening with batterers. Almost everyone cited GALs they know who, on their own initiative, have sought additional training to better prepare them to address complex issues like domestic violence. Participants in this survey recommended making such training mandatory and standardized for all GALs. To further support this idea, participants noted the positive impact that education about domestic violence has already had within Family and Probate Courts.

NOTES AND QUESTIONS

1. **The Importance of Adequate Training.** Given that judges rely very heavily on the recommendations of GALs, it is essential that GALs be trained in the dynamics and effects of violence within intimate relationships. In 1995 the Family Violence Project of the National Council of

Juvenile and Family Court Judges reported that guardians ad litem, along with custody evaluators, were "the professionals least trained about domestic violence of any actors in the civil justice system." *Family Violence in Child Custody Statutes—An Analysis of State Codes and Legal Practice*, 29 Fam.L.Q. 197 (1995).

2. **Qualifications to Be a GAL.** Should only professionals be appointed as GALs? If so, what profession? Would you limit GAL appointments to lawyers, psychiatrists, psychologists, social workers, teachers, or some other profession? In *In re Custody of Krause*, 19 P.3d 811 (Mont. 2001), the Montana Supreme Court upheld the appointment of a lay volunteer as a guardian ad litem. The Court said "any person whose appointment would be in the best interests of the child" could be appointed as a GAL. The person was not even required to be completely disinterested or neutral. Does this imply that a parent could be appointed as a GAL? What do you think should be the limits on who can be appointed?

Many states allow almost any adult of "good moral character" to be a G.A.L. New Hampshire simply requires that one be 18 years old, hold a bachelor's or associate degree, and never have been convicted of any of a list of specific crimes. http://www.gencourt.state.nh.us/Rules/gal300.html. Does this seem like an adequate background to you? Do you think your classmates would make good G.A.L.s?

3. **Training to Be a GAL.** States differ tremendously on what specific training, if any, a person appointed as a GAL must have. For example, prior to 2001, Massachusetts required only that the appointee have sufficient malpractice insurance and be in good standing in his or her profession. Massachusetts now requires 6 hours of professional development training before beginning the appointment. Massachusetts Senate Committee on Post Audit and Oversight, *Guarding our Children: A Review of Massachusetts' Guardian Ad Litem Program within the Probate and Family Court* (March 2001). In contrast, Minnesota requires 40 hours of training before the first appointment and 8 hours of training every year thereafter. *Id.* There is also an internship requirement in Minnesota. State of Minnesota, *Supreme Court Rules of Guardian Ad Litem Procedure* (Jan. 1, 1999). What information would you consider essential for a training program for future or continuing GALs?

B. EXPERT WITNESSES IN DOMESTIC VIOLENCE FAMILY LAW CASES

As we have seen, some courts treat guardians ad litem similar to expert witnesses. However, there are innumerable other roles that expert witnesses might play in a family law case. Sometimes experts are appointed by the court to evaluate the parties and make a recommendation as to where the child's best interests lie. Sometimes treating physicians or therapists are called to testify on behalf of one of the parties or about the child. In addition, a party may call an expert witness to testify as to the dynamics or effects of domestic violence or child abuse.

Since child custody decisions are particularly difficult and emotional and since judges often feel that they are not trained in determining a child's psychological needs, courts often rely very heavily on these experts. Two commentators have gone so far as to say, "[J]udges and litigators have become dependent upon the expert opinions of mental-health professionals such as psychologists and psychiatrists." Thomas A. Gionis and Anthony S. Zito, Jr., *A Call for the Adoption of Federal Rule of Evidence 702 for the Admissibility of Mental–Health Professional Expert Testimony in Illinois Child–Custody Cases*, 27 S. ILL. U. L. J. 1 (2002).

As you read the following case, consider whether the "expert" witness had expertise in all of the subjects as to which he testified. The notes that follow the case explore the different roles and backgrounds of expert witnesses in custody cases involving domestic violence.

Keesee v. Keesee

Florida District Court of Appeals, 1996.
675 So.2d 655.

■ W. SHARP, JUDGE.

Willard (Craig) Keesee appeals from a final judgment of dissolution of marriage. He argues on appeal that the trial court erred in awarding primary residential custody of the parties' six-year-old daughter and two-year-old son to the former wife, Karen Keesee.... We affirm....

Counsel for Craig asserted at oral argument in this case that there was no competent evidence in the record upon which the trial court could reasonably have based its ruling. Counsel for Karen assured us there was more than a sufficient basis in the record. Under such circumstances, we have no choice except to read the entire record. Both attorneys cannot be right.

This case was vigorously litigated over a three-day period. Numerous witnesses appeared for both sides. There were expert witnesses, family members, neighbors, social friends, school teachers and acquaintances, a guardian ad litem, and the parties themselves.... After reviewing the record in this case, we conclude that there was sufficient competent evidence to support the trial judge's rulings, and we cannot hold he abused his discretion. We choose to write an opinion in this case because we wish to warn appellate counsel not to make such arguments without good cause. However partisan the lawyer, and however intense the litigation below has been, candor with the appellate court is the only option. In the future, such extreme positions which prove to be without substance, may be grounds for this court to impose sanctions or take other measures to discourage such practice.

I. Determination of Primary Residential Custody in Former Wife's Favor

... Numerous witnesses testified Karen is a loving, concerned parent, who had been the children's primary caretaker since birth. She was the parent who took them to their pediatricians for regular checkups, and for various illnesses. She participated in an unusually large number of programs and activities with the children: a parent-run preschool co-op ... the PTA; volunteering as an Addition in the public school; sports programs ... and religious instruction at the Holy Family Catholic Church. Not until appellant had temporary custody of the children did he participate to any extent in such programs.

Further, the testimony established that Karen was by far the more supporting, nurturing and loving parent. She put the children's interests and concerns before any other matter. She tried to educate herself to be a better parent by taking parenting classes and reading books about subjects relating to the children.... During the marriage, appellee's job kept him away from home long hours, and he did not participate in such activities.

The court-appointed psychologist, Dr. Fleischmann, who did a custody evaluation for the court of the parties and the daughter (the son was too young) and the guardian ad litem, both concluded that appellee had by far the greater insight into the children's feelings and emotional needs and had met this responsibility well in the past.... She also evidenced a superior willingness and desire to foster a continuing and close relationship with appellant, and the two sets of grandparents. There was evidence in this record that the daughter was much more closely bonded to appellee, and that although she loved her father, she was fearful and insecure with him, due to having witnessed his physical and emotional abuse of her mother.

Neither party in this case was free from blame or fault. Karen was shown to have abused taking diet pills.... She was a rather messy housekeeper, and did not handle the family finances in a responsible manner.... In contrast, appellant denied he had any problems, or that he needed any kind of counseling. There was contrary evidence. Based on it, the court could have found that appellant had committed physical and emotional spouse abuse during the course of the marriage, more particularly, during the last two years the parties lived together. His ugly conduct escalated from threats and yelling, to pushing and hitting, and at the end of the marriage, such conduct took place in front of the children, causing damage to the daughter's feelings for him.

A pivotal piece of the evidence was a Christmas morning tape made by appellee of their home, Christmas tree, and children opening their presents. The trial judge, the guardian ad litem, and Dr. Fleischmann all viewed the tape. So did we.

In the tape, the appellant and appellee begin to argue about finances. Karen asks Craig to back off and let the children enjoy their Christmas. But Craig says he cannot. Things escalate. The tape records Craig threatening to smash Karen's face in because she is "pissing" him off. She tells him she just recorded that threat on tape. Craig grabs the camcorder from her, hits her in the head with it (she testified) and breaks it. The picture vanishes but the sound continues to record. The children can be heard, terrified and screaming in the background. Craig then walks out of the house and is gone for days without letting them know where he is. One witness who saw the tape said Craig's depicted behavior did not surprise her. It was not unusual for him.

Dr. Fleischmann said in his report, and at the trial, that this taped incident showing appellant as sullen, angry, cursing and ultimately aggressive, illustrated appellant's lack of concern about the children's emotional well-being. He said the tape struck him powerfully as an "appalling display of insensitivity to the kid's needs."

. . . There was also testimony that appellant, during the time he had temporary custody of the children, slammed the door in appellee's face so that the daughter could not kiss her Mom goodbye, and that he limited or restricted telephone contact by appellee with the children while they were in his household. He denied this behavior also. . . .

At the end of the case, the court stated it had relied on [Dr. Fleischmann's] reports in making its decision, and without objection, it placed the written reports in evidence as the court's exhibits. . . .

[E]ven without Dr. Fleischmann's reports and testimony, there was abundant sufficient evidence to support the judgment being appealed. . . .

■ GRIGGIN, JUDGE, concurring specially.

I vote to affirm in this case, as I necessarily do in any such case where I can identify evidence in the record that the lower court judge, as the finder of fact, could have chosen to believe. I am bound to say, however, that I am increasingly concerned about the proliferating and extensive use of psychologists in these family law cases and the extreme reliance trial courts appear to place on their opinions. These experts conduct interviews, sometimes do tests and then are allowed to render opinions on an extraordinary range of subjects. They have been allowed to offer opinions on why a child nestles with its parent (no, it's not necessarily love), whether someone is prone to domestic violence, who is telling the truth and who is "in denial." Yet, no one seems to be able to muster any measure of the competence or the reliability of these opinions. On the one hand, it is certainly desirable to bring before the court as much evidence as possible to assist the trial court in making the best decision concerning the raising of children in families torn by divorce. On the other hand, rules of evidence exist for a reason, and the issue of competency of such a broad reach of expert testimony is not something that should be taken lightly-particularly in such cases where there is frequently little other objective or disinterested evidence on which the court can rely. These psychological evaluations in many cases amount to no more than an exercise in human lie detection. For example, in this case, the psychologist testified that husband's test results were not valid because he described himself as a moral and virtuous person, which put him at the "pathological" level on the "lie scale." Wife, on the other hand, was described as "forthcoming." On the hotly contested issue of her substance abuse, he testified that she scored within "normal limits" insofar as predisposition to engage in substance abuse and that you "can't fake that scale." This same psychologist was vehemently attacked in another case by the same counsel who here represents the wife on the ground that this psychologist's own addictive behavior makes him "unable to pass judgment as to the addiction of another." . . .

After several years of reading records in these cases, my own confidence in such evidence has fallen very low.

NOTES AND QUESTIONS

1. **Should an Expert Witness Draw Conclusions?** The GAL and the court-appointed psychologist in *Keesee v. Keesee* both concluded that the mother had greater insight into the children's emotional state than the father. The psychologist also testified that the tape showed an "appalling display of insensitivity to the kid's needs" on the part of the father. Is it appropriate for experts to state such conclusions? On what are they based? Judge Griffin, concurring, complains that there is no standard of statistical reliability for expert opinions such as these. Do you agree that experts' conclusions need to be scientifically based to be admissible as expert testimony? If they are no different from the opinions of lay people, why should they be admitted? Would it have been appropriate for either the evaluator or the GAL to make recommendations as to who should have residential custody of the children?

Thomas Gionis and Anthony Zito offer the following caution in dealing with expert testimony:

> The testimony offered by mental-health experts in child-custody cases pertaining to the best interest of a particular child generally takes the form of "hybrid" expert testimony. Hybrid expert testimony is based partially on scientific research, and partially on the expert's less-than-scientific opinion.... It is important to note that mental-health professionals have no scientific research to guide them in making evaluations concerning numerous factors relative to the determination of a child's best interest. For example, although state child-custody statutes often include factors like parental moral fitness and financial capability, there is no scientific research on these components to aid mental health professionals. On the other hand, psychological research does exist as a foundation for some, albeit limited, opinions when statutory factors such as: (1) the mental health of the parent and child; (2) the child's wishes; (3) the child's adjustment to home, school, and community; and (4) the relationship among the child, the parents, and the siblings are considered.... Because most mental-health professional expert testimony is largely based on the unverified, and often unverifiable, observations and experiences of the expert, the distinction between expert testimony based on clinical judgment and expert testimony based on scientific research must be carefully considered in any child-custody litigation involving expert opinion testimony. Clinical judgment (untested opinions) and decision-making characteristically rely upon the practitioner's reliance on personal experience instead of statistically analyzed data drawn from valid and reliable research....
> In light of the inherent unreliability of clinical judgment and decision making of mental-health professionals in child-custody claims, it must be recalled that the certainty experts bring to their conclusions, or the earnestness with which experts hold them, reveals nothing about the

likelihood the conclusions are correct. Thomas Gionis and Anthony Zito, *A Call for the Adoption of Federal Rule of Evidence 702 for the Admissibility of Mental–Health Professional Expert Testimony in Illinois Child–Custody Cases*, 27 S. ILL. U. L.J. 1 (2002).

2. **Using Expert Witnesses to Establish Social Context.** In some cases it may be desirable to offer expert testimony as to why victims of intimate violence act the way they do, why victims engage in specific parenting behaviors, or even whether victims who have suffered particular emotional problems as a result of the violence will be able to be good parents in the future. Sometimes a lawyer may want to call an expert witness to explain why victims remain in the relationship, why they return home with the children after leaving, or the connections between abuse and victims' alcohol or drug abuse. Experts who testify to such general characteristics of abusive relationships may never have examined the particular victim in the case under consideration. As Jane Aiken and Jane Murphy say, "Too often lawyers offer clinically based testimony but overlook useful social framework testimony." Jane H. Aiken and Jane C. Murphy, *Evidence Issues in Domestic Violence Civil Cases*, 34 FAM.L.Q. 43 (2000). Should "social context" expert testimony be excluded on the grounds that it does not add anything that the court and other non-experts do not already know?

3. **Who Qualifies as an Expert Witness?** Federal Rule of Evidence 702 allows a person to testify as an expert witness if specialized knowledge will be useful to the trier of fact and if the proposed witness is qualified as an expert by virtue of "knowledge, skill, experience, training, or education." Notice that this would allow someone who works at a shelter or domestic violence program to testify about domestic violence so long as the witness has sufficient experience to be considered an expert. It is not necessary to obtain an expensive expert witness with many degrees after his or her name. The Montana Coalition against Domestic and Sexual Violence is taking advantage of this to create a pool of experienced advocates who can serve as expert witnesses in court. As one participant said, "Many advocates have specialized expertise in the dynamics of domestic violence and understand the many ways batterers' behavior can affect their victims.... They have a wealth of knowledge: they've been working in the field for years, they've attended countless trainings, and have, in turn, provided trainings at the local and state level." State Bar of Montana, *Organization Offers Expert Witnesses*, 29 MONT. LAW. 23 (March 2004). Just as we saw in Chapter Eight, the broad standard of admissibility for expert testimony allows for a wide range of professionals to be qualified as an expert.

4. **Expert Witnesses and Neutrality.** In an omitted portion of the *Keesee* opinion the court notes that the psychologist, Dr. Fleischmann, shared an office with the wife's treating therapist. Should this be enough to disqualify Dr. Fleischmann on the grounds that he is interested? The Court held that it was not. The Court also held that it was proper for Dr. Fleischmann to have talked to the treating therapist as part of the process of investigating the case. The neutrality of expert witnesses is also often attacked on the grounds that they are frequent witnesses. Should this be a

basis for not admitting the witness's testimony? For impeaching the witness's credibility?

C. MEDIATION IN THE CONTEXT OF ABUSE

At least 42 states have statutes that envision the use of mediation in custody disputes. Jane C. Murphy and Robert Rubinson, *Domestic Violence and Mediation*, 39 FAM. L.Q. 53 (2005). In some states mediation is mandatory; in others courts have the discretion to order mediation. Of course, parties can also turn to private mediators and present the court with a mediated settlement for approval. The use of court ordered mediation has increased dramatically since the early 1980s.

There are a number of reasons why courts, parties, and legislators have turned to mediation in the past quarter century. First, there is the dramatic growth in family law cases over this time period. Domestic relations cases represent the fastest growing segment of a civil court's caseload. Between 1984 and 1995, the number of domestic relations cases increased by 70%. Estimates are that half of all civil cases today are family law cases. Bill Ezzell, *Inside the Minds of America's Family Law Courts: The Psychology of Mediation Versus Litigation in Domestic Disputes*, 25 LAW & PSYCHOL. REV. 119 (2001). Furthermore, divorce and custody cases often take a year or more to try. This is tied to the increase in the caseload of civil courts and family courts. Busy, understaffed courts are likely to grant continuances and to have clogged calendars. Mediation of custody disputes may appear an attractive option to the parties because courts are often seen as impersonal and very public. In courts in which the judges rotate through sessions, litigants may end up seeing many different judges in the course of their cases. No one judge is likely under those circumstances to become familiar with the details of the case or with the personalities of the people involved. Similarly, courts are open to the public; many litigants are not anxious to wash their dirty linen in public. Finally, policy makers recognize that litigation is often polarizing. The adversarial process often encourages parties to paint their opponents as being extremely bad parents. The negative things that get said in court or in pleadings are not easily forgotten after the litigation. Parties may have a hard time relating to one another both during and after the litigation. This is certainly not good for their children. All of these are reasons often given for preferring mediation to litigation of custody cases. Carol J. King, *Burdening Access to Justice; The Cost of Divorce Mediation on the Cheap*, 73 ST. JOHN'S L. REV. 375 (1999).

Unlike litigation which resolves a conflict in accordance with a set of externally imposed rules, mediation is aimed at producing a voluntary settlement according to norms determined by the parties. Mediation proclaims self-determination and empowerment of the parties as two of its goals. Mediation is touted as a flexible dispute resolution system, both procedurally and substantively. The mediator's job is to remain neutral and not to take sides on the debates between the parties. Instead, the mediator is to facilitate better communication between the parties. Advocates of mediation in custody cases support it because it is quicker than litigation, because it is more personal, because it is more private, and because it is less adversarial and polarizing. Nancy Ver Steegh, *Yes, No, and Maybe: Informed Decision Making About Divorce Mediation in the Presence of Domestic Violence,* 9 WM. & MARY J. WOMEN & L. 145 (2003).

Despite all of these ostensible advantages, advocates for victims of domestic violence have voiced doubts about the appropriateness of mediation for couples whose relations have involved violence. It is important to remember that there is evidence of violence in approximately half of the cases referred to Family Court mediation programs. Jessica Pearson, *Mediating When Domestic Violence is a Factor,* 14 MEDIATION Q. 319 (1997). The readings that follow describe the arguments for and against the use of mediation in cases in which there has been domestic violence. In addition to posing the question of whether mediation is appropriate, they raise a number of questions including what type of training is appropriate for mediators, how to screen for domestic violence, and who should participate in mediation sessions.

Trina Grillo

The Mediation Alternative: Process Dangers for Women

100 YALE L. J. 1545 (1991).

There is little doubt that divorce procedure needs to be reformed, but reformed how? Presumably, any alternative should be at least as just, and at least as humane, as the current system, particularly for those who are least powerful in society. Mediation has been put forward, with much fanfare, as such an alternative. The impetus of the mediation movement has been so strong that in some states couples disputing custody are required by statute or local rule to undergo a mandatory mediation process if they are unable to reach an agreement on their own. Mediation has been embraced for a number of reasons. First, it rejects an objectivist approach to conflict resolution, and promises to consider disputes in terms of relationships and responsibility. Second, the mediation process is, at least in theory, cooperative and voluntary, not coercive. The mediator does not make a decision: rather, each party speaks for himself. Together they reach an agreement that meets the parties' mutual needs. In this manner, the process is said to enable the parties to exercise self-determination and eliminate the hierarchy of dominance that characterizes the judge/litigant and the lawyer/client relationships. Third, since in mediation there are no rules of evidence or legalistic notions of relevancy, decisions supposedly may be informed by context rather than by abstract principle. Finally, in theory at least, emotions are recognized and incorporated into the mediation process. . . .

The movement for voluntary mediation of divorce disputes began several decades ago as lawyers and therapists offered to help their clients settle their cases in a non-adversarial manner. . . . As mediation caught on, it began to be heralded as the cure for the various ills of adversary divorce.... Consumers, however, were not embracing the mediation cure. Whether because of lack of familiarity with the process, the hostility of the organized bar, or some more considered reluctance, few divorcing couples chose to enter mediation. In order to bypass this consumer resistance, some state legislatures established court-annexed mediation programs, requiring that couples disputing custody mediate prior to going to court.

Karla Fischer, Neil Vidmar and Rene Ellis
The Culture of Battering and the Role of Mediation in Domestic Violence Cases
46 S.M.U. L. REV. 2117 (1993).

Consider the widely quoted definition of mediation set forth by Folberg and Taylor:

"Mediation is an alternative to violence, self-help, or litigation.... It can be defined as the process by which the participants, together with the assistance of a neutral person or persons, systematically isolate disputed issues in order to develop options, consider alternatives, and reach a consensual settlement that will accommodate their needs. Mediation is a process that emphasizes the participants' own responsibility for making decisions that affect their lives. It is therefore a self-empowering process."

The definition itself reflects what Laura Nader has labeled the "harmony ideology" underlying mediation as it is currently practiced in the alternative dispute resolution (ADR) movement. In contrast to the adversary system which is based on the notion of justice and on the understanding of power differentials, the harmony model values consensus settlement and management of disputes through "healing" processes that "minimize power differentials of class, race, economics, and gender; it articulates the notion that disputes are generated in relationships by the failure of individuals to act as they should." Nader's critique addresses the social and legal systems as a whole. She argues that the ADR movement has become increasingly coercive and "values means over ends, harmony over justice, and efficiency over due process."

Nader's critique is shared by others who have analyzed the implicit and explicit assumptions underlying mediation theory. The objections to it are brought into sharpest focus when mediation assumptions are contrasted with our analysis of the culture of battering....

... Below we consider eight purported advantages of the mediation forum and weigh them against our insights about the culture of battering.

1. IDEOLOGY OF MEDIATION: Abuse arises out of conflict

   CULTURE OF BATTERING: Conflict is only the pretext for abuse.

   ... [C]ulture of battering relationships are not about conflict, but rather about domination and control. To the extent that conflict is present it is only a symptom. The conflict is manufactured by the abuser in the relationship. To structure mediation sessions as if the cause of abuse is conflict is to artificially frame the problem of battering. . . .

For divorce cases where child custody or property settlements are disputed, these conflicts may be equally likely to be manufactured by the batterer, as he may raise the issues as a pretext for regaining power in the relationship and exerting his usual system of control and domination. Martha Mahoney warned of this possibility: "[T]he custody action is part of an ongoing attempt, through physical violence and legal manipulation, to force the woman to make concessions or return to the violent partner." Because batterers use threats against the children—especially to take them away from their mothers—and abuse the children to control the woman, it is plausible to view custody "disputes" as suspicious in cases where a culture of battering has been established. Similar dynamics may operate in property settlements. Batterers use family financial resources to control their victims both physically and psychologically. Mediation sessions may simply become another forum for this coercion. Whether the issue is property or children, the mediation model of ameliorating conflict presumes, and therefore imposes, a conflict structure on a situation where these issues may not be truly disputed. The danger for battered women who have recently extracted themselves from a culture of battering is that the batterers' domination and control tactics will flourish in the mediation environment and not be recognized as such.

2.   IDEOLOGY OF MEDIATION: Focus on future, not past behavior.

CULTURE OF BATTERING: Ignoring past behavior denies victims' experiences of violence.

According to Bethel and Singer, "[u]nlike legal remedies, mediation is prospectively rather than retrospectively centered and is not concerned with determining rights and wrongs" but is focused on "future conduct." This component of the mediation ideology is partially responsible for the policy of many mediation centers to exclude attorneys from the mediation session even though the victim's attorney may be the primary source of support and protection for the victim's rights.

Yet, the culture of battering is ineluctably tied to an escalating history of domination and control. The batterer and the victim cannot, and should not, be separated from their history. The specific failure to consider right and wrong allows an assumption that the victim may be responsible for her plight. The mediation process then treats the victim as though she shares responsibility, in essence subtly classifying her as a perpetrator. . . .

Consider Bethel and Singer's response to the argument for setting history aside: "[m]ediation is not therapy. Mediation's goal is to help effect behavioral change, because it is specific behavior, assaultive behavior or threatening behavior, that one or both parties cannot tolerate. Attitudinal change . . . is not the paramount goal of mediation." "[F]undamental personality or attitudinal change is not required to prevent many forms of domestic violence." They go on to state that the process of mediation "requires the parties to focus on crucial rather than peripheral issues, and it allows little room for excuses."

Two interrelated problems are inherent in this aspect of mediation ideology. First, the assumption that attitude change is not a goal of mediation shifts the process away from the root cause of abuse. Second, it assumes that problem is a specific conflict or set of conflicts and that peripheral incidents are of no consequence. Yet, the peripheral matters are reflective of the total relationship between the two parties.... Being battered involves more than the specific acts of violence committed by the abuser; it means living in a relationship with a partner who systematically dominates and controls your activities, your relationships with other people, your beliefs and values, and your body. Labeling this experience as "peripheral" delegitimizes the victim's right to bring the abuse up as an issue in mediation even though it may be extremely relevant to how custody and visitation should be arranged, or how property should be divided.

3.   IDEOLOGY OF MEDIATION: Each party participates equally in the search for a mutual agreement.

CULTURE OF BATTERING: Equal participation is impossible

Another of Bethel and Singer's ideological statements addresses the process of mediation: "The parties are treated as responsible adults and in turn are expected to participate actively in the search for a mutually acceptable agreement."

This expectation ... is also problematic. Mediation theorists consistently evoke the theme that participation is a self empowering process. They assert that helping to shape the outcome that is the subject matter of the forum compels even a weak party to find new strength. However, to participate and become self empowered the weaker party must be able to articulate needs and desires. This may be extremely difficult for a victim of spousal abuse because she may not even understand her position, may have been consistently silenced by her partner, and may fear the consequences of speaking out. Further, the task of negotiating an agreement runs a grave risk of simply mimicking the battering culture. The mediation may in fact be a safe as well as powerful setting for the abuser to intimidate and control his victim through hidden symbols of impending violence. Even his mere presence may be intimidating, particularly if she is attempting to escape from the relationship; contact with the abuser is often the last thing that victims want.

The issue for battered women is consistent with the general problems that women may have when they are involved in domestic issues mediation. Trina Grillo has argued that mediation's emphasis on joint needs may push the woman away from an attempt to define herself as a person with needs and rights that are independent of the spousal relationship. The mediation process may evoke feelings of guilt and socialized tendencies to subordinate self needs to relationships with others and acquiesce in the face of social pressure. Clearly, abused women may often experience certain characteristics in the extreme, such as feelings of dependency, uncertainty about self worth, and self-censoring tendencies to deny their own needs. Thus, the mediation process, with its emphasis on compromise and healing relationships may actually serve to undo the abused woman's initial steps to find empowerment as an individual person.

Finally, the emphasis of mediation ideology on joint participation may make the mediator insensitive to the needs of an abused woman or even cause the mediator to view the woman as uncooperative. . . .

Bethel and Singer further state that "[m]ediation relies on a rough parity in bargaining power between the parties to be successful. If one side dominates the other there is much less chance that any agreement will be truly voluntary or that it will accurately reflect the parties' needs." Indeed! And by its very nature the culture of battering makes the couple unequal in subtle and pervasive ways.

4.   IDEOLOGY OF MEDIATION: Avoid blame and findings of fact.

CULTURE OF BATTERING: Avoidance of abuse issues perpetuates status quo of victim responsibility and abuser domination.

"Mediation is an informal, participatory method of conflict resolution. The mediator . . . has no higher authority to invoke, and rebuffs requests to make findings of fact or decisions about blameworthiness." If followed, this tenet of mediation ideology eschews any actions by mediators relating to the parties as anything but equals and prevents mediators from looking for elements in the relationship that might indicate a culture of battering. The tenet forces the mediator to treat spousal abuse and domination neutrally. Because batterers place the responsibility and blame for the assaults on the victim, frequently tying the abuse to her inability to live up to his rules, the status quo of the relationship is left in place when his belief system is left unchallenged. By ignoring the context of the abuse under the guise of avoiding blame, the mediator leaves behind any opportunity to learn about how the abuser might attempt to control and dominate the victim during mediation sessions.

5.   IDEOLOGY OF MEDIATION: Private caucuses will encourage the victim to speak her needs.

CULTURE OF BATTERING: Private caucuses will not assist victims who are afraid of the consequences of speaking their needs.

"The process is participatory, but the nature of the participation is controlled by the mediator. . . ." Bethel and Singer recognize that the mediator may communicate individually, through caucuses with the parties, to develop the agreement. It is assumed that getting the victim alone will allow her to state her true feelings, wants and needs. This assumption naively ignores the fear and psychological control that develops in culture of battering relationships and extends beyond the immediate physical presence of the abuser. If the relationship has been one where the victim has been punished for having or speaking her needs, she may be justifiably afraid of the consequences of doing so, even if she is unable to articulate this fear. Spending five minutes alone with the victim . . . will not substantially reduce the reality of this fear or enhance her trust of the mediators. In fact, it is absurd to believe that a five minute caucus can uncover and rectify the effects of being silenced through months or years of abuse—

presuming, of course, that the mediator earns the trust of the victim who truly wishes to disclose her history and experiences.

6. IDEOLOGY OF MEDIATION: Batterers need to be coerced into mediation.

CULTURE OF BATTERING: Batterers may coerce victims into mediation.

As explained by Erickson and McKnight, "[m]ediation is to some extent a voluntary process, but one party may participate only because it is the least objectionable of several alternatives. The prospect of court action, or further police involvement, or retaliation from the other party, may have substantial coercive effect." This assertion seems to focus on the inducements to bring the batterer to the mediation forum. It ignores the possibility that the batterer may prefer mediation because it places him in a situation where he can continue to dominate. Moreover, it clearly glosses over the pressures that may force the reluctant victim into mediation. Some women may go to mediation only because it is cheaper, or it is their only recourse because a judge or other authority has ordered it, or they cannot receive legal support unless they submit to mediation first.

7. IDEOLOGY OF MEDIATION: The novelty of a written agreement detailing the rules of the relationship will end the violence.

CULTURE OF BATTERING: Rules in a battering relationship may justify the batterer's further abuse.

The culmination of the mediation ideology is usually a written agreement specifying the rules and obligations of the parties' relationship. Each of several examples provided by Bethel and Singer articulates rules. Yet [a culture of battering relationship] is already filled with rules imposed on the victim by the batterer. It is the violation of these rules that leads to the violence and abuse. Because the agreements place obligations on the victim as well as the batterer, any minor infraction of these rules by the victim may provide the batterer with an excuse to abandon his obligations. Moreover, he now has a written text to help justify his outrage.

8. IDEOLOGY OF MEDIATION: The process of mediation can protect battered women from future violence.

CULTURE OF BATTERING: Battered women will not disclose abuse to mediators, during or after sessions.

... The notion that the process of mediation will "heal" the relationship is anchored in the abuse-is-conflict framework. Changing the couple's communication strategies to include non-abusive ones will only be effective outside mediation if those "strategies" are the cause of the abuse. Because much of the violence in battering relationships occurs "out of the blue," or at the end of manufactured arguments, the healing power of the mediation session is likely to be limited.

The ideological statement that mediation will end the violence also has an underlying assumption that mediators will somehow know if the victim is currently being abused. The culture of battering involves an element of hiding, denying, and minimizing the abuse. Much abuse is itself hidden, leaving no visible marks: sexual assaults, emotional abuse and threats, familial abuse. Even physical abuse may not leave marks if the batterer chooses to hit where the bruises on the victim's body will not be revealed to others. The parties may cancel mediation sessions until the bruises fade away (in the event that mediation lasts for more than one session) in much the same way that battered women stay home from work or school until their injuries heal. If mediators send the message that abuse is irrelevant or peripheral, this may intensify the victim's feelings of shame, and she may be even less likely to disclose the abuse.

As a final thought on the ideology of mediation with violent couples, in cases where the couple is separated ..., the risk for serious violence is heightened. The abuser's ability to dominate and control his partner through abuse becomes more limited as his access to her decreases. Consequently, his motivation for obtaining access to her through any means possible, including formal interaction with the legal system through court-mandated mediation sessions, is quite high. Sadly, scheduled court proceedings can lead to an opportunity to kill, as they were in one recent death for a battered woman: Shirley Lowery was killed by her estranged husband as she arrived in a Wisconsin courthouse lobby to wait for the hearing for her second order of protection. Mediators must never forget that separation is the most dangerous time for battered women, and avoid allowing the contact that the sessions require to become the abuser's safe opportunity to strike out with violence against his partner.

NOTES AND QUESTIONS

1. **Victim's Advocates' Opposition to Mediation.** Fischer, Vidmar, and Ellis provide a comprehensive account of the mismatch between the philosophical underpinnings of mediation and the dynamics of partner abuse. To this account we need to add the flavor of actual disputes between the mediation community and the battered women's community. Battered women's advocates accuse mediators of ignorance with respect to the dynamics of abuse and of naivete with respect to abusers' efforts to manipulate the legal process. They point to mediator misconceptions about those who abuse or are abused; misconceptions which can lead to ineffective screening and inappropriate decisions about who is and who is not a suitable candidate for mediation. They are incensed by many mediators' commitment to joint custody or other shared parenting arrangements, arguing that it violates the precept of mediator neutrality, as well as endangering the women and children who, through such arrangements, become more vulnerable to further abuse.

2. **Reasons to Consider Mediation for Violent Relationships.** Despite the prevailing hostility toward mediation of those who advocate for battered women, there are some important reasons to resist the categorical conclusion that mediation is never an acceptable process for women separating from an abusive relationship. First, as Jessica Pearson reminds her readers, in her article, *Mediating When Domestic Violence is a Factor*, 14 MEDIATION Q. 319 (1997):

[S]ome critics have compared the best possible litigation with the worst examples of mediation ...; many of the shortcomings attributed to mediation are also present during attorney-assisted negotiations and litigation. Indeed, by encouraging parties to adopt extreme positions in negotiations or attempting to portray the other parent in the least favorable light in court documents, the judicial system can escalate and prolong conflict in ways that increase the level of danger for the victim. Because the client is usually the passive recipient of the lawyer's expertise, this can reinforce patterns of domination for women.

Perhaps the most significant way the judicial system fails victims of domestic abuse is by frequently neglecting to provide them with any legal representation. Increasingly, divorcing parents are self-represented and have no attorney. The incidence of self-representation ranges from 40 percent in Alameda County, California to 90 percent in Maricopa County, Arizona. It is clearly unrealistic to compare mediation to a system of strong, assertive advocacy when the absence of advocacy is increasingly the norm.

Second, mediation and litigation are not the only two alternatives. There are other processes that may be called into play and potentially combined with mediation or litigation to provide a richer range of options. In the same article, Pearson describes some of these possibilities:

[S]ome high-conflict and violent couples need court interventions other than those currently available to resolve their disputes. This includes more intensive therapeutic and legal interventions that combine mediation with counseling, evaluation, and long-term therapy. Another recommended approach is arbitration, where trained and experienced mental health professionals assess issues and make binding decisions in disputes that involve children. Still a third approach to decision making used by custody evaluators in Tucson is a hybrid of evaluation and mediation wherein mental health professionals conduct an assessment, make recommendations, present them to parents and their attorneys, and use the feedback phase to stimulate parties to engage in decision-making regarding their postseparation parenting arrangements. Arbitration, case management and mediation-evaluation hybrids are less formal and stressful than litigation, are more evaluative and structured than regular mediation, and may offer more protections for victims of domestic violence.

Third, mediation programs have never followed a uniform blueprint, and there is room to ask whether mediation could be reconceived and redesigned to be more attentive to the issues raised by domestic violence, and more useful to those who are separating from abusive relationships. It is an encouraging sign that in some collaborations, such as the Maine Mediation and Domestic Abuse Project (1990–1992) and the Toronto Forum on Woman Abuse and Mediation (1993), members of the mediation and domestic violence communities have begun to bridge the gulf that has traditionally separated them.

3. **Mandated Mediation.** In some states, like California, mediation is statutorily required before a contested custody case can be litigated. The

following excerpt describes California's efforts to make its mediation program as hospitable as possible to victims of violence, without endangering them or making their situation worse.

Lauri Boxer–Macomber

Revisiting the Impact of California's Mandatory Custody Mediation Program on Victims of Domestic Violence through a Feminist Positionality Lens

15 ST. THOMAS L. REV. 883 (2003).

In 1981, California became the first state in the country to enact mandatory child custody mediation legislation. Today, all family law cases, even those with histories or allegations of domestic violence, are subject to mediation. . . .

CALIFORNIA'S RESPONSE TO CONCERNS ABOUT THE MANDATORY CUSTODY MEDIATION PROGRAM

This section [reviews the] concerns [of opponents of mandatory mediation in domestic violence cases] and looks at how California is presently handling each concern. In some cases, the California legislature and judiciary have actively sought to protect the rights of victims of domestic violence during the mediation process by adopting prescriptive statutes and rules. In other cases, the state has failed to respond to relevant concerns. . . .

Mandatory Mediation

California's policy of mandatory custody mediation has persisted for over two decades. Despite significant criticism of the legislation's impact on victims of domestic violence, the law remains. . . . [T]he California Rules of Court, allow for an exemption from mediation when "the mediator believes that he or she is unable to achieve a balanced discussion between the parties." However, in some courts, mediators rarely, if ever, employ this rule to excuse a case from mediation.

Protecting the Physical Safety of Victims of Domestic Violence

There are presently several laws and rules in place to protect victims of domestic violence while they are participating in mandatory mediation. First, the California Rules of Court require courts to use "a detailed intake process that screens for, and informs the mediator about, any restraining orders or safety-related issues affecting any party or child named in the proceedings. . . ."

In addition, victims of domestic violence may elect to bring an attorney or victim advocate to the mediation. . . . Unfortunately, however, a victim's right to have an attorney or advocate present during mediation is stifled by the presiding mediator's right to exclude attorneys or advocates at his or her discretion.

Regardless of whether an attorney or advocate is present during the mediation, the California custody mediation process is designed to allow victims to play active roles in defining custody and visitation plans that will not compromise their physical safety and/or well-being. Competent mediators who "check in" with victims throughout the mediation process can take preventative measures to protect victims from agreeing to a custody or visitation plan that will place them at risk for future harm.

Another way that California attempts to protect the physical safety of victims of domestic violence during the mediation process is by either placing them in, or allowing them to elect, separate mediation. Where there is a protective order in place, California law mandates separate mediation. In addition, in cases where a victim of domestic violence is worried about safety and the victim does not have a protective order, the California Family Code allows the victim or the victim's attorney to request separate mediation. In such cases, independent mediations usually take place in different rooms of the courthouse or at the mediator's office. In the alternative, if victims without protective orders prefer, they may elect joint mediation. Joint mediation is often used when victims feel that face-to-face mediation will put them at less risk of future violence, when victims would prefer to hear what the other party is discussing with the mediator, or when victims are concerned that their perpetrators will attempt to manipulate the mediation process to their advantage. . . .

Process Dangers Explored

The California mandatory custody mediation process is designed to address the power imbalances between victims of domestic violence and their perpetrators, as well as to prevent further emotional harm to victims of domestic violence. California's Uniform Standards for the Practice of Mediation require that mediators conduct negotiations "in such a way as to equalize power relationships between the parties." . . .

Another way that the California custody mediation process lends itself to balancing power inequities is through its flexibility. As mentioned earlier, if victims are unwilling to meet with their offenders, they may elect for independent caucuses with their mediators. Similarly, victims of domestic violence may bring attorneys and/or advocates with them to mediation. The physical presence of these individuals may be able to offset some of the power imbalance between victims of domestic violence and their perpetrators. In addition, when victims are unable to assert themselves and make specific requests about custody and visitation, their attorneys and/or advocates are able to speak in their places.

When appropriate, California mediation laws also offer opportunities for victims of domestic violence to participate in the legal decision making process without the assistance of counsel. Under a traditional adversarial system, victims' attorneys may take complete control of litigation. As a result, victims' attorneys may end up repeating the pattern of dominance that victims of domestic violence previously experienced in their relationships with their abusers. In California, however, if a mediator feels that it would be more advantageous for a victim to work without an attorney, the mediator will exercise his or her right to exclude counsel. Similarly, mediators are allowed to exclude opposing counsel from mediation. The statutory authority granted upon mediators to exercise this option allows them to prevent victims from being subjected to re-victimization.

Finally, the California custody mediation program attempts to mitigate the emotional damage to victims of domestic violence by providing them with a safe environment in which to speak. In California, all mediation sessions are held in private and are confidential. The confidential process affords victims of domestic violence the opportunity to speak freely about domestic violence and safety concerns.

Mediator Competency

California has taken significant steps to ensure that its Family Court mediators are prepared to identify and handle custody mediations where there are histories or allegations of domestic violence. First, to become a family court mediator, an individual must have the following minimum qualifications:

1.   A master's degree in psychology, social work, marriage, family and child counseling, or other behavioral science substantially related to marriage and family interpersonal relationships.

2.   At least two years of experience in counseling or psychotherapy. . . .

3.   Knowledge of the court system of California and the procedures used in family law cases.

4.   Knowledge of other resources in the community. . . .

5.   Knowledge of adult psychopathology and the psychology of families.

6.   Knowledge of child development, child abuse, clinical issues relating to children, the effects of divorce on children, the effects of domestic violence on children, and child custody research sufficient to enable a counselor to assess the mental health needs of children.

In addition, California law mandates that all family court mediators participate in programs of continuing instruction on domestic violence. Mediators must complete sixteen hours of advanced domestic violence training within the first twelve months of employment and four hours of domestic violence training each year thereafter. . . . Areas of instruction include, but are not limited to the effects of domestic violence on children, the nature and extent of domestic violence, the social and family dynamics of domestic violence, and techniques for identifying and assisting families affected by domestic violence. . . .

If, despite this training, a mediator acts or seems unprepared to handle custody mediation where there is a history or allegations of domestic violence, victims and their attorneys may request that the court assign them a new mediator. Each family court is required to have rules in place that parties may employ to change mediators.

Batterers are Not Exculpated

California's decision to place perpetrators of domestic violence in a custody mediation setting in no way exonerates them from liability for their abusive behavior. The California Code makes it clear that custody mediation is about developing a custody plan that is in the best interests of the child. However, given that a parent's history of abuse is a factor taken into consideration when determining custody, the fact that domestic violence is ancillary to the custody mediation does not make it irrelevant.

In addition, the California Code prevents batterer exoneration by limiting the scope of child custody mediation agreements to the resolution of issues relating to parenting plans, custody, visitation, or a combination of these issues. Therefore, even if a batterer or a victim of domestic violence wanted to negotiate an agreement related to the batterer's abusive behavior, such an agreement would not be permissible in the custody mediation setting.

NOTES AND QUESTIONS

1. **Mediation and Exoneration of the Abuser.** As indicated in the above excerpt, California has tried to be responsive to the criticisms of those who think that mediation is inappropriate for couples whose relationships have involved violence. Do you agree that a focus specifically on custody, visitation, and parenting plans avoids exonerating the abuser? Fischer, Vidmar, and Ellis argued in the earlier excerpt that mediation's focus on setting rules for specific interactions shifts the attention away from the abuse as a cause of the difficulties and implies that the conflict itself is the problem as opposed to its underlying causes. Another commentator has argued that the requirement that a mediator remain neutral makes it difficult for the mediator to condemn the abuse. As a result, "the batterer's belief that his behavior is acceptable is maintained and the battered woman is disempowered." Laurel Wheeler, *Mandatory Family Mediation and Domestic Violence*, 26 S. ILL. U. L. J. 559 (2002).

2. **Mediation and Power Imbalances.** How well do you think California's mediation process addresses the power imbalances that the abuser has tried to create? There are at least three different ways that one might think about these power imbalances.

First, the dynamics of abusive relationships often result in victims who are easily manipulated by the abuser and in abusers who are used to manipulating others, including the victim. Mediation may play right into this imbalance by creating a setting in which the victim may falsely believe that the abuser will finally change. For example, as the parties to mediation discuss their needs and flexible points, the victim may be thinking, "Surely he would be sorry if only he could see how he is destroying me." A victim's hope that the relationship can be restructured may not only be unrealistic, but it may also keep her disempowered. See Jennifer P. Maxwell, *Mandatory Mediation of Custody in the Face of Domestic Violence*, 37 FAM. & CONCIL. CTS. REV. 335 (1999). The abuser may be using the mediation to maintain his dominant position. It ensures that he will have regular access to his partner and the opportunity to continue to manipulate and intimidate her. Furthermore, his willingness to participate may also make him appear like a very attractive and concerned parent to the mediator, increasing his chances of gaining significant custodial time with his children. Laurel Wheeler, *Mandatory Family Mediation and Domestic Violence*, 26 S. ILL. U. L. J. 559 (2002).

Mediation may also be unable to equalize the power relationship between the parties if the domestic violence has affected the victim's ability to function. This might happen in any of three ways that are crucial to mediation: the victim might be unable to think rationally about the situation, she may be unable to establish and implement her own priorities, or she may not be able to conform her behavior to the ground rules of the mediation. See Connie J.A. Beck and Lynda E. Frost, *Defining a Threshold for Client Competence to Participate in Divorce Mediation*, 12 PSYCHOL. PUB. POL'Y & L. 1 (2006).

Finally, the very flexibility that is central to mediation's ability to respond to individual parties' needs and goals may undermine its ability to establish equality of power between the parties. As two commentators have pointed out:

> [M]any of the characteristics of litigation that mediation seeks to avoid—formality, decision making by neutral fact finder, the constraining influence of a set of neutral principles embodied in "law," even the institutional naming of actions as wrong and illegal—can act to equalize the playing-field in the presence of power differentials between or among parties. The absence of such safeguards could thus render mediation a more dangerous process in the presence of power imbalances between parties. Jane C. Murphy and Robert Rubinson, *Domestic Violence and Mediation*, 39 FAM. L.Q. 53 (2005).

Given what you know about relationships in which there has been domestic violence, are you concerned that mediation might exacerbate instead of reduce power imbalances? Are there other sources of power imbalances that should be considered in relation to mediation of relationships that have involved violence? Do you think the California system described in the excerpt above, including separate mediation sessions, adequately deals with these power imbalances?

3. **Participation of Advocates in the Mediation Process.** The above description of mediation in California raises the question as to whether attorneys or other advocates for the parties ought to be allowed to participate in the mediation. If attorneys or advocates are allowed in for one party, must they also be allowed in for the other party? Do you think the mediator should have the discretion to determine whether or not to allow people other than the parties to participate in mediation? Under what circumstances are victims of abuse likely to have attorneys or other advocates who can attend the mediation with them?

4. **The Cost of Mediation.** In many states, the cost of mediation is also an issue. If the only type of mediation available is private mediation, it may be very expensive. This could easily result in one system of dispute resolution for the rich and another for the non-rich. In some jurisdictions costs for mediation may be as high as $150/hour or more. Of course, litigation costs are likely to be significantly higher. On the other hand, if

the mediation is not successful, the parties will end up litigating anyway. In that case, the money that was spent on mediation is simply lost. Carol J. King, *Burdening Access to Justice: The Cost of Divorce Mediation on the Cheap,* 73 ST. JOHN'S L. REV. 375 (1999).

5. **Mediation and Confidentiality.** Another issue in relation to mediation and domestic violence is the question of confidentiality. In some jurisdictions, if the mediation is unsuccessful, the mediator will make a report and perhaps a recommendation to the court. What risks do you see here given that mediation involves one party's unproven allegations against the other? Mediators are not investigators; they rely on the parties for information. Carol J. King, *Burdening Access to Justice: The Cost of Divorce Mediation on the Cheap,* 73 ST. JOHN'S L. REV. 375 (1999).

Confidentiality becomes an issue in another way also: victims who would otherwise be unwilling to share certain information may be induced to share it with the mediator. This information might include allegations of abuse or other information that the victim had given to the mediator. Even if the mediator never explicitly refers to the information, the abuser may be able to deduce from other aspects of the mediation that it has been disclosed. Furthermore, in some states, including California, the parties are entitled to cross-examine the mediator if he or she makes a recommendation. If the abusive party chooses to cross-examine the mediator, any information that the victim thought had been revealed confidentially is likely to come out. Similarly, if the batterer chooses not to cross-examine the mediator, the victim may want to do so, depending on the mediator's recommendation. The victim's decision to examine the mediator makes it more likely that the abuser will also, even if initially disinclined to do so. All of this may put the victim at risk. See Alana Dunnigan, *Restoring Power to the Powerless,* 37 U.S.F.L. REV. 1031 (2003). Do you think that California has dealt adequately with these risks? Is there any way to create safeguards against them in a mediation program?

6. **Screening for Domestic Violence.** One of the most difficult aspects of mediating domestic relations disputes is whether and how to screen for domestic violence. Some states, like Alabama, provide that custody or visitation cases involving domestic violence cannot be sent to mediation. Ala. Code § 6–6–20 (2006). In other states, the court has more discretion as to whether to allow mediation of domestic violence cases or not. For, example, in Maine the relevant statute provides that before hearing a contested custody case, the court "shall" refer the parties to mediation, but that this requirement may be waived "for extraordinary cause shown." 19–A M.R.S.A. § 251 (2006). Either of these approaches places the burden of showing the domestic violence on the victim of the violence. Can you think of reasons why she might be reluctant to undertake that showing? Indeed, fewer than 5% of cases are excluded from mediation due to domestic violence. Jennifer P. Maxwell, *Mandatory Mediation of Custody in the Face of Domestic Violence,* 37 FAM. & CONCIL. CTS. REV. 335 (1999). The two excerpts that follow offer different approaches to screening for domestic violence prior to mediation.

Carol J. King

Burdening Access to Justice: The Cost of Divorce Mediation on the Cheap

73 ST. JOHN'S L. REV. 375 (1999).

... This Article presents the findings of a new empirical research project examining three different models of divorce mediation in three different Ohio court systems (the "Descriptive Study"). All of the court systems studied encouraged settlement of contested custody cases, but each court approached this goal in different ways. In both the Toledo (Lucas County) and Columbus (Franklin County) metropolitan areas, divorcing parents were encouraged to resolve child custody issues by participation in face-to-face negotiations guided by a trained mediator. . . .

[A] Columbus mediation program coordinator individually screened litigants to determine whether or not to recommend mediation. Mediation was thought to be contraindicated in cases with histories of severe domestic violence, child abuse, and chronic drug and alcohol abuse. In practice, very few cases were found to be unsuitable for participation in mediation. . . . Many of the custody disputes sent to mediation did involve spousal abuse issues. The Descriptive Study does not confirm the fears of critics that battered women, in general, are detrimentally impacted by participation in mediation. Overall, 58.7% of the respondents, including 20% of the men, reported violence in the home ranging from some to a great deal. Of the women, 26.7% reported high levels of domestic violence before the divorce. . . . Of the women reporting very high levels of abuse, 90% felt they had the opportunity to tell their side of the story in mediation. Also, 70% stated that it was their choice to go to mediation, although half felt pressured to attend. Similarly, 70% said they participated thoroughly in the mediated discussions, and 60% did not feel hurried in the process. Half the abused women reported that the discussions focused on problem-solving, 30% were undecided, and 20% disagreed. In addition, 70% said discussion of the issues was thorough, and 80% felt the mediator conducted the sessions fairly. Furthermore, 60% disagreed or strongly disagreed with the statement that they felt pressured to settle in mediation. There was also no correlation between satisfaction with the outcome and the presence of domestic violence in the home. Of the women reporting high levels of family violence, 60% were encouraged by their attorneys to use mediation, and 40% of these women said mediation helped them reach settlement on contested issues. Overall, women who came from very violent homes reported slightly more favorable impressions towards mediation than women reporting a range of none to moderately high levels of domestic abuse. These differences, however, were statistically insignificant.

Process satisfaction reports from domestic violence victims using mediation compared favorably with similar measures relating to attorney-negotiated settlements. In the group of women who reported high levels of violence and who did not mediate, 63.6% disagreed or strongly disagreed with the statement that they participated thoroughly in the discussions.

More women reported feeling pressure to settle outside mediation than in mediation.

The Descriptive Study's findings are consistent with prior reports that found no correlation between the existence of domestic violence and satisfaction with or pressure to settle in mediation. One study found that 45% of abused women, and 40% of women reporting no abuse, felt empowered by mediation.

Impasse is more common in domestic violence cases, indicating that walking away from the table, rather than giving in, is often the reaction to power imbalances. To date, research provides no strong empirical support for policies fostering the blanket exclusion of all domestic violence cases from mediation. Some cases, however, do present significant power imbalances that can cause bargaining inequality. Moreover, mediation in some domestic violence cases can endanger the victim's safety by facilitating the abuser's access to her. Physical abuse is not the only factor that can lead to bargaining imbalances, and thus, the presence or absence of domestic violence is too crude a screening measure for evaluating mediation programs. Instead, mediators must assess the parties' ability to meaningfully engage in negotiations on a case by case basis. Parties should be able to opt out of mediation when there is cause for concern. Additionally, mediation programs can screen for significant power imbalances, address safety issues, provide training on domestic violence issues, use shuttle negotiation instead of direct party negotiation where indicated, and provide victims with information about community resources.

Pearson v. District Court

Supreme Court of Colorado, 1996.
924 P.2d 512.

■ JUSTICE SCOTT delivered the Opinion of the Court.

The trial court ordered the petitioner, Karen K. Pearson, n/k/a Karen K. Sanders (Sanders), and her former husband, Scott R. Pearson (Pearson), to mediate disputes raised in post-dissolution of marriage proceedings. Sanders, the petitioner before us and in the dissolution proceedings below, seeks relief from the respondent trial court's orders mandating mediation. The [case] turns on whether section 13–22–311 permits a court to refer a case to mediation where one party claims it has been the victim of abuse. Because we conclude the statutory provision expressly limits a trial court's referral authority when a party claims he or she has been subjected to abuse, we make the rule absolute. Accordingly, we direct the trial court to vacate its orders for mediation.

In 1990, the trial court entered its decree of dissolution terminating the marriage of Sanders and Pearson. By that decree, Sanders was granted sole custody of their two minor children, while Pearson was granted rights to parenting time with the children....

In March 1995, Pearson filed a motion to modify his parenting time rights.... By order dated October 10, 1995, the trial court directed the parties to obtain mediation services to resolve the dispute regarding parenting time.... On October 30, 1995, Sanders filed a motion to reconsider. In support of her motion to reconsider, Sanders claimed that "during the course of the marriage [Pearson] was physically and emotionally abusive. During the latter four years of the marriage, there were numerous incidents of physical violence." Sanders further asserted that prior to the termination of their marriage, one "incident involved [Pearson] hitting [Sanders] and throwing her against a wall" resulting in injury to Sanders, including a bruised eye and a partially torn bicep. Sanders' motion stated that, as a result, Pearson was charged and convicted of assault and domestic violence. According to her motion, Sanders now "suffers severe anxiety episodes when interacting" with her former husband and "shake[s] uncontrollably" when in his presence....

IV

Section 13–22–311(1) grants the trial court authority to order mediation. That statute provides in pertinent part:

> Any court of record may, in its discretion, refer any case for mediation services or dispute resolution programs ... *except that the court shall not refer the case to mediation services or dispute resolution programs where one of the parties claims that it has been the victim of physical or psychological abuse by the other party and states that it is thereby unwilling to enter into mediation services* or dispute resolution programs. In addition, the court may exempt from referral any case in which a party files with the court, within five days of a referral order, a motion objecting to mediation and demonstrating compelling reasons why mediation should not be ordered. Compelling reasons may include, but are not limited to, that the costs of mediation would be higher than the requested relief and previous attempts to resolve the issues were not successful....

The generally accepted and familiar meaning of "shall" indicates that this term is mandatory.... Section 13–22–311(1) permits a court, "in its discretion," to refer a case to mediation "except that the court shall *not* refer the case to mediation services ... where one of the parties *claims* that it has been the victim of physical or psychological abuse by the other party and states that it is thereby unwilling to enter into mediation services...." (Emphasis added.) The plain and obvious statutory language forbids a court from ordering mediation where a party claims physical and psychological abuse.

In the present case, Sanders filed a verified, uncontroverted claim of physical and psychological abuse by Pearson and established an unwillingness to participate in mediation. Under the circumstances asserted here, the trial court "shall not refer" such a case to mediation.

Respondent contends that a party may be excused from mediation in only two situations: (1) when a party files a declaration of abuse and an unwillingness to participate in mediation *prior* to the entry of a court order to mediate; or (2) when a party, within five days of entry of a court order to mediate, files a motion demonstrating compelling reasons why mediation should not be ordered, the trial court may, in its discretion, rescind the order. Initially, we note that nothing in section 13–22–311 requires a party to anticipate a mediation order. Petitioner asserts and respondent does not dispute that the trial court entered its orders referring the dispute to mediation *sua sponte*. While the question of whether a court may *sua sponte* refer a matter to mediation is not before us, when seeking excusal from mediation for physical or psychological abuse, a party need not file a declaration of abuse prior to the entry of a mediation order. Regarding the second situation, we find no basis in the statute to uphold such a five-day rule where a party claims physical or psychological abuse.

Respondent argues that the trial court was not obligated to review Sanders' motion to reconsider mediation orders because it was filed more than five days after the entry of the mediation order. However, section 13–22–311(1) covers two distinct circumstances. First, section 13–22–311(1) contains a mandatory command that a court "shall not refer" a case to mediation services where a party claims physical or psychological abuse. This requirement contains no time limitations. Therefore, so long as a court receives notice of such a claim, a party that alleges abuse shall not be referred to mediation. . . .

Second, in cases where a party does not claim abuse, section 13–22–311(1) provides a distinct procedure for excusal from mediation. Section 13–22–311(1) provides that "[i]n addition, the court may exempt from referral any case in which a party files with the court, within five days of a referral order, a motion objecting to mediation and demonstrating compelling reasons why mediation should not be ordered." The use of the phrase "in addition" and the word "may" show the General Assembly's intent to establish a separate and alternative method for excusal from mediation that applies only in situations where the mandatory excusal for abuse is not triggered. The discretionary "compelling reasons" excusal, subject to the five-day rule, exists independently of the mandatory excusal for physical or psychological abuse.

V

. . . Accordingly, we direct the trial court to vacate its orders for mediation. . . .

NOTES AND QUESTIONS

1. **Evidence of Domestic Violence.** In *Pearson*, the Court accepted a verified, uncontroverted claim of violence as sufficient evidence to divert the case from mediation under Colorado law. Do you agree that this should be a sufficient basis for avoiding mediation that would otherwise be mandatory? In California, where mediation is mandatory but the process of mediation varies depending on whether there has been domestic violence, the Court Rules suggest that mediators consider the following in screening for domestic violence: 1) the presence of a protective order, 2) the pleadings and other court papers, 3) telephone interviews, 4) intake forms, and 5)information from attorneys, shelters, hospital reports, Child Protective

Services, police reports, or criminal record checks. The Court Rule requires asking questions to ascertain information on the following: 1) the date of separation, 2) the frequency and severity of the violence, 3) specific incidents of past and recent violence, 4) the identities of children and others exposed to or present during incidents of violence, and 5) fears of future violence. Cal. Rules of Court, Rule 5.215 (2006). Which screening system do you think is preferable in domestic violence cases, California's or Colorado's? Do you think that the differences in the level of screening could be related to the fact that Colorado does not require mediation of cases in which there has been violence while California does? Can you think of other sources of information that you think would be important in screening for domestic violence prior to mediation?

2. **Mandatory Mediation.** As should be clear to you by now, California requires mediation of child custody or visitation cases. Cal. Family Code § 3170 (2004). Approximately 10 other states also require, as opposed to permit, mediation of child custody or visitation cases, but all of these other states exempt couples whose relationship has involved domestic violence, at least under some circumstances. Given the readings above, including the findings from the study described in Carol King's article, do you think it is necessary to provide for exemption of some domestic violence cases from mandatory mediation or can the mediation process be adjusted to accommodate those cases successfully?

If you think that some exemption is necessary, how would you draft a statute or a rule providing for the exemption? Delaware exempts from mediation cases in which one of the parties has been found by a court to have committed an act of domestic violence against the other or in which one party has obtained a protective order against the other. 13 Del. Code 711A (2006). Should an exemption be available only if a court has already found that there was domestic violence? Florida exempts from mediation cases in which the court finds "a history of domestic violence that would compromise the mediation process." Fla. Stat. § 44–102 (2005). Are more cases likely to go to mediation under the Florida statute or the Delaware statute? Which provision do you think is preferable? Furthermore, the Florida statute requires that the exemption consideration be initiated by a motion or request of a party. Are there reasons why a victim of domestic violence might not make such a request? On the other hand, given the varying levels of severity of domestic violence and the differing effects that it can have on its targets, is an automatic exemption from mediation for cases involving domestic violence desirable? What do you think of the Alaska law quoted below?

> The court may not order or refer parties to mediation in a divorce proceeding if a protective order ... is in effect. The court may not order or refer parties to mediation if a party objects on the grounds that domestic violence has occurred between the parties.... If the court proposes or suggests mediation under this subsection,
>
> (1) mediation may not occur unless the victim of the alleged domestic violence agrees to the mediation; and

(2) the court shall advise the parties that each party has the right to not agree to mediation and that the decision of each party will not bias other decisions of the court. Alaska Stat. § 25.24.060 (2005).

3. **Mediation and the Reprivatization of Domestic Violence.** As we have seen, concepts of family privacy traditionally protected against state intervention when there was domestic violence. This left victims of violence, usually women, at the mercy of their abusers. The recent criminalization of intimate violence and the development of protective orders recognizes that this violence is not just a private matter for the couple to resolve but that it has public policy implications, including recognition of women's equality with men. Elizabeth M. Schneider, *The Synergy of Equality and Privacy in Women's Rights*, 2002 U. CHI. LEGAL F. 137. Alana Dunnigan argues that mediation reprivatizes domestic violence and that this reprivatization has negative consequences:

> The danger of taking a serious social problem like domestic violence out of public discourse and hiding it in the corners of mediation rooms is that it minimizes the importance of the problem and operates as a setback to the movements of the 1970s that brought the private family problem of abuse into public scrutiny. One critic cautions that "the privatization of domestic violence through mediation can ... diminish[] the judicial development and vindication of legal rights for disadvantaged groups such as battered women." A mandatory mediation policy, with no exemptions for battered women, gives the State imprimatur to treat domestic violence as a peripheral issue that is not important enough to justify spending precious court time or money remedying. One commentator remarked: When public matters are funneled into [mediation], the American people lose, among other things, the opportunity to vindicate and develop the legal rights of the oppressed. But most importantly, it is American society itself that must bear the burden of knowing that it and its institutions are turning their backs on those segments of the population most in need of protection. Alana Dunnigan, *Restoring Power to the Powerless*, 37 U.S.F.L. REV. 1031 (2003).

Do you agree with Dunnigan? In what ways does mediation reprivatize domestic violence? Is this reprivatization problematic only when there are no exemptions for battered women from the mediation requirement or is it also a problem if victims of violence must claim and prove the violence in order to obtain an exemption from mediation?

D. PARENTAL EDUCATION PROGRAMS WHEN THERE HAS BEEN DOMESTIC VIOLENCE

Over the last 30 years or so family law courts have begun to require divorcing families to attend parental education programs.

Interest in parent education programs is spurred by several factors. One is the growing recognition of the long-term implications of postdivorce parental conflict for both families and courts. Parental conflict is often intense after divorce and has been identified in previous studies as a cause of postdivorce litigation; nonpayment of child support; visitation disputes; nonvisitation by the noncustodial parent; and poor child adjustment to divorce. Parent education programs represent a new approach—a preventive approach—to such problems. By focusing on the postdivorce needs of children and the consequences of parental conflict, these programs strive to reach parents before full-scale disputes emerge. Sanford L. Braver, Peter Salem, Jessica Pearson, and Stephanie R. DeLuse, *The Content of Divorce Education Programs: Results of a Survey*, 34 FAM. & CONCIL. CTS. REV. 41 (1996).

Parent education programs focus on teaching parents to reduce the conflict to which their children might be exposed after divorce. Their curricula usually aim to inform parents of the significant negative effects that divorce-related conflict can have on children. One theory that underlies these programs is that it is not the divorce itself that is harmful to children, but rather the conflict that children witness as a result of the divorce. Parent education programs strive to teach parents to communicate better and more easily with each other, not to put the children in the middle of the parents' disagreements, and not to denigrate each other in the presence of the children.

One study described a widely-used program, Children in the Middle (CIM), in the following manner:

CIM covered divorce information, communication skills, and parenting skills. Divorce information included effects of divorce on preschool, elementary school, and adolescent children; described the difficulties of single and long-distance parenting; and described how reduced conflict and high-quality parenting can improve child adjustment. In addition, CIM focused on specific parenting skills, such as keeping children out of the middle of parental conflict (e.g., children not carrying messages, parents not "putting down" the other parent, parents not involving children in money problems, and parents not using children to spy on the other parent). CIM also included training and practice in communication skills, including using nonthreatening "I" messages, discussing one topic at a time, and staying on the topic.

Kevin M. Kramer, Jack Arbuthnot, Donald A. Gordon, Nicholas J. Rousis and Joann Hoza, *Effects of Skill–Based Versus Information– Based Divorce Education Programs on Domestic Violence and Parental Communication*, 36 FAM. & CONCIL. CTS. REV. 5 (1998)

Some parent education programs focus more on conveying information about the effects of conflict on children while others focus more on teaching parents the skills to avoid engaging in battle in front of the children. Most parent education programs meet only once or twice for a total of anywhere between one and four hours.

There are more than 1,500 parent education programs in existence now in counties across the country. At least eleven states require divorcing families to participate in some form of parent education. Other states, and some individual county programs, make participation voluntary. Surprisingly, although parent education programs have been in existence now for approximately two decades, there are few good studies of their effectiveness in reducing parental conflict, particularly in front of children. Most evaluations of these programs rely on parental self-reports. Very few have obtained data on the effects on children by actually studying the children or by interviewing third parties like teachers or therapists who might be able to provide information. Similarly, many do not include comparison groups. The studies that do exist indicate high levels of parental satisfaction with the programs, but their effectiveness in reducing levels of conflict is less clear.

One review of studies of particular programs concluded that there is "some evidence that the Children in the Middle program [described above] influences interparental conflict, but only a sparse amount of evidence to suggest that other parenting programs affect interparental conflict." Matthew Goodman, Darya Bonds, Irwin Sandler and Sanford Braver, *Parent Psychoeducational Programs and Reducing the Negative Effects of Interparental Conflict Following Divorce*, 42 FAM. CT. REV. 263 (2004). Another review of several studies found that parents in the two programs studied were less likely to report interparental conflict around the children than parents in comparison groups. This same review found that participating parents in a third study returned to court for modifications of the terms of the divorce and custody less frequently than those in the comparison group. Finally, the review noted that three other studies of parent education programs indicated that the three programs had no effect on reducing levels of interparental conflict, on improving parent-child relations or on assisting the parents in dealing with the effects of the divorce. Jeffrey T. Cookston, Sanford Braver, Irwin Sandler and M. Toni Genalo, *Prospects for Expanded Parent Education Services for Divorcing Families with Children*, 40 FAM. CT. REV. 190 (2002). For an even more recent, but equally skeptical, evaluation of parent education programs, see John H. Grych, *Interparental Conflict as a Risk Factor for Child Maladjustment*, 43 FAM. CT. REV. 97 (2005).

Advocates of parent education programs usually focus on the effects on children of exposure to parents' post-divorce conflict. They hope that this conflict can be reduced by parent education programs. In order to accomplish this, they support programs that focus on trying to induce parents to cooperate with one another, to rebuild the trust between them, and to facilitate the children's relationship with the other parent. These types of objectives scare victims' advocates who are focused on victims' and children's safety and on separating the victim, physically and emotionally, from the abuser. As a result, there are often disagreements between those involved in providing services to victims of abuse and their families and those involved in parent education. These disagreements are summarized by Geri Fuhrmann and her colleagues in the following imaginary conversation:

> Parent Educator (PE): Your domestic violence service providers are throwing the baby out with the bath water. By boycotting programs and interfering with legislation that could mandate attendance, you are

depriving women of parts of the programs that are beneficial and applicable.

Domestic Violence Service Provider (DVSP): You people think all you are doing is teaching folks who just can't quite get along. Well, you know what? In those classrooms of yours, there are women who have been seriously abused and threatened and the men who are looking to abuse them again. I guarantee it.

PE: It's not the role of parent educators to evaluate the participants. We have enough respect for the parents in our audiences to let them rise to the occasion and take the pieces of what we teach that are best for their children and use what works for them in their particular situations.

DVSP: You tell women who've been beaten and threatened that they're supposed to cooperate with the men who beat and threatened them. That's a really great idea! Then you tell them that if they don't cooperate they are going to hurt their children.

PE: Unlike the domestic violence community, parent educators do not assume that the alleged victim is telling the truth. She is telling her truth, and there are two sides to the story.

DVSP: Oh good! Don't you see how you undermine the victim when you tell her that her version of reality may be all wrong? In her mind, you're siding with her abuser, just like everybody else. Batterers can be very charming—and very believable. And no one knows that better than the victim.

PE: Domestic violence service providers place such strong emphasis on the victim's role, like it's the sole role as parent. Parent educators strive to treat parents as equally important contributors to their children's well-being.

DVSP: You treat men who beat their wives just like men who are model husbands and fathers. Everybody gets contact with their kids. With you, "no" is never an option.

PE: The domestic violence service community often assumes that what is best for women is best for children and, consequently, you put women's needs before kids' needs even if that means no contact with Dad.

DVSP: You tell a woman to go sit in the same room with the man who threatened her life. There's another of your great ideas!

They conclude by saying, "Though each participant in this mock battle has taken some cheap shots, each side has also contributed something very important that the other side needs to hear and understand. As with all stereotypes, there are grains of truth in the epithets hurled above. To move beyond the impasse between the two communities, parent educators must address the appropriate concerns raised by domestic violence service providers." Geri S.W. Fuhrmann, Joseph McGill and Mary O'Connell, *Parent Education's Second Generation*, 37 FAM. & CONCIL. CTS. REV. 24 (1999).

There are at least two ways to deal with the tension between those who are focused on the results of domestic violence and those who are focused on the need to educate parents about the effects of conflict and divorce on children. One possibility is to screen the participating population so that victims of abuse are excluded from attending the classes. This is problematic, as noted in the discussion about screening for mediation, because victims of domestic violence often do not self-identify and because, even if they do, they may not be able to meet the evidentiary burden for proving the violence. A second solution is to structure the parent education program so that attendance at the program is safe for victims and so that the messages are tempered by the knowledge that some in the class are victims of violence.

The following excerpt articulates some standards for increasing the safety of victims of domestic violence while attending parent education programs. Do you think these measures are sufficient?

Victoria L. Lutz and Cara E. Gady

Necessary Measures and Logistics to Maximize the Safety of Victims of Domestic Violence Attending Parent Education Programs

42 FAM. CT. REV. 363 (2004).

... A parent's safety when attending a parent education program must be ensured in many ways. Administrators of parent education programs should assume that classes will contain victims or perpetrators of domestic abuse because divorced or separated persons are subject to an unusually high rate of domestic violence, as compared to other marital statuses. The following logistical, administrative, and content-based requirements put the safety of domestic violence victims first, while ensuring the effectiveness of parent education programs for all attendees, regardless of their level of conflict.

NECESSARY MEASURES AND LOGISTICS REQUIRE THAT PARENTS ATTEND SEPARATE SESSIONS ON SEPARATE DAYS

Generally speaking, the optimal benefit of parent education programs is obtained when both parents attend the program, because both parents are usually involved in parenting. However, when there is domestic violence, victims need to be circumspect about coming into contact with the abusive parent to protect themselves and the physical and emotional health of their children.

The safety of victims must be secured by requiring that parents attend separate sessions on separate days.... Attendance at the same session should not be permitted even if parents express their desire to do so because there is no assurance that one parent's expressed desire to attend with the other parent is a voluntary choice rather than the coerced decision of an abused partner. Forcing cooperation by mandating concurrent attendance is not safe for victims of abuse and their children. Attempting to facilitate cooperation at an early point in separation or divorce proceedings by having parents attend the same presentation session is inappropriate, regardless of whether domestic violence is present, because partners are often engaged in litigation because of their inability to cooperate with one another. . . .

KEEP THE LOCATION OF PARENT EDUCATION CLASSES CONFIDENTIAL

There should be a presumption against any publication of logistical information about classes that would assist stalkers or batterers in knowing yet another place where their victims could be found. To practically implement this, the general location of the class may be disclosed in the program literature with the specific address communicated to the parent in a letter or other communication confirming enrollment. Additionally, information about the participants, such as the names and addresses of attendees, must be kept confidential to ensure that victims of domestic violence cannot be tracked by their abusers. . . .

TAKE SECURITY PRECAUTIONS

The following security precautions should be taken:

Have security on the premises, at the sign up desk, and within earshot of the participants. . . . Conduct classes in a courthouse or at a hospital or college/university, where there is more of a public presence. . . . Security staff should also be trained to understand domestic violence and to ensure that they protect the confidentiality of attendees' names and addresses. Security staff should be aware of and vigilant in watching out for the high risk factors of domestic violence. . . .

STANDARDS AT EACH SESSION

. . . Even where there are screening and/or waiver provisions, victims and perpetrators of abuse will be present in parent education programs because many perpetrators and victims of abuse do not accurately self disclose or may choose to attend. . . . Therefore, information addressing the problem and repercussions of domestic abuse should be a standard part of parent education programs. For example, topics should include how battering affects family functioning and the obstacles faced by a battered mother in maintaining parental control, as well as the tendency of batterers to distort course concepts for their own purposes by using insights from parent education as excuses to criticize the mother's parenting skills rather than to examine their own. Domestic violence information must be available at each class to help parents self identify and ensure that victims and perpetrators are aware that their violent situation means that some parenting approaches and ways of interacting are more appropriate for them than others.

To help victims and perpetrators of domestic violence accurately self identify, parent education programs must give an accurate definition of domestic violence to all attendees, focusing on power, control, and the different forms of abuse. . . . [P]arent education programs must not support the agendas of the abusers in the class by ignoring domestic violence. Programs must promote dialogue about domestic violence to reduce the risk of abuse to victims and children by enabling victims and perpetrators to self identify and access resources....

Educators should provide frequent reminders that parts of the program are not appropriate for domestic violence victims because some generally recommended methods of parenting are inappropriate when there is abuse. For example, during discussions regarding negotiation as an alternative to litigation, educators should encourage parents to understand that victims of domestic violence must talk to their attorneys about their abusive situation and evaluate whether a victim of domestic violence can ever be on equal grounds with an abuser during a negotiation proceeding. Additionally, educators should advise against anger management as a technique to end domestic violence; because domestic violence is not the result of anger, anger management will not work to curtail it.

Attendees should be informed that a number of children benefit from divorce and custody battles in situations of domestic violence because the divorce releases children from the toxic environment of abuse. Similarly, during discussions comparing cooperative parenting to parallel parenting, all attendees should be informed that parallel parenting is more appropriate than cooperative parenting in high conflict relationships or in relationships where there is a history of domestic violence because of the need to avoid face to face encounters. Parallel parenting (parenting autonomously and separately) contrasts sharply with cooperative parenting (working together and communicating). If a victim of domestic violence hears from the parent educator that the goal is for parents to cooperate, achieving this goal might jeopardize his or her safety and that of the children. Yet to not pursue that goal would suggest that the victim is a less than model parent.... Every statement and every message at parent education programs must be viewed through the eyes of a victim of domestic violence and adapted to ensure that the wrong message is not inadvertently delivered. Additionally, program materials should not contain any messages that may make victims feel as though they must attempt to cooperate and continue in an abusive relationship for the sake of their children.

ALL PRESENTERS SHOULD BE EDUCATED IN THE DYNAMICS OF DOMESTIC VIOLENCE

... To provide safe and effective parent education, all educators should be trained in the dynamics of domestic violence, because it is inevitable that many of the parents they educate will be victims or perpetrators.... Educators must also be aware that domestic violence is control instigated violence, not conflict instigated violence, and is therefore rooted in learned behavior that parent education programs are very unlikely to affect.... Furthermore, educators must be trained to understand that actions that are discouraged for parents in general, such as litigation, might be optimal when there is domestic violence....

Educators must presume that victims and perpetrators of domestic violence are attendees at each class and exercise the same care for them and their children as for other attendees by understanding their situation and educating them accordingly.

NOTES AND QUESTIONS

1. **Special Focus Parent Education Programs.** Lutz and Gady advocate changing the nature of parent education programs so that they are appropriate for victims of violence and for abusers. Would it be a better idea to have specialized parent education programs that were aimed only at victims of violence or only at abusers?

2. **Managing Intractable Conflict After Divorce.** Most parent education programs involve only a very limited number of sessions, although some programs are now experimenting with a dozen or more sessions spread out over months. Matthew Goodman, Darya Bonds, Irwin Sandler and Sanford Braver, *Parent Psychoeducational Programs and Reducing the Negative Effects of Interparental Conflict Following Divorce*, 42 FAM. CT. REV. 263 (2004). Are programs that last only a few hours likely to be able to achieve their goals, including conveying how to modify the recommendations in situations in which there has been violence?

Another option for managing long-term conflict is a parent coordinator. Parent coordinator positions have only come into existence in the last decade or so, but more than a dozen states, including California, Massachusetts, North Carolina, and Ohio, authorize them. Parent coordinators are appointed by courts to manage the difficult issues around the implementation of family court orders relating to custody and child support in "high conflict" cases. Thus, parent coordinators are generally expected to resolve issues relating to court ordered time sharing arrangements, transportation, exchange of the child, a child's extra-curricular activities, etc. Parents who are in high levels of conflict with each other over this type of issue can meet together or separately with the parent coordinator. Sometimes "meetings" are done by telephone. The parents can also communicate *ex parte* with the coordinator; generally communications are not confidential. Parent coordinator positions were developed to help manage parental relations that involve unusual levels of conflict. In the absence of a parent coordinator, these couples resort frequently to the courts. Association of Family and Conciliation Courts (AFCC) Task Force on Parenting Coordination, *Parenting Coordination*, 41 FAM. CT. REV. 533 (2003).

"High conflict" can mean a variety of things. It can apply to couples with a high instance of motion filings in court, couples who "bad mouth" each other to the children, couples who think it is necessary to "win" all disagreements with their ex-spouses, couples whose relationships have been marked by physical violence and verbal abuse, or couples who engage in more than one of these behavior patterns. Do you think that parent coordinators will be more successful in dealing with couples in which one partner has been physically abusive to the other or with couples who are trying to "win" in every disagreement with a spouse? Why? Where there has been or may have been domestic violence, what training should a parent coordinator have? What concerns would you have about an official whose job it is to resolve disputes between the parents without considering a past history of abuse within the relationship?

CHAPTER TWELVE

DOMESTIC VIOLENCE AND THE CHILD PROTECTIVE SYSTEM

Introduction

This poem, written by a young client of the Children's Safety Project in New York, is reprinted in Bonnie Rabin, *Violence Against Mothers Equals Violence Against Children: Understanding the Connections,* 58 ALB. L. REV. 1109 (1995).

I am 17 years old

I live in a group home

I've been here for 3 years

My step-father used to beat up my mother

And he used to rape me

He didn't touch my little brothers

But he made them feel like shit

Calling them faggots assholes and shitheads

One night he beat my mother real bad

She was laying on the floor all curled up

She couldn't stop crying

She said "God give me the strength to leave him"

That's when I broke

I couldn't hold it no more

I told her he been raping me since I was 12

We both cried and screamed

She slept with me that night

He came home drunk but he left us alone

Next day she told me to tell the counselor at school

It got reported

BCW[1] told my mother she got to take us and leave

She said "How my going to do that I got nothing"

They took my brothers and me

They left my mother with him

They said my mother knew or should have

---

1. The Bureau of Child Welfare.

They said she was neglectful

She needed a lawyer they was charging her

We went to court so many times

Two of them she had a black eye

Nobody said nothing about that

They sent my brothers back home

Everybody acts like I'm the problem

Nobody did nothing to help my mother

It became them against me

Should have been us against him

I know in my heart

Give my mother a place to be with her kids

She would leave him for good

Tell them that

NOTES AND QUESTIONS

1.   **Understanding This Poem.** The villain of this piece is the Bureau of Child Welfare, New York's child welfare agency. "It became them against me," says the poem's author, referring to the agency's decision to separate her from her family, and place her in a group home, where she has lived from the age of 14 to the age of 17. When she says, "Should have been us against him," she expresses her conviction that what the agency *should* have done was to set limits with the father who sexually abused her, physically abused her mother, and emotionally abused her brothers, and protect the rest of the family from him. As the story ends, her mother and brothers are still vulnerable to the father's abuse, and she is deprived of her mother's support and of her relationships with her brothers.

How did things go wrong? This chapter explores this question. As the poet describes it, the involvement of the child welfare agency was prompted by a report from a teacher to whom the poet had revealed the abuse. The teacher would have had no choice in the matter; teachers are commonly mandated to report child abuse that comes to their attention. The Bureau of Child Welfare reacted by giving the mother a Hobson's choice—if she did not leave the father, taking the children with her, they would hold her responsible for the abuse. There was apparently no helpful response to her question: "How my going to do that I got nothing?" Nor was there any consideration, apparently, of a different strategy—that the mother should stay put, while the father was required to leave. The mother was then charged with neglect, and the children taken away. Indeed, having decided that the children were at risk, and having failed to provide the mother with either an alternative place to take them, or a way of keeping the father away from them, the agency was in a sense forced to bring charges—to provide a legal basis for the removal. In the subsequent legal proceedings, the focus remained stubbornly on the child who had been abused; no one was looking at the mother's black eyes, or asking whether the child could be protected by first protecting the mother.

As you will see in this chapter, child protective workers are faced with a number of complicated decisions to which there may be no obvious answer. Domestic violence is, as indicated in Chapter Ten, frequently accompanied by some risk of injury—physical or psychological—to children in the family. However, removal of children from the family is not without risks also. Furthermore, children in foster care are significantly more likely to be abused than children in the population in general. Furthermore, there is a question of whether some acts that remove children from the home in domestic violence situations might violate the parental rights of the non-violent parent. Finally, there is always the question of whether the same objective—child safety in a non-violent environment—might be achieved by some means other than removing the child. For example, can the abuser be removed from the situation effectively?

2. **The Risks to Children from Living in Families in Which One Parent Abuses the Other.** As we have already seen in Chapter Ten during our discussion of parental custody battles, if a child lives in a family setting in which there is domestic violence between the adults, that child is likely to suffer also. Approximately half of those who abuse their intimate partners also abuse their children. Even children who are not directly abused by their mothers' abusers are likely to suffer trouble in school, trouble making friends, regressive or other inappropriate behavior, or even PTSD as a result of the violence in their homes. Finally, some children are injured when they try to intervene in the violence to protect their mothers from its full effects. See Judith G. Greenberg, *Domestic Violence and the Danger of Joint Custody Presumptions*, 25 N. ILL. U. L. REV. 403 (2005).

Despite widespread agreement that many abusers put both their children as well as their adult targets at risk, the physical injuries to children may not be serious. Studies in both Connecticut and New York City show that police rarely charge abusers in domestic violence cases with injury to their children. Evan Stark has noted, "the rate of harm to children that rises to the level of abuse in domestic violence cases (between 3% and 4%) is only slightly higher than the rate in the general population, (about 2.5% ...), and less than the comparable risk in foster families (about 5% ...)." Evan Stark, *The Battered Mother in the Child Protective Service Caseload: Developing an Appropriate Response*, 23 WOMEN'S RTS. L. REP. 107 (2002).

3. **The Risks to Children of Living in Foster Care.** As indicated above, life in foster care is not without its own risks to children. Once moved to foster care, the majority of children remain there for more than a year. Adults who have spent time in foster care experience high rates of PTSD, depression, panic syndrome, and anxiety disorders. Rates of physical abuse, sexual abuse, and neglect are higher among foster families than among other families. See Clare Huntington, *Rights Myopia in Child Welfare*, 53 UCLA L. REV. 637 (2006). This means that child welfare workers are constantly faced with the need to balance the possible risks of

injury to children in families in which there is domestic violence with the risks to children in foster care.

4. **Options Other Than Removal to Foster Care.** What other options do child protective workers have aside from removing the child from the home or leaving the child in the home? How effective do you think it would be to require the mother to obtain a protective order against the abuser? Suppose she does not want to seek such an order? What about the option of seeking criminal charges against the abuser? How likely is this actually to remove him from the home? What other options might the child protective worker have?

5. **Introduction to the *Nicholson* Case.** The next excerpt is from *Nicholson v. Williams,* 203 F.Supp.2d 153 (E.D.N.Y. 2002). In this case, a number of plaintiffs, ultimately certified as a class for class action purposes, challenged the policy of New York City's Administration for Children's Services (ACS) of automatically removing children on the grounds of neglect from homes in which there was domestic violence. Can you see why, given the overlap between domestic violence and child abuse, ACS may have decided to use the presence of domestic violence as an indicator of child abuse? Do you think this was warranted?

Different opinions in the *Nicholson* case are excerpted or discussed at various points in this chapter. The excerpt immediately below describes the facts of the case to give you a feel for ACS's policy. The District Court found this policy to be unconstitutional. The portion of the opinion analyzing the policy's constitutionality is discussed below. That decision was appealed to the United States Court of Appeals for the Second Circuit which in turn certified to the New York Court of Appeals the question of whether New York law authorized such a policy. A portion of the New York Court of Appeals opinion is provided in Section B. Some of the opinions in the *Nicholson* litigation are extremely lengthy, thus you have only very brief excerpts here.

The remaining sections of this chapter discuss the processes of child removal and termination of parental rights, removal policies in situations where there is domestic violence, constitutional issues raised by these removal policies, criminal actions against victims of domestic violence whose children may be endangered by the violence, and interactions between child protective services workers and domestic violence advocates.

Nicholson v. Williams

United States District Court for the Eastern District of New York, 2002.
203 F.Supp.2d 153.

Background

Sharwline Nicholson is a thirty-two year old working mother of two. For the past two years, Ms. Nicholson has both worked full-time as a cashier at Home Depot and taken classes full-time at Mercy College, where she is pursuing a degree in Behavioral Sciences. While she manages this busy schedule, Ms. Nicholson has made arrangements for her children to be cared for. When she is working, her son is in school and her daughter is at day care. When she is at school, she takes her son with her and leaves her daughter with a baby-sitter. Ms. Nicholson has lived at the same address in Brooklyn for the past seven years.

This plaintiff has always been a single mother. Ms. Nicholson's son, Kendell Coles, is eight years old. His father has never been a part of his life. Ms. Nicholson's daughter, Destinee Barnett, is three years old. Destinee's father, Mr. Barnett, never lived with Ms. Nicholson but traveled from his home in South Carolina to visit with Ms. Nicholson and Destinee on a monthly basis for the first nine months of Destinee's life.

Prior to an attack by Mr. Barnett on Ms. Nicholson in 1999, ACS [Administration for Children's Services] had only had contact with Ms. Nicholson once before [as a result of Mr. Barnett's having struck Kendell in the face]. . . .

b. Domestic Violence Against Ms. Nicholson

Early in 1999, during one of his visits, Ms. Nicholson told Mr. Barnett that she was breaking off their relationship. . . . Mr. Barnett, who had never previously assaulted or threatened Ms. Nicholson, flew into a rage. He punched her, kicked her, and threw objects at her. When he left, her head was bleeding profusely.

Throughout the assault, Destinee was in her crib in another room. Kendell was at school. After the attack, Mr. Barnett left the apartment. Her head bleeding, Ms. Nicholson called 911. Before the ambulance arrived, Ms. Nicholson asked her neighbor, Anna Thomas, a baby-sitter who[m] Ms. Nicholson had relied on in the past, to care for her children while she was away at the hospital. Anna agreed to pick up Kendell at his bus stop when he returned from school.

At the Kings County emergency room, CAT scans and X-rays revealed that Ms. Nicholson had suffered a broken arm, fractured ribs, and head injuries. . . .

c. Removal

On January 27, the same evening as the assault, the evening branch of ACS (ECS) directed the 70th Precinct to take Ms. Nicholson's children from the babysitter and to transport them to ECS. The children stayed that night in the nursery at ECS. The following day, January 28, an ACS worker called Ms. Nicholson at the hospital. The worker informed Ms. Nicholson that ACS had possession of her children and that if she wanted to see them she had to appear in court the following week. The worker refused to tell Ms. Nicholson where her children were. Ms. Nicholson testified that this news left her "very upset . . . [and] devastated." Ms. Nicholson demanded that the hospital discharge her immediately so that she could get more information about her children. She was discharged, but the hospital informed her that the police had left word that she was not to return to her apartment. Ms. Nicholson made arrangements to stay with a cousin. . . .

CPM Williams was assigned to oversee the Nicholson case.... CPM Williams testified that he believed that the children were in "imminent risk if they remained in the care of Ms. Nicholson because she was not, at that time, able to protect herself nor her children because Mr. Barnett had viciously beaten her."

CPM Williams [rejected Ms. Nicholson's suggestions as to cousins who might care for the children.] Instead, he decided to place the children in foster care with strangers.

d.   Court Proceedings

Although the children were placed in foster care by ACS on January 28, a Thursday, no petition was filed in court until February 2, the following Tuesday. Williams conceded that, as of January 28, he knew that the children were in ACS's care without legal authorization. He explained that ... in domestic violence cases, it is common to wait a few days before going to court in order to "try to work things out with the mother" ... [and that] after a few days of the children being in foster care, the mother will usually agree to ACS's conditions for their return without the matter ever going to court....

When the petition was filed with the Family Court on February 2—five days after ACS had seized the children—it was filed as a neglect petition against Ms. Nicholson as well as Mr. Barrett. CPM Williams testified that, as of the filing of the petition, he did not believe that Ms. Nicholson was actually neglectful; he hoped that "once she got before the Judge, that the Judge would order her to cooperate with realistic services to protect herself and the two children...." It was CPM Williams' belief that Ms. Nicholson was an inadequate guardian, because she was "refusing to deal with the reality of the situation" ... and that it would be unsafe for her to return to her Brooklyn residence with her children. Had he made inquiry, he would have learned that Mr. Barnett, the abuser, had never lived at the Brooklyn apartment with Ms. Nicholson, that he did not have a key to the apartment, and that he lived in South Carolina. Another basis for CPM Williams' attempted justification was that Ms. Nicholson had failed to follow ACS's instruction that she obtain an order of protection from a local police precinct. Ms. Nicholson had in fact attempted to do so, but had been denied an order because Mr. Barnett lived out of state and she did not know his address. She had informed CPM Williams of this fact.

The petition of neglect filed by ACS against Ms. Nicholson and Mr. Barnett included three allegations of neglect. The first count, directed solely against Mr. Barnett, alleged excessive corporal punishment. The second count, directed against both parents, alleged that "[r]espondents engage in acts of domestic violence in the presence of the subject child, Destinee. As a result of one such fight, on or about January 27, 1999, the respondent mother suffered a broken left arm and a head injury caused when the father struck her with a gun." This count made no distinction between the culpability of batterer and victim. The final count was directed solely against Ms. Nicholson, and alleged simply that she "fails to cooperate with offered services designed to insure the safety of the children." There were no specific indications of what services she had failed to cooperate with, or how any failure constituted neglect.

As she had been directed to do by ACS, Ms. Nicholson appeared at Family Court in Brooklyn on Tuesday, February 2.... The Family Court ordered the children remanded to the custody of ACS.... Ms. Nicholson testified that she was not even aware that this order was issued....

On February 4, after she had been separated from the children for a full week, Ms. Nicholson appeared in Family Court a second time, now represented by ... counsel. The Family Court ordered that Ms. Nicholson's children be paroled to her, on the condition that she and the children not return to Ms. Nicholson's address in Brooklyn, but instead live with her Bronx cousin.

On February 5, eight days since she had last been permitted to see or speak with her children, Ms. Nicholson was at last permitted by ACS to visit with them. The supervised visit occurred at the ACS foster agency in Queens. Ms. Nicholson was able to locate her daughter within the building by following the sounds of her crying. When Ms. Nicholson found her daughter she was "sitting on a chair by herself with tears running down." Destinee had a rash on her face, yellow pus running from her nose, and she appeared to have scratched herself. Her son had a swollen eye ... because the foster mother had slapped his face. Following Ms. Nicholson's report, ACS arranged for a different foster mother to have Ms. Nicholson's children. When the new foster mother arrived at the agency to take Ms. Nicholson's children at the end of the visit, her boy, Kendell, asked the new foster mother, "You are not going to hit me, are you?" ...

On February 18, twenty-one days after the separation and fourteen days after the Family Court had paroled Ms. Nicholson's children to her, ACS returned her children to her....

NOTES AND QUESTIONS

1. **Thinking about the Facts of _Nicholson_.** Why do you think ACS instituted a policy of removing children from homes in which there had been domestic violence? From what you learned in the chapter on family law about the effects of domestic violence on children, what are the risks to a child in a home in which there has been domestic violence? Were Ms. Nicholson's children exposed to these risks? In what ways are the factors to be considered in failure to protect cases different from in divorce and custody cases?

Why did case workers often wait a few days before filing papers with the court? Does strategic behavior on the part of caseworkers like those in this case make it more or less likely that survivors of domestic violence will seek out child protective service workers as their allies? Given the facts of this case, can you see why domestic violence survivors in custody battles with their abusers are often reluctant to mention the domestic violence?

2. **More on the Effects of Children's Exposure to Domestic Violence.** In _Nicholson_, the Court heard from a number of experts on the

effects on children of exposure to domestic violence. It concluded, "The consensus of the experts was that the children can be—but are not necessarily—negatively affected by witnessing domestic violence." *Nicholson v. Williams*, 203 F.Supp.2d 153 (E.D.N.Y.2002). Furthermore, the experts in front of the court disagreed about the long-term effects of children's exposure to adult intimate violence. For some children, there may be a long-term tendency to use violence in their own relationships in the future. Others may develop a pessimistic view of the world. But Evan Stark testified that studies show that many children, even if exposed to serious domestic violence will, after a relatively short period of time, test normal. According to him, "well over 80 percent, and sometimes over 90 percent, tested psychologically normal, were self-confident, had positive images of themselves, and were emotionally well off." Furthermore, he said, that even among children exposed to the most severe violence, "95 to 97 percent . . . do not become delinquent, do not develop alcohol or drug problems, and about 90 percent do not become violent adults." *Nicholson v. Williams*, 203 F.Supp.2d 153 (E.D.N.Y.2002).

Does this testimony undermine the ACS policy of automatically removing children from homes in which there is domestic violence? Does it equally undermine the policies beneath the statutes that create a presumption against giving custody to a batterer in a custody dispute between the child's parents?

For more detailed descriptions of the studies on which Evan Stark was relying, see Evan Stark, *The Battered Mother in the Child Protective Service Caseload*, 25 WOMEN'S RTS. L. REP. 107 (2002) and Evan Stark, *Nicholson v. Williams Revisited*, 82 DENV. U. L. REV. 691 (2005).

3. **Effects of Placing Children Who Have Been Exposed to Domestic Violence in Foster Care.** In *Nicholson*, the Court also heard from several experts who testified about the risks of foster care placement for children who have been exposed to domestic violence in their families of origin. Several witnesses testified to the importance of the parent-child bond to children in general and the anxiety that a child can feel when this is disrupted. One witness testified that the separation may be even more traumatic for a child exposed to domestic violence because the child may worry that " 'a parent might not be OK, may be injured, may be vulnerable. . . . They feel that they should somehow be responsible for the parent and if they are not with the parent, then it's their fault.' " *Nicholson v. Williams*, 203 F.Supp.2d 153 (E.D.N.Y.2002).

4. **Race, Ethnicity, and Foster Care Placement.** Studies of the rates of placement of children in foster care show that foster care systems in the United States disproportionately serve minority populations. One author wrote:

> "[A]t the end of 2002, Black individuals made up only 13 percent of the greater population, whereas they comprised 37 percent of the foster care population. The 1998 statistics for New York City show that 1 in every 22 Black children was in foster care, as compared with only 1 in every 385 white children. Another statistic showed that at the end of 1997, out of 42,000 children in the New York City child welfare system

only 1,300 (3 percent) were white." Beth A. Mandel, *The White Fist of the Child Welfare System*, 73 U. Cin. L. Rev. 1131 (2005).

Similarly, a federal study determined that "even when families have the same characteristics and lack of problems, African–American children, and Hispanic children to a lesser extent, are more likely than white children to be placed in foster care." Zanita E. Fenton, *Colorblind Must Not Mean Blind to the Realities Facing Black Children*, 26 B.C. Third World L.J. 81 (2006).

What explanations, other than overt racism, might account for these statistics? We'll return to the subject of the child protective system, foster care, and race at several additional points below.

A.   The Workings of the Child Welfare System

The following excerpt tracks the actual process by which a child abuse investigation is launched, legal proceedings initiated, and the "case" brought to resolution.

Amy Sinden
"Why Won't Mom Cooperate?": A Critique of Informality in Child Welfare Proceedings

11 Yale J.L. & Feminism 339 (1999).

The Anatomy of a Child Welfare Case

. . . [S]tate agencies typically employ hundreds of social workers to investigate reports of suspected child abuse and neglect and work with families when such reports are substantiated. These agency social workers usually serve as case managers, contracting with other private non-profit agencies to provide particular services, such as intensive social work or foster care.

The typical case proceeds as follows. First, a hotline administered by the child welfare agency receives an anonymous report of suspected child abuse or neglect. The agency then assigns a social worker to investigate the report. The social worker begins by knocking on the family's door and attempting to interview the parent and other adults that live in the household, as well as the child who is the subject of the report. If the child attends school, the social worker may go to the school to interview her. Depending on the nature of the allegations, the social worker may also talk to school personnel, medical providers, neighbors or others who may have relevant information.

Based on her investigation, the social worker then makes one of several decisions. She may determine that the alleged abuse or neglect did not occur and close the case. Or she may determine that it did occur but did not sufficiently endanger the child to warrant removing the child from the home. In that case she will usually seek to have the family placed under agency supervision to provide those social services she thinks will help to alleviate the problem she has identified. Or, if she determines that someone in the home has perpetrated abuse or neglect sufficient to endanger the safety of the child, she may seek to have the child removed from the family and placed in foster care.

Under any of these scenarios, the social worker can seek court intervention at various stages of the case if the parent does not accede voluntarily to the social worker's plan. If, when the social worker first knocks on the family's door, the parent refuses to let her in, refuses to talk to her, or refuses to allow her to talk privately with the child, the social worker may ask the agency's attorneys to file a petition seeking a court order compelling the parent to cooperate with the investigation. If the social worker completes her investigation and determines that the family needs agency supervision and services but the parent refuses to submit to supervision or cooperate with the provision of services, the social worker may ask the agency's attorneys to file a petition seeking court-ordered supervision of the family.

Finally, if the social worker concludes that the situation warrants the removal of the child from her parents, the social worker will try to accomplish this in one of two ways. First, she will try to convince the parent to sign a voluntary placement agreement. Such an agreement will typically authorize the state to keep the child in foster care for some specified amount of time (30 days to six months), at the expiration of which a court hearing will be scheduled to determine whether the placement should continue. Second, if the parent refuses to consent to placement, the social worker will seek to have the agency's attorneys petition the court to remove the child.

Child welfare agencies will often remove children from their homes on an emergency basis. All states authorize social workers (or in some instances police) to immediately remove children from their homes where they are deemed to be in imminent danger. In some states the social worker must first obtain an ex parte order from a judicial officer, and in others the social worker acts independently in making the initial removal decision. In either case, the court holds a preliminary hearing at which the parents are entitled to appear (often called a "detention" hearing) within a prescribed period of time, generally ranging from three days to six days, but sometimes as long as two weeks. At this hearing, the court addresses only the limited issue whether the evidence warrants holding the child in foster care until a full hearing can be held.

Once in court, and following any preliminary hearing on emergency removal, cases usually proceed in two phases. At the first phase, in some states termed the "adjudicatory" hearing, the court determines whether the allegations of abuse or neglect rise to a level warranting state interference with the parent-child relationship and, if so, whether they are true. If the court finds that the state has made a sufficient showing on these issues, it makes a finding to that effect, in some jurisdictions termed an "adjudication of dependency." If the court makes such a finding, it then moves on to the second phase, usually termed the "dispositional" hearing. At this hearing the court determines where the child should be placed. Choices may include leaving the child in the home with agency supervision and provision of services, placement in foster care, or placement with a relative or friend.

... At the adjudicatory phase, the state must show parental unfitness by proving acts or omissions on the part of the parent that bring the child within the statutory definition of a "dependent" child or a "child in need of assistance." Even at the dispositional stage, after the court has already made a finding of parental unfitness, some states require a stronger showing than the best interests of the child in order to remove a child from her parents.

Following a dispositional hearing, the court reviews the case periodically, often every six months. Except in certain exceptional cases of severe abuse, once a child is placed outside the home, state agencies must make "reasonable efforts" to reunify children with their families in order to receive federal funding for foster care. Accordingly, when a child welfare agency first removes a child, the agency social worker meets with the parent and draws up a plan for reunification of the family. This plan specifies steps the parent needs to take and services the agency needs to provide to meet that goal. Tasks identified for the parent may include completing a parenting course or a program of mental health or drug treatment, or finding a suitable place to live. Services to be provided by the agency may include referrals to or payments for drug or mental health treatment or logistical or financial help finding housing.

If reunification does not occur within a certain period of time, the agency may try to have the child adopted. This requires the agency's lawyers to first petition the court for an order terminating the natural parent's rights. To obtain such an order, the agency must generally prove in court that the parent is unable or unwilling to care for the child presently and in the foreseeable future. With the passage of the Adoption and Safe Families Act of 1997, the pressures on agencies to move quickly toward termination of parental rights once removal has occurred have increased substantially. Under the Act, the agency must file a petition for termination twelve months after placement in most instances. Where the court finds "aggravated circumstances," the agency must move for termination in just 30 days.

State statutes and case law interpreting constitutional due process protections direct trial courts to conduct dependency and termination proceedings at an intermediate level of formality. These proceedings therefore include most of the standard trappings of the traditional adversarial model of dispute resolution. The state must set forth its allegations in a petition and serve it on the parent. Cases are heard by judges. Witnesses testify under oath. A court reporter transcribes the proceedings. Rules of evidence apply, with some exceptions. The parties may be represented by lawyers and may appeal adversarial decisions.

However, parents in dependency and termination proceedings do not receive many of the procedural rights that criminal defendants—even those facing minor charges—enjoy. Thus, as a matter of federal Constitutional law, an indigent parent in a dependency or termination case has no right to appointed counsel. A number of states provide a right to appointed counsel by statute, but even in those states, courts have held that parents have no right to effective assistance of counsel because the right to counsel is not constitutionally mandated. An indigent parent facing termination of parental rights has a right to a free transcript on appeal but she does not have this right in a dependency proceeding. The constitutionally required standard of proof in a termination of parental rights proceeding is the intermediate clear and convincing evidence standard. The civil "preponderance of the evidence" standard governs dependency proceedings in many states. Although termination and dependency cases generally provide the parent an opportunity to confront and cross-examine witnesses (with exceptions for child witnesses), courts in many instances apply relaxed evidentiary rules. For example, many jurisdictions allow social workers' hearsay reports to be admitted into evidence. Courts do not construe the due process rights of parents and children in dependency and termination proceedings to include rights analogous to the criminal prohibition on double jeopardy or the right against self-incrimination contained in the Fifth Amendment.

NOTES AND QUESTIONS

1. **Mandatory Reporting Statutes.** One significant aspect of the child protection system that is not mentioned in the above description is the regime of mandatory reporting statutes. Since the 1960s, many states have required certain people who might learn of child abuse or neglect to report it to the appropriate state agency. Beginning in 1974, the federal Child Abuse Prevention and Treatment Act (CAPTA) required every state to have a mandatory reporting mechanism as a condition of receiving federal funding for child protection. In most states, the statutes require medical personnel, school personnel, social workers, and therapists who have reason to believe a child has been abused or neglected to report that abuse or neglect.

For example, the Alabama statute requires doctors and other medical personnel, teachers, law enforcement personnel, social workers, mental health professionals, members of the clergy, and any other person called to aid a child to report. Ala. Code § 26–14–3 (2006). Some states are even more inclusive as to who is required to report. Illinois requires the same categories as Alabama, but it also requires personnel in domestic violence programs and "homemakers" to report. 325 Ill. Comp. Stat. 5/4 (2006). Texas and Mississippi both include attorneys among those who are required reporters. Tex. Fam. Code Ann. § 261.101 (2006); Miss. Code Ann. § 43–21–353 (2006). Finally, the Oklahoma statute lists a number of specific groups of people who must report and then adds a general provision that any person with reason to believe there has been abuse or neglect must report. Okla. Stat. Ann. Tit. 10, § 7103 (2005).

What difficulties do you see arising from the inclusion of domestic violence workers, homemakers, attorneys, and any one with reason to believe there has been abuse? For a discussion of the problems attached to including attorneys as mandatory reporters, see Brooke Albrandt, *Turning in the Client: Mandatory Child Abuse Reporting Requirements and the Criminal Defense of Battered Women,* 81 TEX. L. REV. 655 (2002). Alaska requires that employees of domestic violence agencies report, but it exempts them from reporting mental injury to a child as a result of the domestic violence so long as the reporter "has reasonable cause to believe that the child is in safe and appropriate care and not presently in danger of mental injury as a result of exposure to domestic violence." Alaska Stat. § 47.17.020 (2005). What are the advantages and disadvantages of a provision like Alaska's?

Some commentators have argued that the mandatory reporting statutes are structured in such a way as to encourage over-reporting of child abuse and neglect. The average substantiation rate of abuse and neglect reports is between 31% and 44%. Brooke Albrandt, *Turning in the Client: Mandatory Child Abuse Reporting Requirements and the Criminal Defense of Battered Women,* 81 TEX. L. REV. 655 (2002). Steven J. Singley, *Failure to Report Suspected Child Abuse,* 19 J. JUV. L. 236 (1998). Most statutes impose a misdemeanor criminal penalty for failure to report as required and many also include a civil liability provision. In addition, although the reporter is not usually anonymous to the agency to which the report is made, the parent who is the target of the report is usually unable to ascertain the name of the reporter. Do these facts imply to you that there is over-reporting? If there is, do you think it should be curbed? Why are adult victims of domestic violence likely to be particularly concerned about reports being made?

2. **Burdens of Proof.** As the above excerpt indicates, the state's burden of proof is different in initial dependency hearings than it is in subsequent termination hearings. In dependency hearings (to determine the accuracy of claims of abuse or neglect), states are not constitutionally required to use any standard beyond the usual civil "preponderance of the evidence" standard. As a result, many do use the preponderance standard although some use a higher "clear and convincing" standard. If a child is adjudicated to be abused or neglected, there will be a dispositional hearing to determine the child's placement. At this point, a child could be placed back in his or her home with conditions attached, or the child could be placed in foster care, or in some other placement deemed appropriate. Usually, there is no guiding standard of proof applicable to placement decisions; they are ordinarily not reviewable because they are seen as interim decisions instead of final judgments. Ellen Marrus, *Fostering Family Ties: The State as Maker and Breaker of Kinship Relationships,* 2004 U. CHI. LEGAL F. 319. The Child Protective Agency is required in most circumstances both to make efforts at reuniting the child with her or his parents and to plan for termination of parental rights. Federal law requires that a petition to terminate parental rights be filed within 12 months of the foster care placement. In proceedings to terminate parental rights, the state agency bears a burden of proving its case by "clear and convincing evidence." *Santosky v. Kramer,* 455 U.S. 745 (1982).

3. **Representation in Child Protective Proceedings.** Another provision of CAPTA, the federal Child Abuse Prevention and Treatment Act, provides that states are only eligible for certain federal child welfare grants as long as they provide guardians ad litem (GALs) or court appointed special advocates (CASAs) to all children involved in child protective proceedings. 42 U.S.C. § 5106, et seq. Every state therefore has a statutory framework for at least some form of representation for all court-involved abused and neglected children. Most states are currently appointing attorneys to serve the dual role of GAL and legal counsel for children, though CAPTA allows for lay volunteers to fill these roles too. Astra Outley, *Representation for Children and Parents in Dependency Proceedings*, available at http://pewfostercare.org/research/docs/Representation.pdf. However, as we have seen previously, GALs most frequently are mandated to advocate for the child's "best interests" as understood by the GAL, not to represent the child's wishes as to placement.

Some states require that every court-involved child have a volunteer CASA to represent the child's interests instead of a lawyer acting as a GAL. While exact training procedures for CASA volunteers vary among the states, the usual requirements are approximately 40 hours of training and "a big heart." Although some CASAs are lawyers, a background in law is not required. For examples of training requirements, see http://www.geocities.com/alabamacasa/casado.html (Alabama), http://casahelpskids.org/main.asp?id=30 (Oregon), and http://www.courts.state.me.us/jobs/casa/index.html (Maine).

In contrast, most states, either by statute or by case law, provide counsel for parents. Martin Guggenheim, *The Right To Be Represented But Not Heard: Reflections on Legal Representation for Children*, 59 N.Y.U.L. REV. 76 (1984). Some commentators and judges have concluded that although the parent and child are likely to be represented in some manner, the representation is often inferior. This is usually as a result of limited training or inadequate pay.

4. **Race, Class, and Poverty.** Some scholars and activists are critical of child protective proceedings as being overly protective of parents' constitutional rights to raise their children. Richard J. Gelles and Ira Schwartz, *Children and the Child Welfare System*, 2 U. PA. J. CONST. L. 95 (1999). Others, however, have leveled a different criticism, suggesting that the state accords deference to the privacy of some families, but not all; and that poor families, families of color, and female-headed households are the most likely to suffer both the intrusions of the state, and the imposition of values and norms insensitive to the economic and social realities these families confront:

> The mothers and children "served" by the public, protective system are overwhelmingly poor and disproportionately of color. Poor families are more susceptible to state intervention because they lack power and resources and because they are more directly involved with governmental agencies. For example, the state must have probable cause to enter the homes of most Americans, yet women receiving aid to families with dependent children (AFDC) are not entitled to such privacy. In addi-

tion to receiving direct public benefits (like AFDC and Medicaid), poor families lead more public lives than their middle-class counterparts: rather than visiting private doctors, poor families are more likely to attend public clinics and emergency rooms for routine medical care; rather than hiring contractors to fix their homes, poor families encounter public building inspectors; rather than using their cars to run errands, poor mothers use public transportation.

Of course, the vast majority of the parents involved in the child protective system are mothers. Men are rarely brought into court, held accountable, or viewed as resources for their children. When fathers are involved in the proceedings, they are usually subject to lower expectations and are significantly less likely to be criminally charged with neglect or passive abuse of their children. Annette R. Appell, *Protecting Children or Punishing Mothers: Gender, Race, and Class in the Child Protection System*, 48 S.C.L. Rev. 577 (1997).

As you read the cases and materials that follow think about whether you agree that poverty and minority status make these families more vulnerable to the intervention of the child protective system. If you agree, do you think the intervention is likely to be helpful or damaging to the children involved?

B.   How the System Works Against Battered Women

In Re Glenn G.

Family Court, Kings County, New York, 1992.
587 N.Y.S.2d 464.

■ Sara P. Schecter, J.

Respondent parents in the proceeding before the court are charged with sexually abusing their children—Josephine, born in 1985 and now six years of age, and Glenn, born in 1987 and now almost five years old.... [The] father is charged with having improperly touched the genitals and rectums of both children, conduct which would constitute sexual abuse in the third degree, a violation of Penal Law § 130.55. Respondent mother is charged with having allowed the abuse, in that the acts occurred in her presence and she failed to protect the children. In addition, both respondents are charged with sexually abusing the children by having taken pornographic photographs of the children, a violation of Penal Law § 263.05.... In the alternative, it is alleged that the children are neglected in that the foregoing conduct constitutes improper supervision of the children by the respondents.

This case came to the attention of the authorities on April 12, 1991 when the respondent mother went to the 68th Police Precinct to seek assistance after an incident of domestic violence. There she was referred to a worker with the Victim Services Agency, Barbara Anselmo. Ms. Anselmo testified that upon arrival respondent mother was pale, shaking, crying and incoherent. After about an hour, respondent mother became calm enough to speak and, in the ensuing discussion, asked if it was normal for a father to grab his children in the groin area, dance naked with them and take photos of them naked. Ms. Anselmo said, "No." After further discussion respondent mother was relocated to a battered women's shelter. The children were medically examined at Bellevue Hospital on April 19, 1991, following which a report of suspected child abuse or maltreatment . . . was called in by the Bellevue social worker. The Child Welfare Administration (hereinafter CWA) was already involved, however, as a result of two [abuse reports] it had received on April 18, 1991, relaying allegations made by the father against the mother. Upon investigation those allegations proved to be unfounded.

The CWA caseworker, Edris Juandoo, interviewed the respondent mother and the children on April 22, 1991. Josephine told the caseworker that the father plays with her and touches her in the "tushie and in the front, in the hole." Respondent mother recounted to the caseworker the same sort of touching she had described to Ms. Anselmo, and she told the caseworker that when she confronted the father about it, he threatened to kill her. . . .

. . . One photograph . . . depicts Glenn, who appears to be between three and four years old, lying on his back on a couch, clad in a shirt and pants. In this photo the child's underwear and jeans are pulled down to his knees, exposing him from waist to mid-thighs. He has an erection, which is conspicuous due to the angle of the photograph.

. . . [R]espondent father took the lewd photograph. The child Josephine spontaneously told Dr. April Kuchuk, a psychologist who interviewed the child at Bellevue Hospital, that her father would take pictures of her and her brother with their clothes off, and specifically stated that her mother did not. Furthermore, the taking of this photo is consistent with the respondent father's over-all approach to the children as sex objects. . . . Accordingly, the court finds the child Glenn to have been sexually abused by the respondent father by reason of the father's having used him in a sexual performance. . . .

On the basis of the respondent mother's testimony and Josephine's out-of-court statements, which were amply corroborated by the physical findings of Dr. McHugh and the psychological findings of Dr. Kuchuk, the court finds that the respondent father sexually abused both children by touching their intimate parts for the purpose of his sexual gratification.

The Respondent Mother's Culpability

Respondent mother is charged with sexual abuse, and, in the alternative, neglect, based on her failure to protect the children from the father's conduct described above. She asserts as a defense that she was a battered woman during the period when the abuse was occurring and asks that the charges against herself be dismissed. CWA and the Law Guardian argue that whether the mother was a battered woman is irrelevant, since they contend that the Family Court Act child protective article is a strict liability statute. . . .

The analysis of respondent mother's defense must commence with a preliminary review of the legal responsibility of the passive parent of a child who has been sexually abused. The passive parent is guilty of child abuse when she "allows" the abuse to be inflicted.... Petitioner and the Law Guardian urge this court to adopt an objective standard for the conduct of the passive parent, by which the passive parent would be held to have "allowed" the abuse if she failed to act as a reasonable and prudent parent would have acted to protect the child.... This argument fails to distinguish between a finding of abuse and one of neglect....

In a recent case which addresses the distinction between abuse and neglect it was held that when the passive parent is merely careless or negligent and inattentive, and by her failure to exercise a minimum degree of care leaves the child unprotected from the abusive parent, her conduct constitutes child neglect....

The conduct of the passive parent of a sexually abused child may range across a wide spectrum. At one extreme is the parent who actually instigates the abuse or encourages the abuser; at the other extreme is the parent who has failed to notice nonspecific symptoms in the child such as frequent rashes or recurrent urinary tract infections. In between lie countless scenarios.... To label such variegated behavior as monolithic "abuse" would be arbitrary and insensitive and, in many instances, would needlessly stigmatize the passive parent without providing any greater protective or dispositional alternatives than would be available upon a finding of neglect. Instead, in determining where on the abuse-neglect spectrum the liability of a particular respondent lies, the court should use two coordinates: the passive parent's knowledge or awareness of the actions of the abusive parent, and second, the passive parent's actual ability to intervene to protect the child.

The first is not in dispute in the instant case.... The issue of her ability to protect the children, however, is heavily contested.... In the case at bar, respondent mother ... asserts that she was unable to take appropriate action because she was suffering from "Battered Woman's Syndrome."

Respondent mother established by convincing evidence that during her relationship with respondent father she was a battered woman. She testified to an escalating pattern of abuse, which began soon after the couple began living together. In the early days ... more upsetting than the insults and invective were what Mrs. G. called "mind games," in which Mr. G. convinced Mrs G. that he spied on her at work and actually supplied details of what she had done during the day to prove that he was having her watched....

After the birth of their first child, Mr. G. became more menacing.... The first instance of actual physical abuse occurred when Mrs. G. returned from ... an errand and found Mr. G. inappropriately touching Josephine. When she grabbed the baby away and began to yell at the father, he hit her in the mouth, causing her lip to bleed. At that point Mrs. G. realized that she should get away, and within a few weeks, in May 1987, she took Josephine and went to the home of her sister in Florida.

While in Florida she gave birth to the second child, Glenn. Mr. G., who had located the mother by phoning around to hospitals in the area ... arrived at the mother's bedside the day after Glenn's birth. He was tearful and apologetic, said he knew the problems were his fault and that he was getting counseling. After the mother returned to her sister's house, he kept up such a campaign of telephonic harassment that the mother finally felt she was imposing on her sister. Mr. G. sent a ticket, and Mrs. G. and the children returned to New York around the end of June 1987.

Following the return to New York, the domestic situation worsened....

In November of 1990 Mrs. G. sought medical treatment in the emergency room of St. Vincent's Medical Center of Richmond for headaches, blurred vision and black lines in her left eye sustained as a result of an assault by Mr. G. Although St. Vincent's responded appropriately by giving Mrs. G. a referral to the Victim Services Agency, she signed herself out against medical advice and failed to follow through on the referral.

Respondent mother's efforts to protect herself and the children after her return from Florida were meager. She began to call 911 once, but did not give the operator her address. She confided in her mother-in-law, who said she should just endure her situation and that Mr. G.'s father had been the same way. She stayed for days at a time at her mother-in-law's home with the children. She mentioned Josephine's frequent vaginal rashes to the pediatrician, but did not tell him of any sex abuse. She attempted to intervene when Mr. G. was behaving inappropriately with the children, but he told her, "Butt out, that's how you get hurt so much."

Respondent mother's testimony concerning Mr. G.'s abuse of her was totally credible, while Mr. G.'s denials were unworthy of belief.... The original attorney for respondent mother, the original Law Guardian, two former attorneys for respondent father and the Judge to whom this matter was originally assigned all withdrew from the case after conduct by Mr. G. which they perceived as threatening....

Respondent mother produced two expert witnesses who testified about the condition known as "Battered Woman's Syndrome." Ms. Anselmo ... described the syndrome as "a breaking down of a woman's self confidence and self respect to the point where she no longer knows if she is crazy or not." ... Based on her observations of Mrs. G. in the police station and in the days immediately following, Ms. Anselmo testified that in her opinion Mrs. G. had been a battered woman for a long period of time.

The second expert on the subject was Valerie Bryant.... Ms. Bryant ... stated her opinion that the role of the mother-in-law in urging Mrs. G. to "bear with it" was very instrumental in undermining respondent mother's sense of self-worth and in reinforcing her sense of helplessness, particularly because she was estranged from her own family. Mrs. G., therefore, came to see herself as having few options. She lost the ability to protect herself, and thus lost the ability to protect the children as well. Ms. Bryant also noted that Mrs. G.'s dilemma is not uncommon, as a correlation between spousal abuse and child abuse is generally recognized among professionals who work with battered women and that in her opinion the two forms of abuse share very similar psychodynamics. . . .

The court is in accord with those who have recognized that Battered Woman's Syndrome is a condition which seriously impairs the will and the judgment of the victim. The abused should not be branded as abuser. Respondent mother in the case at bar clearly did not condone the sexual abuse of the children by the respondent father, but rather, due to her affliction with Battered Woman's Syndrome, was powerless to stop it. She cannot be said to have "allowed" the abuse within the meaning of Family Court Act § 1012(e)(iii). Accordingly, the child abuse charges against the respondent mother are dismissed. The neglect statute, however, imposes strict liability. As respondent mother's actions were manifestly inadequate to protect the children from the father's ongoing abuse, of which she was well aware, a finding of neglect must be entered against her.

NOTES AND QUESTIONS

1. **Reasonable Battered Woman Standard and Child Abuse.** The court's willingness to hear expert testimony with respect to "battered woman's syndrome," and its conclusion that Mrs. G. had not "allowed" the sexual abuse of her children, and was therefore not herself guilty of child abuse, demonstrates both understanding of, and sympathy for, the battered wife and mother's situation. At the same time, the "battered women's syndrome" framework may limit the judge from seeing Mrs. G's repeated and affirmative efforts, although unsuccessful, to try to leave. The CWA and the children's law guardian had argued both that the abuse statute should be understood as creating strict liability, and that it should be read as imposing an "objective" standard—abuse would be measured by the failure to act as a reasonable and prudent parent would have acted in protecting the child. Does that mean that the court, in exonerating Mrs. G. of the charge of abuse, is using a "subjective" standard? Or only that the court is applying, in the context of the abuse statute, an objective standard modified to reflect the realities of life for a reasonable mother living in a battering relationship and suffering from "battered woman's syndrome?" Has the court, in other words, adopted the "reasonable battered mother" standard for use in interpreting the abuse statute?

Again, as we have seen in Chapters Five and Nine, the issue of the use of testimony on battering is a complicated one. Do you feel differently about the use of expert testimony on battering here than in the criminal context? Does it assist the judge in evaluating the ways in which Mrs. G. attempted to extricate herself from the relationship?

2. **Neglect and the Strict Liability Standard.** If a "reasonable battered mother" standard is used in child abuse proceedings, why is it not also used when the parent is charged with neglect of the child? In neglect proceedings, as *In Re Glenn G.* makes quite clear, the standard is one of strict liability. Indeed, parents who are unable to protect their children from harm because of mental illness or retardation can still be liable for neglect. Under the strict liability standard, the statement "Mrs. G. neglect-

ed to protect her children" means nothing more than "Mrs. G. did not prevent her children from being abused." It would be possible to argue that, interpreted in this light, a finding of neglect carries no moral judgment C it is just a statement of fact. We do not usually understand neglect in this way, of course, since our legal system overwhelmingly equates negligence with unreasonableness and fault.

One could argue that this strict liability standard is the appropriate standard. If our goal is to protect children, why should we care whether a parent was or was not at fault in exposing them to risk? We want steps taken to eliminate that risk; at a minimum we want services made available to the family, and if that will not ensure the child's safety, we are willing to contemplate the possibility that the child (or possibly one of the parents) should be removed. As long as we are not adjudicating criminal liability, where a strict liability standard would be considerably more problematic, why should we resist a finding of neglect if it will provide a basis for protecting a child?

One answer to that question is that findings of neglect, even under a strict liability standard, do still carry overtones of blame. The tendency to blame is strongly evident in child welfare investigations and adjudications, where child welfare workers and judges routinely condemn mothers for failing to save their children from abuse, not understanding or crediting the supreme difficulty of that task when the mother herself is a victim of abuse, who understands the dangers posed by her abuser and who may have experienced an increase rather than a decrease in the violence directed at both her and the children when she has tried to intervene. One of the reasons to resist findings of neglect in these circumstances is to combat the woman-blaming attitudes that accompany them. One commentator who has argued strongly for a "reasonable battered mother" standard in child protective proceedings is G. Kristian Miccio, *A Reasonable Battered Mother? Redefining, Reconstructing, and Recreating the Battered Mother in Child Protective Proceedings*, 22 HARV. WOMEN'S L.J. 89 (1999).

Another reason to reject strict liability in neglect proceedings is the fear that a finding of neglect will lead, ultimately, to a termination of parental rights, so that a loving parent with much to offer a child will be permanently written out of that child's life, because the mother was not able to keep the child safe from another's abuse. Surely this is the moment to ask who else might have helped to keep both mother and child safe, and whether we would be better off laying blame at the door of others with more resources to bring to the task of controlling the abuser's behavior.

Is there a compromise? Could we invoke the system on the child's behalf without finding that the mother has either abused or neglected her child? In cases in which the abuser is also the father of the child, or a legal guardian, the answer would appear to be "yes," since the culpable party is also one against whom the child welfare system has authority to proceed. But, frequently, the abusive man is the mother's partner, but not otherwise related to or responsible for the children. Usually, the child welfare authorities have no authority to proceed against such a person. Two commentators have tried to explain why child welfare authorities may bring charges against an abused mother in this situation:

> ... In most states, the jurisdiction of the juvenile court in child maltreatment cases is limited to those situations in which the child's parent or legal guardian has created, or failed to protect the child from, the conditions deemed by the court to be harmful to the child. Thus, in most states, the juvenile court, and thus CPS [child protective services], cannot intervene in direct response to the conduct of an adult who is not the child's parent or guardian, even when the adult has regular contact with the child because of a close personal relationship with the child's parent. In situations in which such an individual is perpetrating the violence, substantiating the case by charging the nonabusive parent with failure to protect becomes the only way to obtain dependency jurisdiction over the child. Fortunately, state policies are beginning to change to address this problem. Michigan law, for example, now allows the juvenile court to assert jurisdiction and authorize CPS intervention in cases involving non-parent adults, whether or not such adults reside in the same household as the child. However, CPS has relied on the possibility of a child being removed for encouraging changes in adult behavior so that the risk of harm to the child is reduced. A violent adult who is not a custodial or biological parent may not care enough about the possible loss of the child to change his behavior. Ultimately, the CPS worker may have no choice but to use the failure-to-protect argument, if intervention is necessary to protect the child. But it should be a last resort. In situations in which the battered mother is not abusing the children, perpetrators of domestic violence should be held responsible for the violence in the household. Janet E. Findlater and Susan Kelly, *Child Protective Services and Domestic Violence,* 9 THE FUTURE OF CHILDREN 84 (1999).

What do you make of the argument that even when charges could be brought directly against the abuser, the threat of removing the children from the mother may provide her with the necessary impetus for changing her situation? Was this part of the strategy that the ACS caseworker used in Sharwline Nicholson's case, described at the beginning of this chapter? What strategies would you recommend CPS try before using this strategy of last resort?

3. *Nicholson* **and the Presence of Domestic Violence as Grounds for Neglect.** As mentioned above, the New York City Administration for Children's Services (ACS) adopted a policy that incidents of domestic violence witnessed by children were sufficient as grounds for a neglect petition and for the removal of the children from the home. This is described in the *Nicholson* excerpt in Section A of this chapter. Is this a strict liability interpretation of neglect? The policy was challenged in the *Nicholson* case. The District Court found the policy unconstitutional, 203 F.Supp.2d 153 (E.D.N.Y. 2002), and the Second Circuit Court of Appeals certified questions of state law interpretation to the N.Y. Court of Appeals so as to avoid ruling on the constitutional issues, *Nicholson v. Scoppetta,*

344 F.3d 154 (2nd Cir.2003). The New York Court of Appeals' opinion interpreting the underlying law and the policy follows.

Nicholson v. Scoppetta

Court of Appeals of New York, 2004.
820 N.E.2d 840.

■ KAYE, CHIEF JUDGE.

In this federal class action, the United States Court of Appeals for the Second Circuit has certified ... questions centered on New York's statutory scheme for child protective proceedings. The action is brought on behalf of mothers and their children who were separated because the mother had suffered domestic violence, to which the children were exposed, and the children were for that reason deemed neglected by her.

... Plaintiffs alleged that ACS, as a matter of policy, removed children from mothers who were victims of domestic violence because, as victims, they "engaged in domestic violence" and that defendants removed and detained children without probable cause and without due process of law. That policy, and its implementation—according to plaintiff mothers— constituted, among other wrongs, an unlawful interference with their liberty interest in the care and custody of their children in violation of the United States Constitution....

In January 2002, the District Court granted a preliminary injunction.... The District Court concluded that ACS's practices and policies violated both the substantive due process rights of mothers and children not to be separated by the government unless the parent is unfit to care for the child, and their procedural due process rights....

On appeal, the Second Circuit held that the District Court had not abused its discretion in concluding that ACS's practice of effecting removals based on a parent's failure to prevent his or her child from witnessing domestic violence ... may raise serious questions of federal constitutional law.... The court hesitated, however, before reaching the constitutional questions, believing that resolution of uncertain issues of New York statutory law would avoid ... the substantial federal constitutional issues presented.

Given the strong preference for avoiding unnecessary constitutional adjudication ... the Second Circuit ... chose to put the open state statutory law issues to us for resolution. We accepted certification and now proceed to answer those questions.

Certified Question No. 1: Neglect

"Does the definition of a 'neglected child' under N.Y. Family Ct. Act § 1012(f), (h) include instances in which the sole allegation of neglect is that the parent or other person legally responsible for the child's care allows the child to witness domestic abuse against the caretaker?" ... That question must be answered in the negative....

[The] Family Court Act is explicit in [requiring that] ... a party seeking to establish neglect must show, by a preponderance of the evidence first, that a child's physical, mental or emotional condition has been impaired or is in imminent danger of becoming impaired and second, that the actual or threatened harm to the child is a consequence of the failure of the parent or caretaker to exercise a minimum degree of care in providing the child with proper supervision or guardianship....

The first statutory element requires proof of actual (or imminent danger of) physical, emotional or mental impairment to the child. This prerequisite to a finding of neglect ensures that the Family Court, in deciding whether to authorize state intervention, will focus on serious harm or potential harm to the child, not just on what might be deemed undesirable parental behavior....

Assuming that actual or imminent danger to the child has been shown, "neglect" also requires proof of the parent's failure to exercise a minimum degree of care.... Notably, the statutory test is "minimum degree of care"—not maximum, not best, not ideal—and the failure must be actual, not threatened.

Courts must evaluate parental behavior objectively: would a reasonable and prudent parent have so acted, or failed to act, under the circumstances then and there existing? Thus, when the inquiry is whether a mother—and domestic violence victim—failed to exercise a minimum degree of care, the focus must be on whether she has met the standard of the reasonable and prudent person in similar circumstances.

As the ... [plaintiff-mothers] point out, for a battered mother—and ultimately for a court—what course of action constitutes a parent's exercise of a "minimum degree of care" may include such considerations as: risks attendant to leaving, if the batterer has threatened to kill her if she does; risks attendant to staying and suffering continued abuse; risks attendant to seeking assistance through government channels, potentially increasing the danger to herself and her children; risks attendant to criminal prosecution against the abuser; and risks attendant to relocation. Whether a particular mother in these circumstances has actually failed to exercise a minimum degree of care is necessarily dependent on facts such as the severity and frequency of the violence, and the resources and options available to her.

Only when a petitioner demonstrates, by a preponderance of evidence, that both elements ... are satisfied may a child be deemed neglected under the statute. When "the sole allegation" is that the mother has been abused and the child has witnessed the abuse, such a showing has not been made. This does not mean, however, that a child can never be "neglected" when living in a household plagued by domestic violence. Conceivably, neglect might be found where a record establishes that, for example, the mother acknowledged that the children knew of repeated domestic violence by her paramour and had reason to be afraid of him, yet nonetheless allowed him several times to return to her home, and lacked awareness of any impact of the violence on the children....

In such circumstances, the battered mother is charged with neglect not because she is a victim of domestic violence or because her children witnessed the abuse, but rather because a preponderance of the evidence establishes that the children were actually or imminently harmed by reason of her failure to exercise even minimal care in providing them with proper oversight. . . .

NOTES AND QUESTIONS

1. *Nicholson* **and the Standard in Neglect Proceedings.** Does *Nicholson* use a reasonable person standard, a reasonable battered woman standard, a strict liability standard, or yet another standard? Is it possible for a mother to fail, without fault, to meet the "minimum" degree of care required by the statute? Justine Dunlap argues that in many common situations, mothers who have been abused by their intimate partners may not be able to meet this "minimum care" requirement. *Judging Nicholson: An Assessment of Nicholson v. Scoppetta,* 82 DENV. U. L. REV. 671 (2005). What frequent settings can you imagine in which victims of family violence might be found to have neglected a child without any fault on the part of the victim? Would *In Re Glenn G.* have been decided differently if it had been decided after *Nicholson?*

2. **Neglect Proceedings and Domestic Violence, Post-***Nicholson.* For a finding of neglect, *Nicholson* requires that there be actual injury to the child (or that injury be imminent) and that the injury result from the parent's failure to exercise a "minimum" amount of care. In considering what constitutes a "minimum" amount of care, the New York Court of Appeals instructed trial courts to consider the circumstances that are part of a battered mother's life. Prior to actually removing a child from the home, the Court of Appeals said later in the opinion, the trial court must consider not only whether the child has been neglected, but also whether it would be in the child's best interests to remove him or her from the home.

Since *Nicholson* is quite recent, there are not many reported cases and even fewer studies of what has happened since the decision. The reported cases do not present a clear picture. In two post-*Nicholson* cases, the Appellate Division reversed trial court determinations of neglect. In the first, the determination had been based on a finding that the mother "engaged in" domestic violence by being attacked by her boyfriend. Citing *Nicholson,* the Appellate Division noted that there was no finding that the mother was "responsible for neglect." *In re Ravern H.,* 789 N.Y.S.2d 563 (N.Y.A.D. 4th Dept. 2005). The facts were more complicated in the second of these cases. The children had been adjudicated neglected based on extensive domestic violence against the mother. However, at her request the police arrested the abuser, she obtained a restraining order protecting the children and herself, and she moved out of the home and into a shelter. Shortly thereafter, the order of protection was modified; she then returned home so as to facilitate visitation between the children and their father, the abuser. When police saw the abuser near the marital home, the children were removed on the basis of the history of domestic violence. The

Appellate Division reversed the trial court's finding of neglect, basing its decision on *Nicholson*. *In re Eryck N.*, 791 N.Y.S.2d 857 (N.Y.A.D. 3rd Dept. 2005).

In two other post-*Nicholson* cases, the Appellate Division upheld findings of neglect against the mother based primarily on the fact that she was a victim of domestic violence. In one case, the child had witnessed both the father's violence toward the mother and his drug use. Furthermore, the mother was unaware of the effects of the violence and drug use on the child. The Court found that this was sufficient evidence to sustain the neglect finding. *In re Christopher B.*, 809 N.Y.S.2d 202 (N.Y.A.D. 2nd Dept. 2006). In yet another case, post-*Nicholson* case the Appellate Division upheld a finding of neglect on the grounds that the mother had attempted to leave the child with the father against whom she had an order of protection that included the child. She said she did not have the resources to care for the child financially. *In re Paul U.*, 785 N.Y.S.2d 767 (N.Y.A.D. 3rd Dept. 2004). See also *In re Alan FF.*, 811 N.Y.S.2d 158 (N.Y.A.D. 3rd Dept. 2006) (Court noted that one of the allegations in neglect petition against mother was that she had allowed children to be exposed to domestic violence and that this, with other allegations, would be sufficient if proven to support finding of neglect.) One might wonder whether there were alternative strategies for supporting the mother financially so that she could have kept the child with her. Indeed, one might wonder whether facts similar to those in *Christopher B.* and *Paul U.* are sufficiently common that a court that believed the presence of domestic violence was deleterious for the children could usually find facts on which to base its decision instead of relying on the mere fact of abuse.

Not surprisingly, *Nicholson* has also created changes in many areas that are not reflected in the reported cases. One of the attorneys for the plaintiffs in *Nicholson* claims that, as a result of the case, ACS "stopped removing children from battered mothers." Jill M. Zuccardy, *Nicholson v. Williams: The Case*, 82 Denv. U. L. Rev. 655 (2005). Although ACS may no longer remove children solely on the grounds that the mother has been abused, the cases cited above indicate that abuse by an intimate partner may still create circumstances that lead to a neglect finding. Another result of *Nicholson* is that ACS caseworkers are now required to be trained about the effects of domestic violence. Finally, compensation for attorneys involved in protective proceedings has increased. Hopefully, this will encourage more attorneys to take on this type of case. Justine A. Dunlap, *Judging Nicholson, An Assessment of Nicholson v. Scoppetta*, 82 Denv. U. L. Rev. 671 (2005).

3. **Gender Norms and Definitions of Neglect.** To what extent do gendered expectations as to women's roles as mothers influence courts' willingness to adjudicate a child to be neglected? Are mothers expected to be all-knowing when it comes to their children's welfare? Are mothers expected to sacrifice their own safety in order to provide for their children's? G. Kristian Miccio argues,

> "[T]he socially constructed paradigm of mothering leaves no accommodation for the battered mother. Within this construct, the 'good mother' is selfless and deferential. The needs and desires of fathers and children define her existence. The 'bad' or 'evil' mother is one who

insinuates her independent self into the familial picture, permitting her needs to co-exist with those of familial members." G. Kristian Miccio, *A Reasonable Battered Mother? Redefining, Reconstructing, and Recreating the Battered Mother in Child Protective Proceedings*, 22 HARV. WOMEN'S L.J. 89 (1999).

Think about the cases you have read, especially the trial courts' decisions. Do you agree with Miccio? Do courts have a tendency to emphasize mothers' concern for their own safety, financial security, etc., while ignoring both the mothers' efforts to extricate themselves from the situation and the system's failures to help? G. Kristian Miccio, *In the Name of Mothers and Children: Deconstructing the Myth of the Passive Battered Woman and the "Protected Child" in Child Neglect Proceedings*, 58 ALB. L. REV. 1087 (1995).

4.   **The Adoption and Safe Families Act.** The federal government has continued to shape state child welfare policy by conditioning the receipt of federal funding of state programs on compliance with federal law. In 1997, concerned that child welfare policy permitted children to remain in the limbo of foster care for too long, Congress passed the Adoption and Safe Families Act (ASFA), 42 U.S.C. § 671(a)(15)(A). The goal of ASFA is to ensure children's health and safety through permanent placements whenever possible. Thus, the statute requires reasonable efforts at reunifying most children with their parents. However, if these are not successful in a short period of time, the focus switches to planning for permanent care for the child elsewhere. Under the statute, a state is to move to terminate parental rights if a child has been in foster care for fifteen of the last twenty-two months. Do you agree that this "creates an implicit presumption that a parent who allows a child to linger in foster care for fifteen months is unfit?" Catherine J. Ross, *The Tyranny of Time*, 11 VA. J. SOC. POL'Y & L. 176 (2004). Under ASFA, states must schedule a permanency hearing within twelve months of the time a child enters foster care, rather than the previously mandated eighteen months.

The short time frames imposed by ASFA have their greatest effect on parents wrestling with the most complex and intractable problems. These are likely to be cases involving drug abuse, including domestic violence cases complicated by substance abuse. Catherine J. Ross, *The Tyranny of Time*, 11 VA. J. SOC. POL'Y & L. 176 (2004). There is some evidence to indicate that in these difficult cases, AFSA is resulting in the termination of parental rights whereas previously reunification might ultimately have been possible. Richard P. Barth, Fred Wulczyno and Tom Crea, *From Anticipation to Evidence: Research on the Adoption and Safe Families Act*, 12 VA. J. SOC. POL'Y & L. 371 (2005). Finally, it is important to remember that the large majority of families affected by the termination requirements of AFSA are families of color. Jane C. Murphy, *Protecting Children by Preserving Parenthood*, 14 WM. & MARY BILL RTS. J. 969 (2006).

C.   CONSTITUTIONAL ISSUES IN *NICHOLSON V. WILLIAMS*

The Federal District Court, in *Nicholson v. Williams*, 203 F.Supp.2d 153 (E.D.N.Y. 2002), found the practice of removing children from their homes because they had been exposed to domestic violence to be an unconstitutional practice. The Court relied on three main grounds for this decision. It found violations of the Fourteenth Amendment's procedural due process requirements, of the Fourteenth Amendment's substantive due process requirements, and of the Fourth Amendment's search and seizure clause. The Second Circuit, on appeal, agreed that "the removals may raise serious questions of federal constitutional law," *Nicholson v. Scoppetta*, 344 F.3d 154 (2d Cir.2003), but it was able to avoid a decision on the constitutional questions by certifying questions of state law to the New York Court of Appeals. Nonetheless, since protective decisions from other states sometimes sound like they are relying on the mere fact that the child witnessed violence as a basis on which to remove the child, it is worth our while to explore the constitutional claims.

The Federal District Court in *Nicholson* found that the removals violated procedural due process in that they presumed that parents whose children are exposed to domestic violence are unfit parents. Invoking *Stanley v. Illinois*, 405 U.S. 645 (1972), the Court said that states were required to provide individualized hearings to determine unfitness, instead of "relying on presumptions about categories of people." In *Stanley*, the U.S. Supreme Court declared that it was unconstitutional to remove an unmarried man's children from his care without a hearing when the basis for the removal was that, as an unmarried man, he was an unfit parent. Was the situation in *Nicholson* analogous to *Stanley*? Should it matter that the children in *Stanley* were removed permanently whereas the removals in *Nicholson* were for a limited period of time unless a hearing was held?

The Federal District Court also found that the removals infringed on the mothers' fundamental liberty interests in raising their children as they wished and on the mothers' and children's fundamental liberty interests in having the family remain together. These are substantive due process claims. The mothers' interests in raising their own children flow from *Pierce v. Society of Sisters*, 268 U.S. 510 (1925), *Meyer v. Nebraska*, 262 U.S. 390 (1923), and *Wisconsin v. Yoder*, 406 U.S. 205 (1972). These relatively old U.S. Supreme Court cases all struck down state efforts to restrict parents' choices as to their children's education. More recently, in *Troxel v. Granville*, 530 U.S. 57 (2000), the Court held that a state statute that permitted grandparent visitation over the mother's objection was an unconstitutional infringement on a fit mother's right to raise the children as she wished. Do you agree that these decided cases show that the mothers in the *Nicholson* litigation had a fundamental interest in directing their own children's upbringing? Do you think the cases about education are distinguishable? The opinion in *Troxel* was a plurality opinion; it is unclear what weight to give the parental interest in raising the children. Even a fundamental interest can be infringed upon if the state has a compelling reason for doing so. The District Court found no compelling reason because "the evidence proves that the challenged policies of ACS work against the state interest in protecting the safety of children," 203 F.Supp.2d at 251. Do you agree that the ACS policy worked against the state interest in protecting children's safety? Note that the right protected in these cases is a parental right. It is not an interest that children can enforce.

The District Court also found that both the mothers and children had a fundamental liberty interest in "family integrity." Although there are several cases that refer to a parent's right to direct her own children's upbringing, there are fewer that recognize a right to family integrity. The closest case to the situation in *Nicholson* is *Duchesne v. Sugarman*, 566 F.2d 817 (2d Cir. 1977). In *Duchesne*, the Court found a constitutional violation in the Bureau of Child Welfare's refusal to return children to their mother's care when they had been taken on an emergency basis without her consent and held without any hearing to determine that they were dependent children. In *Nicholson,* the Court cited to *Duchesne* for the proposition that "The right of the family to remain together without the coercive interference of the awesome power of the state is the most essential and basic aspect of familial privacy." The *Nicholson* Court also relied on the U.S. Supreme Court case of *Quilloin v. Walcott*, 434 U.S. 246 (1978). In *Quilloin*, the Supreme Court held that a child could not be adopted by the mother's new husband without the consent of the child's unmarried father where the father had actually lived with and helped to raise the child for several years. The Court referred to this as an unconstitutional effort to break up a "natural" family. Is this good precedent for a finding of a fundamental right to "family integrity" in *Nicholson* or is the right recognized in *Quilloin* a more limited right to veto a step-parent adoption? Is the right to family integrity one that can be invoked by children or only by adults? In 1998, the Massachusetts Supreme Judicial Court upheld a trial court's decision to place a child for adoption with his aunt whom he had rarely met instead of in a foster home with his biological sister to whom he looked for support and with whom he was strongly bonded. *Adoption of Hugo*, 700 N.E.2d 516 (Mass. 1998).

Both the right to raise one's child as one sees fit and the right to family integrity unimpeded by the state are aspects of the right of privacy. As we have already seen, the right to privacy has often been used as a means of maintaining male power over women and as a rationale for preventing the state from protecting women who have been abused. One of the many ways that the concept of privacy has been harmful to women is in its devaluation of women and the roles they traditionally play. In situating women in the private sector, the concept of privacy implies that women are not important enough to merit the state's attention and protection. Elizabeth M. Schneider, *The Violence of Privacy*, 23 Conn. L. Rev. 973 (1991). Of course, privacy can also have a positive meaning for women: it can protect a realm of individual choice. Elizabeth M. Schneider, *The Synergy of Equality and Privacy in Women's Rights*, 2002 U. Chi. Legal F. 137. Which of these meanings do you see in *Nicholson's* use of the idea of privacy? Suzanne Kim argues that the *Nicholson* Court adopted a view of privacy that protects women who have suffered abuse and recognizes the need for state intervention on their behalves, while it also shields women from governmental and social coercion in their relations with their children. However, she also worries that it empowers parents at the expense of children. Suzanne Kim, *Reconstructing Family Privacy*, 57 Hastings L.J. 557 (2006). Do you agree?

Child protective cases like *Nicholson v. Williams* also raise Fourth Amendment issues. Eight federal circuit Courts of Appeals have faced questions about whether ACS is subject to the same probable cause requirements as police conducting a search and seizure for a criminal investigation. The Second, Third, Fifth, Ninth, and Tenth Circuits have held or indicated through dicta that child welfare agencies will usually be held to probable cause requirements. The First and Fourth Circuits have been more willing to find that child welfare agencies should be held to a "special needs" standard that is not as burdensome as the probable cause standard. The Seventh Circuit has found each standard to apply in different cases. Doriane Coleman, *Storming the Castle to Save the Children: The Ironic Costs of a Child Welfare Exception to the Fourth Amendment*, 47 WM. & MARY L. REV. 413 (2005). Few state courts have had to address this issue and those that have addressed it have generally agreed with the majority of the federal Courts of Appeals that the Fourth Amendment is fully applicable. *State in Interest of A.R.*, 937 P.2d 1037 (Utah App. 1997); *In re Petition to Compel Cooperation with Child Abuse Investigation*, 875 A.2d 365 (Pa. Super. 2005). But in *Matter of Pima County Juvenile Delinquency Action No. 102091–01* the Arizona Court of Appeals held that the Fourth Amendment does not apply in child welfare situations if an officer reasonably believes that a child is in peril. 783 P.2d 1213 (1989). There is a question as to whether anyone other than the child has standing to raise a claim that the Fourth Amendment has been violated. *Osborne v. County of Riverside*, 385 F.Supp.2d 1048 (C.D.Cal. 2005).

D.   PROSECUTING BATTERED MOTHERS FOR FAILURE TO PROTECT

Under what circumstances will a mother who has "allowed" her child to be abused, or failed to prevent the abuse, be criminally prosecuted, rather than simply called to account through the child welfare system? There are no good statistical studies to answer this question.

The irony, of course, is that the very same constituencies that welcome a heightened police response to domestic violence and a recognition of its impact on children are highly critical of efforts to guard the welfare of abused children by prosecuting non-abusive, and abused, mothers. From the perspective of those who understand the dangerous and disempowering dynamics of abusive relationships, holding the abused mother accountable for failing to protect her children when she has manifestly not been able to protect herself appears profoundly unjust. This injustice is compounded when prosecutors overlook both the efforts the mother *has* made to keep her children safe or the violence directed at them at a minimum, and the failure of other helping systems to respond to the mother's or the children's needs. To blame the mother for being unable to keep her batterer away from her home when police fail to enforce the restraining order she has taken out—to give just one scenario from the reported cases—seems both hypocritical and vindictive.

Those critical of increased prosecutions of mothers who have been unable to protect their children also argue that if we are first and foremost concerned with the wellbeing of a child, and the child is still alive, we should consider carefully whether the child's wellbeing, in the aftermath of abuse, will be better served by the foster care system, or by the mother. Both mother and child should now be safe from their abuser, assuming he is prosecuted, convicted, and incarcerated. Both may well need assistance in recovering from the trauma of abuse; but if there is a bond of affection between them (as there frequently is), being able to enjoy their relationship in safety may help in that recovery. Certainly the mother understands better than most what her child has been through.

Finally, from a practical standpoint, prosecuting mothers for failure to protect provides a perverse incentive. Imagine being the woman who discovers that her child has been physically or sexually abused. Imagine knowing that making efforts to report the abuse to the authorities, or to take the child for medical care, would not only put you and the child in further danger from the abuser, but would be likely to result in the child being removed from your care, and in your being criminally prosecuted for failure to protect. Might you not decide that the better course of action would be to continue to make whatever efforts you could to keep the child safe without ''help'' from the outside?

These prosecutions occur in three types of situations: where the mother was present when the child was abused and did not prevent or halt the abuse, where the mother left the child in the care of a known abuser, and where the mother failed to seek assistance for a child for abuse-related injuries. In practice, criminal justice system involvement can come about in two ways. If police respond to an incident of child or partner abuse, they may report on their findings in the home in a fashion that triggers an investigation and a prosecution, in addition to triggering an intervention by the child welfare system. Alternatively, the child welfare authorities may be the first to respond to an allegation of child abuse and neglect, but may refer the matter to a prosecutor if the circumstances seem to warrant the consideration of criminal charges. The criminal charges are likely to be charges of child abuse, neglect, or endangerment; in many jurisdictions the same statutory definitions serve both to identify criminal conduct and to frame the jurisdiction of child welfare authorities. If the child is dead, the charges may be murder or manslaughter.

The materials that follow provide an opportunity to think about criminal prosecutions of mothers who have been abused and whose children have been neglected or abused. These materials are intended to raise questions in three important areas: what are the requirements for proving these criminal cases, what defenses are available to abused mothers, and, to what extent do racial and gender norms influence how we and the courts think about these cases.

Campbell v. State

Supreme Court of Wyoming, 2000.
999 P.2d 649.

■ GOLDEN, JUSTICE.

Appellant Casey Campbell appeals her conviction for felony child endangerment.... We affirm....

FACTS

In 1992, Casey Campbell's eight-month-old daughter, HC, suffered severe injuries at the hands of Campbell's live-in boyfriend, Floid Boyer. The Department of Family Services (DFS) removed HC from Campbell's custody and placed her in foster care. Campbell was convicted of misdemeanor child endangerment. HC was returned to her mother's care on September 16, 1994. Campbell still lived with Boyer and her two other children that he had fathered since HC was removed. On June 27, 1995, while left alone with Boyer, HC received second and third degree burns over eighteen percent of her body. . . .

Boyer admitted causing the burns but claimed the burns were inflicted when he tripped and spilled coffee on the child sometime during the day. Shortly after 7:00 p.m. that evening, Campbell arrived home from work with a friend and the friend's fourteen-year-old daughter who planned to baby sit Campbell's children that evening. The three observed the burns and at least one large blister. The friend recommended that Campbell take HC to the doctor. Campbell and Boyer decided not to follow that advice and, without providing medications for the babysitter, left to play darts at a local bar. The babysitter observed that HC was in pain that evening and dressed her in a large t-shirt. . . . Campbell and Boyer returned home at midnight. By 2:00 a.m., HC's pain was severe, and Campbell decided the burns were serious and required that she take HC to the hospital. Campbell wrapped the child, placed her in a stroller, and walked the few blocks to the hospital.

The treating physician . . . believed the injuries were not consistent with hot liquid as the source. The police were contacted, and a criminal investigation began. Police went to the home and checked the carpet where Boyer alleged that he had spilled the coffee, finding no signs of a spill because the carpet was dry as was the padding underneath, and there was a layer of chalky dust underneath the pad. Boyer agreed to questioning at the police station, and DFS was contacted. . . . The conditions of the home were deemed deplorable, and DFS decided that Campbell's other two children should be placed in protective custody . . . with Boyer's parents.

Campbell was arrested on charges of child abuse and [felony] child endangerment, [and] released on bond . . . Before Campbell's trial, Boyer pled guilty to misdemeanor child endangerment.

At trial, the State alleged that Campbell had failed to protect HC from Boyer although she knew Boyer was abusive to the child and failed to get immediate medical care for HC after observing her injuries. The State contended that the unclean condition of Campbell's home required immediate attention because of the risk of infection to a burn victim. . . . [T]he State contended that Campbell knew Boyer was a danger to HC because he disliked HC because he was not her father and because HC was of a different race. In Campbell's defense, Boyer testified that he thought he was HC's father, and had spilled coffee on the child accidentally, causing the burns. He testified that Campbell wanted to take the child to the hospital at 7:00 p.m. that evening, but that he believed the burns were not serious enough to require them to forgo playing darts. He testified that he had been physically abusive to Campbell for years, and he believed that Campbell played darts that night to avoid angering him. Campbell testified that she had been abused by her brother since she was seven years old, by her stepfather since a teenager, and by Boyer since she was sixteen years old, and Boyer had violently assaulted her with knives and guns on past occasions. At the time of HC's injuries, she feared for herself and HC if she defied Boyer that night by refusing to play darts. By 2:00 a.m., she believed that HC's condition had changed because she now had blistered severely, and Boyer and Campbell both testified that they agreed that the child should be taken to the hospital for medical care. . . .

Campbell . . . contends that the [child endangerment] statute is vague as applied to her. . . . The State contends that Campbell endangered HC's life or health by failing to immediately seek medical care after seeing the burns when the lack of cleanliness in her home necessitated medical care without delay. The babysitter and her mother both saw the burns at the same time that Campbell first saw them and testified they believed the child required medical care and had so advised Campbell. Campbell herself testified that she believed the child needed medical care but was too afraid of Boyer to insist upon it at the time. The treating physician testified that the burns required immediate medical attention because of the risk of infection. Campbell did not seek immediate medical care but instead delayed for an eight hour period. Her testimony establishes that she understood that HC probably required immediate medical care and that she as the parent had the duty to provide that care. On this theory of child endangerment, the statute is not unconstitutionally vague as applied.

The State's failure to protect theory is more difficult to resolve. The State contends that "[t]he statute points squarely at any mother who would fail to take reasonable steps to protect her child from known abuse." The State contends that the "known abuse" is the past abuse that HC suffered at the hands of Boyer and that Campbell "fully realized that she had a duty to protect [HC]. . . ." Our concern with the State's contentions is that, if accepted, we would in essence be finding that Campbell was guilty of child endangerment as soon as she accepted the return of custody of her child because she still lived with Boyer. The State, however, also knew that a potentially abusive situation remained at Campbell's home for HC because of Boyer's presence, and, despite that knowledge, DFS agreed that physical custody should be returned to Campbell, and the district court granted legal custody to Campbell. Upon these particular facts, we do not think that Campbell would know that accepting the return of HC's custody would violate the child endangerment statute. Accepting custody of one's child from the State while living with the abuser of whom the State knows does not violate the child endangerment statute.

One's suspicion that the abuser would again harm the child and failure to act despite the suspicion, however, is child endangerment, and evidence at trial established that Campbell held this belief. Campbell testified that

Boyer continued to abuse her and she suspected that Boyer was abusing HC as well. . . .

Despite these fears, Campbell did leave HC alone with Boyer on the day that Boyer burned the child, and then permitted Boyer's further abuse of HC by agreeing with him that she would not seek medical care. Inaction, complicity, or permitting child abuse constitutes child endangerment for failing to protect a child from a dangerous situation, and Campbell's testimony establishes she knew that her conduct was prohibited. Under this theory, the statute is not unconstitutionally vague as applied.

Coercion and Duress

. . . Campbell requests that this Court recognize that her status as a battered woman alters the elements of a coercion or duress defense. The trial court denied the defense's requested instruction on the defense of coercion and duress, finding no evidence of imminent bodily harm. Campbell contends that her years of abuse established evidence of her belief of an imminent danger of death or great bodily harm if she refused Boyer's demand that she leave HC to play darts. . . .

Coercion or duress has been recognized as a defense to criminal charges. . . . Coercion or duress must be present, imminent or impending, and of such a nature so as to induce a well-grounded fear of death or serious bodily harm if the otherwise criminal act is not done. . . .

Campbell contends that she demonstrated that Boyer's past abuse of her reasonably put her in fear of imminent death or serious bodily harm if she did not agree to go play darts that night. . . . She argues that her apprehension was objectively reasonable because she acted "under threats or conditions that a person of ordinary firmness would have been unable to resist". . . . She contends that her years of abuse reasonably caused her to decide that a coffee burn with little visible blistering did not justify provoking an argument with her abuser, and an abused woman of ordinary firmness would have feared for her life that night if she acted to care for HC. . . .

[T]he issue is whether she presented evidence that she faced present, imminent or impending death or serious bodily harm if she acted to care for the child on the night burned. . . . The evidence established that others were present in the house at the time Campbell made her decision and did not witness Campbell's refusing to play darts or witness Boyer's threatening Campbell if she cared for her child. Campbell made no attempt to seek medical advice, take her daughter to the hospital, dress her in loose clothing, or give her medications either for pain or to prevent infection. Campbell testified that she recognized that the burns were extensive and serious and required medical care, and she decided not to seek medical care because her past abuse caused her to realize that she would provoke Boyer. We agree with the district court that this record does not establish that she faced present, imminent or impending death or serious bodily harm, and the district court did not err in refusing to give her defense instruction. . . .

Prosecutorial Misconduct

Campbell claims that the prosecutor improperly made appeals to racial bias.... The prosecutor did make many references to the fact that Boyer is white and HC's father is black as the reason that Boyer disliked the child and his motive for abusing the child in 1992 and upon her return to the home. The prosecution established this motive to prove that Campbell knew Boyer would abuse HC because of her parentage.... Our review of the record confirms the prosecution's use of HC's racial difference to establish motive, and we find no attempt to appeal to racial bias....

In her last argument, Campbell claims that several times the prosecutor suggested to the jury that Campbell had the obligation to present affirmative evidence of her past injuries at the hands of Boyer.... [T]he following was argued by the prosecutor:

> ... Casey did nothing to protect [HC]. That is why we are here.... Casey never did anything to get out of this relationship. She didn't do anything at all.... She got slapped, but where were her broken bones? Where were her burns and what is it that she did to protect this child? It is not there. The evidence wasn't presented.

This argument was made after defense counsel's closing argument declared that Boyer was the abuser and Campbell the victim and the atrocious abuse she suffered was reason enough for the jury to return a verdict of not guilty.... Viewed in its entirety, we find no prejudice to Campbell....

NOTES AND QUESTIONS

1. **Culpability for Child Abuse and Neglect.** Do you think Floid Boyer or Casey Campbell is more responsible for the injuries to HC? Does it make sense to you that Boyer ultimately pled to a misdemeanor while Campbell was found guilty of a felony?

2. **Who is Prosecuted for Child Abuse and Child Neglect?** You might wonder how common this pattern is of a male being responsible for the actual injury and a mother being held responsible, appropriately or not, for neglect of the child. According to the Child Welfare Information Gateway, a service of the U.S. Department of Health and Human Services:

> There is no single profile of a perpetrator of fatal child abuse, although certain characteristics reappear in many studies. Frequently the perpetrator is a young adult in his or her mid–20s without a high school diploma, living at or below the poverty level, depressed, and who may have difficulty coping with stressful situations. In many instances, the perpetrator has experienced violence first-hand. Most fatalities from *physical abuse* are caused by fathers and other male caretakers. Mothers are most often held responsible for deaths resulting from child neglect. http://www.childwelfare.gov/pubs/factsheets/fatality.cfm.

3. **Protective Custody for Campbell's Two Uninjured Children.** Notice that Campbell's two younger children were taken into custody by DFS despite the fact that neither of them was injured. How can you explain

this? They were placed with Boyer's parents. Is this a reasonable placement? What aspects of this placement might worry you?

4. **Mens Rea.** Most crimes have three elements: mens rea, an act, and a
causal relation between the act and the result. In the various forms of
criminal child neglect or endangerment the "act" is a failure to act or an
omission. How would you show mens rea? In criminal law in general, the
mens rea requirement establishes the defendant's culpability. In most
criminal child neglect or endangerment statutes, this requirement is satisfied by showing that the passive parent had knowledge of the likelihood of
abuse. Did Campbell have knowledge that Boyer would abuse HC when she
left the child with him? Did Campbell have knowledge when she left to play
darts that HC's injuries would become worse if she did not receive immediate medical treatment? Is the standard what Campbell understood or what
a reasonable person would have understood under the circumstances? For a
fuller discussion of these issues, see Ricki Rhein, *Assessing Criminal
Liability for the Passive Parent*, 9 CARDOZO WOMEN'S L.J. 627 (2003).

5. **Defenses to Failure to Protect Prosecutions.** Casey Campbell's
attorney tried to claim the defense of duress, arguing that Campbell had
repeatedly been seriously abused by Boyer and that she feared renewed
violence if she took HC to the hospital immediately instead of playing darts
with Boyer. The trial court ruled that she had not carried her burden of
showing that she would have been faced with "imminent" death or serious
injury if she had provided assistance to the child. Do you think that the
trial court ruled correctly or not? Why does the court emphasize that she
did not even provide medicine or a loose T-shirt to HC before going to play
darts? Does this mean that she was not concerned about the child or that
she was genuinely afraid of what Boyer might do to her or HC? The
prosecutor implied that the fact that she had no broken bones or serious
burns meant that she was not at risk of serious injury. Is this accurate?
Think back to Chapter Nine and the use of testimony on battering in other
duress cases. Would expert testimony have helped Ms. Campbell? Why
would it have been relevant? Many courts have refused to admit this
testimony in failure to protect cases. Jeanne A. Fugate, *Who's Failing
Whom? A Critical Look at Failure-to-Protect Laws*, 76 N.Y.U.L. REV. 272
(2001).

Why do you think courts are reluctant to accept expert testimony in
these cases? Wyoming has a statute that permits a defendant to introduce
expert testimony on "battered woman syndrome" if the defendant is
charged with a crime involving the use of force against another and if the
defendant is raising a claim of self-defense. In an omitted portion of the
opinion in *Campbell v. State*, the Court rejected the defendant's argument
that she should be permitted to introduce expert testimony because her
situation was analogous to that mentioned in the statute. Does this make
you think again of Joan Meier's argument, excerpted in Chapter Ten, that
although courts are now comfortable accepting claims as to the effects of

abuse in many criminal proceedings, they are uneasy with them in proceedings that involve family relations? Why is this?

Some states provide statutory defenses if the accused fears that intervention on behalf of the child would result in physical injury to herself or would increase the danger to the child. For example, Iowa law provides that a parent is guilty of child endangerment if he or she "knowingly permits the continuing physical or sexual abuse of a child or minor. However, it is an affirmative defense to this subsection if the person had a reasonable apprehension that any action to stop the continuing abuse would result in substantial bodily harm to the person or the child or minor." I.C.A. § 726.6(e) (2006). Would a provision like this have assisted Ms. Campbell? If you were asked to testify to the legislature, would you recommend the adoption of a defense like Iowa's?

Dorothy E. Roberts
Mothers Who Fail to Protect their Children

From MOTHER TROUBLES (Julia E. Hanigsberg and Sara Ruddick, eds. 1999).

Accounting for Private and Public Responsibility

Mothers are held responsible for the harm that befalls their children even when they do not inflict it. The duty imposed on mothers to protect their children is unique and enormous. . . .

I first grasped the extraordinary scope of maternal responsibility when I began teaching criminal law. To find evidence of this duty, one need only open first-year criminal law casebooks to the omission liability section. The doctrine of omission liability bases criminal culpability on a person's failure to perform a legal duty rather than the usual requirement that she perform an affirmative act. Most of the cases on omission liability, if not all, concern mothers (or women in mothering roles) who failed to care properly for their children. . . .

Overwhelming evidence of the connection between men's battering of women and the battering of children reveals that power relationships, rather than mothers' infirmities, are responsible for family violence. Women who fail to protect their children from violence are often victims of violence themselves. Numerous studies show that in most families in which the father batters the mother, the children are also battered. . . .

Courts, however, have not asked how this web of violence affects the mother's culpability. They presume that a woman's obligation to her children always takes precedence over her own interest in independence and physical safety. They presume that a woman's maternal instinct can always prevail over the harmful aspects of her children's lives. . . .

This view of the protective mother, however, repeats the assumption that mothers' interests and children's interests are always complementary. There are also many mothers who . . . ignore or paper over the child abuse they witness in order to maintain their relationship with the batterer. . . . [T]he truth is that mothers' interests and children's interests often conflict. And mothers sometimes choose against their children in order to be safe, to pursue their own ambitions, to hold on to a man. Recognizing this conflict allows us to see that women have an identity apart from their children. Part of the quandary raised by maternal failures is determining how mothers may retain their own identity without violating their moral duty to protect their children from harm.

Punishing Mothers' Resistance

While some mothers who stay with their batterer sacrifice their children's interests for self-destructive reasons, others put their children at risk by resisting domination in the home. One approach that takes negligent mothers' situations into account argues that battered mothers are physically and emotionally incapable of controlling or escaping violence in their homes. Legal scholar Nancy Erickson, for example, proposes that a battered mother charged with failing to protect her child should be allowed to present expert testimony that "by reason of her battered condition, she was unable to prevent the battering of her children." Several states provide an affirmative defense to a charge of allowing child abuse to defendants who feared that acting to prevent the abuse would risk greater harm to the child or to the defendant. This is an important legal strategy because it forces courts to consider the real limits on a mother's ability to guard her children from violence.

I believe that the law should go further to situate mothers' failure to protect their children in its *political* context. Rather than seeing battering as an excuse for mothers' failure to protect their children, we need to rethink the relationship between motherhood and family violence. Battering arises out of a struggle for power in the home.... Many men respond to women's attempts to resist male privilege in the home by violently subjugating both women and children. The typical pattern of assault suggests that male violence is not random, but "is directed at a woman's gender identity." ... Battering typically is evoked by struggles around gender issues, such as sex, housework, child care, the woman's employment outside the home, and her involvement in family finances. Batterers often justify their assaults with complaints about the woman's inadequate performance of household chores. A batterer's violence is his attempt to control the boundaries of the woman's role in the family....

When the criminal law punishes battered mothers for failing to fulfill their maternal role ... it may be punishing women's resistance. Let me be clear. I am not arguing that permitting child abuse is a means of resisting a subjugating maternal role. Rather, I am arguing that child abuse for which mothers are punished is often triggered by the mothers' resistance in the home. These battered mothers are faced with the dilemma that their fight for greater power exacerbates the violence not only against themselves but also against their children.

Judges' decisions in child abuse cases support my proposition that the criminal law punishes mothers' resistance. Courts treat mothers who appear pathetically weak or deranged more leniently than mothers who were struggling to retain power in their homes. Perhaps the most well-known example is the case of Hedda Nussbaum, whose live-in companion, Joel Steinberg, killed their six-year-old illegally adopted daughter, Lisa

Steinberg, in New York City in 1987. Nussbaum must have been aware of the danger to Lisa for some time: At the time of her death, Lisa's hair was heavily matted, her skin was dirty and scaling, and her body was covered with bruises. Yet Nussbaum was never convicted for failing to protect Lisa. The press depicted Nussbaum as hunched over, demented, and totally subservient to Joel Steinberg's psychological spell. Prosecutors dropped manslaughter charges against Nussbaum after she underwent months of intensive, residential therapy at a psychiatric hospital. . . .

By contrast, courts consider more rational mothers' experience of battering to support a finding of guilt because it evidenced their knowledge of their husbands' potential for violence. . . .

Maternal Failure in the Context of Idealized Motherhood

Not only do courts ignore the context of family violence, but they judge mothers in relation to biased expectations. Courts often seem less concerned with protecting children from abuse than with imposing an idealized and racialized standard of selfless motherhood. . . .

Judging mothers who fail to protect their children according to this standard tends to disadvantage Black women. . . . Black women are burdened with myths about their unfitness as mothers, which distort the public's view of their maternal failures. From the image of the lascivious jezebel during the antebellum era to the contemporary mythical welfare queen, Black mothers are supposed to pass on a culture of depravity, dependency, and criminality to their children. It is easily assumed that they didn't stop the violence in their homes because they are generally careless about raising their children.

In [a] front-page article reporting the death of a 5–month–old baby from burns inflicted by the mother's boyfriend, the New York Times devoted an entire page to exploring the cause of the tragedy. Although the mother claimed that the boyfriend had beaten her and the baby, the article focused solely on the failure of city welfare workers to supervise the Black mother adequately. Perhaps images of Black mothers' depravity influenced the reporter's obsession with maternal regulation. The article also appeared to chastise the mother for raising her children in a poor, inner-city neighborhood, noting that "[l]ater in 1990, Ms. Harden and her children moved into a crumbling, drug-infested building in Harlem, where young men peddled crack and most of the tenants were, like herself, formerly homeless families from city shelters." It was there that her son would be fatally burned. In this way, blaming mothers for failure to protect their children becomes a way of justifying stepped-up state supervision of poor Black mothers. . . .

The ideal of mothers' exclusive responsibility for children also justifies punishing Black mothers in particular. Black women's style of mothering is often misinterpreted as child neglect precisely because it violates this standard. Black mothers have a long-standing cultural tradition of sharing child raising with other women in the community. These cooperative networks include members of the extended family (grandmothers, sisters, aunts, and cousins), as well as non blood kin and neighbors. . . . Social workers and judges often believe that Black children raised in these arrangements are neglected because they do not have the constant, exclusive attention of their mother. This is yet another way in which the law punishes women's resistance to an oppressive maternal role, thwarting the potential of alternative visions of motherhood.

The Case of Julia Cardwell

Commonwealth v. Cardwell [515 A.2d 313 (Pa. Super. 1986)] illustrates the complicated interweaving of these considerations of private and public responsibility. Julia Cardwell was charged with failing to protect her daughter Alicia from sexual abuse by Clyde Cardwell, her husband and Alicia's stepfather. Clyde sexually abused Alicia for five years, beginning when Alicia was about eleven years old. Ten months passed between the time that Julia became aware of the danger to her child and the date Alicia finally ran away from home.... During those ten months, Julia did take steps to try to escape with Alicia. Julia wrote two letters to Clyde, expressing her awareness of the abuse and her plan to leave him. She made an unsuccessful attempt to move to her parents' house, moving some of her and Alicia's clothing and applying for Alicia to transfer schools. The destruction of her parents' house by fire, killing her father, frustrated Julia's plans.

Were Julia's actions enough to relieve her of criminal or moral culpability? Clyde's violence, combined with the setbacks Julia encountered, might explain Julia's failure to do more to save Alicia. Alicia testified at the trial that she and her mother were afraid of Clyde. He had beaten Julia, smashed objects in the house, punched holes in the walls, and kept a pistol on the mantel piece. Violence often escalates and becomes lethal when battered women attempt to leave the batterer....

Julia may have also feared social workers as much as Clyde.... Reporting Clyde's criminal conduct ... might have triggered an investigation of Julia, possibly leading a judge to remove Alicia from her care or even to terminate her parental rights. Facing the possible loss of her child, Julia may have decided to try to evade Clyde on her own.

For Black women, the stakes are heightened. Too often when police are summoned to a Black home, they end up injuring family members and even shooting someone to death. Too often social workers are especially quick to remove Black children from their parents. Given the history of racism in the administration of criminal justice and child protective services, Black women may be reluctant to utilize government agencies as a means of solving their domestic problems. Black legal scholar Kimberle Crenshaw identifies this reluctance as "a community ethic against public intervention, the product of a desire to create a private world free from the diverse assaults on the public lives of racially subordinated people." Of course, being beaten should not be the price of allegiance to one's community. It is a lie that Black women who defy a violent partner are disloyal to their race. But resistance to an oppressive legal system or the plain fear of police terror is yet another piece of the complicated puzzle a battered mother must put in place to protect her children.

Even without the threat of death or separation, the decision to leave may be difficult. Protecting the child from abuse is one of many factors the mother must consider in deciding what is best for her child. The abuse may be sporadic, and may seem less hazardous than the consequences of leaving home C losing the main source of income, moving into shoddy housing or a dangerous shelter, ripping the child from friends and family, finding childcare, and depriving the child of the father's positive features. Taking all of these factors into account, then, transforms what first appeared as a mother's inaction into an intricate resistance strategy.

I can also imagine, on the other hand, that Julia ignored for years the signs that Alicia was being abused and could have tried harder to leave Clyde once she knew he was raping her daughter. There are usually clues even before the incest begins. Before Clyde began having sex with Alicia, he bought her sexually suggestive clothing, photographed her in sexual positions, and wrote sexually explicit notes to Alicia nearly every day. Did Julia not ever come across the clothing, the photographs, the letters? Sexual abuse usually marks a child's behavior. Alicia became pregnant twice and had two abortions. I also wonder why Julia chose to write to Clyde to express her disapproval, suggesting a hope for reconciliation. Perhaps Julia's desire to maintain a relationship with her husband superseded her concern for her child. Perhaps her accommodation to patriarchal ideals, rather than resistance to them, caused her maternal failure.

It is impossible to explore these possibilities, however, unless the inquiry attends to the mother's social circumstances in failure to protect cases. The court in Cardwell did not even consider whether Clyde's terrorization of Julia and Alicia mitigated Julia's criminal liability. Ironically, the court only used Julia's efforts to challenge Clyde's abuse as evidence against her, finding that Julia's letters to Clyde established her awareness of the abuse and its endangerment of her daughter's welfare. Because courts are concerned only with a woman's compliance with an idealized standard of selfless, exclusive motherhood, they neglect to examine the power struggle typically underlying family violence. A political focus would enable courts to question the expectation that mothers alone are responsible for children and to recognize mothers' oppositional acts. Understanding how maternal failures originate in family power struggles, themselves embedded in structures of racism, sexism, and poverty, rather than in mothers' pathologies, will help us direct mothers' opposition toward more liberating forms of resistance and direct social resources toward creating better conditions for mothers.

Political Support for Mothers

I can only explain my position as a political stand on behalf of mothers. I have asked myself whether my reluctance to blame mothers stems from my own stereotypical belief in maternal love. Do I, too, hold fast to the myth that no mother would willingly allow her child to be harmed, and therefore look for some social explanation for any maternal failure? No: My reluctance is based not on a romantic faith in mothers, but on a realistic assessment of the conditions of mothering and a desire to make them more equitable. Although not all mothers are treated the same or treat their children the same, all mothers struggle, to various degrees, against oppressive social circumstances. The dominant culture and legal system place the bulk of child rearing on mothers' shoulders without the compensation, power, and support they need and deserve. And it is those very mothers who are most likely to be charged with crimes or to have their children taken away C poor women of color C who also face the greatest obstacles. They are the ones I identify with the most....

My allegiance to mothers does not mean taking sides against children....

Protecting children depends far more on addressing social inequities by identifying with mothers than on pronouncing mothers' guilt.

NOTES AND QUESTIONS

1. ***Campbell v. State* and Women's Resistance.** One of Dorothy Roberts's many powerful claims in this article is that domestic violence is often an effort by the abuser to maintain power within the family and in the relationship with her partner. Thus, when the woman begins to get a little "uppity" and rejects the role of the passive house servant, she is likely to get abused as a result. Does this hold true in *Campbell*, excerpted above? Consider the following. The hot liquid "spills" on HC while her mother is at work and while HC is with Boyer who is to care for her. Furthermore, the prosecutor implies that Boyer has a particular animus toward HC because she is the issue of an interracial sexual relationship between Campbell, currently Boyer's girlfriend, and another man. Could Boyer's abuse of HC be a means of disciplining Campbell for working and leaving him in charge of the child, those reversing traditional gender roles? Could it be a way of retaliating against her for having had sexual relations with other men? How does Roberts's theory work in connection with other domestic violence cases you have read?

2. **Gender Stereotypes and Failure to Protect Prosecutions.** Roberts claims that rational mothers are likely to be found guilty of failing to protect their children because they understand, from the abuse aimed at them, their partners' capacity for violence. Roberts's argument is that women who act like stereotypical weak women—timid, afraid, and unable to cope with the situation—are more likely to be "saved" by the legal system from a conviction. How convincing did you find her arguments?

Roberts is by no means alone in believing that gender norms and stereotypes affect courts' views of mothers' culpability when their children are injured by someone else. Jeanne Fugate has argued that mothers are supposed to be all-knowing, all-sacrificing, and nurturing (as opposed to being financial providers.) *Who's Failing Whom? A Critical Look at Failure-to-Protect Laws*, 76 N.Y.U.L. REV. 272 (2001). See also Elizabeth M. Schneider, BATTERED WOMEN AND FEMINIST LAWMAKING (2000). Do you see these stereotypes at work in any of the cases that you've read in this chapter?

3. **The Impact of Race on Failure to Protect Prosecutions.** Elsewhere, Dorothy Roberts has written:

> The disproportionate number of black children in America's child welfare system is staggering. Black children make up more than two-fifths of the foster care population, although they represent less than one-fifth of the nation's children. In Chicago, ninety-five percent of children in foster care are black. The racial imbalance in New York City's foster care population is truly mind-boggling: out of 42,000 children in the system at the end of 1997, only 1,300 were white.... A national study of child protective services by the U.S. Department of Health and Human Services reported that "[m]inority children, and in particular African American children, are more likely to be in foster care placement than receive in-home services, even when they have the same problems and characteristics as white children." ... Once removed from their homes, black children remain in foster care longer, are moved more often, receive fewer services, and are less likely to be either returned home or adopted than any other children. Dorothy E. Roberts, *Child Welfare and Civil Rights*, 2003 U. ILL. L. REV. 171.

Some have argued that there are two family law systems in the U.S.: The divorce and custody system that serves white, middle-class families and the child protective services system that serves poor, minority families. Another commentator tells of a visit of someone from South Africa to the Juvenile Court in Philadelphia. After spending a day observing the Juvenile Court, the visitor turned to his American host and said, "Where's the white Juvenile Court?" Martin Guggenheim, *The Rights of Parents and Children in Foster Care*, 6 N.Y. CITY L. REV. 61 (2003).

One way to explain the disproportionate number of black children (and other minority children) in the foster care system is by reference to the stereotypes of Black mothers that pervade society. For decades, black women have been seen as likely to "breed carelessly and disastrously" with the result that motherhood is likely to be the lot of those "least able to rear children properly." Beth A. Mandel, *The White Fist of the Child Welfare System*, 73 U.CIN. L. REV. 1131 (2005) (quoting Margaret Sanger.) Similarly, black women have been considered inadequate mothers because they have been part of the employed labor force and thus not home full-time with their children. They have also been viewed as inadequate mothers because as single mothers, they have not provided their children with the idealized two-parent family. Finally, as single mothers, they have also been charged with responsibility for the problems of black families. To the extent that caseworkers and courts accept these stereotypes, even unconsciously, it is understandable that they would not want to leave a child in the care of such a person. Given the cases and other materials you have read, do you think racism and racial stereotypes play a role in the disproportionate number of removals of children from the homes of mothers of color?

4. **The Impact of Poverty on Failure to Protect Prosecutions.** Poverty also is a clear factor in the removal of children from their homes. It overlaps with minority status. Again, quoting from Dorothy Roberts:

The child welfare system is designed to address mainly the problems of poor families. Because black children are disproportionately poor, we would expect a corresponding racial disparity in the child welfare caseload. The Illinois Department of Children and Family Services prepares a multicolored map that shows the distribution of abuse and neglect cases in Chicago. Neighborhoods with the highest concentration of cases form an L-shaped pattern colored in red. There is another map of Chicago with the same color coding that shows levels of poverty across the city. The poorest neighborhoods in the city form an identical red L-shaped pattern. A third map shows the distribution of ethnic groups in Chicago. The red-colored section marking the city's segregated black neighborhoods is virtually a perfect match. In Chicago, there is a geographical overlap of child maltreatment cases, poverty and black families. Dorothy E. Roberts, *Child Welfare and Civil Rights*, 2003 Univ. Ill. L. Rev. 171.

Another study has shown that the major reason children are removed from their parents' homes is not abuse, but rather inadequate parental income. Martin Guggenheim, *Somebody's Children*, 113 Harv. L. Rev. 1716 (2000). Most of these are neglect cases, not abuse cases, and they frequently involve the problems of poverty: inadequate medical care, inadequate child care while the parent works, or inadequate housing including a lack of heat. Dorothy E. Roberts, *Child Welfare and Civil Rights*, 2003 Univ. Ill. L. Rev. 171. Inadequate housing would be a particular problem for parents who are victims of violence and have left their abusers but have nowhere to go.

The welfare system, with its emphasis on forcing recipients into work, may also contribute to child abuse. In a context in which mothers must work to continue to receive state assistance and in which there is inadequate child care, it should not be surprising that children are often left in the care of people who poses risks to them. Morgan B. Ward Doran and Dorothy E. Roberts, *Welfare Reform and Families in the Child Welfare System*, 61 Md. L. Rev. 386 (2002). For more information on the interplay between the welfare system and impoverished mothers' decisions about child care see Dorothy E. Roberts, *Welfare Reform and Economic Freedom: Low Income Mothers' Decisions about Work at Home and in the Market*, 44 Santa Clara L. Rev. 1029 (2004).

Most of the work on the relationship between poverty and child removals in minority communities has been gathered in the context of child protective actions, not criminal prosecutions for failure to protect. Is there any reason, however, to think that the overlap between prosecutions, minority racial status, and poverty would not be equally great if not greater? Furthermore, a recent study of prosecutions of parents for child neglect found that in hyperthermia cases in which the parent had left the child in the car and the child died as a result, 85.7% of working class or poor parents were prosecuted whereas only 23.3% of white collar professionals were. Jennifer M. Collins, *Crime and Parenthood*, 100 Nw. U. L. Rev. 807 (2006). Again, this study reinforces the significance of poverty in parental prosecutions.

5. **Roberts's Political Stance on Behalf of Mothers.** Why does Roberts think that admission of testimony on the effects of battering on women is a desirable but inadequate remedy for the problems of abused mothers whose children are neglected? To what degree do you think the injuries to children stem, at least in part, from inequitable conditions of mothering and from society's refusal to take the actions necessary to support poor mothers and children?

Two United States Supreme Court cases that you will read later in this book exemplify this refusal. In *DeShaney v. Winnebago County Department of Social Services*, 489 U.S. 189 (1989), the Court held that a child's liberty interests had not been unconstitutionally invaded by the Department in a situation in which the child was subject to serious abuse at home and the Department had been informed of the abuse but took no action. In dissent, Justice Blackmun lamented, "Poor Joshua! Victim of repeated attacks by an irresponsible, bullying, cowardly, and intemperate father, and abandoned by [the Department] . . . who knew or learned what was going on, and yet did essentially nothing. . . ." More recently, in a reaffirmation of *DeShaney* that you read in Chapter One and will read more in depth in Chapter Fourteen, the Court ruled that even a restraining order that contained within it a specific message to the police stating "you shall" arrest a violator of the order did not create a property interest in the holder of the order within the meaning of the Fourteenth Amendment's due process clause. *Town of Castle Rock v. Gonzales*, 545 U.S. 748 (2005). The restraining order protected its holder from further abuse by her estranged husband and provided limited visitation for the abuser with their children whom he abducted one afternoon. When she realized the children had been kidnapped, the mother pled several times with the police to arrest the abuser and return the children. At one point, she even informed the police where the husband was with the children, but the police did nothing. Ultimately, the abuser came to the police, shooting. The police killed him in a firefight and found the bodies of the children in the cab of the truck. Do you agree with Roberts that society is failing mothers who have been abused?

Do you agree that society places "the bulk of child rearing on mothers' shoulders without the compensation, power, and support they need and deserve"? What does Roberts mean when she says that she takes a political stand on behalf of mothers?

E. TRADITIONAL TENSIONS AND NEW COLLABORATIONS

As you may have gathered from the materials above, there have traditionally been tensions between those who work with abused and neglected children and those who advocate on behalf of their abused mothers. The child welfare workers have seen mothers as adults who fail to provide protection for their innocent children. The mothers' advocates have viewed mothers as caught in an impossible, dangerous situation and have seen the child welfare workers as yet another threat to their clients. Just in the past decade a few agencies and individuals from both sides have come together, often with Juvenile and Family Court judges, to try to overcome their mutual distrust and find ways of advancing children's welfare through improving the lives of the mothers.

The following excerpts show the tensions between advocates for these different constituencies and then an effort to bring their work together. The second excerpt is a joint effort of the National Resource Center on Domestic Violence, the Child Welfare League of America, and other organizations committed to promoting the well-being of children and victims of domestic violence. This report is intended to be a resource for advocates of battered women whose children have been abused or neglected.

Janet Findlater and Susan Kelly
Child Protective Services and Domestic Violence
9 The Future of Children 84 (1999).

For years, domestic violence service providers and CPS have worked with families experiencing both forms of abuse, but until recently they had not begun working together to create safe, appropriate, and effective responses to family violence. The relationship between child welfare workers and battered women's advocates has been difficult, at best. Mistrust has been common, noncollaboration the rule.

A significant obstacle to collaboration has been the tension caused by the different historical developments and missions of the domestic violence and child welfare movements.... Some battered women and their advocates viewed CPS as yet another public institution that overlooked domestic violence and the needs of battered women, or blamed battered women for the harm their batterers caused to their children.

The mistrust has existed on both sides. Because of CPS's focus on the safety of the child, caseworkers did not consider the identification of domestic violence to be important to accomplishing CPS goals. When domestic violence was identified, CPS workers have often misunderstood its dynamics and held battered mothers responsible for ending it. Furthermore, as the domestic violence movement has focused primarily on the needs of battered women, and been slower to address the needs of these women's children, CPS workers have not viewed battered women's advocates as potential allies in their efforts to protect children....

Linda Spears
Building Bridges Between Domestic Violence Organizations and Child Protective Services
Violence Against Women Online Resources (2000) http://www.vaw.umn.edu/documents/dvcps/dvcps.html#id76318.

Principles for domestic violence-child protection collaboration

Successful collaboration requires a shared framework for the response to battered women and their children. Core principles already guide collaborative efforts in communities across the country. The following discussion explains each principle and raises key policy challenges that face advocates and child protection workers as they practice together to keep children and their battered mothers safe.

- Principle 1: The safety of children is the priority.

    Every procedure, policy or practice of an integrated response to child maltreatment and domestic violence must ensure that children are protected. For example, services to support a battered mother's safety and autonomy must not compromise safety for children. Commitment to this principle can provide essential common ground as child protection workers and domestic violence advocates work through the complex issues of building a collaborative response.

    Policy challenges raised by Principle 1:

    Does a child's s witnessing domestic violence constitute abuse/neglect?

    There is growing consensus that witnessing domestic violence is harmful to children. However, the harm will not be the same for every child, because the level of violence and each child's s experience of the violence are different. Therefore, there is much less agreement about when the harm from witnessing domestic violence is serious enough by itself to constitute possible child abuse and neglect that should be reported to authorities.

    While it is clear that situations in which children are physically injured or sexually assaulted during a domestic violence incident should be reported, other situations are less straightforward and require a careful assessment of danger and risk. For most child protection agencies, the threshold for the finding of emotional abuse and even neglect is quite high, and many domestic violence cases, therefore, will be inappropriate for a referral to CPS. Typically, CPS intervention requires independent corroboration that documents that the neglect and emotional harm is significant and is caused by the actions of the parent.

    When domestic violence cases fall below the threshold for child protection intervention, community-based services are needed to address the problems that children may experience.

- Principle 2: Child safety can often be improved by helping the mother to become safe and by supporting the mother's efforts to achieve safety.

    Child protection strategies should include efforts to enhance a battered mother's s safety.

    Policy challenges raised by Principle 2:

    Should CPS routinely assess for domestic violence at intake?

    Among many child protection workers and domestic violence advocates there is a great deal of concern about whether or not routine child protection service intake assessment for domestic violence should be done. Child protection agencies fear that this assessment will overwhelm the agency with even more new cases. Domestic violence advocates fear that child protection may fail to address, or, even worse, compromise the mother's safety during the intake process. In reality, assessing for domestic violence is already a part of the investigation and risk assessment procedures for many child protection agencies. There is growing consensus that child protection should develop the skills and protocols needed to effectively assess for domestic violence, to determine which cases require child protection intervention and which should be referred to community agencies, and to offer services that promote safety for mother and child.

How do we resolve confidentiality issues in child protection?

Privacy and confidentiality are cornerstones of domestic violence advocacy with battered women. In contrast, child protection agencies are often bound by policies that mean that information contained in safety plans, service plans and case records may be accessible to perpetrators. A batterer may use this information in custody proceedings or to thwart safety plans developed to protect a woman and her children. Confidentiality issues and misunderstandings often hinder collaboration. To avoid unnecessary conflict, advocates and CPS should work together to understand existing policy and look for ways to improve it. Confidentiality policies must balance the CPS's need for information with the battered mother's right to privacy and with advocates' legal/ethical requirements to keep certain information confidential.

- Principle 3: Safety for battered mothers and their children can be supported by holding the batterer, not the adult victim, accountable for the domestic abuse.

  By focusing on perpetrator accountability, we open a new range of resources that can protect children—including restraining orders, prosecution of domestic assaults, and batterer intervention programs. By focusing on perpetrator accountability, we are less likely to blame one victim for harm to another. Batterers must be held accountable for their abuse of women and children, and they must have access to services that eliminate violence and that appropriately and safely support their role as parents.

  While most would agree with this principle, in practice the issues become more complicated.

    [Consider the following scenario: *Last night Gina's boyfriend Mark came home drunk again. They started arguing about money, and Mark slapped and punched Gina. Seven-year-old Sammy ran into the kitchen and started hitting Mark and yelling, "Stop hurting my Mommy!" Mark picked Sammy up by the seat of his pants and yelled, "Stay out of this, you little bastard, you're just like your father—a real loser." He then dropped Sammy, who crashed to the floor. Sammy started crying, and Gina yelled at him to get out of the kitchen. Gina and Mark's one-year-old daughter Jessie started crying in the other room. Mark told Gina to just "let her cry, or she'll grow up to be a stupid baby like you."*

A neighbor called the child abuse hotline to report that there was fighting in the apartment next door and that she could hear the children crying again and worried that they were being hit.

A caseworker subsequently interviewed Gina and Sammy. He decided that Gina has a problem with excessive use of alcohol and is depressed. Sammy appeared scared of Mark. Gina told the caseworker that Mark has come home drunk more frequently in the last year. Gina agreed to get a restraining order against Mark who moved out of the home and began attending a Batterer's Program.]

Gina, for example, did not hit Sammy or Jessie, nor was she the one who dropped Sammy. In fact, Gina tried to get Sammy to leave the kitchen and get out of Mark's way. However, Gina is also a parent who is responsible for making decisions about her kids' lives. When Gina decided that Mark could move back in, after he dropped out of the substance abuse/batterer intervention program, she made a decision that could place her kids at risk. Her decision to let Mark move back in was based on her need for financial support. It is important to understand that Gina did not decide, "Yes, I want Mark to move back in so that Sammy and Jessie are at risk," but, rather, "I have to let him back in or else we'll be homeless."

Given Gina and her children's need for financial support, she had little other choice but to let him move back in. The key to keeping Gina safe is to look beyond the decision she made to fully understand why that was her decision. As CPS and other agencies make efforts to help Gina and her children meet their financial needs, Gina's responsibility is to accept and work with those who are trying to help her. (In Gina's case, financial independence through employment may take awhile, and she may need temporary support from the government along with opportunities to address her substance abuse and depression.)

At the same time, Mark needs to be mandated back to substance abuse treatment and batterer intervention programs. If Mark is once again living with the children and, as a result, the children are in danger, child protection and the courts may have no choice but to remove them from Gina's care.

Understanding the basis for battered mothers' decision-making about their lives and the lives of their children will provide the information necessary to effectively safety plan with them. Understanding a battered mother's decision-making also points out that strategies to protect children that hold mothers like Gina liable for "failure to protect"—either in juvenile or criminal courts—will be counterproductive. For example, arresting Gina for getting access to Mark's financial support would not make Jessie or Sammy safe, nor would it change her decision, as she believed she had no other choice. Such strategies will actually decrease a woman's options (thereby increasing her danger and her partner's control) and may subject children to unnecessarily being taken from their homes and families.

Policy challenges raised by Principle 3:

Decision-making in Child Protection

A decision to substantiate or confirm a report of abuse and neglect is typically made in the context of several key questions: (1) Did the reported incident occur? (2) Is the child at continued risk of harm? (3) Who is responsible for the maltreatment? and (4) Who can protect the child?

The last few questions pose some unique challenges in cases involving domestic violence.

- How do we minimize allegations of failure to protect?

   When child protection workers substantiate maltreatment, they must typically identify what type of abuse occurred (e.g., physical abuse, neglect, sexual abuse, or emotional maltreatment) and how the parent is responsible for the harm. Often a substantiated neglect decision is based on the mother's "failure to protect," when the actual harm to the child is the result of actions by the father or the mother's partner. Neglect allegations due to failure to protect may also be the basis for the petition for juvenile court involvement. In cases of domestic violence, basing substantiation decisions or petition allegations on neglect due to failure to protect can mean that the ultimate cause of the risk, the abuser, is not being addressed.

   Collaborators have worked to achieve mother/child safety without making "failure-to-protect" allegations. Typically, these efforts have been successful when service to the family integrates safety interventions for both victims. We must further consider how a system of case decision-making and substantiation can better reflect the real source of harm to the child. New categories for case findings exist in a few states, including New Jersey and North Dakota, that allow a family to be considered "in need of services" when there is no need for placement. This finding does not require that a parent be blamed for maltreatment but acknowledges that services are needed to protect the child. As these new frameworks evolve, they may help us to resolve this concern.

- How do we hold batterers accountable when they are responsible for child maltreatment?

Typically, this would be done through the criminal legal system process, as many juvenile courts do not have the same authority to criminally punish. In addition, when batterers are not the parent, they are usually not a party to the child protection legal case and therefore the juvenile court has no authority over them. New strategies for connecting criminal and juvenile proceedings may be one solution to this dilemma. However, criminal court involvement may raise other legal and safety issues for battered mothers and their children. For example, a criminal proceeding may delay the juvenile proceeding and result in an escalation in the batterer's s violence, or it may lessen the likelihood that he will agree to voluntary interventions. In additional, criminal court actions will not guarantee that the battered mother or her child will be safe.

Batterers intervention services should also be integrated in the CPS response. Given the legal framework guiding child protection, workers typically have a responsibility to work with fathers who may also be batterers. These services are typically intended to strengthen the father's ability to parent and provide safe visitation with children. We must consider how to provide workers with a framework for deciding what services to provide to these men and what criteria to use for determining when and how these fathers should be part of their children's lives.

- What do we do when battered women abuse and neglect their children?

Sometimes battered women abuse or neglect their children. Reluctance to discuss these concerns has limited our ability to fully consider how to address the safety needs of women and children in these cases.

We are also learning that domestic violence, depression, and substance abuse are interrelated. For children living in these situations, the risk of abuse and neglect is elevated. We must thoughtfully consider how these circumstances place children at risk and work with child protection agencies to develop guidance for properly identifying and appropriately helping these families. In each of these circumstances, safety planning for battered mothers and children will need different yet coordinated strategies.

NOTES AND QUESTIONS

1. **Questions about Building Bridges' Principles.** As part of its first principle, Building Bridges says that it is clear that if a child is injured during an incident of domestic violence a report should be made to the child protective service (CPS). Do you agree? If Sammy had chipped a tooth or been bumped on the head when Mark dropped him, should that be reported? The Alabama statute, which is similar to others in its reporting requirements, says that mandated reporters must report if "the child is known or suspected to be a victim of child abuse or neglect." Ala. Code § 26–14–3 (2006). Neglect is defined as "[n]egligent treatment or maltreat-

ment of a child, including the failure to provide adequate food, medical treatment, supervision, clothing, or shelter." Ala. Code § 26–14–1 (2006).

Are the confidentiality provisions sufficient? Why might information given to CPS possibly need to be made available to the mother's abuser? If the child protective proceeding (against the mother) is aimed at protecting the child, can you imagine circumstances in which the father would have a legitimate interest in obtaining the information? For example, what about information relating to the child's health or educational plan? What if the father denied the abuse? Most advocates for victims of domestic violence would agree that the batterer should be held accountable for the results of his violence. However, as Building Bridges notes, traditionally CPS has not had jurisdiction to pursue criminal charges against the abuser. Under these circumstances, what does it mean to hold the batterer accountable for the violence?

2. **Early Collaborative Undertakings.** Massachusetts was one of the first states to educate Department of Social Service workers to recognize that the safety of abused or neglected children and the safety of the battered mothers are frequently intertwined. As early as 1992, the Massachusetts Department of Social Services developed a protocol for caseworkers to assess risks and plan services for families in which there was a history of domestic violence. The protocol specifically focuses on protecting children by including their mothers in safety planning and by holding the abusers accountable. Furthermore, by the late 1990s, the Department had hired eleven advocates experienced in domestic violence and two domestic violence coordinators to provide training and assistance to its caseworkers, as well as direct services and consultations on particular cases.

In 1988, the Michigan Department of Social Services began its Families First program. This program was aimed at providing services to families with abused or neglected children that would make it safe to retain the children within the family. By the early 1990s, Families First had begun providing services to victims of domestic violence. These include safety planning, transportation, child care, and other assistance so that children can remain safely with their mothers. In 1997, a program assessment found that children and battered mothers could stay together safely in 95% of the cases. Janet Findlater and Susan Kelly, *Child Protective Services and Domestic Violence,* 9 THE FUTURE OF CHILDREN 84 (1999).

3. **The Green Book Initiative.** Recognizing the need for children's advocates and battered women's advocates to learn to work together whenever possible, the National Council of Juvenile and Family Court Judges brought experts from each field together to discuss what they could do. In 1999, they released the "Green Book," which offered suggestions for collaborative practices. The Greenbook National Evaluation Team, The Greenbook Demonstration Initiative: Interim Evaluation Report (2004). In 2000, the federal government provided grants for six demonstration sites nationwide. Joan Meier has noted the importance of the Green Book Initiative.

> The most significant development in this area to date has been the 1999 publication of the so-called "Green Book," a set of joint recom-

mendations developed over approximately two years of organized discussion and debate among child welfare and domestic violence experts,
advocates and judges. The collaboration which spawned the Green
Book was radical; it was the first time that domestic violence and child
welfare advocates had systematically sought (at a national level) to
actively bridge their profound gulfs and mutual mistrust. This process,
designed to assist the government in improving child abuse and neglect
proceedings, created a model of collaboration for child protection,
domestic violence and court officials. The Green Book (and projects it
has spawned) represents a paradigm shift with the potential for transforming the practice of child protection agencies. At root, it seeks to
replace such agencies' conventional perspective, which typically treats
any harm to children as the fault of mothers, with a more domestic
violence-savvy perspective, which places responsibility on male abusers
when appropriate, recognizes that children's interests require the
safety of their mothers, and forms alliances with battered women to
protect both their children and themselves. Joan Meier, *Domestic
Violence, Child Custody, and Child Protection*, 11 AM. U. J. GENDER SOC.
POL'Y & L. 657 (2003).

The results of the Green Book Initiative in the six demonstration sites
were evaluated in 2004, approximately mid-way through the five year
initiative. Not surprisingly, the evaluators found "[i]nstitutional empathy—
the degree to which stakeholders understand and appreciate the mandates,
environments, and policies of other systems—continued to challenge the
collaborations." In general, the projects had been successful in increasing
the active screening for co-occurring issues. This was particularly true of
the child welfare system. The programs had also improved the training that
the various participating agencies offered about the joint occurrence of
domestic violence and child maltreatment. Furthermore, the language of
many official documents, especially child abuse or neglect petitions, had
been changed so as not to blame victimized mothers. The evaluation noted
many other changes; it emphasized that this was only the mid-way point in
the demonstrations so there was time for much more work. It ended by
saying, "[D]irect service staff are reporting that they think about 'cases'
differently—no longer in the context of one family violence incident or
victim, but in the context of all family members and all family strengths
and needs." The Greenbook: Interim Evaluation Report (2004).

CHAPTER THIRTEEN

DOMESTIC VIOLENCE AND TORT LAW

Introduction

This chapter addresses tort actions available to those who suffer, physically and/or emotionally, at the hands of abusive partners. While many abused women do not have the resources to bring tort actions, and many of their abusers are virtually judgment-proof, there are still situations in which a tort claim is a potential source of redress, and of vindication, for someone who has been abused. The symbolic value of such cases also goes well beyond their practical impact—they send a clear message to those batterers with substantial resources that their behavior is not merely condemned by law, but may be costly as well.

This area of law is still in its infancy, for several reasons. Most generally, the problem of accidental injury, and the choice between negligence and strict liability in that arena, has been the central concern of modern tort law. Intentional torts have not, by and large, captured the intellectual interest or imagination of torts theorists. This has begun to change, with the development of the relatively new tort of intentional infliction of emotional distress or outrage, and the realization that it has a potentially significant role to play in addressing issues of contemporary concern, such as discrimination and harassment in the workplace, and domestic violence. But the change is recent, and the field still underdeveloped.

More specifically, the development of domestic tort law has been significantly slowed by the tradition of interspousal tort immunity, the tendency of lawyers to focus on negligently caused injuries instead of intentional tort, the time constraints imposed by statutes of limitations, and the confusion and conflict about the relationship between domestic tort actions and divorce proceedings. In 1992 one researcher reported:

> Among approximately 2600 reported cases of battery, assault, or both, from 1981 through 1990, only fifty-three involved adult parties in domestic relationships. Similarly, during the same time frame, only four reported federal cases involved a claim or counterclaim between adult parties in a domestic relationship. From 1958 through 1990 slightly more than 6000 intentional infliction of emotional distress cases were reported from all state and federal courts. Evaluation of these cases revealed a total of eighteen in which courts have applied the tort action to a domestic abuse fact pattern. Douglas D. Scherer, *Tort Remedies for Victims of Domestic Abuse,* 43 S.C. L. REV. 543 (1992).

The fact that reform has been focused on the threshold issue of access to the tort system has meant that the system has been slow to adapt to the needs of "domestic" claimants:

> Their somewhat specialized experiences of injury and violation were previously excluded from the courts, remaining unheard and unconsidered by the judges who built modern tort law, necessarily, out of the cases that came before them. A parallel could be drawn here with women's experiences in the workplace. The first goal of reformers was to overcome the discrimination that kept women out of so many work environments. The second phase of reform has been to work for change in those environments to make them practically, rather than merely theoretically, accessible to women. In both cases the first step must, of necessity, precede the second, and has enormous symbolic importance. But in both cases the second step may turn out to be the harder struggle, requiring a level of change that stirs up resistance, and offers resisters many fronts on which to fight. Clare Dalton, *Domestic Violence, Domestic Torts and Divorce: Constraints and Possibilities,* 31 NEW ENG. L. REV. 319 (1997).

The succeeding sections look first at interspousal immunity, and its slow demise; then at existing and new causes of action that might be applicable in the context of a battering relationship; then at new actions that abusers have tried in response to victims' actions against them; next at the very considerable barriers to victims' claims imposed by statutes of limitation; and finally at the vexed relationship between tort actions and divorce proceedings. Remember, most tort law is state law. That means there can be significant variations in the law from state to state.

A. INTERSPOUSAL TORT IMMUNITY

The historical rule that one spouse could not sue another gave way slowly over the last half century. For example, Missouri did not finally abolish interspousal immunity for intentional torts until 1986. *Townsend v. Townsend,* 708 S.W.2d 646 (Mo. 1986). *Townsend* recounts the varying rationales that supported interspousal immunity. Initially, it was justified on the basis that a husband and wife were one person at law since women's legal rights belonged to their husbands during marriage. After the passage of the Married Women's Property Acts gave women the right to sue and be sued, courts often argued for the continuation of the immunity on the grounds that allowing a wife to sue her husband for injuries committed during marriage would undermine the harmony essential to a good marriage. These courts did not pay attention to the fact that if the wife wanted to sue her husband, the marriage was probably no longer harmonious. In Chapter One you read an excerpt from Reva Siegel's *The Rule of Love*: *Wife Beating as Prerogative and Privacy,* 105 YALE L. J. 2117 (1996), in which she used the evolution of rules and rhetoric restricting the freedom of women to sue their partners to demonstrate how apparent "reforms" can serve to disguise the perpetuation of status hierarchy, and the subordination of women. *Townsend* is an excellent illustration of the process Siegel describes.

This section adds additional background on the gradual demise of interspousal immunity, and the surprising resilience of some of the more contemporary policy arguments offered in its support.

Clare Dalton

Domestic Violence, Domestic Torts, and Divorce: Constraints and Possibilities

31 NEW ENG. L. REV. 319 (1997).

From the perspective of many modern commentators, interspousal tort immunity has long seemed an anachronism. This has perhaps obscured from modern audiences just how durable the immunity has proved to be in many states, and how very recent its demise. Georgia and Louisiana are still hanging on stubbornly to their immunities. Florida's Supreme Court capitulated, finally, to the demand for its total abolition only in 1993. In the same year Delaware abolished the immunity for negligence cases, with the implication that cases involving intentional torts would be treated similarly, and Hawaii passed legislation generally abolishing the immunity. Missouri made the move only in 1986. . . . Other states could be added to this list of late and reluctant abolitionists, while still others, like Massachusetts, have taken confusingly piecemeal steps toward reform, with the first steps coming early, but the last coming late. When you add to this the crucial fact that not many domestic tort suits are brought, for some obvious and some not-so-obvious reasons, it becomes apparent that there has been relatively little opportunity for state courts to "develop" their domestic tort law to fit current understandings and needs, or to tinker creatively with the fit between tort litigation and divorce proceedings, even if inclined to do so. . . .

Back in the nineteenth century the immunity was understood to flow from the even earlier idea that a woman was merged with her husband in marriage, so that as an indivisible marital unit, neither partner could sue the other on any cause of action, tortious or otherwise. The husband, of course, was the legal representative of this marital unit, and the only partner endowed with legal capacity to pursue its goals or protect its interests in court. This highly legalized explanation served to distance the legal profession from another enduring ideology—that as head of the household, the husband, father and master was in fact privileged to discipline those under his sovereignty, whether wife, children or servants, which privilege extended to the use of reasonable physical "chastisement."

By the end of the nineteenth century, however, the Married Women's Property Acts and Earnings Acts, supported by an energetic women's movement, had made significant inroads on the "marital unity" ideology, endowing women with legal personality and capacity, and thereby recognizing their individuality. . . .

While it was possible to hang on to interspousal tort immunity simply through obdurately restrictive interpretations of Married Women's Property Acts or related legislation, reformulated policy arguments were usually brought in to provide a second line of defense. The two most crucial arguments, often used in tandem, were the "domestic harmony" argument and the "privacy" argument. Domestic harmony, the argument goes, requires that a state committed to the institution of marriage—as all states are—should encourage the maintenance of marital relationships, and not provide discontented partners with opportunities for blowing their domestic grievances out of all proportion, exacting revenge for minor slights and injuries, rather than kissing and making up. Family life, the privacy argument goes, is an essential feature of society, but at the same time fragile, requiring protection from the incursions of the state. To some extent, both arguments propose, we are better off tolerating abuses within that private sphere than we would be trying to micromanage family relationships.

Both domestic harmony and privacy arguments have proved vulnerable, over time, to the feminist critique that they privilege men over women in relationships in which privacy can too easily become a license for abuse, and in which the illusion of "harmony" is too frequently maintained by male dominance and female subservience. In the often extreme cases in which state Supreme Courts have done away with interspousal tort immunity, it would have been preposterous to argue that there was any "harmony" left to preserve, and recognizing the "privacy" argument would have made a mockery of the state's power to protect its citizens against private violence. Nonetheless, these arguments, unlike the older "marital unity" argument, still exert residual influence on the legal system, just as they do on popular thinking, complicating the impetus for reform.

NOTES AND QUESTIONS

1. **The Privacy Argument.** Political theorist Carole Pateman said in 1989: "The dichotomy between the private and the public is central to almost two centuries of feminist writing and struggle; it is, ultimately, what the feminist movement is about." Carole Pateman, THE DISORDER OF WOMEN: DEMOCRACY, FEMINISM AND POLITICAL THEORY (1989). For a survey of feminist analysis of the public/private distinction, and its role in the subordination of women, see Frances Olsen, *Constitutional Law: Feminist Critiques of the Public/Private Distinction,* 10 CONST. COMMENT 319 (1993) and Ruth Gavison, *Feminism and the Public/Private Distinction,* 45 STAN. L. REV. 1 (1992). Catharine MacKinnon points out that privacy arguments do more than simply deprive women of remedies for the violence that subordinates them. Such arguments actually exacerbate women's situation. According to MacKinnon, the "right to privacy is a right of men 'to be let alone' to oppress women one at a time." Catharine MacKinnon, TOWARDS A FEMINIST THEORY OF THE STATE (1989).

Most recently, arguments about "public" responses to "private" violence against women have centered around the contested constitutionality of the federal civil rights provision enacted as part of the 1994 Violence Against Women Act. See, for example, Sally F. Goldfarb, *Violence Against Women and the Persistence of Privacy,* 61 OHIO ST. L.J. 1 (2000). This provision and the *Morrison* case declaring it unconstitutional receive extensive discussion in Chapter Sixteen.

2. **Interspousal Immunity in Georgia and Louisiana.** As the text notes, Georgia and Louisiana appear to be the only states that are "still hanging on stubbornly to their immunities." In Georgia, the common law doctrine of interspousal tort immunity is codified in Ga. Code. Ann. § 19–3–8 (2006). In 2003, the Georgia Supreme Court refused to allow a divorcing wife to sue her husband for injuries that she had suffered in a motorcycle accident prior to the marriage. *Gates v. Gates,* 587 S.E.2d 32 (Ga.2003). It held that if the immunity were to be abridged or abolished, it should be done by the legislature, not the court. The Court applied the common law doctrine that marriage extinguished any tort action that one spouse might have against the other.

The situation in Louisiana is different. In *Duplechin v. Toce,* 497 So.2d 763 (La. Ct. App. 1986), the court found that the state's immunity statute only suspended the right to sue until the parties were legally separated or divorced. Ironically, this position may provide better protection for some women than outright abrogation of the immunity, because it allows more time after separation for a suit to be brought.

3. **Partial Abolition of Interspousal Tort Immunity.** Some states like Vermont and Nevada have only abolished interspousal tort immunity for negligence actions involving automobile accidents. Those accidents usually involve insurance that can pay the judgment. See *Richard v. Richard,* 300 A.2d 637 (Vt. 1973) and *Rupert v. Stienne,* 528 P.2d 1013 (Nev. 1974). In *Ward v. Ward,* 583 A.2d 577 (Vt. 1990), the court allowed an intentional tort action to go forward, "assuming, but not deciding," that such an action could be brought. Are there situations in which victims of domestic violence might be injured in an automobile accident and might want to sue the driver? Are these likely to be negligence or intentional tort actions?

4. **Civil Suits for Marital Rape.** The marital rape immunity, shielding rape within marriage from criminal liability, has proven even more resistant to change than interspousal tort immunity. While some (surprisingly few) states have done away with it altogether, many others retain significant distinctions between rape and sexual assault inside and outside of marriage. See Jill Elaine Hasday, *Contest and Consent: A Legal History of Marital Rape,* 88 CAL. L. REV. 1373 (2000). Chapter Four discussed marital rape in more detail.

A separate question is whether the existence of criminal immunity will affect civil liability for rape or sexual assault of a spouse. In their treatise, Domestic Torts, Family Violence, Conflict and Sexual Abuse (1989 & Supp. 1996), Leonard Karp and Cheryl Karp, suggest:

> In jurisdictions that have abrogated the marital rape exemption in criminal cases, there should now be no impediment to bringing a tort case in a civil action based upon the rape. Moreover, regardless of

whether the jurisdiction in question has abrogated the marital rape exemption, in criminal cases, one should always consider a civil action for assault and battery, as these jurisdictions may not necessarily preclude the civil action.

Karp and Karp's position is supported by *Lusby v. Lusby*, 390 A.2d 77 (Ct. App. Md. 1978), in which the court allowed a battery action in tort to proceed against the plaintiff's husband on the grounds that he had raped her. Maryland had, and continues to have, a criminal marital rape exemption. MD. CODE, Criminal Law § 3–318 (2006).

5. **The Constitutionality of Interspousal Tort Immunities.** Most states have abolished their interspousal tort immunities through legislation, or through decisions in which the highest court of the state has exercised its prerogative to adapt the common law to changing social conditions. For most litigants, therefore, there has been no need to invoke constitutional doctrine to support the argument that interspousal tort immunities have no place in late twentieth century tort jurisprudence. However, it can certainly be argued that interspousal tort immunities discriminate against married people in violation of the equal protection guarantees of the Fourteenth Amendment. In 1984 the Seventh Circuit invalidated Illinois' immunity on that basis. *Moran v. Beyer*, 734 F.2d 1245 (7th Cir. 1984). Since the discrimination was, on its face, between married and unmarried people, and not between men and women (although we might argue that its impact is disproportionately felt by women), the lowest level of equal protection scrutiny, "rational basis" scrutiny, was applied, rather than the intermediate level of scrutiny adopted by the Supreme Court for gender-based discrimination. Nonetheless, the immunity was held to flunk even this least stringent of tests. In contrast, the Georgia Supreme Court has repeatedly found the doctrine of interspousal immunity to be constitutional on the grounds that it is reasonably related to the promotion of domestic harmony and treats men and women equally. *Robeson v. International Indem. Co.*, 282 S.E.2d 896 (Ga.1981); *Gates v. Gates*, 587 S.E.2d 32 (Ga.2003).

6. **Reinstating Interspousal Immunity through Insurance.** For many people, tort actions are only worth pursuing if there is a possibility of recovering money damages. Insurance is often the source of these funds. Jennifer Wriggins has shown how insurance contracts recreate many of the same barriers to recovery that previously existed through the immunities doctrine.

> Insurance (or the lack of it) is extremely important in all aspects of tort litigation. Torts and insurance cannot be understood in isolation from one another. Litigation for harms from domestic violence is no exception. There is very little third-party liability insurance coverage for defendants accused of domestic violence torts. Lack of insurance is a major contributor to the scarcity of tort claims for domestic violence injuries.
>
> The most common types of liability insurance policies issued to individuals, such as homeowners, renters, and automobile policies, typically exclude coverage for "intentional acts" of the insured. As a

result of this "intentional acts exclusion," if a plaintiff brings a claim for intentional torts and the insured is a homeowner or renter with liability insurance, the insurance company is likely to claim (successfully) that the suit is not covered by the policy.

A second common barrier to liability insurance coverage is the "family member exclusion." Often with jointly owned property, homeowners liability policies name all owners or residents as insureds, and exclude all claims by insureds against one another. Thus, a tort claim of any sort between insureds would not be covered by such a policy. If a husband inadvertently left a shoe on the stairs and his wife slipped on it and was injured, the policy would not cover him for her negligence claim against him. If the husband did the same act but a guest slipped and was injured, however, the policy would cover the guest's negligence claim. Family member exclusions were once standard in automobile policies but have been struck down in many jurisdictions in recent years.

These insurance barriers limit or in many instances, vitiate, insurance coverage. Even if litigation would likely be successful on the merits, these insurance issues present hurdles that discourage filing lawsuits even in cases of clear liability and serious injury. Jennifer Wriggins, *Domestic Violence Torts*, 75 S. Cal. L. Rev. 121 (2001).

As Wriggins says, family member exclusions in automobile insurance policies have recently been struck down. This has been because they run contrary to the mandatory insurance schemes that underlie auto insurance in many states. In her article, Wriggins proposes requiring the inclusion of domestic violence insurance in these mandatory plans. She argues this would benefit victims of domestic violence because "[p]ersons harmed by domestic violence torts would be more likely to receive compensation than they are now. Liability policies would require that insureds reimburse insurers for payments they make for domestic violence torts. Insurers would pursue such reimbursement, and thus the assets of domestic violence tortfeasors would be at risk. The deterrence of domestic violence torts should be greater than it is currently because threats of liability and threats to assets will be real." Do you think that an insurance provision like this would be likely to have a significant deterrent effect? Do you think that it could be of significant benefit to victims of domestic violence regardless of whether it has a deterrent effect? Would the insurance provision need to extend to intentional torts as well as negligent ones in order to be meaningful?

B. Existing Causes of Action

Now that tort actions are more freely available between married people, it is important to think creatively about precisely which causes of action may be effective in the context of partner violence. Two valuable resources on this topic are Fredrica L. Lehrman's Domestic Violence

PRACTICE AND PROCEDURE, 2–1 to 2–236 (1996) and Jennifer Wriggins, *Domestic Violence Torts*, 75 S. CAL. L. REV. 121 (2001).

Assault and battery are obvious candidates for the battered litigant. When they are not available it is often because the applicable statute of limitations, usually quite short, has run. The relatively new tort of intentional infliction of emotional distress is also an important candidate for consideration, especially for cases in which an abuser has relied more on psychological and emotional abuse than physical abuse, or in which the major injuries are the consequence of emotional rather than physical abuse. This cause of action receives extensive coverage below. Wrongful or false imprisonment is a less obvious choice, but may fit the reality of battering relationships in which the battered partner is essentially held prisoner by her abuser, isolated from friends and family, and able to leave the house or apartment only with, or with the permission of, her abuser.

Other causes of action may also be available. When an abuser verbally humiliates his partner in public, making false accusations of infidelity or substance abuse, or when he tries to poison his partner's professional relationship with a school or an employer by blackening her reputation, she may have an action in defamation. Illegal wiretapping may be civilly actionable. If children are themselves abused or threatened, physically or sexually, they have their own assault and battery claims. If they witness a parent's violence, the psychological consequences for them may provide a basis for a claim of negligent, reckless or intentional infliction of emotional distress. If their access to one parent is manipulated by the other as part of his campaign to control or terrorize his partner, there may be claims, called by various names in different jurisdictions, such as child snatching, obstruction of visitation rights, or interference with custody. A child hurt accidentally by violence aimed at his or her parent can pursue a straightforward negligence action.

Survival and Wrongful Death Actions

Survival and wrongful death actions are possible in cases in which the abuse has ended in the victim's death. In the case of a wrongful death action, there must also be qualified survivors—most often the victim's minor children. In the survival action the victim herself is the plaintiff, although the suit is brought on her behalf by a representative of her estate. Recovery is for injuries and losses the victim experienced between the time of her injury and the time of her death. These are called survival actions because the cause of action survives the plaintiff's death. In most wrongful death actions, on the other hand, others sue for their derivative losses; the financial support they are now deprived of, the services the deceased can no longer perform for them, and, in a minority of states, the loss of companionship or other emotional damages.

A number of state courts authorized wrongful death actions against batterers, or the estates of batterers, even before any more general abolition of interspousal tort immunity. More than one of these cases involved a situation in which the abusive partner had killed his wife and then himself, which is why the suit was brought against his estate, rather than against him personally. For some courts, the critical consideration was that the suit, while it depended on the primary claim of the dead spouse, was protecting the interests of others—almost always the victim's children. For other courts the critical consideration was that whatever arguments could be made about protecting domestic harmony or the privacy of the relationship while the husband and wife lived, those arguments plainly had no bearing in a situation in which one or both of the partners was dead. See *Jones v. Pledger*, 363 F.2d 986 (D.C. Cir. 1966).

In the 1990s, after O.J. Simpson was acquitted of the murders of Nicole Brown Simpson and Ronald Goldman, the Brown and Goldman families brought survival and wrongful death actions against him, seeking both compensatory and punitive damages. Under the civil "preponderance of the evidence" standard, the jury found O.J. Simpson responsible for the deaths, and brought back substantial verdicts; $8,500,000 for the wrongful death claim brought by the survivors of Ronald Goldman, and punitive damage awards of $12,500,000 in each of the survival actions. The punitive damage award to the estate of Ronald Goldman was attached to property damages in the amount of $100, and the award to the estate of Nicole Brown Simpson was attached to property damages in the amount of $250. *Judgment on Jury Verdict in Favor of Plaintiff Louis H. Brown as Executor and Personal Representative of the Estate of Nicole Brown Simpson, Against Orenthal James Simpson* [C.C.P. ¶ 664], 1997 WL 114570 (Cal. Super. Doc.); *Judgment on Jury Verdict in Favor of Plaintiff Fredric Goldman and Against Defendant Orenthal James Simpson* [C.C.P. ¶ 664], 1997 WL 114574 (Cal. Super. Doc.). For further discussion of the O.J. Simpson case see POSTMORTEM—THE O.J. SIMPSON CASE: JUSTICE CONFRONTS RACE, DOMESTIC VIOLENCE, LAWYERS, MONEY AND THE MEDIA (Jeffrey Abramson, ed. 1996).

Intentional Infliction of Emotional Distress

Intentional infliction of emotional distress is a tort that might well be useful to many victims of intimate violence. To succeed in a case for intentional infliction of emotional distress, a plaintiff must prove that the defendant "by extreme and outrageous conduct intentionally or recklessly cause[d] severe emotional distress." Section 46, Restatement 2d of Torts. Since the courts usually accept recklessness as satisfying the intent requirement, the difficult element for many plaintiffs is proving that the defendant's conduct was extreme and outrageous, and not merely insulting, annoying, or trivial. As Comment d to the Restatement says, "The rough edges of our society are still in need of a good deal of filing down, and in the meantime plaintiffs must necessarily be expected and required to be hardened to a certain amount of rough language, and to occasional acts that are definitely inconsiderate and unkind." Many courts agree, rejecting intentional infliction of emotional distress actions by one spouse against the other on the grounds that a measure of abuse and indignity is just part of married life. Robert G. Spector, *Domestic Torts*, 27 FAM. ADVOC. 6 (Spring, 2005). The following excerpt focuses on the difficulty of articulating a standard for what is extreme and outrageous conduct within a marriage.

Ira Mark Ellman and Stephen D. Sugarman
Spousal Emotional Abuse as a Tort?

55 Md. L. Rev. 1268 (1996).

In *Massey v. Massey*, [807 S.W.2d 391 (Tex. Ct. App. 1991), writ denied, 867 S.W.2d 766 (Tex. 1993),] the wife claimed that her husband, a bank president, denied her any independent access to funds and doled out money to her in small amounts, belittled her in front of others, had outbursts that sometimes included property destruction and that caused her to experience "intense anxiety and fear," and threatened to tell her children and friends of her extramarital affair and take custody of her youngest daughter from her. The wife's psychologist testified that the wife dealt with the husband by "walking on egg shells so as not to trigger [his] rage." The wife made no claim of personal physical violence, and the jury ultimately found that the husband "had not assaulted [the wife] by threat of imminent injury nor acted with malice." Although the husband portrayed most facts differently than his wife, he conceded that he often used threats in both his business and his marriage "to get his way." The husband claimed that the wife was an alcoholic, and that he had been devastated by her extramarital affair. The parties had been married for twenty-two years. The distress claim, tried with the divorce action, resulted in a judgment against the husband for $362,000 in compensatory damages, with no punitive damages award. A Texas appeals court affirmed the award....

Massey is troubling to us for two reasons. First, it seems wrongly decided and thereby portends further inappropriate decisions if the tort of spousal emotional abuse is unleashed. Second, the way the appellate court in *Massey* envisioned how "outrageousness" is to be determined in individual cases seems ultimately misguided.

In rejecting the arguments that the husband's conduct was outrageous as a matter of law, the appeals court in *Massey* approved the following instruction that the trial judge had given the jury:

> The bounds of decency vary from legal relationship to legal relationship. The marital relationship is highly subjective and constituted by mutual understandings and interchanges which are constantly in flux, and any number of which could be viewed by some segments of society as outrageous. Conduct considered extreme and outrageous in some relationships may be considered forgivable in other relationships. In your deliberation on the questions, definitions and instructions that follow, you shall consider them only in the context of the marital relationship of the parties to this case.

In short, by accepting the proposition that the "bounds of decency vary" among marital relationships, the court seemed thereby drawn to the conclusion that the same acts could be found "outrageous" in the context of one marriage but not in another. Put differently, the court approved a jury instruction that seeks to avoid imposing fixed societal standards of conduct on intimate personal relationships, asking the jury, in effect, to apply the couple's own standards. The instruction tells the jurors not to focus on what they would find outrageous in their own marriage, nor to search for some community consensus as to what marital behavior is completely out of bounds. Rather, they are to decide whether the complaining spouse can fairly label as "outrageous" the complained of acts in the setting of her own marriage.

The policy issue here—shall the outrageousness of spousal conduct be judged by external or internal standards—seems fundamental. The apparent justification for the choice expressed by the approved jury instruction is that the imposition of external standards on an intimate relationship may risk inappropriate, and possibly even unconstitutional, intrusion on marital privacy. But while we agree that such intrusion should be avoided, we doubt that Massey's resort to internal standards offers a promising solution.

Presumably, any effort to judge a spouse's conduct by the couple's own standards must look for those standards in the parties' understanding at the time their marriage began, or as they mutually adjusted it at some later time, rather than in the unilateral expressions of one party after the marriage has fallen apart. Consider, then, some possible interpretations of the *Massey* facts. On the one hand, the opinion portrays the husband as an insensitive, domineering bully in his personal relations, a man whose conduct might be judged to fit precisely the classic fault-divorce standard of mental cruelty. Yet his marriage lasted over twenty years, and perhaps close scrutiny would have shown that during much of the marriage his wife enjoyed compensating benefits in her relationship with him. Possibly his behavior became more extreme during the course of the marriage. Or possibly when they first married both were poorly socialized and incapable of "normal" relationships, but later the wife matured. Still, their earlier understanding, even if "unhealthy," functioned for two decades or more, perhaps meeting each other's needs as well as either of them could. On this last understanding of the couple's marriage, the court's jury instruction would seem to require a verdict for the defendant.

Consider also the husband's claim in *Massey* that his wife was an alcoholic and that he had been devastated by her extramarital affair. Although ... the wife's affair would not give the husband an IIED [intentional infliction of emotional distress] action for her violation of her marital vows, under the approved jury instruction ought not the wife's adultery and excessive drinking in *Massey*, if proved, at least provide a context in which his behavior, even if still wrongful, should not be deemed outrageous? Indeed, on close examination, this couple's "mutual understanding" might well have condemned adultery more than the husband's behavior of which the wife complained.

What is going on here? In the first place, it appears that the kind of close examination of the couple's entire marriage history called for by the judge's instruction did not actually take place in *Massey*. Indeed, we find it highly questionable whether it is either realistic or desirable to ask the jury to make such an inquiry in order to determine exactly what standards the parties had set for themselves. To do so requires a great deal of nuanced detective work at a time when the parties have every incentive to cast earlier words and actions in an altogether false light. Moreover, to successfully make the inquiry requires a deep intrusion into the spouses' intimate affairs, thereby flying in the face of a central argument in favor of the internal standard in the first place—that it is supposed to respect their privacy by refraining from imposing outside standards on them.

It appears, then, that despite what both courts said, the jury and both levels of the judiciary are doing something different than what is called for by the appellate court's legal reasoning. Rather, it seems the jurors were permitted to deem the husband's conduct unacceptable for whatever reasons of their own they might have had, and, following the trial court, the reviewing court simply shrank from overturning that verdict as a matter of law. At the appellate level this means either that the court, applying its own values, decided that the husband's behavior was outrageous despite the wife's adultery and drinking, or that, by approving the internal standard, the court put itself in a position where appellate reversal of the jury determination becomes all but impossible.

The most disturbing implication for us is that standardless instructions combined with toothless appellate review add up to enormous jury discretion to impose on the couple just about any decision they wish. This not only threatens uneven justice and unpredictable outcomes, but also invites virtually all discontented, divorcing spouses to try their chance at the lottery.

There is an additional consequence of allowing marital IIED claims based upon internal standards: they can create liability as well as avoid it. Suppose, for example, that [a] couple . . . at the time of their marriage were both staunch members of an orthodox religious group in whose sacred texts adultery was clearly viewed as an outrage. The use of internal standards would then seem to require judgment for the plaintiff even though, as a general matter, IIED claims by spouses harmed by their partners' extramarital affairs would fail. Go a step further. Suppose a marrying couple solemnly vows never to tell each other even the smallest of "white lies" on the mutual understanding that to do so would be to rip the very heart out of their relationship. Should the victimized spouse in this marriage be entitled to recover in tort when the other tells a fib concerning a rather unimportant subject? Although a positive answer is implied by the internal standard, using tort law to police such private codes of behavior would seem to take us far away from what section 46 is supposed to be about.

Even if a jury wanted to be faithful to the *Massey* instruction, the implementation difficulties with internal standards seem irremediable. All too often it will be hopeless to derive internal marital standards from a postmarriage investigation of the typically informal and unarticulated understandings that once existed in the now-defunct relationship. Consider our last two examples again. Even commitments to well-defined fundamentalist religious beliefs about adultery, and even written commitments about honesty made at the time of the wedding, may well have been mutually adjusted (or at least reasonably believed to have been so by one party) during the course of the marriage. As a result, at the crucial moment when the plaintiff claims an outrageous breach took place, the couple's unique "deal" may be fairly understood to be different from what it was at the outset. But it hardly seems realistic to expect the jury to determine accurately the terms of that "deal" in the wake of the lawsuit.

Because of this, it seems to us inevitable that Massey illustrates that judges and juries instead will apply their own values as they carry out post hoc inquiries into now-dissolved intimate relationships. The internal standard will become a mirage as the subtle interactions of facts and values in these cases will usually render it impossible to tell what standards the decision-maker actually applied. Yet the values that juries and judges wind up applying may not be consistent with the understanding upon which the marriage was built—the central thrust of the Massey jury instruction in the first place.

We conclude, therefore, that the approach to these cases envisioned by the Massey appeals court is misguided, and that if section 46 of the Restatement were made applicable to interspousal claims, one would at least have to start with external standards. Yet we also agree that the Massey court was emphasizing an important consideration. Because marital understandings do vary, important privacy norms can be violated if tort law were to impose liability after the marriage for conduct that was within the bounds of the marriage as the spouses then understood it. This means that the external standard only should reach conduct that is highly unlikely to have been part of any couple's mutual understanding, or in any event is sufficiently malevolent to justify overriding these privacy norms. Indeed, one might argue that the outrage standard is meant to incorporate this very idea: marital conduct crosses the line into outrageousness at just the point when it becomes so extreme that it is not credible to think it was part of any reasonable couple's marital understanding.

The preeminent example of such conduct is battery. In holding spouses liable for the physical injuries they intentionally inflict on one another, a court has no occasion to remind the jury that "bounds of decency vary from marital relationship to marital relationship." We normally do not believe that couples meaningfully agree that one may batter the other in return for, say, providing financial support; and the social norm against spousal beating is sufficiently strong that we are prepared to condemn it anyway, notwithstanding any alleged mutual understanding of the couple....

But what alleged spousal emotional abuse, if any, would be included? There's the rub. In contrast to battery, it is much more difficult to establish satisfactory standards to identify when emotional mistreatment is completely out of bounds. First of all, intimate relationships often involve complex emotional bargains that make no sense to third parties with different needs or perceptions. People often remain in marriages that look to others to be unhealthy. Although staying married is sometimes the result of coercion or delusion, often what may seem to outsiders as, say, intolerably extreme verbal harshness, is instead a feature of the particular relationship with which the parties, at least on balance, are content. In short, in many matters some couples arrive at solutions that depart from the social conventions that govern most of their acquaintances. Because those who sufficiently dislike their spouse's behavior can seek a divorce, it becomes more difficult to justify the conclusion that their marital relationship was so unacceptably uncivilized as to require tort damages when they wait many years to do so.

For example, was Mrs. Massey the victim of an extremely cruel husband who fiendishly exploited her personal insecurity in order to keep her trapped in an abusive relationship? Or was she someone who willingly accepted verbal unkindness and a loss of independence in return for relief from many ordinary responsibilities, who later changed her mind and wants compensation? We doubt that jurors can really tell. . . . The upshot is that while we are content to tell the batterer that he acts at his peril, we feel much less comfortable with a legal regime that says the same to Mr. Massey.

Turning away from the peculiarities of any specific couple, and looking generally at marital conduct that can be emotionally distressing, it is critical to recognize that by requiring "outrageous" conduct the Restatement clearly means to exclude from liability the common incivilities of everyday life. The idea is that such rude, insensitive, or mean-spirited behavior is better regulated, at least in the usual case, by social mechanisms or through self-help resort to divorce rather than through tort law. Although one reason for seeking to restrict recovery to extreme cases is to prevent a flood of litigation, surely another reason for a high threshold is the disparity between our aspirations and our conduct. Few if any of us consistently can avoid violating the norms of appropriate, sensitive social conduct that we endorse. The gap between societal aspiration and individual reality may be especially great in marital relations.

Yet, without clear guidelines as to what meets the threshold, the risk is that at least some juries will measure outrageousness against an ideal standard of marital relations—in effect lowering the threshold. This tendency is facilitated if outrageousness is left a flexible, open-ended concept. In this way, the outrage standard could yield liability for a much wider swath of marital conduct than for conduct by employers toward their employees, creditors toward their debtors, and landlords toward their tenants. . . .

NOTES AND QUESTIONS

1. **Intentional Infliction of Emotional Distress (I.I.E.D.) in Intimate Relationships.** Do you think the "outrageousness" of the conduct between a couple that is intimate should be judged by a standard that is internal to the relationship or that is external and based on an objective social standard? In responding to this question, would it matter to you if there had been domestic violence in the relationship? Do you think the husband in the *Massey* case described above engaged in domestic violence? How easy do you think it will be for a court in a tort action to determine if there has been domestic violence?

2. **Restricting I.I.E.D. Suits in Intimate Relationships.** Ellman and Sugarman ultimately recommend that I.I.E.D. suits be allowed for actions during a marriage only if the "outrageous" conduct involves conduct that is

also criminal, e.g. a battery or a violation of federal wiretapping laws. Do you agree with this limitation? Think back to the discussion in Chapter Seven about the criminal law's difficulty in capturing the breadth of the experience in violent relationships.

As a test of their position, they cite *Twyman v. Twyman*, 855 S.W.2d 619 (Tex. 1993) in which the Texas Supreme Court remanded for consideration of whether there was intentional infliction of emotional distress. In *Twyman*, the wife claimed the husband "pursued sadomasochistic bondage activities with her, even though he knew that she feared such activities because she had been raped at knife-point before their marriage." She also claimed that he told her he had sexual relations with other women because of her reluctance to engage in sexual bondage. When she finally tried the sadomasochistic sex that he desired, she felt humiliated and emotionally devastated. Should his efforts to convince her to engage in bondage sex even after he knew of her earlier rape be considered the intentional infliction of emotional distress?

In another portion of the article excerpted above, Ellman and Sugarman argue that they should not be: "[W]e ... conclude that if consensual 'bondage' between married couples is not a crime, it should not be actionable in tort either. It seems to us that the objecting spouse's remedy in these situations should be separation, not grudging consent followed by litigation." 55 Md. L. Rev. 1268 (1996). Do you agree?

3. **I.I.E.D. and Divorce.** One of the important issues in these cases is how a suit for intentional infliction of emotional distress relates to modern no-fault divorce rules. Ellman and Sugarman note, in discussing *Twyman*, that Texas law has traditionally been reluctant to grant alimony. They suggest that Texas's willingness to allow intentional infliction actions appears to reflect a common law system under which "alimony at divorce was allowed exclusively to the 'innocent' wife." 55 Md. L. Rev. 1268 (1996).

As you read the following case, try to decide for yourself whether you think there should be a tort of intentional infliction of emotional distress between spouses (or non-married intimate couples), how "outrageousness" should be defined, and what the relationship should be between the tort and divorce. This latter issue will be discussed in more detail later in this chapter.

Feltmeier v. Feltmeier

Supreme Court of Illinois, 2003.
798 N.E.2d 75.

▲ Justice Rarick delivered the opinion of the court:

Plaintiff, Lynn Feltmeier, and defendant, Robert Feltmeier, were married on October 11, 1986, and divorced on December 16, 1997. The judgment for dissolution of marriage incorporated the terms of a December 10, 1997, marital settlement agreement. On August 25, 1999, Lynn sued Robert for the intentional infliction of emotional distress. According to the allegations contained in the complaint, Robert engaged in a pattern of domestic abuse, both physical and mental in nature, which began shortly after the marriage and did not cease even after its dissolution. . . .

The first matter before us for review is whether Lynn's complaint states a cause of action for intentional infliction of emotional distress. . . .

According to the allegations contained in Lynn's complaint, since the parties' marriage in October 1986, and continuing for over a year after the December 1997 dissolution of their marriage:

"[Robert] entered into a continuous and outrageous course of conduct toward [Lynn] with either the intent to cause emotional distress to [Lynn] or with reckless disregard as to whether such conduct would cause emotional distress to [Lynn], said continuing course of conduct, including but not limited to, the following:

A.   On repeated occasions, [Robert] has battered [Lynn] by striking, kicking, shoving, pulling hair and bending and twisting her limbs and toes.

* * *

B.   On repeated occasions, [Robert] has prevented [Lynn] from leaving the house to escape the abuse.

* * *

C.   On repeated occasions, [Robert] has yelled insulting and demeaning epithets at [Lynn]. Further, [Robert] has engaged in verbal abuse which included threats and constant criticism of [Lynn] in such a way as to demean, humiliate, and degrade [Lynn].

* * *

D.   On repeated occasions, [Robert] threw items at [Lynn] with the intent to cause her harm.

* * *

E.   On repeated occasions, [Robert] attempted to isolate [Lynn] from her family and friends and would get very upset if [Lynn] would show the marks and bruises resulting from [Robert's] abuse to others.

F.   On repeated occasions since the divorce, [Robert] has engaged in stalking behavior.

* * *

G.   On at least one occasion, [Robert] has attempted to interfere with [Lynn's] employment by confiscating her computer. Additionally, [Robert] broke into [Lynn's] locked drug cabinet for work on or about March 23, 1997."

The complaint further alleged, as examples of conduct within the categories set forth above, dozens of episodes of abusive behavior, including specific details and time frames for the various physical and emotional attacks. . . .

In the case at bar, Robert first contends that the allegations of Lynn's complaint do not sufficiently set forth conduct which was extreme and outrageous when considered "[i]n the context of the subjective and fluctuating nature of the marital relationship." ... [W]hile we agree that special caution is required in dealing with actions for intentional infliction of emotional distress arising from conduct occurring within the marital setting, our examination of both the law of this state and the most commonly raised policy concerns leads us to conclude that no valid reason exists to restrict such actions or to require a heightened threshold for outrageousness in this context.

One policy concern that has been advanced is the need to recognize the "mutual concessions implicit in marriage," and the desire to preserve marital harmony. However, in this case, brought after the parties were divorced, there is clearly no marital harmony remaining to be preserved. Moreover, we agree with the Supreme Judicial Court of Maine that "behavior that is 'utterly intolerable in a civilized society' and is intended to cause severe emotional distress is not behavior that should be protected in order to promote marital harmony and peace." *Henriksen [v. Cameron]*, 622 A.2d [1135] at 1139 [(Me. 1993)].

Indeed, the Illinois legislature, in creating the Illinois Domestic Violence Act of 1986 (Act) has recognized that domestic violence is "a serious crime against the individual and society" and that "the legal system has ineffectively dealt with family violence in the past, allowing abusers to escape effective prosecution or financial liability." However ... while the Act created the crime of domestic battery and "provides a number of remedies in an effort to protect abused spouses and family members, it did not create a civil cause of action to remedy the damages done." Thus, it would seem that the public policy of this state would be furthered by recognition of the action at issue.

A second policy concern is the threat of excessive and frivolous litigation if the tort is extended to acts occurring in the marital setting. Admittedly, the likelihood of vindictive litigation is of particular concern following a dissolution of marriage, because the events leading to most divorces involve some level of emotional distress. However, we believe that the showing required of a plaintiff in order to recover damages for intentional infliction of emotional distress provides a built-in safeguard against excessive and frivolous litigation. As the appellate court herein stated: "When conduct is truly extreme and outrageous, it is more likely that severe emotional distress suffered by the victim was actually caused by that conduct."

Another policy consideration which has been raised is that a tort action for compensation would be redundant. However, as earlier noted, while our legislature has recognized the inadequacy of our legal system in allowing abusers to escape financial liability for domestic violence, the laws of this state provide no compensatory relief for injuries sustained. An action for dissolution of marriage also provides no compensatory relief for domestic abuse. In Illinois, as in most other states, courts are not allowed to consider marital misconduct in the distribution of property when dissolving a marriage.

After examining case law from courts around the country, we find the majority have recognized that public policy considerations should not bar actions for intentional infliction of emotional distress between spouses or former spouses based on conduct occurring during the marriage. . . .

Further, this court [has] identified several factors that may be considered in determining whether a defendant's conduct is extreme and outrageous. We find . . . such factor to be particularly relevant when examining, as alleged herein, outrageous conduct in the light of a marital relationship:

"It is thus clear * * * that the degree of power or authority which a defendant has over a plaintiff can impact upon whether that defendant's conduct is outrageous. The more control which a defendant has over the plaintiff, the more likely that defendant's conduct will be deemed outrageous, particularly when the alleged conduct involves either a veiled or explicit threat to exercise such authority or power to plaintiff's detriment. Threats, for example, are much more likely to be a part of outrageous conduct when made by someone with the ability to carry them out than when made by someone in a comparatively weak position."

Indeed, Illinois cases in which the tort of intentional infliction of emotional distress has been sufficiently alleged have very frequently involved a defendant who stood in a position of power or authority relative to the plaintiff. While these past cases have generally involved abuses of power by employers, creditors, or financial institutions, we see no reason to exclude the defendant at issue here, a spouse/former spouse, from the many types of individuals who may be positioned to exercise power over a plaintiff.

Therefore, we conclude that neither the policy considerations commonly raised nor the law of this state support a conclusion that an action for intentional infliction of emotional distress based upon conduct occurring in the marital setting should be barred or subject to any heightened threshold for establishing outrageousness. With this background in mind, we now examine the allegations set forth in Lynn's complaint to determine whether Robert's conduct satisfies the "outrageousness" requirement.

As earlier stated, to qualify as outrageous, the nature of the defendant's conduct must be so extreme as to go beyond all possible bounds of decency and be regarded as intolerable in a civilized community. Here, Robert contends that "Lynn's allegations are not sufficiently repeated and pervasive so as to justify a claim for intentional infliction of emotional distress." However, the . . . "outrageousness of a defendant's conduct must be determined in view of all the facts and circumstances pleaded and proved in a particular case." A pattern, course, and accumulation of acts can make an individual's conduct "sufficiently extreme to be actionable, whereas one instance of such behavior might not be."

The issue of whether domestic abuse can be sufficiently outrageous to sustain a cause of action for intentional infliction of emotional distress is apparently one of first impression in Illinois. Other jurisdictions, however, have found similar allegations of recurring cycles of physical and verbal abuse, wherein the conduct went far beyond the "trials of everyday life between two cohabiting people," to be sufficiently outrageous to fall within the parameters of section 46 of the Restatement (Second) of Torts.

In the instant case, we must agree with the appellate court that, when the above-summarized allegations of the complaint are viewed in their entirety, they show a type of domestic abuse that is extreme enough to be actionable:

> "It combines more than a decade of verbal insults and humiliations with episodes where freedom of movement was deprived and where physical injury was often inflicted. The alleged pattern of abuse, combined with its duration, worked a humiliation and loss of self-esteem. Regardless of the form in which it arrived, violence was certain to erupt, and when seasons of spousal abuse turn to years that span the course of a decade, we are unwilling to dismiss it on grounds that it is unworthy of outrage."

Therefore, where we find that a reasonable trier of fact could easily conclude that Robert's conduct was so outrageous as to be regarded as intolerable in a civilized community, we reject his contention that the complaint fails to sufficiently allege this element.

It is equally clear, and Robert does not argue to the contrary, that Lynn's complaint adequately pleads the second element necessary to state a cause of action for intentional infliction of emotional distress, *i.e.,* that Robert either intended to inflict, or knew that his conduct was likely to inflict, severe emotional distress upon Lynn. However, Robert does contest the adequacy of the complaint as to the third necessary element, that his conduct in fact caused severe emotional distress. He argues that Lynn's complaint "contains no factual allegations from which the level of severity of the emotional distress could be inferred." We must disagree.

Lynn's complaint specifically alleges that, "[a]s a direct and proximate result of the entirety of [Robert's] course of conduct, [she] has sustained severe emotional distress including, but not limited to, loss of self-esteem and difficulty in forming other relationships, and a form of Post Traumatic Stress Disorder sustained by battered and abused women as a result of being repeatedly physically and verbally abused and harassed over a long period of time." The complaint also alleges that Lynn has suffered depression and a "fear of being with other men," and that her enjoyment of life has been substantially curtailed. Finally, it is alleged that Lynn has incurred, and will continue to incur, medical and psychological expenses in an effort to become cured or relieved from the effects of her mental distress. . . .

Here, we find that Lynn has sufficiently alleged that as a result of enduring Robert's physical and psychological abuse for the duration of their 11–year marriage and beyond, she suffered severe emotional distress. Therefore, where the complaint sets forth sufficient facts which, if proven, could entitle Lynn to relief, we conclude that she has stated a cause of action for intentional infliction of emotional distress. We, of course, express no opinion on the substantive merits of Lynn's complaint. We simply hold that, taking the allegations of the complaint as true, as we are required to do for purposes of our review, the complaint is sufficient to survive a motion to dismiss. . . .

NOTES AND QUESTIONS

1. **Defining "Outrageousness."** Do you think each of this case was correctly decided? What particular facts would you rely on in making your decision? Can you imagine a case in which there would be intentional infliction of emotional distress without a battery, kidnapping, or some other clearly criminal act on the part of the defendant? Do you think that Ellman and Sugarman are correct that in a marital or post-marital relationship there must be a criminal action in order to meet the outrageousness requirement?

As you know, many relationships with domestic violence do not involve frequent physical violence. Instead, abusers rely on other means of control. Do you think the abuser's conduct in such a relationship is "outrageous?" In *Sudan v. Sudan*, 145 S.W.3d 280 (Tex. App. 2004), rev'd on other grounds, 199 S.W.3d 291 (Tex. 2006), the ex-husband used his control over the ex-wife's finances to cause her to lose her job and her house and to threaten that if she did not pay additional funds she would be unable to see her children. Is this an example of a relationship in which there is domestic violence? Was the husband's conduct "outrageous?" The Court held that the ex-husband's conduct was not "so outrageous in character and extreme in degree as to go beyond all possible bounds of decency, and to be regarded as atrocious, and utterly intolerable in a civilized society." Do you agree with this? If not, how would you define "outrageousness" in the context of an intimate relationship? In *Christians v. Christians*, 637 N.W.2d 377 (S.D. 2001), the Court held that non-physical conduct on the husband's part that caused the wife to lose her job supported an award of damages for intentional infliction of emotional distress because the "actions . . . extended over and above the grounds for divorce[] and were intended to harm" the wife. What do you think of this standard?

Common carriers have traditionally been held to higher levels of responsibility in relation to patrons than most people are to others. This means that they are liable for levels of discourtesy to patrons that would not be actionable in others. Section 48, Restatement 2d of Torts. According to the Restatement's Comments, the rationale behind this rule "lies in the incentive which it provides for . . . employees . . . not [to] be grossly discourteous to those who must come in contact with them. . . ." Comment a. Could one argue that individuals should similarly be liable for insulting or abusive conduct or language toward their intimates in an effort to promote family harmony and courtesy? In other words, should it be easier, not harder, to hold an intimate liable for intentional infliction of emotional distress?

2.   **Non–Marital Intimate Relationships.** Should the standard for out-rageousness be different in non-marital relationships? Do the policy grounds that concerned the court in *Feltmeier*—marital harmony, the possibility of vindictive litigation, and the redundancy of tort and divorce actions—apply equally to non-marital relationships?

C.   Abusers' Defensive Actions to Tort Suits

Abusers have frequently engaged in two different strategies in an effort to fend off tort liability. First, they have claimed that the tort actions are barred by statutes of limitations. Many victims of intimate abuse do not sue until after they have extracted themselves from the relationship. This means that the violence that might support a battery or false imprisonment action may no longer be actionable because of a statute of limitations. If the plaintiff is suing for intentional infliction of emotional distress, it may be that the outrageousness of the defendant's conduct is only apparent if abuse stretching back many years is included to show a pattern of threatening, demeaning, or other humiliating conduct. In either case, evidence of necessary events may not be admitted because of statutes of limitations.

Second, some abusers have decided that the best defense is a good offense. These abusers have begun their own tort actions against the targets of their abuse. Some have sued their victims, making them the defendants in suits for malicious prosecution, defamation, etc. Other abusers have chosen to sue third party professionals who have supported the victim's efforts to get free of the abuse or to create an independent life.

Statutes of Limitation

In cases in which a victim of partner abuse has been in a long-term relationship with her abuser, she is highly unlikely to sue until she is leaving or has left him. At this point, the statute of limitations may already have run with respect to many of the incidents of abuse in which she suffered injury. Actions for battery or assault must usually be brought within one or two years. Sometimes emotional distress claims carry the same limitations period, and sometimes a longer one; the range is between one and six years. The more standard period for negligence actions is three years. The reasons for these distinctions are generally not articulated, and not obvious; their variability from state to state suggests that the choice of period may in fact be quite arbitrary.

Ironically, while interspousal tort immunity was still the rule, reformist courts could argue that the immunity ended with the end of the marriage, and that the statute of limitations was also tolled until that time. Once the immunity is abolished, the abused partner has no technical reason to postpone suit, and may lose the advantage of that tolling rule. From a policy perspective, this may be a mistake:

> [T]o the extent victims remain in abusive relationships out of the desire to make them work—seeking to end the violence without ending the relationship—they are expressing the very values that supported

the old interspousal tort immunity. In essence, they are seeking to restore marital harmony to a relationship disrupted by violence. The immunity was flawed in imposing that value on marital partners, whether or not they shared it. But to the extent an abused partner embraces that value as her own, we should not penalize her by jeopardizing her ability to recover for her injuries if her efforts are sabotaged by further abuse. Rather, the legal system should recognize her efforts by preserving her right to sue. Clare Dalton, *Domestic Violence, Domestic Torts and Divorce: Constraints and Possibilities,* 31 NEW ENG. L. REV. 321 (1997).

Parties to recent suits have tried in a variety of ways to overcome the substantial barriers created by restrictive limitation periods. One strategy is to focus on traditional tolling doctrines, e.g. duress or insanity. Another is to claim a continuing tort that requires the court to review a course of conduct that may have begun before the period covered by the statute of limitations. This strategy would require plaintiffs to concentrate on torts like intentional infliction of emotional distress rather than one-time torts like battery. Here, we describe first the arguments for tolling the statutes and then the arguments for a continuing course of conduct.

Duress or Insanity

If an abused partner fails to take action against her abuser because she is afraid of him, her argument for tolling applicable statutes of limitation is an argument based on duress. Even if her abuser does not say in so many words: "Sue me and you are dead," or: "Tell anyone what I've done to you and you'll pay for it," the underlying theory is the same. In this situation the abused partner fears, often with reason, that any action taken to separate herself from her abuser, or confront him with his abuse, will result in serious injury or death to her, and for the time being she chooses what appears to be the lesser of two evils. You have read enough of battered women's attempts to invoke duress in both the child welfare context and the criminal justice context, to know that judges and juries often require express threats of imminent violence before they will exonerate battered women of criminal wrongdoing on the basis of duress. The more subtle and pervasive atmosphere of terror created by an abusive partner often fails to meet standards for duress established in cases of the "gun to the head" model of coercion. So too in this different context; it is often hard for women to persuade judges that their fear was both strong and imminent enough, over an extended period of time, to prevent them from filing suit. This difficulty is exacerbated when the woman continues to delay the filing of a suit, even after she has separated from her abuser. Perhaps because of these difficulties, it is hard to find cases in which victims of domestic violence argue duress as a basis for tolling a statute of limitations.

Plaintiffs in various types of sexual abuse cases, however, have argued that statutes of limitation should be tolled because of duress. In *Jones v. Jones,* 576 A.2d 316 (N.J. Super. A.D. 1990), the plaintiff claimed that the defendant, her father, had sexually abused her for years. She also alleged that he threatened to kill her if she disclosed the abuse. She further alleged that he beat her regularly and occasionally tried to suffocate her in order to enforce the threats. As a result, she claimed that the duress exerted by the defendant prevented her from filing suit within the prescribed statutory period. The Appellate Division reversed the trial court's summary judgment order for the parents, holding

> [A] subjective and an objective standard must be satisfied in order for the plaintiff to prevail. Specifically, the duress and coercion exerted by the prospective defendant must have been such as to have actually deprived the plaintiff of his [sic] freedom of will to institute suit in a timely fashion, and it must have risen to such a level that a person of reasonable firmness in the plaintiff's situation would have been unable to resist.

Similarly, in *Jane Doe One v. Garcia*, 5 F.Supp.2d 767 (D. Ariz. 1998), involving claims of sexual abuse by a school administrator against a student, the Court said that in order for duress to toll a statute of limitations the "plaintiff must show some act or threat by the defendant that precluded the exercise of her free will and judgment and prevented her from exercising her legal rights." In this case also the Court found that plaintiff's claim of duress was entitled to a hearing. The Court cited the facts that the defendant, as a school administrator, had a lot of control over the plaintiff, that he had a gun and she was aware of that fact, that he stalked her even after she left the school, and that he led her to believe that he had killed her boyfriend. In contrast, in *Doe v. Holy See*, 793 N.Y.S.2d 565 (N.Y.A.D. 3rd Dept. 2005), the New York Court rejected a claim of duress to toll a statute of limitations in a case involving claims of sexual abuse of children by priests. The Court said, "Plaintiffs fail to demonstrate that any duress they may have experienced continued after they attained majority or broke all ties with the church."

NOTES AND QUESTIONS

1. **Showing Duress.** How useful do you think these cases are for adult victims of domestic violence who want to file suits some number of years after they have separated from or divorced their former partners? Under what circumstances would you expect adult victims of domestic violence to be able to meet the joint subjective/objective test of *Jones*? Would you expect a plaintiff who is claiming to have been a victim of abuse to need to introduce expert testimony to meet this test? To what would you think the expert would need to testify? In what types of situations would you think that the separation from the abusive partner would prohibit a claim of tolling based on duress and in what situations would it not?

2. **Analogies to Child Sexual Abuse.** Does it disturb you to need to make analogies between adult victims of intimate abuse and child victims of sexual abuse? What are or might be your concerns about such analogies?

3. **Insanity and Tolling the Statute of Limitations.** Insanity also usually tolls a statute of limitations. The following cases provide examples of such an approach in the context of domestic violence.

Giovine v. Giovine

Superior Court of New Jersey, 1995.
663 A.2d 109.

Plaintiff and defendant were married on May 1, 1971. Three children were born of this marriage on August 17, 1975, July 5, 1979, and July 7, 1983.

On approximately December 31, 1978, defendant separated from plaintiff. In May 1980, he filed a complaint seeking to establish visitation rights with the two children of the marriage.... Plaintiff filed an answer and counterclaim for divorce, alleging habitual drunkenness and extreme cruelty.... Additionally, that counterclaim contained three counts for damages predicated upon the following torts: a specific act of assault and battery in March 1972 and a final act of assault and battery on December 28, 1978; infliction of emotional distress based upon the same acts of assault and battery; and "a continuous and unbroken wrong commencing on or about March 1972 and continuing down until December 28, 1978." ... In July 1982, while their matrimonial action was pending, the parties reconciled and resumed living together. On July 26, 1982, both parties directed their respective attorneys to discontinue the litigation.... The couple separated again in September 1993.... [P]laintiff filed her present complaint on July 1, 1994 ...

II—PRESENT LITIGATION

On August 8, 1994, defendant filed a motion to strike certain causes of action contained within plaintiff's complaint.... [T]he motion judge granted defendant's motion, striking all tortious claims occurring prior to June 30, 1992 based upon the applicable statute of limitations, and limiting plaintiff's proofs on her claims for emotional distress or negligence to those acts alleged to have occurred after June 30, 1992....

In [an earlier case], the Supreme Court held that *N.J.S.A.* 2A:14–21 "foreclose[d] a tolling of the running of [the limitations period] unless plaintiff was [insane] at the time the cause of action accrued...." The Court carved out an equitable exception, however, where defendant's "negligent act brings about [a] plaintiff's insanity." Applying equitable considerations, the Court concluded:

> [I]f plaintiff's insanity was caused by defendant's wrongful act, it may be said that such act was responsible for plaintiff's failure or inability to institute her action prior to the running of the statute of limitations. We feel that justice here requires us to carve out an equitable exception to the general principle that there is no time out for the period of time covered by the disability if the disability accrued at or after the cause of action accrued. Thus, a defendant whose negligent act brings about plaintiff's insanity should not be permitted to cloak himself with the protective garb of the statute of limitations....

"Insane," ... means "such a condition of mental derangement as actually prevents the sufferer from understanding his [or her] legal rights or instituting legal action."

In *Jones v. Jones,* 576 A.2d 316 (App.Div.), *certif. denied,* 585 A.2d 412 (1990), we applied equitable considerations to abrogate the running of the statute of limitations against an incest victim. We noted the victim's emotional condition as a justification for tolling the statute of limitations, as well as the fact that the victim plaintiff was placed under physical and psychological duress by the defendant. Plaintiff's expert psychologist opined that "individuals subjected to childhood sexual abuse often find it impossible to communicate and describe such misconduct." *Jones* likened plaintiff's condition to the condition of insanity, which tolls the statute of limitations. . . .

We are able to draw an analogy between the status of the plaintiff in *Jones* to the status of a victim of repeated violence within the marital setting, who may "sink into a state of psychological paralysis and become unable to take any action at all to improve or alter the situation." . . .

[I]n [an earlier case], the Supreme Court directed:

A trial court shall itself without a jury hear and determine (1) whether insanity developed on or subsequent to the date of the alleged act of defendant and within the period of limitation and if so, whether that insanity resulted from the defendant's acts; and (2) whether plaintiff's suit was started within a reasonable time after restoration of sanity. . . .

That same mandate will be applicable in the trial of this matter. It will be incumbent upon plaintiff to establish pretrial, by medical, psychiatric or psychological evidence, that she suffers from battered woman's syndrome, which caused an inability to take any action to improve or alter the circumstances in her marriage unilaterally, so as to warrant a conclusion by the trial judge that the statute of limitations should be tolled.

We construe the clear legislative statement in the preamble to *N.J.S.A.* 2C:25–18 as justification for the decision we reach: "the Legislature encourages . . . the broad application of the remedies available under this act in the civil and criminal courts of this State." The motion judge . . . mechanistically and totally ignored the invitation of the Legislature. We . . . reverse the motion judge's decision and direct that plaintiff shall be entitled to present proof that she has the medically diagnosed condition of battered woman's syndrome. Plaintiff shall be entitled to sue her husband for damages attributable to his continuous tortious conduct resulting in her present psychological condition, provided she has medical, psychiatric, or psychological expert proof to establish that she was caused to have an inability "to take any action at all to improve or alter the situation." . . .

Nussbaum v. Steinberg

Supreme Court of the State of New York, 1994.
618 N.Y.S.2d 168.

[In 1988 Hedda Nussbaum sued her abuser, Joel Steinberg, for assault, battery, and intentional infliction of emotional distress, on the basis of his conduct toward her between 1978 and 1987. At the time that she sued him, he was incarcerated for the murder of Lisa Steinberg, the young girl whom they had unofficially adopted. The relevant period of limitations for all of Nussbaum's claims was one year. She argued that the statute should be tolled on the grounds of insanity. In 1997 the special referee assigned to the case determined that she met the standard, and allowed her case to go forward. An excerpt from the referee's decision follows.]

■ STEVEN E. LIEBMAN, SPECIAL REFEREE.

. . . It must be recognized that domestic violence, by its very nature, is much more insidious and complex than even other intentional torts or crimes involving assault, or other abuse, in that the abuser and the victim are generally found to be in a close or intimate relationship. The destructive impact of violence in such an intimate relationship may be so complete that the victim is rendered incapable of independent judgment even to save one's own life. In various forms, the victim may very well turn to the tormentor for connection and support. Significantly, because of the usual close proximity and/or relationship of the domestic violence abuser and the victim, the abused and battered person is often less able than other intentional tort victims to obtain legal protection or recourse after being abused or assaulted. The emotional commitments and the psychological attachments that domestic violence victims usually have to their abusers provide a significant impediment to the victims being capable of seeking help or assistance, even where the abuser does not appear to be actively restraining them from seeking aid. These factors, in various combinations, confirm the devastating effect that such prolonged psychological and physical abuse can have on the victims; including a demonstration that such a person would be clearly incapacitated and incapable of recognizing or asserting their legal rights. In instances where a batterer's primary goal is often absolute control over every aspect of the victim's life, the combination of such extensive control and violence may disable one's independent judgment and functioning so as to place that person within the insanity definition. . . .

Plaintiff testified on her own behalf detailing, through her own testimony, her story of her relationship with Joel Steinberg for over a ten year period that only ended because of the intervening and tragic death of Lisa Steinberg. Plaintiff's testimony recounted the years of the horrific physical abuse and violence and total emotional and psychological domination over every aspect of her life and being. The magnitude of this traumatic, brutal and destructive relationship was dramatically illustrated by the New York City Police Department videotape of the plaintiff, shortly after her arrest, evidencing physical injuries to virtually every part of her body. . . . No less evident than the condition of her ravaged and mutilated body were her significant psychological disorders and mental defects that undoubtedly were the consequences of her relationship with Joel Steinberg.

Plaintiff also offered the testimony of her treating psychiatrist Dr. Samuel C. Klagsbrun and a prominent expert in psychological trauma Professor Bessel van der Kolk, M.D. The defendant relied on the offer of the expert testimony of Dr. Daniel Schwartz, a retired forensic psychiatrist.

Dr. Schwartz offered his opinion that throughout the entire period of 1975 through 1987, the plaintiff never became incapable of protecting her legal rights or functioning overall in society. Dr. Schwartz characterized plaintiff as having made bad choices or used very poor judgment, but that she still retained the ability to exercise her free will and make decisions. Dr. Schwartz described his former practice as primarily examining criminal defendants to establish their competency to stand trial. . . . He admitted that he had no clinical knowledge about the psychology or life experience of battered women, nor received any training in physical or psychological trauma. Dr. Schwartz conceded that he had never worked with any professionals who treated victims of domestic violence; and he was unaware of his own former institution's protocols for the treatment of battered women. He eventually concluded that plaintiff suffered from what he described as a dependent personality disorder, and that she retained power to extricate herself from the control of the defendant if she wanted to.

The testimony offered by Dr. Klagsbrun and Dr. van der Kolk confirmed their respective expert opinions that Hedda Nussbaum decisively demonstrated that her behavior was consistent with prolonged and extensive psychological and physical abuse. The result of such exposure, they concluded, made the plaintiff incapable of functioning independently of the defendant to the extent of making her unable to make her own judgments about her life or the protection of her interests. Dr. Klagsbrun testified that at the time the plaintiff was admitted to his hospital for treatment she was still delusional and still suffering from a psychotic disorder. He also described Ms. Nussbaum as continuing to display ''robotic'' impaired functioning and to even talk about the defendant in an adoring manner. Dr. Klagsbrun further stated that the plaintiff believed that she was responsible for the abuse; a perception confirmed as common among trauma victims by Dr. van der Kolk. The testimony of Dr. Klagsbrun emphasized that the impact on Hedda of the defendant's violence so impaired her judgment that she was unable to make judgments and decisions which were basic to human life. Dr. van der Kolk concluded that the plaintiff had even lost her capacity to escape or take independent action; and for all intents and purposes, the plaintiff was ''dead to the world.'' Both physicians maintained that the plaintiff's process to recovery was slow and painful. Notwithstanding the opinion of Dr. Schwartz in this case, it appears that every competent psychiatrist who had examined the plaintiff found that she was not functioning in society, and that this incapacity was the result of chronic trauma inflicted upon her by the defendant.

It was only after plaintiff separated from the defendant that she began to first experience, as reported by Dr. Klagsbrun, conflicting feelings about the defendant. It was not until May 1988, that plaintiff made known that she was experiencing these conflicting feelings. Dr. van der Kolk testified that the ties are so strong that it can take from six months to a year for a battered woman to develop enough strength to remain away from her abuser permanently. In the professional opinions of the plaintiff's experts, Hedda Nussbaum lacked the capacity to function overall in society to the extent of being out of the control and influence of the defendant to at least October 1988. Both doctors conjectured that the earliest the plaintiff had any real ability to function without her incapacity was September 1988, but that she still lacked such ability in August 1988. Dr. Klagsbrun stated that even in October 1988, when Hedda Nussbaum instituted the instant action against Joel Steinberg, there was still significant concern about the plaintiff's capacity to see it through. . . .

Accordingly, I hereby report my findings that the plaintiff, Hedda Nussbaum, was under a disability because of insanity within the meaning of CPLR § 208 through the period of September 1988, thereby rendering her underlying action timely upon the appropriate application of the tolling statute. I herein order that the defendant's underlying motion for summary judgment to dismiss the Complaint, as time-barred by the Statute of Limitations and held in abeyance, is denied and plaintiff is permitted to proceed on her causes of action alleged in her Complaint. . . .

NOTES AND QUESTIONS

1. **Duress and Insanity.** What do you see as the relative advantages of each of these two grounds for tolling statutes of limitations? What are the disadvantages of each? Does the insanity claim play into notions that domestic violence is caused by a personality deficiency in the victim, or, even more crudely, that victims are crazy? Does duress imply a complete lack of agency on the part of the victim? Which claim will be more difficult to prove? Are either of these claims likely to prejudice a victim's effort to win or retain custody of children?

2. **Duress, Insanity, and Rebuilding a Life.** How will claims of insanity or duress affect victims of domestic violence who are trying to rebuild their lives, post-separation? Many victims continue for some period of time to be confused about the nature of their relationships with their abusers and about who properly bears the responsibility for the abuse they have suffered. They may well be too fearful of further interactions with their abusers to bring suit. However, they may otherwise be rebuilding their lives and managing their affairs. Will efforts to stabilize and rebuild portions of their lives undermine victims' ability to meet the demanding definitions of "insanity" or "duress?"

3. **The Discovery Rule.** A related but somewhat different argument, one that in a sense "splits the difference" between insanity and duress, is that the abuser's continuing psychological hold on his partner may prevent her from being able to frame her abuse as a wrong for which he is responsible. She may need some distance from the inherently unequal relationship to see the exploitation for what it is and to summon the independence to challenge it.

Such claims have sometimes been made successfully in cases involving sexual abuse by therapists. The analogy to sexual abuse by therapists is not a perfect one, because those courts that have allowed tolling in that context, usually by applying a "discovery" rule (the period of limitations begins to run at the point where the plaintiff is capable of recognizing the wrongful nature of the therapist's conduct, and acting on it), have emphasized the professional "tools" that make the patient vulnerable to exploitation (the phenomena of transference and counter-transference). However, the equally effective "tools" of the batterer could be viewed as giving his victim's claim just as much force. For decisions favoring tolling in cases involving sexual abuse by therapists, see *Simmons v. United States*, 805 F.2d 1363 (9th Cir. 1986); *Greenberg v. McCabe*, 453 F.Supp. 765 (E.D. Pa. 1978), aff'd 594 F.2d 854 (3d Cir. 1979); *Riley v. Presnell*, 565 N.E.2d 780 (Mass. 1991).

4. **Legislation to Toll Statutes of Limitations.** Another problem with relying on an analogy to cases involving sexual abuse by therapists is that many courts have refused to toll statutes of limitation in this context. Adult survivors of childhood sexual abuse have had similarly mixed success in arguing for tolling under the various common law doctrines and equitable principles you have been introduced to in the last several pages. Some states have responded with tolling legislation specific to suits based on childhood sexual abuse. William A. Gray, *A Proposal for Change in Statutes of Limitations in Childhood Sexual Abuse Cases*, 43 BRANDEIS L.J. 493 (2005). It is therefore worth considering whether the plight of battered partners who need a period of healing before pursuing legal remedies is one that should be addressed by state legislatures rather than, or in addition to, state courts.

If you were crafting such legislation, how would you frame it? What would be the benefits of arguing for a fixed additional term during which someone emerging from a battering relationship might bring suit? What would be the appropriate term—five years, or three, or seven? Would it be better to leave the term undefined, but articulate the circumstances under which the running of the statute of limitations would be suspended? Would this new legislation preclude the plaintiff from arguing any other applicable tolling rule or principle, or simply provide additional ammunition? From a political perspective, what choices would give your legislation the best chance of being adopted?

Continuing Torts

Courts have long recognized that some torts are of a recurrent nature. This is particularly true of the torts of trespass and nuisance, but recently some courts have recognized that civil rights violations, tortious damage to property, trademark infringements, and violations of the antitrust laws may also occur continuously over a period of time. Many courts have found that where a tort is of a continuous nature, the statute of limitations will not bar an action if the tort has continued until within the statutory period. Thus, even if some of the injury caused by the continuing tort happened too far before filing to be actionable under the statute of limitations, the statute will not bar a tort that has continued into the statutory period. *Thorndike v. Thorndike*, 910 A.2d 1224 (N.H. 2006). Some states have also applied the continuing tort concept to allow legal and accounting malpractice actions that would otherwise have been barred by the statute of limitations. In so holding, one court explained its position by saying, "[A] person seeking professional assistance has a right to repose confidence [throughout the course of the representation] in the professional's ability and good faith, and realistically cannot be expected to question and assess the techniques employed or the manner in which the services are rendered...." *Bambi's Roofing, Inc. v. Moriarty, Dahms and Yarian,* 859 N.E.2d 347 (Ind. App. 2006) In the context of violent relationships, some courts have recognized intentional infliction of emotional distress as a continuing tort. The following excerpt is from the *Feltmeier* case. You read another excerpt from this same case above in which the court recognized intentional infliction of emotional distress as actionable in the spousal context. One of the issues not discussed in the prior excerpt is "[w]hether the plaintiff's claims for intentional infliction of emotional distress based on conduct prior to August 25, 1997, are barred by the applicable statute of limitations." 798 N.E.2d 75. This is the question discussed in the excerpt below.

Feltmeier v. Feltmeier

Supreme Court of Illinois, 2003.
798 N.E.2d 75.

[The facts and the portion of this case discussing intentional infliction of emotional distress are excerpted above.]

... Generally, a limitations period begins to run when facts exist that authorize one party to maintain an action against another. However, under the "continuing tort" or "continuing violation" rule, where a tort involves a continuing or repeated injury, the limitations period does not begin to run until the date of the last injury or the date the tortious acts cease.

At this juncture, we believe it important to note what does *not* constitute a continuing tort. A continuing violation or tort is occasioned by continuing unlawful acts and conduct, not by continual ill effects from an initial violation. Thus, where there is a single overt act from which subsequent damages may flow, the statute begins to run on the date the defendant invaded the plaintiff's interest and inflicted injury, and this is so despite the continuing nature of the injury....

A continuing tort, therefore, does not involve tolling the statute of limitations because of delayed or continuing injuries, but instead involves viewing the defendant's conduct as a continuous whole for prescriptive purposes....

In the instant case, Robert ... maintains that "each of the alleged acts of abuse inflicted by Robert upon Lynn over a 12 year period are separate and distinct incidents which give rise to separate and distinct causes of action, rather than one single, continuous, unbroken, violation or wrong which continued over the entire period of 12 years." We must disagree. While it is true that the conduct set forth in Lynn's complaint could be considered separate acts constituting separate offenses of, *inter alia,* assault, defamation and battery, Lynn has alleged, and we have found, that Robert's conduct *as a whole* states a cause of action for intentional infliction of emotional distress. Further ... there are unjust results in the present case ... which would militate in favor of applying the continuing tort rule in an action for intentional infliction of emotional distress.

As did the appellate court below, we find the case of *Pavlik v. Kornhaber,* 761 N.E.2d 175 (2001), to be instructive. In *Pavlik,* the court first found that plaintiff's complaint stated a cause of action for intentional infliction of emotional distress, where the defendant's persistent notes, sexually explicit comments, insistence on meetings to discuss his desire for sexual contact and lewd behavior in their employer-employee relationship were such that a reasonable person would perceive them to be sufficiently offensive and sinister to rise to the level of extreme and outrageous behavior. The court in *Pavlik* then found that the trial court had erred in dismissing the plaintiff's claim as untimely. While the defendant argued that his sexual advances took place outside the two-year statute of limitations for personal injury, the plaintiff had alleged an ongoing campaign of offensive and outrageous sexual pursuit that established a continuing series of tortious behavior, by the same actor, and of a similar nature, such that the limitations period did not commence until the last act occurred or the conduct abated.

We find the following passage, wherein the *Pavlik* court explains its reasons for applying the continuing tort rule to the plaintiff's action for intentional infliction of emotional distress, to be particularly cogent:

> Illinois courts have said that in many contexts, including employment, repetition of the behavior may be a critical factor in raising offensive acts to actionably outrageous ones. It may be the pattern, course and accumulation of acts that make the conduct sufficiently extreme to be actionable, whereas one instance of such behavior might not be. It would be logically inconsistent to say that each act must be independently actionable while at the same time asserting that often it is the cumulative nature of the acts that give rise to the intentional infliction of emotional distress. Likewise, we cannot say that cumulative continuous acts may be required to constitute the tort but that prescription runs from the date of the first act. Because it is impossible to pinpoint the specific moment when enough conduct has occurred to become actionable, the termination of the conduct provides the most sensible place to begin the running of the prescriptive period. . . .

We believe the appellate court herein properly applied this reasoning to the facts of this case where:

> "The alleged domestic violence and abuse endured by Lynn ... spanned the entire 11–year marriage. No one disputes that the allegations set forth the existence of ongoing abusive behavior. Lynn's psychologist, Dr. Michael E. Althoff, found that Lynn suffered from the 'battered wife syndrome.' He described the psychological process as one that unfolds over time. The process by which a spouse exerts coercive control is based upon 'a systematic, repetitive infliction of psychological trauma' designed to 'instill terror and helplessness.' Dr. Althoff indicated that the posttraumatic stress disorder from which Lynn suffered was the result of the entire series of abusive acts, not just the result of one specific incident." . . .

Therefore, based upon the foregoing reasons, we agree ... that the continuing tort rule should be extended to apply in cases of intentional infliction of emotional distress.

We note, however, that embracing the concept of a continuing tort in the area of intentional infliction of emotional distress does not throw open the doors to permit filing these actions at any time. As with any continuing tort, the statute of limitations is only held in abeyance until the date of the last injury suffered or when the tortious acts cease. Thus, we find that the two-year statute of limitations for this action began to run in August 1999, because Lynn's complaint includes allegations of tortious behavior by Robert occurring as late as that month. Applying the continuing tort rule to the instant case, Lynn's complaint, filed August 25, 1999, was clearly timely and her claims based on conduct prior to August 25, 1997, are not barred by the applicable statute of limitations.

Robert contends that even if the acts of alleged abuse are considered to be a continuing tort, the discovery rule should apply to determine when the statute of limitations began to run. Contrary to Robert's contention, the discovery rule is inapplicable here. The discovery rule, like the continuing tort rule, is an equitable exception to the statute of limitations. However, under the discovery rule, a cause of action accrues, and the limitations period begins to run, when the party seeking relief knows or reasonably should know of an injury and that it was wrongfully caused.

By contrast, in the case of a continuing tort, such as the one at bar, a plaintiff's cause of action accrues, and the statute of limitations begins to run, at the time the last injurious act occurs or the conduct is abated. Thus, as previously stated, a continuing tort does not involve tolling the statute of limitations because of delayed or continuing injuries, but instead involves viewing the defendant's conduct as a continuous whole for prescriptive purposes. We therefore have no need to consider application of the discovery rule here, because we have found that Lynn's complaint was filed within two years of the accrual of her action for the continuing tort of intentional infliction of emotional distress.

NOTES AND QUESTIONS

1. **Continuing Tort v. Separate and Distinct Torts.** Is it clear to you, after reading this excerpt from *Feltmeier* how to distinguish a continuing tort from separate and distinct torts? Why was Robert not correct in claiming that the various batteries, assaults, defamations, and other torts involved in his abuse of Lynn were separate and that those that occurred before August 25, 1997 were barred by the statute of limitations?

In the early 1990s the marriage of Yankee coach Jack Satter to Nancy Bernard unraveled amidst claims on her part that he often beat her and abused her psychologically. Ultimately, she filed a $10 million tort action against him for the physical and emotional abuse. The court found that the statute of limitations barred all of the claims except one. It took the entirely male jury less than an hour to decide against compensating the plaintiff at all. Sarah M. Buel, *Access to Meaningful Remedy: Overcoming*

Doctrinal Obstacles in Tort Litigation Against Domestic Violence Offenders, 83 OR. L. REV. 945 (2004). Why wasn't this an appropriate case for the continuing tort doctrine? Do you think the court's refusal to apply the doctrine in this setting represents yet again its reluctance to "interfere" in private family matters? Do you think the jury's failure to find the defendant liable even for a single incident of violence indicates that society still believes that relations between spouses must be given more leeway than those between strangers?

Plaintiffs are particularly likely to be unsuccessful in convincing a court to apply the continuing tort doctrine in jurisdictions in which courts do not recognize the possibility of intentional infliction of emotional distress between partners to a marriage. In *Galvin v. Francis*, 2003 WL 21696740 (N.Y.Sup.), plaintiff sought damages for her husband's abusive conduct from 1992 to 1999. The court allowed her action to go forward only for one claim of battery in 1999. It said,

> While the prohibition of a cause of action for intentional infliction of emotional distress within a matrimonial action is supported by clear appellate authority, the same is not true for other torts. In general, there is no longer any impediment to an interspousal non-matrimonial action for personal injury.... Although a cause of action for assault and battery may be asserted, incidents occurring prior to the one-year limitations period may not be included pursuant to a continuing tort exception. Causes of action for assault and battery accrue immediately upon the occurrence of the tortious act and thus, are not appropriate for the continuing tort violation exception.... Accordingly ... Plaintiff's claim for money damages for assault and battery is limited to the December 25, 1999 incident.

2. **Tort of Domestic Abuse.** In 1995, in *Giovine v. Giovine*, 663 A.2d 109 (N.J.Super. A.D.1995) (partially excerpted above), the New Jersey Appellate Division took what appeared to be the first step toward the recognition of a tort of domestic violence. The Court said:

> We ... conclude that a wife diagnosed with battered woman's syndrome should be permitted to sue her spouse in tort for the physical and emotional injuries sustained by continuous acts of battering during the course of the marriage, *provided* there is medical, psychiatric, or psychological expert testimony establishing that the wife was caused to have an inability to take any action to improve or alter the situation unilaterally. In the absence of expert proof, the wife cannot be deemed to be suffering from battered woman's syndrome, and each act of abuse during the marriage would constitute a separate and distinct cause of action in tort, subject to the statute of limitations.

As is apparent from the above quotation, one of the advantages of this tort is that it would draw on the continuing tort doctrine so as to delay the barring effect of statutes of limitations. Commentators have argued that another advantage of recognizing a tort of domestic violence would be that the entire story of the abuse could be told in a coherent fashion without having to break it down to fit the elements of a variety of other torts. Another argument in favor of creating a new domestic violence tort is that the mere act of naming the tort could provide victims with credibility and result in more attention to the subject from the bar and legal academia. On the other hand, scholars in the field worry that the creation of a new tort might result in rigid requirements for recovery that are inconsistent with an understanding of the variety of practices and experiences that constitute abusive relationships. This could mean that some victims of abuse are yet again excluded from legal benefits intended to benefit victims in general. Clare Dalton, *Domestic Violence, Domestic Torts and Divorce: Constraints and Possibilities,* 31 NEW ENG. L. REV. 319 (1997); Sarah M. Buel, *Access to Meaningful Remedy: Overcoming Doctrinal Obstacles in Tort Litigation Against Domestic Violence Offenders,* 83 OR. L. REV. 945 (2004). Given these arguments, would you advocate the creation of a new tort of domestic violence? It is perhaps worth noting that other courts, including other New Jersey courts, have not been rushing to endorse *Giovine.* For a discussion of torts and domestic violence, see Jennifer Wriggins, *Domestic Violence Torts,* 75 S. CAL. L. REV. 121 (2001).

Abusers' Tort Actions Against Victims of Domestic Violence

Defendants in criminal domestic violence actions, in divorces in which domestic violence is alleged, or in motions for civil protective orders sometimes turn around and sue the plaintiffs or instigators of those actions. In some cases they also sue third parties who have, they believe, participated in the "wrongful" actions against them.

As the following case indicates, these suits often claim intentional infliction of emotional distress or malicious prosecution. Although these suits are frequently unsuccessful, they do require the defendant (usually the person claiming victimization as a result of the alleged domestic violence) to defend against the litigation. That can be expensive, time-consuming, and nerve-wracking even if the case is dismissed on summary judgment.

Celley v. Stevens

Court of Appeals of Michigan, 2004.
2004 WL 134000.

■ PER CURIAM.

Plaintiff appeals as of right the trial court's decision to grant defendant's motion for summary disposition. We affirm in part and reverse in part.

I. Facts and Proceedings

Plaintiff married defendant on May 6, 2000. Shortly thereafter, their relationship deteriorated. According to plaintiff, when he refused to leave the marital home, defendant created a "phony story" about domestic violence, which eventually formed the basis for plaintiff's claims. On July 3, 2000, defendant sought treatment in the emergency room at Saline Community Hospital, alleging that she had been assaulted. She also called the Ann Arbor police department and informed the police that plaintiff had assaulted her. Plaintiff was subsequently prosecuted for domestic violence and acquitted following a jury trial in October 2000.

In 2001, plaintiff filed a complaint against defendant . . . in which he alleged that on July 3, 2000, defendant Stevens wrongfully filed a domestic assault charge against him for which he faced criminal charges. Plaintiff's complaint asserted claims of negligence, defamation, intentional infliction of emotional distress, [abuse of process,] and malicious prosecution against defendant. . . .

The trial court granted defendant's motion [for summary judgment], dismissing plaintiff's claims with prejudice. This appeal followed. . . .

III.   Analysis

Plaintiff first claims that the trial court erred in dismissing his defamation claim on the basis that defendant's reports of domestic assault were absolutely privileged. In part, we agree.

Statements made by a witness as part of a judicial proceeding are absolutely privileged. This privilege extends to all stages of the proceeding, including providing information to police officers regarding criminal activity. Accordingly, defendant's allegations of domestic violence made to Ann Arbor police officers cannot form the basis of a defamation claim by plaintiff.

This privilege does not extend, however, to the reports of domestic assault defendant made to individuals outside of the judicial process, as alleged in plaintiff's amended complaint. Moreover, defendant did not request summary disposition on plaintiff's claims that defendant defamed him to individuals other than law enforcement personnel. Accordingly, the trial court erred by dismissing all of plaintiff's claims of defamation on the basis of defendant's immunity as a witness. When evaluating claims of defamation, each allegedly false publication amounts to a separate cause of action, and, therefore, must be evaluated individually. We remand this matter to the trial court for reinstatement of plaintiff's remaining defamation claims that defendant has not yet challenged.

Plaintiff next contends that the trial court erred in granting summary disposition to defendant on plaintiff's negligence claim. We disagree. "To establish a prima facie case of negligence, a plaintiff must prove four elements: (1) a duty owed by the defendant to the plaintiff, (2) a breach of that duty, (3) causation, and (4) damages."

Here, the trial court concluded that plaintiff had not established the existence of a duty owed to him by defendant. Plaintiff argues that a fiduciary duty, including the duty not to make a false domestic violence allegation, arises out of the relationship between a husband and wife, and that the existence of such a duty supports his cause of action for negligence. We disagree. A fiduciary relationship arises "only when there is a reposing of faith, confidence and trust and the placing of reliance by one upon the judgment and advice of another." Plaintiff's claim against defendant does not arise out of his placement of reliance upon defendant's judgment and advice, and, therefore, cannot be premised on the duty imposed in a fiduciary relationship.

The duty necessary to sustain a claim of negligence, however, is defined as "an obligation to perform to a specific standard of care toward another as recognized under the law." Here, plaintiff alleges that defendant had a duty not to make a false report of domestic violence and breached that duty, causing foreseeable harm. Examined closely, these allegations do not support a claim of negligence but merely restate plaintiff's defamation claims. Accordingly, the trial court did not err by dismissing plaintiff's negligence claim.

Plaintiff next contends that the trial court erred in granting summary disposition to defendant on his claim of intentional infliction of emotional distress. We disagree. To sustain a claim of intentional infliction of emotional distress, a plaintiff must establish the following: "(1) extreme and outrageous conduct, (2) intent or recklessness, (3) causation, and (4) severe emotional distress." Liability for such a claim has been found only where the conduct complained of has been so outrageous in character, and so extreme in degree, as to go beyond all possible bounds of decency and to be regarded as atrocious and utterly intolerable in a civilized community.

Plaintiff based his claim of intentional infliction of emotional distress on defendant's reports of domestic violence to the police. In light of our conclusion that these reports were absolutely privileged, we likewise conclude that the trial court properly granted defendant's motion for summary disposition on plaintiff's claim of intentional infliction of emotional distress. Additionally, we conclude that defendant's conduct was not sufficiently "extreme and outrageous," as a matter of law, to permit recovery. The conduct plaintiff complained of would not cause a member of the community to respond "Outrageous!" and would not be regarded as atrocious.

Plaintiff also contends that the trial court erred in granting summary disposition to defendant on plaintiff's malicious prosecution claim. We disagree. To prevail on a claim of malicious prosecution, the plaintiff has the burden of proving: (1) that the defendant has initiated a criminal prosecution against him, (2) that the criminal proceedings terminated in his favor, (3) that the private person who instituted or maintained the prosecution lacked probable cause for his actions, and (4) that the action was undertaken with malice or a purpose in instituting the criminal claim other than bringing the offender to justice.

Moreover, a claim asserted against a private person requires proof that the private person instituted or maintained the prosecution and that the prosecutor acted on the basis of information submitted by the private person that did not constitute probable cause. The prosecutor's exercise of his independent discretion in initiating and maintaining a prosecution is a complete defense to an action for malicious prosecution.

In the present case, plaintiff cannot demonstrate that defendant initiated the prosecution. As the Court stated [previously], institution of criminal charges lies within the prosecutor's exclusive discretion. Unless the prosecutor acts on the information provided by the private person, exclusive of conducting an independent investigation, the private person has not procured the prosecution. Here, plaintiff testified that he did not know whether the prosecution instituted an independent investigation prior to prosecuting him. This is not sufficient to show that the prosecution acted without conducting an independent investigation before exercising its discretion to prosecute plaintiff. We therefore conclude that the trial court properly granted summary disposition to defendant on this claim as well.

Finally, plaintiff contends that the trial court erred in granting summary disposition to defendant on his abuse of process claim. We disagree. A successful claim of abuse of process requires proof of "(1) an ulterior purpose, and (2) an act in the use of the process that is improper in the regular prosecution of the proceeding." A claim of abuse of process will not succeed unless the plaintiff shows "some irregular act in the use of the process." Merely harboring bad motives without manifesting those motives does not amount to abuse of process.

The trial court granted summary disposition on the basis that plaintiff had not produced evidence of a corroborating act or ulterior purpose. Plaintiff, however, contends that corroborating evidence exists because defendant told him that if he did not leave the marital home on July 3, 2000, and participate in a quick, no-fault divorce, she would embarrass him and ruin him. In the trial court, however, defendant did not assert the existence of any substantively admissible evidence to support his claim of abuse of process. Accordingly, the trial court properly granted summary disposition. . . .

The gravamen of plaintiff's claim is that defendant maliciously caused the institution of criminal proceedings against him for her advantage in the divorce proceeding. However, an action for abuse of process lies for the improper use of process after it has been issued, not for maliciously causing it to issue. Although plaintiff argues that defendant informed him that she would ruin him if he did not participate in a quick divorce proceeding, he does not demonstrate through substantively admissible evidence that she actually used the criminal proceedings to accomplish that purpose. His claim for abuse of process consequently fails.

Affirmed in part, reversed in part, and remanded for proceedings consistent with this opinion. . . .

NOTES AND QUESTIONS

1. **Variety of Tort Actions that an Abuser May Try to Use.** Notice the large number of different causes of action on which an alleged abuser can sue the claimed victim of domestic violence. It appears to be increasingly common for accused abusers who have won the claimed victim's case against them to turn around and sue the victim. People in Celley's position frequently use these same torts. *Davis v. Remy*, 2006 WL 2780114 (Ohio App. 4 Dist.) involved an action for malicious prosecution, while *Franco v. Mudford*, 802 N.E.2d 129 (Mass. App. 2004), involved actions for malicious prosecution and abuse of process. In *Price v. Dyke*, 2001 WL 127871 (Ohio

App. 2 Dist.), the plaintiff sued for slander, libel, and intentional infliction of emotional distress.

Not surprisingly, the defendants in these cases, like defendant Stevens in the above case, all tried to dispose of the cases by motion prior to trial. Some succeeded, while others did not. *Price v. Dyke*, 2001 WL 127871 (Ohio App.) is an example of a case in which the court found summary judgment against the plaintiff inappropriate. How do you think the possibility that the alleged abuser may file a tort action against the claimed victim of domestic violence will affect the claimed victim's willingness to seek the protection of the police or civil protective orders? Do you think there should be a mechanism for discouraging those who have been the subject of claims of abuse from filing tort claims against their alleged victims or do you think those alleged abusers are merely engaging in the protection of their own legal rights?

2. **Issue Preclusion and Claim Preclusion as Barring Further Litigation.** In some instances the torts on which the alleged batterer wishes to sue a former partner can be disposed of by use of the doctrines of issue preclusion (also known as collateral estoppel) or claim preclusion (also known as res judicata.) In order to establish a claim of issue preclusion, the party seeking to use the doctrine must show (1) the issue to be precluded has already been litigated, (2) the issue was actually decided in the previous litigation, (3) the issue's determination was necessary to the decision in the previous litigation, (4) the judgment in the previous litigation is final, and (5) the party against whom the preclusion is asserted had a full opportunity to litigate the issue in the previous proceeding. *Collins v. Pond Creek Mining Co.*, 468 F.3d 213 (4th Cir. 2006). Claim preclusion means that not only the issue has been precluded by previous decision, but the entire claim has been.

One example of how this can work is *Riemers v. Peters–Riemers*, 684 N.W.2d 619 (N.D. 2004). There, the plaintiff, after being divorced from his ex-wife, sued her for intentional infliction of emotional distress on the grounds that she had been violent against him and that he had acted in self-defense. The North Dakota Supreme Court upheld the trial court's dismissal of the action on the grounds that the question of who had initiated the violence had been decided against the ex-husband as part of prior divorce and protective order proceedings and that the ex-husband (the plaintiff) was estopped from relitigating the question. The Court noted that Riemers, the ex-husband, was a party to those proceedings and had "multiple" chances to litigate the issue during those proceedings. The Court rejected Riemers's claim that the issues had not been adequately addressed previously because the trial court judge had merely "flipped through" the materials and had not given them adequate attention. Of course, often the relevant issues will not have been previously litigated in the underlying divorce or other action.

3. **Anti–SLAPP Act Litigation.** At least 14 states have specific statutes that permit the rapid dismissal of suits filed with the objective of limiting the defendant's right to exercise first amendment rights of speech or petition. These statutes are usually known as statutes to prevent Strategic

Litigation Against Public Participation (anti-SLAPP acts.) For example, Massachusetts law permits a party who asserts that civil claims or counterclaims against him are based on his exercise of the "right to petition" under the state or federal constitution to bring a special motion to dismiss. M.G.L. Ch. 231 § 59H (2007). Under the statute, the court is required to grant the motion to dismiss unless the movant's exercise of the right to petition lacked either "any reasonable factual support" or an "arguable basis in the law." The statute also provides for the award of costs and attorneys' fees in instances in which the motion to dismiss under the anti-SLAPP Act is granted. This is a powerful tool and in Massachusetts those who claim to be victims of domestic violence have been able to use it to protect themselves against what they claim are their partners' abusive, retaliatory actions.

The case of *McLarnon v. Jokisch*, 727 N.E.2d 813 (Mass. 2000), is an example of the use of the Massachusetts anti-SLAPP Act in the context of allegations of domestic violence. Virginia Jokisch had a restraining order against her ex-husband which she alleged he had violated. The court rejected that claim. He then filed an action against her for malicious prosecution, intentional infliction of emotional distress, and alienation of their child's affections. He alleged that she had made false allegations against him in obtaining the restraining order. Pursuant to the anti-SLAPP act, the Massachusetts Supreme Judicial Court upheld the trial court's dismissal of McLarnon's actions against Jokisch on the grounds that the statute is broad enough to cover filings for restraining orders and does not require that the protected acts of petition be of public concern. For further examples of the use of the Massachusetts anti-SLAPP Act in the context of claims of domestic violence, see *Franco v. Mudford*, 802 N.E.2d 129 (Mass. App. Ct. 2004) and *Fabre v. Walton*, 802 N.E.2d 1030 (Mass. 2004).

Although more than a dozen states besides Massachusetts have anti-SLAPP Acts, some are considerably narrower than the Massachusetts statute. The anti-SLAPP Acts do not appear to have been used to prevent harassing litigation in domestic violence situations other than in Massachusetts. For a summary of the various anti-SLAPP acts, see The California Anti–SLAPP Project, www.casp.net.

4. **The Costs of Litigation.** Suits by alleged abusers against victims of domestic violence are traditional tort actions. Most tort litigation is done on a contingency fee basis. Thus, abusers' tort suits against victims are likely to be prosecuted either pro se or on a contingency basis. The victim, however, will need to find an attorney to represent her on a normal fee for service basis. This will be extremely difficult unless she has funds to pay for the services. Legal services offices are overwhelmed with cases, and as a result, unable to take these. David Luban, *Taking Out the Adversary: The Assault on Progressive Public–Interest Lawyers,*, 91 Cal. L. Rev. 209 (2003). For example, Greater Boston Legal Services provides representation for the poor in a wide range of administrative cases, as well as representation for victims of domestic violence in custody, divorce, and paternity cases. However, it does not provide any representation, even defensively, in tort cases. Greater Boston Legal Services, www/gbls.org/services.html.

5. **Suits by Alleged Abusers against Third Parties who Assist their Claimed Victims.** Abusers also use the litigation process to try to intimidate third parties from assisting their victims. If successful, this tactic would be yet another way of isolating the victim. For example, in *Riemers v. Peters–Riemers*, 684 N.W.2d 619 (N.D. 2004), the Court noted that Reimers had previously challenged unsuccessfully a restraining order that his ex-wife, Reimers–Peters had brought against him. He had also been unsuccessful in challenging his eviction from the former marital dwelling, although he had managed to get several contempt actions against him relating to the divorce dismissed. In this action, he sued his ex-wife for a variety of torts that he claimed occurred during the marriage. He also sued her law firm for conspiring with her to give false testimony, deceive the court, and delay settlement of the divorce. He sought in excess of $200 million against the defendants in this action. The trial court granted summary judgment for the defendants and Reimers appealed to the North Dakota Supreme Court which affirmed the trial court's decision.

Abusers may also sue therapists and others who assist the victim. In an action separate from the one described above, Reimers sued local officials who had responded to an incident of domestic violence between himself and his wife. He alleged that the officials had falsely arrested him. Ultimately, the North Dakota Supreme Court affirmed dismissal of the claims as barred by collateral estoppel and "not having any basis in law or fact." *Riemers v. Anderson*, 680 N.W.2d 280 (N.D. 2004). For another example, see *Riccobene v. Scales*, 19 F.Supp.2d 577 (N.D.W.Va. 1998) (suit against attorney who represented wife in divorce and domestic violence proceedings.) In *Lawrence v. Roberdeau*, 665 N.W.2d 719 (N.D. 2003), a father, whose conduct had earlier been found *not* to meet the statutory requirements for domestic violence, sued an employee of Lutheran Social Services and others for recommending in the earlier custody and visitation action that the father participate in a domestic violence program before the court granted unsupervised visitation with his son. The claims against the therapists were ultimately dismissed on the basis of witness and state employee immunity. In suits like these, the fact that they are ultimately dismissed is probably less important than their value in harassing the defendants and in encouraging them to think twice before aligning themselves in any way with the victim of the violence.

6. **Suits by Alleged Abusers Against Academics Who Write about Domestic Violence.** In one instance, a law professor wrote a law review article about custody issues in domestic violence cases. She cited one case and one of the parties to the case threatened to sue her. Both the university at which she worked and the law review that had published the article declined to defend her despite an outside expert's assurances that she would eventually win in court. Ultimately, she was forced to remove the offending reference from the article. *Twisting in the Wind*, INSIDE HIGHER ED. (Nov. 30, 2005) http://insidehighered.com/news/2005/11/30/ liability. If the threat of suit can have this effect on the legal academy, imagine its effect on non-lawyers like therapists, doctors, and shelter personnel.

D. THE RELATIONSHIP BETWEEN TORT ACTIONS AND DIVORCE PROCEEDINGS

In many abusive relationships, the first time the abused partner will be able even to contemplate a tort action is when she decides to separate from her abuser. At this moment, something has happened to tip the balance, to make separation feel either safe, or in any event less dangerous, physically and emotionally, than trying to maintain the relationship. Perhaps the level of violence has become life-threatening. Perhaps it is spilling over onto the children. Perhaps the police have come to the house and, through a restraining order or criminal process, the woman has made contact with an advocate who has expanded her sense of the options available to her. Perhaps a friend's patient insistence that she does not deserve to be beaten has eroded her partner's hold on her. For whatever reason, she has shifted from efforts to minimize and contain the abuse, to invoking the legal system to help her put it behind her. If she has, in addition, retained the services of a family lawyer, she also has, or should have, access to new information, not only about the dissolution of her marriage, if she *is* married, but also about her rights and options with respect to a tort claim.

On the other hand, the barriers to suit we have already identified are still there. And if she has been married to her partner, a new set of questions about the relationship between the divorce proceedings and any cause of action in tort will have to be answered. Thus far, courts around the country have responded in a bewildering variety of ways to the question of whether, and under what circumstances, the civil cause of action can be pursued simultaneously with, or subsequent to, the divorce. If the actions can be pursued simultaneously, there is the additional question of how an award of tort damages should affect the division of the marital estate. If the tort action is pursued after the divorce is completed, there is always the question as to whether the tort issues were waived in the divorce determination. Similarly, the tort action may be barred by either claim or issue preclusion.

The materials that follow address the above issues, beginning with the question of the timing of the divorce and tort actions.

Twyman v. Twyman

Supreme Court of Texas, 1993.
855 S.W.2d 619.

■ CORNYN, JUSTICE.

In this case we decide whether a claim for infliction of emotional distress can be brought in a divorce proceeding. Because the judgment of the court of appeals is based on negligent infliction of emotional distress, and cannot be affirmed on that or any other basis, we reverse the judgment of that court and remand this cause for a new trial in the interest of justice. We deem a new trial appropriate because of our recent decision that no cause of action for negligent infliction of emotional distress exists in Texas. Today, however, we expressly adopt the tort of intentional infliction of emotional distress, and hold that such a claim can be brought in a divorce proceeding.

I.

Sheila and William Twyman married in 1969. Sheila filed for divorce in 1985. She later amended her divorce petition to add a general claim for emotional harm without specifying whether the claim was based on negligent or intentional infliction of emotional distress. In her amended petition, Sheila alleged that William "intentionally and cruelly" attempted to engage her in "deviate sexual acts."[1] Following a bench trial, the court rendered judgment dissolving the marriage, dividing the marital estate, awarding conservatorship of the children to Sheila, ordering William to pay child support, and awarding Sheila $15,000 plus interest for her claim for emotional distress. William appealed that portion of the judgment based on emotional distress. . . .

II.

We now consider whether the cause of action for intentional infliction of emotional distress may be brought in a divorce proceeding. . . . Under the rules [previously] established . . . there appears to be no legal impediment to bringing a tort claim in a divorce action based on either negligence or an intentional act such as assault or battery.

The more difficult issue is when the tort claim must be brought and how the tort award should be considered when making a "just and right" division of the marital estate. Of the states that have answered this question, several have held that the tort case and the divorce case must be litigated separately. Other states require joinder of the two actions.

We believe that the best approach lies between these two extremes. As in other civil actions, joinder of the tort cause of action should be permitted, but subject to the principles of res judicata. Of course, how such claims are ultimately tried is within the sound discretion of the trial court. But joinder of tort claims with the divorce, when feasible, is encouraged. Resolving both the tort and divorce actions in the same proceeding avoids two trials based at least in part on the same facts, and settles in one suit "all matters existing between the parties."

When a tort action is tried with the divorce, however, it is imperative that the court avoid awarding a double recovery. When dividing the marital estate, the court may take into account several factors, including the fault of the parties if pleaded. . . . However, a spouse should not be allowed to

---

1. At trial, Sheila testified that William pursued sadomasochistic bondage activities with her, even though he knew that she feared such activities because she had been raped at knife-point before their marriage. The trial court found that William "attempted to emotionally coerce [Sheila] in 'bondage' on an ongoing basis . . .'" and "engaged in a continuing course of conduct of attempting to coerce her to join in his practices of 'bondage' by continually asserting that their marriage could be saved only by [Sheila] participating with him in his practices of 'bondage.' "

recover tort damages and a disproportionate division of the community estate based on the same conduct. Therefore, when a fact finder awards tort damages to a divorcing spouse, the court may not consider the same tortious acts when dividing the marital estate.... The court may still award a disproportionate division of property for reasons other than the tortious conduct. To avoid the potential problem of double recovery, the fact finder should consider the damages awarded in the tort action when dividing the parties' property....

■ PHILLIPS, CHIEF JUSTICE, concurring and dissenting.

I join in the Court's recognition of the tort of intentional infliction of emotional distress.... [However] recognition of this tort in the context of a divorce unnecessarily restricts the trial court's discretion in dividing the marital estate. Prior to today's opinion, the trial court could, but was not required to, consider fault in dividing the community property. The court had broad discretion to weigh any fault along with other appropriate factors, such as relative financial condition, disparity of ages, and the needs of the children. Now, however, where fault takes the form of "outrageous" conduct intentionally or recklessly inflicted, it becomes a dominant factor that must be considered at the expense of the other factors....

NOTES AND QUESTIONS

1. **Tort and Divorce Actions: Mandatory Joinder?** Some jurisdictions have held that claims "arising out of or relating to the same transactional circumstances [between the same parties] ... be joined in a single action." *Brennan v. Orban*, 678 A.2d 667 (N.J. 1996). This raises the issue of whether the plaintiff in the tort action is thereby required to give up her right to a trial by jury. Divorce is an action in equity and there is no right to a jury. In *Brennan v. Orban*, the New Jersey Supreme Court found that if the trial court determined that the social interest in vindicating the wrong done by the tortious action is the "dominant interest," the marital tort could be transferred out of equity and tried separately with a jury.

There are also states that have held that the tort claim cannot be joined with the divorce action. For example, in *McCulloh v. Drake*, 24 P.3d 1162 (Wyo. 2001), the Court held that spousal tort cases could not be heard with the parties' divorce because the two types of actions are so different. A divorce is to terminate the parties' relationship whereas a tort case is to provide money damages for the commission of a wrong. Furthermore, in a tort case, the plaintiff is usually entitled to a jury and frequently will have numerous witnesses to present. Tort cases may also involve insurance carriers and joint tortfeasors whose presence is likely to be time-consuming and complicating in terms of resolving the divorce.

Finally, there are a number of jurisdictions like *Twyman* that permit but do not require joinder of tort and divorce claims. Clare Dalton has written:

> The most crucial argument in favor of allowing a woman to wait until her divorce is resolved before she brings a tort action against her

abuser is that unless the legal system preserves this option, a tort remedy will be foreclosed altogether for any woman who feels that pursuing a claim is simply too dangerous, until such time as her separation from her abuser has been successfully accomplished.... If she is forced to pursue the tort claim together with the divorce, or even to notify the probate court that she is bringing it, or plans to bring it, in another court, she may well forfeit the claim to buy her safety. But if the legal system encourages or facilitates this choice, it rewards her abuser; reinforcing his belief that violence, or the threat of violence, is an effective strategy to secure his interests. *Domestic Violence, Domestic Torts, and Divorce*, 31 NEW ENG. L. REV. 319 (1997).

Which approach do you think is best and why?

2. **The Defense of Claim Preclusion.** The doctrine of claim preclusion precludes a party from litigating a claim when there has been previous litigation under the following circumstances:

> (1) the two cases must involve the same claim ... (2) the parties to the two suits must be identical or in "privity"; and (3) the first case must have ended in a valid final judgment "on the merits." [(4) there must have been an opportunity to bring the claim in the first action.] Richard D. Freer and Wendy Collins Perdue, CIVIL PROCEDURE 651 (3d ed. 2001).

Most of the issues around claim preclusion in relation to torts claims and divorce cases involve the first requirement: when are two claims the same? The answer to this question initially appears to depend on the abused spouse's litigation strategy in the divorce action. If the victimized spouse is seeking in the divorce either a fault-based determination of grounds for divorce, a disproportionate division of assets because of the abuser's actions, or special damages because of injury done by the abuse, the court is likely to find that a subsequent tort action is not permitted because of claim preclusion. For example, in *Ex Parte Mardis Howle*, 776 So.2d 133 (Ala. 2000), the ex-wife sought and received in the divorce decree $1,500 for dental and doctor bills incurred as a result of her ex-husband's hitting her. When she subsequently tried to sue in tort for battery, the Court held that the doctrine against claim splitting prohibited her from "recovering medical expenses in one action and additional damages in a separate action based on the same evidence that supported the award of compensation for medical expenses." Similarly, in *Brinkman v. Brinkman*, 966 S.W.2d 780 (Tex. App. 1998), Ms. Brinkman sought a divorce and disproportionate allocation of the marital assets based on cruelty. She also asked for both temporary support and a civil protective order based on her claims of abuse and its effects. Like the *Howle* Court, the *Brinkman* Court ruled that the plaintiff should have litigated her tort claims in the divorce action and that she was barred from doing so subsequently. The court reasoned:

> When Ms. Brinkman chose to allege cruel treatment as grounds for divorce in order to receive a disproportionate share of community property, she was bound to assert all of her claims for cruel treatment arising out of the marriage. To hold otherwise would enable a spouse to

use one instance of abuse as grounds for receiving a large amount of temporary spousal support or a greater share of community property, and then another instance of abuse to obtain actual and punitive damages from the former spouse.

Cases like *Howle* and *Brinkman* imply that if the abused spouse does not seek a fault-based divorce or disproportionate distribution of assets, support, or damages in the divorce on the basis of the abuse, she should be able to sue for damages in tort after the divorce action is finished. And, some courts have so found. For example, in *Roussel v. Roussel*, 2003 WL 22951910 (Va. Cir. Ct.), the Court found that the parties had agreed during the divorce trial that they would not present evidence of abuse, but would limit evidence of fault to adultery. As a result, the Court held that the plaintiff's separate tort action was not precluded. Similarly, in *Stuart v. Stuart*, 410 N.W.2d 632 (Wis. App. 1987), aff'd. 421 N.W.2d 505 (Wis. 1988), overruled on other gnds. in *Kruckenberg v. Harvey* 694 N.W.2d 879 (Wis. 2005), the court ruled that since no mention of the plaintiff's possible tort claims was made in the divorce proceedings, she was not barred from asserting them later. The Wisconsin Court of Appeals noted that in Wisconsin, the Court can divorce a couple without the need for any determination of fault. For yet another case that holds that a divorce decree that does not rely on the presence of abuse for aspects of its final judgment does not preclude the separate litigation of a tort action, see *Sotirescu v. Sotirescu*, 52 S.W.3d 1 (Mo.App. 2001).

Despite the fact that one might decide from the above description that the abused spouse has a strategic choice as to whether to bring the tort claims to the divorce court's attention and allow them to be settled along with the divorce, thereby precluding later tort litigation, or to remain silent about them while in divorce court and only litigate them later, that may be an overly rationalistic understanding of the situation. Frequently actions of the divorce court, sometimes on the petition of the abusive spouse, preclude completely the litigation of the tort claims. In *Brinkman*, Ms. Brinkman had joined the tort causes of action with the action for divorce, only to have the former claims severed by the divorce court on Mr. Brinkman's motion. When she subsequently filed a tort action, the Court found that it was barred. In *Howle*, the plaintiff sued for divorce and for assault and battery and the circuit judge severed the torts claims and transferred them to another court. At the divorce trial, the plaintiff testified to the facts of the battery and was awarded a share of the marital assets, lump sum alimony, and the $1,500 for medical and dental bills. The divorce decree stated that the award was to serve as a "full settlement of all claims now existing between [the] parties." The plaintiff then moved to amend the judgment since her tort claims were still pending in another court. Her motion was denied. On appeal of that denial, the Court of Appeals said that she might have a "viable claim for assault and battery" and that the divorce decree referred only to "those claims still before the judge after the assault and battery claim had been severed." It also noted that the judge presiding in the tort action would have to determine whether those claims were barred. As noted above, the judge in the tort action subsequently determined that they were barred. In both the *Brinkman* and *Howle* cases, the plaintiffs had originally tried to bring the divorce and tort actions together but had been prevented by the courts. In both they were then barred from pursuing the separate tort action.

If you were representing an abused spouse who wanted a divorce and also wanted to pursue damages for her injuries, would you bring the two actions simultaneously or would you bring them separately? If you brought them separately, would you inform the divorce court that you intended to bring tort claims subsequently or would you remain silent about the tort claims? What are the risks of pursuing your strategy?

3. **The Defense of Issue Preclusion.** Even if a spouse is not barred by the doctrine of claim preclusion from bringing the tort claim after the resolution of the divorce, she may still face objections on the grounds of issue preclusion. One is legally estopped from making a particular claim if one has taken an action (or has not acted) and that action (or failure to act) has reasonably induced reliance by the other party. In *Stuart v. Stuart*, 410 N.W.2d 632 (Wis. App. 1987), aff'd. 421 N.W.2d 505 (Wis. 1988), *overruled on other gnds.* in *Kruckenberg v. Harvey* 694 N.W.2d 879 (Wis. 2005), the court held that the failure to disclose plans to sue in tort after the divorce was not a representation that no tort claim existed. Even if the failure to give notice of the impending tort action were taken to represent that no tort claim existed, there was no showing that the allegedly abusive husband had relied to his detriment on any such representation. Thus, the abused wife was not barred from asserting her tort claim. In contrast, in *Heacock v. Heacock*, 568 N.E.2d 621 (Mass. App. 1991), the Court found that the husband had relied on the silence in the divorce action and had subsequently not appealed the divorce decree and had thrown away potentially relevant documents. The trial court had found that the plaintiff's actions had been taken in order to obtain "unfair tactical advantage." The Court of Appeals affirmed the decision that the wife was barred from pursuing her tort claim after the divorce.

These cases are clearly very sensitive to the facts. As a result, can an abused spouse ever be certain that silence in the divorce proceedings about a possible tort claim will not subsequently be found to bar her from asserting that claim? Is it a better legal strategy to announce that she is reserving her rights to sue in tort after the conclusion of the divorce proceedings? Are there safety risks to such a strategy?

4. **The Defense of Waiver.** Most divorce settlements include a "zipper" clause that indicates that the settlement resolves all of the claims between the parties. The parties in *Flugge v. Flugge*, 681 N.W.2d 837 (S.D. 2004), had included such a clause in their settlement and the Court held that the husband had thereby waived his right to sue subsequently for what he claimed was abuse of process on the wife's part in obtaining restraining orders. However, in many cases the abuse continues after the divorce. Since a waiver cannot be valid without knowledge of what one is waiving, one cannot waive a right to sue for future tortious actions that have not yet occurred. Similarly, the *Flugge* Court held that a continuing tort, like intentional infliction of emotional distress, cannot be waived because it does not accrue as a claim until the last tortious act that contributes to the

tort. This is another strength of the continuing tort theory. It allows a plaintiff to recover despite a waiver for abuse that begins before the divorce but which continues afterwards.

Finally, one remaining question about the relation of divorce actions to tort actions involves the interaction of the division of property on divorce with the money judgment that might result from a tort action. The following excerpt describes several possibilities.

5.   **The Relationship Between a Judgment in Tort and Division of Assets on Divorce.** If the tort action is litigated in the same proceeding as the divorce, there is a question of how any recovery in tort affects the division of assets on divorce. Some courts that require joinder of the claims also stay the divorce proceeding until the tort recovery, if any, has been established. Of course, that has the effect of keeping the parties married longer than they would otherwise have been. Furthermore, if the court takes the abused partner's tort recovery into account when dividing the assets, the abused partner may receive less of the parties' marital assets and the abuser may receive more than might otherwise have been awarded. On the other hand, if the assets are divided before the recovery in tort is determined, should the tort claim be considered as an asset of the abused partner and thus considered in the division of the assets? These, and additional possibilities, are discussed in Clare Dalton, *Domestic Violence, Domestic Torts and Divorce*, 31 New Eng. L. Rev. 319 (1997).

CHAPTER FOURTEEN

LAW ENFORCEMENT AND EMPLOYER LIABILITY FOR DOMESTIC VIOLENCE

Introduction

This chapter looks at two contexts that have generated claims by victims of domestic violence against third parties. The first involves police or other law enforcement officers or agencies who fail to protect victims from their abusers. The second involves situations in which abuse follows victims to work, and employers become implicated, either by their failure to offer protection, or by taking adverse action against victimized employees. In the first context, recent cases demonstrate increasing reluctance to impose liability, at both the federal and the state level. In the second, the parameters of potential liability are only now being worked out.

Both contexts present complex doctrinal questions. Failures of law enforcement can be challenged under federal civil rights law, as constitutional torts—violations of constitutional guarantees of due process or equal protection. However, the Supreme Court has narrowly interpreted both the substantive and procedural due process owed by state actors to those threatened by private violence. Furthermore, demanding levels of proof of discrimination have created significant barriers for plaintiffs. Alternatively, failures of law enforcement can be challenged under state tort law, as breaches of a duty of care owed to those threatened by violence. But issues of sovereign immunity, coupled with judicial reluctance to recognize specific duties of protection, make this road equally difficult.

In the workplace context, those seeking redress from employers must grapple with a variety of regulatory schemes, and risk that their claims will fall through the cracks. Workers' compensation schemes generally provide an exclusive remedy for claims arising out of and in the course of employment. While these "no-fault" schemes offer compensation without any proof of fault on the employer's part, recovery is usually significantly less generous than it would be in a comparable tort claim. Depending on the state's interpretation of its workers' compensation statute, and the precise circumstances of the case, a plaintiff may find herself shut out of the statutory scheme, and then may or may not find that she has an alternative remedy under state tort law. If her abuser is a fellow employee, there is even a possibility that Title VII's guarantees against gender discrimination and sexual harassment may come into play. If her employer takes adverse action against her, and her workplace is unionized, her claim is likely to be processed through a grievance procedure and decided by an arbitrator under federal labor relations law. Outside the union context, her only recourse against adverse action by an employer because of her status as a victim of partner abuse is under state contract law, which is likely to offer only very limited protection.

A.   WHEN LAW ENFORCEMENT FAILS TO PROTECT

Challenges to police inaction in the face of domestic violence have a venerable history within the battered women's movement; they were among the earliest strategies deployed by lawyers working with battered women to change policing policy and force public recognition of the criminal, and often lethal, nature of partner abuse. In this first reading, Joan Zorza describes the early challenges, and their impact.

Joan Zorza
The Criminal Law of Misdemeanor Domestic Violence, 1970–1990

83 J. CRIM. L. & CRIMINOLOGY 46 (1992).

In the 1970s, Americans gradually became aware that millions of women were being brutally abused by their husbands. A few women had started organizing around the issue of battered women. Some opened their homes to victims or started shelters. Others proposed legislation to assist battered women. It was clear, however, that neither of these approaches would have much effect if the police did not enforce the new laws. As women [became] increasing[ly] frustrated by the failure of police to arrest even husbands who committed even felony assaults, it became clear that they needed to concentrate their efforts on forcing the police to enforce the few laws that did exist to help battered women.

In 1972, the executor of Ruth Bunnell's estate filed a wrongful death action against the San Jose Police Department (46 Cal.App.3d 6, 120 Cal.Rptr. 5 (1975)). Mrs. Bunnell had called the police at least twenty times in the year before her death to complain that her husband was abusing both her and her two daughters. Only once did they arrest her husband. In September of 1972, she called the police for help, telling them that her husband was on his way to the house to kill her. They told her to wait until he arrived. By the time police came in response to a neighbor's call, her husband had stabbed her to death. The California Court of Appeals upheld the trial court's dismissal of the case, reasoning that the police had never "induced decedent's reliance on a promise, express or implied, that they would provide her with protection."

Legal aid and legal service lawyers, who had always known that the vast majority of their female divorce clients were being violently abused by their husbands, were experiencing the same frustrations. Fearing that another tort action for damages against the police would probably meet with little success, two groups of legal services lawyers on opposite shores of the country decided to adopt a different approach. They filed for declaratory and injunctive relief against the police in order to force them to do what the law empowered them to do to protect battered women.

The first to file suit was a group of five attorneys in the Legal Aid Society of Alameda County in Oakland. They filed a complaint in October of 1976 in the Northern District of California. The suit, which was captioned *Scott v. Hart* [No. C–76–2395 (N.D. Cal., filed Oct. 28, 1976)] was in the form of a class action against George T. Hart, Chief of the Oakland Police Department. They filed on behalf of "women in general and black women in particular who are victims of domestic violence." All five of the named plaintiffs were black women who had repeatedly called the Oakland police for protection when they were beaten up by their husbands, ex-husbands or boyfriends. The officers had either failed to respond or had responded in an ineffectual or, in one case, a threatening manner. By bringing their suit on behalf of black victims of domestic violence who were getting less adequate police responses than were white victims, the legal aid lawyers were able to allege a denial of the equal protection mandated by the Fourteenth Amendment. They also claimed that the police had breached their duty to arrest the abusers "when a felony [had] been committed such as felony wife beating" and that a "police policy that de-emphasizes and discourages arresting assailants . . . is arbitrary, capricious, discriminatory, and deprives plaintiffs and the plaintiff class of the right to equal protection of the laws." The complaint asked the court to: (1) permanently enjoin the police from refusing to respond adequately to battered women's calls; (2) affirmatively order the police to respond adequately; (3) order the police "to arrest when they know that a felony has been committed or when the woman requests the arrest of the assailant"; (4) order the police to "advise women of their right to make citizens' arrests and [of the fact] that the police [will] effectuate those arrests by taking the assailant into custody"; (5) order the police to "take assailants to a mental facility for 72–hour observation" when appropriate; (6) order the police to train officers in "how to best handle these incidents"; (7) order the police to start a batterer treatment program; (8) order the city to establish a shelter for women; and (9) force defendants to pay plaintiffs' "court costs, expenditures and reasonable attorneys' fees."

The first hurdle which plaintiffs needed to overcome was . . . that supervisory officials must have actual knowledge of and responsibility for promulgating discriminatory polices before an aggrieved party could get injunctive relief in federal court. This hurdle, however, proved to be not much of an obstacle. . . . The existence within the Oakland Police Department of a clear arrest-avoidance policy which was known to the watch commanders and other supervisors persuaded the court to allow the case to survive a motion to dismiss. Not until November 14, 1979, however, more than three years after the class had filed its complaint, did the parties agree to a settlement. The settlement granted most of the plaintiffs' requested relief: the police agreed to a new policy in which they would respond quickly to domestic violence calls. The police also agreed to make an arrest whenever an officer had probable cause to believe that a felonious assault had occurred or that a misdemeanor had been committed in his presence. This new policy required the police to make their arrest decisions without looking to factors traditionally used to justify inaction. The police also agreed not to use the threat of adverse financial consequences for the couple to justify inaction or to urge the victim not to pursue the case. The settlement also required police to inform each battered woman that she had a right to make a citizen's arrest, and required police to help her to do so. Officers would thereafter refer victims to supportive agencies for counseling and other assistance. Furthermore, the department acknowledged that it had an affirmative duty to enforce civil restraining and "kick out" orders. While Oakland was not required to provide a shelter and counseling for victims (or assailants), the city agreed to apply for federal funding for any support services available to battered women, and to pay the plaintiffs' attorney fees and court costs. . . .

The . . . lawsuits made clear to police departments throughout the United States that they were vulnerable to being sued if they failed to protect the rights of battered women. Battered women's advocates soon learned how many police chiefs knew that both of the departments had "lost." As a result, police departments in many towns and cities agreed to revamp their policies and practices without any suit having to be filed. The possibility that the town or city might be liable for attorney fees and even for damages in a case by injured women became a persuasive bargaining chip to many battered women's lawyers and advocates.

The case law took one more important step forward in *Thurman v. City of Torrington, Conn.,* 595 F.Supp. 1521 (D.Conn. 1984) where a federal jury awarded Tracey Thurman and her son $2.3 million because the police were negligent in failing to protect her from her abusive husband. The court found that Torrington's policy of indifference amounted to sex discrimination.

The effect of the case was dramatic. As one commentator observed,

> The Thurman case was widely reported in the popular press and in academic journals. It graphically confirmed the extreme financial penalty that could be imposed on police departments when they abjectly fail to perform their duties. In addition, it confirmed that in appropriate cases, these massive liability awards would be upheld.

Many police departments that did not get the message from *Scott* were forced by *Thurman's* threat of huge liability to change their policies.

Federal Civil Rights Claims under 42 U.S.C. § 1983

42 U.S.C. § 1983, the federal civil rights law on which some of these early challenges were based, provides a cause of action against government officials whose actions deprive individuals of a constitutionally protected right. It was originally enacted as part of the Ku Klux Klan Act of 1871 as a federal response to state inaction in the face of private racially-motivated violence—in particular the violence of the Klan's nightriders against former slaves. In the 1960s, after decades of disuse, § 1983 was reinvigorated to protect against police misconduct. See *Monroe v. Pape*, 365 U.S. 167 (1961).

To establish a claim, a plaintiff must show: (1) that the conduct complained of was committed by a person acting under color of state law; (2) that the conduct deprived the plaintiff of a constitutional right; and (3) that the deprivation proximately caused the plaintiff's injury. The defendant may be an individual, or a municipality or municipal agency, such as a police department. States and state agencies can be sued only for prospective relief, not damages, because of state sovereign immunity under the Eleventh Amendment. Individual state employees can be sued for damages, but only in their personal rather than their official capacities, so that any judgment against them will be satisfied out of their personal assets. Municipalities are not vicariously liable for the actions of their employees under § 1983, but only for their own policies or practices. Individual municipal employees can be sued in either their personal or their official capacities. If they are sued in their official capacities, any judgment against them will be satisfied by their employer. Individual defendants are also protected by certain immunities. Judges and prosecutors have absolute immunity for acts within the scope of their official duties. Police officers and other officials have qualified immunity for discretionary actions, meaning that they are protected from individual liability unless their conduct violates clearly established law, and is unreasonable, based on the knowledge they had at the time.

Plaintiffs in § 1983 actions can recover attorneys' fees, compensatory damages, punitive damages for reckless or callously indifferent conduct, and declaratory or injunctive relief.

There are three constitutional claims that can be made on behalf of victims of domestic violence when the police fail to enforce a protective order or fail to arrest a domestic abuser: the failure violates the equal protection clause of the 14th Amendment; the failure violates the substantive due process clause of the 14th Amendment; and the failure violates the procedural due process clause of the 14th Amendment. Consider how each of these arguments has fared.

Equal Protection

Thurman v. Torrington

United States District Court for the District of Connecticut, 1984.
595 F.Supp. 1521.

■ Blumenfeld, Senior District Judge.

The plaintiffs have brought this action pursuant to 42 U.S.C. §§ 1983, 1985, 1986 and 1988, as well as the fifth, ninth, and fourteenth amendments to the Constitution, alleging that their constitutional rights were violated by the nonperformance or malperformance of official duties by the defendant police officers. In addition, the plaintiffs seek to hold liable the defendant City of Torrington (hereinafter, the "City"). The defendant City has filed a motion to dismiss the plaintiffs' complaint. . . .

Between early October 1982 and June 10, 1983, the plaintiff, Tracey Thurman, a woman living in the City of Torrington, and others on her behalf, notified the defendant City through the defendant police officers of the City of repeated threats upon her life and the life of her child, the plaintiff Charles J. Thurman, Jr., made by her estranged husband, Charles Thurman. Attempts to file complaints by plaintiff Tracey Thurman against her estranged husband in response to his threats of death and maiming were ignored or rejected by the named defendants and the defendant City.

An abbreviated chronology of the plaintiff's attempted and actual notifications of the threats made against her and her son by her estranged husband to the defendant City and police officers is appropriate for consideration of this motion.

In October 1982, Charles Thurman attacked plaintiff Tracey Thurman at the home of Judy Bentley and Richard St. Hilaire in the City of Torrington. Mr. St. Hilaire and Ms. Bentley made a formal complaint of the attack to one of the unnamed defendant police officers and requested efforts to keep the plaintiff's husband, Charles Thurman, off their property.

On or about November 5, 1982, Charles Thurman returned to the St. Hilaire–Bentley residence and using physical force took the plaintiff Charles J. Thurman, Jr. from said residence. Plaintiff Tracey Thurman and Mr. St. Hilaire went to Torrington police headquarters to make a formal complaint. At that point, unnamed defendant police officers of the City of Torrington refused to accept a complaint from Mr. St. Hilaire even as to trespassing.

On or about November 9, 1982, Charles Thurman screamed threats at Tracey while she was sitting in her car. Defendant police officer Neil Gemelli stood on the street watching Charles Thurman scream threats at Tracey until Charles Thurman broke the windshield of plaintiff Tracey Thurman's car while she was inside the vehicle. Charles Thurman was arrested after he broke the windshield, and on the next day, November 10, 1982, he was convicted of breach of peace. He received a suspended sentence of six months and a two-year "conditional discharge," during which he was ordered to stay completely away from the plaintiff Tracey Thurman and the Bentley–St. Hilaire residence and to commit no further crimes. The court imposing probation informed the defendants of this sentence.

On December 31, 1982, while plaintiff Tracey Thurman was at the Bentley–St. Hilaire residence, Charles Thurman returned to said residence and once again threatened her. She called the Torrington Police Department. One of the unnamed police officer defendants took the call, and, although informed of the violation of the conditional discharge, made no attempt to ascertain Charles Thurman's whereabouts or to arrest him.

Between January 1, 1983 and May 4, 1983, numerous telephone complaints to the Torrington Police Department were taken by various unnamed police officers, in which repeated threats of violence to the plaintiffs by Charles Thurman were reported and his arrest on account of the threats and violation of the terms of his probation was requested.

On May 4 and 5, 1983, the plaintiff Tracey Thurman and Ms. Bentley reported to the Torrington Police Department that Charles Thurman had said that he would shoot the plaintiffs. Defendant police officer Storrs took the written complaint of plaintiff Tracey Thurman who was seeking an arrest warrant for her husband because of his death threat and violation of his "conditional discharge." Defendant Storrs refused to take the complaint of Ms. Bentley. Plaintiff Tracey Thurman was told to return three weeks later on June 1, 1983 when defendant Storrs or some other person connected with the police department of the defendant City would seek a warrant for the arrest of her husband.

On May 6, 1983, Tracey filed an application for a restraining order against Charles Thurman in the Litchfield Superior Court. That day, the court issued an ex parte restraining order forbidding Charles Thurman from assaulting, threatening, and harassing Tracey Thurman. The defendant City was informed of this order.

On May 27, 1983, Tracey Thurman requested police protection in order to get to the Torrington Police Department, and she requested a warrant for her husband's arrest upon her arrival at headquarters after being taken there by one of the unnamed defendant police officers. She was told that she would have to wait until after the Memorial Day holiday weekend and was advised to call on Tuesday, May 31, to pursue the warrant request.

On May 31, 1983, Tracey Thurman appeared once again at the Torrington Police Department to pursue the warrant request. She was then advised by one of the unnamed defendant police officers that defendant Schapp was the only policeman who could help her and that he was on vacation. She was told that she would have to wait until he returned. That same day, Tracey's brother-in-law, Joseph Kocsis, called the Torrington Police Department to protest the lack of action taken on Tracey's complaint. Although Mr. Kocsis was advised that Charles Thurman would be arrested on June 8, 1983, no such arrest took place.

On June 10, 1983, Charles Thurman appeared at the Bentley–St. Hilaire residence in the early afternoon and demanded to speak to Tracey. Tracey, remaining indoors, called the defendant police department asking that Charles be picked up for violation of his probation. After about 15 minutes, Tracey went outside to speak to her husband in an effort to persuade him not to take or hurt Charles Jr. Soon thereafter, Charles began to stab Tracey repeatedly in the chest, neck and throat.

Approximately 25 minutes after Tracey's call to the Torrington Police Department and after her stabbing, a single police officer, the defendant Petrovits, arrived on the scene. Upon the arrival of Officer Petrovits at the scene of the stabbing, Charles Thurman was holding a bloody knife. Charles then dropped the knife and, in the presence of Petrovits, kicked the plaintiff Tracey Thurman in the head and ran into the Bentley–St. Hilaire residence. Charles returned from within the residence holding the plaintiff Charles Thurman, Jr. and dropped the child on his wounded mother. Charles then kicked Tracey in the head a second time. Soon thereafter, defendants DeAngelo, Nukirk, and Columbia arrived on the scene but still permitted Charles Thurman to wander about the crowd and to continue to threaten Tracey. Finally, upon approaching Tracey once again, this time while she was lying on a stretcher, Charles Thurman was arrested and taken into custody.

It is also alleged that at all times mentioned above, except for approximately two weeks following his conviction and sentencing on November 10, 1982, Charles Thurman resided in Torrington and worked there as a counterman and short order cook at Skie's Diner. There he served many members of the Torrington Police Department including some of the named and unnamed defendants in this case. In the course of his employment Charles Thurman boasted to the defendant police officer patrons that he intended to "get" his wife and that he intended to kill her.

I. *Motion to Dismiss the Claims of Tracey Thurman*

The defendant City now brings a motion to dismiss the claims against it. The City first argues that the plaintiff's complaint should be dismissed for failure to allege the deprivation of a constitutional right. Though the complaint alleges that the actions of the defendants deprived the plaintiff Tracey Thurman of her constitutional right to equal protection of the laws, the defendant City argues that the equal protection clause of the fourteenth amendment "does not guarantee equal application of social services." ... Rather, the defendant City argues that the equal protection clause "only prohibits intentional discrimination that is racially motivated"....

The defendant City's argument is clearly a misstatement of the law. The application of the equal protection clause is not limited to racial classifications or racially motivated discrimination.... Classifications on the basis of gender will be held invalid under the equal protection clause unless they are substantially related to an important governmental objective. And lastly, the equal protection clause will be applied to strike down classifications which are not rationally related to a legitimate governmental purpose.

In the instant case, the plaintiffs allege that the defendants use an administrative classification that manifests itself in discriminatory treatment violative of the equal protection clause. Police protection in the City of Torrington, they argue, is fully provided to persons abused by someone with whom the victim has no domestic relationship. But the Torrington police have consistently afforded lesser protection, plaintiffs allege, when the victim is (1) a woman abused or assaulted by a spouse or boyfriend, or (2) a child abused by a father or stepfather. The issue to be decided, then, is whether the plaintiffs have properly alleged a violation of the equal protection clause of the fourteenth amendment.

Police action is subject to the equal protection clause and section 1983 whether in the form of commission of violative acts or omission to perform required acts pursuant to the police officer's duty to protect. ... City officials and police officers are under an affirmative duty to preserve law and order, and to protect the personal safety of persons in the community.... This duty applies equally to women whose personal safety is threatened by individuals with whom they have or have had a domestic relationship as well as to all other persons whose personal safety is threatened, including women not involved in domestic relationships. If officials have notice of the possibility of attacks on women in domestic relationships or other persons, they are under an affirmative duty to take reasonable measures to protect the personal safety of such persons in the community. Failure to perform this duty would constitute a denial of equal protection of the laws.

Although the plaintiffs point to no law which on its face discriminates against victims abused by someone with whom they have a domestic relationship, the plaintiffs have alleged that there is an administrative classification used to implement the law in a discriminatory fashion. It is well settled that the equal protection clause is applicable not only to discriminatory legislative action, but also to discriminatory governmental action in administration and enforcement of the law.... Here the plaintiffs were threatened with assault in violation of Connecticut law. Over the course of eight months the police failed to afford the plaintiffs protection against such assaults, and failed to take action to arrest the perpetrator of these assaults. The plaintiffs have alleged that this failure to act was pursuant to a pattern or practice of affording inadequate protection, or no protection at all, to women who have complained of having been abused by their husbands or others with whom they have had close relations.... Such a practice is tantamount to an administrative classification used to implement the law in a discriminatory fashion.

If the City wishes to discriminate against women who are the victims of domestic violence, it must articulate an important governmental interest for doing so.... In its memorandum and at oral argument the City has failed to put forward any justification for its disparate treatment of women....

A man is not allowed to physically abuse or endanger a woman merely because he is her husband. Concomitantly, a police officer may not knowingly refrain from interference in such violence, and may not "automatically decline to make an arrest simply because the assaulter and his victim are married to each other." Such inaction on the part of the officer is a denial of the equal protection of the laws.

In addition, any notion that defendants' practice can be justified as a means of promoting domestic harmony by refraining from interference in marital disputes, has no place in the case at hand. Rather than evidencing a desire to work out her problems with her husband privately, Tracey pleaded with the police to offer her at least some measure of protection. Further, she sought and received a restraining order to keep her husband at a distance. Finally, it is important to recall ... that "whatever may be said as to the positive values of avoiding intrafamily controversy, the choice in this context may not lawfully be mandated solely on the basis of sex." Accordingly, the defendant City of Torrington's motion to dismiss the plaintiff Tracey Thurman's complaint on the basis of failure to allege violation of a constitutional right is denied.

II. *Motion to Dismiss the Claims of Charles Thurman, Jr.*

Plaintiff Charles Thurman, Jr. also claims that the City of Torrington denied him the equal protection of the laws. He alleges that the defendants fail to protect children against the domestic violence of fathers and stepfathers. This claim fails on several grounds. Other than the June 10, 1983 assault, Charles Thurman, Jr. has alleged no attacks made against him. . . . Thus Charles Thurman Jr. did not suffer from a continuous failure of the police to provide him protection as did his mother, Tracey Thurman. The isolated failure of the defendants to prevent the June 10, 1983 assault on Charles Thurman, Jr. does not violate any constitutional rights. . . .

III. *Have the Plaintiffs Properly Alleged a Custom or Policy on the Part of the City of Torrington?*

The plaintiffs have alleged in paragraph 13 of their complaint as follows:

> During the period of time described herein, and for a long time prior thereto, the defendant City of Torrington acting through its Police Department, condoned a pattern or practice of affording inadequate protection, or no protection at all, to women who have complained of having been abused by their husbands or others with whom they have had close relations. Said pattern, custom or policy, well known to the individual defendants, was the basis on which they ignored said numerous complaints and reports of threats to the plaintiffs with impunity.

While a municipality is not liable for the constitutional torts of its employees on a *respondeat superior* theory, a municipality may be sued for damages under section 1983 when "the action that is alleged to be unconstitutional implements or executes a policy statement, ordinance, regulation, or decision officially adopted and promulgated by the body's officers" or is "visited pursuant to governmental 'custom' even though such a custom has not received formal approval through the body's official decisionmaking channels."

In the instant case . . . the plaintiff Tracey Thurman has specifically alleged in her statement of facts a series of acts and omissions on the part of the defendant police officers and police department that took place over the course of eight months. From this particularized pleading a pattern emerges that evidences deliberate indifference on the part of the police department to the complaints of the plaintiff Tracey Thurman and to its duty to protect her. Such an ongoing pattern of deliberate indifference raises an inference of "custom" or "policy" on the part of the municipality. . . . Furthermore, this pattern of inaction climaxed on June 10, 1983 in an incident so brutal that under the law of the Second Circuit that "single brutal incident may be sufficient to suggest a link between a violation of constitutional rights and a pattern of police misconduct." Accordingly, defendant City of Torrington's motion to dismiss the plaintiffs claims against it, on the ground that the plaintiffs failed to properly allege a custom or policy on the part of the municipality, is denied.

NOTES AND QUESTIONS

1. **Gender Discrimination vs. Discrimination Against Victims of Domestic Violence.** Tracey Thurman's claim resulted in a jury award of $2.3 million. Subsequent efforts to invoke equal protection as the basis for challenges to police inaction, however, have fared less well. To succeed, the plaintiff must demonstrate: (1) the existence of a policy or a practice that leads police to respond differently to domestic violence situations than they do to other similar incidents of violence, affording victims of domestic violence less protection; and (2) that the policy or practice purposefully, or intentionally, discriminates against women. As the court in *Thurman* suggested, there will often be a question whether the policy or practice in question discriminates between women and men, or rather between domestic violence and other victims. If the discrimination is not gender-based, it will be subject only to a deferential "rational basis" scrutiny. See, for example, *Cellini v. City of Sterling Heights*, 856 F.Supp. 1215 (E.D. Mich. 1994), in which the court applied a rational relationship test because even though the complaint alleged gender discrimination, the plaintiff's response to a summary judgment motion only articulated discrimination against domestic violence victims. Similarly, the Second Circuit in *Eagleston v. Guido*, 41 F.3d 865 (2d Cir. 1994) noted that there were differences between domestic disputes and nondomestic disputes that could reasonably result in disparate treatment, without discriminatory intent. In addition, the First Circuit ruled that the testimony of officers that they "shied away from" domestic violence cases established a discriminatory policy, but not gender discrimination. *Soto v. Flores*, 103 F.3d 1056 (1st Cir. 1997), *cert. den.* 522 U.S. 819 (1997).

2. **Difficulties in Proving Gender Discrimination.** Proving an intent to discriminate on the basis of gender has become increasingly difficult in the context of § 1983 actions, as it has in both equal protection challenges more generally and in Title VII cases. Courts generally require evidence beyond the facts of plaintiff's own case, contrary to the finding in *Thurman* that a sufficient history in a single case, or even a single brutal incident, could at least raise an inference of a discriminatory custom or policy. On the other hand, in *Balistreri v. Pacifica Police Department*, 901 F.2d 696 (9th Cir. 1988), where the police officer who responded to the plaintiff made disparaging remarks, the Ninth Circuit found those remarks enough to suggest an equal protection violation, an intent to treat domestic violence less seriously than other assaults, and an animus against abused women.

It would seem that statistical proof, aggregating information about police handling of different classes of case, could support the argument that the plaintiff's treatment was not aberrant, but was indeed part of a pattern of discriminatory conduct. However, the statistics are unlikely to do more than prove that domestic disputes receive different treatment than non-domestic disputes, which is not enough, as noted above, to demonstrate denial of equal protection. Furthermore, courts have in a number of cases found fault with the statistical evidence offered by the plaintiff. In *McKee v. City of Rockwall*, 877 F.2d 409 (5th Cir. 1989), for example, the Fifth

Circuit found that the statistics proffered by the plaintiff were mathematically inaccurate, and that even if they had been accurate they would not have accounted for a wide variety of factors that might influence the likelihood of arrest. In a more recent district court case, *Soto v. Carrasquillo*, 878 F.Supp. 324 (D.P.R. 1995) the court ruled that the statistics offered were insufficient, because the expert did not explain how they had been compiled, and because the plaintiff did not compare arrest rates under the domestic violence law with arrest rates for other cases of abuse or violence.

The difficulties of proof are illustrated in this excerpt from the opinion in *Ricketts v. City of Columbia*, 36 F.3d 775 (8th Cir. 1994):

> When a widespread custom of a municipality impacts disproportionately on one gender, an equal protection violation arises "only if that impact can be traced to a discriminatory purpose." The disproportionate impact is only relevant to the extent that it "reflects a discriminatory purpose." A discriminatory purpose is more than a mere "awareness of the consequences." The law or custom must be found to have been implemented "at least in part 'because of,' not merely 'in spite of,' its adverse effects upon an identifiable group." Id.

> When a municipal custom employs a facially neutral classification and its disproportionate impact on one gender is not susceptible to a neutral explanation, "impact itself would signal that the real classification made by the law was in fact not neutral." *Feeney*, 442 U.S. at 275. However, in only a few cases, where a facially neutral policy impacted exclusively against one suspect class and that impact was unexplainable on neutral grounds, has the impact alone signalled a discriminatory purpose. When there is a rational, neutral explanation for the adverse impact and the law or custom disadvantages both men and women, then an inference of discriminatory purpose is not permitted.

> When the adverse consequences of a law [or custom] upon an identifiable group are as inevitable as the gender-based consequences . . . a strong inference that the adverse effects were desired can reasonably be drawn. But in this inquiry—made as it is under the Constitution—an inference is a working tool, not a synonym for proof. When, as here, the impact is essentially an unavoidable consequence of a [legitimate neutral policy or custom] the inference simply fails to ripen into proof.

> In sum, when determining whether there is a showing of discriminatory intent, disproportionate impact is but one factor to consider along with the inferences that rationally may be drawn from the totality of the other relevant facts. . . .

> The plaintiffs offered the expert testimony of Dr. Eve Buzawa who had gathered statistics indicating that the Columbia police department makes fewer arrests in domestic abuse cases than in nondomestic cases. Dr. Buzawa's opinion was based upon assault reports from portions of the previous year. Dr. Buzawa testified that the custom of disparate treatment for victims of domestic abuse adversely impacts women to a greater extent than men because over 90% of the victims of domestic abuse are women. The disproportionate impact is not exclu-

sively suffered by women, however, because the classification itself is facially neutral and includes male victims of domestic abuse. There is no evidence that male victims of domestic abuse are treated differently than female victims of domestic abuse.

We must discern whether there is a rational explanation for the disparate impact on women. Because of the inherent differences between domestic disputes and nondomestic disputes, legitimately different factors may affect a police officer's decision to arrest or not to arrest in any given situation. Dr. Buzawa's statistics took into account some of the variables that affect a decision to arrest in domestic disputes, but we believe that not all of the differences that enter into the discretionary decision of whether to arrest can be properly assessed and quantified through statistics. . . . Police "discretion is essential to the criminal justice process." "Where the discretion that is fundamental to our criminal process is involved, we decline to assume that what is unexplained is invidious."

Because the statistical disparity alone does not signal an intent to discriminate against women, we look to whether the plaintiffs submitted any other evidence of a discriminatory intent. The plaintiffs introduced hearsay statements from members of the Ricketts family, but this evidence is insufficient. Kimberly's sister-in-law testified to statements allegedly made by a police officer to the effect that one man accused of domestic abuse should have been arrested before but was not. Kimberly's father testified that he heard that one officer had been instructed not to arrest Sonny because Kimberly had gone back to him before and probably would again. . . . These statements are unreliable hearsay. More importantly, while they might offer support for a discriminatory intent toward domestic disputes, they do not evidence an intent to discriminate against women.

The plaintiffs also offered evidence of a historic tolerance of domestic abuse in society and of one fairly recent newspaper statement. A Columbia officer was quoted as blaming a woman victim of domestic abuse for bringing on the assault herself. The officer explained that the context of the statement related only to one particular case where he had seen that happen.

. . . These were the only factors directly bearing on gender discrimination, and they do not combine to create a submissible inference of a discriminatory animus toward women by the Columbia police department. Although we are sympathetic to the plaintiffs and we acknowledge that they have suffered greatly from the criminal acts of Sonny Stephens, we conclude that the plaintiffs have failed to present evidence of an equal protection violation on the basis of gender.

3. **Evidence of Police Inaction.** Based on your reading of these materials, what do you think might qualify as proper evidence of a discriminatory intent underlying police inaction in domestic violence cases? How likely do you think it is that an individual plaintiff could offer that proof?

Substantive Due Process

Before considering police liability for failure to protect victims of domestic violence, first consider the general theory that the state does have a duty to protect those people with whom it has developed a "special relationship." Below is an excerpt from *DeShaney v. Winnebago County Dept. of Social Services,* 489 U.S. 189 (1989), in which the Supreme Court considered whether there was a substantive due process right when the state undertakes to help a victim of violence. Although the case involves a victim of child abuse, not domestic violence, the case is an important development in the jurisprudence of third-party liability and has direct implications for victims of domestic violence.

DeShaney v. Winnebago County Dept. of Social Services

United States Supreme Court, 1989.
489 U.S. 189.

■ CHIEF JUSTICE REHNQUIST delivered the opinion of the Court.

The facts of this case are undeniably tragic. Petitioner Joshua DeShaney was born in 1979. In 1980, a Wyoming court granted his parents a divorce and awarded custody of Joshua to his father, Randy DeShaney. The father shortly thereafter moved to Neenah, a city located in Winnebago County, Wisconsin, taking the infant Joshua with him. There he entered into a second marriage, which also ended in divorce.

The Winnebago County authorities first learned that Joshua DeShaney might be a victim of child abuse in January 1982, when his father's second wife complained to the police, at the time of their divorce, that he had previously "hit the boy causing marks and [was] a prime case for child abuse." The Winnebago County Department of Social Services (DSS) interviewed the father, but he denied the accusations, and DSS did not pursue them further. In January 1983, Joshua was admitted to a local hospital with multiple bruises and abrasions. The examining physician suspected child abuse and notified DSS, which immediately obtained an order from a Wisconsin juvenile court placing Joshua in the temporary custody of the hospital. Three days later, the county convened an ad hoc "Child Protection Team"—consisting of a pediatrician, a psychologist, a police detective, the county's lawyer, several DSS caseworkers, and various hospital personnel—to consider Joshua's situation. At this meeting, the Team decided that there was insufficient evidence of child abuse to retain Joshua in the custody of the court. The Team did, however, decide to recommend several measures to protect Joshua, including enrolling him in a preschool program, providing his father with certain counselling services, and encouraging his father's girlfriend to move out of the home. Randy DeShaney entered into a voluntary agreement with DSS in which he promised to cooperate with them in accomplishing these goals.

Based on the recommendation of the Child Protection Team, the juvenile court dismissed the child protection case and returned Joshua to the custody of his father. A month later, emergency room personnel called the DSS caseworker handling Joshua's case to report that he had once again been treated for suspicious injuries. The caseworker concluded that there was no basis for action. For the next six months, the caseworker made monthly visits to the DeShaney home, during which she observed a number of suspicious injuries on Joshua's head; she also noticed that he had not been enrolled in school, and that the girlfriend had not moved out. The caseworker dutifully recorded these incidents in her files, along with her continuing suspicions that someone in the DeShaney household was physically abusing Joshua, but she did nothing more. In November 1983, the emergency room notified DSS that Joshua had been treated once again for injuries that they believed to be caused by child abuse. On the caseworker's next two visits to the DeShaney home, she was told that Joshua was too ill to see her. Still DSS took no action.

In March 1984, Randy DeShaney beat 4–year–old Joshua so severely that he fell into a life-threatening coma. Emergency brain surgery revealed a series of hemorrhages caused by traumatic injuries to the head inflicted over a long period of time. Joshua did not die, but he suffered brain damage so severe that he is expected to spend the rest of his life confined to an institution for the profoundly retarded. Randy DeShaney was subsequently tried and convicted of child abuse.

Joshua and his mother brought this action under 42 U.S.C. § 1983 in the United States District Court for the Eastern District of Wisconsin against respondents Winnebago County, DSS, and various individual employees of DSS. The complaint alleged that respondents had deprived Joshua of his liberty without due process of law, in violation of his rights under the Fourteenth Amendment, by failing to intervene to protect him against a risk of violence at his father's hands of which they knew or should have known. . . .

Petitioners contend . . . that even if the Due Process Clause imposes no affirmative obligation on the State to provide the general public with adequate protective services, such a duty may arise out of certain "special relationships" created or assumed by the State with respect to particular individuals. . . .

Petitioners argue that such a "special relationship" existed here because the State knew that Joshua faced a special danger of abuse at his father's hands, and specifically proclaimed, by word and by deed, its intention to protect him against that danger. Having actually undertaken to protect Joshua from this danger—which petitioners concede the State played no part in creating—the State acquired an affirmative "duty," enforceable through the Due Process Clause, to do so in a reasonably competent fashion. Its failure to discharge that duty, so the argument goes, was an abuse of governmental power that so "shocks the conscience," as to constitute a substantive due process violation. . . .

[W]hen the State takes a person into its custody and holds him there against his will, the Constitution imposes upon it a corresponding duty to assume some responsibility for his safety and general well-being. The rationale for this principle is simple enough: when the State by the affirmative exercise of its power so restrains an individual's liberty that it renders him unable to care for himself, and at the same time fails to provide for his basic human needs—*e.g.,* food, clothing, shelter, medical care, and reasonable safety—it transgresses the substantive limits on state action set by the Eighth Amendment and the Due Process Clause. The affirmative duty to protect arises not from the State's knowledge of the individual's predicament or from its expressions of intent to help him, but from the limitation which it has imposed on his freedom to act on his own behalf. In the substantive due process analysis, it is the State's affirmative act of restraining the individual's freedom to act on his own behalf— through incarceration, institutionalization, or other similar restraint of personal liberty—which is the "deprivation of liberty" triggering the protections of the Due Process Clause, not its failure to act to protect his liberty interests against harms inflicted by other means.

. . . Petitioners concede that the harms Joshua suffered occurred not while he was in the State's custody, but while he was in the custody of his natural father, who was in no sense a state actor. While the State may have been aware of the dangers that Joshua faced in the free world, it played no part in their creation, nor did it do anything to render him any more vulnerable to them. That the State once took temporary custody of Joshua does not alter the analysis, for when it returned him to his father's custody, it placed him in no worse position than that in which he would have been had it not acted at all; the State does not become the permanent guarantor of an individual's safety by having once offered him shelter. Under these circumstances, the State had no constitutional duty to protect Joshua.

Judges and lawyers, like other humans, are moved by natural sympathy in a case like this to find a way for Joshua and his mother to receive adequate compensation for the grievous harm inflicted upon them. But before yielding to that impulse, it is well to remember once again that the harm was inflicted not by the State of Wisconsin, but by Joshua's father. The most that can be said of the state functionaries in this case is that they stood by and did nothing when suspicious circumstances dictated a more active role for them. In defense of them it must also be said that had they moved too soon to take custody of the son away from the father, they would likely have been met with charges of improperly intruding into the parent-child relationship, charges based on the same Due Process Clause that forms the basis for the present charge of failure to provide adequate protection.

■ JUSTICE BRENNAN, with whom JUSTICE MARSHALL and JUSTICE BLACKMUN join, dissenting.

Each time someone voiced a suspicion that Joshua was being abused, that information was relayed to the Department for investigation and possible action. When Randy DeShaney's second wife told the police that he had " 'hit the boy causing marks and [was] a prime case for child abuse,' " the police referred her complaint to DSS. When, on three separate occasions, emergency room personnel noticed suspicious injuries on Joshua's body, they went to DSS with this information. When neighbors informed the police that they had seen or heard Joshua's father or his father's lover beating or otherwise abusing Joshua, the police brought these reports to the attention of DSS. And when respondent Kemmeter, through these reports and through her own observations in the course of nearly 20 visits to the DeShaney home compiled growing evidence that Joshua was being abused, that information stayed within the Department—chronicled by the social worker in detail that seems almost eerie in light of her failure to act upon it. (As to the extent of the social worker's involvement in, and knowledge of, Joshua's predicament, her reaction to the news of Joshua's last and most devastating injuries is illuminating: " 'I just knew the phone would ring some day and Joshua would be dead.' " . . .)

Even more telling than these examples is the Department's control over the decision whether to take steps to protect a particular child from suspected abuse. While many different people contributed information and advice to this decision, it was up to the people at DSS to make the ultimate decision (subject to the approval of the local government's Corporation Counsel) whether to disturb the family's current arrangements. When Joshua first appeared at a local hospital with injuries signaling physical abuse, for example, it was DSS that made the decision to take him into temporary custody for the purpose of studying his situation—and it was DSS, acting in conjunction with the corporation counsel, that returned him to his father. Unfortunately for Joshua DeShaney, the buck effectively stopped with the Department.

In these circumstances, a private citizen, or even a person working in a government agency other than DSS, would doubtless feel that her job was done as soon as she had reported her suspicions of child abuse to DSS. Through its child-welfare program, in other words, the State of Wisconsin has relieved ordinary citizens and governmental bodies other than the Department of any sense of obligation to do anything more than report their suspicions of child abuse to DSS. If DSS ignores or dismisses these suspicions, no one will step in to fill the gap. Wisconsin's child-protection program thus effectively confined Joshua DeShaney within the walls of Randy DeShaney's violent home until such time as DSS took action to remove him. Conceivably, then, children like Joshua are made worse off by the existence of this program when the persons and entities charged with carrying it out fail to do their jobs.

It simply belies reality, therefore, to contend that the State "stood by and did nothing" with respect to Joshua. Through its child-protection program, the State actively intervened in Joshua's life and, by virtue of this intervention, acquired ever more certain knowledge that Joshua was in grave danger. . .

My disagreement with the Court arises from its failure to see that inaction can be every bit as abusive of power as action, that oppression can result when a State undertakes a vital duty and then ignores it. Today's opinion construes the Due Process Clause to permit a State to displace private sources of protection and then, at the critical moment, to shrug its shoulders and turn away from the harm that it has promised to try to prevent. Because I cannot agree that our Constitution is indifferent to such indifference, I respectfully dissent.

■ JUSTICE BLACKMUN, dissenting.

Like the antebellum judges who denied relief to fugitive slaves, the Court today claims that its decision, however harsh, is compelled by existing legal doctrine. On the contrary, the question presented by this case is an open one, and our Fourteenth Amendment precedents may be read more broadly or narrowly depending upon how one chooses to read them. Faced with the choice, I would adopt a "sympathetic" reading, one which comports with dictates of fundamental justice and recognizes that compassion need not be exiled from the province of judging. . . .

Poor Joshua! Victim of repeated attacks by an irresponsible, bullying, cowardly, and intemperate father, and abandoned by respondents who placed him in a dangerous predicament and who knew or learned what was going on, and yet did essentially nothing except, as the Court revealingly observes, "dutifully recorded these incidents in [their] files." It is a sad commentary upon American life, and constitutional principles—so full of late of patriotic fervor and proud proclamations about "liberty and justice for all"—that this child, Joshua DeShaney, now is assigned to live out the remainder of his life profoundly retarded. Joshua and his mother, as petitioners here, deserve—but now are denied by this Court—the opportunity to have the facts of their case considered in the light of the constitutional protection that 42 U.S.C. § 1983 is meant to provide.

NOTES AND QUESTIONS

1. **Protection Orders and Victim Safety.** Caitlin Borgmann has argued that the situation of a battered woman with a restraining order can be distinguished from the situation of Joshua DeShaney. She suggests first that an order of protection does involve the state in a custodial relationship with its holder, because that individual must remain within the sphere of protection created by the order in order to secure her safety. Caitlin E. Borgman, *Battered Women's Substantive Due Process Claims: Can Orders of Protection Deflect DeShaney?*, 65 N.Y. U.L. REV. 1280 (1990). Unfortunately, this argument has been undermined by the Violence Against Women Act, which essentially makes orders of protection national in scope by requiring that each state give full faith and credit to a sister state's orders. 18 U.S.C.A. § 2265. In one case, a court found no custodial relationship where a domestic violence victim was killed by her estranged husband outside a courtroom, even though the court mandated her attendance, and had offered her specific assurances of safety. *Duong v. County of Arapahoe*, 837 P.2d 226 (Colo. Ct. App. 1992). In *Losinski v. County of Trempealeau*, 946 F.2d 544 (7th Cir. 1991), the Seventh Circuit found that a woman was not in protective custody for purposes of § 1983 when a deputy accompanied her to her home, since she had not been coerced or persuaded to accept protection.

Second, Borgmann argues that when a state issues a protective order and fails to enforce it, it creates an affirmative danger:

> In cases in which the state has granted an order of protection to a battered woman, the state affirmatively "play[s] a part" in the creation of a dangerous situation. Thus, a state's conduct in granting an order

of protection to a battered woman gives rise to an affirmative duty to protect her. The requirement of causation, namely that the state played a role in causing the woman's danger, may be satisfied in two ways when an order of protection goes unenforced. First, the state gives the woman reason to forgo self-defense and other self-help remedies in reliance on the order. Second, the issuance of an order of protection results in a high likelihood of retaliation by the batterer.

How would you assess the strength of these arguments? Does she make her case that these factors differentiate the battered woman from the abused child in whose case a Department of Social Services makes a preliminary intervention, but then fails to prevent further abuse?

Since *DeShaney,* substantive due process claims brought by battered women have focused on showing that the state increased the danger they faced from their batterers, rather than just failing to protect them from violence. Suppose, for example, that the state promised to put or keep an abuser in custody, or to notify his victim before his release; that the promise was relied upon by the victim in her own safety planning, and then broken. In this situation the argument that the state's actions increased the victim's vulnerability seems a strong one. Unfortunately, this very scenario was found insufficient to ground a due process claim in *Pinder v. Johnson*, 54 F.3d 1169 (4th Cir. 1995). In *Pinder* an officer assured a woman that her abuser, who had been arrested, would not be released until the following day. The officer provided this information in response to her specific question whether it would be safe for her to return to work, leaving her three children in the house. After she had gone back to work the officer was persuaded by the abuser to release him on his own recognizance. The abuser promptly returned to the plaintiff's house and set it on fire, killing her three children.

Another scenario that has led to litigation is where the abuser is himself a law enforcement officer, and his peers or inferiors, out of solidarity or fear of the consequences of intervention, fail to provide appropriate protection to his victim. Substantive due process claims along these lines survived motions to dismiss in *Wright v. Village of Phoenix*, 2000 WL 246266 (N.D. Ill. 2000), and *Freeman v. Ferguson*, 911 F.2d 52 (8th Cir. 1990).

It could also be argued that where police reinforce the batterer's behavior by failing to take his victim's complaints seriously, or to hold him accountable, they increase his sense of entitlement, and correspondingly increase his victim's danger. This argument was successful in defeating a summary judgment motion in *Smith v. City of Elyria*, 857 F.Supp. 1203 (N.D. Ohio 1994). However, in *Ricketts v. City of Columbia*, 36 F.3d 775 (8th Cir. 1994), the Eighth Circuit found the argument that the police had repeatedly failed to arrest the defendant, and had therefore "emboldened" him to continue his campaign of violence, insufficient to show a proper causal connection between the conduct of the police and the ultimate injury to the plaintiff.

2. **Language and Violence.** In response to the *DeShaney* decision, Martha Minow wrote an article examining the current use of words by

judges, the media, and others in describing family violence. In particular, she is critical of the language in *DeShaney* that describes the violence as private, as well as the abstract language the court uses to obscure the facts of the case. See Martha Minow, *Words and the Door to the Land of Change: Law, Language, & Family Violence,* 43 VAND.L.REV. 1665 (1990).

Procedural Due Process

While some plaintiffs have been successful in distinguishing *DeShaney,* the case effectively forecloses most *substantive* due process claims when the police fail to enforce a protective order. However, *DeShaney* never addressed any *procedural* due process claims. In *Castle Rock v. Gonzales,* the Supreme Court considered whether a victim of domestic violence who had restraining order was entitled to some procedural due process if the order was not going to be enforced. This case is one of the most important Supreme Court cases concerning the rights of domestic violence victims.

Castle Rock v. Gonzales

United States Supreme Court, 2005.
545 U.S. 748.

■ SCALIA, J., delivered the opinion of the Court, in which REHNQUIST, C.J., and O'CONNOR, KENNEDY, SOUTER, THOMAS, and BREYER, JJ., joined. SOUTER, J., filed a concurring opinion, in which BREYER, J., joined. STEVENS, J., filed a dissenting opinion, in which GINSBURG, J., joined.

We decide in this case whether an individual who has obtained a state-law restraining order has a constitutionally protected property interest in having the police enforce the restraining order when they have probable cause to believe it has been violated.

I.

. . . The restraining order had been issued by a state trial court several weeks earlier in conjunction with respondent's divorce proceedings. The original form order, issued on May 21, 1999, and served on respondent's husband on June 4, 1999, commanded him not to "molest or disturb the peace of [respondent] or of any child," and to remain at least 100 yards from the family home at all times. The bottom of the pre-printed form noted that the reverse side contained "IMPORTANT NOTICES FOR RESTRAINED PARTIES AND LAW ENFORCEMENT OFFICIALS." (emphasis deleted). The preprinted text on the back of the form included the following:

> "**WARNING**":
>
> "**A KNOWING VIOLATION OF A RESTRAINING ORDER IS A CRIME** . . . A VIOLATION WILL ALSO CONSTITUTE CONTEMPT OF COURT. **YOU MAY BE ARRESTED** WITHOUT NOTICE IF A LAW ENFORCEMENT OFFICER HAS PROBABLE CAUSE TO BELIEVE THAT YOU HAVE KNOWINGLY VIOLATED THIS ORDER."

The preprinted text on the back of the form also included a "**NOTICE TO LAW ENFORCEMENT OFFICIALS,**" which read in part:

"YOU SHALL USE EVERY REASONABLE MEANS TO ENFORCE THIS RESTRAINING ORDER. YOU SHALL ARREST, OR, IF AN ARREST WOULD BE IMPRACTICAL UNDER THE CIRCUM- STANCES, SEEK A WARRANT FOR THE ARREST OF THE RE- STRAINED PERSON WHEN YOU HAVE INFORMATION AMOUNTING TO PROBABLE CAUSE THAT THE RESTRAINED PERSON HAS VIOLATED OR ATTEMPTED TO VIOLATE ANY PROVISION OF THIS ORDER AND THE RESTRAINED PERSON HAS BEEN PROPERLY SERVED WITH A COPY OF THIS ORDER OR HAS RECEIVED ACTUAL NOTICE OF THE EXISTENCE OF THIS ORDER."

On June 4, 1999, the state trial court modified the terms of the restraining order and made it permanent. The modified order gave respon- dent's husband the right to spend time with his three daughters (ages 10, 9, and 7) on alternate weekends, for two weeks during the summer, and, " 'upon reasonable notice,' " for a mid-week dinner visit " 'arranged by the parties' "; the modified order also allowed him to visit the home to collect the children for such "parenting time."

According to the complaint, at about 5 or 5:30 p.m. on Tuesday, June 22, 1999, respondent's husband took the three daughters while they were playing outside the family home. No advance arrangements had been made for him to see the daughters that evening. When respondent noticed the children were missing, she suspected her husband had taken them. At about 7:30 p.m., she called the Castle Rock Police Department, which dispatched two officers. The complaint continues: "When [the officers] arrived . . ., she showed them a copy of the TRO and requested that it be enforced and the three children be returned to her immediately. [The officers] stated that there was nothing they could do about the TRO and suggested that [respondent] call the Police Department again if the three children did not return home by 10:00 p.m."

At approximately 8:30 p.m., respondent talked to her husband on his cellular telephone. He told her "he had the three children [at an] amuse- ment park in Denver." She called the police again and asked them to "have someone check for" her husband or his vehicle at the amusement park and "put out an [all points bulletin]" for her husband, but the officer with whom she spoke "refused to do so," again telling her to "wait until 10:00 p.m. and see if" her husband returned the girls.

At approximately 10:10 p.m., respondent called the police and said her children were still missing, but she was now told to wait until midnight. She called at midnight and told the dispatcher her children were still missing. She went to her husband's apartment and, finding nobody there, called the police at 12:10 a.m.; she was told to wait for an officer to arrive. When none came, she went to the police station at 12:50 a.m. and submitted an incident report. The officer who took the report "made no reasonable effort to enforce the TRO or locate the three children. Instead, he went to dinner."

At approximately 3:20 a.m., respondent's husband arrived at the police station and opened fire with a semiautomatic handgun he had purchased earlier that evening. Police shot back, killing him. Inside the cab of his pickup truck, they found the bodies of all three daughters, whom he had already murdered.

II

The Fourteenth Amendment to the United States Constitution provides that a State shall not "deprive any person of life, liberty, or property, without due process of law." In 42 U.S.C. § 1983, Congress has created a federal cause of action for "the deprivation of any rights, privileges, or immunities secured by the Constitution and laws." Respondent claims the benefit of this provision on the ground that she had a property interest in police enforcement of the restraining order against her husband; and that the town deprived her of this property without due process by having a policy that tolerated nonenforcement of restraining orders.

As the Court of Appeals recognized, we left a similar question unanswered in *DeShaney v. Winnebago County Dept. of Social Servs.*, 489 U.S. 189 (1989), another case with "undeniably tragic" facts: Local child-protection officials had failed to protect a young boy from beatings by his father that left him severely brain damaged. We held that the so-called "substantive" component of the Due Process Clause does not "requir[e] the State to protect the life, liberty, and property of its citizens against invasion by private actors." We noted, however, that the petitioner had not properly preserved the argument that—and we thus "decline[d] to consider" whether—state "child protection statutes gave [him] an 'entitlement' to receive protective services in accordance with the terms of the statute, an entitlement which would enjoy due process protection."

The procedural component of the Due Process Clause does not protect everything that might be described as a "benefit": "To have a property interest in a benefit, a person clearly must have more than an abstract need or desire" and "more than a unilateral expectation of it. He must, instead, have a legitimate claim of entitlement to it." Such entitlements are " 'of course, . . . not created by the Constitution. Rather, they are created and their dimensions are defined by existing rules or understandings that stem from an independent source such as state law.' " . . .

The critical language in the restraining order came not from any part of the order itself (which was signed by the state-court trial judge and directed to the restrained party, respondent's husband), but from the preprinted notice to law-enforcement personnel that appeared on the back of the order. That notice effectively restated the statutory provision describing "peace officers' duties" related to the crime of violation of a restraining order. At the time of the conduct at issue in this case, that provision read as follows:

"(a) Whenever a restraining order is issued, the protected person shall be provided with a copy of such order. *A peace officer shall use every reasonable means to enforce a restraining order.*

"(b) *A peace officer shall arrest, or, if an arrest would be impractical under the circumstances, seek a warrant for the arrest of a restrained person* when the peace officer has information amounting to probable cause that:

"(I) The restrained person has violated or attempted to violate any provision of a restraining order; and

"(II) The restrained person has been properly served with a copy of the restraining order or the restrained person has received actual notice of the existence and substance of such order.

"(c) In making the probable cause determination described in paragraph (b) of this subsection (3), a peace officer shall assume that the information received from the registry is accurate. *A peace officer shall enforce a valid restraining order whether or not there is a record of the restraining order in the registry.*"

The Court of Appeals concluded that this statutory provision—especially taken in conjunction with a statement from its legislative history, and with another statute restricting criminal and civil liability for officers making arrests—established the Colorado Legislature's clear intent "to alter the fact that the police were not enforcing domestic abuse retraining orders," and thus its intent "that the recipient of a domestic abuse restraining order have an entitlement to its enforcement." Any other result, it said, "would render domestic abuse restraining orders utterly valueless."

This last statement is sheer hyperbole. Whether or not respondent had a right to enforce the restraining order, it rendered certain otherwise lawful conduct by her husband both criminal and in contempt of court. The creation of grounds on which he could be arrested, criminally prosecuted, and held in contempt was hardly "valueless"—even if the prospect of those sanctions ultimately failed to prevent him from committing three murders and a suicide.

We do not believe that these provisions of Colorado law truly made enforcement of restraining orders *mandatory*. A well established tradition of police discretion has long coexisted with apparently mandatory arrest statutes.

"In each and every state there are long-standing statutes that, by their terms, seem to preclude nonenforcement by the police.... However, for a number of reasons, including their legislative history, insufficient resources, and sheer physical impossibility, it has been recognized that such statutes cannot be interpreted literally.... [T]hey clearly do not mean that a police officer may not lawfully decline to make an arrest. As to third parties in these states, the full-enforcement statutes simply have no effect, and their significance is further diminished." ...

Against that backdrop, a true mandate of police action would require some stronger indication from the Colorado Legislature than "shall use every reasonable means to enforce a restraining order" (or even "shall arrest ... or ... seek a warrant"). That language is not perceptibly more mandatory than the Colorado statute which has long told municipal chiefs of police that they "shall pursue and arrest any person fleeing from justice in any part of the state" and that they "shall apprehend any person in the act of committing any offense . . . and, forthwith and without any warrant, bring such person before a . . . competent authority for examination and trial." It is hard to imagine that a Colorado peace officer would not have some discretion to determine that—despite probable cause to believe a restraining order has been violated—the circumstances of the violation or the competing duties of that officer or his agency counsel decisively against enforcement in a particular instance. The practical necessity for discretion is particularly apparent in a case such as this one, where the suspected violator is not actually present and his whereabouts are unknown.

The dissent correctly points out that, in the specific context of domestic violence, mandatory-arrest statutes have been found in some States to be more mandatory than traditional mandatory-arrest statutes. The Colorado statute mandating arrest for a domestic-violence offense is different from but related to the one at issue here, and it includes similar though not identical phrasing. . . . Even in the domestic-violence context, however, it is unclear how the mandatory-arrest paradigm applies to cases in which the offender is not present to be arrested. As the dissent explains, much of the impetus for mandatory-arrest statutes and policies derived from the idea that it is better for police officers to arrest the aggressor in a domestic-violence incident than to attempt to mediate the dispute or merely to ask the offender to leave the scene. Those other options are only available, of course, when the offender is present at the scene. . . .

Respondent does not specify the precise means of enforcement that the Colorado restraining-order statute assertedly mandated—whether her interest lay in having police arrest her husband, having them seek a warrant for his arrest, or having them "use every reasonable means, up to and including arrest, to enforce the order's terms." Such indeterminacy is not the hallmark of a duty that is mandatory. Nor can someone be safely deemed "entitled" to something when the identity of the alleged entitlement is vague. The dissent, after suggesting various formulations of the entitlement in question, ultimately contends that the obligations under the statute were quite precise: either make an arrest or (if that is impractical) seek an arrest warrant. The problem with this is that the seeking of an arrest warrant would be an entitlement to nothing but procedure—which we have held inadequate even to support standing. After the warrant is sought, it remains within the discretion of a judge whether to grant it, and after it is granted, it remains within the discretion of the police whether and when to execute it. Respondent would have been assured nothing but the seeking of a warrant. This is not the sort of "entitlement" out of which a property interest is created.

Even if the statute could be said to have made enforcement of restraining orders "mandatory" because of the domestic-violence context of the underlying statute, that would not necessarily mean that state law gave *respondent* an entitlement to *enforcement* of the mandate. Making the actions of government employees obligatory can serve various legitimate ends other than the conferral of a benefit on a specific class of people. The serving of public rather than private ends is the normal course of the criminal law because criminal acts, "besides the injury [they do] to individuals, . . . strike at the very being of society; which cannot possibly subsist, where actions of this sort are suffered to escape with impunity." This principle underlies, for example, a Colorado district attorney's discretion to prosecute a domestic assault, even though the victim withdraws her charge.

Respondent's alleged interest stems only from a State's *statutory* scheme—from a restraining order that was authorized by and tracked precisely the statute on which the Court of Appeals relied. She does not assert that she has any common-law or contractual entitlement to enforcement. If she was given a statutory entitlement, we would expect to see some indication of that in the statute itself. Although Colorado's statute spoke of "protected person[s]" such as respondent, it did so in connection with matters other than a right to enforcement. It said that a "protected person shall be provided with a copy of [a restraining] order" when it is issued, that a law enforcement agency "shall make all reasonable efforts to contact the protected party upon the arrest of the restrained person,"; and that the agency "shall give [to the protected person] a copy" of the report it submits to the court that issued the order. Perhaps most importantly, the statute spoke directly to the protected person's power to "initiate contempt proceedings against the restrained person if the order [was] issued in a civil action or request the prosecuting attorney to initiate contempt proceedings if the order [was] issued in a criminal action." The protected person's express power to "initiate" civil contempt proceedings contrasts tellingly with the mere ability to "request" initiation of criminal contempt proceedings—and even more dramatically with the complete silence about any power to "request" (much less demand) that an arrest be made.

The creation of a personal entitlement to something as vague and novel as enforcement of restraining orders cannot "simply g[o] without saying." We conclude that Colorado has not created such an entitlement.

III.

In light of today's decision and that in *DeShaney,* the benefit that a third party may receive from having someone else arrested for a crime generally does not trigger protections under the Due Process Clause, neither in its procedural nor in its "substantive" manifestations. This result reflects our continuing reluctance to treat the Fourteenth Amendment as " 'a font of tort law,' does not mean States are powerless to provide victims with personally enforceable remedies." Although the framers of the Fourteenth Amendment and the Civil Rights Act of 1871, (the original source of § 1983), did not create a system by which police departments are generally held financially accountable for crimes that better policing might have prevented, the people of Colorado are free to craft such a system under state law.

■ Justice Souter, with whom Justice Breyer joins, concurring.

I agree with the Court that Jessica Gonzales has shown no violation of an interest protected by the Fourteenth Amendment's Due Process Clause, and I join the Court's opinion. The Court emphasizes the traditional public focus of law enforcement as reason to doubt that these particular legal requirements to provide police services, however unconditional their form, presuppose enforceable individual rights to a certain level of police protection. The Court also notes that the terms of the Colorado statute involved here recognize and preserve the traditional discretion afforded law enforcement officers. Gonzales's claim of a property right thus runs up against police discretion in the face of an individual demand to enforce, and discretion to ignore an individual instruction not to enforce (because, say, of a domestic reconciliation); no one would argue that the beneficiary of a Colorado order like the one here would be authorized to control a court's contempt power or order the police to refrain from arresting. These considerations argue against inferring any guarantee of a level of protection or safety that could be understood as the object of a "legitimate claim of entitlement." Consequently, the classic predicate for federal due process protection of interests under state law is missing. . . .

Just as a State cannot diminish a property right, once conferred, by attaching less than generous procedure to its deprivation, neither does a State create a property right merely by ordaining beneficial procedure unconnected to some articulable substantive guarantee. This is not to say that state rules of executive procedure may not provide significant reasons to infer an articulable property right meant to be protected; but it is to say that we have not identified property with procedure as such. State rules of executive procedure, however important, may be nothing more than rules of executive procedure.

■ JUSTICE STEVENS, with whom JUSTICE GINSBURG joins, dissenting.

Police enforcement of a restraining order is a government service that is no less concrete and no less valuable than other government services, such as education. The relative novelty of recognizing this type of property interest is explained by the relative novelty of the domestic violence statutes creating a mandatory arrest duty; before this innovation, the unfettered discretion that characterized police enforcement defeated any citizen's "legitimate claim of entitlement" to this service. Novel or not, respondent's claim finds strong support in the principles that underlie our due process jurisprudence. In this case, Colorado law *guaranteed* the provision of a certain service, in certain defined circumstances, to a certain class of beneficiaries, and respondent reasonably relied on that guarantee. . . . Surely, if respondent had contracted with a private security firm to provide her and her daughters with protection from her husband, it would be apparent that she possessed a property interest in such a contract. Here, Colorado undertook a comparable obligation, and respondent—with restraining order in hand—justifiably relied on that undertaking. Respondent's claim of entitlement to this promised service is no less legitimate than the other claims our cases have upheld, and no less concrete than a hypothetical agreement with a private firm. The fact that it is based on a statutory enactment and a judicial order entered for her special protection, rather than on a formal contract, does not provide a principled basis for refusing to consider it "property" worthy of constitutional protection. . . .

Because respondent had a property interest in the enforcement of the restraining order, state officials could not deprive her of that interest without observing fair procedures. Her description of the police behavior in this case and the department's callous policy of failing to respond properly to reports of restraining order violations clearly alleges a due process violation. At the very least, due process requires that the relevant state decision-maker *listen* to the claimant and then *apply the relevant criteria* in reaching his decision. The failure to observe these minimal procedural safeguards creates an unacceptable risk of arbitrary and "erroneous deprivation[s]." According to respondent's complaint—which we must construe liberally at this early stage in the litigation,—the process she was afforded by the police constituted nothing more than a "sham or a pretense."

NOTES AND QUESTIONS

1. **Police Training.** Police Departments nationwide feared an onslaught of lawsuits had Jessica Gonzales prevailed. Now advocates must continue to work with the police to encourage them to arrest or immediately issue warrants. Is better police training the answer, or would the fear of lawsuits have made a difference? Kris Miccio has argued that procedural due process requires, among other things, that the police receive specialized training in domestic violence and that they undertake a moral duty of care. See G. Kristian Miccio, *Exiled from the Province of Care: Domestic Violence, Duty & Conceptions of State Accountability*, 37 RUTGERS L.J. 111 (2005).

2. **Just a Piece of Paper?** Advocates often report that the police do not enforce restraining orders. When *Castle Rock* was decided, many claimed that it was huge setback for victims of domestic violence, giving the police less incentive to take domestic violence seriously. But do advocates focus too much on what the police do wrong, and not enough on what they do right? After all, there are many police officers that do take restraining orders seriously and do respond appropriately to violations. Are advocates sending the wrong message when they claim restraining orders are "just a piece of paper?"

Some scholars have argued that not only is a restraining order "just a piece of paper," but also that the state has created a danger to the victim by issuing it, and that "state-created danger" ought to give rise to police liability for failure to protect. How does the state arguably endanger victims by issuing restraining orders? See Laura Oren, *Some Thoughts on the State–Created Danger Doctrine: DeShaney is Still Wrong and Castle Rock is More of the Same*, 16 TEMP. POL. & CIV. RTS. L. REV. 47 (2006).

3. **Federalism.** There are many ways in which to interpret *Castle Rock*. One way is to suggest that the Court retreats from its understanding of domestic violence by refusing to recognize the rights of victims to have their orders enforced. The other is to see this decision as part of the Rehnquist Court's long-standing commitment to federalism and states' rights. In *Castle Rock*, state discretion is paramount. Thus, just as in *United States v. Morrison,* in which the Court struck down the civil rights provisions of the Violence Against Women Act, it could be argued that

Castle Rock has little to do with domestic violence and much more to do with states' rights. Do you agree? For an analysis of this issue see Megan Grill, *Walking the Line: The Rehnquist Court's Reverence for Federalism and Official Discretion in DeShaney and Castle Rock,* 10 Lewis & Clark L. Rev. 487 (2006).

It is interesting to note that the Bush Administration filed a brief on behalf of the Town of Castle Rock, in which it argued that a ruling for Gonzales would undermine law enforcement by opening the door for increased and unnecessary litigation, thus drawing resources away from other urgent situations. *Brief for the United States as Amicus Curiae Supporting Petitioner, Town of Castle Rock v. Gonzales,* 545 U.S. 748 (2005). Does such an intervention suggest that this case was about state's rights, or were there other national interests involved?

4.   **The Inter–American Commission on Human Rights.** Following the decision in *Castle Rock*, the American Civil Liberties Union, the Columbia Law School Human Rights Clinic and other organizations filed a petition with the Inter–American Commission on Human Rights on behalf of Jessica Gonzales, asserting that the failure to enforce her restraining order, the failure to protect her and her children, and the failure to provide a legal remedy violates the obligations of the United States under international human rights treaties. See *Gonzales v. United States,* Brief Before the Inter–American Commission on Human Rights, available at http://www.aclu-co.org/docket/200410/Inter_American_Comm.n_Gonzales_brief_12_11_06.pdf. In October 2007, the Inter–American Commission ruled that the petition was "admissible," akin to finding jurisdiction, rejecting arguments by the U.S. Department of State that the Commission should not hear the case. http://www.cidh.org/annualrep/2007/eng/htm. See Marcia Coyle, Rights Panel to Hear U.S. Domestic Violence Case, Nat'l L.J., October 15, 2007. We examine other issues related to domestic violence and international human rights in Chapter Seventeen.

State Tort Claims

After *Castle Rock v. Gonzales*, victims must increasingly rely on state tort claims when the police fail to enforce a domestic violence law. If an action is available, it will lie in negligence, and depend on a showing that the defendant or defendants owed the plaintiff a duty of care, and breached that duty, causing the plaintiff injury. There are two preliminary obstacles to suit that a plaintiff will have to overcome. The first is sovereign immunity, which protects government entities from tort liability. Each state defines which state actors and what actions are immune from claims of negligence. Some states grant sovereign immunity only for those acts which are discretionary, and generally protect the police from liability so long as they act in good faith. However, if acts are ministerial or operational in nature, meaning the officer has no discretion but is mandated by law to act in a certain way, then liability can be imposed. The policy justification for this distinction is to prevent the judiciary from intervening in policy decisions that are better left to the executive or legislative branches of government. It also prevents the fear of law suits from interfering with appropriate law enforcement. See Fredrica L. Lehrman, DOMESTIC VIOLENCE PRACTICE & PROCEDURE, §§ 6:23–6:26 (1997) (Supp. 2005). The distinction between discretionary and ministerial acts was heavily relied upon by Justice Scalia in *Castle Rock v. Gonzales*.

The second major barrier to tort liability under state law is the traditional "public duty" or "no duty" common law doctrine, under which law enforcement officers and agencies have a general duty to the public to provide protection, but no specific duty to safeguard any individual, unless the case falls within a recognized exception to the rule. The rationale for the rule is the same as the rationale for sovereign immunity: the importance of preserving separation of powers, and not allowing the judicial branch to question allocative and policy decisions made by the legislative or executive branches. Nonetheless, in most jurisdictions the two bodies of law are distinct; the plaintiff must establish *both* that the conduct of the state and its agents is not immunized from liability, *and* that the case falls within an exception to the public duty rule.

Consider below how other states have addressed police liability for failure to act in domestic violence cases.

Massee v. Thompson

Montana Supreme Court, 2004.
90 P.3d 394.

■ JUSTICE PATRICIA O. COTTER, delivered the Opinion of the Court.

Vickie Sue Massee (Vickie) and Ray Doggett (Ray) were married in October 1990. Prior to Vickie's marriage to Doggett, Vickie had been married to Raymond Massee (Massee). She had three sons during her marriage to Massee, James, Michael and Marcus. For most of the times at issue, the three boys lived with Vickie and Ray.

Over the course of the Doggetts' tumultuous marriage, members of the Broadwater County Sheriff's Office (BCSO or Sheriff's Office), and most notably Thompson, became intimately involved in the lives of Ray and Vickie. BCSO's first involvement with the couple occurred approximately one year after Vickie and Ray got married, when the Sheriff's Office responded to a domestic violence disturbance at the Doggetts' home. Vickie and Ray had each struck and injured the other. They were sentenced to counseling which they completed.

From the record, it appears that the marriage had frequent ups and downs, with the downs generally occurring after Ray and/or Vickie had been drinking. Ray became unable to work shortly after he and Vickie married and he began suffering from bouts of depression. With his depression came binge drinking, accusations of infidelity, and threats of suicide or murder.

Just before midnight on October 29, 1994, the Broadwater County Undersheriff responded to a call from Vickie. She was at a Townsend bar and asked that an officer come get her, collect her sons, and then drive them all to the county line to be picked up by the children's grandparents.

Vickie indicated that she and Ray were arguing and that she wanted to be away from Ray. Undersheriff Ludwig responded. On the way to the county line, Vickie decided she would let the boys go with their grandparents, and she would return home. Undersheriff Ludwig, after confirming there had been no physical violence in the earlier argument, convinced Vickie that she and Ray should spend the night apart while each sobered up. Vickie ultimately conceded.

On Ludwig's return to Townsend, she was then dispatched to Ray's house. Ray had called the BCSO threatening suicide if Ludwig did not tell him where Vickie was. When Ludwig arrived at the Doggetts' home with a reserve deputy, Ray was sitting at a table with a loaded .44 magnum pistol. Ludwig assured him that Vickie was safe, and while the reserve deputy talked with Ray in an effort to calm him, the Undersheriff took Ray's pistol for safekeeping. The record is unclear as to when the weapon was returned to Ray.

On December 10, 1994, the BCSO received another domestic dispute call from the Doggetts' home, and two deputies were dispatched. According to the Sheriff's Office log, Vickie and Ray were intoxicated and engaged in a serious argument. When the two deputies arrived, they could hear the argument escalating. Upon entering the home, they discovered that one of Vickie's teenage sons was also present. The officers ushered him outside to safety and then returned inside, at which time Ray threatened them with bodily harm. Thompson was then called and advised of the situation. The Sheriff immediately telephoned Ray and began talking to him. At that time, one of the responding officers was called away to another incident. When the remaining officer got on the telephone to talk to Thompson, Ray left the room, ostensibly to go to the bathroom, but moments later emerged from the bedroom with the .44 magnum revolver (the same revolver that had been earlier confiscated). The deputy reported this to the Sheriff who told the deputy to leave the house immediately. The deputy obeyed. Shortly thereafter, the BCSO dispatcher called the Doggett home and Vickie told her that Ray was holding a gun to her head. Within minutes, the officer who had responded to another call returned with a third officer. The three deputies stayed outside and awaited the Sheriff's arrival a few minutes later.

Thompson and a deputy entered the home while the other officers remained outside. Ray was agitated, drunk and wielding his .44 magnum handgun. After talking to the Sheriff for a short period of time, Ray put the gun to his own head. The Sheriff and his deputy were able to wrestle the loaded pistol from him. After several minutes of calming discussion, the deputies were told they could leave and the Sheriff remained to counsel Ray. Two deputies left. The third deputy waited in the car parked in a location that allowed him to see inside the Doggetts' home where Ray and the Sheriff were talking.

At trial, there was substantial testimony presented that one of the responding officers, as recorded in his official report, had seen Ray holding the gun to Vickie's head. This deputy also indicated in his report that the Sheriff decided not to arrest Ray but did confiscate Ray's gun. The Sheriff testified that he did not know that Ray had held the gun to Vickie's head until some later date, and that during the time he was at the Doggett residence, Ray had not done anything that would warrant arrest. The Sheriff's report of this event, however, differs from the Sheriff's testimony. Thompson's official report dated December 11, 1994, states, "While on the way into town, I heard the officers at the scene talking to dispatch and telling her that Ray was pointing the gun at Vickie."

After these events, the marriage appeared to stabilize somewhat. However, on October 6, 1996, the BCSO's log reflects three calls between 4:00 a.m. and 4:30 a.m. from Ray Doggett during which he sounded depressed and requested that the Sheriff come visit him because he needed a friend. Then, again, in the early morning hours of December 18, 1996, Ray called for a deputy. When two deputies arrived, they found Ray alone and drunk. He was complaining, as he had before, that Vickie was being unfaithful. The officers then received an unrelated call, and Ray told them he would be all right and that they could leave.

About ten days later, Ray asked that the BCSO send a particular deputy to his home. When the deputy arrived, Ray was drunk and claiming that Vickie wanted him dead. Vickie told the officer that Ray was always threatening to kill himself and she was considering leaving the marriage because of the overwhelming stress. Vickie's son Marcus was also present, and informed the deputy that Ray had a revolver in the back of his pants. The deputy warned Ray that if Ray touched his gun, he would shoot him. The deputy stayed and talked with Ray until he was calm. Vickie and Marcus left the house during this time, upon suggestion of the deputy.

Within a few minutes of the deputy's departure, Ray called the BCSO to tell them he was going to the local bar. Meanwhile, Vickie and Marcus had arrived at the home of Roger Reiman, a friend of Vickie's sons. James and Michael were also present. She told them she wanted to spend the night in Helena, but was afraid to return to the house for the overnight items she would need. James and Roger went to get the items for her. When they arrived at the house and walked inside, Ray, who had returned from the bar and whose back was to the door, turned, pulled his gun and pointed it at them. He lowered it after about 5 seconds. James, who was quite frightened by the experience, retrieved his own .38 pistol while getting his mother's toiletry items, and hid it under his jacket in case he needed to protect himself while leaving the house. While James was out of the room, Ray pulled his gun on Roger and suggested that they go outside. Just then, however, the BCSO called and Ray answered the phone. While Ray was on the phone with the Sheriff's Office, James and Roger left.

James and Roger immediately went to the BCSO to report what had occurred, but did not sign a formal complaint. Vickie and her sons left Roger's house, and spent the night with friends in Helena. James gave his gun to Roger before leaving because Roger was afraid Ray would come looking for him when he realized Vickie was not coming home that night.

Later that night, Roger called the BCSO to report that Ray had called and threatened to kill him and to hunt down Vickie, James and Michael and kill them for taking Marcus away. Shortly thereafter, Roger went to the Sheriff's Office and signed a Voluntary Statement regarding these threats. He did not sign a Complaint because, he later testified, he was afraid that Ray might hurt him. The deputy who took Roger's statement called and informed the Sheriff. Thompson said he would look into it the following day, but according to his own testimony, he failed to do so. Vickie, her sons, and Roger were never questioned about this incident and no investigation appears to have occurred. The BCSO's log indicates that when Vickie returned from Helena the following day, she made arrangements for the boys to temporarily stay with their grandparents in White Sulphur Springs.

During the ensuing four months, Ray and Vickie did not seek the services of the BCSO. However, at about 2:00 a.m. on April 20, 1997, then eight-year old Marcus called the BCSO reporting that Ray and Vickie were having an argument and that he and his fourteen-year old brother, Michael, were in their bedroom with their .22 rifle on the bed for protection. According to the Sheriff's Office log, the dispatcher instructed the boys to put the gun away. The Sheriff and a deputy then went to the Doggetts' residence. According to the deputy's report, he immediately went to the bedroom with the boys and found the unloaded rifle put away in the closet. He reported that the boys said that the rifle was unloaded at all times during this event.

The boys told the officers that Ray's gun was in his bedroom. The deputy found Ray's gun on his bedside table, unloaded it and left the bullets on Ray's dresser. The deputy did not confiscate Ray's pistol but left it at the residence. Vickie, Michael and Marcus left the residence, followed shortly thereafter by the police officers. Vickie and the boys once again stayed with a friend in Helena.

At trial, Michael testified to a more detailed and slightly different version of the events of that evening. He stated that Ray and Vickie had returned home that night and were arguing. Michael saw Ray holding his .44 magnum pistol, waving it and pointing it at Vickie while arguing. He returned to his bedroom where Marcus was waiting, loaded his .22 rifle, and after listening to the escalating argument for about fifteen minutes, had Marcus call the BCSO. He stated at trial that during the course of the argument, Vickie, scared and crying, had come into their bedroom and shut the door. Ray opened the door and Michael saw that he was still carrying his .44 magnum pistol. However, according to Michael's testimony and the testimony of the officers involved, no one subsequently investigated the incident; therefore, they did not learn from Michael or Vickie that Ray had threatened Vickie with a loaded pistol that night.

On May 5, 1997, Ray stopped by the BCSO at 2:00 a.m., in an extremely depressed state. He later called the Sheriff's Office at 3:00 a.m. and again at 3:15 a.m. also quite depressed, triggering serious concerns that he was suicidal. The Sheriff's fears were realized when, less than three weeks later, on May 24, the BCSO responded to the Doggetts' home and discovered that Ray had shot and killed Vickie with his .44 magnum pistol, and then fatally turned the gun on himself.

Vickie's sons sued Sheriff Thompson for negligently failing to take appropriate action to prevent Ray from killing their mother.... The jury concluded that Sheriff Thompson was negligent as defined by the jury instructions, and that his negligence was the cause of Vickie's death. The jury awarded a total of $358,000 to Vickie's sons.

DISCUSSION

[A]t all times between 1994 and 1997, while discretionary, the statutorily-preferred response in domestic abuse situations was to arrest the alleged abuser; 2) in 1994, the Sheriff was required to give Vickie notice of her victim's rights only if he arrested Ray; 3) after 1995, the Sheriff was required to give Vickie notice of her victim's rights whenever he responded to a domestic dispute call generated by Vickie, Ray or the boys; and 4) in 1996 and 1997, the Sheriff was required to seize any weapon used or threatened to be used in a domestic assault, and could only return the weapon upon acquittal or by Court order....

When considering negligence claims against a public entity or person, such as Sheriff Thompson, it is necessary to consider the "public duty doctrine." The public duty doctrine provides that a governmental entity cannot be held liable for an individual plaintiff's injury resulting from a governmental officer's breach of a duty owed to the general public rather than to the individual plaintiff. An exception to the public duty doctrine's immunity provision arises when a "special relationship" between the victim and officer has been created....

The Massees maintain that the Sheriff had a special duty to Vickie by virtue of a special relationship ... They contend that the domestic abuse statutes were written specifically to protect domestic violence victims, a class of which Vickie was a member. Indeed, these statutes were enacted to prevent domestic abuse from escalating to a point of serious injury or death-Vickie's exact fate. Significantly, Thompson agreed that Vickie was a member of the protected class of domestic violence victims. Moreover, during the trial, the District Court expressly concluded, "that Vickie falls within that statutorily protected class of victims of domestic violence ... She is clearly a member of that class. And so [Sheriff Thompson] would have a duty to her under that." ...

The Sheriff testified that under the 1993 version of § 46–6–602, MCA, he was required to give Vickie notice only if he arrested Ray, and that because he did not arrest Ray, failure to give notice was not a violation. This testimony, however, was undermined by the Sheriff's further testimony that during the December 1994 incident, he had substantial grounds to arrest Ray and, inexplicably, chose not to do so. He admitted that the preferred response under the law would have been arrest, at which time his obligation to give Vickie her notice rights would have become mandatory. The Sheriff also agreed that the 1995 version of the statute made it mandatory that he give notice whenever responding to a domestic abuse call, or a call which he suspected was a domestic abuse call. Moreover, the Sheriff repeatedly testified that despite having the notice forms available to him and having given them to numerous other Broadwater County abuse victims, he did not give Vickie notice of her victim's rights at any time between 1994 and 1997. There was, therefore, substantial evidence from which the jury could conclude that, by failing to comply with the 1995 mandatory notice statute, the Sheriff was negligent, and arguably, negligent per se.

We now examine the Massees' argument that the Sheriff breached his duty to arrest Ray and to seize Ray's .44 magnum handgun on more than one occasion, and that such breach of duty caused Vickie's death. We note that the jury was correctly instructed that the Sheriff's negligence was a cause of Vickie's death if "it was a substantial factor in bringing it about."

Throughout the trial, the Massees presented substantial evidence describing Ray wielding his pistol and making threats to kill himself and others. . . .

Over the course of the trial, several deputies testified that they believed Ray should have been arrested and taken into custody for his own protection or the protection of others, and that his handgun should have been seized and kept in accordance with the statute. . . .

In addition, and importantly to our analysis, the Sheriff himself testified that the purpose of notifying victims of their rights is to help them understand the dangerousness of their situation. He agreed that domestic abuse victims rarely recognize this danger but, nonetheless, look to law enforcement for protection. . . .

Lastly, we address the concern that a ruling for the Massees would "signify an erosion of law enforcement's discretion" and render such discretion "illusory." Amicus Montana Sheriffs and Peace Officers Association argues that Thompson acted within his lawful discretion in this case and that this Court should not "second-guess law enforcement officers when they are acting within their lawful discretion." We are not engaging in any such endeavor. We reiterate that while the "arrest" statute bestows discretion, the Sheriff's duties under both §§ 46–6–602 and –603, MCA, were not discretionary but mandatory.

NOTES AND QUESTIONS

1. **Differences in State Immunity Laws.** In connection with domestic violence arrest laws, some states only immunize officers from liability when they make an arrest in good faith and in the exercise of due care. See, for example, Ark. Code § 16–81–113(3) (2005); Minn. Stat. § 629.341(2) (2005). Other states have gone further, and immunized officers with respect to good faith decisions either to arrest or not to arrest. See, for example, N.J. Stat. § 2C:25–22 (2007); Wis. Stat. § 968.075(6m) (2006). For a decision noting that a broad interpretation of immunity language contained in a statute would undermine the purpose of the domestic violence act, see *Roy v. City of Everett*, 823 P.2d 1084 (Wash. 1992).

In contrast, *Nearing v. Weaver*, 670 P.2d 137 (Or. 1983) the Oregon Supreme Court held that officers may not claim immunity under a statute providing immunity for making good faiths arrests when they fail to make an arrest in a domestic violence case, even if done in good faith. Thus, police officers who knowingly fail to enforce a judicial order under the abuse prevention act are potentially liable for any resulting harm to the psychic and physical health of the intended beneficiary of the order. See also Kathryn E. Litchman, *Punishing the Protectors: The Illinois Domestic Violence Act Remedy for Victims of Domestic Violence Against Police Misconduct*, 38 Loy. U. Chi. L.J. 765 (2007); G. Kristian Miccio, *Exiled from the Province of Care: Domestic Violence, Duty & Conceptions of State Accountability*, 37 Rutgers L.J. 111 (2005).

2. **Exceptions to the Public Duty Rule.** Despite the ruling in *Massee*, the public duty doctrine remains firmly in place. In litigation, the question therefore becomes whether the circumstances of an individual case can fit within one of the exceptions to that doctrine. The exceptions can all be viewed as answers to the question: "What is special about the relationship between this plaintiff, and the public actors who failed to keep her safe?" In this respect there is a close parallel between case law at the state level developing exceptions to the public duty rule, and case law at the federal level developing exceptions to the rule that state *inaction* is insufficient to ground a substantive due process claim under § 1983. In *Riss v. City of New York*, 22 N.Y.2d 579 (1968), the New York Court of Appeals refused to find that there was a general duty of protection police officers owed the general public. As in federal law, the court refused to find inaction on the part of the police actionable.

3. **Examples Where a Court Found "Special Relationships".** In the domestic violence arena, special relationships can be created by statute, mandatory arrest laws that require specific action on the part of police, or even by abuse prevention legislation. In another New York case, *Sorichetti v. City of New York*, 482 N.E. 70 (N.Y.1985), the court found a special relationship where police had knowledge of and failed to enforce a valid order of protection, and where, in addition, they knew the level of danger potentially posed by the abuser. The Illinois Supreme Court reached a similar decision in 1995, in *Calloway v. Kinkelaar*, 659 N.E.2d 1322 (Ill. 1995):

> To give effect to the legislature's purposes and intent in enacting the Domestic Violence Act, we believe judicial recognition of a right of action for civil damages is necessary, provided that the injured party can establish that he or she is a person in need of protection under the Act, the statutory law enforcement duties owed to him or her were breached by the willful and wanton acts or omissions of law enforcement officers, and such conduct proximately caused plaintiff's injuries.

The Domestic Violence Act itself had limited the liability of public officials, requiring a showing of willful or wanton negligence, rather than simple negligence.

In *Simpson v. City of Miami*, 700 So.2d 87 (Fla. Dist. App. 1997), an abuser who had violated a protective order was detained at his victim's home by a police officer, but then released after promising to leave the plaintiff alone. The following day he returned and shot her. The trial court dismissed the complaint on the basis of sovereign immunity (arguing that the officer's decision to release the perpetrator was a discretionary one), and the lack of any special relationship between the plaintiff and the police. In a per curiam opinion, the court of appeals reversed and remanded, in order to allow the plaintiff to amend her complaint to allege that the officer's initial detention of the perpetrator was an arrest. If she could do that, the court said, the officer's subsequent decision to release the abuser violated a clear statutory directive to hold the violator in custody until he could be brought before a court. FLA. STAT. § 741.30(9)(b) (1993). Presumably the court felt that the statute would operate both to defeat the argument that the officer had discretion, and to create the necessary special relationship. A concurring opinion instead grounded the special relationship in Florida's abuse prevention legislation more generally:

> Although the legislature, perhaps unadvisedly, did not expressly state that police officers have an affirmative duty to arrest domestic violence injunction violators, it created a special category of crime victim and established a special relationship between the decedent in this case and the responsible governmental entity. The concurring judge also noted that the Miami Police Department was well aware of the "discordant relations" between the plaintiff and her abuser, having responded to previous calls.

See also *Campbell v. Campbell*, 682 A.2d 272 (N.J. Super. 1996) (officers who failed to arrest a guest subject to a domestic violence restraining order not immune from tort liability); *Matthews v. Pickett County*, 996 S.W.2d 162 (Tenn. 1999) (failure to arrest under state domestic violence statute breached a duty owed the victim).

4. **Negligence Liability as a Public Actor.** Some jurisdictions recognize separate exceptions to the public duty rule in situations in which the public actor affirmatively puts the plaintiff in danger, or increases her danger; or commits to act on her behalf and then carries out his or her duties in a negligent way. Other jurisdictions incorporate these scenarios into the "special relationship" exception. In *Hutcherson v. City of Phoenix*, 961 P.2d 449 (Ariz. 1998), for example, the plaintiffs recovered well in excess of $1 million from the City of Phoenix, when negligent handling of a 911 call resulted in the deaths of the perpetrator's ex-partner and her new boyfriend. The 911 operator told the victim that an officer would be sent to her apartment, but gave the lowest priority rating to the call, even though the operator was told that the abuser had threatened lethal violence, that he was on his way to the apartment, and that he was less than five minutes away. Twenty-two minutes after the 911 call, the damage was done. When witnesses of the shootings called 911 to report them, the police arrived within seven minutes. There was direct contact between one of the victims and the operator, enough information for the operator to understand that the situation was serious, a specific commitment on the part of the operator, and a basis to believe that the victims of the shooting might have acted differently (by leaving the apartment, for example) if they had known that the police were not going to arrive. But the case can also be framed as one in which the operator increased the danger to the victims by promising protection that did not materialize, or as one in which an intervention was

begun (the call taken, and action promised), and then negligently continued.

5. **Respondeat Liability.** If a plaintiff is able to surmount the hurdles created by sovereign immunity and the public duty doctrine, they still have to establish actual and proximate cause, as in any other negligence action. Significantly, respondeat superior, which does not apply in § 1983 actions, is applicable in state tort actions, so that police departments or other governmental entities will be liable for the negligence of their employees.

Even if police officers owe a special duty to domestic violence victims, when does their mandate to arrest end, and their discretion to follow-up begin? Consider the following case:

Donaldson v. City of Seattle

Court of Appeals of Washington, 1992.
831 P.2d 1098.

■ FORREST, JUDGE.

FACTS

Leola Washington had a long history of drug abuse and failed drug treatment. During her life she had several relationships in which she was physically abused. In 1982 Leola was introduced to Steven Barnes. Both Barnes and Leola were seriously addicted to drugs, which created continuous pressure on their personal, financial, and employment relationships. Barnes's assaultive behavior toward Leola began early in their relationship.

In January 1983 Leola was so badly beaten she was taken to Harborview Medical Center. Although the medical personnel suspected domestic violence, Leola refused to discuss the situation. In January 1985 the police were dispatched to Leola and Barnes's residence. The police could see that Leola was injured and found Barnes upstairs. In spite of Leola's protestations, Barnes was arrested and Leola was given a domestic violence information sheet.

While Leola was in drug treatment in March 1985 she met another patient, Kenny Williams. Barnes was also in treatment in another center. In May of 1985 Barnes returned to the home he shared with Leola to find Kenny Williams' clothing. Outraged, Barnes tore up the house. Leola called the police and Barnes was arrested and jailed on charges of malicious mischief. On May 29, 1985 Leola filed for a temporary order of protection against Barnes. The order was granted but never entered into the Washington Criminal Information System. On August 30, 1985 Barnes was sentenced for malicious mischief, was ordered to pay restitution and have no contact with Leola. Again, the no contact portion of the sentence was not entered on the state information system.

Barnes and Leola continued contacts following this incident, even though it was in violation of the no-contact order. On September 11, 1985 the two got together and spent that evening and the next morning taking drugs. On September 12 Leola loaned Barnes her mother's car. Later that day he robbed a Value Village store. The police traced the license number of the car seen at Value Village to Leola and a witness to the robbery saw the car parked at Leola's. One of the officers that arrived at Leola's home to investigate the robbery had also answered the January 1985 domestic violence call and questioned Leola about Barnes' possible involvement in the robbery. Apparently Leola did not cooperate in the investigation and hid Barnes from the police. Barnes was not arrested for this robbery.

In December 1985 Barnes and Leola were together again and heavily involved with drugs. On Thursday, December 12, 1985 Barnes received an $1,800 settlement in a lawsuit. Leola and Barnes spent the money on drugs and spent the night together. On Saturday morning, December 14, Leola went to see Barnes at his mother's home. While there the two argued. They returned to Leola's house, where they continued to argue. Barnes pushed Leola to the couch, started to unbutton her pants and said he intended to "make love" to her. She told him it was not a good time since their son was still out in the car. Barnes then released Leola, she got up and went out of the house screaming. Leola ran to the neighbor's house, Barnes followed, allegedly saying "I'm going to kill you for ruining my life." Barnes then left the area.

Leola called the police. Officers Burrows and Baker answered the call. Baker got a description of Barnes and began an area search. Burrows took a statement from Leola. Leola informed Burrows of the no-contact order, but a radio check by Burrows revealed no order on the computer. Leola was unable to provide Burrows with a copy of the order. Leola gave Burrows Barnes's mother's address but told Burrows Barnes would not likely go there. Burrows also completed an area search and returned to Leola's home. Informing Leola that Barnes could not be found, Burrows offered to take her to a shelter or to a family member. Leola declined the offer.

Kenny Williams spent Saturday night with Leola at her home. The next morning, Sunday, December 15, 1985, Leola, Williams and Leola's brother, were moving Leola to her mother's home. Immediately after Williams and Leola's brother left the house Barnes entered the home and stabbed Leola to death. Barnes was subsequently arrested and convicted of first degree murder.

La Vern Donaldson, administratrix of Leola's estate, brought a wrongful death action against the State, Barnes's probation officer, and the City of Seattle. The State and the probation officer were granted summary judgment on the basis of immunity. The court denied the City's motion for summary judgment. A 3–week jury trial began on November 20, 1989. At the close of plaintiff's case and the conclusion of the trial the City moved to dismiss the claims. The court denied the motions, holding there was sufficient evidence the City owed Leola a statutory duty. The jury was instructed on the statutory duty to arrest and that violation of a statute is negligence per se. The jury returned a verdict in favor of the plaintiff, less 35 percent comparative negligence. The court denied post-trial motions for judgment notwithstanding the verdict and a new trial.

DUTY TO CONTINUE INVESTIGATION

[The Court of Appeals first agreed that the Domestic Violence Prevention Act imposes a duty on the City to protect victims of domestic violence. It went on to conclude that if Barnes had been found at the scene, the officers were not entitled to walk away but would in fact have a duty to arrest him.]

While the DVPA clearly establishes a mandatory duty to arrest, this case presents a question as to what the scope of that duty is. Statutory interpretation is for the court and it is proper for the court to consider public policy in defining the scope of the duty created in the statute. Donaldson argues that the existence of a mandatory duty to arrest when the abuser is on the premises also generates a mandatory duty to conduct a follow-up investigation by searching for the absent violator. She further contends that any negligence in the course of such investigation exposes the City to liability. We disagree.

The most important consideration is that the act does not so provide. Nowhere in the original act, nor any of the subsequent amendments, did the legislature create a special duty to conduct follow up investigations after the initial response where the violator is absent. Washington does not recognize the tort of negligent investigation. Liability for negligent investigation would be a substantial change in the law and is certainly not required as a necessary inference from the duty to make a mandatory arrest.

There is a vast difference between a mandatory duty to arrest and a mandatory duty to conduct a follow up investigation. In the arrest situation the officer is on the scene, the arrest is merely a matter of deciding to do so and a few minutes to physically effectuate the arrest. A mandatory duty to investigate, on the other hand, would be completely open-ended as to priority, duration and intensity. Would it entail ignoring other calls for a domestic violence response, ignoring other reported crimes, ignoring response to a report of an injury traffic accident? How long does such duty continue? To the end of the officer's shift? Or is the department obligated to detail another officer to take over? Merely to state such obvious practical problems is to demonstrate the extraordinary difficulty that would follow in attempting to implement any such mandatory duty of investigation. Law enforcement must be vested with broad discretion to allocate limited resources among the competing demands.

It is true that in this case Donaldson complains only of a failure to go to Barnes's mother's home, but such duty must be part of a general duty applicable in other similar situations. What if Barnes's mother gave the police another address and so on ad infinitum?

The act's focus on the immediate situation and prompt removal of an abuser from the home is apparent in the 4–hour time limitation. This provision sharply curtails the mandatory duty to arrest contained in the statute. Consider the following scenario: The husband commits an assault on the wife at breakfast, the wife does not request law enforcement help at the time, the husband returns and at dinner a verbal dispute arises with no

threats and no physical assault, and the wife then requests law enforcement help. By the explicit terms, the officer would have no mandatory duty
to arrest because more than 4 hours had elapsed since the incident. A
fortiori the officer would have no mandatory duty to arrest if he found the
abuser elsewhere after the 4 hours have passed. His authority to arrest
under those circumstances is limited to his general statutory authority to
arrest where he has probable cause to believe that a person has committed
a felony and there would, of course, be no power to arrest for a misdemean-
or since none was committed in his presence. In and of itself this 4–hour
limitation is not decisive as to the present case since if the officer had gone
to Barnes's mother's house, the opportunity to arrest would have occurred
within the 4 hours. It does, however, appear to put an outer limit on the
mandatory arrest duty and shows that the act is focused on addressing the
situation when the officer confronts an abuser in the house and not
creating an on-going duty to conduct a mandatory investigation.

The emphasis of the statute is on prompt intervention and removal of
the abuser, not on long-term protection. The statute recognizes that the
abuser may be released on personal recognizance or on other terms and we
can take judicial notice of the fact that this may happen promptly. As
emphasized in the brief of amicus curiae, Northwest Women's Legal
Center, the statutory amendments were aimed at insuring that domestic
violence assaults were dealt with in a similar manner to assaults between
other parties, and in effect, to make equal protection a reality. The statute
does not generate new or special long-term protection. The legislature
designed the act to address the "under-enforcement" of the criminal laws.
The law does not give a priority to domestic violence laws, but aims to have
all laws equally enforced without regard to the relationship of the parties.

In the past, a common police response to domestic violence calls was to
treat the matter as a family quarrel, try to mediate the situation and walk
the abuser around so he could "cool off." Mandatory arrest policies
eliminate this practice and require the police to treat domestic assaults the
same as any other assault, arresting the offender and removing him/her
from the scene. However, there will be situations when no arrest is
possible, such as when the alleged abuser is not in the home. In such a case
the law directs the police to offer alternate means to protect the victim.

It is not necessary to attempt to precisely define the scope of the
mandatory duty to arrest in responding to a domestic violence call when
the abuser is no longer present. Here, the officers did conduct a search of
the immediate area and reported to Leola that they were unable to locate
Barnes. Although the officers secured a possible address for Barnes, Leola
told them that he would not be present at that address. The officers further
properly exercised their responsibility by offering to take Leola to a place of
safety. Under these circumstances we hold that the special relationship
created by the statute terminated when Leola declined the offer. We attach
great significance to the officers' offer to take Leola to a place of safety
because the overriding purpose of the statute is to protect victims of
domestic violence from further violence. Where the offender is present his
arrest and removal serves that function. Where he is not present, taking

the victim to a place of safety serves the same function. The special responsibilities placed on the police in responding to complaints of domestic violence are fulfilled when continuation or escalation of the abuse is prevented.

Police responsibility in regard to any further investigation becomes part of their overall law enforcement function and does not generate a right to sue for negligence. We hold the Domestic Violence Protection Act limits the mandatory duty to arrest to cases where the offender is on the scene and does not create an on-going mandatory duty to conduct an investigation. The claim should have been dismissed at the close of plaintiff's case and the judgment is therefore reversed.

■ COLEMAN, JUDGE (dissenting).

. . . Inasmuch as the majority relies upon certain facts to justify part of its analysis, I will address whether this court can, under those facts, determine as a matter of law that the officers did all that was required under the provisions of the DVPA. Because Leola declined the officers' invitation to take her to a place of safety, the majority holds that the special relationship created by the statute terminated. I disagree. The act focuses on the importance of arresting violators in order to promote the safety of victims. Indeed, the majority acknowledges that the overriding purpose of the statute is to protect domestic violence victims from further violence. When the offender is present, arrest and removal serves that function.

However, the majority concludes that taking the victim to a place of safety serves the same function of protecting domestic violence victims when the violator is not present. That latter conclusion is not supportable and, in itself, is insufficient to satisfy the officers' duties under the act. Further, it overlooks the effect that an arrest may have. In the first place, while the suspect is in custody the victim is safe. If the suspect is to be released, conditions of release may be imposed, including supervision. Moreover, an arrest emphasizes to the arrestee the gravity of the situation and may, in and of itself, serve a deterrent function. Simply taking the victim to a safe place does not effectively accomplish the purposes intended by the DVPA. As noted in RCW 10.99.010,

> [t]he purpose of this chapter is to recognize the importance of domestic violence as a serious crime against society and *to assure the victim of domestic violence the maximum protection from abuse which the law and those who enforce the law can provide. . . . It is the intent of the legislature that the official response to cases of domestic violence shall stress the enforcement of the laws to protect the victim* and shall communicate the attitude that violent behavior is not excused or tolerated.

(Italics mine.) In those cases where it is reasonably possible to locate the suspect and effectuate an arrest, taking a victim to a place of safety—while commendable and to be encouraged—does not assure the victim of domestic violence the maximum protection from abuse which the law can provide. Likewise, offering a safe haven for the victim is not enough in itself to demonstrate an official response to domestic violence aimed at enforcing the laws to protect the victim. . . .

While I appreciate the majority's desire to determine limits in a difficult area, neither the facts nor the law supports the conclusion reached here. In short, I would affirm the judgment entered by the Superior Court.

NOTES AND QUESTIONS

1. **Clarifying the Role of a Police Officer.** The facts of this case are strikingly similar to *Castle Rock v. Gonzales* in that the police officers did little to find the defendant once they learned an order of protection had been violated. How can state legislatures, in drafting civil protection order statutes, make clear what officers should do in these cases if the defendant is not at the scene? Should liability extend to failure to investigate, or failure to seek a warrant? What policy arguments exist for mandating officers continue to investigate? What arguments dictate against such a policy?

2. **Will the Legislatures Act?** In light of *Castle Rock v. Gonzales*, there will be increased pressure on state legislatures to draft specific statutes subjecting the police to liability for failure to act in domestic violence cases. It remains to be seen whether the states will take affirmative steps to create liability, or whether they will leave such decisions, as they have done thus far, in the hands of the courts. See Jennifer Dieringer and Carolyn Grose, *Judicial Deference or Bad Law: Why Massachusetts Courts Will Not Impose Municipal Liability for Failure to Enforce Restraining Orders*, 38 SUFFOLK U.L.REV. 557 (2005). As of 2007, no states had expanded police liability for failure to protect victims of domestic violence.

B.   DOMESTIC VIOLENCE AT THE WORKPLACE

Introduction

According to a report published by the Bureau of National Affairs, domestic abuse is costing businesses between 3 and 5 billion dollars annually in lost productivity in the forms of higher health care costs, lost wages, sick leave, absenteeism and higher turnover rates, and liability for injuries inflicted in the workplace by abusers on their partners or co-workers. One small pilot study of employed battered women found that more than half missed three days of work each month because of abuse. Lucy Friedman and Sarah Cooper, *The Costs of Domestic Violence*, (New York Victim Services Agency, 1987). In another study of domestic violence victims, 96% of those who were employed reported experiencing severe problems in the workplace as a result of their abuse or abuser; 60% were often late, more than 50% missed work; 70% had difficulty performing job-related tasks; 60% were reprimanded for problems associated with the abuse, and 30% lost their jobs. *Domestic Violence: An Occupational Impact Study* (Domestic Violence Intervention Services, Inc., Tulsa, Oklahoma, July 27, 1992). More recently, a women's rights organization reported that up to half of all victims of domestic violence had been fired or had to leave a job, at least partially because of the domestic violence. Legal Momentum, *State Law Guide: Employment Discrimination Against Victims of Domestic and Sexual Violence* (2006), avail. at http://www.legalmomentum.org. Yet another study showed that almost 2/3 of domestic violence survivors said their ability to work was adversely affected by the domestic violence. Deborah A. Widiss and Robin R. Runge, *Advocating for the Employment Rights of Victims of Domestic Violence and Sexual Assault*, COMMISSION ON DOMESTIC VIOLENCE QUARTERLY E–NEWSLETTER, AMERICAN BAR ASSOCIATION (Spring 2007). See also Nina W. Tarr, *Employment and Economic Security for Victims of Domestic Abuse*, 16 S.CAL.REV.L. & SOC. J. 371 (2007).

In addition, domestic violence threatens the physical safety of victims and victims' co-workers on the job. In the New York study referenced above, 75% of women said they had been harassed by their batterers while at work. In 17% of the cases in which women are murdered at work, the alleged assailant is a current or former husband or boyfriend. A nationwide study found that 44% of employed adults had been affected at work by domestic violence against themselves or others. Deborah A. Widiss and Robin R. Runge, *Advocating for the Employment Rights of Victims of Domestic Violence and Sexual Assault*, COMMISSION ON DOMESTIC VIOLENCE QUARTERLY E–NEWSLETTER, AMERICAN BAR ASSOCIATION, (Spring 2007). Recently, for example, a Vermont teacher's former boyfriend killed one of her colleagues and injured another at the elementary school where they all taught while seeking her. Christian Avard, *Beyond the Abuse,* VT. GUARDIAN (Sept. 1, 2006) Workplace safety may be a particularly important issue for lawyers whose advocacy on behalf of victims of domestic violence can infuriate abusers. Kathleen M. Schoen and Janet Mickish, *Workplace Violence: Issues for Lawyers in Colorado,* 34 COLO. LAWYER 37 (June 2005).

Stephanie Perrin has summarized the wide-ranging effects of domestic violence in the workplace:

> Because it is easy to assume that domestic violence is a private family problem, one reaction of employers confronted with battered employees may be to tell them to leave their personal problems behind when they come to work. This is exactly the response one Chicago woman got when she went to her boss for help. Although she had received harassing phone calls from her boyfriend while at work, her boss informed her that her situation was not a company problem and that she should deal with it herself. However, it became a company problem that evening when her boyfriend appeared in the company parking garage and opened fire. He injured her, killed a parking attendant, and then killed himself.
>
> All too often it is not only the battered employee, but also her coworkers and supervisors that may be in the line of fire when an abuser shows up at the office. For example, an owner of an answering service was shot in the face when an employee's former boyfriend showed up at work. He had been stalking the employee up to the very day that he found her at work and killed her. A coworker who tried to stop him was also killed. In California, a woman was at work when her

ex-husband arrived. He killed three of her coworkers and badly injured six others. She had previously informed her employer that her ex-husband threatened to find her at work and kill her. The employer failed to take action.... In yet another case, two employees were killed and nine employees were injured when a coworker's husband showed up at the office, assembled a shotgun, and opened fire.... Although the building owners and occupants had knowledge that the husband had made threats to kill his wife at work, they refused to tighten security at their offices. Stephanie L. Perin, *Employers May Have to Pay When Domestic Violence Goes to Work*, 18 REV. LITIG. 265 (1999).

In contrast, some employers have made enormous efforts to assist employees who have been abused. Liz Claiborne, Inc. (LCI), for example, is a leader in responding to the needs of battered women at work. LCI has trained counselors to provide counseling and referrals to victims of domestic violence. It has also trained personnel from its human resources, health services and security departments to respond to the needs of victimized employees. Employees who have been victims of partner violence may take the time they need to seek safety or services, to attend court appearances, and to arrange for new housing. LCI also provides flexible hours, special parking spaces, short-term paid leaves, and extended leaves without pay. Safe@work Coalition, www.safeatworkcoalition.org. Many firms also work hard to make employees aware of their options if they are victimized by domestic violence. Marshalls Stores puts the hotline numbers for domestic violence in employees' bathrooms; Target Stores sponsors educational workshops on domestic violence for employees. Comment, *Employer Liability for Domestic Violence in the Workplace,* 31 TEX. TECH.L.Rev. 139 (2000).

Many employers are aware that domestic violence is costing them money. In a study of senior executives of Fortune 1000 companies, 47% said that domestic violence has a harmful effect on employee attendance, and 44% said that it increases insurance and medical costs. Liz Claiborne, Inc., *Addressing Domestic Violence: A Corporate Response* (Roper Starch Worldwide, 1994). However, only 12% of those surveyed said that corporations should play a significant role in addressing the issue, while 96% said that responsibility should ideally fall to the family. In the minds of most business leaders domestic violence is still a private matter. A 1997 study supported by the National Institute of Justice found that only 14% of larger U.S. companies addressed domestic violence in their workplace policies or guidelines, although 75% had policies or guidelines addressing workplace violence more generally. Despite the fact that employers tend to see the effects of domestic violence as private, the study found that a large majority of providers had dealt with specific partner abuse scenarios within the previous year, including employees with restraining orders and employees stalked at work. Nancy Isaac, *Corporate Sector Responses to Domestic Violence,* VIOLENCE AGAINST WOMEN ACT NEWS, Volume II, No.3 (U.S. Department of Justice, Violence Against Women Office, June/July 1997).

There are a number of possible causes of action for domestic violence related to the workplace. Employees who are injured while working may be able to make claims under workers' compensation statutes, Title VII, or the tort of wrongful discharge. In addition, they may be entitled to leave time to deal with the effects of the violence. Unfortunately, such employees may also find themselves fired from their jobs because of the violence against them. When this happens they may have few remedies, although unemployment insurance may be available. The materials that follow discuss all of these issues, as well as the question of whether employers or professional organizations can discipline employees or members who are abusive.

Remedies for Abuse at Work—Workers' Compensation

The vast majority of on-the-job injuries are channeled through state statutory workers' compensation schemes which supplant tort recovery. On the one hand, recovery under workers' compensation does not depend on finding the employer at fault, but on the other hand, workers' compensation recovery is less generous than the tort system. Notably, neither punitive damages nor pain and suffering are usually recoverable. In almost every state, injuries are governed by the Workers' Compensation Act if they arise out of and in the course of employment. The workers' compensation remedy is usually the exclusive remedy, precluding any common law action in tort against the employer. The first question in a suit for workers' compensation payments by an employee who has been abused on the job is usually whether or not the injury is covered by the workers' compensation statute. Most courts have answered that question in the negative, as the following case illustrates.

Dildy v. MBW Investments, Inc.

North Carolina Court of Appeals, 2002.
566 S.E.2d 759.

■ CAMPBELL, JUDGE.

. . . In June 1996, plaintiff was employed as a cashier at an Amoco gas station and convenience store in Wilson, North Carolina, owned by MBW Investments, Inc. ("defendant-employer"). Plaintiff was responsible for operating the store's cash register, which primarily involved ringing up sales of gasoline and merchandise. . . .

Prior to her employment with defendant-employer, plaintiff had lived with her boyfriend, Vernon Farmer. Due to the abusive nature of their relationship, plaintiff left Farmer in late 1995. Following the couple's separation, Farmer began threatening plaintiff. In March 1996, plaintiff was seen by a psychiatrist . . . for depression and anxiety caused by her fear of being attacked by Farmer. . . . Plaintiff subsequently obtained a restraining order against Farmer, but he continued to harass and threaten her. In early May 1996, plaintiff was voluntarily admitted to the psychiatric unit of a local hospital as a result of the anxiety caused by her fear of Farmer. Finally, on 18 June 1996, plaintiff reported to her psychiatrist that Farmer had blown up her current boyfriend's truck. Plaintiff's psychiatrist recommended that she consider relocating.

Despite the violent nature of their relationship and the fact that Farmer continued to threaten and harass her, plaintiff did not tell her co-workers or supervisors about her relationship with Farmer.

On 21 June 1996, Farmer came into the convenience store while plaintiff was working. Plaintiff was unaware of his presence in the store until he placed a six-pack of beer on the counter. After paying for the beer, Farmer forcefully threw the six-pack at plaintiff, hitting her in the chest. Farmer then left the store. Plaintiff, frightened by Farmer's attack, began repeatedly exclaiming that Farmer was going to come back to the store to kill her. Plaintiff asked Ronnie Braziel, the store supervisor on duty at the time, to call the police. Braziel told plaintiff to put the beer back in the beer cooler and to continue waiting on customers. As plaintiff continued working, she repeatedly asked Braziel to call the police because she was scared that Farmer would come back to the store to kill her. Braziel told plaintiff that Farmer would not be back and refused to honor plaintiff's requests to call the police.

Several minutes later, Farmer telephoned the store and plaintiff answered. Farmer threatened to come back to the store to kill plaintiff if she hung up the phone. Plaintiff reported this threat to Braziel while she was still on the phone with Farmer. Plaintiff asked Braziel to call the police or allow her to leave the store. Braziel refused plaintiff's request and told her to hang up the phone and resume waiting on customers. Approximately twenty minutes after he had first entered the store, Farmer returned with a handgun. Farmer walked up to the counter and shot at plaintiff three times, hitting her once in the right hand and once in the leg. Farmer later pled guilty to assault with a deadly weapon inflicting serious injury.

Plaintiff filed a claim for workers' compensation benefits for the injuries she received as a result of the shooting.... Plaintiff's claim was heard by a Deputy Commissioner [who denied] plaintiff's claim. The Deputy Commissioner found that Farmer's assault on plaintiff was entirely personal to her and had nothing to do with her employment. However, the Deputy Commissioner did find that the employment contributed to the assault on plaintiff to some degree in that plaintiff's supervisor, knowing of the threats being made by Farmer, instructed plaintiff to continue working and did not call the police, thereby failing to take an opportunity to reduce the risk. Nonetheless, the Deputy Commissioner concluded that the risk of assault was not attributable to the employment and that plaintiff's injuries did not arise out of her employment.

Upon appeal by plaintiff, the Full Industrial Commission upheld the denial of benefits to plaintiff.... Plaintiff appeals....

In order to be compensable under the Act, an injury must result from an accident arising out of and in the course of employment.... Within the meaning of the Act, an accident is an unlooked for and untoward event which is not expected or designed by the employee and which interrupts the employee's normal work routine and introduces unusual conditions likely to result in unexpected consequences. An assault may be an accident within the meaning of the Act when it is unexpected and without design on the part of the employee who suffers from it. The phrase "in the course of the employment" refers to the time, place and circumstances under which an accidental injury occurs. In the instant case, plaintiff was shot, without design on her part, during working hours while performing her duties as an employee on the premises of the employer. Thus, plaintiff's injuries were the result of an injury by accident occurring during the course of employment. Accordingly, the only issue presented by this appeal is whether the shooting that injured plaintiff arose out of her employment with defendant-employer.

The phrase "arising out of the employment" refers to the origin or causal connection of the accidental injury to the employment. The controlling test of whether an injury "arises out of" the employment is whether the injury is a natural and probable consequence of the nature of the employment. An injury "arises out of the employment" if a contributing proximate cause of the injury is a risk to which the employee was exposed because of the nature of the employment, and to which the employee would not have been equally exposed apart from the employment. This test has been referred to as the "increased risk" analysis, and focuses on whether the nature of the employment creates or increases a risk to which the employee is exposed. . . .

[Previous cases indicate] that an injury is not compensable when it is inflicted in an assault upon an employee by an outsider as the result of a personal relationship between them, and the attack was not created by and not reasonably related to the employment. This is true even though the employee was engaged in the performance of his duties at the time, for even though the employment may have provided a convenient opportunity for the attack it was not the cause. For an injury inflicted in an assault by an outsider to be compensable, the assault must have had such a connection with the employment that it can be logically found that the nature of the employment created the risk of the attack.

In the instant case, the evidence tends to show that plaintiff and Farmer were involved in an abusive relationship. Following their breakup, Farmer began threatening to harm plaintiff. After plaintiff obtained a restraining order against him, Farmer continued to threaten and harass her. The fact that Farmer blew up plaintiff's current boyfriend's truck further illustrates the danger posed by Farmer to plaintiff and those associated with her. Thus, Farmer's assault on plaintiff at the convenience store was entirely unrelated to the nature of plaintiff's employment; it did not stem from the type of work plaintiff was required to do for defendant-employer. It was a personal risk that plaintiff brought with her from her domestic and private life and the motive that inspired the assault was likely to assert itself at any time and in any place.

Plaintiff argues that . . . in the case before us defendant-employer, through the supervisor on duty at the store when plaintiff was shot (Braziel), had knowledge of an outside peril that immediately endangered plaintiff, had an opportunity to protect plaintiff from this outside peril, and failed to act appropriately to reduce or eliminate the risk of peril, thereby making the assault a risk incident to the employment. . . . Under the circumstances present here, Braziel was under no duty to call the police or let plaintiff leave the store merely because a customer had thrown beer at her and she had expressed fear that the customer would return to kill her. Braziel knew nothing about the nature of plaintiff and Farmer's relationship and had no basis for understanding and appreciating the seriousness of the threat posed by Farmer. The fact that Braziel failed to call the police and refused to let plaintiff leave the store did not make the risk that Farmer would come back and assault plaintiff a risk arising out of the nature of the employment. While we agree with the Commission that the conduct of Braziel contributed in some degree to plaintiff being shot while performing her job duties in the store, the fact that Braziel did not take plaintiff seriously when she warned that Farmer would come back to the store to kill her was not a risk arising out of the nature of plaintiff's employment. . . .

In sum, notwithstanding the events at the convenience store on the day of the shooting, the risk to plaintiff that her former boyfriend would shoot her was not one which a rational mind would anticipate as incident to her employment with defendant-employer. The risk that her boyfriend would carry out his previous threats against her was a hazard common to the neighborhood and not peculiar to her employment; it was independent of the relation between employer and employee.

Although the Workers' Compensation Act should be liberally construed to the end that the benefits thereof should not be denied upon technical, narrow and strict interpretation, the rule of liberal construction cannot be employed to attribute to a provision of the Act a meaning foreign to the plain and unmistakable words in which it is couched. The Act was not intended to establish general insurance benefits. To grant compensation in the instant case would effectively remove the "arising out of the employment" requirement of the Act.

Accordingly, we find that the evidence was sufficient to support the Commission's findings of fact and that these findings support the Commission's denial of plaintiff's claim for workers' compensation benefits since plaintiff's injury did not arise out of her employment.

NOTES AND QUESTIONS

1. **Workers' Compensation Statutes.** Most states' workers' compensation statutes, like the North Carolina statute in *Dildy*, require that a compensable accident both occur in the course of the injured party's employment and arise out of that employment. A few are different however. The Washington State workers' compensation statute provides compensation for any injury sustained in the course of employment, without any additional requirement that the injury "arise out of" the employment. WASH. REV. CODE § 51.32.010. The Maryland statute specifically defines "accident" to include injuries caused by an assault by a third party if they occur in the course of employment. MD. CODE, LAB. & EMPL. § 9–101(b)(2). Do you think that *Dildy* would have been decided differently if it had taken place in Washington or Maryland instead of North Carolina?

In some states, the *Dildy* case would have been decided in the same way, but on the basis of an express statutory defense, providing that employees will not be compensated for assaults at the workplace if they stem from personal disputes. Alabama (Ala. Code 1975 § 25–5–1), Georgia (Ga. Code Ann. § 34–9–1 (2000)), Delaware, Iowa (I.C.A. § 85.16 (1996)), Minnesota (M.S.A. § 176.011 (2006)), Pennsylvania (77 P.S. § 411(1) (2002)), and Texas (V.T.C.A., Labor Code § 406.032 (2006)) all have such defenses. Similarly, Missouri provides that injuries will not be compensable if they arise from a risk unrelated to employment, to which the employee would be equally exposed in his or her life outside the workplace. Mo. Rev. Stat. § 287.020(3) (2005). In those states that have considered this issue without the benefit of express statutory provisions, most, like North Carolina, have concluded that injuries sustained at work, but arising out of an abusive personal relationship, are not compensable under workers' compensation schemes. For other examples see *Temple v. Denali Princess Lodge*, 21 P.3d 813 (Alaska 2001), *Foster v. Cleveland Clinic Fdn.*, 2004 WL 2914985 (Ohio App.), *Stone v. Traylor Bros.*, 600 S.E.2d 551 (S.C.App. 2004).

2. **Injuries to Other Employees.** What if the person hurt in *Dildy* had been a security guard? What if, instead, it had been the on-duty supervisor? Could those injuries be said to "arise out of" the coworker's employment? Would they be covered by the express statutory defenses described in the previous note? In one disturbing case in North Carolina an employee was being harassed at work by her violent boyfriend. Responding to concerns expressed by other employees who were afraid for their own safety, the employer decided to monitor the abused employee's performance, in order to justify firing her. A co-worker was given the task of keeping a record of the victim's working hours, and because of that assignment was injured by the boyfriend when he appeared at the workplace and shot and killed his partner. The Court of Appeals decided that the co-worker's injury was not compensable, because it was caused by the criminal act of a third party that did not arise out of employment. *Hemric v. Reed and Prince Manufacturing Co.*, 283 S.E.2d 436 (N.C. App. 1981). Do you agree that the court should have focused on whether the boyfriend's violent *act* arose out of the employment or do you think its focus should have been on whether the co-worker's *injury* arose out of the employment assignment? Unlike the abused employee herself, the coworker had no private relationship with his assailant, and was in the line of fire solely because of workplace responsibilities imposed by his employer. For another co-worker case that also denies workers' compensation benefits, see *Kmart Corp. v. Workers' Comp. Bd.*, 748 A.2d 660 (Pa. 2000) (injured employee was on lunch break in Kmart lunch area).

3. **Exacerbation of Vulnerability.** Could Dildy have claimed that her employer increased the level of risk she faced by assigning her to work at an easily accessible place instead of in, for example, a rear storage area? Could she thereby have made a claim that her injury "arose out of" her employment? In *Guillory v. Interstate Gas Station*, 653 So.2d 1152 (La. 1995), a Louisiana court held that a gas station employee who was shot by her husband while she was at work could not recover workers' compensa-

tion benefits because her injuries arose out of a non-employment related dispute. The employee had filed for a divorce from her husband and taken out a restraining order. She was afraid for her life, and had asked her employer both whether she could keep a gun with her at work and whether she could work the day shift rather than her customary evening shift so that she would be less accessible to her husband. Her employer refused both of these requests. Could you make the argument that her vulnerability to her husband's assault was exacerbated by her employment? Would a decision for Guillory on such a claim mean that most victims of partner violence at work would be entitled to workers' compensation benefits using the same argument?

The argument that the victim's employment is an exacerbating factor in her injury is more commonly used when the assault is perpetrated by a fellow employee, whose attentions, and violence, cannot be evaded because the employment environment forces victim and perpetrator into proximity, or precipitates the violent incident. See for example, *Torres v. Triangle Handbag Manufacturing*, 211 N.Y.S.2d 992 (N.Y.A.D. 3rd Dept. 1961).

4. **The Effects of Economic Class in the Workplace.** We know that victims of domestic violence can be rich or poor, CEOs of major corporations or unskilled hourly workers. Do you think that the differences in working conditions are likely to affect employee vulnerabilities to domestic violence? For example, would Dildy have been more able to protect herself if she had not been subject to such close supervision or if she had a more flexible work day?

5. **Liability in Tort.** Theoretically, a finding that an injury is not compensable under the applicable workers' compensation statute simultaneously opens the door to a substantially greater award of damages through the mechanism of a tort claim. The next case gives you a sense of just how likely recovery in tort is.

Carroll v. Shoney's, Inc., d/b/a Captain D's Restaurant

Supreme Court of Alabama, 2000.
775 So.2d 753.

■ MADDOX, J.

The facts, viewed in the light most favorable to Carroll, as the nonmovant, suggest the following: On the evening of September 22, 1995, Mildred Harris was working at Captain D's. Adrian Edwards, the relief manager, was also working that evening. Ms. Harris told Edwards that, the night before, her husband, Ronnie Harris, had beaten and choked her and that he had threatened her. Ms. Harris told Edwards that she was afraid of Ronnie Harris and that she did not want to talk to him. Ms. Harris asked Edwards to telephone the police if Ronnie Harris appeared at the restaurant that evening.

Around 10 o'clock that evening, while Ms. Harris was working in the rear of the restaurant, Ronnie Harris came in. He pushed his way past Edwards and went to the back of the restaurant, where he confronted Ms.

Harris. He told Ms. Harris that he was going to "get her." Edwards and another employee repeatedly told Ronnie Harris to leave, but he continued yelling at Ms. Harris. Edwards telephoned the police; the officer who responded to the call escorted Ronnie Harris from the restaurant. The police detained him briefly; they released him after learning that Captain D's was not going to press charges. Evidence was presented indicating that after that confrontation Ms. Harris asked employees of Captain D's to help her hide from her husband; there was evidence indicating that she was taken to a motel in Montgomery and that her fellow employees lent her enough money to pay for the motel room.

The next day, September 23, 1995, Edwards reported for work and told the restaurant manager, Rhonda Jones, about the incident that had occurred the night before, i.e., that Ronnie Harris had threatened Ms. Harris, and that the police had to be called to remove Ronnie Harris from the restaurant. Edwards also told Jones that Ms. Harris had said that she was afraid to return to work. At some point after the conversation, Ms. Harris telephoned Jones and asked to be excused from work that evening. Ms. Harris told Jones that she and her husband had been fighting and that she was afraid of him. Jones told Ms. Harris to come into work; and she also told Ms. Harris that if Ronnie Harris showed up, she would telephone the police. Ms. Harris went to work that evening, and was working at the front counter. At some point during her shift, Ronnie Harris walked into the restaurant, pulled out a pistol, and shot Ms. Harris in the back of the head. Ms. Harris died as a result of the gunshot wound....

The general rule is that an employer is not liable to its employees for criminal acts committed by third persons against an employee....

It is well settled that absent a special relationship or special circumstances a person has no duty to protect another from criminal acts of a third person.... We recognize, of course, that this Court has held that there is a singular exception to this general rule, which arises where the particular criminal conduct was foreseeable....

We believe that Carroll has failed to show how this case falls outside the general rule that a person has no duty to protect another from criminal acts of a third person. Alabama law requires a plaintiff to show three elements to establish a duty that would be the basis for a cause of action such as the one presented in this case.... First, the particular criminal conduct must have been foreseeable. Second, the defendant must have possessed "specialized knowledge" of the criminal activity. Third, the criminal conduct must have been a probability.

Viewing the facts most favorably to Carroll, as we are required to do, and applying the law to those facts, we conclude that the plaintiff has not presented evidence creating a genuine issue of material fact as to Captain D's liability. The particular criminal conduct in this case was a murder.... [T]here was no evidence in this case that any employee of Captain D's was told, or should have reasonably foreseen, that Ronnie Harris would enter the Captain D's restaurant and murder his wife. Admittedly, there was evidence that Mildred Harris and her husband had been fighting, and that she had requested permission to be away from work for that reason, but the evidence also indicated that she had made similar requests on other occasions for the same reason. During his deposition, Carroll, who is Mildred Harris's father, admitted that he had no reason to think that Ronnie Harris would shoot Mildred Harris. Based on the foregoing, we fail to see how Captain D's can be held responsible for Ms. Harris's death. Consequently, we affirm the judgment of the trial court.

■ JOHNSTONE, J. (dissenting).

The crucial issue is not whether the murder was foreseeable, but whether violence and injury, fatal or not, were foreseeable. Had the husband slapped the deceased, would anyone say the slapping was not foreseeable? If he had blackened her eye or broken her nose or knocked her teeth down her throat, would anyone say any of these batterings was not foreseeable? Is the defendant less liable because the husband killed her? "[A plaintiff] is not required to prove 'that the particular consequence should have been anticipated, but rather that some general harm or consequence could have been anticipated.' " . . .

On the day of the killing . . . Jones was informed of the decedent's husband's angry trespass into the back of the restaurant and angry threat against the deceased during the preceding night. Jones was informed that the incident was so bad the restaurant personnel needed to call the police in order to remove the husband. Jones was informed that the deceased had told her coworkers that her husband had beaten her two days earlier and that she thought that he would kill her. Nonetheless, Jones refused the deceased's plea to be excused from work, ordered the deceased to report to work, and promised to protect the deceased at work. Jones then assigned the deceased to work at the counter, where she was more exposed to violence from her husband than she would have been on virtually any other assignment within the restaurant. The husband's injuring the deceased was not just foreseeable but was expectable. . . .

As already discussed, violence by the husband was so obviously foreseeable that the manager of the restaurant expressly promised to protect the deceased from the husband. Second, the manager had specialized knowledge of the husband's trespass, abuse, and threat the preceding night, the battery he had committed on the deceased two days earlier, and the deceased's perception of the danger he posed. Third, the husband's criminal conduct was a probability if not a certainty: the night before, he had pushed his way past a restaurant employee and trespassed into the back of the store in order to threaten the deceased that he was going to "get her."

To absolve the defendant of liability, the main opinion [reiterates] "that crime can and does occur despite society's best efforts to prevent it." . . . Society did not exert its best efforts to prevent the crime committed on the deceased in the case before us. Rather the defendant, through its managerial personnel, demonstrated a preoccupation with the logistics of fast food and an irresponsible disregard for the notorious dangers of spouse abuse and the public policy of this state, expressed in a number of recent statutes, against spouse abuse.

Foreseeability is a matter of common sense. The decision of this Court in this case will send a message whether we think common sense entails recognizing the danger of demonstrated spouse abuse.

NOTES AND QUESTIONS

1.   **Assessing the Analysis in *Carroll v. Shoney's, Inc.*** Who do you think has the better of this argument, the majority or the dissent? Does it seem surprising, given all that society has learned about the nature of abusive relationships, that a court would find violence unforeseeable to an employer, even when the employer has witnessed threatening conduct?

In an omitted portion of the opinion, the court cited *Guerrero v. Memorial Medical Center of East Texas*, 938 S.W.2d 789 (Tex. App. 1997) in support of its position that the third party's criminal conduct needs to be not only foreseeable, but probable, for liability to attach. *Guerrero* is another case in which an employee was killed by her abusive husband while she was at work and the court found that the employer was not liable. In *Guerrero*, there was no evidence that the victim had ever informed her employer of her partner's physical abuse, or that his behavior in the workplace prior to the shooting provided any indication of his violent propensities. The majority in *Carroll* thought that *Guerrero* was an analogous case. Do you agree that it should be followed in *Carroll* or is it distinguishable?

The claim against Shoney's was essentially a negligent security claim, analogous to well-established lines of cases brought by tenants against landlords, and customers against store owners. In all these cases the focus is on the foreseeability of the risk created by criminal third parties to the class of people represented by the plaintiff, and on whether the defendant has the kind of control over the environment that puts it in the best position to guard against the risk. Although the focus of these materials is on an employer's responsibilities towards its employees, it is worth noting that the same arguments could be used by victims of domestic violence terrorized in schools and on college campuses, in hospitals, and while using public transportation. To the extent these facilities are run by public rather than private entities, issues of sovereign immunity may complicate the analysis.

Once the foreseeability of the risk establishes that a duty of care is owed, the next question will be whether the steps taken by the defendant were reasonable, or whether the plaintiff is right to claim that they were inadequate. In the *Guerrero* case cited by the majority, the employer's security personnel had escorted the abusive husband off of the employer's premises the day before the murder, after another employee heard yelling in a stairwell. Similarly, the morning of the shooting, when the abused employee was afraid that her husband might be waiting in the employee lot, the security personnel met her there. On neither of these occasions was the husband violent. When you look at the facts of *Guerrero*, do you think the defendant acted reasonably, given what it knew about the situation? Is that another basis for distinguishing *Guerrero* from *Carroll*?

Finally, even if a plaintiff were able to establish a duty and a foreseeable risk of harm, she would still have to worry about defenses that the employer might claim to the action. For example, in one case, the employee walked on her own to the employee's parking lot without asking for assistance from the employer's security because she thought her boyfriend had calmed down. Apparently he had not and he shot her. The court treated the employee's decision to walk on her own almost as if she had assumed the risk of the injury. *Griffin v. AAA Auto Club South, Inc.*, 470 S.E.2d 474 (Ga. App. 1996).

Despite the strength of Justice Johnstone's dissenting opinion in *Carroll*, most courts continue to grant summary judgment for the employer in suits in which an employee is suing for injuries that result from domestic violence on the employer's premises. See *Midgette v. Wal–Mart Stores, Inc.*, 317 F.Supp.2d 550 (E.D.Pa. 2004).

2. **Tort Theories if the Abuser is a Co-employee of the Victim.** Different tort theories of liability may come into play if the perpetrator of workplace violence is another employee, or a supervisor. If the conduct is intentional, as it almost certainly will be, the employer will not be liable on a respondeat superior basis. However, the employer could potentially be liable for negligent hiring, negligent supervision, or negligent retention of the abusive employee. A negligent hiring claim focuses on whether the employer properly investigated the employee's background prior to hiring him or her; a negligent supervision claim focuses on whether the employer has exercised appropriate control over the employee's conduct on the job; and a negligent retention claim focuses on whether, as problems come to light, the employer has taken appropriate action to investigate charges of misconduct, reassign an employee who is causing trouble for a specific fellow worker, or terminate the abusive employee's employment. In all these actions the key questions will again be whether the risk created by the employer was foreseeable, and whether, under the specific circumstances of the case, the employer's conduct was or was not reasonable. In at least one recent case involving an abusive co-employee summary judgment for the employer was denied on the grounds that a fact-finder might find the abusive employee posed a foreseeable danger to the victimized employee. *Panpat v. Owens–Brockway Glass Container, Inc.*, 71 P.3d 553 (Or. App. 2003).

3. **Claims under Title VII.** An employee who is threatened, harassed, or assaulted by another employee or by a supervisor at work may also be able to invoke Title VII of the Civil Rights Act of 1964, 42 U.S.C. § 2000e–2, claiming sexual harassment as a form of gender discrimination. Title VII claims are not precluded by workers' compensation schemes. Remediable sexual harassment in the workplace falls into two categories. The first is quid pro quo harassment—unwelcome conduct on the basis of an employee's sex affecting a term or condition of employment. Classic examples are making a promotion or favorable assignment conditional on the employee's granting sexual favors, or threatening discharge or demotion if those favors are withheld. The second category is hostile work environment harassment, which requires that an employee show she was, based on her gender,

subject to unwelcome conduct sufficiently severe or pervasive that it affected the conditions of her employment and created an abusive working environment. It seems likely that partner abuse would more often manifest itself in the workplace in this second way.

In order to recover, the employee must show that the employer knew or had reason to know about the harassment and failed to take appropriate action to end it. In Title VII cases the perpetrator of the abusive or harassing behavior is usually a fellow employee, over whose behavior the employer has control. However, there have been cases in which employers have been held liable for failing to protect employees from harassment by customers, so that some precedent exists for bringing a Title VII claim even when the primary perpetrator is not employed by the defendant. For a more thorough discussion of Title VII suits in the context of partner violence, see Fredrica L. Lehrman, DOMESTIC VIOLENCE PRACTICE AND PROCE-DURE, §§ 10:19–10:21 (1997 & Supp. 2005).

In some jurisdictions, courts have used the existence of Title VII or parallel state civil rights legislation to preclude tort actions based on sexual or racial harassment. Illinois, for example, requires that all claims based on intentionally discriminatory conduct must be brought under the state's Human Rights Act, rather than in tort. *Daulo v. Commonwealth Edison,* 938 F.Supp. 1388 (N.D. Ill. 1996). Similarly, a federal district court in New York has held that under New York law no tort claim for negligent hiring and retention will lie when the gravamen of the claim is racial harassment by a coworker. *Brown v. Bronx Cross County Medical Group,* 834 F.Supp. 105 (S.D.N.Y. 1993). Other courts have allowed discrimination-based negligence actions to go forward. See for example, *Cox v. Brazo,* 303 S.E.2d 71 (Ga.App. 1983), judgment affirmed 307 S.E.2d 474 (Ga. 1983); *Kerans v. Porter Paint Co.,* 575 N.E.2d 428 (Ohio 1991). See also Fredrica L. Lehrman, DOMESTIC VIOLENCE PRACTICE AND PROCEDURE, § 10:21.3 (Supp. 2005). In the context of partner violence at work, the practical response to this problem may be to frame the claim squarely as a negligence claim, without reference to discrimination, in those states in which the discrimination framework may preclude other alternatives.

4. **OSHA.** The Federal Occupational and Safety Health Act (OSHA) imposes a duty on employers to provide a workplace that is "free from recognized hazards." 29 U.S.C. § 654(a)(1) (2006). Violations are subject to fines. OSHA does not create a private right of action for employees injured while at work. At the moment, according to the OSHA website, there are no particular standards on workplace violence, much less any dealing specifically with domestic violence. www.osha.gov. Of course, if one could prove that a particular injury occurred as a result of a violation of OSHA, it would probably be considered negligence per se in a tort suit.

When Employers Punish Victims

When an employee's abusive partner sets out to sabotage her ability to perform her job, or carries his campaign of harassment to her workplace, he frequently jeopardizes her employment. Sometimes employers are simply unaware that the reason the employee is late, distracted, or unreliable is that she is coping with violence at home. Sometimes they know, but simply decide that the problem is one personal to the employee. If the abusive partner begins to make his presence felt at work, either by appearing at the worksite, or by making harassing calls, other employees may begin to worry about their own safety or have their own work performance disrupted. In all too many situations, the result is that the employee loses her job or suffers other adverse job action. The question in this section of the materials is whether she has any recourse against the employer who seeks to punish her for her abuser's behavior.

More than half of the states have laws on the books that make it illegal for an employer to fire, or otherwise discriminate against, any victim of a crime who takes time off from work to testify in a criminal proceeding, pursuant to a subpoena. This protection, albeit somewhat limited, would certainly extend to victims of domestic violence in those states, if they were cooperating in criminal proceedings against their batterers. Similarly, nine states permit victims of domestic violence to take time off from work to obtain civil protective orders. Eight states offer more targeted protection to domestic violence victims who need to miss work for medical treatment or other reasons related to the violence. Finally, New York City requires that employers provide "reasonable accommodations" to victims of domestic violence. This might include such things as time off to change the locks or, where feasible, a shift change or new telephone number at work. Deborah A. Widiss and Robin R. Runge, *Advocating for the Employment Rights of Victims of Domestic Violence and Sexual Assault*, COMMISSION ON DOMESTIC VIOLENCE QUARTERLY E–NEWSLETTER, AMERICAN BAR ASSOCIATION (Spring 2007).

Except for the narrow coverage provided by the statutes mentioned above, very little protects employees who are victims of domestic violence.

Green v. Bryant

Eastern District of Pennsylvania, 1995.
887 F.Supp. 798.

■ DITTER, J.

The primary question in this case is whether Pennsylvania's public policy protects an at-will employee who is the victim of spousal abuse from discharge by her employer. For the reasons stated below, I find that it does not.

I. FACTS

Defendant, Dr. Winston Murphy Bryant, employed plaintiff, Philloria Green, from December 1992 through August 1993. Plaintiff asserts that during her last week of work, her estranged husband raped and severely beat her with a pipe at gun point. She received medical treatment and returned to work shortly thereafter. Ms. Green informed another doctor in the office about the attack. The doctor informed defendant, who then terminated plaintiff's employment. Ms. Green asserts that Dr. Bryant told her that the discharge had nothing to do with plaintiff's performance at work, but was based solely upon her being the victim of a violent crime. . . .

A. Wrongful Discharge

Plaintiff asserts . . . that defendant wrongfully discharged her from employment in violation of Pennsylvania public policy. Plaintiff admits she was an at-will employee of Dr. Bryant's. The general rule in Pennsylvania is that an at-will employee may be dismissed with or without cause, for good reason, bad reason, or no reason. . . . Some courts have recognized a narrow exception, "in only the most limited of circumstances," where discharge of an at-will employee would threaten clear mandates of public policy. . . . The cases in Pennsylvania where the public policy exception has been recognized all involve a constitutionally or legislatively established prohibition, requirement, or privilege; e.g., firing an employee who made a nuclear safety report required by law, not hiring someone whose criminal conviction had been pardoned, and firing an employee who was absent due to jury duty. . . . In sum, the exception is most frequently applied when the discharge results from an employee's compliance with or refusal to violate the law, or where the employee did something he or she was privileged to do. . . . [T]he public policy exception does not exist to protect the employee. . . . Rather, it protects society from public harm or vindicates fundamental individual rights. . . .

Ms. Green argues that her dismissal violates dual public policies: protecting an employee's right to privacy and protecting victims of crime or spousal abuse. In support of her first contention, plaintiff notes that the Third Circuit has recognized a strong policy favoring a right to privacy. . . . In this case, plaintiff states that she revealed to another employee, Dr. Brown, that she had been raped and severely beaten. There is no allegation that defendant initiated the conversation, required disclosure of the information, questioned plaintiff about her marital situation, inquired into personal or private details, or in any way sought to intrude upon plaintiff's privacy in a substantial and highly offensive manner. . . . I find that defendant's discharge of plaintiff did not violate the public policy favoring a right to privacy. Plaintiff also argues that her discharge is in violation of Pennsylvania's policy to protect victims of crime and domestic abuse, as embodied in the state's criminal code, Protection from Abuse Act, and the establishment of the Crime Victim's Compensation Board. The flaw in plaintiff's argument is that while these statutes provide certain procedures and protections, they do not thereby create a protected employment class. In the statutes to which plaintiff refers, the legislature included certain programs or safety measures, but excluded others. For example, the Protection from Abuse Act specifies that a defendant may be directed to pay a plaintiff for economic losses incurred as a result of the abuse. It does not, however, say that a complainant is entitled to any kind of employment rights or benefits. Similarly, a crime victim may be eligible for compensation . . . but the statute does not create employment rights or privileges. It might be a different case, and a closer question as to the public policy exception, if plaintiff alleged that she was discharged because she had applied for victim compensation or had sought a protective order. That, however, is not her allegation. Plaintiff was not discharged because she refused to violate the law, because she complied with the law, or because she exercised a right or privilege granted by the law. Therefore, in the absence of any indication that Pennsylvania has established a clear mandate that crime victims generally, or spousal abuse victims specifically, are entitled to benefits or privileges beyond those enumerated in the laws, I must conclude that plaintiff's dismissal was not in violation of public policy. Because plaintiff has not alleged facts sufficient to state a claim that her discharge from at-will employment was in violation of public policy, defendant's motion to dismiss . . . must be granted.

B.   Negligent Infliction of Emotional Distress

. . . As the Supreme Court of Pennsylvania has pointed out, the first point of inquiry is whether the defendant owed plaintiff a duty of care. . . . While [prior cases] suggest[] . . . that there is a pre-existing duty between an employer and employee, the cases do not imply that simply terminating a worker's employment breaches that duty. . . . Therefore, because plaintiff has not alleged that defendant breached any duty to her, and because I found above that defendant committed no wrong in discharging plaintiff, I find that Ms. Green has not sufficiently alleged a claim for [negligent infliction of emotional distress]. . . .

C.   Intentional Infliction of Emotional Distress

. . . Under Pennsylvania law, the conduct complained of in a claim for IIED [intentional infliction of emotional distress] must be extreme or clearly outrageous, a determination initially made by the court. . . . It is rare within the employment context that the conduct will reach a sufficient level of outrageousness. . . . Ms. Green asserts that because of her status as an abused spouse, Dr. Bryant's termination of her employment was extreme and outrageous. While I can contemplate circumstances where this might be the case, Ms. Green's complaint does not allege such a circumstance. Rather, she alleges only that she was fired because she was the victim of a violent crime. Although any involuntary discharge from employment is unpleasant, defendant's conduct was not so outrageous in character or extreme in degree as to exceed all bounds of decency. Because plaintiff has not alleged facts that would support a claim for IIED, defendant's motion to dismiss . . . must be granted.

D.   Breach of Covenant of Good Faith and Fair Dealing

Finally, plaintiff alleges . . . that defendant has breached the implied covenant of good faith and fair dealing, arguing that "all employment contracts, including those construed to be at-will, contain an implied covenant of good faith." . . . In this case, it is unnecessary to explore the boundaries of employer-employee good faith in the at-will context. It is sufficient to say that there is no bad faith when an employer discharges an at-will employee for good reason, bad reason, or no reason at all, as long as no statute or public policy is implicated. . . .

NOTES AND QUESTIONS

1.   **At–Will Employment.** Notice that the court's decision that the employer had the right to fire the plaintiff operates to undermine the rest of her claims. If he has the right to terminate her employment, his conduct cannot be construed as outrageous or unreasonable for purposes of her emotional distress claims (unless, perhaps, he communicated that decision in a particularly outrageous or unreasonable way). Nor can he breach a covenant of good faith, if he is acting within his legal rights. For a more recent case, also finding no wrongful discharge, see *Imes v. City of Asheville,* 594 S.E.2d 397 (N.C.App. 2004) (plaintiff-husband was shot by his wife who claimed he was having an extra-marital affair).

As noted above, many jurisdictions provide protection to employees who are victims of criminal activity and must, as a result, take time off from work to appear in court. A few places even provide such protection specifically to domestic violence victims. These statutes are discussed in more detail in the following note. A victim of domestic violence who was fired for missing work to go to court might be able to invoke such a statute in a wrongful discharge suit. This strategy was successful in a Massachusetts case in which an employer allegedly fired the employee, a victim of domestic violence, for missing a day of work during which she had renewed a restraining order, appeared at the arraignment of her abuser, and changed her locks at the suggestion of the police. The trial court found that these actions were protected pursuant to public policies of assisting in law enforcement and protecting victims of domestic violence under the Massachusetts Abuse Prevention Act. *Apessos v. Memorial Press Group,* 2002 WL 31324115 (Mass.Super. 2002).

2.   **Disclosure of Domestic Violence.** If you represented a victim of domestic violence would you encourage her to disclose the violence to her supervisor? To her co-workers?

In a manual for attorneys for domestic violence victims, Deborah A. Widiss and Robin R. Runge wrote:

> You should help your client understand the pros and cons of disclosing to her employer that she is a victim of domestic violence or sexual assault. There are some significant advantages. Disclosing may make it possible for your client to work with her employer to take steps to address the violence and to help keep the workplace safe. It may also be necessary to disclose the violence to access certain kinds of leave or take advantage of other policies. It can be helpful ... to explain a period of poor performance, especially if she has taken steps to address the violence so that there is reason to believe that issues affecting her performance will abate.
>
> There are some real downsides to disclosing as well. <u>You need to warn her that she may be fired simply for having the conversation or because of perceived security threats, and if this happens she may have little or no recourse.</u> ... For some victims, possible firing is not as much of a deterrent to disclosure as it first seems; if she knows she will be forced to quit or be fired if she cannot get time off or changes at

work, she may have little to lose. Moreover, increasingly, employers are sympathetic and want to be supportive of victims of domestic violence in their workplace. Nonetheless, she needs to understand the risk. Other possible downsides of disclosure include potential pressure from her employer to obtain a protective order (which may not be the best course of action for her at that time) or the possibility of her situation becoming common knowledge at work.

After discussing these issues, your client may tell you that she does not want anyone at work to know about the violence. Many victims value their workplace as a place (often the only place) where they are not identified as domestic violence victims. Deborah A. Widiss and Robin R. Runge, *Advocating for the Employment Rights of Victims of Domestic Violence and Sexual Assault*, COMMISSION ON DOMESTIC VIOLENCE QUARTERLY E–NEWSLETTER, AMERICAN BAR ASSOCIATION (Spring 2007).

3. **Statutes Providing a Measure of Protection to Victims of Domestic Violence.** Over half the states provide that employees who participate in criminal trials cannot be fired or disciplined by their employers for so doing. Arkansas's statute is a little broader than many of the others in protecting not only employees who participate in a trial at the prosecutor's summons, but also those who participate in a criminal proceeding for their own safety. Ark. Stat. § 16–9–1105 (2005). In Alaska, an employer who violates the applicable statute may be liable for actual damages and for punitives at three times actual damages. Alaska Stat. § 12.61.017 (2005). In other states, the penalty for violation is a misdemeanor, Mich. Comp. Laws § 780.790 (1998), while in still other states, the penalties are unstated, Colo. Rev. Stat. § 24–4.1–303 (2006). Although these statutes are helpful, they will not protect an employee who needs to take time away from work to obtain a civil restraining order or to see a doctor or talk with a child's teacher. Several states have broader statutes that would protect the victim in these kinds of situations. Calif. Labor Code § 230 (2004) (employee must use sick leave or vacation or compensatory time); Colo. Rev. Stat. § 24–34–402.7 (2006) (up to three days leave annually); 820 Ill. Comp. Stat. 180/1 *et seq.* (2006) (up to 12 weeks of leave annually.)

The federal Family and Medical Leave Act (FMLA), 29 U.S.C.A. 2611 *et seq.* (2004), provides eligible employees with up to twelve weeks of unpaid leave to attend to their own or their children's serious health conditions. This could be of assistance to victims of domestic violence. The Alaska Supreme Court recently held the Anchorage Police Department violated the FMLA by denying leave to a victim of domestic violence who was suffering from post-traumatic stress disorder. *Municipality of Anchorage v. Gregg*, 101 P.3d 181 (2004).

4. **Unemployment Compensation.** State unemployment insurance programs generally provide a limited period of benefits for eligible employees who have either been dismissed from their jobs without misconduct on their parts or who have had to resign for good cause. As of early 2006, twenty-eight states and the District of Columbia provided benefits to otherwise eligible employees who were either fired or had to quit because of

domestic violence. John E. Matejkovic, *Which Suit Would You Like*, 33 Cap. U. L. Rev. 409 (2004); Employment and Housing Rights for Victims of Domestic Violence Project, Legal Momentum, www.legalmomentum.org. However, these employees would need to show that they are available and actively seeking work in order to obtain benefits. Some states define suitable work to mean only full-time work. L'Nayim A. Shuman–Austin, *Is Leaving Work to Obtain Safety "Good Cause" to Leave Employment?* 23 Seattle U. L. Rev. 797 (2000). Why might these last requirements be particularly difficult for victims of domestic violence?

5. **Labor Grievance Processes.** Currently a small percentage of employees work in unionized workplaces. These usually have grievance processes established as a result of collective bargaining between the union and the employer. Frequently these grievance procedures call for an arbitrator to make the ultimate decision on whether an employee has been treated fairly. What concerns would you have about the arbitration process if you represented an employee who had been dismissed either because domestic violence was interfering with her job performance or because she had attempted to defend herself against violence on the job in contravention of the employer's policies against fighting or weapons in the workplace? Jennifer Atterbury noted that arbitrators and unions, like employers, are often uninformed about the effects of domestic violence on employees. She warns that although employees were frequently reinstated by arbitration decisions, the employees rarely received full back pay awards. See Jennifer Atterbury, *Employment Protection and Domestic Violence: Addressing Abuse in the Labor Grievance Process*, 1998 J. Disp. Resol. 165 (1998).

6. **Welfare–to–Work Requirements.** In 1996, Congress passed the Personal Responsibility and Work Opportunity Reconciliation Act (PRWORA). It replaced the earlier program of cash grants to support individuals and families in need with block grants to states that could then provide the support to families. The block grants to the states came with requirements that the states move recipients off of welfare and into the workforce within five years. Congress understood that welfare recipients who had been abused by intimate partners might face particular barriers in moving to employment. Thus, it created the Family Violence Option (FVO) that would allow states to create exceptions to the rules for victims of domestic violence. As of 2004, 41 states and the District of Columbia had adopted the FVO. Legal Momentum, *Family Violence Option: State by State Summary,* avail. at www.legalmomentum.org. States that adopt the FVO are required to screen all applicants to identify domestic violence victims, provide appropriate referrals for the identified clients, and waive any requirements with which the client cannot comply because of the domestic violence. These might include the time limits on receipt of welfare, the requirements related to child support enforcement, and the work requirements, among others.

Early studies of the implementation of the FVO indicate that waivers were granted to one-half of 1% of participants in one Texas program and to 5% in N.Y. Considering that between 20% and 32% of welfare recipients report current abuse and between 50% and 65% report current or past abuse, these numbers appear very low. See Taryn Lindhorst and Julianna D. Padgett, *Disjunctures for Women and Frontline Workers: Implementation of the Family Violence Option*, 79 Soc. Serv. Rev. 405 (2005); Judy L. Postmus, *Battered and on Welfare: The Experiences of Women with the Family Violence Option*, 31 J. Sociology & Soc. Welf. 113 (2004).

It may be that the FVO has not been very successful at identifying victims of intimate violence and providing them with waivers because the objective of the 1996 welfare reform was to move recipients off of welfare and into work settings. Welfare case workers will be evaluated on how well they achieve this and are encouraged in numerous ways to ensure that the transition occurs. Every waiver that they give to victims of domestic violence will work against this goal of reducing the number of people receiving welfare funds. Perhaps because granting waivers is not a high priority, forms relating to domestic violence are complicated and difficult for recipients with low literacy levels to read; furthermore, case workers often do not ask about domestic violence because they think it is up to the clients to disclose its presence and because the workers have high case loads and very little time with each client. In addition, clients are often unwilling to disclose the violence because it is uncomfortable and demeaning to do so, because they worry that confidentiality will not be maintained and the abuser will be angry upon learning that they have told someone, and because disclosing that they have a relationship with a man may cause their benefits to be reduced. Even when clients do disclose the violence, they often do not receive waivers of burdensome requirements. Welfare workers often think the clients are undeserving of the assistance and do not believe them. Taryn Lindhorst and Julianna Padgett, authors of one study, found, "Some workers expressed the belief that battered women should demonstrate their commitment to ending the abusive relationship before they became eligible for assistance through the welfare department." Indeed, they quote one worker who said, "I think if they are in a shelter and they are fleeing, that's a legitimate exemption. I don't think that everybody that just comes in here and says they are a victim of domestic violence should be exempt." Taryn Lindhorst and Julianna D. Padgett, *Disjunctures for Women and Frontline Workers: Implementation of the Family Violence Option*, 79 Soc. Serv. Rev. 405 (2005). See also Judy L. Postmus, *Battered and on Welfare: The Experiences of Women with the Family Violence Option*, 31 J. Sociology & Soc. Welf. 113 (2004).

Do you think the PRWORA work requirement may have the effect of increasing the risks of violence for some domestic violence victims?

Employer and Professional Discipline of Abusers

As employers and professional organizations become more sensitive to issues of partner violence, and more willing to participate in broader societal responses, some have focused not only on providing assistance to victims, but also on disciplining perpetrators. The easiest case is presented by the abusive employee who is harassing a co-worker on the job. Here the employer's responsibility is clear, and failure to act, as we have seen, may expose the employer to substantial liability, whether under a workers' compensation scheme, through tort litigation, or through a Title VII action. On the other hand, employers must still be attentive to their employees' rights. The issues are more complex if the abuse is perpetrated by the employee outside the workplace. Of course, many abusers, like those they abuse, have employment at-will contracts. However, a batterer may still try to bring a variety of actions against an employer who has dismissed him. In the following excerpt, Fredrica Lehrman summarizes the possible challenges an employee might bring against the employer who disciplines him for abuse either at work or at home.

Fredrica Lehrman

Domestic Violence Practice and Procedure

§§ 10:26–10:30 (Supp. 2005).

Employers who act rashly against employees suspected of engaging in acts of domestic violence can find themselves liable to these employees. Employees discharged or disciplined for committing acts of domestic violence may attempt to sue the employer for any number of torts, including defamation, wrongful discharge, [and] invasion of privacy. The employer may be liable under the Americans with Disabilities Act. Employers should take appropriate sanctions against employees who perpetrate acts of domestic violence; however, employers need to respect the legal rights of these employees.

Defamation

An employer who accuses an employee suspected of committing domestic violence [of being] a "wifebeater" ... may find itself liable for defamation. Employee meetings, internal memos, conversations with clients or customers, and post-employment references all can be the backdrop of a defamatory statement. To prove liability, the defamed employee must show:

1. The employer made a false and defamatory statement about the employee;

2. An unprivileged publication to a third party;

3. Fault amounting to at least negligence on the part of the publisher; and

4. Either actionability of the statement regardless of special harm or the existence of special harm caused by the publication.

To be published, a statement simply must be made to a third party. The statement published by the employer must be false. Truth is an absolute defense to a claim of defamation. However, the publication of a truthful statement can lead to lawsuits under other tort theories, including intentional infliction of emotional distress, invasion of privacy, or interference with contractual relations.

Employers have a qualified privilege in the area of defamation. This qualified privilege allows an employer to publish a false and defamatory statement about an employee if the employer can show that the statement:

1. Was made with a good faith belief in its truth;

2. Served a business interest or had a business purpose;

3. Was limited to a business interest or purpose to be served; and

4. Was made on a proper occasion.

Additionally, the employer must properly verify the facts underlying the defamatory statement. If an employer abuses its qualified privilege, it is likely to lose the privilege. Thus, the employer must keep confidential all inquiries into an employee's possible commission of domestic violence, informing other employees on a need-to-know basis only.

Some jurisdictions have recognized the tort of "self-defamation" or "compelled defamation." Compelled defamation arises when an employee is discharged on false or defamatory ground and must explain the grounds for termination to potential future employers. In these jurisdictions, an employer can find itself liable when it knew or should have foreseen that the discharged employee would be compelled to repeat the defamatory statement.

Wrongful Discharge

An employee who is fired because he or she committed an act of domestic violence may argue that he or she was wrongfully discharged.... A wrongful discharge claim can arise when an employee is fired in contravention of public policy; a covenant of good faith and fair dealing; or promises made orally, through a course of performance, or in employer policies or handbooks.

Invasion of Privacy

An employer who investigates charges that an employee has engaged in acts of domestic violence should do so with the employee's privacy rights in mind. State courts have recognized four different types of invasion of privacy torts:

- appropriation of another's name or likeness;
- false light publicity;
- public disclosure of private facts;
- intrusion upon seclusion.

The first type ... will probably not be at issue in the case of an employee discharged for committing an act of domestic violence. The others, however, may be implicated.

False light publicity is similar to defamation. A plaintiff in a defamation action seeks to vindicate his or her reputation; however, in a false light invasion of privacy tort, a plaintiff seeks to protect his or her right to be left alone. An employer can be held liable for placing an employee in a false light if the false light into which the employee was placed was highly offensive to a reasonable person, and the employer acted in a reckless disregard of the falseness of the publicized matter. To be actionable, the statement or statements in question must be communicated to the public at large so as to become a matter of public knowledge.

An employer also could be sued for public disclosure of private facts if the matter publicized would be highly offensive to a reasonable person and is not of legitimate concern to a reasonable person. As with the false light tort, this tort requires a public disclosure, not a mere communication to a third party, as in defamation.

Intrusion upon seclusion, the final type of privacy tort, occurs when one intentionally intrudes, physically or otherwise, on the seclusion of another, or on the other's private affairs or concerns, if the intrusion would be offensive to a reasonable person. As with defamation, an employer has a qualified privilege in privacy tort cases.

Americans with Disabilities Act

The Americans with Disabilities Act (ADA) prohibits employers from discriminating against a qualified individual with a disability on the basis of the disability. An employee who commits an act of domestic violence against a coworker or other intimate partner may claim that such behavior is the result of a mental illness. Mental illnesses, such as depression, can qualify as disabilities for the purposes of the ADA. However, the ADA does not require the employment of a disabled individual if that individual poses a direct threat to the health and safety of others. Therefore, an employer must evaluate carefully the employee's conduct and determine appropriate remedial measures to take in light of a claim of disability. If there is no direct threat, the employer may be required to make reasonable accommodations for the mentally ill employee. Examples of such accommodations include providing for leave or flexibility in scheduling, job restructuring, part-time work, working from home, reassignment to a vacant position, [or] providing for or monitoring medication.

NOTES AND QUESTIONS

1. **Abusers' Claims of "Privacy."** Clearly the best protection for an employer is to ensure that any information about an employee's abusive behavior that is shared with others inside or outside the workplace is accurate, and that the information is disseminated only to those who have a need to know. Beyond these parameters, to what extent do you think an employee should be able to claim that his abusive behavior outside the workplace is a "private" matter? Is the claim that the abusive behavior is "private" based on its lack of relevance, arguably, to the employee's job performance or on the fact that until the information was publicized by the employer, no one in the employee's work environment knew about it? Does it make a difference whether there were witnesses to any of the incidents of abuse, whether police reports exist, or whether a protection order has issued? In other words, are there situations in which it could be said that an individual has waived his privacy rights by drawing public attention to his abuse? Or is the stronger argument that the lesson of the last twenty-

five years is precisely that domestic violence is no longer a private issue, even when it happens behind closed doors?

2.   **Dismissal of Police Officer for Domestic Violence.** In *Chesser v. City of Hammond*, 725 N.E.2d 926 (Ind. Ct. App. 2000), the Court of Appeals of Indiana upheld the dismissal of a police officer for abuse of his wife. At the time of the incident Chesser was on probation following a citizen complaint about his use of violent force, and had been ordered not to violate any rules or regulations of the police department. During that period, however, police responded to a report of domestic violence at his home, and found his wife with scratches and red marks on her neck and lumps on her head. Chesser was dismissed even though the charge of domestic battery against him was dropped when Mrs. Chesser chose not to proceed, and even though she testified at his disciplinary hearing that she had attacked him, and inflicted her injuries on herself. The court found that Mr. Chesser had been accorded due process, and that the evidence was sufficient to support his dismissal.

3.   **Using the ADA as a Batterer's Defense.** Lehrman briefly discusses the possibility that batterers might use the ADA to defend themselves against employers' disciplinary actions subsequent to their abusing co-employees.

To claim protection under the ADA, 42 U.S.C. § 12101 et seq., courts require an employee to prove that he or she is or is perceived as (1) disabled, (2) qualified to perform his or her job with or without reasonable accommodation, and (3) that the disability was the cause of termination or other disciplinary action by the employer. *Doyal v. Oklahoma Heart, Inc.*, 213 F.3d 492 (10th Cir. 2000). A disability under the ADA is "a physical or mental impairment that substantially limits one or more of the [individual's] major life activities." 42 U.S.C. § 12101(2). A batterer who had been disciplined by his employer for abusive actions toward another employee might try to claim the protection of the ADA if he were depressed, had a personality disorder, or some other condition that qualified as a "disability." A batterer is unlikely to seek accommodation under the ADA unless disciplined by the employer since this would require him not only to recognize that he is a batterer, but to willingly share this fact with his employer.

Although the ADA does not require an employer to retain an employee who is an immediate danger to others, an abuser could claim that if he were given reasonable accommodation—which the ADA requires employers to provide to disabled employees—the threat could be eliminated. Such accommodation might include transferring the employee to a different department or shift or granting a reduced workload. 29 C.F.R. § 1630.2(*o*)(2) (2006). For an accommodation to be reasonable, it must not pose an undue economic hardship on the employer or have a significant negative impact on coworkers. 29 C.F.R. § 1630.2(p) (2006).

Not every medical condition that negatively affects an employee's life counts as a disability under the ADA. In order for there to be a "disability," the impairment must significantly limit a major life activity. "Major life activities" include such functions as interacting successfully with others and engaging in sexual relations. Even if a condition, such as depression or a personality disorder, impairs these major life activities, the abuser must still show that his ability to engage in these activities is "substantially" limited. In *McAlindin v. County of San Diego*, 192 F.3d 1226 (9th Cir. 1999), the court held that the activity of interacting with others would only be considered significantly impaired by a strong showing of antisocial behavior such as frequent hostility or complete social withdrawal. However, the court in *Jacques v. DiMarzio, Inc.*, 386 F.3d 192 (2d Cir. 2004), criticized the Ninth Circuit's approach as rewarding the most dangerous employees with the highest level of job security. Which court has the more persuasive argument? Since activities such as engaging in sexual relations usually have nothing to do with employment qualifications, is it fair for a batterer to claim protection under the ADA for such a disability? Could it equally be argued that abusing one's wife/girlfriend/co-employee has little to do with the job and therefore should not serve as a basis for disciplinary action? Is the batterer's defense in line with the purposes for which the Act was enacted?

4. **Attorney Discipline for Intimate Partner Abuse.** In recent years state bar associations and state courts have been asked with increasing frequency to discipline lawyers who abuse their partners, and lawyers have been subject to a wide range of sanctions, from reprimand to suspension to disbarment. In these cases, the attorneys often claim that their conduct should not be subject to discipline because it is "private." In one Maryland case, in which the disciplined attorney had a sixteen year history of abusing his wife, the state Supreme Court said:

> [Respondent argues] what happened behind closed doors has had no impact on his fitness as an attorney.... Rather than being related to his law practice, involving a client or directly implicating the traits so closely associated with the legal profession—honesty, trustworthiness, truthfulness and reliability—or fitness to practice law, the respondent's conduct consisted of abusing physically, verbally, and psychologically, his wife and his children. In other words, what is involved in this case is domestic violence. We have not heretofore been presented with the question of the appropriate discipline when an attorney has engaged in such misconduct.... It is patent ... that an attorney's conduct in engaging in spousal abuse, domestic violence, is viewed by the courts addressing the issue as prejudicial to the administration of justice and maybe even as impacting adversely [on] that attorney's fitness to practice law.... [I]t is a morally reprehensible crime to engage in domestic abuse assault....
>
> [U]nder the circumstances, an attorney, an officer of the court, who has committed acts of violence, to some of which he pled guilty, on both his wife and children, contrary to the policy of this State, which abhors such acts, and violated court ordered probation, at the very least, engage[s] in conduct that is prejudicial to the administration of justice.... [T]he appropriate sanction to be imposed is disbarment. *Attorney Grievance Commission of Maryland v. Painter*, 739 A.2d 24 (1999).

Some courts have imposed significantly lesser sentences. In *Matter of Margrabia*, 695 A.2d 1378 (N.J.1997), an attorney was suspended for two years rather than being disbarred, even though he had violated the protection order taken out by his wife more than fifteen times, served several jail terms for those violations, and on at least one occasion threatened to break down her door and shoot her. One important issue in suspension cases is whether the court imposes suspension with an automatic reinstatement once the period has run, or continues to monitor the situation, requiring the attorney to petition for reinstatement and to demonstrate that he is no longer abusing his partner, or that he has completed a batterers' treatment program. This was the approach taken by the Colorado Supreme Court in *People v. Musick*, 960 P.2d 89 (Colo. 1998).

CHAPTER FIFTEEN

Domestic Violence, Immigration and Asylum

Introduction

Living in the United States as a battered woman is difficult. As you have seen throughout this book, immigrants face a multitude of challenges, from language barriers to cultural beliefs and traditions that make leaving abusive relationships even more difficult. Living in the United States as a battered woman who is not a citizen is even more challenging. An immigrant living in the United States without documentation—passport, visa, work permit, United States birth certificate etc.—constantly faces the threat of deportation. If she is undocumented, she must guard not only against potential deportation, but also against the danger posed by her abuser. If she was abused in her native country, seeking asylum in the United States may be the only way to avoid returning to the abuse. Furthermore, as Lesyle Orloff and her colleagues have argued, "Immigrant women who encounter language barriers, cultural differences, and stereotyping by mainstream society are often invisible to the anti-domestic violence movement. The pervasive lack of understanding of the life experiences of battered immigrant women by the systems designed to protect battered women and immigrant victims greatly reduces the likelihood that immigrant victims will be able to escape the violence in their lives." Leslye E. Orloff, Mary Ann Dutton, Giselle Aguilar Hass, and Nawal Ammar, *Battered Immigrant Women's Willingness to Call for Help and Police Response,* 13 UCLA Women's L.J. 43 (2003).

This chapter focuses on the specific legal challenges that non-citizen victims of domestic violence and women who seek asylum in the United States face. This area of work is highly specialized as it can involve intricate federal administrative law, as well as other areas, such as constitutional, criminal, and family law.

The first section on immigration briefly reviews many of the social and barriers that immigrant women face that we have already touched upon in other chapters. The section describes the current status of immigration law. We next turn to the Violence Against Women Act and its efforts to remedy the problems created by the immigration system. In particular, we focus on the ways in which battered immigrant women can petition courts for immigration status without the assistance of their abusers. We then examine the problem of trafficking, and how many of its victims also face intimate violence.

The second section of this chapter looks at issues related to asylum. Domestic violence is a significant problem world-wide. Yet, many countries do little, if anything, to protect women. Thus, many women seek asylum in the United States. We survey the current legal barriers these women face and ask what the legal standards govern the grant of asylum ought to be. As in other areas in the law related to domestic violence, think about how some legal strategies, such as VAWA petitions, make visible victims who might otherwise have remained invisible.

A.   THE IMMIGRANT VICTIM OF DOMESTIC VIOLENCE

To effectively represent a battered woman, advocates must be cognizant of the legal, social, familial, and economic barriers their clients face. Every client is unique. But immigrant battered woman often present problems that an advocate might not face when representing other victims of domestic violence. The following excerpt by Julie Dinnerstein reminds us of some barriers that are specific to battered immigrants.

Julie Dinnerstein
Working with Immigrant Victims of Domestic Violence, in Immigration Remedies for Domestic Violence Victims: VAWA Self–Petitions and Battered Spouse Waivers

SANCTUARY FOR FAMILIES CENTER FOR BATTERED WOMEN'S LEGAL SERVICES (2006).

Working with immigrant victims of domestic violence presents a series of challenges. Battered immigrant women may fear deportation more than they fear their batterers, and fear of deportation means that a battered immigrant woman may initially fear you, the service provider and representative of the outside world, as much as, or even more than, the batterer himself. Hand in hand with fear is a lack of knowledge about immigration law, about non-immigration-related supports and protection that may be available to a battered immigrant woman and her children (shelter, counseling, police protection, public assistance, etc.), and about her own immigration status.

Your work with an immigrant victim of domestic violence, as with any victim of domestic violence, must begin with her trust. You can do so by both listening to her concerns and priorities, which may not be the same as your own, and by letting her know that you are there to help her find solutions that work for her, not to tell her what to do or to contact immigration authorities. Understanding both common barriers faced by immigrant victims fleeing domestic violence and possible immigration law remedies and resources will put you in the best position to serve your immigrant clients.

Economic Barriers

Lack of money is a primary reason immigrant domestic violence victims cannot escape. According to the National Organization for Women Legal Defense and Education Fund (NOW LDEF, now known as Legal

Momentum) study, 67.1% of battered immigrants (as compared with 40% of US citizens) cite lack of money as a reason they stay with their abusers. Immigrant (as opposed to US citizen) victims of domestic violence are particularly vulnerable to stay with the batterer because they are:

- More likely to have limited or no English proficiency;
- Less likely to have immigration status and thus less likely to be authorized to work legally in the United States;
- More likely to be ineligible for public benefits or, if eligible, fear immigration consequences of seeking public benefits and face wrongful denials of public benefits;
- More likely to be rejected by their community for leaving;
- Less likely to have back-up child care from friends and family; and
- Less likely to have education, training or work experience necessary for employment.

Fear of Consequences in the Home Country

Immigrants leave friends and family members behind when they [come] to the United States, and abusive partners may well have long arms that reach all the way back to their home country. Even if an immigrant victim of domestic violence is able to find adequate protection from her abuser here in the United States, chances are slim that she can protect her children, siblings, parents and friends back home from an abusive partner who has connections in their home country or an ability and will to travel there. Realize that while you are engaged in safety planning for the woman sitting in your office, she may be calculating the safety risks for friends and family back home.

Fear of Losing Custody of the Children

Immigrants often fear that if they separate from an abusive partner, they will lose their children. In many countries, when a couple splits, children, either by custom or law, go to their father, not the mother. Regardless of the rules and practices in the home country, many immigrants assume that their abusive partners will be awarded custody because of their superior command of English, superior economic resources, stronger family and community supports, and above all, immigration status. Immigrant victims are often told (and just as often believe) that judges adjudicating custody will have them deported and that they will be banished while their children remain behind with their abusers.

Fear of Deportation

Woven in the fabric that noncitizen victims of violence experience, is the terror at the prospect of deportation. Many noncitizens cannot distinguish between immigration officials and other government officials, particularly those who wear uniforms (the police) or robes (the judges) or work at imposing buildings (the courts). While the risk to domestic violence victims of government officials alerting federal immigration authorities about presence varies from location to location and is quite limited in New York City, the fear that all government officials are in collusion to deport immigrants is real and overwhelming to the vast majority of noncitizen victims of domestic violence. When serving this population, it is critical to know whether government officials in your area are likely to report suspected immigration law violators to the federal immigration authorities. . . .

NOTES AND QUESTIONS

1. **Documentation.** The barriers that an undocumented battered woman faces are often lessened once the victim is able to secure documentation. An undocumented battered woman can secure lawful permanent residency status in one of several ways. First, if the undocumented victim is married to her abuser, the victim can potentially obtain lawful permanent residency, provided her abuser is a citizen or lawful permanent resident of the United States, under the Violence Against Women Act. Second, an undocumented victim may secure lawful permanent residency if she assists the authorities in prosecuting her batterer for trafficking, or more generally, a criminal act under the Trafficking Victims Protection Act (TVPA), passed in 2000 to protect trafficking victims by providing them with immigration relief. Trafficking Victims Protection Act of 2000, Pub. L. No. 106–386, div. A, 114 Stat. 1466 (codified as amended at 22 U.S.C. §§ 7101–7110 (2000)). Third, there can also be Cancellation of Removal. The specific requirements of each of these provisions are discussed below.

2. **Immigrants and Domestic Homicide.** A recent study in New York City found that 51% of intimate partner homicide victims were foreign-born, while 45% were born in the United States. Femicide in New York City: 1995–2002. New York City Department of Health and Mental Hygeine, October 2004, available at http://www.ci.nyc.ny.us/html/doh/html/public/press04/pr145–1022.html. This data suggests that immigrant women may be at much higher risk of homicide because of the multitude of barriers that they face when trying to leave a violent intimate relationship.

3. **Shelters and Immigrant Women.** Seeking shelter is often difficult for immigrant women because of language barriers and other concerns. Many battered immigrant women fear that shelters will notify government officials of their immigration status. Also, some shelters are under the mistaken assumption that if they serve undocumented victims, they risk losing federal funding. However, under federal law, non-profit charitable organizations are not required to inquire into immigration status or ensure that applicants are "qualified aliens' before providing them with services." Furthermore, shelters that refuse to offer services to battered immigrant women may be in violation of Title VIII, which prohibits discrimination on the basis of immigrant status. The 2005 reauthorization of VAWA further strengthened these laws by prohibiting the Department of Homeland Security from seizing immigrants from shelters and by providing greater confidentiality protections. For an overview of these issues see Leslye E. Orloff and Rachel Little, *Somewhere to Turn: Making Domestic Violence Services Available to Battered Immigrant Women. A "How–To" Manual for Battered Women's Advocates and Service Providers*, AYUDA INC. (1999),

available at http://www.vawnet.org/DomesticViolence/ServicesAndProgram Dev/ServiceProvAndProg/BIW99toc.php#toctp. See also *Guidance on Inquiries to Immigration & Citizenship Status, Access to HHS–Funded Services for Immigrant Survivors of Domestic Violence, Office of Civil Rights Fact Sheet*, January 2001, available at http://www.hhs.gov/ocr/immigration/ bifsltr.html; *National Task Force to End Sexual and Domestic Violence Against Women, Violence Against Women Act 2005, Title VIII–Immigration Issues* (2005), available at http://www.endabuse.org/vawa/factsheets/ Immigration.pdf.

4. **Legal Services for Battered Immigrant Women.** Most legal aid offices are funded by the Legal Services Corporation (LSC), a private, non-profit organization that allocates federal funds to organizations that represent indigent clients in civil matters. LSC has placed numerous restrictions on the ability of recipients of its funds to represent certain categories of immigrants. These restrictions have made it very difficult for many battered immigrant women to receive legal services despite the fact that VAWA does provide federal funds for the legal representation of battered immigrant women. For an overview of this issue see E. Lesleigh Varner, *Funding Opportunities for Legal Services Programs Offer Hope for Battered Immigrants: A Call for Strides in Community Collaborations*, 10 ILSA J. INT'L & COMP. L. 179 (2003).

The Contours of Current Immigration Law

The mechanisms for obtaining lawful permanent residency under VAWA and the TVPA are not without limitations. Each element a petitioner must satisfy to secure lawful permanent residency under VAWA and the TVPA represents a hurdle, some more significant than others, for undocumented battered women. In the following article Linda Kelly provides a brief history of immigration law as it relates to battered immigrant women.

Linda Kelly

Stories From the Front: Seeking Refuge for Battered Immigrants in the Violence Against Women Act

92 N.W.U. L. REV. 665 (1998).

By incorporating the doctrines of coverture and chastisement, immigration law has been recognized to perpetuate the no longer viable assumption that a wife belongs to her husband. Early immigration law allowed otherwise inadmissible female aliens who were married to U.S. citizens or residents to enter the United States because legal provisions exempted them from various grounds of exclusion. By contrast, no parallel exceptions existed for the foreign-born husbands of female citizens. In fact, a U.S. female citizen's marriage to an alien male was an expatriating act. Legally stripping the woman of her U.S. citizenship, the law presumed she would follow her husband to his country . . . .

In 1986, the Immigration Marriage Fraud Amendments (IMFA) strengthened the power of the U.S. citizen or resident spouse. Due to widespread legislative and administrative fear of marriage-based fraud, IMFA mandated that the spouse of a U.S. citizen or resident married for less than two years initially be provided with "conditional residence." In such status, the alien is considered to be a permanent resident for virtually all purposes and is entitled to all the benefits and privileges that accompany residency, such as the right to work, live legally in the United States, and travel abroad and re-enter. However, within the 90–day period immediately preceding the second anniversary of being accorded conditional residency, the immigrant and his or her spouse must jointly petition for the removal of the conditional status in order for the alien to maintain permanent residency. Both spouses also may be required to attend another interview.

As IMFA complicated an already burdensome system, the alien became more dependent upon his or her spouse. Under IMFA, the petitioning spouse was now required to execute numerous affirmative duties to secure his or her spouse's residency: complete the initial petition, attend the preliminary interview, sign and participate in the completion of the petition to remove conditions on residency, and attend any required second interview. Failure to cooperate in any of these critical steps could result in the denial of residency and ultimate deportation for the alien spouse.

Driven by stereotypical images of devious male aliens, rather than a realistic portrayal of the female aliens affected by this legislation, Congress failed to realize the dangerous consequences of its 1986 amendments. In legislating a two-year trial period, Congress ignored the control IMFA provided to the abusive, petitioning husband. Caught in limbo, many battered women were reluctant to leave their abusive spouses, as without their husbands' legal assistance the women risked losing permanent residency and facing deportation.

As accurately told by Kevin Johnson, "IMFA spoke in gender-neutral terms but had gender-specific impacts." Responding to such criticisms, Congress ameliorated IMFA by providing an exception to joint filing for battered spouses through the Immigration Act of 1990. Upon proof that the "qualifying marriage" had been entered into in "good faith" and that the alien spouse or child was "battered or subject to extreme cruelty," the alien spouse can now have the conditions on her residency removed without the cooperation of the U.S. citizen spouse.

The 1990 Act did not, however, extract all the threads of coverture so inextricably woven into the fabric of U.S. immigration law. Indeed, after the 1990 Act, the alien spouse still had to depend upon her lawful spouse in order to initially acquire residency through the marriage. The domestic violence exception created by the 1990 Act only provided relief to battered immigrants who have successfully obtained conditional residency. Such provisions, therefore, did nothing to help undocumented battered women whose lawful husbands had not yet petitioned for their residency. Undocumented and beaten, these women remained hostages to their abusive spouses, choosing physical and emotional battery over the greater threat of deportation that faced them if they left.

Passed in 1994, the Violence Against Women Act is the culmination of efforts to fill the void remaining in the law's commitment to battered immigrants. It was not, however, until 1996, when the Immigration and Naturalization Service (INS) [currently the United States Citizen and Immigration Service (USCIS)] finally released its administrative regulations, that the first VAWA self-petitioning cases were adjudicated.

The two-year delay in the implementation of VAWA was met with mixed feelings of relief and resentment by battered immigrants and their advocates. Such ambivalence foreshadowed the difficulties to come. While some of VAWA's requirements are difficult for the victim of domestic violence to document, others can be impossible. Such inherent problems in the legislation and administrative regulations do not facilitate a woman's efforts to leave her abusive spouse. In practice, the law therefore fails to provide a realistic alternative to more than a handful of battered immigrant women.

NOTES AND QUESTIONS

1. **Immigrant Women and Welfare Reforms.** Public benefits can be a critical safety net for abused women and children. For a discussion on the ability of battered immigrants to access public benefits and the challenges that they face in doing so, see Leslye E. Orloff, *Lifesaving Welfare Safety Net Access for Battered Immigrant Women and Children: Accomplishments and Next Steps*, 7 WM. & MARY J. WOMEN & L. 597 (2001).

Violence Against Women Act Immigration Petitions

There are three provisions in the Violence Against Women Act that create special routes to immigration for undocumented victims of battering. First, there is the VAWA Self–Petition (INA § 204(a)(1)). Second, there is the VAWA Cancellation of Removal (INA § 240A(b)(2)). Third, there is the Battered Spouse Waiver (INA § 216(c)(4)(C)). The section that follows details the eligibility requirements for each of the three provisions.

1. **VAWA Self–Petition (INA § 204(a)(1)).** In order to be eligible for a self-petition, the petitioner must satisfy six requirements. First, the petitioner must show she has a qualifying relationship with her abuser. Because self-petitions can be filed by individuals who are abused by a parent, child, or marital partner, for a battered spouse to satisfy this first element, she must show that she is married to her abuser and explain why she believes that marriage is valid. Second, the petitioner must show that her abuser is either a legal permanent resident or a citizen of the United States. Third, the petitioner must show that she has suffered abuse. This element can be satisfied by a showing of either battery or extreme cruelty. Fourth, the petitioner must show that she has good moral character. This element is generally evaluated with an eye to the petitioner's criminal record. Significantly, criminal violations found to be related to the abuse will be disregarded. Fifth, the petitioner must show she married her abuser in good faith. Specifically, the petitioner must demonstrate that she did not marry her spouse for the sole purpose of gaining entrance into the United

States. Finally, the petitioner must show that she currently resides in the United States. If the abuser works abroad, the petitioner must show that (a) the abuser works for the United States or (b) the abuser is a member of the United States military or (c) the abuser subjected the petitioner to violence in the United States.

2. **VAWA Cancellation of Removal (INA § 240A(b)(2)).** Where the petitioner has already been placed in deportation proceedings, the only option available to her under VAWA is to apply for a Cancellation of Removal. To obtain legal permanent residency in this way, the petitioner must satisfy the first five elements required under the self petition— qualifying relationship with a United States citizen, marriage to a legal permanent resident or citizen of the United States, battery or extreme cruelty, good moral character and good faith marriage. In addition, the petitioner must satisfy two additional elements. First, she must show that leaving the United States would subject her or her children to "extreme hardship." This can be proven in one of four ways: (a) petitioner needs access to US courts to obtain criminal prosecutions against her abuser, child support or custody, or to enforce any protective orders; (b) petitioner needs access to social, medical, mental health and other services for herself or her child that are not reasonably accessible in her home country; (c) the laws and customs of petitioner's home country would penalize or punish the petitioner or her children for being victims of abuse, leaving the relationship, seeking a divorce, or for any other actions she took in ending the abuse; (d) petitioner would not be protected from her abuser or his family and friends in her home country; and/or (e) any other justifications petitioner may be able to use to show extreme hardship. Second, the petitioner must show three years of continuous physical presence in the United States prior to application.

3. **The Battered Spouse Waiver (INA § 216(c)(4)(C)).** Battered immigrants who are married to citizen abusers generally have conditional lawful permanent residency. Such immigrants are at the mercy of their abusive spouse, who alone has the power to file papers to change that residency status from conditional to permanent. Often, abusers will use the fact that they hold the key to their victim's immigration status as a method of maintaining power and control. The Battered Spouse Waiver enables these immigrants to remove the condition on their residency status and become lawful permanent residents. The criteria for this waiver is the same as the criteria under a VAWA self-petition.

NOTES AND QUESTIONS

1. **VAWA Process.** All VAWA self-petitions and cancellations of removal are filed at the Citizenship and Immigration Services Center (USCIS), formerly the Immigration and Naturalization Service (INS) in Vermont. Thus, applicants have no opportunity to be interviewed by the decision-maker. However, the advantage of centralized processing is that Vermont has a special group of officers who receive training on domestic violence.

2. **What Does Extreme Cruelty Mean?** The requirement of either "battery or extreme cruelty" under the VAWA self-petition and cancellation of removal petition has recently been broadly interpreted in a decision by the Ninth Circuit in *Hernandez v. Ashcroft*, 345 F.3d 824 (9th Cir. 2003). When *Hernandez v. Ashcroft* was decided, VAWA required a petitioner to demonstrate that she had suffered battery or extreme cruelty within the United States. Shortly after the *Hernandez* decision, the requirement that the petitioner must suffer battery or extreme cruelty within the United States was eliminated. Now, a petitioner is able to satisfy the battery or extreme cruelty prong of her petition regardless of where the battery or extreme cruelty has taken place.

In *Hernandez v. Ashcroft*, the only contact the petitioner, Laura Hernandez, had with her abuser, Refugio Gonzales, while the petitioner was in the United States was in the form of phone calls. Specifically, Gonzales called Hernandez from Mexico, imploring her to return home, after Hernandez had fled to the United States following a particularly brutal physical attack committed by Gonzales. There was a long history of physical violence committed by Gonzales against Hernandez while the two were in Mexico. But at the time of this decision, the court could only look to acts of battery or extreme cruelty that took place within the United States. Thus, the controlling question in the case was whether phone calls from Gonzales in Mexico to Hernandez in the United States constituted a form of extreme cruelty. The court found that they did. In relevant part, the court wrote:

> Understood in light of the familiar dynamics of violent relationships, Refugio's seemingly reasonable actions take on a sinister cast. Following Refugio's brutal and potentially deadly beating, Hernandez fled her job, home, country, and family. Hernandez believed that if she had not fled, Refugio would have killed her. Unwilling to lose control over Hernandez, Refugio stalked her, convincing the very neighbor who helped Hernandez to escape, to give him her phone number and calling her sister repeatedly until Hernandez finally agreed to speak with him. Once Refugio was able to speak with Hernandez, he emanated remorse, crying and telling Hernandez that he needed her. Refugio promised not to hurt Hernandez again, and told her that if she would go back to him he would seek counseling. Wounded both emotionally and physically by someone she trusted and loved, Hernandez was vulnerable to such promises. Moreover, Hernandez was well aware of Refugio's potential for violence. Behind Refugio's show of remorse, there also existed the lurking possibility that if Hernandez adamantly refused, Refugio might resort to the extreme violence or murder that commonly results when a woman attempts to flee her batterer. Refugio successfully manipulated Hernandez into leaving the safety that she had found and returning to a deadly relationship in which her physical and mental well-being were in danger.

The Court notes that Congress distinguished "extreme cruelty" from "battery" when it drafted the immigration provision in VAWA. It suggests that Congress's intent was to distinguish overt acts of physical violence (battery) from something other than physical assault, such as psychological abuse (extreme cruelty). Significantly, the opinion falls just short of directly stating that any form of psychological abuse, when in the context of the "cycle of violence," constitutes "extreme cruelty."

3. **Scope of *Hernandez v. Ashcroft*.** At first glance, *Hernandez v. Ashcroft* appears to open the door for battered women who have not experienced physical abuse to still be able to satisfy the "extreme cruelty" prong of a VAWA immigration petition. But how far does the court open the door? Alexandra Blake Flamme examines this question:

> Although the Hernandez court's construction of extreme cruelty is both novel and broad, it is not likely to result in a significant number of immigrants who will be successful in claiming protection under the extreme cruelty provision of VAWA. In determining that Hernandez had been subjected to extreme cruelty in the United States at the hands of her husband, the Ninth Circuit was careful to limit the scope of its holding. The court stated at the outset, "an abuser's behavior during the 'contrite' phase of domestic violence may, and in circumstances such as those present here does, constitute 'extreme cruelty.'" In describing extreme cruelty as an "alternative measure of domestic violence," the court confined its holding to those situations in which non-physical acts occur in the context of a physically abusive relationship.
>
> In so doing, the court explained that "Congress's intent in allowing a showing of either battery or extreme cruelty was to protect survivors of domestic violence." The battered immigrant women provision in VAWA aims to protect women from manipulative tactics intended to maintain dominance, not to protect from "mere unkindness." Emotional abuse—or mere unkindness—is distinguishable from psychological violence and extreme cruelty because the former involves no reasonable threat of violence. The same behavior displayed in two different relationships may have very different effects on the recipient of that behavior, depending upon whether she has experienced violence at the hands of her partner previously. Thus, non-physical behavior by the batterer will rise to the level of domestic violence when the batterer combines control tactics with threats of physical harm in order to maintain dominance. Alexandra Blake Flamme, *Hernandez v. Ashcroft: A Construction of "Extreme Cruelty" Under the Violence Against Woman Act and Its Potential Impact on Immigration and Domestic Violence Law*, 40 NEW ENG. L. REV. 571 (2006).

4. ***Hernandez* and Non–Physical Abuse.** Domestic violence advocates have long argued that courts should take seriously forms of domestic violence that are not just physical and that courts should place individual acts of violence in the greater context of a cycle of violence. Indeed, a theme throughout our readings has been the need for courts to take this broader view. The Ninth Circuit does that in *Hernandez*. Consider whether there are cases that you have read where the court should have employed reasoning similar to that which the Ninth Circuit uses in *Hernandez*?

5. **Good Moral Character.** To secure legal permanent residency under VAWA, the petitioner must show she has good moral character. Immigration officers evaluate this prong with an eye to the petitioner's criminal record. Though immigration officers are generally instructed to disregard criminal offenses related to domestic violence, such offenses might not be easy to spot. For example, in order to cope with violence in the home, a battered woman might turn to alcohol or drugs. How likely is it that an immigration officer, even if trained in the dynamics of domestic violence, will regard a criminal charge of narcotics possession as related to domestic violence? Some battered women turn to prostitution in order to financially support themselves and their children. Again, how likely is it for an immigration officer to regard a charge of prostitution as related to the domestic violence? Immigration officers who review VAWA petitions are trained on issues of domestic violence. But so are many judges who refuse to grant battered women civil protection orders where such orders are clearly warranted. Even if immigration officers are trained in the dynamics of domestic violence, they may not understand these dynamics in context. We have seen throughout our readings that training in the dynamics of domestic violence is only a first step.

The Trafficking Victims Protection Act: T and U Visas

In order to apply for immigration relief under VAWA, the petitioner must be married to her abuser and her abuser must be a legal permanent resident or a citizen of the United States. Where an undocumented battered woman is not married to her abuser or if her abusive spouse is undocumented, The Trafficking Victims Protection Act (TVPA) may offer relief where VAWA does not. Under the TVPA a battered woman can find relief under both its U Visa and T Visa Provisions. While the T Visa is designed to provide immigration relief for victims of human trafficking not married to their partner, or in a partnered relationship, traffickers often subject their victims to domestic violence. Thus, to the extent that an undocumented victim of domestic violence also meets the definition of trafficking under the TVPA, she is eligible for relief under the T Visa. Like the T Visa, the U Visa is not designed specifically for victims of domestic violence. The U Visa is designed to provide immigration relief to undocumented victims of crime. However, the U Visa can be a useful tool for victims of domestic violence to the extent that their abusers are also guilty of other crimes against them. The material below describes each of these forms of relief.

Julie Dinnerstein

Working with Immigrant Victims of Domestic Violence, in Immigration Remedies for Domestic Violence Victims: VAWA Self–Petitions and Battered Spouse Waivers

SANCTUARY FOR FAMILIES CENTER FOR BATTERED WOMEN'S LEGAL SERVICES (2006).

1. **U Visa (8 U.S.C. § 1101(a)(15)(U)).** The U Visa is for unmarried abuse victims who have been the victims of certain crimes, including

domestic violence, who have suffered substantial physical or mental harm as a result of the crime and who have been or are likely in the future to be, helpful to the investigation or prosecution of the crime. U Visa holders are granted temporary residence status, and the end of three years upon a showing of extreme hardship, may apply for lawful permanent residency status. Unfortunately, although President Clinton signed a law creating U Visas, as of the date of this writing, no U Visas have been issued because no regulations have been promulgated. Nonetheless, immigrants who can show that they are prima facie eligible for U visas are eligible for deferred action status, which allows them to live and work lawfully in the United States. A key element of the prima facie case, includes certification from a government official attesting to the immigrants "helpfulness" in the investigation or prosecution of a crime. Thus, domestic violence victims who wish to pursue a U Visa should report crimes committed against them to police and cooperate with the District Attorney's office in the prosecution of the crime.

2. **T Visa (8 INA § 1101(a)(15)(T)).** Some immigrant victims of domestic violence are also victims of trafficking, and are thus eligible for T Visas for victims of trafficking. This visa has much more stringent criteria than the U Visa and numerical limits on how many visas can be granted. To obtain a T Visa, the applicant must show that she is a victim of "severe" trafficking and "would suffer extreme hardship involving extreme and unusual harm" if returned to her home country. The requirement for cooperation with government authorities is also higher; adult victims must cooperate with any reasonable requests for assistance in the investigation or prosecution of traffickers. T Visa holders, like U Visa holders, are granted temporary residency for three years and, at the end of that time, may apply for lawful permanent resident status. Since the requirements are more stringent, a woman who could qualify for a T Visa could get a U Visa.

NOTES AND QUESTIONS

1. **What is Trafficking?** Under the TVPA, to be eligible for a T Visa, the petitioner must show she was subjected to a "severe form of trafficking." Trafficking can include domestic violence but may have somewhat different elements. Severe trafficking is defined as follows:

> sex trafficking in which a commercial sex act is induced by force, fraud, or coercion, or in which the person induced to perform such act has not attained 18 years of age; or (B) the recruitment, harboring, transportation, provision, or obtaining of a person for labor or services, through the use of force, fraud, or coercion for the purpose of subjection to involuntary servitude, peonage, debt bondage, or slavery. http://www.state.gov/documents/organization/10492.pdf.

By way of comparison, the United Nations Protocol to Prevent, Suppress and Punish Trafficking in Persons, Especially Women and Children offers quite a different definition of trafficking and is the only internationally agreed upon definition of trafficking. Under the Protocol, trafficking is defined as follows:

> the recruitment, transportation, transfer, harbouring or receipt of persons, by means of the threat or use of force or other forms of coercion, of abduction, of fraud, of deception, of the abuse of power or of a position of vulnerability or of the giving or receiving of payments or benefits to achieve the consent of a person having control over another person, for the purpose of exploitation. Exploitation shall include, at a minimum, the exploitation of the prostitution of others or other forms of sexual exploitation, forced labour or services, slavery or practices similar to slavery, servitude or the removal of organs. The definition also excludes victims' consent as a relevant factor, and it includes children who were recruited, transported, transferred, harbored, or received by any means, not just by the enumerated means. U.N. Protocol, art. III, para. (a), at 32.

Compare the TVPA definition of trafficking with the UN Protocol definition. Presumably, an Act that defines "severe" forms of trafficking would also define non-severe forms of trafficking. But the TVPA does not do so. Why do you think the TVPA definition is so stringent? Do you think it makes sense? What would you think if our law made statutory distinctions between "severe" and "non-severe" rape? Would that make sense?

2. **When the Victim Does Not Want Her Abuser Deported.** The battered immigrant woman is no exception to the general rule that leaving an abuser can be very hard to do. Like all victims of battering, she may love her abuser. In consequence, she may not want her abuser deported, but at the same time, desire relief from the abuse and legal residency in the United States. Even where the battered immigrant may want to leave her abuser, she may not want him deported for a number of reasons, such as not wanting to deprive her children of their father or the fact that she will not survive financially without her abuser. In cases where she is only eligible for a U Visa or a T Visa, she is faced with a difficult choice. If she does not cooperate with the government against her abuser, she is ineligible for relief. If she does cooperate with the government, her abuser might be deported, provided he is in the United States illegally.

3. **Protections for the Battered Immigrant Defendant.** In *United States v. Maswai*, 419 F.3d 822 (8th Cir. 2005), Lilian Maswai traveled from Kenya to the United States on a visitor's visa. She then stayed in the country and married a legal permanent resident. She obtained a job at a bank and signed an I–9 employment form stating that she was a citizen of the United States. Her husband was abusive throughout the marriage and he was eventually arrested for beating her while pregnant. From jail, he wrote a letter to Iowa Senator Charles Grassley explaining that Maswai was living and working in the country illegally. Sen. Grassley turned over the information to immigration authorities, and Maswai was arrested. On appeal to the Eighth Circuit, Maswai argued that the letter from her husband could not be used as evidence against her, as doing so would violated 8 U.S.C. § 1367(a)(1)(A) and § 1367(a)(2). These sections state:

[I]n no case may the Attorney General, or any other official or employee of the Department of Justice (including any bureau or agency of such Department)—

(1) make an adverse determination of admissibility or deportability of an alien under the Immigration and Nationality Act [8 U.S.C. § 1101 et seq.] using information furnished solely by—

(A) a spouse or parent who has battered the alien or subjected the alien to extreme cruelty.

. . . .

[Or] (2) permit use by or disclose to anyone (other than a sworn officer or employee of the Department, or bureau or agency thereof, for legitimate Department, bureau, or agency purposes) of any information which relates to an alien who is the beneficiary of an application for relief . . . as an alien (or the parent of a child) who has been battered or subjected to extreme cruelty.

Because Maswai was charged with falsely claiming U.S. citizenship, the government argued that the above law only applied to violations of Title 8 of the U.S. Code, not Title 18. The Eighth Circuit agreed, and held that evidence from her abusive husband could be used against her. For an analysis of this case see Laura Jontz, *Eighth Circuit to Battered Kenyan: Take a Safari—Battered Immigrants Face New Barrier When Reporting Domestic Violence*, 55 DRAKE L. REV. 195 (2006).

4. **Barriers to Government Cooperation.** For both the T and U Visas government cooperation is essential to obtain relief. Accordingly, how might you advise a client who has come to you seeking relief under either a T or U visa? If the battered woman reports her partner for domestic violence, the partner might be convicted of a crime and he will be deported. This raises issues of the "unintended consequences" of mandatory arrest that we have previously discussed in Chapter Seven. With a T Visa, would your answer change if your client tells you that her trafficker, who has been battering her, is a member of an extended trafficking network with members in your client's country of residence? How would you advise this client if her abuser has threatened to harm your client's family in their home country? Consider these questions while reading the following excerpt.

Jayashri Srikantiah

Perfect Victims and Real Survivors: The Iconic Victim in Domestic Human Trafficking Law

87 B.U.L REV. 157 (2007).

The iconic victim concept contemplates a victim who is passive until rescued, but whose free will is restored upon rescue. Just as blamelessness prior to rescue required demonstrated passivity, blamelessness post-rescue requires active cooperation with law enforcement. Once the victim is understood to possess the ability to choose, she must exercise that choice to cooperate with prosecutorial demands. If a victim fails to cooperate because she fears reprisals against herself or her family, or is still under the trafficker's psychological control, her legitimacy as a victim is in question.

Contrary to the conception of victimhood embodied in the iconic victim narrative, a trafficking victim may still be under the psychological control of the trafficker when she is "liberated" by law enforcement. Although the narrative envisions rescue followed by trusting cooperation with law enforcement, victims may feel more loyalty to their trafficker than to law enforcement. They may believe that the trafficker will not be prosecuted and that they will simply return to pre-raid exploitation after the law enforcement investigation is complete. In such cases, failure to cooperate stems from the ongoing effect of trafficker control. The idea that a "liberated" victim will exercise her newfound free will to cooperate with law enforcement may be inconsistent with the nature of the control she experienced during trafficking exploitation.

Imagine, for instance, a young woman trafficked for sex work who, after a decade of exploitation, is "rescued" by law enforcement during a large-scale raid. Over the preceding decade, the traffickers repeatedly told her that if the immigration authorities found her, they would jail and deport her. During the raid, as she is taken away by law enforcement, the traffickers tell her that they will provide her with lawyers and that she should be loyal to the trafficker or her family will be harmed abroad. Prosecutors and law enforcement agents take the woman to a federal facility, which she is not permitted to leave. Agents interview her through an interpreter, promising that she is safe and that her only role now is to cooperate in locking up the trafficker. The woman, still believing that the trafficker will provide her with a lawyer and get her out of custody, fearing harm to her family, and feeling loyal to the trafficker, lies to the agents, telling them that she voluntarily migrated and that the trafficker did nothing wrong. The agents see her as an accomplice to the trafficker and place her in removal proceedings. In their eyes she is not a victim.

A victim's loyalty to the trafficker and refusal to cooperate with law enforcement is consistent with current understandings of trafficking victims' post-exploitation psychological state. As psychiatrist Jose Hidalgo explains, many trafficking victims suffer "chronic traumatic stress" during their exploitation because "their lives and bodies are under constant threat." Traffickers "may alternate between kindness and viciousness; for psychological survival, the victim may form positive feelings for that part of the perpetrator that is kind and ignore the vicious side." Hidalgo terms this syndrome "traumatic attachment" and suggests that the attachment can result in seemingly illogical victim behavior, where a recently rescued or escaped victim does not want law enforcement assistance. Hidalgo observes that "[a] victim may even become protective of the perpetrator and excuse violent behavior as an aberration."

Particularly given the psychological state of trafficking victims post-rescue or escape, law enforcement's assessment of cooperation is not a principled or accurate way to distinguish between trafficking victims and other undocumented migrants. The decision by a victim to cooperate does not necessarily correlate to her authenticity as a victim. The victims we might characterize as most worthy of relief—those most under the control of the trafficker, or those subjected to the most horrific abuse—may in fact be the least likely to cooperate with law enforcement.

The prosecutorial concern is a collective one: to reduce trafficking through prosecution and ultimately protect future victims. Even if linking the T visa to prosecutors' assessment of victim cooperation functions to encourage such cooperation, however, the visa is more than simply a law enforcement tool. It also serves a humanitarian purpose, allowing victims to recover from the trauma of trafficking, restore their autonomy, and begin new, independent lives. The prosecutorial interest in an individual victim is retrospective—the focus is on the victim's past exploitation—whereas the humanitarian interest in the victim is mostly prospective: the focus is on victim rehabilitation and recovery. A regulatory implementation that centers on prosecutorial goals fails to balance the TVPA's dual purposes of serving prosecutorial interests and protecting individual trafficking victims.

NOTES AND QUESTIONS

1. **Cooperation with Law Enforcement.** The state has an interest in prosecuting traffickers and the trafficking victim has an interest in obtaining immigration relief. Superficially, it seems that both these interests can be satisfied when the victim chooses to cooperate with the government in prosecuting the trafficker. However, as the excerpt above shows, the risks and interests that the trafficking victim must weigh in contemplation of cooperating with the government are far more nuanced than the choice to cooperate with the government and receive legal permanent residency, or not to cooperate with law enforcement and be deported. How might the government accomplish its goal of prosecution while also addressing the legitimate concerns of a trafficking victim who fears cooperating with the prosecution? Is this even possible given the interests of both parties?

2. **Sex Workers.** Jayashri Srikantiah describes three dimensions of trafficking: domestic workers; migrant workers in restaurants, hotels, farm work and factories; and forced sex work. While domestic violence is especially prevalent among domestic and sex workers, it is also likely that domestic violence affects forced labor as well.

As Sarah Buel pointed out in Chapter Nine, we often overlook the fact that many sex workers are victims of domestic violence. Sex work, trafficking, and domestic violence are often interrelated, and yet we often fail to understand that link. Thus, many women may be deported for sex work even though they may have been eligible to petition under VAWA. If law enforcement is not sensitive to the nuances of domestic violence, and lawyers don't screen for it in these cases, many immigrant women are not able to exercise their rights.

3. **Domestic Trafficking.** While the focus of this chapter is on international trafficking, many women and children are often trafficked within the United States to be sex workers. These victims are also at high risk for

intimate partner and other violence. For a discussion of the link between domestic trafficking and intimate violence, see Cheryl Hanna, *Somebody's Daughter: The Domestic Trafficking of Girls for the Commercial Sex Industry & the Power of Love,* 9 WM. & MARY J. WOMEN & L. 1 (2002).

4. **Mail–Order Brides.** It is not clear how many women enter the United States as "mail-order brides." Yet, these women can suffer high rates of domestic violence. As one author details:

> Although there are no national figures on abuse of mail-order brides, authorities agree that domestic violence in these marriages can be expected at higher levels than in other marriages. Documentation to show the extent of the mail-order bride domestic abuse problem is quite difficult to find because "[m]arriages arranged by IMBs [international mail order brides] are not tracked separately from other immigrant marriages."

> Also, it is currently difficult to find statistics on mail-order bride domestic abuse because many of the women do not complain. Mail-order brides do not complain for a variety of reasons—they do not know their rights, they are fearful of deportation, or they are isolated. Grace Lyu–Volckhausen, a women's rights activist and a member of the New York City Commission on the Status of Women, says that she receives "late-night phone calls from mail-order brides who have been beaten by their husbands" but are too fearful of deportation to seek help. Lyu–Volckhausen expands, "[The mail-order bride] has to tell [the public] everything is fine, . . . [because] she has to live with her husband."

> Even with the absence of firm national statistics on mail-order bride domestic abuse, there is strong evidence that the abuse is far too common. When mail-order brides and consumer-husbands meet through IMBs, the women have little opportunity to get to know their prospective husbands or assess their potential for violence, unlike most American women or even foreign-born fiancées who have dated their husbands and gone through the "normal" courtship ritual. The consumer-husband has the benefit of a complete background check on the mail-order bride (a requirement for the immigration process), but the foreign woman does not have that privilege. The mail-order bride gets only the information that the consumer-husband wants to share and has little, if any, knowledge of her rights as a victim of domestic abuse in the United States. Because these women typically immigrate alone, they have no support system other than their husbands. Such dependency and fear of deportation can make it difficult for women to report abuse and leave the marriage. Researchers agree that isolation and dependency put mail-order brides at greater risk for domestic abuse. All of these factors lead to a growing epidemic of domestic abuse among couples who meet using IMBs.

> An immigration service report entitled The Mail–Order Bride Industry and Its Impact on U.S. Immigration states, "[T]here is every reason to believe that the [incident of wife abuse] is higher in this population than for the nation as a whole." Holli B. Newsome, *Mail Dominance: A*

Critical Look at the International Marriage Broker Regulation Act and It's Sufficiency in Curtailing Mail–Order Bride Domestic Abuse, 29 CAMPBELL L. REV. 291 (2007).

In 2005, in response to many deaths of mail-order brides at the hands of their American husbands, Congress passed the International Marriage Broker Act of 2005, as part of VAWA reauthorization. 8 U.S.C.S. §§ 1375a(d)(3)(A)(iii)(II), (III) (2007). This law requires those who arrange such marriages to provide brides with the criminal violent histories of those men who use international marriage brokers, as well as about rights and resources for victims of domestic violence in the United States. For further information about mail-order brides, see Marie–Claire Belleau, *Mail–Order Brides in a Global World*, 67 ALB. L. REV. 595 (2003); Vanessa Brocato, *Profitable Proposals: Explaining and Addressing the Mail–Order Bride Industry Through International Human Rights Law*, 5 SAN DIEGO INT'L L. J. 225 (2004); Linda Kelly, *Marriage for Sale: The Mail Order Bride Industry & the Changing Value of Marriage*, 5 J. GENDER RACE & JUST. 175 (2001); Suzanne H. Jackson, *Marriages of Convenience: International Marriage Brokers, "Mail Order Brides," and Domestic Servitude*, 38 U. TOL. L. REV. 895 (2007).

5. **Further Discussion.** For further discussion of the issues raised by domestic violence in immigration., see Sarah Ignatius and Elisabeth S. Stickney, IMMIGRATION LAW AND THE FAMILY (2d ed. 2002, database updated June 2007); Laura Jontz, *Eighth Circuit To Battered Kenyan: Take a Safari—Battered Immigrants Face New Barrier When Reporting Domestic Violence*, 55 DRAKE L. REV. 195 (2006); Indira K. Balram, *The Evolving, Yet Still Inadequate, Legal Protections Afforded Battered Immigrant Women*, 5 U. MD. L.J. RACE, RELIGION, GENDER & CLASS 387 (2005); Sarah M. Wood, *VAWA's Unfinished Business: The Immigrant Women Who Fall Through the Cracks*, 11 DUKE J. GENDER L. & POL'Y 141 (2004); *Zelda B. Harris, The Predicament of the Immigrant Victim/Defendant: "VAWA Diversion" and Other Considerations in Support of Battered Women*, 23 ST. LOUIS U. PUB. L. REV. 49 (2004); Nimish R. Ganatra, *The Cultural Dynamic in Domestic Violence: Understanding the Additional Burdens Battered Immigrant Women of Color Face in the United States*, 2 J. L. SOCIETY 109 (2001); Leslye E. Orloff and Janice V. Kaguyutan, *Offering a Helping Hand: Legal Protections for Battered Immigrant Women: A History of Legislative Responses*, 10 AM. U. J. GENDER SOC. POL'Y & L. 95 (2001); Lori A. Nessel, *Forced to Choose: Torture, Family Reunification, and the United States Immigration Policy*, 78 TEMP. L.REV. 897 (2005).

B. ASYLUM

Next we turn to the related question of asylum. If a woman from outside the United States claims that she has been beaten, and that her country has failed to protect her, can she claim refugee status in this country? Domestic violence is a global epidemic. By way of example, in Korea, 38% of women reported being abused by their spouses; in Pakistan, 52% of women in urban areas admitted to being beaten by their husbands;

in Egypt, 35% of a nationally representative group of women reported being beaten by their husbands at least once during their marriage; in Uganda 41% of women in a representative sample reported being beaten by their partners and 41% of husbands in this same sample reported beating their partners; in Nicaragua 57% of women reported being abused by a partner at least once; and in Poland 60% of divorced women reported being hit by their ex-husbands at least once. Rebecca Adams, *Violence Against Women and International Law: The Fundamental Right to State Protection from Domestic Violence*, 20 N.Y. Int'l L. Rev. 57 (2007). Many victims of gender-based violence from across the globe seek asylum in the United States.

There have been both grants and denials of asylum claims brought on grounds of domestic violence. The central policy issue here is whether the United States should recognize intimate violence as a basis for asylum. The *Matter of Kasinga* case, mentioned in *In Re R–A–*, the case that follows, is one decision that recognized that private violence such as female genital mutilation, involving gender as a social group, could be a basis for an asylum claim. The best known of these cases is a 1999 decision, *In Re R–A–*, in which the United States Board of Immigration Appeals (BIA) denied asylum to a domestic violence victim from Guatemala.

While reading the *In Re R–A–* decision below, bear in mind (1) the five grounds for asylum and (2) the manner in which a court will analyze a request for asylum. The five grounds for asylum are race, religion, nationality, social group status and political opinion. In order to be granted asylum, the applicant must meet the statutory definition of a refugee. To meet this definition, the applicant (a) must have a fear of persecution, (b) the fear must be well founded, (c) the persecution feared must be on account of race, religion, nationality, membership in a particular social group or political opinion and (d) the applicant must be unable or unwilling to return to her country of nationality or to the country where she last resided because of persecution or her well-founded fear of persecution.

In *In Re R–A–*, a Guatemalan woman sought asylum to escape ten years of brutal spousal violence from which she claimed the Guatemalan government had failed to protect her. In a ten-to-five ruling, the BIA overturned a grant of asylum on the ground that, despite her undisputed suffering, she did not meet the legal standards for refugee status and establish that she was persecuted on account of her membership in a social group or her political opinion.

In reaching its decision, the BIA refused to recognize a social group based on gender, relationship to an abusive partner, and the asylum seeker's opposition to domestic violence. The BIA also failed to credit her claim that her husband's abuse was at least in part in response to her political opinion that her husband had no right to beat her—reversing the immigration judge's finding that her husband's violence had escalated in response to her resistance and futile attempts to seek official aid.

The BIA decision was vacated and remanded in 2001 by then-Attorney General Janet Reno, and since that time there have been both grants and denials of asylum claims based on domestic violence. The BIA opinion and the dissent present the common arguments for and against granting asylum based on a state's failure to protect from domestic violence.

In Re R–A–

Respondent Interim Decision 3403 Board of Immigration Appeals, 1999.

I. Issues

The question before us is whether the respondent qualifies as a "refugee" as a result of the heinous abuse she suffered and still fears from her husband in Guatemala. Specifically, we address whether the repeated spouse abuse inflicted on the respondent makes her eligible for asylum as an alien who has been persecuted on account of her membership in a particular social group or her political opinion. We find that the group identified by the Immigration Judge has not adequately been shown to be a "particular social group" for asylum purposes. We further find that the respondent has failed to show that her husband was motivated to harm her, even in part, because of her membership in a particular social group or because of an actual or imputed political opinion. Our review is de novo with regard to the issues on appeal. . . .

II. Factual Background

A. Testimony and Statements of Abuse

The respondent is a native and citizen of Guatemala. She married at age 16. Her husband was then 21 years old. He currently resides in Guatemala, as do their two children. Immediately after their marriage, the respondent and her husband moved to Guatemala City. From the beginning of the marriage, her husband engaged in acts of physical and sexual abuse against the respondent. He was domineering and violent. The respondent testified that her husband "always mistreated me from the moment we were married, he was always . . . aggressive."

Her husband would insist that the respondent accompany him wherever he went, except when he was working. He escorted the respondent to her workplace, and he would often wait to direct her home. To scare her, he would tell the respondent stories of having killed babies and the elderly while he served in the army. Oftentimes, he would take the respondent to cantinas where he would become inebriated. When the respondent would complain about his drinking, her husband would yell at her. On one occasion, he grasped her hand to the point of pain and continued to drink until he passed out. When she left a cantina before him, he would strike her. As their marriage proceeded, the level and frequency of his rage increased concomitantly with the seeming senselessness and irrationality of his motives. He dislocated the respondent's jaw bone when her menstrual period was 15 days late. When she refused to abort her 3–to 4–month–old fetus, he kicked her violently in her spine. He would hit or kick the respondent "whenever he felt like it, wherever he happened to be: in the house, on the street, on the bus." The respondent stated that "as time went on, he hit me for no reason at all."

The respondent's husband raped her repeatedly. He would beat her before and during the unwanted sex. When the respondent resisted, he would accuse her of seeing other men and threaten her with death. The rapes occurred "almost daily," and they caused her severe pain. He passed on a sexually transmitted disease to the respondent from his sexual relations outside their marriage. Once, he kicked the respondent in her genitalia, apparently for no reason, causing the respondent to bleed severely for 8 days. The respondent suffered the most severe pain when he forcefully sodomized her. When she protested, he responded, as he often did, "You're my woman, you do what I say."

The respondent ran away to her brother's and parents' homes, but her husband always found her. Around December 1994, the respondent attempted to flee with her children outside the city, but her husband found her again. He appeared at her door, drunk, and as she turned to leave, he struck her in the back of her head causing her to lose consciousness. When she awoke, he kicked her and dragged her by her hair into another room and beat her to unconsciousness.

After 2 months away, her husband pleaded for the respondent's return, and she agreed because her children were asking for him. One night, he woke the respondent, struck her face, whipped her with an electrical cord, pulled out a machete and threatened to deface her, to cut off her arms and legs, and to leave her in a wheelchair if she ever tried to leave him. He warned her that he would be able to find her wherever she was. The violence continued. When the respondent could not give 5,000 quetzales to him when he asked for it, he broke windows and a mirror with her head. Whenever he could not find something, he would grab her head and strike furniture with it. Once, he pistol-whipped her. When she asked for his motivation, he broke into a familiar refrain, "I can do it if I want to."

Once, her husband entered the kitchen where the respondent was and, for no apparent reason, threw a machete toward her hands, barely missing them. He would often come home late and drunk. When the respondent noted his tardiness, he punched her. Once, he asked where the respondent had been. When she responded that she had been home waiting for him, he became enraged, struck her face, grabbed her by her hair, and dragged her down the street. One night, the respondent attempted to commit suicide. Her husband told her, "If you want to die, go ahead. But from here, you are not going to leave."

When asked on cross-examination, the respondent at first indicated that she had no opinion of why her husband acted the way he did. She supposed, however, that it was because he had been mistreated when he was in the army and, as he had told her, he treated her the way he had been treated. The respondent believed he would abuse any woman who was his wife. She testified that he "was a repugnant man without any education," and that he saw her "as something that belonged to him and he could do anything he wanted" with her.

The respondent's pleas to Guatemalan police did not gain her protection. On three occasions, the police issued summons for her husband to appear, but he ignored them, and the police did not take further action.

Twice, the respondent called the police, but they never responded. When the respondent appeared before a judge, he told her that he would not interfere in domestic disputes. Her husband told the respondent that, because of his former military service, calling the police would be futile as he was familiar with law enforcement officials. The respondent knew of no shelters or other organizations in Guatemala that could protect her. The abuse began "from the moment [they] were married," and continued until the respondent fled Guatemala in May 1995. One morning in May 1995, the respondent decided to leave permanently. With help, the respondent was able to flee Guatemala, and she arrived in Brownsville, Texas, 2 days later.

A witness, testifying for the respondent, stated that she learned through the respondent's sister that the respondent's husband was "going to hunt her down and kill her if she comes back to Guatemala."

We struggle to describe how deplorable we find the husband's conduct to have been.

B. Country Conditions

Dr. Doris Bersing testified that spouse abuse is common in Latin American countries and that she was not aware of social or legal resources for battered women in Guatemala. Women in Guatemala, according to Dr. Bersing, have other problems related to general conditions in that country, and she suggested that such women could leave abusive partners but that they would face other problems such as poverty. Dr. Bersing further testified that the respondent was different from other battered women she had seen in that the respondent possessed an extraordinary fear of her husband and her abuse had been extremely severe.

Dr. Bersing noted that spouse abuse was a problem in many countries throughout the world, but she said it was a particular problem in Latin America, especially in Guatemala and Nicaragua. As we understand her testimony, its roots lie in such things as the Latin American patriarchal culture, the militaristic and violent nature of societies undergoing civil war, alcoholism, and sexual abuse in general. Nevertheless, she testified that husbands are supposed to honor, respect, and take care of their wives, and that spouse abuse is something that is present "underground" or "underneath in the culture." But if a woman chooses the wrong husband her options are few in countries such as Guatemala, which lack effective methods for dealing with the problem.

The Department of State issued an advisory opinion as to the respondent's asylum request. The opinion states that the respondent's alleged mistreatment could have occurred given its understanding of country conditions in Guatemala. The opinion further indicates:

> Spousal abuse complaints by husbands have increased from 30 to 120 a month due to increased nationwide educational programs, which have encouraged women to seek assistance. Family court judges may issue injunctions against abusive spouses, which police are charged with enforcing. The [Human Rights Ombudsman,] women's rights depart-

ment and various non-governmental organizations provide medical and legal assistance.

The respondent has submitted numerous articles and reports regarding violence against women in Guatemala and other Latin American countries. One article, prepared by Canada's Immigration and Refugee Board, indicates that Guatemala has laws against domestic violence, that it has taken some additional steps recently to begin to address the problem, and that "functionaries" in the legal system tend to view domestic violence as a violation of women's rights. Nevertheless, the article indicates that Guatemalan society still tends to view domestic violence as a family matter, that women are often not aware of available legal avenues, and that the pursuit of legal remedies can often prove ineffective.

III. IMMIGRATION JUDGE'S DECISION

The Immigration Judge found the respondent to be credible, and she concluded that the respondent suffered harm that rose to the level of past persecution. The Immigration Judge also held that the Guatemalan Government was either unwilling or unable to control the respondent's husband. The balance of her decision addressed the issue of whether the respondent's harm was on account of a protected ground.

The Immigration Judge first concluded that the respondent was persecuted because of her membership in the particular social group of "Guatemalan women who have been involved intimately with Guatemalan male companions, who believe that women are to live under male domination." She found that such a group was cognizable and cohesive, as members shared the common and immutable characteristics of gender and the experience of having been intimately involved with a male companion who practices male domination through violence. The Immigration Judge then held that members of such a group are targeted for persecution by the men who seek to dominate and control them.

The Immigration Judge further found that, through the respondent's resistance to his acts of violence, her husband imputed to the respondent the political opinion that women should not be dominated by men, and he was motivated to commit the abuse because of the political opinion he believed her to hold.

IV. ARGUMENTS ON APPEAL

On appeal, the Service argues that "Guatemalan women who have been involved intimately with Guatemalan male companions, who believe that women are to live under male domination" is not a particular social group, and that the respondent was not harmed because she belonged to such a group. The Service also contends that the respondent's husband did not persecute the respondent because of an imputed political opinion.

The respondent's brief supports the Immigration Judge's conclusions and advances additional arguments. The Refugee Law Center and the International Human Rights and Migration Project filed a joint amicus curiae brief. The thorough and well-prepared amicus brief argues that the Immigration Judge's decision is supported not only by United States asylum law, but also by international human rights laws, and that the respondent's asylum claims should be analyzed against the fundamental purpose of refugee law: to provide surrogate international protection when there is a fundamental breakdown in state protection resulting in serious human rights violations tied to civil and political status.

V. THE LAW

An asylum applicant bears the burden of proof and persuasion of showing that he or she is a refugee.... The term "refugee" refers to:

> any person who is outside any country of such person's nationality ... and who is unable or unwilling to return to, and is unable or unwilling to avail himself or herself of the protection of, that country because of persecution or a well-founded fear of persecution on account of race, religion, nationality, membership in a particular social group, or political opinion....

We have held that members of a particular social group share a "common, immutable characteristic" that they either cannot change, or should not be required to change because such characteristic is fundamental to their individual identities.... The United States Court of Appeals for the Ninth Circuit, the circuit within which this case arises, defines a particular social group as:

> a collection of people closely affiliated with each other, who are actuated by some common impulse or interest. Of central concern is the existence of a voluntary associational relationship among the purported members, which impart some common characteristic that is fundamental to their identity as a member of that discrete social group.

The asylum applicant bears the burden of providing evidence, either direct or circumstantial, from which it is reasonable to conclude that her persecutor harmed her at least in part because of a protected ground. The Court in Elias–Zacarias pointed out that overcoming or punishing a protected characteristic of the victim, and not the persecutor's own generalized goals, must be the motivation for the persecution....

VI. ANALYSIS

... [W]e agree with the Immigration Judge that the severe injuries sustained by the respondent rise to the level of harm sufficient (and more than sufficient) to constitute "persecution." We also credit the respondent's testimony in general and specifically her account of being unsuccessful in obtaining meaningful assistance from the authorities in Guatemala. Accordingly, we find that she has adequately established on this record that she was unable to avail herself of the protection of the Government of Guatemala in connection with the abuse inflicted by her husband. The determinative issue, as correctly identified by the Immigration Judge, is whether the harm experienced by the respondent was, or in the future may be, inflicted "on account of" a statutorily protected ground.

It is not possible to review this record without having great sympathy for the respondent and extreme contempt for the actions of her husband. The questions before us, however, are not whether some equitable or prosecutorial authority ought to be invoked to prevent the respondent's deportation to Guatemala. Indeed, the Service has adequate authority in the form of "deferred action" to accomplish that result if it deems it appropriate. Rather, the questions before us concern the respondent's eligibility for relief under our refugee and asylum laws. And, as explained below, we do not agree with the Immigration Judge that the respondent was harmed on account of either actual or imputed political opinion or membership in a particular social group.

A.   Imputed Political Opinion

The record indicates that the respondent's husband harmed the respondent regardless of what she actually believed or what he thought she believed. The respondent testified that the abuse began "from the moment [they] were married." Even after the respondent "learned through experience" to acquiesce to his demands, he still abused her. The abuse took place before she left him initially, and it continued after she returned to him. In fact, he said he "didn't care" what she did to escape because he would find her. He also hurt her before her first call to the police and after her last plea for help.

The respondent's account of what her husband told her may well reflect his own view of women and, in particular, his view of the respondent as his property to do with as he pleased. It does not, however, reflect that he had any understanding of the respondent's perspective or that he even cared what the respondent's perspective may have been. According to the respondent, he told her, "You're my woman and I can do whatever I want," and "You're my woman, you do what I say." In fact, she stated that "as time went on, he hit me for no reason at all," and that he "would hit or kick me whenever he felt like it."

Nowhere in the record does the respondent recount her husband saying anything relating to what he thought her political views to be, or that the violence towards her was attributable to her actual or imputed beliefs. Moreover, this is not a case where there is meaningful evidence that this respondent held or evinced a political opinion, unless one assumes that the common human desire not to be harmed or abused is in itself a "political opinion." The record before us simply does not indicate that the harm arose in response to any objections made by the respondent to her husband's domination over her. Nor does it suggest that his abusive behavior was dependent in any way on the views held by the respondent. Indeed, his senseless actions started at the beginning of their marriage and continued whether or not the respondent acquiesced in his demands. The record reflects that, once having entered into this marriage, there was nothing the respondent could have done or thought that would have spared her (or indeed would have spared any other woman unfortunate enough to have married him) from the violence he inflicted....

B. *Particular Social Group*

1. Cognizableness

Initially, we find that "Guatemalan women who have been involved intimately with Guatemalan male companions, who believe that women are to live under male domination" is not a particular social group. Absent from this group's makeup is "a voluntary associational relationship" that is of "central concern" in the Ninth Circuit. . . .

Moreover, regardless of Ninth Circuit law, we find that the respondent's claimed social group fails under our own independent assessment of what constitutes a qualifying social group. We find it questionable that the social group adopted by the Immigration Judge appears to have been defined principally, if not exclusively, for purposes of this asylum case, and without regard to the question of whether anyone in Guatemala perceives this group to exist in any form whatsoever. The respondent fits within the proposed group. But the group is defined largely in the abstract. It seems to bear little or no relation to the way in which Guatemalans might identify subdivisions within their own society or otherwise might perceive individuals either to possess or to lack an important characteristic or trait. The proposed group may satisfy the basic requirement of containing an immutable or fundamental individual characteristic. But, for the group to be viable for asylum purposes, we believe there must also be some showing of how the characteristic is understood in the alien's society, such that we in turn may understand that the potential persecutors in fact see persons sharing the characteristic as warranting suppression or the infliction of harm.

Our administrative precedents do not require a voluntary associational relationship as a social group attribute. But we have ruled that the term "particular social group" is to be construed in keeping with the other four statutory characteristics that are the focus of persecution: race, religion, nationality, and political opinion. . . . These other four characteristics are ones that typically separate various factions within countries. They frequently are recognized groupings in a particular society. The members of the group generally understand their own affiliation with the grouping, as do other persons in the particular society.

In the present case, the respondent has shown that women living with abusive partners face a variety of legal and practical problems in obtaining protection or in leaving the abusive relationship. But the respondent has not shown that "Guatemalan women who have been involved intimately with Guatemalan male companions, who believe that women are to live under male domination" is a group that is recognized and understood to be a societal faction, or is otherwise a recognized segment of the population, within Guatemala. The respondent has shown neither that the victims of spouse abuse view themselves as members of this group, nor, most importantly, that their male oppressors see their victimized companions as part of this group. . . .

On the record before us, we find that the respondent has not adequately established that we should recognize, under our law, the particular social group identified by the Immigration Judge.

2.   Nexus

... In this case, even if we were to accept as a particular social group "Guatemalan women who have been involved intimately with Guatemalan male companions, who believe that women are to live under male domination," the respondent has not established that her husband has targeted and harmed the respondent because he perceived her to be a member of this particular social group. The record indicates that he has targeted only the respondent. The respondent's husband has not shown an interest in any member of this group other than the respondent herself. The respondent fails to show how other members of the group may be at risk of harm from him. If group membership were the motivation behind his abuse, one would expect to see some evidence of it manifested in actions toward other members of the same group....

When the Immigration Judge correctly identifies the husband as the persecutor whom the Guatemalan Government failed to control, her nexus finding is both too broad and too narrow. It is too broad in that he did not target all (or indeed any other) Guatemalan women intimate with abusive Guatemalan men. It is too narrow in that the record strongly indicates that he would have abused any woman, regardless of nationality, to whom he was married....

The respondent's statements regarding her husband's motivation also undercut the nexus claims. He harmed her, when he was drunk and when he was sober, for not getting an abortion, for his belief that she was seeing other men, for not having her family get money for him, for not being able to find something in the house, for leaving a cantina before him, for leaving him, for reasons related to his mistreatment in the army, and "for no reason at all." Of all these apparent reasons for abuse, none was "on account of" a protected ground, and the arbitrary nature of the attacks further suggests it was not the respondent's claimed social group characteristics that he sought to overcome. The record indicates that there is nothing the respondent could have done to have satisfied her husband and prevented further abuse. Her own supposition is that he abused her because he was abused himself in the military.

The respondent was not at particular risk of abuse from her husband until she married him, at which point, given the nature of his focus, she was in a "group" by herself of women presently married to that particular man. Such a group, however, would fail to qualify as a "particular social group" under the Act....

The Immigration Judge nevertheless found, and the respondent argues on appeal, that her various possible group memberships account for her plight, in large measure because the social climate and the Government of Guatemala afford her no protection from her husband's abuse. Societal attitudes and the concomitant effectiveness (or lack thereof) of governmental intervention very well may have contributed to the ability of the respondent's husband to carry out his abusive actions over a period of many years. But this argument takes us away from looking at the motivation of the husband and focuses instead on the failure of the government to offer protection.

Focusing on societal attitudes and a particular government's response to the infliction of injury is frequently appropriate in the adjudication of asylum cases. It is most warranted when the harm is being inflicted by elements within the government or by private organizations that target minority factions within a society. But governmental inaction is not a reliable indicator of the motivations behind the actions of private parties. And this is not a case in which it has been shown that the Government of Guatemala encourages its male citizens to abuse its female citizens, nor in which the Government has suddenly and unreasonably withdrawn protection from a segment of the population in the expectation that a third party will inflict harm and thereby indirectly achieve a governmental objective.

The record in this case reflects that the views of society and of many governmental institutions in Guatemala can result in the tolerance of spouse abuse at levels we find appalling. But the record also shows that abusive marriages are not viewed as desirable, that spouse abuse is recognized as a problem, and that some measures have been pursued in an attempt to respond to this acknowledged problem. In this context, we are not convinced that the absence of an effective governmental reaction to the respondent's abuse translates into a finding that her husband inflicted the abuse because she was a member of a particular social group. The record does not support such a conclusion, as a matter of fact, when the husband's own behavior is examined. And Guatemala's societal and governmental attitudes and actions do not warrant our declaring this to be the case as a matter of law. . . .

The adequacy of state protection is obviously an essential inquiry in asylum cases. But its bearing on the "on account of" test for refugee status depends on the facts of the case and the context in which it arises. In this case, the independent actions of the respondent's husband may have been tolerated. But, as previously explained, this record does not show that his actions represent desired behavior within Guatemala or that the Guatemalan Government encourages domestic abuse.

Importantly, construing private acts of violence to be qualifying governmental persecution, by virtue of the inadequacy of protection, would obviate, perhaps entirely, the "on account of" requirement in the statute. We understand the "on account of" test to direct an inquiry into the motives of the entity actually inflicting the harm. . . .

In the end, we find that the respondent has failed to show a sufficient nexus between her husband's abuse of her and the particular social group the Immigration Judge announced, or any of the other proffered groups.

3. The Kasinga Decision

Our decision in Matter of Kasinga, [Interim Decision 3278 (BIA 1996)], does not prescribe a different result. In that case, the alien belonged to the Tchamba–Kunsuntu tribe in Togo in which young women normally underwent female genital mutilation ("FGM") before the age of 15. Under tribal custom, the alien's aunt and husband planned to force her to submit to FGM before she was to be married. Following her escape from Togo, the Togolese police were looking for her. The record included a letter from a cultural anthropologist indicating that women from the Tchamba people probably would be expected to undergo FGM prior to marriage. A Department of State report in the record indicated that FGM was practiced by some Togo ethnic groups, that as many as 50% of Togolese females may have been mutilated, and that violence against women in Togo occurs with little police intervention. We held that FGM was persecution, that "young women of the Tchamba–Kunsuntu Tribe who have not had FGM, as practiced by that tribe, and who oppose the practice" constitute a particular social group, that the alien was a member of such a group, and that she possessed a well-founded fear of persecution on account of her membership in that group.

In contrast to our ruling in Matter of Kasinga, the Immigration Judge in the instant case has not articulated a viable social group. The common characteristic of not having undergone FGM was one that was identified by Kasinga's tribe, and motivated both her family and the tribe to enforce the practice on Kasinga and other young women. Indeed, the tribe expected or required FGM of women prior to marriage, signifying the importance of the practice within that tribal society. The record in Kasinga indicated that African women faced threats or acts of violence or social ostracization for either refusing the practice or attempting to protect female children from FGM. Moreover, although the source of Kasinga's fear of physical harm was limited to her aunt and husband, she established that FGM was so pervasive that her tribal society targeted "young women of the Tchamba–Kunsuntu Tribe who have not had FGM, as practiced by that tribe, and who oppose the practice."

The respondent in this case has not demonstrated that domestic violence is as pervasive in Guatemala as FGM is among the Tchamba–Kunsuntu Tribe, or, more importantly, that domestic violence is a practice encouraged and viewed as societally important in Guatemala. She has not shown that women are expected to undergo abuse from their husbands, or that husbands who do not abuse their wives, or the nonabused wives themselves, face social ostracization or other threats to make them conform to a societal expectation of abuse. While the respondent here found no source of official protection in Guatemala, the young woman in Kasinga testified that the police in Togo were looking for her and would return her to her family to undergo FGM.

VII.   CONCLUSION

In sum, we find that the respondent has been the victim of tragic and severe spouse abuse. We further find that her husband's motivation, to the extent it can be ascertained, has varied ... Absent other evidence, we accept the respondent's own assessment that the foundations of the abuse she suffered lay in the abuse her husband had experienced in his own life. We are not persuaded that the abuse occurred because of her membership in a particular social group or because of an actual or imputed political opinion. . . .

The respondent in this case has been terribly abused and has a genuine and reasonable fear of returning to Guatemala. Whether the district director may, at his discretion, grant the respondent relief upon humanitarian grounds—relief beyond the jurisdiction of the Immigration Judge and this Board—is a matter the parties can explore outside the present proceedings. We further note that Congress has legislated various forms of relief for abused spouses and children. The issue of whether our asylum laws (or some other legislative provision) should be amended to include additional protection for abused women, such as this respondent, is a matter to be addressed by Congress. In our judgment, however, Congress did not intend the "social group" category to be an all-encompassing residual category for persons facing genuine social ills that governments do not remedy. The solution to the respondent's plight does not lie in our asylum laws as they are currently formulated....

DISSENT:

I respectfully dissent. I agree with the thorough and well-reasoned decision of the Immigration Judge that the respondent has demonstrated past persecution and a well-founded fear of future persecution based on her membership in a particular social group and upon her express and imputed political opinion.

I.   ISSUES PRESENTED

This case presents two questions: (1) whether a woman trapped in a long-term relationship with an abusive spouse, in a country in which such abuse is tolerated by society and ignored by governmental officials, is a member of a particular social group entitled to the protection of asylum law; and, (2) whether the domestic abuse in the instant case was at least partially motivated by an actual or imputed political opinion.

II.   OVERVIEW

This is not merely a case of domestic violence involving criminal conduct. The respondent's husband engaged in a prolonged and persistent pattern of abuse designed to dominate the respondent and to overcome any effort on her part to assert her independence or to resist his abuse. His mistreatment and persecution of her in private and in public was founded, as the majority states, on his view that it was his right to treat his wife as "his property to do as he pleased." He acted with the knowledge that no one would interfere. His horrific conduct, both initially and in response to her opposition to it, was not that of an individual acting at variance with societal norms, but one who recognized that he was acting in accordance with them.

The harm to the respondent occurred in the context of egregious governmental acquiescence. When the respondent sought the aid and assistance of government officials and institutions, she was told that they could do nothing for her. This is not a case in which the government tried, but failed, to afford protection. Here the government made no effort and showed no interest in protecting the respondent from her abusive spouse. Thus, when the respondent went to the police or to the court to seek relief from threats, physical violence, broken bones, rape, and sodomy inflicted by her husband, Guatemalan police officials and the judge refused to inter-vene. . . .

III.   PERSECUTION ON ACCOUNT OF MEMBERSHIP IN A PARTICULAR SOCIAL GROUP

. . . The respondent has a fundamental right to protection from abuse based on gender. When domestic abuse based on gender occurs, as here, with state acquiescence, the respondent should be afforded the protection of asylum law.

A.   *The Immigration Judge's Finding of a Particular Social Group is Consistent With Board Precedent*

The Immigration Judge found that the respondent was a member of a social group comprised of "Guatemalan women, who have been involved intimately with Guatemalan male companions, who believe that women are to live under male domination." In so finding, she carefully analyzed the facts of the case and correctly applied the law . . .

We first set forth the requirements for a particular social group in Matter of Acosta. There we interpreted the phrase "membership in a particular social group" in a manner consistent with the other enumerated grounds for asylum. As each of the other grounds (race, religion, nationali-ty, and political opinion) refers to a common, immutable characteristic which a person either cannot change, or should not be required to change, because it is "fundamental to individual identity or conscience," we deter-mined that the phrase "particular social group" also should be defined by this type of characteristic. The shared immutable characteristic "might be an innate one such as sex, color, or kinship ties, or in some circumstances it might be a shared past experience such as former military leadership or land ownership." We concluded that such determinations must be made on a case-by-case basis. Applying this test to the record in Acosta, we found that members of a taxi cooperative and persons engaged in the transporta-tion industry of El Salvador did not constitute a particular social group, because the characteristics defining the group were not immutable. . . .

Under Acosta, then, immutability is of the essence. . . .

In Matter of Kasinga, a case involving a young Togolese woman who fled her country to avoid the practice of female genital mutilation practiced by her tribe, we considered a social group partly defined by gender. We found that the applicant had a well-founded fear of persecution based on her membership in the social group of young women of the Tchamba–Kunsuntu tribe who have not been mutilated and who oppose the practice. In so holding, we ruled that Ms. Kasinga's gender and ethnic affiliation were characteristics she could not change, and the characteristic of having intact genitalia was so fundamental that she should not be required to change it.

The Immigration Judge decided the case before her consistent with our precedent decision in Kasinga. In both cases, the social group was defined by reference to gender in combination with one or more additional factors. In Kasinga, the social group was defined by gender, ethnic affiliation, and opposition to female genital mutilation ("FGM"). In the instant case, the social group is based on gender, relationship to an abusive partner, and opposition to domestic violence. As the Immigration Judge below correctly observed, the respondent's relationship to, and association with, her husband is something she cannot change. It is an immutable characteristic under the Acosta guidelines, which we affirmed in Kasinga.

There are a number of other striking similarities between the instant case and Kasinga. Both cases involve a form of persecution inflicted by private parties upon family members. In both cases, the victims opposed and resisted a practice which was ingrained in the culture, broadly sanctioned by the community, and unprotected by the state. In both cases, the overarching societal objective underlying the cultural norm was the assurance of male domination. . . .

In attempting to distinguish this case from Kasinga, the majority contends that domestic violence in Guatemala, unlike FGM in Togo, is not so pervasive or "societally important" that the respondent will face "social ostracization" for refusing to submit to the harm. The majority's distinction is flawed. The facts of Kasinga did not suggest that Kasinga would face severe social ostracization for her refusal to submit to FGM; rather, as a member of a social group defined by her unique circumstances, she faced harm only because she lost the protection of her father. In Kasinga, a family member, Kasinga's aunt, targeted her after the death of her father who, as the primary authority figure in her family, had previously protected her from FGM. In other words, the practice was not so pervasive in Togo that her father, also a member of the ethnic group which had targeted her, had been unable to identify the practice as harmful. Some persons within Togo viewed FGM as an acceptable practice; other persons, even those within the same ethnic group (such as Kasinga's father, mother, and sister), did not. We extended asylum protection to Kasinga not because she faced societal ostracization, but because she demonstrated a well-founded fear of harm on account of her membership in a group composed of persons sharing her specific circumstances.

In the end, there are no meaningful distinctions that justify recognizing the social group claim in Kasinga while refusing to recognize such a social group claim in the instant case. The gender-based characteristics shared by the members of each group are immutable, the form of abuse resisted in both cases was considered culturally normative and was broadly sanctioned by the community, and the persecution imposed occurred without possibility of state protection. . . .

D.   The Respondent Was Harmed and Has a Well–Founded Fear of Harm on Account of Membership in a Particular Social Group

. . . [T]o assess motivation, it is appropriate to consider the factual circumstances surrounding the violence. The factual record reflects quite clearly that the severe beatings were directed at the respondent by her husband to dominate and subdue her, precisely because of her gender, as he inflicted his harm directly on her vagina, sought to abort her pregnancy, and raped her. . . .

[W]e should attempt to identify why such horrific violence occurs at all. In Kasinga, we determined that FGM exists as a means of controlling women's sexuality. So too does domestic violence exist as a means by which men may systematically destroy the power of women, a form of violence rooted in the economic, social, and cultural subordination of women.... The fundamental purpose of domestic violence is to punish, humiliate, and exercise power over the victim on account of her gender....

It is reasonable to believe, on the basis of the record before us, that the husband was motivated, at least in part, "on account of" the respondent's membership in a particular social group that is defined by her gender, her relationship to him, and her opposition to domestic violence....

IV. Persecution on Account of Actual or Imputed Opinion Opposing Domestic Abuse and Violence Against Women

... Opposition to male domination and violence against women, and support for gender equity, constitutes a political opinion.... Such opposition is not restricted to those who have not been victims of domestic violence, but constitutes a political opinion that may also be held by victims of domestic violence themselves. Both the respondent's status as a battered spouse in an intimate relationship with a man who imposes such domination and her actual or perceived opinion opposing domestic violence trigger continuing abuse from the persecutor who seeks to dominate her....

V. Conclusion

For the foregoing reasons, I would dismiss the Service's appeal. The Immigration Judge was correct in determining that the respondent is eligible for asylum pursuant to section 208 of the Act, 8 U.S.C. § 1158 (1994). I, therefore, respectfully dissent.

NOTES AND QUESTIONS

1. **Gender as a Social Group and Domestic Violence as Persecution.** After considerable public outcry over the decision, the USCIS in 2000 proposed new regulations that would formally recognize gender as a particular social group, and domestic violence as persecution, so long as certain circumstances were met. 65 Fed. Reg. 76,588 (Dec. 7, 2000). Excerpts of these regulations appear below. In January 2001, following a national campaign by asylum advocates, then-Attorney General Janet Reno vacated the Bureau of Immigration Appeals (BIA) decision and directed the BIA to reconsider, but to stay reconsideration until after finalization of the proposed regulations. In 2003, with the proposed regulations still not finalized, Attorney General John Ashcroft recertified the case to himself, prompting a storm of advocacy by NGOs, professors and legislators to try to persuade him to affirm the original grant of asylum.

Significantly, in February 2004, the Department of Homeland Security (DHS), which had taken over the functions of the Immigration and Naturalization Service, recommended to Ashcroft that asylum be granted. In its brief, DHS argued that "under some limited circumstances, a victim of domestic violence can establish eligibility for asylum on the basis of having a well-founded fear of persecution on account of membership in a particular social group." Since both parties were now in agreement that asylum should be granted, DHS said it believed the case to be moot, and moved the Attorney General to remand the case to the BIA with the instruction to summarily grant asylum. The brief of the Department of Homeland Security, which analyzes both the social group and political opinion arguments, appears at http://cgrs.uchastings.edu/documents/legal/dhs_brief_ra.pdf. Instead of following the DHS recommendation, however, in January 2005 Attorney General Ashcroft remanded the case to the BIA for reconsideration following final publication of the proposed asylum regulations.

The proposed regulations have yet to be finalized. As of January 2007, Rodi Alvarado is in legal limbo, still awaiting a decision, separated from her children, and without any of the legal rights that would come from being granted asylum.

The proposed regulations cited by both Reno and Ashcroft state, in part:

> . . .
>
> The Board's particular social group analysis in *In re R–A–* . . ., requires some clarification.
>
> As an evidentiary matter, it often would be reasonable to expect that a person who is motivated to harm a victim because of a characteristic the victim shares with others would be prone to harm or threaten others who share the targeted characteristic. Such a showing should not necessarily be required as a matter of law, however, in order for an applicant to satisfy the "on account of" requirement. In some cases, a persecutor may in fact target an individual victim because of a shared characteristic, even though the persecutor does not act against others who possess the same characteristic. For example, in a society in which members of one race hold members of another race in slavery, that society may expect that a slave owner who beats his own slave would not beat the slave of his neighbor. It would nevertheless be reasonable to conclude that the beating is centrally motivated by the victim's race. Similarly, in some cases involving domestic violence, an applicant may be able to establish that the abuser is motivated to harm her because of her gender or because of her status in a domestic relationship. This may be a characteristic that she shares with other women in her society, some of whom are also at risk of harm from their partners on account of this shared characteristic. Thus, it may be possible in some cases for a victim of domestic violence to satisfy the "on account of" requirement, even though social limitations and other factors result in the abuser having the opportunity, and indeed the motivation, to harm only one of the women who share this characteristic, because only one of these women is in a domestic relationship with the abuser.
>
> To allow for this possibility, this rule provides that, when evaluating whether an applicant has met his or her burden of proof to establish that the harm he or she suffered or fears is "on account of" a protected

characteristic, "[b]oth direct and circumstantial evidence may be relevant to the inquiry." The rule further provides that "[e]vidence that the persecutor seeks to act against other individuals who share the applicant's protected characteristic is relevant and may be considered but shall not be required." . . .

As this rule underscores, both direct and circumstantial evidence may be relevant to this determination. As in any asylum or withholding case, evidence about the persecutor's statements and actions will be considered. In addition, evidence about patterns of violence in the society against individuals similarly situated to the applicant may also be relevant to the "on account of" determination. For example, in the domestic violence context, an adjudicator would consider any evidence that the abuser uses violence to enforce power and control over the applicant because of the social status that a woman may acquire when she enters into a domestic relationship. This would include any direct evidence about the abuser's own actions, as well as any circumstantial evidence that such patterns of violence are (1) supported by the legal system or social norms in the country in question, and (2) reflect a prevalent belief within society, or within relevant segments of society, that cannot be deduced simply by evidence of random acts within that society. Such circumstantial evidence, in addition to direct evidence regarding the abuser's statements or actions, would be relevant to determining whether the abuser believes he has the authority to abuse and control the victim "on account of" her status in the relationship. . . .

2. **Legal Limbo.** Because these proposed regulations have not yet been finalized, many battered women seeking asylum have found themselves in a sort of "legal purgatory." As a result, many of these women have been forced to put their lives on hold. And it could be years before the issue is ultimately resolved, according to Philip Hwang, Staff Attorney for the Lawyers' Committee for Civil Rights, which provides *pro bono* legal services for indigent asylum seekers. Tresa Baldas, *Waiting for Asylum: Battered Women Stuck in Legal Limbo*, Nat'l L. J., Mar. 13, 2006, at 1–2.

3. **Characterization of "Social Group."** In its brief to Attorney General Ashcroft, the Department of Homeland Security characterized "social group" very narrowly, as "married women in Guatemala who are unable to leave the relationship." How would "social group" be characterized under the proposed regulations? If you were to submit comments on the proposed regulations with suggestions for change or adoption, what remarks would you submit and why?

The dissent in *In Re R–A–* accuses the majority of making an "unacceptable," as well as "outdated and improper" distinction between the "supposedly" more private forms of persecution suffered by women and the more public forms of persecution suffered by men. Does the majority or the dissent have the better of this argument? How does the dissent frame domestic violence as a "political" and "public" matter? How exactly does the majority consign domestic violence to the private sphere? As both opinions make clear, the abuse suffered by an applicant can provide a basis for asylum if it is inflicted on either of two grounds: membership in a particular social group, or an actual or imputed political opinion. The majority finds that R–A–qualifies on neither ground, while the dissent argues that she qualifies on both. Do you find one basis more persuasive than the other? For a discussion of what constitutes a social group see Michael G. Heyman, *Asylum, Social Group Membership, and the Non–State Actor: The Challenge of Domestic Violence*, 36 U. Mich. J.L. Reform 767 (2003).

4. **Asylum, Global Violence, Floodgates or Call to Action.** You have seen that domestic violence is widespread around the world. What do these statistics mean for refugee and asylum claims made in the United States? In light of the critical perspectives that you have read on treatment of domestic violence in the United States, is it puzzling that there are so many domestic violence victims from around the world seeking refuge in the United States? By granting asylum to victims of gender-based violence, is the United States opening the door to a flood of abused immigrants from across the globe, as some fear? Or is it, as others claim, that by granting asylum in cases of gender-based violence the United States sends a much-needed "principled message" to states that refuse to protect such victims? While reading the excerpt below, consider these questions:

> After World War II the nations of the world made a commitment to protect individuals fleeing persecution. In the last half-century the Cold War has come to an end, much of the movement of asylum seekers is from the global south to global north, and the types of claims, as well as the complexion of those seeking protection, has changed. As a consequence, countries have become less welcoming of asylum seekers, and have erected various barriers—some procedural, and some substantive. It is in this climate that gender asylum claims— which vary from the historically traditional claims—have given rise to controversy, and resistance from States that fear an inundation of asylum seekers.... [T]he inextricable relationship between human rights violations and refugee claims for protection points to another solution to countries wary that the acceptance of gender claims will lead to waves of asylum seekers. This solution is to simultaneously extend protection to those in need of it, while taking measures to address the underlying causes of refugee flows. Such a response is not only principled, but it is consistent with commitments undertaken in the wake of World War II. Furthermore, such an approach is both pragmatic and feasible. The claim of Rodi Alvarado provides an opportunity to put this model to the test—instead of denying her protection, the United States should recognize her valid claim to asylum, and turn its attention to Guatemala to help bring an end to impunity for violence against women." Karen Musalo, *Protecting Victims of Gendered Persecution: Fear of Floodgates or Call to (Principled) Action?*, 14 Va. J. Soc. Pol'y & L. 119 (2007).

5. **Domestic Violence, Gender Claims and Political Opposition.** We have focused on asylum claims that are based on domestic violence, but it is important to note that there may also be asylum petitions in which political

opposition claims are made in addition to claims concerning gender and domestic violence.

6. **Further Discussion.** For further discussion of the issues raised by the application of asylum doctrine to the context of domestic or other gender-based violence, see Deborah Anker, Lauren Gilbert and Nancy Kelly, *Women Whose Governments are Unable or Unwilling to Provide Reasonable Protection from Domestic Violence May Qualify as Refugees Under United States Asylum Law,* 11 Geo. Immigr. L.J. 709, 713 (1997); Kristin E. Kandt, *United States Asylum Law: Recognizing Persecution Based on Gender Using Canada as a Comparison,* 9 Geo. Immigr. L.J. 137, 145 (1995); Nancy Kelly, *Gender–Related Persecution: Assessing the Asylum Claims of Women,* 26 Cornell Int'l L.J. 625 (1993); Pamela Goldberg, *Anyplace But Home: Asylum in the United States for Women Fleeing Intimate Violence,* 26 Cornell Int'l L.J. 565, 591–92 (1993); Joan Fitzpatrick, *Flight from Asylum: Trends Towards Temporary "Refuge" and Local Responses to Forced Migration,* 35 Va. J. Int'l L. 13 (1994); Angélica Cházaro and Jennifer Casey, *Getting Away with Murder: Guatemala's Failure to Protect Women and Rodi Alvarado's Quest for Safety,* Ctr. for Gender and Refugee Studies (Nov. 2005), available at http://cgrs.uchastings.edu/documents/cgrs/cgrs_guatemala_femicides.pdf; Audrey Macklin, *Disappearing Refugees: Reflections on the Canada–U.S. Safe Third Country Agreement,* 36 Colum. Hum. Rts. L. Rev. 365 (2005). The Center for Refugee and Asylum Studies at Hastings College of Law is an important general resource (http://cgrs.uhastings.edu).

CHAPTER SIXTEEN

DOMESTIC VIOLENCE AS A VIOLATION OF CIVIL RIGHTS

Introduction

Our starting point in Chapter One was that domestic violence, like other forms of violence against women, has historically been, and is still, a public practice as well as a private practice. It is public in the sense that it has historically enforced, and still enforces, broadly accepted or tolerated norms about what women are for, where they belong, and what they may and may not do, even as it exacts a terrible and often excruciatingly private price from individual women.

If we were looking for support for the idea that private violence is still attached to ideas about male entitlement and power, we might note how often it continues by other means. Restrictions on women's freedom were legally sanctioned or enforced, such as the exclusion of women from participation in the professions and many other forms of employment, and the legal subordination of women to men in marriage. John Stuart Mill, writing about the subjection of women in 1869, saw a progression from the exercise of brute force against women to the more legally-based restrictions of his own day. John Stuart Mill, THE SUBJECTION OF WOMEN (S.M. Okin ed. 1988). As we do away with this overt, state-sanctioned machinery of women's subordination, it seems we are leaving to private enforcers the last ditch efforts to sustain the old order.

To the extent that practices of violence against women, including domestic violence, still function to subordinate women to men, public failure to curb that violence has particular consequences. First, as long as "the state" in its official capacity, and society more generally, continue to tolerate private violence, women are not, in reality, the full and equal citizens the constitution and laws promise they will be; nor are women the full and equal citizens we imagine they are. They are not, in other words, receiving their full "due" from the state. At the same time, violence against women, in its daily and mundane exercise, concretely impedes women's participation in civic and political life, and diminishes their contribution to it. Women are not in a position, in other words, to give the full measure of what they have to offer to society. This may in turn explain why we are not, as a society, making faster progress towards eradicating practices of violence against women.

Feminist scholars have consistently stressed this political and public aspect of women's private oppression, offering frameworks that reflect both the richness of feminist legal interpretations of battering and the expressive dimensions of rights claims. Within this literature, domestic violence has been interpreted as a perpetuation of coverture, as a denial of equal

849

protection, as involuntary servitude, and as terrorism and torture. All these formulations underscore the problem of woman abuse as political, and identify the underlying issues of liberty, autonomy, equality and women's citizenship, which have become important in feminist social theory. The use of political imagery highlights the degree to which domestic violence is understood within a broader public-private dichotomy and challenges this dichotomy to describe the "personal" and "domestic" problem of partner violence as a problem of public dimension, implicating issues of citizenship and political rights.

Significantly, no sooner does law confront one of the contested arenas in which "private" violence against women still flourishes, and begin to elaborate new norms, or make new demands on behalf of women, than these efforts are discredited, ridiculed and attacked, in a highly public and political way. It could be that this is because the efforts are consistently wrongheaded, or misdirected, or clumsy, or trample on "rights" of higher priority than women's full and equal participation as citizens in society. It may surely be the case that individual initiatives on behalf of women sometimes miss the mark, or prove blunt instruments in need of refinement or adjustment. But the intensity of the opposition may have much more to do with the fact that as a society we do still resist, at a fundamental level, the idea that women's concerns, their needs, their perceptions and even their rights are as valid, as legitimate, as deserving of recognition and protection, as men's. The intensity of that resistance may not have changed much since J.S. Mill wrote about it in 1869:

> So long as an opinion is strongly rooted in the feelings, it gains rather than loses in stability by having a preponderating weight of argument against it. For if it were accepted as a result of argument, the refutation of the argument might shake the solidity of the conviction; but when it rests solely on feeling, the worse it fares in argumentative contest, the more persuaded its adherents are that their feeling must have some deeper ground, which the arguments do not reach; and while the feeling remains, it is always throwing up fresh intrenchments of argument to repair any breach made in the old. And there are so many causes tending to make the feelings connected with this subject the most intense and most deeply rooted of all those which gather round and protect old institutions and customs, that we need not wonder to find them as yet less undermined and loosened than any of the rest by the progress of the great modern spiritual and social transition; nor suppose that the barbarisms to which men cling longest must be less barbarous than those which they earlier shake off.

The opening section of this chapter introduces some scholarly theorizing about the political and public nature of domestic violence. The next section traces the history of the first federal effort to define violence against women as a violation of women's civil rights. In the opposition to the provision's passage, in the compromises reached in order to secure its enactment, and in the subsequent legal challenges which resulted in the Supreme Court's decision that Congress had no power to enact it, you will see replayed the contest over what is public and what private, and the contest over whether we are willing to reorder our priorities to give precedence to women's freedom from violence. The final materials in this chapter offer a glimpse of how the next round of the contest may be shaping up and provide some thoughts about the full implications of gender equality for the society at large.

A.   VIOLENCE, EQUALITY AND CITIZENSHIP

Isabel Marcus has argued, as the next reading illustrates, that abusive relationships continue the practice of coverture; the legal structure which denied the separate legal existence of married women, and merged their identities with those of their husbands, who had exclusive control of their property and earnings, and exclusive authority over the children of the marriage.

Isabel Marcus
Reframing Domestic Violence as Terrorism in the Home
in The Public Nature of Private Violence (M.A. Fineman and R. Mykitiuk, eds. 1994).

Coverture was a designation of limitation and exclusion. It encoded beliefs regarding women's capacity and competence to act in the world. It confirmed and validated a sex-based locus of virtually unaccountable control in a marital relationship. It was a manifestation of cultural consciousness and a statement about the condition of citizenship. . . .

Both political and economic theory reinforced the theologically ordained structure of family. Political theory identified the family as the building block or basis of society and the state, though women, even as family members, are virtually absent from the works of Western political theorists. Like a polity, a family must possess a hierarchical structure. Logically, there must be one designated head for a family whose will prevails by virtue of an assigned place in the structure. The absence of a clear rule designating a head would create disharmony and strife in the family and, consequently, both in the polity and in the market which were best served by *a priori* clear—that is—sex-based—designations of competence in civic matters and in commercial transactions.

Separately, or in combination, these beliefs spoke to the self-evident "naturalness" of the family structure of coverture. Even a skeptic might be convinced by the array of theology, political theory, and economics which proffered dire predictions of societal disorder and chaos in the wake of any proposed separate legal identity for married women. No wonder that contesting this seemingly closed belief system was the first important task of nineteenth-century American feminism.

While the most economically disempowering aspects of the doctrine of coverture were officially abolished by the end of the nineteenth century, it was not until the final quarter of the twentieth century that the last formal vestiges of the doctrine in a commercial setting were eliminated. . . .

The demise of the formal doctrine of coverture did not signal the eradication of beliefs regarding the "naturalness" or appropriateness of sex-based power in marital relationships and the use of coercive means, including violence and abuse ..., for securing or maintaining that power. In the interval between the formal elimination of coverture and the present, there is no reason to believe that the violence abated.

When the second wave of feminism began to interrogate the status of women ..., emphasis was placed initially on pay equity, sexuality, and personal freedom. With the emergence in the seventies of rape and pornography as issues, contemporary feminists rediscovered battered women, and the, at times, lethal level of resistance on the part of men to efforts to divest them of privilege. I argue that the continuation of the violence, and the widespread failure of the state to address and punish it, are contemporary manifestations of the practice of coverture in the United States; the men who abuse or batter their spouse or partner practice that domination and control which is the *sine qua non* of coverture. I recognize that this claim is open to several challenges: ahistoricism, or at least the blurring or conflating of historical boundaries, or, worse yet, engagement in a mere semantic dispute. My answer is that this response is shortsighted and parochial. In no other relationship established and "privileged" by law or contract is such physical violence condoned; in no other relationship enjoying the protection of the state is such physical violence minimized or denied. Simply put, coverture cannot be said to have disappeared when its essential enforcement mechanism is available and widely used to maintain power and control in a marriage. That the structures of subordination persist in reshaped form is not unique to women's subordination in families. Critical race theorists understand well the premise that "contemporary inequalities and social institutional practices are linked to earlier periods in which the intent and cultural meaning of such practices were clear."

NOTES AND QUESTIONS

1. **Enforcing Coverture through Terrorism.** Marcus argues further that modern day coverture is imposed by a strategy that approximates terrorism:

> Regimes or groups seeking to terrorize populations utilize three tactics to enhance their credibility: unannounced and seemingly random but actually calculated attacks of violence; psychological as well as physical warfare aimed at silencing protests and minimizing retaliatory responses from the targets of violence; and the creation of an atmosphere of intimidation in which there is no safe place of escape....

> There are strong and striking parallels and similarities between terrorism as a strategy used to destabilize a community or society consisting both of women and men, and the abuse and violence perpetrated against women in intimate or partnering situations. Like terror directed at a community, violence against women is designed to maintain domination and control, to enhance or reinforce advantages, and to defend privileges. Like other individuals or communities who experience politically motivated terrorism, women whose partnering and

intimate relationships are marked by violence directed against them live in a world similarly punctuated by traumatic and or catastrophic events, such as threats and humiliation, stalking and surveillance, coercion and physical violence.

There is a powerful connection between Marcus's suggestion that modern-day enforcers of coverture are terrorists, and the terrorism practiced in the post Civil War era by those unwilling to yield the privileges of slave ownership.

2. **Similarities Between the Life of Abused Women and Involuntary Servants.** Joyce McConnell, in the article from which the next reading is drawn, likens the situation of abused women to the plight of those relieved from "involuntary servitude" by the passage of the Thirteenth Amendment. While she properly resists the analogy to slavery, calling it both inaccurate and inherently racist, she suggests multiple ways in which the life of an abused woman parallels a life under involuntary servitude: the creation of slave-like conditions through the private use of force; the control of all aspects of the woman's life; the forced performance, not only of economic production and domestic tasks, but of personal services such as sex and reproduction; the abuser's controlling of food, water, medicinal care, movement, formal education, religion and familial affiliation; deprivation, beatings, maimings, whippings, rape, murder, torture, starvation, and the ever present threat of any of them, and the constant threat and actual separation of mothers from children, and other family members from one another.

Joyce McConnell
Beyond Metaphor: Battered Women, Involuntary Servitude and the Thirteenth Amendment

4 Yale J.L. and Feminism 207 (1992).

When Congress debated the Thirteenth Amendment and its prohibitions against slavery and involuntary servitude, anxious members inquired whether it would alter the traditional relationship of husband and wife. Their concern materialized out of a political context in which those who sought abolition of African American chattel slavery and the establishment of women's rights were applying the norm of individual freedom beyond the narrow scope of landed white men. At that time, the metaphor "women are slaves" had rhetorical currency, and suggested that white women shared with African American men and women a similar legal and social status of non-identity and disability. No matter how rhetorically useful this metaphor may have seemed then or may seem now, it was and remains grossly inaccurate and inherently racist. It obscured the fact that white women were slaveholders or beneficiaries of the slave system. It failed to recognize that even though there were significant political and social constraints on white women, they did not as a class suffer in the way that African Americans did under slavery. Finally, it ignored the fact that African American women were slaves and that other women were not, no matter what their subordinate legal or socio-economic status. So, the metaphor was and is fundamentally flawed both by its generality and its exclusion.

It was not slavery, as metaphor or term, however, that evoked the concern of some Congressmen that their dominant positions in their families were in jeopardy. Rather, their uneasy recognition of the Amendment's potential to reach into marital relationships was sparked by the term "involuntary servitude," which was explicitly included in the Thirteenth Amendment to prohibit the creation of slave-like conditions through the private use of force. Although the Congressmen's anxiety was treated as absurd by sponsors of the Amendment, an examination of the Thirteenth Amendment's prohibition against involuntary servitude in the context of the conditions to which women who are battered in intimate relationships such as marriage are subjected reveals that their anxiety was well-founded. . . .

To fully understand the potential reach of the Thirteenth Amendment's prohibition, it is best to dispense, if only for a minute, with the mind's attempt to define slavery and to permit the soul to explore the horror of what it meant to be owned as human property. The owner of human chattel could freely use this human property as she or he would any other piece of property, animate or inanimate. Although there were some legal sanctions against some egregious acts, such as unjustified murder of a slave, they were seldom enforced and had little if any impact on slaveholders' conduct. Their freedom was essentially unbridled.

As important as legal ownership was, the slaveholders' belief in their moral right of ownership, in their natural superiority, and in the African–Americans' natural inferiority provided the justification for daily degradation and subjugation. Thus, the system of American slavery is best understood as the absolute control by white slaveholders over all aspects of the lives of their slaves. This is not to diminish the ways in which the slaves manifested their free will, but rather to acknowledge the legal right and the power of the slaveholders to attempt to break it and to supplant it with their own. Understood in this way, the concept of the servitude contemplated by slavery as being just like that exchanged by the free worker for wages becomes absurd. The owner of humans was free to demand whatever he or she pleased, and what pleased was not confined to existing market equivalents. Thus, along with forced economic production and domestic tasks, with their obvious counterparts in the free wage-labor system, came other personal services such as sex and reproduction.

Furthermore, there were services demanded through coercion that should be categorized as such, but which are more typically thought of as aspects of the coercion itself. For example, splitting families, removing children, controlling food, water, medical care, movement, formal education, religion and familial affiliation are all coercive techniques. They involve services of the body, mind, heart and spirit, all outside the bounds of the free marketplace, but completely and legitimately within the private sphere of the master/slave relationship. Viewed in historical context, the concept of the servitude embodied in the Thirteenth Amendment is an expansive one with roots in both the public and private spheres.

Congress recognized that the system of absolute control existing in slavery flowed from the legal status of slaves as chattel. Thus, when

Congress prohibited slavery, it started from the premise that one person should not be permitted by law to own another. But Congress also recognized that, even without the imprimatur of the state, an evil similar to slavery could exist. The system of chattel slavery provided proof of the abuses springing from the actual ownership of, or the belief in the right of domination over, other human beings. The nature and level of coercion used against slaves was violent and horrific. It included deprivation, beatings, maimings, whippings, rape, murder, torture, starvation, and the ever present threat of any or all of them. In addition, it included the constant threat and actual separation of mothers from children and other family members from one another.

Congress sought to abolish not just slavery, but the characteristics of slavery created through coercion. Thus, in adopting the Thirteenth Amendment, Congress not only forbade the legal ownership of human chattel (slavery) but prohibited anyone from treating another as if such ownership existed (involuntary servitude). The Thirteenth Amendment sought to preserve the tenet of free will and prohibited the use of coercion sufficient to break it.

NOTE AND QUESTIONS

1. **Enforcing Freedom through the Fourteenth Amendment.** A third theorist, Robin West, looks not at the Thirteenth Amendment but the Fourteenth. The passage of the Thirteenth Amendment was not enough, as a practical matter, to abolish slavery; the continued enforced subordination of former slaves through economic coercion and private violence allowed the continuation of slavery by other means, and law enforcement, at the state level, turned a blind eye. The passage of the Fourteenth Amendment, she argues, was viewed as a necessary next step; enabling the federal government to step in and ensure that state authority was not complicit in upholding the private authority of former slave owners.

Robin West argues that, historically, the equal protection clause was understood as challenging the "dual sovereignty" under which slaves lived, and that the situation of women subject to violence at the hands of their partners, and deprived of legal remedy, can also be understood as a situation of dual sovereignty. She urges that the Fourteenth Amendment should be interpreted to allow those deprived of meaningful state protection against private violence to challenge this public inaction, while acknowledging that Fourteenth Amendment jurisprudence has strayed far from this original "abolitionist" interpretation.

Robin West
Toward an Abolitionist Interpretation of the Fourteenth Amendment
94 W. VA. L. REV. 111 (1991).

... [T]he citizen lives under the rule of only one sovereign—the state—while the slave lives under the rule of at least two sovereigns—the state and the master—the commands of both to be endured under the threat of unchecked violence. The citizen must abide by the commands of the state if he wishes to avoid its violent sanctions, but must not abide the commands of any other. He is protected by the state and more specifically by its criminal law against all non-state violence: this protection is certainly a part of what it means to have rights. The slave, in marked contrast, must abide by the commands of two sovereigns, the state and the master, if he wishes to avoid violence or deprivation: this is *what it is* to be denied the protection of the state's law. Where one citizen, but not others, is denied protection, then protection is obviously unequal. The inequality of *protection*, unlike the unequal application of general laws ..., gives rise not only to the evil of formal injustice but to the much more concrete, pervasive, and pernicious evil of slavery.

... [T]he plainest possible meaning of the Fourteenth Amendment mandate ... is that no state may deny to any citizen the protection of its criminal and civil law against private violence and private violation. Put differently, no state may, through denials of protection, permit any citizen to live in a state of "dual sovereignty." ... Only the state shall have access to the use of unchecked and uncheckable violence to effectuate its will (and then, of course, only with due process). No citizen shall be subject to uncheckable violence by anyone other than the state; no citizen shall be under the will and command of anyone other than the state. Inversely, no entity, no individual, no group, no race, no gender, and no class other than the state shall have recourse to uncheckable violence as a means of effectuating his, her, or its will. No one other than the state shall have the power, backed by the credible threat of violence, to command and dominate the will of others.... Any relationship of sovereignty between a subject and master, other than that between state and citizen, that exists through state acquiescence—a refusal of the state to deter the credible threat of violence on which sovereignty depends—is evidence that the state has violated this guarantee of protection....

... The abolitionists, above all else, understood that it was precisely a denial of the protection of the state against private violence and private violation of trust that facilitated and even defined the status of the slave. After the passage of the Thirteenth Amendment, it became apparent to the abolitionists, their advocates, and fellow travelers in Congress that although a denial of equal protection is a necessary condition of slavery, eradication of slavery is not tantamount to a guarantee of equal protection. The wave of Ku Klux Klan violence of whites against blacks and abolitionists, the refusal of the southern states (and in many instances the northern states), to punish, check or deter that violence, and the states' refusal to extend to the freed slaves the legal forms of contract and property that were essential to their participation in the community's economic life ... engendered precisely the relationship of sovereign and subject, dominance and subservience, command and obedience, which the unchecked violence and violation of one group against another can predictably insure....

Thus, the need for yet another amendment: one outlawing not just the symptom of slavery but the disease itself—the denial of the protection of the state against private violence and violation, of which slavery is one, but only one, possible manifestation. The equal protection clause of the Fourteenth Amendment was thus intended by the abolitionists, and at least some of its proponents, to abolish not only slavery *per se*, but also the "dual sovereignty" which facilitates it. . . .

As far as I can tell, this particular history is not controversial; indeed, this can fairly be called the *uncontested* meaning of the Fourteenth Amendment. . . .

. . . [T]he marital rape exemption still in force, albeit in an attenuated form, in several states, constitutes as literal a modern withdrawal of the states' protection against violent assault as did the states' failure to protect against murder during the heyday of Klan violence. The consequences are also not dissimilar. A woman who can be forcibly and physically intruded upon without recourse to legal protection or remedy is not a victim of crime, with the remedies and rights pertinent thereto; rather, she is, and will most likely regard herself, as subject to the sovereign whim of he who can, without fear of state reprisal, coerce her consent through legitimate threats of force and violence. Such a woman . . . lives under the will of two sovereigns rather than one: the state and her husband against whose violence there is no recourse. Consequently, the husband's commands must be obeyed if violence is to be avoided. The marital rape "exemption" is in a very literal sense a denial of the state's promise of protection against violent assault and, as such, given an abolitionist understanding of the phrase, is clearly and unproblematically unconstitutional. . . .

. . . [I]t follows that a number of the [Supreme] Court's recent decisions, whether grounded in the Fourteenth Amendment's equal protection clause or not, are wrong, or, if not wrong in their outcome, wrong in some aspect of their reasoning. The major premise of the Court's recent decision in *DeShaney v. Winnebago County Department of Social Services,* and the sizeable number of similar cases that followed and preceded it, that there is no constitutional right to a police force, is squarely wrong. The right to a police force, or, more specifically, the right to the state's protection against the subjugating effects of private violence, are the paradigm Fourteenth Amendment rights. It is precisely these rights which make us "equal" in the eyes of the law. Given our right to police protection against private violence, we are equally subject to the commands of only one sovereign, the rule of law, and given that right we are equally free because we are equally free of subjection to the commands of any other. It follows that little Joshua DeShaney, brutally, repeatedly, and privately assaulted by his father, suffering massive and permanent brain damage as a result, did indeed suffer a constitutional deprivation. This violation was not *because* the state had sufficiently intervened into the family's life so as to satisfy the state action requirement as (indirectly) argued by the dissent, but, rather, because it did not intervene *enough*. Through its inaction, not its action, the state failed to provide equal protection of the law. . . .

It also follows from the abolitionists' minimalist understanding of equal protection that the so-called "state action" requirement, at least as presently understood by the court, and according to some of its various definitions, is drastically misconceived. The equal protection clause, under an abolitionist interpretation, targets states' refusal to protect citizens against profoundly private action which results in subordination or enslavement. The "state action," then, which is the object of the Amendment, is the breach of an affirmative duty to protect the rights of citizens to be free, minimally, of the subordinating, enslaving violence of other citizens.... The state breach that constitutes the violation may take the form either of action or inaction, feasance or malfeasance: the state may simply fail to protect one group from the violence of others (as in the case of unpunished and undeterred Klan or domestic violence), or the state may do something far more visible, such as pass legislation explicitly removing one group from the reach of the state's protection against the violence of others (such as in the case of marital rape exemption laws). Whether the state's failure to protect constitutes an action or inaction, however, is not determinative. What is determinative are the consequences of the state's conduct: whether by virtue of the state's action or inaction there exists a separate state of sovereignty in which one citizen is subjected to the will of another citizen as well as to the sovereignty of the state.

NOTES AND QUESTIONS

1. **Applying the Abolitionist Interpretation of the Fourteenth Amendment.** You have encountered equal protection claims, successful and unsuccessful, elsewhere in this book. Remember the case of *Moran v. Beyer*, 734 F.2d 1245 (7th Cir. 1984), excerpted in Chapter Thirteen above, in which the Seventh Circuit struck down Illinois' interspousal tort immunity as violative of equal protection for married people. Remember also the constitutional tort claims based on police failures to protect abused women, discussed in Chapter Fourteen. To what extent might these claims have been more successful had Robin West's proposed abolitionist interpretation of the Fourteenth Amendment guided the development of Fourteenth Amendment jurisprudence? Are there other contexts in which this interpretation might support litigation against state action or inaction in response to domestic violence?

2. **The Nineteenth Amendment.** Another scholar, Reva Siegel, has suggested that women have been handicapped in their quest for equality under the Constitution by the necessity of relying on the Fourteenth Amendment, which offers no legislative history specific to issues of gender. She wonders whether the debates surrounding the passage of the Nineteenth Amendment might have more to offer than is commonly appreciated. We understand the Nineteenth Amendment as doing nothing more than guaranteeing women the right to vote. Her argument is that read in the light of its history, that Amendment could instead be understood as incorporating a sex-equality norm bearing on a wide range of institutions and practices. "In particular," she suggests, "those who advocated and opposed enfranchising women understood woman suffrage to raise questions concerning the family, and the link between voting and family structure shaped debates over enfranchising women as a matter of state and federal law." Reva B. Siegel, *Collective Memory and the Nineteenth*

Amendment: Reasoning About "the Woman Question" in the Discourse of Sex Discrimination, in HISTORY, MEMORY AND THE LAW (A. Sarat and T. Kearns, eds. 1999).

3. **VAWA Civil Rights Provision.** One relatively recent context in which the connections between "private" violence against women and women's political and civil rights have again been debated is the civil rights provision of the 1994 Violence Against Women Act. This is the topic of the next section.

B.   THE CIVIL RIGHTS REMEDY CREATED BY THE VIOLENCE AGAINST WOMEN ACT OF 1994

In 1994, the Violence Against Women Act passed by Congress included a civil rights provision. Many women's rights and civil rights organizations and domestic advocacy groups around the country worked to develop this legislation and struggled mightily for many years to achieve its passage. The provision was controversial, and as soon as it was invoked as the basis for litigation, it was challenged on constitutional grounds. In May 2000, the United States Supreme Court held the provision unconstitutional in *United States v. Morrison*, 529 U.S. 598 (2000).

This section examines the history and meaning of the VAWA civil rights provision, and its demise. The section begins with a statement made prior to the provision's passage by the NOW Legal Defense Fund, one of the legislation's major proponents, and a discussion of the concerns and compromises that shaped the legislative process. The section continues with the provision as it was ultimately enacted, looks at commentary on the significance of the controversies surrounding the provision and the constitutional challenges it faced, and ends with an excerpt from the Supreme Court's opinion in *Morrison*. The following section turns to the future of alternative federal and state civil rights provisions in light of *Morrison*.

Sally Goldfarb
STATEMENT OF THE NOW LEGAL DEFENSE AND EDUCATION FUND ON THE VIOLENCE AGAINST WOMEN ACT

BEFORE THE SUBCOMMITTEE ON CIVIL AND CONSTITUTIONAL RIGHTS, COMMITTEE OF THE JUDICIARY, HOUSE OF REPRESENTATIVES, UNITED STATES CONGRESS, PRESENTED NOVEMBER 16, 1993.

The Violence Against Women Act's Civil Rights Provision

. . . The NOW Legal Defense and Education Fund strongly supports Title III of H.R. 1133 in its present form. We feel that the definition of "crime of violence motivated by gender" furnished in the bill is clear, workable, and sound public policy. . . .

[T]he civil rights remedy extends only to acts that would rise to the level of a felony under state or federal law. It does not cover random acts of violence unrelated to gender. Thus it is amply clear that not every crime against a women would qualify. Indeed, the civil rights remedy is gender-neutral and is available to male or female victims of serious gender-motivated crimes.

The burden rests on the plaintiff to prove by a preponderance of the evidence that the crime was motivated by gender. Proving that a crime was gender-motivated under the new law will presumably be analogous to proving that a crime was racially motivated under existing laws. Evidence typically presented in civil rights cases alleging racial violence include: racially derogatory epithets used by the assailant, membership of the victim in a different racial group than the assailant, a history of similar attacks by the assailant against other members of the victim's racial group, a pattern of attacks against victims of a certain race in a certain neighborhood and time period, lack of provocation, use of force that is excessive in light of the absence of other motivations, etc. By substituting "gender" for "race" in the foregoing list, it becomes apparent that many—but not all—crimes against women will qualify as crimes of violence motivated by gender.

Recognizing the gender-discriminatory element in some violent crimes is not radical or unprecedented. Not only does federal law already contain civil remedies for racially-discriminatory violence, but the Hate Crimes Sentencing Enhancement Act of 1993 (H.R. 1152), passed by the House in September and under consideration as part of the Senate crime bill, provides increased sentences for defendants convicted in federal court of having selected a victim because of gender. The Violence Against Women Act simply takes this principle and applies it to a civil, rather than criminal, remedy. Moreover, unlike the Hate Crimes Sentencing Enhancement Act, application of the Violence Against Women Act is not limited to crimes occurring on federal lands.

To the extent that questions remain about how this cause of action will work in practice, this is to be expected with any cutting-edge legislation. As Judge Stanley Marcus, chair of the U.S. Judicial Conference Ad Hoc Committee on Gender–Based Violence, has helpfully pointed out, it is inevitable that there are some questions about legislation that cannot be answered until cases are litigated and judges have the opportunity to apply the law to specific facts.

What Title III Will Accomplish

Because of gender-based violence, American women and girls are relegated to a form of second-class citizenship. Just as a democratic society cannot tolerate violence motivated by the victim's membership in a minority racial group, and must pass special laws to combat such oppression, so too we need effective federal laws to combat violent crimes motivated by the victim's gender.

The enactment of civil rights legislation would convey a powerful message: that violence motivated by gender is not merely an individual crime or a personal injury, but is a form of discrimination, an assault on a publicly-shared ideal of equality. When half of our citizens are not safe at home or on the streets because of their sex, our entire society is diminished.

The impact of the legislation would not be purely symbolic, however. Federal recognition that gender-based violence is a form of discrimination is likely to alter the way both men and women regard sexual assault and domestic violence. The impact of this attitudinal change will be felt in homes, streets, and workplaces. It will also be felt in courtrooms. Currently, jury studies and research on gender bias in the judiciary have shown that the "boys will be boys"/"she must have asked for it" mentality that prevails in most sectors of our society has a direct, measurable effect on the outcome of cases involving sexual assault, domestic violence, and a host of other issues where men's violence toward women is directly or tangentially involved. Thus, the educational power of the VAW Act is of immense practical importance to the development of American law.

In addition, many victims who are currently unable to succeed in state criminal and civil proceedings would, for the first time, have access to legal redress.

It is not true that all men who beat or rape women lack the resources to pay damages. In fact, violence against women is found at every socioeconomic level in America. For some victims, even a damages judgment that cannot be collected (or a judgment granting only declaratory or injunctive relief) will be seen as an immensely valuable vindication of their rights.

Enactment of the Violence Against Women Act will not eliminate rape, domestic violence, and other sex-based attacks on women, any more than passage of the civil rights legislation of the 19th century and the mid–20th century has eliminated racism. Nevertheless, the power of this proposed federal civil rights law to improve the prospects for social justice and equality are substantial.

State Criminal and Civil Laws Are Not Adequate to Protect Victims of Gender–Motivated Crime

The existence of state criminal and tort laws covering rape and domestic violence does not do away with the need for a federal civil rights remedy. First, a federal civil rights law would redress a different injury than the injuries that are at issue in state criminal and tort proceedings.

In addition, gender-motivated crimes are currently not being adequately addressed in state courts.

- A woman is forcibly raped by her husband. In over half the states he is immune from prosecution under many or most circumstances—for example, if the couple is living together and no divorce or separation papers have been filed.

- A young woman is sexually assaulted by her boyfriend. Several states have statutes exempting cohabitants and dating companions from sexual assault laws.

- A man brutally beats his wife, causing her severe injuries. Interspousal immunity doctrines in at least seven states prevent her from suing him to recover damages for her medical expenses and pain and suffering.

- A teenage girl is subjected to incestuous sexual abuse by her father. In some states, strict statutes of limitations require her to bring suit within a few years—which is virtually impossible for an emotionally and economically dependent young person—or else lose forever the chance to pursue a civil legal remedy.

- It was recently revealed that the Oakland, California Police Department closed over 200 rape cases with little or not investigation in 1989 and 1990. The complaints involved rapes of prostitutes and drug users, as well as allegations of acquaintance rape.

- A recent Senate Judiciary Committee study showed that only one in 100 forcible rapes results in a sentence of more than one year in prison.

- State rape shield laws do not apply in civil cases. Thus, women bringing tort actions for sexual assault are routinely subjected to intrusive questions about consensual sexual activity unrelated to the attack.

The laws on the books are only part of the problem. In states throughout the country, prosecutors, juries, and judges routinely subject female victims of rape and domestic violence to a wide range of unfair and degrading treatment that contributes to the low rates of reporting and conviction that characterize these crimes. Although federal courts are not immune from these problems, the fact that federal judges are not elected, are subjected to a more rigorous selection process, and typically exercise greater control over courtroom procedures such as jury voir dire help to minimize these problems.

Federal civil rights laws passed since the mid–19th century have typically prohibited acts that were already illegal under state law. The reason for this is that federal remedies are needed to reinforce state remedies and to provide a "back-up" when the state justice system is unable to protect victims' rights adequately. In an eloquent testimony to the need for federal intervention, 41 state attorneys general have signed a letter to members of this House urging passage of the Violence Against Women Act.

The Violence Against Women Act Builds on and Complements Existing Federal Civil Rights Laws

Currently, American women are being attacked and killed because they are women. Over 100 years ago, following the Civil War, Congress responded to an epidemic of race-based violence by passing a series of federal laws to provide remedies against private individuals who deprive citizens of their civil rights. Similar legislation is needed today to protect citizens from an epidemic of gender-based violence.

Title III of the Violence Against Women Act is modeled on well-established federal civil rights laws. For example, the key phrase "because of . . . gender or on the basis of gender," which describes crimes of violence that are covered, is modeled on language found in Title VII of the Civil Rights Act of 1964, which is the leading federal statute prohibiting discrimination in employment.

Similarly, the basic concept of Title III resembles that of the Reconstruction-era civil rights laws. Like those earlier laws (42 U.S.C. §§ 1981, 1982, and 1985(3)), the Violence Against Women Act provides a federal civil remedy for deprivation of certain rights. The "animus" requirement, which has been added to S. 11, is derived from caselaw decided under 42 U.S.C. § 198. Title III is not identical to its predecessors, however. Each law has different technical legal requirements. For example, unlike § 1983, Title III does not require that the challenged actions were taken "under color of state law," and unlike § 1985(3), it does not require more than one wrongdoer. While Title III is thus broader in some respects than other civil rights laws, it is far narrower in some other respects: it protects *only* against gender-motivated crimes of violence that rise to the level of a felony, whereas 42 U.S.C. §§ 1983 and 1985(3) protect disadvantaged groups from virtually any deprivations of rights, privileges and immunities.

The differences between Title III of the Violence Against Women Act and the nineteenth-century federal civil rights laws are necessary because gender-based violence typically differs from the types of racial violence directed against men. For instance, § 1985(3) was drafted to combat the Ku Klux Klan and similar conspiracies. The dangers confronting women of all races are often quite different. Conspiratorial group attacks on women are not the primary cause of gender violence. In fact, *women are six times more likely than men to suffer a crime at the hands of someone they know.*

The Reconstruction-era civil rights laws were not designed with women in mind. For 120 years since they were passed, "women of all races have lacked a meaningful civil rights remedy to protect them from pervasive anti-female violence." While §§ 1983 and 1985(3) fall short of providing ideal protection against discrimination based on race, religion, or national origin, they at least provide a meaningful remedy for a significant percentage of such cases. The fact that these two statutes require the plaintiff to prove conspiracy or color of state law virtually eliminates the possibility that women of any race can redress what is arguably the most common and most damaging form of gender discrimination: acts of gender-motivated violence committed by private individuals.

This defect in existing civil rights laws has meant, among other things, that rape by individual white men acting in a private capacity, which has historically been a widespread form of oppression of African–American women, has never been actionable under the civil rights laws ostensibly designed to protect all African–Americans from racial terrorism. In short, most of the victimization that women experience because of their gender alone, or because of their gender in combination with their race, remains ignored by the federal civil rights laws currently on the books....

The Impact of Title III on the Courts

Some have suggested that lawsuits brought under the Violence Against Women Act will overwhelm the federal courts. In fact, the legislation will provide a significant new remedy without generating a large number of new cases.

... The inhospitality of state courts to such claims (see above) is doubtless one reason why this figure is so low, but there are other reasons that would be equally applicable to cases brought under federal law.... Women do not now, and will not in the future, rush to proclaim themselves as victims of sex crimes or of violence inflicted by family members.

Sexual harassment provides a useful analogy. A major study by the U.S. Merit Systems Protection Board found that 42% of women employed by the federal government had experienced sexual harassment, but despite the availability of legal remedies, only 5% of those who had been sexually harassed made any kind of formal complaint (including complaints in the workplace); an even smaller number actually filed a legal action.

Moreover, a certain number of potential VAW Act defendants (though by no means all) are indigent, and many women and their attorneys may be unwilling to bring suit if there is no hope of collecting damages. And of course, a large number of violent gender-motivated crimes are committed by assailants who are never caught. As Prof. Cass Sunstein has pointed out, the fact that few cases will probably be filed under Title III of the VAW Act does not detract from its importance as an addition to the civil rights legal arsenal.

The fact that a bill to enhance the rights of women is met with a concern for overloading the federal courts adds a disturbing note of sexism to the debate. In recent decades, when Congress was considering the Americans With Disabilities Act and other civil rights legislation that created private rights of action, this concern was heard only from staunch opponents of civil rights. In any event, the fact that violence against women is widespread would seem to argue in favor of, not against, passing legislation to remedy it.

The true burdens on the federal courts are a heavy criminal caseload, particularly drug-related cases, together with a large number of vacant judgeships. Keeping civil rights cases out of federal court will not solve these problems.

It should be noted that in March 1993, the U.S. Judicial Conference revoked its previous opposition to the Violence Against Women Act and specifically adopted a position of neutrality on this bill, with the exception that the organization now actively supports the portions of the bill regarding task forces on gender bias in the courts. The National Association of Women Judges also supports the principles of Title III. A recent Congressional Budget Office report estimates the cost of Title III to be far lower than previously projected . . . . .

Conclusion

The Congress has a historic opportunity to play a crucial role in the effort to reduce crime and combat discrimination against women. This long overdue legislation will recognize that violence motivated by gender is a deprivation of civil rights. We urge you to support the Violence Against Women Act. Thank you.

NOTES AND QUESTIONS

1. **Violence Against Women is a Public Matter.** Implicit in this carefully crafted advocacy statement is the argument that violence against women is a "public" issue—one that implicates society's commitment to gender equality, and to women's full participation in society. In the next reading, Sally Goldfarb elaborates on the role of "public-private dichotomies in the debate over the Violence Against Women Act," providing a richer and more robust account of the arguments advanced by the provision's proponents, and also by its opponents.

Sally F. Goldfarb

Violence Against Women and the Persistence of Privacy

61 Ohio St. L.J. 1 (2000).

When VAWA was pending in Congress, the civil rights provision was its most controversial aspect. To attain its passage, supporters of the legislation had to overcome opposition based on the longstanding attitude that violence against women is a private matter, not a suitable subject for federal judicial attention. During congressional deliberations on the Act, the controversy over the civil rights provision focused in large part on whether federal courts should concern themselves with violence committed by private individuals—particularly when such violence takes place in the context of family relationships. The bill's opponents, including organizations representing the federal and state judiciaries, advanced arguments that relied heavily on traditional concepts of the split between the market and family and the split between the state and civil society. In fact, one of the primary goals of supporters of the Act was to overcome centuries of assumptions about the public and private spheres that have operated to deny women full equality under the law. Passage of VAWA seemed to signal a major victory for feminist efforts to bring violence against women out from behind the veil of privacy....

A.   Rhetoric of Public and Private Among Supporters of VAWA

... The first report on the legislation by the Senate Judiciary Committee described its purpose as bringing domestic violence out from "behind closed doors." In its report a year later, the Committee stated:

> Historically, crimes against women have been perceived as anything but crime—as a "family" problem, as a "private" matter, as sexual miscommunication.... Vast numbers of these crimes [rape and domestic violence] are left unreported to police or other authorities. Both literally and figuratively, these crimes remain hidden from public view. A House of Representatives subcommittee hearing on the bill was entitled "Domestic Violence: Not Just a Family Matter."

Similar themes were sounded by the bill's co-sponsors and by witnesses who testified in support other legislation.

Proponents of the legislation directly attacked the legal legacy of the market-family dichotomy as reflected in state law. For example, in congressional testimony supporting the legislation, the NOW Legal Defense and Education Fund (NOW LDEF) argued that federal intervention was necessary in light of trends in the state courts that denied justice to victims of domestic violence and rape. Among the trends cited by NOW LDEF were judges who trivialized domestic violence with comments like "Let's kiss and make up and get out of my court"; criminal court judges who denied relief for domestic violence on the ground that it is "merely a domestic problem that belongs in family court"; rape immunities for husbands, cohabitants, and social companions; interspousal and parental tort immunity doctrines; the unwillingness of police to enforce orders of protection; and judicial reluctance to take nonstranger rape seriously. As we have seen, all of these trends are traceable to the split between market and family and the concomitant assumption that the law should not interfere in the domestic sphere.

VAWA's supporters also attempted to counter the view that violence against women is purely a domestic matter by proving the massive effects of such violence on interstate commerce. The Senate Judiciary Committee noted that domestic violence alone is estimated to cost society between five and ten billion dollars a year. Congress heard extensive testimony on the effect of violence on women's workforce participation and productivity, income, health care expenses, consumer spending, and interstate travel. Based on the evidence before it, the Senate Judiciary Committee concluded that gender-based violence bars women from full participation in the national economy. According to the Committee, the experience of gender-based violence interferes with women's ability to obtain and keep employment, travel, and engage in other economic activities, and the fear of gender-motivated violence has a deterrent effect that prevents women from taking available, well-paying jobs.

In addition to helping establish Congress's constitutional authority to enact the civil rights provision under the Commerce Clause, this economic evidence was a direct challenge to the conventional view that domestic matters, including domestic violence, have no impact on the public sphere of the marketplace. By indicating that violence against women has a prominent place in the market, VAWA's supporters sought to show that violence against women also deserves to have a prominent place in the law.

In another indication of the relevance of the market-family split to the debate over VAWA, the bill's supporters repeatedly emphasized that the civil rights provision would not create a federal domestic relations law. This strategy was necessitated by two ways in which the market-family dichotomy is reflected in federal law: first, the federal judiciary's staunch resistance to hearing family-related cases, and second, the tendency to assume that all cases concerning women are really about the family.

Another way in which supporters of the civil rights remedy positioned violence against women as a public issue was by emphasizing that gender-motivated violence is a group-based denial of equality. Patricia Ireland, president of the National Organization for Women, testified:

It's very clear to all of us who see the bombings of NAACP offices, the vandalizing of synagogues, that these are more clearly political and public violence. But because so much of the violence against women is behind closed doors, is ... private violence, ... the political aspect of it has often been ignored. It's not just a problem that an individual woman faces ... but rather a systemic problem that all women face.

Echoing this analysis, the Senate Judiciary Committee described violence motivated by gender as "not merely an individual crime or a personal injury, but ... a form of discrimination," "an assault on a publicly shared ideal of equality." The Committee characterized the civil rights provision as "an effective anti-discrimination remedy for violently expressed prejudice."

In addition to highlighting the discriminatory impact of individual acts of gender-motivated violence, the bill's supporters also emphasized the discrimination inherent in the state legal systems' responses to such violence. Testimony of individual witnesses and committee reports repeatedly stressed the fact that states have condoned violence against women through legal doctrines that treat crimes against women less seriously than crimes against men; through inadequate enforcement of existing laws by police, prosecutors, and judges; and through overtly discriminatory treatment of female crime victims. Thus, the bill's supporters identified causes of violence against women in the public sphere of the state, not merely in the private sphere of civil society. After reviewing a series of reports from official state task forces on gender bias in the courts, the Senate Judiciary Committee concluded that there was "overwhelming evidence that gender bias permeates the court system and that women are most often its victims." ...

B.   Rhetoric of Public and Private Among Opponents of VAWA

While VAWA was pending in Congress, much of the opposition to the civil rights provision was premised on a group of attitudes associated with orthodox adherence to the public-private distinctions: the idealization of family privacy and legal nonintervention in the family; the tendency to equate women with the domestic sphere; the belief that matters involving the family belong only in state court; and resistance to the recent trend of applying federal constitutional and civil rights to nonstate actors. The clearest expressions of these attitudes came from the judiciary, who lobbied actively against the bill. An examination of statements made by VAWA's opponents reveals the lingering influence of traditional conceptions of public and private.

In a particularly striking evocation of the ideology of legal nonintervention in the family, the Conference of Chief Justices, which represents the state judiciary, criticized VAWA's civil rights provision on the ground that it would conflict with the marital rape exemption. Similarly, lawyer Bruce Fein, who testified against the legislation, specifically objected to the fact that VAWA would interfere with a state's choice not to criminalize spousal rape—a choice that, according to Fein, states should be free to make based on "local customs." Although the marital rape exemption survives, it is rare to see it openly defended; the fact that VAWA's opponents did so reveals the depth of their immersion in the world view of the market-family split.

Much of the opposition to the civil rights provision took the form of assertions that federal courts should not interfere in the private, domestic sphere. Chief Justice Rehnquist, for example, used his 1991 Year–End Report on the Federal Judiciary to urge Congress not to pass the Violence Against Women Act because it would create an influx of "domestic relations disputes" into the federal courts. Similarly, the Conference of Chief Justices opposed the statute on the basis that it would constitute an unwarranted federal intrusion into the domain of the state courts. Like its state counterpart, the Judicial Conference of the United States, representing the federal judiciary, adopted a resolution in 1991 opposing VAWA's civil rights provision because of "its potential to disrupt traditional jurisdictional boundaries between the federal and state courts."

Implicit in these objections are the familiar assumptions that all violence against women is "domestic" and that domestic issues do not belong in federal court. In fact, VAWA's scope encompasses any "crime of violence motivated by gender"; the fact that an act of violence took place in the home or among family members is neither necessary nor sufficient to make out a cause of action. Viewed objectively, VAWA is not a domestic relations law. It explicitly does not confer pendent jurisdiction over state law claims seeking establishment of divorce, alimony, marital property, and custody decrees. VAWA is a civil rights law, modeled on other federal civil laws. . . .

Both the Conference of Chief Justices and the Judicial Conference of the United States expressed concern that women would use VAWA as a bargaining chip to extort larger settlements in divorces. The President of the Conference of Chief Justices complained that VAWA "would add a new count to many if not most divorce and other domestic relations cases, further complicating their adjudication and making them more difficult to settle peacefully." This emphasis on "peaceful[ ]" settlement of domestic relations cases echoes nineteenth-century cases arguing against judicial intrusion in the marriage relationship. Settlement, like mediation, is a way to keep family disputes out of court even when legal recourse is technically available.

In addition to raising arguments based on the split between market and family and corresponding assumptions about federal and state jurisdiction, the Conference of Chief Justices also invoked the split between the state and civil society. The Conference objected that VAWA's civil rights provision "appears to eliminate, or at least vitiate, the 'state action' requirement for civil rights litigation." Because VAWA's scope is not limited to actions taken under color of state law, the Conference argued, it is inconsistent with existing federal civil rights laws. In other words, civil rights statutes can protect private individuals only from the state, not from each other. As noted earlier, the preceding three decades had seen a proliferation of federal cases and statutes prohibiting discrimination by private actors. The fact that the organization representing the leading state jurists in the country argued repeatedly and forcefully that federal civil rights laws apply exclusively to state actors, without acknowledging the growing number of exceptions to that general rule, demonstrates the lingering power of the state-civil society dichotomy over the judicial imagination.

NOTES AND QUESTIONS

1.   **Narrowing the Scope of the Law to Allay Concerns.** Ultimately, as indicated by the NOW LDEF (now Legal Momentum) statement excerpted above, the Judicial Conference of the United States withdrew its opposition to the legislation, and adopted a position of neutrality. In essence, the Conference allowed its concerns about "federalizing" "private" arenas of violence against women to be allayed by compromises that limited the scope of the legislation: making explicit that nothing in the provision would give federal courts jurisdiction over domestic relations law; requiring that violence must be at the level of a felony to trigger the provision, and adding a gender animus requirement. The text of the provision, as enacted, follows.

Violence Against Women: Civil Rights for Women, 42 USCS § 13981 (2000)

(a) Purpose. Pursuant to the affirmative power of Congress to enact this subtitle under section 5 of the Fourteenth Amendment to the Constitution, as well as under section 8 of Article I of the Constitution, it is the purpose of this subtitle to protect the civil rights of victims of gender motivated violence and to promote public safety, health, and activities affecting interstate commerce by establishing a Federal civil rights cause of action for victims of crimes of violence motivated by gender.

(b) Right to be free from crimes of violence. All persons within the United States shall have the right to be free from crimes of violence motivated by gender (as defined in subsection (d)).

(c) Cause of action. A person (including a person who acts under color of any statute, ordinance, regulation, custom, or usage of any State) who commits a crime of violence motivated by gender and thus deprives another of the right declared in subsection (b) shall be liable to the party injured, in an action for the recovery of compensatory and punitive damages, injunctive and declaratory relief, and such other relief as a court may deem appropriate.

(d) Definitions. For purposes of this section—

(1) the term "crime of violence motivated by gender" means a crime of violence committed because of gender or on the basis of gender, and due, at least in part, to an animus based on the victim's gender; and

(2) the term "crime of violence" means—

(A) an act or series of acts that would constitute a felony against the person or that would constitute a felony against property if the conduct presents a serious risk of physical injury to another, and that would come within the meaning of State or Federal offenses described in section 16 of title 18,

United States Code, whether or not those acts have actually resulted in criminal charges, prosecution, or conviction and whether or not those acts were committed in the special maritime, territorial, or prison jurisdiction of the United States; and

(B) includes an act or series of acts that would constitute a felony described in subparagraph (A) but for the relationship between the person who takes such action and the individual against whom such action is taken.

(e) Limitation and procedures.

(1) Limitation. Nothing in this section entitles a person to a cause of action under subsection (c) for random acts of violence unrelated to gender or for acts that cannot be demonstrated, by a preponderance of the evidence, to be motivated by gender (within the meaning of subsection (d)).

(2) No prior criminal action. Nothing in this section requires a prior criminal complaint, prosecution, or conviction to establish the elements of a cause of action under subsection (c).

(3) Concurrent jurisdiction. The Federal and State courts shall have concurrent jurisdiction over actions brought pursuant to this subtitle.

(4) Supplemental jurisdiction. Neither section 1367 of title 28, United States Code, nor subsection (c) of this section shall be construed, by reason of a claim arising under such subsection, to confer on the courts of the United States jurisdiction over any State law claim seeking the establishment of a divorce, alimony, equitable distribution of marital property, or child custody decree.

2.   **Passage of VAWA Celebrated.** The passage of the Violence Against Women Act, and specifically of the civil rights provision, was greeted with jubilation by feminist activists and scholars. In the words, again, of Sally Goldfarb:

The passage of this legislation had great practical and symbolic value. On a practical level, VAWA offers a remedy that in some cases is the only source of legal redress for violence against women and in many others is vastly superior to other available legal options. VAWA avoids the restrictive effects of state tort immunities, marital rape exemptions, and unduly short statutes of limitations. Unlike most previous federal civil rights laws, VAWA does not require a showing of action taken under color of state law or proof of a conspiracy to deny the plaintiff an independent, federally protected right. VAWA civil rights claims brought in federal court are covered by Rule 412 of the Federal Rules of Evidence which, as amended elsewhere in VAWA, extends rape shield protections to civil cases; few states offer such protections. For cases of gender-motivated violence in the workplace, VAWA provides a desirable alternative to Title VII because it permits unlimited awards of compensatory and punitive damages; has a far longer statute of limitations; does not require exhaustion of administrative remedies; and applies to workplaces with fewer than fifteen employees. As a civil rather than criminal action, VAWA empowers women by placing control over the litigation in their own hands and sidesteps the obstacles of gender bias among police and prosecutors. Also, unlike criminal cases, VAWA permits plaintiffs to collect money damages and applies the preponderance of the evidence standard rather than the more onerous standard of beyond a reasonable doubt.

On a symbolic level, VAWA was a major victory for women's equality and seemed to displace rigid conceptions of privacy that had for so long hidden violence against women from public recognition and public response. A federal civil rights remedy places the issue of violence against women squarely in the domain of public law rather than relegating it to private law remedies or no legal remedies at all. Notably, VAWA's challenge to traditional distinctions between public and private was applauded by a range of feminist writers whose views on privacy otherwise differ profoundly, from those who have emphasized the negative impact of privacy ideology on women to those who have celebrated privacy as a potential source of freedom and autonomy for women. If indeed the public-private distinction is what the feminist movement is all about, it would seem that the enactment of VAWA's civil rights remedy advanced the movement's agenda significantly. Sally F. Goldfarb, *Violence Against Women and the Persistence of Privacy*, 61 OHIO ST. L.J. 1 (2000).

3. **Federalism Eventually Limits the Protections of the Act.** Despite the jubilation, however, no one expected that the provision would go unchallenged. As Sally Goldfarb put it: "There was still the danger that despite VAWA's successful journey through the legislative process, the judiciary's privacy-based opposition would reassert itself in interpretations of the statute." There were, however, two different schools of thought about the form those challenges would take. In the following reading, Reva Siegel, in 1996, was predicting that the struggle would be over the definition of "crime motivated by gender," as adversaries of civil rights for women victimized by violence shifted their ground from the federalism arguments that characterized debate over the passage of the statute to the interpretive arguments that would limit its impact. In fact, as the subsequent readings demonstrate, the attack was instead framed as an assault on the constitutionality of the provision, an assault in which arguments about the limits of federal authority were again predominant. Precisely because federalism continues to limit women's quest for freedom from violence, Siegel's analysis, which provides a rich historical account of the connection between federalism and women's subordination within marriage, remains relevant to the contemporary debate—more relevant even than she imagined it would be.

Reva B. Siegel
The Rule of Love: Wife Beating as Prerogative
105 YALE L.J. 2117 (1996).

While VAWA's civil rights remedy drew many critics, not one critic of the civil rights remedy disparaged the statute's goal of protecting women from rape and domestic violence. Rather, critics argued that creating a federal cause of action to vindicate such injuries usurped a traditional regulatory interest of the states and threatened to flood the federal courts with cases the federal judiciary was ill-equipped to handle.

For example, in January of 1991, the Conference of Chief Justices announced its opposition to Title III on the grounds that the provision could "cause major state-federal jurisdictional problems and disruptions in the processing of domestic relations cases in state courts." The state chief justices reasoned that the "right will be invoked as a bargaining tool within the context of divorce negotiations and add a major complicating factor to an environment which is often acrimonious as it is." They continued:

> The issue of inter-spousal litigation goes to the very core of familial relationships and is a very sensitive policy issue in most states. It does not appear that S. 15 is meant to plunge the federal government into this complex area which has been traditionally reserved to the states, but this might well be the result if the current language stands. It should be noted that the volume of domestic relations litigation in state courts is enormous.

> It should also be noted that the very nature of marriage as a sexual union raises the possibility that every form of violence can be interpreted as gender-based.

Observing that "the federal cause of action . . . would impair the ability of state courts to manage criminal and family law matters traditionally entrusted to the states," the Conference of Chief Justices resolved that the provision should be eliminated.

By September of 1991, the Judicial Conference of the United States joined the Conference of Chief Justices in opposing Title III. The federal judges complained that the new civil rights remedy would burden an already overcrowded federal docket; they also echoed the concern voiced by the state judges that the civil rights cause of action " 'will be invoked as a bargaining tool within the context of divorce negotiations [complicating] an environment which is often acrimonious as it is.' " The Judicial Conference then observed that the "subject of violence based on gender and possible responses is extremely complex," and promised to work with Congress "to fashion an appropriate response to violence directed against women." It was in this context that Chief Justice Rehnquist raised his objections to Title III, complaining that the "new private right of action [is] so sweeping that the legislation could involve the federal courts in a whole host of domestic relations disputes."

Facing opposition to Title III, VAWA's original sponsor, Senate Judiciary Committee Chairman Senator Joseph Biden, joined with Senator Orrin Hatch (then ranking minority member of the Committee) to draft a version of the civil rights remedy that could allay the federalism concerns voiced by the bill's critics. In order to defer to the states' traditional role in regulating matters of marriage and divorce and to shield federal dockets from overcrowding, Senator Hatch sought to limit the range of assaults that might fall within the ambit of Title III's protections. . . .

The same federalism concerns that critics raised in opposition to the civil rights remedy presumably will shape its interpretation, as courts attempt to identify which acts of violence are "gender-motivated" within the meaning of the act, and which are not. But how is it that courts are to determine which acts of rape and domestic violence are "gender-motivated" and which are not? Here the meaning given the phrase "an animus based on the victim's gender" will be pivotal in the interpretation of the new civil rights remedy. Will courts construe "animus" to mean something akin to *"purpose"* or *"malice"*? Those, such as Senator Hatch, who seek a more restrictive construction of the civil rights remedy will argue that animus means malice, while those more receptive to a federal role in remedying violence against women will construe animus as a form of purpose. To appreciate how the interpretive struggle will unfold in more concrete terms, it is helpful to consider how Senator Hatch described for the *New Republic* the injuries the statute covers:

> "We're not opening the federal doors to all gender-motivated crimes. Say you have a man who believes a woman is attractive. He feels encouraged by her and he's so motivated by that encouragement that he rips her clothes off and has sex with her against her will. Now let's say you have another man who grabs a woman off some lonely road and in the process of raping her says words like, 'You're wearing a skirt! You're a woman! I hate women! I'm going to show you, you woman!' Now, the first one's terrible. But the other's much worse. *If a man rapes a woman while telling her he loves her, that's a far cry from saying he hates her. A lust factor does not spring from animus."* [Emphasis added.]

In the controversy over the scope of VAWA's civil rights remedy, we can see the law of intimate assault undergoing modernization. The bill's proponents sought to provide women relief from intimate assault, treating it as a form of sex discrimination—as "gender-motivated violence." The bill's opponents raised a series of federalism objections to the cause of action, first resisting and then accepting with reservations, the antidiscrimination framework of the statute. Although both groups now espouse a commitment to ending gender-motivated violence, their understanding of what that violence is differs. Accordingly, there will be a struggle over the scope of the civil rights remedy, focusing on the meaning of "crime of violence motivated by gender." What is "a crime of violence committed because of gender or on the basis of gender, and due, at least in part, to an animus based on the victim's gender"? The answer to this question will depend in part on the weight given the federalism arguments raised by critics of the civil rights remedy. If we examine these federalism objections, it is possible to see how they gain persuasive power as they draw on the discourse of affective privacy, using it as a basis for restricting the meaning of "gender motivated violence," and thus the protections afforded women by the Act. In short, the struggle over VAWA's civil rights remedy resembles the struggle over the tort provisions of the married women's property acts, not only in structure, but in substance: Federalism objections to the civil rights remedy acquire persuasive power as they draw on the traditional modes of reasoning about intimate assault.

There are several levels at which we can discern the discourse of affective privacy operating in disputes over the civil rights remedy. The first involves the characterization question on which the whole federalism dispute hinges. Suppose a man rapes, beats, or knifes his wife. Does a woman's ability to secure relief for such injuries bear on her status as an equal citizen of this nation? Or is this question properly of local concern, implicating matters of family law and criminal law, but not matters of sex discrimination or equal protection? The assertion that VAWA interferes with traditional state regulatory concerns implicitly, and explicitly, adopts the latter view. In these objections the issue of gender bias that prompted VAWA's enactment recedes from view, and sexualized assault appears as a problem concerning "family matters." As Chief Justice Rehnquist succinctly expressed his objections to the civil rights remedy, the statute "could involve the federal courts in a whole host of domestic relations disputes." When the Conference of Chief Justices asserted that "the issue of interspousal litigation goes to the very core of familial relationships and is a very sensitive policy issue in most states," it was characterizing intimate assaults in the idiom of the interspousal immunity doctrine.... It is only by virtue of this historical tradition that significant audiences of lawmakers and jurists find it at all persuasive to characterize acts of rape or battery as matters of "domestic relations" law, or the stuff of "acrimonious" "divorce negotiations," or as "sensitive policy issues," or "matters traditionally entrusted to the states." In short, it is because critics of the civil rights remedy are still reasoning within the common law tradition the statute seeks to disestablish that they can characterize VAWA as intruding in regulatory domains that are not properly of federal concern.

Just as history plays a role in characterizations of VAWA's regulatory objectives, it also plays a role in the federalism story that characterization sets in motion. Under our system of federalism, states have historically regulated matters of family law. And in federalism claims about the family, that history typically assumes dispositive weight: Congress should not disturb the allocation of regulatory responsibilities that this nation has forged under the federal constitutional system. But as the paradigm case of slavery teaches us, before we defer to the weight of tradition in such matters, we need at least to consider the normative underpinnings of that initial allocation of federal and state regulatory responsibilities. In the case of family law, uncritical perpetuation of past practice is likely to prove normatively problematic for reasons that, upon reflection, are not terribly surprising: Federalism discourses about the family grew up in intimate entanglement with the common law of marital status. Indeed, as we examine the claim that marriage is a state-law concern, it begins to appear that federalism discourses about marriage bear strong family resemblances to common law privacy discourses about marriage, and in some instances are even direct descendants of the discourse of affective privacy.

The claim that marriage is properly a matter of state-law concern has important roots in nineteenth-century deliberations of Congress and the Court. One prominent source of this notion is the "domestic-relations exception" to federal diversity jurisdiction, announced in the 1858 case of Barber v. Barber. But if we read *Barber* closely, it turns out that the claim that husband and wife cannot be diverse for federal jurisdictional purposes was itself an outgrowth of the doctrine of marital unity. Under the common law of marital status, a wife's domicile was her husband's; thus, following the logic of the common law, the Supreme Court reasoned that husband and wife could not be diverse (i.e., citizens of different states) for federal jurisdictional purposes. Both the majority and dissenting opinions in *Barber* affirm that proposition. The *Barber* dissent then goes on to translate that precept of marital unity doctrine into the discourse of affective privacy:

> It is not in accordance with the design and operation of a Government having its origin in causes and necessities, political, general, and external, that it should assume to regulate the domestic relations of society; should, with a kind of inquisitorial authority, enter the habitations and even into the chambers and nurseries of private families, and inquire into and pronounce upon the morals and habits and affections or antipathies of the members of every household.... The Federal tribunals can have no power to control the duties or the habits of the different members of private families in their domestic intercourse. This power belongs exclusively to the particular communities of which those families form parts, and is essential to the order and to the very existence of such communities. [Emphasis added.]

This passage from *Barber* should sound somewhat familiar. It discusses the role of the federal and state government in regulating domestic relations much as the *Rhodes* opinion discussed the role of state government and "family government" in regulating domestic relations. As this passage from *Barber* might suggest, much of the idiom used to designate marriage as a "local" matter within discourses of federalism either echoes or can be traced to ... common law doctrines of marital privacy....

The conviction that marriage is a matter for states to regulate can also be traced to efforts to protect the common law of marital status from reform in the aftermath of the Civil War, an era when Congress was first beginning to exercise its new power to regulate race discrimination in the states. As several historians have recounted, Congress sought to draft the Fourteenth Amendment and the 1866 Civil Rights Act so as to protect emancipated slaves from race discrimination while shielding from reform certain features of gender status law: specifically, restrictions on woman suffrage and the marital status doctrines that, for example, prohibited wives from forming contracts, filing suit, or otherwise exercising legal capacity independently of their husbands.

Thus, the notion that family law is a matter of state, not federal, concern can be traced to gendered domicile rules of the common law of marital status, as well as to efforts to preserve other gender-specific aspects of the common law of marital status—law that is now deemed unconstitutional. In addition, as our examination of *Barber* reveals, the claim that marriage is a state-law concern acquires persuasive force at least in part because it draws upon discourses of affective privacy that grew out of the doctrine of marital unity. Claims about federal intervention in domestic relations reiterate more generalized anxieties about governmental interference in family life.

Thus far I have shown how traditions of common law reasoning have shaped federalism claims about regulating domestic relations raised by critics of VAWA's civil rights remedy. But the discourse of affective privacy plays another important role in disputes over the scope of the civil rights remedy, supplying normative criteria for identifying the types of assaults to which the cause of action applies. Here historical connection is by no means as direct, and yet some notion of affection in intimate relationships seems to be regulating intuitions about what kinds of sexualized assaults are "gender-motivated" within the meaning of the Act. It is easier to appreciate this connection once we examine the narratives that Senator Hatch and others employ to separate the acts of rape and domestic violence considered of "local" regulatory concern from those properly considered of "federal" regulatory concern.

Senator Hatch differentiates the roles of federal and state government in regulating intimate assaults by looking to the motivation animating the conduct. When such acts are motivated by hate, he reasons, they are properly matters of federal concern, but when they are motivated by love, they are not. As Senator Hatch succinctly put it: "If a man rapes a woman while telling her he loves her, that's a far cry from saying he hates her. A lust factor does not spring from animus." Restating this distinction, those acts of rape and domestic violence that are motivated by hate properly concern women's status as equal citizens of the United States, while those acts of rape and domestic violence that are motivated by love (or lust) are matters of purely local concern having no bearing on women's status as federal citizens or persons entitled to equal protection of the laws. The structure of this claim depends in part on an assumption that gender bias will manifest itself as race discrimination manifests itself: in an emotional state called "hate." But the claim also draws force from specifically gendered assumptions about intimate relations of the sort manifested in the discursive tradition of affective privacy. As in the nineteenth-century interspousal immunity cases, assertions about love and intimacy in a relationship rhetorically efface the violence of sexualized assault. We might distill the logic of this tradition to the following maxim: Where love is, law need not be. Intimacy occurs in a domain having no bearing on matters of citizenship.

I believe that federalism claims about VAWA's civil rights remedy are persuasive in significant part because they perpetuate traditional discourses of marital status in new idiomatic form. But one need not trace the lineage of these federalism claims to appreciate how the controversy over regulation of "gender-motivated violence" that we are examining will function to modernize discourses of gender status. A civil rights initiative intended to dismantle elements of a centuries-old status regime declares that violence against women is a form of sex discrimination, and soon thereafter becomes the object of political controversy. Those who wish to prevent enactment of the law raise a series of objections to it, couched in "legitimate, nondiscriminatory" reasons. They prevail to the extent of imposing an as yet indeterminate limit on the reach of the new antidiscrimination statute. Now courts are about to implement a law that requires them to determine which acts of rape and domestic violence are gender-motivated, hence violative of women's civil rights as equal citizens of this nation, and which acts of rape and domestic violence are purely local, presumably personal matters, attributable to love or lust, but not gender-based animus. The very struggle over the interpretation of VAWA's civil rights remedy will, of necessity, modernize gender status discourse, altering the rules and rhetoric governing intimate assaults in such a way as to make the distinctions VAWA draws "reasonable" for our day. Considered in larger historical perspective, controversy over the civil rights remedy contained in the Violence Against Women Act has set in motion a legal regime that will restate sexual assault law in the gender mores of American society at the dawn of the twenty-first century.

NOTES AND QUESTIONS

1. **Examples of Cases Brought under the Civil Rights Provision.** After VAWA was enacted in 1994, plaintiffs brought claims under the new civil rights provision alleging various types of gender-motivated violence, including rape, sexual assault, nonsexual assault, sexual abuse of minors, partner abuse, and murder. For examples of cases involving domestic violence, see: *Kuhn v. Kuhn*, 1999 WL 519326 (N.D. Ill.1999) (physical and sexual abuse by husband); *Bergeron v. Bergeron*, 48 F.Supp.2d 628 (M.D. La. 1999) (battery, assault and attempted rape by husband); *Wright v. Wright*, No. Civ. 98–572–A (W.D. Okla. Apr. 27, 1999) (physical violence by defendant against both wife and daughter); *Culberson v. Doan*, 65 F.Supp.2d 701 (S.D. Ohio 1999) (beating murder of girlfriend); *Ziegler v. Ziegler*, 28 F.Supp.2d 601 (E.D. Wash. 1998) (assault, threats and harassment by husband); *Timm v. Delong*, 59 F.Supp.2d 944 (D. Neb. 1998) (physical and sexual abuse by husband); *Seaton v. Seaton*, 971 F.Supp. 1188 (E.D. Tenn. 1997) (physical and sexual abuse by husband); *Doe v. Doe*, 929 F.Supp. 608 (D. Conn. 1996) (physical and mental abuse by husband). In all these cases except *Bergeron*, the civil rights provision was found to be a constitutional exercise of the Commerce Clause. In *Wright* and *Timm*, the courts also found the provision constitutional under § 5 of the Fourteenth Amendment.

2. **Constitutional Challenges Brought by Defendants.** In response to the early claims brought under VAWA's civil rights provision, a growing number of defendants challenged its constitutionality. These challenges revived the public-private distinctions that VAWA itself was designed to transcend:

> First, the challenges claim that the civil rights provision is not a legitimate exercise of Congress's Commerce Clause power because violence against women does not have sufficiently close ties to the market. Second, they argue that Congress lacked authority to enact the civil rights remedy under section 5 of the Fourteenth Amendment because violence against women does not have sufficiently close ties to the state. These constitutional challenges, by invoking the image of an irreconcilable division between family and market and between civil society and the state, simply recapitulate the public-private split in

both its forms. Relying on the familiar public-private dichotomies, the defendants bringing these challenges, and the judges who agree with them, would isolate violence against women in the private sphere and thereby exclude those injuries from federal civil rights relief. In addition, the litigants and judges who embrace these arguments bring to bear a set of assumptions that, as we have seen, arise naturally from rigid adherence to conventional rubrics of public and private, such as the assumptions that women exist only in the domestic sphere and that cases affecting the family belong exclusively in state courts. Their arguments, in short, echo the judiciary's unsuccessful opposition to VAWA during the legislative process. Sally F. Goldfarb, *Violence Against Women and the Persistence of Privacy*, 61 OHIO ST. L.J. 1, 59 (2000).

The first constitutional challenge to reach a federal court of appeals was *Brzonkala v. Virginia Polytechnic Institute & State University,* 169 F.3d 820 (4th Cir. 1999). The Fourth Circuit issued an en banc decision striking the provision down as unconstitutional under both the Commerce Clause and section 5 of the Fourteenth Amendment. The Supreme Court granted certiorari, and affirmed the Fourth Circuit in the decision that follows.

United States v. Morrison

Supreme Court of the United States, 2000.
529 U.S. 598.

■ REHNQUIST, C.J., delivered the opinion of the Court, in which O'CONNOR, SCALIA, KENNEDY, and THOMAS, JJ., joined. THOMAS, J., filed a concurring opinion. SOUTER, J., filed a dissenting opinion, in which STEVENS, GINSBURG, and BREYER, JJ., joined. BREYER, J., filed a dissenting opinion, in which STEVENS, J., joined, and in which SOUTER and GINSBURG, JJ., joined as to Part I–A.

■ CHIEF JUSTICE REHNQUIST delivered the opinion of the Court. . . .

I.

Petitioner Christy Brzonkala enrolled at Virginia Polytechnic Institute (Virginia Tech) in the fall of 1994. In September of that year, Brzonkala met respondents Antonio Morrison and James Crawford, who were both students at Virginia Tech and members of its varsity football team. Brzonkala alleges that, within 30 minutes of meeting Morrison and Crawford, they assaulted and repeatedly raped her. After the attack, Morrison allegedly told Brzonkala, "You better not have any . . . diseases." In the months following the rape, Morrison also allegedly announced in the dormitory's dining room that he " 'liked' to get girls drunk and. . . ." The omitted portions, quoted verbatim in the briefs on file with this Court, consist of boasting, debased remarks about what Morrison would do to women, vulgar remarks that cannot fail to shock and offend.

Brzonkala alleges that this attack caused her to become severely emotionally disturbed and depressed. She sought assistance from a university psychiatrist, who prescribed antidepressant medication. Shortly after the rape Brzonkala stopped attending classes and withdrew from the university.

In early 1995, Brzonkala filed a complaint against respondents under Virginia Tech's Sexual Assault Policy. During the school-conducted hearing on her complaint, Morrison admitted having sexual contact with her despite the fact that she had twice told him "no." After the hearing, Virginia Tech's Judicial Committee found insufficient evidence to punish Crawford, but found Morrison guilty of sexual assault and sentenced him to immediate suspension for two semesters.

Virginia Tech's dean of students upheld the judicial committee's sentence. However, in July 1995, Virginia Tech informed Brzonkala that Morrison intended to initiate a court challenge to his conviction under the Sexual Assault Policy. University officials told her that a second hearing would be necessary to remedy the school's error in prosecuting her complaint under that policy, which had not been widely circulated to students. The university therefore conducted a second hearing under its Abusive Conduct Policy, which was in force prior to the dissemination of the Sexual Assault Policy. Following this second hearing the Judicial Committee again found Morrison guilty and sentenced him to an identical 2–semester suspension. This time, however, the description of Morrison's offense was, without explanation, changed from "sexual assault" to "using abusive language."

Morrison appealed his second conviction through the university's administrative system. On August 21, 1995, Virginia Tech's senior vice president and provost set aside Morrison's punishment. She concluded that it was " 'excessive when compared with other cases where there has been a finding of violation of the Abusive Conduct Policy.' " Virginia Tech did not inform Brzonkala of this decision. After learning from a newspaper that Morrison would be returning to Virginia Tech for the fall 1995 semester, she dropped out of the university.

In December 1995, Brzonkala sued Morrison, Crawford, and Virginia Tech in the United States District Court for the Western District of Virginia. Her complaint alleged that Morrison's and Crawford's attack violated § 13981 and that Virginia Tech's handling of her complaint violated Title IX of the Education Amendments of 1972. Morrison and Crawford moved to dismiss this complaint on the grounds that it failed to state a claim and that § 13981's civil remedy is unconstitutional. The United States, petitioner in No. 99–5, intervened to defend § 13981's constitutionality.

[The district and circuit courts granted defendants' motion to dismiss the VAWA claims on the ground that the law exceeded Congress's authority under either the Commerce Clause or the Fourteenth Amendment.]

II.

As we observed in [United States v. Lopez, 514 U.S. 549 (1995) (holding that Congress does not have constitutional authority to criminalize possession of firearms near schools)], modern Commerce Clause jurisprudence has "identified three broad categories of activity that Congress may regulate under its commerce power." "First, Congress may regulate the use of the channels of interstate commerce." "Second, Congress is empowered to regulate and protect the instrumentalities of interstate commerce, or persons or things in interstate commerce, even though the threat may come only from intrastate activities." . . . "Finally, Congress' commerce authority includes the power to regulate those activities having a substantial relation to interstate commerce, . . . *i.e.*, those activities that substantially affect interstate commerce." . . .

[Petitioners United States and Brzonkala argued that § 13981 fell under the third category, which was also the focus of *Lopez*.]

. . . [A] fair reading of *Lopez* shows that the noneconomic, criminal nature of the conduct at issue was central to our decision in that case. . . . *Lopez*'s review of Commerce Clause case law demonstrates that in those cases where we have sustained federal regulation of intrastate activity based upon the activity's substantial effects on interstate commerce, the activity in question has been some sort of economic endeavor. . . .

The second consideration that we found important in analyzing [the statute at issue in Lopez] was that the statute contained "no express jurisdictional element which might limit its reach to a discrete set of firearm possessions that additionally have an explicit connection with or effect on interstate commerce." . . . Such a jurisdictional element may establish that the enactment is in pursuance of Congress' regulation of interstate commerce.

Third, we noted that neither [the statute] " 'nor its legislative history contains express congressional findings regarding the effects upon interstate commerce of gun possession in a school zone.' " . . . While "Congress normally is not required to make formal findings as to the substantial burdens that an activity has on interstate commerce," . . . the existence of such findings may "enable us to evaluate the legislative judgment that the activity in question substantially affects interstate commerce, even though no such substantial effect [is] visible to the naked eye." . . .

Finally, our decision in *Lopez* rested in part on the fact that the link between gun possession and a substantial effect on interstate commerce was attenuated. . . . The United States argued that the possession of guns may lead to violent crime, and that violent crime "can be expected to affect the functioning of the national economy in two ways. First, the costs of violent crime are substantial, and, through the mechanism of insurance, those costs are spread throughout the population. Second, violent crime reduces the willingness of individuals to travel to areas within the country that are perceived to be unsafe." . . . The Government also argued that the presence of guns at schools poses a threat to the educational process, which in turn threatens to produce a less efficient and productive workforce, which will negatively affect national productivity and thus interstate commerce. . . .

We rejected these "costs of crime" and "national productivity" arguments because they would permit Congress to "regulate not only all violent crime, but all activities that might lead to violent crime, regardless of how tenuously they relate to interstate commerce." . . . We noted that, under this but-for reasoning:

> "Congress could regulate any activity that it found was related to the economic productivity of individual citizens: family law (including marriage, divorce, and child custody), for example. Under these theories . . ., it is difficult to perceive any limitation on federal power, even in areas such as criminal law enforcement or education where States historically have been sovereign. Thus, if we were to accept the Government's arguments, we are hard pressed to posit any activity by an individual that Congress is without power to regulate." . . .

With these principles underlying our Commerce Clause jurisprudence as reference points, the proper resolution of the present cases is clear. Gender-motivated crimes of violence are not, in any sense of the phrase, economic activity. While we need not adopt a categorical rule against aggregating the effects of any noneconomic activity in order to decide these cases, thus far in our Nation's history our cases have upheld Commerce Clause regulation of intrastate activity only where that activity is economic in nature. . . .

In contrast with the lack of congressional findings that we faced in *Lopez*, § 13981 *is* supported by numerous findings regarding the serious impact that gender-motivated violence has on victims and their families. But the existence of congressional findings is not sufficient, by itself, to sustain the constitutionality of Commerce Clause legislation. . . .

In these cases, Congress' findings are substantially weakened by the fact that they rely so heavily on a method of reasoning that we have already rejected as unworkable if we are to maintain the Constitution's enumeration of powers. Congress found that gender-motivated violence affects interstate commerce:

> "by deterring potential victims from traveling interstate, from engaging in employment in interstate business, and from transacting with business, and in places involved in interstate commerce; . . . by diminishing national productivity, increasing medical and other costs, and decreasing the supply of and the demand for interstate products."

Given these findings and petitioners' arguments, the concern that we expressed in *Lopez* that Congress might use the Commerce Clause to completely obliterate the Constitution's distinction between national and local authority seems well founded. The reasoning that petitioners advance seeks to follow the but-for causal chain from the initial occurrence of violent crime (the suppression of which has always been the prime object of the States' police power) to every attenuated effect upon interstate commerce. If accepted, petitioners' reasoning would allow Congress to regulate any crime as long as the nationwide, aggregated impact of that crime has substantial effects on employment, production, transit, or consumption. Indeed, if Congress may regulate gender-motivated violence, it would be able to regulate murder or any other type of violence since gender-motivated violence, as a subset of all violent crime, is certain to have lesser economic impacts than the larger class of which it is a part.

Petitioners' reasoning, moreover, will not limit Congress to regulating violence but may, as we suggested in *Lopez*, be applied equally as well to family law and other areas of traditional state regulation since the aggregate effect of marriage, divorce, and childrearing on the national economy is undoubtedly significant. Congress may have recognized this specter when it expressly precluded § 13981 from being used in the family law context. Under our written Constitution, however, the limitation of congressional authority is not solely a matter of legislative grace....

We accordingly reject the argument that Congress may regulate non-economic, violent criminal conduct based solely on that conduct's aggregate effect on interstate commerce. The Constitution requires a distinction between what is truly national and what is truly local.... In recognizing this fact we preserve one of the few principles that has been consistent since the Clause was adopted. The regulation and punishment of intrastate violence that is not directed at the instrumentalities, channels, or goods involved in interstate commerce has always been the province of the States.... Indeed, we can think of no better example of the police power, which the Founders denied the National Government and reposed in the States, than the suppression of violent crime and vindication of its victims....

III.

[Because the Court rejected Congress's Commerce Clause authority, it also considered, but rejected the claim that § 5 of the Fourteenth Amendment provided constitutional authority for § 13981.]

Petitioners' § 5 argument is founded on an assertion that there is pervasive bias in various state justice systems against victims of gender-motivated violence. This assertion is supported by a voluminous congressional record. Specifically, Congress received evidence that many participants in state justice systems are perpetuating an array of erroneous stereotypes and assumptions. Congress concluded that these discriminatory stereotypes often result in insufficient investigation and prosecution of gender-motivated crime, inappropriate focus on the behavior and credibility of the victims of that crime, and unacceptably lenient punishments for those who are actually convicted of gender-motivated violence.... Petitioners contend that this bias denies victims of gender-motivated violence the equal protection of the laws and that Congress therefore acted appropriately in enacting a private civil remedy against the perpetrators of gender-motivated violence to both remedy the States' bias and deter future instances of discrimination in the state courts.

As our cases have established, state-sponsored gender discrimination violates equal protection unless it " 'serves "important governmental objectives and ... the discriminatory means employed" are "substantially related to the achievement of those objectives." ' " United States v. Virginia (1996).... However, the language and purpose of the Fourteenth Amendment place certain limitations on the manner in which Congress may attack discriminatory conduct. These limitations are necessary to prevent the Fourteenth Amendment from obliterating the Framers' carefully crafted balance of power between the States and the National Government. Foremost among these limitations is the time-honored principle that the Fourteenth Amendment, by its very terms, prohibits only state action. The principle has become firmly embedded in our constitutional law that the action inhibited by the first section of the Fourteenth Amendment is only such action as may fairly be said to be that of the States. That Amendment erects no shield against merely private conduct, however discriminatory or wrongful....

Shortly after the Fourteenth Amendment was adopted, we decided two cases interpreting the Amendment's provisions, United States v. Harris (1883), and the Civil Rights Cases (1883). In *Harris*, the Court considered a challenge to § 2 of the Civil Rights Act of 1871. That section sought to punish "private persons" for "conspiring to deprive any one of the equal protection of the laws enacted by the State." We concluded that this law exceeded Congress' § 5 power because the law was "directed exclusively against the action of private persons, without reference to the laws of the State, or their administration by her officers."

We reached a similar conclusion in the *Civil Rights Cases*. In those consolidated cases, we held that the public accommodation provisions of the Civil Rights Act of 1875, which applied to purely private conduct, were beyond the scope of the § 5 enforcement power. 109 U.S. at 11 ("Individual invasion" of individual rights is not the subject-matter of the [Fourteenth] Amendment.)

[Rejecting a broad reading of United States v. Guest, 383 U.S. 745 (1966), the Court dismissed the petitioners' argument that the Fourteenth Amendment could justify federal regulation of private actions.]

Petitioners alternatively argue that, unlike the situation in the Civil Rights Cases, here there has been gender-based disparate treatment by state authorities, whereas in those cases there was no indication of such state action. There is abundant evidence, however, to show that the Congresses that enacted the Civil Rights Acts of 1871 and 1875 had a purpose similar to that of Congress in enacting § 13981: There were state laws on the books bespeaking equality of treatment, but in the administration of these laws there was discrimination against newly freed slaves....

But even if that distinction were valid, we do not believe it would save § 13981's civil remedy. For the remedy is simply not "corrective in its character, adapted to counteract and redress the operation of such prohibited state laws or proceedings of state officers." ... Section 13981 is not aimed at proscribing discrimination by officials which the Fourteenth Amendment might not itself proscribe; it is directed not at any State or state actor, but at individuals who have committed criminal acts motivated by gender bias.

In the present cases, for example, § 13981 visits no consequence whatever on any Virginia public official involved in investigating or prosecuting Brzonkala's assault. The section is, therefore, unlike any of the § 5 remedies that we have previously upheld. For example, in Katzenbach v. Morgan (1966), Congress prohibited New York from imposing literacy tests as a prerequisite for voting because it found that such a requirement disenfranchised thousands of Puerto Rican immigrants who had been educated in the Spanish language of their home territory. That law, which we upheld, was directed at New York officials who administered the State's election law and prohibited them from using a provision of that law. In South Carolina v. Katzenbach (1966), Congress imposed voting rights requirements on States that, Congress found, had a history of discriminating against blacks in voting. The remedy was also directed at state officials in those States. Similarly, in Ex parte Virginia, (1880), Congress criminally punished state officials who intentionally discriminated in jury selection; again, the remedy was directed to the culpable state official.

Section 13981 is also different from these previously upheld remedies in that it applies uniformly throughout the Nation. Congress' findings indicate that the problem of discrimination against the victims of gender-motivated crimes does not exist in all States, or even most States. By contrast, the § 5 remedy upheld in Katzenbach v. Morgan, supra, was directed only to the State where the evil found by Congress existed, and in South Carolina v. Katzenbach, supra, the remedy was directed only to those States in which Congress found that there had been discrimination.

IV

Petitioner Brzonkala's complaint alleges that she was the victim of a brutal assault. But Congress' effort in § 13981 to provide a federal civil remedy can be sustained neither under the Commerce Clause nor under § 5 of the Fourteenth Amendment. If the allegations here are true, no civilized system of justice could fail to provide her a remedy for the conduct of respondent Morrison. But under our federal system that remedy must be provided by the Commonwealth of Virginia, and not by the United States.

■ JUSTICE SOUTER, with whom JUSTICE STEVENS, JUSTICE GINSBURG, and JUSTICE BREYER join, dissenting.

Our cases, which remain at least nominally undisturbed, stand for the following propositions. Congress has the power to legislate with regard to activity that, in the aggregate, has a substantial effect on interstate commerce.... The fact of such a substantial effect is not an issue for the courts in the first instance, ... but for the Congress, whose institutional capacity for gathering evidence and taking testimony far exceeds ours. By passing legislation, Congress indicates its conclusion, whether explicitly or not, that facts support its exercise of the commerce power. The business of the courts is to review the congressional assessment, not for soundness but simply for the rationality of concluding that a jurisdictional basis exists in fact.... Any explicit findings that Congress chooses to make, though not dispositive of the question of rationality, may advance judicial review by identifying factual authority on which Congress relied. Applying those propositions in these cases can lead to only one conclusion.

One obvious difference from United States v. Lopez is the mountain of data assembled by Congress, here showing the effects of violence against women on interstate commerce. Passage of the Act in 1994 was preceded by four years of hearings, which included testimony from physicians and law professors; from survivors of rape and domestic violence; and from representatives of state law enforcement and private business. The record includes reports on gender bias from task forces in 21 States, and we have the benefit of specific factual findings in the eight separate Reports issued by Congress and its committees over the long course leading to enactment

With respect to domestic violence, Congress received evidence for the following findings:

"Three out of four American women will be victims of violent crimes sometime during their life." H. R. Rep. No. 103–395 p. 25 (1993) (citing U.S. Dept. of Justice, Report to the Nation on Crime and Justice 29 (2d ed. 1988)).

"Violence is the leading cause of injuries to women ages 15 to 44...." S. Rep. No. 103–138, p. 38 (1993) (citing Surgeon General Antonia Novello, From the Surgeon General, U.S. Public Health Services, 267 JAMA 3132 (1992)).

"As many as 50 percent of homeless women and children are fleeing domestic violence." S. Rep. No. 101–545, p. 37 (1990) (citing E. Schneider, Legal Reform Efforts for Battered Women: Past, Present, and Future (July 1990)).

"Since 1974, the assault rate against women has outstripped the rate for men by at least twice for some age groups and far more for others." S. Rep. No. 101–545, at 30 (citing Bureau of Justice Statistics, Criminal Victimization in the United States (1974) (Table 5)).

"Battering 'is the single largest cause of injury to women in the United States.'" S. Rep. No. 101–545, at 37 (quoting Van Hightower and McManus, Limits of State Constitutional Guarantees: Lessons from Efforts to Implement Domestic Violence Policies, 49 Pub. Admin. Rev. 269 (May/June 1989)).

"An estimated 4 million American women are battered each year by their husbands or partners." H. R. Rep. No. 103–395, at 26 (citing Council on Scientific Affairs, American Medical Assn., Violence Against Women: Relevance for Medical Practitioners, 267 JAMA 3184, 3185 (1992)).

"Over 1 million women in the United States seek medical assistance each year for injuries sustained [from] their husbands or other partners." S. Rep. No. 101–545, at 37 (citing Stark and Flitcraft, Medical Therapy as Repression: The Case of the Battered Woman, Health & Medicine (Summer/Fall 1982).)

"Between 2,000 and 4,000 women die every year from [domestic] abuse." S. Rep. No. 101–545, at 36 (citing Schneider, *supra*).

"Arrest rates may be as low as 1 for every 100 domestic assaults." S. Rep. No. 101–545, at 38 (citing Dutton, Profiling of Wife Assaulters:

Preliminary Evidence for Trimodal Analysis, 3 Violence and Victims 5–30 (1988)).

"Partial estimates show that violent crime against women costs this country at least 3 billion—not million, but billion—dollars a year." S. Rep. No. 101–545, at 33 (citing Schneider, *supra,* at 4).

"Estimates suggest that we spend $5 to $10 billion a year on health care, criminal justice, and other social costs of domestic violence." S. Rep. No. 103–138, at 41 (citing Biden, Domestic Violence: A Crime, Not a Quarrel, Trial 56 (June 1993)).

The evidence as to rape was similarly extensive . . .

Congress thereby explicitly stated the predicate for the exercise of its Commerce Clause power. Is its conclusion irrational in view of the data amassed? True, the methodology of particular studies may be challenged, and some of the figures arrived at may be disputed. But the sufficiency of the evidence before Congress to provide a rational basis for the finding cannot seriously be questioned.

Indeed, the legislative record here is far more voluminous than the record compiled by Congress and found sufficient in two prior cases upholding Title II of the Civil Rights Act of 1964 against Commerce Clause challenges. In Heart of Atlanta Motel, Inc. v. United States (1964), and Katzenbach v. McClung, (1964), the Court referred to evidence showing the consequences of racial discrimination by motels and restaurants on interstate commerce. Congress had relied on compelling anecdotal reports that individual instances of segregation cost thousands to millions of dollars. Congress also had evidence that the average black family spent substantially less than the average white family in the same income range on public accommodations, and that discrimination accounted for much of the difference.

While Congress did not, to my knowledge, calculate aggregate dollar values for the nationwide effects of racial discrimination in 1964, in 1994 it did rely on evidence of the harms caused by domestic violence and sexual assault, citing annual costs of $3 billion in 1990. Equally important, though, gender-based violence in the 1990's was shown to operate in a manner similar to racial discrimination in the 1960's in reducing the mobility of employees and their production and consumption of goods shipped in interstate commerce. Like racial discrimination, "gender-based violence bars its most likely targets—women—from full participation in the national economy." . . .

If the analogy to the Civil Rights Act of 1964 is not plain enough, one can always look back a bit further. In *Wickard*, we upheld the application of the Agricultural Adjustment Act to the planting and consumption of homegrown wheat. The effect on interstate commerce in that case followed from the possibility that wheat grown at home for personal consumption could either be drawn into the market by rising prices, or relieve its grower of any need to purchase wheat in the market. . . . The Commerce Clause predicate was simply the effect of the production of wheat for home consumption on supply and demand in interstate commerce. Supply and demand for goods in interstate commerce will also be affected by the deaths of 2,000 to 4,000 women annually at the hands of domestic abusers, . . . and by the reduction in the work force by the 100,000 or more rape victims who lose their jobs each year or are forced to quit. . . . Violence against women may be found to affect interstate commerce and affect it substantially.

II

The Act would have passed muster at any time between *Wickard* in 1942 and *Lopez* in 1995, a period in which the law enjoyed a stable understanding that congressional power under the Commerce Clause, complemented by the authority of the Necessary and Proper Clause, Art. I. § 8 cl. 18, extended to all activity that, when aggregated, has a substantial effect on interstate commerce. As already noted, this understanding was secure even against the turmoil at the passage of the Civil Rights Act of 1964, in the aftermath of which the Court not only reaffirmed the cumulative effects and rational basis features of the substantial effects test . . . but declined to limit the commerce power through a formal distinction between legislation focused on "commerce" and statutes addressing "moral and social wrongs," . . . .

The fact that the Act does not pass muster before the Court today is therefore proof, to a degree that *Lopez* was not, that the Court's nominal adherence to the substantial effects test is merely that. Although a new jurisprudence has not emerged with any distinctness, it is clear that some congressional conclusions about obviously substantial, cumulative effects on commerce are being assigned lesser values than the once-stable doctrine would assign them. These devaluations are accomplished not by any express repudiation of the substantial effects test or its application through the aggregation of individual conduct, but by supplanting rational basis scrutiny with a new criterion of review. . . .

. . . Today's majority . . . finds no significance whatever in the state support for the Act based upon the States' acknowledged failure to deal adequately with gender-based violence in state courts, and the belief of their own law enforcement agencies that national action is essential.

The National Association of Attorneys General supported the Act unanimously, . . . and Attorneys General from 38 States urged Congress to enact the Civil Rights Remedy, representing that "the current system for dealing with violence against women is inadequate," . . . . It was against this record of failure at the state level that the Act was passed to provide the choice of a federal forum in place of the state-court systems found inadequate to stop gender-biased violence. . . . The Act accordingly offers a federal civil rights remedy aimed exactly at violence against women, as an alternative to the generic state tort causes of action found to be poor tools of action by the state task forces. As the 1993 Senate Report put it, "The Violence Against Women Act is intended to respond both to the underlying attitude that this violence is somehow less serious than other crime and to the resulting failure of our criminal justice system to address such violence. Its goals are both symbolic and practical. . . ." . . .

The collective opinion of state officials that the Act was needed continues virtually unchanged, and when the Civil Rights Remedy was challenged in court, the States came to its defense. Thirty-six of them and the Commonwealth of Puerto Rico have filed an *amicus* brief in support of petitioners in these cases, and only one State has taken respondents' side. It is, then, not the least irony of these cases that the States will be forced to enjoy the new federalism whether they want it or not. For with the Court's decision today, Antonio Morrison, like *Carter Coal*'s James Carter before him, has "won the states' rights plea against the states themselves."

All of this convinces me that today's ebb of the commerce power rests on error, and at the same time leads me to doubt that the majority's view will prove to be enduring law. . . .

■ JUSTICE BREYER, with whom JUSTICE STEVENS joins, . . . dissenting.

[The portion of the dissent addressing the Commerce Clause, and joined also by Justices Souter and Ginsburg is omitted.]

Given my conclusion on the Commerce Clause question, I need not consider Congress' authority under § 5 of the Fourteenth Amendment. Nonetheless, I doubt the Court's reasoning rejecting that source of authority. The Court points out that . . . § 5 does not authorize Congress to use the Fourteenth Amendment as a source of power to remedy the conduct of *private persons*. That is certainly so. The Federal Government's argument, however, is that Congress used § 5 to remedy the actions of *state actors*, namely, those States which, through discriminatory design or the discriminatory conduct of their officials, failed to provide adequate (or any) state remedies for women injured by gender-motivated violence—a failure that the States, and Congress, documented in depth. . . .

The Court responds directly to the relevant "state actor" claim by finding that the present law lacks " 'congruence and proportionality' " to the state discrimination that it purports to remedy. That is because the law, unlike federal laws prohibiting literacy tests for voting, imposing voting rights requirements, or punishing state officials who intentionally discriminated in jury selection, . . . is not "directed . . . at any State or state actor." . . .

But why can Congress not provide a remedy against private actors? Those private actors, of course, did not themselves violate the Constitution. But this Court has held that Congress at least sometimes can enact remedial "legislation . . . [that] prohibits conduct which is not itself unconstitutional." The statutory remedy does not in any sense purport to "determine what constitutes a constitutional violation." It intrudes little upon either States or private parties. It may lead state actors to improve their own remedial systems, primarily through example. It restricts private actors only by imposing liability for private conduct that is, in the main, already forbidden by state law. Why is the remedy "disproportionate"? And given the relation between remedy and violation—the creation of a federal remedy to substitute for constitutionally inadequate state remedies—where is the lack of "congruence"?

The majority adds that Congress found that the problem of inadequacy of state remedies "does not exist in all States, or even most States." But Congress had before it the task force reports of at least 21 States documenting constitutional violations. And it made its own findings about pervasive gender-based stereotypes hampering many state legal systems, sometimes unconstitutionally so.... The record nowhere reveals a congressional finding that the problem "does not exist" elsewhere. Why can Congress not take the evidence before it as evidence of a national problem? This Court has not previously held that Congress must document the existence of a problem in every State prior to proposing a national solution. And the deference this Court gives to Congress' chosen remedy under § 5, suggests that any such requirement would be inappropriate.

Despite my doubts about the majority's § 5 reasoning, I need not, and do not, answer the § 5 question, which I would leave for more thorough analysis if necessary on another occasion. Rather, in my view, the Commerce Clause provides an adequate basis for the statute before us. And I would uphold its constitutionality as the "necessary and proper" exercise of legislative power granted to Congress by that Clause

NOTES AND QUESTIONS

1. **Analyzing the Majority's Opinion.** Do you find yourself more persuaded by Rehnquist's opinion for the Court or by the dissenters? Do you think the outcome in *Morrison* was predetermined by the Court's earlier decision in *Lopez*? Does the fact that *Lopez* preceded *Morrison* persuade you that the Court had an agenda (the reassertion of limits on federal authority) quite distinct from any concern about framing violence against women as a public rather than a private issue?

2. **Justices' Current Views of Federalism.** *Morrison* provided a heated forum on the current debates over federalism. During the oral argument, Justice Scalia stated that the "right to regulate was the right to preempt." He went on to state that the Fourteenth Amendment does not provide "as a remedy for the state's failure to abide by the Constitution, the federal government's abolition of the federal system." Justice Kennedy suggested that individuals could be provided with private remedies for state failure to provide equal protection of the law, noting that the federal government should be able to say to the states, "state, you have not done this, so we will force you to do this." These are two very different views of the proper balance of power between the federal government and the states. In the dissent, Justice Breyer presented a third view of federalism, which he described as cooperation between state and federal governments to solve a mutual problem. This view is labeled "cooperative federalism." In the except below, Sally Goldfarb explains why VAWA is a model of cooperative federalism:

> VAWA's civil rights provision entailed federal-state cooperation on a number of levels ... VAWA as a whole was a broad-ranging statute designed to respond in numerous ways to the national epidemic of rape, domestic violence, and other forms of violence against women.

This epidemic, and the difficulty of combating it, were a source of profound concern to the states as well as to the federal government. Taken in its entirety, VAWA created a series of coordinated measures in which the federal and state governments worked in concert, with both playing indispensable roles. Many sections of VAWA were aimed at strengthening the ability of the states to provide their own civil and criminal legal remedies for violence against women. Others created joint federal-state collaborations. Still others addressed the distinctively federal aspects of a multifaceted problem that had both federal and state dimensions.

The civil rights remedy was integrated with and complementary to VAWA's other provisions. The civil rights remedy enhanced the rest of the statute by condemning gender-motivated violence in the uniquely powerful terms of a federal civil rights guarantee. This message had the potential to reinforce the educational and deterrent effects of other sections of the bill. VAWA's civil rights remedy also had the potential to change attitudes among state actors and spur them to improve the states' legal response to violence against women.

The civil rights remedy left the laws of the states intact. Contrary to the assertions of some judges, the civil rights remedy did not usurp the role of the states in regulating family law, torts, or criminal law. Rather, it established a parallel, alternative remedy for a different injury. The wrong for which VAWA provided redress was the discrimination inherent in gender-motivated violence, as distinct from the interests that are remedied by traditional domestic relations, personal injury, or criminal proceedings under state law. Sally Goldfarb, *The Supreme Court, the Violence Against Women Act, and the Use and Abuse of Federalism*, 71 FORDHAM L.REV. 57 (2002).

3. **Recent Commerce Clause Cases.** After *Morrison*, the Supreme Court considered two more cases involving Congressional power under the Commerce Clause. The first was *Gonzales v. Raich*, 545 U.S. 1 (2005), in which the Court held that the Federal Government could prosecute those who use medical marijuana even in states which legalized its use. In the 6–3 opinion, the court found that unlike *Morrison* and *Lopez*, the production and use of marijuana was economic in nature, even if the marijuana was home grown only for personal medical use, and thus was properly regulated under the Commerce Clause. Justices O'Connor, Rehnquist, and Thomas dissented, arguing that this case was exactly like *Morrison*—the government had not shown how growing marijuana for private medical use "substantially effected" interstate commerce.

The following year, in *Gonzales v. Oregon*, 546 U.S. 243 (2006), the Court considered whether the federal government could prosecute doctors who provided drugs to patients under Oregon's Death with Dignity Act. The Act allows doctors to legally prescribe certain lethal substances to assist in the painless death of competent yet terminally ill individuals. Oregon's was the first, and by 2006, the only, physician-assisted suicide law in any state. Former Attorney General John Aschroft viewed assisting suicide as an "illegitimate medical purpose" under the Controlled Dangerous Substance Act (CSA) and ordered that doctors who assisted suicide either have their registration to deliver controlled substances revoked, or be prosecuted under federal law. Oregon claimed the Attorney General's position violated the Commerce Clause as an over-reaching of federal government power into an area traditionally left to the states. In a 6–3 decision, Justice Kennedy ruled that the CSA did not give the Attorney General the power to regulate medical practices. In his dissent joined by Justice Thomas and the then newly appointed Chief Justice John Roberts, Justice Scalia argued that if "legitimate medical purpose" meant anything, it certainly could not mean administering death. Whether *Gonzales v. Oregon* signals a change back to pre-*Lopez* days, or is a more narrow case involving statutory, rather than constitutional principles, remains to be seen.

Feminist lawmakers and civil rights advocates have asserted that, historically, the state's rights argument has been most closely associated with the denial of individual rights. Indeed, the southern states relied upon the state's rights argument during the Civil War, reconstruction, the Jim Crow era, and the civil rights era to resist providing African–Americans with their legal rights. But given *Raich* and *Oregon*, it may be that in a modern era, state's rights might lead to more individual rights, safeguarding against a more oppressive federal regime and allowing individuals more political decision-making about their private, personal lives. Take, for example, the debate over gay marriage. Some states, including Massachusetts, Connecticut, and Vermont, have given same-sex couples greater rights, either through marriage or civil unions, than would be permitted under federal law. The fear is that the federal government could try to strip same-sex couples of the rights won at the state level. From this perspective, the federalism argument may be helpful in curbing federal power.

Furthermore, consider the argument that federalism is really about responsibility. Returning to *Morrison*, it can be argued that legislation such as VAWA encourages the states to rely on the benefits of the federal government while avoiding responsibility for ensuring that victims of domestic violence have proper legal recourse locally. Arguably, by increasing state and local responsibility for solving social problems, such as domestic violence, individual rights and personal accountability will ultimately be enhanced.

4. Amending the Act to Comply with Constitutional Restrictions. In the aftermath of *Morrison,* new civil rights legislation was introduced in Congress. The Violence Against Women Civil Rights Restoration Act of 2000, H.R. 5021, 106th Cong. (2000), amends Section 40302 of the Violence Against Women Act, 42 U.S.C. § 13981, in two critical respects. First, it adds a requirement that, in connection with the crime of violence for which the victim seeks redress either:

(A) the defendant or the victim travels in interstate or foreign commerce;

(B) the defendant or the victim uses a facility or instrumentality of interstate or foreign commerce;

OR:

(C) the defendant employs a firearm, explosive, incendiary device, or other weapon, or a narcotic or drug listed pursuant to section 202 of the Controlled Substances Act, or other noxious or dangerous substance, that has traveled in interstate or foreign commerce;

OR:

(2) the offense interferes with commercial or other economic activity in which the victim is engaged at the time of the conduct;

OR:

(3) the offense was committed with intent to interfere with the victim's commercial or other economic activity.

Second, the bill adds an entirely new provision:

DISCRETIONARY AUTHORITY OF ATTORNEY GENERAL— Whenever the Attorney General has reasonable cause to believe that any State or political subdivision of a State, official, employee, or agent thereof, or other person acting on behalf of a State or political subdivision of a State has discriminated on the basis of gender in the investigation or prosecution of gender-based crimes and that discrimination is pursuant to a pattern or practice of resistance to investigating or prosecuting gender-based crimes, the Attorney General, for or in the name of the United States, may institute a civil action in any appropriate United States district court against such party for such equitable relief as may be appropriate to ensure the elimination of such discriminatory practices.

This bill was never voted out of committee during VAWA's 2005 reauthorization. Nevertheless, based on a careful reading of Rehnquist's opinion for the Court in *Morrison*, do you believe the new provisions would pass constitutional muster? Do they impose significant limits on the scope of the redress provided? Has the cause of action against "state actors" been included with the expectation that such suits would actually be brought, or simply to shore up the claim that the legislation is designed to address discrimination that women experience when they pursue their claims at the state level?

5. **Educational Institutions May be Liable for Indifference.** Christy Brzonkala, the plaintiff in *Morrison*, was the victim of a campus sexual assault. She had only known the defendants for thirty minutes before they raped her. While the Civil Rights provision of VAWA gave Brzonkala the right to sue her assailants, it did not provide a remedy for her to sue Virginia Polytechnic Institute, which arguably did very little to protect Brzonkala from her assailants. However, Brzonkala may have had a claim against Virginia Tech under Title IX. In 1972, using the spending power granted to Congress under the Constitution, Congress enacted Title IX, making non-discrimination by sex a condition of participation in federally funded education programs. Under Title IX, schools can be held liable for student-student, as well as teacher-student, sexual harassment if the school was deliberately indifferent to the sexual harassment, had knowledge of it,

and the harassment was severe, persuasive and objectively offensive to the point of denying access to educational opportunities of benefits provided by the institution. See *Davis v. Monroe County Bd. of Educ.*, 526 U.S. 629 (1999).

Some colleges, such as the University of Colorado, have been accused of fostering an atmosphere that is hostile to women by having parties for football recruits where there is an expectation of sexual favors. For example, in 2001, three women who claimed that they were raped by football players or recruits at, or after, an official campus party filed a lawsuit under Title IX alleging that the University knew and even encouraged the practice. Other schools, including the University of Alabama and Oklahoma State have also been sued under Title IX for alleged sexual assaults by football players, but those cases settled out of court. See Erik Brady, *Colorado Scandal Could Hit Home at Other Colleges*, U.S.A. Today, May 26, 2004.

6. **Schools Reinforcing Violence Against Women.** It could be argued that there is a "custom" of sexually assaulting women that is connected to a sense of entitlement among young males, especially athletes. When schools provide prostitutes or women at parties to bestow sexual favors, it exacerbates the message that women are disposable objects for the sexual pleasure and gratification of men. Do such practices reinforce a culture of female subordination that not only results in rape and sexual assault, but domestic violence as well? Think back to Chapter Three and Lundy Bancroft's argument that culture encourages violence against women. Do such practices at the college level ultimately encourage violence against one's intimate partner?

7. **Circumventing the Constitutional Questions Raised by the Commerce Clause.** Should there be federal legislation giving domestic violence victims the right to sue state actors who fail to stop domestic violence, similar to Title IX? As we saw in Chapter Fourteen, such theories of third party liability have not been successful when based on due process challenges. However, Title IX ties the civil rights remedy to federal spending, thus avoiding some of the more difficult constitutional questions about either the Commerce Clause or the Fourteenth Amendment. If schools want to discriminate against women, they need not accept federal funds, although as a practical matter, that is incredibly difficult to do. Thus, under Title IX, the Federal government is using the powers of the purse to provide victims of school-based sexual discrimination a federal civil rights remedy. Could there be other strategies to combat domestic violence as sex discrimination? See Julie Goldscheid, *Domestic and Sexual Violence as Sex Discrimination: Comparing American and International Approaches*, 28 T. JEFFERSON L. REV. 355 (2006).

The majority opinion in *Morrison* suggested that the Civil Rights provision of VAWA was disproportionate in that it did not provide remedies that would address state actors in situations where rights were denied. Are there adequate laws that address judges who show gender bias in their decisions or police departments that mishandle domestic violence calls? If you were a United States Senator, how might you craft legislation to reach such state actors? Think about all the federal spending now related to Homeland Security after September 11, 2001. Would there be a way to link domestic terrorism with domestic violence enforcement as a way to grant Congressional authority in this area?

C. STATE CIVIL RIGHTS REMEDIES

Civil rights legislation modeled on VAWA's original civil rights provision has also been introduced at the state and local level. The following excerpt describes some of those efforts and the current civil rights opportunities under state law.

Julie Goldscheid
The Civil Rights Remedy of the 1994 Violence Against Women Act: Struck Down But Not Ruled Out
39 FAM. L.Q. 157 (2005).

III.   State and Local Legislative Responses to the Morrison Decision

In the course of striking the law on federalism grounds, the Morrison majority declared that the Court could "think of no better example of the police power, which the Founders ... reposed in the States, than the suppression of violent crime and vindication of its victims." With that reasoning, the Court essentially invited states and localities to enact comparable civil rights legislation. California, Illinois, New York City, and Westchester followed up on this invitation and enacted civil rights remedies that were modeled after the now-defunct federal law. Other states have introduced legislative proposals that sought to fill the gap left by the Morrison opinion but have not yet been enacted. Other than restricting plaintiffs to a state versus federal forum, these laws provide virtually identical substantive relief, with similar elements of proof, to that which was provided for in the now-unavailable federal law. At least as a theoretical matter, these laws should serve as a rough substitute for the VAWA civil rights remedy in the jurisdictions in which they have been enacted.

In addition to these state reforms, members of Congress have introduced post-Morrison civil rights remedy legislation. These proposals would retain the essential civil cause of action but would amend the language of the 1994 law to avoid the aspects the Supreme Court found constitutionally infirm. To date, however, none of the federal proposals has been enacted.

The state statutes enacted after the *Morrison* decision have received little public attention and do not yet appear to be widely used. One can speculate about the reasons for the laws' limited use, although it is difficult to determine whether any underutilization reflects a lack of general awareness about the law's availability, some structural limitation of an approach that provides a private cause of action for a civil rights violation, or the relative superiority of a federal forum. To date, only one reported decision involves a survivor's attempt to use any of these new laws. In *Cadiz–Jones v. Zambetti,* a domestic violence survivor brought a claim against her former fiancé based on allegations of his ongoing physical abuse and violence. She brought suit under New York City's then-recently enacted law after her VAWA civil rights remedy claim in federal court was dismissed in response to the Morrison decision. The court rejected the defendant's arguments that the local law would not apply retroactively, and that the new city law was preempted by state legislation governing statutes of limitations for intentional torts. It reviewed the law's legislative history and concluded that the New York City Council had enacted the law to fill the void created when the United States Supreme Court struck the VAWA civil rights remedy, and that the City Council sought to restore a cause of action for victims of gender-motivated violence. According to the court, it could give effect to the legislative purpose driving the law only by allowing the plaintiff's claim to proceed, since her VAWA civil rights claim was struck and dismissed before a federal court could adjudicate her claims. Although the decision currently stands alone, it demonstrates that these state laws hold potential for survivors seeking civil recovery from their abusers.

IV. State Civil Rights Remedies for Gender–Motivated Violence

Although the VAWA civil rights remedy was the first express federal legislative acknowledgment that violence against women violates women's rights, many state and local laws provided similar relief even before VAWA was enacted. Many states had, and continue to have, laws on the books that provide civil as well as criminal remedies for bias-motivated violence. Since many of these laws are part of the state's bias crime statutes, they will be referenced here as the "state gender-bias crime" laws. Currently, eleven states and the District of Columbia include "sex" or "gender" as one of the categories that can give rise to civil recovery under those state bias crime frameworks.

Not unlike the state civil rights laws enacted after *Morrison*, these laws are neither widely used nor widely publicized. Their relative lack of use may similarly reflect the public's general lack of awareness about the laws' existence and the redress they authorize. Although these laws authorize suit in a state rather than a federal forum, and although they offer only a patchwork of protection nationwide, as a substantive matter, these laws provide relief that is similar to, if not broader than, that provided by either the VAWA civil rights remedy or the state civil rights statutes that were modeled after the VAWA provision.

Several substantive and procedural comparisons highlight the state laws' potential reach. For example, in contrast to the VAWA civil rights remedy, which contained a relatively complex formulation for proving gender-motivation, many of the state statutes allow recovery based on the more simple proof that the individual suffered an injury based on her actual or perceived sex or gender. Most of the state statutes authorize a broad range of remedies like those Congress authorized under the VAWA civil rights remedy. For example, most of these state laws allow plaintiffs to recover damages for emotional distress as well as punitive damages. Most also expressly authorize injunctive relief in addition to money damages. Virtually all of the state statutes allow successful plaintiffs to recover attorneys' fees. Many state laws are governed by statutes of limitations that are longer than what a victim would be bound by in a traditional tort action. Some mirror the VAWA civil rights remedy in specifying that the burden of proof is a preponderance of the evidence. Given this comparable if not broader coverage, to the extent that the VAWA civil rights remedy held both practical and transformational potential, these analogous state laws should hold similar, if not identical, promise.

What is remarkable about the body of decisions under these laws, beyond its small size, is that none of the reported decisions analyze the merits of the claim of gender-motivated harm. The majority of decisions involve allegations of sexual harassment at work in which the threshold question concerning the state civil rights statute was whether that law authorized recovery that was duplicative of recovery available under other state laws. Courts upheld claims under the state civil rights statute where the alleged wrongdoing was not covered by another state law, such as the state statute prohibiting employment discrimination based on sex. Yet even those decisions upholding claims have focused on procedural issues, rather than analyzing the merits of the claims.

Cases outside of the sexual harassment context also have hinged on procedural rather than substantive analyses. For example, a case arising out of domestic violence that included a claim under the VAWA civil rights remedy contained, and upheld, a claim under the state statute prohibiting malicious harassment "motivated by the perpetrator's perception of the victim's gender." The court rejected an argument that the claim was time-barred and upheld the state civil rights claim without addressing its merits. A claim that a male National Guard member sexually assaulted a fellow (male) guard member during a hazing ritual was upheld against an immunity challenge, and the plaintiff's claim for attorneys' fees was sustained. Similarly, a tenant who was sexually harassed by her apartment manager was able to proceed with her claim under the California civil statute authorizing damage relief from gender-motivated violence based on the court's determination that respondent superior liability could apply....

The relative lack of use of these state statutes stands in stark contrast to the interest and attention generated by the federal law. Yet some have suggested that VAWA was underutilized as well. In addition to litigants' lack of awareness of what the law would offer, this phenomenon could also reflect the constitutional controversy that surrounded the VAWA civil rights remedy since its enactment or the narrow crafting of its statutory terms. The apparent limited use of the more broadly crafted state laws raises the question whether the utility of a civil remedy in this context may be limited by systemic factors, such as domestic violence victims' reluctance to re-engage with the batterer, or their fears that the batterer will use the civil litigation context as a further device for perpetuating a pattern of coercion and control over her. The laws may be underutilized as well due to the difficulty victims of domestic and sexual violence continue to face in obtaining counsel notwithstanding fee-shifting provisions. In addition, these laws may not offer the remedies most victims of domestic and sexual violence seek, such as financial assistance (from sources other than the batterer), jobs, childcare, immigration assistance, and legal representation. Nevertheless, to the extent that civil remedies can offer practical assistance and can be a catalyst for the transformation the VAWA civil rights remedy's drafters hoped to inspire, the state statutes may in time advance both goals for victims of gender-based violence.

NOTES AND QUESTIONS

1. **State and Local Civil Rights Laws.** In 2002, California became the first state to enact a civil rights statute modeled on the civil rights provision of VAWA. It provides that a person who commits gender-motivated violence, such as domestic violence or sexual assault, has violated the civil rights of the victim and can, in turn, be sued for actual, compensatory, and punitive damages, as well as attorney's fees. Plaintiffs have three years from the date of the act to bring suit. See CAL. CIV. CODE § 52.4 (WEST 2003).

In 2004, Illinois passed the "Gender Violence Act," which provides, "Any person who has been subjected to gender-related violence . . . may bring a civil action for damages, injunctive relief, or other appropriate relief against a person or persons perpetrating that gender-related violence." 72 ILL. COMP. STAT. 82/10 (2004). Gender-motivated violence is defined as:

> (1) One or more acts of violence or physical aggression satisfying the elements of battery the laws of Illinois that are committed, at least in part, on the basis of a person's sex, whether or not those acts have resulted in criminal charges, prosecution, or conviction.

> (2) A physical intrusion or physical invasion of a sexual nature under coercive conditions satisfying the elements of battery under the laws of Illinois, whether or not the act or acts resulted in criminal charges, prosecution, or conviction.

> (3) A threat of an act described in item (1) or (2) causing a realistic apprehension that the originator of the threat will commit the act.

Plaintiffs can recover actual damages, damages for emotional distress, punitive damages, attorneys' fees, and costs, thus providing victims with far more available forms of relief than under traditional tort law. Although an original version of this law was introduced prior to the *Morrison* decision, the legislative history makes clear that the statute was needed after *Morrison* held that states alone have the authority to grant civil relief to the survivors of sexually motivated violence.

New York, Arizona, and Arkansas have also considered bills which would give victims of domestic violence a civil cause of action. Additionally, at least three states, including California, Vermont, and Michigan, have passed hate crime statutes that provide for civil remedies for victims of gender-motivated hate crimes. See Sarah F. Russell, *Covering Women & Violence: Media Treatment of VAWA's Civil Rights Remedy*, 9 MICH. J. GENDER & L. 327 (2003).

In December 2000, New York City passed the Victims of Gender–Motivated Violence Protection Act, N.Y., N.Y., Admin. Code §§ 8–901 to –905 (2002). This ordinance amended the "civil rights" title of New York City's Administrative Code. It allows for victims of domestic violence to sue their attackers for civil damages. In fact, the citizens of New York City were the first in the nation to have such a right. Victims now have seven years to bring a law suit, instead of one to two years under traditional tort law, and may sue to recover attorney's fees and punitive damages, as well as compensation. Westchester County in New York has also passed an almost identical ordinance creating a civil remedy for victims of gender-motivated violence. Westchester County Laws, § 701 (2005).

What are the advantages and disadvantages of enacting civil rights legislation at the state rather than the federal level? If the federal legislation was prompted in part by the inadequacy of state responses to violence against women, will additional legislation, which must still be interpreted and implemented by state courts, produce significant changes in the climate within which women seek redress? Note that seven years after *Morrison*, very few states have even considered, let alone passed, legislation providing civil remedies for victims of domestic violence. Some argue that such laws will do little to help poor women, who often lack the resources to even exercise their most basic rights. Other critics contend that such laws are excessive and unnecessary, and create a special class of victims who will get more relief than other victims of assault and battery. Yet, for all the fear that such cases will clog the court system, there is very little evidence that victims of domestic violence are, in fact, suing under state or local statutes.

2.   **Gender Neutral Legislation.** When Sally Goldfarb represented the position of NOW LDEF on the Violence Against Women Act civil rights provision, she was careful to point out that the legislation was in fact gender-neutral—it offered men as well as women the prospect of suing those who used violence against them when that violence was motivated by gender animus. It is not our experience, however, that men are the targets of violence because they are men—except, perhaps, when men are victimized by other men because they fail to conform to "manly" stereotypes (because they are effeminate, or gay, or transsexual, or in their behavior or dress otherwise fail to observe gender boundaries). Ironically, our gender-discrimination jurisprudence has not as yet recognized that this male-on-male violence *is* gender-motivated; these cases tend to be viewed as cases involving discrimination based on sexuality rather than gender, and as such they fall outside the scope of protection offered by gender discrimination laws.

There is another way, however, in which civil rights legislation addressing discrimination against women, or more narrowly violence against women, benefits men as well as women, and therefore society at large. John Stuart Mill said it as well as anyone, in describing the costs to society of inequality, and the corresponding gains associated with eradicating that inequality:

If no authority, not in its nature temporary, were allowed to one human being over another, society would not be employed in building up propensities with one hand which it has to curb with the other. The child would really, for the first time in man's existence on earth, be trained in the way he should go, and when he was old there would be a chance that he would not depart from it. But so long as the right of the strong to power over the weak rules in the very heart of society, the attempt to make the equal right of the weak the principle of its outward actions will always be an uphill struggle; for the law of justice ... will never get possession of men's innermost sentiments; they will be working against it, even when bending to it.

... The love of power and the love of liberty are in eternal antagonism. Where there is least liberty, the passion for power is the most ardent and unscrupulous. The desire of power over others can only cease to be a depraving agency among mankind, when each of them individually is able to do without it: which can only be where respect for liberty in the personal concerns of each is an established principle. John Stuart Mill, The Subjection of Women (S.M. Okin ed. 1988).

Jane Maslow Cohen puts the same thought in more contemporary language:

[N]othing about the model of patriarchy even begins to suggest how the mothers into whose care the males of our society entrust our future citizens can likely inculcate in them a love of the liberty and equality that these same women have been denied.... [I]t is remarkable that the young of this society ever grow up to be democrats.... From a practical standpoint, therefore, it can be nothing other than a mistake for democracy to be married to patriarchy, since patriarchy is barren of democratic values and cannot, therefore, reproduce them. Jane Maslow Cohen, *Private Violence and Public Obligation: The Fulcrum of Reason*, The Public Nature of Private Violence 349 (M.A. Fineman and R. Mykitiuk, eds. 1994).

When women are full civic participants in both the senses discussed in these pages; when they both receive their full due from the state, and are free to make their maximum contribution to it, we will have left far behind the notion that power is society's first organizing principle, and be well on our way to embracing respect, the foundation of democratic governance, as its replacement. While civil rights legislation is only one of the many tools available to move society towards this goal, it does have the advantage of framing the debate in a fashion that clarifies what is at stake.

CHAPTER SEVENTEEN

DOMESTIC VIOLENCE AS A VIOLATION OF INTERNATIONAL HUMAN RIGHTS

Introduction

This chapter addresses the issue of domestic violence as a violation of international human rights. Like many other areas that we have explored, developments in this chapter are very recent. It is only in the last two decades that the human rights of women have emerged as a major focus of international advocacy efforts. Largely due to the work of an active global women's movement, what international human rights lawyer and scholar Rhonda Copelon has called "the coalescence of women as a global presence," the scope of protection of international treaties and covenants has expanded to victims of domestic violence. Important accomplishments include: the appointment in 1994 of a Special Rapporteur on Violence Against Women, Causes and Consequences; the adoption of an individual complaint procedure for alleging a violation of the Convention on the Elimination of All Forms of Discrimination Against Women (CEDAW); and acknowledgment by a range of United Nations human rights bodies that domestic violence is a human rights violation.

Framing violence against women as a violation of international human rights raises issues parallel to those explored in the last chapter, which looked at domestic violence as a violation of women's civil rights. The international human rights effort has established within the international community that violence against women is a public issue, and an issue of state dereliction of responsibility toward its citizenry, rather than a purely or merely private problem faced by individual women in their relationships with individual men. On the other hand, whereas the ill-fated civil rights remedy enacted as part of the Violence Against Women Act gave victims private rights of action against perpetrators, international efforts are aimed at increasing state responsiveness to the needs of women. As with any other international regulatory effort, however, the issue of enforcement is crucial. Do any of the increasingly specific international mandates in this area have any teeth? Are they important nonetheless in establishing global norms against violence against women? This chapter documents the history of the inclusion of women's concerns in the international arena and suggests the extent of the barriers that still exist.

Domestic violence can be understood as a human rights violation in several related ways: as a consequence of discrimination and lack of equal protection, as torture, and as state failure to exercise due diligence to protect, prosecute, and punish. This chapter begins with several articles that set out theoretical frameworks for understanding domestic violence as a violation of international human rights. In the first article published in 1995, Dorothy Thomas and Michele Beasley provide an historical overview of the arguments that paved the way for women's international human rights advocacy and offer examples of early advocacy efforts. In the second, more recent article, Rhonda Copelon describes the current situation of women's international human rights work in the United States and then, in a third article, argues that domestic violence can be understood within one of the most important and conventional frameworks of international human rights, the prohibition against torture. Then, we include an excerpt from The Secretary–General's In–Depth Study on All Forms of Violence Against Women which was submitted to the General Assembly in 2006 and adopted this human rights framework. We turn next to examination of some of the basic international human rights documents relevant to intimate partner violence: the Convention on the Elimination of All Forms of Discrimination Against Women (CEDAW); CEDAW Committee General Recommendation Number 19, specifically addressing violence; the General Assembly Resolution "Declaration on the Elimination of Violence Against Women;" Reports of the Special Rapporteur on Violence Against Women; and an excerpt of a contemporary report on violence from the Women's Rights Division of Human Rights Watch. Finally, we consider the significance of international human rights work for, and its impact on, domestic violence advocacy in the United States.

A.   DOMESTIC VIOLENCE AS A VIOLATION OF INTERNATIONAL HUMAN RIGHTS

Dorothy Q. Thomas and Michele E. Beasley
Domestic Violence As a Human Rights Issue
58 ALB. L.REV. 1119 (1995).

Maria was brutally assaulted in her own kitchen in England by a man wielding two knives. He held one of the weapons at her throat, while raping her with the other. After he finished, the man doused her with alcohol and set her alight with a blow torch. Maria lived through the assault to prosecute the man, although seventy percent of her body is now covered with scars. But because they were married, he could not be charged with rape. He received a ten-year sentence for bodily injury, of which he will serve only five years.

Between 1988 and 1990 in the Brazilian state of Maranhio, women registered at the main police station over 4,000 complaints of battery and sexual abuse in the home. Of those complaints, only 300—less than eight percent—were forwarded to the court for processing, and only two men were ever convicted and sent to prison.

In Pakistan, Muhammad Younis killed his wife, claiming that he found her in the act of adultery. The court found his defense untrue, in part because the woman was fully dressed when she was killed, and sentenced him to life imprisonment. However, on appeal the Lahore High Court reduced his sentence to ten years at hard labor stating that the "accused had two children from his deceased wife and when accused took the extreme step of taking her life by giving her repeated knife blows on different parts of her body she must have done something unusual to enrage him to that extent."

It has been observed that "the concept of human rights is one of the few moral visions ascribed to internationally." Domestic violence violates the principles that lie at the heart of this moral vision: the inherent dignity and worth of all members of the human family, the inalienable right to freedom from fear and want, and the equal rights of men and women. Yet until recently, it has been difficult to conceive of domestic violence as a human rights issue under international law.

Rhonda Copelon
International Human Rights Dimensions of Intimate Violence: Another Strand in the Dialectic of Feminist Law Making

11 AM. U. J. GENDER SOC. POL'Y & L. 865 (2003).

In 1990, womens' human rights issues were barely on the margin of the international human rights agenda. The Convention on the Elimination of All Forms of Discrimination Against Women ("CEDAW") was consigned to little more than window-dressing. Violence against women was almost never addressed in either official or non-governmental human rights documentation and reporting. Even when the state was responsible for rape, for example, it was usually was treated as a personal matter, rendered invisible and immunized from accountability. Rape in war was also on shaky ground as it had evolved in international humanitarian law only as implicit in the crime of "humiliating and degrading treatment" or in the "offense against honor and dignity" rather than as an explicit, named crime of violence.

In response, a burgeoning and irrepressible international feminist women's human rights movement coalesced and identified violence against women, by intimates and officials alike, as a priority issue of human rights in its preparations for the 1993 World Conference on Human Rights in Vienna ("Vienna Conference"). In the early stages, the allies were visionaries or renegades from mainstream thinking or women, in various positions in and out of governments, who themselves were survivors of rape or battering.

Leading mainstream human rights non-governmental advocates, however, adhered to a state-centric approach to human rights and were just beginning to recognize the severity of gender-based violence. With narrow exceptions like slavery, the traditional view was that human rights address only the actions of the state, not private individuals. In this view, state action which inflicts violence of sufficient gravity upon women would constitute a human rights violation. But privately inflicted violence, while appropriate for condemnation by municipal criminal laws, did not, they argued, present a human rights concern apart from some form of active state involvement. . . .

But the notion of treating the phenomenon of private violence against women as discrimination per se, or as torture or enslavement, or even as a violation of the international protection of life, liberty or personal security when tolerated by the state, was taking matters too far. Including private gendered violence, it was said, would "dilute" the human rights framework. Thus feminists had to challenge this incarnation of the public/private distinction, and discovered, in the process, that the international human rights process was not impenetrable to global organizing and that basic human rights principles include certain positive state responsibilities that should apply to private gender violence.

The Vienna Conference was a watershed. Testimonies as to the gravity and pervasiveness of gender violence, the force of women's broad organizing, and the very concrete fact, brought home by the participation of women from Bosnia and the former Yugoslavia, that women were being raped systematically in Bosnia—just hours from the site of the Conference—prevailed over objections to incorporating gender violence as a human rights problem. They also prevailed over the vigorous chorus of "nos" from defenders of archly patriarchal religions and cultures, who may condemn violence against women but who also contend that it is not an international problem and that sexual subordination in the home should be excluded from the human rights framework. The new consensus is reflected in the official document, the Vienna Declaration and Programme of action.

The historic achievement of Vienna Conference was two-fold: the recognition of violence against women as a human rights issue and the setting into motion of a process of integrating or "mainstreaming" issues of women's rights and gender equality into the international system at all levels. . . .

While the UN human rights system operates primarily through various shaming techniques, the recent Rome Treaty creating the International Criminal Court ("ICC") is different. Despite vigorous objections from the Vatican and some Islamist countries, the ICC's jurisdiction encompasses rape, sexual slavery, forced pregnancy, enforced sterilization and other sexual violence in time of peace as well as war as crimes against humanity when such violence is widespread or systematic and is the consequence of state or organizational policy. The ICC exists not only as an institution of justice but as an incentive to states to adopt and prosecute these crimes domestically. Thus, for example, acceptance or encouragement of marital rape or battering by law or by organizational leaders is one example of the ICC's potential reach.

At the same time, intimate gender-based violence seems intractable and the obstacles endure. In United Nations arenas, a small band of countries, representing various fundamentalisms, and now joined by representatives of the Bush Administration, continues to challenge the Vienna framework. In addition to outright obstruction, the full implementation of the obligation to eliminate gender-based violence in international or domestic policy has yet to be achieved in practice as the implementers commonly lack commitment or know-how. Beyond that, having just passed through the first stage of recognition, the problems ... of de-politicization and fragmentation, the tension between victimization and agency, the need for collaboration with and dangers of cooptation by the state, and the cultural embeddedness of violence against women, are also among the dilemmas faced by international activists.

Nonetheless, there are a number of important ways in which the international human rights recognition of gender-based violence, and particularly intimate violence, should strengthen and inspire the struggle here as well as abroad. The fact that intimate violence is now clearly a human rights issue is itself significant and heightens the demand for vigorous and multifaceted preventive and remedial action by the state.... [W]e not only enhance the significance of the problem of intimate violence and bring home some of the more capacious and positive aspects of international human rights obligations; we also reinforce the over-arching importance of universal principles and multilateral frameworks for human security and human rights generally.

International acceptance of the concept that gender violence as per se gender discrimination [is significant]. International recognition of gender violence as a human rights violation does not depend upon showing that the state inflicted it or that the state treated violence against women differently from violence against men. Rather, gender violence is viewed as inherently discriminatory in that it both reflects inequality and perpetuates it. This approach is rooted in an acknowledgment of the impact of this systemic practice and the necessity to prioritize its elimination. It entrains the positive obligation of the state under the International Covenant on Political and Civil Rights ("ICCPR") to ensure people against attack on their rights by others and the obligation, set forth in CEDAW and the Convention on the Elimination of All Forms of Racial Discrimination ("CERD"), to both eliminate discrimination and take positive steps to achieve full equality.

Recognition by the international human rights system is an important step in transforming private gender violence from a personal to a political issue. Paralleling right-wing anti-federalist opposition to the federal Violence Against Women Act here, opponents of recognizing privately inflicted gender violence as a human rights violation argued that this is a municipal or "domestic" law matter inappropriate for international scrutiny, sanction or redress. Internationally, the argument that addressing domestic battering transcends the proper scope of the state-centric human rights system had superficial plausibility. The focus of human rights on the wrongs committed by states was already a significant inroad into state sovereignty. State wrongdoing, it was argued, is the appropriate target because the state has a greater capacity to harm and where the state is the wrongdoer, the victim has no recourse. However, feminist advocates around the globe insisted upon and demonstrated—through women's tribunals, testimonies, documentation, statistical compilations, scholarship, and manifestations—that the harm done by the batterer is no less grave than that perpetrated by the state. Further, as Celina Romany elucidated in her classic article on the public/private distinction in international human rights, women in battering relationships, when denied meaningful recourse to the state, are relegated by the state to rule by a private, and equally absolute "parallel state"—the rule of the batterer. In other words, neither human rights law, nor the state, can claim to be neutral when it does nothing to prevent private abuse, because the impact in fact is to empower the abuser.

Further, ... to elucidate the gravity and political nature of private gender violence, feminist human rights advocates and scholars analogized battering to enslavement and torture. The issue of torture, for example, was first brought to the table by Latin American women who, while fighting dictatorial repression in their countries, recognized that what they or their sisters were suffering at home had far too much in common with the violence inflicted on political prisoners in the jails. The analogy to torture and slavery challenges the traditional trivialization of private violence as well as shifts the responsibility from the blameful woman to the batterer. These arguments provide an additional lens, illuminating women's dependency, not as a product of their own weakness or pathology, but as a function of the exercise of political power and control. By probing the relevance of torture and enslavement and utilizing these terms to characterize severe battering and marital rape, feminists challenged the tendency to see this violence as somehow permissible or inevitable....

Again, traditional human rights advocates originally argued that the concept of torture had no bearing on violence against women at least unless the violence was state-inflicted or explicitly state-sanctioned. Nonetheless, women persisted and the notion that rape and battering can constitute torture or enslavement gained ground in official documents as well as in the jurisprudence of the ad hoc International Criminal Tribunals. It also is very significant that ... Amnesty International has begun a domestic violence campaign that relies heavily on the analogy to torture....

The international human rights system also helps us to understand the nature of battering as a "cultural practice." Western media tend to focus on "cultural practices"—honor killings, female genital mutilation, and dowry deaths, for example—as human rights violations. But these are simply ritualized and openly legitimated versions of the implicitly accepted violence in the everyday—the intimidation, humiliation, beating, rape and killing of women in intimate relationships for some form of resistance to their gender-determined role or for no reason at all. In other words, throughout the world, as well as in the United States, intimate battering of women is a pervasive "cultural practice," rooted in patriarchal norms of male superiority and control and female inferiority and obedience, encased in familial and social and economic structures of inequality, terrorizing women and perpetuating gender conformity and oppression. A culturally embedded practice requires also a cultural response. CEDAW, for example, requires states to "take appropriate measures to ... modify the social and cultural patterns of conduct of men and women, with a view to achieving the elimination of prejudices and customary and all other practices which are based on the idea of the inferiority or superiority of either of the sexes or on stereotyped roles for men and women.''

Contrary to our constitutional system, the international human rights system—including political and civil rights—imposes positive as well as negative state responsibilities. Under our federal constitutional system, claims that the state is responsible for failing to protect, prevent or punish have no force. In *DeShaney v. Winnebago County*, the Supreme Court crystallized the extreme and cruel form of negative constitutional protection that dominates our system in denying redress for the state's knowing failure to protect a helpless child from his father's violence. . . . Excepting essentially custodial situations, the state has only the duty to refrain from actively harming a person. As a federal constitutional matter, we are often reminded that the state has no obligation to enact murder laws or to stop a murder or a battering apart from the rare case where selectivity renders the omission discriminatory.

The international human rights framework, however, does require murder laws and much more. The ICCPR identifies two concepts of state responsibility: the duty to respect (negative) or do no harm and the duty to ensure (positive) the protection of these rights as against private interference as well as the means to exercise basic rights. Acquiescence in privately inflicted torture renders the state directly responsible. Thus, the state has, at least, the obligation to exercise due diligence to protect women from the harm of intimate violence just as it is obligated to protect the life, liberty and personal security of all its citizenry. Under CEDAW, a state has a broader obligation to take positive measures to eliminate gender-based violence as part and parcel of the obligation to eliminate both intentional and disparate impact discrimination. Thus the positive responsibilities of the state under human rights law to protect even what our Supreme Court has labeled negative rights are, in theory, far reaching. They include not only the duty to investigate and punish, but also to prevent, protect, rehabilitate and develop and implement a plan to eliminate such violence in every sphere. . . .

To the extent that our constitutional system embraces international law, the positive obligations of the international framework should eventually bear concrete fruit here despite persistent objections from successive administrations. Consider a familiar and narrow example—the provision of a federal judicial remedy for gender-based discrimination such as legislated by Congress under the Violence Against Women Act ("VAWA").Under the ICCPR, which the United States has ratified, the state has the duty to provide appropriate remedies for gender violence, including judicial remedies ... [S]tudents at CUNY's International Women's Human Rights Clinic, ... sought to defend the VAWA cause of action on international law grounds through submitting the Brief Amicus Curiae on Behalf Of International Law Scholars and Human Rights Experts to the Supreme Court in *United States v. Morrison*. The amicus argued that Congress' power to implement treaty obligations and to confer Article III jurisdiction on the federal courts over treaty-based and customary international law claims, enables Congress to enact remedies against gender-based violence irrespective of whether it has authority to do so under the Commerce Clause or Fourteenth Amendment. The Clinton Administration had already touted VAWA as implementing legislation pursuant to the ICCPR and we emphasized that VAWA also implemented the United States' obligation under federal common law created by customary norms to provide appropriate remedies for gender-based violence.

The Court, and, most disappointingly, the dissenters in *Morrison*, did not even note this argument as one for the future, which would have been appropriate since the issue had neither been addressed by Congress nor argued below. . . .

The Vienna Convention's mandate to "mainstream" gender in the human rights system also applies to nations and has been an important tool for local activists. Gender mainstreaming is pro-active. In theory, all governmental and inter-governmental entities are required to take initiative to examine the impact of their policies on women, search out the invisibilized harms and inequalities that result, and develop alternative approaches and remedies. To do this, agencies and institutions are to have a gender focal point—someone who has expertise in the subtleties of gender—with authority to investigate, critique, jump start and implement reforms in a continuing process of consultation with women affected and their representatives. While this approach is not unknown in United States domestic processes, it tends to become quickly marginalized when separated from a positive human rights mandate. Taking the positive obligations seriously calls for a far more systematic approach to eliminating gender violence than is demanded by our negative Constitution or by remedies that depend upon individual cases. Gender-mainstreaming, gender analysis, and gender budgeting would make a difference if adopted as domestic policy. Along with heightening awareness of the human rights system and the seriousness of intimate gender violence, these mainstreaming strategies are among the goals of current efforts in the U.S. to enact CEDAW and CERD on a state or local basis. As local initiatives, they emphasize the importance of the human rights framework generally and of national ratification CEDAW, in terms both of the definition of discrimination and the reach of state responsibility.

While the international system can inspire and legitimate change, international initiatives and impact will wane or rise with the strength of the continued mobilization and monitoring by the women's movement. The long overdue but rapid progress in women's human rights in the 1990s also spawned the proverbial backlash, to slow down or block advances by women both domestically and internationally. . . . Because of the tremendous power of the United States in the United Nations system, it is critical that the women's anti-violence movement, and the women's and progressive movements generally, keep the pressure on the U.S. Administration at home and utilize human rights principles and the human rights system to bring attention to its failures. The impact will be felt both domestically and internationally.

All of this is not to deny that the international human rights system still operates more in rhetoric than in reality. [A] range of problems and contradictions also plague the official international human rights approaches. While it is undeniably progress that the international system has finally recognized gender violence as a human rights matter, the remedies are primarily state-centric. This raises, in turn, the limitations and dangers of transferring reliance for protection to, and, thereby, enhancing, the policing power of the state. What happens to women's alternative remedies—the protective whistles used in Nicaragua and the shaming tactics, picketing, etc., with which movement in many places, including here, began? Casting women as victims draws attention and support, but victimization approaches can undermine rather than advance the goal of women's empowerment. And dealing only with violence rather than with the broader underlying social, economic, cultural and racial discrimination, as well as poverty, all of which perpetuate the conditions for gender violence, is to focus on the tip of the iceberg.

[It is necessary] to reinvigorate the struggle against the separation of the problem of gender violence from gender equality.... For example, the mandate of the Special Rapporteur on Violence against Women, Its Causes and Consequences was the product of women's demand for a rapporteur on violence and discrimination. Closely linked to the separation of gender violence from discrimination is the even greater chasm between the commitment progressively to implement economic and social rights, which is also crucial to addressing the cycle of gender violence and dependency as well as women's inequality....

The Secretary General's In–Depth Study on All Forms of Violence Against Women (2006).

Consequences of Addressing Violence Against Women as a Human Rights Concern

The first Special Rapporteur on violence against women described the violence against women movement as "perhaps the greatest success story of international mobilization around a specific human rights issue, leading to the articulation of international norms and standards and the formulation of international programmes and policies". There are important consequences that flow from categorizing violence against women as a matter of human rights. Recognizing violence against women as a violation of human rights clarifies the binding obligations on States to prevent, eradicate and punish such violence and their accountability if they fail to comply with these obligations. These obligations arise from the duty of States to take steps to respect, protect, promote and fulfill human rights. Claims on the State to take all appropriate measures to respond to violence against women thus move from the realm of discretion and become legal entitlements. The human rights framework provides access to a number of tools and mechanisms that have been developed to hold States accountable at the international and regional level. These include the human rights treaty bodies and international criminal tribunals, as well as the African, European and inter-American human rights systems. Human rights provide a unifying set of norms that can be used to hold States accountable for adhering to their obligations, to monitor progress and to promote coordination and consistency. Addressing violence against women as a human rights issue empowers women, positioning them not as passive recipients of discretionary benefits but as active rights-holders. It also enhances the participation of other human rights advocates, including men and boys, who become stakeholders in addressing violence against women as part of building respect for all human rights. Recognizing violence against women as a human rights issue has also enabled human rights discourse and practice to become more inclusive by encompassing the experiences of women. When women's particular experiences remain invisible, they do not inform the understanding of human rights violations and remedies for them. Human rights norms therefore must take into account the particular circumstances of women in order to be fully universal. An integrated and inclusive human rights regime should take into account not only gender perspectives but also the wide variety of factors that shape and reinforce women's, and men's, experiences of discrimination and violence, including race, ethnicity, class, age, sexual orientation, disability, nationality, religion and culture. Understanding violence against women as a human rights concern does not preclude other approaches to preventing and eliminating violence, such as education, health, development and criminal justice efforts. Rather, addressing violence against women as a human rights issue encourages an indivisible, holistic and multisectoral response that adds a human rights dimension to work in all sectors. It calls for strengthening and accelerating initiatives in all areas to prevent and eliminate violence against women, including in the criminal justice, health, development, humanitarian, peacebuilding and security sectors.

NOTES AND QUESTIONS

1. **Human Rights and the Need for Gender–Specific Initiatives.** Rhonda Copelon indicates that the human rights community was traditionally reluctant to include domestic violence within its definition of human rights violations. Dorothy Thomas and Michele Beasley make this point in more detail:

> At least four interrelated factors have caused the exclusion of domestic violence in particular from international human rights practice: (1) traditional concepts of state responsibility under international law and practice, (2) misconceptions about the nature and extent of domestic violence and states' responses to it, (3) the neglect of equality before and equal protection of the law without regard to sex as a governing human rights principle, and (4) the failure of states to recognize their affirmative obligation to provide remedies for domestic violence crimes. These factors, independently and in relationship to one another, are beginning to change and, with them, so is the treatment of domestic violence under international law. Dorothy Q. Thomas and Michele E. Beasley, *Domestic Violence As a Human Rights Issue,* 58 ALB. L.R. 1119 (1995)

Women's advocates argued that human rights guarantees, such as those established by the Universal Declaration of Human Rights, were applied in gender-biased ways, despite their facial gender-neutrality or universality. This explains the perceived necessity for gender-specific initiatives such as the Convention for the Elimination of All Forms of Discrimination Against Women, and the General Assembly's Declaration on the Elimination of Violence Against Women. Is there a parallel here to the situation in the United States, where dissatisfaction with the protection accorded women under the Fourteenth Amendment led to the (ultimately unsuccessful) campaign to ratify a separate Equal Rights Amendment and to the civil rights remedy declared unconstitutional in *Morrison*?

2. **The Link Between Human Rights and Women's Rights.** For a discussion critical of the ways in which law text books fail to develop the rights of women within an international human rights context, see Stephanie Farrior, *The Rights of Women in International Human Rights Law Textbooks: Segregation, Integration, or Omission?* 12 COLUM. J. GENDER & L. 587 (2003). Have you studied women's issues in your courses that address international human rights? We return to broader questions of legal education and domestic violence in the last chapter.

3. **The Secretary–General's In–Depth Study.** As you can see, the Secretary–General's In–Depth Study on All Forms of Violence Against Women adopts a human rights framework as the basis of discussion of global violence against women. This is an important first step in a document directed at nation-states because the focus was state responsibility.

Current efforts on the part of human rights activists and scholars are not limited, however, to pursuing new remedies for women. In addition, these reformers are revisiting traditional human rights doctrine, and arguing that unbiased analysis demands its application to certain harms suffered by women. This tension between seeking to frame women's claims within existing structures, and seeking to establish new ones, has been a theme running through much of what you have read in prior chapters. It is not surprising to see it resurface in this new context.

4. **Violence as a Form of Torture.** One powerful claim made by Rhonda Copelon in the article above is that domestic violence is a form of torture. In an earlier article, Copelon stated that international documents define torture as having four elements: (1) severe physical and/or mental pain and suffering; (2) intentional infliction; (3) specified purposes; and (4) some degree of official or quasi-official involvement, whether active or passive. She continued:

> ... [P]sychologists and advocates for battered women have analogized the condition of POWs to that of battered women. Batterers manipulate and create stress in much the same way as official torturers. ... women are isolated from family, friends and others, which is a form of "house arrest." They are subjected to verbal insult, sexual denigration and abuse. Their lives and those of their loved ones are threatened and they are made to fear the loss of their children. At the same time, at least early in the battering cycle, they are occasionally showered with apologies, promises and kindness. Even so, the possibility of explosion

over the smallest domestic detail places battered women in a condition of severe and unremitting dread. For some women the psychological terror is the worst part. . . .

In regard to psychological suffering, the comparison between survivors of official torture and imprisonment and battered women makes clear that submission is not a particularity of women's pathology. Rather, it is a consequence of terroristic efforts at domination. And, just as we do not excuse torture that fails to accomplish the complete submission of the victim, neither must battering result in complete surrender to violate international law. As we condemn the practitioners of terror, we must recognize the heroism of women's efforts to endure and survive, just as we have begun to recognize that of POWs and victims of dictatorships. Rhonda Copelon, *Recognizing the Egregious in the Everyday: Domestic Violence as Torture,* 25 COLUM. HUM. RTS L. R. 291 (1994).

5. **The Significance of Treating Domestic Violence as Torture.** Treating domestic violence as torture has significance in a number of ways. Because the United Nations Convention against Torture spells out a series of measures that states must implement, if domestic violence is classified as torture under that treaty states would have to act to prevent domestic violence through training, investigation and prosecution or extradition of offenders. In addition, victims would have the right to be free from retaliation and to receive fair and adequate compensation. Aggressors could still be prosecuted, even if they left the country. Finally, a victim would not be faced with expulsion, return or extradition to another state where it was probable she would be subject to torture. States ratifying the U.N. Convention against Torture make their own decisions on just what legislative and administrative measures may be necessary to implement these obligations. However, these obligations are certainly more specific and more robust than any obligations listed in the Convention on the Elimination of All Forms of Discrimination against Women, discussed below.

Domestic violence has been treated as falling within the meaning of torture or other cruel treatment under Article 7 (prohibition of torture) of the International Covenant on Civil and Political Rights, a treaty the United States has ratified. See, e.g., U.N. Doc. CCPR/C/21/Rev.1/Add.10, General Comment No. 28: *Equality of rights between men and women (article 3)* (2000). See also General Comment No. 20 (1992): "It is the duty of the State party to afford everyone protection through legislative and other measures as may be necessary against the acts prohibited by article 7 [prohibiting torture and other cruel, inhuman and degrading treatment], whether inflicted by people acting in their official capacity, outside their official capacity or in a private capacity."

In the United States, both civil and criminal causes of action for torture are available. A victim of torture who has minimum contacts with the U.S. (either through residence or a current visit) can bring a civil suit against the perpetrator in federal court under the Torture Victim Protection Act of 1991, 28 U.S.C. § 1350. S.Rep. 102–249, pt. (iv)(c) (1991). Actions brought under the Torture Victim Protection Act may only be brought against an individual, not a state. Further, the Act does not allow actions against former leaders "merely because an isolated act of torture occurred somewhere in that country." S. Rep. 102–249, pt. (iv)(E) (1991). Torture is also a criminal offense in the United States under the Torture Convention Implementing Legislation, 18 U.S.C. §§ 2340–2340B (2000). Under this authority, federal courts have jurisdiction for torture committed outside the U.S. so long as the alleged perpetrator is a U.S. national or is in the U.S. 18 U.S.C. § 2340A (2000). Neither the alleged victim nor offender need be citizens of the U.S. for the court to have jurisdiction.

6. **Traditional Practices.** The 2006 Secretary–General's study enumerates a number of traditional practices involving women that it defines as harmful. These include: female genital mutilation; the preference for sons, including female infanticide, female sex selection, and the systematic neglect of girls; early and forced marriage of girls; violent or coercive demands for dowry; and so-called "honour killings" of women. Do you think these qualify as torture? *The Secretary–General's In–Depth Study on All Forms of Violence Against Women* (2006).

B. INTERNATIONAL HUMAN RIGHTS DOCUMENTS AND REPORTS ON DOMESTIC VIOLENCE

Advocacy efforts concerning women's human rights have had a significant impact on institutional responses. The subject of women's human rights received prominent attention in the Declaration and Programme of Action adopted at the United Nations World Conference on Human Rights in Vienna in 1993. In 1994, the U.N. Commission on Human Rights appointed a Special Rapporteur on Violence Against Women and in 1995, the United Nations sponsored a World Conference on Women in Beijing. Out of that conference came the Beijing Declaration and Platform for Action, and a Beijing + 5 meeting held in the year 2000 as a Special Session of the United Nations General Assembly. And then in 2006, we have the Secretary–General's Report on Global Violence.

The first international document that dealt specifically with gender-based discrimination was a special treaty, the Convention on the Elimination of All Forms of Discrimination against Women, ("Women's Convention" or CEDAW). The Women's Convention was adopted by the United Nations General Assembly in 1979, and entered into force two years later. In order for a treaty like CEDAW to have effect, States must ratify it. Some States, however, are uncomfortable with some provisions of a treaty. In order to ratify the treaty without being bound by those provisions, States may make reservations to a treaty, so long as the treaty does not prohibit it and the reservations are not incompatible with the overall purpose of the treaty. Reservations qualify or negate any provisions in the treaty that the State sees as undesirable. A State will consider a treaty, decide which provisions pose a problem and make reservations to deal with them. The State will then ratify the treaty with those reservations. Reservations to human rights treaties are unilateral—only the obligations of the State making the reservation are affected. Other States that have ratified the same treaty are not affected by another State's reservations. See Vienna Convention on the Law of Treaties, art. 60(5). CEDAW is notorious for having the most reservations of any human rights treaty.

The United States is the only industrialized state that has not ratified CEDAW. As of November 2006, 185 States had ratified the treaty. Despite the fact the President Carter signed CEDAW in 1980, the U.S. Senate has still not given its consent to ratification of the treaty. Efforts to gain Senate consent in 1980, 1994, 2000 and 2002 did not meet with success, though twice the treaty made it through the first step of Senate approval. In 1994, the Senate Foreign Relations Committee voted 13 to 5 (with one abstention) in favor of sending the treaty to the full Senate for its consent to ratification, but several Republican Senators blocked a floor vote. In 2002, the Senate Foreign Relations Committee voted the treaty favorably out of committee 12 to 7, but a full Senate vote was not scheduled before the Congressional session came to an end.

The following readings discuss CEDAW and the arguments why the United States should ratify it.

The Secretary General's In-Depth Study on All Forms of Violence Against Women

(2006).

Violence against women: a form of discrimination and human rights violation

Evidence gathered by researchers of the pervasive nature and multiple forms of violence against women, together with advocacy campaigns, led to the recognition that violence against women was global, systemic and rooted in power imbalances and structural inequality between men and women. The identification of the link between violence against women and discrimination was key. The work of the Committee on the Elimination of Discrimination against Women, the treaty body established in 1982 to monitor implementation of the Convention on the Elimination of All Forms of Discrimination against Women, contributed significantly to the recognition of violence against women as a human rights issue. The Convention does not explicitly refer to violence against women, but the Committee has made clear that all forms of violence against women fall within the definition of discrimination against women as set out in the Convention. The Committee regularly calls on States parties to adopt measures to address such violence. In its general recommendation No. 12 (1989), the Committee noted States' obligation to protect women from violence under various articles of the Convention, and requested them to include information on the incidence of violence and the measures adopted to confront it in their periodic reports to the Committee. General recommendation No. 19 (1992) decisively established the link: it asserted unequivocally that violence against women constitutes a form of gender-based discrimination and that discrimination is a major cause of such violence. This analysis added the issue of violence against women to the terms of the Convention and the international legal norm of non-discrimination on the basis of sex and, thus, directly into the language, institutions and processes of human rights. The inquiry and individual complaints procedures under the Optional Protocol to the Convention, in force since 2000, allow the Committee to develop jurisprudence in this area

Harold Hongju Koh
Why America Should Ratify the Women's Rights Treaty
34 Case W. Res. J. Int'l L. 263 (2002).

CEDAW is drafted with the reality of women's lives in mind. It focuses particularly upon the economic, social and cultural areas in which women suffer the most, the confluence of discriminations that has led to the feminization of global poverty. The treaty defines and condemns discrimination against women and announces an agenda for national action to end such discrimination. By ratifying the treaty, states do nothing more than commit themselves to undertaking "appropriate measures" toward ending discrimination against women, steps our country has already begun in numerous walks of life. CEDAW then lays a foundation for realizing equality between women and men in these countries by ensuring women's equal access to education, employment, healthcare, marriage and family relations, and other areas of economic and social life. CEDAW also ensures opportunities in public and political life—including the right to vote, to stand for election, to represent their governments at an international level, and to enjoy equal rights "before the law." The Convention directs States Parties to "take into account the particular problems faced by rural women," and permits parties to take "temporary special measures aimed at accelerating de facto equality" between men and women, a provision analogous to one also found in the Convention on the Elimination of All Forms of Racial Discrimination, which our country has already ratified.

Ratifying this treaty would send the world the message that we consider eradication of these various forms of discrimination to be solemn, universal obligations. The violent human rights abuses we recently witnessed against women in Afghanistan, Bosnia, Haiti, Kosovo, and Rwanda painfully remind us of the need for all nations to join together to intensify efforts to protect women's rights as human rights. Because much of the discrimination against women goes on behind multiple veils of family privacy, culture, religion, and sovereignty, available governmental statistics are notoriously inaccurate in their undercounting of acts of gender discrimination. Yet even so, the facts are haunting. As Amartya Sen has reminded us, around the world, more than 100 million women are likely missing. In all parts of the world, women are subject to stunning abuses resulting from deeply entrenched cultural and religious norms, and family and community practices are often shielded from external scrutiny by claims of privacy or sovereignty. To take just one example, more than 115 million women have been forced to undergo genital mutilation, and some two million still risk this harmful procedure every year. The same goes for another traditional practice: the ironically named "honor killings"—a practice better called "arbitrary killings"—whereby family members take it upon themselves to kill their sisters or cousins if they suspect them of bringing shame upon the family. In almost every part of the globe, women are far less likely to be literate; they lag far behind men in access to higher education; and they enjoy many fewer job opportunities. Even in the 21st century, a modern form of slave trade persists under the label of trafficking in persons, especially women and children.

At the State Department, where I supervised the production of the annual country reports on human rights conditions worldwide, I found that a country's ratification of the CEDAW is one of the surest indicators of the strength of its commitment to internalize the universal norm of gender equality into its domestic laws. Let me emphasize that in light of our ongoing national efforts to address gender equality through state and national legislation, executive action, and judicial decisions, the legal requirements imposed by ratifying this treaty would not be burdensome. Numerous countries with far less impressive practices regarding gender equality than the United States have ratified the treaty, including countries whom we would never consider our equals on such matters, including Iraq, Kuwait, North Korea, and Saudi Arabia.

At the same time, from my direct experience as America's chief human rights official, I can testify that our continuing failure to ratify CEDAW has reduced our global standing, damaged our diplomatic relations, and hindered our ability to lead in the international human rights community. Nations that are otherwise our allies, with strong rule-of-law traditions, histories, and political cultures, simply cannot understand why we have failed to take the obvious step of ratifying this convention. In particular, our European and Latin American allies regularly question and criticize our isolation from this treaty framework both in public diplomatic settings and private diplomatic meetings.

Our nonratification has led our allies and adversaries alike to challenge our claim of moral leadership in international human rights, a devastating challenge in this post-September 11 environment. Even more troubling, I have found, our exclusion from this treaty has provided anti-American diplomatic ammunition to countries who have exhibited far worse record on human rights generally, and women's rights in particular. Persisting in the aberrant practice of nonratification will only further our diplomatic isolation and inevitably harm our other foreign policy interests.

NOTES AND QUESTIONS

1. **U.S. Failure to Ratify CEDAW.** At a hearing on CEDAW held in 2002 by the Senate Committee on Foreign Relations, Senator Chris Dodd (D–CT) stated:

> [T]he United States is among a small number of countries, including Afghanistan, Iran, and Sudan, that have not yet taken the important step of ratification. . . . The United States made ratification of the Women's Convention by the year 2000 one of its public commitments

at the U.N. Conference on Women in Beijing in 1995. It is now up to us to honor this commitment. . . .

In our country, domestic violence is and has been an issue of nation-wide concern. Only 44% of all rural counties have full time prosecutors for violent crimes against women, and women in these areas do not even have sufficient legal representation to combat domestic violence if they choose to seek it. Ratification of the treaty would encourage the United States to provide more sufficient social and legal services.

In early 2002, the State Department notified the Senate Foreign Relations Committee that the CEDAW treaty was "generally desirable and should be ratified." Previously, the State Department had emphasized in its testimony (in both 1994 and 2000) that CEDAW is well within the bounds of already established U.S. law and that any provisions exceeding these bounds have been contained by the U.S. proposed reservations, understandings and declarations (RUDS).

The U.S. has, for example, proposed a reservation that states that ratifying CEDAW will not obligate the U.S. to pass legislation mandating equal pay for women. Also among the RUDS proposed by the U.S. is a non-self executing declaration which would bar the use of CEDAW as an independent cause of action in U.S. federal court. Malvina Halberstam argues that CEDAW "would, in fact, be without any legal effect whatsoever domestically if ratified with the present RUDS." Malvina Halberstam, *United States Ratification of the Convention on the Elimination of All Forms of Discrimination Against Women,* 31 GEO. WASH. J. INT'L L. & ECON. 49 (1997). This has led advocates to use a strategy of urging cities, counties and states adopt and implement the provisions of CEDAW. San Francisco was the first to do so, adopting an ordinance in 1998 implementing CEDAW locally. Berkeley's City Council followed, with a resolution adopting the operative articles of CEDAW into the Berkeley Municipal Code. New York City is working on an ordinance based on the San Francisco model that will also incorporate the International Convention on the Elimination of All Forms of Racial Discrimination.

2. **CEDAW's Enforcement Mechanisms and the New Optional Protocol.** The Committee on the Elimination of Discrimination Against Women (CEDAW Committee) is the treaty body that monitors States parties' compliance with the Women's Convention. The Committee's primary means of supervising compliance is through consideration of reports that States parties are required to submit on a periodic basis. Traditionally, the powers and procedures of this Committee have been weak compared with those of the other human rights treaty bodies, but this changed in 2000 when an Optional Protocol to CEDAW entered into force that authorizes the CEDAW Committee to consider complaints of violations of the Convention in those States that have ratified the optional protocol.

Article 1 of CEDAW defines discrimination against women as "any distinction, exclusion or restriction made on the basis of sex which has the effect or purpose of impairing or nullifying the recognition, enjoyment or exercise by women, irrespective of their marital status, on a basis of equality of men and women, of human rights and fundamental freedoms in the political, economic, social, cultural, civil or any other field." Article 3 requires States parties to take all appropriate measures "to ensure the full development and advancement of women." Article 5(a) requires States parties "(t)o modify the social and cultural patterns of conduct of men and women, with a view to achieving the elimination of prejudices and customary and all other practices which are based on the inferiority or superiority of either of the sexes or on stereotyped roles for men and women."

In 2005, CEDAW examined a domestic violence case brought under the Optional Protocol. The petitioner, a Hungarian woman who had undergone years of violence at the hands of her common law husband, alleged that Hungary violated her rights under CEDAW by failing to provide her with effective protection from the serious risk to her physical integrity, physical and mental health and her life from her husband. In its decision, the Committee noted that CEDAW and General Recommendation 19 require that the state exercise due diligence: "The state may be responsible for private acts if they fail to exercise due diligence to prevent violations of rights or to investigate and punish acts of violence, and for providing compensation." The Committee determined that the State party had failed to fulfil its obligations under the Women's Convention and had thereby violated the rights of the petitioner under article 2(a), (b) and (e) and article 5(a) in conjunction with article 16 of the Women's Convention. It also listed a set of recommended steps for the State to implement in order to protect against domestic violence. CEDAW, *Ms. A. T. v. Hungary*, Communication no. 2/2003 (views adopted 26 Jan. 2005), U.N. Doc. A/60/38 (Part I).

Although the text of CEDAW is silent about violence, the Committee has interpreted the Convention to prohibit violence against women. In 1992, the Committee issued a General Recommendation (an authoritative interpretation of the treaty) stating that gender-based violence that nullifies or impairs the enjoyment of human rights by women constitutes discrimination within the meaning of article 1 of the Women's Convention. This General Recommendation on Violence Against Women is excerpted below. The General Assembly Resolution from 1993 follows. As you read these documents, consider the gravity of these recommendations, and the failure of most states to adopt them.

General Recommendation No. 19: Violence against Women

CEDAW Committee, U.N. Doc. A/47/38 (1992)

1. Gender-based violence is a form of discrimination that seriously inhibits women's ability to enjoy rights and freedoms on a basis of equality with men....

4. ... The full implementation of the Convention require(s) States to take positive measures to eliminate all forms of violence against women....

6.   The Convention in article 1 defines discrimination against women. The definition of discrimination includes gender-based violence, that is, violence that is directed against a woman because she is a woman or that affects women disproportionately. It includes acts that inflict physical, mental or sexual harm or suffering, threats of such acts, coercion and other deprivations of liberty. Gender-based violence may breach specific provisions of the Convention, regardless of whether those provisions expressly mention violence.

7.   Gender-based violence, which impairs or nullifies the enjoyment by women of human rights and fundamental freedoms under general international law or under human rights conventions, is discrimination within the meaning of article 1 of the Convention. These rights and freedoms include:

(a) The right to life;

(b) The right not to be subject to torture or to cruel, inhuman or degrading treatment or punishment;

(c) The right to equal protection according to humanitarian norms in time of international or internal armed conflict;

(d) The right to liberty and security of person;

(e) The right to equal protection under the law;

(f) The right to equality in the family;

(g) The right to the highest standard attainable of physical and mental health;

(h) The right to just and favourable conditions of work.

8.   The Convention applies to violence perpetrated by public authorities. Such acts of violence may breach that State's obligations under general international human rights law and under other conventions, in addition to breaching this Convention.

9.   It is emphasized, however, that discrimination under the Convention is not restricted to action by or on behalf of Governments (see articles 2(e), 2(f) and 5). For example, under article 2(e) the Convention calls on States parties to take all appropriate measures to eliminate discrimination against women by any person, organization or enterprise. Under general international law and specific human rights covenants, States may also be responsible for private acts if they fail to act with due diligence to prevent violations of rights or to investigate and punish acts of violence, and for providing compensation. . . .

11.   Traditional attitudes by which women are regarded as subordinate to men or as having stereotyped roles perpetuate widespread practices involving violence or coercion, such as family violence and abuse, forced marriage, dowry deaths, acid attacks and female circumcision. Such prejudices and practices may justify gender-based violence as a form of protection or control of women. The effect of such violence on the physical and mental integrity of women is to deprive them of the equal enjoyment, exercise and knowledge of human rights and fundamental freedoms. While this comment addresses mainly actual or threatened violence, the underly-

ing consequences of these forms of gender-based violence help to maintain women in subordinate roles and contribute to the low level of political participation and to their lower level of education, skills and work opportunities. . . .

23.   Family violence is one of the most insidious forms of violence against women. It is prevalent in all societies. Within family relationships women of all ages are subjected to violence of all kinds, including battering, rape, other forms of sexual assault, mental and other forms of violence, which are perpetuated by traditional attitudes. Lack of economic independence forces many women to stay in violent relationships. The abrogation of their family responsibilities by men can be a form of violence, and coercion. These forms of violence put women's health at risk and impair their ability to participate in family life and public life on a basis of equality.

General Assembly Resolution 48/104 of 20 December 1993

U.N.Doc. A/RES/48/104 (1994).

[The year after CEDAW adopted General Recommendation No. 19, the United Nations General Assembly adopted by consensus the Declaration on the Elimination of Violence against Women, the first international instrument to explicitly address violence against women.]

Article 1

For the purposes of this Declaration, the term "violence against women" means any act of gender-based violence that results in, or is likely to result in, physical, sexual or psychological harm or suffering to women, including threats of such acts, coercion or arbitrary deprivation of liberty, whether occurring in public or in private life.

Article 2

Violence against women shall be understood to encompass, but not be limited to, the following:

(a) Physical, sexual and psychological violence occurring in the family, including battering, sexual abuse of female children in the household, dowry-related violence, marital rape, female genital mutilation and other traditional practices harmful to women, non-spousal violence and violence related to exploitation;

(b) Physical, sexual and psychological violence occurring within the general community, including rape, sexual abuse, sexual harassment and intimidation at work, in educational institutions and elsewhere, trafficking in women and forced prostitution;

(c) Physical, sexual and psychological violence perpetrated or condoned by the State, wherever it occurs.

Article 4

States should condemn violence against women and should not invoke any custom, tradition or religious consideration to avoid their obligations with respect to its elimination. States should pursue by all appropriate means and without delay a policy of eliminating violence against women and, to this end, should:

(a) Consider, where they have not yet done so, ratifying or acceding to the Convention on the Elimination of All Forms of Discrimination against Women or withdrawing reservations to that Convention; . . .

(b) Refrain from engaging in violence against women;

(c) Exercise due diligence to prevent, investigate and, in accordance with national legislation, punish acts of violence against women, whether those acts are perpetrated by the State or by private persons;

(d) Develop penal, civil, labour and administrative sanctions in domestic legislation to punish and redress the wrongs caused to women who are subjected to violence; women who are subjected to violence should be provided with access to the mechanisms of justice and, as provided for by national legislation, to just and effective remedies for the harm that they have suffered; States should also inform women of their rights in seeking redress through such mechanisms; . . .

(f) Develop, in a comprehensive way, preventive approaches and all those measures of a legal, political, administrative and cultural nature that promote the protection of women against any form of violence, and ensure that the re-victimization of women does not occur because of laws insensitive to gender considerations, enforcement practices or other interventions;

(g) Work to ensure, to the maximum extent feasible in the light of their available resources and, where needed, within the framework of international cooperation, that women subjected to violence and, where appropriate, their children have specialized assistance, such as rehabilitation, assistance in child care and maintenance, treatment, counselling, and health and social services, facilities and programmes, as well as support structures, and should take all other appropriate measures to promote their safety and physical and psychological rehabilitation; . . .

(j) Adopt all appropriate measures, especially in the field of education, to modify the social and cultural patterns of conduct of men and women and to eliminate prejudices, customary practices and all other practices based on the idea of the inferiority or superiority of either of the sexes and on stereotyped roles for men and women;

(k) Promote research, collect data and compile statistics, especially concerning domestic violence, relating to the prevalence of different forms of violence against women and encourage research on the causes, nature, seriousness and consequences of violence against women and on the effectiveness of measures implemented to prevent and redress violence against women; those statistics and findings of the research will be made public;

(l) Adopt measures directed towards the elimination of violence against women who are especially vulnerable to violence;

(m) Include, in submitting reports as required under relevant human rights instruments of the United Nations, information pertaining to violence against women and measures taken to implement the present Declaration; . . .

(o) Recognize the important role of the women's movement and non-governmental organizations world wide in raising awareness and alleviating the problem of violence against women;

(p) Facilitate and enhance the work of the women's movement and non-governmental organizations and cooperate with them at local, national and regional levels; . . .

NOTES AND QUESTIONS

1. **Affirmative State Duties.** General Recommendation 19 and General Assembly Recommendation are presented here at length because of their importance in calling on States to take affirmative action to protect women. Notice how different this approach to state obligations is when compared to *DeShaney*, which held that there is no constitutional duty on states to protect children, let alone abused adults. Also note that General Recommendation 19 affirmatively links violence against women and the material conditions in which women live. Finally, it suggests that the state is responsible for human rights abuses against non-state actors, a concept that American law has largely rejected in the domestic violence context. For a discussion of state responsibility for non-state actors see Stephanie Farrior, *State Responsibility for Human Rights Abuses by Non–State Actors*, 92 Am. Soc'y Int'l L. Proc. 299 (1998).

2. **The Force of General Assembly Resolutions.** What is the legal weight of a General Assembly Resolution? Here is an analysis by Oscar Schachter, from his article *United Nations Law*, 88 A.J.I.L. 1 (1994):

> The legal arguments that resolutions may be authoritative evidence of binding international law usually rest on characterizing them as (1) "authentic" interpretations of the UN Charter agreed by all the parties, (2) affirmations of recognized customary law, or (3) expressions of general principles of law accepted by states. These reasons fit into the three sources of international law contained in Article 38 of the Statute of the International Court of Justice. The Court itself has recognized the legal force of several UN declarations in some of its advisory opinions. But some caution is called for. Even a UN declaration adopted unanimously will have diminished authority as law if it is not observed by states particularly affected. Negative votes by a few concerned states to a declaratory resolution also cast doubt on its authority as presumptive evidence of existing law. We cannot apply a categorical rule to all cases; distinctions must be drawn that take into account the nature and importance of the legal rule in question. Declarations that affirm the prohibitions against aggression, genocide, torture or systematic racial discrimination would not be deprived of their legal value because they were not uniformly observed. On the other hand, declarations asserting or affirming legal rules of a less

peremptory character would not prevail over evidence that such rules were not generally observed by affected states.

UN recourse to recommendatory authority to declare law is a reflection of the perceived need for more law in many fields. The traditional case-by-case process of customary law cannot meet the necessity for common action to deal with the numerous problems raised by technological developments, demographic and environmental impacts, changing attitudes as to social justice, or the many requirements of international business. While all of these matters could be dealt with by multilateral treaties, the treaty processes are often complicated and slow. In contrast, UN resolutions can be more readily attained.... [T]he curious result is that new law is often considered as "custom" or as based on already-recognized general principles. The law-declaring resolutions are not only a response to felt needs; they are also a consequence of the opportunity afforded by voting rules in the UN system. Weaker states, which constitute a majority in UN bodies, use their voting strength for lawmaking to improve their position vis-a-vis the more powerful states. However, these efforts are often limited by the realities of power and politics. It has come to be recognized that resolutions by majorities on economic matters are likely to remain "paper" declarations without much effect unless genuinely accepted by states with the requisite resources to carry them out.

Do you think that the U.N. Declaration on the Elimination of Violence against Women might, like resolutions on economic matters, be a "paper" declaration? What might make you think so? Even though it is not a binding treaty, how might advocates use this Declaration in their strategies to end domestic violence?

3. **Regional Treaties.** Two regional treaties directly address violence against women, one in the Americas and one in Africa. The Inter–American Convention on the Prevention, Punishment and Eradication of Violence Against Women, known as the "Convention of Belém do Pará," was adopted by the Organization of American States (OAS) in 1994. With 32 States parties, every member of the OAS has ratified this treaty except for Canada and the United States. Like the U.N. Declaration, the preamble recognizes that violence against women is "a manifestation of the historically unequal power relations between women and men" and defines violence against women as encompassing "physical, sexual and psychological violence." Article 3 specifies that a woman's rights are "to be free from violence in both the public and private sphere." Under Article 7, States agree "to pursue, by all appropriate means and without delay, policies to prevent, punish and eradicate such violence." To help achieve implementation and accountability, this treaty contains a reporting mechanism as well as a procedure by which an individual, group or non-governmental organization may lodge a petition complaining of a violation with the Inter–American Commission on Human Rights.

Violence against women is also addressed in the Protocol to the African Charter on Human and Peoples' Rights on the Rights of Women in Africa, which entered into force in 2005. Article 1 of the Protocol on the Rights of

Women defines "violence against women" as "all acts perpetrated against women which cause or could cause them physical, sexual, psychological, and economic harm, including the threat to take such acts; or to undertake the imposition of arbitrary restrictions on or deprivation of fundamental freedoms in private or public life in peace time and during situations of armed conflicts or of war." The Right to Dignity (Art. 3) includes the right of women to protection from violence, "particularly sexual and verbal violence." Article 4 on the Rights to Life, Integrity and Security sets out a series of measures states should take to protect women from violence. These include a requirement that States "enact and enforce laws to prohibit all forms of violence against women including unwanted or forced sex whether the violence takes place in private or public," as well as "such other legislative, administrative, social and economic measures as may be necessary."

4. **Special Rapporteurs on Violence.** Further acknowledgment that violence against women is a human rights violation of international concern was signaled in 1994, when the U.N. followed its adoption of the Declaration on Violence against Women with the establishment of a Special Rapporteur on Violence Against Women, its causes and consequences. That same year, the Inter–American Commission on Human Rights established the Special Rapporteur on the rights of women, and in 1998 the African Commission on Human and Peoples' Rights appointed a Special Rapporteur on the rights of women in Africa. The first U.N. Special Rapporteur on violence against women was Radhika Coomaraswamy from Sri Lanka; she served until the appointment in 2003 of Yakin Ertürk of Turkey. The U.N. Special Rapporteur is authorized to engage in field missions, to work with other rapporteurs and working groups, to seek and to receive information from governments, other treaty bodies, specialized agencies of the U.N. and nongovernmental organizations (NGO's) and to consult with the CEDAW Committee. Significantly, her reports go beyond the information provided by states themselves pursuant to their obligations under the Women's Convention. The Special Rapporteur has submitted annual reports to the Commission since 1994. Portions of those reports are excerpted below.

5. **The Role of Culture in Human Rights Campaigns.** Culture is often used as a "defense" to argue against change that would empower women. The claim made by opponents to change is that Western norms and values should not be imposed in an imperialistic way on non-Western cultures. The following materials grapple with this issue.

Preliminary Report of the Special Rapporteur on Violence Against Women, Its Causes and Consequences, Radhika Coomaraswamy, Commission on Human Rights

U.N. Doc. E/CN.4/1995/42 (1994).

49. ... [V]iolence against women is a manifestation of historically unequal power relations between men and women. Violence is part of a historical process and is not natural or born of biological determinism. The system of male dominance has historical roots and its functions and

manifestations change over time. . . . The oppression of women is therefore a question of politics, requiring an analysis of the institutions of the State and society, the conditioning and socialization of individuals, and the nature of economic and social exploitation. The use of force against women is only one aspect of this phenomenon, which relies on intimidation and fear to subordinate women.

50.   Women are subject to certain universal forms of abuse. . . . It is argued that any attempt to universalize women's experience is to conceal other forms of oppression such as those based on race, class or nationality. This reservation must be noted and acknowledged. And yet it must be accepted that there are patterns of patriarchal domination which are universal, though this domination takes a number of different forms as a result of particular and different historical experiences. . . .

54.   The institution of the family is . . . an arena where historical power relations are often played out. On the one hand, the family can be the source of positive nurturing and caring values where individuals bond through mutual respect and love. On the other hand, it can be a social institution where labour is exploited, where male sexual power is violently expressed and where a certain type of socialization disempowers women. Female sexual identity is often created by the family environment. The negative images of the self which often inhibit women from realizing their full potential may be linked to familial expectation. The family is, therefore, the source of positive humane values, yet in some instances it is the site for violence against women and a socialization process which may result in justifying violence against women. . . .

57.   In the context of the historical power relations between men and women, women must also confront the problem that men control the knowledge systems of the world. Whether it be in the field of science, culture, religion or language, men control the accompanying discourse. Women have been excluded from the enterprise of creating symbolic systems or interpreting historical experience. It is this lack of control over knowledge systems which allows them not only to be victims of violence, but to be part of a discourse which often legitimizes or trivializes violence against women. . . .

64.   The ideologies which justify the use of violence against women base their discussion on a particular construction of sexual identity. The construction of masculinity often requires that manhood be equated with the ability to exert power over others, especially through the use of force. Masculinity gives man power to control the lives of those around him, especially women. The construction of femininity in these ideologies often requires women to be passive and submissive, to accept violence as part of a woman's estate. Such ideologies also link a woman's identity and self-esteem to her relationship to her father, husband or son. An independent woman is often denied expression in feminine terms. In addition, standards of beauty, defined by women, often require women to mutilate themselves or damage their health, whether with regard to foot binding, anorexia nervosa and bulimia. It is important to reinvent creatively these categories of masculinity and femininity, devoid of the use of force and ensuring the full development of human potential. . . .

67. Certain customary practices and some aspects of tradition are often the cause of violence against women. Besides female genital mutilation, a whole host of practices violate female dignity. Foot binding, male preference, early marriage, virginity tests, dowry deaths, sati, female infanticide and malnutrition are among the many practices which violate a woman's human rights. Blind adherence to these practices and State inaction with regard to these customs and traditions have made possible large-scale violence against women. States are enacting new laws and regulations with regard to the development of a modern economy and modern technology and to developing practices which suit a modern democracy, yet it seems that in the area of women's rights change is slow to be accepted.

NOTES AND QUESTIONS

1. **The Secretary–General's In–Dept Study on "Culture."** The Secretary–General's In–Depth Study on All Forms of Violence Against Women (2006) discusses the problem of "culture" very broadly. Consider its observations:

> Cultural justifications for restricting women's human rights have been asserted by some States and by social groups within many countries claiming to defend cultural tradition. These defences are generally voiced by political leaders or traditional authorities, not by those whose rights are actually affected. Cultural relativist arguments have been advanced in national contexts and in international debates when laws and practices that curtail women's human rights have been challenged. The politicization of culture in the form of religious "fundamentalisms" in diverse geographic and religious contexts has become a serious challenge to efforts to secure women's human rights. Tension between cultural relativism and the recognition of women's human rights, including the right to be free from violence, has been intensified as a result of the current heightened attention to State security issues. The resort to cultural relativism has been "made worse by the policies adopted since 11 September 2001 by many groups and societies that feel threatened and under siege". This tension poses a notable challenge in ensuring that violence against women is kept firmly on the international and national agendas with the priority it requires. The role of culture as a causal factor for violence against women must therefore be investigated within diverse cultural settings, taking into account the many ways in which the concept of culture is used. Culture can be most usefully viewed as a shifting set of discourses, power relations and social, economic and political processes, rather than as a fixed set of beliefs and practices. Given the fluidity of culture, women's agency in challenging oppressive cultural norms and articulating cultural values that respect their human rights is of central importance. Efforts to address the impact of culture on violence should therefore take direction from the women who are seeking to ensure their rights within the cultural communities concerned. *The Secretary–General's In–Depth Study on All Forms of Violence Against Women* (2006).

The Report is premised upon the notion that culture is always changing. Do you agree? How then do you evaluate the arguments about cultural relativism? Do you agree that the events of September 11, 2001 have created new tensions about the role of culture that makes it more difficult for States to do act to end violence against women?

2. The Role of Culture in International Proceedings. Sally Engle Merry is an anthropologist who has studied international decisionmaking on gender and violence at the United Nations. Consider her observations about the role that culture plays in decision-making within the context of CEDAW:

> [C]ommittee members and NGO representatives recognize the importance of building on national and local cultural practices and religious beliefs to promote transformations of marriage, family, and gender stereotypes. They argue that reforms need to be rooted in existing practices and religious systems if they are to be accepted. Thus, alongside the portrayal of culture as an unchanging and intransigent obstacle lies another more fluid conception of culture. The former view is, as scholars have noted, often connected to racialized understandings of "others" forged during the colonial era. The latter is closer to the current anthropological theorization of culture. In other words, there is an old vision of culture as fixed, static, bounded, and adhered to by rote juxtaposed to a more modern understanding of culture as a process of continually creating new meanings and practices that are products of power relationships and open to contestation among members of the group and by outsiders. In CEDAW discussions, when culture is raised as a problem, its old meaning is invoked. This is, of course, the way the term is used in the convention itself, which explicitly condemns cultural practices that discriminate against women in articles 2 and 5. When culture is discussed as a resource, or when there is recognition that the goal of the CEDAW process is cultural reformulation, the second meaning is implied. Needless to say, the coexistence of these two quite different understandings of culture in the same forum is confusing. I think it obscures the creative cultural work that the CEDAW process accomplishes. Sally Engle Merry, *Constructing A Global Law—Violence Against Women and the Human Rights System*, 28 LAW & SOC. INQUIRY 941 (2003)

3. **Human Rights Activism and "Western Values."** The activities of women's rights activists have often been criticized as inappropriate applications of Western values to other cultures or even worse, cultural imperialism. Activists themselves are acutely aware of this tension and have long debated how to balance the feminist valuation of difference with efforts to advance women's rights internationally. Tracy Higgins, *Anti–Essentialism, Relativism, and Human Rights*, 19 HARV. WOMEN'S L.J. 89 (1996). At the same time, they have made the argument that cultural justifications are used selectively to preserve State power and further argue that culture is not the monolithic, static force that States might claim. Notice that Paragraph 50 of Coomaraswamy's 1994 report makes an effort to address the tension between the universalist nature of women's rights and cultural relativism. Coomaraswamy addresses this issue even more explicitly in

Paragraph 32 of her 1999 report, which follows. The Declaration on the Elimination of Violence against Women, adopted by the U.N. General Assembly by consensus, specifies that States may not "invoke custom, tradition, or religious considerations to avoid their obligations with respect to the elimination of discrimination against women."(Article 4). Women's rights advocates in the global South often face claims of culture and religion aimed at undermining their work to end violence against women. For an example of strategies NGOs use to confront these claims, see Asia Pacific Women for Law and Development (www.apwld.org) whose workshops have addressed cultural practices and religious claims related to violence against women. For discussion of the translation of universal principles into local contexts, see Sally Engle Merry, HUMAN RIGHTS AND GENDER VIOLENCE: TRANSLATING INTERNATIONAL LAW INTO LOCAL JUSTICE (2006).

4. **Concrete Results of Women's Human Rights Advocacy.** Despite the increasing recognition of women's human rights claims, and the increase in "official" monitoring of violence against women around the world by a variety of international agencies, there has been widespread criticism of the lack of concrete results of women's human rights advocacy. In her 1999 report, Coomaraswamy criticized governments for "lack of strategies of implementation on commitments to eradicate violence." Although she observed that many countries have "acknowledged domestic violence as an important human rights issue," she concluded that states have "overwhelmingly" failed in their international obligations to prevent, investigate, and prosecute domestic abuse. Hilary Charlesworth, a leading feminist legal scholar on women's international human rights, concurs, concluding that "the human rights system appears to have learned that the art of politically correct rhetoric is an effective tool in silencing potential critics. It finds it very hard, however, to institute significant change." Hilary Charlesworth, *The Mid–Life Crisis of the Universal Declaration of Human Rights*, 55 WASH. & LEE L. REV. 781 (1998). See also Hilary Charlesworth, *Not Waving But Drowning, Gender Mainstreaming and Human Rights in the United Nations*, 18 HARV. HUM. RTS. J. 1 (2005).

5. **Strategies to Create Change.** The following materials discuss efforts to create change through the development of the concept of "due diligence," namely the responsibility of States to prevent, investigate, and punish international law violations of violence against women whether those acts are perpetrated by the state or private persons.

Report of the Special Rapporteur on Violence Against Women, Its Causes and Consequences, Radhika Coomaraswamy, Commission on Human Rights

U.N. Doc. E/CN.4/1999/68/Add.4 (1999).

III. An Evolving Legal Framework

22. Violence against women in the family raises the jurisprudential issue of State responsibility for private, non-State actors. In her previous report on violence in the family the Special Rapporteur outlined three

doctrines put forward by scholars and experts in international law in attempting to deal with this issue of violence against women by private actors. The first, taken from the international law doctrine of State responsibility, was that States have a due diligence duty to prevent, investigate and punish international law violations and pay just compensation. The second doctrine is related to the question of equality and equal protection. If it can be shown that law enforcement discriminates against the victims in cases involving violence against women, then States may be held liable for violating international human rights standards of equality. Finally, scholars have also argued that domestic violence is a form of torture and should be dealt with accordingly.

23.   The principle of "due diligence" is gaining international recognition. In accordance with article 4 of the Declaration on the Elimination of Violence against Women, States must "exercise due diligence to prevent, investigate and, in accordance with national legislation, punish acts of violence against women, whether those acts are perpetrated by the State or by private persons." General Recommendation 19 of CEDAW states that "under general international law and specific human rights covenants, States may also be responsible for private acts if they fail to act with due diligence to prevent violations of rights, or to investigate and punish acts of violence, and for providing compensation."

24.   The due diligence standard of State responsibility for private actors was discussed in detail by the Inter–American Court of Human Rights in the judgement of the Velasquez–Rodriguez case handed down on 29 July 1988. In that case, the Government of Honduras was held responsible for violating human rights in the case of disappearances. The Court found that:

> An illegal act which violates human rights and which is initially not directly imputable to the State (for example, because it is the act of a private person or because the person responsible has not been identified) can lead to international responsibility of the State, not because of the act itself but because of the lack of due diligence to prevent the violation or to respond to it as required by the Convention.

Further, the Court held that:

> The State has a legal duty to take reasonable steps to prevent human rights violations and to use the means at its disposal to carry out a serious investigation of violations committed within its jurisdiction, to identify those responsible, to impose the appropriate punishment and to ensure the victim adequate compensation. This obligation implies the duty of State parties to organize the governmental apparatus and, in general, all the structures through which public power is exercised, so that they are capable of juridically ensuring the free and full enjoyment of human rights.

25.   On her field visits concerning violence against women by private actors, the Special Rapporteur has attempted to assess State adherence to the due diligence standard. In so doing, she has relied upon the Declaration on the Elimination of Violence against Women and upon General Recommendation 19 of CEDAW and has considered information provided in response to the following questions:

(i) Has the State Party ratified all the international human rights instruments including the Convention on the Elimination of All Forms of Discrimination against Women?

(ii) Is there constitutional authority guaranteeing equality for women or the prohibition of violence against women?

(iii) Is there national legislation and/or administrative sanctions providing adequate redress for women victims of violence?

(iv) Are there executive policies or plans of action that attempt to deal with the question of violence against women?

(v) Is the criminal justice system sensitive to the issues of violence against women? In this regard, what is police practice? How many cases are investigated by the police? How are victims dealt with by the police? How many cases are prosecuted? What type of judgements are given in such cases? Are the health professionals who assist the prosecution sensitive to issues of violence against women?

(vi) Do women who are victims of violence have support services such as shelters, legal and psychological counselling, specialized assistance and rehabilitation provided either by the Government or by non-governmental organizations?

(vii) Have appropriate measures been taken in the field of education and the media to raise awareness of violence against women as a human rights violation and to modify practices that discriminate against women?

(viii) Are data and statistics being collected in a manner that ensures that the problem of violence against women is not invisible?

IV.   Findings

A.   General trends

28.   In the Spring of 1998, the Special Rapporteur sent a note verbale to Governments, requesting them to provide her with information about initiatives taken with regard to violence against women in the family. Subsequently, she sought the same information from non-governmental sources. In both governmental and non-governmental responses, there were common trends, positive and negative. Overwhelmingly, Governments presented a picture which suggested that they are taking steps, as small as they may sometimes be, to address violence in the family. Governments have begun to acknowledge that violence against women in the family is a serious social issue that should be confronted. Formal provisions and policies have been adopted in many States.

29.   The Special Rapporteur would like to highlight the encouraging trend in Latin America and the Caribbean to adopt specific legislation on domestic or intra-family violence. Thus far in the 1990s, 12 Latin American and Caribbean countries have adopted such legislation. The Special Rapporteur welcomes these initiatives and encourages Governments to ensure effective implementation.

30.   Generally, as testified to in non-governmental submissions from all regions, however, there is a lack of coordination between the State and

civil society in working towards the effective implementation of formal provisions and policies. While some States make an active attempt to consult and include civil society representatives in the process of developing and implementing laws and policies, others have maintained a distant and, at times, antagonistic relationship with NGOs. Overwhelmingly, Governments lack the necessary expertise to develop and implement policy relating to violence against women. Government actors generally, and those within the criminal justice system in particular, continue to subscribe to outdated myths about the role of women in society and the family, and about causes of violence in the family. Systematic training and gender awareness programmes are essential if policies are to be implemented by the criminal justice system.

31.   Many States continue to make the erroneous link between alcohol and violence. While alcohol does in many cases exacerbate violence, alcohol does not itself cause violence against women. The focus on alcohol or drugs, rather than on male patriarchal ideology, which has as its ultimate expression male violence against women, undermines the anti-violence movement. . . .

32.   Increasingly, States are using cultural relativist claims to avoid responsibility for positive, anti-violence action. The recognition of heterogeneous or multicultural communities is not at odds with developing comprehensive and multifaceted strategies to combat domestic violence. In all communities, the root causes of domestic violence are similar, even when the justifications for such violence or the forms of such violence vary.

33.   Many Governments continue to classify women, children, the elderly, the disabled or any combination of these together as one social group. This arises from the paternal nature of the State, which seeks to protect "vulnerable" groups. While distinct measures must be developed to combat violence against women and provide remedies and support to victim-survivors, the emphasis must be on empowerment rather than care—on social justice rather than social welfare. Women must be treated, in fact and in law, as full citizens, endowed with rights and reason.

34.   There is a continuing emphasis on mediation and counselling by police or mediation boards in cases of violence in the family. Police efforts to counsel victims in such cases, which often includes mediation between victim and perpetrator, may serve to undermine the seriousness of crimes of violence against women and, in many instances, may heighten the risk for the victim.

The Due Diligence Standard as a Tool for the Elimination of Violence against Women

Report of the Special Rapporteur on Violence against Women, its Causes and Consequences, Yakin Ertürk, Commission on Human Rights

U.N. Doc. E/CN.4/2006/61 (2006).

14.   The Declaration on the Elimination of Violence against Women adopted by the General Assembly in 1993 urges States, in its article 4(c), to

"exercise due diligence to prevent, investigate and, in accordance with national legislation, punish acts of violence against women, whether those acts are perpetrated by the State or by private persons". As such, the concept of due diligence provides a yardstick to determine whether a State has met or failed to meet its obligations in combating violence against women. However, there remains a lack of clarity concerning its scope and content.

15.   The application of the due diligence standard, to date, has tended to be limited to responding to violence against women when it occurs and in this context it has concentrated on legislative reform, access to justice and the provision of services. There has been relatively little work done on the more general obligation of prevention, including the duty to transform patriarchal gender structures and values that perpetuate and entrench violence against women. On the other hand, the exclusively State-centric nature of the due diligence obligation has failed to take into account the changing power dynamics and the challenges these pose for State authority as well as the new questions they raise about accountability.

16.   The current challenge in combating violence against women is the implementation of existing human rights standards to ensure that the root causes and consequences of violence against women are tackled at all levels from the home to the transnational arena. The multiplicity of forms of violence against women as well as the fact that this violence frequently occurs at the intersection of different types of discrimination makes the adoption of multifaceted strategies to effectively prevent and combat this violence a necessity.

17.   This report aims to reconsider the due diligence standard in order to (a) focus on State obligation to transform the societal values and institutions that sustain gender inequality while at the same time effectively respond to violence against women when it occurs, and (b) examine the shared responsibilities of State and non-State actors with respect to preventing and responding to violence and other violations of women's human rights. . . .

57.   . . . Since the 1980s, women's rights activists have been working within the existing framework to expand the vision of rights to respond to the violations inherent in women's experiences, thereby transforming the understanding of international human rights law and the doctrine of State responsibility. This paved the way for the recognition of violence against women as a human rights violation for which States could be held responsible, regardless of whether the perpetrator is a public or private actor.

58.   The quest for such a vision continues to confront diverse challenges. While a comprehensive analysis of these is not intended here, three main areas are highlighted: (a) the public/ private dichotomy; (b) the resurgence of identity politics based on cultural specificity, challenging State authority from below; (c) the emergence of translational power blocks with the right to command global governance, challenging State authority from above. Thus, international law, which has traditionally centered on the State as its primary subject is now confronted with other powerful actors. . . .

100.   ... [I]n practice, the response to the issue of violence against women has been fragmented and treated in isolation from the wider concern for women's rights and equality.

101.   This report has argued that this is caused by a narrow interpretation and application of human rights law. In this regard, the potentials of the due diligence standard have been explored to overcome the shortcomings in this regard.

102.   If we confine ourselves to the current conception of due diligence as an element of State responsibility, then obstacles relative to the capacity of the State will be determinative. If, on the other hand, we continue to dare to push the boundaries of due diligence in demanding the full compliance of States with international law, including the obligation to address the root causes of violence against women and to hold non-State actors accountable for their acts, then we will move towards a conception of human rights compatible with our aspirations for a just world free of violence

NOTES AND QUESTIONS

1.   **Due Diligence.** Due diligence is one of the most important issues in women's international human rights law because it emphasizes the importance of state responsibility for violence committed by individuals and highlights the importance of state obligations to comply with international law.

2.   **The Secretary–General's In–Depth Study.** The Secretary–General's In–Depth Study on All Forms of Violence Against Women in 2006 concretizes the steps States must take to fulfill their international obligations. It calls for action in the following ways, among others:

- Ratification of all international human rights instruments, including the Convention on the Elimination of all Forms of Discrimination against Women and its Optional Protocol, and withdrawal of reservations

- Establishment of constitutional frameworks guaranteeing substantive equality for women and prohibiting violence against women

- Adoption, periodic review and effective implementation, in a gender-sensitive manner, of legislation that criminalizes all forms of violence against women

- Investigation in a prompt, thorough, gender-sensitive and effective manner of all allegations of violence against women, including by keeping official records of all complaints; undertaking investigation and evidence-gathering expeditiously; collecting and safeguarding evidence, with witness protection where needed; and providing the opportunity for women to make complaints to, and deal with, skilled and professional female staff

- Punishment of the perpetrators of all forms of violence against women in a manner commensurate with the severity of the offence

• Implementation of training and awareness-raising programmes to familiarize judges, prosecutors and other members of the legal profession with women's human rights in general, and the Convention on the Elimination of All Forms of Discrimination against Women and its Optional Protocol in particular

• Creation of services, in cooperation with civil society organizations as appropriate, in the following areas: access to justice, including free legal aid when necessary; provision of a safe and confidential environment for women to report violence against women; adequately funded shelters and relief services; adequately funded health-care and support services, including counselling; linguistically and culturally accessible services for women requiring such services; and counselling and rehabilitation programmes for perpetrators of violence against women

• Systematic collection of data disaggregated by sex and other factors such as age, ethnicity and disability detailing the prevalence of all forms of violence against women; the causes and consequences of violence against women; and the effectiveness of any measures implemented to prevent and redress violence against women. *The Secretary–General's In–Depth Study on All Forms of Violence Against Wowen* (2006).

If asked to assess United States progress towards meeting international obligations, what would you cite? Do you think the United States has taken important steps?

3. **The Role of NGOs.** In the face of recalcitrance on the part of state governments, the role of NGOs, who may be less inhibited in their denunciation of violence and state participation in violence, remains a crucial one. In 1991 the Women's Rights Project of Human Rights Watch joined with Americas Watch to send a delegation to Brazil, to assess the government's response to domestic violence. The subsequent report was the first issued by an international human rights organization to analyze systematic non-prosecution of domestic violence crimes by the state as a violation of equal protection under human rights law. Dorothy Thomas and Michele Beasley describe the report's findings as follows. It indicated that:

[W]ife-murder is a common crime in Brazil, and reveals a pattern of impunity or undue mitigation of sentence in homicides where the victim is a woman. In cases of spousal murder, men are able to obtain an acquittal based on the theory that the killing was justified to defend the man's "honor" after the wife's alleged adultery. The reverse is rarely true. . . .

[It also showed that] despite the prevalence of violence in the home, police rarely investigated such crimes prior to 1985. Studies from 1981 and 1983 show that "when [women] tried to report aggressions" to the police, the police often turned them away on the grounds that domestic violence was "a private problem." When the police did register domestic abuse crimes they frequently failed to follow standard procedures, leaving out pertinent information about the circumstances of the abuse or subjecting the victim to abusive treatment aimed at implicating her in the crime. These biased police attitudes greatly deterred women from seeking the government's protection.

The joint report of Human Rights Watch and Americas Watch exposed the situation in Brazil, putting pressure on the government to react. The following report describes more recent NGO efforts to bring about change through publicizing the results of their investigations.

Human Rights Watch
Women's Human Rights World Report 2000

In 1999, Human Rights Watch continued to investigate the state response to sexual assault and domestic violence against women in Peru, Russia, South Africa, and Pakistan. We also monitored the state response to "honor killings" in Jordan and to the sexual abuse of female prisoners in the United States. Despite some positive efforts by state and non-state actors, abuses against women were carried out frequently and with virtual impunity, as states largely failed to fulfill their obligations to prevent and provide redress for such crimes. States were particularly negligent in addressing violence in the family. This problem received widespread international attention in recent years, but concrete action was slow in coming. Japan, for example, only began to consider specific legislation and support services to combat domestic violence in mid–1999. There were also disturbing indications that such violence was increasing. UNICEF reported in 1999 that violence against women was rising in post-communist countries as economic crises increased women's financial dependence upon men. In many of these states, domestic violence was not prohibited by law and marital rape was not recognized as a crime. Speaking on a more global level, in her 1999 report to the U.N. Commission on Human Rights, the special rapporteur on violence against women noted the "growing prevalence of violence against women generally and domestic violence specifically," and concluded that "[o]verwhelmingly, States are failing in their international obligations to prevent, investigate and prosecute violence against women in the family."

. . . In Russia, where women continued to be subject to domestic violence, attempts to pass national legislation on the topic failed, and little was done to improve the state response to the abuse. The federal government did not make financial resources available for combating violence against women. Activists, expressing frustration with the lack of progress nationally, focused their attention on local level initiatives, establishing cooperative links with local law enforcement, city officials, and journalists. The number of nongovernmental crisis centers grew across the country, while the few existing government-sponsored centers and shelters closed due to budget cuts. Crisis center leaders traveled throughout Russia, training judges, police, and activists on rape and domestic violence issues. The Russian Association of Crisis Centers for Women officially registered in 1999 and held a national meeting in September to coordinate its activities. But according to crisis center workers, despite educational campaigns and continuing advocacy, police still failed to report cases of rape and domestic violence, and few such cases made it to court.

As South Africa celebrated its fifth year of democratic rule, it continued to face staggering levels of domestic and sexual violence against women. In a 1999 study by the South African Medical Council, 25 percent of the women interviewed in three rural provinces had been assaulted by an intimate partner. Victims of rape and domestic violence confronted significant obstacles to legal redress. Even at a handful of new one-stop rape crisis centers, women were often unable to receive adequate examinations by forensic doctors, whose reports were needed for a legal case. These doctors were criticized—by NGOs and the head of forensic medicine at a leading South African medical school—for being poorly trained and often biased against rape victims. Proposals for reform of the forensic medical service moved forward only slowly. On National Women's Day, President Mbeki tied judgment of the country's progress toward total liberation to advancement in combating violence against women. Still, to the dismay of women's groups, South Africa's ground-breaking 1998 Domestic Violence Act languished, its implementation delayed, according to the government, by the cost of drafting regulations and training personnel to implement the legislation in the courts. At this writing, the government was still using a flawed 1993 domestic violence law.

In Pakistan, it was estimated that eight women were raped every twenty-four hours and 70 to 95 percent of women had experienced domestic or familial violence. Extreme forms of familial violence included so-called honor killings and bride burnings, with both practices claiming the lives of hundreds of women every year. In April 1999, Samia Sarwar was gunned down in a much publicized honor killing at the behest of her parents for seeking a divorce. Other women were attacked, by or at the instigation of family members, for choosing their spouses. The government appeared uninterested in combating impunity for these acts. Women victims of violence who turned to the criminal justice system confronted a discriminatory legal regime, venal and abusive police, untrained doctors, incompetent prosecutors, and skeptical judges. As a result, few women reported crimes of violence, and fewer still saw their attackers punished. In the case of Sarwar's murder, a police report was registered, but as of October 1999 her killers remained free despite exceptionally strong and credible evidence against them. In August 1999, Pakistan's Senate refused even to consider a resolution sparked by Sarwar's murder condemning the practice of honor killing, sending a clear message of government acquiescence in the climate of impunity surrounding acts of violence against women.

NOTES AND QUESTIONS

1. **Reports on Violence Against Women.** This report was also critical of the United States, but with respect to custodial sexual misconduct in state and federal prisons, not with respect to its response to domestic violence. The Amnesty International report issued in 2004 to launch its global campaign "Stop Violence against Women" includes an analysis of

domestic violence, with data and stories from around the world including in the United States, and places this analysis in an international human rights framework. Amnesty International, *It's in our hands: Stop violence against women*, AI Index ACT 77/001/2004 (http://web.amnesty.org/actforwomen/reports-index-eng). Reports can be found from such United States groups as the Center for Women's Global Leadership (CWGL), Equality Now, Human Rights Watch, Women's Economic and Development Organization and Amnesty International, and on the websites of the United Nations Division for the Advancement of Women and UNIFEM.

2. **Effects of NGO Reports.** How much of an effect would you expect NGO reports and investigations to have in bringing about change? Can you imagine conditions under which they might backfire?

C. LINKING THE INTERNATIONAL TO THE DOMESTIC

As with the VAWA civil rights remedy examined in the last chapter, the international human rights perspective presented here links violence explicitly with issues of gender discrimination and women's equality. Within this framework, violence against women is inextricably linked with issues of reproductive choice and sexual equality, workplace discrimination, wage equity, child care and health care. Some have argued that in the aftermath of *Morrison*, domestic violence advocates in the United States need "to bring Beijing home," in the words of Rhonda Copelon, and work harder to promote an understanding of domestic violence as just one among many practices that enforce women's continuing subordination in American society. The next excerpt explores these links between the work of international and national activists and scholars, and the ways in which international human rights perspectives could impact work on domestic violence in the United States.

Elizabeth M. Schneider
Transnational Law as a Domestic Resource: Thoughts on the Case of Women's Rights
38 NEW ENG. L. REV. 689 (2004).

Why the interest in global perspectives? First, as already suggested, activists and lawyers have an increased understanding about globalization and its impact on women everywhere. The internet, international meetings, foreign travel and increased access to legal materials around the world have facilitated global contacts, information and influences. Another reason is that U.S. women's rights activists and lawyers recognize limits to women's rights legal reform in this country. Global perspectives provide cross-country critical insights, experiences and personal affiliations, and offer an opportunity to energize the women's rights movement. They contribute important comparative insights that can change the language, the strategies and advocacy terrain. Especially for younger people, global perspectives may provide a "transformative" opportunity for women's rights.

In the United States, there have been some important successes but also some serious problems in the development of women's rights litigation.... Despite continuing wage and occupational discrimination in the area of women's employment rights, "first generation" problems of overt discrimination and facial exclusion on the basis of sex are rare. There are, however, serious obstacles in reforming the more complex aspects of "second generation" gender-based litigation in employment and constitutional equality. Many national legal groups that focus on women's rights, such as the NOW Legal Defense and Education Fund, the ACLU Women's Rights Project, and Equal Rights Advocates, deal with a range of issues from employment discrimination to Title IX, and have won some important cases, but progress is slow. At the same time, many national reproductive rights organizations, such as the Center for Reproductive Rights, Planned Parenthood, NARAL Pro–Choice America and the ACLU Reproductive Rights Project, focus exclusively on women's reproductive rights, which is a deeply contested issue and faces constant and serious attack. While many national and local organizations around the country address violence against women and involve themselves in state and federal law reform efforts, pro-criminalization efforts and resistance to understanding domestic violence in the context of gender equality have undermined some of the core principles that shaped early feminist work on violence. The United States Supreme Court's decision in *United States v. Morrison*, which held the civil rights remedy of the Violence Against Women Act (VAWA) unconstitutional on the ground that violence against women was a "local" problem, not a national one, reflected these limits. Although Laura Bush criticized the treatment of women under the Taliban, President Bush closed the White House Office on Women's Issues, an office created by President Clinton.

Historically, U.S. national organizations addressing women's rights have tended to work separately from international organizations working on similar issues. Dorothy Thomas has suggested several reasons for this division between domestic civil rights and international human rights advocacy. Thomas argues that historical resistance in the United States to international standards and scrutiny "has effectively shut down the human rights dimension of [United States] rights advocacy," that this resistance is the result of "persistent tensions in domestic women's and civil rights advocacy," tensions that arise from the broad-based indivisibility of civil, political, economic, social, and cultural rights that shape much of human rights work in the United States, in contrast with a civil rights approach. She observes that "[d]ecades of isolationist U.S. policy have produced a bifurcated rights reality in the United States," one that implies that "civil rights applies to 'us' and human rights to 'them.'"

However, this dichotomy is beginning to change, partially as a result of greater participation of domestic women's rights lawyers with activists in international conferences and projects. Some national organizations even have international departments; for example, the Center for Reproductive Rights in New York has maintained separate domestic and international units for several years. The Women's Rights Network in Boston was established specifically to provide international resources for domestic violence programs in the United States. Frustration with the complex problems associated with litigating women's rights cases in this country and incrementalism, on the one hand, and the internationalization of domestic organizations, on the other, has challenged activists and lawyers to develop new international human rights arguments. The result: an increased use of international human rights arguments in domestic women's rights litigation and increased campaigning to urge the United States to ratify CEDAW.

It is unclear what impact the consideration or integration of international perspectives could have on domestic lawmaking. Arguing for consideration or integration does not guarantee any particular result. Some claim that introducing international human rights arguments and perspectives into domestic law has the potential to transform the very conceptual bases of the problems and issues that are presented and could lead to the reconceptualization of the way these problems are dealt within domestic courts. For some activists and scholars, international human rights arguments challenge the framework of domestic rights-based arguments in several ways: they present a more indivisible perspective that relates economic and social and civil rights; they present a more intersectional perspective that links race, gender, ethnicity; they recognize a positive state responsibility with "strong substantive support for non-discrimination and social welfare and affirmative action initiatives;" and they challenge the Rehnquist Court's view that the United States Constitution imposes only negative and no positive obligations on government.

At a minimum, international human rights has the potential to offer new perspectives to "old" issues, or issues that appear to be "old" in this country. There are many examples. Many countries around the world now have more generous family leave and child care polices than the United States, and comparative perspectives are frequently used to attempt to shame United States policymakers. A recent book looks at sexual harassment from "Capitol Hill to the Sorbonne" and draws new insights from France for the American experience. Legal treatment of workers in the Maquiladoras, the United States manufacturing export zones in northern Mexico, has received considerable human rights attention, although in the United States most people consider issues of excluding pregnant workers from jobs on the ground of reproductive hazards in the workplace settled because it was litigated and argued in the 1970s in cases like *UAW v. Johnson Controls, Inc.* or *Oil, Chem. & Atomic Workers Int'l Union v. Am. Cyanamid Co.* Yet little has changed here in the United States; we have not had protests, activist efforts, litigation or public education concerning reproductive hazards in the workplace for many years. International human rights perspectives on this issue provide an opportunity to revitalize this issue domestically, and thus view the problem through a different lens. Finally, international human rights concern with the "honor" defense in Muslim countries to punish, kill or control women who have violated local gender norms can be viewed in light of the long history of the "heat of passion" defense in this country: only a few years ago it was the basis for a Maryland judge's expression of empathy for a man who killed his wife after finding her in bed with another man. Put simply, the U.S. judicial system can benefit from the internationalization and universalization of these problems that international human rights arguments and perspectives provide. As Vicki Jackson notes, comparison with other laws "can illuminate paths not taken and choices made that constitute a challenge" to United States perspectives.

Several recent attempts have been made to encourage the Supreme Court to consider international human rights standards in women's rights cases. In an amicus brief in *Brzonkala v. Morrison*, a group of international law scholars and human rights experts put forth an extensive human rights argument in support of the federal civil rights cause of action provided by the Violence Against Women Act (VAWA). The brief focused on the International Covenant on Civil and Political Rights (ICCPR), ratified by the United States in 1992, arguing that the United States was obligated under this treaty to provide remedies for victims of gender-based violence. They emphasized that Congress is authorized by the Constitution to enact laws to implement international treaties, such as the ICCPR. In a press release announcing the filing of the brief, Rhonda Copelon, co-author of the brief and Director of the International Women's Human Rights Law Clinic at CUNY School of Law, expressed the importance of making these arguments:

The international legal recognition of gender violence, both official and private, as among the gravest human rights violations, as well as the participation of eminent international law scholars and human rights experts in this amicus brief are very significant developments. For the Court to recognize these international arguments would be a critical step in the process of implementing human rights in the United States, an idea whose time—50 years after the signing of the Universal Declaration of Human Rights—has finally come....

International human rights standards are being presented in lower court cases on women's rights as well, and sometimes judges even invoke them in their decisions. In 2002, District Judge Jack Weinstein held that New York's Administration of Children's Services' (ACS) practice of removing children from the care of battered mothers solely because of domestic violence violated the constitutional rights of both the mothers and the children. In his opinion, Judge Weinstein cited numerous international treaties in support of his holding that mothers and children have a constitutionally recognized liberty interest in familial integrity:

This interest is not only a fundamental value of American society and constitutional law, but also is protected by international law. International law instruments, of which the United States is a party and signatory, provide that the state must use extreme care when making decisions which could threaten familial integrity.

On appeal in *Nicholson*, an amicus brief reasserted international human rights arguments offered in Judge Weinstein's decision. The New York Legal Assistance Group argued that battered women are a protected class under international human rights standards and that ACS's policy of removing their children "clearly disregards" these standards, although the Court of Appeals decision did not reach it....

On the state legislative level, the Battered Mothers' Testimony Project was developed in Massachusetts by the international human rights group Women's Rights Network "to document and address the injustices inflicted on battered mothers and their children during family court child custody and visitation litigation." It used "human rights fact-finding, qualitative research, advocacy and community organizing," and according to its website, was the "first human rights initiative to address child custody and domestic violence issues." The website refers to the United Nations Declaration on the Elimination of Violence against Women, Articles 2 and 4, and to the United Nations Convention on the Rights of the Child as international sources for these arguments.

NOTES AND QUESTIONS

1. **The Global and the Local.** One example of the way in which international human rights advocacy on domestic violence can enrich local efforts and assist in struggles against violence in the United States is the amicus curiae brief filed in 2005 by International Law Scholars and Women's, Civil Rights and Human Rights Organizations in the United States Supreme Court in *Town of Castle Rock v. Gonzales*, 545 U.S. 748 (2005). The brief argued two points: first, that the Court's consideration of the due process question in the case should be informed by the international customary norm that has evolved that women and children have a fundamental human right both to be protected from family violence and to have effective remedies when such protection fails; second, that the terms of the International Covenant on Civil and Political Rights are recognized to encompass States parties' obligations to ensure persons, particularly women and children, the right to freedom from domestic violence. The brief argued that recognizing Ms. Gonzales' right of action under 42 U.S.C. § 1983 would be consistent with the federal obligations undertaken when U.S. ratified that treaty. The more recent effort to file a petition with the Inter–American Commission on Human Rights on behalf of Jessica Gonzales, described in Chapter Fourteen, takes international human rights advocacy in United States cases of domestic violence to a new level. The Inter–American Commission ruled in October 2007 that the petition was "admissible", akin to finding jurisdiction, and that it would hear the Gonzales case. http://www.cidh.org/annualrep/2007/eng/htm. See Marcia Coyle, Rights Panel to Hear U.S. Domestic Violence Case, Nat'l L.J., October 15, 2007.

Another example of the use of international law arguments in domestic violence litigation is the amicus curiae brief filed by International Law Scholars and Human Rights Experts in the United States Supreme Court in *Morrison*, excerpted in Chapters One and Sixteen. This brief argued that Congress had the authority to enact legislation such as the civil rights remedy of the Violence Against Women Act to meet both international treaty obligations and customary law obligations and that United States ratification of the International Covenant on Civil and Political Rights (ICCPR) and other treaties meant that the United States was required to provide protection from gender-based violence from both private persons and public officials.

For other examples of the ways in which international human rights argumentation can assist in U.S. domestic struggles, see Martin A. Geer, *Human Rights and Wrongs In Our Own Backyard: Incorporating International Human Rights Protections Under Domestic Civil Rights Law—A Case Study of Women in United States Prisons,* 13 Harv. Hum. Rts. J. 71 (2000) and Carrie Cuthbert and Kim Slote, *Bridging the Gap Between Battered Women's Advocates in the US and Abroad,* 6 Tex. J. Wmn & L. 287 (1997). International human rights meetings organized by groups such as the Center for Women's Global Leadership at Rutgers University and others already mentioned have resulted in the generation and sharing of strategies that can support advocacy on behalf of victims of violence around the world and in the United States.

CHAPTER EIGHTEEN

DOING THE WORK

Introduction

Throughout this book, you have read about both the failures and the successes of lawyers when handling domestic violence cases. We have encountered situations in which lawyers and advocates have failed their battered clients. We have read about family lawyers who have not taken their clients' abuse seriously, or advocated effectively for their safety or the safety of their children; about prosecutors who have failed to understand why victims might have difficulty cooperating with law enforcement, and failed to hold batterers accountable; and about criminal defense lawyers who have not understood how to use testimony about abuse to present a strong self-defense claim. Some of these failures of representation are lodged in failures of strategy, and some in failures of relationship. The failures of strategy often reflect a lack of understanding of the dynamics of abusive relationships, of those who perpetrate and those who live with abuse, of what legal interventions are appropriate, and of how to procure them. Unfortunately, these failures of understanding have characterized not only traditional approaches to violence in intimate relationships, but even some of the newer approaches advocated by feminist activists and theorists; think back, for example, on the controversy surrounding policies of mandatory arrest and no-drop prosecution. The failures of relationship can result either from the inadequacies of the model of lawyer-client relationship within which a particular lawyer or advocate is working, or from more specific difficulties introduced by the experiences a particular client brings to the relationship, and the responses those experiences evoke.

There are also many stories of hope throughout this book: attorneys convincing courts to extend protections under restraining orders to same-sex couples; advocacy groups providing new approaches to serving victims with disabilities or with language barriers; and legislators redefining a multitude of laws that have provided victims with greater protections. These successes have been aided by better training of lawyers and other policy makers on the dynamics of abuse. They also reflect the growing number of women in the legal profession, who have brought to the law their experiences, concerns, and commitment to ending violence, as well as a growing number of men in the profession who are committed to ending intimate violence.

This chapter explores in more detail some of the barriers and bridges that have led to failures and successes. We explore the complicated dynamics between client and attorney, and the policies shaping representation. We end the book by examining the changing landscape of domestic violence practice and the many challenges and rewards lawyers undertaking this work will experience.

A.   Representing Clients Who Have Been Abused

Since the 1970's, activists, advocates and lawyers have been working to transform the legal system's responses to intimate partner violence, and the attitudes towards victims of violence that guided those responses. Specifically, as you have read, the goal was to dislodge old stereotypes of women as provocateurs of violence, as masochistic participants in their own abuse, or as deceitful manipulators who fabricate tales of abuse to achieve other ends. Although those stereotypes are slow to die, the work of the last thirty years has created competing images that have been successful in prompting legal reform, and have resulted in many women receiving more sympathetic treatment within the legal system. The accomplishments of the battered women's movement, and the many committed individuals who have contributed to these changes, should not be minimized. However, within the last two decades we have begun to see new tendencies toward stereotype, and to appreciate the limitations of the reform strategies that guided work in the seventies and eighties. You have seen these new stereotypes at work, and discussed, earlier in this book, but this next reading provides a useful summary.

Ann Shalleck
Theory and Experience in Constructing the Relationship Between Lawyer and Client: Representing Women Who Have Been Abused
64 Tenn. L. Rev. 1019 (1997).

Without rejecting the importance of many of the cultural, social, political and legal developments of the last quarter century, or the recognition of the oppression of women underlying the efforts to secure these changes, some feminist theorists and activists have identified limitations, contradictions and dangers embedded in the theoretical constructs that have dominated both the discourse about, and the institutional developments affecting, the experience of abused women in an intimate relationship. They have seen the harms women who have been abused suffer under the legal regime resulting from the changes that have been implemented, and confronted the conceptual problems revealed in the actualization of the new legal landscape. Against this background, these feminist theorists and activists have begun to articulate new ways to conceive and approach the issue of abuse of women in intimate relationships. Although not all of those who have engaged in this critique embrace all of the following elements, several overlapping and intersecting themes characterize this emerging feminist critique.

First, these theorists see the construct of the "battered woman" as essentializing. It makes one characteristic of a woman's experience define her entire identity, thereby marginalizing or trivializing other aspects of her identity. Those aspects of her life that she may have insulated from the impact of the violence in her life become invisible. Her strengths and her accomplishments become submerged under the label of "battered woman." Her relationship with a violent person entirely defines her.

Second, these critics also view the construct of "battering" as essentializing because this framework treats intimate abuse as a single, uniform experience. Within dominant theories of domestic violence, the "cycle of violence" is presented as having a powerful, internal dynamic that, of necessity, replicates itself in all battered women's lives. Experiences that do not fit into the cycle are denied, diminished, or interpreted to make them fit into the model. If a woman's experience does not fit the cycle, it must not be "battering." In addition, this view of "battering" is constructed out of the experiences of primarily white, heterosexual women. "Battering" of women of color or of lesbians is understood as a variant of the dominant model. Their experiences of intimate abuse and their understanding of those experiences are not used to alter the model or to challenge its validity, but are assimilated into it.

Third, "battered women" are portrayed as victims, as powerless and passive objects of another's violence, helpless to free themselves from the constraints imposed by the "batterer." Women whose actions seem to fit into the stereotypical portrait are denied affirmation of their attempts to resist, to survive, to protect their children, or to create space to maneuver within the constraints they face. The reasonableness of the choices made within the constraints they face is obliterated. In addition, the stereotype of "battered women" as passive victims might secure them help or protection in one context, but may boomerang to harm them in another. Other women, whose actions challenge the stereotypical portrait, who wish to assert their capacity to shape or control the violent situation in some way, are often left outside of the sphere of protection offered by the legal developments regarding domestic violence.

Fourth, the power of the construct of the "battered woman" tends to put the focus on the woman, rather than the man who is violent. This focus has two consequences. First, the common question asked about abused women is "Why didn't she leave?" This question tends to obscure the inquiry about why she had to face the violence at all. Second, the twin constructs of "battering" and "battered woman" are dependent upon the demonization of the "batterer." Seen solely as the instrument or incarnation of violence, he is rarely a real, complex human being for whom a woman might have felt or still feel affection. When differences among men who abuse women are minimized or the complexities of a particular woman's history with a man are invisible, women's differential responses to varying situations are more difficult to comprehend. Therefore, women's efforts to find help for or to protect the person who has abused them are understood, at best, as misguided and, at worst, demented. Other women's efforts to protect their children's relationship with a parent who may be loving, or at least adequate, by staying in an abusive situation or resisting punishment of an abusive partner are demeaned, ignored, or treated as irrational.

Fifth, these four characteristics of the concepts of "battering" and "battered woman" lead many women not to recognize themselves or their experiences in the standard narrative of domestic violence. In order to secure what legal protections exist, they often must violate their own understanding of themselves and conform to the dominant stereotype. In making this strategic maneuver, a woman can feel additional powerlessness at her inability to explain her own situation as she experienced it. If she refuses to participate in this violation of her self-understanding, a woman may forego the limited protections that the legal system offers. She may decide to withdraw from the legal system that seems to demand adherence to the stereotype, incurring the wrath or the pity of many participants in that system. She may even end up jailed or punished for failing to play her appointed role. Alternatively, if she proceeds in the legal system but refuses to adopt the standard story, she may find herself denied the protection that she sought.

Sixth, using legal remedies may create additional dangers for women who have been abused rather than ensuring or even increasing their safety or the safety of their children. This feminist critique is directed not just at the partial nature of most legal tools, but also at the site of the decision about whether to use available legal mechanisms. Beyond the debates about whether or not civil protection orders, arrests, criminal prosecutions and incarceration actually decrease the incidence or level of violence in the aggregate, these critics are concerned that those who work with or counsel the women, initiate legal actions, or make decisions in those cases disregard and belittle an individual woman's evaluation of the danger she or her children face when she participates in legal action.

These feminist theorists and activists seek first to reveal and challenge the assumptions behind and consequences of legal reforms, many of which they themselves originally sought. Second, they attempt to place these reforms in a historical and political perspective, in order to further our understanding of how visions implicit in legal reforms may not be apparent until those reforms are realized and how the consequences of legal change may not be predictable or intended. Third, these theorists and activists are engaged in a search for new legal strategies that provide abused women with legal accounts of abuse by an intimate partner that resonate with their own experiences, that create additional space for successfully challenging that abuse, and that do not separate social policies regarding domestic violence from the complex and multiple realities of women who must find ways to cope with violence in their intimate relationships.

NOTES AND QUESTIONS

1. **Unintended Consequences.** It is worth pausing to consider how much of the "backfiring" of legal reforms designed to address partner abuse has been due to mistakes of characterization or conceptualization on the part of activists and theorists, and how much has been due to the translation process by which accurate and nuanced characterizations and conceptualizations are filtered through mainstream cultural assumptions and attitudes before being integrated into the legal system. You might decide, for example, that it is legal readings of Lenore Walker's early work that have created problems for battered women who do not fit the "helpless" stereotype, rather than the work itself. On the other hand, it does seem that policies like mandatory arrest and no-drop prosecution have been

guided by an "essentializing" and paternalistic (or perhaps in this case maternalistic) impulse that it is *always* better for women if their batterers are held accountable for their abuse within the criminal justice system, even if the women themselves resist that outcome.

2. **Who Knows Best?** Is it ever appropriate for those working in the domestic violence field, whether as theorists, activists, advocates or lawyers, to claim that they know what is best for victims of partner violence, either in the aggregate, or individually? At the policy level it is of course necessary to advocate for solutions at a generic level, even knowing that they will not serve every individual equally, and that there may be individuals who are not helped at all, and may even be hurt, by proposed reform. Responsible policy advocacy consists of careful listening, study and learning, so that proposals grow out of a wide and solid base of information, and aim for solutions flexible enough to accommodate the needs of the vast majority of those who will be affected by them. Even after more than twenty years of study, the body of empirical research on the impact of reforms in the domestic violence arena is dangerously thin; there is too much room, still, for advocacy based more on conviction than knowledge.

The next reading provides a summary of what has been written on this subject, again drawn from the work of Ann Shalleck. Her account draws from articles by Susan Bryant and Maria Arias, *Case Study: A Battered Women's Rights Clinic: Designing a Clinical Program Which Encourages a Problem–Solving Vision of Lawyering that Empowers Clients and Community*, 42 WASH. U. J. URB. & CONTEMP. L. 207 (1992); Leslie G. Espinoza, *Legal Narratives, Therapeutic Narratives: The Invisibility and Omnipresence of Race and Gender*, 95 MICH. L. REV. 901 (1997), Peter Margulies, *Representation of Domestic Violence Survivors as a New Paradigm of Poverty Law: In Search of Access, Connection and Voice*, 93 GEO. WASH. L. REV. 1071 (1995); Joan S. Meier, *Notes From the Underground: Integrating Psychological and Legal Perspectives on Domestic Violence in Theory and Practice*, 21 HOFSTRA L. REV. 1295 (1993); Linda Mills, *Intuition and Insight: A New Job Description for the Battered Woman's Prosecutor and Other More Modest Proposals*, 7 U.C.L.A. WOMEN'S L. J. 183 (1997); and Linda Mills, *On the Other Side of Silence: Affective Lawyering for Intimate Abuse*, 81 CORNELL L. REV. 1225 (1996).

For a more recent discussion of the ethics involved in representing battered women, see Leigh Goodmark, *Going Underground: The Ethics of Advising a Battered Woman Fleeing an Abusive Relationship*, 75 U.M.K.C.L.REV. 999 (2007).

Ann Shalleck
Theory and Experience in Constructing the Relationship between Lawyer and Client: Representing Women Who Have Been Abused
64 TENN. L. REV. 1019 (1997).

Several theorists of practice have identified elements that they think are essential to effective representation of women who have been abused.

Although these various efforts ... have differences, certain recurring characteristics emerge from these models. Identifying these characteristics can be helpful in increasing our awareness of the assumptions we bring to representation for women who have been abused, evaluating our emerging conceptions of this representation, fashioning alternative models, identifying lawyering practices through which the models can be realized, and exploring pedagogical methods that would enable students to learn how to provide and critique the practices that the aspirational models describe.

In different ways, these theorists of practice are particularly attentive to the affective components of the lawyer-client relationship. Two of them, Peter Margulies and Linda Mills, have explicitly characterized their models as "affective." A third, Leslie Espinoza, has characterized hers as "therapeutic." A fourth, Joan Meier, in the creation of a model integrating both legal and psychological theory and practice, has made the affective component central to her vision of lawyering. Finally, while Susan Bryant and Maria Arias are deeply concerned abut making a client's understanding of her situation and definition of her needs a critical component in the interaction between lawyer and client, they also stress the importance of other aspects of client representation....

A.   Reflection on Experience

First, these models of lawyering encourage lawyers representing women who have been abused to identify and reflect upon, both before and during their representation, their own experiences of and feelings about violence or powerlessness in intimate relationships. This reflection is needed for three interrelated reasons. First, understanding his or her own vulnerability and powerlessness within intimate relationships is part of a lawyer's ability to experience empathy with the client's situation. Although the lawyer may not have gone through the same type of experience as the client, the lawyer needs to find within his or her own experience a basis for beginning to understand the situation of a client on an emotional level. For these theorists, the discovery of common experiential ground is necessary, not primarily for instrumental reasons of gaining the trust of or increasing rapport with a client, but for the construction of a relationship built explicitly on the shared recognition of the similarities and differences in their situations. From a relationship characterized by this sort of understanding comes the lawyer's abilities to act effectively with and for the client.

For these theorists, self-reflection is important for more than empathic understanding, however. Reflection by the lawyer on his or her own experiences is part of the process of understanding the pervasive nature and complex dynamics of intimate violence. The lawyer needs to see intimate abuse not as a single category within which one fits or not, but as a complex mixture of experiences involving not just physical violence, but also coercive behavior and the exercise of power and control, as well as other, yet unnamed, forms of domination and dependency. From this identification of commonalities of experience, lawyers can see that abuse is not a problem of the "other," but a shared experience, even if the experience is different.

Within these models, reflection by the lawyer furthers a third goal. Only with reflection can the lawyer respond respectfully to both the client's understanding of, and the decision-making affecting, her life. Lawyers must confront and overcome any barriers in their own reactions to and understanding of a client that could prompt them to disregard or overwhelm a client's own thoughts and decisions about how to proceed in a case. For these theorists, the lawyer's ability to not impose his or her own assumptions, ways of thinking, stereotypes, or biases on a client is grounded in reflection on the lawyer's own experience. A lawyer's views of and feelings about intimate abuse cannot just be left outside the door to the lawyer's office. A lawyer can "shed" those attitudes only by reaching into his or her own experience and finding commonalities, as well as differences, with the client. The lawyer, by appreciating, or at least sensing, the ways in which he or she shares in the vulnerabilities of the client ... may avoid judging the client. As the lawyer perhaps becomes increasingly uncertain about what he or she would have done if in the client's situation, the lawyer becomes less likely to impose on the client a course of action that arises from the lawyer's imposition of his or her own framework of understanding on the client.

As with the development of empathy, the process of not judging the client is a part of understanding the nature of intimate violence. For these theorists, the uni-dimensional conception of "battering" within the dominant theories of domestic violence has masked the complexities and contradictions of the interactional structures within which intimate violence occurs. It has permitted and even encouraged participants in all parts of the legal system to judge harshly women who have experienced abuse. By failing to see and respect an individual woman's sometimes shifting and contradictory ways of dealing with and interpreting the violence in her relationship, a lawyer may easily impose his or her own understanding of the violence on the client as the client makes the multiple decisions involved in taking any legal action at all, including meeting with a lawyer. The lawyer can come to understand the dynamics involved in continuing in an intimate relationship in which there is abuse only if he or she accepts the conflicted and unstable accounts that the woman has of her relationships and experiences.

B.   Recognition of the Fluidity of the Lawyer–Client Relationship

The second characteristic of these models of lawyering is their explicit recognition of the fluidity of the lawyer-client relationship. A woman who is or has been in an abusive relationship and has entered the legal system is often in a long process of coming to understand the relationship and herself within that relationship. As her understanding of the complex dynamics of the relationship changes, and her vision of herself alters over time, she can bring great instability to the relationship with her lawyer. In addition, the relationship between the client and her lawyer can become an element affecting her concepts of her life and herself. Therefore, the lawyer needs to see his or her role not as furthering a stable goal of the client, but as creating an opportunity for a client to explore multiple possibilities, as well as her own changing desires to further any of them.

The fluid character of the lawyer-client relationship, therefore, has two components of particular importance for women who have been in abusive relationships. First, it helps to affirm within the process of representation the non-judgmental attitude of the lawyer. If the woman can experience a space within which she can examine multiple possibilities and shift among them freely without fear of being judged as unstable or indecisive, she is then better able to figure out, within the contours of that relationship, what she thinks is best for her to do. If most people in the legal system are telling her that she ought to leave, she has at least one place where the desirability of leaving is not assumed and the complexities of separating are acknowledged not just in words, but throughout the multiple aspects of the lawyer-client interactions.

Second, by explicitly recognizing the unstable character of the client's goal, the lawyer is better able to accept the seemingly non-instrumental character of the representation. The purpose of the representation is not just to help the client achieve what she wants, but to work with the client to help her figure out what she wants. The client's ambivalence is not a moment to be confronted and worked through, but an important and continuing aspect of a case. The process of deciding what she wants may even be bound up for the client with the process of attempting to bring about an articulated goal. When concrete actions are taken to move towards a goal, a client may see that the goal is not what she understood it to be abstractly, or that the goal has consequences she did not foresee. As the client shifts in what she wants, the lawyer can come to understand the multiple meanings that each step within the legal system has for a woman who is abused within an intimate relationship.

C. Working Collaboratively with Clients

The lawyer and client operate collaboratively within these models of lawyering. This collaboration is grounded in two principles. First, this model rejects the pre-eminence of legal solutions for women who are abused in their intimate relationships. Not only are legal remedies limited in their effectiveness in stopping or reducing violence, but they can inter-fere with a woman's ability to develop for herself both an understanding of the violence in her intimate relationships and responses that enable her to alter the situation in ways that meet her changing needs. At their worst, legal actions can further harm women. If the lawyer treats legal under-standing of violence and legal remedies as not better than any other possible understanding or response, and if the lawyer views a woman's decision to pursue a legal remedy as constantly fluid, then the lawyer has no special claims to expertise. Within this framework, a client must be treated as an equal participant in shaping both the understanding of what type of action should be taken and how it should be pursued.

Second, the lawyer's ability to act effectively for his or her client is dependent upon a relationship within which lawyer and client recognize each other as jointly involved in a common enterprise. For some of the theorists of this model of lawyering, the lawyer not only takes on a client's goal, but participates with the client in achieving a goal that has significance for both of them. For some advocates of this model of lawyering, this collaboration entails at least some form of self-disclosure by the lawyer. Advocates of this approach stress the importance of the respect and shared commitment that come from mutual self-disclosure that is part of a collaborative effort despite the dangers of manipulation, imposition of a lawyer's understandings and responses on a client, and the inequality that may be part of the lawyer's having and exercising discretion about how and when to disclose aspects of his or her life to the client.

D.   Developing Responses that Enable Clients to Take Steps that Are Viable Within Their Particular Situations

This model of lawyering is particularly attentive to the limitations of remedies available through the legal system to women who have been in abusive relationships. Even the legal system's more innovative efforts of the last few years fail to respond to the needs of most women who are attempting to figure out ways to deal with the violence in their intimate relationships. Because of the legal system's emphasis upon eradicating violence rather than understanding it or helping women find ways to address the intimate violence in their own lives, as well as the system's emphasis upon the termination of a woman's relationship with the person who has abused her, the remedies available through the legal system often do not provide women an opportunity to make the changes in their lives that they need. When the inadequacies of these remedies are combined with the need to conform to the stereotypical image of a "battered woman" that the legal system reinforces, many women seek to escape from the system once they enter it or are deterred from even approaching it at all.

Within this legal context, lawyers for women who have been abused face several challenging tasks in their relationship with a client. The lawyer needs to work with the client to develop a variety of actions that both fit within the client's sense of her own capacity for acting and respond to the shifting and conflicting needs that the client feels. Also, the lawyer needs to explore with the client how each of those responses might work if implemented. Each response might or might not have a legal component to it. The lawyer needs to respect the client's judgments about the dangers that any action might pose, as well as the disruption of the client's life that each action could entail. In identifying and explaining various legal actions that could be part of a client's plan, the lawyer needs to be particularly careful not to favor legal action over other kinds of actions, either implicitly or explicitly. Furthermore, in describing the nature of the legal actions, as well as the multiple consequences that might flow from them, the lawyer needs to draw upon his or her understanding of the client in anticipating the meaning that those consequences could have for the client in her own struggle to deal with the violence in her relationship.

E.   Making Time

Often, for lawyers, time assumes the quality of a commodity. While it feels like the most precious thing we have, it also feels like the one over which we have the least control. Lawyers can feel that they are constantly in a responsive mode, answering to multiple demands.... Against this backdrop, lawyering in this model requires that lawyers recognize the centrality of time in the process of representing women who have been in abusive relationships. Each of the elements of lawyering identified above demands significant and often unpredictable allocations of time. In order to be self-reflective in a serious and meaningful way, the lawyer must set aside time to explore his or her own feelings and experiences. Developing empathic understanding of the relationships surrounding the violence in someone's life involves becoming familiar with the details and texture of her experiences and thoughts. Accepting the constant changes in a client's desires regarding her situation requires patience and attention to the reasons for the shifts in understanding and decisions. The mutual recognition of shared understanding and mutual projects that characterizes a collaborative relationship comes only after multiple interactions and much exploration in the search for common ground. Developing with a client creative and specifically tailored responses to her situation is a process that results only after lawyer and client have imagined and explored multiple possibilities.

NOTES AND QUESTIONS

1. **Rethinking the Lawyering Model.** As Ann Shalleck suggests, the model of lawyering with and on behalf of victims of domestic violence she describes is deeply informed by psychological theory and insight. One of the most helpful theorists in the domestic violence field is psychiatrist Judith Lewis Herman. In her pathbreaking 1992 book TRAUMA AND RECOVERY, Herman draws on the experiences of combat veterans, prisoners of war and battered women to explain the consequences of prolonged and chronic exposure to violence and abuse for those who suffer it, and also for those who work with survivors:

> This is a book about restoring connections: between the public and private worlds, between the individual and the community, between men and women. It is a book about commonalities: between rape survivors and combat veterans, between battered women and political prisoners, between the survivors of vast concentration camps and the survivors of small, hidden concentration camps created by tyrants who rule their homes.

An important focus for Herman is the survivor's path to recovery, and the ways in which helping professionals can assist, or hinder, that process. The next reading is an excerpt from the chapter of Herman's book called *A Healing Relationship*, which focuses on the work of therapy, and the task of the therapist, in the context of abuse. Lawyers and advocates are not therapists, and there are obviously important distinctions between the types of assistance and support they can provide a survivor of domestic violence. Nonetheless, much of what Herman says about the client-therapist relationship may have application to the lawyer-client, or advocate-client, relationship. As you read the next pages, ask yourself what aspects of Herman's analysis have relevance for the lawyer or advocate, and how many of her admonitions and recommendations have value, even in the different context of legal advocacy. One way to do that is to ask to what extent her analysis supports the model of lawyering described in the previous reading by Ann Shalleck.

Judith Lewis Herman
Trauma and Recovery (1992)

The core experiences of psychological trauma are disempowerment and disconnection from others. Recovery, therefore, is based upon the empowerment of the survivor and the creation of new connections. Recovery can take place only within the context of relationships; it cannot occur in isolation. In her renewed connections with other people, the survivor re-creates the psychological faculties that were damaged or deformed by the traumatic experience. These faculties include the basic capacities for trust, autonomy, initiative, competence, identity and intimacy. . . .

The first principle of recovery is the empowerment of the survivor. She must be the author and arbiter of her own recovery. Others may offer advice, support, assistance, affection and care, but not cure. Many benevolent and well-intentioned attempts to assist the survivor founder because this fundamental principle of empowerment is not observed. No intervention that takes power away from the survivor can possibly foster her recovery, no matter how much it appears to be in her immediate best interest. . . .

In exceptional circumstances, where the survivor has totally abdicated responsibility for her own self-care or threatens immediate harm to herself or to others, rapid intervention is required with or without her consent. But even then, there is no need for unilateral action; the survivor should still be consulted about her wishes and offered as much choice as is compatible with the preservation of safety. . . .

The therapy relationship is unique in several respects. First, its sole purpose is to promote the recovery of the patient. . . . Second, the therapy relationship is unique because of the contract between patient and therapist regarding the use of power. . . . It is the therapist's responsibility to use the power that has been conferred upon her only to foster the recovery of the patient, resisting all temptations to abuse. This promise, which is central to the integrity of any therapeutic relationship, is of special importance to patients who are already suffering as the result of another's arbitrary and exploitative exercise of power. . . .

The alliance of therapy cannot be taken for granted; it must be painstakingly built by the effort of both patient and therapist. Therapy requires a collaborative working relationship in which both partners act on the basis of their implicit confidence in the value and efficacy of persuasion rather than coercion, ideas rather than force, mutuality rather than authoritarian control. These are precisely the beliefs that have been shattered by the traumatic experience. Trauma damages the patient's ability to enter into a trusting relationship; it also has an indirect but powerful impact on the therapist. As a result, both patient and therapist will have predictable difficulties coming to a working alliance. These difficulties must be understood and anticipated from the outset.

TRAUMATIC TRANSFERENCE

Patients who suffer from a traumatic syndrome form a characteristic type of transference in the therapy relationship. Their emotional responses to any person in a position of authority have been deformed by the experience of terror. For this reason, traumatic transference reactions have an intense, life-or-death quality unparalleled in ordinary therapeutic experience. . . .

The traumatic transference reflects not only the experience of terror but also the experience of helplessness. . . . The greater the patient's emotional conviction of helplessness and abandonment, the more desperately she feels the need for an omnipotent rescuer. Often she casts the therapist in this role. She may develop intensely idealized expectations of the therapist. . . . When the therapist fails to live up to these idealized expectations—as she inevitably will fail—the patient is often overcome with fury. Because the patient feels as though her life depends upon her rescuer, she cannot afford to be tolerant; there is no room for human error. . . .

Though the traumatized patient feels a desperate need to rely on the integrity and competence of the therapist, she cannot do so, for her capacity to trust has been damaged by the traumatic experience. . . . The patient enters the therapeutic relationship prey to every sort of doubt and suspicion. She generally assumes that the therapist is either unable or unwilling to help. Until proven otherwise, she assumes that the therapist cannot bear to hear the true story of the trauma. Combat veterans will not form a trusting relationship until they are convinced that the therapist can stand to hear the details of the war story. Rape survivors, hostages, political prisoners, battered women, and Holocaust survivors feel a similar mistrust of the therapist's ability to listen. In the words of one incest survivor, "These therapists sound like they have all the answers, but they back away from the real shitty stuff." . . .

Patients who have been subjected to chronic trauma and therefore suffer from a complex post-traumatic syndrome also have complex transference reactions. The protracted involvement with the perpetrator has altered the patient's relational style, so that she not only fears repeated victimization, but also seems unable to protect herself from it, or even appears to invite it. The dynamics of dominance and submission are reenacted in all subsequent relationships, including the therapy.

Chronically traumatized patients have an exquisite attunement to unconscious and nonverbal communication. Accustomed over a long time to reading their captors' emotional and cognitive states, survivors bring this ability into the therapy relationship. . . .

The patient scrutinizes the therapist's every word and gesture, in an attempt to protect herself from the hostile reactions she expects. Because she has no confidence in the therapist's benign intentions, she persistently misinterprets the therapist's motives and reactions. The therapist may eventually react to these hostile attributions in unaccustomed ways. Drawn into the dynamics of dominance and submission, the therapist may inadvertently reenact aspects of the abusive relationship....

TRAUMATIC COUNTERTRANSFERENCE

Trauma is contagious. In the role of witness to disaster or atrocity, the therapist at times is emotionally overwhelmed. She experiences, to a lesser degree, the same terror, rage, and despair as the patient. This phenomenon is known as "traumatic countertransference" or "vicarious traumatization." ...

Engagement in this work thus poses some risk to the therapist's own psychological health. The therapist's adverse reactions, unless understood and contained, also predictably lead to disruptions in the therapeutic alliance with patients and to conflict with professional colleagues. Therapists who work with traumatized people require an ongoing support system to deal with these intense reactions. Just as no survivor can recover alone, no therapist can work with trauma alone....

In addition to suffering vicarious symptoms of post-traumatic stress disorder, the therapist has to struggle with the same disruptions in relationship as the patient. Repeated exposure to stories of human rapacity and cruelty inevitably challenges the therapist's basic faith. It also heightens her sense of personal vulnerability. She may become more fearful of other people in general and more distrustful even in close relationships.... The therapist also empathetically shares the patient's experience of helplessness....

As a defense against the unbearable feeling of helplessness, the therapist may try to assume the role of a rescuer. The therapist may take on more and more of an advocacy role for the patient. By so doing, she implies that the patient is not capable of acting for herself. The more the therapist accepts the idea that the patient is helpless, the more she perpetuates the traumatic transference and disempowers the patient.

Many seasoned and experienced therapists, who are ordinarily scrupulously observant of the limits of the therapy relationship, find themselves violating the bounds of therapy and assuming the role of a rescuer, under the intense pressures of traumatic transference and countertransference. The therapist may feel obliged to extend the limits of therapy sessions or to allow frequent emergency contacts between sessions. She may find herself answering phone calls late at night, on weekends, or even on vacations. Rarely do these extraordinary measures result in improvement; on the contrary, the more helpless, dependent, and incompetent the patient feels, generally the worse her symptoms become....

Emotional identification with the experience of the victim does not exhaust the range of the therapist's traumatic countertransference. In her role as a witness, the therapist is caught in a conflict between victim and perpetrator. She comes to identify not only with the feelings of the victim but also with those of the perpetrator.... The therapist may find herself becoming highly skeptical of the patient's story, or she may begin to minimize or rationalize the abuse. The therapist may feel revulsion and disgust at the patient's behavior, or she may become extremely judgmental and censorious when the patient fails to live up to some idealized notion of how a "good" victim ought to behave. She may begin to feel contempt for the patient's helplessness or paranoid fear of the patient's vindictive rage....

Traumatic transference and countertransference reactions are inevitable. Inevitably, too, these reactions interfere with the development of a good working relationship. Certain protections are required for the safety of both participants. The two most important guarantees of safety are the goals, rules and boundaries of the therapeutic contract and the support system of the therapist.

THE THERAPY CONTRACT

The alliance between patient and therapist develops through shared work. The work of therapy is both a labor of love and a collaborative commitment. Though the therapeutic alliance partakes of the customs of everyday contractual negotiations, it is not a simple business arrangement. And though it evokes all the passions of human attachment, it is not a love affair or a parent-child relationship. It is a relationship of existential engagement, in which both partners commit themselves to the task of recovery.

This commitment takes the form of a therapy contract. The terms of this contract are those required to promote a working alliance. Both parties are responsible for the relationship. Some of the tasks are the same for both patient and therapist, such as keeping appointments faithfully. Some tasks are different and complementary: the therapist contributes knowledge and skill, while the patient pays a fee for treatment; the therapist promises confidentiality, while the patient agrees to self-disclosure; the therapist promises to listen and bear witness, while the patient promises to tell the truth. The therapy contract should be explained to the patient explicitly and in detail....

The patient enters the therapy relationship with severe damage to her capacity for appropriate trust. Since trust is not present at the outset of the treatment, both therapist and patient should be prepared for repeated testing, disruption, and rebuilding of the therapeutic relationship. As the patient becomes involved, she inevitably re-experiences the intense longing for rescue that she felt at the time of the trauma. The therapist may also wish, consciously or unconsciously, to compensate for the atrocious experiences the patient has endured. Impossible expectations are inevitably aroused, and inevitably disappointed. The rageful struggles that follow upon disappointment may replicate the initial, abusive situation, compounding the original harm.

Careful attention to the boundaries of the therapeutic relationship provides the best protection against excessive, unmanageable transference and countertransference reactions. Secure boundaries create a safe arena where the work of recovery can proceed. The therapist agrees to be available to the patient within limits that are clear, reasonable, and tolerable for both. The boundaries of therapy exist for the benefit and protection of both parties and are based upon a recognition of both the therapist's and the patient's legitimate needs. These boundaries include an explicit understanding that the therapy contract precludes any other form of social relationship, a clear definition of the frequency and duration of therapy sessions, and clear ground rules regarding emergency contact outside of regularly scheduled sessions. . . .

The therapist does not insist upon clear boundaries in order to control, ration, or deprive the patient. Rather, the therapist acknowledges from the outset that she is a limited, fallible human being, who requires certain conditions in order to remain in an emotionally demanding relationship. . . .

Therapists usually discover that some degree of flexibility is also necessary; mutually acceptable boundaries are not created by fiat but rather result from a process of negotiation and may evolve to some degree over time. A patient describes her view of the process: "My psychiatrist has what he calls 'rules,' which I have defined as 'moving targets.' The boundaries he has set between us seem flexible, and I often try to bend and stretch them. Sometimes he struggles with these boundaries, trying to balance his rules against his respect for me as a human being. As I watch him struggle, I learn how to struggle with my own boundaries, not just the ones between him and me, but those between me and everyone I deal with in the real world." . . .

THE THERAPIST'S SUPPORT SYSTEM

The dialectic of trauma constantly challenges the therapist's emotional balance. The therapist, like the patient, may defend against overwhelming feelings by withdrawal or by impulsive, intrusive action. The most common forms of action are rescue attempts, boundary violations, or attempts to control the patient. The most common constrictive responses are doubting or denial of the patient's reality, dissociation or numbing, minimization or avoidance of the traumatic material, professional distancing, or frank abandonment of the patient. Some degree of intrusion or numbing is probably inevitable. The therapist should expect to lose her balance from time to time with such patients. She is not infallible. The guarantee of her integrity is not her omnipotence but her capacity to trust others. The work of recovery requires a secure and reliable support system for the therapist.

Ideally, the therapist's support system should include a safe, structured, and regular forum for reviewing her clinical work. This might be a supervisory relationship or a peer support group, preferably both. The setting must offer permission to express emotional reactions as well as technical or intellectual concerns related to the treatment of patients with histories of trauma. . . .

Unless the therapist is able to find others who understand and support her work, she will eventually find her world narrowing, leaving her alone with the patient. The therapist may come to feel that she is the only one who understands the patient, and she may become increasingly arrogant and adversarial with skeptical colleagues. As she feels increasingly isolated and helpless, the temptations of either grandiosity or flight become irresistible. Sooner or later she will indeed make serious errors. It cannot be reiterated too often: *no one can face trauma alone.* If a therapist finds herself isolated in her professional practice, she should discontinue working with traumatized patients until she has secured an adequate support system. . . .

The reward of engagement is the sense of an enriched life. . . . By constantly fostering the capacity for integration, in themselves and their patients, engaged therapists deepen their own integrity. Just as basic trust is the developmental achievement of earliest life, integrity is the developmental achievement of maturity. . . .

Integrity is the capacity to affirm the value of life in the face of death, to be reconciled with the finite limits of one's own life and the tragic limitations of the human condition, and to accept these realities without despair. Integrity is the foundation upon which trust in relationships is originally formed, and upon which shattered trust may be restored. The interlocking of integrity and trust in caretaking relationships completes the cycle of generations and regenerates the sense of human community which trauma destroys.

NOTES AND QUESTIONS

1. **Empowerment.** In suggesting that the first principle of recovery for survivors is empowerment, Herman acknowledges that: "Caregivers schooled in a medical model of treatment often have difficulty grasping this fundamental principle and putting it into practice." Do you think lawyers would have more or less difficulty than doctors? What about non-lawyer advocates? What has your legal education taught you so far about the nature of the relationships with clients you should anticipate, or work toward?

2. **Overriding the Victim's Empowerment.** Herman states very categorically that: "no intervention that takes power away from the survivor can possibly foster her recovery." She then suggests that there may be exceptional cases where the survivor's safety, or the safety of others, may justify overriding the principle of empowerment. Might there be situations when a lawyer or advocate would similarly be justified in overriding a client's autonomy? What would those situations be? Should they be as exceptional in the legal context as Herman argues they should be in the context of therapy? For a discussion of how lawyers might handle the ethical dilemmas involved in representing abused clients, see Dana Harrington Conner, *To Protect or to Serve: Confidentiality, Client Protection, & Domestic Violence*, 79 TEMP. REV. 877 (2006).

3. **Disengaged Therapists.** Herman argues that the ideal stance of the therapist is one of disinterest and neutrality. Taken out of context, those characteristics sound unappealing, and even inappropriate. How would you

explain their meaning, and their importance, to someone who had not read Herman's account?

4.   **Relevance to the Lawyer–Client Relationship.** How much of what Herman has to say about the therapist-patient relationship do you think is relevant to the lawyer-client, or advocate-client relationship? If you believe that the dynamics of the relationships are similar enough in some respects that the lawyer or advocate should expect to experience some of the same difficulties as the therapist, are Herman's prescriptions realistic for the lawyer or advocate? Is there a difference in this regard between the professional who works exclusively, or almost exclusively, with battered women, and the family lawyer, prosecutor or criminal defense lawyer who works on occasion with a survivor of partner violence, but does not maintain a specialized practice?

In the next reading Joan Meier suggests ways in which the roles of psychological and legal professionals are similar and different, and what the differences may imply for how those roles will play out.

Joan S. Meier

Notes From the Underground: Integrating Psychological and Legal Perspectives on Domestic Violence in Theory and Practice

21 HOFSTRA L. REV. 1295 (1993).

. . . The analogy between therapists and lawyers stems from their common commitment to "helping" or serving individuals who are their clients. This commonality is profound; indeed, the lawyer's role as "advocate" for the client is probably the most essential aspect of her role, and the fundamental attribute of the therapeutic role is the therapist's unconditional acceptance of and commitment to the patient on a psychological level. Nonetheless, the methods which lawyers and therapists use to help their clients differ profoundly. At root, the lawyer's role is to act as an advocate for the client vis a vis other people and institutions in the world. The therapist's role is characterized primarily by his or her limitation to private, confidential communication only with the patient, as a supportive listener in an isolated one-on-one interaction, without communication or advocacy in the larger world on the patient's behalf. . . .

From this fundamental difference flow several potential differences in the way the professional roles must be played out with clients.

a.   Goals and Methods of Information–Gathering

First, the difference in methods means that psychologists and lawyers need information for different purposes. Psychological professionals need information to a large extent as an end in itself. . . . Lawyers, on the other hand, need information so that they may take legal action on the client's behalf in the legal system to achieve the client's goals. . . .

In short, the lawyer's role in "interviewing" the client is both narrower and broader than the therapist's role. It is narrower, in that only a limited portion of the client's life, feelings, or concerns are relevant to the legal matter. It is broader in that the lawyer needs to go beyond the client, to explore other sources of information. . . .

With respect to the broader aspect, i.e., the lawyer's need to search for "proof," corroboration, and contradictions of the client's point of view, the lawyer's investigations into the external facts is potentially more alienating to the client than the ideal therapeutic exchange. . . . [I]n the legal context, unlike the therapeutic context, confrontations of the client (albeit sympathetic and gentle ones) are often necessary. . . .

b. The Need for Lawyers to Take Action on Behalf of Clients

. . . Insofar as the lawyer's role requires her to act "expressively" on behalf of the client, in ways that both affect her own reputation and professional relationships, and also affect third parties, she is personally involved in and affected by client decisions far more than the typical therapist. The lawyer thus must frequently discuss decisions, actions, and tactics with clients, sometimes engaging in persuasion or expressing her own views. In addition, the morally engaged lawyer may need to engage the client in "moral dialogue" with respect to actions desired by the client but about which the lawyer feels moral qualms. . . .

c. The Need for Clients to Make Decisions

The action orientation of legal representation also means that a central part of the lawyer-client relationship entails assisting clients in making decisions, often quickly. This is in complete contrast to the therapeutic relationship in which decisions regarding action by the client are, if not discouraged, certainly not considered an integral element of most mainstream types of psychotherapy. Most directly, this means that the lawyer-client relationship typically entails far more "counseling" or input by the lawyer, than the typical therapist-patient relationship. Lawyers must, at a minimum, describe and interpret legal procedures and options, and the risks and consequences of different tactics, so the client can make a timely "informed" choice about these actions. Stephen Ellman suggests that one consequence of this greater involvement of the professional in client decisions is that overt expression of "approval" may be more appropriate and beneficial in the lawyer-client relationship than it has traditionally been considered to be in the therapeutic relationship. It may be posited that another consequence is, very simply, the need for greater input by the legal professional than the psychological professional. In short, lawyers must learn how to "advise" clients. This means they must develop their own abilities to assess legal options and consequences, but also means developing a sensitivity to the boundaries between appropriate "informing," "counseling" or "advising" and inappropriate control over decisions which should be made by the clients.

NOTES AND QUESTIONS

1. **Differences Between Lawyer and Therapist.** Do you agree with this assessment of the differences between the roles of therapist and lawyer or advocate? To the extent you do, do you think the differences affect the applicability of the principles outlined by Judith Herman to good legal advocacy on behalf of battered women clients? How would Herman react, do you think, to the idea of a lawyer or advocate explicitly "approving" a client's decision?

2. **Why Women May Not Want Help.** Herman comments that battered women may approach relationships with helping professionals "prey to every sort of doubt and suspicion." In the legal arena, those doubts and suspicions are too often based in a recalcitrant reality. However, Herman's insight makes it easier to understand why women who have been victims of abuse might abandon their efforts to secure help from the legal system, or law enforcement, after just one negative experience—where individuals who have a greater capacity for trust might persist in their help-seeking efforts. On the other hand, Herman also notes that victims' "intense perceptiveness," when combined with doubt and suspicion, can result in misinterpretations of a helping professional's motives and reactions.

3. **Empowering Clients.** The final reading in this section is drawn from a manual used at Northeastern University School of Law in a clinical program training law students to advocate for battered women. As you read it, ask yourself whether it implements Judith Herman's vision of a client-empowering relationship, and incorporates the lessons she teaches about the impact of trauma.

Lois H. Kanter and V. Pualani Enos
Client–Centered Interviewing and Counseling Skills

DOMESTIC VIOLENCE MANUAL: VOLUME ONE.
(DOMESTIC VIOLENCE INSTITUTE, NUSL, 1999).

1. *Client Empowering Interviewing Skills for the Battered Women's Advocate*

Many women will readily talk about the violence if they feel safe and supported. The purpose of this section is to aid the interviewer in creating a safe and supportive environment in which to assist the woman in exploring her options while respecting her right to self-determination. It is crucial that the interviewer consistently remind the woman that violence is unacceptable and that she is not to blame. In order to empower and assist her in making an informed choice, the following steps are suggested: . . .

a. Validating the woman's experience:

Empathize with her and validate her feelings. Because the abuser blames her for the violence and because society frequently does nothing to stop the assaults, many battered women feel that they are responsible for the violence. The advocate needs to take a stand against the violence and make an alliance with the battered woman so that she can talk about her confusion, fear, guilt, anger and pain. The advocate must also articulate a clear set of beliefs about the unacceptability of violence. However, it is important to remember that you cannot define the experience for her or suggest that you know more about this than she does.

Take some time to explain the interview process to her and to let her know that she should stop you at any point to ask questions, make comments or simply tell you that she's not comfortable continuing the interview. You'll be asking her some very personal questions dealing with experiences that she may not even have revealed to those closest to her. Talking about the violence and coercion can be embarrassing, humiliating and even frightening and you are virtually a stranger to her. Therefore, it's important that you take the time necessary to make her feel as comfortable with you as possible.

However, to reassure the novice interviewer, we've found that once your initial explanations are made, the simple statement "I'm here because I am most concerned about your safety. Can you explain to me what happened to bring you here (to the court, to the office, etc.) today?" is often an easy way to begin a two-way conversation. Thereafter, by asking short, simple questions which encourage the woman to "think aloud" about her situation, her concerns and her objectives, the novice will frequently discover that the task of exploring options while respecting the client's right to make decisions is not quite as difficult as it first appears.

It is important to listen carefully to what she says and to make no assumptions. Give her plenty of time to answer each of your questions and to ask her own. Understand that some of the information will be very difficult for her to convey.

Ask her directly about the violence, If the advocate avoids talking about it, so will the woman. . . . Do not lapse into "legalese." Support her for telling her story. If English is not her native language, and she feels more comfortable speaking in her native language, consider asking her to bring a friend to interpret or arrange for an interpreter if possible. . . .

Convey that you do not believe that she is responsible for the violence. No matter what she's done, including striking back, drinking or taking drugs, the assailant is responsible for the abuse. Advocates need to reiterate that the violence is criminal and wrong, and no one deserves to be abused.

Universalize the information. Let her know that she's not alone, that many women have been trapped in violent relationships feeling isolated, discouraged and ashamed. . . .

b.   Reminding her of and building her strengths:

Many women who are battered have extremely poor or no self-esteem. Anyone who is consistently and repeatedly told that he or she is worthless, while being isolated from other people who could contradict this information, will in time doubt his or her own worth. Since women in our society are often treated less respectfully to begin with, a woman is even more vulnerable to attacks on her self-confidence and self-worth.

Battered women, though doubting themselves, are actually strong and courageous, but they need to be reminded of this. Battered women are not passive recipients of abuse. Rather, they constantly try to stop the violence and protect themselves and their children. Their thoughtfulness is often invisible to the outsider because frequently, in the face of erratic and irrational assault, it is best to proceed very cautiously and by means tailored to meet the needs of the individual woman's situation.

Acknowledge her strengths, the specific ways that she has protected herself and her children, methods she used to leave the abuse or maintain her sanity, the courage she demonstrates by telling you about the violence or calling for help.

c.   Avoiding victim-blaming:

One of the most common and damaging mistakes an advocate can make is to frame a question or statement in such a way as to appear to be blaming the victim for the violence. Questions that suggest that her behavior can trigger the violence or that she is in any way responsible for the violence are offensive, inappropriate and even dangerous; they can help to perpetuate the woman's feeling that she should take partial (or even sole) responsibility for the violence.

Do not ask questions that blame the victim like "What keeps you with a man like that? Do you get something out of the violence? Is all this worth the financial security? What did you do at that moment that caused him to hit you? What could you have done to de-escalate the situation? Is there any way you participate in the escalation of the violence?"

If the children have been abused as well or were witnesses to her abuse, do not blame her for his abuse even indirectly. Avoid questions such as "How can you keep your children in this situation? How can you allow your children to go through this? How could you not know what was happening to your child? or How could you let him do that to your child?"

d.   Exploring her options while advocating for her safety:

1.   *Identifying Support Systems:* Ask her about support she may have from friends, relatives or co-workers. Are there people who would help her in terms of temporary housing, child care or even appearing in court as a witness on her behalf. Find out if she knows about shelters and/or support groups in her area. Give her referral numbers to these programs if she doesn't already have them . . . .

2.   *Identifying Legal Options:* The advocate should explain both criminal and civil options available so that the woman can make an informed choice about how she wants to proceed if she chooses to use the legal system.

3.   *Assistance If She Chooses to Take No Legal Action*: It is important to tell every battered woman that you are concerned about her safety and to plan together for her protection.

Remember that *she is an expert about the batterer*, and that she, not you, must live with her choices. Do not choose for her. Rather, help her assess her options and the potential consequences of her decisions. When battered women choose to live with their partners, safety is still a priority. If you are not developing a formal safety plan with her, ask some of the following questions as you discuss safety:

- How can we help ensure safety? What do you feel you need in order to be safe?

- Can I safely call you? How should I identify myself when I call? What should I do if the abuser answers the telephone?

- If the violence escalates, can you leave for a few days? Do you have a place to go and the telephone numbers for shelters?

- Is there a car available; have you a hidden set of keys? Do you have any money that you can hide in case of emergency?

- Can you run to a neighbor's or work out a signal so that the neighbor calls the police?

- Do you understand how you can request protective orders on an emergency basis in the evening or on weekends?

e.   Respecting her right to self-determination:

Once the advocate has explored with the battered woman the options available to her, the woman must make a choice as to what course of action she wishes to take. Sometimes the choice will be to do nothing. While it is the advocate's role to lay out the options available to her, and even, if asked, to recommend a course of action, once the woman has made her choice the advocate must respect it. It is inappropriate, for instance, to communicate even indirectly or nonverbally that you are disappointed or dissatisfied with her choice.

Battered women are adults who are making virtually impossible choices under extremely difficult circumstances. They must be allowed to make decisions for themselves. Be sure that you are sensitive to this and keep the following suggestions in mind during your conversations with her:

- Do not bully the woman or mandate conditions for your help. Do not say things such as "I can't do anything for you unless you leave him." Instead, ask questions like: "In what way can I be helpful to you?" and "What do you want to do?"

- Allow women to talk about their ambivalence toward the batterer. No one gives up a relationship without a struggle. "How will it feel if he moves out?" and "Is it sad to think about not being with him?"

- Respect her pace in the process. Frequently we urge the impossible. By pressuring her, we may do more damage than good by making her feel out of control in the process and, therefore, more vulnerable, or by placing her in a position of greater danger because we haven't listened to her assessment of what action is safe and appropriate. Encourage her to trust her gut by saying things like, "You seem to make choices which are good for you and your kids," and "It's OK to take it one step at a time." Also remember that some battered women leave and return to their partners several times. Then it is important to say, "Someone will always be available to talk if you want to."

- Accept that each woman must find solutions that she can live with.... Be sensitive and respectful of cultural, class and religious differences which may affect the choices she makes.

Conclusion: Many of the interviewing techniques described above are appropriate and helpful in any legal interview. However, in cases involving battered women, these techniques are even more crucial because of the level of danger involved and the vulnerability of the women being interviewed. It is absolutely critical that the woman feel as comfortable and safe as possible in order to ensure that she can discuss every aspect of her case, even those experiences which are painful, humiliating and extremely intimate. Good interviewing skills can make a tremendous difference in the case in the long run and are worth the extra time and sensitivity required.

2. *Additional Tips Applicable to Interviewing Battered Women*

Listening and Giving Support

- Be real. People in crisis are very sensitive to others; they will catch you hiding behind a role.

- You need to decide when to set limits. You can set them by bartering or by standing firm on your own determination. Trust your gut.

- A woman may need space to freak out before calming down and talking.

- A lot of crisis counseling is bearing witness to her pain—allowing her to go through it but staying with her.

- Maintain eye contact, even if she doesn't she will be aware of it.

- Maintain a respectful, non-judgmental attitude toward the woman (not necessarily toward her actions).

- Give criticism in a form of "I feel . . . when you do. . . ."

- Show empathy by feeding back what you hear. Paraphrase.

- Look for subtitles—e.g., "I am so tired of it all" may be subtitled "I want to kill myself"; figure out what is behind what she is talking about, especially if time is a problem.

- Take all she said and make it simpler, classify and present it back to her.

- Prioritize together; decide what needs to be dealt with first and start with that. Either deal with items in turn or give some idea of when others might be dealt with.

- Try to present options. People in crisis often think they don't have options.

- Don't get into "why" during crisis, it may avoid getting to closure.

- Watch when she seems to have gone through the needed crisis and is holding onto crisis. Use your own sense of fatigue or boredom. Lay it out that you are tired and need to set limits.

- Make sure you get back to her, touch base again within the next few days.

- Take part in peer supervision; get feedback on your own process, feelings, places you felt you did well or not well.

Contradict the Batterer

Frequently battered women come to us with messages their partners have worked hard to instill. These messages may be supported by the media and other members of the community. Every interaction with a survivor provides an opportunity to provide an alternative message, one which encourages help-seeking and supports the skills women do have. The following are examples of ways in which an advocate can contradict the batterer's disempowering and abusive messages:

Batterer says: "No one cares about you"

We say: "I AM WORRIED ABOUT YOU" "IS THERE ANYTHING YOU WANT TO TALK ABOUT"

Batterer says: "This is all your fault. If only you didn't . . ."

We say: "NO ONE DESERVES TO BE HURT. YOU DIDN'T DO ANYTHING TO CAUSE THIS"

Batterer says: "No one will believe you"

We say: "IT SOUNDS LIKE YOU HAD VERY GOOD REASON TO BE AFRAID" "I AGREE THAT WHAT HE DID WAS VERY DANGEROUS" "I AM VERY CONCERNED FOR YOUR SAFETY" "I KNOW HOW DIFFICULT IT IS TO TALK ABOUT THESE ISSUES. THANK YOU FOR TRUSTING ME WITH SOMETHING SO IMPORTANT"

Batterer says: "If you leave me, you'll have nowhere to go"

We say: "THERE IS SOMEONE HERE FOR YOU TO TALK TO BOTH DURING THE DAY AND AT NIGHT. YOU CAN COME ANYTIME" "WE CAN TELL YOU ABOUT OTHER RESOURCES AND SERVICES AND SUPPORT YOU TO ACCESS THEM"

Batterer says: "You are crazy"

We say: "ANYONE FACING THOSE CIRCUMSTANCES WOULD HAVE FELT AND REACTED THE WAY YOU DID"

Batterer says: "You are stupid. You need me. You wouldn't survive without me"

We say: "I TRUST YOU TO MAKE THE RIGHT DECISIONS" "I BELIEVE THAT YOU KNOW WHAT IS BEST FOR YOU" "I HAVE FAITH IN YOUR ABILITY TO MAKE DECISIONS AND ACT ON YOUR OWN BEHALF"

Batterer says: "You are weak"

We say: . . . "WE ADMIRE YOUR STRENGTH AND COURAGE"

Batterer says: "You will do as I say or you will suffer"

We say: "WE WILL SUPPORT ANY DECISIONS YOU MAKE" "WE RESPECT YOUR RIGHT TO CHOOSE"

NOTES AND QUESTIONS

1. **Self–Care and Client Counseling.** Judith Herman is adamant about the need for professionals working with those who have experienced trauma to engage in "self-care." Specifically, she talks about setting appropriate limits with clients, about guarding against over-commitment, about finding room in one's life for relaxation and pleasure, and about working in an environment in which there is sufficient support, ideally among peers, but at a minimum from a clinical supervisor. These conditions may be harder for lawyers and legal advocates to secure than for those working in the mental health field, where concepts of self-care are better established, and clinical supervision traditionally includes attention to the clinician's own emotional state. Ironically, lawyers and legal advocates working with domestic violence victims may have chosen their work in part because it gave them the freedom to reject overly distanced and professionalized models of lawyering—they may, that is to say, be particularly vulnerable to the temptations of doing too much for their clients and not maintaining appropriate boundaries.

On the other hand, anyone who has worked in this field has either experienced, or witnessed, burnout, and Herman offers a compelling explanation both of why this happens, and of what to do to guard against it. She is also clear that self-care by professionals enhances rather than detracts from the service they provide to their clients. It is worth careful attention, therefore, on the part of students, advocates and lawyers in the many different settings in which they work, to the ways in which they can create and maintain a working environment sufficiently attentive to their own needs.

2. **Lawyers and Substance Abuse.** According to the American Bar Association, Commission on Lawyer Assistance Programs, while approximately 10% of the population has problems with alcohol abuse, anywhere between 15–18% of lawyers suffer from these problems. There is no evidence that the type of law one practices has an impact on substance abuse. Those who practice law in a domestic violence field do not have higher rates of substance abuse or depression than those who focus on other areas. Yet it is important for all lawyers to have support systems in place to help them deal with the stresses of practice that can lead to depression and substance abuse. For more information on how lawyers can find support services, see http://www.abanet.org/legalservices/colap/.

3. **Representing Abusers.** Many lawyers, be they public defenders, family law attorneys, civil lawyers, or private defense counsel, will find themselves representing someone accused of abuse. There is very little written about dilemmas lawyers may face in these situations. In a recent article, *Representing Defendants in Domestic Violence Prosecutions: Interview with a Public Defender*, 11 J. CONTEMP. LEGAL ISSUES 63 (2000), Renee Harrison interviews Marian Gaston of the San Diego Public Defender's

Office who specializes in domestic violence cases. As noted earlier, San Diego has one of the most aggressive prosecution programs in the country. Gaston stresses the importance of keeping an open mind and not becoming too jaded when representing those accused of abuse. She also suggests that there are some cases in which the state gets it wrong and the allegations of abuse are untrue. What do you think the role of attorneys in these situations ought to be? Is the goal to find the truth, or zealously represent your client's wishes? What kind of support ought to be available to public defenders who routinely represent those accused of intimate violence?

4.   **The Duty to Warn.** Assume that you are a public defender representing Brett Jones, a 35 year-old male accused of stalking his ex-girlfriend Susan Stafford. While the couple was together, Jones allegedly hit Stafford and threatened to kill her. She received a restraining order against him, but never filed criminal charges. Since the couple broke-up, Jones has been following Stafford, calling her constantly at home and at work, and has been telling her friends and family how he wants her back. Stafford filed criminal charges. Jones was arrested and released on bail. Jones has remarked to you on three occasions that he can't live without Stafford, and that not being with her is making him crazy. He has also told you that Stafford seems to be dating someone else, although how he knows this he refused to disclose. Yesterday, when you called to tell him the date of the pretrial hearing, he told you that he had a dream that he killed Stafford. He then says, "If I do it, it's only because she has driven me mad." This remark alarmed you, given Jones' tone and anxious demeanor. You suspect that Jones has access to a gun. What ethical or moral obligations, if any, do you have to either report your client to the police or the court, or to warn Stafford that she could be in further danger? How can you be sure that Jones is serious? How would your duty to warn conflict with your duty of rigorous representation of your client? For a discussion of the lawyer's obligation in this situation, see John M. Burman, *Lawyers and Domestic Violence: Raising the Standard of Practice*, 9 MICH.J. GENDER & L. 207 (2003).

In *Don't Ask, Do Tell: Rethinking the Lawyer's Duty to Warn in Domestic Violence Cases*, 75 U. Cin. L. Rev. 447 (2006), Sarah Buel and Margaret Drew argue that in the context of these cases, lawyers have an affirmative duty to screen clients who have a likelihood for harming others, to attempt to dissuade them from carrying out their planned attacks, and to warn victims whom their clients have threatened. They argue:

> A lawyer's silence constitutes collusion with the batterer and likely malpractice for it reflects an unethical position that is no longer acceptable. Most lawyers and members of the public express outrage when yet another battered woman is murdered, but that disdain appears short-lived. In reference to intimate partner abuse, Professor Kristian Miccio asserts,

> [I]t is more than cultural amnesia that facilitates violence. It is a failure of will.... However, the perpetuation of such violence requires more than the act of an individual male. It requires state condonation of such violence.... Although we speak of accountability, we have

neither the collective will nor the inclination to hold our selves or the architects of such violence accountable.

As lawyers we are facilitators of a legal system premised on a duty to do justice and engage in ethical practice. It is difficult to imagine how that foundation can be squared with maintaining silence while in possession of information that can save a victim's life. Attorney inaction may reflect troublesome minimization and denial about the potential danger to victims, but ignorance about the issue demands remedial education—it in no way relieves the lawyer of responsibility to avoid complicity in a pending crime.

Do you agree that lawyers are complicit in domestic violence when they do not warn potential victims? How does such a view square with lawyer-client confidentiality? How can lawyers be sure the threats their clients make are credible?

B.   LEGAL ADVOCACY: A CHANGED AND CHANGING LANDSCAPE

There has been much progress made on behalf of battered victims and their families since the inception of the modern battered women's movement. As we have seen throughout this book, lawyers have not been alone in those efforts, but have worked side-by-side with advocates, social workers, health care professionals, psychologists, and many others. In this next excerpt, Emily Sack describes the innovative approaches now being used throughout the country.

Emily J. Sack

Battered Women and the State: The Struggle for the Future of Domestic Violence Policy

2004 WIS.L.REV. 1657 (2004).

An important lesson learned from initial implementation of the new laws and policies has been that they are far less effective when utilized in isolation. For example, mandatory arrest does not have much deterrent effect if the batterer is not prosecuted for the offense. Prosecutions have little impact if the court provides minimal or no sanctions for domestic violence convictions. None of these policies will be effective if there is no monitoring of defendants' compliance with court-imposed sanctions and imposition of consequences for failures to comply.

Similarly, although a growing number of states passed laws that criminalized the violation of civil protection orders, in many jurisdictions, these violations were infrequently detected by law enforcement if they did not occur in conjunction with a new substantive criminal offense. Even where charges on violations were brought, the violators were rarely prosecuted. Policymakers and practitioners came to recognize that an effective domestic violence response required the coordination and integration of all parts of the justice system, as well as community-based victim advocates who could provide counseling and services to domestic violence victims. Diverse members of the community who interact with domestic violence victims are part of the response under this approach. In addition, public education campaigns for the community at large are also part of a community response. These campaigns raise public awareness, help to change societal norms about domestic violence, and provide support to battered women, as well as aid in domestic violence prevention efforts.

By the 1990s, "coordinated community response" became the catchword that embodied this policy, which was supported by battered women's advocates as well as institutional actors. The DOJ has demonstrated its support of this policy by requiring communities seeking grants under the VAWA to show interagency coordination and integrated response to domestic violence that, in particular, includes collaboration with nongovernmental victim advocacy organizations. The policy of coordinated community response has had barely a decade to take effect throughout the country. The funding support through the Office on Violence Against Women of the DOJ has been highly influential in bringing this policy to many jurisdictions nationwide, but there are still many areas that have not undertaken this effort. Moreover, a truly coordinated response is a complex and ongoing project, and even in those jurisdictions that are implementing such policies, they continue to be works-in-progress.

Preliminary studies have demonstrated that this coordinated response has greater impact in reducing domestic violence than any single reform implemented in isolation, and is currently the most promising response to domestic violence. For example, Professors Maryann Syers and Jeffrey Edleson have published a study of the Minneapolis Intervention Project, which coordinated efforts on misdemeanor domestic violence assault cases in two police precincts. This project included mandatory arrest upon probable cause of domestic assault or violation of a protection order, and coordination with victim advocates who reached out to victims and offered a variety of services. Local jails also held the arrested men for several hours or until the following morning to provide increased protection to the victims, and give time for victim advocates to reach out to victims. Prosecutors worked with other partners to proceed on these cases aggressively. Probation officers conducted comprehensive presentence investigations for the court, which adopted consistent and more stringent sentencing policies. Advocates worked with victims throughout the court process, linked them to various services including housing and job training, and assisted them with civil matters, such as protection orders, custody, and child support.

The study collected data from several sources, including follow-up with victims at six and twelve months after the incident. At the twelve-month point, those batterers arrested and court-mandated to treatment were least likely to be reported as recidivating. The authors conclude: "The results appear to support the combination of police making arrests on first visits with the use of mandated treatment by the courts as a consequence. The strength of this finding appears to increase the longer men are monitored." The follow-up by the court after arrest appeared to be significant for the outcomes and the "combination of interventions . . . appears to be the most consistent model for predicting lower recidivism rates."

An important component of a coordinated response is the recognition that there are several opportunities for contact with domestic violence victims throughout the community, all of which provide the potential for outreach and access to comprehensive services. Contact can be achieved through the pediatrician to whom a domestic violence victim takes her children, as well as through a local hospital. It can also be through the criminal justice system, when a perpetrator is arrested. Criminal justice intervention provides an important point of entry for victims, and an effective coordinated response will utilize that critical moment to provide services to the victim and her children. Many effective coordinated responses have linked victim advocates to either police or prosecutors so that the advocates can reach out to victims very early in a criminal case to offer them counseling, safety planning, and emergency services, as well as longer-term assistance and referrals. This includes community-based advocates who are not affiliated with any governmental agency, who are simply utilizing the arrest as a point of contact with the victim. These advocates routinely provide services, referrals, and counseling, whether a victim wants to proceed with the criminal case or not.

The federal government has also continued to expand its funding for battered women's services that are part of a coordinated and community-based response. The VAWA-funded grants were never devoted exclusively to support of criminal justice agencies, and from the start included extensive funding for independent battered women's advocacy organizations. These grants have expanded over the years to include significant funding for civil legal assistance for battered women, as well as support of supervised visitation services in domestic violence cases. The DOJ has also recognized the importance of bringing a broad array of services together in one locale to make them more accessible and provide better coordination for battered women. In July of 2004, the DOJ awarded over twenty million dollars to support the creation of Family Justice Centers in several jurisdictions nationwide. Victims of domestic violence will no longer have to travel from agency to agency to obtain services and navigate numerous different systems. The Family Justice Centers will bring several services "together under one roof," including independent victim advocates, civil legal assistance, prosecutors, and police.

. . . When their jobs require that they become involved in the handling of domestic violence cases, law enforcement, prosecutors, and judges begin to recognize the need to work with advocates for battered women. While they may have come to the table somewhat reluctantly, in many communities these institutional partners have come to value the expertise and insights offered by community-based advocates, as well as numerous other community partners. And, as they work with diverse elements of the community, these institutional actors begin to identify with the coordinated project, and become committed to it. In another study of a coordinated community response in several communities, Denise Gamache and her coauthors identified the development of this critical component, which is not captured by quantitative data:

Those in the police and judicial systems cooperate more fully as they begin to see their own role in the CIPs [community intervention projects] as helping to carry out the law to the fullest extent. By creating this shared goal, many in participating police departments and judicial systems begin to see themselves as partial owners of CIPs and begin to invest in their success.

Mandatory policies have direct effects, measured in increased arrests and prosecutions. But, they also have indirect impacts—greater sensitivity to domestic violence by the criminal justice system, and recognition of the need to work in concert with advocates and other parts of the community. Coordinated community response means more than the criminal justice system, but without these institutional partners, it cannot work effectively. There are additional benefits to a coordinated community response that includes law enforcement and the court system, such as the reduction of a batterer's ability to manipulate the justice system, the creation of ongoing collaboration among diverse community groups, and increased understanding of the dynamics of domestic violence among both institutional and community-based partners.

1. Reduction in Manipulation of the Justice System by Batterers.

A serious concern raised by advocates who criticize the mandatory policies is the ability of batterers to exploit the lack of coordination in the justice system. When the justice system increased its response to domestic violence, including improved access to protection orders and mandatory arrest policies, it also created a wealth of additional options for abusers determined to manipulate the system to control their partners. This lack of coordination has permitted batterers to manipulate the increased response to domestic violence to intimidate or harass their victims.

An integrated community response also includes coordination among court systems, as well as among the agencies that work with the court. Communication among judges, connection between databases, and coordination between agencies can help to identify this manipulation when it exists and respond to it quickly and effectively. For example, a civil protection order court can access a database for child custody and visitation cases to see if there is a related custody matter involving the parties. Databases providing protection order history that are accessible to law enforcement can help them to determine who the primary physical aggressor in a domestic violence incident is, helping to reduce dual arrests and arrests of actual victims. A coordinated community response, including coordination of the criminal justice and other justice system components, can help to reduce some negative outcomes of the mandatory policies that are caused, in part, by batterer manipulation.

2. Prevention Strategies

Efforts to educate community members about the dynamics of domestic violence and the creation of programs designed to aid in the prevention of this violence are other elements integral to a comprehensive community response. For example, school-based programs for children at different age levels have been developed, which focus on personal safety and injury prevention in trusting relationships; for older children, these programs also include direct discussion of domestic violence, sexual assault, alternatives to violence, and personal responsibility. Preliminary evaluations of such programs have been encouraging.

3. Procedural Justice

There has also been promising work done on the effects of procedural fairness in the criminal justice system on defendant compliance. In addition, the manner in which law enforcement, prosecutors, and judges treat the victims of domestic violence may be an important factor in their decision-making process and their acceptance of assistance and services. One study analyzed data on 825 cases from April of 1987 to August of 1988 originally collected for one of the Minneapolis experiment replication studies. The results showed that abusers' perceptions of procedural justice and fair treatment by the police are important factors in the propensity for future conduct, and have a statistically significant recidivism-inhibiting effect. For those suspects who were arrested, there was no evidence that the length of the suspects' detention or their "stake in conformity" affected the beneficial impact on outcomes of perceived procedural justice. Several researchers and commentators have noted that victims' satisfaction with police response is related, at least in part, to the actual quality of the personal conduct and demeanor of the officer. This is also true of victims' contact with judges. In a substantial review of battered women's experiences with the court system, Professor James Ptacek concluded that judicial demeanor toward both the domestic violence victim and the batterer was important to the victim's perception of whether she had received justice.

Procedural justice improvements are far easier to achieve when a coordinated community response is in place. Part of the integrated response is ongoing training and education on domestic violence issues for all involved in this response. Law enforcement, prosecutors, and judges with an understanding of domestic violence dynamics and experience in working on these issues, are more likely to handle these cases with greater sensitivity. In addition, because of the ongoing communication and coordination among partners, protocols that are respectful and perceived as fair by both victims and offenders can be implemented more quickly and consistently.

4. Civil Legal Assistance and Economic Self–Sufficiency for Battered Women

Despite the increase in services for victims of domestic violence, and expanded government funding in this area, advocates and attorneys working with victims emphasize the tremendous need that remains in several areas, particularly for legal assistance with custody, divorce, and child support and protection issues; adequate housing; job training; and educational programs. All of these services facilitate economic self-sufficiency. While battered women may have several reasons for ambivalence about leaving an abusive relationship, economic dependency is repeatedly cited as a primary reason for staying with their batterers. Barbara Hart, a long-time attorney and advocate for battered women, has argued: "Economic viability appears to be a critical factor in the decision-making of battered women deliberating on separation from the batterer. The most likely predictor of whether a battered woman will permanently separate from her abuser is whether she has the economic resources to survive without him." If they receive assistance in achieving economic independence, more victims will be able to gain safety.

Some critics of the mandatory policies have argued that the focus on criminal justice has deflected resources into the criminal area that could have been targeted for this type of victim assistance. On the contrary, the focus on domestic violence as a problem demanding community attention from the criminal justice system, as well as many components of governmental and nongovernmental organizations, has been central in bringing more resources and attention to the need for additional services for battered women. Attention has never focused solely on criminal justice response, either in policy or funding decisions. However, attention to the criminal justice response, valuable in and of itself, has also led central governmental actors to become involved and invested in addressing domestic violence. As they have worked in the field, through both their relationships with battered women's advocates and their own experience with domestic violence victims, many have come to recognize the importance of community-wide collaboration and attention to additional assistance for victims.

NOTES AND QUESTIONS

1. **Coordinated Community Responses.** Emily Sack describes the enormous benefits for both victims and abusers when the community works together to coordinate appropriate responses. Many jurisdictions have now implemented such programs including San Diego, Pittsburgh, and Seattle. The earliest of these collaborations was the Duluth Domestic Violence Intervention Project (DAIP). In their introduction to Coordinating Community Responses to Domestic Violence: Lessons from Duluth and Beyond, (Melanie F. Shepard & Ellen L. Pence, eds. 1999), Shepard and Pence describe the DAIP, and offer an account of eight key components of a community intervention project:

> The Domestic Abuse Intervention Project (DAIP), located in Duluth, Minnesota, was initiated in 1980 after legal advocates in other cities had effected changes in every aspect of criminal court intervention, from dispatching to sentencing. The DAIP gained national recognition as the first community-based reform project to successfully negotiate an agreement with the key intervening legal agencies to coordinate their interventions through a series of written policies and protocols that limited individual discretion on the handling of cases and subjected practitioners to minimum standards of response.... The Duluth project's most well-known accomplishments have been its work with the Duluth Police Department to develop a mandatory arrest policy in the early 1980s and the creation of an educational curriculum for

batterers that focuses on power and control as the purpose and function of battering. . . .

Many domestic violence agencies have adopted what has been termed the *Duluth model.*

Eight Key Components of Community Intervention Projects

Community intervention projects engage in a fairly complex set of activities that occur simultaneously. The staff of the Duluth DAIP have identified eight key components that comprise a community intervention project:

    1. Creating a coherent philosophical approach centralizing victim safety

    2. Developing ''best practice'' policies and protocols for intervention agencies that are part of an integrated response

    3. Enhancing networking among service providers

    4. Building monitoring and tracking into the system

    5. Ensuring a supportive community infrastructure for battered women

    6. Providing sanctions and rehabilitation opportunities for abusers

    7. Undoing the harm violence to women does to children

    8. Evaluating the coordinated community response from the standpoint of victim safety.

For further readings on coordinated community responses, see Denise Gamache and Mary Asmus, *Enhancing Networking Among Service Providers: Elements of Successful Coordination Strategies* in COORDINATING COMMUNITY RESPONSES TO DOMESTIC VIOLENCE: LESSONS FROM DULUTH AND BEYOND (Melanie F. Shepard & Ellen L. Pence, eds. 1999).

2. **Partnering with Other Professionals.** Another strategy has been for lawyers to team with other professionals, even in the absence of community-wide programs. Consider the following description of such an approach:

Not a model frequently taught in law schools, a solid attorney-advocate partnership can transform the nature of client interactions and dramatically impact case dispositions. Several public defender offices have created such partnerships, sometimes with the assistance of social workers and counselors. Solo, small firm, and pro bono practitioners can contact their local shelters to locate the advocates within their communities who may be able to assist with complex or problematic cases. As a survivor who is also an experienced, empathetic, and assertive advocate, Beth Ledoux taught me that in partnership, we could do far more for the terrified battered women with whom we worked than either of us could alone. As a trial attorney, it is easy to become consumed with the minutiae of legal doctrine while ignoring the fact that legal strategy must be dictated by client-specific concerns and facts. Ledoux's gentle persistence could elicit from battered women detailed histories of abuse, depression, substance abuse, the impact of abuse on their children, current fears, job losses due to stalking, abuser harassment from jail, and prolific witness intimidation.

As a juvenile court prosecutor, I worked closely with another effective advocate, Pam Ellis. Not surprisingly, a substantial majority of our cases involved family violence, though most often the charged offenses were burglary, drug sales or possession, stolen cars, property destruction, and assaults on teachers, girlfriends, and parents. First, Ellis and I would meet with the arrested juvenile and his or her attorney. After explaining that we were not going to discuss the present case, I would say to the youth, "I'm an adult in your community who loves and cares about you. Tell me how I can help." We would discuss safety planning for home, school, and on the street, then ask the youth his or her life aspirations and create a chronological list for the juvenile to complete in order to achieve the goals. Subsequently, either Ellis or I would meet with a parent or guardian if one had appeared in court. Sarah M. Buel, *Effective Assistance of Counsel for Battered Women Defendants: A Normative Construct*, 26 HARV.WOMEN'S L.J. 217 (2003)

An interdisciplinary approach serving domestic violence victims can have enormous benefits. Yet, in law school, as Buel notes, students are not trained to work with or use professionals outside of the legal profession to serve their clients. Given what you have studied in this course, how might you help law students understand the value of partnering with advocates and social workers in addressing the needs of abused clients? What would be effective? Guest speakers, or possibly more intense training that advocates themselves receive? What does the possibility of partnering with other professions tell us about the limitations of lawyers and legal training?

3. **Possibilities of Different Models.** Thinking back on all the issues we have covered in this book, as well as learning from the Duluth experience, what partners would you seek to bring to the table if you were the grant-funded Executive Director of a coordinated community response project? Remember that you have to decide not only which organizations are going to be represented, but at what level—are you going to invite the City Police Chief, for example, or the domestic violence detective from your particular precinct? Or will you structure your Roundtable, or Coordinating Council, or Advisory Board, so that different representatives are involved in different ways? Other than law enforcement, which legal institutions will you seek to involve?

Sarah M. Buel

Effective Assistance of Counsel for Battered Women Defendants: A Normative Construct

26 HARV.WOMEN'S L.J. 217 (2003).

E. The Politics and Ethics of Language

In discussing the institutionalization of an ethical model of practice, it is necessary to discuss both the politics and ethics of the language used in domestic violence discourse. As part of the effort to hold perpetrators of domestic violence accountable, the use of passive voice must be eliminated from feminist discourse on battered women. When stating that, "four women per day were killed in 2001," the passive construct takes the focus away from typically male offenders. The more accurate statement is: "In 2001, men murdered four women per day." This construct provides a more accurate picture of the true nature of domestic violence. The term "violence against women" is also problematic because, again, the actual concept being voiced is "men's violence against women." However, the use of the more precise terminology causes feminists to be labeled "male bashers"—a term that itself connotes violence. This label is an interesting choice since women are not only the targets of the slur but also the underlying abuse. The phrase "male basher" is an overt attempt to silence honest discourse and represents what can be called "Orwellian Doublespeak." Just as George Orwell's novel 1984 highlighted inaccurate use of language, the doublespeak surrounding domestic violence is a thinly disguised effort to de-gender the discourse of men's violence against women. In 1984, all words challenging the power of the government were eliminated, and severe sanctions resulted from their use. Similarly, batterers seek eradication of words likely to hold them responsible for their abusive conduct.

Terms such as "domestic violence" encourage the dialogue to be inclusive of female and male victims, in part to ensure those who are lesbian and gay are not made invisible. But, as educator Jackson Katz points out, the term "male basher" is unfair to men, because men are most often victimized by other men and deserve to have their experiences accurately characterized, and also because it implies that men will not tolerate true reporting of criminal activity.

VII.   UNINTENDED CONSEQUENCES

Anticipating the unintended consequences of insisting on minimum standards of professional practice will enable lawyers to diffuse some of the potential negative repercussions of reform, and will help them decide, on balance, which of the remaining consequences are necessary evils. Such foresight includes an analysis of how minimum standards can best be utilized to achieve the desired results of attorney competence and access to fair trials for battered defendants.

Given that many attorneys are reluctant to represent abuse victims at present, insistence upon minimum standards could make obtaining counsel even more difficult. However, there are several explanations for attorneys' hesitation that must be addressed prior to condemning minimum standards as counterproductive. First, some attorneys fear that domestic violence cases will be never-ending, with recurring emergencies and contested matters dragging the case on for years.

Second, there exists a common stereotype that the battered client is unstable, prone to hysteria, and will generally be difficult. Third, attorneys may fear that the perpetrator will retaliate against the victim's lawyer with violent or harassing behavior and refuse to comply with agreed upon court orders. Fourth, a number of attorneys may be concerned that, as an emerging area of practice, there is simply too much to learn and no adequate guidance from statutory or case law, creating potential liability. While there are additional reasons why lawyers are reluctant to take on domestic violence cases, these four will be addressed as the most commonly articulated concerns.

The imposition of a minimum threshold of practice would necessitate comprehensive trainings affording the opportunity to address the above concerns and, in the process, actually increase the number of attorneys accepting domestic violence case referrals. With regard to the first apprehension that the case will be prolonged, the training could offer guidance as to how tenacious advocacy can expedite cases. The second issue, reflecting the misconception that abuse victims will inevitably be problematic, can best be described as erroneous, unjustified, and without merit in most cases. For example, when dealing with difficult business or estate planning clients, lawyers develop strategies for either coping with or, in extreme cases, withdrawing from such matters. Additionally, if a lawyer feels overwhelmed by the emotional frailty, confusion, or ambivalence of her battered client, she can request (with her client's permission) assistance from the experienced domestic violence advocates in her community. The third cause of trepidation, fearing the batterer, is an emotion worth heeding but can be overcome by taking precautions, including safety planning for self and staff. However, such planning should be undertaken in every law practice, as disgruntled clients or adversarial parties in virtually any case can become dangerous. The fourth area of concern, liability for practicing without adequate knowledge, can be remedied by skills training, practice manuals, and advice of experienced practitioners.

Thus, while there may be problems incorporating domestic violence cases into one's practice, there are advantages as well. Many lawyers and judges express genuine satisfaction, albeit tempered by the presence of distressing facts, in handling cases involving battered defendants when the dispositions render some degree of ameliorative justice. Attorney Kris Davis–Jones says, "I think lawyers ought to relish these cases; they provide so much more to work with than many criminal matters. They give lawyers the chance to express the same kind of righteous indignation that prosecutors so often unleash on so many of their other clients."

NOTES AND QUESTIONS

1. **The Use of Language and the Complications of Politics.** Do you agree with Buel that the way in which we describe experiences with domestic violence impacts the politics of the movement? By stating "men murdered women" instead of "women were murdered" does one invite criticism that advocates against domestic violence are fueled by a larger feminist agenda? Does that criticism matter politically? Practically?

2. **Domestic Violence in the Media.** As Buel suggests, and as many prior discussions in this book have confirmed, the ineffectiveness of reform measures often has to do with the attitudes or the ignorance of those charged with implementing them. Attitudes hostile to women's autonomy, and women's claims, are still deeply embedded in our culture; passed from

one generation to another in our families, confirmed by our peers in educational and work environments, and reinforced by our exposure to the music, television, movies, newspapers and magazines that comprise our popular culture. Ann Jones offers harsh criticism of the media, and their contribution to societal perceptions of domestic violence:

> The murders of Nicole Brown Simpson and Ron Goldman in June 1994 and the indictment of O.J. Simpson prompted a flood of calls to the new National Resource Center on Domestic Violence from journalists nationwide, many of whom subsequently produced informative background stories on domestic violence. That early coverage of the Simpson case—before the trial started and the case went up in sensational smoke—surely raised public awareness of the issue. It is a good example of the role responsible journalism can play in stimulating, informing, and elevating public discourse on social issues. But too often reporters covering domestic violence assaults, femicides, and trials, pressed by deadlines, fall back on sexist cliches and ready-made sexist sex-and-violence scenarios to get their copy out. It happens so easily, so "naturally"; they may not even realize that instead of investigating and accurately reporting the facts, they've masked rape and battering in the language of "love." They quote police and lawyers as authoritative sources but rarely consult battered women's advocates who could provide valuable background information, a different perspective, and an alternative scenario. Sometimes journalists seem willfully to throw fairness and balance to the winds.... [A]s long as routine press coverage presents rape, assault, and femicide from the perspective of the offender, the press will be part of the problem women and children are up against. Ann Jones, NEXT TIME SHE'LL BE DEAD: BATTERING AND HOW TO STOP IT, 244 (2000).

Think back to the many, many recent instances in which domestic violence related cases have been portrayed in the media. Do you agree with Jones that the media is biased against the interests of women and their children? How should journalists cover these cases? Is the general public well-educated and understanding about the dynamics of abuse? How can you help change public misperceptions? Letters to the editor? Blogging? Sharing what you have learned with your classmates, your rugby team family, your church, synagogue or mosque,?

3. **Lawyer Competency.** Buel writes from the perspective of a criminal defense attorney who represents clients who have been battered, yet her suggestions on how to improve lawyering on behalf of battered clients is universal. She suggests that lawyers receive specialized training in domestic violence to overcome some of the challenges. Many jurisdictions now offer continuing legal education courses on domestic violence and related topics. The ABA Commission on Domestic Violence also has an abundance of resources for attorneys representing clients who have been battered. See http://www.abanet.org/domviol//. Do you think that lawyers need more ongoing training and support in this area? Have you imagined yourself practicing with victims of domestic violence? How do you think that you might handle the challenges that these cases can present?

4. **Educating Judges.** As you have seen throughout this book, judges play a key role in how the law responds to domestic violence. Some judges are very sensitive to the issues involved in abusive relationships, while others cling to stereotypes and troublesome assumptions. Many judges have taken a key leadership role in reaching out to the bench on these issues. See e.g. Hon. Laurence D. Kay, *On Open Letter to the California Judiciary Administration of Justice in Domestic Violence Cases*, 6 J. CENTER FOR FAMILIES, CHILD. &CTS. 163 (2005).

Judicial education has been key to the law's development. Many states have implemented judicial training programs. For example, the New Mexico Judicial Education Center, University of New Mexico School of Law has been a leader in this area. It developed, among other resources, the NEW MEXICO DOMESTIC VIOLENCE BENCH BOOK, which aids judges in adjudicating domestic violence cases. It is available at http://jec.unm.edu/resources/benchbooks/dv/. See also Emily J. Sack, CREATING A DOMESTIC VIOLENCE COURT: GUIDELINES AND BEST PRACTICES, STATE JUSTICE INSTITUTE (2002). The National Judicial Education Program has done judicial trainings on domestic violence and is developing a web-based, asynchronous curriculum on co-occurring sexual assault and domestic violence, which, as was noted in Chapter Four, is far more common than often realized. Dangerous Intersection: Sexual Assault in the Context of Domestic Violence—What the Courts Need to Know will be available at http://www.legalmomentum.org/legalmomentum/programs/njep/. The National Association of Women Judges (www.nawj.org) is another resource for judicial training.

5. **Educating Professionals.** The helping professions—legal, mental health and medical—have a special opportunity, and a special obligation, to educate their members. For all members of the legal profession, the need to understand the nature of abusive relationships, and law's relationship to abuse, is acute. In its 1997 report, WHEN WILL THEY EVER LEARN? EDUCATING TO END DOMESTIC VIOLENCE, the ABA Commission on Domestic Violence summarized the situation as follows:

> Domestic violence has a tremendous impact on the legal profession. Whether or not lawyers recognize it, domestic violence permeates the practice of law in almost every field. Corporate lawyers, bankruptcy lawyers, tort lawyers, real property lawyers, criminal defense lawyers, and family lawyers, regularly represent victims or perpetrators of domestic violence. Criminal and civil judges preside over a range of cases involving domestic violence as an underlying or a hotly contested issue. Failure to fully understand domestic violence legal issues threatens the competency of individual lawyers and judges, as well as the legal profession as a whole.

> Legal professionals who are uninformed about domestic violence issues may endanger the safety of victims or contribute to a society which has historically condoned the abuse of intimate partners. In Maryland, for example, a victim was killed by her intimate partner after a judge refused to grant her a civil protection order. Recently, another judge expunged a batterer's criminal record for wife abuse in order to allow him to join a country club; the judge reversed his ruling only in

response to public outcry. Still another judge modified a custody order and awarded custody of the child to the child's father, despite the fact that the father had abused the child's mother, and had been convicted of murdering his first wife.

The vast majority of telephone calls received by the American Bar Association Commission on Domestic Violence indicate that lawyers, too, are not representing victims of domestic violence according to the standards dictated by the profession. Callers report that many family and criminal lawyers fail to address a client's safety needs where there is a history of domestic violence or refuse to introduce evidence of the violence in court, despite the legal consequences. This hesitation to handle domestic violence cases, or to address domestic violence issues when they arise, stems in part from lack of legal training. It is time for law schools to fill this desperate gap in legal education by incorporating domestic violence law into core curricula courses, upper level courses, and clinical programs. WHEN WILL THEY EVER LEARN? EDUCATING TO END DOMESTIC VIOLENCE: A LAW SCHOOL REPORT (ABA Commission on Domestic Violence, 1997).

Legal education in domestic violence needs to begin, as the ABA Commission concluded, in law school. Certainly much progress has been made on that front in the last decade. When Mithra Merryman conducted the first national survey in 1993, she found only one school offering a seminar on domestic violence on an annual basis—Boalt Hall School of Law at the University of California–Berkeley. There were more schools offering clinical courses; a total of thirteen courses at twelve schools. Mithra Merryman, *A Survey of Domestic Violence Programs in Legal Education*, 28 NEW ENG. L. REV. 383 (1993). By 1997, when the ABA Commission conducted a similar survey, it found twenty-two schools offering an upper-level seminar or course, and a grand total of forty-two schools offering clinical programs either dedicated exclusively to serving victims of domestic violence, or offering a substantial amount of domestic violence casework. An additional two schools were reported as offering entirely student-run programs representing battered women; there may be more schools in this category who were not counted in the survey. Nine schools offered both a specialized course and clinical education in domestic violence, and two schools offered more than one clinical opportunity. The development of domestic violence clinics has been assisted by funding authorized by the Violence Against Women Act, and administered through the U.S. Department of Justice.

In 2003, the ABA Commission on Domestic Violence released TEACH YOUR STUDENTS WELL: INCORPORATING DOMESTIC VIOLENCE INTO LAW SCHOOL CURRICULA, A LAW SCHOOL REPORT. The report, gathered by hosting regional conferences with legal educators, contains sample syllabi, teaching notes, and models of clinics. By 2006, a significant number of law schools had added seminars or courses on domestic violence, as well as established clinics to assist victims. For descriptions of various programs integrating domestic violence in the law school curriculum, see Mary Beck, *Spotlight: Response to Violence Against Women at the University of Missouri at*

Columbia, 23 St. Louis U. Pub. L. Rev. 227 (2004); Leigh Goodmark and Catherine F. Klein, *Deconstructing Teresa O'Brien: A Role Play for Domestic Violence Clinics,* 23 ST. LOUIS U. PUB. L. REV. 253 (2004); Jacqueline St. Joan and Nancy Ehrenreich, *Putting Theory Into Practice: A Battered Women's Clemency Clinic,* 8 CLINICAL L. REV. 171 (2001). For an overview of the efforts of the ABA Commission on Domestic Violence to promote education both in law schools and through continuing legal education, see Bette Garlow, *Ginger Rogers Dancing Backward in Red High Heels– Feminist Lawmaking and Domestic Violence,* 11 AM. U. J. GENDER SOC. POL'Y & L. 401 (2003).

Much harder to gauge is the extent to which education in domestic violence issues has permeated into the mainstream law school curriculum, and is being addressed in both core courses (in the first year and beyond), and relevant specialty courses. The ABA Commission recommends that all law students should be taught to screen for domestic violence, and to conduct safety planning with victims. It also suggests ways in which domestic violence issues can be introduced into criminal law, civil procedure, torts, property, contracts, constitutional law, professional responsibility, legal research and writing, trial advocacy and moot court. "While domestic violence issues could be raised in virtually every course," the Report continues, it is "vital" that they be included in evidence, family law, and advanced criminal courses.

Today, it is hard to imagine teaching either welfare law or immigration law without reference to domestic violence, given the new developments in those fields discussed in earlier chapters. The advantages of integrating domestic violence throughout the curriculum are clear; every law student will be exposed, and there will be multiple opportunities to refine and extend the student's learning. There are also disadvantages, however; the time given to the subject may be insufficient to help students acquire sufficient knowledge, or to overcome their preconceptions, and teachers may themselves be unprepared to offer a thorough or accurate description or analysis of the issue at hand.

Much work remains to be done in providing students with the material they need to foster discussion and learning about domestic violence. In 1984 Catherine Klein, then Director of the Family Abuse Project at Columbus School of Law, Catholic University of America, conducted an informal survey of family-law casebooks, and discovered that only one raised the issue of spouse abuse. While many more casebooks now include some mention of domestic violence, it remains unclear the extent to which students are learning about these issues outside of specialized courses. Think back on those courses you have taken. How often did you discuss domestic violence issues, and in what contexts? Now that you have studied the law in more depth, how might you incorporate issues of domestic violence throughout the law school curriculum?

6. **Bar Examinations.** Would law schools and students consider the study of domestic violence and legal issues more relevant if the subject was tested on bar examinations? Sarah Buel, a professor at the University of Texas notes the following: "In July 1998, one Texas Bar Exam essay

question asked for a full recitation of the state's protection order laws, including available remedies and enforcement provisions. I received many calls from angry students, shocked that relevant domestic violence issues had been neglected in law school. Since 1998, many of my students studying for the bar exam have reported references to domestic violence law in several sections of their bar review courses, from civil procedure and family law to evidence and criminal law." Sarah M. Buel, *Effective Assistance of Counsel for Battered Women Defendants: A Normative Construct*, 26 HARV.WOMEN'S L.J. 217 (2003).

7. **Ongoing Conversations about Domestic Violence and Legal Education.** For a discussion of how integration of domestic violence issues in all aspects of legal education might improve the representation of abused clients, see, Kristin Bebelaar, Stacy Caplow, Patricia Fersch, Betty Levinson, Jennifer L. Rosato, Elizabeth M. Schneider, Anthony J. Sebok and Lisa L. Smith, *Domestic Violence in Legal Education and Legal Practice: A Dialogue Between Professors and Practitioners*, 11 J.L. & POL'Y 409 (2003). The article contains many different perspectives on both substantive and pedagogical approaches that could be incorporated into the law school experience. For student perspectives, see also John F. Mahon and Daniel K. Wright, *The Missing Ingredient: Incorporating Domestic Violence Issues into the Law School Curriculum*, 48 ST.LOUIS U.L.J. 1351 (2004). See also ABA Commission on Domestic Violence, TEACH YOUR STUDENTS WELL: INCORPORATING DOMESTIC VIOLENCE INTO LAW SCHOOL CURRICULA, A LAW SCHOOL REPORT (2003), available at http://www.abanet.org/domviol/teach_students. pdf.

8. **Returning to the Earlier Goals of the Battered Women's Movement.** A new book by Lisa A. Goodman and Deborah Epstein focuses on the need to go back to the principles of the early battered women's movement and make battered women's experiences the central starting-point for reforms for battered women. In LISTENING TO BATTERED WOMEN: A SURVIVOR-CENTERED APPROACH TO THE ADVOCACY, MENTAL HEALTH AND JUSTICE SYSTEMS (2007), the authors write "Despite early attempts by feminist advocates to highlight the fundamental political and social determinants of partner violence, much research has focused on the personal characteristics of victims and perpetrators. Although such research has yielded important information, it also has contributed to the widespread belief that intimate partner violence is rooted in individual pathology rather than gender-based power hierarchies and the societal norms and institutions that support and reinforce women's subordination. Although a wide range of personal and familial factors affect the odds that a particular man will commit an act of domestic violence, the dominance of male power in our culture facilitates and legitimizes such violence. Our analysis leads us to advocate solutions that entail fundamental change in both our public agencies and in civil society".

The book makes three major points. First, that battered women's individual voices need to be brought to the forefront of reform efforts. Second, that advocates need to recognize the critical importance of women's community ties and individual relationships, since existing services frequently fail to promote connection and often actively undermine it. Third, that as advocates expand the options available to battered women, they should focus particularly on those whose socioeconomic status limits their opportunities to achieve safety.

9. **The Future of Domestic Violence Advocacy.** Author Ann Jones concludes her book NEXT TIME SHE'LL BE DEAD: BATTERING AND HOW TO STOP IT (2d ed. 2000) with a grim assessment and a call to action. Looking at recent manifestations of society's attitudes towards battering and its victims, she concedes that there has been change, but questions whether that change genuinely reflects a desire to put an end to intimate partner violence, or to keep its victims safe. The other disturbing possibility, she suggests, is that society still depends on battered women, carefully defined as "other," to absorb male violence—imagining, or fearing, that the violence might otherwise spill out and find other (more vulnerable or less deserving) targets. Perhaps, Jones argues, we do not, despite our protestations to the contrary, want to disturb the status quo. This provocative thesis is the topic of the first reading below.

If we reject this hypothesis, then Jones asserts that we could, and should, demonstrate the sincerity of our commitment to ending domestic violence by making substantially greater progress towards that goal. The goal is not out of reach, she argues; we need only to intensify our efforts, and in some instances redirect or refocus them. Her suggestions for how that could and should be done provide a springboard for the rest of this section, which looks at some of the key components of a broadly based societal response to domestic violence.

Ann Jones

Next Time She'll Be Dead: Battering and How to Stop It (2000)

To measure change, it helps to take the long view of history. Then one can see that in the last century and a half public opinion about battered women has undergone a fundamental shift. During the nineteenth century and a good part of this one, when a woman left her husband, the public asked: Why did she leave? The question was not merely inquisitive but judgmental, suggesting other loaded questions: What kind of woman walks out on her husband and family, the sacred duty entrusted to her by God and nature? How could she abandon her obligations, her destiny? Throw away her life? Her children's happiness? Is she deranged? Irreligious? Unnatural?

Today, family, friends, clergy, courts and counselors still urge a woman's duty upon her, but when a woman complains too loudly, or some "real" trouble occurs—a homicide, perhaps, or the battery of a child—the public wants to know: Why didn't she leave? A century ago a dutiful wife's place was with her husband, even a brutal one, though she herself was blameless. Today she is still supposed to stand by her man, but only up to a point—a point always more easily discerned in retrospect, and by others. . . .

It is also clear that today in the mainstream culture of this country a woman's duty to her child is supposed to take precedence over her duty to her husband. This judgment too represents a fundamental shift away from an older, purely patriarchal order which valued nothing so much as the privilege of the patriarch himself. Marilyn French tells an old story from India, one of those instructive moral tales designed to teach women how they are supposed to *be*. French writes: "The story presenting an exemplary Indian wife tells of a woman sitting with her sleeping husband's head in her lap, watching over him and her baby playing in front of the fire. The baby wanders near the fire, but the woman does not move lest she disturb her sleeping lord. When the child actually enters the flames, she prays, begging Agni not to harm the baby. Agni rewards her wifely devotion by letting the child sit among the flames unscathed." . . .

Thus it happens that the big question—Why didn't she leave?—cuts two ways. On one hand, it shifts the blame from the "nature" of men in general and the societal attitudes and institutions that abet male violence to the character of the individual victim; it blames the victim for the abuse she suffers. On the other hand, it suggests that women now have more options and should make use of them. It implies a widespread belief that women *should* leave abusers, that living with brutality (or, as some would say, "excessive" brutality) is no longer a good wife's duty. Taken in the context of a century and a half of struggle, this is progress.

Yet nothing makes it easy for a woman to leave. Many factors—from low wages and inadequate child care to the unresponsive criminal justice system and a Congress unwilling adequately to fund victim services—conspire to keep the abused woman in her place within the "traditional" family. Abused women leave anyway, but often they are strictly on their own. Many flee one problem—battering—only to become part of another: "the feminization of poverty." These days 65 percent of black children live in a family headed by a single mother, and 45 percent of all American families headed by a single mother live in poverty. When Aid to Families with Dependent Children benefits were suspended in 1996, 60 percent of the poor women receiving them were victims of "domestic violence." [Former United States Vice–President] Dan Quayle pointed to abortion, divorce, and these single-parent families as grievous *causes* of "the disintegration of the American family." But we can attribute this "disintegration" in part to violence, just as we can attribute the "feminization of poverty" in part to woman and child abuse, a cause economists and politicians never cite. Today experts name battery as a "major cause" of homelessness; large numbers of the nation's growing band of homeless are women on their own with children—women and children who, despite the social and economic obstacles, ran from male violence at home. (Reflect for a moment on conventional explanations for the feminization of poverty—*her* youth, *her* lack of education, *her* lack of job skills, *her* sexual activity, *her* insistence upon becoming a single mother, heedless of Quayle's righteous admonitions—and you'll see that we blame the victim for poverty too. Men, especially men of color, are blamed for "abandoning" women and children—but not for the violence that drives women and children away.) Today most people recognize that women have a right—even a responsibility—to leave abusive men, and many individuals feel an impulse to help them, but we don't yet recognize our responsibility as a society to rise to their aid: our duty as a society to safeguard the right of every woman to be free from bodily harm.

Our public attitude—damned if you don't leave, damned if you do—is not simple hypocrisy. Two conflicting views come down to us from nineteenth-century debates, and we've never sorted them out. To radical women in the mid-nineteenth century, questions of marriage and divorce were, as Elizabeth Cady Stanton put it, "at the very foundation of all progress" on women's rights. After all, as Stanton wrote in 1860 in a letter to the editor of the *New York Tribune:* "We decide the whole question of slavery by settling the sacred rights of the individual. We assert that man cannot hold property in man, and reject the whole code of laws that conflicts with the self-evident truth of the assertion." How then can man hold property in woman? Has woman no sacred rights as an individual?

As Stanton and her colleague Susan B. Anthony saw it, marriage was an institution devised by men, and backed by all the authority of church and state, to give husbands absolute authority over wives.... Fundamental to Stanton's "radical" view, of course, is the assumption (never shared by American law) that women and men are equal beings in the eyes of God and should enjoy equal rights and responsibilities in all things.

For women in the nineteenth century the catch was this: marriage made in heaven maintained on earth the rights and privileges of the husband, the man, as Stanton correctly said, and so did all other social institutions. Divorce might be the way out of domestic tyranny, but for most women it looked like a dead end, depriving them as it did at the time of their children, home, livelihood, reputation and prospects. Consequently, more conservative advocates of women's rights tried not to get women out of marriage but to protect them within it. Temperance leaders battled drunkenness, always considered a cause of brutality and violence, while moral reformers sought to curb male "animal" lust and to "improve" men with an infusion of female "purity." More to the point, Lucy Stone and her husband Henry Blackwell campaigned in Massachusetts from 1879 to 1891 for legislation modeled on laws already passed in England in response to Frances Power Cobbe's revelations about "wife-torture." The new legislation provided legal separation (not divorce) and financial maintenance for wives whose husbands were convicted of assaulting them; but even that modest proposal, seen as an attack upon the family, failed.

The same attitudes persist today, both within the family and outside it. Some battered women are as dedicated as any conservative congressman to keeping the family, their own family, together; they want only to stop the violence. Other battered women are ready to strike out for freedom and self-determination, for themselves and their kids. All these women, whether they struggle under the banner of *Family Values,* the flag of *Women's*

Rights, or the colors of *Women's Liberation,* need protection from violence, and institutional supports to help them.

In the public arena, "radical" feminists go on arguing for the rights of women, though we live in what conservatives wishfully call a "postfeminist" age. Never mind that for a pile of economic and social reasons the "traditional" family is as scarce these days as the blue whale. Never mind Elizabeth Cady Stanton's observation that "A legislative act cannot make a unit of a divided family." Policy makers and legislators backed by custom, the church and "modern" psychology, and beholden to the far right, still try to keep "the family" alive. Consequently, our economic and social arrangements still impede a woman's departure, especially if she has children. Some federal reimbursement programs require child welfare agencies to try to keep "families" intact; and although most such agencies now consider a woman and her children to *be* "a family," some abused women may be pressured to enter counseling or mediation with their assailants, while their abused children may be left at his mercy, sometimes in his household. If a woman reports that her husband or boyfriend abuses the children, she may see them removed not only from his custody but from hers to be placed in a *family* of foster parents. If she and the kids set up their own household, they may get poorer, while the abusive husband (unless he is trapped in poverty himself) is likely to get relatively richer. And even the prospect of that supposedly inevitable financial decline, much trumpeted in the media, serves to intimidate the woman who considers setting out on her own. On the other hand, the battered woman who wants to help stop the violence while preserving her marriage and family may find the proffered alternatives—arrest, prosecution, shelter—of no use at all.

Nevertheless, today's battered woman has options her sisters struggled in the last century and in this to win for her. She may not be formally married at all. If married, she can divorce, provided her religion and her pocketbook permit. She may get custody of her children, if she can afford the lawyers she'll need to persuade a judge that a violent man is not fit to be a custodial parent. She can work, albeit for lower wages than a man doing the same job—that is, if she can find a job. She may even get some public assistance, though only for a short term. And she hears, as her nineteenth-century sister did not, the nagging question: "Why doesn't she leave?"

The danger now is that we overestimate society's changes. Implicit in the question, "Why doesn't she leave?" is the assumption that social supports are already in place to help the woman who walks out: a shelter in every town, a cop on every beat eager to make that mandatory arrest, a judge in every courtroom passing out well-enforced restraining orders and packing batterers off to jail and effective re-education programs, legal services, social services, health care, child care, child support, affordable housing, convenient public transportation, a decent job free of sexual harassment, a living wage. The abused woman, wanting to leave, encouraged to think she will find help, yet finding only obstacles at every turn, may grow disheartened and doubt herself. If it's supposed to be so easy, and it's *this* hard, she must be doing something wrong. What seemed to be a social problem—judging by all the reports about "domestic violence" in the news—becomes a personal problem after all. For the abused woman, it's just one more turn of the screw.

Public opinion, too, can easily turn backward—without even changing the dialogue. When we ask "Why doesn't she leave?" do we mean to be helpful, encouraging, cognizant of her rights, and ready with our support? Or do we mean once again to blame her for her failure to avail herself of all the assistance we mistakenly think our society provides? Lucy Stone and Henry Blackwell thought wife abuse would cease when women got the vote—because women would vote off the bench judges who failed to punish wife beaters. That didn't work. The battered women's movement has organized for more than twenty-five years against "domestic violence," yet the violence continues. Could it be that individual women are to blame after all?

Or could it be rather that battered women play some indispensable part in this society that we've overlooked? Could it be that battered women have some function, some role or social utility we haven't taken into account? Thus far ... we've looked at the problem from the point of view of battered women—women who almost invariably ask for help. But perhaps we should look again from the point of view of "society"—if we can try for a moment to imagine that this many-headed abstraction has something like a point of view. Perhaps we should put a different question: What are battered women *for?*

Asking a different question puts a new light on the problem right away: battered women are *for battering.* The battered woman is a woman who may be beaten; she is a *beatable* woman; If you doubt that society views battered women as, by definition, "beatable," then how do you explain the fact that we almost always put responsibility for woman beating on the woman? Why else would we probe her psyche to reveal the secret self within, yearning for abuse, if not to set her apart as a *beatable* woman, unlike ourselves? In our society there are millions of these beatable women. Many of them live within "the family" which entitles only the "head" of the family to beat them. Many others live outside "the family"—in which case anyone may beat them who will. Many live and work in industries that rent or sell beatable women and children to the male "public" prostitution, for example, and pornography....

In the aggregate, battered women are to sexism what the poor are to capitalism—always with us. They are a source of cheap labor and sexual service to those with the power to buy and control them, a "problem" for the righteous to lament, a topic to provide employment for academic researchers, a sponge to soak up the surplus violence of men, a conduit to carry off the political energy of other women who must care for them, an exemplum of what awaits all women who don't behave as prescribed, and a pariah group to amplify by contrast our good opinion of ourselves. And for all their social utility, they remain largely, and conveniently, invisible.

NOTES AND QUESTIONS

1. **Challenges for the Future.** If we take seriously all the admonitions and advice contained in this book about what it takes to work as a lawyer

with victims of domestic violence, the job seems a daunting one indeed. It requires a thorough grounding in the psychological dynamics of abuse, and how those can affect the lawyer's relationship with the women she seeks to assist. It requires resisting the comfort and sense of control that can attach to "paternalistic" (or even "maternalistic") lawyering, in favor of partnerships with women whose control over their own lives is tenuous, and whose lives may even be at risk. It requires a broad interdisciplinary education as well as a careful and intensive legal education. It requires working within a legal system in which a lawyer who advocates for victims of partner violence may still encounter hostility and resistance, and experience attacks on her credibility and competence that uncannily resemble the parallel attacks on her client's reliability and integrity. It requires crossing disciplinary boundaries; working with and depending on other professionals who will not always be welcoming or responsive. And it involves participation in the often bewildering politics of community organization.

Of course, not every lawyer-in-training who seeks to educate him or herself about domestic violence will practice in this field. For those who do not, there will be ample opportunities, commensurate with whatever resources they have to give, to contribute to a profession, and a society, in which the needs of victims are understood and met. It may be as simple as setting someone straight about battered women's self-defense claims at a dinner party, or advocating for a firm's *pro bono* practice to include work on behalf of adult and child victims of domestic violence, and making sure that the firm provides adequate training. It may be standing ready to advise a corporate client or employer about developing a responsible policy to govern those situations where domestic violence comes to work. It may be as personal, and as sensitive, as seeking out a friend or a colleague who is showing the signs of abuse, to offer support.

For those who do decide that this work is their vocation, there will be rewards that match the demands; indeed the rewards are inextricably bound up with the demands. Involvement with community partners and colleagues from other disciplines makes the work less lonely, and adds a public and policy dimension to a practice that might otherwise be too consistently close to other people's pain. Engagement with other service providers also helps the lawyer remind herself, or himself, that the responsibility for the safety of clients is one lawyers share with others, and neither can, nor should, shoulder alone. A grounding in the psychological and emotional dimensions of the work demands a level of self-knowledge, self-awareness and self-care that will stand the lawyer in good stead not only in his or her work with clients, but in every aspect of his or her life. And then finally there is the reward of knowing that the work, done well, contributes both to the safety and well-being of those in need, and to a future, to paraphrase John Stuart Mill, in which the love of liberty has overtaken the love of power as the organizing principle of our society. "The reward of engagement," as Judith Herman has said, "is the sense of an enriched life."

2. **Closing Comments.** We have explored many aspects of domestic violence and the legal system's response to it throughout this book. We

have been confronted with hard issues for which there are often no easy answers. Yet, every day, thousands of lawyers and advocates representing victims, lobby legislatures to change laws, raise money for shelters and advocacy programs, and are involved in other important and meaningful activities. They may be motivated by their own life experiences, their desire for interesting and challenging legal work, or simply by their own sense of justice. There are many ways to go about doing this work either as one's primary professional focus or through *pro bono* or philanthropic commitments. To the extent that this book and your legal studies have inspired you to find how you can best contribute your skills and talents to ending domestic violence, we are grateful that the work will continue.

*

INDEX

References are to Pages.

ABORTION
Generally, 171–178
Coerced, 179–180
Minors, 177–178
Prevented by batterer, 176–177
Spousal notification, 171–176

ADVOCACY
ABA reports, 979–980
Bar examinations, 981–982
Civil Gideon/court-appointed attorneys, 245–247
Counseling, 966
Indigent defendants, obtaining experts for, 478–470
Ineffective assistance of counsel, 458–461, 478–479, 485–487
Interpreters, 244
Interviewing skills, 960–966
Lay advocates, 240–245
Lawyer-client relationship, 943–952
Legal education, 979–983
Pro se litigants, 564, 735
Responsibilities of the legal profession, 335–337, 810–811, 952–960
Therapist-client relationships and lawyer-client relationships compared, 952–960
Victims' advocates programs, 327–328, 331–332

AFRICAN–AMERICANS
See also Race and Battering
Generally, 98–101, 325–326, 484
Stereotypes, 98–101, 207–208, 307–308

AGE
Generally, 127–136
Elder abuse, 132–136
Teen dating violence, 127–132

ALCOHOL AND DRUGS
Generally, 104, 346–350, 462–463, 966

ANIMALS/PETS
Protective orders for, 219–220
Shelters for, 328

ARREST
Generally, 298–314
Dual arrests, 308–314
Efficacy of, 303
Mandatory arrest policies, 299–308
Victim desirability, 304–305

ASIAN–AMERICANS
See also Race and Battering
Impact of abuse on, 101–102, 106–111

ASYLUM
Generally, 812–813, 829–848
Cognizable social group, women as comprising, 829–848
DOJ Guidelines, 844–847
Female genital mutilation, 830

BATTERED WOMAN SYNDROME (BWS)
Generally, 63–66, 191–198, 200–209, 398–402, 404–407, 424–427
Defense, 424–427, 430–458
Expert Testimony, 191–199, 398–402, 404–407, 424–427, 430–458, 468–472

BATTERED WOMEN
Terminology, analysis of, 22, 191–195, 281, 975–977

BATTERED WOMEN AS CRIMINAL DEFENDANTS
Generally, 423–501
Crimes committed by, 461–465
Gender bias in the criminal justice system, 424–461

BATTERED WOMEN'S MOVEMENT
Generally, 18–23, 24–28
Anti-rape movement, 18–21
Feminism, 18–25, 983–987
Nineteenth century reform movement, 14–17
Political consciousness movement of 1970s, 18–21
Shelter movement, 22–23

BATTERER TREATMENT PROGRAMS
Generally, 78, 339–355
Efficacy of, 343–344

BATTERERS
Generally, 72–84, 344
Bio-medical factors, 75–76
Childhood origins of, 80
Culture of violence, 81–84
Distinguishable types, 78
Evolutionary theory, 78–79, 183

BATTERERS—Cont'd
Representing, 231–232, 388, 966–968
Unemployment, 77–78, 104, 114–115

BIRTH CONTROL
Generally, 164–171
Sabotage, 167–169

CHILD ABUSE AND NEGLECT
See also Children
Generally, 645–696
Gender and prosecutions for failure to protect, 680–685
Prosecutions for failure to protect, generally, 680–685, 686–687
Relationship between domestic violence and, 645–646, 648–651, 659–669

CHILD ABUSE PREVENTION AND TREATMENT ACT (CAPTA)
Generally, 656

CHILD PROTECTIVE SERVICES
Generally, 645–696
Adoption and Safe Families Act (ASFA), 670
Burden of proof, 657
Emergency removals, 654
Representation, 658

CHILDREN
See also Child Protective Services
Abandonment under threats of battering, 576
Child Abuse Prevention and Treatment Act, 656
Correlations between partner and child abuse, 645–646, 648–561, 659–669
Exposure to partner violence, impact of, 522–524, 647, 651–652
Failure to protect, prosecutions for, 659–663, 673–680
Fetal protection, 183–190
Foster care, 647–648, 651, 652–653
Kidnapping, 581–583, 597
Molestation by abuser, 518–522

CIVIL PROTECTIVE ORDERS
Generally, 212–273
Assisting victims, 240–248
Burden of proof, 222–226
Civil liability of police for failing to enforce, 744–785
Compliance monitoring, 261–263
Constitutional issues, 237
Criminal Protective Orders, 313–314
Dating relationships, applicability to, 212–218
Defendants' rights in relation to, 231–232, 267–268
Dismissal of orders, 253–254
Duration of orders, 249–254
Efficacy, 269–273
Emergency and ex parte orders, 238–240
Enforcement
Generally, 257–263, 265–269, 744–785
Double jeopardy, 266–267
Interstate enforcement, 232–237
Sanctions, 267–268

CIVIL PROTECTIVE ORDERS—Cont'd
Forms of relief, 220–221
Interstate enforcement, 232–237
Mutual orders, 254–257
Parties subject to, 212–218
Process, issuance of, 237–240
Purposes of, 212–216
Relief available, 227–232
Same-sex abuse, applicability to, 218
Scope of protection, 221
Service of process and orders, 212–218, 248
VAWA protections, 232–237
Withdrawal of orders, 249–254

CIVIL REMEDIES
See also Violence Against Women Act
ANTI–SLAPP Lawsuits, 734–735
Divorce proceedings, tort claims in, 737–743
Federal Occupational and Safety Health Act (OSHA), 798–799
Immunity, 698–703
Limitations of actions, 717–730
Marital rape, 701
Police failure to protect
Generally, 745–785
Immunity, 777–778
Indifference as discrimination, 748–757
Procedural due process claims, 763–771
Public duty doctrine, 772–778
Section 1983 claims, 747–756
State tort claims, 771–777
Substantive due process claims, 757–763
Punitive damages, 754
Section 1983 actions, 747–754
Third party liability
Generally, 745–811
Physician liability for failure to report, 422
Police failure to protect, 745–785
Workplace violence, 876–811
Title VII, 797–798
Title IX, 892–894
Tort actions
Generally, 697–743
Assault and battery, 704
Domestic abuse tort, 729–730
Intentional infliction of emotional distress, 705–717
Wrongful death, 705–706
Wrongful discharge, 798–805

CIVIL RIGHTS
See also Human Rights
Generally, 849–899
Coverture and violence, 871–877
Fourteenth Amendment rights of battered women, 858, 882–884, 887–889
State and local civil rights laws, 894–899
Thirteenth Amendment rights of battered women, 853–859
VAWA civil rights provision, 859–894

CLASS AND BATTERING
See also Poverty and Battering
Generally, 140–153
Arrest, relationship to, 305–306
Socio-economic status, 114–115, 145–146, 461–465

CLEMENCY FOR BATTERED WOMEN
Generally, 485–501

COMMERCE CLAUSE
See also Federalism
Generally, 878–891

CONFRONTATION CLAUSE
Generally, 375–391

CONSTITUTIONAL RIGHTS
Fourth Amendment/Search and Seizure, 292–297
Fourteenth Amendment/Equal Protection, 141–151, 748–757, 855–859
Procedural Due Process, 763–771
Sixth Amendment/Confrontation Clause, 375–391
Substantive Due Process, 757–763
Thirteenth Amendment, 852–855
Nineteen Amendment, 858–859

COORDINATED COMMUNITY RESPONSES
Generally, 969–975

COURTS
Specialized domestic violence, 291–292, 349–350, 979

COVERTURE
Violence as perpetuation of 14–18, 851–853

CRIMINAL JUSTICE SYSTEM
See also Child Welfare Systems
Generally, 274–372
Charging options in battering cases, 275–276
Child abuse, prosecutions for failure to protect, 659–663, 673–680, 680–685, 686–687
Crimes committed by victims, 461–465
Criminal Protective Orders, 313–314
Cultural defenses, 109–112
Domestic violence specific statutes, 277–280
Duress, 465–475, 479–485
Equal rights to trial, 424–430
Evidence, 373–422
Federal domestic violence laws, 355–372
Mandatory victim participation, 329–335
No-drop prosecutions, 328–329
Post-conviction relief, 485–501
Prosecution
Generally, 314–339
Mandatory victim participation, 329–335
No-drop policies, 328–329
Sentencing
Generally, 339–355
Alternative, 350–355
Counseling programs, 342–344
Cultural considerations, 344–345
Firearm restrictions, 345–346
Parole, 487–497
Probation, 342–345
Stalking, 282–290

CRIMINAL JUSTICE SYSTEM—Cont'd
Treatment programs for batterers, 339–355
Victim support programs, 327–328, 331–332

CULTURE AND BATTERING
Generally, 97–118
Asian American women, impact of abuse on, 101–102, 106–111
Blaming culture, 107–111
Haitians, 107, 126
Hispanic Americans, 102–106
Immigrants, 106–107, 812–829
Native Americans, 111–115, 237, 403

CUSTODY
See also Family Law Systems, Relocation
Generally, 530–597
Best interest of the child standard
Generally, 503
Battering of parent as factor, 531–535
Child's preference for abuser, 537–538
Education of divorcing parents, 637–644
Effects of abuse on ability to parent, 535
Friendly parent provisions, 546, 551–552
Guardians Ad Litem, 598–611
Joint, 546, 550–554
Jurisdiction, 583–588, 589–597
Kidnapping, 581–583, 597
Mutual abuse, 545
Parental alienation, 561–562
Parental Kidnapping Prevention Act (PKPA), 583–588
Presumption against batterer, 534, 538–545

CYCLE OF VIOLENCE
Generally, 49–72
Phases of, 56–58
Separation assault, 63
Theories of, 63–68

DEFENDANT'S RIGHTS
See also Constitutional Rights and Confrontation Clause
Generally, 136–140, 338–339, 389, 408

DISABILITIES, VICTIMS WITH
Generally, 136–140
Restraining orders to protect, 140
Sexual abuse, 138–139
Shelters, 139–140

DIVORCE AND DISSOLUTION
See also Family Law Systems, Custody
Division of Assets, 513–517
Grounds, 502, 504–505, 507–511

DURESS
Generally, 461–485
Burden of proof, 479–484

DYNAMICS OF ABUSIVE RELATION-SHIPS
Generally, 5–7, 38–42, 49–55, 59–62
Cycles of Violence, 55–68
Early warnings of violence, 42–49

DYNAMICS OF ABUSIVE RELATION-SHIPS—Cont'd
Female batterers, 11–13, 69
Learned helplessness, 64–69
Power and control wheel, 58
Separation assault, 63
Survivor hypothesis, 66–69

EDUCATION
ABA call for domestic violence education, 979–981
Casebooks, failures of, 981
Divorcing parents. See Family Law Systems

ELDER ABUSE
Generally, 132–136

EMPLOYERS
Discrimination against abuse victims, 799–803
Domestic violence at workplace
    Generally, 785–811
    Assistance programs, 787
Tort liabilities
    Generally, 793–797
    Batterers, civil actions by, 806–809
    Discrimination against abuse victims, 799–803
    Title VII, 797–798
    Unemployment compensation, 803–804
    Workers compensation, 788–793
    Wrongful discharge action by abuse victim, 799–803

ETHICAL CONCERNS
Generally, 966–968, 975–979

EVIDENCE
    Generally, 373–422
BWS evidence, 396–409
Child Witnesses, 412–416
Confrontation Clause, 375–391
Expert Testimony, 191–209, 395–407, 435–436, 442–443, 468–475, 485
Expert Witnesses, 191–209, 403–407, 478–479, 611–617
Impeachment, 390–391
Medical evidence, 416–422
Photographs, 373–391
Prior statements, 375–391
Prior acts, 391–395, 407–409, 472–474
Scientific evidence, 395–401, 402–403
Testimonial privileges, 409–412

EXPERT WITNESSES
    See Evidence

FAILURE TO PROTECT CHILDREN
    See Child Welfare Systems

FAMILY LAW SYSTEMS
    Generally, 524–530
Custody in divorce proceedings, 524–530
Education of divorcing parents
    Generally, 637–644

FAMILY LAW SYSTEMS—Cont'd
Education of divorcing parents—Cont'd
Domestic violence, programs dealing with, 641–644
    Efficacy, 639
Guardians Ad Litem, 598–608
Mediation
    Generally, 617–637
    Confidentiality, 631
    Costs, 630–631
    Culture of battering and, 619–624
    Dangers of, 618–619
    Mandated mediation, 625–629, 633–637
    Screening and safety, 631
Parent Coordinators, 644
Visitation, 554–564

FATHERS' RIGHTS
Generally, 176, 221, 560

FEDERALISM
    Generally, 770
Commerce Clause authority, 365–368, 889–891
Fourteenth Amendment as support for, VAWA 871–877
Interstate activities basis for VAWA, 365–372

FEMALE BATTERERS
Generally, 69–70

FETAL PROTECTION
Generally, 183–190

FIREARMS
    Generally, 268–269, 345–346
Lautenberg Amendment, 231, 345

GUARDIANS AD LITEM
    Generally, 598–611
Confidentiality of sources, 608
Qualifications, 611
Roles, 601–608
Training, 609–611

GUNS
    See Firearms

HAUGE CONVENTION ON THE CIVIL ASPECTS OF INTERNATIONAL CHILD ABDUCTION
Generally, 589–597

HISPANIC AMERICANS
    See also Culture and Battering
    Generally, 102–106

HOMELESSNESS
Generally, 146

HOUSING
    Generally, 146–151
Fair Housing Act, 147–149
Public Housing, 147–151

HOUSING—Cont'd
Right to call police and emergency services, 150
Sex discrimination, 149–150
State statutes, 149–150
VAWA protections, 150–151

HUMAN RIGHTS VIOLATIONS
  See also Civil Rights Violations
  Generally, 900–940
Asylum Rights, 829–848
Convention on the Elimination of All Forms of Discrimination Against Women, 900–940
Conventions, 900–940
Cultural relativist challenges, 925–927
Declaration on the Elimination of Violence Against Women, 919–923
Documents and reports, 912–936
Domestic application of international protections, 936–940
Dowry deaths, 912
Female Genital Mutilation, 830–912
Gender neutral international law, disparate application, 901–902
Globalization, 936–940
Honour killings, 912, 934–935
Inter–American Commission on Human Rights, 771, 940
Mail Order Brides, 828–829
Rape, 900–940
Scope of international human rights law, 900–940
Special Rapporteur, 900–940
Torture, 902–912
Treaties, 900–940
Universal Declaration of Human Rights, 900–940
Vienna Conference, 902–903

IMMIGRANTS & IMMIGRATION
  Generally, 812–829
Arrest, 308
Asylum, 812–813, 829–898
Divorce, 511–513
Police assistance, reluctance to request, 106–107, 812
Reporting reluctance, 106–107, 812
Stereotypes and abuse assumptions, 107–109
VAWA protections, 511–513, 813, 816–829
VISAs, 818–829

INEFFECTIVE ASSISTANCE OF COUNSEL
Generally, 458–461, 478–479, 485–487

INTERNATIONAL HUMAN RIGHTS
  See Human Rights Violations

JUDGES
Judicial education, 979

JURORS AND JURIES
Instructions, 198, 457–461
Voir dire, 458–461

KIDNAPPING
Child, by abused parent, 581–583, 597
Parental Kidnapping Prevention Act (PKPA), 583–588

LAW ENFORCEMENT
  See Police

LAWYERS
  See Advocacy

LEGAL EDUCATION
Generally, 975–983

MANDATORY REPORTING LAWS
Generally, 170–171, 656–657

MARITAL RAPE
  See Rape

MEDIATION
  See Family Law Systems

MEDICAL PROFESSION
Generally, 9–10, 418–422

MINORS
  See Children

NATIVE AMERICANS
  See also Culture and Battering
  Generally, 111–115, 403
Jurisdictional concerns, 112–113, 237
Peace-making, 352–355

POLICE
  Generally, 298–314
Battering by, 80
Efficacy of arrests, 330
Gender discrimination, 754–756
Homophobia affecting, 89–91
Immigrants, reluctance to request assistance, 106–107, 308
Investigations, 313, 375–391
Liability for failure to protect, 313, 745–785
Mandatory arrest policies, 299–314
Public duty doctrine 772–778
Racial minorities, reluctance to request assistance, 306–308, 325–326
Special relationship, 780–785

POVERTY
  See also Welfare
  Generally, 140–153, 247–248
Rural poverty, 151–153

PREGNANCY
Battering during, 178–190
Fetal rights, 187–190
Fetal protection, 189–190

PROSECUTION
  See Criminal Justice System

PUBLIC BENEFITS
  See Welfare

RACE AND BATTERING
  See also Culture and Battering
  Generally, 97–119, 325–327
Intersectionality, 115–119

RAPE
    Generally 155–164
Anti-rape movement, 18–21
Disabilities, sexual abuse of victims with, 138–139
Human Rights Violations
Marital rape, 155–164, 165–167
Prisoners, human rights violations
Shield laws, 162

RELIGION
    Generally, 119–127
Christianity, 126–127
Islam, 120–121, 123–126
Judaism, 121–122

RELOCATION
    See also Custody
    Generally, 503, 564–597
Jurisdiction over custody, 583–597
Confidentiality of information, 587–588

RESTRAINING ORDER SYSTEMS
    See Civil Protection Orders

RURAL COMMUNITIES
Generally, 151–153

SAME–SEX BATTERING
    Generally, 85–97
Arrests, 305, 312–313
Equal protection, 92–95
Homophobia, 89–90
Restraining orders, availability of, 92–94
Same-sex marriage amendments, 96
Solidarity feelings of victims, 90–91
Substantive due process rights, 95–96

SELF–DEFENSE
    Generally, 423–461
BWS, 423–461
    Daubert test applicable to opinions re, 395–401
    Explanations of, 63–69
    Jury instructions, 455
    Social vs. psychological analysis, 63–63
    Terminology, difficulties with
Gender bias in application of, 424–430
Indigent defendants, obtaining experts for, 478
Reasonableness requirement, 434–446, 453–454
Statutes governing, 446–448
Terrorism, compared to, 454–455

SENTENCING
    See Criminal Justice System

SEXUAL HEALTH
Generally, 169–171

SEXUAL OFFENSES
    See also Rape
Evidence of, 394
Marital Rape, 154–161

SEXUAL OFFENSES—Cont'd
Prostitution, 464–465, 827–828
Sadomasochism, 163–164

SHELTERS
Confidentiality, 147, 162–163
Disabled women's access to, 139–140
Language and cultural barriers, 125–126

STALKING
    Generally, 282–290
Constitutional challenges to statutes, 286–287
Cyber-stalking, 285–286
Evidentiary problems in prosecutions, 287
Federal statute, 283
VAWA provision, 283–285

STATISTICS
Generally, 8–11, 781, 342, 464–465

SUBSTANCE ABUSE
    See Alcohol and Drugs

SURVIVORS
Battered women as, 66–68

TEEN DATING VIOLENCE
Generally, 127–132

TERMINATION OF PARENTAL RIGHTS
    See Child Welfare Systems

TITLE VII
    See Civil Remedies

TITLE IX
    See Civil Remedies

TORTS
    See also Civil Remedies
    Generally, 697–743
Assault and battery, 704
Domestic abuse tort, 729–730
Intentional infliction of emotional distress, 705–717
Physician liability for failure to report, 422
Wrongful death, 705–706
Wrongful discharge, 798–805

TORTURE
    See Human Rights Violations

TRAFFICKING
    Generally, 823–829
Mail Order Brides, 828–829
Sex workers/prostitutes, 827–828

VIOLENCE AGAINST WOMEN ACT (VAWA)
    Generally, 22, 24–25, 235–236, 248, 266–276, 283, 357–368, 813, 816–829, 859–894
Civil Rights provision, 859–865
Constitutional challenges, 364–372, 877–889
Federalism challenges, 871–891
Housing, 150

VIOLENCE AGAINST WOMEN ACT (VAWA)—Cont'd
Immigrant women, protections for, 813, 816–829
Interstate enforcement of restraining orders, 232–237, 364
Legislative history, 865–871
Restraining orders, 232–237
Stalking provision, 282–285

VISITATION
Generally, 554–564
Best interests standard, 554
Constitutional right to, 560

VISITATION—Cont'd
Parental alienation, 561–562
Supervised 555–559, 562–564

WELFARE
See also Poverty and Battering
Generally, 142–145
Family Violence Option, 143–144
Reform pressure, 144–145
TANF benefits for abuse victims, 142–144

WORKPLACE
See also Employers
Safety, 798

†